# VW Polo
## Service and Repair Manual

RM Jex

**Models covered** *(3500 - 320 - 5AC2)*

VW Polo models with four-cylinder petrol and diesel engines, including special/limited editions; 3- and 5-door Hatchbacks

1.0 litre (999 cc), 1.05 litre (1043 cc), 1.3 litre (1296 cc), 1.4 litre (1390 cc) and 1.6 litre (1598 cc) SOHC petrol engines

1.7 litre (1716 cc) and 1.9 litre (1896 cc) diesel engines

*Does not cover Polo Classic (Saloon) or Polo Caddy models, or 16-valve engines*

ABCDE
FGHIJ
KLMNO

A book in the **Haynes Service and Repair Manual Series**



ISBN **1 85960 598 2**

**British Library Cataloguing in Publication Data**
A catalogue record for this book is available from the British Library.

Printed in the USA

**Haynes Publishing**
Sparkford, Yeovil, Somerset BA22 7JJ, England

**Haynes North America, Inc**
861 Lawrence Drive, Newbury Park, California 91320, USA

**Editions Haynes**
4, Rue de l'Abreuvoir
92415 COURBEVOIE CEDEX, France

**Haynes Publishing Nordiska AB**
Box 1504, 751 45 UPPSALA, Sweden

# Contents

## LIVING WITH YOUR VW POLO

# Contents

## REPAIRS & OVERHAUL

The VW Polo range covered by this Manual was introduced to the UK market in September 1994. Originally, the Polo was available with a choice of 1.05 litre (1043 cc), 1.3 litre (1296 cc) and 1.6 litre (1598 cc) petrol engines, in three-door and five-door Hatchback form. The range attracted very favourable press reports at its launch, with many commenting on its 'big-car' feel, offered in a small-car package.

In July 1995, the 1.3 litre engine was superseded by a 1.4 litre (1390 cc) unit.

February 1996 saw the introduction of the 1.9 litre (1896 cc) diesel engine, while in September 1996, the 1.05 litre engine was replaced by a new all-alloy 1.0 litre (999 cc) engine, offering an increase in power output from a slightly smaller capacity.

For 1997, the diesel engine was available with direct injection and electronic diesel engine management, for improved economy and lower emissions. In April 1997, a new 1.7 litre version of the diesel engine was introduced.

All engines are derived from the well-proven engines which have appeared in many VW/Audi vehicles. The engine is of four-cylinder overhead camshaft design, mounted transversely, with the transmission mounted on the left-hand side. All models have a five-speed manual transmission or four-speed automatic transmission.

All models have fully-independent front suspension. The rear suspension is semi-independent, with suspension struts, trailing arms and a torsion beam axle.

A wide range of standard and optional equipment is available within the Polo range to suit most tastes, including central locking, electric windows, and air bags; ABS and air conditioning were available as options.

Provided that regular servicing is carried out in accordance with the manufacturer's recommendations, the VW Polo should prove a reliable and economical small car. The engine compartment is well-designed, and most of the items needing frequent attention are easily accessible.

**VW Polo 1.4 CL (1996 model)**

## Your VW Polo manual

The aim of this manual is to help you get the best value from your vehicle. It can do so in several ways. It can help you decide what work must be done (even should you choose to get it done by a garage). It will also provide information on routine maintenance and servicing, and give a logical course of action and diagnosis when random faults occur. However, it is hoped that you will use the manual by tackling the work yourself. On simpler jobs it may even be quicker than booking the car into a garage and going there twice, to leave and collect it. Perhaps most important, a lot of money can be saved by avoiding the costs a garage must charge to cover its labour and overheads.

The manual has drawings and descriptions to show the function of the various components so that their layout can be understood. Tasks are described and photographed in a clear step-by-step sequence. The illustrations are numbered by the Section number and paragraph number to which they relate - if there is more than one illustration per paragraph, the sequence is denoted alphabetically.

References to the 'left' or 'right' of the vehicle are in the sense of a person in the driver's seat, facing forwards.

## The VW Polo Team

Haynes manuals are produced by dedicated and enthusiastic people working in close co-operation. The team responsible for the creation of this book included:

| | |
|---|---|
| **Author** | **Bob Jex** |
| **Editor & Page Make-up** | **Steve Churchill** |
| **Workshop manager** | **Paul Buckland** |
| **Photo Scans** | **Steve Tanswell<br>John Martin** |
| **Cover illustration & Line Art** | **Roger Healing** |
| **Wiring diagrams** | **Matthew Marke** |

**We hope the book will help you to get the maximum enjoyment from your car. By carrying out routine maintenance as described you will ensure your car's reliability and preserve its resale value.**

## Acknowledgements

Thanks are due to Champion Spark Plug, who supplied the illustrations showing spark plug conditions, and to Duckhams Oils, who provided lubrication data. Thanks are also due to Draper Tools Limited, who provided some of the workshop tools, and to all those people at Sparkford who helped in the production of this manual.

This manual is not a direct reproduction of the vehicle manufacturers' data, and its publication should not be taken as implying any technical approval by the vehicle manufacturers or importers.

**We take great pride in the accuracy of information given in this manual, but vehicle manufacturers make alterations and design changes during the production run of a particular vehicle of which they do not inform us. No liability can be accepted by the authors or publishers for loss, damage or injury caused by any errors in, or omissions from, the information given.**

Working on your car can be dangerous. This page shows just some of the potential risks and hazards, with the aim of creating a safety-conscious attitude.

# General hazards

### Scalding

- Don't remove the radiator or expansion tank cap while the engine is hot.
- Engine oil, automatic transmission fluid or power steering fluid may also be dangerously hot if the engine has recently been running.

### Burning

- Beware of burns from the exhaust system and from any part of the engine. Brake discs and drums can also be extremely hot immediately after use.

### Crushing

- When working under or near a raised vehicle, always supplement the jack with axle stands, or use drive-on ramps. ***Never venture under a car which is only supported by a jack.***

- Take care if loosening or tightening high-torque nuts when the vehicle is on stands. Initial loosening and final tightening should be done with the wheels on the ground.

### Fire

- Fuel is highly flammable; fuel vapour is explosive.
- Don't let fuel spill onto a hot engine.
- Do not smoke or allow naked lights (including pilot lights) anywhere near a vehicle being worked on. Also beware of creating sparks (electrically or by use of tools).
- Fuel vapour is heavier than air, so don't work on the fuel system with the vehicle over an inspection pit.
- Another cause of fire is an electrical overload or short-circuit. Take care when repairing or modifying the vehicle wiring.
- Keep a fire extinguisher handy, of a type suitable for use on fuel and electrical fires.

### Electric shock

- Ignition HT voltage can be dangerous, especially to people with heart problems or a pacemaker. Don't work on or near the ignition system with the engine running or the ignition switched on.

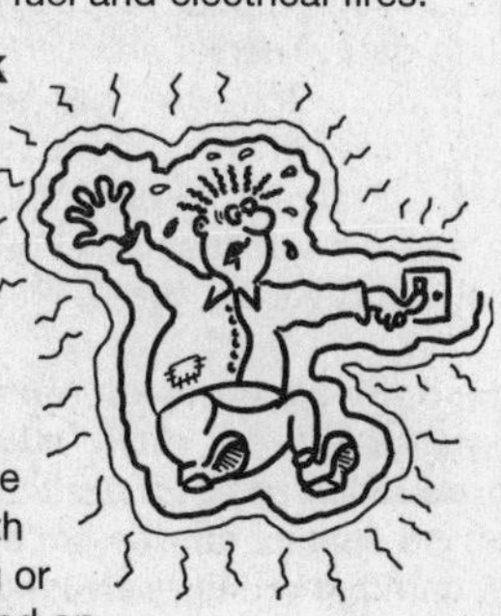

- Mains voltage is also dangerous. Make sure that any mains-operated equipment is correctly earthed. Mains power points should be protected by a residual current device (RCD) circuit breaker.

### Fume or gas intoxication

- Exhaust fumes are poisonous; they often contain carbon monoxide, which is rapidly fatal if inhaled. Never run the engine in a confined space such as a garage with the doors shut.
- Fuel vapour is also poisonous, as are the vapours from some cleaning solvents and paint thinners.

### Poisonous or irritant substances

- Avoid skin contact with battery acid and with any fuel, fluid or lubricant, especially antifreeze, brake hydraulic fluid and Diesel fuel. Don't syphon them by mouth. If such a substance is swallowed or gets into the eyes, seek medical advice.
- Prolonged contact with used engine oil can cause skin cancer. Wear gloves or use a barrier cream if necessary. Change out of oil-soaked clothes and do not keep oily rags in your pocket.
- Air conditioning refrigerant forms a poisonous gas if exposed to a naked flame (including a cigarette). It can also cause skin burns on contact.

### Asbestos

- Asbestos dust can cause cancer if inhaled or swallowed. Asbestos may be found in gaskets and in brake and clutch linings. When dealing with such components it is safest to assume that they contain asbestos.

# Special hazards

### Hydrofluoric acid

- This extremely corrosive acid is formed when certain types of synthetic rubber, found in some O-rings, oil seals, fuel hoses etc, are exposed to temperatures above 400°C. The rubber changes into a charred or sticky substance containing the acid. *Once formed, the acid remains dangerous for years. If it gets onto the skin, it may be necessary to amputate the limb concerned.*
- When dealing with a vehicle which has suffered a fire, or with components salvaged from such a vehicle, wear protective gloves and discard them after use.

### The battery

- Batteries contain sulphuric acid, which attacks clothing, eyes and skin. Take care when topping-up or carrying the battery.
- The hydrogen gas given off by the battery is highly explosive. Never cause a spark or allow a naked light nearby. Be careful when connecting and disconnecting battery chargers or jump leads.

### Air bags

- Air bags can cause injury if they go off accidentally. Take care when removing the steering wheel and/or facia. Special storage instructions may apply.

### Diesel injection equipment

- Diesel injection pumps supply fuel at very high pressure. Take care when working on the fuel injectors and fuel pipes.

***Warning: Never expose the hands, face or any other part of the body to injector spray; the fuel can penetrate the skin with potentially fatal results.***

# Remember...

### DO

- Do use eye protection when using power tools, and when working under the vehicle.
- Do wear gloves or use barrier cream to protect your hands when necessary.
- Do get someone to check periodically that all is well when working alone on the vehicle.
- Do keep loose clothing and long hair well out of the way of moving mechanical parts.
- Do remove rings, wristwatch etc, before working on the vehicle – especially the electrical system.
- Do ensure that any lifting or jacking equipment has a safe working load rating adequate for the job.

### DON'T

- Don't attempt to lift a heavy component which may be beyond your capability – get assistance.
- Don't rush to finish a job, or take unverified short cuts.
- Don't use ill-fitting tools which may slip and cause injury.
- Don't leave tools or parts lying around where someone can trip over them. Mop up oil and fuel spills at once.
- Don't allow children or pets to play in or near a vehicle being worked on.

The following pages are intended to help in dealing with common roadside emergencies and breakdowns. You will find more detailed fault finding information at the back of the manual, and repair information in the main chapters.

## If your car won't start and the starter motor doesn't turn

- ☐ If it's a model with automatic transmission, make sure the selector is in 'P' or 'N'.
- ☐ Open the bonnet and make sure that the battery terminals are clean and tight.
- ☐ Switch on the headlights and try to start the engine. If the headlights go very dim when you're trying to start, the battery is probably flat. Get out of trouble by jump starting (see next page) using a friend's car.

## If your car won't start even though the starter motor turns as normal

- ☐ Is there fuel in the tank?
- ☐ Is there moisture on electrical components under the bonnet? Switch off the ignition, then wipe off any obvious dampness with a dry cloth. Spray a water-repellent aerosol product (WD-40 or equivalent) on ignition and fuel system electrical connectors like those shown in the photos. Pay special attention to the ignition coil wiring connector and HT leads. (Note that Diesel engines don't normally suffer from damp.)

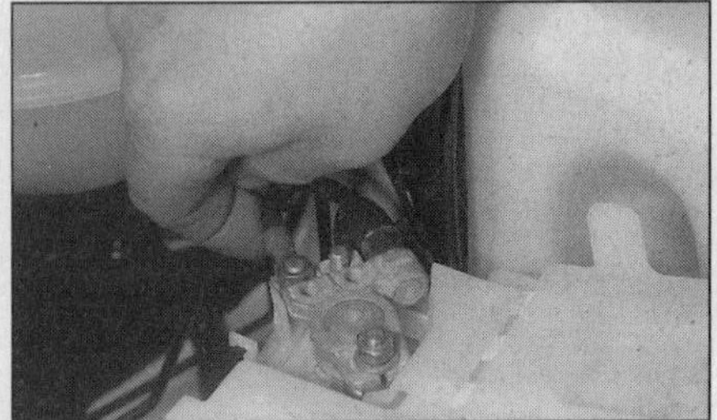

A Check the security and condition of the battery terminals.

B Check that the HT leads are securely connected to the distributor cap (petrol engine models).

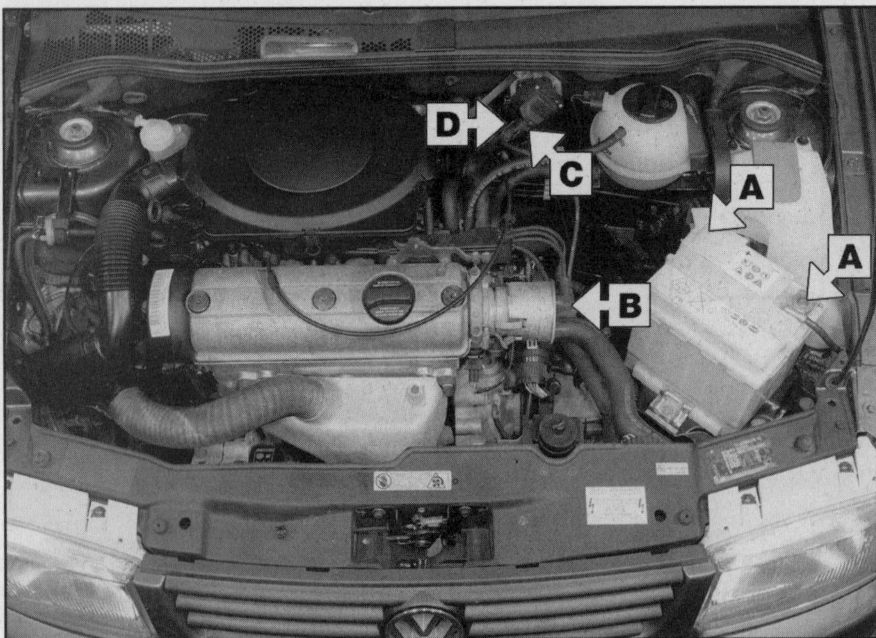


Check that electrical connections are secure (with the ignition switched off). On petrol engine models, check the four spark plug leads and the ignition coil connections at the rear of the engine compartment. Spray the connector plugs with a water-dispersant spray like WD40 if you suspect a problem due to damp.

C Check that the HT lead to the ignition coil is securely connected (petrol engine models).

D Check that the LT wiring plug at the ignition coil is securely connected (petrol engine models).

# Jump starting

**HAYNES HiNT** ***Jump starting will get you out of trouble, but you must correct whatever made the battery go flat in the first place. There are three possibilities:***

***1 The battery has been drained by repeated attempts to start, or by leaving the lights on.***

***2 The charging system is not working properly (alternator drivebelt slack or broken, alternator wiring fault or alternator itself faulty).***

***3 The battery itself is at fault (electrolyte low, or battery worn out).***

When jump-starting a car using a booster battery, observe the following precautions:

- ✔ Before connecting the booster battery, make sure that the ignition is switched off.
- ✔ Ensure that all electrical equipment (lights, heater, wipers, etc) is switched off.
- ✔ Take note of any special precautions printed on the battery case.
- ✔ Make sure that the booster battery is the same voltage as the discharged one in the vehicle.
- ✔ If the battery is being jump-started from the battery in another vehicle, the two vehicles MUST NOT TOUCH each other.
- ✔ Make sure that the transmission is in neutral (or PARK, in the case of automatic transmission).

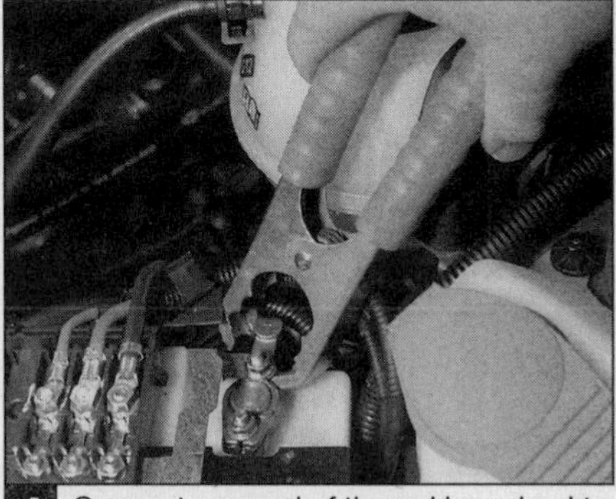

**1** Connect one end of the red jump lead to the positive (+) terminal of the flat battery

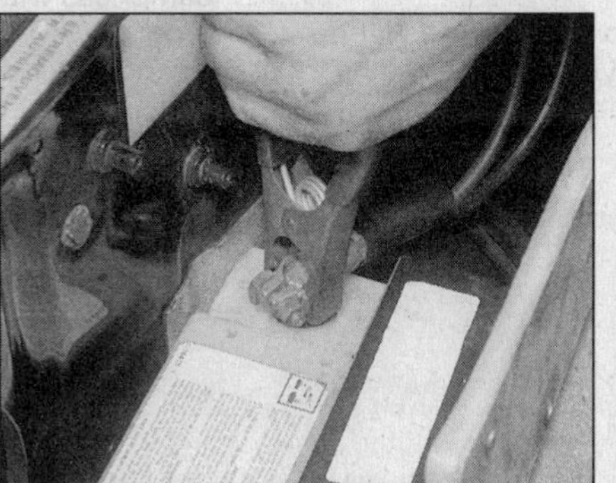

**2** Connect the other end of the red lead to the positive (+) terminal of the booster battery.

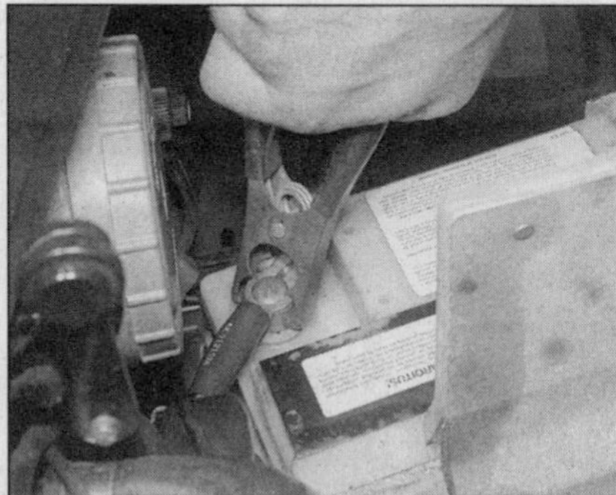

**3** Connect one end of the black jump lead to the negative (-) terminal of the booster battery

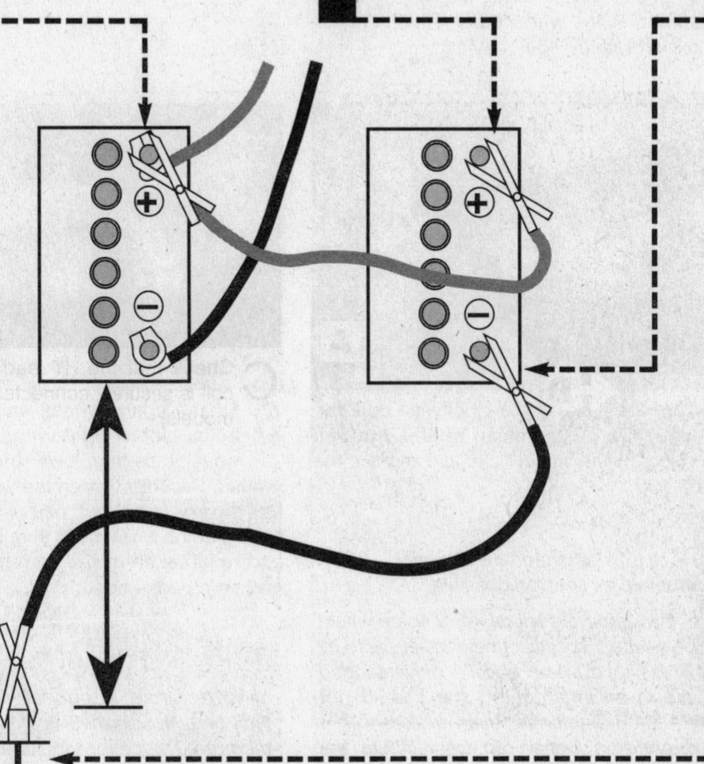

**4** Connect the other end of the black jump lead to a bolt or bracket on the engine block, well away from the battery, on the vehicle to be started.

**5** Make sure that the jump leads will not come into contact with the fan, drive-belts or other moving parts of the engine.

**6** Start the engine using the booster battery and run it at idle speed. Switch on the lights, rear window demister and heater blower motor, then disconnect the jump leads in the reverse order of connection. Turn off the lights etc.

# Wheel changing

Some of the details shown here will vary according to model. For instance, the location of the spare wheel and jack is not the same on all cars. However, the basic principles apply to all vehicles.

⚠ ***Warning: Do not change a wheel in a situation where you risk being hit by another vehicle. On busy roads, try to stop in a lay-by or a gateway. Be wary of passing traffic while changing the wheel - it is easy to become distracted by the job in hand.***

## Preparation

- ☐ When a puncture occurs, stop as soon as it is safe to do so.
- ☐ Park on firm level ground, if possible, and well out of the way of other traffic.
- ☐ Use hazard warning lights if necessary.
- ☐ If you have one, use a warning triangle to alert other drivers of your presence.
- ☐ Apply the handbrake and engage first or reverse gear (or Park on models with automatic transmission.
- ☐ Chock the wheel diagonally opposite the one being removed – a couple of large stones will do for this.
- ☐ If the ground is soft, use a flat piece of wood to spread the load under the jack.

## Changing the wheel

**1** The spare wheel and tools are stored in the luggage compartment, under the floor covering. A warning triangle may be provided on the right-hand side of the luggage compartment, behind a trim panel. Release the retaining strap, and lift out the jack and wheel changing tools from the centre of the wheel. Unscrew the retaining nut and lift the wheel out of the vehicle.

**2** Remove the wheel trim/hub cap (on some models, a wire hook is provided, which is inserted through one of the holes in the wheel trim, and used with the wheelbrace handle to pull off the trim). On lower-specification models, plastic caps may be fitted over the wheel bolts, which can be hooked off with the tool provided.

**3** Slacken each wheel bolt by a half turn, using the wheelbrace. If the bolts are too tight, DON'T stand on the wheelbrace to undo them - call for assistance from one of the motoring organisations.

**4** Only attempt to jack up the vehicle on firm, level ground. Locate the jack below the reinforced point on the sill, indicated by the triangular indentations (don't jack the vehicle at any other point of the sill).

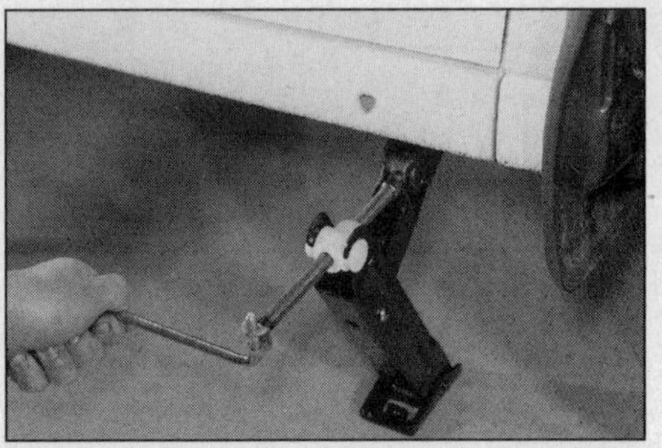

**5** Turn the jack handle clockwise until the wheel is raised clear of the ground. Unscrew the wheel bolts and remove the wheel.

**6** Fit the spare wheel, and screw in the bolts. Lightly tighten the bolts with the wheelbrace then lower the vehicle to the ground. Securely tighten the wheel bolts, then refit the wheel trim/hub cap or the bolt covers. Note that the wheel bolts should be slackened and retightened to the correct torque at the earliest possible opportunity.

# Finally...

- ☐ Check the tyre pressure on the wheel just fitted. If it is low, or if you don't have a pressure gauge with you, drive slowly to the nearest garage and inflate the tyre to the right pressure.
- ☐ Remove the wheel chocks.
- ☐ Stow the jack and tools in the correct locations in the car.
- ☐ Have the damaged tyre or wheel repaired as soon as possible.

**Note:** *If a temporary space-saver spare wheel has been fitted, special conditions apply to its use. This type of spare wheel is only intended for use in an emergency, and should not remain fitted any longer than it takes to get the punctured wheel repaired. While the temporary wheel is in use, do not exceed 50 mph (80 km/h), and avoid harsh acceleration, braking or cornering. Note that, besides being narrower than a normal roadwheel, the temporary spare wheel is of smaller diameter; therefore, since ground clearance will be slightly reduced with the temporary spare in use, take care when travelling over rough ground.*

# Identifying leaks

Puddles on the garage floor or drive, or obvious wetness under the bonnet or underneath the car, suggest a leak that needs investigating. It can sometimes be difficult to decide where the leak is coming from, especially if the engine bay is very dirty already. Leaking oil or fluid can also be blown rearwards by the passage of air under the car, giving a false impression of where the problem lies.

***Warning: Most automotive oils and fluids are poisonous. Wash them off skin, and change out of contaminated clothing, without delay.***

***The smell of a fluid leaking from the car may provide a clue to what's leaking. Some fluids are distinctively coloured. It may help to clean the car carefully and to park it over some clean paper overnight as an aid to locating the source of the leak.***

***Remember that some leaks may only occur while the engine is running.***

## Sump oil

Engine oil may leak from the drain plug...

## Oil from filter

...or from the base of the oil filter.

## Gearbox oil

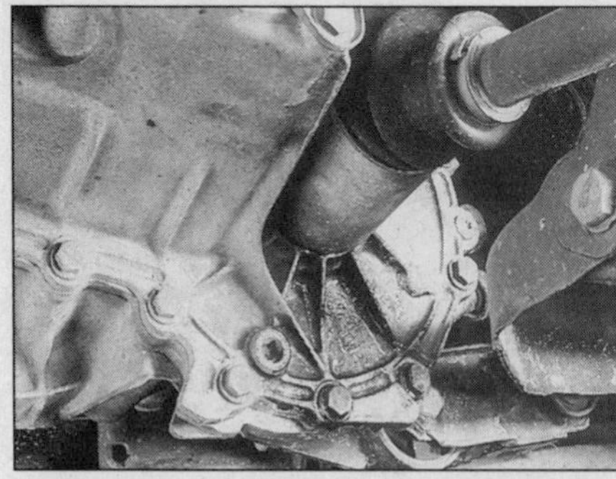

Gearbox oil can leak from the seals at the inboard ends of the driveshafts.

## Antifreeze

Leaking antifreeze often leaves a crystalline deposit like this.

## Brake fluid

A leak occurring at a wheel is almost certainly brake fluid.

## Power steering fluid

Power steering fluid may leak from the pipe connectors on the steering rack.

# Towing

When all else fails, you may find yourself having to get a tow home – or of course you may be helping somebody else. Long-distance recovery should only be done by a garage or breakdown service. For shorter distances, DIY towing using another car is easy enough, but observe the following points:

☐ Use a proper tow-rope – they are not expensive. The vehicle being towed must display an 'ON TOW' sign in its rear window.

☐ Always turn the ignition key to the 'on' position when the vehicle is being towed, so that the steering lock is released, and that the direction indicator and brake lights will work.

☐ A rear towing eye is provided below the rear bumper. The front towing eye is provided in the vehicle tool kit, and is screwed into the front bumper after prising out the trim cover .

☐ Before being towed, release the handbrake and select neutral on the transmission.

☐ Note that greater-than-usual pedal pressure will be required to operate the brakes, since the vacuum servo unit is only operational with the engine running.

☐ On models with power steering, greater-than-usual steering effort will also be required.

☐ The driver of the car being towed must keep the tow-rope taut at all times to avoid snatching.

☐ Make sure that both drivers know the route before setting off.

☐ Only drive at moderate speeds and keep the distance towed to a minimum. Drive smoothly and allow plenty of time for slowing down at junctions.

☐ On models with automatic transmission, special precautions apply. If in doubt, do not tow, or transmission damage may result.

## Introduction

There are some very simple checks which need only take a few minutes to carry out, but which could save you a lot of inconvenience and expense.

These "Weekly checks" require no great skill or special tools, and the small amount of time they take to perform could prove to be very well spent, for example;

☐ Keeping an eye on tyre condition and pressures, will not only help to stop them wearing out prematurely, but could also save your life.

☐ Many breakdowns are caused by electrical problems. Battery-related faults are particularly common, and a quick check on a regular basis will often prevent the majority of these.

☐ If your car develops a brake fluid leak, the first time you might know about it is when your brakes don't work properly. Checking the level regularly will give advance warning of this kind of problem.

☐ If the oil or coolant levels run low, the cost of repairing any engine damage will be far greater than fixing the leak, for example.

## Underbonnet check points

◀ **1.4 litre petrol**

**A** *Engine oil level dipstick*
**B** *Engine oil filler cap*
**C** *Coolant expansion tank*
**D** *Brake fluid reservoir*
**E** *Power steering fluid reservoir*
**F** *Screen washer fluid reservoir*
**G** *Battery*

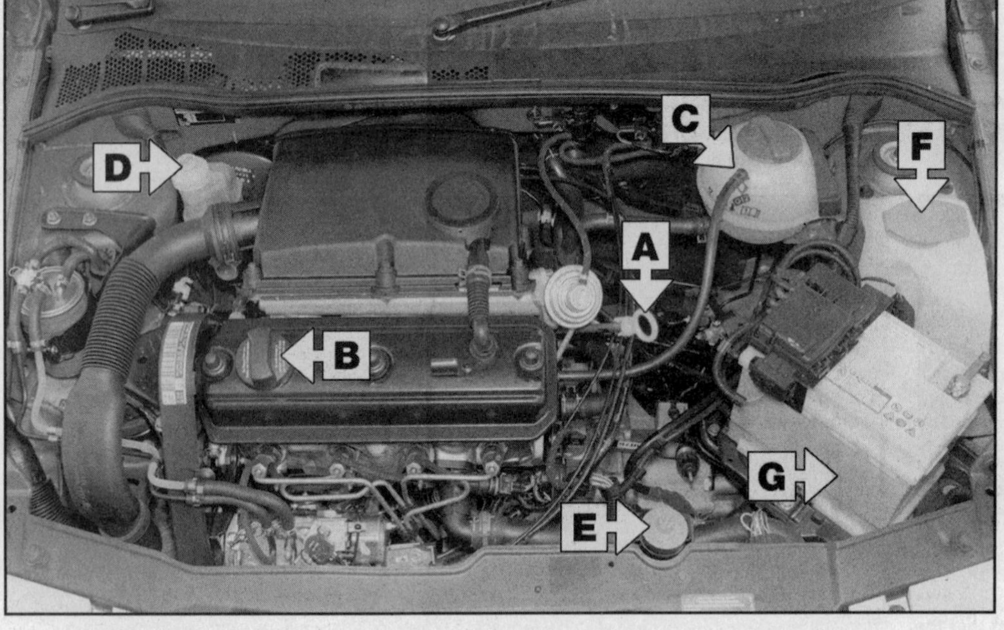


◀ **1.9 litre diesel**

**A** *Engine oil level dipstick*
**B** *Engine oil filler cap*
**C** *Coolant expansion tank*
**D** *Brake fluid reservoir*
**E** *Power steering fluid reservoir*
**F** *Screen washer fluid reservoir*
**G** *Battery*

# Engine oil level

## Before you start

✔ Make sure that your car is on level ground.
✔ Check the oil level before the car is driven, or at least 5 minutes after the engine has been switched off.

***If the oil is checked immediately after driving the vehicle, some of the oil will remain in the upper engine components, resulting in an inaccurate reading on the dipstick!***

## The correct oil

*Modern engines place great demands on their oil. It is very important that the correct oil for your car is used (See "Lubricants, fluids and tyre pressures").*

## Car Care

● If you have to add oil frequently, you should check whether you have any oil leaks. Place some clean paper under the car overnight, and check for stains in the morning. If there are no leaks, the engine may be burning oil *(see "Fault Finding").*

● Always maintain the level between the upper and lower dipstick marks (see photo 3). If the level is too low severe engine damage may occur. Oil seal failure may result if the engine is overfilled by adding too much oil.

1 The dipstick top is often brightly coloured for easy identification (see *Underbonnet check points* on pages 0•10 for exact location). Withdraw the dipstick.

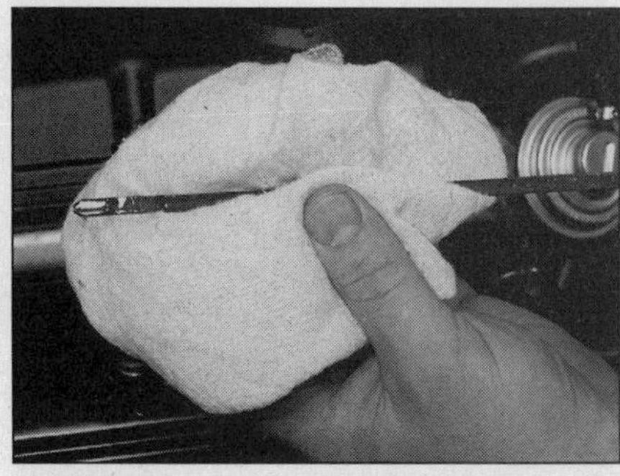

2 Using a clean rag or paper towel remove all oil from the dipstick. Insert the clean dipstick into the tube as far as it will go, then withdraw it again.

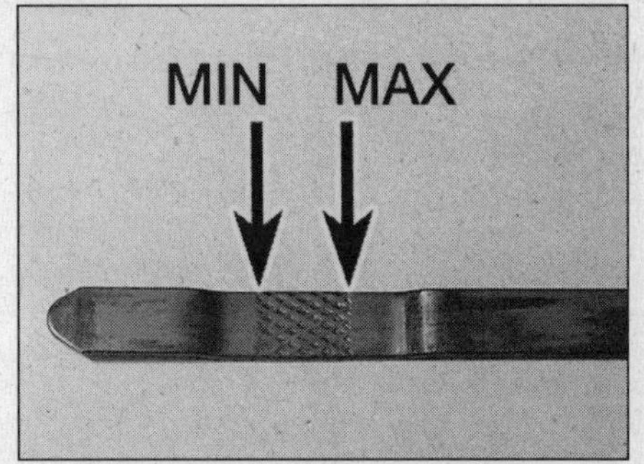


3 Note the oil level on the end of the dipstick, which should be within the hatched area marked. If the oil level is at the bottom of, or below, the hatched area, topping-up is required.

4 Oil is added through the filler cap. Unscrew the cap and top-up the level; a funnel may help to reduce spillage. Add the oil slowly, checking the level on the dipstick often. Don't overfill (see *"Car Care" left*).

# Coolant level

***Warning: DO NOT attempt to remove the expansion tank pressure cap when the engine is hot, as there is a very great risk of scalding. Do not leave open containers of coolant about, as it is poisonous.***

## Car Care

● With a sealed-type cooling system, adding coolant should not be necessary on a regular basis. If frequent topping-up is required, it is likely there is a leak. Check the radiator, all hoses and joint faces for signs of staining or wetness, and rectify as necessary.

● It is important that antifreeze is used in the cooling system all year round, not just during the winter months. Don't top-up with water alone, as the antifreeze will become too diluted.

● The manufacturer states that if the coolant in the expansion tank is red in colour (VW G12 coolant) or blue in colour (VW G11 coolant), on no account should this be mixed with any other type of coolant, even the small amounts likely to be required for topping-up. Refer to your VW dealer for the latest advice.

1 The coolant level varies with engine temperature. When cold, the coolant level should be between the "MAX" and "MIN" marks. When the engine is hot, the level may rise slightly above the "MAX" mark.

2 If topping up is necessary, **wait until the engine is cold**. Slowly unscrew the expansion tank cap, to release any pressure present in the cooling system, and remove it.

3 Add coolant to the expansion tank until the level is halfway between the level marks. Refit the cap and tighten it securely.

## Brake fluid level

***Warning:***
- ***Brake fluid can harm your eyes and damage painted surfaces, so use extreme caution when handling and pouring it.***
- ***Do not use fluid that has been standing open for some time, as it absorbs moisture from the air, which can cause a dangerous loss of braking effectiveness.***

- ***Make sure that your car is on level ground.***
- ***The fluid level in the reservoir will drop slightly as the brake pads wear down, but the fluid level must never be allowed to drop below the "MIN" mark.***

### Safety First!

- If the reservoir requires repeated topping-up this is an indication of a fluid leak somewhere in the system, which should be investigated immediately.
- If a leak is suspected, the car should not be driven until the braking system has been checked. Never take any risks where brakes are concerned.

1 The brake fluid reservoir is located on the right-hand side of the engine compartment, next to the suspension strut top mounting.

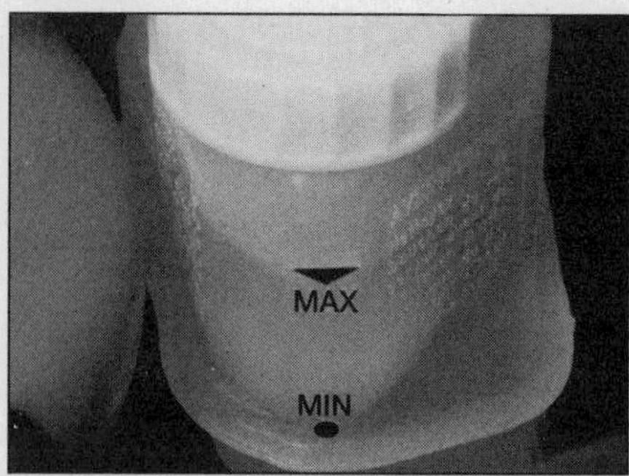



2 The MAX and MIN marks are indicated on the front of the reservoir. The fluid level must be kept between the marks at all times. If topping-up is necessary, first wipe clean the area around the filler cap to prevent dirt entering the hydraulic system.

3 Unscrew the reservoir cap and carefully lift it out of position, taking care not to damage the level switch float. Place the cap and float on a piece of clean rag. Inspect the reservoir; if the fluid is dirty, the hydraulic system should be drained and refilled (see Chapter 1).

4 Carefully add fluid, taking care not to spill it onto the surrounding components. Use only the specified fluid; mixing different types can cause damage to the system. After topping-up to the correct level, securely refit the cap and wipe off any spilt fluid.

## Screen washer fluid level*

***On models with a headlight washer system, the screen wash is also used to clean the headlights. The underbonnet reservoir also serves the tailgate washer.***

Screenwash additives not only keep the winscreen clean during foul weather, they also prevent the washer system freezing in cold weather - which is when you are likely to need it most. Don't top up using plain water as the screenwash will become too diluted, and will freeze during cold weather. ***On no account use coolant antifreeze in the washer system - this could discolour or damage paintwork.***

1 The screen washer fluid reservoir is located in the left-hand rear corner of the engine compartment, behind the battery.

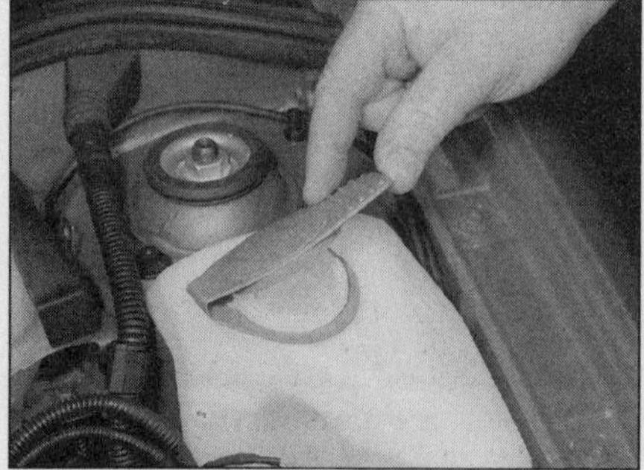

2 The screen washer level can be seen through the reservoir body. If topping-up is necessary, open the cap.

3 When topping-up the reservoir, add a screenwash additive in the quantities recommended on the additive bottle.

# Power steering fluid level

## Before you start:

- ✔ Park the vehicle on level ground.
- ✔ Set the steering wheel straight-ahead.
- ✔ If the system is cold, the fluid level should be checked with the engine switched off.
- ✔ If the system is at operating temperature, the fluid level should be checked with the engine running.

***For the check to be accurate, the steering must not be turned once the engine has been stopped.***

## Safety First!

- The need for frequent topping-up indicates a leak, which should be investigated immediately.

1 The reservoir is located in the front left-hand side of the engine compartment, behind the lock carrier panel.

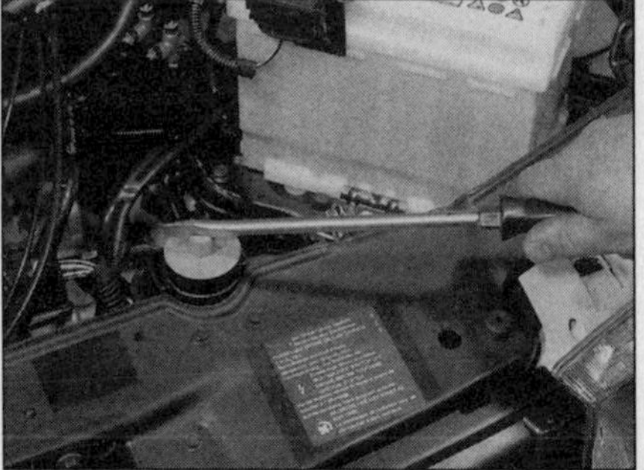

2 Wipe clean the area around the reservoir filler neck and unscrew the filler cap/dipstick from the reservoir, using a flat-bladed screwdriver in the slot provided on the reservoir cap.

3 Wipe the fluid dipstick attached to the cap clean with a clean non-fluffy rag, then screw the cap fully back into position, hand-tight. Unscrew the cap once more, and note the reading on the dipstick. When the system is cold, the fluid level should be up to the MIN mark; when hot, it should be between the MAX and MIN marks.

4 When topping-up, use the specified type of fluid and do not overfill the reservoir. Note that all models require special VW hydraulic oil in the system. When the level is correct, securely refit the cap.

# Wiper blades

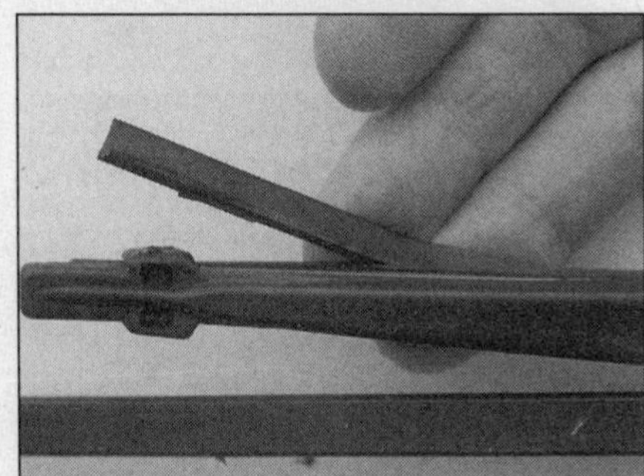

1 Check the condition of the wiper blades; if they are cracked or show any signs of deterioration, or if the glass swept area is smeared, renew them. Wiper blades should be renewed annually.

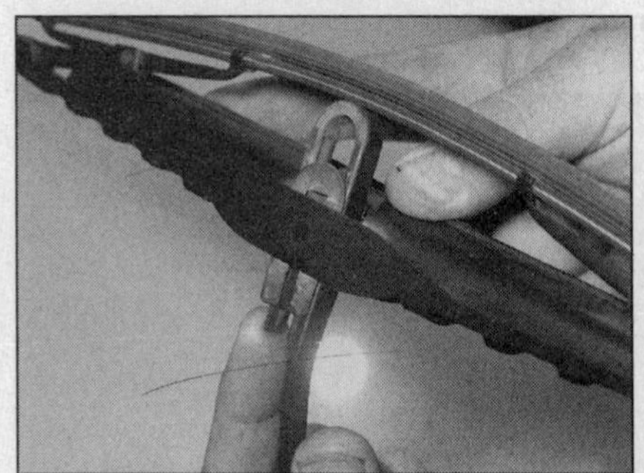

2 To remove a windscreen wiper blade, pull the arm fully away from the screen until it locks. Swivel the blade through 90°, press the locking tab with your fingers and slide the blade out of the arm's hooked end.

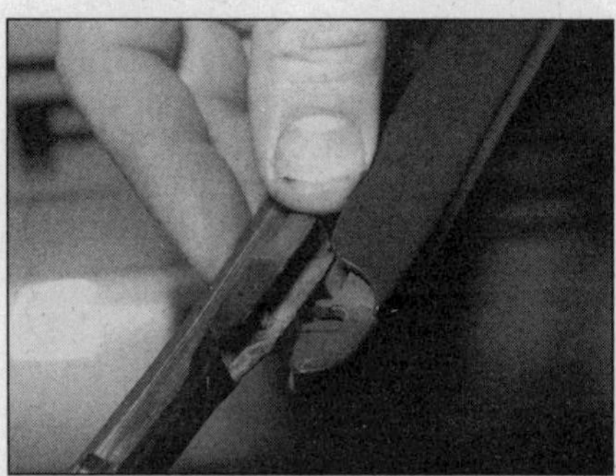

3 Don't forget to check the tailgate wiper blade as well. To remove the blade, simply slide the blade out of the hooked end of the arm.

## Tyre condition and pressure

It is very important that tyres are in good condition, and at the correct pressure - having a tyre failure at any speed is highly dangerous. Tyre wear is influenced by driving style - harsh braking and acceleration, or fast cornering, will all produce more rapid tyre wear. As a general rule, the front tyres wear out faster than the rears. Interchanging the tyres from front to rear ("rotating" the tyres) may result in more even wear. However, if this is completely effective, you may have the expense of replacing all four tyres at once!

Remove any nails or stones embedded in the tread before they penetrate the tyre to cause deflation. If removal of a nail does reveal that the tyre has been punctured, refit the nail so that its point of penetration is marked. Then immediately change the wheel, and have the tyre repaired by a tyre dealer.

Regularly check the tyres for damage in the form of cuts or bulges, especially in the sidewalls. Periodically remove the wheels, and clean any dirt or mud from the inside and outside surfaces. Examine the wheel rims for signs of rusting, corrosion or other damage. Light alloy wheels are easily damaged by "kerbing" whilst parking; steel wheels may also become dented or buckled. A new wheel is very often the only way to overcome severe damage.

New tyres should be balanced when they are fitted, but it may become necessary to re-balance them as they wear, or if the balance weights fitted to the wheel rim should fall off. Unbalanced tyres will wear more quickly, as will the steering and suspension components. Wheel imbalance is normally signified by vibration, particularly at a certain speed (typically around 50 mph). If this vibration is felt only through the steering, then it is likely that just the front wheels need balancing. If, however, the vibration is felt through the whole car, the rear wheels could be out of balance. Wheel balancing should be carried out by a tyre dealer or garage.

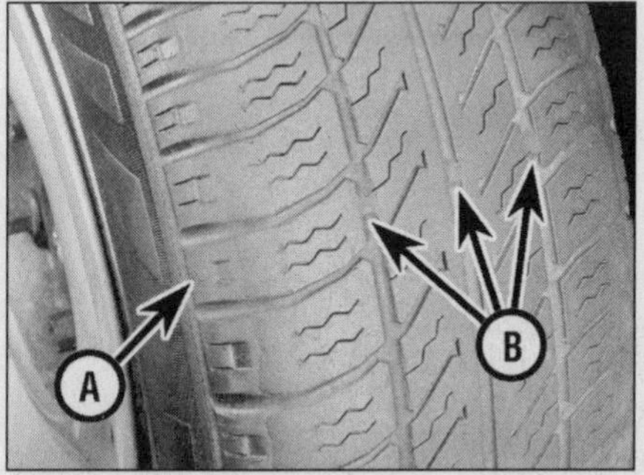


1 ***Tread Depth - visual check***
The original tyres have tread wear safety bands (B), which will appear when the tread depth reaches approximately 1.6 mm. The band positions are indicated by a triangular mark on the tyre sidewall (A).

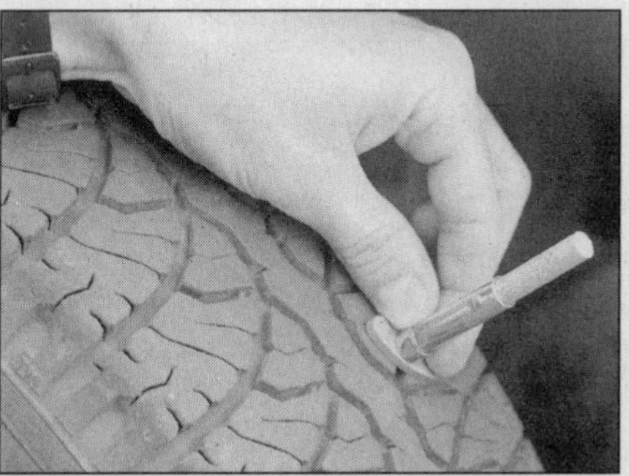

2 ***Tread Depth - manual check***
Alternatively, tread wear can be monitored with a simple, inexpensive device known as a tread depth indicator gauge.

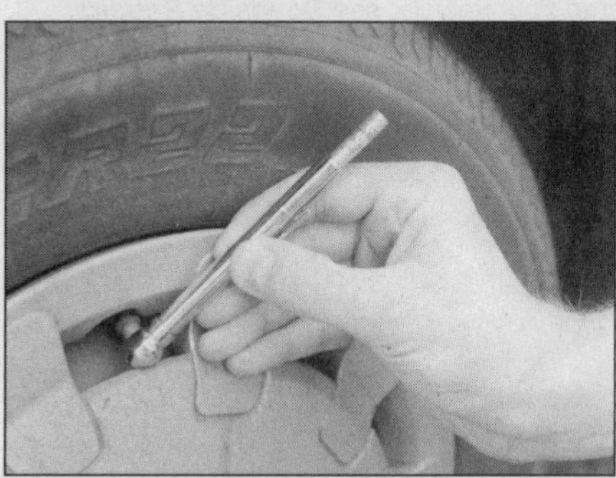

3 ***Tyre Pressure Check***
Check the tyre pressures regularly with the tyres cold. Do not adjust the tyre pressures immediately after the vehicle has been used, or an inaccurate setting will result.

## Tyre tread wear patterns

### *Shoulder Wear*

**Underinflation (wear on both sides)**
Under-inflation will cause overheating of the tyre, because the tyre will flex too much, and the tread will not sit correctly on the road surface. This will cause a loss of grip and excessive wear, not to mention the danger of sudden tyre failure due to heat build-up.
*Check and adjust pressures*
**Incorrect wheel camber (wear on one side)**
*Repair or renew suspension parts*
**Hard cornering**
*Reduce speed!*

### *Centre Wear*

**Overinflation**
Over-inflation will cause rapid wear of the centre part of the tyre tread, coupled with reduced grip, harsher ride, and the danger of shock damage occurring in the tyre casing.
*Check and adjust pressures*

*If you sometimes have to inflate your car's tyres to the higher pressures specified for maximum load or sustained high speed, don't forget to reduce the pressures to normal afterwards.*

### *Uneven Wear*

Front tyres may wear unevenly as a result of wheel misalignment. Most tyre dealers and garages can check and adjust the wheel alignment (or "tracking") for a modest charge.
**Incorrect camber or castor**
*Repair or renew suspension parts*
**Malfunctioning suspension**
*Repair or renew suspension parts*
**Unbalanced wheel**
*Balance tyres*
**Incorrect toe setting**
*Adjust front wheel alignment*
**Note:** *The feathered edge of the tread which typifies toe wear is best checked by feel.*

# Battery

***Caution:*** *Before carrying out any work on the vehicle battery, read the precautions given in "Safety first" at the start of this manual.*

✔ Make sure that the battery tray is in good condition, and that the clamp is tight. Corrosion on the tray, retaining clamp and the battery itself can be removed with a solution of water and baking soda. Thoroughly rinse all cleaned areas with water. Any metal parts damaged by corrosion should be covered with a zinc-based primer, then painted.

✔ Periodically (approximately every three months), check the charge condition of the battery as described in Chapter 5A.

✔ If the battery is flat, and you need to jump start your vehicle, see ***Roadside Repairs***.

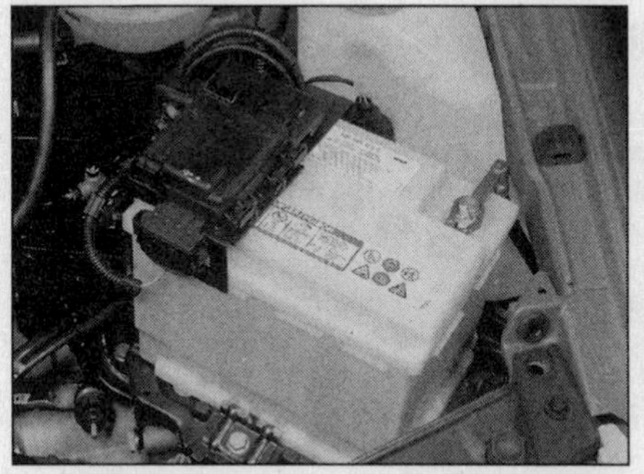

1 The battery is located on the left-hand side of the engine compartment. The exterior of the battery should be inspected periodically for damage such as a cracked case or cover.

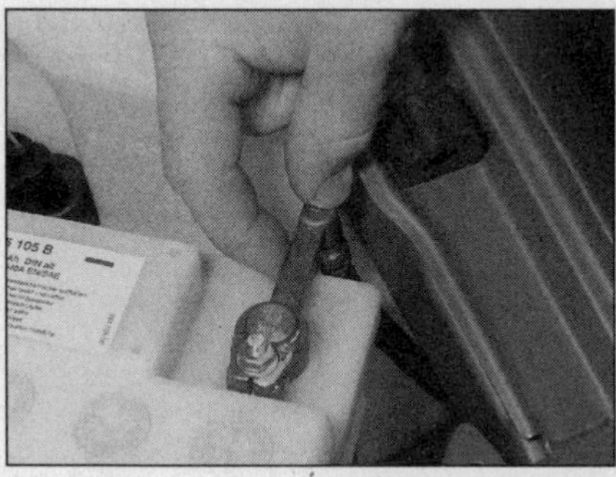

2 Check the tightness of battery clamps to ensure good electrical connections. You should not be able to move them. Also check each cable for cracks and frayed conductors.

***Battery corrosion can be kept to a minimum by applying a layer of petroleum jelly to the clamps and terminals after they are reconnected.***

3 If corrosion (white, fluffy deposits) is evident, remove the cables from the battery terminals, clean them with a small wire brush, then refit them. Automotive stores sell a tool for cleaning the battery post . . .

4 . . . as well as the battery cable clamps

# Bulbs and fuses

✔ Check all external lights and the horn. Refer to the appropriate Sections of Chapter 12 for details if any of the circuits are found to be inoperative.

✔ Visually check all accessible wiring connectors, harnesses and retaining clips for security, and for signs of chafing or damage.

***If you need to check your brake lights and indicators unaided, back up to a wall or garage door and operate the lights. The reflected light should show if they are working properly.***

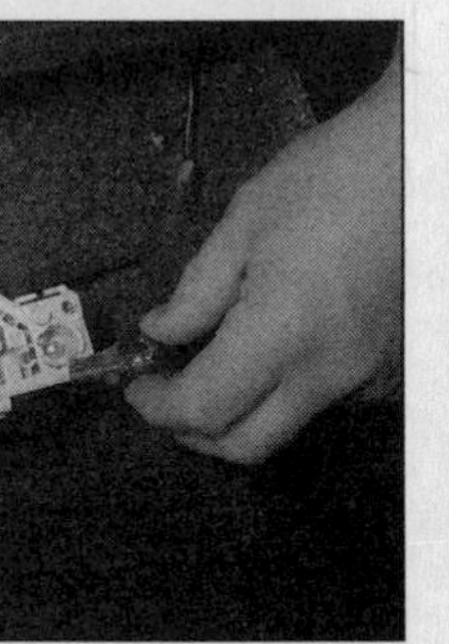

1 If a single indicator light, stop-light or headlight has failed, it is likely that a bulb has blown and will need to be replaced. Refer to Chapter 12 for details. If both stop-lights have failed, it is possible that the switch has failed (see Chapter 9).

2 If more than one indicator light or tail light has failed it is likely that either a fuse has blown or that there is a fault in the circuit (see Chapter 12). The fuses are located behind the driver's side glovebox, which should be removed for access (see Chapter 11).

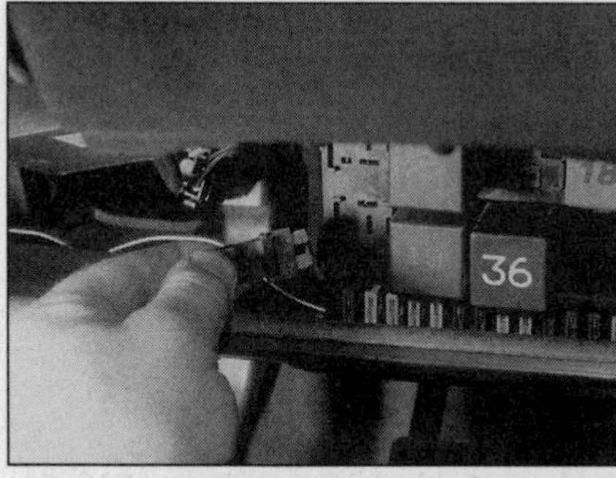


3 To replace a blown fuse, simply pull it out and fit a new fuse of the correct rating (see Chapter 12). If the fuse blows again, it is important that you find out why - a complete checking procedure is given in Chapter 12.

## Lubricants and fluids

| | |
|---|---|
| **Engine (petrol)** | Multigrade engine oil, viscosity SAE 10W/40, 15W/40, 15W/50 or 20W/50, to VW spec 500 00 *(Duckhams QXR Premium Petrol Engine Oil)* |
| **Engine (diesel)** | Multigrade engine oil, viscosity SAE 10W/40, 15W/40, 15W/50 or 20W/50 *(Duckhams QXR Premium Diesel Engine Oil, or Duckhams Hypergrade Diesel Engine Oil)* |
| **Cooling system** | Ethylene glycol-based antifreeze with corrosion inhibitor - VW G11 or G12* |
| **Manual transmission and final drive** | Gear oil, viscosity SAE 80, to API GL4, or VW gear oil G50, SAE 75W/90 *(Duckhams Hypoid Gear Oil 80W GL-4, or Duckhams Hypoid Gear Oil 75W-90 GL-4)* |
| **Automatic transmission and final drive**** | VW ATF G 052 990 A2 |
| **Brake hydraulic system** | Hydraulic fluid to FMVSS 116 DOT 4 *(Duckhams Universal Brake & Clutch Fluid)* |
| **Power steering** | VW hydraulic oil G 002 000 |

** Refer to "Coolant renewal" in Chapter 1A or 1B.*
*** The automatic transmission is "filled for life". Topping-up or changing the fluid can only be undertaken using VW equipment - see Chapter 1A.*

## Choosing your engine oil

Engines need oil, not only to lubricate moving parts and minimise wear, but also to maximise power output and to improve fuel economy. By introducing a simplified and improved range of engine oils, Duckhams has taken away the confusion and made it easier for you to choose the right oil for your engine.

### HOW ENGINE OIL WORKS

• ***Beating friction***

Without oil, the moving surfaces inside your engine will rub together, heat up and melt, quickly causing the engine to seize. Engine oil creates a film which separates these moving parts, preventing wear and heat build-up.

• ***Cooling hot-spots***

Temperatures inside the engine can exceed 1000° C. The engine oil circulates and acts as a coolant, transferring heat from the hot-spots to the sump.

• ***Cleaning the engine internally***

Good quality engine oils clean the inside of your engine, collecting and dispersing combustion deposits and controlling them until they are trapped by the oil filter or flushed out at oil change.

### OIL CARE - FOLLOW THE CODE

To handle and dispose of used engine oil safely, always:

- ***Avoid skin contact with used engine oil. Repeated or prolonged contact can be harmful.***
- ***Dispose of used oil and empty packs in a responsible manner in an authorised disposal site. Call 0800 663366 to find the one nearest to you. Never tip oil down drains or onto the ground.***



## Tyre pressures

| **Up to half load (normal usage)** | **Front** | **Rear** |
|---|---|---|
| 1.0 and 1.05 litre models: | | |
| 155/70 R 13 tyres | 2.1 bar (30 psi) | 2.1 bar (30 psi) |
| All other tyre sizes | 1.9 bar (28 psi) | 1.9 bar (28 psi) |
| 1.3 and 1.4 litre models: | | |
| 155/70 R 13 tyres | 2.2 bar (32 psi) | 2.2 bar (32 psi) |
| All other tyre sizes | 2.1 bar (30 psi) | 2.1 bar (30 psi) |
| 1.6 litre models, and all diesel models | 2.1 bar (30 psi) | 2.1 bar (30 psi) |

| **Up to full load** | **Front** | **Rear** |
|---|---|---|
| 1.0 and 1.05 litre models: | | |
| 155/70 R 13 tyres | 2.4 bar (35 psi) | 2.9 bar (42 psi) |
| All other tyre sizes | 2.1 bar (30 psi) | 2.4 bar (35 psi) |
| 1.3 and 1.4 litre models: | | |
| 155/70 R 13 tyres | 2.5 bar (36 psi) | 3.0 bar (44 psi) |
| All other tyre sizes | 2.3 bar (33 psi) | 2.6 bar (38 psi) |
| 1.6 litre models, and all diesel models | 2.3 bar (33 psi) | 2.6 bar (38 psi) |

**Note:** *Pressures apply to original-equipment tyres, and may vary if any other make of tyre is fitted; check with the tyre manufacturer or supplier for the correct pressures if necessary. Note that the correct pressures for each individual vehicle are given on a sticker which is either inside the glovebox lid or inside the fuel filler flap. The information on this sticker may vary slightly with that quoted above - if so, consult your VW dealer for the latest recommendations.*

*The spare wheel may be of conventional or space-saver type. A conventional spare wheel should be maintained at the highest full-load pressure for the vehicle. The space-saver spare runs at a pressure of 4.2 bar (61 psi) - this pressure should be marked on the tyre sidewall.*

# Chapter 1 Part A:
# Routine maintenance & servicing - petrol models

## Contents

## Degrees of difficulty

| | | | | |
|---|---|---|---|---|
| **Easy,** suitable for novice with little experience 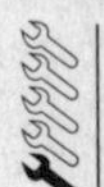 | **Fairly easy,** suitable for beginner with some experience  | **Fairly difficult,** suitable for competent DIY mechanic | **Difficult,** suitable for experienced DIY mechanic  | **Very difficult,** suitable for expert DIY or professional |

## Lubricants and fluids

Refer to end of *Weekly checks*

## Capacities

**Engine oil (including filter)**

| | |
|---|---|
| All engines | 3.5 litres |

**Cooling system (approximate)**

| | |
|---|---|
| All engines | 5.6 litres |

**Transmission (approximate)**

| | |
|---|---|
| Manual transmission: | |
| Filler/level plug on side of transmission housing | 3.1 litres |
| Filler level plug on front of transmission housing | 2.7 litres |
| Automatic transmission (fluid change) | 3.0 litres |

**Fuel tank**

| | |
|---|---|
| All models (approximate) | 45 litres |

**Washer reservoir**

| | |
|---|---|
| Models with headlight washers | 7.0 litres |
| Models without headlight washers | 2.5 litres |

## Engine

| | |
|---|---|
| Oil filter | Champion C161 |

## Cooling system

| | |
|---|---|
| Antifreeze mixture: | |
| 40% antifreeze | Protection down to -25°C |
| 50% antifreeze | Protection down to -35°C |

**Note:** *Refer to antifreeze manufacturer for latest recommendations.*

## Fuel system

| | |
|---|---|
| Air filter element | Champion W222 |
| Fuel filter | Champion L201 |

## Ignition system

| | |
|---|---|
| Ignition timing | Refer to Chapter 5B |
| Spark plugs*: | |
| 1.0 litre and 1.3 litre engines | Champion RN8VTYC4 |
| 1.6 litre engine (up to July 1995) | Champion RN8VTYC4 |
| 1.4 litre engine, and 1.6 litre engine (August 1995 on) | Champion RN10VTYC4 |
| Electrode gap | Not adjustable |

**The spark plug recommendations are those supplied by Champion Spark Plug. If spark plugs of any other type are to be fitted, consult their manufacturers for plug gap information.*

## Brakes

| | |
|---|---|
| Brake pad minimum thickness (including backing plate) | 7.0 mm |
| Brake shoe friction material minimum thickness | 2.5 mm |

## Torque wrench settings

| | Nm | lbf ft |
|---|---|---|
| Manual transmission filler/level plug | 25 | 18 |
| Roadwheel bolts | 110 | 81 |
| Spark plugs | 25 | 18 |
| Sump drain plug | 30 | 22 |

The maintenance intervals in this manual are provided with the assumption that you, not the dealer, will be carrying out the work. These are the minimum intervals recom-mended for vehicles driven daily. If you wish to keep your vehicle in peak condition at all times, you may wish to perform some of these procedures more often. We encourage frequent maintenance, since it enhances the efficiency, performance and resale value of your vehicle.

When the vehicle is new, it should be serviced by a dealer service department, in order to preserve the factory warranty.

## Every 250 miles (400 km) or weekly

- ☐ Refer to *Weekly checks*

## Every 10 000 miles (15 000 km) - OEL on interval display

*In addition to the items listed in the previous services, carry out the following:*

- ☐ Renew the engine oil and filter (Section 3)

**Note:** *Frequent oil and filter changes are beneficial for the engine. We recommend changing the oil at half the mileage specified here or at least twice a year.*

- ☐ Check the front brake pad thickness (Section 4)
- ☐ Reset the service interval display (Section 5)

## Every 12 months - IN 01 on interval display

- ☐ Check operation of all lights and horn (Section 6)
- ☐ Check the condition of the airbag unit(s) (Section 7)
- ☐ Check the operation of the washer system(s) (Section 8)
- ☐ Lubricate all hinges, locks and door check straps (Section 9)
- ☐ Check engine management and other systems for fault codes (Section 10)
- ☐ Check battery electrolyte level - where applicable (Section 11)
- ☐ Check all underbonnet components and hoses for fluid leaks (Section 12)
- ☐ Check the transmission and driveshaft gaiters for leaks and damage (Section 13)
- ☐ Check the braking system for leaks and damage (Section 14)
- ☐ Check the rear brake shoe lining thickness (Section 15)
- ☐ Check the condition of the exhaust system and its mountings (Section 16)
- ☐ Check the steering and suspension components for condition and security (Section 17)
- ☐ Check the headlight beam adjustment (Section 18)
- ☐ Carry out a road test (Section 19)
- ☐ Reset the service interval display (Section 5)

## Every 20 000 miles (30 000 km) - IN 02 on interval display

**Note:** *If the vehicle is covering more than 20 000 miles (30 000 km) a year, also carry out all the operations described above*

- ☐ Lubricate folding fabric sunroof guide rail (Section 20)
- ☐ Renew the spark plugs (Section 21)
- ☐ Renew the pollen filter element (Section 22)
- ☐ Check the condition of the auxiliary drivebelt(s), and renew if necessary (Section 23)
- ☐ Check the manual transmission oil level (Section 24)
- ☐ Check underbody protection for damage (Section 25)
- ☐ Reset the service interval display (Section 5)

## Every 40 000 miles (60 000 km) or 2 years

*In addition to the items listed in the previous services, carry out the following:*

- ☐ Renew the air filter element (Section 26)
- ☐ Check the automatic transmission fluid level (Section 27)
- ☐ Renew the fuel filter (Section 28)
- ☐ Renew the timing belt (Section 29)

**Note:** *VW specify a timing belt renewal interval of 60 000 miles (90 000 km). However, if the vehicle is used mainly for short journeys or a lot of stop-start driving, we recommend that this shorter interval is adhered to. The actual belt renewal interval is very much up to the individual owner but, bearing in mind that severe engine damage will result if the belt breaks in use, we recommend you err on the side of caution.*

## Every 2 years (regardless of mileage)

*In addition to the items listed in the previous services, carry out the following:*

- ☐ Renew the coolant (Section 30)
- ☐ Renew the brake fluid (Section 31)
- ☐ Check exhaust emissions (Section 32)

## Underbonnet view of a 1.0 litre engine model

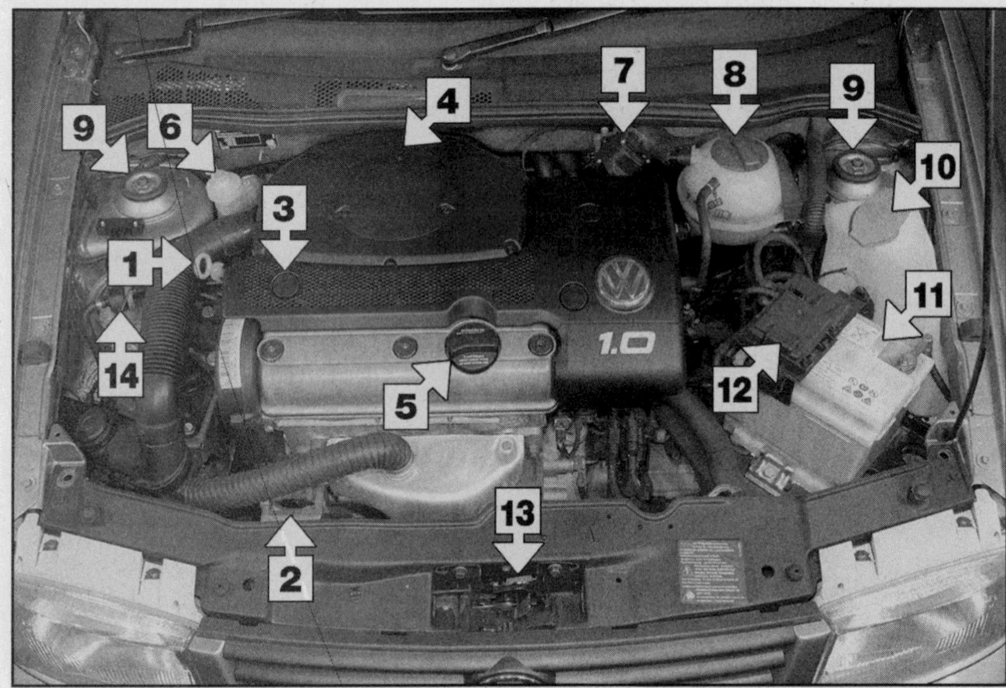


1 *Engine oil dipstick*
2 *Alternator*
3 *No 1 spark plug (under engine top cover)*
4 *Air cleaner housing*
5 *Engine oil filler cap*
6 *Brake fluid reservoir*
7 *Ignition HT coil*
8 *Coolant expansion tank*
9 *Suspension strut upper mounting*
10 *Washer fluid reservoir*
11 *Battery*
12 *Engine compartment fusebox*
13 *Bonnet lock*
14 *Charcoal filter solenoid valve*

## Underbonnet view of a 1.4 litre engine model

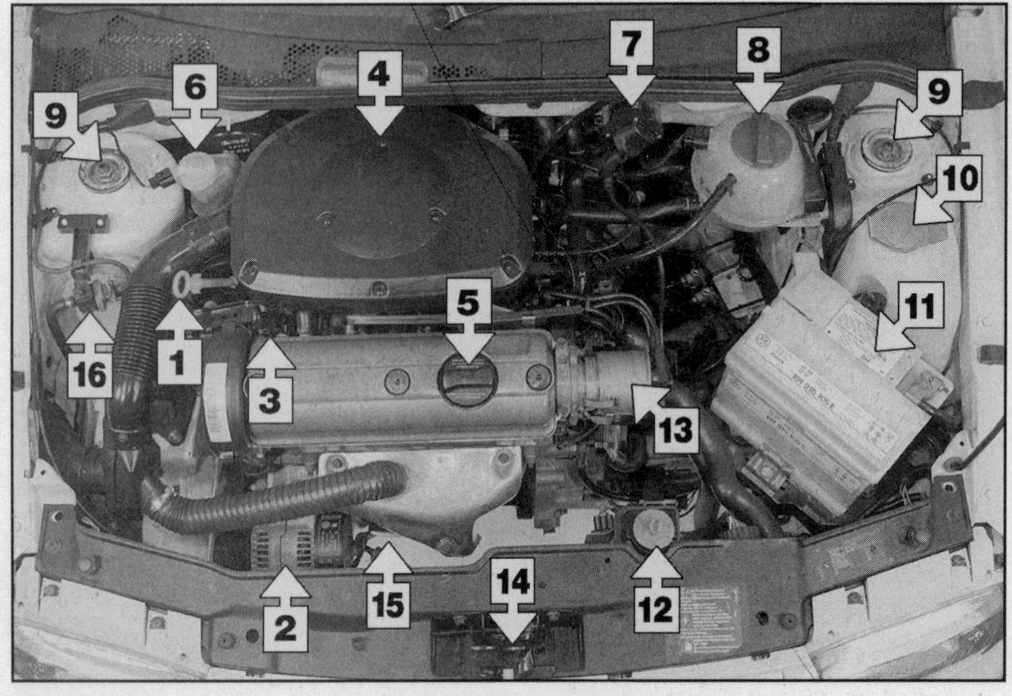


1 *Engine oil dipstick*
2 *Alternator*
3 *No 1 spark plug*
4 *Air cleaner housing*
5 *Engine oil filler cap*
6 *Brake fluid reservoir*
7 *Ignition HT coil*
8 *Coolant expansion tank*
9 *Suspension strut upper mounting*
10 *Washer fluid reservoir*
11 *Battery*
12 *Power steering fluid reservoir*
13 *Distributor*
14 *Bonnet lock*
15 *Oil filter*
16 *Charcoal filter solenoid valve*

## Front underbody view

1 *Engine oil drain plug*
2 *Front brake caliper*
3 *Track rod*
4 *Oil filter*
5 *Lambda sensor*
6 *Radiator cooling fan motor*
7 *Reversing light switch*
8 *Gearchange cables*
9 *Horn*
10 *Wishbone/lower arm*
11 *Engine/transmission rear mounting*
12 *Catalytic converter*
13 *Subframe*
14 *Driveshaft*
15 *Charcoal canister*

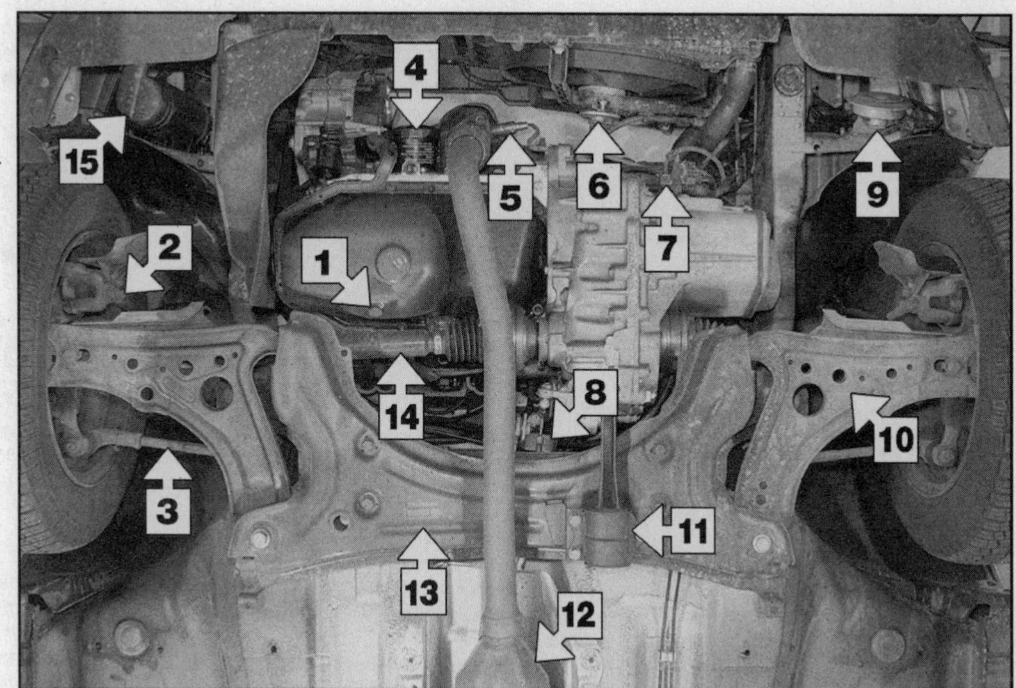


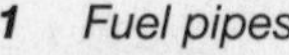



## Rear underbody view

1 *Fuel pipes*
2 *Fuel tank*
3 *Rear axle*
4 *Fuel filter*
5 *Brake pressure regulator*
6 *Handbrake cable*
7 *Exhaust mounting*
8 *Exhaust rear silencer*
9 *Rear strut lower mounting bolt*

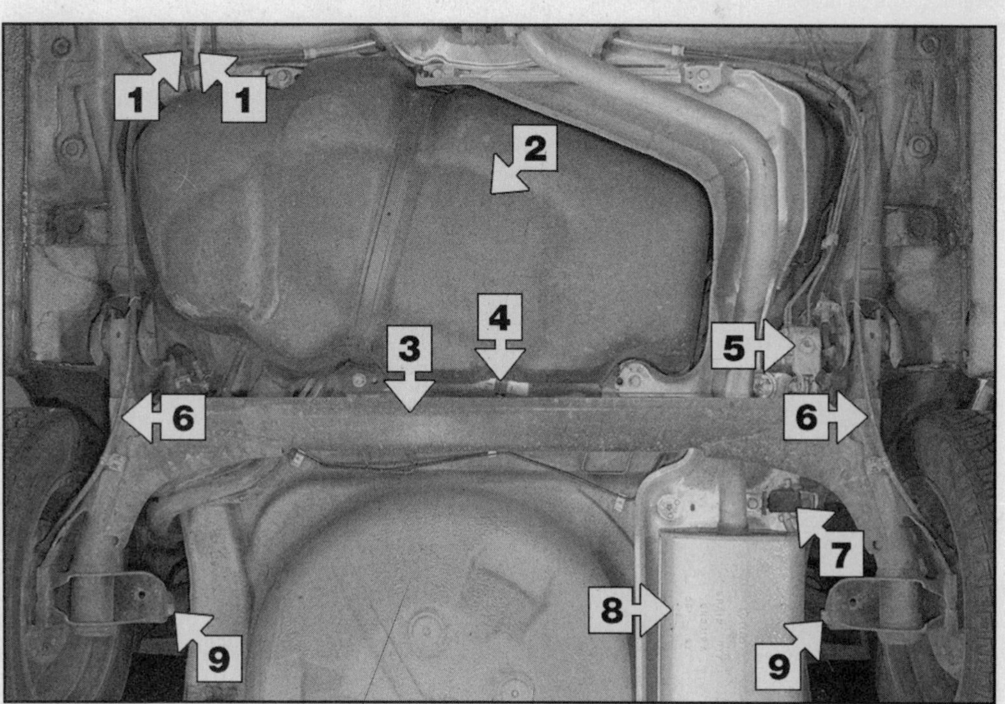

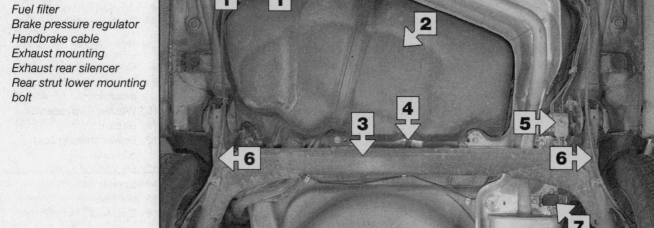

## 1 Introduction

### General information

This Chapter is designed to help the home mechanic maintain his/her vehicle for safety, economy, long life and peak performance.

The Chapter contains a master maintenance schedule, followed by Sections dealing specifically with each task in the schedule. Visual checks, adjustments, component renewal and other helpful items are included. Refer to the accompanying illustrations of the engine compartment and the underside of the vehicle for the locations of the various components.

Servicing your vehicle in accordance with the mileage/time maintenance schedule and the following Sections will provide a planned maintenance programme, which should result in a long and reliable service life. This is a comprehensive plan, so maintaining some items but not others at the specified service intervals, will not produce the same results.

As you service your vehicle, you will discover that many of the procedures can - and should - be grouped together, because of the particular procedure being performed, or because of the proximity of two otherwise unrelated components to one another. For example, if the vehicle is raised for any reason, the exhaust can be inspected at the same time as the suspension and steering components.

The first step in this maintenance programme is to prepare yourself before the actual work begins. Read through all the Sections relevant to the work to be carried out, then make a list and gather all the parts and tools required. If a problem is encountered, seek advice from a parts specialist, or a dealer service department.

### Service interval display

#### Up to 1998 model year

All VW Polo models are equipped with a service interval display indicator in the instrument panel. Every time the engine is started, the panel will illuminate for a few seconds, providing a handy reminder of when the next service is required:

*Display shows IN 00 - no service required.*
*Display shows OEL - 10 000 mile (15 000 km) service required.*
*Display shows IN 01 - 12 monthly service required.*
*Display shows IN 02 - 20 000 mile (30 000 km) service required.*

#### 1998 model year onwards

The service display on later models is similar to the earlier type, but the display is different:

*Display clear - no service required.*
*Display shows 'service OIL' - 10 000 mile (15 000 km) service required.*
*Display shows 'service INSP' - 12 monthly or 20 000 mile (30 000 km) service required.*
*Display shows 'service' when ignition is switched off - switch on ignition to determine which service is required.*

#### All models

The display should not necessarily be used as a definitive guide to the servicing needs of your Polo, but it is useful as a reminder, to ensure that servicing is not accidentally overlooked. Owners of older cars, or those covering a small annual mileage, may feel inclined to service their car more often, in which case the service interval display is perhaps less relevant.

The display should be reset whenever a service is carried out, and the procedure for this is described in Section 5.

## 2 Regular maintenance

**1** If, from the time the vehicle is new, the routine maintenance schedule is followed closely, and frequent checks are made of fluid levels and high-wear items, as suggested throughout this manual, the engine will be kept in relatively good running condition, and the need for additional work will be minimised.

**2** It is possible that there will be times when the engine is running poorly due to the lack of regular maintenance. This is even more likely if a used vehicle, which has not received regular and frequent maintenance checks, is purchased. In such cases, additional work may need to be carried out, outside of the regular maintenance intervals.

**3** If engine wear is suspected, a compression test (refer to the relevant Part of Chapter 2) will provide valuable information regarding the overall performance of the main internal components. Such a test can be used as a basis to decide on the extent of the work to be carried out. If, for example, a compression test indicates serious internal engine wear, conventional maintenance as described in this Chapter will not greatly improve the performance of the engine, and may prove a waste of time and money, unless extensive overhaul work is carried out first.

**4** The following series of operations are those most often required to improve the performance of a generally poor-running engine:

### Primary operations

*a) Clean, inspect and test the battery (See Weekly checks and Section 11, where applicable).*
*b) Check all the engine-related fluids (See Weekly checks).*
*c) Check the condition and tension of the auxiliary drivebelt (Section 23).*
*d) Renew the spark plugs (Section 21).*
*e) Inspect the distributor cap and rotor arm (see Chapter 5B).*
*f) Check the condition of the air filter, and renew if necessary (Section 26).*
*g) Check the fuel filter (Section 28).*
*h) Check the condition of all hoses, and check for fluid leaks (Section 12).*
*i) Check the exhaust gas emissions (Section 32).*

**5** If the above operations do not prove fully effective, carry out the following secondary operations:

### Secondary operations

All items listed under Primary operations, plus the following:

*a) Check the charging system (see Chapter 5A).*
*b) Check the ignition system (see Chapter 5B).*
*c) Check the fuel system (see relevant Part of Chapter 4).*
*d) Renew the distributor cap and rotor arm (see Chapter 5B).*
*e) Renew the ignition HT leads (see Chapter 5B)*

# Every 10 000 miles (15 000 km)

## 3 Engine oil and filter renewal

**1** Frequent oil and filter changes are the most important maintenance procedures which can be undertaken by the DIY owner. As engine oil ages, it becomes diluted and contaminated, which leads to premature engine wear. The oil change interval given in this Manual is the same as quoted by the manufacturer, but we recommend changing the oil and filter more frequently, perhaps every 5000 miles, or every 6 months. This is particularly relevant to owners of older vehicles (or those covering a small annual mileage).

**2** Before starting this procedure, gather all the necessary tools and materials. Also make sure that you have plenty of clean rags and newspapers handy, to mop up any spills. Ideally, the engine oil should be warm, as it will drain better, and more built-up sludge will be removed with it. Take care, however, not to touch the exhaust or any other hot parts of the engine when working under the vehicle. To avoid any possibility of scalding, and to protect yourself from possible skin irritants and other harmful contaminants in used engine oils, it is advisable to wear gloves when carrying out this work.

**3** Access to the underside of the vehicle will be greatly improved if it can be raised on a lift, driven onto ramps, or jacked up and supported on axle stands (see *Jacking and vehicle support*). Whichever method is chosen,

3.3 Noise insulation tray fastener locations (arrowed)

make sure that the vehicle remains level, or if it is at an angle, that the drain plug is at the lowest point. Where applicable, release the fasteners and remove the noise insulation tray from under the engine **(see illustration)**.

**4** Using a socket and handle or a ring spanner, slacken the drain plug (at the rear of the sump) about half a turn **(see illustration)**. Position the draining container under the drain plug, then remove the plug completely **(see Haynes Hint)**. Recover the sealing ring from the drain plug.

**5** Allow some time for the old oil to drain, noting that it may be necessary to reposition the container as the oil flow slows to a trickle.

**6** After all the oil has drained, wipe off the drain plug with a clean rag, and fit a new sealing washer. Clean the area around the drain plug opening, and refit the plug. Tighten the plug to the specified torque setting.

**7** Move the container into position under the oil filter, which is located on the front of the cylinder block.

**8** Using an oil filter removal tool if necessary, slacken the filter initially, then unscrew it by hand the rest of the way **(see illustration)**. Empty the oil in the filter into the container.

**9** Use a clean rag to remove all oil, dirt and sludge from the filter sealing area on the engine. Check the old filter to make sure that the rubber sealing ring has not stuck to the engine. If it has, carefully remove it.

**10** Apply a light coating of clean engine oil to the sealing ring on the new filter, then screw it into position on the engine. Tighten the filter firmly by hand only - **do not** use any tools.

**11** Remove the old oil and all tools from under the car, then lower the car to the ground (if applicable).

**12** Remove the dipstick, then unscrew the oil filler cap from the cylinder head cover. Fill the engine, using the correct grade and type of oil (see *Lubricants and fluids*). An oil can spout or funnel may help to reduce spillage. Pour in half the specified quantity of oil first, then wait a few minutes for the oil to fall to the sump **(see illustrations)**. Continue adding oil a small quantity at a time until the level is up to the bottom of the hatched area on the dipstick. Adding around 0.5 litres of oil will bring the level into the hatched area on the dipstick. Add a little more oil until the level is up to the top of the hatched area on the dipstick, then refit the dipstick and the filler cap.

**13** Start the engine and run it for a few minutes; check for leaks around the oil filter seal and the sump drain plug. Note that there may be a few seconds delay before the oil pressure warning light goes out when the engine is started, as the oil circulates through the engine oil galleries and the new oil filter before the pressure builds up.

**14** Switch off the engine, and wait a few minutes for the oil to settle in the sump once more. With the new oil circulated and the filter completely full, recheck the level on the dipstick, and add more oil as necessary. Refit the noise insulation tray to the underside of the engine, where applicable.

**15** Dispose of the used engine oil safely, with reference to *General repair procedures* in the *Reference* section of this manual.

HAYNES HiNT

***Keep the drain plug pressed into the sump while unscrewing it by hand last couple of turns. As the plug releases, move it away sharply so the stream of oil issuing from the sump runs into the container, not up your sleeve!***

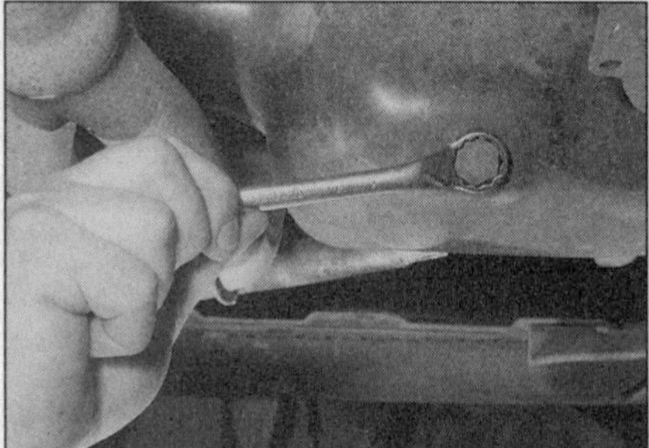

3.4 Slackening the sump drain plug

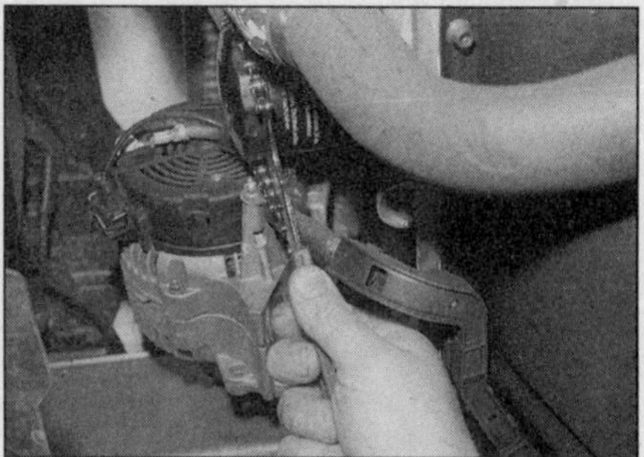

3.8 Loosening the oil filter using a chain-type removal tool

3.12a Remove the oil filler cap . . .

3.12b . . . then fill the engine using the correct grade and quantity of oil

## 4 Front brake pad check

1A

**1** Firmly apply the handbrake, loosen the front roadwheel bolts, then jack up the front of the car and support it securely on axle stands. Remove the front roadwheels.

**2** For a comprehensive check, the brake pads should be removed and cleaned. The operation of the caliper can then also be checked, and the condition of the brake disc itself can be fully examined on both sides. Refer to Chapter 9 **(see Haynes Hint)**.

**3** If any pad's friction material is worn to the specified thickness or less, *all four pads must be renewed as a set.*

HAYNES HiNT

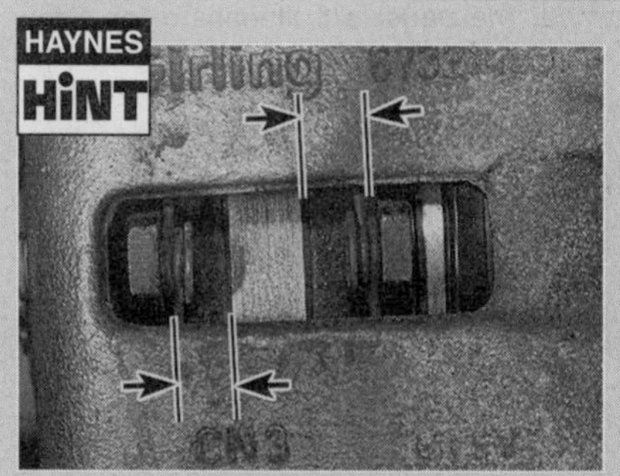

***For a quick check, the thickness of the friction material on each brake pad can be measured through the aperture in the caliper body***

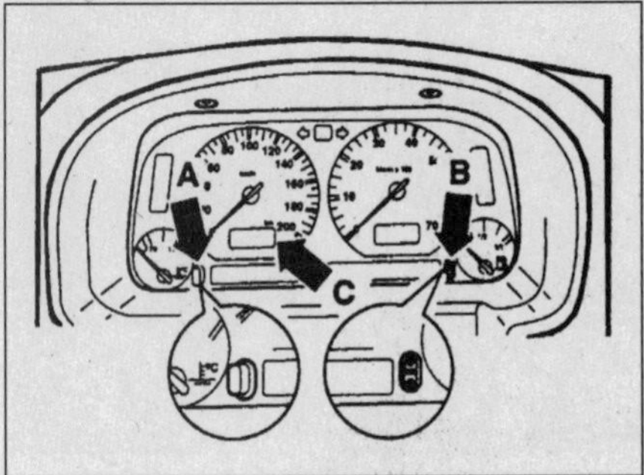


5.2 **Resetting the service interval display**

A *Service selector button (also trip meter selector button)*
B *Service reset button (also digital clock adjustment button)*
C *Service interval display*

## 5 Resetting service interval display

### Up to 1998 model year

**1** Before resetting the service interval display, make sure that the mileometer is displaying the total mileage, and is not in trip mode. Briefly pressing the button to the left of the speedometer will switch the display between total and trip. **Note:** *If the button is pressed and held for longer than one second while in trip mode, the trip meter will be zeroed.*
**2** Switch on the ignition (do not start the engine). Press and hold the button to the left of the speedometer **(see illustration)**.
**3** Switch off the ignition, then release the button. The display should read OEL.
**4** Now press the digital clock lower button on the right-hand side of the instrument panel until five dashes appear on the display. The OEL service is now reset.
**5** By pressing the left-hand button again, the next service interval can be displayed, and then reset by pressing the right-hand button.
**6** Reset as many services as necessary, until switching on the ignition only shows IN 00 (no service required) on the display.

### 1998 model year onwards

**7** The service interval display cannot be reset without special VW fault code reading equipment - refer to your VW dealer.

# Every 12 months

## 6 Lights and horn operation check

**1** With the ignition switched on where necessary, check the operation of all exterior lights.
**2** Check the brake lights with the help of an assistant, or by reversing up close to a reflective door. Make sure that all the rear lights are capable of operating independently, without affecting any of the other lights - for example, switch on as many rear lights as possible, then try the brake lights. If any unusual results are found, this is usually due to an earth fault or other poor connection at that rear light unit.
**3** Again with the help of an assistant or using a reflective surface, check as far as possible that the headlights work on both main and dipped beam.
**4** Replace any defective bulbs with reference to Chapter 12.

***Particularly on older vehicles, bulbs can stop working as a result of corrosion build-up on the bulb or its holder - fitting a new bulb may not cure the problem in this instance. When replacing any bulb, if you find any green or white-coloured powdery deposits, these should be cleaned off using emery cloth.***

**5** Check the operation of all interior lights, including the glovebox and luggage area illumination lights. Switch on the ignition, and check that all relevant warning lights come on as expected - the vehicle handbook should give details of these. Now start the engine, and check that the appropriate lights go out. When you are next driving at night, check that all the instrument panel and facia lighting works correctly. If any problems are found, refer to Chapter 12.
**6** Finally, choose an appropriate time of day to test the operation of the horn.

## 7 Airbag unit check

Where fitted, inspect the airbag(s) exterior condition checking for signs of damage or deterioration. If an airbag shows signs of obvious damage, it must be renewed (see Chapter 12).

## 8 Washer system(s) check

Check that each of the washer jet nozzles is clear, and that each nozzle provides a strong jet of washer fluid. The tailgate and headlight jets (where applicable) should be aimed to spray at a point slightly above the centre of the screen/headlight.

The windscreen washer nozzles have two jets; aim one of the jets slightly above the centre of the screen and the other just below, to ensure complete coverage of the screen. If necessary, adjust the jets using a pin.

Later models may be fitted with additional preset washer jets which only have a limited amount of adjustment. Height adjustment on these later jets is effected by turning an eccentric on the spray jet.

## 9 Hinge and lock lubrication

Lubricate the hinges of the bonnet, doors and tailgate with light general-purpose oil. Similarly, lubricate all latches, locks and lock strikers, and the door check straps with general-purpose oil or grease. At the same time, check the security and operation of all the locks, adjusting them if necessary (see Chapter 11).

Lightly lubricate the bonnet release mechanism and cable with suitable grease.

Do not attempt to lubricate the steering lock.

## 10 Engine management system fault code check

**1** This check is part of the manufacturer's maintenance schedule, and involves 'interrogating' the engine management control unit (and those for the automatic transmission and/or ABS, as applicable) using special dedicated test equipment. Such testing will allow the test equipment to read any fault codes stored in the electronic control unit memory.
**2** Unless a fault is suspected, this test is not essential, although it should be noted that it is recommended by the manufacturers.
**3** It is possible for quite serious faults to occur in the engine management system without the owner being aware of it. Certain engine management system faults will cause the system to enter an emergency back-up mode, which is often so sophisticated that engine performance is not apparently much affected. If a problem has caused the system to enter its back-up mode, this will usually be most apparent when starting and running from cold.

## 11 Battery electrolyte level check

***Warning: The electrolyte inside a battery is diluted acid - it is a good idea to wear suitable rubber gloves. When topping-up, don't overfill the cells so that the electrolyte overflows. In the event of any spillage, rinse the electrolyte off without delay. Refit the cell covers and rinse the battery with copious quantities of clean water. Don't attempt to siphon out any excess electrolyte.***

**1** Some models covered by this Manual may be fitted with a maintenance-free battery as standard equipment, or may have had one fitted as a replacement. If the battery in your vehicle is marked 'Freedom', 'Maintenance-Free' or similar, no electrolyte level checking is required (the battery is often completely sealed, preventing any topping-up).

**2** Batteries which do require their electrolyte level to be checked can be recognised by the presence of removable covers over the six battery cells - the battery casing is also sometimes translucent, so that the electrolyte level can be more easily checked. Make sure you do not have a maintenance-free battery before attempting to top up the electrolyte level.

**3** Remove the cell covers and either look down inside the battery to see the level web, or check the level using any markings provided on the battery casing. The electrolyte should at least cover the battery plates. If necessary, top up a little at a time with distilled (deionised) water until the level in all six cells is correct - don't fill the cells up to the brim. Wipe up any spillage, then refit the cell covers.

## 12 Hose and fluid leak check

**1** Visually inspect the engine joint faces, gaskets and seals for any signs of water or oil leaks. Pay particular attention to the areas around the camshaft cover, cylinder head, oil filter and sump joint faces. Bear in mind that, over a period of time, some very slight seepage from these areas is to be expected - what you are really looking for is any indication of a serious leak **(see Haynes Hint)**. Should a leak be found, renew the offending gasket or oil seal by referring to the appropriate Chapters in this manual.

**2** Also check the security and condition of all the engine-related pipes and hoses. Ensure that all cable-ties or securing clips are in place and in good condition. Clips that are broken or missing can lead to chafing of the hoses, pipes or wiring, which could cause more serious problems in the future.

**3** Carefully check the radiator hoses and heater hoses along their entire length. Renew any hose that is cracked, swollen or deteriorated. Cracks will show up better if the hose is squeezed. Pay close attention to the hose clips that secure the hoses to the cooling system components. Hose clips can pinch and puncture hoses, resulting in cooling system leaks.

**4** Inspect all the cooling system components (hoses, joint faces etc.) for leaks. A leak in the cooling system will usually show up as white- or rust-coloured deposits on the area adjoining the leak. Where any problems of this nature are found on system components, renew the component or gasket with reference to Chapter 3.

**5** Where applicable, inspect the automatic transmission fluid cooler hoses for leaks or deterioration.

**6** With the vehicle raised, inspect the fuel tank and filler neck for punctures, cracks and other damage. The connection between the filler neck and tank is especially critical. Sometimes a rubber filler neck or connecting hose will leak due to loose retaining clamps or deteriorated rubber.

**7** Carefully check all rubber hoses and metal fuel lines leading away from the fuel tank. Check for loose connections, deteriorated hoses, crimped lines, and other damage. Pay particular attention to the vent pipes and hoses, which often loop up around the filler neck and can become blocked or crimped. Follow the lines to the front of the vehicle, carefully inspecting them all the way. Renew damaged sections as necessary.

**8** From within the engine compartment, check the security of all fuel hose attachments and pipe unions, and inspect the fuel hoses and vacuum hoses for kinks, chafing and deterioration.

**9** Where applicable, check the condition of the power steering fluid hoses and pipes.

***A leak in the cooling system will usually show up as white- or rust-coloured deposits on the area adjoining the leak***

## 13 Transmission and driveshaft gaiter check

**1** Raise the front of the vehicle and support on axle stands. Alternatively, drive the car onto ramps.

**2** Inspect around the transmission for any sign of leaks or damage. In particular, check the area around the driveshaft oil/fluid seals for leakage **(see illustration)**. Slight seepage should not be of great concern, but a serious leak should be investigated further, with reference to the relevant Part of Chapter 7.

**3** Check the security and condition of the wiring and wiring plugs on the transmission housing **(see illustration)**.

**4** With the vehicle raised and securely supported on stands, turn the steering onto full lock, then slowly rotate the roadwheel. Inspect the condition of the outer constant velocity (CV) joint rubber gaiters, squeezing the gaiters to open out the folds. Check for signs of cracking, splits or deterioration of the rubber, which may allow the grease to escape, and lead to water and grit entry into the joint **(see illustration)**. Also check the security and condition of the retaining clips.

**13.2 Driveshaft inner CV joint, showing driveshaft seal (arrowed)**

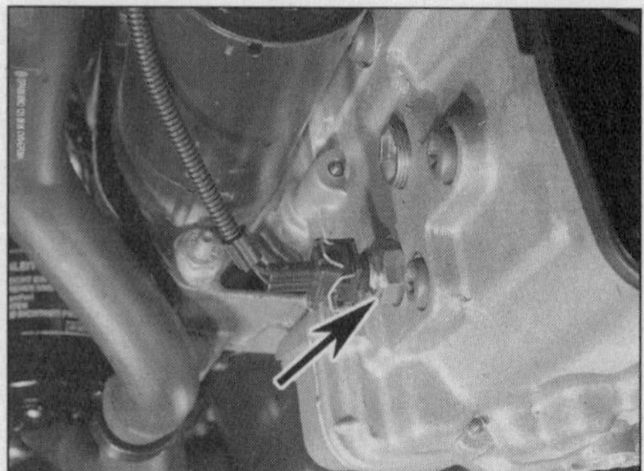

**13.3 Reversing light switch (arrowed) - seen from below**

**13.4 Check the condition of the driveshaft gaiters (arrowed)**

14.4 Rear brake flexible hose

Repeat these checks on the inner CV joints. If any damage or deterioration is found, the gaiters should be renewed (see Chapter 8).

**5** At the same time, check the general condition of the CV joints themselves by first holding the driveshaft and attempting to rotate the wheel. Repeat this check by holding the inner joint and attempting to rotate the driveshaft. Any appreciable movement indicates wear in the joints, wear in the driveshaft splines, or a loose driveshaft retaining nut.

## 14 Braking system check

**1** Starting under the bonnet, examine the brake fluid reservoir and master cylinder for leaks. When a brake fluid leak occurs, it is normal to find blistered or wrinkled paint in the area of the leak. Check the metal pipes from the master cylinder for damage, and check the brake pressure regulator, servo/ABS unit and fluid unions for leaks.

**2** With the vehicle raised and securely supported on stands, first inspect each front brake caliper. In particular, check the flexible hose leading to the caliper for signs of damage or leaks, especially where the hose enters the metal end fitting. Make sure that the hose is not twisted or kinked, and that it cannot come into contact with any other components when the steering is on full lock.

**3** From the caliper, trace the metal brake pipes back along the car. Again, look for leaks from the fluid unions or signs of damage, but

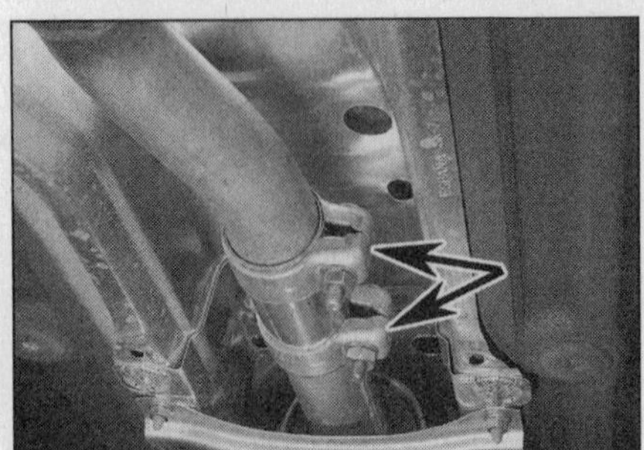

16.2 Typical exhaust system joint clamps (arrowed) - check that the nuts and bolts are tight, with no sign of leaks

15.2 Rear brake backplate inspection hole (arrowed) for assessing brake lining wear

additionally check the pipes for signs of corrosion. Make sure the pipes are securely located by the clips provided on the vehicle underside.

**4** At the rear of the vehicle, inspect each rear brake and its flexible hose, where applicable **(see illustration)**. Examine the handbrake cable, tracing it back from each rear brake and checking for frayed cables or other damage. Lubricate the handbrake cable guides, pivots and other moving parts with general-purpose grease.

**5** If any damage is found, refer to Chapter 9 for further information.

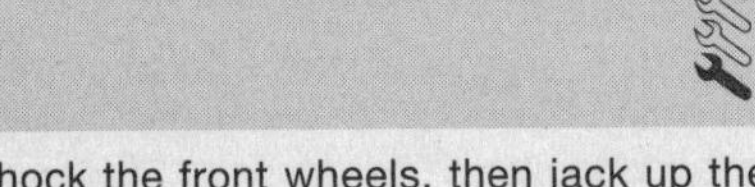

## 15 Rear brake shoe check

**1** Chock the front wheels, then jack up the rear of the vehicle, and support it securely on axle stands.

**2** For a quick check, the thickness of friction material remaining on one of the brake shoes can be observed through the holes in the trailing arm and the brake backplate. The hole in the brake backplate may be plugged with a sealing grommet, which can be prised out **(see illustration)**. If a rod of the same diameter as the specified minimum friction material thickness is placed against the shoe friction material, the amount of wear can be assessed. A torch or inspection light will probably be required, as well as a small mirror if access is difficult. If the friction material on any shoe is worn down to the specified minimum thickness or less, *all four shoes must be renewed as a set.*

**3** For a comprehensive check, the brake drum should be removed and cleaned. This will allow the wheel cylinders to be checked, and the condition of the brake drum itself to be fully examined (see Chapter 9).

17.4 Check for wear in the hub bearings by grasping the wheel and trying to rock it

## 16 Exhaust system check

**1** With the engine cold (at least an hour after the vehicle has been driven), check the complete exhaust system from the engine to the end of the tailpipe. The exhaust system is most easily checked with the vehicle raised on a hoist, or suitably supported on axle stands, so that the exhaust components are readily visible and accessible.

**2** Check the exhaust pipes and connections for evidence of leaks, severe corrosion and damage. Make sure that all brackets and mountings are in good condition, and that all relevant nuts and bolts are tight **(see illustration)**. Leakage at any of the joints or in other parts of the system will usually show up as a black sooty stain in the vicinity of the leak.

**3** Rattles and other noises can often be traced to the exhaust system, especially the brackets and mountings. Try to move the pipes and silencers. If the components are able to come into contact with the body or suspension parts, secure the system with new mountings. Otherwise separate the joints (if possible) and twist the pipes as necessary to provide additional clearance.

## 17 Steering and suspension check

### *Front suspension and steering check*

**1** Raise the front of the vehicle, and securely support it on axle stands. Where necessary for improved access, release the fasteners and remove the noise insulation tray from under the engine (where applicable).

**2** Visually inspect the balljoint dust covers and the steering rack-and-pinion gaiters for splits, chafing or deterioration. Any wear of these components will cause loss of lubricant, together with dirt and water entry, resulting in rapid deterioration of the balljoints or steering gear.

**3** On vehicles with power steering, check the fluid hoses for chafing or deterioration, and the pipe and hose unions for fluid leaks. Also check for signs of fluid leakage under pressure from the steering gear rubber gaiters, which would indicate failed fluid seals within the steering gear.

**4** Grasp the roadwheel at the 12 o'clock and 6 o'clock positions, and try to rock it **(see illustration)**. Very slight free play may be felt, but if the movement is appreciable, further investigation is necessary to determine the source. Continue rocking the wheel while an assistant depresses the footbrake. If the movement is now eliminated or significantly reduced, it is likely that the hub bearings are at fault. If the free play is still evident with the footbrake depressed, then there is wear in the suspension joints or mountings. Before condemning any components, however, check that the roadwheel bolts are tightened to the specified torque.

**5** Now grasp the wheel at the 9 o'clock and 3 o'clock positions, and try to rock it as before. Any movement felt now may again be caused by wear in the hub bearings or the steering track-rod balljoints. If the inner or outer balljoint is worn, the visual movement will be obvious.

**6** Using a large screwdriver or flat bar, check for wear in the suspension mounting bushes by levering between the relevant suspension component and its attachment point **(see illustration)**. Some movement is to be expected as the mountings are made of rubber, but excessive wear should be obvious. Also check the condition of any visible rubber bushes, looking for splits, cracks or contamination of the rubber.

**7** With the car standing on its wheels, have an assistant turn the steering wheel back and forth about an eighth of a turn each way. There should be very little, if any, lost movement between the steering wheel and roadwheels. If this is not the case, closely observe the joints and mountings previously described, but in addition, check the steering column universal joints for wear, and the rack-and-pinion steering gear itself.

### *Suspension strut/shock absorber check*

**8** Check for any signs of fluid leakage around the suspension strut/shock absorber body, or from the rubber gaiter around the piston rod. Should any fluid be noticed, the suspension strut/shock absorber is defective internally, and should be renewed. **Note:** *Suspension struts/shock absorbers should always be renewed in pairs on the same axle.*

**9** The efficiency of the suspension strut/shock absorber may be checked by bouncing the vehicle at each corner. Generally speaking, the body will return to its normal position and stop after being depressed. If it rises and returns on a rebound, the suspension strut/shock absorber is probably suspect. Examine also the suspension strut/shock absorber upper and lower mountings for any signs of wear.

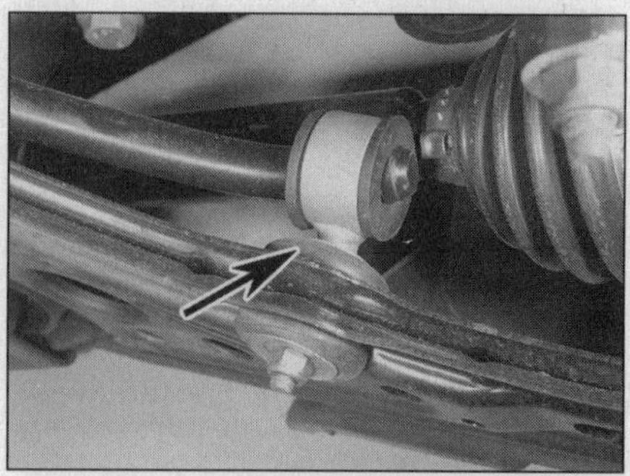

**17.6 Anti-roll bar mounting bushes (arrowed) - only on 1.6 litre models**

## 18 Headlight beam alignment check

Accurate adjustment of the headlight beam is only possible using optical beam-setting equipment, and this work should therefore be carried out by a VW dealer or service station with the necessary facilities. Headlight alignment is checked as part of the MoT test.

Basic adjustments can be carried out in an emergency, and further details are given in Chapter 12.

## 19 Road test

### *Instruments and electrical equipment*

**1** Check the operation of all instruments and electrical equipment.

**2** Make sure that all instruments read correctly, and switch on all electrical equipment in turn, to check that it functions properly.

### *Steering and suspension*

**3** Check for any abnormalities in the steering, suspension, handling or road feel.

**4** Drive the vehicle, and check that there are no unusual vibrations or noises.

**5** Check that the steering feels positive, with no excessive sloppiness, or roughness, and check for any suspension noises when cornering and driving over bumps.

### *Drivetrain*

**6** Check the performance of the engine, clutch (where applicable), transmission and driveshafts.

**7** Listen for any unusual noises from the engine, clutch and transmission.

**8** Make sure the engine runs smoothly at idle, and there is no hesitation on accelerating.

**9** Check that, where applicable, the clutch action is smooth and progressive, that the drive is taken up smoothly, and that the pedal travel is not excessive. Also listen for any noises when the clutch pedal is depressed.

**10** On manual transmission models, check that all gears can be engaged smoothly without noise, and that the gear lever action is not abnormally vague or notchy.

**11** On automatic transmission models, make sure that all gearchanges occur smoothly, without snatching, and without an increase in engine speed between changes. Check that all the gear positions can be selected with the vehicle at rest. If any problems are found, they should be referred to a VW dealer.

**12** Listen for a metallic clicking sound from the front of the vehicle, as the vehicle is driven slowly in a circle with the steering on full-lock. Carry out this check in both directions. If a clicking noise is heard, this indicates wear in a driveshaft joint, in which case renew the joint if necessary.

### *Braking system*



**13** Make sure that the vehicle does not pull to one side when braking, and that the wheels do not lock prematurely when braking hard.

**14** Check that there is no vibration through the steering when braking.

**15** Check that the handbrake operates correctly without excessive movement of the lever, and that it holds the vehicle stationary on a slope.

**16** Test the operation of the brake servo unit as follows. With the engine off, depress the footbrake four or five times to exhaust the vacuum. Hold the brake pedal depressed, then start the engine. As the engine starts, there should be a noticeable give in the brake pedal as vacuum builds up. Allow the engine to run for at least two minutes, and then switch it off. If the brake pedal is depressed now, it should be possible to detect a hiss from the servo as the pedal is depressed. After about four or five applications, no further hissing should be heard, and the pedal should feel considerably harder.

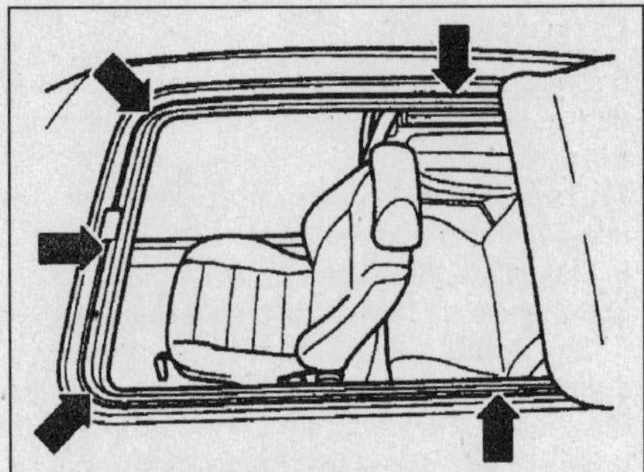

20.1 Folding fabric sunroof guide rail (arrowed)

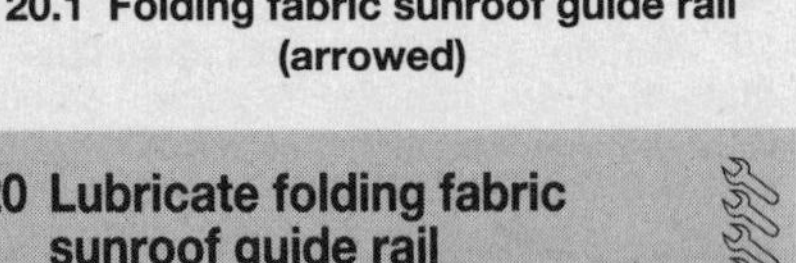

## 20 Lubricate folding fabric sunroof guide rail

**1** Using a clean cloth and a suitable solvent if necessary, thoroughly clean the sunroof guide rail **(see illustration)**.

**2** Apply a little general-purpose grease to the guide rail, then check the sunroof operation.

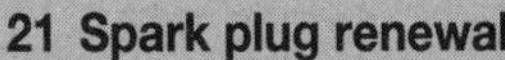

## 21 Spark plug renewal

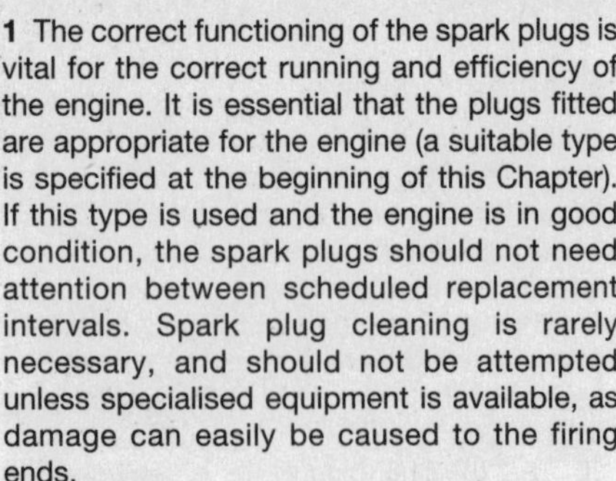

**1** The correct functioning of the spark plugs is vital for the correct running and efficiency of the engine. It is essential that the plugs fitted are appropriate for the engine (a suitable type is specified at the beginning of this Chapter). If this type is used and the engine is in good condition, the spark plugs should not need attention between scheduled replacement intervals. Spark plug cleaning is rarely necessary, and should not be attempted unless specialised equipment is available, as damage can easily be caused to the firing ends.

**2** Before removing the spark plugs, allow the engine time to cool.

**3** To gain access to the spark plugs, refer to Chapter 4A or 4B as applicable, and remove the air filter housing. On some models, it may also be necessary to unclip the accelerator cable.

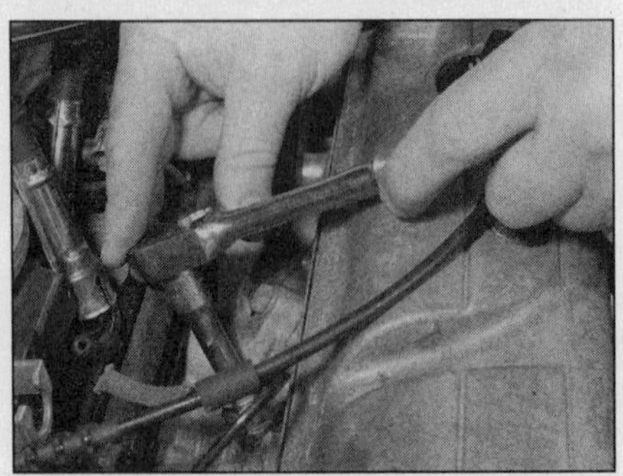

21.7a Unscrew the spark plugs using a suitable socket . . .

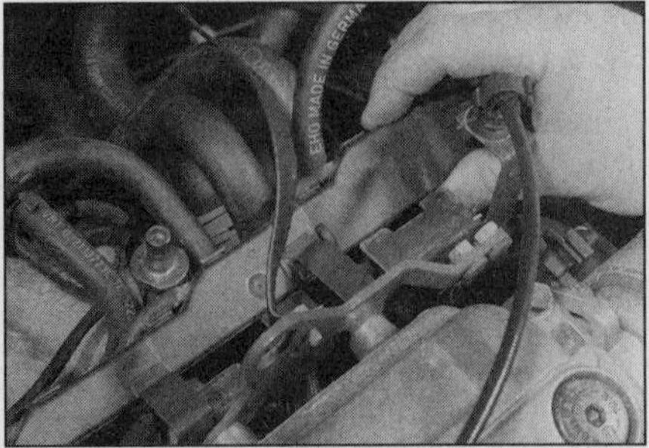

21.4 Pull the HT lead clip out of the retaining brackets on the rear of the cylinder head

**4** Pull the HT lead clip out of the retaining brackets on the rear of the cylinder head, and move the leads back out of the way **(see illustration)**.

**5** If the marks on the original-equipment spark plug (HT) leads cannot be seen, mark the leads 1 to 4, to correspond to the cylinder the lead serves (No 1 cylinder is at the timing belt end of the engine). Where metal heat shields are fitted to the lead end fittings, take care not to burn your hands if the engine is still warm. Pull the leads from the plugs by gripping the end fitting, not the lead, otherwise the lead connection may be fractured **(see illustration)**.

**6** It is advisable to remove the dirt from the spark plug recesses using a clean brush, vacuum cleaner or compressed air before removing the plugs, to prevent dirt dropping into the cylinders.

**7** Unscrew the plugs using a spark plug spanner, suitable box spanner or a deep socket and extension bar **(see illustrations)**. Keep the socket aligned with the spark plug - if it is forcibly moved to one side, the ceramic insulator may be broken off. As each plug is removed, examine it as follows.

**8** Examination of the spark plugs will give a good indication of the condition of the engine. If the insulator nose of the spark plug is clean and white, with no deposits, this is indicative of a weak mixture or too hot a plug (a hot plug transfers heat away from the electrode slowly, a cold plug transfers heat away quickly).

**9** If the tip and insulator nose are covered with hard black-looking deposits, then this is indicative that the mixture is too rich. Should the plug be black and oily, then it is likely that the engine is fairly worn, as well as the mixture being too rich.

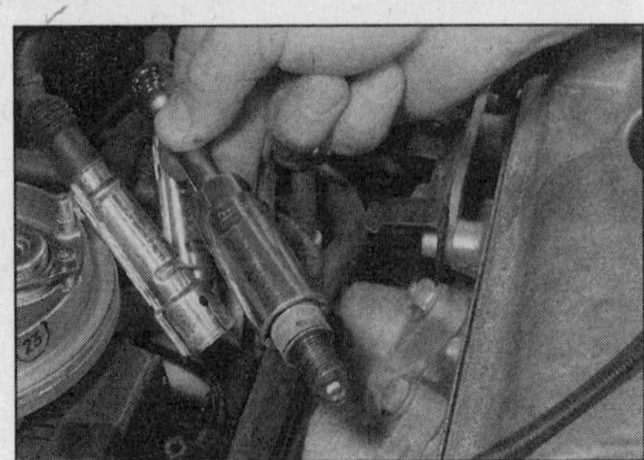

21.7b . . . and remove them from the cylinder head - note multi-earth-electrode spark plug

21.5 Pull the HT lead end fittings off the plugs

**10** If the insulator nose is covered with light tan to greyish-brown deposits, then the mixture is correct and it is likely that the engine is in good condition.

**11** The spark plug electrode gap is of considerable importance as, if it is too large or too small, the size of the spark and its efficiency will be seriously impaired. **Note:** *Spark plugs with multiple earth electrodes are becoming an increasingly common fitment, especially to vehicles equipped with catalytic converters. Unless there is clear information to the contrary, no attempt should be made to adjust the plug gap on a spark plug with more than one earth electrode.*

**12** To set the gap, measure it with a feeler blade and then bend open, or closed, the outer plug electrode until the correct gap is achieved. The centre electrode should never be bent, as this may crack the insulator and cause plug failure, if nothing worse. If using feeler blades, the gap is correct when the appropriate-size blade is a firm sliding fit.

**13** Special spark plug electrode gap adjusting tools are available from most motor accessory shops, or from some spark plug manufacturers.

**14** Before fitting the spark plugs, check that the threaded connector sleeves are tight, and that the plug exterior surfaces and threads are clean. It's often difficult to screw in new spark plugs without cross-threading them - this can be avoided using a piece of rubber hose **(see Haynes Hint)**.

**15** Remove the rubber hose (if used), and tighten the plug to the specified torque using the spark plug socket and a torque wrench. If a torque wrench is not available, tighten the plug by hand until it just seats, then tighten it by no more than a quarter of a turn further with the plug socket and handle. Refit the remaining spark plugs in the same manner.

**16** Clip the HT leads back into the support clip on the rear of the cylinder head, then connect the leads securely in their correct order.

***It is very often difficult to insert spark plugs into their holes without cross-threading them. To avoid this possibility, fit a short length of 5/16 inch internal diameter rubber hose over the end of the spark plug. The flexible hose acts as a universal joint to help align the plug with the plug hole. Should the plug begin to cross-thread, the hose will slip on the spark plug, preventing thread damage to the aluminium cylinder head***

**17** Refer to Chapter 4 and refit the air filter housing.

## 22 Pollen filter renewal

**1** The pollen filter is located beneath the windscreen cowl panels; it is located on the left side on right-hand-drive models, and the right side on left-hand drive models.

**2** Open the bonnet, and lift up the rubber weatherstrip from the relevant end of the top of the engine compartment bulkhead **(see illustration)**.

**3** Peel back the rubber seal at the base of the windscreen, for access to the two cowl panel retaining clips **(see illustration)**. Take care when prising these clips out of position, as they are easily broken.

**4** Remove the cowl panel from the car **(see illustration)**.

**5** Unclip the filter air deflector and remove it **(see illustration)**.

**6** Release the two clips at the front to release the frame, and lift the pollen filter and frame upwards and out from its location **(see illustrations)**. Note which way round the frame is fitted.

**7** Separate the frame from the old filter, noting how it is fitted **(see illustrations)**. Slot the new filter into the frame.

**8** Wipe clean the filter housing, then fit the new filter and frame. Clip the filter securely in position and refit the air deflector and cowl panel.

**9** Refit the rubber seal to the engine compartment bulkhead to complete.

**22.2 Pull off the rubber weatherstrip from the top of the bulkhead**

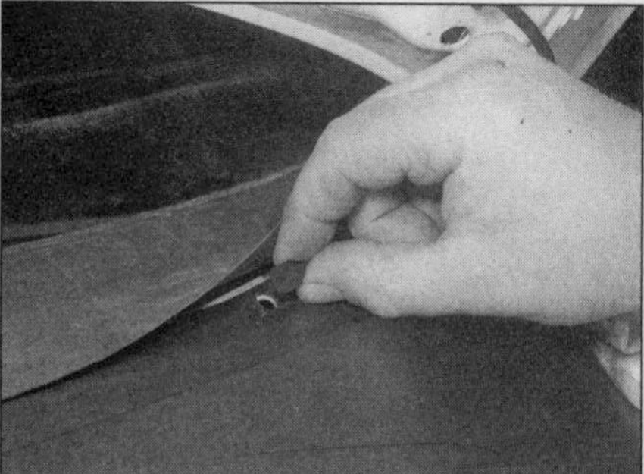

**22.3 Peel back the rubber seal for access to the cowl panel retaining clips**

**22.4 Lifting out the cowl panel**

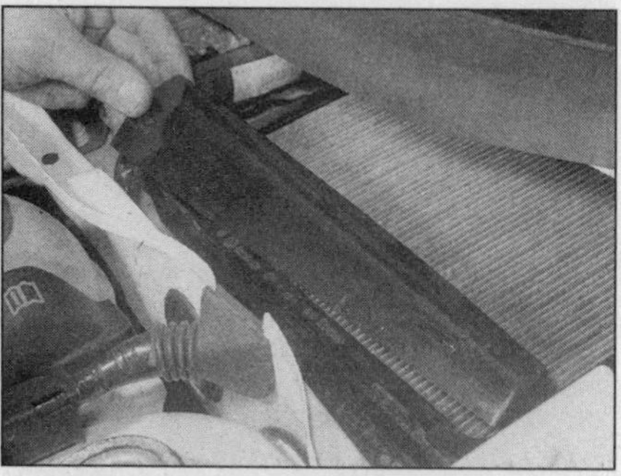

**22.5 Removing the pollen filter air deflector plate**

**22.6a Release the retaining clips at the front . . .**

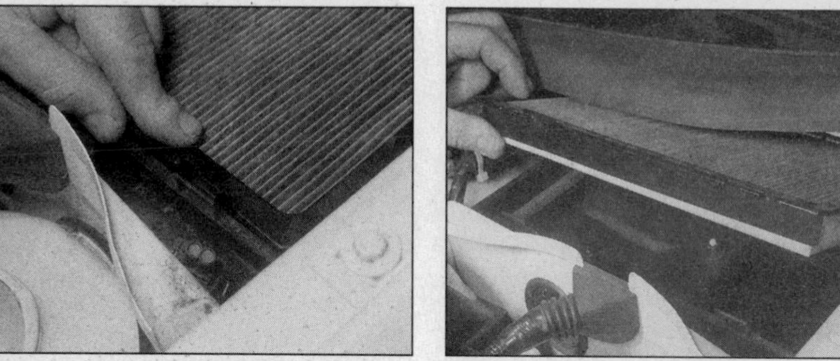

**22.6b . . . then remove the pollen filter and frame**

**22.7a Separating the pollen filter from the frame**

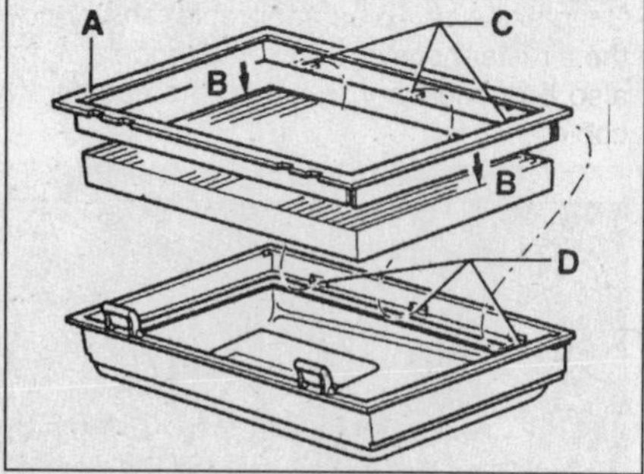


**22.7b Pollen filter, frame and filter housing**

*A Filter frame*
*B Frame fits into first fold of filter at each end*
*C Frame lugs*
*D Frame lug recesses in housing*

1A

24.2 Transmission oil filler/level plug (arrowed) - models up to October 1995

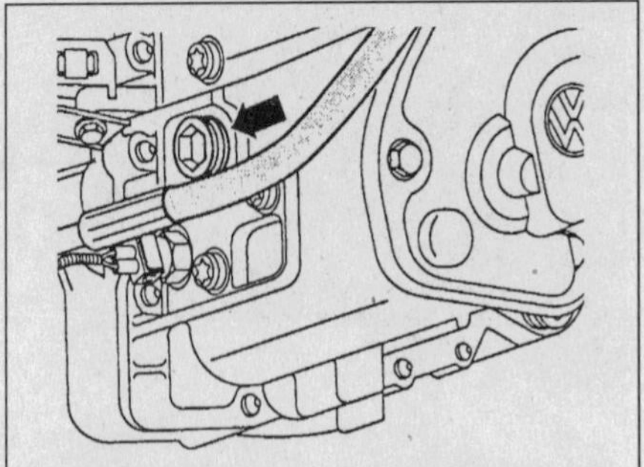
24.3 Transmission oil filler/level plug (arrowed) - models from October 1995

## 23 Auxiliary drivebelt check and renewal

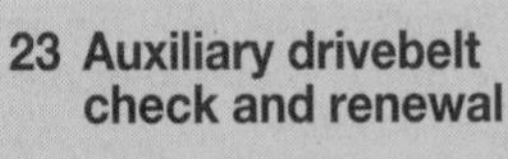

### Checking

**1** Disconnect the battery negative lead and position it away from the terminal. **Note:** *If the vehicle has a security-coded radio, check that you have a copy of the code number before disconnecting the battery. Refer to your VW dealer if in doubt.*

**2** Park the vehicle on a level surface, apply the handbrake and chock the rear wheels. Loosen the right-hand front wheel bolts.

**3** Raise the front of the vehicle, rest it securely on axle stands and remove the right-hand front roadwheel.

**4** Turn the steering to full right-hand lock. Where applicable, remove the fasteners, and lower the wheel arch liner and/or noise insulation tray for access to the drivebelt. Models with power steering may have a cover fitted over the drivebelt - if so, release the fasteners and remove it.

**5** Using a socket and wrench on the crankshaft sprocket bolt, rotate the crankshaft so that the full length of the auxiliary drivebelt can be examined. Look for cracks, splitting and fraying on the surface of the belt; check also for signs of glazing (shiny patches) and separation of the belt plies. If damage or wear is visible, the belt should be renewed. If there is any evidence of contamination by oil, grease or coolant, the reason should be investigated without delay.

**6** Check the drivebelt tension by pressing on the belt at a point midway between two pulleys. Depending on the type of belt, it should move by approximately 5 to 10 mm. If the drivebelt appears excessively taut or slack, refer to Chapter 2A and adjust the belt tension.

**7** On completion, refit the wheel arch liner and noise insulation tray (as applicable), then refit the roadwheel and lower the car to the ground. Tighten the roadwheel bolts to the specified torque.

### Renewal

**8** For details of auxiliary drivebelt renewal, refer to Chapter 2A.

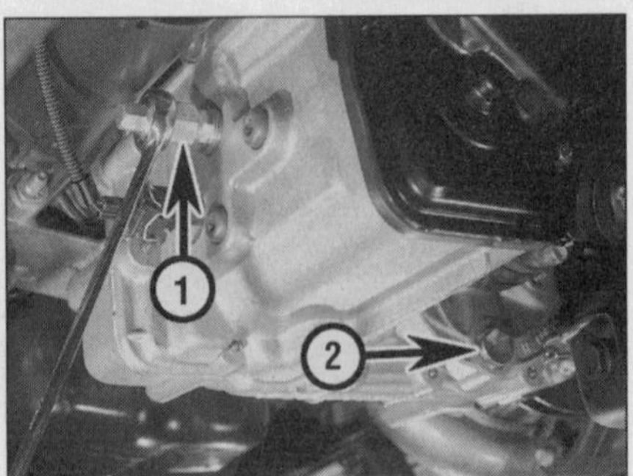

24.4 Loosening the filler/level plug (1) using a hex adapter - also shown is the transmission oil drain plug (2)

## 24 Manual transmission oil level check

**1** Park the car on a level surface. The oil level must be checked before the car is driven, or at least 5 minutes after the engine has been switched off. If the oil is checked immediately after driving the car, some of the oil will remain distributed around the transmission components, resulting in an inaccurate level reading.

**2** On models built up to October 1995, the filler/level plug is located on the left-hand side of the transmission housing, next to the driveshaft **(see illustration)**. For easier access, turn the steering onto full left lock. Do not raise the car, because the level must be checked with the car resting on its wheels, on a level surface.

**3** On models built after October 1995, the filler/level plug is on the front of the transmission housing, and can be accessed from above **(see illustration)**. If preferred, however, the plug can be reached from below, but note that this may mean removing the noise insulation tray (where applicable) from under the engine for access.

**4** Wipe clean the area around the filler/level plug. A 17 mm hexagonal adapter (or a large Allen key) will be required to remove the plug, which will probably be quite tight **(see illustration)**.

**5** The oil level should reach the lower edge of the filler/level hole. A certain amount of oil will have gathered behind the filler/level plug, and will trickle out when it is removed; this does **not** necessarily indicate that the level is correct. To ensure that a true level is established, wait until the initial trickle has stopped, then add oil through the hole as necessary until a trickle of new oil can be seen emerging. The level will be correct when the flow ceases; use only good-quality oil of the specified type.

**6** Filling the transmission with oil is an extremely awkward operation; above all, allow plenty of time for the oil level to settle properly before checking it. If a large amount is added to the transmission, and a large amount flows out on checking the level, refit the filler/level plug; take the vehicle on a short journey so that the new oil is distributed fully around the transmission components, then recheck the level when it has settled again.

**7** If the transmission has been overfilled so that oil flows out when the filler/level plug is removed, check that the car is completely level (front-to-rear and side-to-side), and allow the surplus to drain off into a suitable container.

**8** When the level is correct, refit the plug, tightening it to the specified torque, and wipe off any spilt oil.

## 25 Underbody protection check

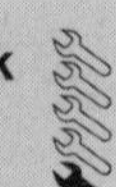

Raise and support the vehicle on axle stands. Using an electric torch or lead light, inspect the entire underside of the vehicle, paying particular attention to the wheel arches. Look for any damage to the flexible underbody coating, which may crack or flake off with age, leading to corrosion. Also check that the wheel arch liners are securely attached with any clips provided - if they come loose, dirt may get in behind the liners and defeat their purpose. If there is any damage to the underseal, or any corrosion, it should be repaired before the damage gets too serious.

## 26 Air filter renewal

### Single-point injection models

**1** Lift up the catches to release the over-centre wire clips around the air cleaner housing, then lift off the top cover. Where applicable, unclip the vacuum hose from the top cover **(see illustrations)**.

### Multi-point injection models

**2** Unscrew and remove the eight screws securing the air cleaner top cover. The screws are of different lengths, so note their locations

**26.1a Release the air filter cover clips . . .**

as they are removed. Depending on model, it may be necessary to pull the housing forwards to allow the top cover to be lifted off **(see illustrations)**.

### *All models*

**3** Lift out the filter element **(see illustration)**.

**4** Remove any debris that may have collected inside the air cleaner.

**5** Fit a new air filter element in position, noting any direction-of-fitting markings and ensuring that the edges are securely seated.

**6** Refit the air cleaner top cover and secure with the screws or clips, as applicable.

## 27 Automatic transmission fluid level check

Checking the fluid level by the DIY mechanic is not advisable; no dipstick is provided. The transmission is regarded as being 'filled for life'. Fluid level checking requires the use of dedicated VW test equipment, and an involved procedure requiring accurate measurement of fluid temperature. In view of this, the car must be taken to a VW dealer for the fluid level to be checked.

**26.2a Unscrew the cover retaining screws . . .**

**26.2b . . . then pull the housing forwards and lift off the cover**

**26.1b . . . then lift off the cover and unclip the vacuum hose (arrowed)**

## 28 Fuel filter renewal

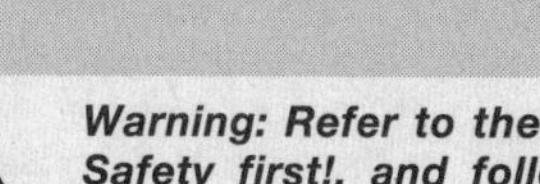

***Warning: Refer to the notes in Safety first!, and follow them implicitly. Petrol is a highly-dangerous and volatile liquid, and the precautions necessary when handling it cannot be overstressed.***

**1** The fuel filter is situated underneath the rear of the vehicle, to the rear of the fuel tank **(see illustration)**. To gain access to the filter, chock the front wheels, then jack up the rear of the vehicle and support it securely on axle stands.

**2** Depressurise the fuel system with reference to the relevant Part of Chapter 4.

**3** If you have them, fit hose clamps to the filter inlet and outlet hoses. These are not essential, but even with the system depressurised, there will still be an amount of petrol in the pipes (and the old filter), and this will siphon out when the pipes are disconnected. Even with hose clamps fitted, the old filter will contain some fuel, so have some rags ready to soak up any spillage.

**26.3 Removing the air filter element - single-point injection model shown**

**4** Release the hose clips and detach the hoses from the filter. If crimp-type clips are used, discard them and fit proper petrol pipe clips when reassembling. Similarly, if the fuel hoses show any sign of perishing or cracking, particularly at the hose ends or where the hose enters the metal end fitting, renew the hoses.

**5** Before removing the filter, note any direction-of-flow markings on the filter body, and check against the new filter - the arrow should point in the direction of fuel flow (towards the black fuel supply pipe leading to the front of the car).

**6** Undo the retaining clamp screw and remove the old filter.

**7** Fit the new filter into position, with the flow marking arrow correctly orientated, and secure with the retaining clamp.

**8** Reconnect the fuel hoses using new clips if necessary. Ensure that no dirt is allowed to enter the hoses or filter connections. Release the hose clamps.

**9** Start the engine (there may be a delay as the system re-pressurises and the new filter fills with fuel). Let the engine run for several minutes while you check the filter hose connections for leaks.

**10** Where applicable, fit the protective undershield and secure with the retaining clips, then lower the vehicle to the ground.

***Warning: Dispose safely of the old filter; it will be highly flammable, and may explode if thrown on a fire.***

1A

## 29 Timing belt renewal

**Note:** *VW specify a timing belt renewal interval of 60 000 miles (90 000 km). However, if the vehicle is used mainly for short journeys or a lot of stop-start driving, we recommend that this shorter interval is adhered to. The actual belt renewal interval is very much up to the individual owner but, bearing in mind that severe engine damage will result if the belt breaks in use, we recommend you err on the side of caution.*

Refer to Chapter 2A.

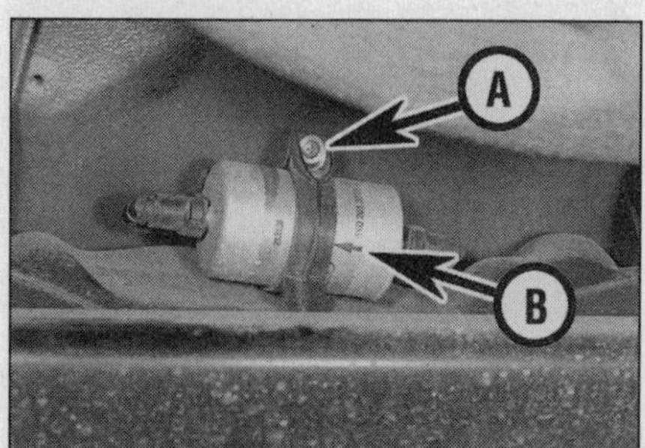


**28.1 Fuel filter location - note retaining clamp screw (A) and direction-of-flow arrow (B)**

## 30 Coolant renewal

**Note:** *VW coolant type G11 or G12 lasts indefinitely. Provided you are sure that this type of coolant has been used and that the concentration is adequate, there is no need to renew it. Most other brands of antifreeze must be renewed every two years. Once the system has been drained, it is as well to flush it and to take the opportunity to renew any rubber hoses whose condition is in doubt. Proceed as follows.*

### Cooling system draining

**Warning: Wait until the engine is cold before starting this procedure. Do not allow antifreeze to come in contact with your skin, or with the painted surfaces of the vehicle. Rinse off spills immediately with plenty of water. Never leave antifreeze lying around in an open container, or in a puddle in the driveway or on the garage floor. Children and pets are attracted by its sweet smell, but antifreeze can be fatal if ingested.**

**1** With the engine completely cold, cover the expansion tank cap with a wad of rag, and slowly turn the cap anti-clockwise to relieve the pressure in the cooling system (a hissing sound will normally be heard). Wait until any pressure remaining in the system is released, then continue to turn the cap until it can be removed.

**2** Where necessary, release the fasteners and remove the noise insulation tray from under the engine. Position a suitable container beneath the radiator bottom hose connection, then release the retaining clip and ease the hose from the radiator stub. If the hose joint has not been disturbed for some time, it will be necessary to gently manipulate the hose to break the joint. Do not use excessive force, or the radiator stub could be damaged. Allow the coolant to drain into the container.

**3** If the coolant has been drained for a reason other than renewal, then provided it is clean and less than two years old, it can be re-used, though this is not recommended (see *Antifreeze type and mixture* later in this Section).

**4** Once all the coolant has drained, reconnect the hose to the radiator and secure it in position with the retaining clip.

### Cooling system flushing

**5** If coolant renewal has been neglected, or if the antifreeze mixture has become diluted, then in time, the cooling system may gradually lose efficiency, as the coolant passages become restricted due to rust, scale deposits, and other sediment. Flushing the system clean can restore the cooling system efficiency.

**6** The radiator should be flushed independently of the engine, to avoid unnecessary contamination.

#### Radiator flushing

**7** To flush the radiator, disconnect the top and bottom hoses and any other relevant hoses from the radiator, with reference to Chapter 3.

**8** Insert a garden hose into the radiator top inlet. Direct a flow of clean water through the radiator, and continue flushing until clean water emerges from the radiator bottom outlet.

**9** If after a reasonable period, the water still does not run clear, the radiator can be flushed with a good proprietary cooling system cleaning agent. It is important that their manufacturer's instructions are followed carefully. If the contamination is particularly bad, insert the hose in the radiator bottom outlet, and reverse-flush the radiator.

#### Engine flushing

**10** To flush the engine, remove the thermostat as described in Chapter 3, then temporarily refit the thermostat cover.

**11** With the top and bottom hoses disconnected from the radiator, insert a garden hose into the radiator top hose. Direct a clean flow of water through the engine, and continue flushing until clean water emerges from the radiator bottom hose.

**12** On completion of flushing, refit the thermostat and reconnect the hoses with reference to Chapter 3.

### Cooling system filling

**13** Before attempting to fill the cooling system, make sure that all hoses and clips are in good condition, and that the clips are tight. Note that an antifreeze mixture must be used all year round, to prevent corrosion of the engine components (see following sub-Section).

**14** Remove the expansion tank filler cap, and fill the system by slowly pouring the coolant into the expansion tank to prevent airlocks from forming.

**15** If the coolant is being renewed, begin by pouring in a couple of litres of water, followed by the correct quantity of antifreeze, then top-up with more water.

**16** Once the level in the expansion tank starts to rise, squeeze the radiator top and bottom hoses to help expel any trapped air in the system. Once all the air is expelled, top-up the coolant level to the MAX mark and refit the expansion tank cap.

**17** Start the engine and run it until it reaches normal operating temperature, then stop the engine and allow it to cool.

**18** Check for leaks, particularly around disturbed components. Check the coolant level in the expansion tank, and top-up if necessary. Note that the system must be cold before an accurate level is indicated in the expansion tank. If the expansion tank cap is removed while the engine is still warm, cover the cap with a thick cloth, and unscrew the cap slowly to gradually relieve the system pressure (a hissing sound will normally be heard). Wait until any pressure remaining in the system is released, then continue to turn the cap until it can be removed.

### Antifreeze type and mixture

**19** The antifreeze should always be renewed at the specified intervals. This is necessary not only to maintain the antifreeze properties, but also to prevent corrosion which would otherwise occur as the corrosion inhibitors become progressively less effective.

**20** Always use ethylene-glycol-based antifreeze suitable for use in mixed-metal cooling systems. The quantity of antifreeze and levels of protection are indicated in the Specifications.

**21** When the car was new, the cooling system will have been filled with either VW G11 (blue colour) or VW G12 (red colour) coolant. At the time of writing, the manufacturer's advice on coolant is as follows:

a) *On no account should the blue G11 coolant be mixed with the red G12 coolant. Thus, if the cooling system was originally filled with G11, ensure that the system is completely drained and the cylinder block flushed before refilling.*
b) *When refilling, the later G12 coolant should be used on all engines.*
c) *In particular, engines with an aluminium cylinder block (engine codes AER and ALL) must be filled only with G12 coolant.*

**22** Before adding antifreeze, the cooling system should be completely drained, preferably flushed, and all hoses checked for condition and security.

**23** After filling with antifreeze, a label should be attached to the expansion tank, stating the type and concentration of antifreeze used, and the date installed. Any subsequent topping-up should be made with the same type and concentration of antifreeze.

**24** Do not use engine antifreeze in the washer system, as it will cause damage to the vehicle paintwork.

## 31 Brake fluid renewal

**Warning: Brake hydraulic fluid can harm your eyes and damage painted surfaces, so use extreme caution when handling and pouring it. Do not use fluid that has been standing open for some time, as it absorbs moisture from the air. Excess moisture can cause a dangerous loss of braking effectiveness.**

1 The procedure is similar to that for the bleeding of the hydraulic system as described in Chapter 9. The brake fluid reservoir should be emptied by siphoning, using a clean poultry baster or similar before starting, and allowance should be made for the old fluid to be expelled when bleeding a section of the circuit.
2 Working as described in Chapter 9, open the first bleed screw in the sequence, and pump the brake pedal gently until nearly all the old fluid has been emptied from the master cylinder reservoir.

***Old hydraulic fluid is often much darker in colour than the new, making it easy to distinguish the two.***

3 Top-up to the MAX level with new fluid, and continue pumping until only the new fluid remains in the reservoir, and new fluid can be seen emerging from the bleed screw. Tighten the screw, and top the reservoir level up to the MAX level line.
4 Work through all the remaining bleed screws in the sequence until new fluid can be seen at all of them. Be careful to keep the master cylinder reservoir topped-up to above the MIN level at all times, or air may enter the system and greatly increase the length of the task.
5 When the operation is complete, check that all bleed screws are securely tightened, and that their dust caps are refitted. Wash off all traces of spilt fluid, and recheck the fluid level.
6 Check the operation of the brakes before taking the car on the road.

## 32 Exhaust emissions check

This check is part of the manufacturer's maintenance schedule, and involves testing the exhaust emissions using an exhaust gas analyser. Unless a fault is suspected, this test is not essential, although it should be noted that it is recommended by the manufacturers. In the majority of cases, adjusting the idle speed and mixture is either not possible, or requires access to dedicated VW test equipment. Exhaust emissions testing is included as part of the MoT test.

# Chapter 1 Part B:
# Routine maintenance & servicing - diesel models

## Contents





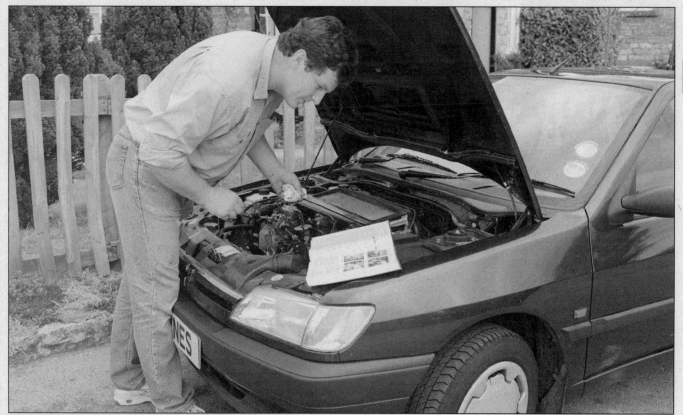

## Degrees of difficulty

**Easy,** suitable for novice with little experience 

**Fairly easy,** suitable for beginner with some experience 

**Fairly difficult,** suitable for competent DIY mechanic

**Difficult,** suitable for experienced DIY mechanic 

**Very difficult,** suitable for expert DIY or professional

# Servicing specifications - diesel models

## Lubricants and fluids
Refer to end of *Weekly checks*

## Capacities

**Engine oil (including filter)**

| | |
|---|---|
| All engines | 5.0 litres |

**Cooling system (approximate)**

| | |
|---|---|
| All engines | 6.5 litres |

**Transmission**

| | |
|---|---|
| Filler/level plug on side of transmission housing | 3.1 litres |
| Filler level plug on front of transmission housing | 2.7 litres |

**Fuel tank**

| | |
|---|---|
| All models (approximate) | 45 litres |

**Washer reservoir**

| | |
|---|---|
| Models with headlight washers | 7.0 litres |
| Models without headlight washers | 2.5 litres |

## Engine

| | |
|---|---|
| Oil filter | Champion C125 |
| Timing belt wear limit: | |
| Engine codes AHG and AKU | 21 mm |
| Engine code AGD | 22 mm |

## Cooling system

| | |
|---|---|
| Antifreeze mixture: | |
| 40% antifreeze | Protection down to -25°C |
| 50% antifreeze | Protection down to -35°C |

**Note:** *Refer to antifreeze manufacturer for latest recommendations.*

## Fuel system

| | |
|---|---|
| Air filter element | Champion type not available |
| Fuel filter | Champion L114 |
| Idle speed (engine code AEF) | 940 ± 20 rpm |

## Brakes

| | |
|---|---|
| Brake pad minimum thickness (including backing plate) | 7.0 mm |
| Brake shoe friction material minimum thickness | 2.5 mm |

## Torque wrench settings

| Torque wrench settings | Nm | lbf ft |
|---|---|---|
| Engine right-hand mounting bolts: | | |
| Upper bolts | 50 | 37 |
| Lower bolts | 25 | 18 |
| Roadwheel bolts | 110 | 81 |
| Sump drain plug | 30 | 22 |
| Timing belt tensioner locknut (engine code AEF) | 20 | 15 |
| Transmission filler/level plug | 25 | 18 |

The maintenance intervals in this manual are provided with the assumption that you, not the dealer, will be carrying out the work. These are the minimum intervals recommended for vehicles driven daily. If you wish to keep your vehicle in peak condition at all times, you may wish to perform some of these procedures more often. We encourage frequent maintenance, since it enhances the efficiency, performance and resale value of your vehicle.

When the vehicle is new, it should be serviced by a dealer service department, in order to preserve the factory warranty.

## Every 250 miles (400 km) or weekly

☐ Refer to *Weekly checks*

## Every 10 000 miles (15 000 km) - OEL on interval display

*In addition to the items listed in the previous services, carry out the following:*

☐ Renew the engine oil and filter (Section 3)

**Note:** *Frequent oil and filter changes are beneficial for the engine. We recommend changing the oil at half the mileage specified here or at least twice a year.*

☐ Check the front brake pad thickness (Section 4)
☐ Drain water from the fuel filter (Section 5)
☐ Reset the service interval display (Section 6)

## Every 12 months - INSP-1 on interval display

☐ Check operation of all lights and horn (Section 7)
☐ Check the condition of the airbag unit(s) (Section 8)
☐ Check the operation of the washer system(s) (Section 9)
☐ Lubricate all hinges, locks and door check straps (Section 10)
☐ Check diesel engine management and other systems for fault codes, where applicable (Section 11)
☐ Check battery electrolyte level - where applicable (Section 12)
☐ Check all underbonnet components and hoses for fluid leaks (Section 13)
☐ Check the transmission and driveshaft gaiters for leaks and damage (Section 14)
☐ Check the braking system for leaks and damage (Section 15)
☐ Check the rear brake shoe lining thickness (Section 16)
☐ Check the condition of the exhaust system and its mountings (Section 17)
☐ Check the steering and suspension components for condition and security (Section 18)
☐ Check the headlight beam adjustment (Section 19)
☐ Carry out a road test (Section 20)
☐ Check the idle speed and adjust if necessary - engine code AEF only (Section 21)
☐ Reset the service interval display (Section 6)

## Every 20 000 miles (30 000 km) - INSP-2 on interval display

**Note:** *If the vehicle is covering more than 20 000 miles (30 000 km) a year, also carry out all the operations described above*

☐ Lubricate folding fabric sunroof guide rail (Section 22)
☐ Renew the fuel filter (Section 23)
☐ Renew the pollen filter element (Section 24)
☐ Check the condition of the auxiliary drivebelt(s), and renew if necessary (Section 25)
☐ Check the condition and tension of the timing belt - engine code AEF (Section 26)
☐ Check the timing belt for condition and wear - engine codes AGD, AHG and AKU (Section 27)
☐ Check the transmission oil level (Section 28)
☐ Check underbody protection for damage (Section 29)
☐ Reset the service interval display (Section 6)

## Every 40 000 miles (60 000 km) or 2 years

*In addition to the items listed in the previous services, carry out the following:*

☐ Renew the air filter element (Section 30)

1B

## Every 40 000 miles (60 000 km)

*In addition to the items listed in the previous services, carry out the following:*

☐ Renew the timing belt and belt tensioner - engine codes AHG and AKU (Section 31)
☐ Renew the timing belt and belt tensioner - engine codes AEF and AGD (Section 32)*

*** Note:** *VW specify a timing belt renewal interval of 60 000 miles (90 000 km). However, if the vehicle is used mainly for short journeys or a lot of stop-start driving, we recommend that this shorter interval is adhered to. The actual belt renewal interval is very much up to the individual owner but, bearing in mind that severe engine damage will result if the belt breaks in use, we recommend you err on the side of caution.*

## Every 2 years (regardless of mileage)

*In addition to the items listed in the previous services, carry out the following:*

☐ Renew the coolant (Section 33)
☐ Renew the brake fluid (Section 34)
☐ Check exhaust emissions (Section 35)

## Underbonnet view of 1.9 litre engine (code AEF)

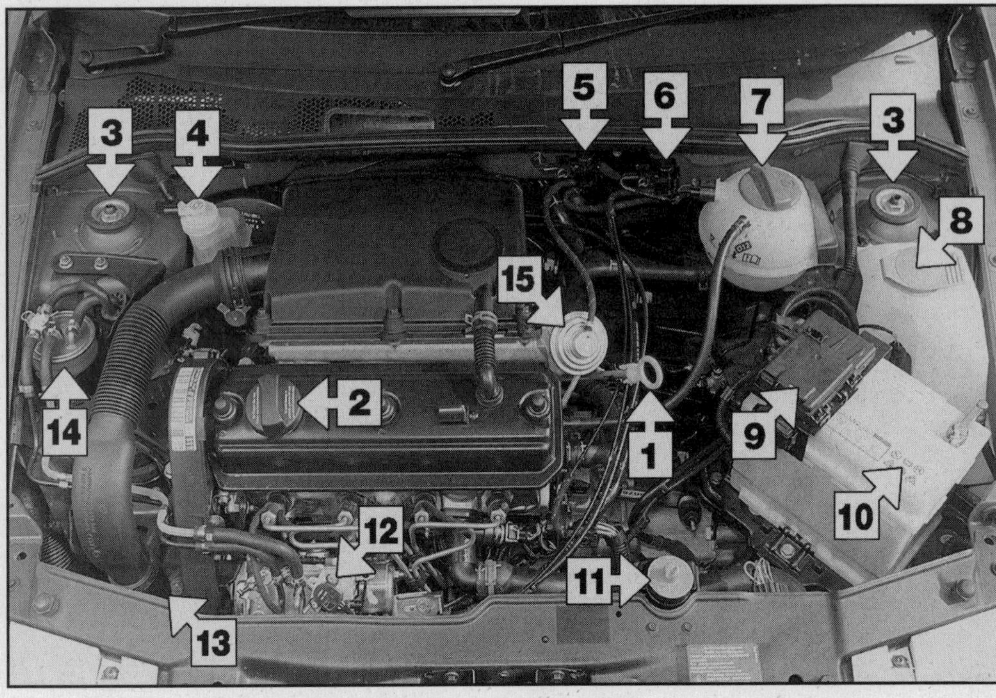


1 Engine oil dipstick
2 Engine oil filler cap
3 Suspension strut upper mounting
4 Brake fluid reservoir
5 EGR solenoid valve
6 Idle speed boost valve (glow plug control unit location on other engine codes)
7 Coolant expansion tank
8 Washer fluid reservoir
9 Engine compartment fusebox
10 Battery
11 Power steering fluid reservoir
12 Fuel injection pump
13 Air cleaner housing (under front wing)
14 Fuel filter
15 EGR valve

## Front underbody view

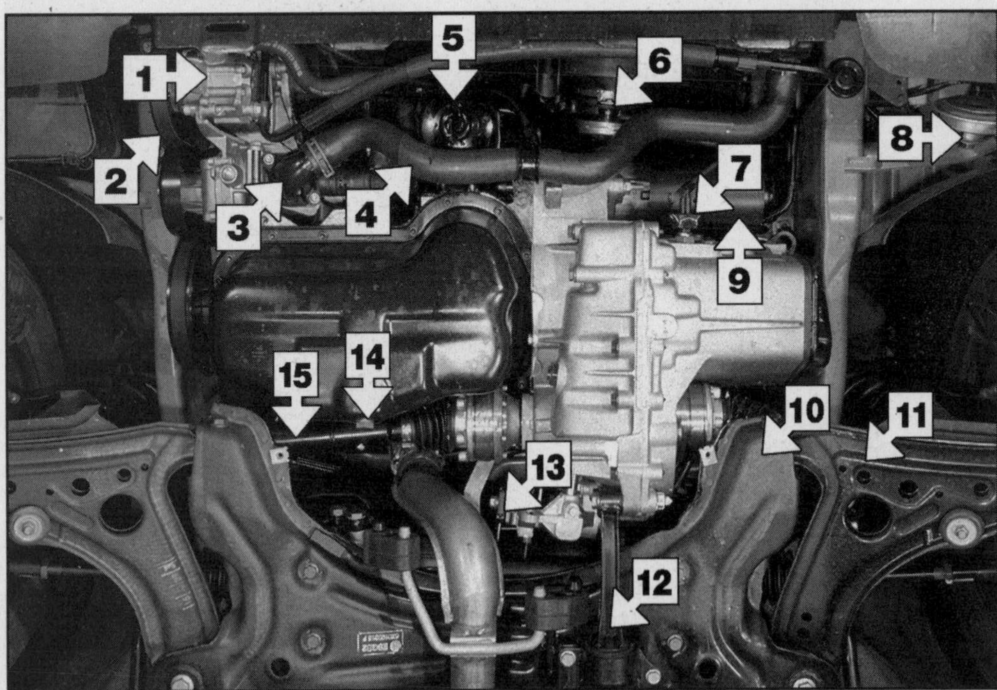


1 Power steering pump
2 Auxiliary drivebelt
3 Thermostat housing
4 Radiator bottom hose
5 Oil filter
6 Radiator cooling fan motor
7 Reversing light switch
8 Horn
9 Starter motor
10 Subframe
11 Wishbone/lower arm
12 Engine/transmission rear mounting
13 Gearchange cables
14 Engine oil drain plug
15 Driveshaft

## Rear underbody view

1 Handbrake cable
2 Fuel tank
3 Rear axle
4 Brake pressure regulator
5 Exhaust mounting
6 Rear strut lower mounting
7 Exhaust rear silencer

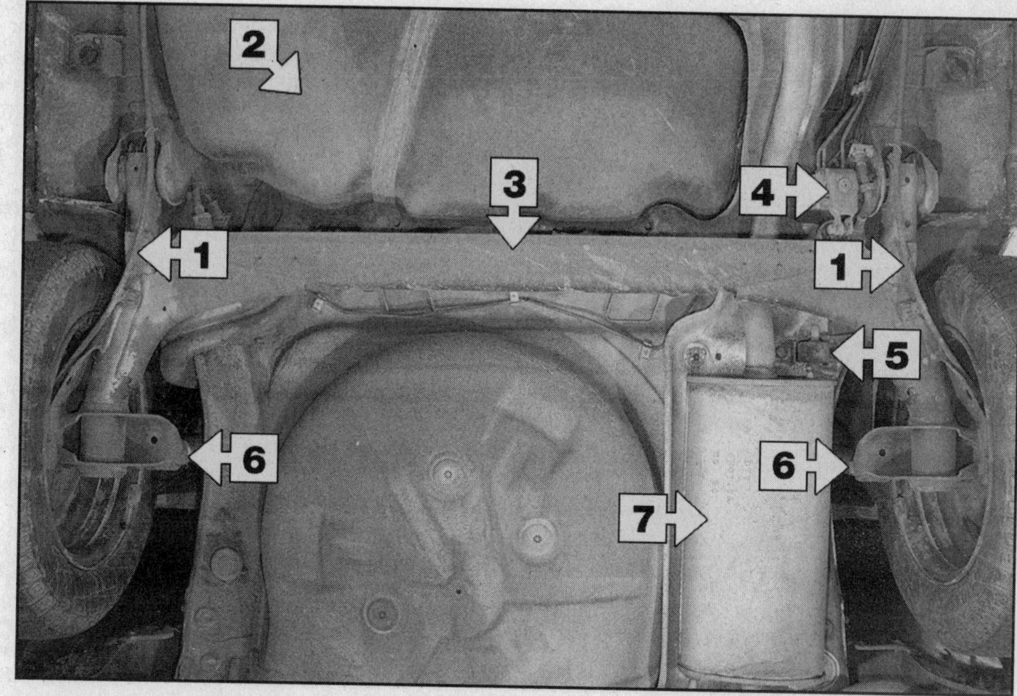




# Maintenance procedures - diesel models

## 1 Introduction

### *General information*

This Chapter is designed to help the home mechanic maintain his/her vehicle for safety, economy, long life and peak performance.

The Chapter contains a master maintenance schedule, followed by Sections dealing specifically with each task in the schedule. Visual checks, adjustments, component renewal and other helpful items are included. Refer to the accompanying illustrations of the engine compartment and the underside of the vehicle for the locations of the various components.

Servicing your vehicle in accordance with the mileage/time maintenance schedule and the following Sections will provide a planned maintenance programme, which should result in a long and reliable service life. This is a comprehensive plan, so maintaining some items but not others at the specified service intervals, will not produce the same results.

As you service your vehicle, you will discover that many of the procedures can - and should - be grouped together, because of the particular procedure being performed, or because of the proximity of two otherwise unrelated components to one another. For example, if the vehicle is raised for any reason, the exhaust can be inspected at the same time as the suspension and steering components.

The first step in this maintenance programme is to prepare yourself before the actual work begins. Read through all the Sections relevant to the work to be carried out, then make a list and gather all the parts and tools required. If a problem is encountered, seek advice from a parts specialist, or a dealer service department.

### *Service interval display*

#### Up to 1998 model year

All VW Polo models are equipped with a service interval display indicator in the instrument panel. Every time the engine is started, the panel will illuminate for a few seconds, providing a handy reminder of when the next service is required:

*Display shows INSP-0 - no service required*
*Display shows OEL - 10 000 mile (15 000 km) service required*
*Display shows INSP-1 - 12 monthly service required*
*Display shows INSP-2 - 20 000 mile (30 000 km) service required*

#### 1998 model year onwards

The service display on later models is similar to the earlier type, but the display is different:

*Display clear - no service required.*
*Display shows 'service OIL' - 10 000 mile (15 000 km) service required.*
*Display shows 'service INSP' - 12 monthly or 20 000 mile (30 000 km) service required.*
*Display shows 'service' when ignition is switched off - switch on ignition to determine which service is required.*

#### All models

On diesel engined Polo models, the display is described as 'flexible', in that it takes note of driving style and engine loading, and uses these factors in calculating the optimum service interval. The display is also useful in ensuring that servicing is not accidentally overlooked. Owners of older cars, or those covering a small annual mileage, may feel inclined to service their car more often, in which case the service interval display is perhaps less relevant.

The display should be reset whenever a service is carried out, and the procedure for this is described in Section 6.

## 2 Regular maintenance

1 If, from the time the vehicle is new, the routine maintenance schedule is followed closely, and frequent checks are made of fluid levels and high-wear items, as suggested throughout this manual, the engine will be kept in relatively good running condition, and the need for additional work will be minimised.
2 It is possible that there will be times when the engine is running poorly due to the lack of regular maintenance. This is even more likely if a used vehicle, which has not received regular and frequent maintenance checks, is purchased. In such cases, additional work may need to be carried out, outside of the regular maintenance intervals.
3 If engine wear is suspected, a compression test (refer to the relevant Part of Chapter 2) will provide valuable information regarding the overall performance of the main internal components. Such a test can be used as a basis to decide on the extent of the work to be carried out. If, for example, a compression test indicates serious internal engine wear, conventional maintenance as described in this Chapter will not greatly improve the performance of the engine, and may prove a waste of time and money, unless extensive overhaul work is carried out first.
4 The following series of operations are those most often required to improve the performance of a generally poor-running engine:

### Primary operations

*a) Clean, inspect and test the battery (See Weekly checks).*
*b) Check all the engine-related fluids (See Weekly checks).*
*c) Drain the water from the fuel filter (Section 5).*
*d) Check the condition and tension of the auxiliary drivebelt(s) (Section 25).*
*e) Check the condition of the air filter, and renew if necessary (Section 30).*
*f) Check the condition of all hoses, and check for fluid leaks (Section 13).*
*g) Check the engine idle speed setting (Section 21 or Chapter 4C).*
*h) Check the exhaust gas emissions (Section 35).*

5 If the above operations do not prove fully effective, carry out the following secondary operations:

### Secondary operations

All items listed under Primary operations, plus the following:

*a) Check the charging system (see Chapter 5A).*
*b) Check the preheating system (see Chapter 5C).*
*c) Renew the fuel filter (Section 23) and check the fuel system (see Chapter 4C).*

# Every 10 000 miles (15 000 km)

## 3 Engine oil and filter renewal

1 Frequent oil and filter changes are the most important maintenance procedures which can be undertaken by the DIY owner. As engine oil ages, it becomes diluted and contaminated, which leads to premature engine wear. The oil change interval given in this Manual is the same as quoted by the manufacturer, but we recommend changing the oil and filter more frequently, perhaps every 5000 miles, or every 6 months. This is particularly relevant to owners of older vehicles (or those covering a small annual mileage).
2 Before starting this procedure, gather all the necessary tools and materials. Also make sure that you have plenty of clean rags and newspapers handy, to mop up any spills. Ideally, the engine oil should be warm, as it will drain better, and more built-up sludge will be removed with it. Take care, however, not to touch the exhaust or any other hot parts of the engine when working under the vehicle. To avoid any possibility of scalding, and to protect yourself from possible skin irritants and other harmful contaminants in used engine oils, it is advisable to wear gloves when carrying out this work.
3 Access to the underside of the vehicle will be greatly improved if it can be raised on a lift, driven onto ramps, or jacked up and supported on axle stands (see *Jacking and vehicle support*). Whichever method is chosen, make sure that the vehicle remains level, or if it is at an angle, that the drain plug is at the lowest point. Where applicable, release the fasteners and remove the noise insulation tray from under the engine **(see illustration)**. This is not necessary for access to the drain plug, but will be required in order to remove the oil filter.
4 Using a socket and handle or a ring spanner, slacken the drain plug (at the rear of the sump) about half a turn **(see illustration)**. Position the draining container under the drain plug, then remove the plug completely **(see Haynes Hint)**. Recover the sealing ring from the drain plug.

***Keep the drain plug pressed into the sump while unscrewing it by hand last couple of turns. As the plug releases, move it away sharply so the stream of oil issuing from the sump runs into the container, not up your sleeve!***

**3.3 Noise insulation tray fastener locations (arrowed)**

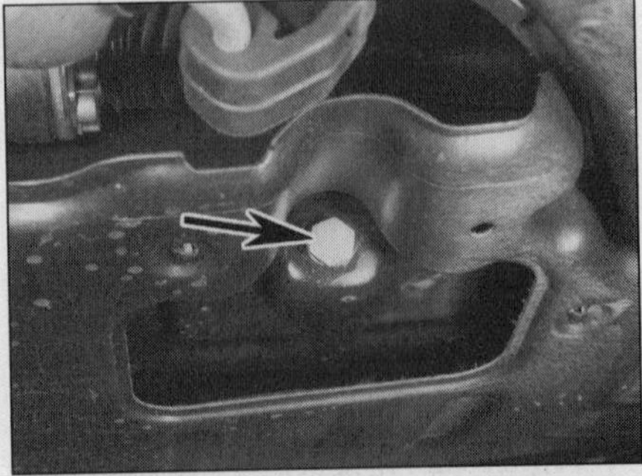

**3.4 Engine oil drain plug (arrowed) - seen with noise insulation tray in place**

5 Allow some time for the old oil to drain, noting that it may be necessary to reposition the container as the oil flow slows to a trickle.
6 After all the oil has drained, wipe off the drain plug with a clean rag, and fit a new sealing washer. Clean the area around the drain plug opening, and refit the plug. Tighten the plug to the specified torque setting.
7 Move the container into position under the oil filter, which is located on the front of the cylinder block, at the flywheel end.
8 Using an oil filter removal tool if necessary

3.8a Oil filter removal using an oil filter removal tool . . .

3.8b . . . or a home-made alternative

3.12a Remove the oil filler cap . . .

slacken the filter initially, then unscrew it by hand the rest of the way. Empty the oil in the filter into the container. Genuine VW filters have a bracket on the base of the filter, for engaging a claw-type removal tool. In the absence of the proper tool, a useful substitute can be made from a strip of thick metal, gripped with a pair of pliers **(see illustrations)**.

**9** Use a clean rag to remove all oil, dirt and sludge from the filter sealing area on the engine. Check the old filter to make sure that the rubber sealing ring has not stuck to the engine. If it has, carefully remove it.

**10** Apply a light coating of clean engine oil to the sealing ring on the new filter, then screw it into position on the engine. Tighten the filter firmly by hand only - **do not** use any tools.

**11** Remove the old oil and all tools from under the car, then lower the car to the ground (if applicable).

**12** Remove the dipstick, then unscrew the oil filler cap from the cylinder head cover. Fill the engine, using the correct grade and type of oil (see *Lubricants and fluids*). A funnel or piece of clean rag wrapped around the filler opening may help to reduce spillage **(see illustrations)**. Pour in half the specified quantity of oil first, then wait a few minutes for the oil to fall to the sump. Continue adding oil a small quantity at a time until the level is up to the bottom of the hatched area on the dipstick. Adding around 0.5 litres of oil will bring the level into the hatched area on the dipstick. Add a little more oil until the level is up to the top of the hatched area on the dipstick, then refit the dipstick and the filler cap.

3.12b . . . and fill the engine with the recommended type and quantity of oil

**13** Start the engine and run it for a few minutes; check for leaks around the oil filter seal and the sump drain plug. Note that there may be a few seconds delay before the oil pressure warning light goes out when the engine is started, as the oil circulates through the engine oil galleries and the new oil filter before the pressure builds up.

**14** Switch off the engine, and wait a few minutes for the oil to settle in the sump once more. With the new oil circulated and the filter completely full, recheck the level on the dipstick, and add more oil as necessary. Refit the noise insulation tray to the underside of the engine, where applicable.

**15** Dispose of the used engine oil safely, with reference to *General repair procedures* in the *Reference* section of this manual.

## 4 Front brake pad check

**1** Firmly apply the handbrake, loosen the front roadwheel bolts, then jack up the front of the car and support it securely on axle stands. Remove the front roadwheels.

**2** For a comprehensive check, the brake pads should be removed and cleaned. The operation of the caliper can then also be checked, and the condition of the brake disc itself can be fully examined on both sides. Refer to Chapter 9 **(see Haynes Hint)**.

HAYNES HiNT

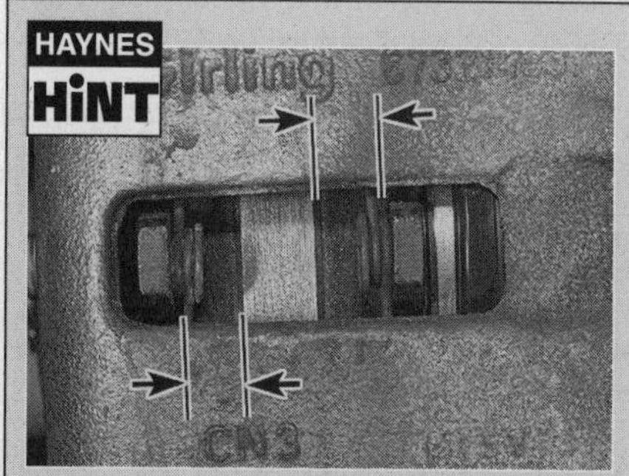

***For a quick check, the thickness of the friction material on each brake pad can be measured through the aperture in the caliper body***

**3** If any pad's friction material is worn to the specified thickness or less, *all four pads must be renewed as a set.*

## 5 Fuel filter water draining

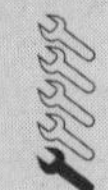

**1** From time to time, the water collected from the fuel by the filter unit must be drained out.

**2** The fuel filter is mounted on the right-hand inner wing. If wished, for improved access, detach the inlet air hose from the inlet manifold and the air cleaner, and move it out of the way.

**3** At the top of the filter unit, pull out the R-clip and lift out the control valve, leaving the fuel hoses attached **(see illustration)**.

**4** Slacken the retaining bracket screw and lift the filter up slightly.

**5** Position a container below the filter unit, and pad the surrounding area with rags to absorb any fuel that may be spilt.

**6** Unscrew the drain valve at the base of the filter unit, until fuel starts to run out into the container **(refer to illustration 23.3)**. Keep the valve open until about 100 cc of fuel has been collected.

**7** Refit the control valve to the top of the filter and insert the retaining clip. Close the drain valve and wipe off any surplus fuel from the nozzle.

**8** Remove the collecting container and rags, then push the filter unit back into the retaining bracket and tighten the bracket screw. Refit the inlet air hose to the air cleaner and inlet manifold, if removed.

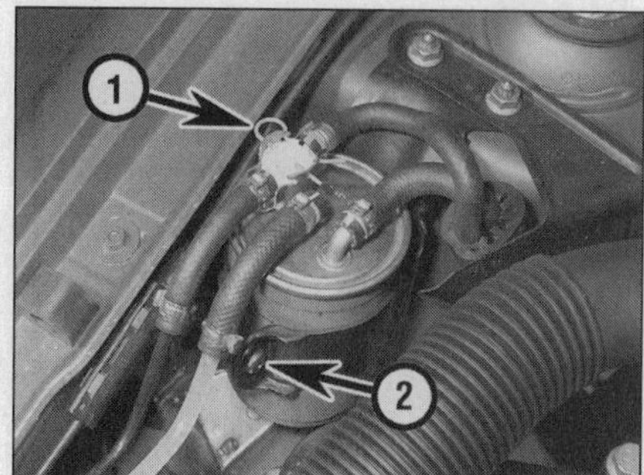

5.3 Fuel filter R-clip (1) and retaining bracket screw (2)

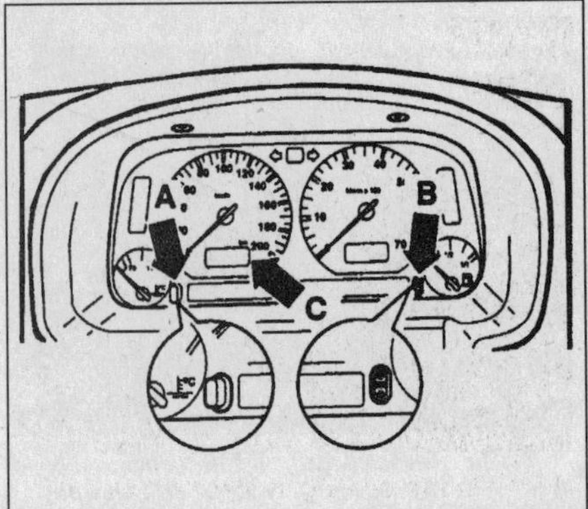


**6.2 Resetting the service interval display**

*A Service selector button (also trip meter selector button)*
*B Service reset button (also digital clock adjustment button)*
*C Service interval display*

**9** Run the engine at idle, and check around the fuel filter for fuel leaks.

**10** Raise the engine speed to about 2000 rpm several times, then allow the engine to idle again. Observe the fuel flow through the transparent hose leading to the fuel injection pump, and check that it is free of air bubbles.

## 6 Resetting service interval display

### Up to 1998 model year

**1** Before resetting the service interval display, make sure that the mileometer is displaying the total mileage, and is not in trip mode. Briefly pressing the button to the left of the speedometer will switch the display between total and trip. **Note:** *If the button is pressed and held for longer than one second while in trip mode, the trip meter will be zeroed.*

**2** Switch on the ignition (do not start the engine). Press and hold the button to the left of the speedometer **(see illustration)**.

**3** Switch off the ignition, then release the button. The display should read OEL.

**4** Now press the digital clock lower button on the right-hand side of the instrument panel until five dashes appear on the display. The OEL service is now reset.

**5** By pressing the left-hand button again, the next service interval can be displayed, and then reset by pressing the right-hand button.

**6** Reset as many services as necessary, until switching on the ignition only shows INSP-0 (no service required) on the display.

### 1998 model year onwards

**7** The service interval display cannot be reset without special VW fault code reading equipment - refer to your VW dealer.

# Every 12 months

## 7 Lights and horn operation check

**1** With the ignition switched on where necessary, check the operation of all exterior lights.

**2** Check the brake lights with the help of an assistant, or by reversing up close to a reflective door. Make sure that all the rear lights are capable of operating independently, without affecting any of the other lights - for example, switch on as many rear lights as possible, then try the brake lights. If any unusual results are found, this is usually due to an earth fault or other poor connection at that rear light unit.

**3** Again with the help of an assistant or using a reflective surface, check as far as possible that the headlights work on both main and dipped beam.

**4** Replace any defective bulbs with reference to Chapter 12.

***Particularly on older vehicles, bulbs can stop working as a result of corrosion build-up on the bulb or its holder - fitting a new bulb may not cure the problem in this instance. When replacing any bulb, if you find any green or white-coloured powdery deposits, these should be cleaned off using emery cloth.***

**5** Check the operation of all interior lights, including the glovebox and luggage area illumination lights. Switch on the ignition, and check that all relevant warning lights come on as expected - the vehicle handbook should give details of these. Now start the engine, and check that the appropriate lights go out. When you are next driving at night, check that all the instrument panel and facia lighting works correctly. If any problems are found, refer to Chapter 12.

**6** Finally, choose an appropriate time of day to test the operation of the horn.

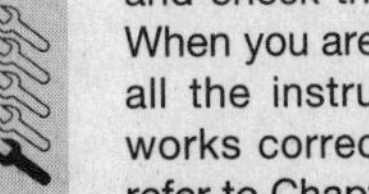

## 8 Airbag unit check

Where fitted, inspect the airbag(s) exterior condition checking for signs of damage or deterioration. If an airbag shows signs of obvious damage, it must be renewed (see Chapter 12).

## 9 Washer system(s) check

Check that each of the washer jet nozzles is clear, and that each nozzle provides a strong jet of washer fluid. The tailgate and headlight jets (where applicable) should be aimed to spray at a point slightly above the centre of the screen/headlight.

The windscreen washer nozzles have two jets; aim one of the jets slightly above the centre of the screen and the other just below, to ensure complete coverage of the screen. If necessary, adjust the jets using a pin.

Later models may be fitted with additional preset washer jets which only have a limited amount of adjustment. Height adjustment on these later jets is effected by turning an eccentric on the spray jet.

## 10 Hinge and lock lubrication

Lubricate the hinges of the bonnet, doors and tailgate with light general-purpose oil. Similarly, lubricate all latches, locks and lock strikers, and the door check straps with general-purpose oil or grease. At the same time, check the security and operation of all the locks, adjusting them if necessary (see Chapter 11).

Lightly lubricate the bonnet release mechanism and cable with suitable grease.

Do not attempt to lubricate the steering lock.

## 11 Fault code check

**1** This check is part of the manufacturer's maintenance schedule, and involves 'interrogating' the diesel engine management control unit (not engine code AEF) and the ABS control unit, as applicable, using special dedicated test equipment. Such testing will allow the test equipment to read any fault codes stored in the electronic control unit memory.

**2** Unless a fault is suspected, this test is not essential, although it should be noted that it is recommended by the manufacturers.

**3** It is possible for quite serious faults to occur in the engine management system without the owner being aware of it. Certain engine management system faults will cause the system to enter an emergency back-up mode, which is often so sophisticated that engine performance is not apparently much affected. If a problem has caused the system to enter its back-up mode, this will usually be most apparent when starting and running from cold.

## 12 Battery electrolyte level check

**Warning: The electrolyte inside a battery is diluted acid - it is a good idea to wear suitable rubber gloves. When topping-up, don't overfill the cells so that the electrolyte overflows. In the event of any spillage, rinse the electrolyte off without delay. Refit the cell covers and rinse the battery with copious quantities of clean water. Don't attempt to siphon out any excess electrolyte.**

**1** Some models covered by this Manual may be fitted with a maintenance-free battery as standard equipment, or may have had one fitted as a replacement. If the battery in your vehicle is marked 'Freedom', 'Maintenance-Free' or similar, no electrolyte level checking is required (the battery is often completely sealed, preventing any topping-up).

**2** Batteries which do require their electrolyte level to be checked can be recognised by the presence of removable covers over the six battery cells - the battery casing is also sometimes translucent, so that the electrolyte level can be more easily checked. Make sure you do not have a maintenance-free battery before attempting to top up the electrolyte level.

**3** Remove the cell covers and either look down inside the battery to see the level web, or check the level using any markings provided on the battery casing. The electrolyte should at least cover the battery plates. If necessary, top up a little at a time with distilled (deionised) water until the level in all six cells is correct - don't fill the cells up to the brim. Wipe up any spillage, then refit the cell covers.

## 13 Hose and fluid leak check

**1** Visually inspect the engine joint faces, gaskets and seals for any signs of water or oil leaks. Pay particular attention to the areas around the camshaft cover, cylinder head, oil filter and sump joint faces. Bear in mind that, over a period of time, some very slight seepage from these areas is to be expected - what you are really looking for is any indication of a serious leak **(see Haynes Hint)**. Should a leak be found, renew the offending gasket or oil seal by referring to the appropriate Chapters in this manual.

**2** Also check the security and condition of all the engine-related pipes and hoses. Ensure that all cable-ties or securing clips are in place and in good condition. Clips that are broken or missing can lead to chafing of the hoses, pipes or wiring, which could cause more serious problems in the future.

**3** Carefully check the radiator hoses and heater hoses along their entire length. Renew any hose that is cracked, swollen or deteriorated. Cracks will show up better if the hose is squeezed. Pay close attention to the hose clips that secure the hoses to the cooling system components. Hose clips can pinch and puncture hoses, resulting in cooling system leaks.

**4** Inspect all the cooling system components (hoses, joint faces etc.) for leaks. A leak in the cooling system will usually show up as white- or rust-coloured deposits on the area adjoining the leak. Where any problems of this nature are found on system components, renew the component or gasket with reference to Chapter 3.

**5** With the vehicle raised, inspect the fuel tank and filler neck for punctures, cracks and other damage. The connection between the filler neck and tank is especially critical. Sometimes a rubber filler neck or connecting hose will leak due to loose retaining clamps or deteriorated rubber.

**6** Carefully check all rubber hoses and metal fuel lines leading away from the fuel tank. Check for loose connections, deteriorated hoses, crimped lines, and other damage. Pay particular attention to the vent pipes and hoses, which often loop up around the filler neck and can become blocked or crimped. Follow the lines to the front of the vehicle, carefully inspecting them all the way. Renew damaged sections as necessary.

***A leak in the cooling system will usually show up as white- or rust-coloured deposits on the area adjoining the leak***

**7** From within the engine compartment, check the security of all fuel hose attachments and pipe unions, and inspect the fuel hoses and vacuum hoses for kinks, chafing and deterioration **(see illustration)**.

**8** Where applicable, check the condition of the power steering fluid hoses and pipes.

## 14 Transmission and driveshaft gaiter check

1B

**1** Raise the front of the vehicle and support on axle stands. Alternatively, drive the car onto ramps.

**2** Inspect around the transmission for any sign of leaks or damage. In particular, check the area around the driveshaft oil seals for leakage **(see illustration)**. Slight seepage should not be of great concern, but a serious leak should be investigated further, with reference to Chapter 7A.

**3** Check the security and condition of the wiring and wiring plugs on the transmission housing **(see illustration)**.

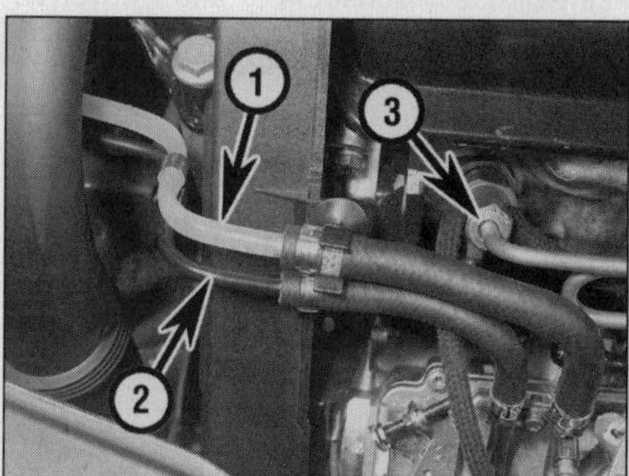


**13.7 Check for leaks around the fuel supply (1) and return (2) pipes, and at the fuel injector unions (3) - one only visible**

**14.2 Driveshaft inner CV joint, showing driveshaft seal (arrowed)**

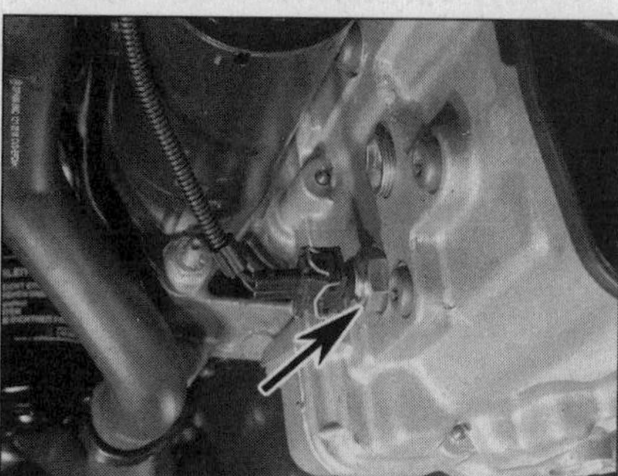

**14.3 Reversing light switch (arrowed) - seen from below**

14.4 Driveshaft outer CV joint gaiter (arrowed)

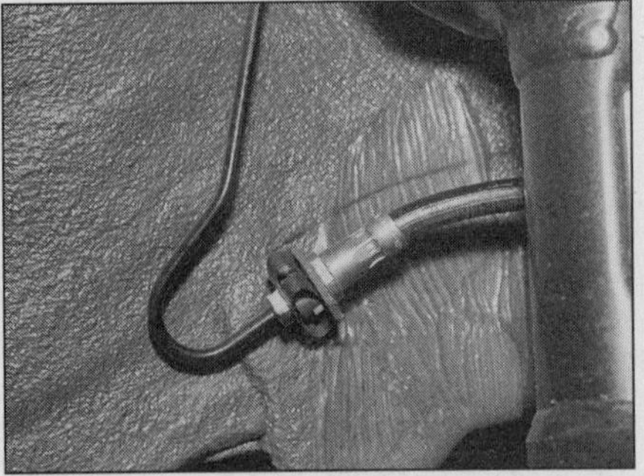
15.4 Rear brake pipe-to-flexible hose union

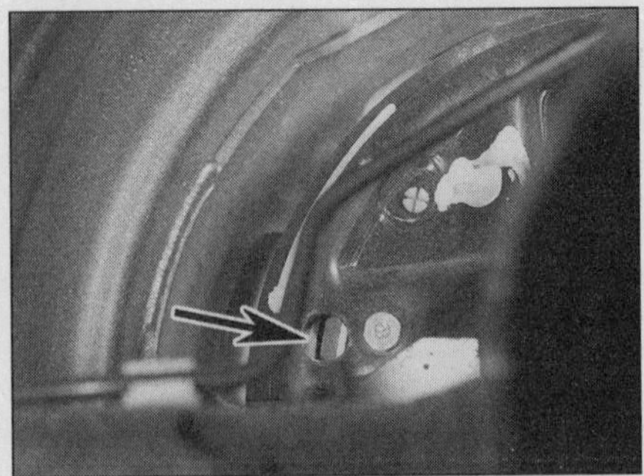
16.2 Rear brake backplate inspection hole (arrowed) for assessing brake lining wear

**4** With the vehicle raised and securely supported on stands, turn the steering onto full lock, then slowly rotate the roadwheel. Inspect the condition of the outer constant velocity (CV) joint rubber gaiters, squeezing the gaiters to open out the folds **(see illustration)**. Check for signs of cracking, splits or deterioration of the rubber, which may allow the grease to escape, and lead to water and grit entry into the joint. Also check the security and condition of the retaining clips. Repeat these checks on the inner CV joints. If any damage or deterioration is found, the gaiters should be renewed (see Chapter 8).

**5** At the same time, check the general condition of the CV joints themselves by first holding the driveshaft and attempting to rotate the wheel. Repeat this check by holding the inner joint and attempting to rotate the drive-shaft. Any appreciable movement indicates wear in the joints, wear in the driveshaft splines, or a loose driveshaft retaining nut.

## 15 Braking system check

**1** Starting under the bonnet, examine the brake fluid reservoir and master cylinder for leaks. When a brake fluid leak occurs, it is normal to find blistered or wrinkled paint in the area of the leak. Check the metal pipes from the master cylinder for damage, and check the brake servo/ABS unit and fluid unions for leaks. Check the vacuum pipe running from the brake vacuum pump on the left-hand end of the cylinder block to the brake servo - look especially for cracks or splits at the hose ends.

17.3 Typical exhaust system rubber mountings - check for security and condition of the rubber

**2** With the vehicle raised and securely supported on stands, first inspect each front brake caliper. In particular, check the flexible hose leading to the caliper for signs of damage or leaks, especially where the hose enters the metal end fitting. Make sure that the hose is not twisted or kinked, and that it cannot come into contact with any other components when the steering is on full lock.

**3** From the caliper, trace the metal brake pipes back along the car. Again, look for leaks from the fluid unions or signs of damage, but additionally check the pipes for signs of corrosion. Make sure the pipes are securely located by the clips provided on the vehicle underside.

**4** At the rear of the vehicle, inspect each rear brake and its flexible hose, where applicable **(see illustration)**. Examine the handbrake cable, tracing it back from each rear brake and checking for frayed cables or other damage. Lubricate the handbrake cable guides, pivots and other moving parts with general-purpose grease.

**5** If any damage is found, refer to Chapter 9 for further information.

## 16 Rear brake shoe check

**1** Chock the front wheels, then jack up the rear of the vehicle, and support it securely on axle stands.

**2** For a quick check, the thickness of friction material remaining on one of the brake shoes can be observed through the holes in the trailing arm and the brake backplate. The hole in the brake backplate is plugged with a sealing grommet, which can be prised out. If a rod of the same diameter as the specified minimum friction material thickness is placed against the shoe friction material, the amount of wear can be assessed. A torch or inspection light will probably be required, as well as a small mirror if access is particularly difficult **(see illustration)**. If the friction material on any shoe is worn down to the specified minimum thickness or less, all four shoes must be renewed as a set.

**3** For a comprehensive check, the brake drum should be removed and cleaned. This will allow the wheel cylinders to be checked, and the condition of the brake drum itself to be fully examined (see Chapter 9).

## 17 Exhaust system check

**1** With the engine cold (at least an hour after the vehicle has been driven), check the complete exhaust system from the engine to the end of the tailpipe. The exhaust system is most easily checked with the vehicle raised on a hoist, or suitably supported on axle stands, so that the exhaust components are readily visible and accessible.

**2** Check the exhaust pipes and connections for evidence of leaks, severe corrosion and damage. Make sure that all brackets and mountings are in good condition, and that all relevant nuts and bolts are tight. Leakage at any of the joints or in other parts of the system will usually show up as a black sooty stain in the vicinity of the leak.

**3** Rattles and other noises can often be traced to the exhaust system, especially the brackets and mountings **(see illustration)**. Try to move the pipes and silencers. If the components are able to come into contact with the body or suspension parts, secure the system with new mountings. Otherwise separate the joints (if possible) and twist the pipes as necessary to provide additional clearance.

## 18 Steering and suspension check

### *Front suspension and steering check*

**1** Raise the front of the vehicle, and securely support it on axle stands. Where necessary for improved access, release the fasteners and remove the noise insulation tray from under the engine (where applicable).

**2** Visually inspect the balljoint dust covers and the steering rack-and-pinion gaiters for splits, chafing or deterioration. Any wear of these components will cause loss of lubricant, together with dirt and water entry, resulting in rapid deterioration of the balljoints or steering gear.

**3** On vehicles with power steering, check the fluid hoses for chafing or deterioration, and the pipe and hose unions for fluid leaks. Also check for signs of fluid leakage under pressure from the steering gear rubber gaiters, which would indicate failed fluid seals within the steering gear.

**4** Grasp the roadwheel at the 12 o'clock and 6 o'clock positions, and try to rock it **(see illustration)**. Very slight free play may be felt, but if the movement is appreciable, further investigation is necessary to determine the source. Continue rocking the wheel while an assistant depresses the footbrake. If the movement is now eliminated or significantly reduced, it is likely that the hub bearings are at fault. If the free play is still evident with the footbrake depressed, then there is wear in the suspension joints or mountings. Before condemning any components, however, check that the roadwheel bolts are tightened to the specified torque.

**5** Now grasp the wheel at the 9 o'clock and 3 o'clock positions, and try to rock it as before. Any movement felt now may again be caused by wear in the hub bearings or the steering track-rod balljoints. If the inner or outer balljoint is worn, the visual movement will be obvious.

**6** Using a large screwdriver or flat bar, check for wear in the suspension mounting bushes by levering between the relevant suspension component and its attachment point. Some movement is to be expected as the mountings are made of rubber, but excessive wear should be obvious. Also check the condition of any visible rubber bushes, looking for splits, cracks or contamination of the rubber **(see illustration)**.

**7** With the car standing on its wheels, have an assistant turn the steering wheel back and forth about an eighth of a turn each way. There should be very little, if any, lost movement between the steering wheel and roadwheels. If this is not the case, closely observe the joints and mountings previously described, but in addition, check the steering column universal joints for wear, and the rack-and-pinion steering gear itself.

### Suspension strut/shock absorber check

**8** Check for any signs of fluid leakage around the suspension strut/shock absorber body, or from the rubber gaiter around the piston rod. Should any fluid be noticed, the suspension strut/shock absorber is defective internally, and should be renewed. **Note:** *Suspension struts/shock absorbers should always be renewed in pairs on the same axle.*

**9** The efficiency of the suspension strut/shock absorber may be checked by bouncing the vehicle at each corner. Generally speaking, the body will return to its normal position and stop after being depressed. If it rises and returns on a rebound, the suspension strut/shock absorber is probably suspect. Examine also the suspension strut/shock absorber upper and lower mountings for any signs of wear.

## 19 Headlight beam alignment check

Accurate adjustment of the headlight beam is only possible using optical beam-setting equipment, and this work should therefore be carried out by a VW dealer or service station with the necessary facilities. Headlight alignment is checked as part of the MoT test.

Basic adjustments can be carried out in an emergency, and further details are given in Chapter 12.

## 20 Road test

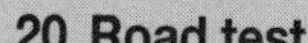

### Instruments and electrical equipment

**1** Check the operation of all instruments and electrical equipment.

**2** Make sure that all instruments read correctly, and switch on all electrical equipment in turn, to check that it functions properly.

### Steering and suspension

**3** Check for any abnormalities in the steering, suspension, handling or road feel.

**4** Drive the vehicle, and check that there are no unusual vibrations or noises.

**5** Check that the steering feels positive, with no excessive sloppiness, or roughness, and check for any suspension noises when cornering and driving over bumps.

### Drivetrain

**6** Check the performance of the engine, clutch (where applicable), transmission and driveshafts.

**7** Listen for any unusual noises from the engine, clutch and transmission.

**8** Make sure the engine runs smoothly at idle, and there is no hesitation on accelerating.

**9** Check that the clutch action is smooth and progressive, that the drive is taken up smoothly, and that the pedal travel is not excessive. Also listen for any noises when the clutch pedal is depressed.

**18.4 Check for wear in the hub bearings by grasping the wheel and trying to rock it**

**10** Check that all gears can be engaged smoothly without noise, and that the gear lever action is not abnormally vague or notchy.

**11** Listen for a metallic clicking sound from the front of the vehicle, as the vehicle is driven slowly in a circle with the steering on full-lock. Carry out this check in both directions. If a clicking noise is heard, this indicates wear in a driveshaft joint, in which case renew the joint if necessary.

### Braking system

**12** Make sure that the vehicle does not pull to one side when braking, and that the wheels do not lock prematurely when braking hard.

**13** Check that there is no vibration through the steering when braking.

**14** Check that the handbrake operates correctly without excessive movement of the lever, and that it holds the vehicle stationary on a slope.

**15** Test the operation of the brake servo unit as follows. With the engine off, depress the footbrake four or five times to exhaust the vacuum. Hold the brake pedal depressed, then start the engine. As the engine starts, there should be a noticeable give in the brake pedal as vacuum builds up. Allow the engine to run for at least two minutes, and then switch it off. If the brake pedal is depressed now, it should be possible to detect a hiss from the servo as the pedal is depressed. After about four or five applications, no further hissing should be heard, and the pedal should feel considerably harder.

**18.6 Anti-roll bar mounting bushes (arrowed)**

21.3 Idle speed adjustment screw (arrowed) - engine code AEF

## 21 Idle speed check - engine code AEF only

1 Start the engine and run it until it reaches its normal operating temperature. With the handbrake applied and the transmission in neutral, allow the engine to idle. Make sure that all electrical equipment (headlights, heated rear window, heater blower, etc) is switched off.

2 Using a diesel tachometer, check the idle speed against the Specifications at the start of this Chapter.

3 To adjust the idle speed, loosen the locknut on the idle speed stop screw, then adjust the screw as necessary **(see illustration)**. On completion, tighten the locknut.

# Every 20 000 miles (30 000 km)

## 22 Lubricate folding fabric sunroof guide rail

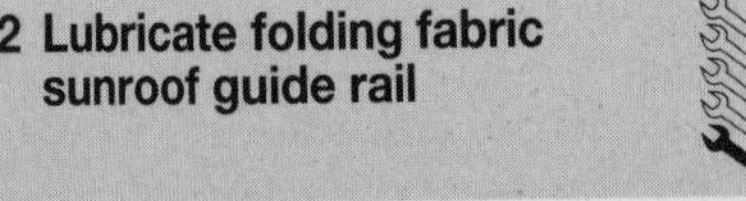

1 Using a clean cloth and a suitable solvent if necessary, thoroughly clean the sunroof guide rail **(see illustration)**.

2 Apply a little general-purpose grease to the guide rail, then check the sunroof operation.

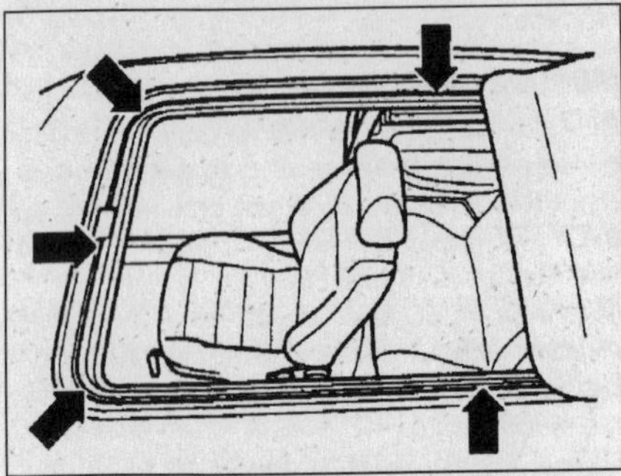

22.1 Folding fabric sunroof guide rail (arrowed)

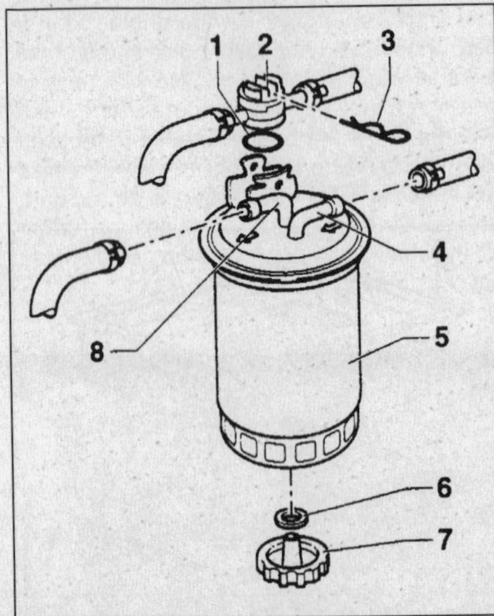


23.3 Fuel filter details

1 *O-ring seal*
2 *Control valve*
3 *R-clip*
4 *Hose connection*
5 *Fuel filter*
6 *Washer*
7 *Water drain tap*
8 *Hose connection*

## 23 Fuel filter renewal

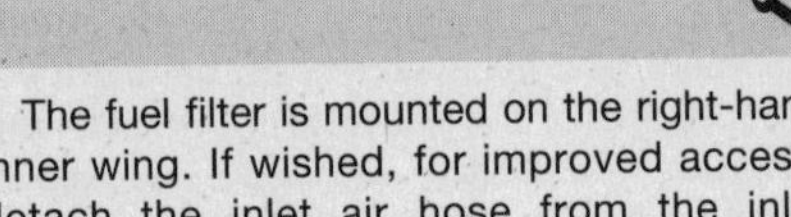

1 The fuel filter is mounted on the right-hand inner wing. If wished, for improved access, detach the inlet air hose from the inlet manifold and the air cleaner, and move it out of the way.

2 Place a container below the filter, and pad the surrounding area with rags to absorb any fuel that may be spilt.

3 At the top of the filter unit, pull out the R-clip and lift out the control valve, leaving the fuel hoses attached **(see illustration)**.

4 Slacken the hose clips, and pull the fuel supply and delivery hoses from the ports on the of the filter unit. If crimp-type clips are fitted, cut them off using snips, and use proper fuel hose clips on refitting. Note the fitted position of each hose, in relation to the direction-of-flow arrows on top of the filter, to aid correct refitting.

***Caution: Be prepared for an amount of fuel loss.***

5 Slacken the retaining bracket screw and lift the filter out.

6 Fill the new fuel filter with clean diesel fuel before fitting - this will make the engine easier to start. Fit the new fuel filter into the retaining bracket, and tighten the screw.

7 Fit a new O-ring seal to the control valve, then refit the control valve to the top of the filter, and insert the retaining clip.

8 Reconnect the fuel supply and delivery hoses, using the notes made during removal - note the fuel flow arrow markings next to each port. Where crimp-type hoses were originally fitted, use screw-type clips on refitting. Remove the collecting container and rags, and refit the inlet air hose to the air cleaner and inlet manifold (where removed).

9 Start and run the engine at idle, then check around the fuel filter for fuel leaks. **Note:** *It may take a few seconds of cranking before the engine starts, especially if the new filter was not primed with fuel before fitting.*

10 Raise the engine speed to about 2000 rpm several times, then allow the engine to idle again. Observe the fuel flow through the transparent hose leading to the fuel injection pump, and check that it is free of air bubbles.

## 24 Pollen filter renewal

1 The pollen filter is located beneath the windscreen cowl panels; it is located on the left side on right-hand-drive models, and the right side on left-hand drive models.

2 Open the bonnet, and lift up the rubber weatherstrip from the relevant end of the top of the engine compartment bulkhead **(see illustration)**.

3 Peel back the rubber seal at the base of the windscreen, for access to the two cowl panel retaining clips **(see illustration)**. Take care when prising these clips out of position, as they are easily broken.

4 Remove the cowl panel from the car **(see illustration)**.

24.2 Pull off the rubber weatherstrip from the top of the bulkhead

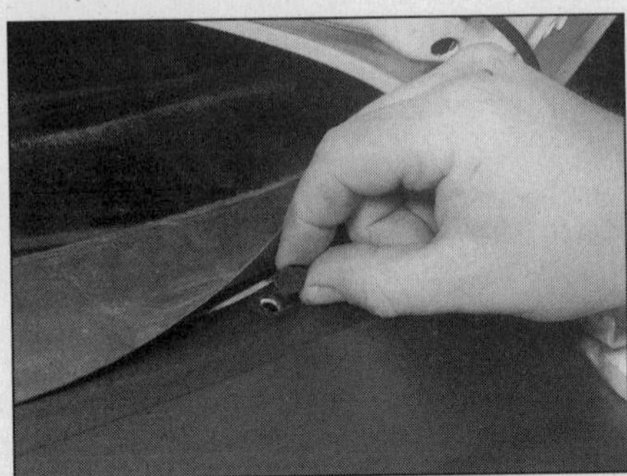

24.3 Peel back the rubber seal for access to the cowl panel retaining clips

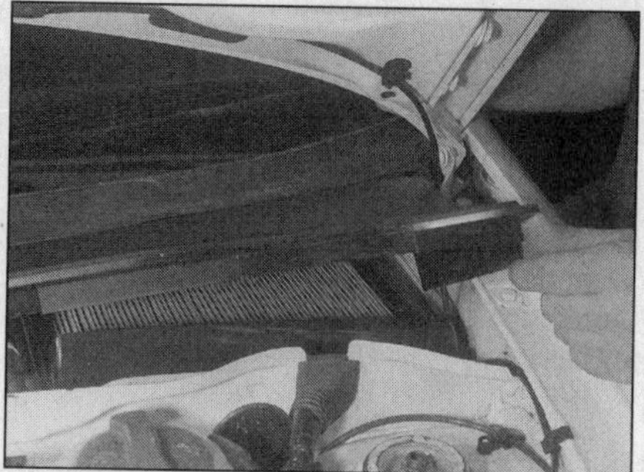
24.4 Lifting out the cowl panel

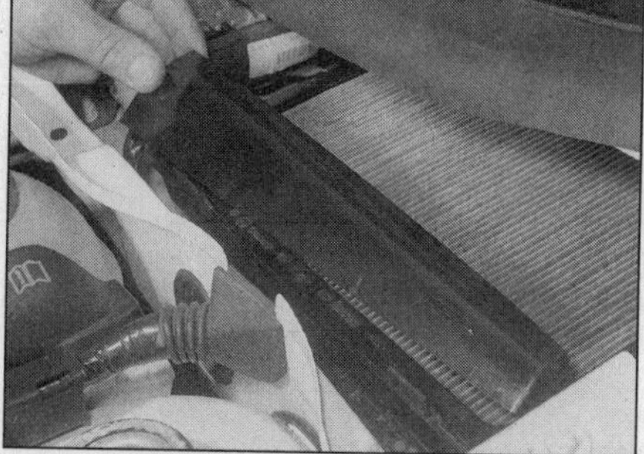
24.5 Removing the pollen filter air deflector plate

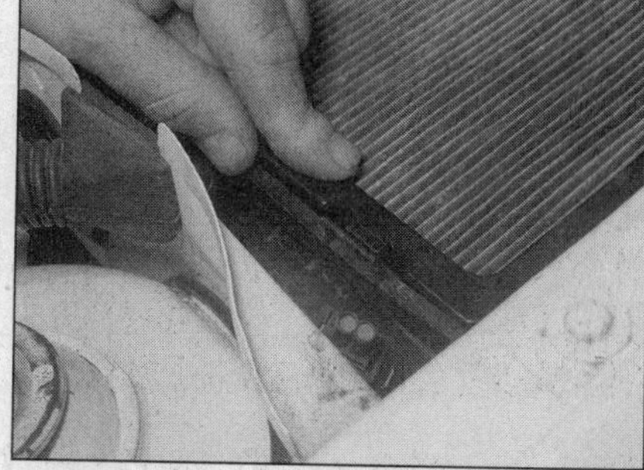
24.6a Release the retaining clips at the front . . .

**5** Unclip the filter air deflector and remove it **(see illustration)**.

**6** Release the two clips at the front to release the frame, and lift the pollen filter and frame upwards and out from its location **(see illustrations)**. Note which way round the frame is fitted.

**7** Separate the frame from the old filter, noting how it is fitted. Slot the new filter into the frame **(see illustrations)**.

**8** Wipe clean the filter housing, then fit the new filter and frame. Clip the filter securely in position and refit the cover.

**9** Refit the rubber seal to the engine compartment bulkhead to complete.

## 25 Auxiliary drivebelt check and renewal

### Checking

**1** Disconnect the battery negative lead and position it away from the terminal. **Note:** *If the vehicle has a security-coded radio, check that you have a copy of the code number before disconnecting the battery. Refer to your VW dealer if in doubt.*

**2** Park the vehicle on a level surface, apply the handbrake and chock the rear wheels. Loosen the right-hand front wheel bolts.

**3** Raise the front of the vehicle, rest it securely on axle stands and remove the right-hand front roadwheel.

**4** Turn the steering to full right-hand lock. Where applicable, remove the fasteners, and lower the wheel arch liner and/or noise insulation tray for access to the drivebelt. Models with power steering may have a cover fitted over the drivebelt - if so, release the fasteners and remove it. To improve access still further, refer to Chapter 4C and remove the air cleaner housing.

**5** Using a socket and wrench on the crankshaft sprocket bolt, rotate the crankshaft so that the full length of the auxiliary drivebelt can be examined. Look for cracks, splitting and fraying on the surface of the belt; check also for signs of glazing (shiny patches) and separation of the belt plies. If damage or wear is visible, the belt should be renewed. If there is any evidence of contamination by oil, grease or coolant, the reason should be investigated without delay.

**6** Check the drivebelt tension by pressing on the belt at a point midway between two pulleys. Depending on the type of belt, it should move by approximately 5 to 10 mm. If the drivebelt appears excessively taut or slack, refer to Chapter 2B and adjust the belt tension.

**7** On completion, refit the wheel arch liner, noise insulation tray and air cleaner housing (as applicable), then refit the roadwheel and lower the car to the ground. Tighten the roadwheel bolts to the specified torque.

### Renewal

**8** For details of auxiliary drivebelt renewal, refer to Chapter 2B.

## 26 Timing belt condition and tension check - engine code AEF only

**1** Refer to Chapter 2B and remove the timing belt upper cover for access to the timing belt. Also prise out the round inspection cover over the timing belt tensioner.

**2** Examine the belt for signs of cracking or splitting, especially around the roots of the teeth, and for signs of fraying or separation of the belt plies. If any damage is noted, the belt should be renewed as described in Chapter 2B.

**3** If there is any sign that the belt is being contaminated with oil or other fluid, the belt should be changed and the source of the leak found and fixed, otherwise the new belt will quickly go the same way.

**4** The timing belt tension can be checked as follows. Using firm thumb pressure, tension the belt and observe the belt tensioner. As tension is applied and then released, the tensioner raised portion and the notch must be seen to move apart, and then back into alignment once more **(see illustration)**. If the marks do not come back into alignment, the belt tension must be reset. The belt tension is critical - if it is slack, there is a danger that the belt might jump a tooth, while a belt which is too tight might wear prematurely.

1B

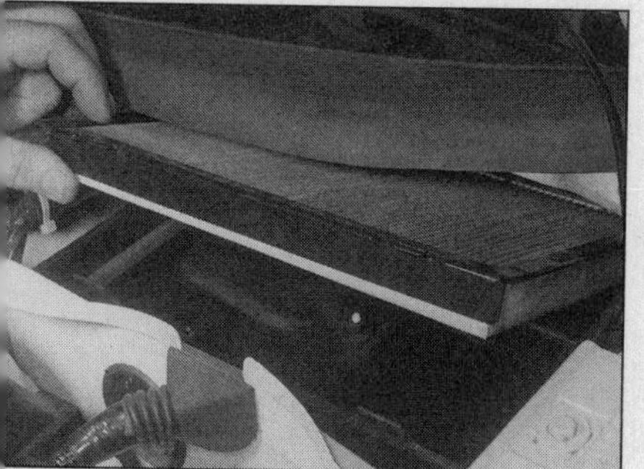
24.6b . . . then remove the pollen filter and frame

24.7a Separating the pollen filter from the frame

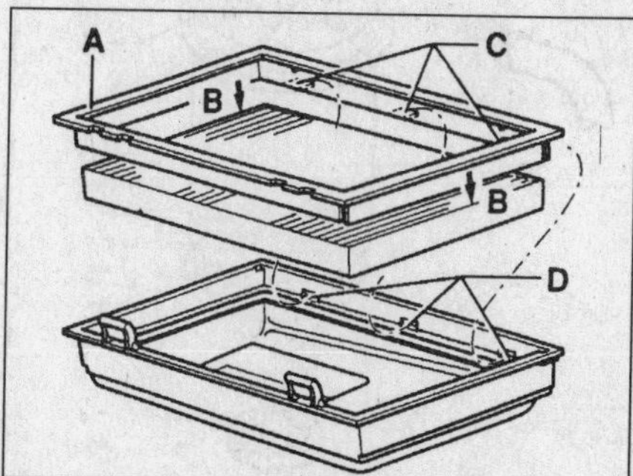

24.7b Pollen filter, frame and filter housing

*A Filter frame*
*B Frame fits into first fold of filter at each end*
*C Frame lugs*
*D Frame lug recesses in housing*

26.4 Timing belt tensioner markings (arrowed)

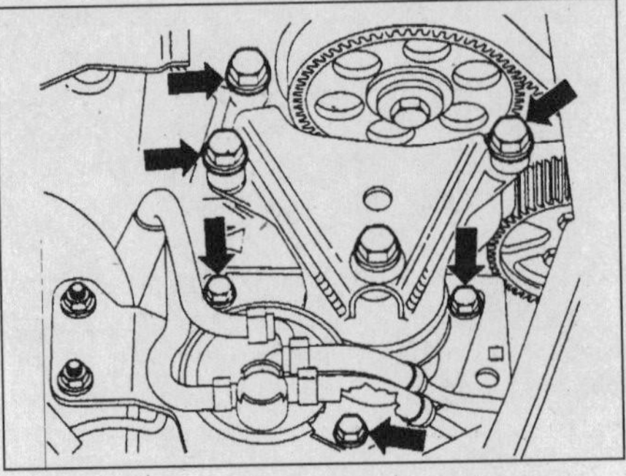

26.6 Engine right-hand mounting bolts (arrowed)

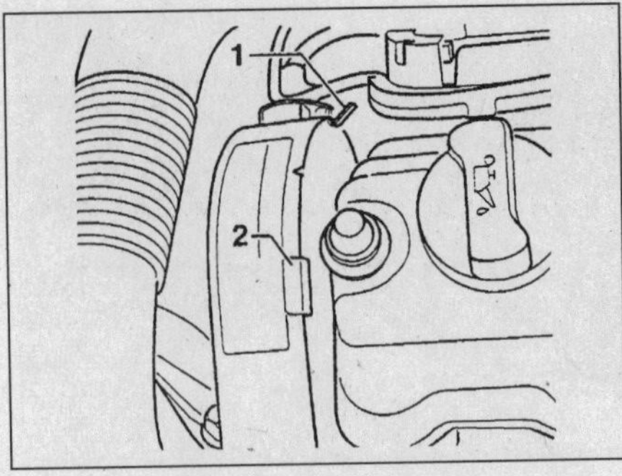


27.1 Timing belt upper cover securing clips (1) and cover (2)

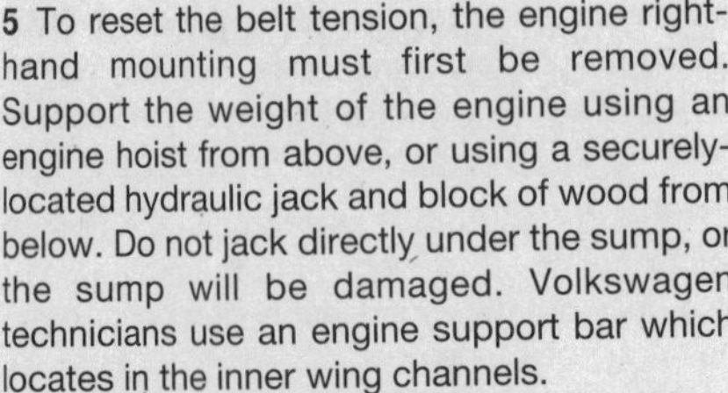

**5** To reset the belt tension, the engine right-hand mounting must first be removed. Support the weight of the engine using an engine hoist from above, or using a securely-located hydraulic jack and block of wood from below. Do not jack directly under the sump, or the sump will be damaged. Volkswagen technicians use an engine support bar which locates in the inner wing channels.

**6** With the engine securely supported, progressively loosen the engine mounting bolts shown **(see illustration)**. Remove the engine mounting from the vehicle.

**7** Loosen the tensioner roller locknut. Tension the belt by turning the eccentrically-mounted tensioner clockwise; two holes are provided in the side of the tensioner hub for this purpose - a pair of sturdy right-angled circlip pliers is a suitable substitute for the correct VAG tool. Turn the tensioner until the notch and the raised portion are aligned, then tighten the locknut to the specified torque.

**8** Repeat the tension check described in paragraph 4, and reset the tension again if necessary. If the belt tensioner is no longer capable of tensioning the belt adequately, it should be renewed as described in Chapter 2B.

**9** Refit the engine mounting using new bolts, and tighten the bolts to the specified torque. Note that the torque setting is different for the smaller, lower bolts. On completion, lower the engine hoist or hydraulic jack.

**10** Refit the timing belt upper cover as described in Chapter 2B, and refit the inspection cover over the belt tensioner.

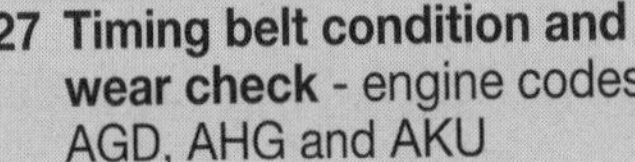

## 27 Timing belt condition and wear check - engine codes AGD, AHG and AKU

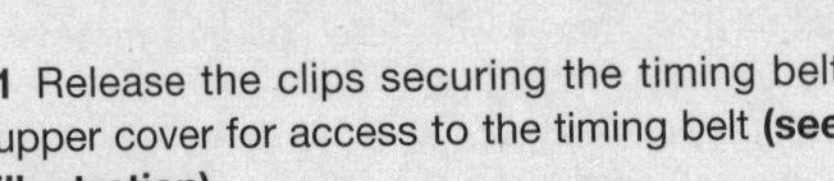

**1** Release the clips securing the timing belt upper cover for access to the timing belt **(see illustration)**.

**2** To assess timing belt wear, the width of the belt must be measured. If you have access to a set of vernier calipers, the width of the belt can be measured to a very high degree of accuracy **(see illustration)**. In the absence of vernier calipers, careful measurement with an accurate ruler will suffice. On completion, refit the timing belt upper cover.

**3** The belt wear limit is given in the Specifications at the start of this Chapter. If the measured width is at or below the wear limit value, the belt should be renewed as described in Chapter 2B.

**4** As far as you can, examine the belt for signs of cracking or splitting, especially around the roots of the teeth, and for signs of fraying or separation of the belt plies. If any damage is noted, the belt should be renewed as described in Chapter 2B.

**5** If there is any sign that the belt is being contaminated with oil or other fluid, the belt should be changed and the source of the leak found and fixed, otherwise the new belt will quickly go the same way.

## 28 Transmission oil level check

**1** Park the car on a level surface. The oil level must be checked before the car is driven, or at least 5 minutes after the engine has been switched off. If the oil is checked immediately after driving the car, some of the oil will remain distributed around the transmission components, resulting in an inaccurate level reading.

**2** On models built up to October 1995, the filler/level plug is located on the left-hand side of the transmission housing, next to the driveshaft **(see illustration)**. For easier access, turn the steering onto full left lock. Do not raise the car, because the level must be checked with the car resting on its wheels, on a level surface.

**3** On models built after October 1995, the filler/level plug is on the front of the transmission housing, and can be accessed from above **(see illustration)**. If preferred, however, the plug can be reached from below, but note that this may mean removing the noise insulation tray (where applicable) from under the engine for access.

**4** Wipe clean the area around the filler/level plug. A 17 mm hexagonal adapter (or a large Allen key) will be required to remove the plug, which will probably be quite tight **(see illustration)**.

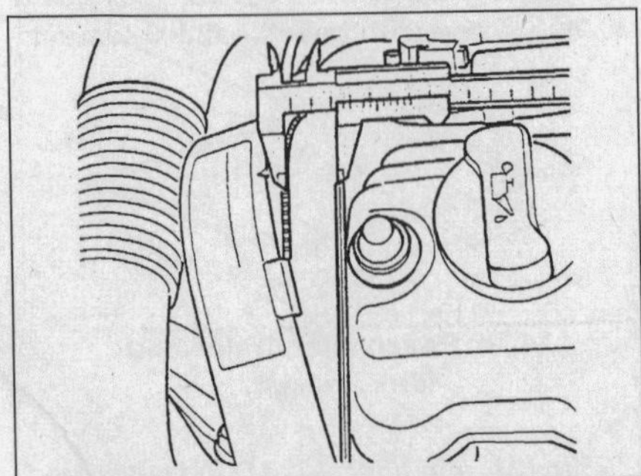

27.2 Measuring the width of the timing belt using vernier calipers

28.2 Transmission oil filler/level plug (arrowed) - models up to October 1995

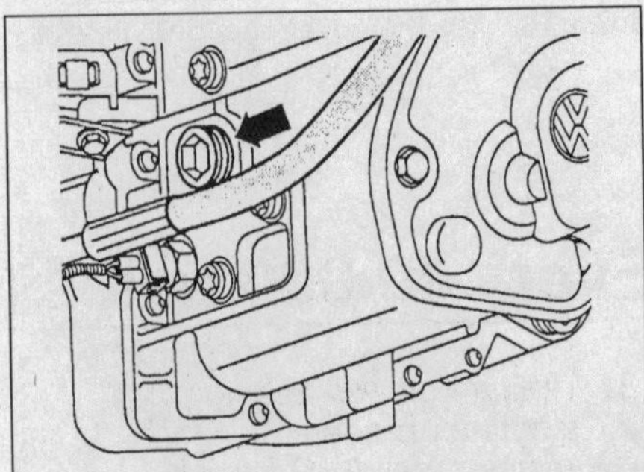

28.3 Transmission oil filler/level plug (arrowed) - models from October 1995

28.4 Loosening the filler/level plug (1) using a hex adapter - also shown is the transmission oil drain plug (2)

5 The oil level should reach the lower edge of the filler/level hole. A certain amount of oil will have gathered behind the filler/level plug, and will trickle out when it is removed; this does **not** necessarily indicate that the level is correct. To ensure that a true level is established, wait until the initial trickle has stopped, then add oil through the hole as necessary until a trickle of new oil can be seen emerging. The level will be correct when the flow ceases; use only good-quality oil of the specified type.

6 Filling the transmission with oil is an extremely awkward operation; above all, allow plenty of time for the oil level to settle properly before checking it. If a large amount is added to the transmission, and a large amount flows out on checking the level, refit the filler/level plug; take the vehicle on a short journey so that the new oil is distributed fully around the transmission components, then recheck the level when it has settled again.

7 If the transmission has been overfilled so that oil flows out when the filler/level plug is removed, check that the car is completely level (front-to-rear and side-to-side), and allow the surplus to drain off into a suitable container.

8 When the level is correct, refit the plug, tightening it to the specified torque, and wipe off any spilt oil.

## 29 Underbody protection check

Raise and support the vehicle on axle stands. Using an electric torch or lead light, inspect the entire underside of the vehicle, paying particular attention to the wheel arches. Look for any damage to the flexible underbody coating, which may crack or flake off with age, leading to corrosion. Also check that the wheel arch liners are securely attached with any clips provided - if they come loose, dirt may get in behind the liners and defeat their purpose. If there is any damage to the underseal, or any corrosion, it should be repaired before the damage gets too serious.

# Every 40 000 miles (60 000 km) or 2 years

## 30 Air filter renewal

1 On diesel engine models, the air cleaner housing is located under the right-hand front wing. Either turn the steering onto full right lock, or jack up the front of the car and remove the right-hand front roadwheel, for better access.

2 Release the cover securing clips around the base of the air cleaner housing, and withdraw the cover and filter element **(see illustrations)**.

3 Wipe clean the inside of the filter housing, and also the outside, if necessary. It is important that no dirt is allowed to enter the housing, or to contaminate the new element when it is fitted.

4 Fit the new element into the housing, observing any direction-of-fitting markings, and secure the cover with the retaining clips.

5 Refit the front wheel and lower the car to the ground, where applicable.

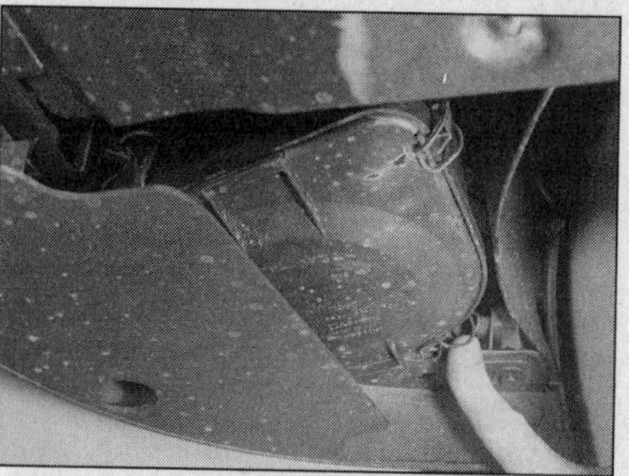

30.2a Release the cover securing clips . . .

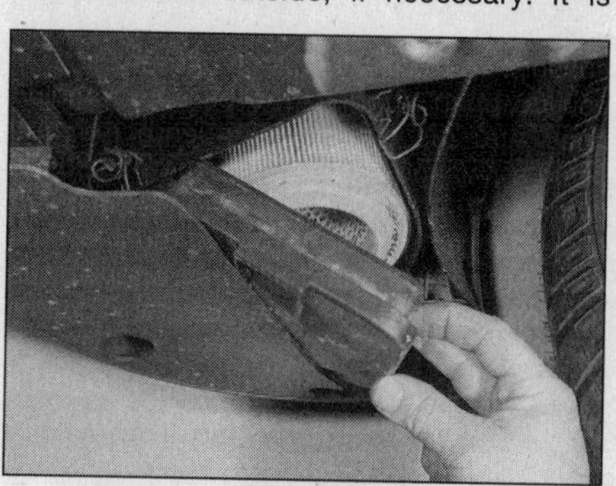

30.2b . . . remove the cover . . .

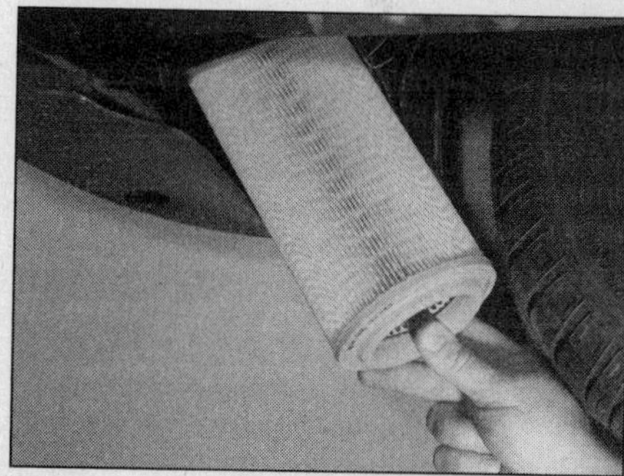

30.2c . . . and withdraw the filter element

1B

# Every 40 000 miles (60 000 km)

## 31 Timing belt and belt tensioner renewal - engine codes AHG and AKU

Refer to Chapter 2B.

## 32 Timing belt and belt tensioner renewal - engine codes AEF and AGD

Refer to Chapter 2B.

## 33 Coolant renewal

**Note:** *VW coolant type G11 or G12 lasts indefinitely. Provided you are sure that this type of coolant has been used and that the concentration is adequate, there is no need to renew it. Most other brands of antifreeze must be renewed every two years. Once the system has been drained, it is as well to flush it and to take the opportunity to renew any rubber hoses whose condition is in doubt. Proceed as follows.*

### Cooling system draining

***Warning: Wait until the engine is cold before starting this procedure. Do not allow antifreeze to come in contact with your skin, or with the painted surfaces of the vehicle. Rinse off spills immediately with plenty of water. Never leave antifreeze lying around in an open container, or in a puddle in the driveway or on the garage floor. Children and pets are attracted by its sweet smell, but antifreeze can be fatal if ingested.***

**1** With the engine completely cold, cover the expansion tank cap with a wad of rag, and slowly turn the cap anti-clockwise to relieve the pressure in the cooling system (a hissing sound will normally be heard). Wait until any pressure remaining in the system is released, then continue to turn the cap until it can be removed.

**2** Where necessary, release the fasteners and remove the noise insulation tray from under the engine. Position a suitable container beneath the radiator bottom hose connection, then release the retaining clip and ease the hose from the radiator stub. If the hose joint has not been disturbed for some time, it will be necessary to gently manipulate the hose to break the joint. Do not use excessive force, or the radiator stub could be damaged. Allow the coolant to drain into the container.

**3** If the coolant has been drained for a reason other than renewal, then provided it is clean and less than two years old, it can be re-used, though this is not recommended (see *Antifreeze type and mixture* later in this Section).

**4** Once all the coolant has drained, reconnect the hose to the radiator and secure it in position with the retaining clip.

### Cooling system flushing

**5** If coolant renewal has been neglected, or if the antifreeze mixture has become diluted, then in time, the cooling system may gradually lose efficiency, as the coolant passages become restricted due to rust, scale deposits, and other sediment. Flushing the system clean can restore the cooling system efficiency.

**6** The radiator should be flushed independently of the engine, to avoid unnecessary contamination.

#### Radiator flushing

**7** To flush the radiator, disconnect the top and bottom hoses and any other relevant hoses from the radiator, with reference to Chapter 3.

**8** Insert a garden hose into the radiator top inlet. Direct a flow of clean water through the radiator, and continue flushing until clean water emerges from the radiator bottom outlet.

**9** If after a reasonable period, the water still does not run clear, the radiator can be flushed with a good proprietary cooling system cleaning agent. It is important that their manufacturer's instructions are followed carefully. If the contamination is particularly bad, insert the hose in the radiator bottom outlet, and reverse-flush the radiator.

#### Engine flushing

**10** To flush the engine, remove the thermostat as described in Chapter 3, then temporarily refit the thermostat cover.

**11** With the top and bottom hoses disconnected from the radiator, insert a garden hose into the radiator top hose. Direct a clean flow of water through the engine, and continue flushing until clean water emerges from the radiator bottom hose.

**12** On completion of flushing, refit the thermostat and reconnect the hoses with reference to Chapter 3.

### Cooling system filling

**13** Before attempting to fill the cooling system, make sure that all hoses and clips are in good condition, and that the clips are tight. Note that an antifreeze mixture must be used all year round, to prevent corrosion of the engine components (see following sub-Section).

**14** Remove the expansion tank filler cap, and fill the system by slowly pouring the coolant into the expansion tank to prevent airlocks from forming.

**15** If the coolant is being renewed, begin by pouring in a couple of litres of water, followed by the correct quantity of antifreeze, then top-up with more water.

**16** Once the level in the expansion tank starts to rise, squeeze the radiator top and bottom hoses to help expel any trapped air in the system. Once all the air is expelled, top-up the coolant level to the MAX mark and refit the expansion tank cap.

**17** Start the engine and run it until it reaches normal operating temperature, then stop the engine and allow it to cool.

**18** Check for leaks, particularly around disturbed components. Check the coolant level in the expansion tank, and top-up if necessary. Note that the system must be cold before an accurate level is indicated in the expansion tank. If the expansion tank cap is removed while the engine is still warm, cover the cap with a thick cloth, and unscrew the cap slowly to gradually relieve the system pressure (a hissing sound will normally be heard). Wait until any pressure remaining in the system is released, then continue to turn the cap until it can be removed.

### Antifreeze type and mixture

**19** The antifreeze should always be renewed at the specified intervals. This is necessary not only to maintain the antifreeze properties, but also to prevent corrosion which would otherwise occur as the corrosion inhibitors become progressively less effective.

**20** Always use ethylene-glycol-based antifreeze suitable for use in mixed-metal cooling systems. The quantity of antifreeze and levels of protection are indicated in the Specifications.

**21** When the car was new, the cooling system will have been filled with VW G11 (blue colour) coolant. Petrol engine models may be filled with G11 coolant or the later G12 (red colour) coolant. At the time of writing, the manufacturer's advice on coolant is as follows:

*a) On no account should the blue G11 coolant be mixed with the red G12 coolant.*

*b) When refilling, G11 coolant should continue to be used on all diesel engines.*

**22** Before adding antifreeze, the cooling system should be completely drained, preferably flushed, and all hoses checked for condition and security.

**23** After filling with antifreeze, a label should be attached to the expansion tank, stating the type and concentration of antifreeze used, and the date installed. Any subsequent topping-up should be made with the same type and concentration of antifreeze.

**24** Do not use engine antifreeze in the washer system, as it will cause damage to the vehicle paintwork.

## 34 Brake fluid renewal

***Warning: Brake hydraulic fluid can harm your eyes and damage painted surfaces, so use extreme caution when handling and pouring it. Do not use fluid that has been standing open for some time, as it absorbs moisture from the air. Excess moisture can cause a dangerous loss of braking effectiveness.***

**1** The procedure is similar to that for the bleeding of the hydraulic system as described in Chapter 9. The brake fluid reservoir should be emptied by siphoning, using a clean poultry baster or similar before starting, and allowance should be made for the old fluid to be expelled when bleeding a section of the circuit.

**2** Working as described in Chapter 9, open the first bleed screw in the sequence, and pump the brake pedal gently until nearly all the old fluid has been emptied from the master cylinder reservoir.

***Old hydraulic fluid is often much darker in colour than the new, making it easy to distinguish the two.***

**3** Top-up to the MAX level with new fluid, and continue pumping until only the new fluid remains in the reservoir, and new fluid can be seen emerging from the bleed screw. Tighten the screw, and top the reservoir level up to the MAX level line.

**4** Work through all the remaining bleed screws in the sequence until new fluid can be seen at all of them. Be careful to keep the master cylinder reservoir topped-up to above the MIN level at all times, or air may enter the system and greatly increase the length of the task.

**5** When the operation is complete, check that all bleed screws are securely tightened, and that their dust caps are refitted. Wash off all traces of spilt fluid, and recheck the fluid level.

**6** Check the operation of the brakes before taking the car on the road.

## 35 Exhaust emissions check

This check is part of the manufacturer's maintenance schedule, and involves checking the exhaust emissions using smoke testing equipment. Unless a fault is suspected, this test is not essential, although it should be noted that it is recommended by the manufacturers. Smoke testing is included as part of the MoT test.

Notes

# Chapter 2 Part A:
# Petrol engine in-car repair procedures

## Contents



## Degrees of difficulty

| | | | | |
|---|---|---|---|---|
| **Easy,** suitable for novice with little experience  | **Fairly easy,** suitable for beginner with some experience  | **Fairly difficult,** suitable for competent DIY mechanic 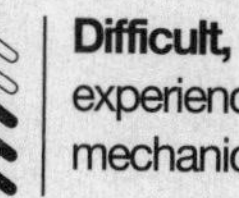 | **Difficult,** suitable for experienced DIY mechanic | **Very difficult,** suitable for expert DIY or professional |

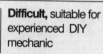

## Specifications



### General

| | |
|---|---|
| Engine code* | |
| 999 cc, Bosch Motronic injection, 37 kW | AER or ALL |
| 1043 cc, Bosch Mono-Motronic injection, 33 kW | AEV |
| 1296 cc, Bosch Mono-Motronic injection, 40 kW | ADX |
| 1390 cc, Bosch Motronic injection, 44 kW | AEX or AKV |
| 1390 cc, Bosch Motronic injection, 40 kW | ANX or APQ |
| 1598 cc: | |
| Bosch Mono-Motronic injection, 55 kW | AEA |
| 1AV injection, 55kW (08/95 on) | AEE |

* **Note:** *See Buying spare parts and vehicle identification for the location of code marking on the engine.*

| | |
|---|---|
| Bore: | |
| AER, ALL | 67.1 mm |
| AEV | 75.0 mm |
| All other engines | 76.5 mm |
| Stroke: | |
| AER, ALL | 70.6 mm |
| AEV | 59.0 mm |
| ADX | 70.6 mm |
| AEX, AKV, ANX | 75.6 mm |
| AEA, AEE | 86.9 mm |
| Compression ratio: | |
| AER, ALL | 10.5:1 |
| AEV, ADX | 10.0:1 |
| AEX, AKV, ANX | 10.2:1 |
| AEA, AEE | 9.8:1 |
| Compression pressures: | |
| Wear limit | 7.0 bar |
| Maximum difference between all cylinders | 3.0 bar |
| Firing order | 1 - 3 - 4 - 2 |
| No 1 cylinder location | Timing belt end |

## Lubrication system

| | |
|---|---|
| Oil pump type | Sump-mounted, chain-driven from crankshaft |
| Normal operating oil pressure | 2.0 bar minimum (at 2000 rpm, oil temperature 80°C) |
| Oil pump backlash | 0.2 mm (wear limit) |
| Oil pump axial clearance | 0.15 mm (wear limit) |
| Oil pump drive chain tension | 4 mm (approx) deflection at mid-point between sprockets |

## Torque wrench settings

| | Nm | lbf ft |
|---|---|---|
| Alternator mounting bolts | 25 | 18 |
| Alternator mounting bracket-to-engine bolts: | | |
| Aluminium cylinder block (engine codes AER, ALL)* | 55 | 41 |
| Cast-iron cylinder block (engine codes except AER, ALL) | 45 | 33 |
| Auxiliary drivebelt tensioner pulley bolt | 45 | 33 |
| Auxiliary drivebelt tensioner-to-bracket bolt | 25 | 18 |
| Camshaft cover bolts: | | |
| Stage 1 | 5 | 4 |
| Stage 2 | Angle-tighten a further 90° | |
| Camshaft sprocket bolt: | | |
| Stage 1 | 20 | 15 |
| Stage 2 | Angle-tighten a further 90° | |
| Crankshaft oil seal housing bolts* | 10 | 7 |
| Crankshaft pulley-to-crankshaft sprocket (socket-head bolts) | 20 | 15 |
| Crankshaft sprocket bolt - oil threads*: | | |
| Hex-head bolt: | | |
| Stage 1 | 90 | 66 |
| Stage 2 | Angle-tighten a further 120° | |
| Splined (bi-hex) bolt: | | |
| Stage 1 | 90 | 66 |
| Stage 2 | Angle-tighten a further 90° | |
| Cylinder head bolts: | | |
| Aluminium cylinder block (engine codes AER, ALL)*: | | |
| Stage 1 | 30 | 22 |
| Stage 2 | Angle-tighten a further 90° | |
| Stage 3 | Angle-tighten a further 90° | |
| Cast-iron cylinder block (engine codes except AER, ALL)*: | | |
| Stage 1 | 40 | 30 |
| Stage 2 | 60 | 44 |
| Stage 3 | Angle-tighten a further 90° | |
| Stage 4 | Angle-tighten a further 90° | |
| Dipstick tube bolts | 10 | 7 |
| Engine right-hand mounting-to-block bolts*: | | |
| Stage 1 | 40 | 30 |
| Stage 2 | Angle-tighten a further 90° | |
| Engine/transmission mountings - oiled threads **(see illustration 13.9)***: | | |
| A | 50 | 37 |
| B | 50 | 37 |
| C: | | |
| Stage 1 | 20 | 15 |
| Stage 2 | Angle-tighten a further 45° | |
| D | 25 | 18 |
| E | 60 | 44 |
| F | 80 | 59 |
| G: | | |
| Stage 1 | 20 | 15 |
| Stage 2 | Angle-tighten a further 45° | |
| H | 50 | 37 |
| I (tighten nut) | 50 | 37 |
| J: | | |
| Up to December 1996 | 35 | 26 |
| December 1996 on: | | |
| Stage 1 | 20 | 15 |
| Stage 2 | Angle-tighten a further 90° | |
| Exhaust manifold | 25 | 18 |
| Exhaust manifold warm air collector plate bolts | 10 | 7 |
| Exhaust pipe-to-manifold: | | |
| M8 | 25 | 18 |
| M10 | 40 | 30 |

| Torque wrench settings (continued) | Nm | lbf ft |
|---|---|---|
| Flywheel bolts*: | | |
| Stage 1 | 60 | 44 |
| Stage 2 | Angle-tighten a further 90° | |
| Knock sensor | 20 | 15 |
| Oil pressure switch | 25 | 18 |
| Oil pump mounting bolts (timing belt end) | 20 | 15 |
| Oil pump pickup bracket bolts | 10 | 7 |
| Roadwheel bolts | 110 | 81 |
| Sump bolts | 15 | 11 |
| Sump drain plug | 30 | 22 |
| Timing belt guard/coolant pump mounting bolts | 20 | 15 |
| Timing belt inner cover-to-cylinder head bolts | 10 | 7 |
| Timing belt lower cover bolts* | 10 | 7 |
| Timing belt tensioner roller locknut | 20 | 15 |

** Use new bolts/nuts*

## 1 General information

### *Using this Chapter*

Chapter 2 is divided into three Parts; A, B and C. Repair operations that can be carried out with the engine in the vehicle are described in Parts A (petrol engines) and B (diesel engines). Part C covers the removal of the engine/transmission as a unit, and describes the engine dismantling and overhaul procedures.

In Parts A and B, the assumption is made that the engine is installed in the vehicle, with all ancillaries connected. If the engine has been removed for overhaul, the preliminary dismantling information which precedes each operation may be ignored.

Access to the engine bay can be improved by removing the bonnet and the front lock carrier assembly; for details, see Chapter 2C, Section 2.

### *Engine description*

Throughout this Chapter, engines are identified and referred to by the manufacturer's code letters, rather than capacity. A listing of all engines covered, together with their code letters, is given in the Specifications.

The engines are water-cooled, single overhead camshaft, in-line four-cylinder units, with aluminium-alloy (engine codes AER and ALL) or cast-iron (all other engine codes) cylinder blocks and aluminium-alloy cylinder heads. All are mounted transversely at the front of the vehicle, with the transmission bolted to the left-hand side of the engine.

The cylinder head carries the camshaft, which is driven by a toothed timing belt. It also houses the inlet and exhaust valves, which are closed by single coil springs, and which run in guides pressed into the cylinder head. The camshaft actuates the valves directly via hydraulic tappets, mounted in the cylinder head. The cylinder head contains integral oilways which supply and lubricate the tappets.

The crankshaft is supported by five main bearings, and on models with a cast-iron cylinder block, crankshaft endfloat is controlled by a thrust bearing fitted between cylinder Nos 2 and 3. On models with an aluminium cylinder block, the crankshaft must not be removed, otherwise the block will distort; the crankshaft and block must therefore be renewed as an assembly.

Engine coolant is circulated by a pump, driven by the camshaft timing belt. For details of the cooling system, refer to Chapter 3.

Lubricant is circulated under pressure by a pump, driven by the crankshaft via a chain. Oil is drawn from the sump through a strainer, and then forced through an externally-mounted, replaceable screw-on filter. From there, it is distributed to the cylinder head, where it lubricates the camshaft journals and hydraulic tappets, and also to the crankcase, where it lubricates the main bearings, connecting rod big- and small-ends, gudgeon pins and cylinder bores.

### *Repairs possible with the engine installed in the vehicle :*

The following operations can be performed without removing the engine:-

*a) Auxiliary drivebelt - removal and refitting.*
*b) Camshaft - removal and refitting.**
*c) Camshaft oil seal - renewal.*
*d) Camshaft sprocket - removal and refitting.*
*e) Coolant pump - removal and refitting (refer to Chapter 3).*
*f) Crankshaft oil seals - renewal.*
*g) Crankshaft sprocket - removal and refitting.*
*h) Cylinder head - removal and refitting.**
*i) Engine mountings - inspection and renewal.*
*j) Oil pump and pickup assembly - removal and refitting.*
*k) Sump - removal and refitting.*
*l) Timing belt, sprockets and cover - removal, inspection and refitting.*

**Cylinder head dismantling procedures are detailed in Chapter 2C, with details of camshaft and hydraulic tappet removal.*

**Note:** *It is possible to remove the pistons and connecting rods (after removing the cylinder head and sump) without removing the engine. However, this is not recommended. Work of this nature is more easily and thoroughly completed with the engine on the bench, as described in Chapter 2C.*

## 2 Locating TDC on No 1 cylinder

### *General information*

**Note:** *This sub-Section has been written with the assumption that the distributor, HT leads and timing belt are correctly fitted.*

**1** The crankshaft and camshaft sprockets are driven by the timing belt, and rotate in phase with each other. When the timing belt is removed during servicing or repair, it is possible for the shafts to rotate independently of each other, and the correct phasing is then lost.

**2** The design of the engines covered in this Chapter is such that potentially damaging piston-to-valve contact may occur if the camshaft is rotated when any of the pistons are stationary at, or near, the top of its stroke.

**3** For this reason, it is important that the correct phasing between the camshaft and crankshaft is preserved whilst the timing belt is off the engine. This is achieved by setting the engine in a reference condition (known as Top Dead Centre or TDC) before the timing belt is removed, and then preventing the shafts from rotating until the belt is refitted. Similarly, if the engine has been dismantled for overhaul, the engine can be set to TDC during reassembly to ensure that the correct shaft phasing is restored. **Note:** *The coolant pump is also driven by the timing belt, but the pump alignment with respect to the crankshaft and camshaft is not critical.*

**4** TDC is the highest position a piston reaches within its respective cylinder - in a four-stroke engine, each piston reaches TDC twice per cycle; once on the compression stroke, and once on the exhaust stroke. In general, TDC normally refers to No 1 cylinder on the compression stroke (the cylinders are numbered 1 to 4, with No 1 being at the timing belt end of the engine).

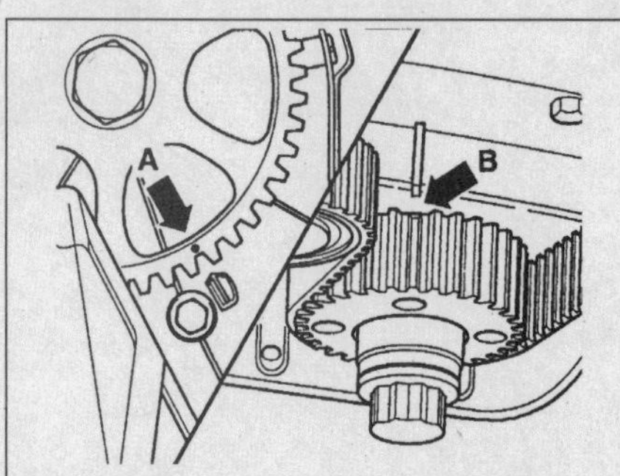


2.5 Camshaft sprocket (A) and crankshaft sprocket (B) TDC timing marks

5 The crankshaft sprocket has a notch ground away from one of its teeth which, when aligned with a reference marking on the crankshaft front oil seal flange, indicates that No 1 cylinder (and hence also No 4 cylinder) is at TDC. However, as the crankshaft sprocket is only visible with the timing belt lower cover removed - there is also a notch in the crankshaft pulley, which, when aligned with a 0 mark moulded into the timing belt lower cover, indicates TDC. The camshaft sprocket is also equipped with a timing mark (a dot punched in its outer face) - when this is aligned with the raised pointer moulded into the timing belt inner cover, the engine is correctly synchronised, and the timing belt can then be refitted and tensioned **(see illustration)**.

6 The following sub-Sections describe setting the engine to TDC on No 1 cylinder.

## *Setting TDC on No 1 cylinder - timing belt fitted*

### All engines

7 Before starting work, disconnect the battery negative lead. **Note:** *If the vehicle has a security-coded radio, check that you have a copy of the code number before disconnecting the battery. Refer to your VW dealer if in doubt.*

8 Prevent any vehicle movement by applying the handbrake and chocking the rear wheels. Ensure that the transmission is in neutral (manual transmission) or P (automatic transmission).

9 On the distributor cap, note the position of the No 1 cylinder HT terminal with respect to the distributor body. On some models, the manufacturer provides a marking in the form of a small cut-out. If the terminal is not marked, follow the HT lead from the No 1 cylinder spark plug back to the distributor cap - No 1 cylinder is at the timing end of the engine - and using chalk or a pen (***not*** a pencil), place a mark on the distributor body directly under the terminal.

10 Remove the distributor cap, as described in Chapter 5B.

11 Disconnect the HT leads from the spark plugs, noting their order of connection.

12 To bring any piston up to TDC, it will be necessary to rotate the crankshaft manually. This can be done by using a wrench and socket on the centre bolt that retains the crankshaft sprocket (refer to Section 5 for more detail).

13 Rotate the crankshaft in its normal direction of rotation until the distributor rotor arm electrode begins to approach the mark that was made on the distributor body.

***Remove all four spark plugs; this will make the engine easier to turn; refer to Chapter 1A for details.***

14 With reference to Section 4, remove the timing belt upper cover to expose the camshaft sprocket beneath.

15 Identify the timing marks on both the camshaft sprocket and the inner section of the timing belt cover. Continue turning the crankshaft clockwise until these marks are exactly aligned with each other **(see illustration)**.

16 At this point, identify the timing marks on the crankshaft pulley and the timing belt lower cover. The cover has a Z and a 0 mark moulded into it - when the notch in the rim of the crankshaft pulley aligns with the 0 mark, the engine is set to TDC.

17 Alternatively, check that the crankshaft sprocket and the crankshaft front oil seal flange timing marks are correctly aligned **(refer to illustration 2.5)**. **Note**: *The crankshaft pulley and the lower timing belt cover must be removed to expose the crankshaft sprocket timing marks.*

18 Check that the centre of the distributor rotor arm electrode is now aligned with the No 1 terminal mark on the distributor body. If it proves impossible to align the rotor arm with the No 1 terminal whilst maintaining the alignment of the camshaft timing marks, refer to Chapter 5B and check that the distributor has been fitted correctly.

19 When all the above steps have been completed successfully, the engine will be set to TDC on No 1 cylinder.

***Caution: If the timing belt is to be removed, ensure that the crankshaft, camshaft and intermediate shaft alignment is preserved by preventing the sprockets from rotating with respect to each other.***

## *Setting TDC on No 1 cylinder - timing belt removed*

20 This procedure has been written with the assumption that the timing belt has been removed and that the alignment between the camshaft and crankshaft has been lost, for example following engine removal and overhaul.

21 On all the engines covered in this manual, it is possible for damage to be caused by the piston crowns striking the valve heads, if the camshaft is rotated with the timing belt removed and the crankshaft set to TDC. For this reason, the TDC setting procedure must be carried out in a particular order, as described in the following paragraphs.

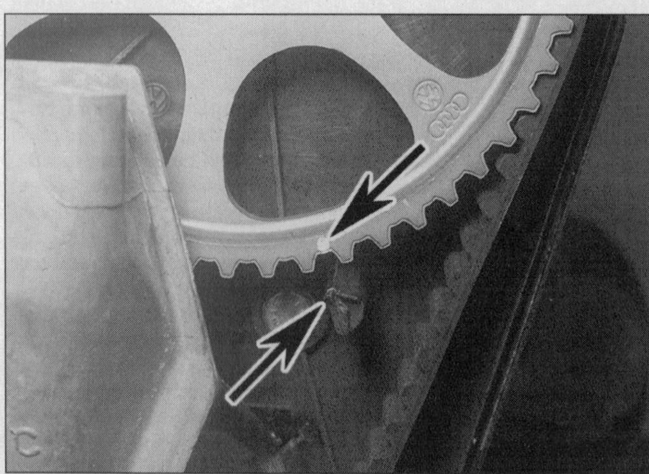

2.15 Camshaft sprocket punched mark and notch in timing belt inner cover aligned (arrowed)

2.25 Crankshaft sprocket chamfered tooth (1) and timing mark (2)

22 Before the cylinder head is refitted, use a wrench and socket on the crankshaft sprocket centre bolt to turn the crankshaft in its normal direction of rotation, until all four pistons are positioned **halfway down** their bores, with No 1 piston on its upstroke - i.e. around 90° before TDC.
23 With the cylinder head and camshaft sprocket fitted, identify the timing marks on both the camshaft sprocket and the inner section of the timing belt cover **(see illustration 2.15)**.
24 Turn the camshaft sprocket in its normal direction of rotation until the timing marks on the sprocket and timing belt inner cover are exactly aligned.
25 Identify the timing marks on the crankshaft sprocket and the crankshaft front oil seal flange **(see illustration)**. Using a socket and wrench on the crankshaft sprocket retaining bolt, turn the crankshaft through 90° (quarter of a turn) in its normal direction of rotation, to bring the timing marks into alignment.
26 Check that the centre of the distributor rotor arm electrode is now aligned with No 1 cylinder terminal marking on the distributor body. If it proves impossible to align the rotor arm with the No 1 terminal whilst maintaining the alignment of the camshaft timing marks, refer to Chapter 5B and check that the distributor has been fitted correctly.
27 When all the above steps have been completed successfully, the engine will be set at TDC on No 1 cylinder. The timing belt can now be fitted as described in Section 4.
***Caution: Until the timing belt is fitted, ensure that the crankshaft, camshaft and intermediate shaft alignment is preserved by preventing the sprockets from rotating with respect to each other.***

## 3 Cylinder compression test

1 When engine performance is down, or if misfiring occurs which cannot be attributed to the ignition or fuel systems, a compression test can provide diagnostic clues as to the engine's condition. If the test is performed regularly, it can give warning of trouble before any other symptoms become apparent.
2 The engine must be fully warmed-up to normal operating temperature, the battery must be fully charged, and all the spark plugs must be removed (refer to Chapter 1). The aid of an assistant will also be required.
3 Disable the ignition system by disconnecting the ignition HT coil lead from the distributor cap and earthing it on the cylinder block. Use a jumper lead or similar wire to make a good connection.
4 To prevent possible damage to the catalytic converter, depressurise and disable the fuel injection system by removing the fuel pump fuse or relay (see Chapter 4).
5 Fit a compression tester to the No 1 cylinder spark plug hole - the type of tester which screws into the plug thread is preferable.
6 Have an assistant hold the accelerator pedal in the full-throttle position, then crank the engine on the starter motor; after one or two revolutions, the compression pressure should build up to a maximum figure, and then stabilise. Record the highest reading obtained.
7 Repeat the test on the remaining cylinders, recording the pressure in each. Keep the accelerator pedal fully depressed.
8 All cylinders should produce very similar pressures; a difference of more than 2 bars between any two cylinders indicates a fault (the manufacturer quotes a maximum difference between the highest and lowest of all four readings). Note that the compression should build up quickly in a healthy engine; low compression on the first stroke, followed by gradually-increasing pressure on successive strokes, indicates worn piston rings. A low compression reading on the first stroke, which does not build up during successive strokes, indicates leaking valves or a blown head gasket (a cracked head could also be the cause). Deposits on the undersides of the valve heads can also cause low compression.
9 Refer to the Specifications section of this Chapter, and compare the recorded compression figures with those stated by the manufacturer.
10 If the pressure in any cylinder is low, carry out the following test to isolate the cause. Introduce a teaspoonful of clean oil into that cylinder through its spark plug hole, and repeat the test.
11 If the addition of oil temporarily improves the compression pressure, this indicates that bore or piston wear is responsible for the pressure loss. No improvement suggests that leaking or burnt valves, or a blown head gasket, may be to blame.
12 A low reading from two adjacent cylinders is almost certainly due to the head gasket having blown between them; the presence of coolant in the engine oil will confirm this.
13 If one cylinder is about 20 percent lower than the others and the engine has a slightly rough idle, a worn camshaft lobe could be the cause.
14 If the compression reading is unusually high, the combustion chambers are probably coated with carbon deposits. If this is the case, the cylinder head should be removed and decarbonised.
15 On completion of the test, refit the spark plugs and restore the ignition and fuel systems.

## 4 Timing belt and outer covers - removal and refitting

### General information

1 The primary function of the toothed timing belt is to drive the camshaft, but it is also used to drive the coolant pump. Should the belt slip or break in service, the valve timing will be disturbed and piston-to-valve contact may occur, resulting in serious engine damage. Similarly, the coolant pump may leak coolant onto the belt, or if the pump is severely worn, the pump may seize and break the belt.
2 For this reason, it is important that the timing belt is tensioned correctly, and inspected regularly for signs of wear or deterioration.
3 Note that the removal of the *inner* section of the timing belt cover is described as part of the camshaft oil seal renewal procedure; see Section 8.

### Removal

4 Before starting work, immobilise the engine and vehicle as follows:

a) *Disconnect the battery negative lead, and position the lead away from the terminal.* **Note:** If the vehicle has a security-coded radio, check that you have a copy of the code number before disconnecting the battery. Refer to your VW dealer if in doubt.
b) *Prevent any vehicle movement by applying the handbrake and chocking the rear wheels. Ensure that the transmission is in neutral (manual transmission) or P (automatic transmission).*
c) *Loosen the right-hand front wheel bolts, then jack up the front of the car and support securely on axle stands (see Jacking and vehicle support).*

5 Access to the timing belt covers can be improved by removing the air cleaner housing, and the air ducting from the exhaust manifold and inner wing. On 1.0 litre models, remove the engine top cover, as described in Section 16. Pull out the engine oil dipstick and place it to one side, out of the way.
6 To renew the belt, the engine right-hand mounting must first be removed. Support the weight of the engine using an engine hoist from above, or using a securely-located hydraulic jack and suitable block of wood from below. Do not jack under the sump without using a block of wood to spread the load, or the sump will be damaged. Volkswagen technicians use an engine support bar which locates in the inner wing channels.
7 With the engine securely supported, progressively loosen the engine mounting bolts and remove the engine right-hand mounting from the vehicle **(see illustrations)**.
8 The engine must now be lowered slightly, to allow the crankshaft pulley to be removed.

4.7a Remove the mounting bolts . . .

4.7b . . . and lift off the engine right-hand mounting

4.10a Loosen the crankshaft pulley bolts, counterholding on the centre bolt . . .

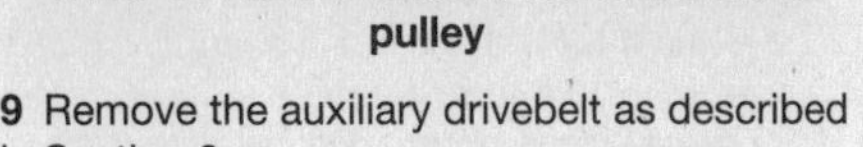

4.10b . . . and withdraw the crankshaft pulley

4.11a Release the timing belt upper cover retaining clips . . .

4.11b . . . then remove the timing belt upper cover

**9** Remove the auxiliary drivebelt as described in Section 6.

**10** Unscrew and remove the four crankshaft pulley retaining bolts - it should be possible to counterhold the pulley using a spanner or socket on the crankshaft sprocket bolt. Remove the crankshaft pulley **(see illustrations)**.

***To prevent the crankshaft drivebelt pulley from rotating whilst the bolts are being slackened, select top gear (manual transmission) or P (automatic transmission) and get an assistant to apply the footbrake firmly. Failing this, grip the sprocket by wrapping a length of old rubber hose or inner tube around it. If top gear is selected to help in removing the pulley, make sure the transmission is returned to neutral before proceeding.***

**11** Release the retaining clips, and remove the timing belt upper cover **(see illustrations)**.

**12** Unscrew and remove the three retaining bolts, release the clips, and remove the timing belt lower cover **(see illustration)**. To improve access to the front bolt, rotate the auxiliary drivebelt tensioner clockwise and hold it out of the way using a spanner on the centre bolt. The tensioner can be removed completely, if preferred, by turning the centre bolt anti-clockwise; remove the bolt, washer and tensioner pulley.

**13** Using the information in Section 2, set the engine to TDC on No 1 cylinder.

**14** Examine the timing belt for manufacturer's markings that indicate the direction of rotation. If none are present, make your own using typist's correction fluid or a dab of paint - do not cut or score the belt in any way.

***Caution: If the belt appears to be in good condition and can be re-used, it is essential that it is refitted the same way around, otherwise accelerated wear will result, leading to premature failure.***

**15** Loosen the tensioner roller locknut, and allow the tensioner to rotate anti-clockwise to relieve the tension on the belt **(see illustration)**.

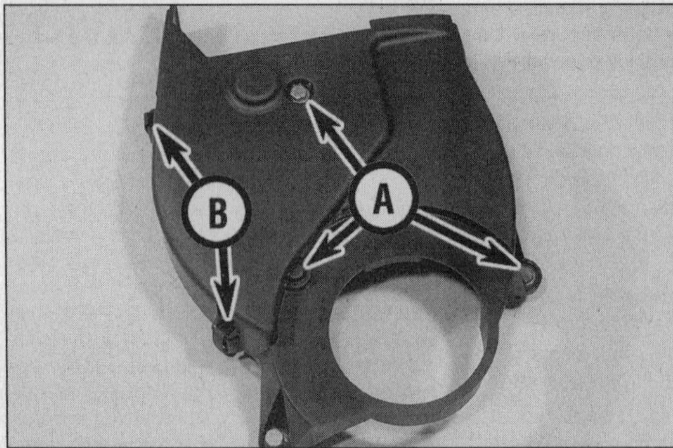



4.12 Timing belt lower cover removed, showing locations of retaining bolts (A) and clips (B)

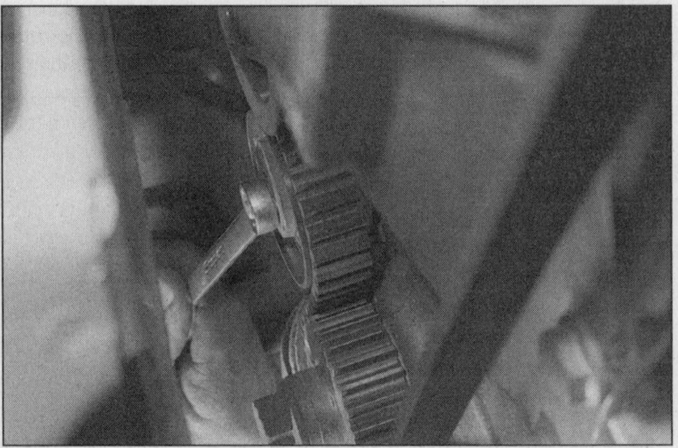

4.15 Loosening the belt tensioner locknut

4.16 Removing the timing belt

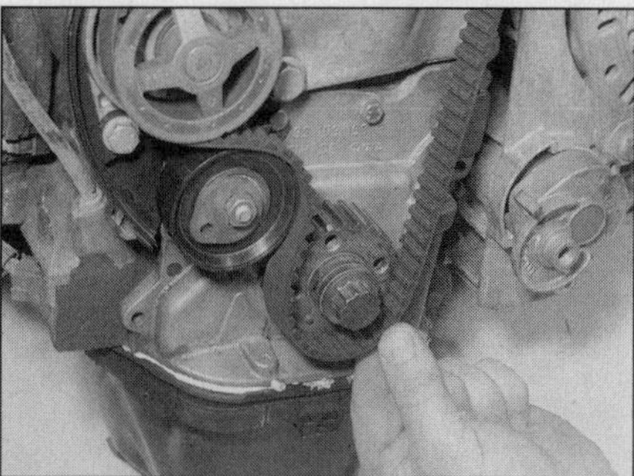
4.20 Engaging the timing belt with the crankshaft sprocket

**16** Slide the belt off the sprockets, taking care to avoid twisting or kinking it excessively **(see illustration)**. Ensure that the sprockets remain aligned with their respective timing markings once the timing belt has been removed.

***Caution: It is potentially damaging to allow the camshaft to turn with the timing belt removed and the engine set at TDC, as piston-to-valve contact may occur.***

**17** Examine the belt for evidence of contamination by coolant or lubricant. If this is the case, identify the source of the contamination before progressing any further. Check the belt for signs of wear or damage, particularly around the leading edges of the belt teeth. Renew the belt if its condition is in doubt; the cost of belt renewal is negligible compared with potential cost of the engine repairs, should the belt fail in service. Similarly, if the belt is known to have covered more than 30 000 miles, it is prudent to renew it regardless of condition, as a precautionary measure.

**18** If the timing belt is not going to be refitted for some time, it is a wise precaution to hang a warning label on the steering wheel, to remind yourself (and others) not to attempt starting the engine. You may wish to further immobilise the engine against being started, perhaps by taping over the ignition switch.

## *Refitting*

**19** Ensure that the timing marks on the camshaft and crankshaft sprockets are correctly aligned with their corresponding TDC reference marks on the timing belt inner cover and crankshaft oil seal flange; refer to Section 2 for details.

**20** Engage the timing belt teeth with the crankshaft sprocket, then manoeuvre it into position over the coolant pump and camshaft sprockets. Observe the direction of rotation markings on the belt **(see illustration)**.

**21** Pass the flat side of the belt over the tensioner roller - avoid bending the belt back on itself or twisting it excessively as you do this. Ensure the front run of the belt is taut - ie all the slack should be in the section of the belt that passes over the tensioner roller.

**22** Tension the belt as follows: tighten the tensioner locknut lightly, then insert an Allen key into the adjustment hole, and turn the eccentrically-mounted tensioner clockwise until the slack in the belt is taken up. Continue turning the tensioner until the sliding pointer lines up with the notch in the tensioner baseplate. On completion, tighten the tensioner locknut to the specified torque **(see illustrations)**.

**23** Using a spanner or wrench and socket on the crankshaft sprocket bolt, rotate the crankshaft through two complete revolutions, and reset the engine to TDC on No 1 cylinder, with reference to Section 2. Re-check the alignment of the tensioner, and adjust it if necessary.

**24** Refer to Section 5 and test the operation of the tensioner.

**25** Refit the lower and upper sections of the timing belt outer cover, refitting the clips and tightening the retaining bolts securely. Use new bolts on the timing belt lower cover.

**26** Refit the pulley for the ribbed auxiliary drivebelt to the crankshaft sprocket, noting that the small hole in the pulley fits over a peg on the crankshaft sprocket **(see illustration)**, then insert and tighten the retaining bolts to the specified torque. Counterhold the sprocket using one of the methods described in paragraph 10.

**27** Working from Section 6, refit and tension the auxiliary drivebelt.

**28** Raise the engine back into a position where the right-hand engine mounting can be refitted.

**29** Refit the engine mounting using new bolts, and tighten the bolts to the specified torque. Note that the mounting upper and lower bolts are tightened to different torques. Lower the hoist or the jack on completion.

**30** Refit the air cleaner warm air ducting to the exhaust manifold and inner wing. Where applicable, restore ignition and fuel systems by reconnecting the coil HT lead and refitting the fuel pump fuse or relay.

**31** Reconnect the battery negative lead.

**32** On completion, refer to Chapter 5B and check the ignition timing.

## 5 Timing belt sprockets and tensioner - removal, inspection and refitting

**1** Before starting work, immobilise the engine and vehicle as follows:

a) *Disconnect the battery negative lead, and position the lead away from the terminal.* **Note:** If the vehicle has a security-coded radio, check that you have a copy of the code number before disconnecting the battery. Refer to your VW dealer if in doubt.

b) *Prevent any vehicle movement by applying the handbrake and chocking the rear wheels. Ensure that the transmission is in neutral (manual transmission) or P (automatic transmission).*

2A

## *Timing belt tensioner*

### Removal

**2** With reference to Section 2, set the engine to TDC on No 1 cylinder.

4.22a Turn the tensioner clockwise using an Allen key until the pointer aligns with the slot in the tensioner baseplate

4.22b When the belt tension is correctly set, tighten the tensioner locknut

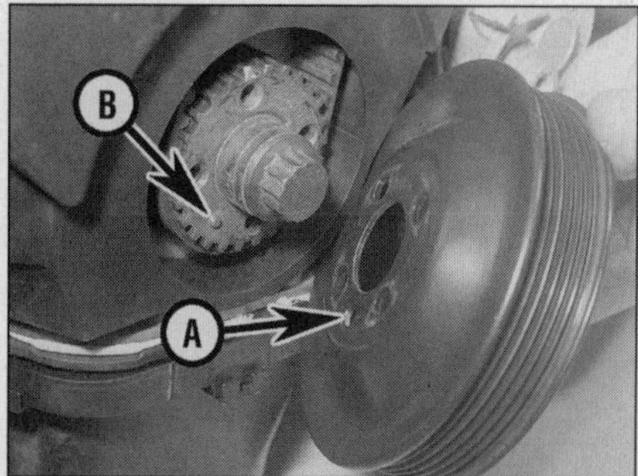

4.26 Refitting the crankshaft pulley - small hole (A) fits over peg (B) on crankshaft sprocket

5.7 Slide tensioner onto its mounting stud, fitting the U-shaped baseplate over the bolt (arrowed)

5.9a Apply pressure to the belt, and the tensioner pointer (arrowed) should move away from the central position . . .

5.9b . . . then return to correct alignment as pressure is released

**3** Referring to Section 4, remove the right-hand engine mounting, then remove the auxiliary drivebelt, crankshaft pulley, and the timing belt upper and lower covers.

**4** Slacken the locknut at the hub of the tensioner pulley, and allow the assembly to rotate anti-clockwise, relieving the tension on the timing belt.

**5** Remove the locknut and slide the tensioner off its mounting stud.

### Inspection

**6** Wipe the tensioner clean, but do not use solvents that may contaminate the bearings. Spin the tensioner pulley on its hub by hand. Stiff movement or excessive freeplay is an indication of severe wear; the tensioner is not a serviceable component, and it should be renewed if its condition is less than perfect.

### Refitting and testing

**7** Slide the tensioner pulley over the mounting stud. The U-shape in the tensioner baseplate fits over the bolt shown **(see illustration)**. Refit the locknut and tighten it lightly - do not fully tighten the nut at this stage.

**8** With reference to Section 4, tension the timing belt.

**9** The operation of the belt tensioner can be tested as follows. Apply finger pressure to the timing belt at a point mid-way between the camshaft and crankshaft sprockets. The sliding pointer that protrudes from behind the tensioner roller should slide away from the alignment notch in the tensioner baseplate as pressure is applied, and then move back as the pressure is removed **(see illustrations)**. Any reluctance to return to the correct position indicates that the tensioner should be renewed - correct tension is critical to the operation of the belt, and the importance of the belt tensioner cannot be overstressed.

**10** Referring to Section 4, refit the timing belt upper and lower covers, the crankshaft pulley, auxiliary drivebelt, and the right-hand engine mounting. Reconnect the battery negative lead.

**11** With reference to Chapter 5B, check the ignition timing.

## *Camshaft timing belt sprocket*

### Removal

**12** With reference to Sections 2 and 4, remove the timing belt covers and set the engine to TDC on No 1 cylinder. Slacken the timing belt tensioner locknut and rotate it anti-clockwise to relieve the tension on the timing belt. Carefully slide the timing belt off the camshaft sprocket.

***Warning: It is potentially damaging to allow the camshaft to turn with the timing belt removed and the engine set at TDC, as piston-to-valve contact may occur. Take care that the camshaft sprocket is not turned as it is removed. As a precaution against damage, VW recommend that the crankshaft be turned back a few degrees, away from TDC, while the camshaft sprocket is removed/refitted. The crankshaft may then be turned back to TDC when the timing belt is to be refitted.***

**13** The camshaft sprocket must be held stationary whilst its retaining bolt is slackened; if access to the correct VAG special tool is not possible, a simple home-made tool using basic materials may be fabricated **(see Tool Tip)**.

***To make a camshaft sprocket holding tool, obtain two lengths of steel strip about 6 mm thick by 30 mm wide or similar, one 600 mm long, the other 200 mm long (all dimensions approximate). Bolt the two strips together to form a forked end, leaving the bolt slack so that the shorter strip can pivot freely. At the end of each 'prong' of the fork, secure a bolt with a nut and a locknut, to act as the fulcrums; these will engage with the cut-outs in the sprocket, and should protrude by about 30mm***

**14** Using the home-made tool, brace the camshaft sprocket. Slacken and remove the retaining bolt **(see illustration)**.

**15** Slide the camshaft sprocket from the end of the camshaft **(see illustration)**. Where applicable, recover the Woodruff key from the keyway.

**16** With the sprocket removed, look for signs of oil leaking from the camshaft oil seal. If necessary, refer to Section 8 and renew it.

**17** Wipe the sprocket and camshaft mating surfaces clean.

### Refitting

**18** Where applicable, fit the Woodruff key into the keyway, with the plain surface facing upwards. Offer up the sprocket to the

5.14 Remove the camshaft sprocket bolt . . .

5.15 . . . and take off the camshaft sprocket - note the alignment tooth and keyway (arrowed)

camshaft, engaging the slot in the sprocket with the Woodruff key. On engines where a key is not used, ensure that the tooth in the sprocket hub engages with the keyway in the end of the camshaft.

**19** Counterholding the camshaft sprocket as for removal, fit and tighten the camshaft sprocket bolt to the specified torque, and then through the specified angle **(see illustration)**.

**20** Working from Sections 2 and 4, check that the engine is still set to TDC on No 1 cylinder, then refit and tension the timing belt. Refit the timing belt covers and all other components removed for access, as described in Section 4. Reconnect the battery negative lead.

## *Crankshaft timing belt sprocket*

### Removal

**21** With reference to Sections 2 and 4, remove the timing belt covers and set the engine to TDC on No 1 cylinder.

**22** The crankshaft sprocket must be held stationary whilst its retaining bolt is slackened. If access to the correct VAG flywheel locking tool is not available, lock the crankshaft in position by removing the starter motor, as described in Chapter 5A, to expose the flywheel ring gear. Then get an assistant to insert a stout lever between the gear teeth and the transmission bellhousing whilst the sprocket retaining bolt is slackened. Refer also to Section 12, paragraph 2.

**23** Holding the engine against rotation as described in the previous paragraph, slacken the crankshaft sprocket bolt - do not remove it yet **(see illustration)**.

**5.19 Tighten the camshaft sprocket bolt to the specified torque, and then through the specified angle**

**5.23 Slacken the crankshaft sprocket bolt**

**24** Ensure that the engine is still set to TDC, then slacken the timing belt tensioner centre nut and rotate it anti-clockwise to relieve the tension on the timing belt. Carefully slide the timing belt off the crankshaft sprocket.

**25** Withdraw the bolt and slide off the crankshaft sprocket **(see illustrations)**.

**26** With the sprocket removed, examine the crankshaft oil seal for signs of leaking. If necessary, refer to Section 9 and renew it.

**27** Wipe the sprocket and crankshaft mating surfaces clean.

### Refitting

**28** Offer up the sprocket, engaging the tooth on the inside of the sprocket with the keyway in the end of the crankshaft **(see illustration)**. Lightly oil and insert a new crankshaft sprocket bolt and tighten it hand-tight at this stage. **Note:** *Due to the high torque to which the sprocket bolt must be tightened, there is a danger that the crankshaft sprocket may turn as it is tightened, particularly if the tool used to lock the flywheel ring gear slips. For this reason, it is recommended that the final tightening of the crankshaft sprocket bolt is delayed until after the timing belt has been fitted.*

**29** Working from Sections 2 and 4, check that the engine is still set to TDC on No 1 cylinder, then refit and tension the timing belt.

**30** Tighten the crankshaft bolt to the specified torque, then through the specified angle, using the method described in paragraph 22 to lock the flywheel **(see illustrations)**. If the engine is out of the car, have an assistant support the engine as the bolt is tightened - a great deal of effort will be required, and the engine may tip over. Note that the final angle-torque depends on the type of bolt fitted, which is either a normal hex-head bolt, or a bi-hex bolt, which has multiple splines.

**31** Refit the timing belt covers and all other components removed for access, as described in Section 4. Reconnect the battery negative lead.

2A

## *Coolant pump timing belt sprocket*

**32** The coolant pump sprocket is an integral part of the coolant pump assembly, and cannot be removed or renewed separately. To remove the coolant pump, refer to Chapter 3.

**5.25a Remove the crankshaft sprocket bolt (this is a bi-hex" type) . . .**

**5.25b . . . then slide the sprocket off the crankshaft**

**5.28 Crankshaft sprocket alignment tooth and keyway (arrowed)**

**5.30a Tighten the bolt to the specified torque . . .**

**5.30b . . . and then through the specified angle - use an angle gauge if available, to ensure accuracy**

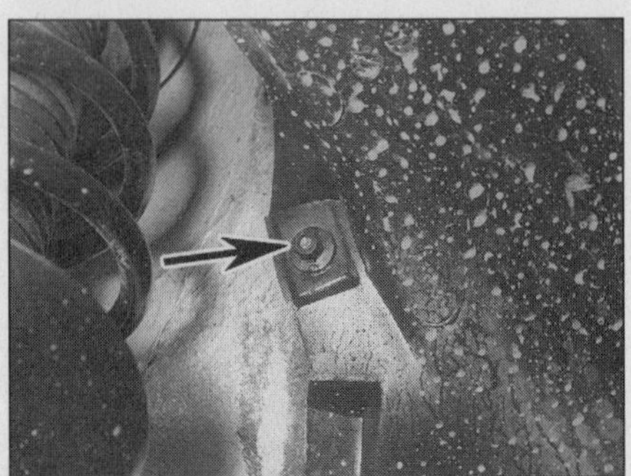
6.6a Typical wheel arch liner retaining bolt (arrowed) . . .

6.6b . . . and washer-type fastener . . .

6.6c . . . which can be unscrewed using a suitable screwdriver in the slots

## 6 Auxiliary drivebelt - removal, refitting and tensioning

### General information

**1** Depending on the vehicle specification, the auxiliary drivebelt, which is driven from a pulley mounted on the crankshaft, will provide drive for the alternator, power steering pump and (on vehicles with air conditioning), the refrigerant compressor.

**2** The ribbed auxiliary belt may be fitted with an automatic tensioning device, depending on its run (and hence the number of components it is driving). Otherwise, the belt is tensioned by the alternator mountings, which have an in-built tensioning spring.

**3** On refitting, the auxiliary belt must be tensioned correctly, to ensure correct operation under all conditions, and for prolonged service life.

### Removal

**4** Park the vehicle on a level surface, apply the handbrake and chock the rear wheels. Loosen the right-hand front wheel bolts.

**5** Raise the front of the car, rest it securely on axle stands and remove the right-hand front roadwheel.

**6** Where applicable, remove the fasteners, and lower the wheel arch liner and/or noise insulation tray for access to the drivebelt **(see illustrations)**. Some models may have a cover fitted over the drivebelt - if so, release the fasteners and remove it.

6.8 Rotate the auxiliary drivebelt tensioner clockwise to relieve the tension on the belt

**7** Examine the ribbed belt for manufacturer's markings, indicating the direction of rotation. If none are present, make some using typist's correction fluid or a dab of paint - do not cut or score the belt in any way.

#### Models with automatic tensioner

**8** Fit a ring spanner to the tensioner centre nut, and rotate the assembly clockwise, against its spring tension **(see illustration)**.

#### Models without automatic tensioner

**9** Slacken the alternator upper and lower mounting bolts by between one and two turns.

**10** Push the alternator down to its stop against the spring tension, so that it rotates around its uppermost mounting.

#### All models

**11** Pull the belt off the alternator pulley, then release it from the remaining pulleys **(see illustration)**.

### Refitting and tensioning

***Caution: Observe the manufacturer's direction of rotation markings on the belt, when refitting.***

**12** Pass the ribbed belt underneath the crankshaft pulley, ensuring that the ribs seat in the channels on the surface of the pulley.

#### Models with automatic tensioner

**13** Fit a ring spanner to the tensioner centre nut, and rotate the assembly clockwise, against its spring tension.

**14** Pass the flat side of the belt underneath the tensioner roller, then fit it over the pulleys.

6.11 Removing the auxiliary drivebelt

Ensure that the belt ribs engage correctly with the pulley grooves.

**15** Release the spanner and allow the tensioner roller to bear against the flat side of the belt.

#### Models without automatic tensioner

**16** Repeatedly push the alternator down to its stop against the spring tension, so that it rotates around its uppermost mounting, and check that it moves back freely when released. If necessary, slacken the alternator mounting bolts by a further half a turn.

**17** Keep the alternator pushed down against its stop, pass the belt over the alternator pulley, then release the alternator and allow it to tension the belt.

**18** Start the engine and allow it to idle for about 10 seconds, leaving the alternator mounting bolts slackened.

**19** Switch the engine off, then tighten first the lower, then the upper alternator mounting bolts to the specified torque.

#### All models

**20** Refit the drivebelt cover, wheel arch liner and noise insulation tray, as applicable.

**21** Refit the right-hand front roadwheel and lower the car to the ground. Tighten the roadwheel bolts to the specified torque.

## 7 Camshaft cover - removal and refitting

### Removal

**1** On models with Mono-Motronic fuel injection, to gain greater working space, refer to Chapter 4A and disconnect the throttle cable from the throttle housing. However, it is possible to remove the camshaft cover by carefully sliding the cover underneath the cable.

**2** On 1.0 litre models, refer to Section 16 and remove the engine top cover.

**3** Slacken and withdraw the three socket-headed camshaft cover retaining bolts **(see illustration)**.

**4** Lift the cover away from the cylinder head **(see illustration)**. If it sticks, do not attempt to lever it off with an implement - instead free it

7.3 Loosen and remove the socket-headed retaining bolts . . .

7.4 . . . and lift off the camshaft cover

by working around the cover and tapping it lightly with a soft-faced mallet.

5 Recover the camshaft cover gasket; renew the gasket if damage or deterioration is evident.

6 Clean the mating surfaces of the cylinder head and camshaft cover thoroughly, removing all traces of oil and old gasket - take care to avoid damaging the surfaces as you do this.

### Refitting

7 Refit the camshaft cover by following the removal procedure in reverse, noting the following points:

a) *Before fitting the gasket, apply a smear of suitable sealant to the joint between the camshaft bearing caps at either end, and the cylinder head.*
b) *Ensure that the gasket is correctly seated on the cylinder head, and take care to avoid displacing it as the camshaft cover is lowered into position.*
c) *Tighten the camshaft cover retaining bolts to the specified torque.*

8.3a Remove two bolts on the end of the engine, and one at the front (arrowed) . . .

8 On completion, refit the throttle cable (if removed). After the engine is next run, check for leaks.

## 8 Camshaft oil seal - renewal

1 Refer to Section 6 and remove the auxiliary drivebelt.

2 With reference to Sections 2, 4 and 5 of this Chapter, remove the crankshaft pulley and timing belt covers, then set the engine to TDC on No 1 cylinder and remove the timing belt, timing belt tensioner and camshaft sprocket.

3 After removing the retaining bolts, lift the timing belt inner cover away from the cylinder head - this will expose the oil seal **(see illustrations)**.

4 Remove the oil seal, using the same method as that described for the crankshaft oil seal removal, in Section 9.

5 Clean out the seal housing and sealing surface of the camshaft by wiping it with a lint-free cloth - avoid using solvents that may enter the cylinder head and affect component lubrication. Remove any swarf or burrs that may cause the seal to leak.

6 Lubricate the lip of the new oil seal with clean engine oil, and push it over the camshaft until it is positioned above its housing.

7 Using a hammer and a socket of suitable diameter, drive the seal squarely into its housing. **Note:** *Select a socket that bears only on the hard outer surface of the seal, not the inner lip which can easily be damaged.*

8 Refit the timing belt inner cover to the cylinder head, and tighten the retaining bolts to the specified torque.

9 With reference to Sections 2, 4 and 5 of this Chapter, refit the camshaft sprocket and the timing belt tensioner, then refit and tension the timing belt. On completion, refit the timing belt outer covers and other removed components.

10 With reference to Section 6, refit and tension the auxiliary drivebelt.

## 9 Crankshaft oil seals - renewal

### Crankshaft front oil seal

1 Drain the engine oil - see Chapter 1A.

2 Refer to Section 6 and remove the auxiliary drivebelt.

3 With reference to Sections 2, 4 and 5 of this Chapter, remove the crankshaft pulley, timing belt outer covers, timing belt and crankshaft sprocket.

4 Note the depth to which the old seal has been fitted, relative to its housing. Drill a small hole into the existing oil seal **(see illustration)**. Take great care to avoid drilling through into the seal housing or the crankshaft sealing surface. It may be necessary to drill another hole, if difficulty is experienced in pulling out the old seal, but we found that one hole was sufficient.

5 Thread a self-tapping screw into the hole, and using a pair of pliers, pull on the head of the screw to extract the oil seal **(see illustrations)**.

6 Clean out the seal housing and sealing surface of the crankshaft by wiping it with a lint-free cloth - avoid using solvents that may enter the crankcase and affect component lubrication. Remove any swarf or burrs that could cause the seal to leak.

7 Tape over the end of the crankshaft, to protect the new oil seal as it is fitted.

8.3b . . . and take off the timing belt inner cover

8.3c Camshaft oil seal (arrowed)

9.4 Drill a small hole into the old seal . . .

9.5a . . . then insert a self-tapping screw . . .

9.5b . . . and pull out the seal using pliers

9.8 Offering up the new oil seal - note the insulating tape over the end of the crankshaft, used to prevent the seal catching on the keyway

**8** Lubricate the lip of the new oil seal with clean engine oil, and position it over the housing **(see illustration)**.

**9** The new seal must be fitted to the same depth as was noted for the old seal. Using a hammer and a socket of suitable diameter, drive the seal squarely into its housing. **Note:** *Select a socket that bears only on the hard outer surface of the seal, not the inner lip which can easily be damaged.* As an alternative, place the old oil seal over the new seal, then fit the sprocket and its bolt, and tighten the bolt a little at a time to press the new seal into position **(see illustrations)**. Be sure to remove the old oil seal before finally fitting and tightening the sprocket and its bolt.

**10** With reference to Sections 2, 4 and 5 of this Chapter, refit the crankshaft sprocket, then refit and tension the timing belt. On completion, refit the timing belt outer covers, crankshaft pulley and other removed components.

**11** The remainder of the refitting procedure is a reversal of removal, as follows:

a) *With reference to Section 6, refit and tension the auxiliary drivebelt.*
b) *Refer to Chapter 1A and refill the engine with the correct grade and quantity of oil.*

## Crankshaft front oil seal housing - gasket renewal

**12** Proceed as described in paragraphs 1 to 3 above, then refer to Section 14 and remove the sump.

**13** Progressively slacken and then remove the oil seal housing retaining bolts from the cylinder block.

9.9a Fit the old seal over the new seal . . .

**14** Lift the housing away from the cylinder block, together with the crankshaft oil seal, using a twisting motion to ease the seal along the crankshaft.

**15** Recover the old gasket from the seal housing and the cylinder block. If it has disintegrated, scrape the remains off with a trimming knife blade. Take care to avoid damaging the mating surfaces.

**16** Recover the sealing bush which fits between the seal housing and the cylinder block. If the bush shows signs of damage or deterioration, lightly oil and fit a new one to the oil seal housing.

**17** Prise the old oil seal from the housing using a stout screwdriver.

**18** Wipe the oil seal housing clean, and check it visually for signs of distortion or cracking. Lay the housing on a work surface, with the mating surface face down. Press in a new oil seal, using a block of wood as a press to ensure that the seal enters the housing squarely.

**19** Smear the crankcase mating surface with multi-purpose sealant, and lay the new gasket in position.

**20** Pad the end of the crankshaft with a layer of PVC tape; this will protect the oil seal as it is being fitted.

**21** Lubricate the inner lip of the crankshaft oil seal with clean engine oil, then offer up the seal and its housing to the end of the crankshaft. Ease the seal along the shaft using a twisting motion, until the housing is flush with the crankcase. Ensure that the sealing bush fitted to the oil seal housing engages correctly with the crankcase.

9.9b . . . then fit the crankshaft sprocket and bolt, and use the sprocket to press the new seal into place

**22** Insert new retaining bolts and tighten them progressively to the specified torque. ***Caution: The housing is fabricated from a light alloy, and may be distorted if the bolts are not tightened progressively.***

**23** Refer to Section 14 and refit the sump.

**24** With reference to Sections 2, 4 and 5 of this Chapter, refit the crankshaft sprocket, then refit and tension the timing belt. On completion, refit the timing belt outer covers, crankshaft pulley and other removed components.

**25** The remainder of the refitting procedure is a reversal of removal, as follows:

a) *With reference to Section 6, refit and tension the auxiliary drivebelt.*
b) *Refer to Chapter 1A and refill the engine with the correct grade and quantity of oil.*

## Crankshaft rear oil seal (flywheel end)

**26** Drain the engine oil - see Chapter 1A.

**27** Refer to Chapter 7A or B as applicable, and remove the transmission from the engine.

**28** On vehicles with manual transmission, refer to Section 12 of this Chapter and remove the flywheel, then refer to Chapter 6 and remove the clutch friction plate and pressure plate.

**29** On vehicles with automatic transmission, refer to Section 12 of this Chapter and remove the driveplate from the crankshaft.

**30** Progressively slacken and then remove the oil seal housing retaining bolts.

**31** Lift the housing away from the cylinder block, together with the crankshaft oil seal, using a twisting motion to ease the seal along the shaft.

**32** The rear oil seal is not available separately from the housing, and the seal and housing must therefore be renewed complete. The original housing had an integral gasket - the replacement part does not, and a separate gasket must be obtained.

**33** Thoroughly clean the mating surface of the cylinder block. Any sealant or old gasket can be scraped off with a trimming knife blade. Take care to avoid damaging the mating surface.

**10.7a Compress the legs of the spring clip to release the radiator hoses . . .**

**34** Smear the crankcase mating surface with multi-purpose sealant, and lay the new gasket in position.

**35** A protective plastic sleeve is supplied with genuine VAG crankshaft oil seals; when fitted over the end of the crankshaft, the sleeve prevents damage to the inner lip of the oil seal as it is being fitted. Use PVC tape to pad the end of the crankshaft if a sleeve is not available.

**36** Lubricate the inner lip of the crankshaft oil seal with clean engine oil, then offer up the seal and its housing to the end of the crankshaft. Ease the seal along the shaft using a twisting motion, until the housing is flush with the crankcase.

**37** Insert new retaining bolts and tighten them progressively to the specified torque. ***Caution: The housing is fabricated from a light alloy, and may be distorted if the bolts are not tightened progressively.***

**10.8b . . . ignition coil earth strap . . .**

**10.7b . . . the expansion tank hose, and all remaining hoses from the thermostat housing**

**38** Refer to Section 14 and refit the sump.

**39** On vehicles with automatic transmission, work from Section 12 of this Chapter and refit the driveplate to the crankshaft.

**40** On vehicles with manual transmission, refer to Section 12 of this Chapter and refit the flywheel, then refer to Chapter 6 and refit the clutch friction plate and pressure plate.

**41** Referring to Chapter 7A or B as applicable, refit the transmission to the engine.

**42** Refer to Chapter 1A and refill the engine with the correct grade and quantity of oil.

## 10 Cylinder head and manifolds - removal, separation and refitting

### Removal

**1** Select a solid, level surface to park the vehicle upon. Give yourself enough space to move around it easily.

**2** Disconnect the battery negative lead, and position It away from the terminal. **Note:** *If the vehicle has a security-coded radio, check that you have a copy of the code number before disconnecting the battery cable. Refer to your VAG dealer if in doubt.*

**3** Referring to Chapter 1A, drain the cooling system.

**4** Remove the air cleaner housing as described in Chapter 4A or B.

**5** Also in Chapter 4, depressurise the fuel injection system.

**10.8a Disconnecting the main engine wiring harness plug connector . . .**

**6** Referring to Chapter 5B, remove the distributor cap, rotor arm and flash shield. This is not essential to allow the cylinder head to be removed (if preferred, just the HT lead to the ignition coil can be disconnected), but it allows easier access, and should prevent damage to the distributor as the head is lifted away.

**7** Referring to Chapter 3 if necessary, loosen the hose clips and disconnect the coolant hoses from the thermostat housing **(see illustrations).**

**8** Disconnect the following electrical connections, labelling as necessary for refitting:

*a) The main engine wiring harness plug connector (below the distributor). This plug typically has a screw fitting - note the red alignment markings* ***(see illustration).*** *Some models have a number of more conventional plug connectors in this location - all should be labelled and disconnected. Unclip the wiring plug(s) from the mounting bracket.*

*b) The ignition coil earth strap, and the earth wires next to it* ***(see illustrations).***

*c) The road speed sensor from the top of the transmission* ***(see illustration).***

*d) The Hall sensor wiring plug from the distributor* ***(see illustration).***

*e) The oil pressure switch from the rear of the cylinder head* ***(see illustration).***

*f) The injector plug(s) and wiring harness from the inlet manifold (refer to Chapter 4A or B as necessary). Unclip and disconnect the harness, and lay it to one side.*

2A

**10.8c . . . additional earth wires . . .**

**10.8d . . . road speed sensor wiring plug . . .**

**10.8e . . . distributor Hall sensor wiring plug . . .**

10.8f . . . and oil pressure switch wire

10.9a Disconnect the charcoal canister hose from the inlet manifold . . .

10.9b . . . and the fuel supply and return hoses - note direction-of-flow arrow markings

g) *Once all the wiring plugs have been disconnected, release the wiring harness from any retaining ties, and move it to one side.*

**9** Disconnect the following hoses:

a) *The inlet manifold hose leading to the charcoal canister solenoid valve on the right-hand inner wing **(see illustration)**.*
b) *The brake servo vacuum hose from the inlet manifold.*
c) *The fuel supply and return hoses from their connections in the engine compartment, noting the direction-of-flow and colour coding markings **(see illustration)**. Anticipate some loss of fuel. Plug or seal off the hose ends, to reduce further fuel loss and prevent the ingress of dirt.*

**10** At the rear of the thermostat housing, slide out the plastic horseshoe clip which joins the thermostat housing to the coolant pump supply pipe running along the back of the engine block **(see illustration)**.

**11** Refer to Section 6 and remove the auxiliary drivebelt.

**12** With reference to Sections 2 and 4 of this Chapter, remove the crankshaft pulley and timing belt outer covers. Disengage the timing belt from the camshaft sprocket.

**13** Once the timing belt has been disengaged, the engine can be raised back into its original position, and the right-hand engine mounting refitted while the cylinder head is removed.

**14** To avoid any possibility of piston-to-valve contact during cylinder head removal, it is recommended that the crankshaft be turned back a few degrees away from the TDC position, to take the pistons down the bores.

**15** Remove the warm air collector plate from the top of the exhaust manifold, then disconnect the exhaust downpipe from the manifold **(see illustrations)**. Recover the gasket.

**16** Slacken and remove the bolt securing the engine oil dipstick tube to the rear of the cylinder head **(see illustration)**. Where applicable, unbolt and remove the inlet manifold support bracket.

**17** Disconnect the accelerator cable as described in Chapter 4. Where applicable, disconnect the wiring from the inlet manifold heater at the connector.

**18** On later models where the lambda sensor is screwed into the exhaust manifold, disconnect the lambda sensor wiring plug at the connector.

**19** Remove the camshaft cover as described in Section 7.

**20** Working in the sequence shown, progressively loosen the cylinder head bolts by half a turn at a time, using a suitable socket, until all bolts can be unscrewed by hand **(see illustrations)**.

**21** Check that nothing remains connected to the cylinder head, then lift the head away from the cylinder block; seek assistance if possible, as it is a heavy assembly, especially if it is being removed complete with the manifolds. Remove the gasket from the top of the block. Do not discard the gasket yet.

**22** If the cylinder head is to be dismantled for overhaul, refer to Chapter 2C.

### Manifold separation

**23** Inlet manifold removal and refitting is described in Chapter 4A or B as applicable.

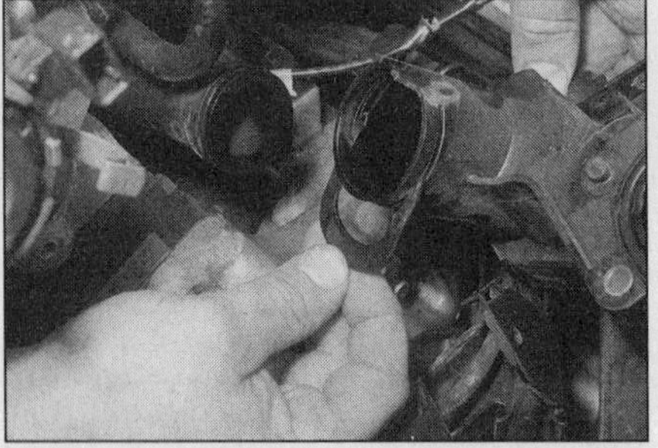
10.10 Pull out the horseshoe clip from the base of the thermostat housing - seen here with the housing removed, for clarity

10.15a Remove the warm air collector plate bolts . . .

10.15b . . . then lift off the plate . . .

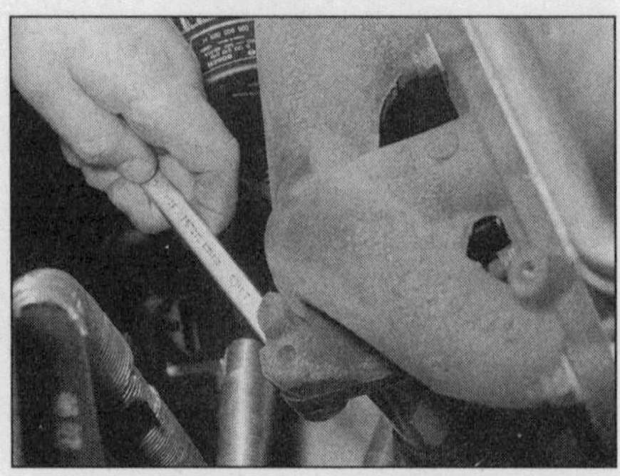
10.15c . . . and remove the three exhaust manifold-to-downpipe nuts

10.16 Remove the dipstick tube securing bolt (arrowed)

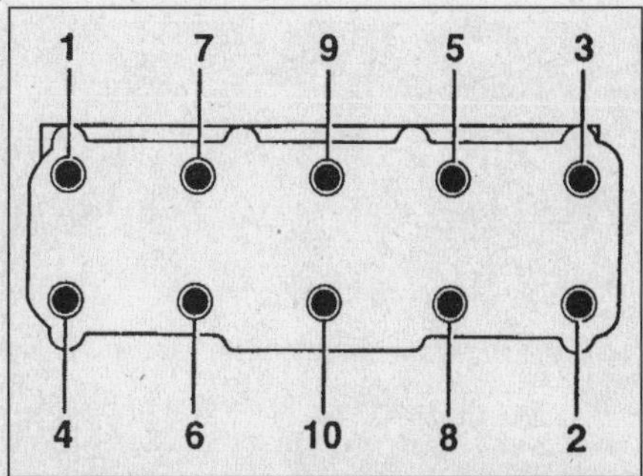


10.20a Cylinder head bolt LOOSENING sequence

10.20b Loosen the bolts by half a turn at a time, using a suitable splined adapter

**24** Progressively slacken and remove the exhaust manifold retaining nuts. Lift the manifold away from the cylinder head, and recover the gaskets.

**25** Ensure that the mating surfaces are completely clean, then refit the exhaust manifold, using new gaskets. Tighten the retaining nuts to the specified torque.

## *Preparation for refitting*

**26** The mating faces of the cylinder head and cylinder block/crankcase must be perfectly clean before refitting the head. Use a hard plastic or wood scraper to remove all traces of gasket and carbon; also clean the piston crowns. Take particular care during the cleaning operations, as aluminium alloy is easily damaged. Also, make sure that the carbon is not allowed to enter the oil and water passages - this is particularly important for the lubrication system, as carbon could block the oil supply to the engine's components. Using adhesive tape and paper, seal the water, oil and bolt holes in the cylinder block/crankcase.

**27** Check the mating surfaces of the cylinder block/crankcase and the cylinder head for nicks, deep scratches and other damage. If slight, they may be removed carefully with a file, but if excessive, machining may be the only alternative to renewal.

**28** If warpage of the cylinder head gasket surface is suspected, use a straight-edge to check it for distortion. Refer to Part C of this Chapter if necessary.

**29** Check the condition of the cylinder head bolts, and particularly their threads, whenever they are removed. Wash the bolts in suitable solvent, and wipe them dry. Check each for any sign of visible wear or damage, renewing any bolt if necessary. Measure the length of each bolt, to check for stretching (although this is not a conclusive test, if all bolts have stretched by the same amount). VW do not actually specify that the bolts must be renewed, however, it is strongly recommended that the bolts should be renewed as a complete set whenever they are disturbed.

**30** Clean out the cylinder head bolt drillings using a suitable tap. If a tap is not available, make a home-made substitute **(see Tool Tip)**.

**31** On all the engines covered in this Chapter, it is possible for the piston crowns to strike and damage the valve heads, if the camshaft is rotated with the timing belt removed and the crankshaft set to TDC. For this reason, the crankshaft must be set to a position other than TDC on No 1 cylinder, before the cylinder head is refitted. Set the crankshaft to TDC on No 1 cylinder, using the information in Section 2, then turn the crankshaft back by a few degrees, away from the TDC position. If preferred, for maximum safety, the pistons can be positioned halfway down their bores, with No 1 piston on its upstroke - ie 90° before TDC.

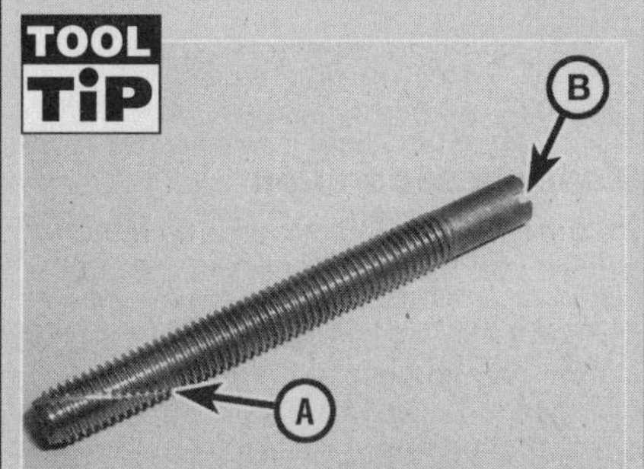


***If a tap is not available, make a home-made substitute by cutting a slot (A) down the threads of one of the old cylinder head bolts. After use, the bolt head can be cut off, and the shank can then be used as an alignment dowel to assist cylinder head refitting. Cut a screwdriver slot (B) in the top of the bolt, to allow it to be unscrewed***

## *Refitting*

**32** Check that the new gasket is the same type as the one which was removed. Lay the new head gasket on the cylinder block, ensuring that the manufacturer's TOP and part number markings are face up **(see illustration)**. Do not handle the gasket excessively before it is fitted, or it may become damaged.

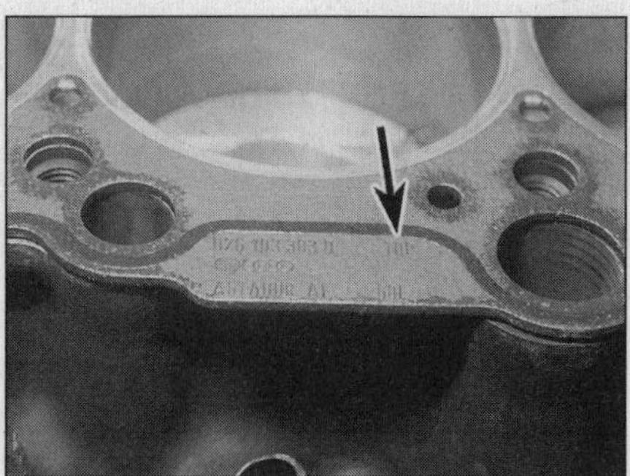

10.32 Ensure that the gasket part number and TOP markings are face up

***Because no locating dowels are fitted, it may prove difficult to accurately align the head on the block when refitting. To overcome this, two of the old cylinder head bolts can be modified to act as locating dowels. Cut the heads off two of the bolts, and then cut a slot in the top of the bolt, so that a flat-bladed screwdriver may be used to unscrew the bolts from the block once the head is placed over them. Screw the two dowels into place either end of the head, then lower the head into position over them. Fit two or more of the new head bolts to locate the head, then unscrew the dowels using a screwdriver.***

**33** Before fitting the cylinder head, check that the camshaft sprocket timing mark is aligned with the mark on the timing belt inner cover, as described in Section 2. Try to avoid turning the camshaft sprocket as the head is refitted.

**34** With the help of an assistant, place the cylinder head and manifolds centrally on the cylinder block. Check that the head gasket is correctly seated before allowing the weight the full weight of the cylinder head to rest upon it.

**35** Apply a smear of grease to the threads, and to the underside of the heads, of the cylinder head bolts; use a good-quality high-melting point grease.

**36** Carefully enter each bolt into its relevant hole (*do not drop them in*) and screw in, by hand only, until finger-tight.

**37** Working progressively and in the sequence shown, tighten the cylinder head bolts to their Stage 1 torque setting, using a torque wrench and suitable socket **(see illustrations)**.

### Cast-iron block engines (all codes except AER and ALL)

**38** Working in the given sequence, tighten the bolts to their Stage 2 torque setting.

**39** Now angle-tighten the bolts, in the same sequence, through the specified Stage 3 angle, using a socket and extension bar. It is recommended that an angle-measuring gauge is used during this stage of the

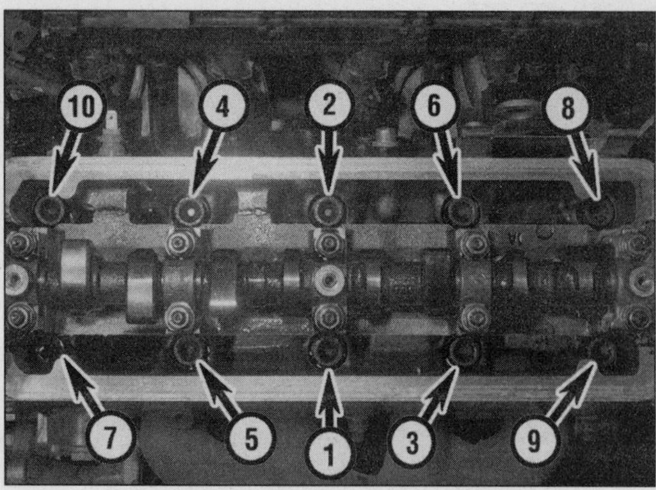

10.37a Cylinder head bolt TIGHTENING sequence

10.37b Tighten all bolts in sequence to the specified torque

tightening, to ensure accuracy **(see illustration)**. If a gauge is not available, use white paint to make alignment marks between the bolt head and cylinder head prior to tightening; the marks can then be used to check that the bolt has been rotated through the correct angle during tightening. Repeat the exercise for the Stage 4 setting.

### Aluminium block engines (codes AER and ALL)

**40** The bolts should now be angle-tightened, in the same sequence, through the specified Stage 2 angle, using a socket and extension bar. It is recommended that an angle-measuring gauge is used during this stage of the tightening, to ensure accuracy. If a gauge is not available, use white paint to make alignment marks between the bolt head and cylinder head prior to tightening; the marks can then be used to check that the bolt has been rotated through the correct angle during tightening. Repeat the exercise for the Stage 3 setting.

### All engines

**41** Refit the camshaft cover (see Section 7).

**42** If removed, refit the distributor components as described in Chapter 5B.

**43** Refit the hose securing clip for the coolant pump supply pipe-to-thermostat housing connection.

**44** Where applicable, reconnect the lambda sensor wiring.

**45** Reconnect the inlet manifold heater, where applicable.

**46** Reconnect the accelerator cable, and adjust if necessary, as described in Chapter 4A or B.

**47** Fit the dipstick tube back onto the head, and tighten the securing bolt.

**48** Reconnect the exhaust front pipe to the manifold, using a new gasket - refer to Chapter 4D.

**49** Refer to Section 2 and follow the procedure for setting the engine to TDC on No 1 cylinder with the timing belt removed.

**50** Support the engine, then disconnect the right-hand engine mounting and lower the engine down slightly. Referring to Section 4, refit the timing belt and outer covers, and the crankshaft pulley.

**51** The engine can now be raised back into position, and the right-hand engine mounting refitted as described in Section 4.

**52** Refit and tension the auxiliary drivebelt as described in Section 6.

**53** The remainder of the refitting sequence is a reversal of the removal procedure, as follows:

*a) Reconnect the fuel hoses, coolant hoses, brake servo vacuum hose and charcoal canister hose.*

*b) Reconnect the injector wiring, road speed sensor, ignition coil earth strap and the other earth wires, then the main engine wiring harness connector plug(s).*

*c) Refit the air cleaner housing as described in Chapter 4A or B.*

*d) Refill the cooling system as described in Chapter 1A, and check the oil level as described in Weekly checks.*

*e) Restore the battery connection.*

## 11 Hydraulic tappets - operation check

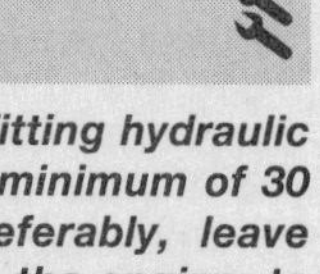

**Warning: After fitting hydraulic tappets, wait a minimum of 30 minutes (or preferably, leave overnight) before starting the engine, to allow the tappets time to settle, otherwise the pistons may strike the valve heads.**

**1** The hydraulic tappets are self-adjusting, and require no attention whilst in service.

**2** If the hydraulic tappets become excessively noisy, their operation can be checked as described below.

**3** Run the engine until it reaches its normal operating temperature. Increase the engine speed to around 2500 rpm (fast idle) for about 2 minutes, then switch off the engine. Refer to Section 7 and remove the camshaft cover.

**4** Rotate the camshaft by turning the crankshaft with a socket and wrench, until the first cam lobe over No 1 cylinder is pointing upwards.

**5** Using a feeler blade, measure the clearance between the base of the cam lobe and the top of the tappet. If the clearance is greater than 0.2mm, then the tappet is defective and must be renewed.

**6** If the clearance is less than 0.2 mm, press down on the top of the tappet, until it is felt to contact the top of the valve stem. Use a wooden or plastic implement that will not damage the surface of the tappet **(see illustration)**.

10.39 Use an angle gauge to ensure accuracy when angle-tightening the cylinder head bolts

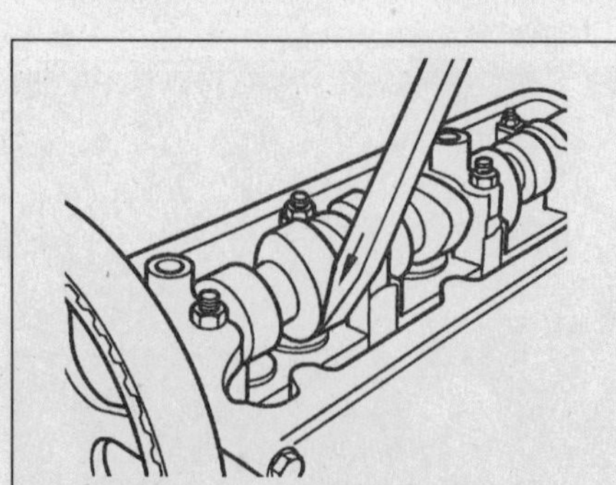
11.6 Press down on the tappet, until it contacts the top of the valve stem

12.2 Flywheel locked in position with a home-made tool

**7** If the tappet travels more than 0.2 mm before making contact, then it is defective and must be renewed.

**8** Hydraulic tappet removal and refitting is described as part of the cylinder head overhaul sequence - see Chapter 2C for details.

## 12 Flywheel/driveplate - removal, inspection and refitting

### *Flywheel*

#### Removal

**1** Remove the manual transmission and clutch as described in Chapter 7A and Chapter 6.

**2** Lock the flywheel in position using a home-made locking tool, fabricated from a piece of scrap metal **(see illustration)**. Bolt it to one of the transmission bellhousing mounting holes. Mark the position of the flywheel with respect to the crankshaft using a dab of paint.

**3** Slacken and withdraw the flywheel mounting bolts, then lift off the flywheel. ***Caution: Get an assistant to help, as the flywheel is extremely heavy.***

#### Inspection

**4** If the flywheel's clutch mating surface is deeply scored, cracked or otherwise damaged, the flywheel must be renewed. However, it may be possible to have it surface-ground; seek the advice of a VAG dealer or engine reconditioning specialist.

**5** If the ring gear is badly worn or has missing teeth, the flywheel must be renewed.

#### Refitting

**6** Clean the mating surfaces of the flywheel and crankshaft. Remove any remaining locking compound from the threads of the crankshaft holes, using the correct-size tap, if available.

***If a suitable tap is not available, cut two slots down the threads of one of the old flywheel bolts with a hacksaw, and use the bolt to remove the locking compound from the threads.***

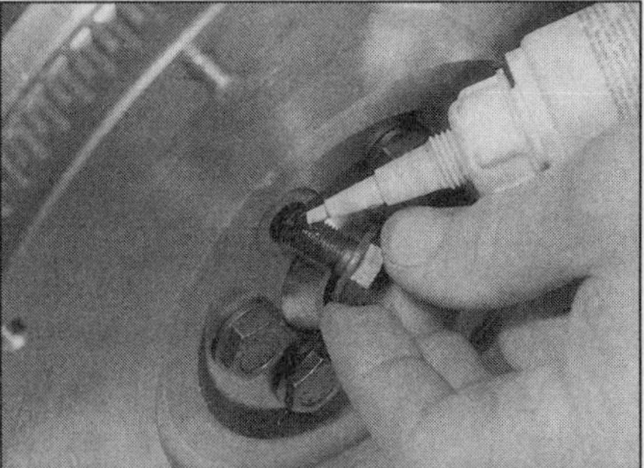

12.7 Apply locking fluid to the new flywheel bolts, if necessary

**7** If the new flywheel retaining bolts are not supplied with their threads already pre-coated, apply a suitable thread-locking compound to the threads of each bolt **(see illustration)**.

**8** Offer up the flywheel to the crankshaft, using the alignment marks made during removal, and fit the new retaining bolts.

**9** Lock the flywheel using the method employed on dismantling, and tighten the retaining bolts to the specified torque **(see illustration)**.

**10** Refit the clutch as described in Chapter 6. Remove the locking tool, and refit the transmission as described in Chapter 7A.

### *Driveplate*

#### Removal

**11** Remove the automatic transmission as described in Chapter 7B.

**12** Lock the driveplate in position by bolting a piece of scrap metal between the driveplate and one of the transmission bellhousing mounting holes. Mark the position of the driveplate with respect to the crankshaft using a dab of paint.

**13** Slacken and withdraw the driveplate mounting bolts, then lift off the driveplate. Recover the packing plate and the shim (where applicable).

#### Refitting

**14** Refitting is a reversal of removal, using the alignment marks made during removal. Fit new mounting bolts and tighten them to the specified torque. Remove the locking tool, and refit the transmission as described in Chapter 7B.

13.7 Engine right-hand mounting

12.9 Tighten the flywheel bolts to the specified torque

## 13 Engine/transmission mountings - inspection and renewal

### *Inspection*

**1** If improved access is required, raise the front of the car and support it securely on axle stands.

**2** Check the mounting rubbers to see if they are cracked, hardened or separated from the metal at any point; renew the mounting if any such damage or deterioration is evident.

**3** Check that all the mounting's fasteners are securely tightened; use a torque wrench to check if possible.

**4** Using a large screwdriver or a crowbar, check for wear in the mounting by carefully levering against it to check for free play. Where this is not possible, enlist the aid of an assistant to move the engine/transmission back and forth, or from side to side, while you watch the mounting. While some free play is to be expected even from new components, excessive wear should be obvious. If excessive free play is found, check first that the fasteners are correctly secured, then renew any worn components as described below.

### *Renewal*

#### Engine right-hand mounting

**5** Disconnect the battery negative lead, and position it away from the terminal. **Note:** *If the vehicle has a security-coded radio, check that you have a copy of the code number before disconnecting the battery. Refer to your VW dealer if in doubt.*

**6** Support the weight of the engine from above using a hoist or lifting beam, or support it from below using a securely-located trolley jack and suitable block of wood underneath the sump. Do not jack directly under the sump without using a block of wood, or the sump may be damaged.

**7** With the engine supported from above or below, slacken and withdraw the upper bolts, and separate the engine mounting **(see illustration)**.

**8** The remaining bolts can now be removed, and the lower part of the mounting removed from the inner wing.

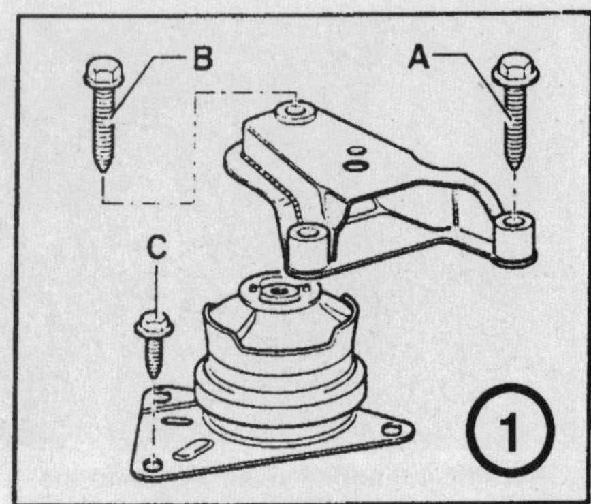


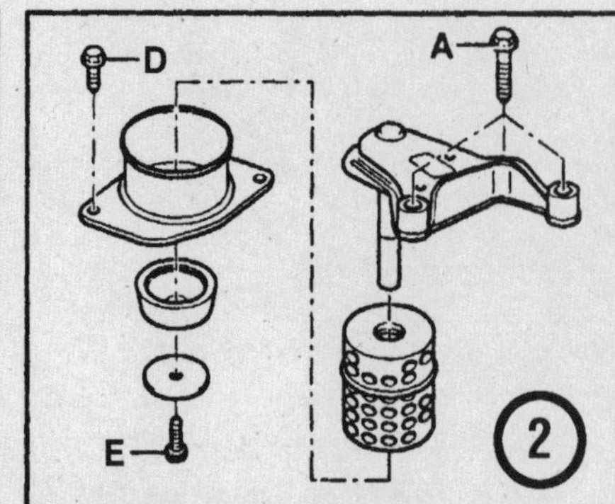


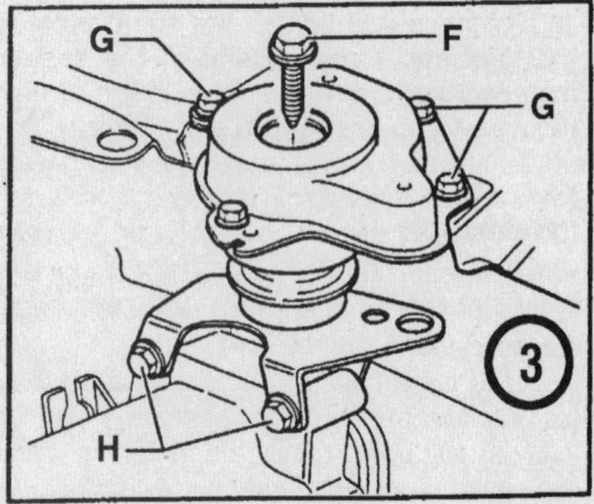


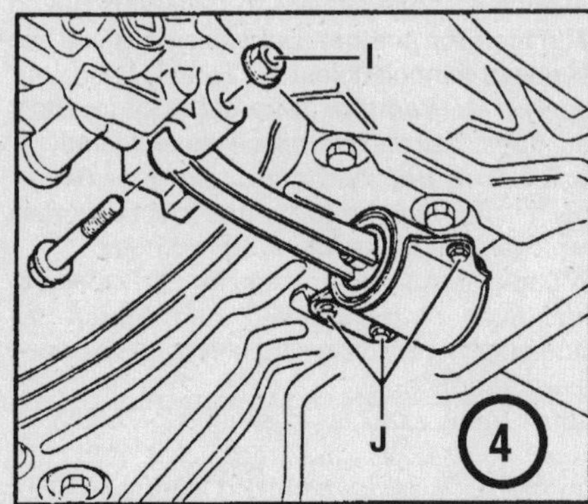


**13.9 Engine/transmission mounting details - for tightening torques (A, B, C, etc.), see Specifications**

1 *Engine right-hand mounting (manual transmission models)*
2 *Engine right-hand mounting (automatic transmission models)*
3 *Transmission left-hand mounting*
4 *Engine/transmission rear mounting*

**13.13a Two of the transmission left-hand mounting bolts are hidden under the wiring harness plastic guide . . .**

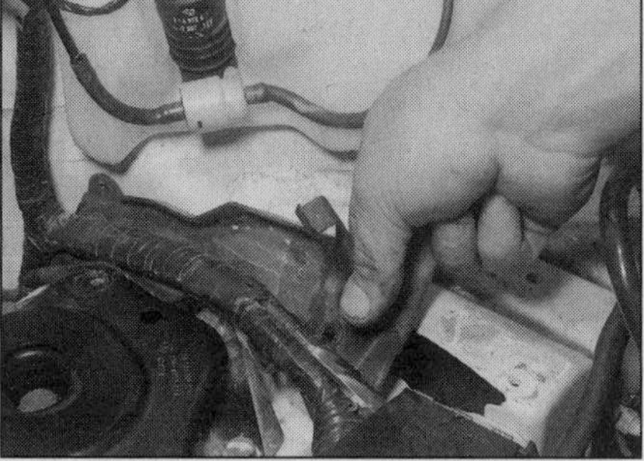
**13.13b . . . which can be unscrewed and removed**

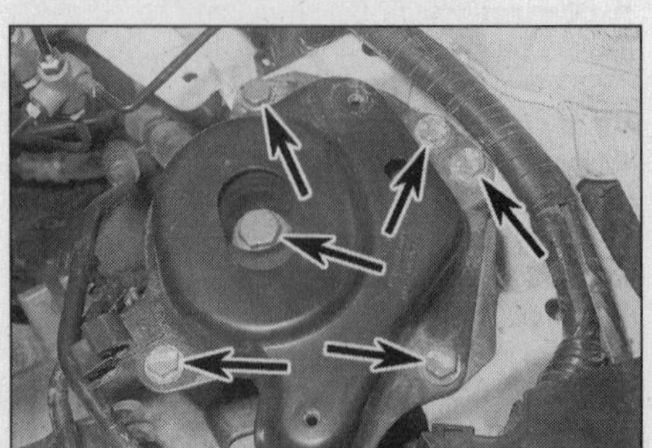
**13.13c With the weight of the engine/transmission securely supported, unscrew the bolts (arrowed) . . .**

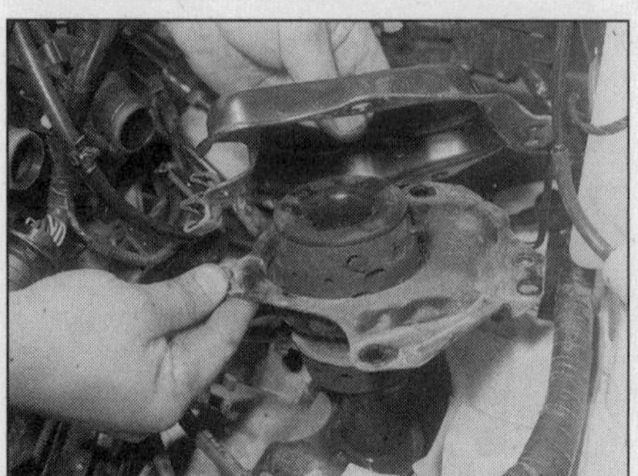
**13.13d . . . and separate the mounting**

**13.18 Engine/transmission rear mounting**

**9** Refitting is a reversal of removal, noting the following points **(see illustration)**:

a) *Use new bolts, and apply a little oil to their threads before fitting.*
b) *Tighten all bolts to the specified torque.*
c) *Note that the tightening torque for the upper and lower bolts is different.*

### Transmission left-hand mounting

**10** Disconnect the battery negative lead, and position it away from the terminal. Refer to the note in paragraph 5.

**11** Support the weight of the engine/transmission from above using a hoist or lifting beam, or support it from below using a securely-located trolley jack and suitable block of wood underneath the bellhousing. Position the jack head directly underneath the engine/bellhousing mating surface. Do not jack directly under the sump without using a block of wood, or the sump may be damaged.

**12** With the engine/transmission supported from above or below, loosen and withdraw the central through-bolt from the mounting on the transmission.

**13** Unbolt the mounting block from the inner wing, and remove it from the engine bay. Note that two of the bolts may be hidden under the wiring harness plastic guide, which is secured by two screws **(see illustrations)**.

**14** Unbolt the mounting bracket from the end of the transmission casing.

**15** Refitting is a reversal of removal, noting the following points **(refer to illustration 13.9)**:

a) *Use new bolts, and apply a little oil to their threads before fitting.*
b) *Tighten all bolts to the specified torque.*

### Engine/transmission rear mounting

**16** Disconnect the battery negative lead, and position it away from the terminal. Refer to the note in paragraph 5.

**17** Support the weight of the engine/transmission from above using a hoist or lifting beam, or support it from below using a securely-located trolley jack and suitable block of wood underneath the bellhousing. Position the jack head directly underneath the engine/bellhousing mating surface. Do not jack directly under the sump without using a block of wood, or the sump may be damaged.

**18** With the engine/transmission supported from above or below, slacken the nut and withdraw the through-bolt from the mounting on the transmission **(see illustration)**.

**19** Remove the three bolts from the subframe, and withdraw the mounting from under the car.

**20** Refitting is a reversal of removal, noting the following points **(refer to illustration 13.9)**:

a) *Use new bolts, and apply a little oil to their threads before fitting.*
b) *Tighten all bolts to the specified torque.*
c) *When tightening the through-bolt, hold the bolt and tighten the nut onto it.*

## 14 Sump - removal and refitting

### *Removal*

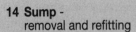

**1** Park the vehicle on a level surface, apply the handbrake and chock the rear wheels.

**2** Raise the front of the vehicle, and rest it securely on axle stands or wheel ramps; refer to *Jacking and vehicle support*.

**3** Disconnect the battery negative lead, and position it away from the terminal. **Note:** *If the vehicle has a security-coded radio, check that you have a copy of the code number before disconnecting the battery. Refer to your VW dealer if in doubt.*

**4** Refer to Chapter 1A and drain the engine oil.

**5** Where applicable, release the fasteners and remove the auxiliary drivebelt cover and the cable guide from the sump.

**6** Disconnect the exhaust system downpipe from the exhaust manifold, as described in Chapter 4D. By releasing the exhaust system from its mountings, it should be possible to lower the system sufficiently to gain clearance to lower the sump.

**7** Refer to Chapter 8 and disconnect the right-hand driveshaft from the transmission output flange.

**8** Working around the outside of the sump, progressively slacken and withdraw the sump retaining bolts **(see illustration)**.

**9** Break the joint by striking the sump with the palm of your hand, then lower the sump and withdraw it from underneath the vehicle.

**10** While the sump is removed, take the opportunity to check the oil pump pick-up/strainer for signs of clogging or disintegration. If necessary, remove the pump as described in Section 15, and clean or renew the strainer.

### *Refitting*

**11** Clean all traces of sealant or old gasket, as applicable, from the mating surfaces of the cylinder block/crankcase and sump, then use a clean rag to wipe out the sump.

#### Engine codes ADX, AEA and AEV

**12** Ensure that the sump and cylinder block/crankcase mating surfaces are clean and dry, then apply a thin coating of suitable sealant to the sump and crankcase mating surfaces.

**13** Lay a new sump gasket in position on the sump mating surface, then offer up the sump and refit the retaining bolts. Tighten the nuts and bolts evenly and progressively to the specified torque.

#### All engines except codes ADX, AEA and AEV

**14** Ensure that the sump and cylinder block/crankcase mating surfaces are clean and dry, then apply a 2 to 3 mm bead of suitable silicone sealant to the sump mating surface. Run the bead of sealant around the inside of the bolt holes.

***Warning: Take care not to apply excessive amounts of sealant, in the hope of obtaining a better seal - if too much is applied, the excess may enter the sump and then block the oil pump strainer, causing oil starvation.***

**15** The sump should be offered into position immediately, and the retaining bolts tightened hand-tight initially.

***To make aligning the sump easier, obtain two or three M6 studs, and screw them by a few threads into opposite sides of the cylinder block/ crankcase mating surface. The sump can be offered into position and fitted over the studs, then the remaining sump bolts can be fitted and hand-tightened. Remove the studs, and fit the rest of the sump bolts.***

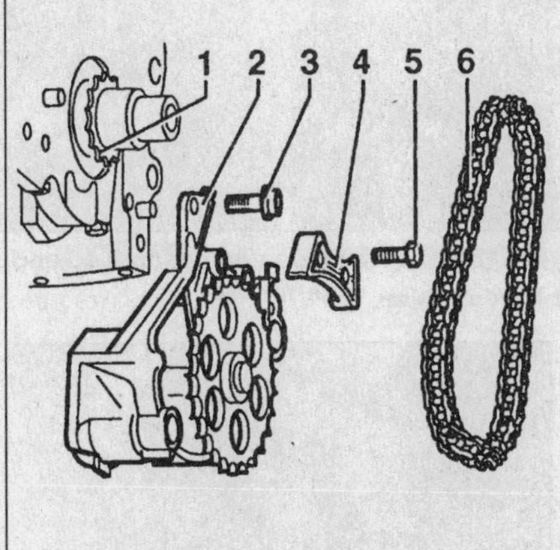


**15.3 Oil pump components**

1. *Crankshaft sprocket*
2. *Oil pump*
3. *Mounting bolts*
4. *Guide rail (not fitted to all models)*
5. *Guide rail bolts*
6. *Drive chain*

**14.8 Removing the sump bolts (seen with engine removed and inverted, for clarity)**

**16** Progressively tighten the sump bolts to the specified torque. Refer to the sealant manufacturer's advice on the length of time required for the sealant to set. Typically, it is advisable to wait for several hours before filling the engine with oil. If the car is to be left for some time with no oil in the sump, ensure that the battery remains disconnected, so that no attempt is made to start the engine.

#### All engines

**17** Refit the driveshaft as described in Chapter 8, and the exhaust downpipe as described in Chapter 4D.

**18** Where applicable, refit the auxiliary drive-belt cover and the cable guide to the sump.

**19** Lower the car to the ground, then refer to Chapter 1A and refill the engine with the specified grade and quantity of oil.

**20** Restore the battery connection, then run the engine and check for leaks.



## 15 Oil pump and pickup - removal, inspection and refitting

### *Removal*

**1** Refer to Section 14 and remove the sump from the crankcase.

**2** With reference to Section 9, remove the front (timing belt end) crankshaft oil seal and housing.

**3** Slacken and remove the bolts securing the oil pump to the timing belt end of the crankcase **(see illustration)**.

**4** Remove the bolts securing the oil pump pickup to the crankcase bracket.

**5** Disengage the pump sprocket from the drive chain, and remove the oil pump and pickup from the engine.

### *Inspection*

**6** Remove the screws from the mating flange, and lift off the pickup tube and oil pump cover. Recover the O-ring seal, where fitted.

**7** Clean the pump thoroughly, and inspect the gear teeth for signs of damage or wear.

**8** Where applicable, check the condition of the oil pump drive chain; if the links appear excessively worn or are particularly loose, renew the chain.

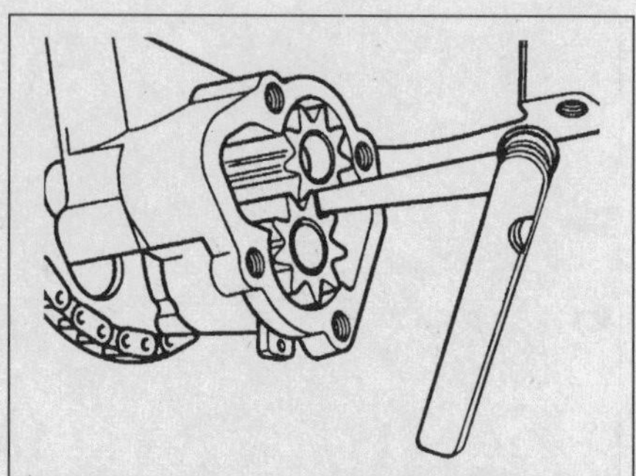
15.9 Checking oil pump backlash

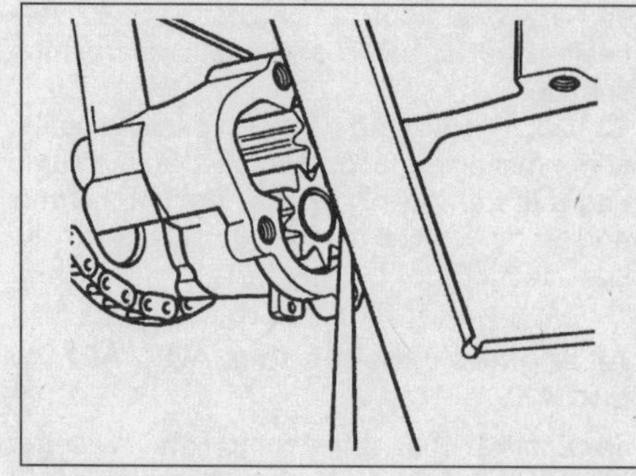
15.10 Checking oil pump axial clearance

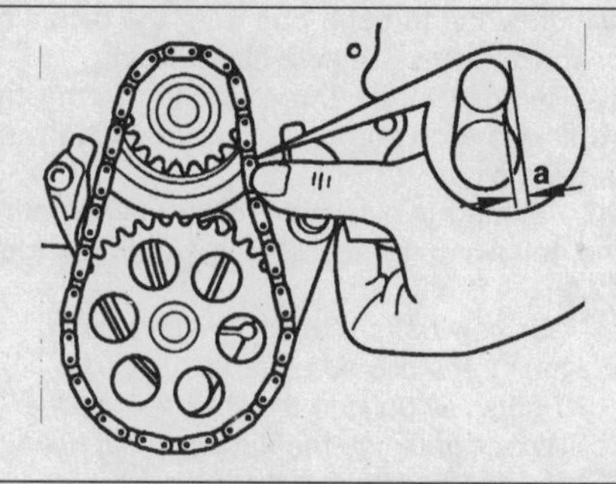

15.15 Tensioning the oil pump drive chain

*For deflection (a), see Specifications*

**9** Check the pump backlash by inserting a feeler blade between the meshed gear teeth; rotate the gears against each other slightly, to give the maximum clearance **(see illustration)**. Compare the measurement with the limit quoted in Specifications.

**10** Check the pump axial clearance as follows. Lay an engineer's straight edge across the oil pump casing, then using a feeler blade, measure the clearance between the straight edge and the pump gears **(see illustration)**. Compare the measurement with the limit quoted in Specifications.

**11** If either measurement is outside of the specified limit, this indicates that the pump is worn and must be renewed.

### Refitting

**12** Reassemble the oil pickup to the oil pump, using a new O-ring seal, where applicable. Tighten the retaining bolts securely.

**13** Offer up the oil pump to the end of the crankcase. Fit the drive chain over the oil pump sprocket, then engage it with the crankshaft sprocket.

**14** Fit the pump mounting bolts to the timing belt end of the engine, and hand-tighten them.

**15** Tension the drive chain by applying finger pressure to it at a point midway between the two sprockets. Adjust the position of the pump on its mountings until the tension is as given in the Specifications **(see illustration)**. On completion, tighten the mounting bolts to the specified torque.

**16** Fit and tighten the fixings for the pickup tube to crankcase bracket.

**17** With reference to Section 9, refit the crankshaft oil seal housing, using a new gasket and oil seal.

**18** Refer to Section 14 and refit the sump.

## 16 Engine top cover (engine codes AER and ALL) - removal and refitting

### Removal

**1** On 1.0 litre aluminium-block engines, a large plastic cover is fitted between the camshaft cover and the air cleaner top cover, secured by three nuts.

**2** Using a flat-bladed screwdriver, prise out the blanking plugs fitted over the three nuts **(see illustrations)**.

**3** Unscrew and remove the nuts and recover the washers (where fitted). Unclip the expansion tank hose from the cover, and lift the cover away from the engine **(see illustrations)**.

### Refitting

**4** Refitting is a reversal of removal.

16.2a Prise out the blanking plugs . . .

16.2b . . . for access to the securing nuts

16.3a Unscrew and remove the nuts and washers . . .

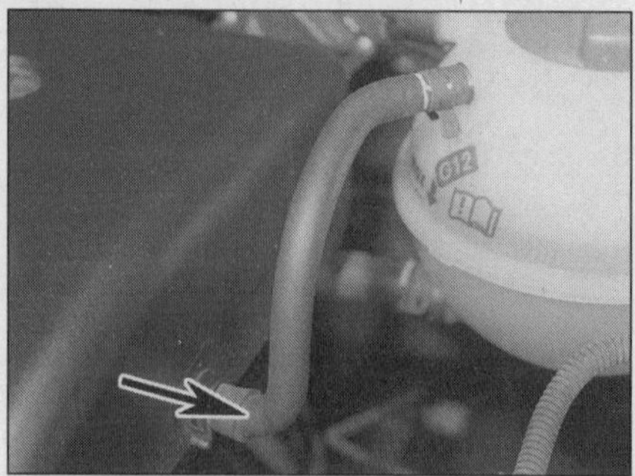

16.3b . . . unclip the expansion tank hose from the cover (arrowed)

16.3c . . . and lift off the top cover

# Chapter 2 Part B:
# Diesel engine in-car repair procedures

## Contents



## Degrees of difficulty

**Easy,** suitable for novice with little experience

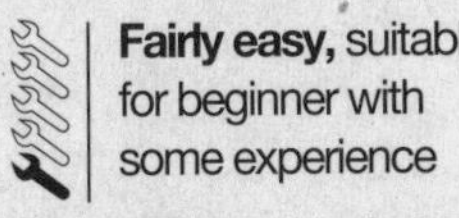

**Fairly easy,** suitable for beginner with some experience

**Fairly difficult,** suitable for competent DIY mechanic

**Difficult,** suitable for experienced DIY mechanic

**Very difficult,** suitable for expert DIY or professional

2B

## Specifications

### General

| | |
|---|---|
| Engine code: * | |
| 1716 cc, electronic direct injection, 42 kW | AHG or AKU |
| 1896 cc, mechanical injection, 47 kW | AEF |
| 1896 cc, electronic direct injection, 47 kW | AGD |

*** Note:** *See Buying spare parts and vehicle identification for the location of the code marking on the engine.*

| | |
|---|---|
| Bore | 79.5 mm |
| Stroke: | |
| Engine codes AHG, AKU | 86.4 mm |
| Engine codes AEF, AGD | 95.5 mm |
| Compression ratio: | |
| AEF | 22.5:1 |
| All other engines | 19.5:1 |
| Compression pressures (wear limit): | |
| AEF | 26 bar |
| All other engines | 19 bar |
| Maximum difference between all four cylinders | 5 bar |
| Firing order | 1 - 3 - 4 - 2 |
| Cylinder No 1 location | Timing belt end |

### Lubrication system

| | |
|---|---|
| Oil pump type | Sump-mounted, driven indirectly from intermediate shaft |
| Normal operating oil pressure | 2.0 bar minimum (at 2000 rpm, oil temperature 80°C) |
| Oil pump backlash | 0.20 mm (wear limit) |
| Oil pump axial clearance | 0.15 mm (wear limit) |

## Torque wrench settings

| | Nm | lbf ft |
|---|---|---|
| Alternator mounting bracket-to-engine bolts | 25 | 18 |
| Auxiliary belt tensioner adjustment bolt | 10 | 7 |
| Auxiliary belt tensioner pulley bolt (left-hand thread) | 20 | 15 |
| Auxiliary belt tensioner-to-bracket bolts | 20 | 15 |
| Camshaft cover nuts | 10 | 7 |
| Camshaft sprocket bolt | 45 | 33 |
| Coolant pump pulley bolts | 25 | 18 |
| Crankshaft front oil seal housing bolts: | | |
| Upper bolt | 10 | 7 |
| Lower bolts | 25 | 18 |
| Crankshaft pulley bolts | 25 | 18 |
| Crankshaft rear oil seal housing bolts | 10 | 7 |
| Crankshaft sprocket bolt (oiled)*: | | |
| Stage 1 | 90 | 66 |
| Stage 2 | Angle-tighten a further 90° | |
| Cylinder head bolts*: | | |
| Stage 1 | 40 | 30 |
| Stage 2 | 60 | 44 |
| Stage 3 | Angle-tighten a further 90° | |
| Stage 4 | Angle-tighten a further 90° | |
| Dipstick tube lower bolt | 45 | 33 |
| Dipstick tube upper bolt | 10 | 7 |
| Engine lifting eye bolt | 20 | 15 |
| Engine right-hand mounting-to-block bolts | 45 | 33 |
| Engine speed sender mounting bolt (not engine code AEF) | 10 | 7 |
| Engine/transmission mountings - oiled threads **(see illustration 14.9)***: | | |
| A | 50 | 37 |
| B | 50 | 37 |
| C | 25 | 18 |
| D | 80 | 59 |
| E | 25 | 18 |
| F | 50 | 37 |
| G (tighten nut) | 50 | 37 |
| H: | | |
| Up to December 1996 | 35 | 26 |
| December 1996 on: | | |
| Stage 1 | 20 | 15 |
| Stage 2 | Angle-tighten a further 90° | |
| Exhaust downpipe-to-manifold nuts | 40 | 30 |
| Exhaust gas recirculation valve bolts | 25 | 18 |
| Exhaust manifold nuts | 25 | 18 |
| Flywheel mounting bolts*: | | |
| Stage 1 | 60 | 44 |
| Stage 2 | Angle-tighten a further 90° | |
| Glow plugs: | | |
| Engine code AEF | 25 | 18 |
| All other engines | 15 | 11 |
| Idler roller bolt (not engine code AEF) | 25 | 18 |
| Injection pump mounting nuts/bolts | 25 | 18 |
| Injection pump sprocket bolts (engine code AEF) | 25 | 18 |
| Injection pump sprocket nut (all other engines) | 55 | 41 |
| Injector pipe unions | 25 | 18 |
| Inlet pipe cover bolts | 10 | 7 |
| Inlet pipe/manifold securing bolts | 25 | 18 |
| Intermediate shaft oil seal housing bolts | 25 | 18 |
| Intermediate shaft sprocket bolt | 45 | 33 |
| Oil cooler retaining nut | 25 | 18 |
| Oil filter mounting bracket bolts | 25 | 18 |
| Oil pressure switch | 25 | 18 |
| Oil pump cover screws | 10 | 7 |
| Oil pump mounting bolts | 25 | 18 |
| Oil pump pickup tube screws | 10 | 7 |
| Sump drain plug | 30 | 22 |
| Sump retaining bolts | 20 | 15 |
| Timing belt tensioner roller locknut | 20 | 15 |
| Timing belt inner cover-to-cylinder head bolts | 10 | 7 |
| Timing belt lower cover bolts | 10 | 7 |
| Vacuum pump clamp bolt | 20 | 15 |

**Use new nuts/bolt(s)*

## 1 General information

### *Using this Chapter*

Chapter 2 is divided into three parts; A, B and C. Repair operations that can be carried out with the engine in the vehicle are described in Parts A (petrol engines) and B (diesel engines). Part C covers the removal of the engine/ transmission as a unit and describes the engine dismantling and overhaul procedures.

In Parts A and B, the assumption is made that the engine is installed in the vehicle, with all ancillaries connected. If the engine has been removed for overhaul, the preliminary dismantling information which precedes each operation may be ignored.

Access to the engine bay can be improved by removing the bonnet and the front lock carrier assembly; these procedures are described in Chapter 11 and Chapter 2C, Section 2 respectively.

### *Engine description*

Throughout this Chapter, engines are identified and referred to by manufacturer's code letters, rather than capacity. A listing of all engines covered, together with their code letters, is given in the Specifications at the start of this Chapter.

The engines are water-cooled, single overhead camshaft, in-line four cylinder units with cast-iron cylinder blocks and aluminium-alloy cylinder heads. All are mounted transversely at the front of the vehicle, with the transmission bolted to the left-hand side of the engine.

The cylinder head carries the camshaft, which is driven by a toothed timing belt. It also houses the inlet and exhaust valves, which are closed by single springs, and which run in guides pressed into the cylinder head. The camshaft actuates the valves directly via hydraulic tappets, mounted in the cylinder head. The cylinder head contains integral oilways which supply and lubricate the tappets.

On engine code AEF (indirect injection engine), the cylinder head incorporates renewable swirl chambers. On all other engines (direct injection), the piston crowns are shaped to form combustion chambers.

The crankshaft is supported by five main bearings, and endfloat is controlled by a thrust bearing fitted between cylinders No 2 and 3.

All diesel engines are fitted with a timing belt-driven intermediate shaft, which provides drive for the brake servo vacuum pump and the oil pump.

Engine coolant is circulated by a pump, driven by the auxiliary drivebelt. For details of the cooling system, refer to Chapter 3.

Lubricant is circulated under pressure by a pump, driven by the intermediate shaft. Oil is drawn from the sump through a strainer, and then forced through an externally-mounted, replaceable screw-on filter. From there, it is distributed to the cylinder head, where it lubricates the camshaft journals and hydraulic tappets, and also to the crankcase, where it lubricates the main bearings, connecting rod big- and small-ends, gudgeon pins and cylinder bores. Oil jets are fitted to the base of each cylinder - these spray oil onto the underside of the pistons, to improve cooling. An oil cooler, supplied with engine coolant, reduces the temperature of the oil before it re-enters the engine.

### *Repairs possible with the engine installed in the vehicle*

The following operations can be performed without removing the engine:

*a) Auxiliary drivebelt - removal and refitting.*
*b) Camshaft - removal and refitting. **
*c) Camshaft oil seal - renewal.*
*d) Camshaft sprocket - removal and refitting.*
*e) Coolant pump - removal and refitting (refer to Chapter 3)*
*f) Crankshaft oil seals - renewal.*
*g) Crankshaft sprocket - removal and refitting.*
*h) Cylinder head - removal and refitting. **
*i) Engine mountings - inspection and renewal.*
*j) Intermediate shaft oil seal - renewal.*
*k) Oil pump and pickup assembly - removal and refitting.*
*l) Sump - removal and refitting.*
*m) Timing belt, sprockets and cover - removal, inspection and refitting.*

**Cylinder head dismantling procedures are in Chapter 2C, and also contain details of camshaft and hydraulic tappet removal.*

**Note:** *It is possible to remove the pistons and connecting rods (after removing the cylinder head and sump) without removing the engine from the vehicle. However, this procedure is not recommended. Work of this nature is more easily and thoroughly completed with the engine on the bench - refer to Chapter 2C.*

## 2 Locating TDC on No 1 cylinder

**1** Remove the camshaft cover, auxiliary drivebelt and timing belt outer covers as described in Sections 7, 6 and 4 respectively.

**2** Remove the inspection bung from the transmission bellhousing. Rotate the crankshaft clockwise with a wrench and socket, or a spanner, until the '0' mark machined onto the edge of the flywheel lines up with pointer on the bellhousing casting **(see illustrations)**.

**3** To lock the engine in the TDC position, the camshaft (not the sprocket) and fuel injection pump sprocket must be secured in a reference position, using special locking tools. Improvised tools may be fabricated, but due to the exact measurements and machining involved, it is strongly recommended that a kit of locking tools is either borrowed or hired from a VW dealer, or purchased from a reputable tool manufacturer - for example, Sykes Pickavant produce a kit of camshaft and fuel injection pump sprocket locking tools specifically for the range of engines covered in this Chapter **(see illustration)**.

**4** Engage the edge of the locking bar with the slot in the end of the camshaft **(see illustration)**.

**5** With the locking bar still inserted, turn the camshaft slightly (by turning the crankshaft clockwise, as before), so that the locking bar rocks to one side, allowing one end of the bar to contact the cylinder head surface. At the



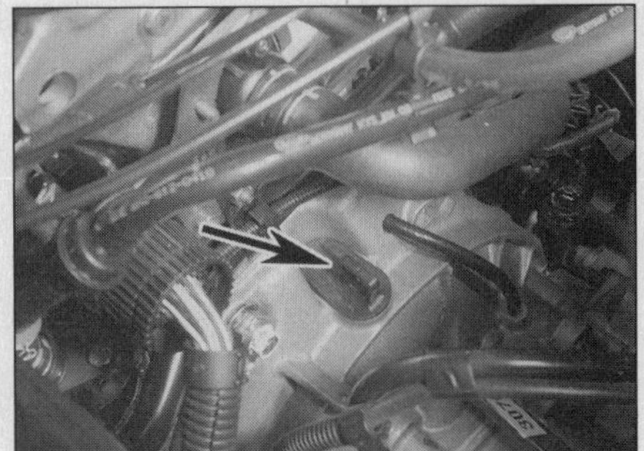

**2.2a Remove the rubber bung from the transmission bellhousing (arrowed) . . .**

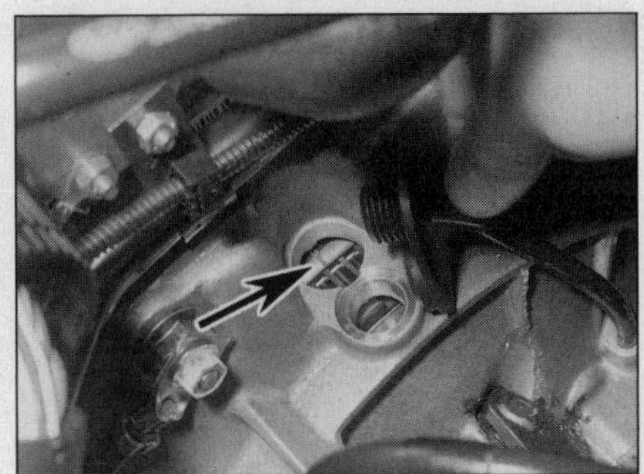

**2.2b . . . to see the TDC 0 marking (arrowed) on the flywheel**

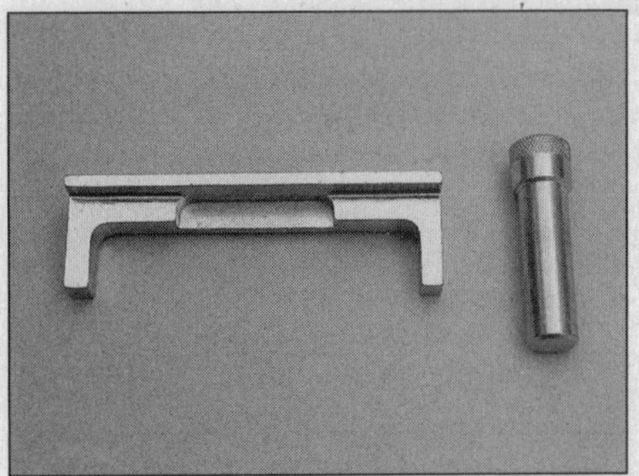

**2.3 Engine locking tools**

2.4 Engage the locking bar with the slot in the camshaft

2.6 Camshaft centred and locked using locking bar and feeler gauges

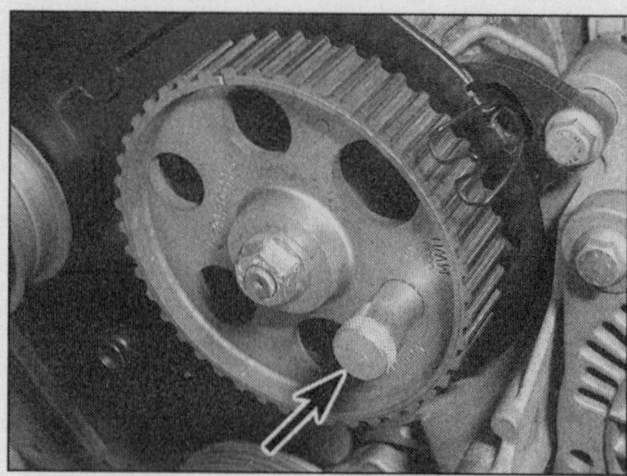

2.7 Injection pump sprocket locked using locking pin (arrowed) - engine code AEF

other side of the locking bar, measure the gap between the end of the bar and the cylinder head using a feeler blade.

**6** Turn the camshaft back slightly, then pull out the feeler blade. The idea now is to level the locking bar by inserting two feeler blades, each with a thickness equal to *half* the originally measured gap, on either side of the camshaft between each end of the locking bar and the cylinder head **(see illustration)**. This centres the camshaft, and sets the valve timing in reference condition.

**7** Insert the locking pin through the fuel injection pump sprocket alignment hole, and thread it into the support bracket behind the sprocket **(see illustration)**. This locks the fuel injection pump in a reference condition.

**8** The engine is now set to TDC on No 1 cylinder.

## 3 Cylinder compression test

### Compression test

**Note:** *A compression tester specifically designed for diesel engines must be used for this test.*

**1** When engine performance is down, or if misfiring occurs, a compression test can provide diagnostic clues as to the engine's condition. If the test is performed regularly, it can give warning of trouble before any other symptoms become apparent.

**2** A compression tester specifically intended for diesel engines must be used, because of the higher pressures involved. The tester is connected to an adapter which screws into the glow plug or injector hole. It is unlikely to be worthwhile buying such a tester for occasional use, but it may be possible to borrow or hire one - if not, have the test performed by a garage.

**3** Unless specific instructions to the contrary are supplied with the tester, observe the following points:

*a) The battery must be in a good state of charge, the air filter must be clean, and the engine should be at normal operating temperature.*

*b) All four injectors (or all four glow plugs) should be removed before starting the test. If removing the injectors, also remove the flame shield washers, otherwise they may be blown out.*

*c) The stop solenoid must be disconnected, to prevent the engine from running or fuel from being discharged.*

*d) On engine code AEF, disconnect the main engine wiring harness connector multi-plug before starting the test.*

*e) On engine codes except AEF, as well as disconnecting the stop solenoid, disconnect the quantity adjuster connector on the injection pump.*

**4** There is no need to hold the accelerator pedal down during the test, because the diesel engine air inlet is not throttled.

**5** VW specify wear limits for compression pressures - refer to the Specifications. Seek the advice of a VW dealer or other diesel specialist if in doubt as to whether a particular pressure reading is acceptable.

**6** The cause of poor compression is less easy to establish on a diesel engine than on a petrol one. The effect of introducing oil into the cylinders (wet testing) is not conclusive, because there is a risk that the oil will sit in the swirl chamber or in the recess on the piston crown, instead of passing to the rings. However, the following can be used as a rough guide to diagnosis.

**7** All cylinders should produce very similar pressures; a difference of more than 5 bar between any two cylinders indicates the existence of a fault. Note that the compression should build up quickly in a healthy engine; low compression on the first stroke, followed by gradually-increasing pressure on successive strokes, indicates worn piston rings. A low compression reading on the first stroke, which does not build up during successive strokes, indicates leaking valves or a blown head gasket (a cracked head could also be the cause).

**8** A low reading from two adjacent cylinders is almost certainly due to the head gasket having blown between them; the presence of coolant in the engine oil will confirm this.

**9** If the compression reading is unusually high, the cylinder head surfaces, valves and pistons are probably coated with carbon deposits. If this is the case, the cylinder head should be removed and decarbonised (refer to Part C of this Chapter).

### Leakdown test

**10** A leakdown test measures the rate at which compressed air fed into the cylinder is lost. It is an alternative to a compression test, and in many ways it is better, since the escaping air provides easy identification of where pressure loss is occurring (piston rings, valves or head gasket).

**11** The equipment needed for leakdown testing is unlikely to be available to the home mechanic. If poor compression is suspected, have the test performed by a suitably-equipped garage.

## 4 Timing belt and outer covers - removal and refitting

### General information

**1** The primary function of the toothed timing belt is to drive the camshaft, but it is also used to drive the fuel injection pump and intermediate shaft. Should the belt slip or break in service, the valve timing will be disturbed, and piston-to-valve contact may occur, resulting in serious engine damage.

**2** For this reason, it is important that the timing belt is tensioned correctly, and inspected regularly for signs of wear or deterioration.

**3** Note that the removal of the *inner* section of the timing belt cover is described as part of the camshaft oil seal renewal procedure; see Section 8.

### Removal

**4** Before starting work, immobilise the engine and vehicle as follows:

*a) Disconnect the battery negative lead, and position the lead away from the terminal.* **Note:** If the vehicle has a security-coded radio, check that you have a copy of the code number before disconnecting the battery. Refer to your VW dealer if in doubt.

*b) Disconnect the fuel cut-off solenoid (see Chapter 4C).*

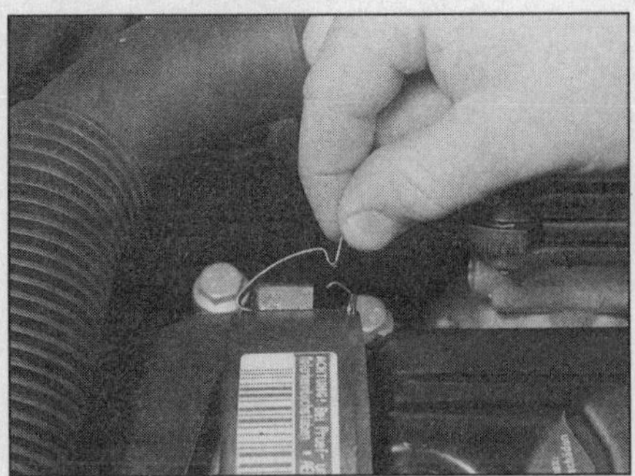
4.14a Prise open the spring clips . . .

4.14b . . . and detach the fuel pipes from the timing belt upper cover

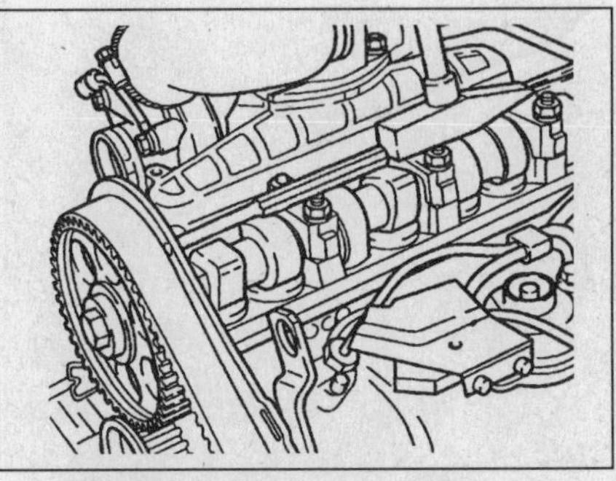
4.24 Releasing the camshaft sprocket from the taper using a pin punch

c) *Prevent any vehicle movement by applying the handbrake and chocking the rear wheels. Ensure that the transmission is in neutral.*

**5** Access to the timing belt covers can be improved by removing the air inlet hose from the inner wing and from the inlet manifold cover - refer to Chapter 4C.

**6** Remove the noise insulation tray from below the engine.

**7** To renew the belt, the engine right-hand mounting and the engine/transmission rear mounting must first be removed. Support the weight of the engine using an engine hoist from above, or using a securely-located hydraulic jack and suitable block of wood from below. Do not jack directly under the sump, or the sump will be damaged. Volkswagen technicians use an engine support bar which locates in the inner wing channels.

**8** With the engine securely supported, progressively loosen the mounting bolts and remove the engine right-hand mounting and the engine/transmission rear mounting from the vehicle (see Section 14). Also unbolt the lower part of the right-hand mounting from the cylinder head.

**9** Refer to Section 2, and using the engine alignment markings, set the engine to TDC on No 1 cylinder.

**10** With reference to Section 6, remove the auxiliary drivebelt.

**11** The engine must now be lowered slightly, to permit removal of the auxiliary drivebelt pulleys.

**12** Slacken and withdraw the bolts, and lift off the coolant pump pulley and the crankshaft pulley.

***To prevent the crankshaft drivebelt pulley from rotating whilst the bolts are being slackened, select top gear and get an assistant to apply the footbrake firmly. Failing this, grip the sprocket by wrapping a length of old rubber hose or inner tube around it. If top gear is selected to help in removing the pulley, make sure the transmission is returned to neutral before proceeding.***

**13** Unscrew and remove the auxiliary drivebelt tensioner pulley bolt, noting that it has a **left-hand thread** (ie it unscrews **clockwise**), and remove the drivebelt tensioner pulley.

**14** Release the uppermost part of the timing belt outer cover by prising open the metal spring clips. Detach the fuel pipes from the locating clip, and move them clear of the work area **(see illustrations)**. Lift the cover away from the engine.

**15** Remove the retaining bolts and clips, and lift off the timing belt lower cover.

**16** On engine code AEF with a two-part fuel injection pump sprocket, ensure that the sprocket locking pin is firmly in position (see Section 2), then loosen the three outer sprocket securing bolts by half a turn.

***Caution: Do not loosen the sprocket centre nut, as this will alter the fuel injection pump's basic timing setting.***

**17** With reference to Section 5, relieve the tension on the timing belt by slackening the tensioner mounting nut slightly, allowing the tensioner to pivot away from the belt.

**18** On all engines except code AEF, slacken and withdraw the bolt and remove the idler roller from the timing belt inner cover.

**19** Examine the timing belt for manufacturer's markings that indicate the direction of rotation. If none are present, make your own using typist's correction fluid or a dab of paint - do not cut or score the belt in any way.

***Caution: If the belt appears to be in good condition and can be re-used, it is essential that it is refitted the same way around, otherwise accelerated wear will result, leading to premature failure.***

**20** Slide the belt off the sprockets, taking care to avoid twisting or kinking it excessively.

**21** Examine the belt for evidence of contamination by coolant or lubricant. If this is the case, find the source of the contamination before progressing any further. Check the belt for signs of wear or damage, particularly around the leading edges of the belt teeth. Renew the belt if its condition is in doubt; the cost of belt renewal is negligible compared with potential cost of the engine repairs, should the belt fail in service. Similarly, if the belt is known to have covered more than 30 000 miles, it is prudent to renew it regardless of condition, as a precautionary measure.

**22** If the timing belt is not going to be refitted for some time, it is a wise precaution to hang a warning label on the steering wheel, to remind yourself (and others) not to try and start the engine. You may wish to further immobilise the engine against being started, perhaps by taping over the ignition switch.

### Refitting

**23** Ensure that the crankshaft is still set to TDC on No 1 cylinder, as described in Section 2.

**24** Refer to Section 5 and slacken the camshaft sprocket bolt by half a turn. Release the sprocket from the camshaft taper mounting by carefully tapping it with a pin punch, inserted through the hole provided in the timing belt inner cover **(see illustration).**

**25** Loop the timing belt loosely under the crankshaft sprocket.

***Caution: Observe the direction of rotation markings on the belt.***

**26** Engage the timing belt teeth with the crankshaft sprocket, then manoeuvre it into position over the camshaft and injection pump sprockets. Ensure the belt teeth seat correctly on the sprockets. **Note:** *Slight adjustments to the position of the camshaft sprocket (and where applicable, injection pump sprocket) may be necessary to achieve this.*

**27** Pass the flat side of the belt over the intermediate shaft pulley and tensioner roller - avoid bending the belt back on itself or twisting it excessively as you do this.

**28** On all engines except code AEF, refit the idler roller to the timing belt inner cover, and tighten the retaining bolt to the specified torque.

**29** On engine codes AHG, AKU and AGD with a single-part fuel injection pump sprocket, remove the locking pin from the fuel injection pump sprocket (see Section 2).

**30** Ensure that the front run of the belt is taut - ie all the slack should be in the section of the belt that passes over the tensioner roller.

**31** Tension the belt by turning the eccentrically-mounted tensioner clockwise; two holes are provided in the side of the tensioner hub for this purpose - a pair of sturdy right-angled circlip pliers is a suitable

4.31a Tensioning the timing belt using a pair of circlip pliers in the belt tensioner

4.31b Timing belt correctly fitted

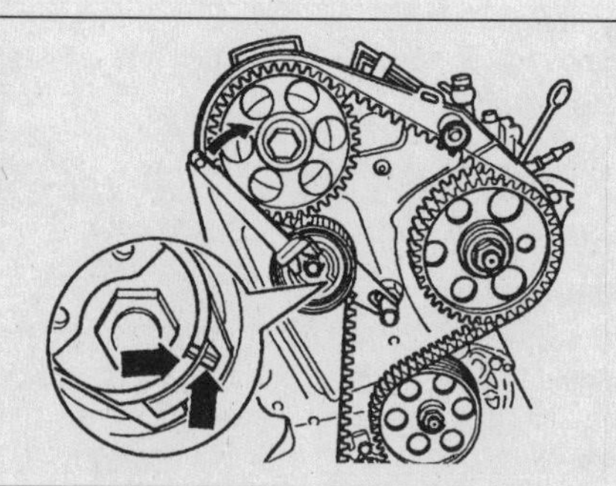
4.31c Alignment marks on pulley and hub - engines with semi-automatic tensioner

substitute for the correct VW tool. Turn the tensioner until the notch and the raised portion are aligned, then tighten the locknut to the specified torque **(see illustrations)**.

**32** At this point, check that the crankshaft is still set to TDC on No 1 cylinder (see Section 2).

**33** Refer to Section 5 and tighten the camshaft sprocket bolt to the specified torque.

**34** On the AEF engine with a two-part fuel injection pump sprocket, tighten the three sprocket outer bolts, then remove the sprocket locking pin.

**35** With reference to Section 2, remove the camshaft locking bar.

**36** Using a spanner or wrench and socket on the crankshaft sprocket bolt, rotate the crankshaft through two complete revolutions. Reset the engine to TDC on No 1 cylinder, with reference to Section 2 and check that the fuel injection pump sprocket locking pin can be inserted. Re-check the timing belt tension and adjust it, if necessary.

**37** Refer to Section 5 and test the operation of the tensioner.

**38** Refit the upper and lower sections of the timing belt outer cover, securing with the clips and tightening the retaining bolts securely.

**39** Refit the auxiliary drivebelt tensioner pulley and tighten the bolt to the specified torque, noting that it has a **left-hand thread** (ie it tightens **anti-clockwise**).

**40** Refit the coolant pump pulley, and tighten the retaining bolts to the specified torque.

**41** Refit the crankshaft auxiliary belt pulley and tighten the retaining bolts to the specified torque, using the method employed during removal. Note that the offset of the pulley mounting holes allows only one fitting position.

**42** Working from Section 6, refit and tension the auxiliary drivebelt.

**43** Raise the engine back into a position where the engine right-hand mounting can be refitted.

**44** Refit the engine right-hand mounting and the engine/transmission rear mounting using new bolts, and tighten the bolts to the specified torque. Lower the hoist or the jack on completion.

**45** Refit the noise insulation tray under the engine, and reconnect the inlet air hose to the inlet manifold cover and the connection on the inner wing.

**46** Restore the fuelling system by reconnecting the fuel cut-off solenoid wiring (see Chapter 4C).

**47** Restore the battery connection.

**48** On completion, refer to Chapter 4C and check the fuel injection pump timing.

## 5 Timing belt tensioner and sprockets - removal and refitting

**1** Before starting work, immobilise the engine and vehicle as follows:

*a) Disconnect the battery negative lead, and position the lead away from the terminal.* **Note:** If the vehicle has a security-coded radio, check that you have a copy of the code number before disconnecting the battery. Refer to your VW dealer if in doubt.

*b) Disconnect the fuel cut-off solenoid (see Chapter 4C).*

*c) Prevent any vehicle movement by applying the handbrake and chocking the rear wheels. Ensure that the transmission is in neutral.*

5.3a Remove the tensioner nut and recover the washer

5.3b Slide the tensioner off its mounting stud

### Timing belt tensioner

#### Removal

**2** With reference to the relevant paragraphs of Sections 2 and 4, set the engine to TDC on No 1 cylinder, then remove the upper and lower sections of the timing belt outer cover.

**3** Slacken the retaining nut at the hub of the tensioner roller and allow the assembly to rotate anti-clockwise, relieving the tension on the timing belt. Remove the nut and slide the tensioner off its mounting stud **(see illustrations)**.

#### Inspection

**4** Wipe the tensioner clean, but do not use solvents that may contaminate the bearings. Spin the tensioner pulley on its hub by hand. Stiff movement or excessive freeplay is an indication of severe wear; the tensioner is not a serviceable component, and should be renewed.

#### Refitting and testing

**5** Slide the tensioner pulley over the mounting stud, and refit the tensioner retaining nut - do not fully tighten the nut at this stage.

**6** With reference to Section 4, refit and tension the timing belt.

**7** The operation of the tensioner can be tested as follows. Apply finger pressure to the timing belt at a point mid-way between the camshaft and crankshaft sprockets. The tensioner pulley alignment marks should move apart as pressure is applied, and then move back and line up again as the pressure is removed **(refer to illustration 4.31c)**. Any reluctance to return to the correct position indicates that the tensioner should be renewed - correct tension is critical to the operation of the belt, and the importance of the belt tensioner cannot be overstressed.

**8** Referring to Section 4, refit the timing belt upper and lower covers, the auxiliary drivebelt pulleys, auxiliary drivebelt, the engine

mountings, and all other components removed for access. Reconnect the battery negative lead.
**9** Restore the fuelling system by reconnecting the fuel cut-off solenoid wiring.

## Camshaft timing belt sprocket

### Removal

**10** Referring to Sections 2 and 4, set the engine to TDC on No 1 cylinder, then remove the timing belt outer covers. Slacken the tensioner centre nut and allow it to rotate anti-clockwise, to relieve the tension on the timing belt. Carefully slide the timing belt off the camshaft sprocket.
**11** The camshaft sprocket must be held stationary whilst its retaining bolt is slackened; if access to the correct VW special tool is not possible, a simple home-made tool may be fabricated using basic materials **(see Tool Tip)**.
**12** Using the home-made tool, brace the camshaft sprocket and slacken and remove the retaining bolt.

***Warning: It is potentially damaging to allow the camshaft to turn with the timing belt removed and the engine set at TDC, as piston-to-valve contact may occur. Take care that the camshaft sprocket is not turned as it is removed. As a precaution against damage, VW recommend that the crankshaft be turned back a few degrees, away from TDC, while the camshaft sprocket is removed/refitted. The crankshaft may then be turned back to TDC when the timing belt is to be refitted.***

**13** Slide the camshaft sprocket from the end of the camshaft **(see illustration)**. Where applicable, recover the Woodruff key from the slot in the camshaft.
**14** With the sprocket removed, examine the camshaft oil seal for signs of leaking. If necessary, refer to Section 8 and renew it.
**15** Wipe the sprocket and camshaft mating surfaces clean.

### Refitting

**16** Where applicable, fit the Woodruff key into the keyway, with the plain surface facing upwards. Fit the sprocket to the camshaft, engaging the slot in the sprocket with the Woodruff key. Where a key is not used, ensure the lug in the sprocket hub engages with recess in the end of the camshaft.

**TOOL TIP**

***To make a camshaft sprocket holding tool, obtain two lengths of steel strip about 6mm thick by 30 mm wide or similar, one 600 mm long, the other 200 mm long (all dimensions approximate). Bolt the two strips together to form a forked end, leaving the bolt slack so that the shorter strip can pivot freely. At the end of each prong of the fork, secure a bolt with a nut and a locknut, to act as the fulcrums; these will engage with the cut-outs in the sprocket, and should protrude by about 30mm***

**17** Working from Sections 2 and 4, check that the engine is still set to TDC on No 1 cylinder, then refit and tension the timing belt.
**18** Referring to Section 4, refit the timing belt upper and lower covers, the auxiliary drivebelt pulleys, auxiliary drivebelt, the engine mountings, and all other components removed for access. Reconnect the battery negative lead.
**19** Restore the fuelling system by reconnecting the fuel cut-off solenoid wiring.

## Crankshaft timing belt sprocket

### Removal

**20** Referring to Sections 2 and 4, set the engine to TDC on No 1 cylinder, then remove the timing belt outer covers. Slacken the tensioner centre hut and allow it to rotate anti-clockwise, to relieve the tension on the timing belt. Carefully slide the timing belt off the camshaft sprocket.

**5.13 Removing the camshaft sprocket**

**21** The crankshaft sprocket must be held stationary whilst its retaining bolt is slackened. If access to the correct VW flywheel locking tool is not available, lock the crankshaft in position by removing the starter motor, as described in Chapter 5A, to expose the flywheel ring gear. Get an assistant to insert a stout lever between the ring gear teeth and the transmission bellhousing whilst the sprocket retaining bolt is slackened. (Refer also to Section 12, paragraph 2 of Chapter 2A).
**22** Withdraw the bolt and lift off the sprocket.
**23** With the sprocket removed, examine the crankshaft oil seal for signs of leaking. If necessary, refer to Section 10 and renew it.
**24** Wipe the sprocket and crankshaft mating surfaces clean.

### Refitting

**25** Offer up the sprocket to the crankshaft, engaging the lug on the inside of the sprocket with the recess in the end of the crankshaft. Oil the threads of a new retaining bolt, then insert and tighten it to the specified torque **(see illustrations)**. **Note:** *If preferred, final tightening of the sprocket bolt may be delayed until after the timing belt has been refitted - this will prevent possible engine damage if the sprocket should turn as the bolt is tightened.*
**26** Working from Sections 2 and 4, check that the engine is still set to TDC on No 1 cylinder, then refit and tension the timing belt.
**27** Referring to Section 4, refit the timing belt upper and lower covers, the auxiliary drivebelt pulleys, auxiliary drivebelt, the engine mountings, and all other components removed for access. Reconnect the battery negative lead.

**5.25a Insert the crankshaft sprocket bolt . . .**

**5.25b . . . tighten it to the Stage 1 torque . . .**

**5.25c . . . then through the Stage 2 angle**

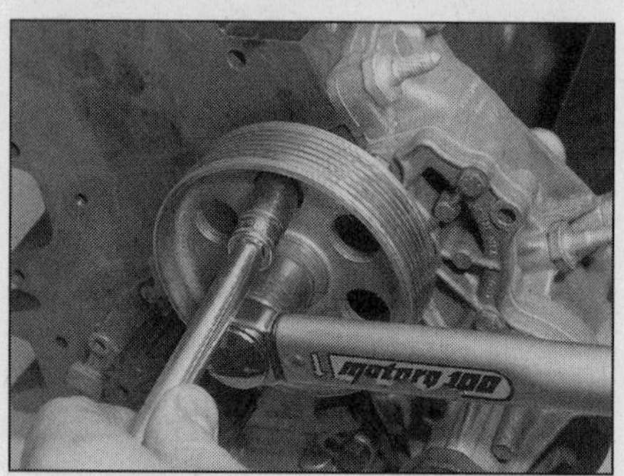

5.31 Brace the intermediate shaft sprocket, then remove the retaining bolt

**28** Restore the fuelling system by reconnecting the fuel cut-off solenoid wiring.

## Intermediate shaft sprocket

### Removal

**29** With reference to Sections 2 and 4, remove the timing belt covers and set the engine to TDC on No 1 cylinder. Slacken the tensioner centre nut and rotate it anti-clockwise to relieve the tension on the timing belt. Carefully slide the timing belt off the camshaft sprocket.

**30** The intermediate shaft sprocket must be held stationary whilst its retaining bolt is slackened; if access to the correct VW special tool is not possible, a simple home-made tool may be fabricated using basic materials as described in the camshaft sprocket removal sub-Section.

**31** Using a socket and extension bar, brace the intermediate shaft sprocket **(see illustration)**. Slacken and remove the retaining bolt, and slide the sprocket from the end of the intermediate shaft. Where applicable, recover the Woodruff key from the keyway.

**32** With the sprocket removed, examine the intermediate shaft oil seal for signs of leaking. If necessary, refer to Section 9 and renew it.

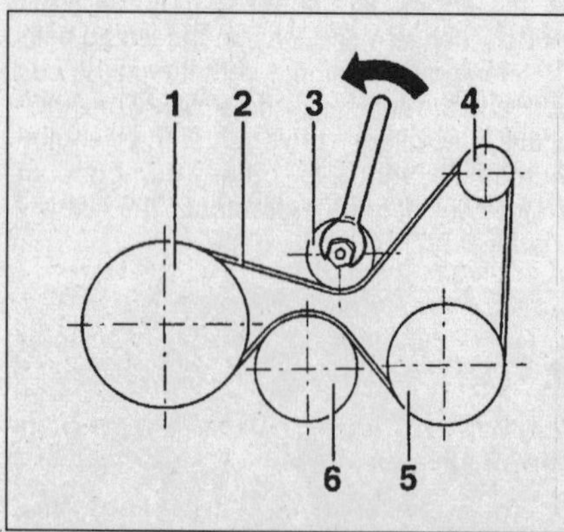


**6.8 Rotate the auxiliary drivebelt tensioner pulley anti-clockwise to relieve the tension on the belt**

*1 Crankshaft pulley*
*2 Auxiliary drivebelt*
*3 Tensioner pulley*
*4 Alternator pulley*
*5 Power steering pump pulley*
*6 Coolant pump pulley*

**33** Wipe the sprocket and shaft mating surfaces clean.

### Refitting

**34** Where applicable, fit the Woodruff key into the keyway, with the plain surface facing upwards. Offer up the sprocket to the intermediate shaft, engaging the slot in the sprocket with the Woodruff key.

**35** Tighten the sprocket retaining bolt to the specified torque; hold the sprocket using the method employed during removal.

**36** With reference to Section 2, check that the engine is still set to TDC on No 1 cylinder. Working from Section 4, refit and tension the timing belt.

**37** Referring to Section 4, refit the timing belt upper and lower covers, the auxiliary drivebelt pulleys, auxiliary drivebelt, the engine mountings, and all other components removed for access. Reconnect the battery negative lead.

**38** Restore the fuelling system by reconnecting the fuel cut-off solenoid wiring.

## Fuel injection pump sprocket

**39** Refer to Chapter 4C.

# 6 Auxiliary drivebelt - removal, refitting and tensioning

## General information

**1** Depending on the vehicle specification, the auxiliary drivebelt, which is driven from a pulley mounted on the crankshaft, will provide drive for the alternator, power steering pump, coolant pump and (on vehicles with air conditioning), the refrigerant compressor.

**2** The ribbed auxiliary belt is usually fitted with an automatic tensioning device. Otherwise, the belt is tensioned by the alternator mountings, which have an in-built tensioning spring.

**3** On refitting, the auxiliary belt must be tensioned correctly, to ensure correct operation under all conditions, and for prolonged service life.

## Removal

**4** Park the vehicle on a level surface, apply the handbrake and chock the rear wheels. Loosen the right-hand front wheel bolts.

**5** Raise the front of the car, rest it securely on axle stands and remove the right-hand front roadwheel.

**6** Where applicable, remove the fasteners, and lower the wheel arch liner and/or noise insulation tray for access to the drivebelt. Some models may have a cover fitted over the drivebelt - if so, release the fasteners and remove it. To improve access still further, refer to Chapter 4C and remove the air cleaner housing.

**7** Examine the ribbed belt for manufacturer's markings, indicating the direction of rotation. If none are present, make some using typist's correction fluid or a dab of paint - do not cut or score the belt in any way.

### Models with automatic tensioner

**8** Fit an open-ended 15 mm spanner (or an adjustable spanner) to the tensioner lever, and rotate the tensioner pulley anti-clockwise, against its spring tension **(see illustration)**.

### Models without automatic tensioner

**9** Slacken the alternator upper and lower mounting bolts by between one and two turns.

**10** Push the alternator down to its stop against the spring tension, so that it rotates around its uppermost mounting.

### All models

**11** Pull the belt off the alternator pulley, then release it from the remaining pulleys.

## Refitting and tensioning

***Caution: Observe the manufacturer's direction of rotation markings on the belt, when refitting.***

**12** Pass the ribbed belt underneath the crankshaft pulley, ensuring that the ribs seat in the channels on the surface of the pulley.

### Models with automatic tensioner

**13** Fit an open-ended 15 mm spanner (or an adjustable spanner) to the tensioner lever, and rotate the tensioner pulley anti-clockwise, against its spring tension.

**14** Pass the flat side of the belt underneath the tensioner roller, then fit it over the pulleys. Ensure that the belt ribs engage correctly with the pulley grooves.

**15** Release the spanner and allow the tensioner roller to bear against the flat side of the belt.

### Models without automatic tensioner

**16** Repeatedly push the alternator down to its stop against the spring tension, so that it rotates around its uppermost mounting, and check that it moves back freely when released. If necessary, slacken the alternator mounting bolts by a further half a turn.

**17** Keep the alternator pushed down against its stop, pass the belt over the alternator pulley, then release the alternator and allow it to tension the belt.

**18** Start the engine and allow it to idle for about 10 seconds, leaving the alternator mounting bolts slackened.

**19** Switch the engine off, then tighten first the lower, then the upper alternator mounting bolts to the specified torque.

### All models

**20** Refit the drivebelt cover, wheel arch liner, noise insulation tray, and air cleaner housing, as applicable.

**21** Refit the right-hand front roadwheel and lower the car to the ground. Tighten the roadwheel bolts to the specified torque. See Chapter 1B.

## 7 Camshaft cover - removal and refitting

### Removal

1 Disconnect the crankcase breather pipe from the camshaft cover. If the sealing grommet is damaged, obtain a new one for reassembly.

2 Prise off the cover caps, then slacken and remove the three camshaft cover retaining nuts - recover the washers and seals, noting their fitted positions. If any of the washers are damaged, new ones should be obtained for reassembly.

3 Lift the cover away from the cylinder head; if it sticks, do not attempt to lever it off - instead free it by working around the cover and tapping it lightly with a soft-faced mallet.

4 Recover the camshaft cover gasket. Inspect the gasket carefully, and renew it if damage or deterioration is evident.

5 Clean the mating surfaces of the cylinder head and camshaft cover thoroughly, removing all traces of oil and old gasket - take care to avoid damaging the surfaces as you do this.

### Refitting

6 Refit the camshaft cover by following the removal procedure in reverse, noting the following points:

a) *Ensure that the gasket is correctly seated on the cylinder head - the projections on the gasket should locate into the holes provided in the cylinder head mating surface.*

b) *Ensure that the sealing cones are still in place on the three camshaft cover studs.*

c) *Take care to avoid displacing the gasket as the camshaft cover is lowered into position.*

d) *Fit the washers and seals in the order noted on removal, then fit and tighten the camshaft cover retaining nuts to the specified torque. Fit the cover caps over the nuts.*

e) *Refit the crankcase breather pipe to the camshaft cover, using a new sealing grommet if necessary.*

## 8 Camshaft oil seal - renewal

1 Refer to Section 6 and remove the auxiliary drivebelt.

2 With reference to Sections 2, 4 and 5 of this Chapter, remove the auxiliary belt pulleys and timing belt upper cover. Set the engine to TDC on No 1 cylinder and remove the timing belt, timing belt tensioner, and the camshaft and fuel injection pump sprockets.

3 After removing the retaining bolts, lift the timing belt inner cover away from the engine.

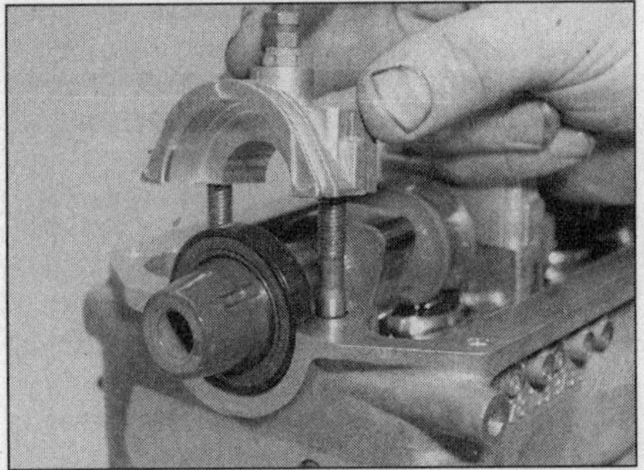

**8.4 Remove the camshaft bearing cap and slide off the oil seal**

4 Working from the relevant Section of Chapter 2C, carry out the following:

a) *Unbolt the camshaft No 1 bearing cap, and slide off the old camshaft oil seal* **(see illustration)**.

b) *Lubricate the surface of a new camshaft oil seal with clean engine oil, and fit it over the end of the camshaft.*

c) *Apply a suitable sealant to the mating surface of the bearing cap, then refit it and tighten its mounting nuts progressively to the specified torque.*

5 With reference to Sections 2, 4 and 5 of this Chapter, refit the timing belt inner cover, belt tensioner and timing sprockets, then refit and tension the timing belt. On completion, refit the timing belt outer covers and all other components removed for access.

6 With reference to Section 6, refit and tension the auxiliary drivebelt.

## 9 Intermediate shaft oil seal - renewal

1 Refer to Section 6 and remove the auxiliary drivebelt.

2 With reference to Sections 2, 4 and 5 of this Chapter, remove the auxiliary belt pulleys and timing belt upper cover. Set the engine to TDC on No 1 cylinder and remove the timing belt, timing belt tensioner and the intermediate shaft sprocket.

3 With reference to Chapter 2C, remove the intermediate shaft flange, and renew the shaft and flange oil seals.

**10.4 Removing the crankshaft front oil seal using self-tapping screws**

4 With reference to Sections 2, 4 and 5 of this Chapter, refit the timing belt tensioner and intermediate shaft sprocket, then refit and tension the timing belt. On completion, refit the timing belt outer covers and all other components removed for access.

5 With reference to Section 6, refit and tension the auxiliary drivebelt.

## 10 Crankshaft oil seals - renewal

### Crankshaft front oil seal

1 Refer to Chapter 1B and drain the engine oil.

2 Refer to Section 6 and remove the auxiliary drivebelt.

3 With reference to Sections 2, 4 and 5 of this Chapter, remove the auxiliary belt pulleys, timing belt outer covers, timing belt and crankshaft sprocket.

4 Drill two small holes into the existing oil seal, diagonally opposite each other. Take great care to avoid drilling through into the seal housing or crankshaft sealing surface. Thread two self-tapping screws into the holes, and using two pairs of pliers, pull on the heads of the screws to extract the oil seal **(see illustration)**.

5 Clean out the seal housing and sealing surface of the crankshaft by wiping it with a lint-free cloth - avoid using solvents that may enter the crankcase and affect component lubrication. Remove any swarf or burrs that could cause the seal to leak.

6 Smear the lip of the new oil seal with clean engine oil, and position it over the housing.

7 Using a hammer and a socket of suitable diameter, drive the seal squarely into its housing. **Note:** *Select a socket that bears only on the hard outer surface of the seal, not the inner lip, which can easily be damaged.*

8 With reference to Sections 2, 4 and 5 of this Chapter, refit the crankshaft sprocket, then refit and tension the timing belt. On completion, refit the timing belt outer covers, auxiliary drivebelt pulleys, and all other components removed for access.

9 The remainder of the refitting procedure is a reversal of removal, as follows:

a) *With reference to Section 6, refit and tension the auxiliary drivebelt.*

b) *Refer to Chapter 1B and refill the engine with the correct grade and quantity of oil.*

### Crankshaft front oil seal housing - gasket renewal

10 Proceed as described in paragraphs 1 to 3 above, then refer to Section 15 and remove the sump.

11 Progressively slacken and then remove the oil seal housing retaining bolts.

12 Lift the housing away from the cylinder block, together with the crankshaft oil seal, using a twisting motion to ease the seal along the shaft.

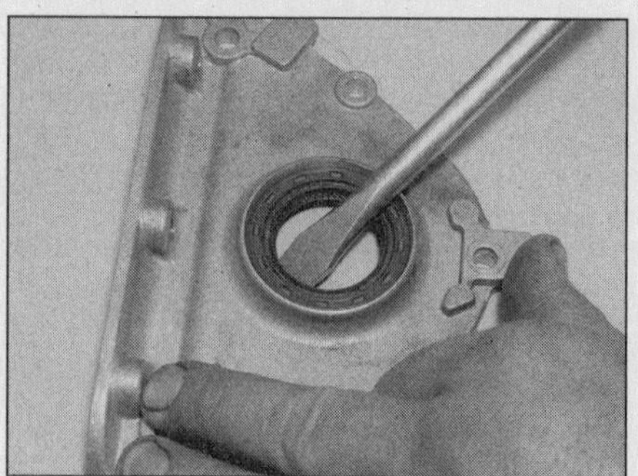
10.14 Prise the old oil seal from the housing

10.16 Locate the new crankshaft front oil seal housing gasket in position

10.18 Offer up the seal and its housing to the end of the crankshaft

**13** Recover the old gasket from the seal housing on the cylinder block. If it has disintegrated, scrape the remains off with a trimming knife blade. Take care to avoid damaging the mating surfaces.

**14** If necessary, prise the old oil seal from the housing using a stout screwdriver **(see illustration)**.

**15** Wipe the oil seal housing clean, and check it visually for signs of distortion or cracking. Lay the housing on a work surface, with the mating surface face down. If removed, press in a new oil seal, using a block of wood as a press to ensure that the seal enters the housing squarely.

**16** Smear the crankcase mating surface with suitable multi-purpose sealant, and lay the new gasket in position **(see illustration)**.

**17** Pad the end of the crankshaft with a layer of PVC tape; this will protect the oil seal as it is being fitted.

10.31 Locate the new crankshaft rear oil seal housing gasket in position

**18** Lubricate the inner lip of the crankshaft oil seal with clean engine oil, then offer up the seal and its housing to the end of the crankshaft **(see illustration)**. Ease the seal along the shaft using a twisting motion, until the housing is flush with the crankcase.

**19** Insert the bolts and tighten them to the specified torque.

***Caution: The housing is light alloy, and may be distorted if the bolts are not tightened progressively.***

**20** Refer to Section 15 and refit the sump.

**21** With reference to Sections 2, 4 and 5 of this Chapter, refit the crankshaft timing belt sprocket, then refit and tension the timing belt. On completion, refit the timing belt outer covers, auxiliary drivebelt pulleys, and all other components removed for access.

**22** The remainder of the refitting procedure is a reversal of removal, as follows:

*a) With reference to Section 6, refit and tension the auxiliary drivebelt.*

*b) Refer to Chapter 1B and refill the engine with the correct grade and quantity of oil.*

## Crankshaft rear oil seal (flywheel end)

**23** Proceed as described in paragraphs 1 to 3 above, then refer to Section 15 and remove the sump.

**24** Refer to Chapter 7A and remove the transmission from the engine.

**25** Refer to Section 13 of this Chapter and remove the flywheel; refer to Chapter 6 and remove the clutch friction plate and pressure plate.

**26** Where applicable, remove the retaining bolts and lift the intermediate plate away from the cylinder block.

**27** Progressively slacken and then remove the oil seal housing retaining bolts.

**28** Lift the housing away from the cylinder block, together with the crankshaft oil seal, using a twisting motion to ease the seal along the shaft.

**29** Recover the old gasket from the seal housing cylinder block. If it has disintegrated, scrape the remains off with a trimming knife blade. Take care to avoid damaging the mating surfaces.

**30** The rear oil seal is not available separately from the housing, and the seal and housing must therefore be renewed complete.

**31** Smear the crankcase mating surface with suitable multi-purpose sealant, and lay the new gasket in position **(see illustration)**.

**32** A protective plastic sleeve is usually supplied with genuine VW crankshaft oil seal housings; when fitted over the end of the crankshaft, the sleeve prevents damage to the inner lip of the oil seal as it is being fitted **(see illustration)**. Use PVC tape to pad the end of the crankshaft if a sleeve is not provided.

**33** Lubricate the inner lip of the crankshaft oil seal with clean engine oil, then offer up the seal housing to the end of the crankshaft **(see illustration)**. Ease the seal along the shaft using a twisting motion, until the housing is flush with the crankcase.

**34** Insert the retaining bolts and tighten them progressively to the specified torque **(see illustration)**.

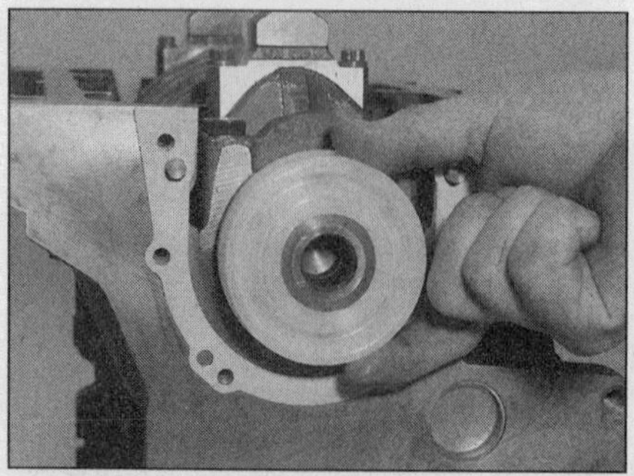
10.32 A protective plastic cap is supplied with genuine VW crankshaft oil seal housings

10.33 Fitting the crankshaft rear oil seal housing

10.34 Tightening the crankshaft rear oil seal housing retaining bolts

**11.6 Disconnecting the inlet air trunking from the inlet manifold cover**

**11.7 Disconnect the heater coolant hoses from the ports on the cylinder head**

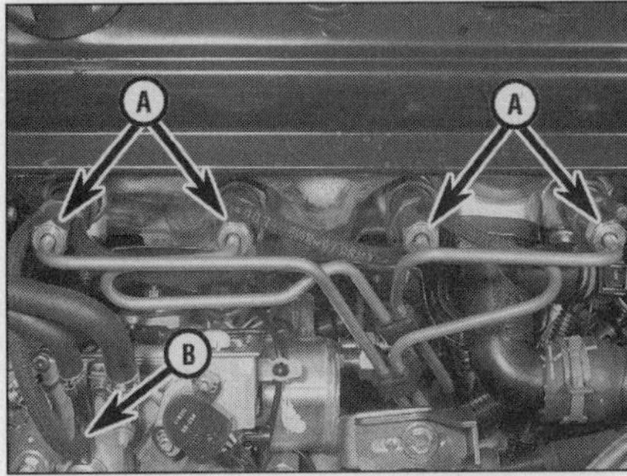


**11.8 General view of the fuel injector pipes (A) and the return hose connection (B)**

***Caution: The housing is light alloy, and may be distorted if the bolts are not tightened progressively.***

**35** Refer to Section 15 and refit the sump.

**36** Refer to Chapter 6 and refit the flywheel, pressure plate and clutch friction plate.

**37** With reference to Chapter 7A, refit the transmission to the engine.

**38** On completion, refer to Chapter 1B and refill the engine with the correct grade and quantity of oil.

## 11 Cylinder head, inlet and exhaust manifolds - removal, separation and refitting

### Removal

**1** Select a level surface to park the vehicle upon. Give yourself enough space to move around it easily.

**2** Disconnect the battery negative lead, and position It away from the terminal. **Note:** *If the vehicle has a security-coded radio, check that you have a copy of the code number before disconnecting the battery cable.*

**3** With reference to Chapter 1B, drain the cooling system.

**4** The lock carrier is a panel assembly comprising the radiator and grille, cooling fan, headlight units, front valance and bonnet lock mechanism. Although its removal is not essential, its does give greatly-improved access to the engine. Its removal is described at the beginning of the engine removal procedure - refer to Chapter 2C for details.

**5** Refer to Section 6 and remove the auxiliary drivebelt.

**6** Compress the legs of the spring clip, and release the inlet air trunking from the inlet manifold cover **(see illustration)**.

**7** Refer to Chapter 3 and perform the following:

a) *Slacken the clips and disconnect the radiator hoses from the ports on the cylinder head.*
b) *Slacken the clips and disconnect the expansion tank hose, and the heater inlet and outlet coolant hoses, from the ports on the cylinder head **(see illustration)**.*

**8** Refer to Chapter 4C and carry out the following:

a) *Disconnect and remove the injector fuel supply pipes from the injectors and the injection pump head **(see illustration)**.*
b) *Disconnect the injector return hose from the injection pump fuel return port.*
c) *Unplug all fuel system electrical cabling at the relevant connectors, labelling each cable to aid refitting later.*

**9** With reference to Sections 2, 4 and 7, carry out the following:

a) *Remove the camshaft cover.*
b) *Remove the timing belt outer covers, and disengage the timing belt from the camshaft sprocket.*
c) *Remove the timing belt tensioner, camshaft sprocket and fuel injection pump sprocket.*

**10** Once the timing belt has been disengaged, the engine can be raised back into its original position, and the engine right-hand mounting refitted while the cylinder head is removed.

**11** To avoid any possibility of piston-to-valve contact during cylinder head removal, it is recommended that the crankshaft be turned back a few degrees away from the TDC position, to take the pistons down the bores.

**12** Slacken and withdraw the retaining screws, and lift off the timing belt inner cover.

**13** With reference to Chapter 3, Section 6, disconnect the wiring plug from the coolant temperature sensor **(see illustration)**.

**14** Refer to Chapter 4D and 5C, and carry out the following:

a) *Working from underneath the car, remove the bolts and separate the exhaust downpipe from the exhaust manifold flange. Alternatively, removing the inlet manifold cover and pipes as described in paragraphs 20 and 21 will provide better access from above.*
b) *Remove the EGR valve and its connecting pipework from the inlet and exhaust manifolds.*
c) *Unbolt the supply cable from the glow plug in cylinder No 4 **(see illustration)**.*

**15** Disconnect the engine harness connector multi-plug, then remove the retaining bolt and detach the engine harness connector bracket from the cylinder head **(see illustration)**.

**16** Progressively slacken the cylinder head bolts, by half a turn at a time, until all bolts can be unscrewed by hand **(see illustration)**. Discard the bolts - new ones must be fitted on reassembly.

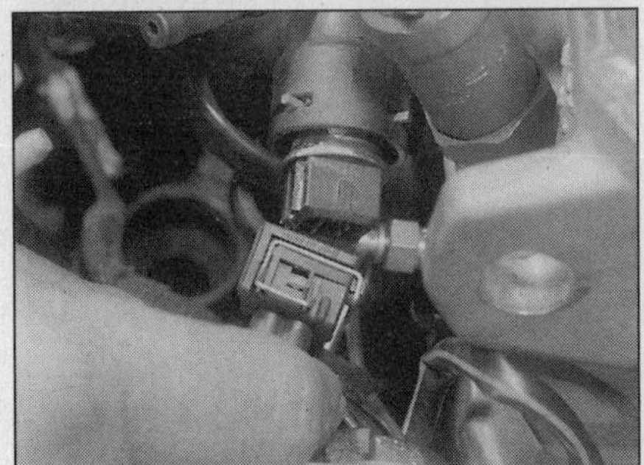

**11.13 Disconnect the wiring plug from the coolant temperature sensor**

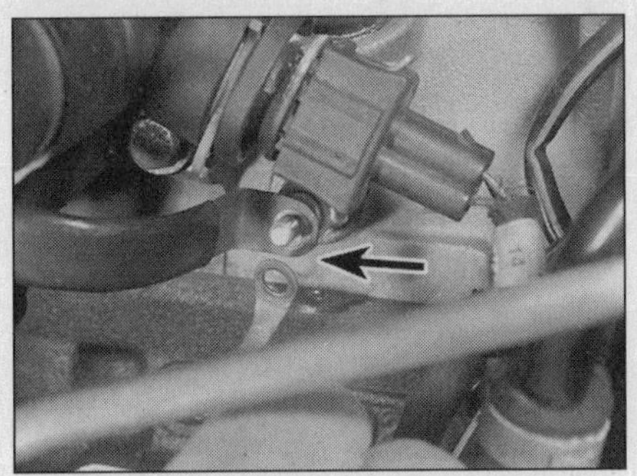

**11.14 Unbolt the electrical supply cable from No 4 cylinder glow plug**

**11.15 Removing the engine harness connector bracket from the cylinder head**

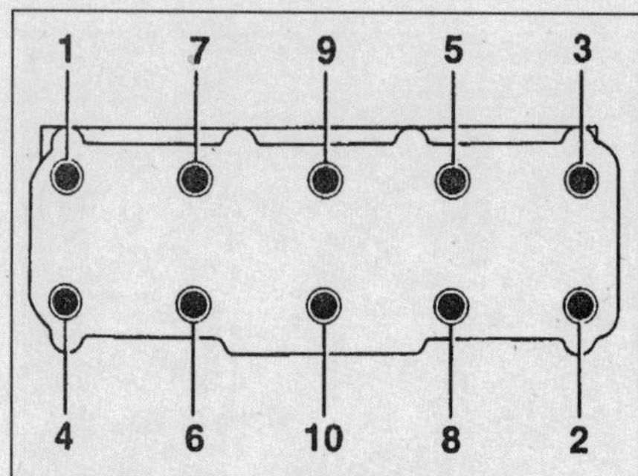


**11.16 Cylinder head bolt LOOSENING sequence**

**17** Check that nothing remains connected to the cylinder head, then lift the head away from the cylinder block; seek assistance if possible, as it is a heavy assembly, especially if it is being removed complete with the manifolds.

**18** Remove the gasket from the top of the block, noting the locating dowels (where fitted). If the dowels are a loose fit, remove them and store them with the head for safe-keeping. Do not discard the gasket yet - it will be needed for identification purposes.

**19** If the cylinder head is to be dismantled for overhaul, refer to Chapter 2C.

## Manifold separation

**20** With the cylinder head on a work surface, slacken and withdraw the five inlet manifold cover bolts. Lift the cover away, and recover the gasket.

**21** Loosen and remove the inlet manifold/inlet pipe retaining bolts, and remove the four pipes and manifold from the cylinder head. Recover the manifold-to-cylinder head gasket.

**22** Unbolt the heat shield (where fitted), then progressively slacken and remove the exhaust manifold retaining nuts. Lift the manifold away from the cylinder head, and recover the gasket.

**23** Ensure that the inlet and exhaust manifold mating surfaces are completely clean. Refit the exhaust manifold, using a new gasket. Tighten the exhaust manifold retaining nuts to the specified torque.

**24** Where applicable, refit the heat shield to the studs on the exhaust manifold, then fit and tighten the retaining nuts.

**25** Fit a new inlet manifold gasket to the cylinder head, then lift the inlet manifold into position. Fitting each inlet pipe in turn, insert the retaining bolts and tighten them to the specified toque.

## Preparation for refitting

**26** The mating faces of the cylinder head and cylinder block/crankcase must be perfectly clean before refitting the head. Use a hard plastic or wood scraper to remove all traces of gasket and carbon; also clean the piston crowns. Take particular care during the cleaning operations, as aluminium alloy is easily damaged. Also, make sure that the carbon is not allowed to enter the oil and water passages - this is particularly important for the lubrication system, as carbon could block the oil supply to the engine's components. Using adhesive tape and paper, seal the water, oil and bolt holes in the cylinder block/crankcase.

**27** Check the mating surfaces of the cylinder block/crankcase and the cylinder head for nicks, deep scratches and other damage. If slight, they may be removed carefully with abrasive paper, but note that head machining will not be possible - refer to Chapter 2C. If warpage of the cylinder head gasket surface is suspected, use a straight-edge to check it for distortion. Refer to Part C of this Chapter if necessary.

**28** Clean out the cylinder head bolt drillings using a suitable tap. If a tap is not available, make a home-made substitute **(see Tool Tip)**.

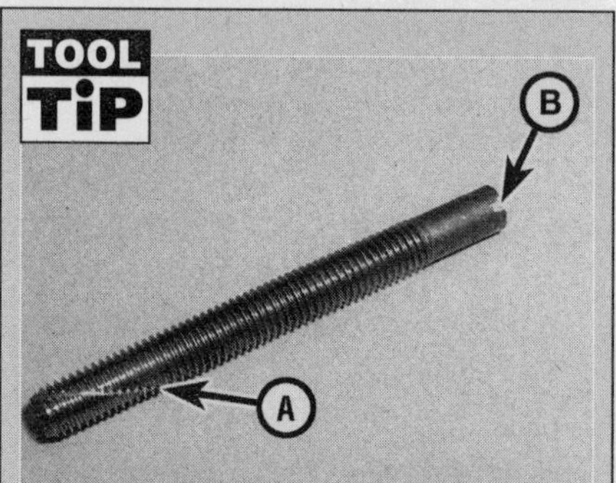


***If a tap is not available, make a home-made substitute by cutting a slot (A) down the threads of one of the old cylinder head bolts. After use, the bolt head can be cut off, and the shank can then be used as an alignment dowel to assist cylinder head refitting. Cut a screwdriver slot (B) in the top of the bolt, to allow it to be unscrewed***

**29** On all the engines covered in this Chapter, it is possible for the piston crowns to strike and damage the valve heads, if the camshaft is rotated with the timing belt removed and the crankshaft set to TDC. For this reason, the crankshaft must be set to a position other than TDC on No 1 cylinder, before the cylinder head is refitted. Set the crankshaft to TDC on No 1 cylinder, using the information in Section 2, then turn the crankshaft back by a few degrees, away from the TDC position. If preferred, for maximum safety, the pistons can be positioned halfway down their bores, with No 1 piston on its upstroke - ie 90° before TDC.

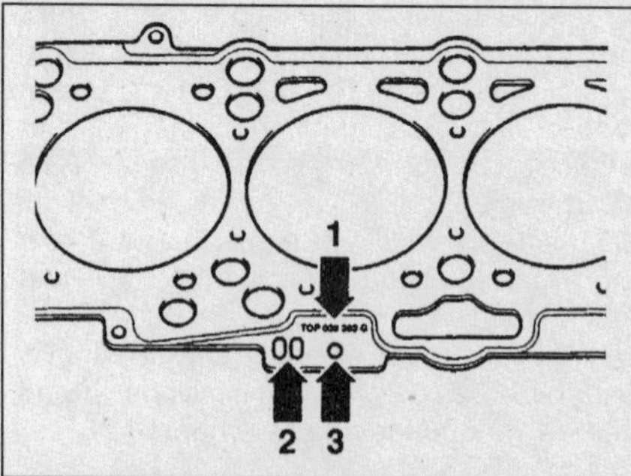


**11.30 Cylinder head gasket identification markings**

*1 Part number*
*2 Production code (disregard)*
*3 Punched hole(s)*

## Refitting

**30** Examine the old cylinder head gasket for manufacturer's identification markings. These will either be in the form of punched holes or a part number, on the edge of the gasket **(see illustration)**. Unless new pistons have been fitted, the new cylinder head gasket must be the same type as the old one.

**31** If new piston assemblies have been fitted as part of an engine overhaul, before purchasing the new cylinder head gasket, refer to Chapter 2C and measure the piston projection. Purchase a new gasket according to the results of the measurement (see Chapter 2C Specifications).

**32** Lay the new head gasket on the cylinder block, engaging it with the locating dowels, where used **(see Tool Tip)**. Ensure that the manufacturer's TOP and part number markings are face up. Do not handle the gasket excessively before it is fitted, or it may become damaged.

***Where no locating dowels are fitted, it may prove difficult to accurately align the head on the block when refitting. To overcome this, two of the old cylinder head bolts can be modified to act as locating dowels. Cut the heads off two of the bolts, and then cut a slot in the top of the bolt, so that a flat-bladed screwdriver may be used to unscrew the bolts from the block once the head is placed over them. Screw the two dowels into place either end of the head, then lower the head into position over them. Fit two or more of the new head bolts to locate the head, then unscrew the dowels using a screwdriver***

**33** With the help of an assistant, place the cylinder head and manifolds centrally on the cylinder block, ensuring that the locating dowels engage with the recesses in the cylinder head. Check that the head gasket is correctly seated before allowing the full weight of the cylinder head to rest upon it.
**34** Apply a little oil to the threads, and to the underside of the heads, of the new cylinder head bolts **(see illustration)**.
**35** Carefully enter each bolt into its relevant hole (*do not drop them in*) and screw in, by hand only, until finger-tight.
**36** Working progressively and in the sequence shown, tighten the cylinder head bolts to their Stage 1 torque setting, using a torque wrench and suitable socket **(see illustration)**. Repeat the exercise in the same sequence for the Stage 2 torque setting.
**37** Once all the bolts have been tightened to their Stage 2 settings, working again in the given sequence, angle-tighten the bolts through the specified Stage 3 angle, using a socket and extension bar. It is recommended that an angle-measuring gauge is used during this stage of the tightening, to ensure accuracy. If a gauge is not available, use white paint to make alignment marks between the bolt head and cylinder head prior to tightening; the marks can then be used to check the bolt has been rotated through the correct angle during tightening. Repeat for the Stage 4 setting.
**38** Refit the timing belt inner cover, tightening the retaining bolts to the specified torque.
**39** Refer to Section 2 and set the engine to TDC on No 1 cylinder.
**40** Support the engine, then disconnect the engine mountings as described in Section 4 and lower the engine down slightly. Referring to Section 5, refit the timing belt sprockets. Using the information in Section 4, refit and tension the timing belt and outer covers, and the crankshaft pulley.
**41** The engine can now be raised back into position, and the engine mountings refitted as described in Section 4.
**42** Refit and tension the auxiliary drivebelt as described in Section 6.
**43** The remainder of refitting is a reversal of the removal procedure, as follows:

- *a) Refer to Chapter 4D and refit the exhaust downpipe, EGR valve and glow plug cabling.*
- *b) Refer to Chapter 4C and refit the injector fuel supply pipes to the injectors and the injection pump head. Reconnect all fuel system electrical cabling. Refit the injector bleed hose to the injection pump fuel return port.*
- *c) Refit the engine harness connector bracket to the cylinder head, and reconnect the multi-plug connector.*
- *d) Refit the camshaft cover (see Section 7).*
- *e) With reference to the information in Chapter 2C, refit the lock carrier assembly, if it was removed for greater access.*

**11.34 Oil the cylinder head bolt threads, then place each bolt into its relevant hole**

- *f) Reconnect the radiator, expansion tank and heater coolant hoses, referring to Chapter 3 for guidance.*
- *g) Reconnect the coolant temperature sensor wiring.*
- *h) Restore the battery connection.*

**44** On completion, refer to Chapter 1B and refill the engine cooling system with the correct quantity of new coolant.

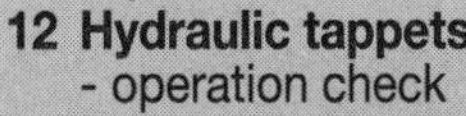

## 12 Hydraulic tappets - operation check

**1** The hydraulic tappets are self-adjusting, and require no attention whilst in service.
**2** If the hydraulic tappets become excessively noisy, their operation can be checked as described below.
**3** Run the engine until it reaches its normal operating temperature. Increase the engine speed to around 2500 rpm (fast idle) for about 2 minutes, then switch off the engine. Refer to Section 7 and remove the camshaft cover.
**4** Rotate the camshaft by turning the crankshaft with a socket and wrench, until the first cam lobe over No 1 cylinder is pointing upwards.
**5** Using a feeler blade, measure the clearance between the base of the cam lobe and the top of the tappet. If the clearance is greater than 0.1mm, then the tappet is defective and must be renewed.
**6** If the clearance is less than 0.1 mm, press down on the top of the tappet, until it is felt to contact the top of the valve stem. Use a wooden or plastic implement that will not damage the surface of the tappet **(see illustration)**.
**7** If the tappet travels more than 1.0 mm before making contact, then it is defective and must be renewed.
**8** Hydraulic tappet removal and refitting is described as part of the cylinder head overhaul sequence - see Chapter 2C for details.

***Warning: After fitting hydraulic tappets, wait a minimum of 30 minutes (or leave overnight) before starting the engine, to allow the tappets time to settle, otherwise the pistons may strike the valve heads.***

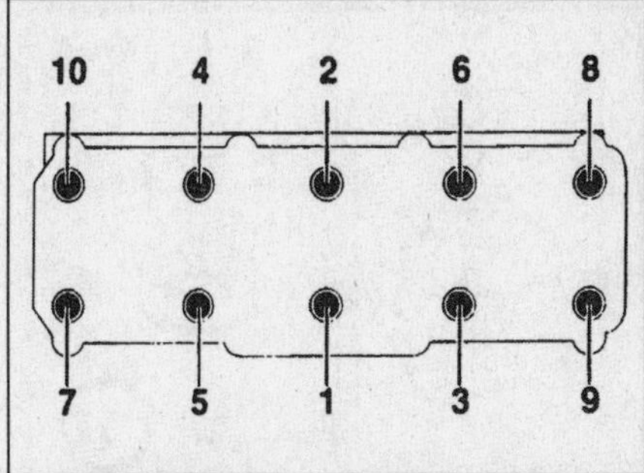


**11.36 Cylinder head bolt TIGHTENING sequence**

## 13 Flywheel - removal, inspection and refitting

Removal of the flywheel is as described in Section 12 of Chapter 2A. Note that the flywheel fitted to the diesel engine may be a conventional type, or a two-part type; procedures are unaffected.

## 14 Engine mountings - inspection and renewal

### *Inspection*

**1** If improved access is required, raise the front of the car and support it securely on axle stands.
**2** Check the mounting rubbers to see if they are cracked, hardened or separated from the metal at any point; renew the mounting if any such damage or deterioration is evident.
**3** Check that all the mounting's fasteners are securely tightened; use a torque wrench to check if possible.
**4** Using a large screwdriver or a crowbar, check for wear in the mounting by carefully levering against it to check for free play. Where this is not possible, enlist the aid of an assistant to move the engine/transmission back and forth, or from side to side, while you watch the mounting. While some free play is to be expected even from new components, excessive wear should be obvious. If

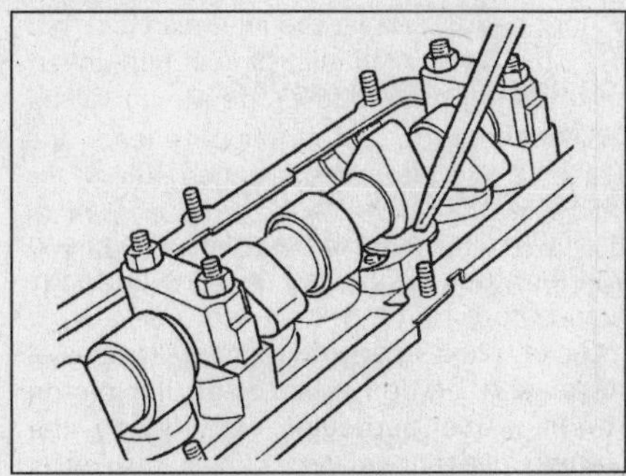

**12.6 Press down on the tappet, until it contacts the top of the valve stem**

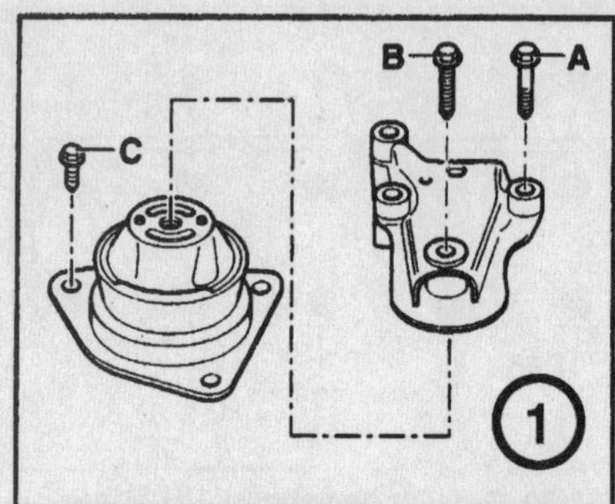


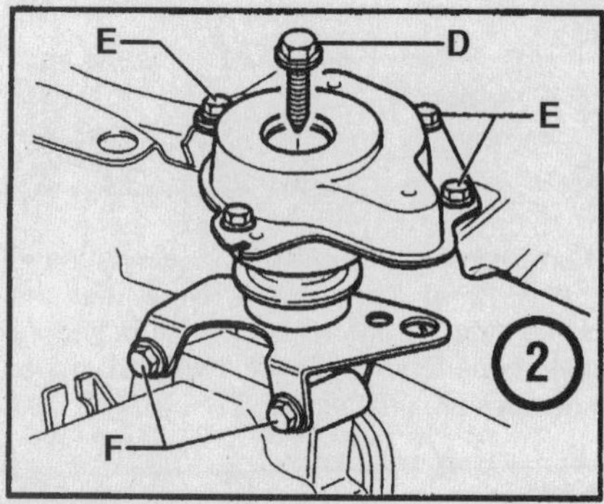


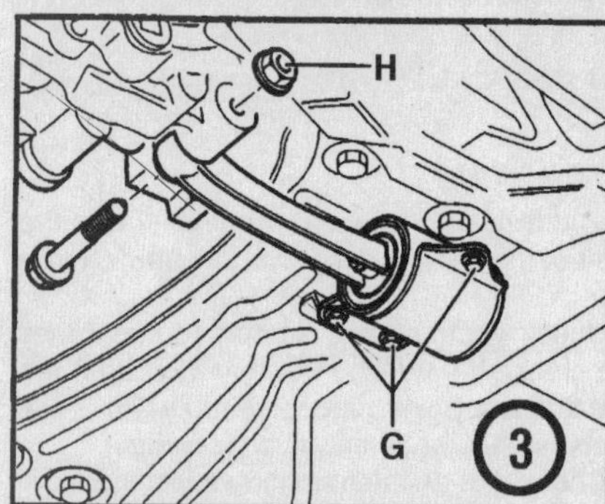


**14.9 Engine/transmission mounting details - for tightening torques (A, B, C, etc.), see Specifications**

1 *Engine right-hand mounting*
2 *Transmission left-hand mounting*
3 *Engine/transmission rear mounting*

excessive free play is found, check first that the fasteners are correctly secured, then renew any worn components as described below.

## *Renewal*

### Engine right-hand mounting

**5** Disconnect the battery negative lead, and position it away from the terminal. **Note:** *If the vehicle has a security-coded radio, check that you have a copy of the code number before disconnecting the battery. Refer to your VW dealer if in doubt.*

**6** Support the weight of the engine from above using a hoist or lifting beam, or support it from below using a securely-located trolley jack and suitable block of wood underneath the sump. Do not jack directly under the sump, or the sump may be damaged.

**7** With the engine supported from above or below, slacken and withdraw the three upper bolts, and separate the engine mounting.

**8** The remaining three bolts can now be removed, and the lower part of the mounting removed from the inner wing.

**9** Refitting is a reversal of removal, noting the following points **(see illustration)**:

a) *Use new bolts, and apply a little oil to their threads before fitting.*
b) *Tighten all bolts to the specified torque.*
c) *Note that the tightening torque for the upper and lower bolts is different.*

### Transmission left-hand mounting

**10** Disconnect the battery negative lead, and position it away from the terminal. Refer to the note in paragraph 5.

**11** Support the weight of the engine/transmission from above using a hoist or lifting beam, or support it from below using a securely-located trolley jack and suitable block of wood underneath the bellhousing. Position the jack head directly underneath the engine/bellhousing mating surface. Do not jack directly under the sump, or the sump may be damaged.

**12** With the engine/transmission supported from above or below, loosen and withdraw the central through-bolt from the mounting on the transmission.

**13** Unbolt the mounting block from the inner wing, and remove it from the engine bay.

**14** Unbolt the mounting bracket from the end of the transmission casing.

**15** Refitting is a reversal of removal, noting the following points **(refer to illustration 14.9)**:

a) *Use new bolts, and apply a little oil to their threads before fitting.*
b) *Tighten all bolts to the specified torque.*

### Engine/transmission rear mounting

**16** Disconnect the battery negative lead, and position it away from the terminal. Refer to the note in paragraph 5.

**17** Support the weight of the engine/transmission from above using a hoist or lifting beam, or support it from below using a securely-located trolley jack and suitable block of wood underneath the bellhousing. Position the jack head directly underneath the engine/bellhousing mating surface. Do not jack directly under the sump, or the sump may be damaged.

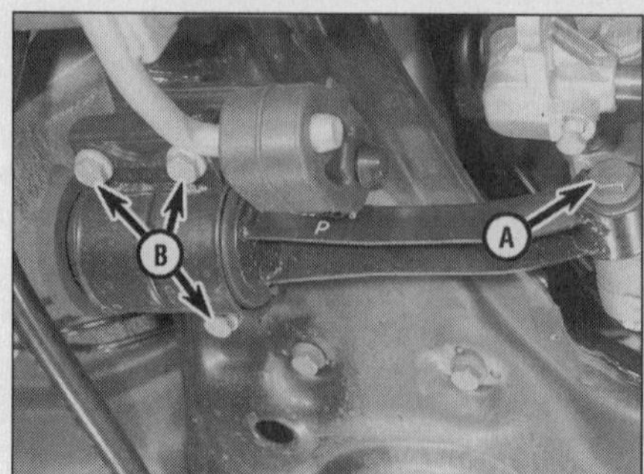


**14.18 Engine/transmission rear mounting through-bolt (A) and mounting-to-subframe bolts (B)**

**18** With the engine/transmission supported from above or below, slacken the nut and withdraw the through-bolt from the mounting on the transmission **(see illustration)**.

**19** Remove the three bolts from the subframe, and withdraw the mounting from under the car.

**20** Refitting is a reversal of removal, noting the following points **(refer to illustration 14.9)**:

a) *Use new bolts, and apply a little oil to their threads before fitting.*
b) *Tighten all bolts to the specified torque.*
c) *When tightening the through-bolt, hold the bolt and tighten the nut onto it.*

## 15 Sump - removal, inspection and refitting

## *Removal*

**1** Disconnect the battery negative cable, and position it away from the terminal. **Note:** *If the vehicle has a security-coded radio, check that you have a copy of the code number before disconnecting the battery. Refer to your VW dealer if in doubt.*

**2** Refer to Chapter 1B and drain the engine oil.

**3** Park the vehicle on a level surface, apply the handbrake and chock the rear wheels.

**4** Raise the front of the vehicle, rest it securely on axle stands or wheel ramps; refer to *Jacking and vehicle support*.

**5** To improve access to the sump, refer to Chapter 8 and disconnect the right-hand driveshaft from the transmission output flange.

**6** Working around the outside of the sump, progressively slacken and withdraw the sump retaining bolts.

**7** Break the joint by striking the sump with the palm of your hand, then lower the sump and withdraw it from underneath the vehicle. Recover and discard the sump gasket. Where a baffle plate is fitted, note that it can only be removed once the oil pump has been unbolted (see Section 16).

**8** While the sump is removed, take the opportunity to check the oil pump pick-up/strainer for signs of clogging or disintegration. If necessary, remove the pump as described in Section 16, and clean or renew the strainer.

## *Refitting*

**9** Clean all traces of sealant from the mating surfaces of the cylinder block/crankcase and sump, then use a piece of clean rag to wipe out the sump.

**10** Ensure that the sump and cylinder block/crankcase mating surfaces are clean and dry, then apply a coating of suitable sealant to the sump and crankcase mating surfaces.

**11** Lay a new sump gasket in position on the sump mating surface, then offer up the sump and refit the retaining bolts. Tighten the nuts and bolts evenly and progressively to the specified torque.
**12** Where applicable, refit the driveshaft as described in Chapter 8, then refit the noise insulation tray under the engine.
**13** Refer to Chapter 1B and refill the engine with the specified grade and quantity of oil.
**14** Restore the battery connection.

## 16 Oil pump and pickup - removal and refitting

### General information

**1** The oil pump and pickup are both mounted in the sump. Drive is taken from the intermediate shaft, which rotates at half crankshaft speed.

### Removal

**2** Refer to Section 15 and remove the sump from the crankcase.
**3** Slacken and remove the bolts securing the oil pump to the base of the crankcase **(see illustration)**.
**4** Lower the oil pump and pickup away from the crankcase. Where applicable, recover the baffle plate.

### Inspection

**5** Remove the screws from the mating flange, and lift off the pickup tube. Recover the O-ring seal. Slacken and withdraw the screws, then remove the oil pump cover.
**6** Clean the pump thoroughly, and inspect the gear teeth for signs of damage or wear.
**7** Check the pump backlash by inserting a feeler blade between the meshed gear teeth; rotate the gears against each other slightly, to give the maximum clearance **(see illustration)**. Compare the measurement with the limit quoted in Specifications.
**8** Check the pump axial clearance as follows. Lay an engineer's straight edge across the oil pump casing, then using a feeler blade, measure the clearance between the straight edge and the pump gears **(see illustration)**. Compare the measurement with the limit quoted in Specifications.
**9** If either measurement is outside of the specified limit, this indicates that the pump is worn and must be renewed.

### Refitting

**10** Refit the oil pump cover, then fit and tighten the screws to the specified torque.
**11** Reassemble the oil pickup to the oil pump, using a new O-ring seal. Tighten the retaining screws to the specified torque.
**12** Where applicable, fit the crankcase baffle plate in place.
**13** Offer up the oil pump to the crankcase, then fit the mounting bolts and tighten them to the specified torque.
**14** Refer to Section 15 and refit the sump.

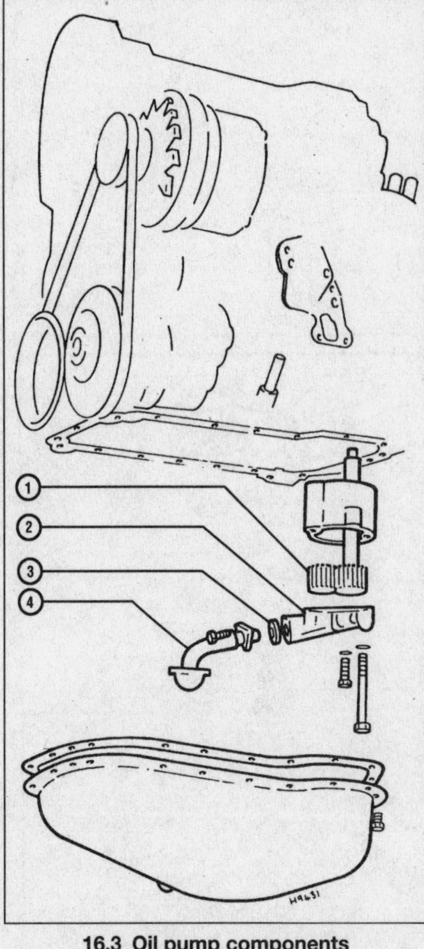


**16.3 Oil pump components**

*1 Oil pump gears*
*2 Oil pump cover*
*3 O-ring seal*
*4 Pickup tube*

**16.7 Checking the oil pump backlash**

**16.8 Checking the oil pump axial clearance**

# Chapter 2 Part C:
# Engine removal and overhaul procedures

## Contents



## Degrees of difficulty

| | | | | |
|---|---|---|---|---|
| **Easy,** suitable for novice with little experience  | **Fairly easy,** suitable for beginner with some experience  | **Fairly difficult,** suitable for competent DIY mechanic | **Difficult,** suitable for experienced DIY mechanic | **Very difficult,** suitable for expert DIY or professional |

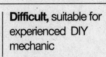

## Specifications

### Engine codes

See Chapter 2A or B

### Cylinder head

| | |
|---|---|
| Cylinder head gasket surface, maximum distortion: | |
| Petrol engines | 0.05 mm |
| Diesel engines | 0.1 mm |
| Minimum cylinder head height: | |
| Petrol engines | 135.6 mm |
| Diesel engines | Head reworking not possible |
| Maximum swirl chamber projection (engine code AEF only) | 0.05 mm |

### Cylinder head gasket

| | |
|---|---|
| Identification markings (punched holes), diesel engines only*: | |
| All diesel engines except engine code AEF: | |
| Piston projection: | |
| 0.91 to 1.00 mm | 1 hole |
| 1.01 to 1.10 mm | 2 holes |
| 1.11 to 1.20 mm | 3 holes |
| Engine code AEF: | |
| Piston projection: | |
| 0.66 to 0.86 mm | 1 hole |
| 0.87 to 0.90 mm | 2 holes |
| 0.91 to 1.02 mm | 3 holes |

*__Note:__ *See text in Chapter 2B and in Sections 4 and 13 of this Chapter for details*

### Valves - petrol engines

| | |
|---|---|
| Valve stem diameter: | |
| Inlet: | |
| Engine codes AER and ALL | 6.967 mm |
| All other engines | 6.963 mm |
| Exhaust: | |
| Engine codes AER and ALL | 6.950 mm |
| All other engines | 6.943 mm |
| Maximum valve head deflection (end of valve stem flush with top of guide): | |
| Inlet | 1.0 mm |
| Exhaust | 1.3 mm |

## Valves - diesel engines

Valve stem diameter:
- Inlet:
  - Engine code AEF ........ 7.97 mm
  - All other engines ........ 6.97 mm
- Exhaust:
  - Engine codes AEF ........ 7.95 mm
  - All other engines ........ 6.95 mm

Maximum valve head deflection
(end of valve stem flush with top of guide) ........ 1.3 mm

## Camshaft

Endfloat, all engine codes ........ 0.15 mm
Maximum runout, all engine codes ........ 0.01 mm
Maximum running clearance:
- Diesel engines ........ 0.11 mm
- Petrol engines ........ 0.10 mm

## Cylinder block - petrol engines

Bore diameter:
- Engine codes AER and ALL:
  - Standard ........ 67.11 mm
  - 1st oversize ........ 67.36 mm
  - 2nd oversize ........ 67.61 mm
  - 3rd oversize ........ 67.86 mm
- Engine code AEV:
  - Standard ........ 75.01 mm
  - 1st oversize ........ 75.26 mm
  - 2nd oversize ........ 75.51 mm
  - 3rd oversize ........ 75.76 mm
- All other petrol engines:
  - Standard ........ 76.51 mm
  - 1st oversize ........ 76.76 mm
  - 2nd oversize ........ 77.01 mm
  - 3rd oversize ........ 77.26 mm
- Diesel engines:
  - Standard ........ 79.51 mm
  - 1st oversize ........ 79.76 mm
  - 2nd oversize ........ 80.01 mm

## Pistons and piston rings

Piston diameter:
- Engine codes AER and ALL:
  - Standard ........ 67.085 mm
  - 1st oversize ........ 67.335 mm
  - 2nd oversize ........ 67.585 mm
  - 3rd oversize ........ 67.835 mm
- Engine code AEV:
  - Standard ........ 74.985 mm
  - 1st oversize ........ 75.235 mm
  - 2nd oversize ........ 75.485 mm
  - 3rd oversize ........ 75.735 mm
- All other petrol engines:
  - Standard ........ 76.470 mm
  - 1st oversize ........ 76.720 mm
  - 2nd oversize ........ 76.970 mm
  - 3rd oversize ........ 77.220 mm
- Engine code AEF:
  - Standard ........ 79.48 mm
  - 1st oversize ........ 79.73 mm
  - 2nd oversize ........ 79.98 mm
- All other diesel engines:
  - Standard ........ 79.47 mm
  - 1st oversize ........ 79.92 mm
  - 2nd oversize ........ 79.97 mm

| | | |
|---|---|---|
| Piston ring-to-groove wall clearance: | | |
| Petrol engines: | | |
| Compression rings | 0.15 mm (wear limit) | |
| Oil scraper ring: | | |
| One-part | 0.15 mm (wear limit) | |
| Three-part | Not measurable | |
| Diesel engines: | | |
| Engine code AEF: | | |
| 1st compression ring | 0.09 to 0.12 mm (wear limit: 0.25 mm) | |
| 2nd compression ring | 0.05 to 0.08 mm (wear limit: 0.25 mm) | |
| Oil scraper ring | 0.03 to 0.06 mm (wear limit: 0.15 mm) | |
| All other engines: | | |
| 1st compression ring | 0.06 to 0.09 mm (wear limit: 0.25 mm) | |
| 2nd compression ring | 0.05 to 0.08 mm (wear limit: 0.25 mm) | |
| Oil scraper ring | 0.03 to 0.06 mm (wear limit: 0.15 mm) | |
| Piston ring end gap: | | |
| Petrol engines: | | |
| Wear limit | 1.0 mm | |
| Diesel engines: | **New** | **Wear limit** |
| 1st compression ring, engine code AEF | 0.20 to 0.40 mm | 1.2 mm |
| 1st compression ring, all other engines | 0.20 to 0.40 mm | 1.0 mm |
| 2nd compression ring, engine code AEF | 0.20 to 0.40 mm | 0.6 mm |
| 2nd compression ring, all other engines | 0.20 to 0.40 mm | 1.0 mm |
| Oil scraper ring, engine code AEF | 0.25 to 0.50 mm | 1.2 mm |
| Oil scraper ring, all other engines | 0.25 to 0.50 mm | 1.0 mm |

## Connecting rods

| | |
|---|---|
| Length: | |
| Diesel engines: | |
| Engine code AEF | 150 mm |
| All other engine codes | 144 mm |
| Petrol engines | N/A |
| Big-end thrust clearance: | |
| Petrol engines: | |
| Engine code AEV | 0.05 to 0.31 mm (wear limit: 0.40 mm) |
| All other engines | N/A |
| Diesel engines: | |
| Wear limit | 0.37 mm |
| Bearing shell pre-tension - minimum (petrol engines only): | |
| Engine code AEV | 0.5 mm |
| All other petrol engines | 1.5 mm |

## Crankshaft*

| | |
|---|---|
| Maximum endfloat: | |
| Petrol engines (cast-iron cylinder block): | |
| New | 0.07 to 0.24 mm |
| Wear limit | 0.26 mm |
| Diesel engines: | |
| New | 0.07 to 0.17 mm |
| Service limit | 0.37 mm |
| Main bearing journal diameters: | |
| All engine codes: | |
| Standard | 54.00 mm |
| 1st undersize | 53.75 mm |
| 2nd undersize | 53.50 mm |
| 3rd undersize | 53.25 mm |
| Tolerance: | |
| Petrol engines | -0.017 to -0.037 mm |
| Diesel engines | -0.022 to -0.042 mm |
| Main bearing running clearances: | |
| Petrol engines (cast-iron cylinder block): | |
| New | 0.02 to 0.07 mm |
| Wear limit | 0.13 mm |
| Diesel engines: | |
| Standard | 0.03 to 0.08 mm |
| Service limit | 0.17 mm |

## Crankshaft* (continued)

| | |
|---|---|
| Crankpin journal diameters: | |
| Engine codes AER, ALL and AEV: | |
| Standard | 42.00 mm |
| 1st undersize | 41.75 mm |
| 2nd undersize | 41.50 mm |
| 3rd undersize | 41.25 mm |
| All other engines: | |
| Standard | 47.80 mm |
| 1st undersize | 47.55 mm |
| 2nd undersize | 47.30 mm |
| 3rd undersize | 47.05 mm |
| Tolerance: | |
| Petrol engines | -0.022 to -0.037 mm |
| Diesel engines | -0.022 to -0.042 mm |
| Big-end running clearance: | |
| Petrol engines: | |
| Engine code AEV: | |
| New | 0.010 to 0.047 mm |
| Wear limit | 0.091 mm |
| All other engines: | |
| New | 0.020 to 0.061 mm |
| Wear limit | 0.091 mm |
| Diesel engines: | |
| Wear limit | 0.08 mm |

***Note:** *Petrol engine codes AER and ALL have an aluminium cylinder block, and the crankshaft on these engines must not be removed, or the block main bearings will distort. Even loosening the main bearing caps will have this effect. For this reason, if crankshaft or main bearing wear is suspected, the crankshaft and cylinder block must be renewed complete, and there are no specifications relating to crankshaft main bearing dimensions provided by the manufacturers. The main bearing specifications quoted for petrol engines do not apply to engines with an aluminium cylinder block.*

## Torque wrench settings

*Also refer to Chapter 2A and 2B Specifications*

| | Nm | lbf ft |
|---|---|---|
| **Petrol engines** | | |
| Big-end bearing caps bolts/nuts*: | | |
| M7 bolts and engine codes AER, ALL: | | |
| Stage 1 | 20 | 15 |
| Stage 2 | Angle-tighten a further 90° | |
| M8 bolts: | | |
| Stage 1 | 30 | 22 |
| Stage 2 | Angle-tighten a further 90° | |
| Camshaft bearing cap bolts | 10 | 7 |
| Camshaft bearing cap nuts: | | |
| Stage 1 | 6 | 4 |
| Stage 2 | Angle-tighten a further 90° | |
| Crankshaft main bearing cap bolts** | 65 | 48 |
| Driveshaft-to-drive flange bolts | 45 | 33 |
| Engine lifting eye bracket bolts | 20 | 15 |
| Engine transmission mountings* | See Chapter 2A | |
| Exhaust front pipe to manifold | 40 | 30 |
| Flywheel cover plate bolts | 10 | 7 |
| Gearshift finger to selector rod | 20 | 15 |
| Lock carrier: | | |
| Front retaining bolts (to chassis legs) | 23 | 17 |
| Upper retaining bolts | 5 | 4 |
| Transmission bellhousing to engine: | | |
| M10 screws | 60 | 44 |
| M12 screws | 80 | 59 |

**Use new nuts/bolts*
***Not engine codes AER, ALL*

| | Nm | lbf ft |
|---|---|---|
| **Diesel engines** | | |
| Big-end bearing caps bolts/nuts*: | | |
| Stage 1 | 30 | 22 |
| Stage 2 | Angle-tighten a further 90° | |
| Camshaft bearing cap nuts | 20 | 15 |
| Crankshaft main bearing cap bolts*: | | |
| Stage 1 | 65 | 48 |
| Stage 2 | Angle-tighten a further 90° | |

| | | |
|---|---|---|
| Driveshaft-to-drive flange bolts | 45 | 33 |
| Engine lifting eye bracket bolts | 20 | 15 |
| Engine transmission mountings* | See Chapter 2B | |
| Exhaust front pipe to manifold | 40 | 30 |
| Gear cable support bracket angle piece bolts | 15 | 11 |
| Gear cable support bracket nut | 20 | 15 |
| Gear/gate selector cables to support bracket | 20 | 15 |
| Gearshift finger to selector rod | 20 | 15 |
| Intermediate shaft sprocket bolt | 45 | 33 |
| Lock carrier: | | |
| Front retaining bolts (to chassis legs) | 23 | 17 |
| Upper retaining bolts | 5 | 4 |
| Piston oil jet (use suitable locking fluid) | 10 | 7 |
| Transmission bellhousing to engine: | | |
| M10 screws | 60 | 44 |
| M12 screws | 80 | 59 |

**Use new nuts/bolts*

## 1 Engine and transmission removal - preparation and precautions

If you have decided that the engine must be removed for overhaul or major repair work, several preliminary steps should be taken

Locating a suitable place to work is extremely important. Adequate work space, along with storage space for the vehicle, will be needed. If a workshop or garage is not available, at the very least a solid, level, clean work surface is required.

If possible, clear some shelving close to the work area, and use it to store the engine components and ancillaries as they are removed and dismantled. In this manner, the components stand a better chance of staying clean and undamaged during the overhaul. Laying out components in groups together with their fixings bolts, screws etc will save time and avoid confusion when the engine is refitted.

Clean the engine compartment and engine/transmission before beginning the removal procedure; this will help visibility and help to keep tools clean.

The help of an assistant should be available; there are certain instances when one person cannot safely perform all of the operations required to remove the engine from the vehicle. Safety is of primary importance, considering the potential hazards involved in this kind of operation. A second person should always be in attendance to offer help in an emergency. If this is the first time you have removed an engine, advice and aid from someone more experienced would also be beneficial.

Plan the operation ahead of time. Before starting work, obtain (or arrange for the hire of) all of the tools and equipment you will need. Access to the following items will allow the task of removing and refitting the engine/transmission to be completed safely and with relative ease: a heavy-duty trolley jack - rated in excess of the combined weight of the engine and transmission, complete sets of spanners and sockets as described in the front of this manual, wooden blocks, and plenty of rags and cleaning solvent for mopping up spilled oil, coolant and fuel. A selection of different-sized plastic storage bins will also prove useful for keeping dismantled components grouped together. If any of the equipment must be hired, make sure that you arrange for it in advance, and perform all of the operations possible without it beforehand; this may save you time and money.

Plan on the vehicle being out of use for quite a while, especially if you intend to carry out an engine overhaul. Read through the whole of this Section and work out a strategy based on your own experience and the tools, time and workspace available to you. Some of the overhaul processes may have to carried out by a VAG dealer or an engineering works - these establishments often have busy schedules, so it would be prudent to consult them before removing or dismantling the engine, to get an idea of the amount of time required to carry out the work.

When removing the engine from the vehicle, be methodical about the disconnection of external components. Labelling cables and hoses as they are removed will greatly assist the refitting process.

Always be extremely careful when lifting the engine/transmission assembly from the engine bay. Serious injury can result from careless actions. If help is required, it is better to wait until it is available rather than risk personal injury and/or damage to components by continuing alone. By planning ahead and taking your time, a job of this nature, although major, can be accomplished successfully and without incident.

On all models described in this manual, the engine and transmission are removed as a complete assembly, upwards and forwards. This involves the removal of the lock carrier, which is the panel assembly that forms the upper front part of the engine bay. Although the lock carrier is a large assembly, its removal is not difficult, and the benefits in terms of ease of access are well worth the effort involved.

Note that the engine and transmission should ideally be removed with the vehicle standing on all four roadwheels, but access to the driveshafts and exhaust system downpipe will be improved if the vehicle can be temporarily raised onto axle stands.

## 2 Engine and transmission - removal, separation and refitting

### *Removal*

2C

#### All models

**1** Select a solid, level surface to park the vehicle upon. Give yourself enough space to move around it easily. Raise the front of the vehicle and support it on axle stands.

**2** Refer to Chapter 11 and remove the bonnet from its hinges. Also remove the noise insulation tray from under the engine (where fitted).

**3** Referring to Chapter 5A, remove the battery and the battery tray.

**4** With reference to Chapter 1A or B as applicable, carry out the following:

*a) If the engine is to be dismantled, drain the engine oil.*

*b) Drain the cooling system.*

**5** The lock carrier is a panel assembly comprising the front valance and bonnet lock mechanism, radiator and grille, cooling fan, and headlight units. Its removal gives greatly-improved access to the engine and transmission, and allows them to be lifted out of the vehicle via the front of the engine bay. To remove the lock carrier, carry out the following:

*a) Remove the front bumper as described in Chapter 11.*

*b) Referring to Chapter 3, disconnect the radiator top and bottom hoses from the radiator.*

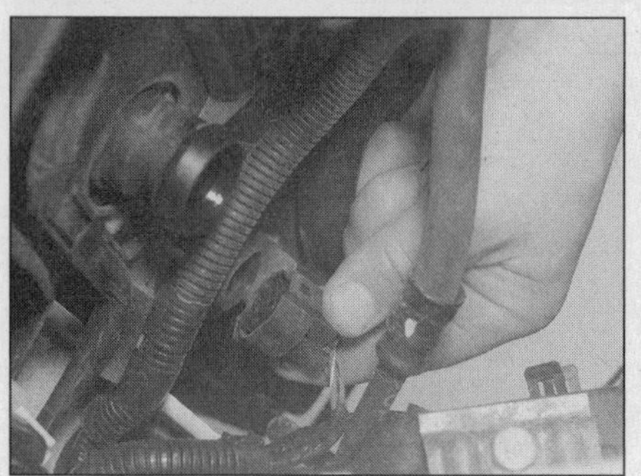
2.5a Disconnect the radiator fan thermo-switch wiring plug . . .

2.5b . . . and the radiator cooling fan motor wiring plug . . .

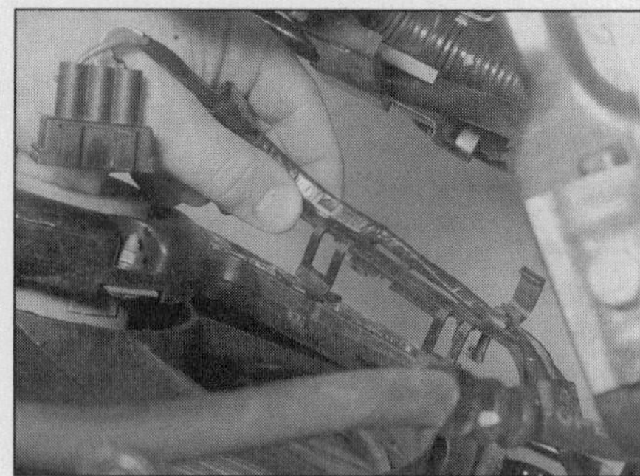
2.5c . . . then unclip the wiring harness from the fan frame

2.5d Unscrew the bayonet-fit harness connector from the rear of the lock carrier

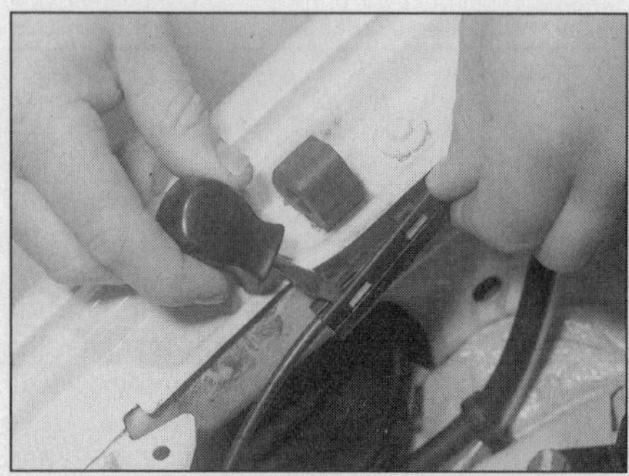
2.5e Unclip the bonnet lock cable connector plastic cover . . .

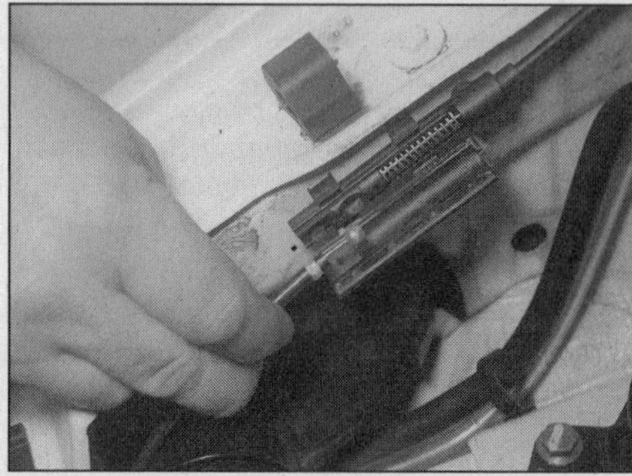
2.5f . . . then unhook the cable end fitting

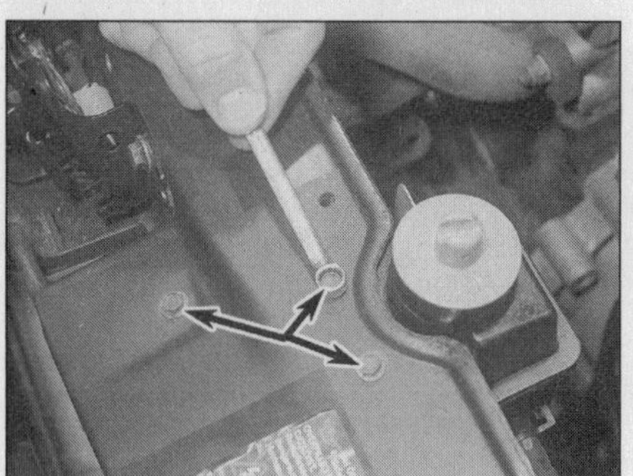
2.5g Remove the power steering reservoir mounting bolts (arrowed) . . .

2.5h . . . then withdraw the reservoir . . .

2.5i . . . and unclip the fluid hoses from the rear of the radiator

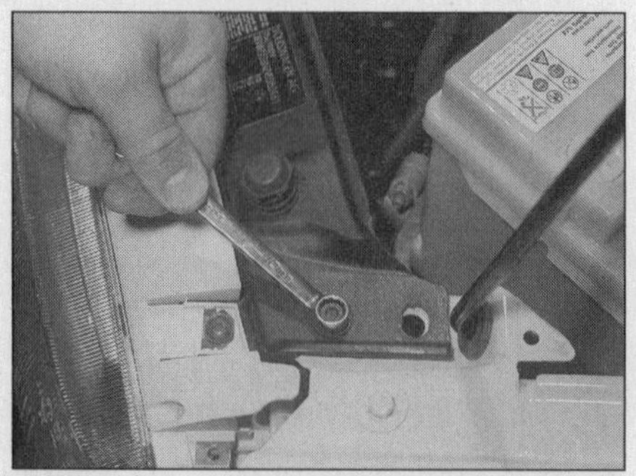
2.5j Remove the flange screws above the headlights . . .

2.5k . . . and the chassis rail bolts (arrowed)

2.5l Lock carrier assembly removed from front of car

c) *Disconnect the wiring plugs from the radiator thermo-switch and cooling fan motor **(see illustrations).***
d) *Unplug the wiring harness at the multiway connector situated at the rear of the lock carrier. The connector is a bayonet fit; twist the housing to unlock the two halves, then pull them apart and recover the internal seal; note the alignment stripe for use when reconnecting **(see illustration)**. Cover the connector housings with a plastic bag to prevent the ingress of dirt or water.*
e) *Detach the bonnet lock release cable at the connector on the left-hand inner wing. Unclip the plastic cover, then release the cable end fitting **(see illustrations).***
f) *Where applicable, disconnect the power steering fluid reservoir from the lock carrier, unclip the fluid pipes and tie it up out of the way, leaving the fluid pipes attached **(see illustrations).***
g) *On models with air conditioning, loosen the refrigerant line securing clamps.*
h) *Remove the lock carrier fixings at the following locations: two flange screws on the uppermost edge above the headlight units, one vertical screw each side at the rear of the front valance, and six bolts (four on the left, two on the right) threaded into the ends of the chassis rails **(see illustrations).***
i) *Lift the lock carrier assembly away from the front of the vehicle and rest it on a dust sheet **(see illustration)**; tilt the assembly forward as you remove it, to avoid spilling any coolant that may remain in the radiator.* **Note:** *On vehicles with air conditioning, the compressor remains connected to the refrigerant condenser by the supply and return hoses, and is removed together with the lock carrier assembly.*

***Caution: Take care to avoid kinking or straining the air conditioning refrigerant hoses.***

**6** Remove the auxiliary drivebelt and the drivebelt pulleys, as described in Chapter 2A or 2B.

**7** Referring to Chapter 6, disconnect the clutch cable from the transmission.

**8** Refer to Chapter 3 and perform the following:
a) *Slacken the clips and disconnect the radiator hoses from the engine, and from the thermostat housing/coolant pump (as applicable) **(see illustration).***
b) *Disconnect the coolant hoses from the expansion tank and heater pipes.*

**9** On vehicles with air conditioning, refer to Chapter 3 and carry out the following additional operations:
a) *Unbolt the air conditioning fluid reservoir from its mountings, and allow it to hang free.*
b) *Remove the retaining bolts from the clips securing the refrigerant condenser supply and return pipes.*

**2.8 Disconnecting a heater hose from the thermostat housing (petrol engine model)**

c) *Unbolt the air conditioning compressor from the engine, and allow it to rest on the floor. Make sure the refrigerant hoses are not under strain.*

**10** On models with power steering, refer to Chapter 10 and remove the pump **(see illustration)**. There's no need to disconnect the fluid lines, as long as the pump is positioned so that the pipes are not under strain (or likely to be damaged during engine removal).

### Petrol models

**11** With reference to Chapters 4A or 4B, unplug the lambda sensor at the multiway connector.

**12** Referring to Chapter 5B, remove the distributor cap, rotor arm and flash shield **(see illustration)**.

**13** On 1.0 litre engines, remove the engine top cover as described in Chapter 2A.

**14** Refer to Chapter 9 and disconnect the brake servo vacuum hose from the port on the inlet manifold.

**15** Refer to Chapter 4D and disconnect the charcoal canister emission control system hose at the connection on the inner wing. Make a careful note of the point of connection to ensure correct refitting.

**16** With reference to Chapter 4, carry out the following operations:
a) *Depressurise the fuel system.*
b) *Remove the exhaust manifold-to-air cleaner and throttle body airbox-to-air cleaner ducting from the engine bay.*
c) *Remove the air cleaner housing from the top of the throttle body; make a note of the vacuum hose connections to ensure correct refitting later.*
d) *Disconnect the accelerator cable from the throttle spindle lever.*
e) *Disconnect the fuel supply and return hoses - observe the precautions at the start of Chapter 4.*
f) *Disconnect the wiring plugs associated with the fuel and ignition system components, labelling the plugs if necessary to aid refitting.*

### Diesel models

**17** Refer to Chapter 9 and disconnect the brake servo vacuum hose from the vacuum pump.

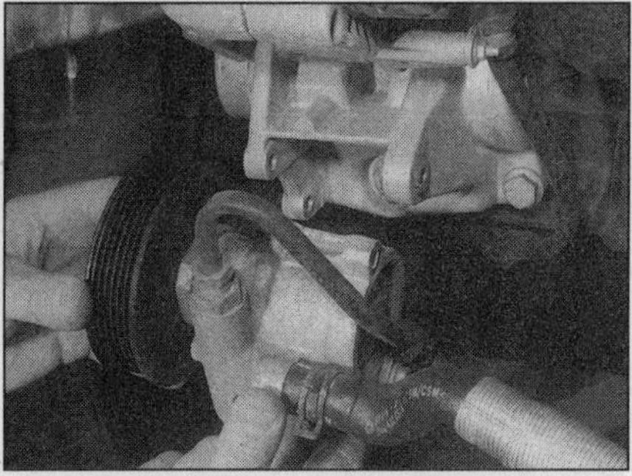
**2.10 Unbolt and remove the power steering pump**

**18** Refer to Chapter 4D and disconnect the vacuum hoses from the connection points on the EGR valve, brake servo vacuum hose, air inlet hose and where applicable, fuel injection pump. Make a careful note of the order of connection to ensure correct refitting.

**19** Refer to Chapter 4C and carry out the following operations:
a) *Slacken and withdraw the banjo bolts, then disconnect the fuel supply and return hoses from the fuel injection pump.*
b) *Release the clip, then disconnect the injector bleed hose from the port on the fuel return union.*
c) *Slacken the clips and remove the inlet air hose from the inlet manifold cover.*

### Engine code AEF

d) *Disconnect the accelerator cable and cold start accelerator cable from the fuel injection pump.*
e) *Disconnect the idle speed boost valve at the bulkhead.*

### All other engine codes

f) *Disconnect the supplementary heater element relay at the bulkhead.*
g) *At the front of the engine, next to No 4 injector, disconnect the multi-plugs for the needle lift sender and the engine speed sender.*
h) *Disconnect the multi-plug located in front of injector Nos 3 and 4. Depending on model, this plug serves various functions.*
i) *Disconnect any further wiring plugs relating to the diesel injection system, labelling them as necessary to aid refitting.*

**2.12 Removing the distributor cap**

**2.20 Unscrew the bayonet-fit main wiring harness connector from the left-hand end of the cylinder head**

**2.21 Later models may have several engine harness plugs at the left-hand end of the cylinder head**

**2.24 Disconnecting the wiring harness from the engine**

## All models

**20** Unplug the wiring harness at the multiway connector situated at the left-hand end of the cylinder block. The connector is a screw fit; twist the housing to unlock the two halves, then pull them apart and recover the internal seal; note the red alignment marking for use when reconnecting **(see illustration)**. Cover the connector housings with a plastic bag to prevent the ingress of dirt or water. Release the harness from all the metal retaining clips.

**21** Later models may have up to four separate plugs mounted in a bracket at the left-hand end of the engine **(see illustration)**. Cover the connector housings with a plastic bag to prevent the ingress of dirt or water. Release the harness from all the metal retaining clips.

**22** Refer to Chapter 5A and disconnect the wiring from the alternator, starter motor and solenoid.

**23** Remove the wiring loom support bracket from the rear of the block.

**24** With reference to Chapter 5B and Chapter 4A, B or C as applicable, identify those sections of the engine, ignition and fuelling system electrical harness that remain connected to sensors and actuators on the engine. Establish which connectors must be separated to permit engine removal, labelling each connector carefully as it is disconnected, to ensure correct refitting **(see illustration)**.

**25** On manual transmission models, refer to Chapter 7A and carry out the following:.

*a) At the front of the transmission casing, disconnect the wiring from the reversing light switch. Also disconnect the wiring plug from the road speed sender on top of the transmission. Depending on model, there may be some additional wiring harness plugs at the front of the transmission - these should be disconnected, and the wiring harness released from any retaining clips **(see illustration)**.*

*b) Disconnect the gear selection mechanism from the transmission.*

*c) On models with cable-operated gear selection, remove the gear selector cable support bracket from the engine block and the bulkhead.*

**26** On automatic transmission models, refer to Chapter 7B and carry out the following:

*a) Select position P, then release the selector cable from the selector lever at the top of the transmission casing. Remove the cable guide rail if necessary.*

*b) Clamp the coolant hoses leading to the transmission fluid cooler, then release the clips and disconnect the hoses from the cooler ports.*

*c) Unplug the wiring harness from the transmission at the connectors; label each connector to aid refitting later.*

*d) Remove the torque converter cover plate and the transmission sump cover plate.*

**27** Refer to Chapter 8 and separate the driveshafts from the transmission differential output shaft flanges. Once the driveshafts have been separated, do not let the shafts hang down at too steep an angle, or the outer CV joints may be damaged. On automatic transmission models, the left-hand driveshaft must be removed completely.

**28** With reference to Chapter 4D, remove the heat shield, then unbolt the exhaust downpipe from the exhaust manifold. Recover and discard the gasket.

**29** Unbolt the engine and transmission earthing straps from the bodywork **(see illustrations)**.

**30** Connect a hoist and raise it so that the weight of the engine and transmission are just supported. Arrange the hoist and sling so that the engine and transmission are kept level when they are being withdrawn from the vehicle.

**31** Unscrew and remove the engine and transmission mounting bolts, referring to Chapter 2A or 2B as necessary. Where possible, leave the bonded rubber mountings attached to the support points; this will avoid the need for realignment during refitting.

**32** Check around the engine and transmission assembly to ensure that all associated attachments are disconnected and positioned out of the way. Engage the services of an assistant to help in guiding the assembly clear of surrounding components, especially the exhaust downpipe and the power steering fluid pipework, where applicable. Carefully raise the engine/transmission assembly so that it is clear of the mountings, and remove the assembly from the front of the vehicle **(see illustration)**.

**2.25 Disconnect any additional wiring harness plugs from the front of the transmission**

**2.29a Remove the securing nut . . .**

**2.29b . . . and disconnect the transmission earth strap**

**33** Once the engine/transmission assembly is clear of the vehicle, move it to an area where it can be cleaned and worked on.

## Separation

**34** Rest the engine and transmission assembly on a firm, flat surface, and use wooden blocks as wedges to keep the unit steady.

### Manual transmission models

**35** The transmission is secured to the engine by a combination of machine screws and studs, threaded into the cylinder block and bellhousing - the total number of fixings depends on the type of transmission and vehicle specification.

**36** Starting at the bottom, remove all the screws and nuts, then carefully draw the transmission away from the engine, resting it securely on wooden blocks. Collect the locating dowels if they are loose enough to be extracted. ***Caution: Take care to prevent the transmission from tilting, until the input shaft is fully disengaged from the clutch friction plate***

**37** Refer to Chapter 6, and remove the clutch release mechanism, pressure plate and friction plate.

### Automatic transmission models

**38** Mark the position of the torque converter with respect to the driveplate, using chalk or a marker pen. Remove the three nuts that secure the driveplate to the torque converter; turn the engine over using a socket and wrench on the crankshaft sprocket to rotate the driveplate and expose each nut in turn.

**39** The transmission is secured to the engine by a combination of machine screws and studs with nuts, threaded into the cylinder block and bellhousing - the total number of fixings depends on the type of transmission and vehicle specification.

**40** Starting at the bottom, remove all the screws and nuts, then carefully draw the transmission away from the engine, resting it securely on wooden blocks. Collect the locating dowels if they are loose enough to be extracted. ***Caution: Take care to prevent the torque converter from sliding off the transmission input shaft - hold it in place as the transmission is withdrawn.***

**41** Place a length of batten across the open face of the bellhousing, fastening it with cable-ties, to keep the torque converter in place in its housing.

## Refitting

**42** If the engine and transmission have not been separated, go to paragraph 48.

### Manual transmission models

**43** Smear a little high-melting-point grease on the splines of the transmission input shaft. Do not use an excessive amount, as there is the risk of contaminating the clutch friction plate. Carefully offer up the transmission to the cylinder block, guiding the dowels into the mounting holes in cylinder block.

**2.32 Engine/transmission assembly being removed from the engine compartment**

**44** Refit the bellhousing bolts and nuts, hand-tightening them to secure the transmission in position. **Note:** *Do not tighten them to force the engine and transmission together.* Ensure that the bellhousing and cylinder block mating faces will butt together evenly without obstruction, before tightening the bolts and nuts to their specified torque.

### Automatic transmission models

**45** Remove the torque converter restraint from the face of the bellhousing. Check that the drive lugs on the torque converter hub are correctly engaged with the recesses in the inner wheel of the automatic transmission fluid pump.

**46** Carefully offer up the transmission to the cylinder block, guiding the dowels into the mounting holes in cylinder block. Observe the markings made during the removal, to ensure correct alignment between the torque converter and the driveplate.

**47** Refit the bellhousing bolts and nuts, hand-tightening them to secure the transmission in position. **Note:** *Do not tighten them to force the engine and transmission together.* Ensure that the bellhousing and cylinder block mating faces will butt together evenly without obstruction, before tightening the bolts and nuts to their specified torque.

### All models

**48** Attach the jib of an engine hoist to the lifting eyelets on the cylinder head, and raise the engine and transmission from the ground.

**49** Wheel the hoist up to the front of the vehicle and with the help of an assistant, guide the engine and transmission in through the front of the engine bay. Rotate the assembly slightly so that the transmission casing enters first.

**50** If necessary, lower the assembly slightly, so that the transmission mounting can slide under the mounting point on the inner wing. When correctly aligned, the assembly can be raised to engage the mounting, and the through-bolt can be fitted and hand-tightened.

**51** Raise the opposite side of the assembly as required, so that the engine right-hand mounting can be aligned and refitted onto the mounting on the inner wing. Insert the bolts and tighten them by hand only at this stage.

**52** Align and reconnect the engine/transmission rear mounting.

**53** Detach the engine hoist jib from the lifting eyelets.

**54** Settle the engine and transmission assembly on its mountings by rocking it backwards and forwards, then tighten the mounting nuts and bolts to their specified torques.

**55** Refer to Chapter 8 and refit/reconnect the driveshafts to the transmission.

**56** The remainder of the refitting sequence is a direct reversal of the removal procedure, noting the following points:

a) *Ensure that all sections of the wiring harness follow their original routing; use new cable-ties to secure the harness in position, keeping it away from sources of heat and abrasion.*

b) *On vehicles with manual transmission, refer to Chapter 7A and reconnect the gear selection mechanism to the transmission, then check the overall operation of the mechanism. If necessary, adjust the gear selection rod/cables.*

c) *Refer to Chapter 6 and reconnect the clutch cable to the transmission, then check the operation of the automatic adjustment mechanism, where applicable.*

d) *On vehicles with automatic transmission, refer to Chapter 7B and reconnect the selector cable to the transmission, then check (and if necessary adjust) the overall operation of the gear selection mechanism.*

e) *Refit the lock carrier assembly to the front of the vehicle; refitting is the reverse of removal as described in paragraph 2 of this Section; ensure that all wiring harness connections are remade correctly and tighten the retaining fixings to the specified torque.*

f) *Ensure that all hoses are correctly routed and are secured with the correct hose clips, where applicable. If the hose clips originally fitted were of the crimp variety, they cannot be used again; proprietary worm-drive clips must be fitted in their place, unless otherwise specified.*

g) *Refill the cooling system as described in Chapter 1A or B.*

h) *Refill the engine with appropriate grades and quantities of oil (Chapter 1A or B).*

### Diesel models

i) *Engine code AEF: with reference to Chapter 4C, Section 8, after reconnecting the cold start accelerator cable to the fuel injection pump, check and if necessary adjust the operation of the cold start acceleration system.*

### Petrol models

j) *With reference to Chapter 4A or B as applicable, reconnect the accelerator cable and adjust it as necessary.*

### All models

**57** When the engine is started for the first time, check for air, coolant, lubricant and fuel leaks from manifolds, hoses etc. If the engine has been overhauled, read the notes in Section 14 before attempting to start it.

## 3 Engine overhaul - preliminary information

***Warning: Petrol engine codes AER and ALL have an aluminium cylinder block, and the crankshaft on these engines must not be removed, or the block main bearings will distort. Even loosening the main bearing caps will have this effect. For this reason, if crankshaft or main bearing wear is suspected, the crankshaft and cylinder block must be renewed complete.***

It is much easier to dismantle and work on the engine if it is mounted on a portable engine stand. These stands can often be hired from a tool hire shop. Before the engine is mounted on a stand, the flywheel should be removed, so that the stand bolts can be tightened into the end of the cylinder block/ crankcase.

If a stand is not available, it is possible to dismantle the engine with it blocked up on a sturdy workbench, or on the floor. Be very careful not to tip or drop the engine when working without a stand.

If you intend to obtain a reconditioned engine, all ancillaries must be removed first, to be transferred to the replacement engine (just as they will if you are doing a complete engine overhaul yourself). These components include the following:

### Petrol engines

*a) Power steering pump (Chapter 10) - where applicable.*
*b) Air conditioning compressor (Chapter 3) - where applicable.*
*c) Alternator (including mounting brackets)and starter motor (Chapter 5A).*
*d) The ignition system and HT components, including all sensors, distributor, HT leads and spark plugs (Chapters 1A and 5B).*
*e) The fuel injection system components (Chapter 4A or B).*
*f) All electrical switches, actuators and sensors, and the engine wiring harness (Chapter 4A or B, Chapter 5B, Chapter 12).*
*g) Inlet and exhaust manifolds (Chapter 2A).*
*h) Engine oil dipstick and tube (Chapter 2A).*
*i) Engine mountings (Chapter 2A).*
*j) Flywheel/driveplate (Chapter 2A).*
*k) Clutch components (Chapter 6) - manual transmission.*

### Diesel engines

*a) Power steering pump (Chapter 10) - where applicable*
*b) Air conditioning compressor (Chapter 3) - where applicable*
*c) Alternator (including mounting brackets)and starter motor (Chapter 5A)*
*d) The glow plug/pre-heating system components (Chapter 5C)*
*e) All fuel system components, including the fuel injection pump, all sensors and actuators (Chapter 4C)*
*f) The brake vacuum pump (Chapter 9).*
*g) All electrical switches, actuators and sensors, and the engine wiring harness (Chapter 4C, Chapter 12).*
*h) Inlet and exhaust manifolds (Chapter 2B)*
*i) The engine oil level dipstick and its tube (Chapter 2B).*
*j) Engine mountings (Chapter 2B).*
*k) Flywheel (Chapter 2B).*
*l) Clutch components (Chapter 6).*

**Note:** *When removing the external components from the engine, pay close attention to details that may be helpful or important during refitting. Note the fitted position of gaskets, seals, spacers, pins, washers, bolts, and other small components.*

If you are obtaining a 'short' engine (the engine cylinder block/crankcase, crankshaft, pistons and connecting rods, all fully assembled), then the cylinder head, sump and baffle plate, oil pump, timing belt (together with its tensioner and covers), auxiliary belt (together with its tensioner), coolant pump, thermostat housing, coolant outlet elbows, oil filter housing and where applicable oil cooler will also have to be removed.

If you are planning a full overhaul, the engine can be dismantled in the order given below:

*a) Inlet and exhaust manifolds.*
*b) Timing belt, sprockets and tensioner.*
*c) Cylinder head.*
*d) Flywheel/driveplate.*
*e) Sump.*
*f) Oil pump.*
*g) Piston/connecting rod assemblies.*
*h) Crankshaft (not engine codes AER, ALL).*

## 4 Cylinder head - dismantling, cleaning, inspection and assembly

**Note:** *New and reconditioned cylinder heads are available from VW, and from engine specialists. Specialist tools are required for the dismantling and inspection procedures, and new components may not be readily available. It may, therefore, be more practical for the home mechanic to buy a reconditioned head, rather than to dismantle, inspect and recondition the original head.*

**4.6 Keep groups of components together in labelled bags or boxes**

### Dismantling

**1** Remove the cylinder head from the engine block, and separate the inlet and exhaust manifolds from it (Part A or B of this Chapter).

**2** On diesel models, remove the injectors and glow plugs (see Chapter 4C and Chapter 5C).

**3** On diesel models, remove the coolant outlet elbow, together with its gasket/O-ring.

**4** Where applicable, unscrew the thermostat housing and oil pressure switch from the cylinder head.

**5** Remove the camshaft timing belt sprocket (Part A or B of this Chapter).

**6** It is important that groups of components are kept together when they are removed and, if still serviceable, refitted in the same groups. If they are refitted randomly, accelerated wear leading to early failure will occur. Stowing groups of components in plastic bags or storage bins will help to keep everything in the right order **(see illustration)**. Label parts according to their fitted location, eg No 1 exhaust, No 2 inlet, etc - note that No 1 cylinder is nearest the timing belt end of the engine.

**7** The principal cylinder head components are as shown **(see illustrations).**

**8** Check that the manufacturer's identification markings are visible on camshaft bearing caps; if none can be found, make your own using a scriber or centre-punch **(see illustration)**. The camshaft bearing cap nuts must be removed progressively and in sequence to avoid stressing the camshaft, as follows.

**9** Slacken the nuts from bearing caps Nos 5, 1 and 3 first, then at bearing caps 2 and 4. Slacken the nuts alternately and diagonally half a turn at a time until they can be removed by hand. **Note:** *Camshaft bearing caps are numbered 1 to 5 from the timing belt end.*

**10** Slide the oil seal from the sprocket end of the camshaft and discard it; a new one must be used on reassembly.

**11** Carefully lift the camshaft from the cylinder head - do not tilt it. Support both ends as it is removed so that the journals and lobes are not damaged.

**12** Lift the hydraulic tappets from their bores and store them with the valve contact surface facing downwards, to prevent the oil from draining out. Alternatively, place the tappets in a tray full of oil, sufficiently deep to prevent the tappets draining. Make a note of the position of each tappet, as they must be fitted to the same valves on reassembly - accelerated wear leading to early failure will result if they are interchanged.

**13** Turn the cylinder head over, and rest it on one side. Using a valve spring compressor, compress each valve spring in turn, extracting the split collets when the upper valve spring seat has been pushed far enough down the valve stem to free them **(see illustrations)**. If the spring seat sticks, tap the upper jaw of the compressor with a hammer to free it.

**14** Release the valve spring compressor and remove the upper spring seat and valve spring.

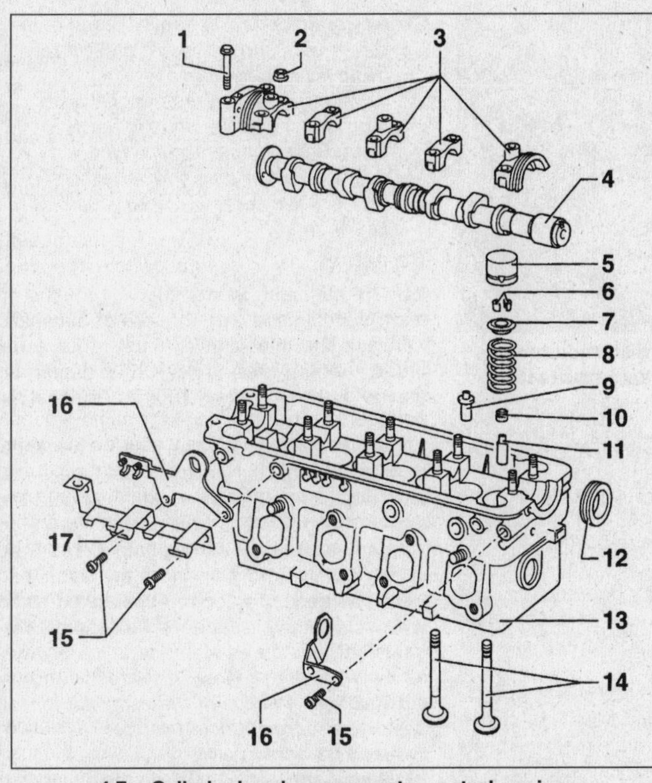

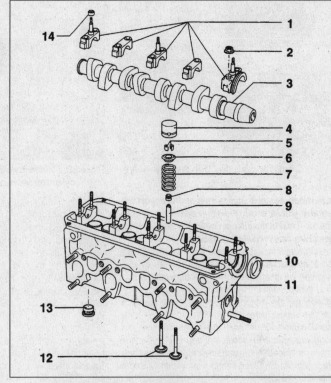

**4.7a Cylinder head components - petrol engines**

1 *Camshaft bearing cap bolt*
2 *Camshaft bearing cap nut*
3 *Camshaft bearing cap*
4 *Camshaft*
5 *Hydraulic tappet*
6 *Cotters*
7 *Upper valve spring seat*
8 *Valve spring*
9 *Valve guide (service part)*
10 *Valve stem oil seal*
11 *Valve guide*
12 *Oil seal*
13 *Cylinder head*
14 *Valves*
15 *Bolt*
16 *Lifting eye*
17 *HT lead bracket*

**4.7b Cylinder head components - diesel engines**

1 *Camshaft bearing cap*
2 *Camshaft bearing cap nut*
3 *Camshaft*
4 *Hydraulic tappet*
5 *Cotters*
6 *Upper valve spring seat*
7 *Valve spring*
8 *Valve stem oil seal*
9 *Valve guide*
10 *Oil seal*
11 *Cylinder head*
12 *Valves*
13 *Swirl chamber (engine code AEF)*
14 *Camshaft cover stud seal*

**4.8 Camshaft bearing cap identification marks**

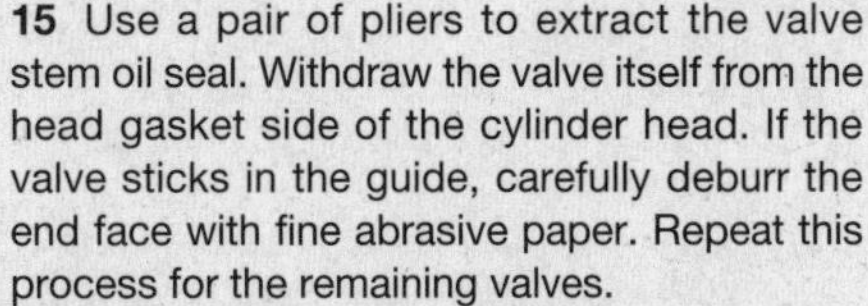

**15** Use a pair of pliers to extract the valve stem oil seal. Withdraw the valve itself from the head gasket side of the cylinder head. If the valve sticks in the guide, carefully deburr the end face with fine abrasive paper. Repeat this process for the remaining valves.

**16** On engine code AEF, if the swirl chambers are badly coked or burned and are in need of renewal, insert a pin punch through each injector hole, and carefully drive out the swirl chambers using a mallet **(see illustration).**

## *Cleaning*

**17** Using a suitable degreasing agent, remove all traces of oil deposits from the cylinder head, paying particular attention to the journal bearings, hydraulic tappet bores, valve guides and oilways. Scrape off any traces of old gasket from the mating surfaces, taking care not to score or gouge them. If using emery paper, do not use a grade of less than 100. Turn the head over and using a blunt blade, scrape any carbon deposits from the combustion chambers and ports.

**4.13a Valve spring compressor jaws located on the upper spring seat . . .**

**4.13b . . . and on the valve head**

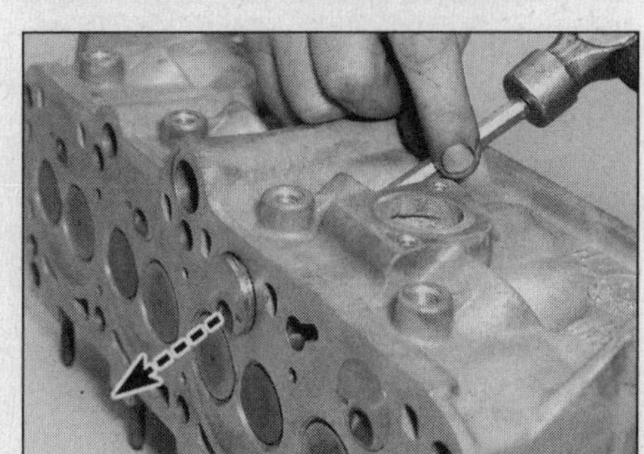

**4.16 Swirl chamber removal (diesel engine code AEF)**

**4.20 Look for cracking between the valve seats**

**4.22 Measuring the distortion of the cylinder head gasketed surface**

***Caution: Do not erode the sealing surface of the valve seat. Finally, wash the entire head casting with a suitable solvent to remove the remaining debris.***

**18** Clean the valve heads and stems using a fine wire brush. If the valve is heavily coked, scrape off the majority of the deposits with a blunt blade first, then use the wire brush.

***Caution: Do not erode the sealing surface of the valve face***

**19** Thoroughly clean the remainder of the components using solvent and allow them to dry completely. Discard the oil seals, as new items must be fitted when the cylinder head is reassembled.

## *Inspection*

### Cylinder head casting

**Note:** *On diesel engines, the cylinder heads and valves cannot be reworked (although valves may be lapped in); new or exchange units must be obtained.*

**20** Examine the head casting closely to identify any damage sustained or cracks that may have developed. Pay particular attention to the areas around the mounting holes, valve seats and spark plug holes. If cracking is discovered between the valve seats, Volkswagen state that the cylinder head may be re-used, provided the cracks are no larger than 0.5 mm wide **(see illustration)**. More serious damage will mean the renewal of the cylinder head casting.

**21** Moderately pitted and scorched valve seats can be repaired by lapping the valves in during reassembly, as described later in this Chapter. Badly worn or damaged valve seats may be restored by recutting; this is a highly specialised operation involving precision machining and accurate angle measurement and as such should be entrusted to a professional cylinder head re-builder.

**22** Measure any distortion of the gasketed surfaces using a straight edge and a set of feeler blades. Take one measurement longitudinally on both the inlet and exhaust manifold mating surfaces. Take several measurements across the head gasket surface, to assess the level of distortion in all planes **(see illustration)**. Compare the measurements with the figures in the Specifications. On petrol engines, if the head is distorted out of specification, it may be possible to repair it by smoothing down any high-spots on the surface with fine abrasive paper.

**23** Minimum cylinder head heights (measured between the cylinder head gasket surface and the cylinder head cover gasket surface), where quoted by the manufacturer, are listed in Specifications. If the cylinder head is to be professionally machined, bear in mind the following:

*a) The minimum cylinder head height dimension (where specified) must be adhered to.*

*b) The valve seats will need to be recut to suit the new height of the cylinder head, otherwise valve-to-piston crown contact may occur.*

*c) Before the valve seats can be recut, check that there is enough material left on the cylinder head to allow repair; if too much material is removed, the valve stem may protrude too far above the top of the valve guide, and this would prevent the hydraulic tappets from operating correctly. Refer to a professional head rebuilder or machine shop for advice.*
**Note:** *Depending on engine type, it may be possible to obtain new valves with shorter valve stems - refer to your VAG dealer for advice.*

### Camshaft

**24** The camshaft is identified by means of markings stamped onto the side of the shaft, between the inlet and exhaust lobes **(see illustration)**. Refer to your VW dealer or engine overhaul specialist for an explanation of the markings.

**25** Visually inspect the camshaft for evidence of wear on the surfaces of the lobes and journals. Normally their surfaces should be smooth and have a dull shine; look for scoring, erosion or pitting and areas that appear highly polished - these are signs that wear has begun to occur. Accelerated wear will occur once the hardened exterior of the camshaft has been damaged, so always renew worn items. **Note:** *If these symptoms are visible on the tips of the camshaft lobes, check the corresponding tappet, as it will probably be worn as well.*

**26** Where applicable, examine the distributor drivegear for signs of wear or damage. Slack in the drive caused by worn gear teeth will affect ignition timing.

**27** If the machined surfaces of the camshaft appear discoloured or 'blued', it is likely that it has been overheated at some point, probably due to inadequate lubrication. This may have distorted the shaft, so check the runout as follows: place the camshaft between two V-blocks and using a DTI gauge, measure the runout at the centre journal. If it exceeds the figure quoted in the Specifications at the start of this Chapter, camshaft renewal should be considered.

**28** To measure the camshaft endfloat, temporarily refit the camshaft to the cylinder head, then fit the first and last bearing caps and tighten the retaining nuts to the specified first stage torque setting - refer to *Reassembly* for details. Anchor a DTI gauge to the timing pulley end of the cylinder head, and align the gauge probe with the camshaft axis **(see illustration)**. Push the camshaft to one end of the cylinder head as far as it will travel, then rest the DTI gauge probe on the end of the camshaft, and zero the gauge display. Push the camshaft as far as it will go to the other end of the cylinder head, and record the gauge reading. Verify the reading by pushing the camshaft back to its original position and checking that the gauge indicates zero again. **Note:** *The hydraulic tappets must **not** be fitted to the cylinder whilst this measurement is being taken.*

**29** Check that the camshaft endfloat measurement is within the limit listed in the Specifications. Wear outside of this limit is

**4.24 Camshaft identification markings**

**4.28 Checking camshaft endfloat using a DTI gauge**

unlikely to be confined to any one component, so renewal of the camshaft, cylinder head and bearing caps must be considered; seek the advice of a cylinder head rebuilding specialist.

**30** The difference between the outside diameters of the camshaft bearing surfaces and the internal diameters formed by the bearing caps and the cylinder head must now be measured, this dimension is known as the camshaft running clearance.

**31** The dimensions of the camshaft bearing journals are not quoted by the manufacturer, so running clearance measurement by means of a micrometer and a bore gauge or internal vernier calipers cannot be recommended in this case.

**32** Another (more accurate) method of measuring the running clearance involves the use of Plastigauge. This is a soft, plastic material supplied in thin sticks of about the same diameter as a sewing needle. Lengths of Plastigauge are cut to length as required, laid on the camshaft bearing journals and crushed as the bearing caps are temporarily fitted and tightened. The Plastigauge spreads widthways as it is crushed; the running clearance can then be determined by measuring the increase in width using the card gauge supplied with the Plastigauge kit.

**33** The following paragraphs describe this measurement procedure step by step, but note that a similar method is used to measure the crankshaft running clearances; refer to the illustrations in Section 11 for further guidance.

**34** Ensure that the cylinder head, bearing cap and camshaft bearing surfaces are completely clean and dry. Lay the camshaft in position in the cylinder head.

**35** Lay a length of Plastigauge on top of each of the camshaft bearing journals.

**36** Lubricate each bearing cap with a little silicone release agent, then place them in position over the camshaft and tighten the retaining nuts down to the specified torque - refer to *Reassembly* later in this Section for guidance. **Note:** *Where the torque setting is expressed in several stages, tighten the cap fixings to the first stage only. Do not rotate the camshaft whilst the bearing caps are in place, as the measurements will be affected.*

**37** Carefully remove the bearing caps again, lifting them vertically away from the camshaft to avoid disturbing the Plastigauge. The Plastigauge should remain on the camshaft bearing surface, squashed into a uniform sausage shape. If it disintegrates as the bearing caps are removed, re-clean the components and repeat the exercise, using a little more release agent on the bearing cap.

**38** Hold the scale card supplied with the kit against each bearing journal, and match the width of the crushed Plastigauge with the graduated markings on the card; use this to determine the running clearances.

**39** Compare the camshaft running clearance measurements with those listed in the Specifications; if any are outside the specified tolerance, the camshaft and cylinder head should be renewed. Note that undersize camshafts with bearing shells may be obtained from VAG dealers, but only as part of an exchange cylinder head package.

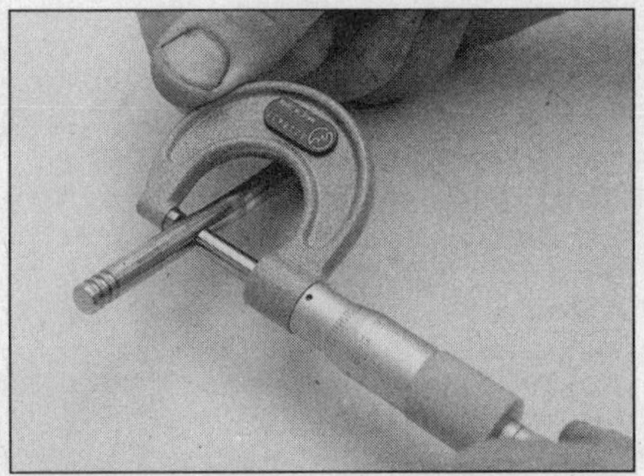

**4.41 Measure the diameter of a valve stem with a micrometer**

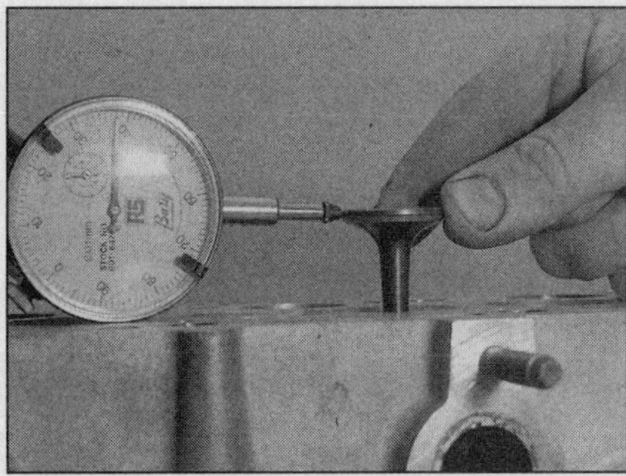

**4.45 Measure the maximum deflection of the valve in its guide, using a DTI gauge**

**40** On completion, remove the bearing caps and camshaft, and clean of all remaining traces of Plastigauge and silicone release agent.

## Valves and associated components

**Note:** *On all engines, the valve heads cannot be re-cut (although they may be lapped in); new or exchange units must be obtained.*

**41** Examine each valve closely for signs of wear. Inspect the valve stems for wear ridges, scoring or variations in diameter; measure their diameters at several points along their lengths with a micrometer **(see illustration).**

**42** The valve heads should not be cracked, badly pitted or charred. Note that light pitting of the valve head can be rectified by grinding-in the valves during reassembly, as described later in this Section.

**43** Check that the valve stem end face is free from excessive pitting or indentation; this would be caused by defective hydraulic tappets.

**44** Place the valves in a V-block and using a DTI gauge, measure the runout at the valve head. A maximum figure is not quoted by the manufacturer, but the valve should be renewed if the runout appears excessive.

**45** Insert each valve into its respective guide in the cylinder head, and set up a DTI gauge against the edge of the valve head. With the valve end face flush with the top of the valve guide, measure the maximum side-to-side deflection of the valve in its guide **(see illustration).**

**46** If the measurement is out of tolerance, the valve and valve guide should be renewed as a pair. **Note:** *Valve guides are an interference fit in the cylinder head, and their removal requires access to a hydraulic press. For this reason, it would be wise to entrust the job to an engineering workshop or head rebuilding specialist.*

**47** Using vernier calipers, measure the free length of each of the valve springs **(see illustration)**. As a manufacturer's figure is not quoted, the only way to check the length of the springs is by comparison with a new component. Note that valve springs are usually renewed during a major engine overhaul.

**48** Stand each spring on its end on a flat surface, against an engineer's square **(see illustration)**. Check the squareness of the spring visually; if it appears distorted, renew the spring. No squareness limits are specified by the manufacturers.

**49** Measuring valve spring pre-load involves compressing the valve by applying a specified weight and measuring the reduction in length. This may be a difficult operation to conduct in the home workshop, so it would be wise to approach your local garage or engineering workshop for assistance. Weakened valve springs will at best, increase engine running noise and at worst, cause poor compression, so defective items should be renewed.

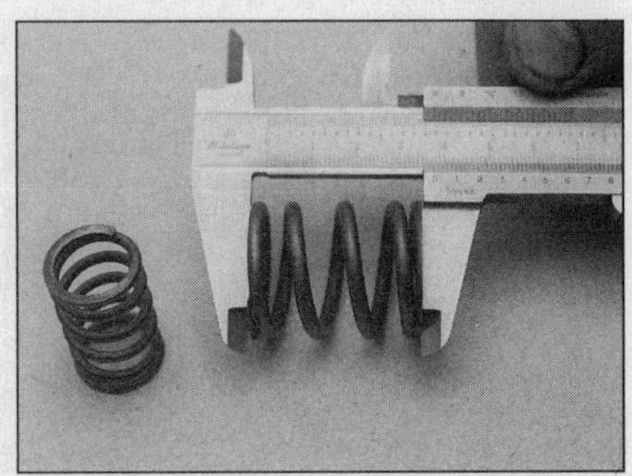

**4.47 Measure the free length of each of the valve springs**

**4.48 Checking the squareness of a valve spring**

2C

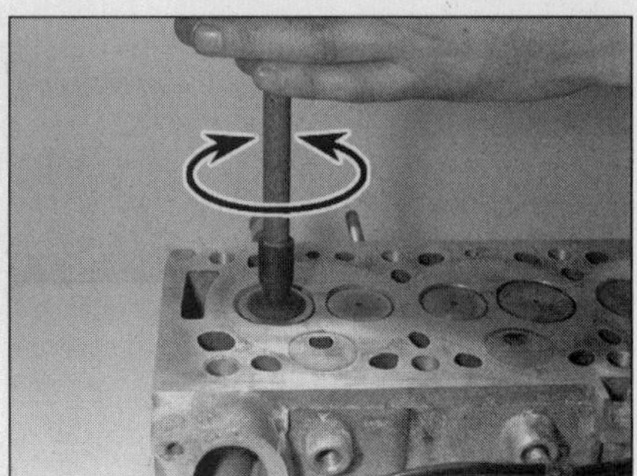
4.51 Grinding-in a valve

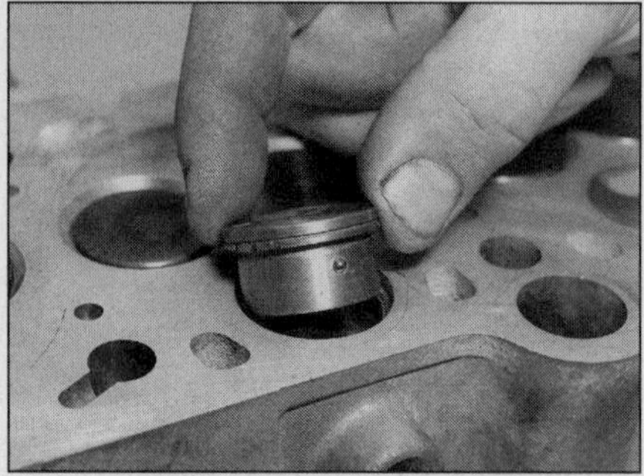
4.56a Fitting a swirl chamber (diesel engine code AEF)

4.56b Swirl chamber locating recess

## Reassembly

***Caution: Unless all new components are to be used, maintain groups when refitting valve train components - do not mix components between cylinders, and ensure that components are refitted in their original positions.***

**50** To achieve a gas-tight seal between the valves and their seats, it will be necessary to grind, or 'lap', the valves in. To complete this process, you will need a quantity of fine/coarse grinding paste and a grinding tool - this can either be of the dowel and rubber sucker type, or the automatic type which are driven by a rotary power tool.

**51** Smear a small quantity of *fine* grinding paste on the sealing face of the valve head. Turn the cylinder head over so that the combustion chambers are facing upwards, and insert the valve into the correct guide. Attach the grinding tool to the valve head and using a backward/forward rotary action, grind the valve head into its seat **(see illustration)**. Periodically lift the valve and rotate it to redistribute the grinding paste.

4.57 Measuring swirl chamber projection using a DTI gauge

**52** Continue this process until the contact between valve and seat produces an unbroken, matt grey ring of uniform width, on both faces. Repeat the operation for the remaining valves.

**53** If the valves and seats are so badly pitted that coarse grinding paste must be used, check first that there is enough material left on both components to make this operation worthwhile - if too little material is left remaining, the valve stems may protrude too far above their guides, impeding the correct operation of the hydraulic tappets. Refer to a machine shop or cylinder head rebuilding specialist for advice.

**54** Assuming the repair is feasible, work as described in the previous paragraph but use the coarse grinding paste initially, to achieve a dull finish on the valve face and seat. Then, wash off coarse paste with solvent and repeat the process using fine grinding paste to obtain the correct finish.

**55** When all the valves have been ground in, remove all traces of grinding paste from the cylinder head and valves with solvent, and allow them to dry completely.

**56** Where necessary on engine code AEF, fit new swirl chambers by driving them squarely into their housings with a mallet - use a block of wood to protect the face of the swirl chamber. Note the locating recess on the side of the chamber and the corresponding groove in the housing **(see illustrations).**

**57** On completion, the projection of the swirl chamber from the face of the cylinder head must be measured using a DTI gauge and compared with the limit quoted in the Specifications **(see illustration)**. If this limit is exceeded, there is a risk that the chamber may be struck by the piston, and in this case the advice of a professional cylinder head rebuilder or machine shop should be sought.

**58** Turn the head over and place it on a stand, or wooden blocks. Where applicable, fit the first lower spring seat into place, with the convex side facing the cylinder head **(see illustration).**

**59** Working on one valve at a time, lubricate the valve stem with clean engine oil, and insert it into the guide. Fit one of the protective plastic sleeves supplied with the new valve stem oil seals over the valve end face - this will protect the oil seal whilst it is being fitted **(see illustrations).**

**60** Dip a new valve stem seal in clean engine oil, and carefully push it over the valve and onto the top of the valve guide - take care not to damage the stem seal as it passes over the valve end face. Use a suitable long-reach socket to press it firmly into position **(see illustrations).**

**61** Locate the valve spring over the valve stem **(see illustration).**

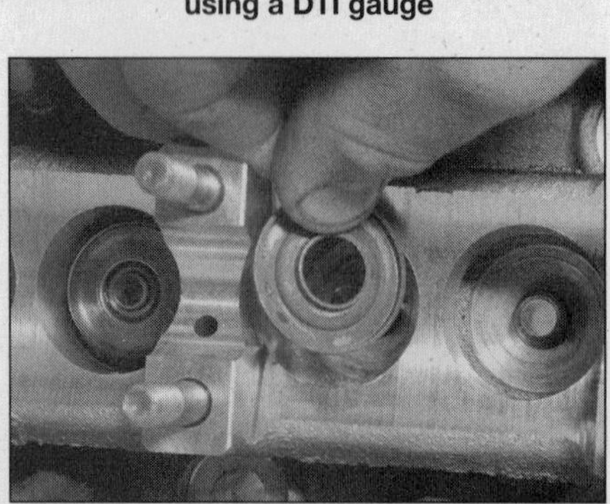
4.58 Fit the lower spring seat in place, with the convex face facing the cylinder head

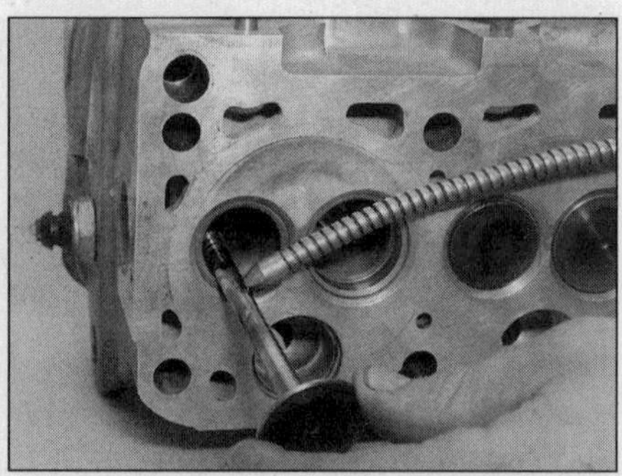
4.59a Lubricate the valve stem with clean engine oil and insert it into the guide

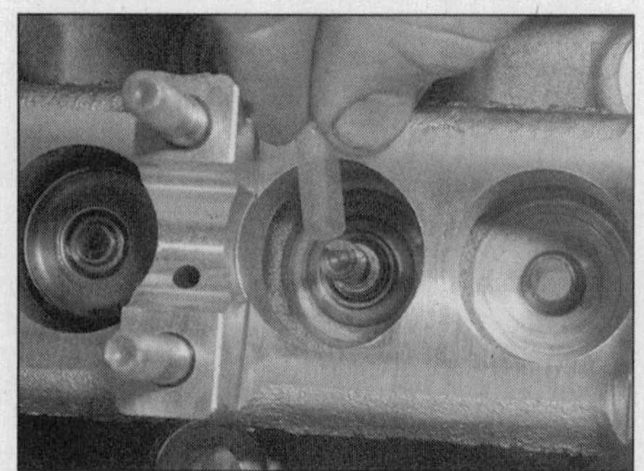
4.59b Fit one of the protective plastic sleeves over the valve end face

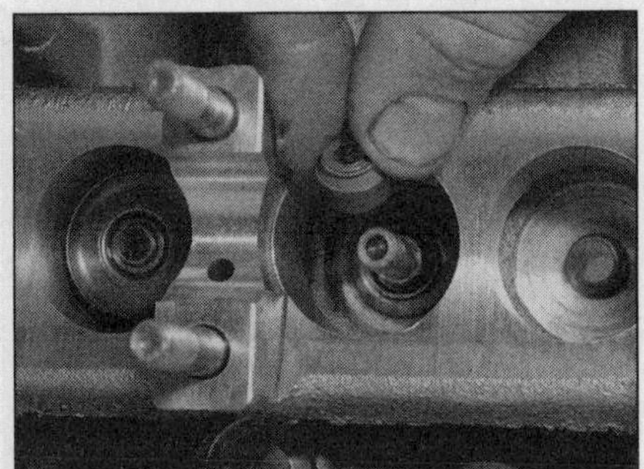
**4.60a Fit a new valve stem seal over the valve**

**4.60b Use a long-reach socket to press on the oil seal**

**4.61 Fitting a valve spring**

**62** Fit the upper seat over the top of the spring, then using a valve spring compressor, compress the spring until the upper seat is pushed beyond the collet grooves in the valve stem. Refit the split collet, using a dab of grease to hold the two halves in the grooves **(see illustrations)**. Gradually release the spring compressor, checking that the collet remains correctly seated as the spring extends. When correctly seated, the upper seat should force the two halves of the collet together, and hold them securely in the grooves in the end of the valve.

**63** Repeat this process for the remaining sets of valve components. To settle the components after installation, strike the end of each valve stem with a mallet, using a block of wood to protect the stem from damage. Check before progressing any further that the spilt collets remain firmly held in the end of the valve stem by the upper spring seat.

**64** Smear some clean engine oil onto the sides of the hydraulic tappets, and fit them into position in their bores in the cylinder head **(see illustration)**. Push them down until they contact the valves, then lubricate the camshaft lobe contact surfaces.

**65** Lubricate the camshaft and cylinder head bearing journals with clean engine oil, then carefully lower the camshaft into position on the cylinder head **(see illustrations)**. Support the ends of the shaft as it is inserted, to avoid damaging the lobes and journals.

**66** On diesel engines, with reference to Chapter 2B, lubricate the lip of a new camshaft oil seal with clean engine oil, and locate it over the end of the camshaft **(see illustration)**. Slide the seal along the camshaft until it locates in the lower half of its housing in the cylinder head.

**67** Oil the upper surfaces of the camshaft bearing journals, then fit the bearing caps in place. Ensure that they are fitted the right way around and in the correct locations, then fit and tighten the retaining nuts, as follows:

### Petrol engines

**68** Note the fitted orientation of the camshaft bearing caps. The wider cast lugs must be positioned on the inlet side of the head, and the bearing cap identification numbers must be readable from the exhaust side **(see illustration)**.

**69** Fit caps Nos 2 and 4 over the camshaft, and tighten the retaining nuts alternately and diagonally to the specified Stage 1 torque.

2C

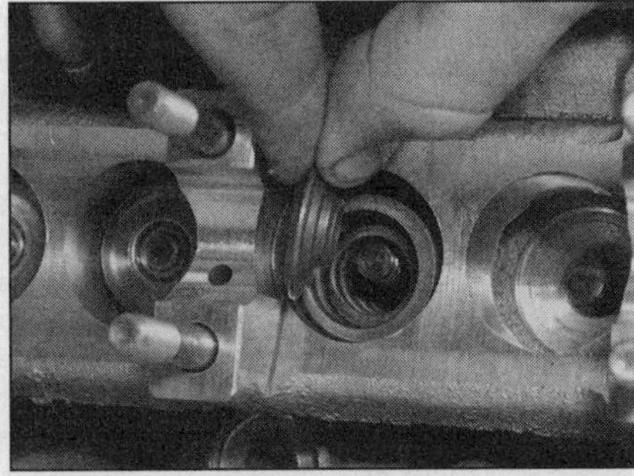
**4.62a Fit the upper seat over the top of the valve spring**

**4.62b Use grease to hold the two halves of the split collet in the groove**

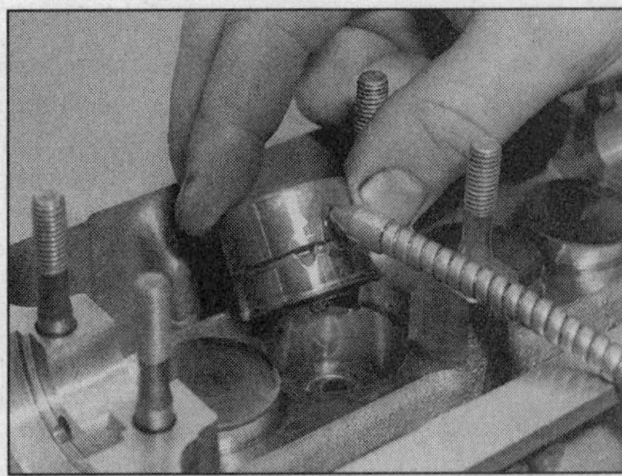
**4.64 Fit the tappets into their bores in the cylinder head**

**4.65a Lubricate the camshaft bearings with clean engine oil . . .**

**4.65b . . . then lower the camshaft into position on the cylinder head**

**4.66 Fitting the camshaft oil seal (diesel engines)**

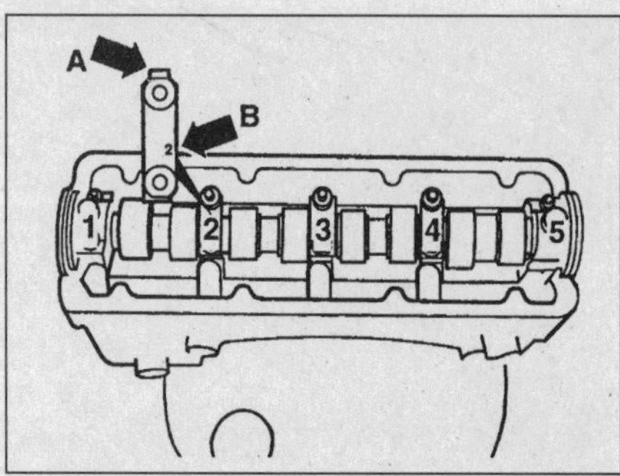

**4.68 Petrol engine camshaft bearing cap orientation**

*A Cast lug*
*B Identification number*

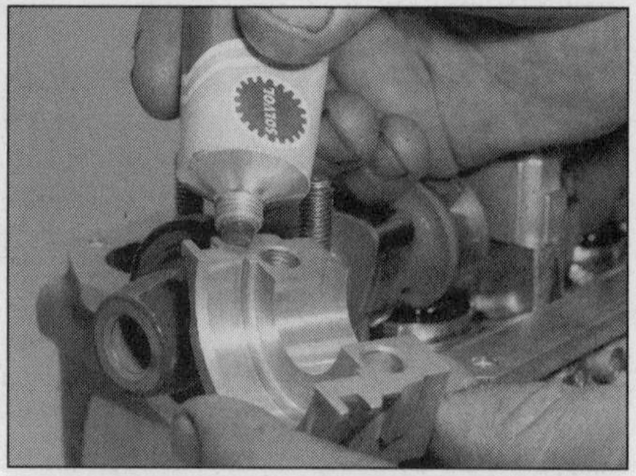
**4.70 Smear the mating surfaces of cap No 1 with sealant**

**4.73 Fitting a new camshaft oil seal**

**70** Smear the mating surfaces of caps Nos 1 and 5 with sealant **(see illustration)**. Locate caps Nos 1, 3 and 5 over the camshaft, then fit and tighten the nuts to the specified Stage 1 torque.

**71** Working in a diagonal sequence, tighten all the bearing cap nuts to the specified Stage 2 angle - use an angle gauge, if available, to ensure accuracy.

**72** Fit the nuts to bearing cap No 5, and tighten to the specified torque.

**73** With reference to Chapter 2A, lubricate the lip of a new camshaft oil seal with clean engine oil, and locate it over the end of the camshaft **(see illustration)**. Using a mallet and a long-reach socket of an appropriate diameter, drive the seal squarely into its housing until it bears against the inner stop - do not attempt to force it in any further.

### Diesel engines

**74** The bearing cap mounting holes are drilled off-centre; ensure that they are fitted the correct way around **(see illustration).**

**75** When fitting the bearing caps, the camshaft lobes for No 1 cylinder must be facing upwards.

**76** Fit caps Nos 2 and 4 over the camshaft, and tighten the retaining nuts alternately and diagonally to the specified torque.

**77** Now fit caps Nos 1, 3 and 5 over the camshaft and tighten the nuts to the specified torque. Ensure that cap No 5 is correctly located by lightly tapping the end of the camshaft.

**78** Refit the coolant outlet elbow, using a new gasket/O-ring as necessary.

**79** Refit the fuel injectors and glow plugs, with reference to Chapters 4C and 5C.

### All engines

**80** Refit the coolant temperature sensor and oil pressure switch.

**81** With reference to Chapter 2A or B as applicable, carry out the following:

*a) Refit the timing belt sprocket to the camshaft.*
*b) Refit the inlet and exhaust manifolds, complete with new gaskets.*

**82** Refer to Chapter 2A or B as applicable and refit the cylinder head to the cylinder block.

## 5 Pistons and connecting rods - removal and inspection

***Warning: Petrol engine codes AER and ALL have an aluminium cylinder block, and the crankshaft on these engines must not be removed, or the block main bearings will distort. Even loosening the main bearing caps will have this effect. Take care, therefore, that only the big-end cap bolts are loosened during the following procedures.***

### Removal

**1** Refer to Part A or B of this Chapter and remove the cylinder head, flywheel, sump and baffle plate, oil pump and pickup, as applicable.

**2** With the pistons sitting halfway down their bores, carefully feel around the tops of the cylinder bores. Any wear ridges found at the point where the pistons reach top dead centre must be removed, otherwise the pistons may be damaged when they are pushed out of their bores. This can be accomplished with a scraper or ridge reamer.

**3** Scribe the number of each piston on its crown, to allow identification later; note that No 1 is at the timing belt end of the engine.

**4** Using a set of feeler blades, measure the big-end to crankpin web thrust clearance at each connecting rod, and record the measurements for later reference.

**5** On diesel engines, remove the retaining screw and withdraw the piston cooling jets from their mounting holes **(see illustrations).**

**6** Rotate the crankshaft until pistons Nos 1 and 4 are at bottom dead centre. Unless they are already identified, mark the big-end bearing caps and connecting rods with their respective piston numbers, using a centre-punch or a scribe **(see illustration)**. Note the orientation of the bearing caps in relation to the connecting rod; it may be difficult to see the manufacturer's markings at this stage, so scribe alignment arrows on them both to ensure correct reassembly. **Note:** *On engine codes AER and ALL, the caps will only fit the correct way round on the correct connecting rod, as the caps are cracked off the rods during production. It is still advisable to mark the caps and rods for location and orientation, however, to save time when reassembling.*

**7** Note the fitted orientation of the connecting rods and caps in relation to the timing belt end

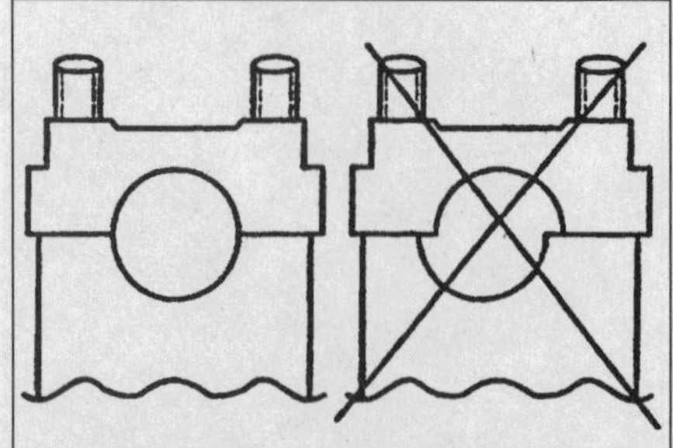
**4.74 The camshaft bearing caps on diesel engines are drilled off-centre, to ensure they are refitted the correct way round**

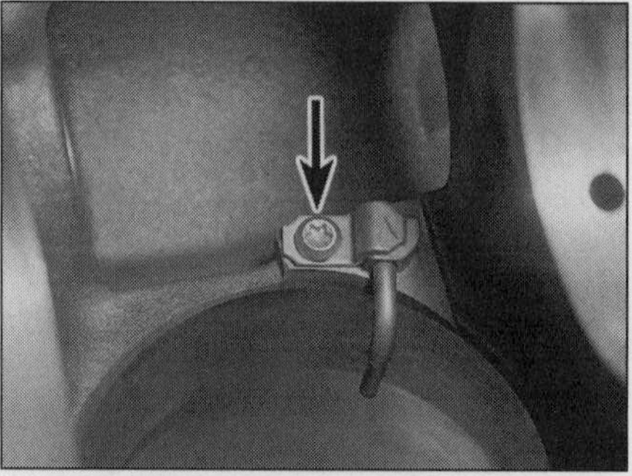
**5.5a Remove the piston cooling jet retaining screw (arrowed) . . .**

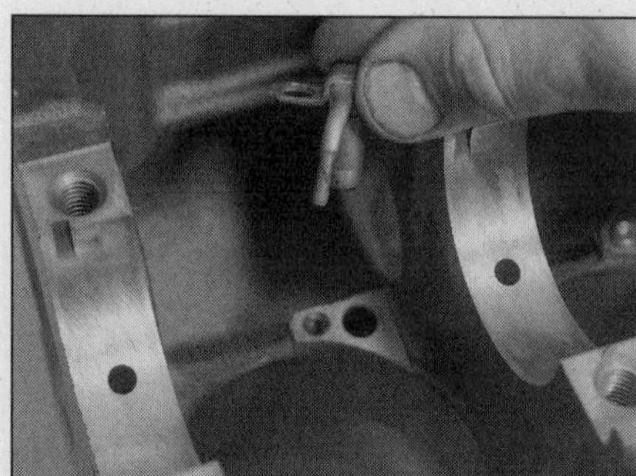
**5.5b . . . and withdraw the jet from its mounting hole**

5.6 Mark the big-end caps and connecting rods with their piston numbers (arrowed)

5.9 Pad the bolt threads with tape

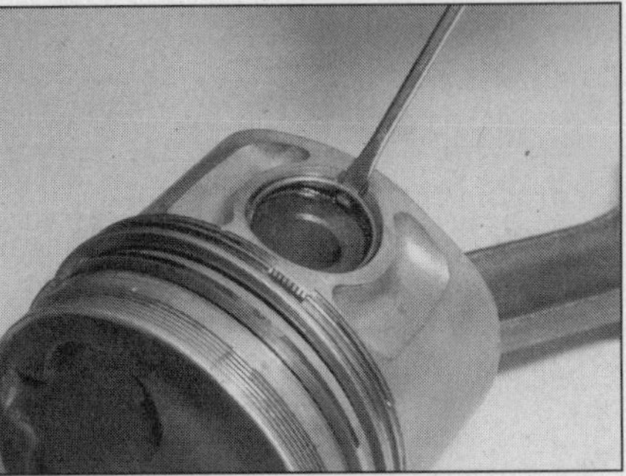
5.12a Insert a small screwdriver into the slot and prise off the gudgeon pin circlips

of the engine. Depending on engine code, there will be some form of marking on the side of rod and cap which faces the timing belt end - this may be a punch mark, cut-out, raised dot or a different profile in the casting. Make your own marks on the timing belt side of the rod and cap if the manufacturer's marks are unclear.

**8** Unbolt the bearing cap bolts/nuts, half a turn at a time, until they can be removed by hand. Recover the bottom shell bearing, and tape it to the cap for safe keeping. Note that if the shell bearings are to be re-used, they must be refitted to the same connecting rod.

**9** On engine code AEV, the bearing cap bolts will remain in the connecting rod; in this case, the threads of the bolts should be padded with insulating tape, to prevent them from scratching the crankpins when the pistons are removed from their bores **(see illustration).**

**10** Drive the pistons out of the top of their bores by pushing on the underside of the piston crown with a piece of dowel or a hammer handle. As the piston and connecting rod emerge, recover the top shell bearing and tape it to the connecting rod for safekeeping.

**11** Turn the crankshaft through half a turn and working as described above, remove Nos 2 and 3 pistons and connecting rods. Remember to maintain the components in their cylinder groups, whilst they are in a dismantled state.

**12** Insert a small flat-bladed screwdriver into the removal slot, and prise the gudgeon pin circlips from each piston. Push out the gudgeon pin, and separate the piston and connecting rod **(see illustrations)**. Discard the circlips, as new items must be fitted on reassembly. If the pin proves difficult to remove, heat the piston to 60°C with hot water - the resulting expansion will then allow the two components to be separated.

## Inspection

**13** Before an inspection of the pistons can be carried out, the existing piston rings must be removed, using a removal/installation tool, or an old feeler blade if such a tool is not available **(see illustration)**. Always remove the upper piston rings first, expanding them to clear the piston crown. The rings are very brittle and will snap if they are stretched too much - sharp edges are produced when this happens, so protect your eyes and hands. Discard the rings on removal, as new items must be fitted when the engine is reassembled.

**14** Use a section of old piston ring to scrape the carbon deposits out of the ring grooves, taking care not to score or gouge the edges of the groove.

**15** Carefully scrape away all traces of carbon from the top of the piston. A hand-held wire brush (or a piece of fine emery cloth) can be used, once the majority of the deposits have been scraped away. Be careful not to remove any metal from the piston, as it is relatively soft. **Note:** *Take care to preserve the piston number markings that were made during removal.*

**16** Once the deposits have been removed, clean the pistons and connecting rods with paraffin or a suitable solvent, and dry thoroughly. Make sure that the oil return holes in the ring grooves are clear.

**17** Examine the piston for signs of terminal wear or damage. Some normal wear will be apparent, in the form of a vertical 'grain' on the piston thrust surfaces and a slight looseness of the top compression ring in its groove. Abnormal wear should be carefully examined, to assess whether the component is still serviceable and what the cause of the wear might be.

**18** Scuffing or scoring of the piston skirt may indicate that the engine has been overheating, through inadequate cooling, lubrication or abnormal combustion temperatures. Scorch marks on the skirt indicate that blow - by has occurred, perhaps caused by worn bores or piston rings. Burnt areas on the piston crown are usually an indication of pre-ignition, pinking or detonation. In extreme cases, the piston crown may be melted by operating under these conditions. Corrosion pit marks in the piston crown indicate that coolant has seeped into the combustion chamber and/or the crankcase. The faults causing these symptoms must be corrected before the engine is brought back into service, or the same damage will recur.

**19** Check the pistons, connecting rods, gudgeon pins and bearing caps for cracks. Lay the connecting rods on a flat surface, and look along the length to see if it appears bent or twisted. If you have doubts about their condition, get them measured at an engineering workshop. Inspect the small-end bush bearing for signs of wear or cracking.

**20** Using a micrometer, measure the diameter of all four pistons at a point 10 mm from the bottom of the skirt, at right-angles to the gudgeon pin axis **(see illustration)**.

5.12b Push out the gudgeon pin and separate the piston and connecting rod

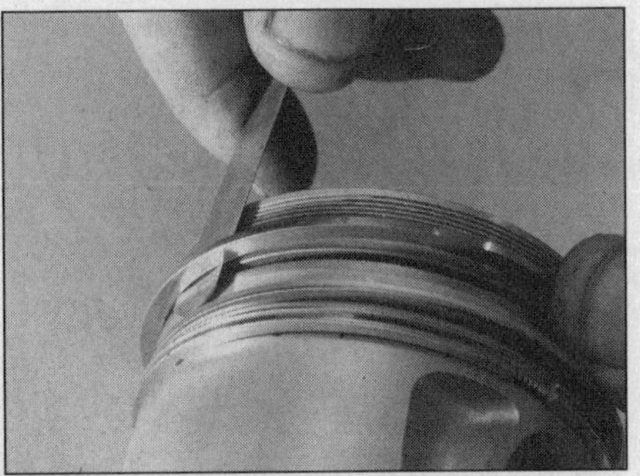
5.13 Piston rings can be removed using an old feeler blade

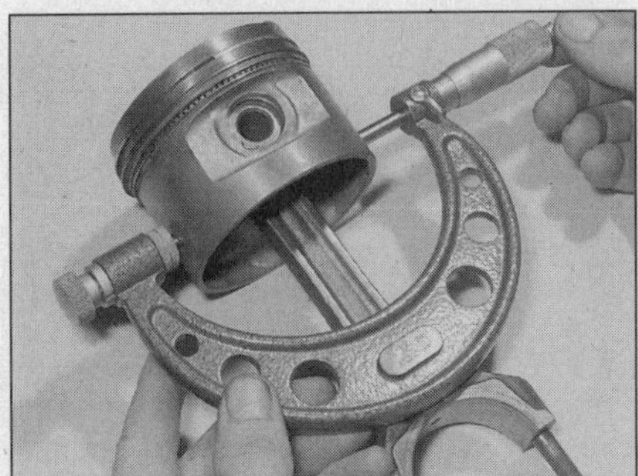
5.20 Using a micrometer, measure the diameter of all four pistons

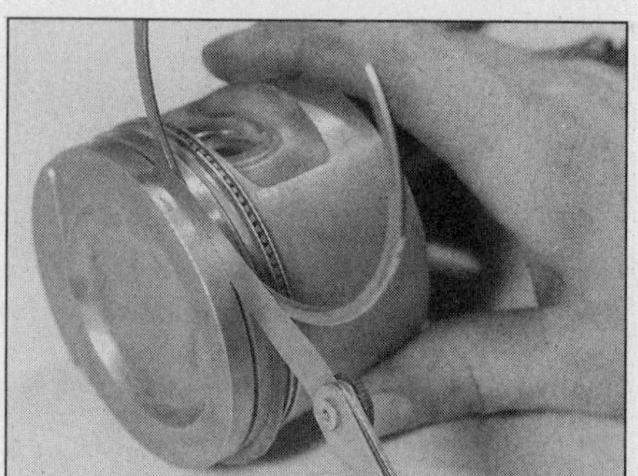
5.21 Measuring the piston ring-to-groove clearance using a feeler blade

6.4 Measuring crankshaft endfloat using a DTI gauge

6.5 Measuring crankshaft endfloat using feeler blades

Compare the measurements with those listed in the Specifications. If the piston diameter is out of the tolerance band listed for its particular size, then it must be renewed. **Note:** *If the cylinder block was re-bored during a previous overhaul, oversize pistons may have been fitted.* Record the measurements and use them to check the piston clearances when the cylinder bores are measured, later in this Chapter.

**21** Hold a new piston ring in the appropriate groove and measure the ring-to-groove clearance using a feeler blade **(see illustration)**. Note that the rings are of different widths, so use the correct ring for the groove. Compare the measurements with those listed; if the clearances are outside of the tolerance band, then the piston must be renewed. Confirm this by checking the width of the piston ring with a micrometer.

**22** Using internal/external vernier calipers, measure the connecting rod small-end internal diameter and the gudgeon pin external diameter. Subtract the gudgeon pin diameter from the small-end diameter to obtain the clearance. If this measurement is outside its specification (where given), then the piston and connecting rod bush will have to be resized and a new gudgeon pin installed. An engineering workshop will have the equipment needed to undertake a job of this nature.

**23** The orientation of the piston with respect to the connecting rod must be correct when the two are reassembled. The piston crown is marked with an arrow (which may be obscured by carbon deposits); this must point towards the timing belt end of the engine when the piston is installed. The connecting rod and its bearing cap both have recesses machined into them, close to their mating surfaces - these recesses must both face the same way as the arrow on the piston crown (ie towards the timing belt end of the engine) when correctly installed. Reassemble the two components to satisfy this requirement.

**24** Lubricate the gudgeon pin and small-end bush with clean engine oil. Slide the pin into the piston, engaging the connecting rod small-end. Fit two new circlips to the piston at either end of the gudgeon pin, such that their open ends are facing 180° away from the removal slot in the piston. Repeat this operation for the remaining pistons.

## 6 Crankshaft - removal and inspection

***Warning: Petrol engine codes AER and ALL have an aluminium cylinder block, and the crankshaft on these engines must not be removed, or the block main bearings will distort. Even loosening the main bearing caps will have this effect. For this reason, if crankshaft or main bearing wear is suspected, the crankshaft and cylinder block must be renewed complete.***

### Removal

**1 Note:** *If no work is to be done on the pistons and connecting rods, then removal of the cylinder head and pistons will not be necessary. Instead, the pistons need only be pushed far enough up the bores so that they are positioned clear of the crankpins. The use of an engine stand is strongly recommended.*

**2** With reference to Chapter 2A or B as applicable, carry out the following:

*a) Remove the crankshaft timing belt sprocket.*
*b) Remove the clutch components, where applicable, and the flywheel/driveplate.*
*c) Remove the sump, baffle plate (where applicable), oil pump and pickup.*
*d) Remove the front and rear crankshaft oil seals and their housings.*

**3** Remove the pistons and connecting rods, as described in Section 5 (refer to the Note above).

**4** Carry out a check of the crankshaft endfloat, as follows. **Note:** *This can only be accomplished when the crankshaft is still installed in the cylinder block/crankcase, but is free to move.* Set up a DTI gauge so that the probe is in line with the crankshaft axis and is in contact with a fixed point on end of the crankshaft **(see illustration)**. Push the crankshaft along its axis to the end of its travel, and then zero the gauge. Push the crankshaft fully the other way, and record the endfloat indicated on the dial. Compare the result with the figure given in the Specifications and establish whether new thrustwashers are required.

**5** If a dial gauge is not available, feeler blades can be used. First push the crankshaft fully towards the flywheel end of the engine, then use a feeler blade to measure the gap between cylinder No 2 crankpin web and the main bearing thrustwasher **(see illustration)**. Compare the results with the Specifications.

**6** Observe the manufacturer's identification marks on the main bearing caps. The number relates to the position in the crankcase, as counted from the timing belt end of the engine **(see illustration)**.

**7** Loosen the main bearing cap bolts one quarter of a turn at a time, until they can be removed by hand. Using a soft-faced mallet, strike the caps lightly to free them from the crankcase. Recover the lower main bearing shells, taping them to the cap for safekeeping. Mark them with indelible ink to aid identification, but do not score or scratch them in any way.

**8** Carefully lift the crankshaft out, taking care not to dislodge the upper main bearing shells **(see illustration)**. It would be wise to get an

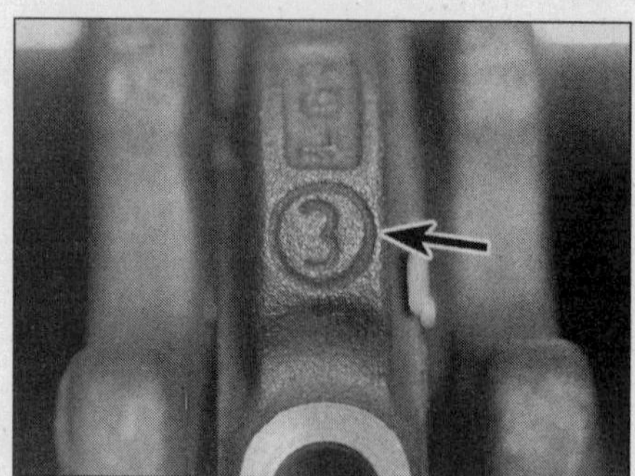

6.6 Manufacturer's identification markings on the main bearing caps (arrowed)

6.8 Lifting the crankshaft from the crankcase

assistant's help, as the crankshaft is heavy. Set it down on a clean, level surface and chock it with blocks to prevent it from rolling.

**9** Extract the upper main bearing shells from the crankcase, and tape them to their respective bearing caps. Remove the two thrustwasher bearings from either side of No 3 crank web.

**10** With the shell bearings removed, observe the recesses machined into the bearing caps and crankcase - these provide location for the lugs which protrude from the shell bearings and so prevent them from being fitted incorrectly.

### Inspection

**11** Wash the crankshaft in a suitable solvent and allow it to dry. Flush the oil holes thoroughly, to ensure that are not blocked - use a pipe cleaner or a needle brush if necessary. Remove any sharp edges from the edge of the hole which may damage the new bearings when they are installed.

**12** Inspect the main bearing and crankpin journals carefully; if uneven wear, cracking, scoring or pitting are evident, the crankshaft should be reground by an engineering workshop, and refitted to the engine with undersize bearings.

**13** Use a micrometer to measure the diameter of each main bearing journal **(see illustration)**. Taking a number of measurements on the surface of each journal will reveal if it is worn unevenly. Differences in diameter measured at 90° intervals indicate that the journal is out of round. Differences in diameter measured along the length of the journal, indicate that the journal is tapered. Again, if wear is detected, the crankshaft must be reground by an engineering workshop, and undersize bearings will be needed (refer to *Reassembly*).

**14** Check the oil seal journals at either end of the crankshaft. If they appear excessively scored or damaged, they may cause the new seals to leak when the engine is reassembled. It may be possible to repair the journal; seek the advice of an engineering workshop or your VW dealer.

**15** Measure the crankshaft runout by setting up a DTI gauge on the centre main bearing and rotating the shaft in V-blocks. The maximum deflection of the gauge will indicate the runout. Take precautions to protect the bearing journals and oil seal mating surfaces from damage during this procedure. A maximum runout figure is not quoted by the manufacturer, but use the figure of 0.05 mm as a rough guide. If the runout exceeds this figure, crankshaft renewal should be considered - consult your VW dealer or an engine rebuilding specialist for advice.

**16** Refer to Section 9 for details of main and big-end bearing inspection.

**6.13 Use a micrometer to measure the diameter of each main bearing journal**

## 7 Intermediate shaft (diesel engines only) - removal and refitting

### Removal

**1** Refer to Chapter 2B and carry out the following:

*a) Remove the timing belt.*

*b) Remove the intermediate shaft sprocket.*

**2** Before the shaft is removed, the endfloat must be checked. Anchor a DTI gauge to the cylinder block, with its probe in line with the intermediate shaft centre axis **(see illustration)**. Push the shaft into the cylinder block to the end of its travel, zero the DTI gauge and then draw the shaft out to the opposite end of its travel. The manufacturers do not quote a figure for intermediate shaft endfloat - as a guide, the figure for camshaft endfloat may be used. Renew the shaft if the endfloat appears excessive.

**3** Slacken the retaining bolts and withdraw the intermediate shaft flange. Recover the O-ring seal, then press out the oil seal **(see illustrations)**.

**4** Withdraw the intermediate shaft from the cylinder block, and inspect the drive gear at the end of the shaft; if the teeth show signs of excessive wear, or are damaged in any way, the shaft should be renewed.

**5** If the oil seal has been leaking, check the shaft mating surface for signs of scoring or damage.

### Refitting

**6** Liberally oil the intermediate shaft bearing surfaces and drive gear, then carefully guide the shaft into the cylinder block and engage the journal at the leading end with its support bearing.

**7** Press a new shaft oil seal into its housing in the intermediate shaft flange, and fit a new O-ring seal to the inner sealing surface of the flange.

**7.2 Check the intermediate shaft endfloat using a DTI gauge**

**7.3a Slacken the retaining bolts (arrowed) . . .**

**7.3b . . . and withdraw the intermediate shaft flange**

**7.3c Press out the oil seal . . .**

**7.3d . . . then recover the O-ring seal**

8.6 To clean the cylinder block threads, run a correct-size tap into the holes

**8** Lubricate the inner lip of the seal with clean engine oil, and slide the flange and seal over the end of the intermediate shaft. Ensure that the O-ring is correctly seated, then fit the flange retaining bolts and tighten them to the specified torque. Check that the intermediate shaft can rotate freely.

**9** With reference to Chapter 2B, refit the timing belt sprocket to the intermediate shaft and tighten the centre bolt to the specified torque.

## 8 Cylinder block/crankcase casting - cleaning and inspection

### Cleaning

**1** Remove all external components and electrical switches/sensors from the block. For complete cleaning, the core plugs should ideally be removed. Drill a small hole in the plugs, then insert a self-tapping screw into the hole. Extract the plugs by pulling on the screw with a pair of grips, or by using a slide hammer.

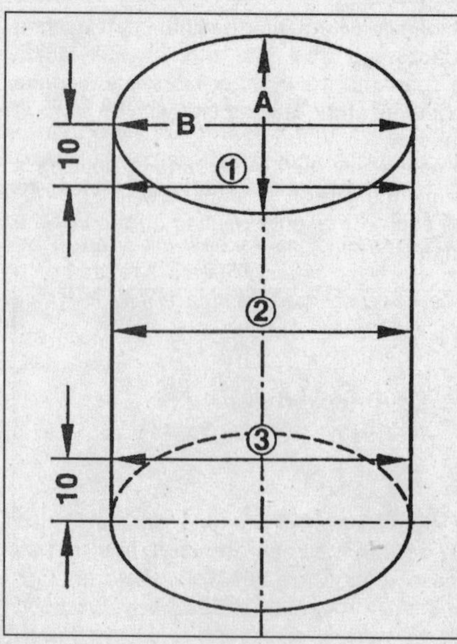


8.12 Bore measurement points

**2** Scrape all traces of gasket and sealant from the cylinder block/crankcase, taking care not to damage the sealing surfaces.

**3** Remove all oil gallery plugs (where fitted). The plugs are usually very tight - they may have to be drilled out, and the holes re-tapped. Use new plugs when the engine is reassembled.

**4** If the casting is extremely dirty, it should be steam-cleaned. After this, clean all oil holes and galleries one more time. Flush all internal passages with warm water until the water runs clear. Dry thoroughly, and apply a light film of oil to all mating surfaces and cylinder bores, to prevent rusting. If you have access to compressed air, use it to speed up the drying process, and to blow out all the oil holes and galleries.

***Warning: Wear eye protection when using compressed air!***

**5** If the castings are not very dirty, you can do an adequate cleaning job with hot, soapy water and a stiff brush. Take plenty of time, and do a thorough job. Regardless of the cleaning method used, be sure to clean all oil holes and galleries very thoroughly, and to dry all components well. Protect the cylinder bores as described above, to prevent rusting.

**6** All threaded holes must be clean, to ensure accurate torque readings during reassembly. To clean the threads, run the correct-size tap into each of the holes to remove rust, corrosion, thread sealant or sludge, and to restore damaged threads **(see illustration)**. If possible, use compressed air to clear the holes of debris produced by this operation. **Note:** *Take extra care to exclude all cleaning liquid from blind tapped holes, as the casting may be cracked by hydraulic action if a bolt is threaded into a hole containing liquid.*

**7** Apply suitable sealant to the new oil gallery plugs, and insert them into the holes in the block. Tighten them securely.

**8** If the engine is not going to be reassembled immediately, cover it with a large plastic bag to keep it clean; protect all mating surfaces and the cylinder bores as described above, to prevent rusting.

### Inspection

**9** Visually check the casting for cracks and corrosion. Look for stripped threads in the threaded holes. If there has been any history of internal water leakage, it may be worthwhile having an engine overhaul specialist check the cylinder block/crankcase with professional equipment. If defects are found, have them repaired if possible; if not, a new block will be required.

**10** Check the cylinder bores for scuffing or scoring. Any evidence of this kind of damage should be cross-checked with an inspection of the pistons: see Section 5 of this Chapter. If the damage is in its early stages, it may be possible to repair the block by reboring it. Seek the advice of an engineering workshop before you progress.

**11** To allow an accurate assessment of the wear in the cylinder bores to be made, their diameter must be measured at a number of points, as follows. Insert a bore gauge into bore No 1, and take three measurements in line with the crankshaft axis; one at the top of the bore, roughly 10 mm below the bottom of the wear ridge, one halfway down the bore and one at a point roughly 10 mm the bottom of the bore. **Note:** *Stand the cylinder block squarely on a workbench during this procedure, inaccurate results may be obtained if the measurements are taken when the engine mounted on a stand.*

**12** Rotate the bore gauge through 90°, so that it is at right-angles to the crankshaft axis and repeat the measurements detailed in paragraph 11 **(see illustration)**. Record all six measurements, and compare them with the data listed in the Specifications. If the difference in diameter between any two cylinders exceeds the wear limit, or if any one cylinder exceeds its maximum bore diameter, then *all four* cylinders will have to be rebored and oversize pistons will have to be fitted. Note that the imbalances produced by not reboring all the cylinders together would render the engine unusable.

**13** Use the piston diameter measurements recorded earlier (see Section 5) to calculate the piston-to-bore clearances. Figures are not available from the manufacturer, so seek the advice of your VAG dealer or engine reconditioning specialist.

**14** Place the cylinder block on a level work surface, crankcase downwards. Use a straight edge and a set of feeler blades to measure the distortion of the cylinder head mating surface in both planes. If the measurement exceeds the specified figures, repair may be possible by machining (on petrol engines) - consult your dealer for advice. On diesel engines, machining the head mating surface is not permissible.

**15** Before the engine can be reassembled, the cylinder bores must be honed. This process involves using an abrasive tool to produce a fine, cross-hatch pattern on the inner surface of the bore. This has the effect of seating the piston rings, resulting in a good seal between the piston and cylinder. There are two types of honing tool available to the home mechanic, both are driven by a rotary power tool, such as a drill. The bottle brush hone is a stiff, cylindrical brush with abrasive stones bonded to its bristles. The more conventional surfacing hone has abrasive stones mounted on spring-loaded legs. For the inexperienced home mechanic, satisfactory results will be achieved more easily using the bottle brush hone. **Note:** *If you are unwilling to tackle cylinder bore honing, an engineering workshop will be able to carry out the job for you at a reasonable cost.*

**16** Carry out the honing as follows; you will need one of the honing tools described above, a power drill/air wrench, a supply of clean rags, some honing oil and a pair of safety glasses.

**17** Fit the honing tool in the drill chuck. Lubricate the cylinder bores with honing oil and insert the honing tool into the first bore, compressing the stones to allow it to fit. Turn on the drill and as the tool rotates, move it up and down in the bore at a rate that produces a fine cross-hatch pattern on the surface. The lines of the pattern should ideally cross at about 50 to 60°, although some piston ring manufacturers may quote a different angle; check the literature supplied with the new rings **(see illustration).**

***Warning: Wear safety glasses to protect your eyes from debris flying off the honing tool.***

**18** Use plenty of oil during the honing process. Do not remove any more material than is necessary to produce the required finish. When removing the hone tool from the bore, do not pull it out whilst it is still rotating; maintain the up/down movement until the chuck has stopped, then withdraw the tool whilst rotating the chuck by hand, in the normal direction of rotation.

**19** Wipe out the oil and swarf with a rag and proceed to the next bore. When all four bores have been honed, thoroughly clean the whole cylinder block in hot soapy water to remove all traces of honing oil and debris. The block is clean when a clean rag, moistened with new engine oil does not pick up any grey residue when wiped along the bore.

**20** Apply a light coating of engine oil to the mating surfaces and cylinder bores to prevent rust forming. Wrap the block in a plastic bag until reassembly.

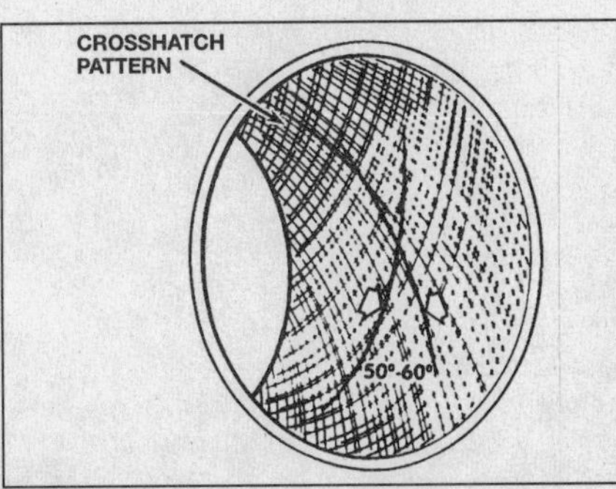


**8.17 Cylinder bore honing pattern**

## 9 Main and big-end bearings - inspection and selection

### *Inspection*

**1** Even though the main and big-end bearings should be renewed during the engine overhaul, the old bearings should be retained for close examination, as they may reveal valuable information about the condition of the engine **(see illustration).**

**2** Bearing failure can occur due to lack of lubrication, the presence of dirt or other foreign particles, overloading the engine, or corrosion. Regardless of the cause of bearing failure, the cause must be corrected before the engine is reassembled, to prevent it from happening again.

**3** When examining the bearing shells, remove them from the cylinder block/crankcase, the main bearing caps, the connecting rods and the connecting rod big-end bearing caps. Lay them out on a clean surface in the same general position as their location in the engine. This will enable you to match any bearing problems with the corresponding crankshaft journal. *Do not* touch any shell's internal bearing surface with your fingers while checking it, or the delicate surface may be scratched.

**4** Dirt and other foreign matter gets into the engine in a variety of ways. It may be left in the engine during assembly, or it may pass through filters or the crankcase ventilation system. It may get into the oil, and from there into the bearings. Metal chips from machining operations and normal engine wear are often present. Abrasives are sometimes left in engine components after reconditioning, especially when parts are not thoroughly cleaned using the proper cleaning methods. Whatever the source, these foreign objects often end up embedded in the soft bearing material, and are easily recognised. Large particles will not embed in the bearing, but will score or gouge the bearing and journal. The best prevention for this cause of bearing failure is to clean all parts thoroughly, and keep everything spotlessly-clean during engine assembly. Frequent and regular engine oil and filter changes are also recommended.

**5** Lack of lubrication (or lubrication breakdown) has a number of interrelated causes. Excessive heat (which thins the oil), overloading (which squeezes the oil from the bearing face) and oil leakage (from excessive bearing clearances, worn oil pump or high engine speeds) all contribute to lubrication breakdown. Blocked oil passages, which usually are the result of misaligned oil holes in a bearing shell, will also oil-starve a bearing, and destroy it. When lack of lubrication is the cause of bearing failure, the bearing material is wiped or extruded from the steel backing of the bearing. Temperatures may increase to the point where the steel backing turns blue from overheating.

**9.1 Typical bearing failures**

**6** Driving habits can have a definite effect on bearing life. Full-throttle, low-speed operation (labouring the engine) puts very high loads on bearings, tending to squeeze out the oil film. These loads cause the bearings to flex, which produces fine cracks in the bearing face (fatigue failure). Eventually, the bearing material will loosen in pieces, and tear away from the steel backing.

**7** Short-distance driving leads to corrosion of bearings, because insufficient engine heat is produced to drive off the condensed water and corrosive gases. These products collect in the engine oil, forming acid and sludge. As the oil is carried to the engine bearings, the acid attacks and corrodes the bearing material.

**8** Incorrect bearing installation during engine assembly will lead to bearing failure as well. Tight-fitting bearings leave insufficient bearing running clearance, and will result in oil starvation. Dirt or foreign particles trapped behind a bearing shell result in high spots on the bearing, which lead to failure.

**9** *Do not* touch any shell's internal bearing surface with your fingers during reassembly; there is a risk of scratching the delicate surface, or of depositing particles of dirt on it.

**10** As mentioned at the beginning of this Section, the bearing shells should be renewed as a matter of course during engine overhaul; to do otherwise is false economy.

### *Selection*

**11** Main and big-end bearings for the engines described in this Chapter are available in standard sizes and a range of undersizes to suit reground crankshafts - refer to Specifications for details.

**12** The running clearances will need to be checked when the crankshaft is refitted with its new bearings (see Section 11).

## 10 Engine overhaul - reassembly sequence

**1** Before reassembly begins, ensure that all new parts have been obtained, and that all necessary tools are available. Read through the entire procedure to familiarise yourself with the work involved, and to ensure that all items necessary for reassembly of the engine are at hand. In addition to all normal tools and

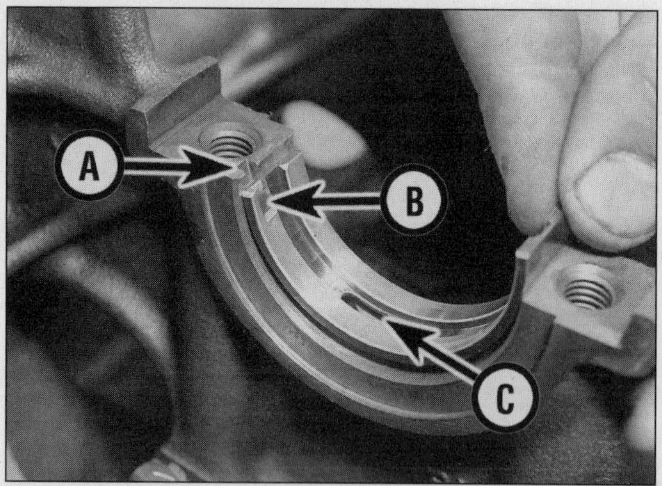


**11.3 Bearing shells correctly refitted**

*A Recess in bearing saddle*
*B Lug on bearing shell*
*C Oil hole*

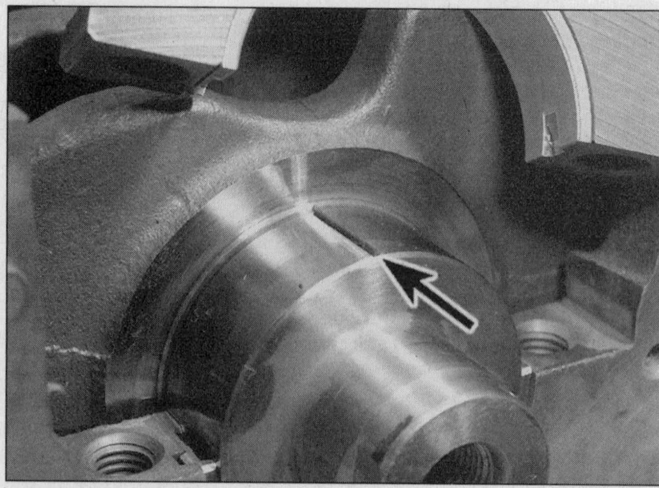

**11.7 Lay a piece of Plastigauge on each journal, in line with the crankshaft axis**

materials, thread-locking compound will be needed. A suitable tube of liquid sealant will also be required for the joint faces that are without gaskets. It is recommended that the manufacturer's own products are used, which are specially formulated for this purpose; the relevant product names are quoted in the text of each Section where they are required.

**2** In order to save time and avoid problems, engine reassembly should ideally be carried out in the following order:

*a) Crankshaft (not engine codes AER and ALL).*
*b) Piston/connecting rod assemblies.*
*c) Oil pump (see Chapter 2A or B).*
*d) Sump (see Chapter 2A or B).*
*e) Flywheel/driveplate (see Chapter 2A or B).*
*f) Cylinder head and gasket (see Chapter 2A or B).*
*g) Timing belt tensioner, sprockets and timing belt (see Chapter 2A or B).*
*h) Engine external components and ancillaries.*
*i) Auxiliary drivebelts, pulleys and tensioners (see Chapter 2A or B).*

**3** At this stage, all engine components should be absolutely clean and dry, with all faults repaired. The components should be laid out (or in individual containers) on a completely clean work surface.

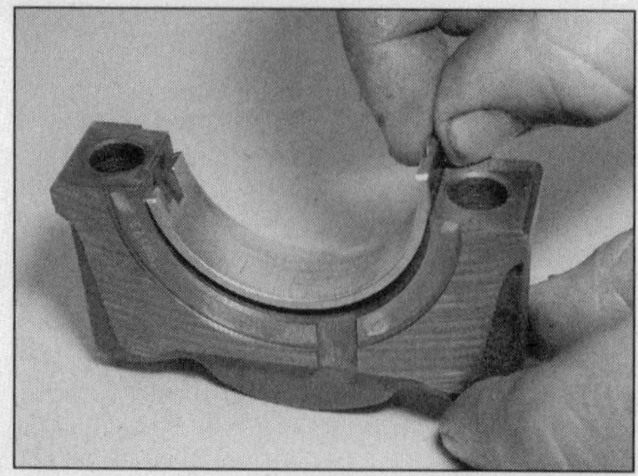

**11.8 Fit the new lower half main bearing shells to the main bearing caps**

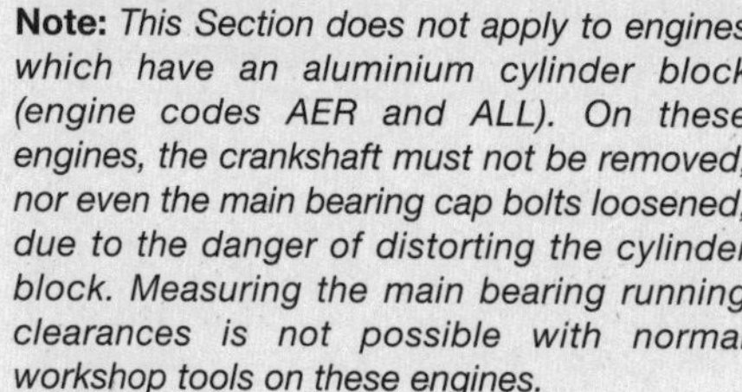

## 11 Crankshaft - refitting and running clearance check

**Note:** *This Section does not apply to engines which have an aluminium cylinder block (engine codes AER and ALL). On these engines, the crankshaft must not be removed, nor even the main bearing cap bolts loosened, due to the danger of distorting the cylinder block. Measuring the main bearing running clearances is not possible with normal workshop tools on these engines.*

**1** Crankshaft refitting is the first stage of engine reassembly following overhaul. At this point, it is assumed that the crankshaft, cylinder block/crankcase and bearings have been cleaned, inspected and reconditioned or renewed.

**2** Place the cylinder block on a clean, level work surface, with the crankcase facing upwards. Unbolt the bearing caps and carefully release them from the crankcase; lay them out in order to ensure correct reassembly. If they are still in place, remove the bearing shells from the caps and the crankcase, and wipe out the inner surfaces with a clean rag - they must be kept spotlessly clean.

**3** Clean the rear surface of the new bearing shells with a rag, and lay them on the bearing saddles. Ensure that the orientation lugs on the shells engage with the recesses in the saddles, and that the oil holes are correctly aligned **(see illustration)**. Do not hammer or otherwise force the bearing shells into place. It is critically important that the surfaces of the bearings are kept free from damage and contamination.

**4** Give the newly-fitted bearing shells and the crankshaft journals a final clean with a rag. Check that the oil holes in the crankshaft are free from dirt, as any left here will become embedded in the new bearings when the engine is first started.

**5** Carefully lay the crankshaft in the crankcase, taking care not to dislodge the bearing shells.

### *Running clearance check*

**6** When the crankshaft and bearings are refitted, a clearance must exist between them to allow lubricant to circulate. This clearance is impossible to check using feeler blades, so Plastigauge is used. This is a thin strip of soft plastic that is crushed between the bearing shells and journals when the bearing caps are tightened up. The change in its width then indicates the size of the clearance gap.

**7** Cut off five pieces of Plastigauge, just shorter than the length of the crankshaft journal. Lay a piece on each journal, in line with its axis **(see illustration).**

**8** Wipe off the rear surfaces of the new lower half main bearing shells and fit them to the main bearing caps, ensuring the locating lugs engage correctly **(see illustration).**

**9** Wipe the front surfaces of the bearing shells, and give them a light coating of silicone release agent - this will prevent the Plastigauge from sticking to the shell. Fit the caps in their correct locations on the bearing saddles, using the manufacturer's markings as a guide. Ensure that they are correctly orientated - the caps should be fitted such that the recesses for the bearing shell locating lugs are on the same side as those in the bearing saddle.

**10** Working from the centre bearing cap, tighten the bolts one half turn at a time until they are all correctly torqued (on diesel engines, tighten only to the Stage 1 torque - no further). Do not let the crankshaft turn at all whilst the Plastigauge is in place. Progressively unbolt the bearing caps and remove them, taking care not to dislodge the Plastigauge.

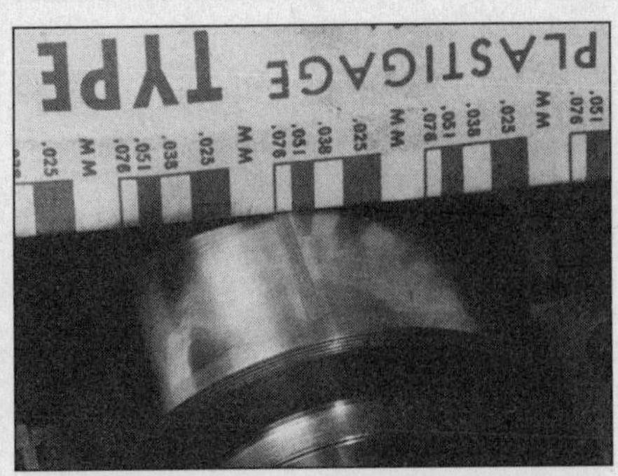


11.11 **Measure the width of the crushed Plastigauge using the scale provided**

**11** The width of the crushed Plastigauge can now be measured, using the scale provided **(see illustration)**. Use the correct scale, as both imperial and metric are printed. This measurement indicates the running clearance - compare it with that listed in Specifications. If the clearance is outside the tolerance, it may be due to dirt or debris trapped under the bearing surface; try cleaning them again and repeat the clearance check. If the results are still unacceptable, re-check the journal diameters and the bearing sizes. If the Plastigauge is thicker at one end, the journals may be tapered, and will require regrinding.

**12** When you are satisfied that the clearances are correct, carefully remove the remains of the Plastigauge from the journals and bearings faces. Use a soft, plastic or wooden scraper as anything metallic is likely to damage the surfaces.

## *Crankshaft - final refitting*

**13** Lift the crankshaft out of the crankcase. Wipe off the surfaces of the bearings in the crankcase and the bearing caps. Fit the thrust bearings either side of the No 3 bearing saddle, between cylinders No 2 and 3. Use a small quantity of grease to hold them in place; ensure that they are seated correctly in the machined recesses, with the oil grooves facing outwards.

**14** Liberally coat the bearing shells in the crankcase with clean engine oil of the appropriate grade.

**15** Lower the crankshaft into position so that No 2 and 3 cylinder crankpins are at TDC; No 1 and 4 cylinder crankpins will then be at BDC, ready for fitting No 1 piston.

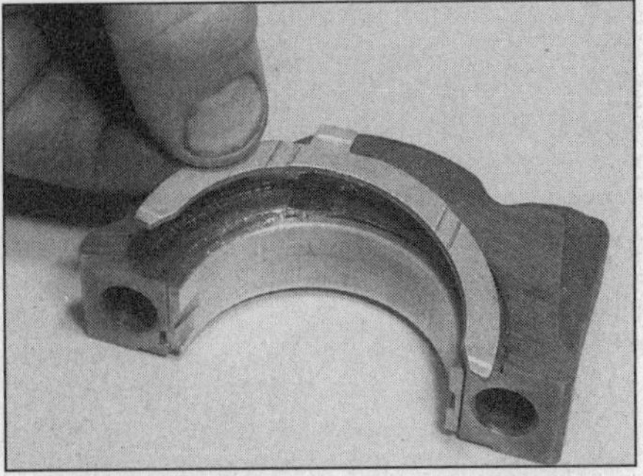

11.16 **Fitting the thrustwashers to No 3 bearing cap**

**16** Lubricate the lower bearing shells in the main bearing caps with clean engine oil, then fit the thrustwashers to either side of bearing cap No 3, noting that the lugs protruding from the washers engage the recesses in the side of the bearing cap **(see illustration)**. Make sure that the locating lugs on the shells are still engaged with the corresponding recesses in the caps.

**17** Fit the main bearing caps in the correct order and orientation - No 1 bearing cap must be at the timing belt end of the engine, and the bearing shell locating recesses in the bearing saddles and caps must be adjacent to each other **(see illustration)**. Insert the bearing cap bolts (new bolts on diesel engines) and hand-tighten them only.

### Petrol engines

**18** Working from the centre bearing cap outwards, tighten the retaining bolts to the specified torque.

### Diesel engines

**19** Working from the centre bearing cap outwards, tighten the retaining bolts to the specified Stage 1 torque **(see illustration).**

**20** Working in the same sequence, tighten the bolts further to the specified Stage 2 angle. Use an angle-measuring gauge, if available, to ensure accuracy.

### All engines

**21** Refit the crankshaft rear oil seal housing, together with a new oil seal; refer to Part A or B (as applicable) of this Chapter for details.

**22** Check that the crankshaft rotates freely by turning it manually. If resistance is felt, re-check the running clearances, as described above.

**23** Carry out a check of the crankshaft endfloat as described at the beginning of Section 6. If the thrust surfaces of the crankshaft have been checked and new thrust bearings have been fitted, then the endfloat should be within specification.

## 12 Pistons and piston rings - assembly

**1** At this point, it is assumed that the pistons have been correctly assembled to their respective connecting rods, and that the piston ring-to-groove clearances have been checked. If not, refer to the end of Section 5.

**2** Before the rings can be fitted to the pistons, the end gaps must be checked with the rings fitted into the cylinder bores.

**3** Lay out the piston assemblies and the new ring sets on a clean work surface so that the components are kept together in their groups during and after end gap checking. Place the crankcase on the work surface on its side, allowing access to the top and bottom of the bores.

**4** Take the No 1 piston top ring and insert it into the top of the bore. Using the No 1 piston as a ram, push the ring close to the bottom of the bore, at the lowest point of the piston travel. Ensure that it is perfectly square in the bore by pushing firmly against the piston crown.

**5** Use a set of feeler blades to measure the gap between the ends of the piston ring; the correct blade will just pass through the gap with a minimal amount of resistance **(see illustration)**. Compare this measurement with the wear limit listed in the Specifications. Check that you have the correct ring before deciding that a gap is incorrect. Repeat the operation for all rings.

**6** If new rings are being fitted, it is unlikely that the end gaps will be too small. If a measurement is found to be undersize, it must be corrected or there is the risk that the ends of the ring may contact each other during operation, possibly resulting in engine damage. Ensure that the ring has been fitted in its correct location, and consult your parts supplier if the ring end gap is still too small.

11.17 **Fitting a main bearing cap in place**

11.19 **Tighten the bearing cap bolts to the specified torque**

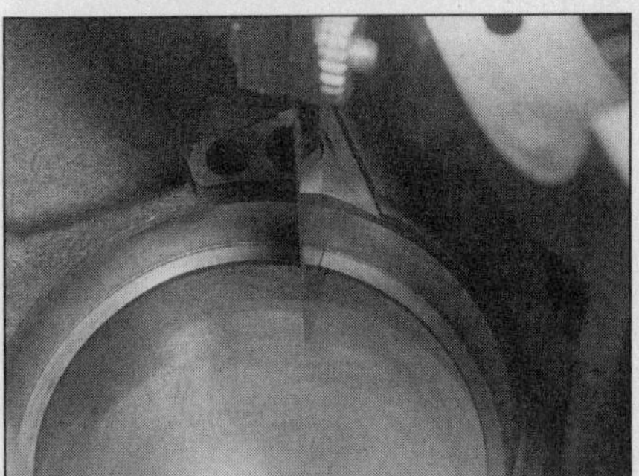

12.5 **Checking a piston ring end gap using a feeler blade**

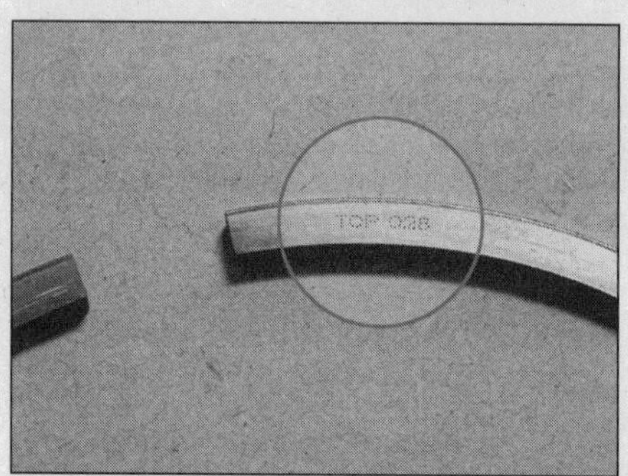


12.7 Piston ring TOP marking

7 When all the piston ring end gaps have been verified, they can be fitted to the pistons. Work from the lowest ring groove (oil control ring) upwards. Note that the oil control ring comprises two side rails separated by a expander ring. Note also that the two compression rings are different in cross-section, and so must be fitted in the correct groove and the right way up, using a piston ring fitting tool. Both of the compression rings have marks stamped on one side to indicate the top facing surface **(see illustration)**. Ensure that these marks face up when the rings are fitted.
8 Distribute the end gaps around the piston, spaced at 120° intervals to the each other. **Note:** *If the piston ring manufacturer supplies specific fitting instructions with the rings, follow these exclusively.*

## 13 Piston and connecting rod assemblies - refitting and big-end bearing clearance check

### Big-end running clearance check

**Note:** *At this point, it is assumed that the crankshaft is fitted to the engine, as described in Section 11.*
1 As with the main bearings (Section 11), a running clearance must exist between the big-end crankpin and its bearing shells to allow oil to circulate. There are two methods of checking the size of the running clearance, as described in the following paragraphs.
2 Place the cylinder block on a clean, level work surface, with the crankcase facing upwards. Position the crankshaft such that crankpins No 1 and 4 are at BDC.
3 The first method is the least accurate and involves bolting bearing caps to the big-ends, away from the crankshaft, with the bearing shells in place. **Note:** *Correct orientation of the bearing caps is critical; refer to the notes in Section 5. The internal diameter formed by the assembled big-end is then measured using internal vernier calipers. The diameter of the respective crankpin is then subtracted from this measurement and the result is the running clearance.*
4 The second method of carrying out this check involves the use of Plastigauge, in the same manner as the main bearing running clearance check (see Section 11) and is much more accurate than the previous method. Clean all four crankpins with a clean rag. With crankpins No 1 and 4 at BDC initially, place a strand of Plastigauge on each crankpin journal.
5 Fit the upper big-end bearing shells to the connecting rods, ensuring that the locating lugs and recesses engage correctly. Temporarily refit the piston/connecting rod assemblies to the crankshaft; refit the big-end bearing caps, using the manufacturer's markings to ensure that they are fitted the correct way around - refer to *Final refitting* for details.
6 Tighten the bearing cap nuts/bolts to the specified Stage 1 torque only - no further. Take care not to disturb the Plastigauge or rotate the connecting rod during the tightening process.
7 Dismantle the assemblies without rotating the connecting rods. Use the scale printed on the Plastigauge envelope to determine the big-end bearing running clearance and compare it with the figures listed in Specifications.
8 If the clearance is significantly different from that expected, the bearing shells may be the wrong size (or excessively worn, if the original shells are being re-used). Make sure that no dirt or oil was trapped between the bearing shells and the caps or connecting rods when the clearance was measured. Re-check the diameters of the crankpins. Note that if the Plastigauge was wider at one end than at the other, the crankpins may be tapered. When the problem is identified, fit new bearing shells or have the crankpins reground to a listed undersize, as appropriate.
9 Upon completion, carefully scrape away all traces of the Plastigauge material from the crankshaft and bearing shells. Use a plastic or wooden scraper, which will be soft enough to prevent scoring of the bearing surfaces.

### Bearing shell pre-tension check - petrol engines

10 Using internal and external vernier calipers, measure the internal diameter of the assembled connecting rod and big-end bearing cap, and the diameter of its bearing shells, as shown **(see illustration)**. Subtract the connecting rod internal diameter from the shell diameter to obtain the shell pre-tension. If the figure obtained is less than the specified minimum, new shells should be fitted.

### Piston and connecting rod assemblies - final refitting

11 Note that the following procedure assumes that the crankshaft main bearing caps are in place (see Section 11).
12 Ensure that the bearing shells are correctly fitted, as described at the beginning of this Section. If new shells are being fitted, ensure that all traces of the protective grease are cleaned off using paraffin. Wipe dry the shells and connecting rods with a lint-free cloth.
13 Lubricate the cylinder bores, the pistons, and piston rings with clean engine oil. Lay out each piston/connecting rod assembly in order on a work surface. On engine code AEV, fit the new bolts to the connecting rods with short sections of rubber hose or tape over the bolt threads, to protect the cylinder bores and crankshaft journals during reassembly.
14 Start with piston/connecting rod assembly No 1. Make sure that the piston rings are still spaced as described in Section 12, then clamp them in position with a piston ring compressor.
15 Insert the piston/connecting rod assembly into the top of cylinder No 1. Lower the big-end in first, guiding it to protect the cylinder bores.
16 Ensure that the orientation of the piston in its cylinder is correct - the piston crown, connecting rods and big-end bearing caps have markings, which must point towards the timing belt end of the engine when the piston is installed in the bore - refer to Section 5 for details.
17 Using a block of wood or hammer handle against the piston crown, tap the assembly into the cylinder until the piston crown is flush with the top of the cylinder.
18 Ensure that the bearing shell is still correctly installed. Liberally lubricate the crankpin and both bearing shells with clean engine oil. Taking care not to mark the cylinder bores, tap the piston/connecting rod assembly down the bore and onto the crankpin. Refit the big-end bearing cap, tightening its new retaining nuts/bolts finger-tight at first. Note that the orientation of the bearing cap with respect to the connecting rod must be correct when the two components are reassembled. The connecting rod and its corresponding bearing cap both have markings machined into them, close to their mating surfaces - these must both face in the same direction as the arrow on the piston crown (ie towards the timing belt end of the engine) when correctly installed - refer to Section 5 for details.

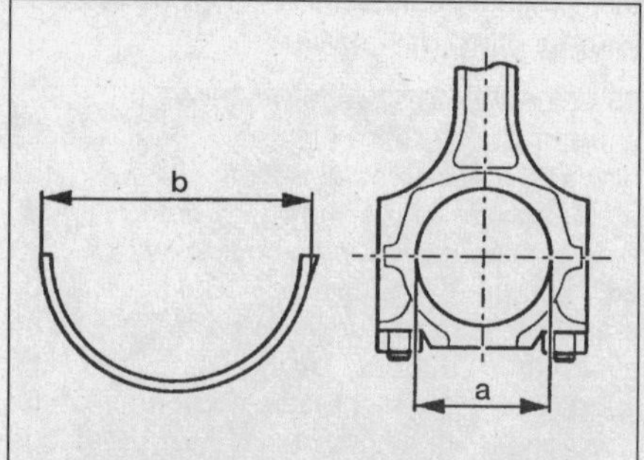


**13.10 Dimensions for calculation of big-end bearing shell pre-tension**

*a Connecting rod internal diameter*
*b Bearing shell diameter*

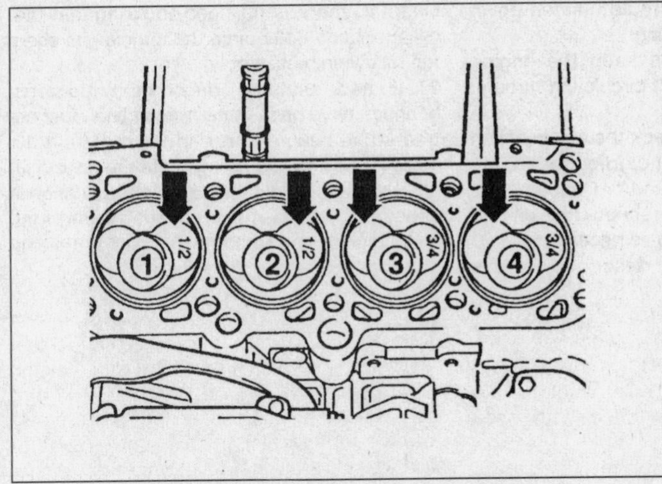


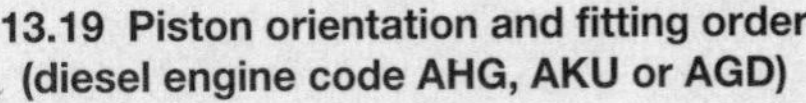
**13.19 Piston orientation and fitting order (diesel engine code AHG, AKU or AGD)**

**13.21 Tightening the big-end bearing cap bolts to the Stage 1 . . .**

**19** On diesel engines except code AEF (direct injection diesel engines), the piston crowns are specially shaped. Because of this, pistons 1 and 2 are different to pistons 3 and 4. When correctly fitted, the larger inlet valve chambers on pistons 1 and 2 must face the flywheel end of the engine, and the larger inlet valve chambers on pistons 3 and 4 must face the timing belt end of the engine **(see illustration)**. New pistons have number markings on their crowns to indicate their type - 1/2 denotes piston 1 or 2, 3/4 indicates piston 3 or 4.

**20** On engine code AEV, remove the hose or tape from the connecting rod bolt threads.

**21** Oil the threads and contact faces of the new retaining nuts/bolts with clean engine oil. Tighten the nuts/bolts half a turn at a time to the specified Stage 1 torque **(see illustration).**

**22** Now tighten the nuts/bolts further to the specified Stage 2 angle. Use an angle-measuring gauge, if available, to ensure accuracy **(see illustration).**

**23** Refit the remaining three piston/ connecting rod assemblies in the same way.

**24** Rotate the crankshaft by hand. Check that it turns freely; some stiffness is to be expected if new parts have been fitted, but there should be no binding or tight spots.

### Diesel engines

**25** If new pistons are to be fitted, or if a new short engine is to be installed, the projection of the piston crowns above the cylinder head at TDC must be measured, to determine the type of head gasket that should be fitted.

**26** Turn the cylinder block over (so that the crankcase is facing downwards) and rest it on a stand or wooden blocks. Anchor a DTI gauge to the cylinder block, and zero it on the head gasket mating surface. Rest the gauge probe on No 1 piston crown and turn the crankshaft slowly by hand so that the piston reaches and then passes through TDC. Measure and record the maximum deflection at TDC.

**27** Repeat the measurement at piston No 4, then turn the crankshaft through 180° and take measurements at pistons Nos 2 and 3.

**28** If the measurements differ from piston to piston, take the highest figure and use this to determine the head gasket type that must be used - refer to the Specifications for details.

**29** Note that if the original pistons have been refitted, then a new head gasket of the same type as the original item must be fitted; refer to Chapter 2B for details of how to identify different head gasket types.

## 14 Engine - initial start-up after overhaul and reassembly

**1** Refit the remainder of the engine components in the order listed in Section 10, referring to Part A or B where necessary. Refit the engine (and transmission) to the vehicle as described in Section 2. Double-check the engine oil and coolant levels and make a final check that everything has been reconnected. Make sure that there are no tools or rags left in the engine compartment.

### *Petrol models*

**2** Remove the spark plugs, referring to Chapter 1A for details.

**13.22 . . . and Stage 2 torque settings**

**3** The engine must be immobilised such that it can be turned over using the starter motor, without starting - disable the fuel pump by unplugging the fuel pump power relay from the relay board; refer to the relevant Part of Chapter 4 for details. Alternatively, identify and remove the fuel pump fuse.

***Caution: On vehicles with a catalytic converter, it is potentially damaging to immobilise the engine by disabling the ignition system without first disabling the fuel system, as unburnt fuel could be supplied to the catalyst. When the engine is later started, the unburnt fuel in the converter may ignite and irreparably damage the converter.*** **2C**

**4** Turn the engine using the starter motor until the oil pressure warning light goes out. If the light fails to extinguish after several seconds of cranking, check the engine oil level and that the oil filter is secure. Assuming these are correct, check the security of the oil pressure switch wiring - do not progress any further until you are satisfied that oil is being pumped around the engine at sufficient pressure.

**5** Refit the spark plugs, and reconnect the fuel pump relay (or refit the fuel pump fuse).

### *Diesel models*

**6** Disconnect the electrical wiring from the fuel cut-off valve (stop solenoid) at the fuel injection pump - refer to Chapter 4C for details.

**7** Turn the engine using the starter motor until the oil pressure warning light goes out.

**8** If the light fails to extinguish after several seconds of cranking, check the engine oil level and that the oil filter is secure. Assuming these are correct, check the security of the oil pressure switch wiring - do not progress any further until you are satisfied that oil is being pumped around the engine at sufficient pressure.

**9** Reconnect the fuel cut-off valve wiring.

### All models

**10** Start the engine, but be aware that as fuel system components have been disturbed, the cranking time may be a little longer than usual

**11** While the engine is idling, check for fuel, water and oil leaks. Don't be alarmed if there are some odd smells and the occasional plume of smoke as components heat up and burn off oil deposits.

**12** The hydraulic tappets may initially run noisily, but the engine should quieten down after a few seconds' running.

**13** Assuming all is well, keep the engine idling until hot water is felt circulating through the top hose.

**14** On diesel models, check the fuel injection pump timing and engine idle speed, as described in Chapter 4C and/or Chapter 1B.

**15** After a few minutes, recheck the oil and coolant levels, and top-up as necessary.

**16** On all the engines described in this Chapter, there is no need to re-tighten the cylinder head bolts once the engine has been run following reassembly.

**17** If new pistons, rings or crankshaft bearings have been fitted, the engine must be treated as new, and run-in for the first 600 miles (1000 km). *Do not* operate the engine at full-throttle, or allow it to labour at low engine speeds in any gear. It is recommended that the engine oil and filter are changed at the end of this period.

# Chapter 3
# Cooling, heating and ventilation systems

## Contents



## Degrees of difficulty

**Easy,** suitable for novice with little experience 

**Fairly easy,** suitable for beginner with some experience 

**Fairly difficult,** suitable for competent DIY mechanic 

**Difficult,** suitable for experienced DIY mechanic

**Very difficult,** suitable for expert DIY or professional 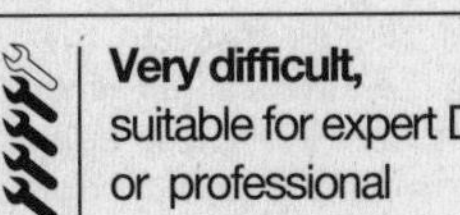

## Specifications

### General

| | |
|---|---|
| Expansion tank cap opening pressure | 1.4 to 1.6 bars |

### Thermostat

| | |
|---|---|
| Opening temperatures: | |
| Petrol engine models: | |
| Starts to open | 84°C |
| Fully open | 98°C |
| Diesel engine models: | |
| Starts to open | 85°C |
| Fully open | 105°C |

### Electric cooling fan(s)

| | |
|---|---|
| Cooling fan(s) cut in: | |
| Stage 1 speed: | |
| Switches on | 92 to 97°C |
| Switches off | 84 to 91°C |
| Stage 2 speed: | |
| Switches on | 99 to 105°C |
| Switches off | 91 to 98°C |

| Torque wrench settings | Nm | lbf ft |
|---|---|---|
| Coolant elbow to cylinder head (diesel engine models) | 10 | 7 |
| Coolant pump bracket bolts (diesel engine models) | 25 | 18 |
| Coolant pump mounting bolts: | | |
| Diesel engine models | 10 | 7 |
| Petrol engine models | 20 | 15 |
| Coolant pump pulley bolts (diesel engine models only) | 25 | 18 |
| Radiator cooling fan bracket bolts | 10 | 7 |
| Radiator cooling fan retaining nuts | 10 | 7 |
| Radiator cooling fan thermostatic switch | 35 | 26 |
| Radiator mounting bolts | 10 | 7 |
| Thermostat cover bolts (diesel engine models) | 10 | 7 |
| Thermostat housing bolts (petrol engine models) | 10 | 7 |

## 1 General information and precautions

### General information

The cooling system is of pressurised type, comprising a pump, an aluminium crossflow radiator, an electric cooling fan, and a thermostat. The system functions as follows. Cold coolant from the radiator passes through the hose to the coolant pump, where it is pumped around the cylinder block and head passages. After cooling the cylinder bores, combustion surfaces and valve seats, the coolant reaches the underside of the thermostat, which is initially closed. The coolant passes through the heater and is returned through the cylinder block to the coolant pump.

When the engine is cold, the coolant circulates only through the cylinder block, cylinder head, expansion tank and heater. When the coolant reaches a predetermined temperature, the thermostat opens and the coolant passes through to the radiator. As the coolant circulates through the radiator it is cooled by the inrush of air when the car is in forward motion. Airflow is supplemented by the action of the electric cooling fan when necessary. Upon reaching the radiator, the coolant is now cooled and the cycle is repeated.

On petrol engine models, the coolant pump is driven by the timing belt, while on diesel engine models, the pump is mounted externally, and is driven by the auxiliary drivebelt.

Coolant temperature information for the gauge mounted in the instrument panel, and for the fuel system, is provided by a single temperature sensor, mounted in the thermostat housing on petrol engine models, and in the coolant outlet elbow on the front of the cylinder head on diesel engine models. A coolant level switch is fitted to the expansion tank.

The electric cooling fan mounted on the rear of the radiator is controlled by a thermostatic switch. At a preset coolant temperature, the switch actuates the fan.

Refer to Section 11 for information on the air conditioning system.

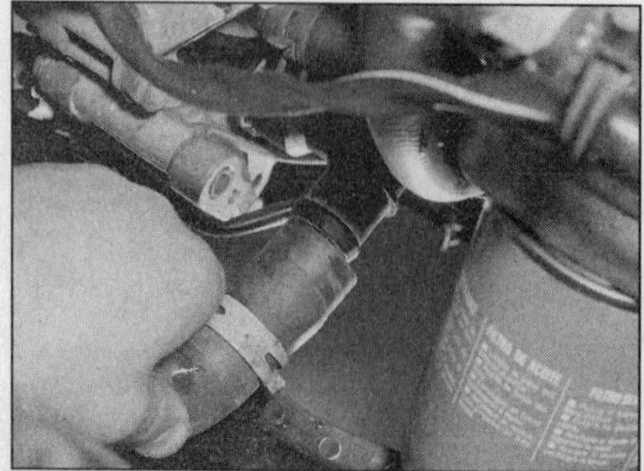

**2.3 Disconnecting the bottom hose from the thermostat housing (diesel engine model)**

### Precautions

***Warning: Do not attempt to remove the expansion tank filler cap or disturb any part of the cooling system while the engine is hot, as there is a high risk of scalding. If the expansion tank filler cap must be removed before the engine and radiator have fully cooled (even though this is NOT recommended) the pressure in the cooling system must first be relieved. Cover the cap with a thick layer of cloth, to avoid scalding, and slowly unscrew the filler cap until a hissing sound can be heard. When the hissing has stopped, indicating that the pressure has reduced, slowly unscrew the filler cap until it can be removed; if more hissing sounds are heard, wait until they have stopped before unscrewing the cap completely. At all times keep well away from the filler cap opening. Be aware that, in certain circumstances, removing the filler cap with the system hot can result in a sudden rush of hot coolant (not just steam) emerging from the system.***

***Do not allow antifreeze to come into contact with skin or painted surfaces of the vehicle. Rinse off spills immediately with plenty of water. Never leave antifreeze lying around in an open container or in a puddle in the driveway or on the garage floor. Children and pets are attracted by its sweet smell. Antifreeze can be fatal if ingested.***

***If the engine is hot, the electric cooling fan may start rotating even if the engine is not running, so be careful to keep hands, hair and loose clothing well clear when working in the engine compartment.***

***Refer to Section 11 for precautions to be observed when working on models with air conditioning.***

## 2 Cooling system hoses - disconnection and renewal

**Note:** *Refer to the warnings given in Section 1 of this Chapter before proceeding.*

**1** If the checks described in Chapter 1 reveal a faulty hose, it must be renewed as follows.

**2** First drain the cooling system (see Chapter 1). If the coolant is not due for renewal, it may be re-used if it is collected in a clean container.

**3** To disconnect a hose, release its retaining clips, then move them along the hose, clear of the relevant inlet/outlet union. Carefully work the hose free **(see illustration)**. While the hoses can be removed with relative ease when new or hot, **do not** attempt to disconnect any part of the system while it is still hot.

**4** Note that the radiator inlet and outlet unions are fragile; do not use excessive force when attempting to remove the hoses. If a hose proves to be difficult to remove, try to release it by rotating the hose ends before attempting to free it.

***If all else fails, cut the hose with a sharp knife, then slit it so that it can be peeled off in two pieces. Although this may prove expensive if the hose is otherwise undamaged, it is preferable to buying a new radiator.***

**5** When fitting a hose, first slide the clips onto the hose, then work the hose into position. If clamp type clips were originally fitted, it is a good idea to replace them with screw type clips when refitting the hose. If the hose is stiff, use a little soapy water as a lubricant, or soften the hose by soaking it in hot water.

**6** Work the hose into position, checking that it is correctly routed, then slide each clip along the hose until it passes over the flared end of the relevant inlet/outlet union, before securing it in position with the retaining clip. If spring-type clips are used to secure the cooling system hoses, note that these can lose their ability to seal the hose ends and prevent leaks over time. It is common practice to replace spring-type clips with the more commonly used worm-drive clips when replacing a coolant hose.

**7** Refill the cooling system (see Chapter 1).

**8** Check thoroughly for leaks as soon as possible after disturbing any part of the cooling system.

## 3 Radiator - removal, inspection and refitting

***If leakage is the reason for wanting to remove the radiator, bear in mind that minor leaks can often be cured using a radiator sealant which is added to the coolant with the radiator in situ.***

### Removal

**1** Disconnect the battery negative lead. **Note:** *If the vehicle has a security-coded radio, check that you have a copy of the code number before disconnecting the battery. Refer to your VW dealer if in doubt.*

**3.4 Disconnecting the radiator top hose**

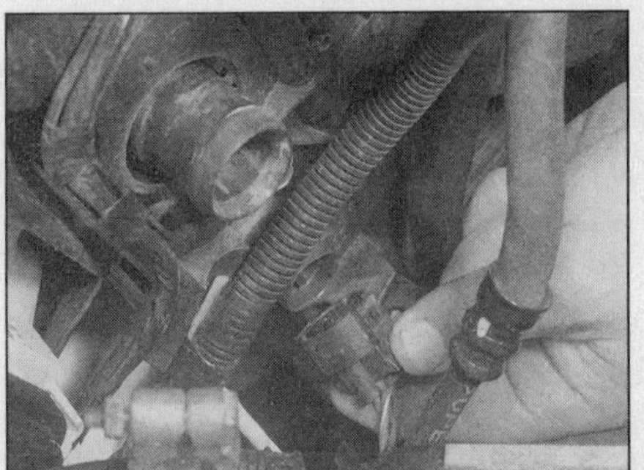
3.5 Disconnecting the radiator cooling fan switch wiring plug

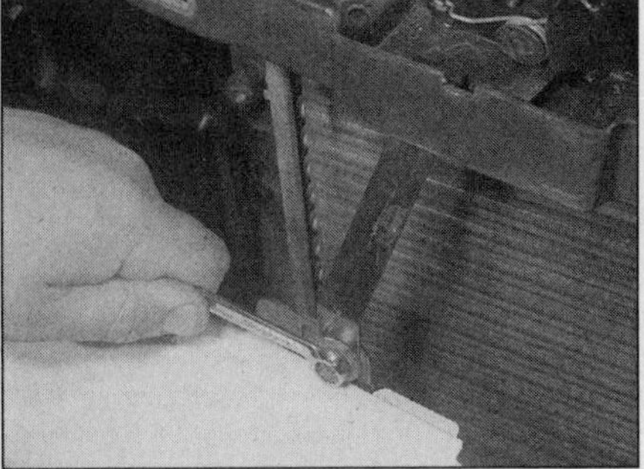
3.6a Remove the bonnet lock support arm securing bolt . . .

3.6b . . . then unhook the arm from the lock carrier, and remove it

2 Drain the cooling system (see Chapter 1).
3 Remove the radiator grille as described in Chapter 11.
4 Release the retaining clips and disconnect the coolant hoses from the radiator **(see illustration)**.
5 Disconnect the wiring connector from the cooling fan switch on the left-hand end of the radiator **(see illustration)**.
6 Unbolt and remove the support arm for the bonnet lock **(see illustrations)**.
7 On models equipped with air conditioning, in order to gain the clearance required to remove the radiator carry out the following. Referring to Chapter 11, remove the front bumper and lower skirt where necessary for access to the condenser lower mounting bolts. Release the refrigerant lines from all the relevant retaining clips, then undo the retaining bolts and move the condenser forwards as far as possible, taking great care not to place any excess strain on the refrigerant lines. **Do not** disconnect the refrigerant lines from the condenser (refer to the warnings given in Section 11). Once the radiator has been removed, secure or support the condenser so that the refrigerant lines are not under strain.
8 On all models, slacken and remove the four retaining bolts from the rear of the radiator, then manoeuvre the radiator out from the front of the vehicle **(see illustrations)**.

### *Inspection*

9 If the radiator has been removed due to suspected blockage, reverse-flush it as described in Chapter 1. Clean dirt and debris from the radiator fins, using an air line (in which case, wear eye protection) or a soft brush. Be careful, as the fins are sharp and easily damaged.
10 If necessary, a radiator specialist can perform a flow test on the radiator, to establish whether an internal blockage exists.
11 A leaking radiator must be referred to a specialist for permanent repair. Do not attempt to weld or solder a leaking radiator, as damage may result.
12 In an emergency, minor leaks from the radiator can be cured using a suitable radiator

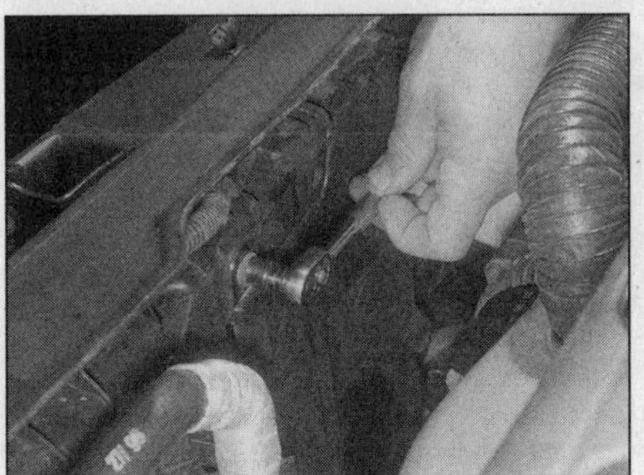
3.8a Loosen and remove the radiator retaining bolts . . .

3.8b . . . then withdraw the radiator from the front

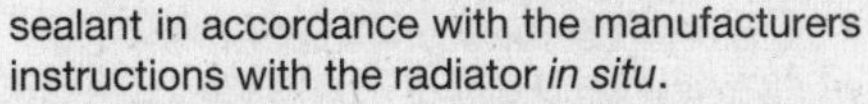
sealant in accordance with the manufacturers instructions with the radiator *in situ*.
13 If the radiator is to be sent for repair or renewed, remove the cooling fan switch from its left-hand end.

### *Refitting*

14 Manoeuvre the radiator into position and refit its retaining bolts, tightening them to the specified torque setting.
15 On models with air conditioning, seat the condenser in position and securely tighten its retaining bolts. Refit the front bumper and skirt (where removed), and ensure that all refrigerant lines are retained by all the relevant clips.
16 The remainder of refitting is a reversal of removal. On completion, refer to Chapter 1 and refill the cooling system.

## 4 Thermostat - removal, testing and refitting

### *Removal*



1 Disconnect the battery negative lead. **Note:** *If the vehicle has a security-coded radio, check that you have a copy of the code number before disconnecting the battery. Refer to your VW dealer if in doubt.*
2 Drain the cooling system (see Chapter 1).

### Petrol engine models

3 On these models, the thermostat housing is on the left-hand end of the cylinder head.
4 Release the retaining clip and disconnect the coolant hose from the thermostat housing **(see illustrations)**.

4.4a Using a suitable pair of pliers, compress and release the hose clip . . .

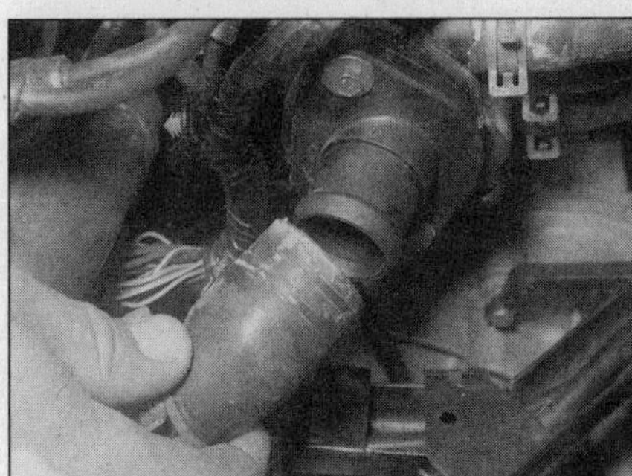
4.4b . . . and disconnect the hose from the thermostat housing

4.5a Loosen and remove the thermostat cover bolts . . .

4.5b . . . and carefully remove the thermostat cover

4.6a Withdraw the thermostat from the housing

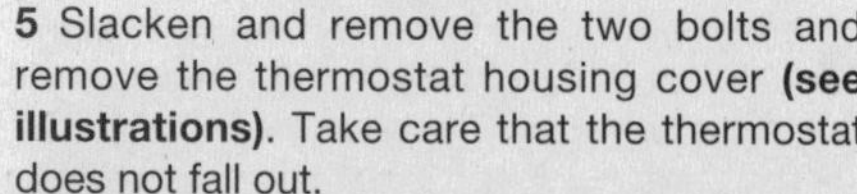

5 Slacken and remove the two bolts and remove the thermostat housing cover **(see illustrations)**. Take care that the thermostat does not fall out.

6 Recover the sealing ring and withdraw the thermostat, noting its fitted position. The thermostat is unusual in that the operating unit can be separated from the spring housing - note which way round it is fitted **(see illustrations)**. The thermostat appears only to be available as an assembled unit, however. Discard the sealing ring; a new one should be used on refitting.

### Diesel engine models

7 On these models, the thermostat is in the base of the coolant pump housing which is on the front, right-hand end of the engine.

8 Release the retaining clip and disconnect the coolant hose from the thermostat cover.

9 Slacken and remove the two retaining bolts and remove the thermostat cover from the coolant pump housing **(see illustration)**.

10 Recover the sealing ring and withdraw the thermostat, noting its fitted position. Discard the sealing ring; a new one should be used on refitting.

## *Testing*

11 A rough test of the thermostat may be made by suspending it with a piece of string in a container full of water. Heat the water to bring it to the boil - the thermostat must open by the time the water boils. If not, renew it.

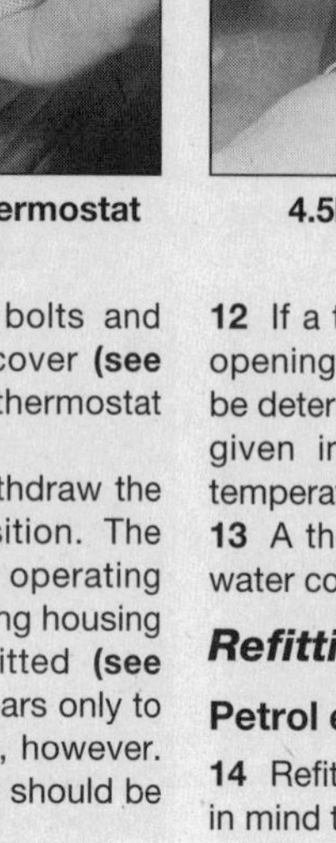

12 If a thermometer is available, the precise opening temperature of the thermostat may be determined, and compared with the figures given in the Specifications. The opening temperature is also marked on the thermostat.

13 A thermostat which fails to close as the water cools must also be renewed.

## *Refitting*

### Petrol engine models

14 Refitting is a reversal of removal, bearing in mind the following points:

a) *Ensure that the thermostat is correctly located in the housing. On early models with engine codes ADX, AEA or AEV, the thermostat bridge support locates in a recess in the cover* ***(see illustration)****.*

b) *Fit a new sealing ring, then fit the thermostat cover and tighten the bolts securely.*

c) *On completion refill the cooling system as described in Chapter 1A.*

### Diesel engine models

15 Refitting is the reverse of the removal sequence, noting the following points:

a) *Ensure that the thermostat is correctly located in the housing, and fit the new sealing ring.*

b) *Tighten the cover bolts to the specified torque setting.*

c) *On completion refill the cooling system as described in Chapter 1B.*

## 5 Electric cooling fan - testing, removal and refitting

## *Testing*

1 The cooling fan is supplied with current through the ignition switch, cooling fan control unit (mounted on the left-hand inner wing), the relay(s) and fuses/fusible link (see Chapter 12). The circuit is completed by the cooling fan thermostatic switch, which is mounted in the left-hand end of the radiator. The cooling fan has two speed settings; the thermostatic switch actually contains two switches, one for the stage 1 fan speed setting and another for the stage 2 fan speed setting. Testing of the cooling fan circuit is as follows, noting that the following check should be carried out on both the stage 1 speed circuit and stage 2 speed circuit (refer to the wiring diagrams at the end of Chapter 12).

2 If the fan does not appear to work, first check the fuses/fusible links. If they are good, run the engine until normal operating temperature is reached, then allow it to idle. If the fan does not cut in within a few minutes, or before the temperature gauge approaches the 110 mark or the red end of the scale, switch off the ignition and disconnect the wiring plug from the cooling fan switch. Bridge the relevant two contacts in the wiring plug using a length of spare wire, and switch

4.6b The thermostat can be separated from its spring housing

4.9 Thermostat cover and retaining bolts (arrowed) seen from below - diesel engine models

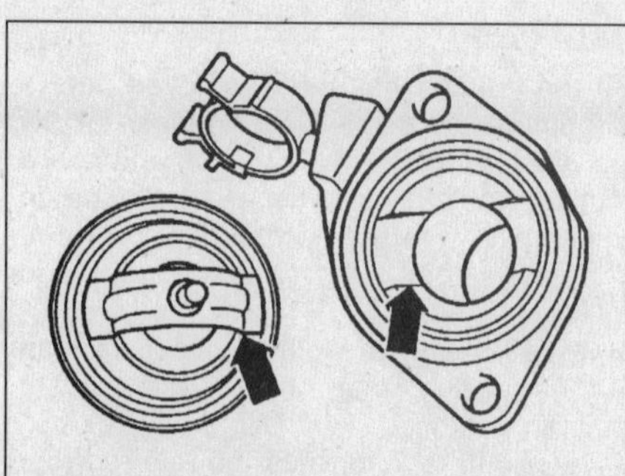

4.14 Thermostat installation details - engine codes ADX, AEA and AEV

*Thermostat bridge support locates in recess in thermostat cover (arrowed)*

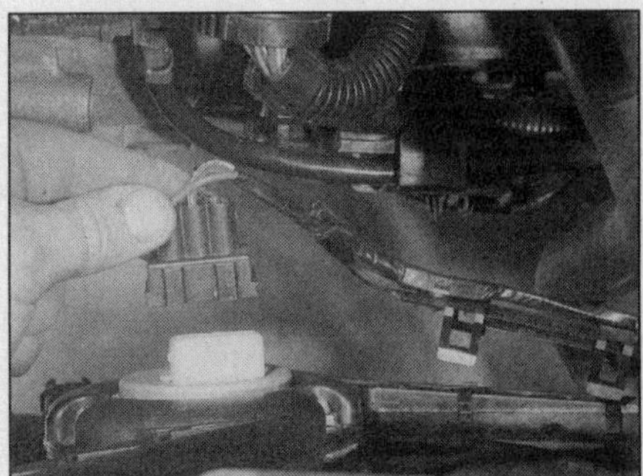

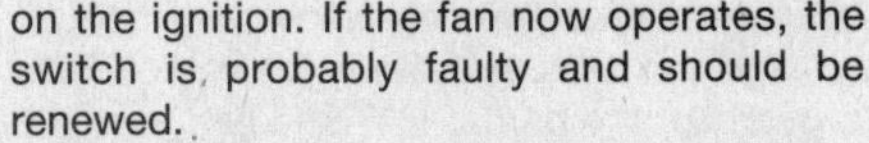
**5.5 Disconnect the cooling fan motor wiring connector**

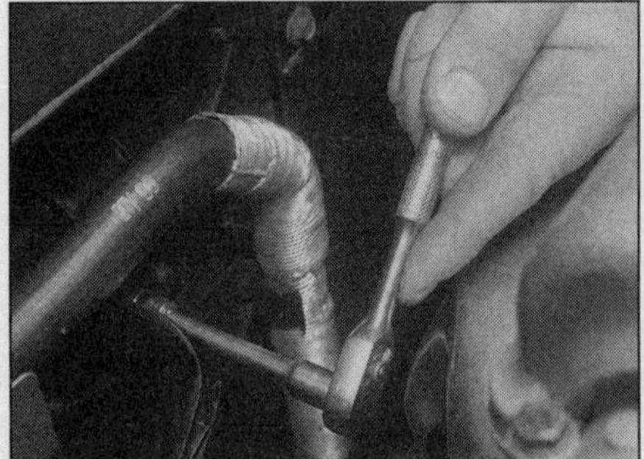
**5.6a Unscrew the mounting nuts . . .**

**5.6b . . . then remove the fan motor and its mounting bracket from the rear of the radiator**

on the ignition. If the fan now operates, the switch is probably faulty and should be renewed.

**3** If the switch appears to work, the motor can be checked by disconnecting the motor wiring connector and connecting a 12 volt supply directly to the motor terminals. If the motor is faulty, it must be renewed, as no spares are available.

**4** If the fan still fails to operate, check the cooling fan circuit wiring (Chapter 12). Check each wire for continuity, and ensure all connections are clean and free of corrosion.

### *Removal*

**5** Disconnect the wiring connector from the cooling fan motor, and unclip the wiring harness from the fan mounting bracket **(see illustration)**.

**6** Unscrew and remove the three nuts securing the cooling fan motor mounting bracket, and remove the cooling fan assembly to the rear **(see illustrations)**. No spare parts are available for the motor, and if the unit is faulty, it must be renewed.

### *Refitting*

**7** Refitting is a reversal of removal, tightening the cooling fan retaining nuts to the specified torque.

**8** Start the engine and run it until it reaches normal operating temperature. Continue to run the engine and check that the cooling fan cuts in and functions correctly.

## 6 Cooling system electrical switches - testing, removal and refitting

### *Radiator cooling fan thermostatic switch*

#### Testing

**1** Testing of the switch is described in Section 5, as part of the electric cooling fan test procedure.

#### Removal

**2** The switch is located in the left-hand side of the radiator. The engine and radiator should be cold before removing the switch.

**3** Disconnect the battery negative lead. **Note:** *If the vehicle has a security-coded radio, check that you have a copy of the code number before disconnecting the battery. Refer to your VW dealer if in doubt.*

**4** Either drain the cooling system to below the level of the switch (as described in Chapter 1), or have ready a suitable plug which can be used to plug the switch aperture in the radiator whilst the switch is removed. If a plug is used, take great care not to damage the radiator, and do not use anything which will allow foreign matter to enter the radiator.

**5** Disconnect the wiring plug from the switch.

**6** Carefully unscrew the switch from the radiator.

#### Refitting

**7** Refitting is a reversal of removal, applying a smear of suitable sealant to the threads of the switch and tightening it to the specified torque setting. On completion, refill the cooling system as described in Chapter 1, or top-up as described in *Weekly checks*.

**8** Start the engine and run it until it reaches normal operating temperature, then continue to run the engine and check that the cooling fan cuts in and functions correctly.

### *Coolant temperature gauge sensor*

#### Testing

**9** The coolant temperature gauge, mounted in the instrument panel, is fed with a stabilised voltage supply from the instrument panel feed (through the ignition switch and a fuse), and its earth is controlled by the sensor.

**10** The sensor unit is clipped into the base of the thermostat housing on petrol engine models, and is clipped into the coolant outlet elbow on the front of the cylinder head on diesel engine models **(see illustrations)**. The sensor contains a thermistor, which consists of an electronic component whose electrical resistance decreases at a predetermined rate as its temperature rises. When the coolant is cold, the sensor resistance is high, current flow through the gauge is reduced, and the gauge needle points towards the cold end of the scale. If the sensor is faulty, it must be renewed.

**11** If the gauge develops a fault, first check the other instruments; if they do not work at all, check the instrument panel electrical feed. If the readings are erratic, there may be a fault in the instrument panel assembly. If the fault lies in the temperature gauge alone, check it as follows.

**12** If the gauge needle remains at the cold end of the scale, disconnect the wiring connector from the sensor unit, and earth the temperature gauge wire (see Wiring diagrams for details) to the cylinder head. If the needle then deflects when the ignition is switched on, the sensor unit is proved faulty, and should be renewed. If the needle still does not move, remove the instrument panel (Chapter 12) and check the continuity of the wiring between the sensor unit and the gauge, and the feed to the gauge unit. If continuity is shown, and the fault still exists, then the gauge is faulty and should be renewed.

**6.10a Coolant temperature sensor (arrowed) - petrol engine models**

**6.10b Coolant temperature sensor (arrowed) - diesel engine models**

6.22 Disconnect the wiring plug from the coolant level sensor

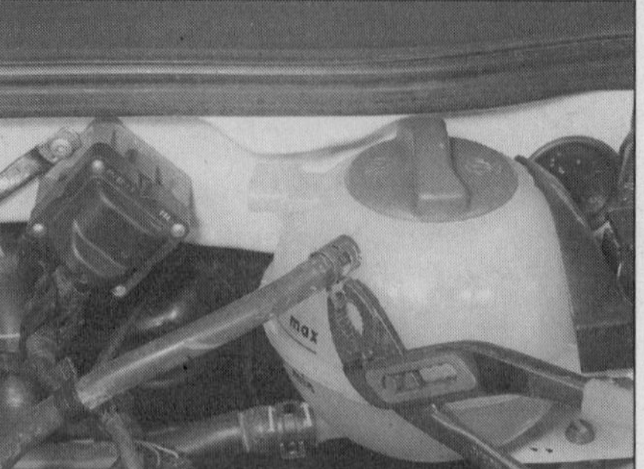
6.23 Release the securing clips using a suitable pair of pliers, then disconnect the expansion tank hoses

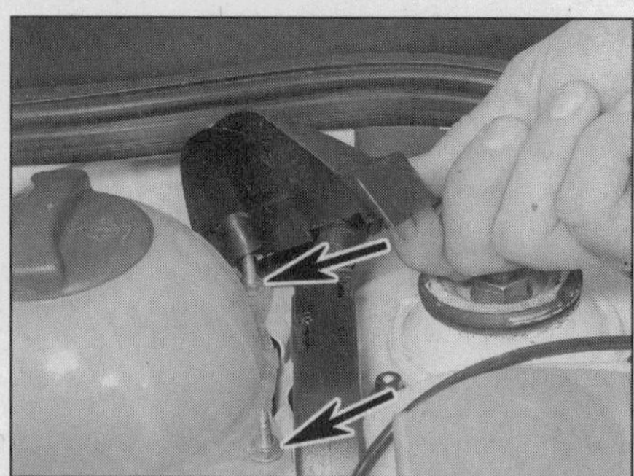
6.24 Unclip the plastic cover next to the expansion tank, for access to the mounting nuts (arrowed)

**13** If the gauge needle remains at the hot end of the scale, disconnect the sensor wire. If the needle then returns to the cold end of the scale when the ignition is switched on, the sensor unit is proved faulty and should be renewed. If the needle still does not move, check the remainder of the circuit as described previously.

### Removal

**14** Either partially drain the cooling system to just below the level of the sensor (as described in Chapter 1), or have ready a suitable plug which can be used to plug the sensor aperture whilst it is removed. If a plug is used, take great care not to damage the sensor unit aperture, and do not use anything which will allow foreign matter to enter the cooling system.
**15** Disconnect the battery negative lead - refer to the note in paragraph 3.
**16** Disconnect the wiring from the sensor.
**17** Depress the sensor unit and slide out its retaining clip. Withdraw the sensor from the coolant elbow and recover its sealing ring.

### Refitting

**18** Fit a new sealing ring to the sensor unit. Push the sensor fully into position and secure it in place with the retaining clip.
**19** Reconnect the wiring connector, then refill the cooling system as described in Chapter 1 or top-up as described in *Weekly checks*.

## *Fuel system coolant temperature sensor*

**20** On all models, the sensor is combined with the coolant temperature gauge sensor (see above). Testing of the sensor should be entrusted to a VW dealer.

## *Coolant level switch*

**21** The switch is incorporated into the expansion tank, and cannot be renewed separately.
**22** To remove the expansion tank, disconnect the wiring plug for the level switch at the top of the tank **(see illustration)**.
**23** Either drain the cooling system as described in Chapter 1, or use pipe clamps to seal off the coolant hoses to the tank, before disconnecting them **(see illustration)**.
**24** Pull off the plastic cover **(see illustration)**, then remove the two mounting nuts and lift the tank away, noting the locating lug on its base.
**25** Refitting is a reversal of removal.

# 7 Coolant pump - removal and refitting

## *Removal*

### Petrol engine models

**1** Drain the cooling system as described in Chapter 1A.
**2** Remove the timing belt as described in Chapter 2A.
**3** Unscrew the two bolts securing the coolant pump and its timing belt guard, and withdraw the coolant pump and guard from the cylinder block **(see illustrations)**.
**4** Discard the sealing ring - a new one should be used on refitting. Note it is not possible to overhaul the pump. If it is faulty, the unit must be renewed.

### Diesel engine models

**Note:** *New coolant pump/thermostat housing bracket retaining studs/bolts will be required on refitting.*
**5** Drain the cooling system as described in Chapter 1B.
**6** Remove the alternator as described in Chapter 5A.
**7** On models equipped with power steering, remove the power steering pump as described in Chapter 10.
**8** On models equipped with air conditioning, unbolt the compressor from its mounting bracket and position it clear of the engine. **Note:** *Do not disconnect the refrigerant lines from the compressor (see Warnings in Section 11).*
**9** Slacken and remove the retaining bolts, and remove the pulley from the coolant pump.
**10** Release the retaining clips and disconnect the coolant hoses from the back of the coolant pump housing and the thermostat housing.
**11** Unscrew the retaining studs/bolts (as applicable) securing the coolant pump mounting bracket to the block and remove the bracket from the engine **(see illustration)**. **Note:** *On some engines it will be necessary to unscrew the bolt(s) that secure the timing belt cover to the bracket.* Recover the sealing ring which is fitted between the bracket and block and discard it; a new one should be used on refitting.

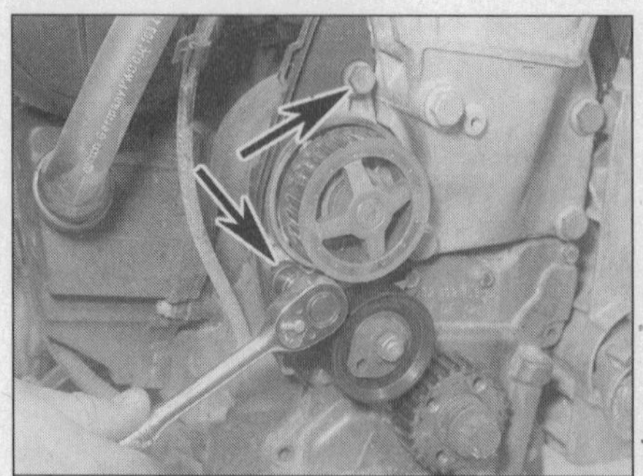
7.3a Remove the two bolts (arrowed) . . .

7.3b . . . and remove the timing belt plastic guard . . .

7.3c . . . and the coolant pump

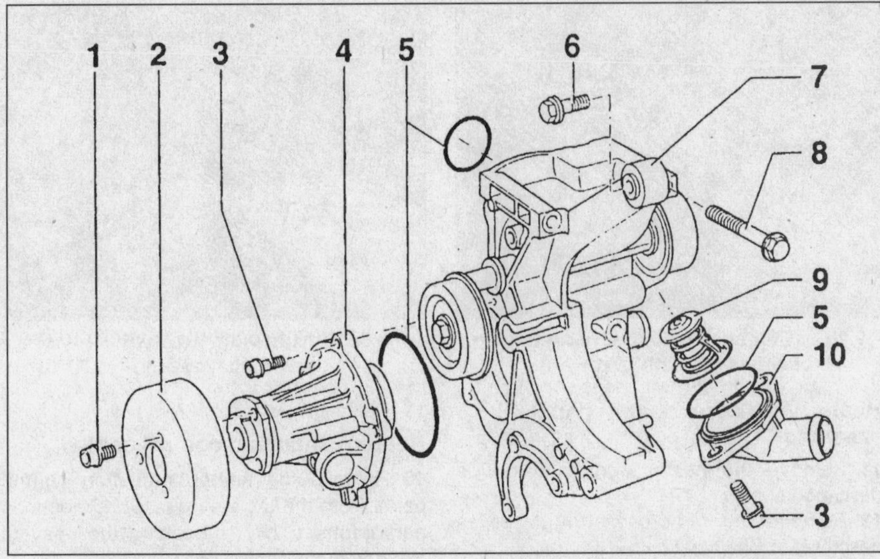


**7.11 Coolant pump, thermostat housing and mounting bracket - diesel engine models**

1 *Pulley bolts*
2 *Auxiliary drivebelt pulley*
3 *Coolant pump mounting (and thermostat cover) bolts*
4 *Coolant pump*
5 *O-ring*
6 *Bolt*
7 *Mounting bracket*
8 *Mounting bracket bolt*
9 *Thermostat*
10 *Thermostat cover*

**12** With the assembly on a bench, unscrew the retaining bolts and remove the pump from the bracket. Discard the O-ring - a new one must be used on refitting. Note it is not possible to overhaul the pump. If it is faulty, the unit must be renewed.

## *Refitting*

### Petrol engine models

**13** Fit a new sealing ring to the rear of the pump **(see illustration)**, then locate the pump in the cylinder block.

**14** Fit the timing belt guard in place, then insert the guard/pump mounting bolts and tighten them to the specified torque.

**15** Refit and tension the timing belt as described in Chapter 2A.

**16** On completion, refill the cooling system as described in Chapter 1A.

### Diesel engine models

**17** Ensure that the pump and bracket mating surfaces are clean and dry.

**18** Fit the coolant pump to the bracket, using a new O-ring, and evenly tighten its retaining bolts to the specified torque setting.

**19** Fit the new sealing ring to the housing assembly recess, and refit the housing to the cylinder block. Fit the retaining bolts and tighten them to the specified torque in the sequence shown **(see illustration)**.

**20** Connect the coolant hoses to the housing and securely tighten their retaining clips.

**21** Refit the pulley to the coolant pump and tighten its retaining bolts to the specified torque setting (this can be done once the drivebelt is refitted and tensioned).

**22** Where necessary, refit the power steering pump as described in Chapter 10 and the air conditioning compressor.

**23** Refit the alternator as described in Chapter 5A.

**24** On completion refill the cooling system as described in Chapter 1B.

**7.13 Fit a new O-ring to the coolant pump**

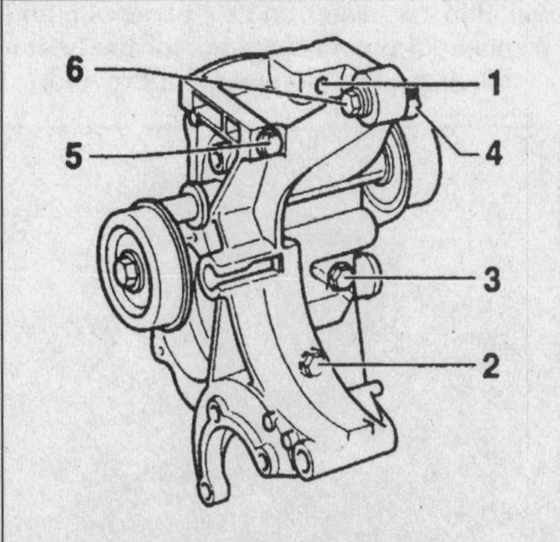


**7.19 Coolant pump mounting bracket bolt tightening sequence**

## 8 Heating and ventilation system - general information

**1** The heating/ventilation system consists of a four-speed blower motor (housed in the passenger compartment), face-level vents in the centre and at each end of the facia, and air ducts to the front and rear footwells.

**2** The control unit is located in the facia, and the controls operate flap valves to deflect and mix the air flowing through the various parts of the heating/ventilation system. The flap valves are contained in the air distribution housing, which acts as a central distribution unit, passing air to the various ducts and vents.

**3** Cold air enters the system through the grille at the rear of the engine compartment. A pollen filter is fitted to the ventilation inlet to filter out dust, soot, pollen and spores from the air entering the vehicle.

**4** The airflow, which can be boosted by the blower, then flows through the various ducts, according to the settings of the controls. Stale air is expelled through ducts at the rear of the car. If warm air is required, the cold air is passed through the heater matrix, which is supplied with coolant from the engine cooling system.

**5** If necessary, the outside air supply can be closed off, allowing the air inside the vehicle to be recirculated. This can be useful to prevent unpleasant odours entering from outside the vehicle, but should only be used briefly, as the recirculated air inside the vehicle will soon deteriorate.

**6** Models for certain export markets may be fitted with heated front seats. The heat is produced by electrically-heated mats in the seat and backrest cushions (see Chapter 12). The temperature is regulated automatically by a thermostat, and cannot be adjusted.

3

## 9 Heater/ventilation components - removal and refitting

## *Models without air conditioning*

### Heater/ventilation control panel

**1** Disconnect the battery negative lead. **Note:** *If the vehicle has a security-coded radio, check that you have a copy of the code number before disconnecting the battery. Refer to your VW dealer if in doubt.*

**2** Carefully unclip the surround from the heater controls, and remove the four heater control panel retaining screws beneath **(see illustrations)**.

**3** Remove the retaining screws, then pull out the switch panel/shelf below the heater control panel **(see illustrations)**. There is no need to disconnect the wiring from the switches.

**4** Pull the heater control panel forwards out of the facia panel **(see illustration)**.

**9.2a Unclip the heater control surround . . .**

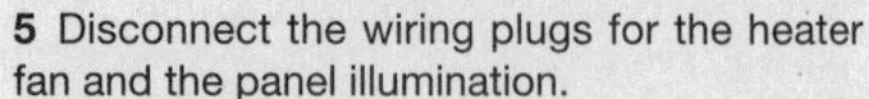

5 Disconnect the wiring plugs for the heater fan and the panel illumination.

6 Note the fitted locations of the heater control cables, attaching labels to identify them if necessary. The cables are colour-coded, to aid identification.

7 Release the retaining clips and disconnect each outer cable from the panel, and each inner cable from its operating lever **(see illustration)**. Remove the control panel from the facia.

8 If required, the panel illumination bulb can be renewed by unclipping the plastic cover behind the central control knob **(see illustrations)**.

9 The illumination bulb can then be pulled out of its holder, and renewed **(see illustration)**.

10 Refitting is a reversal of removal. Ensure that the control cables and/or the illumination bulb are operating correctly before refitting the control panel.

**9.2b . . . for access to the four retaining screws beneath (arrowed)**

## Heater/ventilation control panel surround

11 Remove the heater control panel as described above.

12 Remove the radio/cassette player as described in Chapter 12.

13 Working through the radio/cassette player aperture, press out the switch panel to the right of the central ventilation grilles.

14 Disconnect the wiring plugs from the rear of the switches, noting their fitted positions.

15 Referring to Chapter 11, loosen the fixings for the centre console, and move the console sufficiently to gain access to and remove the three screws below the ashtray.

16 Using thin-nosed pliers, pull out the ventilation grilles above the radio aperture. Remove the two screws now exposed at the top of the central vent surround, and pull the surround out from the facia.

**9.3a Unscrew the two switch panel screws (arrowed) . . .**

17 Refitting is reversal of removal.

## Heater/ventilation control cables

18 Remove the heater/ventilation control panel from the facia as described above in paragraphs 1 to 7, detaching the relevant cable from the control unit.

19 Working in the front passenger footwell, release the retaining clips and remove the cover from underneath the air distribution/blower motor housing.

20 Follow the run of the cable behind the facia, taking note of its routing, and disconnect the cable from the lever on the air distribution/blower motor housing. Note that the method of fastening is the same as that used at the control unit.

21 Fit the new cable, ensuring that it is correctly routed and free from kinks and obstructions.

**9.3b . . . and withdraw the panel from the facia**

**9.4 Pull the heater control panel out, and disconnect the wiring plugs for the heater fan and panel illumination (arrowed)**

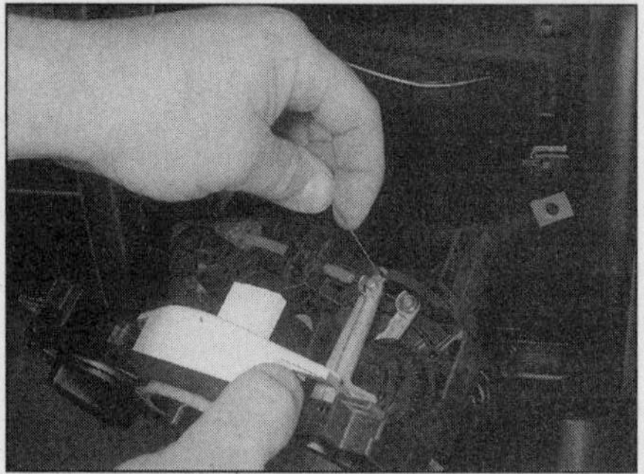

**9.7 Disconnecting a heater control cable inner from its operating lever**

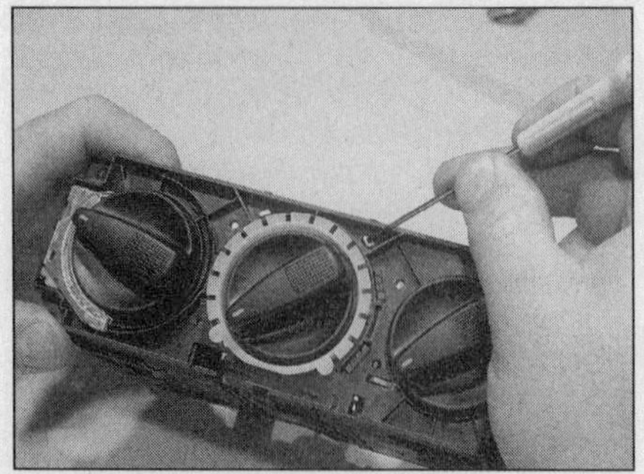

**9.8a Using a small screwdriver, release the cover retaining lugs . . .**

**9.8b . . . then remove the cover from the rear of the heater control panel**

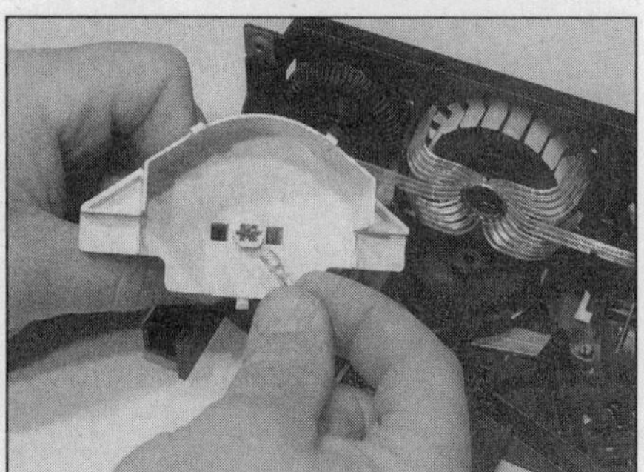

**9.9 The wedge-type bulb is simply pulled from its holder**

9.26a Using pliers, release the hose clips . . .

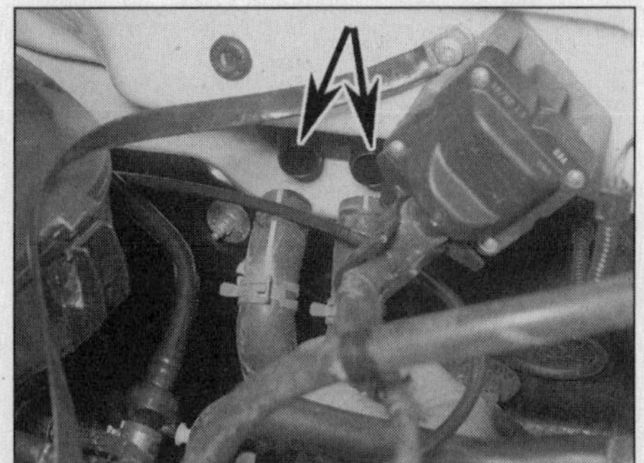
9.26b . . . and pull off the hoses from the heater matrix unions (arrowed) at the engine compartment bulkhead

9.28 Removing the footwell supply duct from the air distribution housing

**22** Connect the cable to the control unit and air distribution/blower motor housing, making sure the outer cable is clipped securely in position.

**23** Check the operation of the control knob, then refit the control panel as described previously in this Section. Finally refit the cover below the air distribution/blower motor housing.

## Heater matrix

**24** Unscrew the expansion tank cap (referring to the Warning note in Section 1) to release any pressure present in the cooling system, then securely refit the cap.

**25** Clamp both heater hoses as close to the bulkhead as possible to minimise coolant loss. Alternatively, drain the cooling system as described in Chapter 1.

**26** Release the retaining clips and disconnect both hoses from the heater matrix unions which are located in the centre of the engine compartment bulkhead **(see illustrations)**.

**27** Remove the facia panel as described in Chapter 12.

**28** Disconnect the front and rear footwell supply duct from the base of the air distribution housing **(see illustration)**.

**29** Remove the screw securing the clutch footrest to the heater housing **(see illustration)**.

**30** Disconnect the earth strap from the left-hand front door pillar **(see illustration)**.

**31** Release the wiring harness from any retaining clips securing it to the facia frame.

**32** Disconnect the wiring plugs from the air distribution housing, and those connected to the blower motor and resistor **(see illustrations)**.

**33** Slacken and remove the four nuts on the engine compartment bulkhead securing the air distribution/blower motor housing in position **(see illustration)**. **Note:** *The nuts may be hidden behind the engine compartment bulkhead sound insulation material; if the insulation material is examined closely it will be seen that access holes are provided.*

**34** From inside the vehicle, manoeuvre the air distribution/blower motor housing assembly out of position **(see illustration)**. **Note:** *Keep the matrix unions uppermost as the matrix is removed, to prevent coolant spillage. Mop up any spilt coolant immediately, and wipe the affected area with a damp cloth to prevent staining.*

**35** Recover the seal which is fitted between the matrix union and bulkhead; the seal should be renewed whenever it is disturbed.

9.29 Removing the screw securing the clutch footrest to the air distribution housing

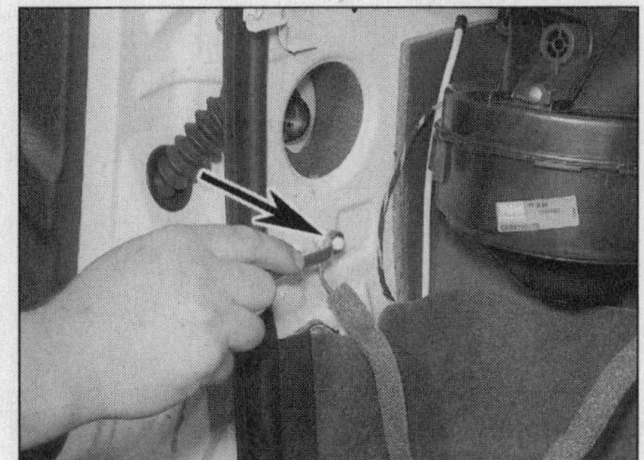
9.30 Remove the nut and disconnect the earth strap

9.32a Disconnect the wiring plugs from the air distribution housing . . .



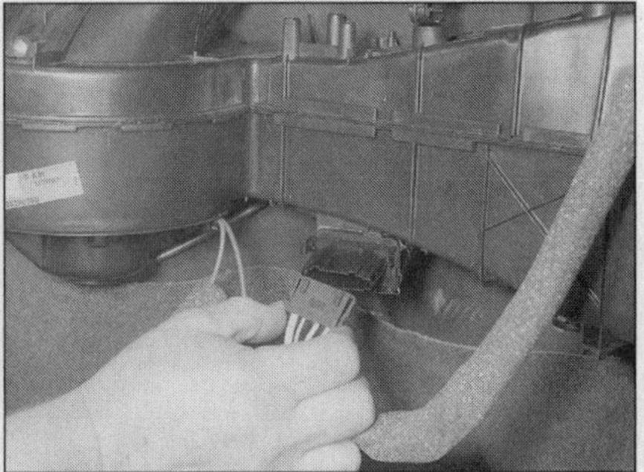
9.32b . . . and from the blower motor

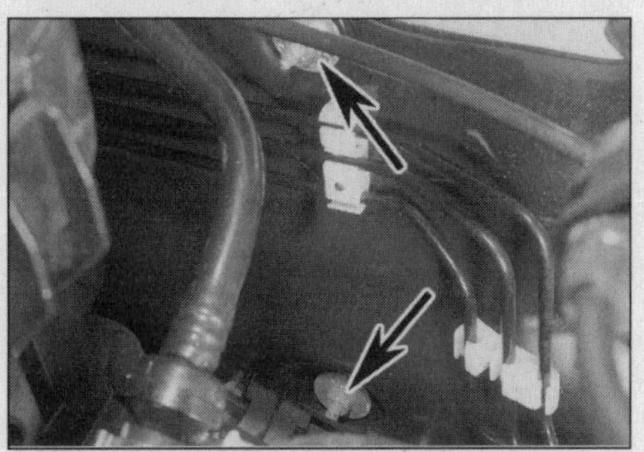
9.33 Two of the four air distribution retaining nuts (arrowed) on the engine compartment bulkhead

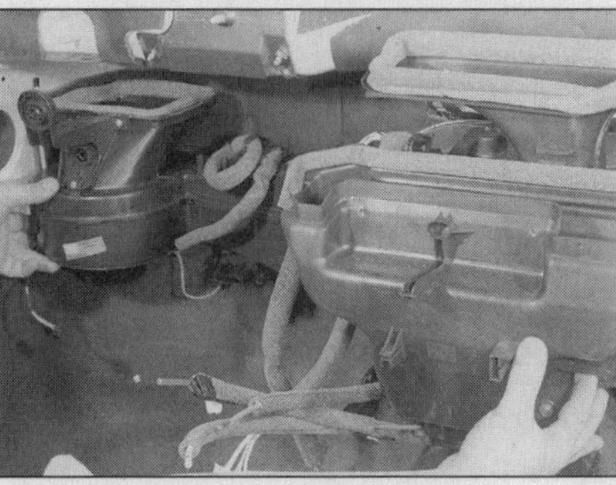
9.34 Removing the air distribution housing

9.36a Release the retaining clips . . .

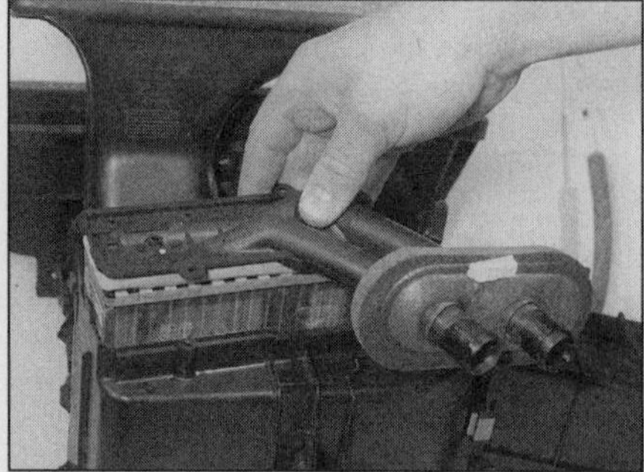

9.36b . . . and withdraw the heater matrix from the air distribution housing

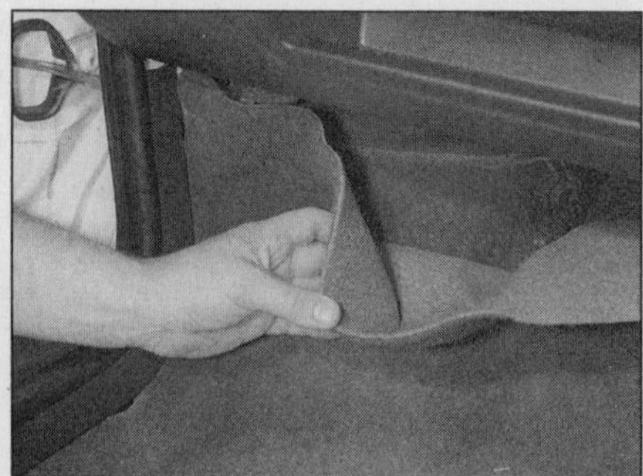

9.39a Fold back the carpet from the passenger footwell . . .

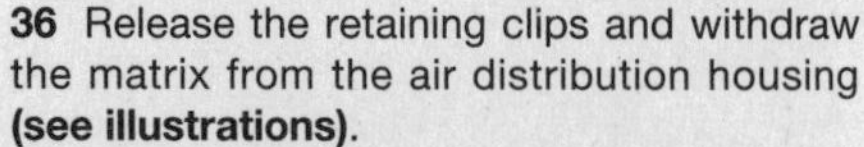

**36** Release the retaining clips and withdraw the matrix from the air distribution housing **(see illustrations)**.

**37** Refitting is a reversal of removal, bearing in mind the following points:

*a) Ensure that the matrix is clipped securely into the air distribution housing. If the clips are no longer effective, the matrix should be located with self-tapping screws. Take great care that the matrix is not punctured if screws are required to locate it.*

*b) Prior to refitting, make sure the foam seals on the top of the housings are in good condition. These foam seals should be glued in place, to form an airtight seal with no gaps. Fit a new seal to the matrix unions.*

*c) When tightening the air distribution/ blower motor housing retaining nuts, have an assistant hold the assembly fully upwards to ensure an airtight seal between the housings and bulkhead.*

*d) On completion, refill the cooling system as described in Chapter 1.*

### Heater blower motor

**38** Disconnect the battery negative lead - refer to the note in paragraph 1.

**39** Working in the front passenger footwell, release the retaining clips and fold back the carpet from the footwell. Withdraw the cover underneath the air distribution/blower motor housing **(see illustrations)**.

**40** Disconnect the motor supply wiring connector, and the earth lead from the left-hand side of the footwell **(see illustrations)**. If required, remove the passenger side glovebox as described in Chapter 11 for improved access.

**41** Twist the motor assembly to release it, and lower it out from the base of the housing **(see illustration)**.

**42** Refitting is a reversal of the removal procedure, making sure the motor is correctly clipped into the housing, and that it sits correctly in the under-dash cover.

### Heater blower motor resistor

**43** Carry out the operations described in paragraphs 29 and 30.

**44** Disconnect the wiring connectors from the resistor then release the side retaining clips and withdraw the resistor from the housing.

**45** Refitting is the reverse of removal.

## *Models with air conditioning*

### Heater control unit

**46** Refer to the information given in paragraphs 1 to 8. As the control panel is removed, the wiring plug for the air conditioning switch must also be disconnected. The switch is released from the control panel by depressing four retaining tabs.

### Heater matrix

**47** On models equipped with air conditioning, it is not possible to remove the heater matrix without opening the refrigerant circuit (see Section 11). Therefore this task must be entrusted to a VW dealer.

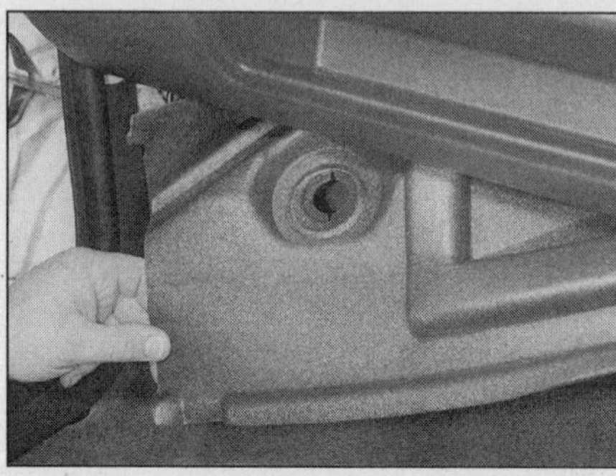

9.39b . . . and withdraw the foam cover below the blower motor

### Heater blower motor

**48** Disconnect the battery negative lead - refer to the note in paragraph 1.

**49** Referring to Chapter 11 or 12, remove the glovebox or passenger airbag unit, as applicable.

**50** Disconnect the wiring connector from the motor then undo five retaining screws and lower the motor assembly out of position.

**51** Refitting is the reverse of removal.

### Heater blower motor resistor

**52** Carry out the operations described in paragraphs 39 and 40.

**53** Disconnect the wiring connector then undo the retaining screw and remove the resistor from the housing.

**54** Refitting is the reverse of removal. The resistor should be sealed into position in the air duct, using a suitable sealant.

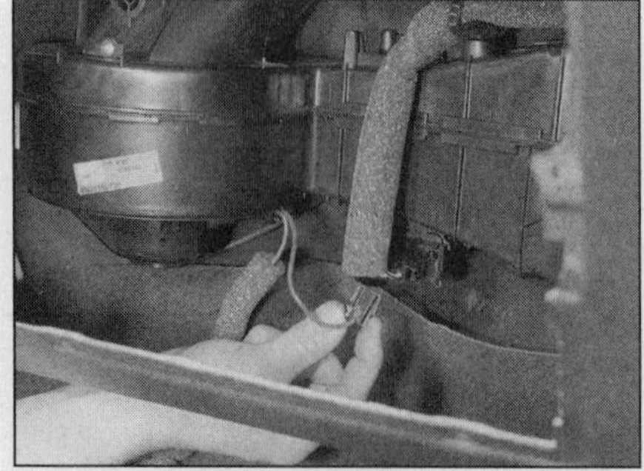

9.40a Disconnect the blower motor supply wiring plug . . .

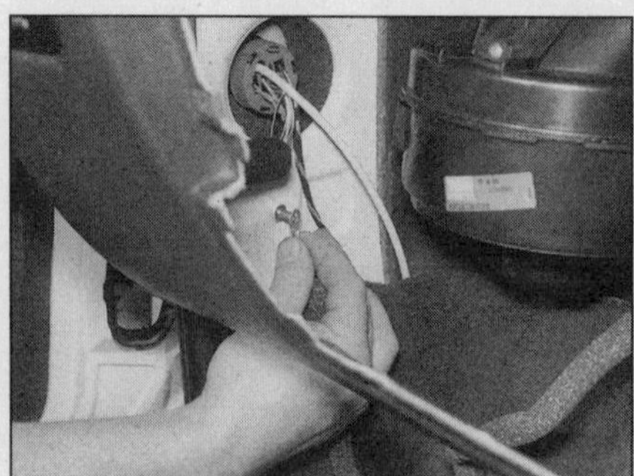

9.40b . . . and the earth lead from the left-hand side of the footwell (seen through the glovebox aperture)

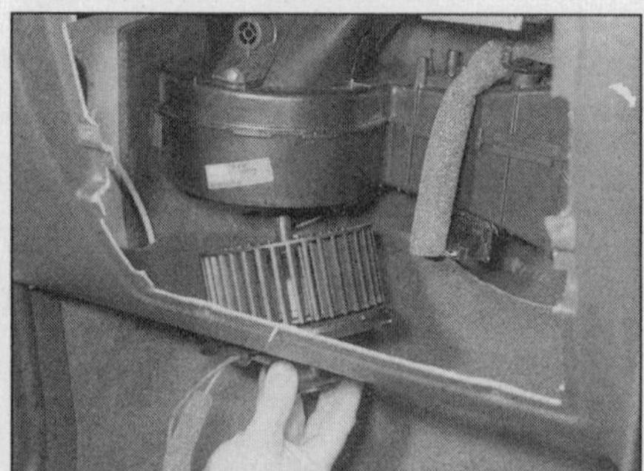

9.41 Twist the blower motor to release it, and lower it out of the housing

## 10 Heater/ventilation vents and housings - removal and refitting

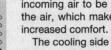

### *Driver's side facia vent housing*

**1** Remove the lighting switch as described in Chapter 12.

**2** Unclip the vent housing from the facia (two clips at the top, one at the bottom).

**3** Do not try to remove the vent grille from its housing, as it is a one-piece unit.

**4** Refitting is the reverse of removal.

### *Passenger's side facia vent housing*

**5** Unclip the vent housing from the facia (two clips at the top, one at the bottom).

**6** Do not try to remove the vent grille from its housing, as it is a one-piece unit.

**7** Refitting is the reverse of removal.

### *Central facia vent housing*

**8** The two ventilation grilles can be pulled out using thin-nosed pliers.

**9** To remove the central vent housing, refer to the procedure in Section 9, paragraphs 2 to 6.

**10** Refitting is the reverse of removal.

## 11 Air conditioning system - general information and precautions

### *General information*

An air conditioning system is available on certain models. It enables the temperature of incoming air to be lowered, and dehumidifies the air, which makes for rapid demisting and increased comfort.

The cooling side of the system works in the same way as a domestic refrigerator. Refrigerant gas is drawn into a belt-driven compressor and passes into a condenser mounted in front of the radiator, where it loses heat and becomes liquid. The liquid passes through an expansion valve to an evaporator, where it changes from liquid under high pressure to gas under low pressure. This change is accompanied by a drop in temperature, which cools the evaporator. The refrigerant returns to the compressor and the cycle begins again.

Air blown through the evaporator passes to the air distribution unit, where it is mixed with hot air blown through the heater matrix to achieve the desired temperature in the passenger compartment.

The heating side of the system works in the same way as on models without air conditioning (see Section 8).

The operation of the system is controlled electronically by coolant temperature switches (see Section 5), and pressure switches which are screwed into the compressor high-pressure line. Any problems with the system should be referred to a VW dealer.

### *Precautions*

***Warning: The refrigeration circuit contains a liquid refrigerant (Freon) and it is therefore dangerous to disconnect any part of the system without specialised knowledge and equipment. The refrigerant is potentially dangerous and should only be handled by qualified persons. If it is splashed onto the skin it can cause frostbite. It is not itself poisonous, but in the presence of a naked flame (including a cigarette) it forms a poisonous gas. Uncontrolled discharging of the refrigerant is dangerous and potentially damaging to the environment. Do not operate the air conditioning system if it is known to be short of refrigerant, as this may damage the compressor.***

When an air conditioning system is fitted, it is necessary to observe special precautions whenever dealing with any part of the system, its associated components and any items which require disconnection of the system. If for any reason the system must be disconnected, entrust this task to your VW dealer or a refrigeration engineer.

## 12 Air conditioning system components - removal and refitting

***Warning: Do not attempt to open the refrigerant circuit. Refer to the precautions given in Section 11.***

**1** The only operation which can be carried out easily without discharging the refrigerant is the renewal of the compressor drivebelt, which is covered in Chapter 1. All other operations must be referred to a VW dealer or an air conditioning specialist.

**2** If necessary the compressor can be unbolted and moved aside, without disconnecting its flexible hoses, after removing the drivebelt.

# Chapter 4 Part A:
# Fuel system - single-point petrol injection

## Contents



## Degrees of difficulty

| | | | | |
|---|---|---|---|---|
| **Easy,** suitable for novice with little experience 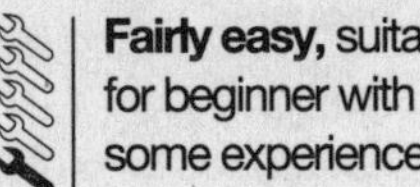 | **Fairly easy,** suitable for beginner with some experience  | **Fairly difficult,** suitable for competent DIY mechanic  | **Difficult,** suitable for experienced DIY mechanic  | **Very difficult,** suitable for expert DIY or professional |

## Specifications

### System type*

| | |
|---|---|
| Engine code AEV | Bosch Mono-Motronic 1.2.3 |
| Engine codes ADX and AEA | Bosch Mono-Motronic 1.3 |

### Fuel system data

| | |
|---|---|
| Fuel pump type | Electric, immersed in fuel tank |
| Fuel pump delivery rate | 1000 $cm^3$ / min (battery voltage of 12.5 V) |
| Regulated fuel pressure | 0.8 to 1.2 bar |
| Engine idle speed | 750 to 850 rpm (non-adjustable, electronically controlled) |
| Idle CO content | 0.5% (non-adjustable) |
| Maximum engine speed | 6300 rpm (governed electronically) |
| Injector electrical resistance | 1.2 to 1.6 ohms at 15 to 30°C |

### Recommended fuel

| | |
|---|---|
| Minimum octane rating (all models) | 95 RON unleaded |

### Inlet manifold heater resistance

0.25 to 0.5 ohms (engine cold)

### Torque wrench settings

| | Nm | lbf ft |
|---|---|---|
| Air cleaner housing nuts/bolts | 10 | 7 |
| Cable/hose guide peg bolt | 15 | 11 |
| Fuel pump/gauge sender unit securing ring | 75 | 55 |
| Fuel tank filler neck screws | 4 | 3 |
| Fuel tank mounting bolts | 25 | 18 |
| Injector cap/inlet air temperature sensor housing screw | 5 | 4 |
| Inlet manifold heater retaining screws | 10 | 7 |
| Inlet manifold retaining nuts/bolts | 25 | 18 |
| Lambda sensor | 50 | 37 |
| Throttle body mounting flange-to-inlet manifold nuts | 10 | 7 |
| Throttle valve positioning module screws | 6 | 4 |

**Refer to Chapter 2A for engine code listings.*

4A

## 1 General information and precautions

### General information

The Bosch Mono-Motronic system is a self-contained engine management system, which controls both the fuel injection and ignition **(see illustration)**. This Chapter deals with the fuel injection system components only - refer to Chapter 5B for details of the ignition system components.

The fuel injection system comprises a fuel tank, an electric fuel pump, a fuel filter, fuel supply and return lines, a throttle body with an integral electronic fuel injector, and an Electronic Control Unit (ECU) together with its associated sensors, actuators and wiring.

The fuel pump delivers a constant supply of fuel through a cartridge filter to the throttle body, at a slightly higher pressure than required - the fuel pressure regulator (integral with the throttle body) maintains a constant fuel pressure at the fuel injector, and returns excess fuel to the tank via the return line. This constant flow system also helps to reduce fuel temperature and prevents vaporisation.

The fuel injector is opened and closed by an Electronic Control Unit (ECU), which calculates the injection timing and duration according to engine speed, throttle position and rate of opening, inlet air temperature, coolant temperature, road speed and exhaust gas oxygen content information, received from sensors mounted on the engine.

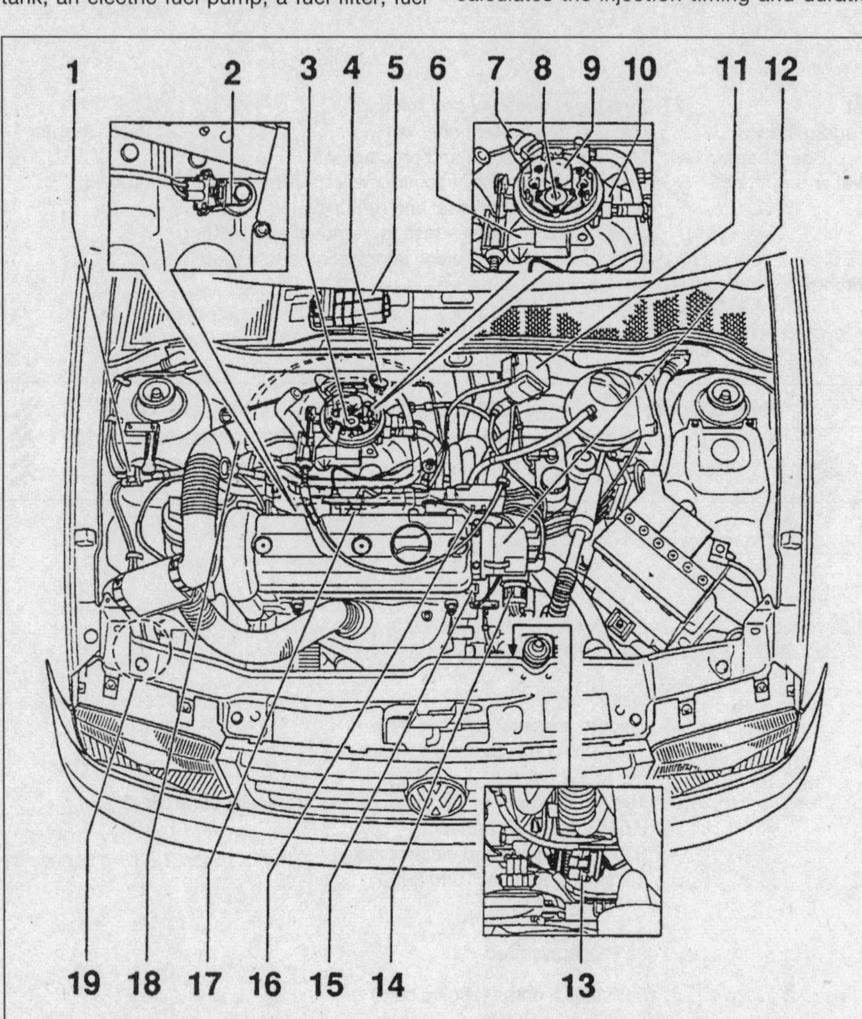


**1.1 Bosch Mono-Motronic engine management system component locations**

1 *Charcoal filter solenoid valve*
2 *Knock sensor - engine codes ADX and AEA only*
3 *Injection unit/throttle body*
4 *Inlet air temperature vacuum switch*
5 *ECU*
6 *Throttle valve positioning module and idle switch*
7 *Inlet air temperature sensor connector*
8 *Fuel pressure regulator*
9 *Fuel injector and inlet air temperature sensor*
10 *Throttle valve potentiometer*
11 *Ignition coil*
12 *Distributor*
13 *Lambda sensor connector*
14 *Main wiring harness connector*
15 *Coolant temperature sender*
16 *Earth connection*
17 *Spark plug*
18 *Air cleaner and air inlet trunking*
19 *Charcoal canister*

Inlet air is drawn into the engine through the air cleaner, which contains a renewable paper filter element. The inlet air temperature is regulated by a vacuum-operated valve mounted in the air cleaner inlet trunking, which blends air at ambient temperature with hot air, drawn from over the exhaust manifold. Vacuum supply to the valve is regulated by a temperature switch mounted in the air cleaner.

The temperature of the air entering the throttle body is measured by a sensor mounted directly above the injector. This information is used by the ECU to fine-tune the fuelling requirements for different operating temperatures.

Idle speed control is achieved partly by an electronic throttle positioning module, mounted on the side of the throttle body and partly by the ignition system, which gives fine control of the idle speed by altering the ignition timing. As a result, manual adjustment of the engine idle speed is not necessary, or possible.

To improve cold starting and idling (and fuel economy), an electric heating element is mounted on the underside of the inlet manifold; this prevents fuel vapour condensation when the engine is cold. Power is supplied to the heater by a relay, which is in turn controlled by the ECU. The heater is sometimes known as the 'hedgehog', due to its appearance.

The exhaust gas oxygen content is constantly monitored by the ECU via the Lambda sensor, which is mounted in the exhaust pipe. The ECU then uses this information to modify the injection timing and duration to maintain the optimum air/fuel ratio - a result of this is that manual adjustment of the idle exhaust CO content is not necessary. All models are fitted with a catalytic converter - see Chapter 4D for details.

In addition, the ECU controls the operation of the activated charcoal filter evaporative loss system - refer to Chapter 4D for further details.

It should be noted that fault diagnosis of the Bosch Mono-Motronic system is only possible with dedicated electronic test equipment. Problems with the system's operation should therefore be referred to a VW dealer for assessment. Once the fault has been identified, the removal/refitting sequences detailed in the following Sections will then allow the appropriate component(s) to be renewed as required.

### Precautions

***Warning: Petrol is extremely flammable - great care must be taken when working on any part of the fuel system.***

2.1a Release the air filter cover clips . . .

2.1b . . . then lift off the cover and unclip the vacuum hose (arrowed)

2.2a Remove the air cleaner housing securing nuts around the top of the throttle body (arrowed) . . .

***Do not smoke, or allow any naked flames or uncovered light bulbs near the work area. Note that gas powered domestic appliances with pilot flames, such as heaters boilers and tumble-dryers, also present a fire hazard - bear this in mind if you are working in an area where such appliances are present. Always keep a suitable fire extinguisher close to the work area, and familiarise yourself with its operation before starting work. Wear eye protection when working on fuel systems, and wash off any fuel spilt on bare skin immediately with soap and water. Note that fuel vapour is just as dangerous as liquid fuel - possibly more so; a vessel that has been emptied of liquid fuel will still contain vapour, and can be potentially explosive.***

***Many of the operations described in this Chapter involve the disconnection of fuel lines, which may cause an amount of fuel spillage. Before commencing work, refer to the above Warning and the information in Safety first! at the beginning of this manual.***

***Residual fuel pressure always remain in the fuel system, long after the engine has been switched off. This pressure must be relieved in a controlled manner before work can commence on any component in the fuel system - refer to Section 9 for details.***

***When working with fuel system components, pay particular attention to cleanliness - dirt entering the fuel system may cause blockages, which will lead to poor running.***

***In the interests of personal safety and equipment protection, many of the procedures in this Chapter suggest that the negative lead be removed from the battery terminal. This firstly eliminates the possibility of accidental short-circuits being caused as the vehicle is being worked upon, and secondly prevents damage to electronic components (eg sensors, actuators, ECUs) which are particularly sensitive to the power surges caused by disconnection or reconnection of the wiring harness whilst they are still live.***

***It should be noted, however, that the engine management systems described in this Chapter (and Chapter 5B) have a learning capability, that allows the system to adapt to the engine's running characteristics as it wears with use. This learnt information is lost when the battery is disconnected, and the system will then take a short period of time to re-learn the engine's characteristics - this may be manifested (temporarily) as rough idling, reduced throttle response and possibly a slight increase in fuel consumption, until the system re-adapts. The re-adaptation time will depend on how often the vehicle is used and the driving conditions encountered.***

## 2 Air cleaner and inlet system components - removal and refitting

### *Removal*

**1** Release the over-centre wire clips around the air cleaner top cover, and lift off the top cover. Where applicable, unclip the vacuum hose from the cover **(see illustrations)**.

**2** Lift out the air cleaner element, then unscrew and remove the three central nuts and three Allen bolts which secure the air cleaner housing to the throttle body **(see illustrations)**.

**3** Lift out the insulated earth strap leading to the ignition coil, which is hooked into a clip on the right-hand side of the air cleaner housing **(see illustration)**.

**4** Slacken the retaining screw and disconnect the air ducting from the air cleaner housing **(see illustration)**.

**5** Unclip the vacuum hose from the front underside of the housing, and the charcoal canister hose from the rear of the housing **(see illustrations)**.

**6** Lift the housing away from the throttle body slightly, then disconnect the vacuum pipes underneath leading to the throttle body and the air inlet temperature control valve housing **(see illustration)**. Label the pipes if necessary for accurate refitting.

2.2b . . . and the Allen bolts around the outside of the housing (arrowed)

2.3 Unhook the ignition coil earth strap from the side of the air cleaner housing

2.4 Slacken the cross-head screw and detach the inlet duct from the housing

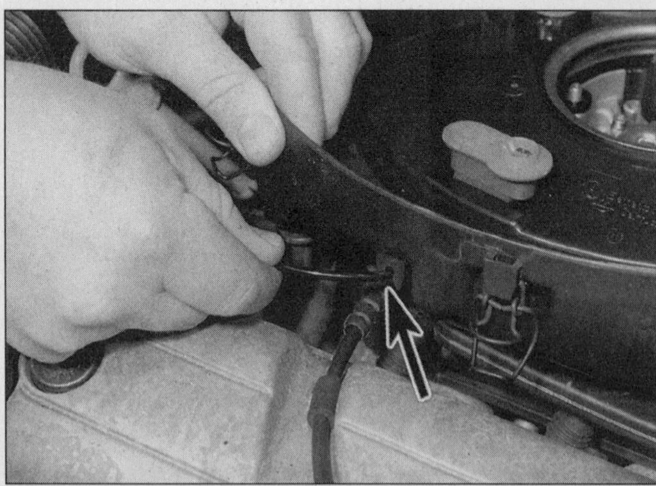
2.5a Unclip the vacuum hose (arrowed) from the front . . .

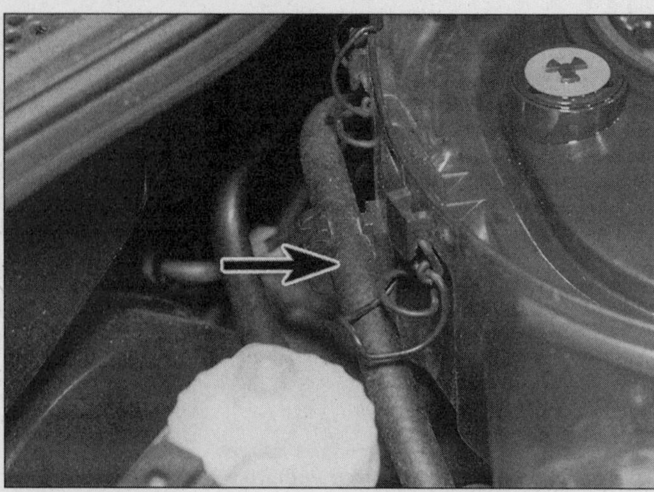
2.5b . . . and the charcoal canister hose (arrowed) from the rear of the housing

**7** Pull off the crankcase breather pipe from the base of the housing **(see illustration)**.

**8** The air cleaner housing can now be removed from the engine compartment **(see illustration)**.

**9** The removal of the rest of the air inlet trunking is fairly self-evident. The trunking is secured to the air inlet temperature valve housing by a single screw at each end, and the valve housing itself is mounted to the inner wing by a single bolt. The air inlet trumpet is attached to the inner wing by a further bolt; once removed, it can then be pulled from the aperture in the inner wing. The duct to the exhaust manifold warm-air collector plate is simply pulled off the pipe stubs **(see illustrations)**.

### Refitting

**10** Refit the air cleaner and air inlet system components by following the removal procedure in reverse. Make sure that the vacuum connections to the throttle body and air inlet temperature valve housing are correctly and securely made. The air cleaner housing must be correctly mounted on the throttle body, to ensure there is no air leakage.

## 3 Inlet air temperature vacuum switch - removal and refitting

### Removal

**1** Remove the air cleaner housing as described in Section 2.

**2** Using a small flat-bladed screwdriver, prise off the retaining plate from below the vacuum switch. The plate will probably be quite stiff, but work carefully, to avoid damaging the pipe stubs.

2.6 Lift up the housing, and disconnect the vacuum pipes from the base of the air temperature vacuum switch

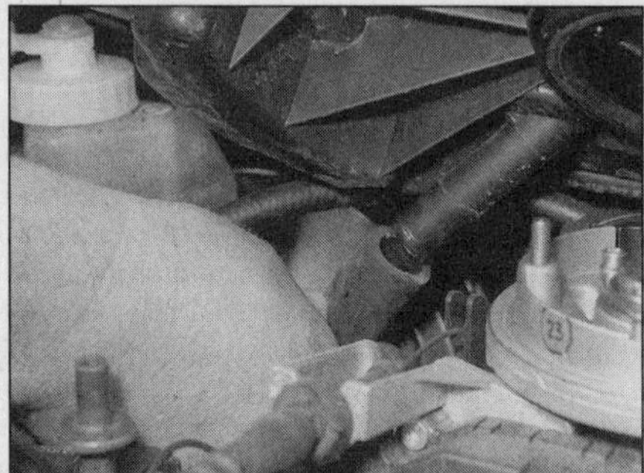
2.7 Pull off the crankcase breather hose from the base of the housing

2.8 Withdraw the air cleaner housing from the engine compartment

2.9a Removing the screw securing the duct to the air temperature control valve housing

2.9b Air temperature control valve housing mounting bolt on inner wing

2.9c Pulling off the warm-air duct from the temperature control valve housing

3 Remove the vacuum switch from the air cleaner housing, and recover the seal.

### Refitting

4 Refit the vacuum switch by following the removal procedure in reverse. If the seal is damaged or deteriorated, fit a new one when reassembling. Press the retaining plate firmly into position over the pipe stubs.

## 4 Accelerator cable - removal, refitting and adjustment

### Removal

1 Remove the air cleaner housing as described in Section 2.
2 At the throttle body, disconnect the accelerator cable inner from the throttle valve spindle plate by pulling on the cable inner and detaching the cable end fitting.
3 Remove the adjustment clip and extract the cable outer from the mounting bracket **(see illustration)**.
4 Refer to Chapter 11 and remove the facia trim panels from underneath the steering column.
5 Working under the facia, depress the accelerator pedal slightly, then unclip the accelerator cable end from the pedal extension lever.
6 At the point where the cable passes through the bulkhead, unscrew the cap from the two-piece grommet so that the cable can move freely.
7 Release the cable from its clips and guide it out through the bulkhead grommet.

### Refitting

8 Refit the accelerator cable by following the removal procedure in reverse.

### Adjustment

9 At the throttle body, fix the position of the cable outer in its mounting bracket by inserting the metal clip in one of the locating slots **(see illustration)**, such that when the accelerator is depressed fully, the throttle valve is just held wide open to its end stop.

## 5 Bosch Mono-Motronic system components - removal and refitting

**Note:** *Observe the precautions in Section 1 before working on any component in the fuel system.*

### Throttle body

#### Removal

1 Refer to Section 2 and remove the air cleaner housing.
2 Refer to Section 9 and depressurise the fuel system, then disconnect the battery negative lead and position it away from the terminal. **Note:** *If the vehicle has a security-coded radio, check that you have a copy of the code number before disconnecting the battery. Refer to your VW dealer if in doubt.*
3 Disconnect the fuel supply and return hoses from the ports on the side of the throttle body. Note the arrows that denote the direction of fuel flow, and mark the hoses accordingly **(see illustrations)**. The fuel supply hose is colour-coded white, and the return hose has blue markings.

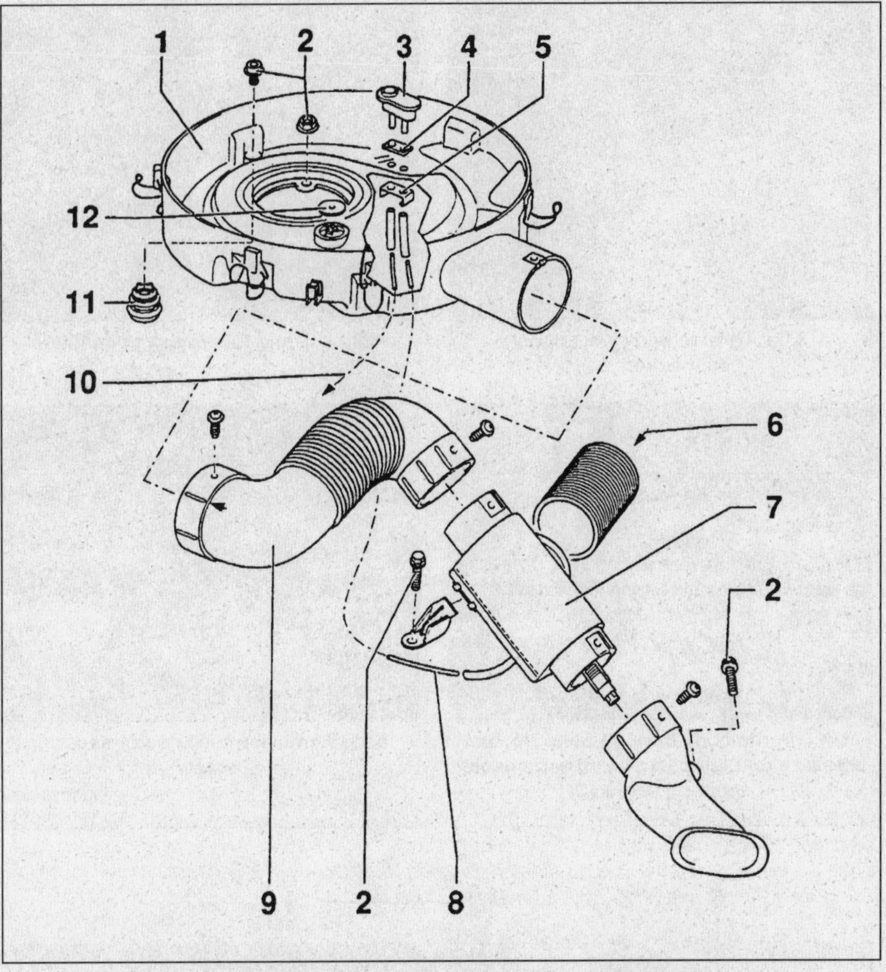


**2.9d Air cleaner housing and inlet system components**

1 Air cleaner housing
2 Mounting nut/bolt
3 Inlet air temperature vacuum switch
4 Seal
5 Retaining plate
6 Warm-air inlet duct
7 Air inlet temperature control valve housing
8 Vacuum hose
9 Air inlet trunking
10 To throttle body connection
11 Grommet
12 Non-return valve for crankcase breather pipe

**4.3 Removing the accelerator cable from the mounting bracket**

**4.9 Adjust the accelerator cable by inserting the metal clip into one of the slots in the cable outer**

5.3a Throttle body fuel supply connection . . .

5.3b . . . and fuel return connection

5.4 Disconnecting the fuel injector wiring plug

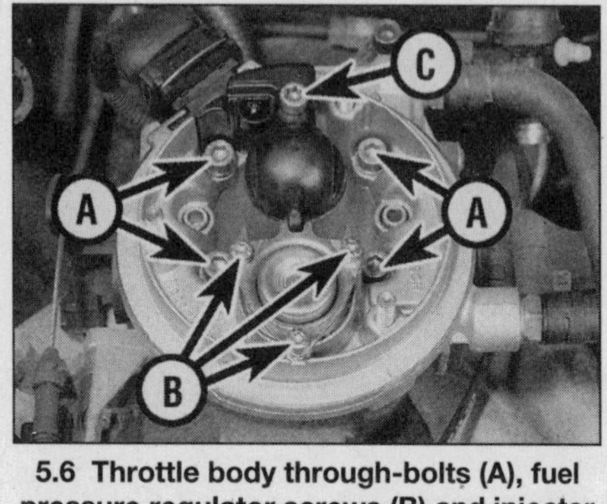


5.6 Throttle body through-bolts (A), fuel pressure regulator screws (B) and injector securing screw (C)

5.11 Removing the injector securing screw

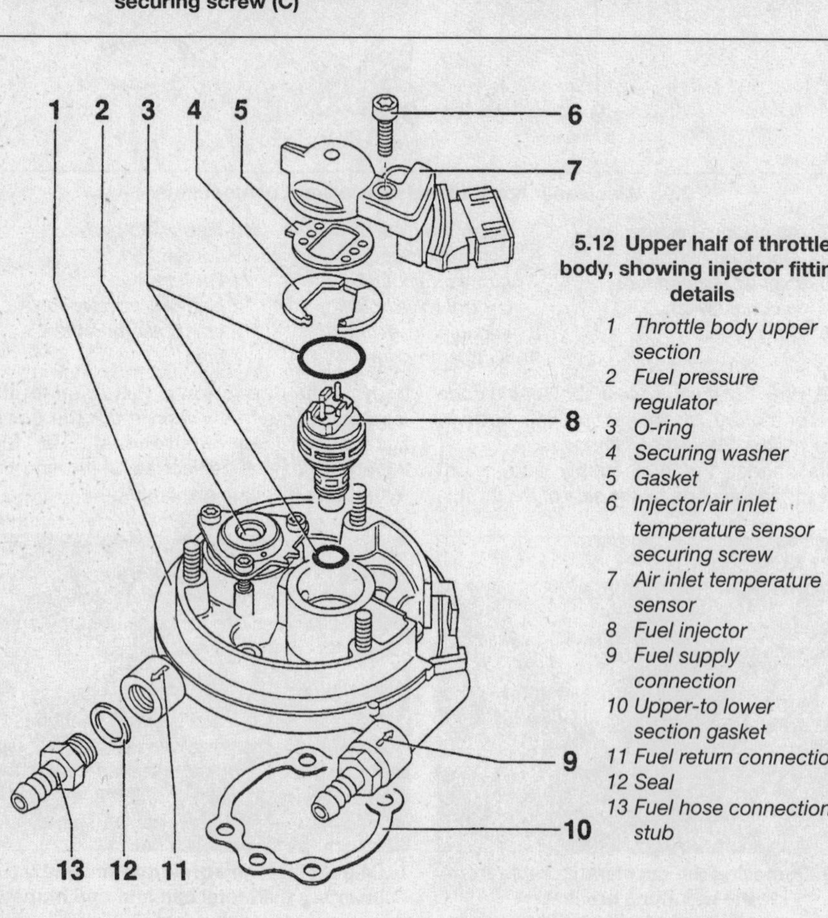


**5.12 Upper half of throttle body, showing injector fitting details**

*1 Throttle body upper section*
*2 Fuel pressure regulator*
*3 O-ring*
*4 Securing washer*
*5 Gasket*
*6 Injector/air inlet temperature sensor securing screw*
*7 Air inlet temperature sensor*
*8 Fuel injector*
*9 Fuel supply connection*
*10 Upper-to lower section gasket*
*11 Fuel return connection*
*12 Seal*
*13 Fuel hose connection stub*

**4** Unplug the wiring harness from the throttle body at the connectors, labelling them to aid correct refitting later **(see illustration)**.

**5** Refer to Section 4 and disconnect the accelerator cable from the throttle body.

**6** Loosen and remove the four through-bolts which secure the throttle body to the inlet manifold **(see illustration)**. Lift the throttle body away from the inlet manifold, recovering the gasket (where applicable). Unless specifically required, it is not recommended that the upper and lower halves of the throttle body are separated - these are held together by two inner through-bolts. If the two halves are split, a new gasket must be used on reassembly.

### Refitting

**7** Refitting is a reversal of removal; renew all gaskets where appropriate. Tighten the through-bolts securely. On completion, check and if necessary adjust the accelerator cable.

## *Fuel injector*

### Removal

**8** Refer to Section 2 and remove the air cleaner housing.

**9** Refer to Section 9 and depressurise the fuel system, then disconnect the battery negative lead and position it away from the terminal - refer to the note in paragraph 2.

**10** Unplug the wiring harness from the injector at the connector(s), labelling them to aid correct refitting later.

**11** Remove the screw and lift off the injector retaining cap/inlet air temperature sensor housing **(see illustration)**. Recover the gasket.

**12** Release the securing washer, then lift the injector out of the throttle body, recovering the O-ring seals **(see illustration)**.

**13** Check the injector electrical resistance using a multimeter and compare the result with the Specifications.

### Refitting

**14** Refit the injector by following the removal procedure in reverse, renewing all O-ring seals and gaskets. Apply a suitable sealant to the screw threads, then insert and tighten the retaining screw to the specified torque.

## *Inlet air temperature sensor*

**15** The inlet air temperature sensor is an integral part of the injector retaining cap.

Removal is as described in the previous sub-Section.

### Fuel pressure regulator

#### Removal

**16** If the operation of the fuel pressure regulator is in question, dismantle the unit as described below, then check the cleanliness and integrity of the internal components. **Note:** *The fuel pressure regulator components are matched to the upper part of the throttle body during manufacture. If the pressure regulator is defective, VW state that the upper part of the throttle body must be renewed complete. Consult your parts supplier for the latest advice.*

**17** Remove the air cleaner housing, with reference to Section 2.

**18** Refer to Section 9 and depressurise the fuel system, then disconnect the battery negative lead and position it away from the terminal - refer to the note in paragraph 2.

**19** With reference to the relevant sub-Section, remove the screw and lift off the inlet air temperature sensor/injector cap.

**20** Slacken and withdraw the three Torx retaining screws and lift off the fuel pressure regulator retaining frame.

**21** Lift out the upper cover, spring and membrane.

**22** Clean all the components thoroughly, then inspect the membrane for cracks or splits.

#### Refitting

**23** Reassemble the pressure regulator by following the removal procedure in reverse.

### Throttle valve positioning module

#### Removal

**24** Disconnect the battery negative lead and position it away from the terminal - refer to paragraph 2. Remove the air cleaner housing, with reference to Section 2.

**25** Refer to Section 4 and disconnect the accelerator cable from the throttle body.

**26** Unplug the connector from the side of the throttle valve positioning module.

**27** Remove the retaining screws **(see illustration)** and lift the module, together with the accelerator cable outer mounting bracket, away from the throttle body.

#### Refitting

**28** Refitting is a reversal of removal. Note that if a new module has been fitted, the adjustment of the idle switch will need to be checked - refer to a VW dealer for advice as this operation requires access to dedicated test equipment.

### Throttle valve potentiometer

**29** Refer to the relevant sub-Section and remove the throttle body. The throttle valve potentiometer is an integral part of the lower section of the throttle body, and cannot be renewed separately.

**5.27 Throttle valve positioning module securing screws**

### Idle switch

**30** Refer to the relevant sub-Section and remove the throttle valve positioning module. The idle switch is an integral part of the module, and cannot be renewed separately.

**31** Where a new throttle valve positioning module has been fitted, the adjustment of the idle switch will need to be checked - refer to a VW dealer for advice as this operation requires access to dedicated test equipment.

### Lambda sensor

#### Removal

**32** The lambda sensor is threaded into the exhaust pipe, ahead of the catalytic converter **(see illustration)**. Refer to Chapter 4D for details.

**33** Disconnect the battery negative lead and position it away from the terminal - refer to the note in paragraph 2. Unplug the wiring harness from the lambda sensor at the connector, which is located in a bracket mounted on the transmission.

**34** **Note:** *As a flying lead remains connected to the sensor after it has been disconnected, if the correct-size spanner is not available, a slotted socket will be required to remove the sensor.* Working under the vehicle, slacken and withdraw the sensor, taking care to avoid damaging the sensor probe as it is removed.

#### Refitting

**35** Apply a little anti-seize grease to the sensor threads only - keep the probe tip clean.

**36** Refit the sensor to its housing, tightening it to the correct torque. Restore the harness connection. Note that the type of lambda sensor fitted depends on vehicle specification - the sensor may not be interchangeable with one obtained from another model.

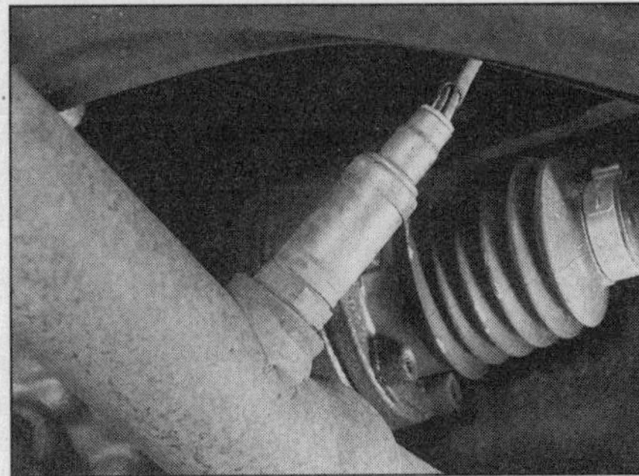

**5.32 Lambda sensor - seen from below**

### Coolant temperature sensor

**37** Refer to Chapter 3, Section 6.

### Inlet manifold heater

**38** Refer to Section 11.

### Road speed sensor

**39** The road speed sensor is mounted on the transmission - refer to Chapter 7A.

### Electronic control unit (ECU)

**40** The ECU is located centrally behind the engine compartment bulkhead, under one of the windscreen cowl panels. To remove the cowl panels, refer to Chapter 12, Section 13. The unit is coded, and should not be removed without consulting a VW dealer, otherwise it may not function correctly when the multi-plug is reconnected.

## 6 Fuel filter - renewal

**Note:** *Observe the precautions in Section 1 before working on any component in the fuel system.*

Refer to Chapter 1A, Section 28.

## 7 Fuel pump and gauge sender unit - removal and refitting

**Note:** *Observe the precautions in Section 1 before working on any component in the fuel system.*

***Warning: Avoid direct skin contact with fuel - wear protective clothing and gloves when handling fuel system components. Ensure that the work area is well-ventilated to prevent the build-up of fuel vapour.***

### General information

**1** The fuel pump and gauge sender unit are combined in one assembly, which is mounted on the top of the fuel tank. Access is via a hatch provided in the load space floor. The unit protrudes into the fuel tank, and its removal involves exposing the contents of the tank to the atmosphere.

### Removal

**2** Depressurise the fuel system (Section 9).

**3** Ensure that the vehicle is parked on a level surface, then disconnect the battery negative lead and position it away from the terminal.

**4** Fold the rear seat forwards, and remove the trim from the load space floor.

**5** Slacken and withdraw the access hatch screws, and lift the hatch away from the floorpan.

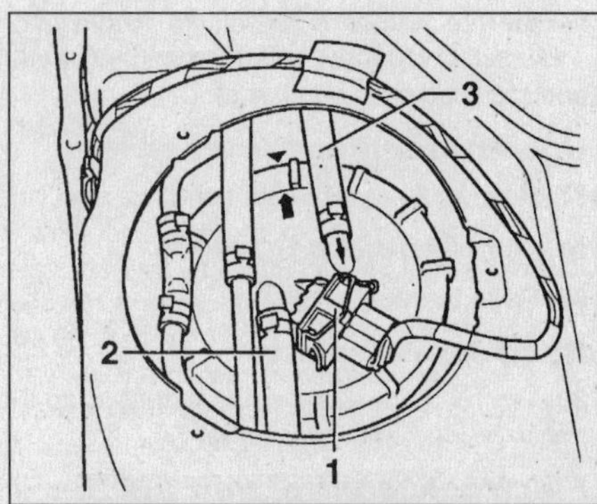


**7.6 Fuel pump/fuel gauge sender unit location - note alignment mark and arrow**

1 *Wiring connector*
2 *Fuel supply hose to engine (colour-coded black)*
3 *Fuel return hose (colour-coded blue)*

**6** Unplug the wiring harness connector from the pump/sender unit **(see illustration)**.

**7** Pad the area around the supply and return fuel hoses with rags to absorb any spilt fuel, then slacken the hose clips and remove them from the ports at the sender unit. Observe the supply and return arrows markings on the ports - label the fuel hoses accordingly to ensure correct refitting later.

**8** Unscrew the plastic securing ring and lift it out. Use a pair of water pump pliers to grip and rotate the plastic securing ring. Recover the flange and seal.

**9** Turn the pump/sender unit to the left to release it from its bayonet fitting and lift it out, holding it above the level of the fuel in the tank until the excess fuel has drained out.

**10** Remove the pump/sender unit from the vehicle and lay it on an absorbent card or rag. Inspect the float at the end of the sender unit swinging arm for punctures and fuel ingress - renew the unit if it appears damaged.

**11** The fuel pick-up incorporated in the assembly is spring-loaded to ensure that it always draws fuel from the lowest part of the tank. Check that the pick-up is free to move under spring tension with respect to the sender unit body.

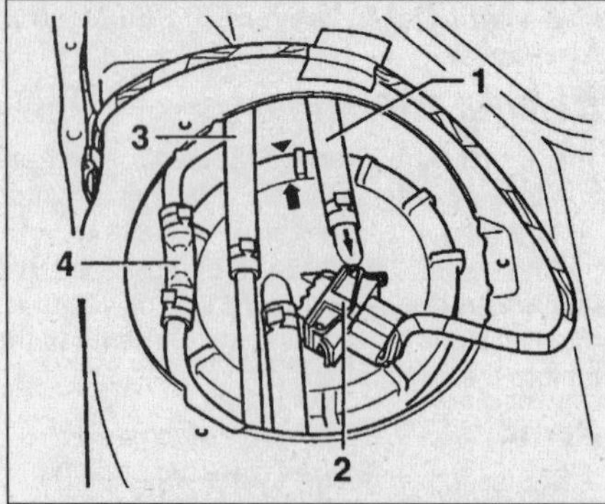


**8.4 Fuel pump/sender unit pipes and wiring to be disconnected for fuel tank removal**

1 *Fuel return hose*
2 *Wiring connector*
3 *Fuel supply hose to tank*
4 *Breather pipe*

**12** Inspect the rubber seal from the fuel tank aperture for signs of fatigue - renew it if necessary.

**13** Inspect the sender unit wiper and track; clean off any dirt and debris that may have accumulated, and look for breaks in the track.

### Refitting

**14** Refit the sender unit by following the removal procedure in reverse, noting the following points:

a) *Take care not to bend the float arm as the unit is refitted.*
b) *When correctly installed, the pump/sender unit float arm must point towards the fuel filler pipe.*
c) *Smear the tank aperture rubber seal with clean fuel before fitting it in position.*
d) *The arrow markings on the sender unit body and the fuel tank must be aligned.*
e) *Reconnect the fuel hoses to the correct ports - observe the direction-of-flow arrow markings.*

## 8 Fuel tank - removal and refitting

**Note:** *Observe the precautions in Section 1 before working on any component in the fuel system.*

### Removal

**1** Before the tank can be removed, it must be drained of as much fuel as possible. As no drain plug is provided, it is preferable to carry out this operation with the tank almost empty.

**2** Disconnect the battery negative lead and position it away from the terminal. **Note:** *If the vehicle has a security-coded radio, check that you have a copy of the code number before disconnecting the battery. Refer to your VW dealer if in doubt.* Using a hand pump or syphon, remove any remaining fuel from the bottom of the tank.

**3** Gain access to the top of the fuel pump/sender unit as described in Section 7, and disconnect the wiring harness from the top of the pump sender unit at the multiway connector.

**4** Disconnect the fuel return hose (colour-coded blue) from the pump/sender unit, along with the fuel supply and breather pipes **(see illustration)**. Label the pipes to ensure accurate refitting.

**5** Loosen the right-hand rear wheel bolts, then jack up the rear of the car and remove the right-hand rear wheel.

**6** Position a trolley jack under the centre of the tank. Insert a block of wood between the jack head and the tank to prevent damage to the tank surface. Raise the jack until it just takes the weight of the tank.

**7** Loosen and remove the two retaining nuts, then detach the tank support bracket from the body **(see illustration)**. Note that this bracket doubles as an exhaust support - be ready to support the exhaust system as the nuts are removed. If wished, the remaining two nuts can also be removed, and the bracket removed completely.

**8** Unhook all the rear exhaust mountings from the body, then lower the exhaust system sufficiently to allow the fuel tank to be lowered. Do not allow the exhaust to hang down unsupported - tie it loosely to the body with wire, or position suitable supports underneath it, to just take its weight.

**9** Working inside the rear right-hand wheel arch, slacken and withdraw the screws that secure the tank filler neck inside of the wheel arch. Open the fuel filler flap and peel the rubber sealing flange away from the bodywork.

**10** Loosen and remove the retaining bolts at the front edge and around the tank, keeping one hand on the tank to steady it as it is released from its mountings.

**11** Lower the jack and tank away from the underside of the vehicle; detach the filler pipes and the outlet pipe from the fuel filter as the tank is lowered. Disconnect the charcoal canister vent pipe from the port on the filler neck as it is exposed. Locate the earthing strap and disconnect it from the terminal at the filler neck.

**12** If the tank is contaminated with sediment or water, remove the fuel pump/sender unit (see Section 7) and swill the tank out with clean fuel. The tank is injection-moulded from a synthetic material, and if damaged, it should be renewed. However, in certain cases it may be possible to have small leaks or minor damage repaired. Seek the advice of a suitable specialist before attempting to repair the fuel tank.

### Refitting

**13** Refitting is the reverse of the removal procedure, noting the following points:

a) *When lifting the tank back into position, make sure the mounting rubbers are correctly positioned, and take care to ensure none of the hoses get trapped between the tank and vehicle body.*
b) *Ensure that all pipes and hoses are correctly routed, are not kinked, and are*

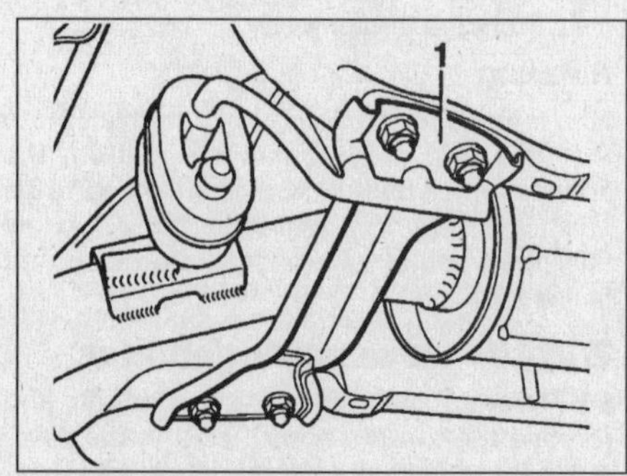


**8.7 Fuel tank support bracket (1)**

securely held in position with their retaining clips.

c) Reconnect the earth strap to its terminal on the filler neck.

d) Tighten the tank retaining bolts to the specified torque.

e) On completion, refill the tank with fuel, and exhaustively check for signs of leakage prior to taking the vehicle out on the road.

## 9 Fuel injection system - depressurisation

**Note:** *Observe the precautions in Section 1 before working on any component in the fuel system.*

***Warning: The following procedure will merely relieve the pressure in the fuel system - remember that fuel will still be present in the system components and take precautions accordingly before disconnecting any of them.***

**1** The fuel system referred to in this Section is defined as the tank-mounted fuel pump, the fuel filter, the fuel injector, the throttle body-mounted fuel pressure regulator, and the metal pipes and flexible hoses of the fuel lines between these components. All these contain fuel, which will be under pressure while the engine is running and/or while the ignition is switched on. The pressure will remain for some time after the ignition has been switched off, and must be relieved before any of these components are disturbed for servicing work. Ideally, the engine should be allowed to cool completely before work commences.

**2** Referring to Chapter 12, locate and remove the fuel pump relay. Alternatively, identify and remove the fuel pump fuse from the fusebox.

**3** With the fuel pump disabled, crank the engine for about ten seconds. The engine may fire and run for a while, but let it continue running until it stops. The fuel injector should have opened enough times during cranking to considerably reduce the line fuel pressure, and reduce the risk of fuel spraying out when a fuel line is disturbed.

**4** Disconnect the battery negative terminal. **Note:** *If the vehicle has a security-coded radio, check that you have a copy of the code number before disconnecting the battery. Refer to your VW dealer if in doubt.*

**5** Place a suitable container beneath the relevant connection/union to be disconnected, and have a large rag ready to soak up any escaping fuel not being caught by the container.

**6** Slowly loosen the connection or union nut (as applicable) to avoid a sudden release of pressure, and position the rag around the connection to catch any fuel spray which may be expelled. Once the pressure has been released, disconnect the fuel line. Insert plugs to minimise fuel loss and prevent the entry of dirt into the fuel system.

## 10 Inlet manifold - removal and refitting

**Note:** *Observe the precautions in Section 1 before working on any component in the fuel system.*

### Removal

**1** Disconnect the battery negative lead and position it away from the terminal. **Note:** *If the vehicle has a security-coded radio, check that you have a copy of the code number before disconnecting the battery. Refer to your VW dealer if in doubt.*

**2** Refer to Chapter 1A and drain the coolant from the engine.

**3** With reference to Section 5, remove the throttle body from the inlet manifold. Recover and discard the gasket, where applicable.

**4** Slacken the clips and remove the coolant hoses from the inlet manifold.

**5** Refer to Chapter 9 and disconnect the brake servo vacuum hose from the port on the inlet manifold.

**6** Disconnect the wiring for the inlet manifold heater at the connector.

**7** To allow the manifold to be withdrawn, the cable/hose guide must be removed. This is secured to the inlet manifold by two spreader pins, and by one of the air cleaner housing peg bolts. The spreader pins may just pull out, or it may be necessary to thread a self-tapping screw into the pin to gain greater purchase. If the pins are damaged on removal, obtain new ones for refitting. The peg bolt may be unscrewed using a pair of self-locking pliers. Lift the cable/hose guide out of position.

**8** Progressively slacken and remove the inlet manifold retaining nuts and bolts, then loosen the manifold from the cylinder head **(see illustration)**. Note that the retaining bolts are of different lengths - to make refitting easier, note the location of each bolt as it is removed.

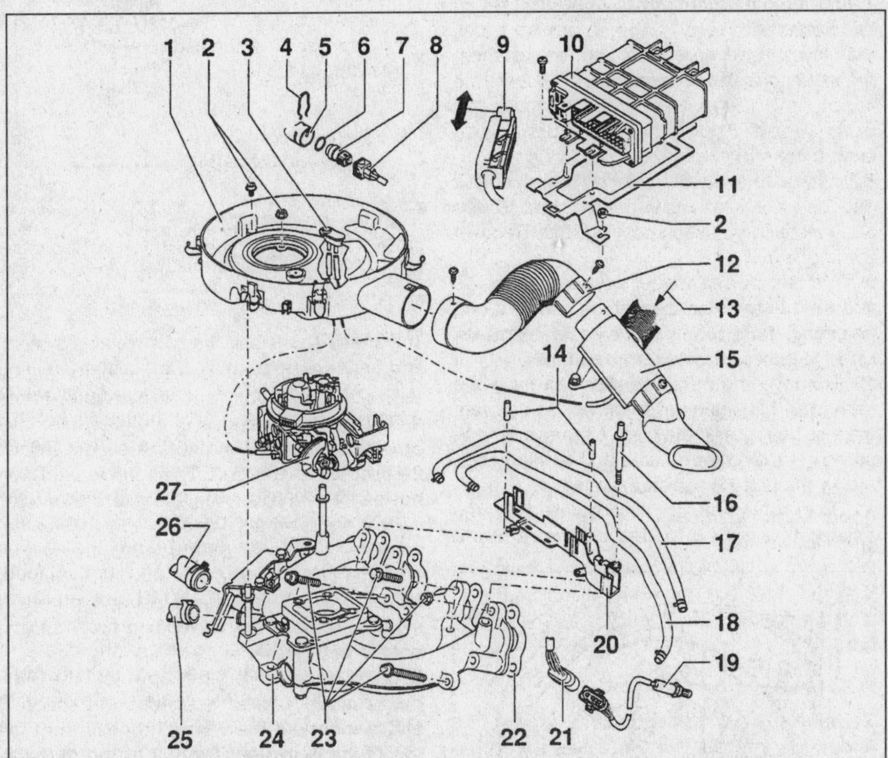


**10.8 Inlet manifold and related fuel system components**

1 Air cleaner housing
2 Housing securing nuts and Allen bolts
3 Air temperature vacuum switch
4 Retaining clip
5 Thermostat housing
6 O-ring
7 Coolant temperature sender
8 Connector
9 ECU multi-plug
10 Fuel injection ECU
11 ECU mounting bracket
12 Inlet air duct
13 Warm-air inlet
14 Spreader pins
15 Air temperature control valve
16 Peg bolt
17 Fuel supply hose
18 Fuel return hose
19 Lambda sensor
20 Cable guide
21 Lambda sensor wiring connector
22 Inlet manifold gasket
23 Inlet manifold securing bolts
24 Inlet manifold
25 Vacuum connection to brake servo
26 Coolant hose to thermostat housing
27 Throttle body

4A

9 Make a final check to ensure that nothing remains connected to the manifold, then manoeuvre it out of the engine bay and recover the gasket. If required, the throttle body mounting flange can be removed by unscrewing the retaining nuts and lifting it from the inlet manifold.

### Refitting

10 Refitting is the reverse of the removal procedure, noting the following points:

a) *Ensure that the manifold and cylinder head mating surfaces are clean and dry. Install the manifold with a new gasket, and tighten its retaining nuts and bolts to the specified torque setting.*
b) *Install the cable/hose guide using new spreader pins if necessary. Ensure that the fuel hoses are not kinked or pinched.*
c) *Ensure that all relevant hoses are reconnected to their original positions and are securely held (where necessary) by their retaining clips.*
d) *Refit the throttle body as described in Section 5.*
e) *On completion, refill the cooling system as described in Chapter 1A.*

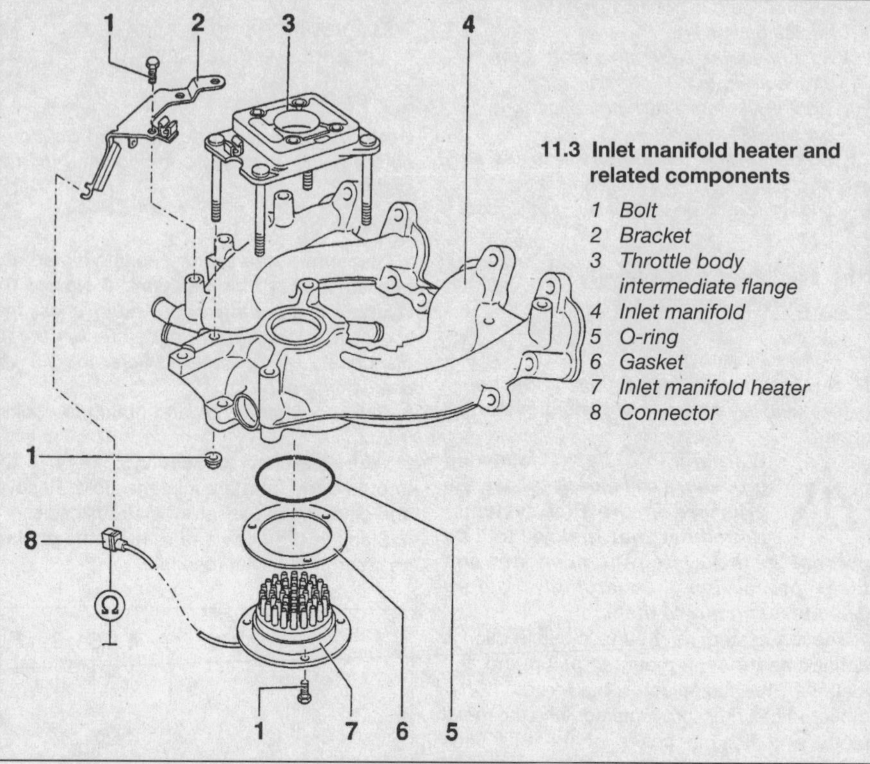


**11.3 Inlet manifold heater and related components**

*1 Bolt*
*2 Bracket*
*3 Throttle body intermediate flange*
*4 Inlet manifold*
*5 O-ring*
*6 Gasket*
*7 Inlet manifold heater*
*8 Connector*

## 11 Inlet manifold heater - testing, removal and refitting

### Testing

1 If the heater is suspected of having failed, first check for a supply to the heater element - refer to the wiring diagrams at the end of Chapter 12, and check that the wiring is not damaged, and that the fuse has not blown. Disconnect the wiring plug for the heater element, and using a suitable multi-meter, check the resistance between the plug and a good earth. Compare the result with the specified value.

2 It is not advisable to check for operation by feeling under the element - if the heater is working normally, it will quickly get extremely hot.

### Removal

3 The inlet manifold heater is secured to the underside of the inlet manifold by three screws **(see illustration)**. With the air cleaner housing and air inlet trunking removed as described in Section 2, it should be possible to access these screws to allow the heater to be removed, but it may be necessary to remove the inlet manifold as described in Section 10.

4 Disconnect the wiring plug for the heater element, and remove the heater from the engine compartment.

### Refitting

5 Refitting is a reversal of removal, tightening the retaining screws to the specified torque.

## 12 Fuel injection system - testing and adjustment

1 If a fault appears in the fuel injection system, first ensure that all the system wiring connectors are securely connected and free of corrosion. Then ensure that the fault is not due to poor maintenance; ie, check that the air cleaner filter element is clean, the spark plugs are in good condition and correctly gapped, the cylinder compression pressures are correct, the ignition timing is correct and the engine breather hoses are clear and undamaged, referring to Chapters 1A, 2A, 4D (Section 3) and Chapter 5B for further information.

2 If these checks fail to reveal the cause of the problem, the vehicle should be taken to a suitably-equipped VW dealer for testing. A diagnostic connector is incorporated in the engine management system wiring harness, into which a dedicated electronic test equipment can be plugged. The test equipment is capable of 'interrogating' the engine management system ECU electronically and accessing its internal fault log. In this manner, faults can be pinpointed quickly and simply, even if their occurrence is intermittent. Testing all the system components individually in an attempt to locate the fault by elimination is a time-consuming operation that is unlikely to be fruitful (particularly if the fault occurs dynamically) and carries high risk of damage to the ECU's internal components.

3 Experienced home mechanics equipped with an accurate tachometer and a carefully-calibrated exhaust gas analyser may be able to check the exhaust gas CO content and the engine idle speed; if these are found to be out of specification, then the vehicle must be taken to a suitably-equipped VW dealer for assessment. Neither the air/fuel mixture (exhaust gas CO content) nor the engine idle speed are manually adjustable; incorrect test results indicate a fault within the fuel injection system.

## 13 Unleaded petrol - general information and usage

**Note:** *The information given in this Chapter is correct at the time of writing, and applies only to petrols currently available in the UK. Check with a VW dealer, as more up-to-date information may be available. If travelling abroad consult one of the motoring organisations (or a similar authority) for advice on the petrols available and their suitability for your vehicle.*

1 The fuel recommended by VW is given in the Specifications of this Chapter.

2 RON and MON are different testing standards; RON stands for Research Octane Number (also written as RM), while MON stands for Motor Octane Number (also written as MM).

# Chapter 4 Part B:
# Fuel system - multi-point petrol injection

## Contents



## Degrees of difficulty

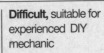

| | | | | |
|---|---|---|---|---|
| **Easy,** suitable for novice with little experience  | **Fairly easy,** suitable for beginner with some experience  | **Fairly difficult,** suitable for competent DIY mechanic | **Difficult,** suitable for experienced DIY mechanic  | **Very difficult,** suitable for expert DIY or professional |

## Specifications

### System type*

| | |
|---|---|
| Engine codes AER, ALL, AEX, AKV, ANX and APQ | Bosch Motronic 9.0 |
| Engine code AEE | Magneti-Marelli 1AV |

### Fuel system data

| | |
|---|---|
| Fuel pump type | Electric, immersed in fuel tank |
| Fuel pump delivery rate | 1100 cm$^3$ / min (battery voltage of 12.5 V) |
| Regulated fuel pressure | 2.5 bar |
| Engine idle speed (non-adjustable, electronically controlled): | |
| Engine codes AER and ALL | 660 to 740 rpm |
| Engine codes AEX, AKV, ANX and APQ: | |
| Manual transmission models: | |
| Control unit 030 906 027A | 600 to 700 rpm |
| Control unit 030 906 027K | 770 to 970 rpm |
| Automatic transmission models | 750 to 850 rpm |
| Engine code AEE: | |
| Manual transmission models | 830 to 930 rpm |
| Automatic transmission models: | |
| Control unit 032 906 030A | 750 to 850 rpm |
| Control unit 032 906 030J | 630 to 730 rpm |
| Idle CO content (non-adjustable, electronically controlled) | 0.5 % max |
| Injector electrical resistance | 14 to 17 ohms |

### Recommended fuel

| | |
|---|---|
| Minimum octane rating (all models) | 95 RON unleaded |

### Torque wrench settings

| Torque wrench settings | Nm | lbf ft |
|---|---|---|
| ECU mounting bracket nuts | 10 | 7 |
| Fuel rail mounting bolts | 10 | 7 |
| Inlet manifold to cylinder head | 20 | 15 |
| Lambda sensor | 55 | 41 |
| Throttle body earth strap bolt | 10 | 7 |

**Refer to Chapter 2A for engine code listings.*

## 1 General information and precautions

### General information

The Bosch Motronic and Magneti-Marelli 1AV systems are self-contained engine management systems, which control both the fuel injection and ignition **(see illustration)**. This Chapter deals with the fuel system components only - see Chapter 5B for details of the ignition system.

The fuel injection system comprises a fuel tank, an electric fuel pump, a fuel filter, fuel supply and return lines, a throttle body, a fuel rail, a fuel pressure regulator, four electronic fuel injectors, and an Electronic Control Unit (ECU) together with its associated sensors, actuators and wiring. The two systems used are essentially very similar - the only significant differences lie within the ECUs.

The fuel pump delivers a constant supply of fuel through a cartridge filter to the fuel rail, at a slightly higher pressure than required - the fuel pressure regulator maintains a constant fuel pressure to the fuel injectors, and returns excess fuel to the tank via the return line. This constant flow system also helps to reduce fuel temperature, and prevents vaporisation.

The fuel injectors are opened and closed by an Electronic Control Unit (ECU), which calculates the injection timing and duration according to engine speed, crankshaft position, throttle position and rate of opening, inlet manifold depression, inlet air temperature, coolant temperature, road speed and exhaust gas oxygen content information, received from sensors mounted on and around the engine.

Inlet air is drawn into the engine through the air cleaner, which contains a renewable paper filter element. The inlet air temperature is regulated by a valve mounted in the air cleaner inlet trunking, which blends air at ambient temperature with hot air, drawn from over the exhaust manifold.

The temperature of the air entering the throttle body is measured by a sensor mounted on the right-hand side of the inlet manifold. This sensor also monitors the pressure in the inlet manifold. This information is used by the ECU to fine-tune the fuelling requirements for different operating conditions.

Idle speed control is achieved partly by an electronic throttle valve positioning module, on the rear of the throttle body and partly by the ignition system, which gives fine control of the idle speed by altering the ignition timing. As a result, manual adjustment of the engine idle speed is not necessary or possible.

The exhaust gas oxygen content is constantly monitored by the ECU via the Lambda sensor, which is mounted in the exhaust pipe. The ECU then uses this information to modify the injection timing and duration to maintain the optimum air/fuel ratio - a result of this is that manual adjustment of the idle exhaust CO content is not necessary or possible. All models are fitted with a catalytic converter - see Chapter 4D.

Where fitted, the ECU controls the operation of the activated charcoal filter evaporative loss system - refer to Chapter 4D for further details.

It should be noted that fault diagnosis of all the engine management systems described in this Chapter is only possible with dedicated electronic test equipment. Problems with the systems operation should therefore be referred to a VW dealer for assessment. Once the fault has been identified, the removal/refitting sequences detailed in the following Sections will then allow the appropriate component(s) to be renewed as required.

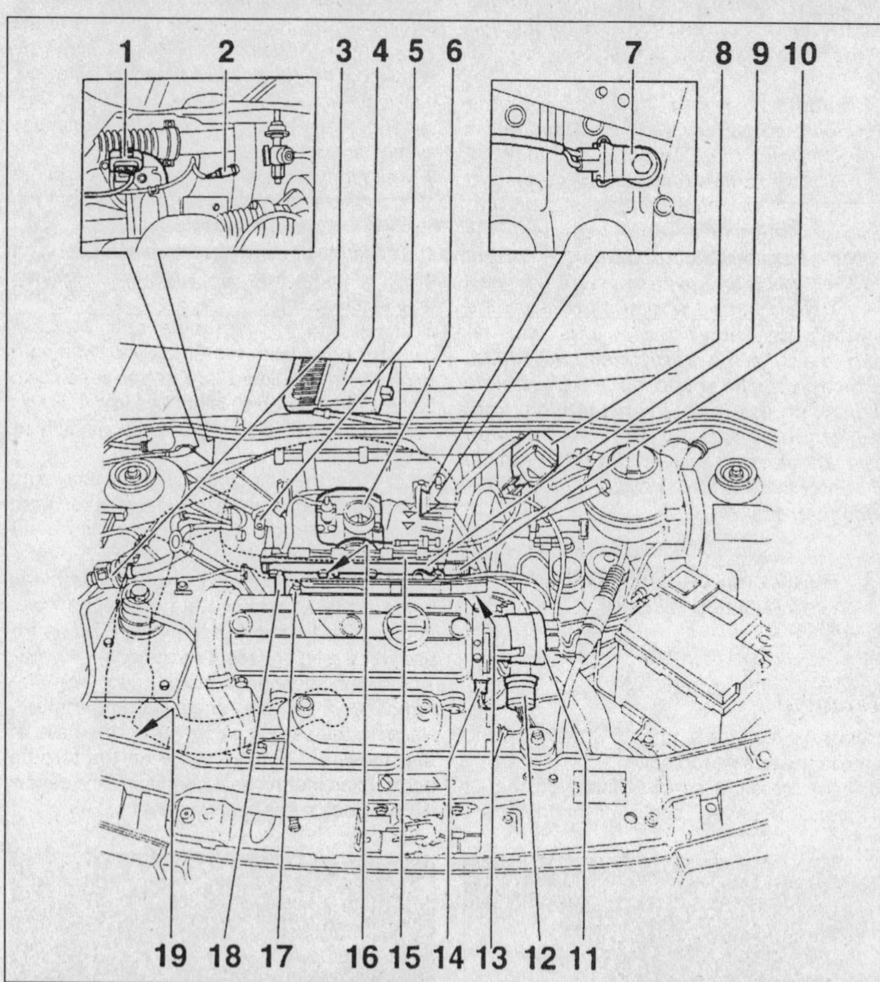


**1.1 Bosch Motronic/Magneti-Marelli 1AV engine management system component locations**

*1 Lambda sensor connector*
*2 Lambda sensor*
*3 Charcoal filter solenoid valve*
*4 ECU*
*5 Inlet manifold pressure and inlet air temperature sensor*
*6 Throttle body*
*7 Knock sensor*
*8 Ignition coil*
*9 Fuel rail*
*10 Fuel pressure regulator*
*11 Distributor*
*12 Main wiring harness connector*
*13 Earth connection*
*14 Coolant temperature sender*
*15 Air cleaner housing*
*16 Fuel injector*
*17 Spark plug*
*18 Oil pressure switch*
*19 Charcoal canister*

### Precautions

***Warning: Petrol is extremely flammable - great care must be taken when working on any part of the fuel system.***

***Do not smoke, or allow any naked flames or uncovered light bulbs near the work area. Note that gas powered domestic appliances with pilot flames, such as heaters boilers and tumble-dryers, also present a fire hazard - bear this in mind if you are working in an area where such appliances are present. Always keep a suitable fire extinguisher close to the work area, and familiarise yourself with its operation before starting work. Wear eye protection when working on fuel systems,***

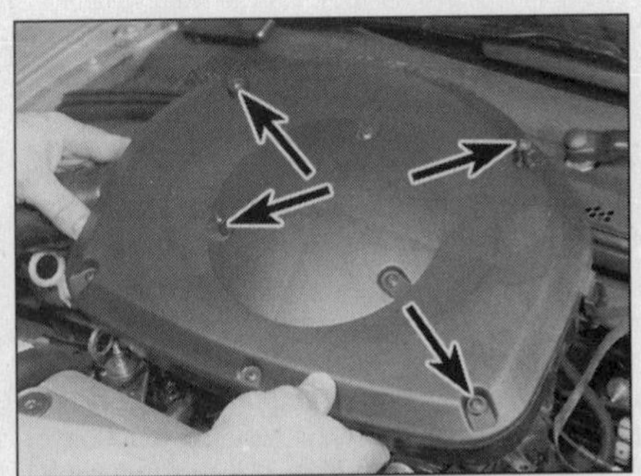

2.2 Top view of air cleaner, showing the four screws which secure the air cleaner housing (arrowed)

2.3 Removing the air cleaner element (not essential, if just the housing is to be removed)

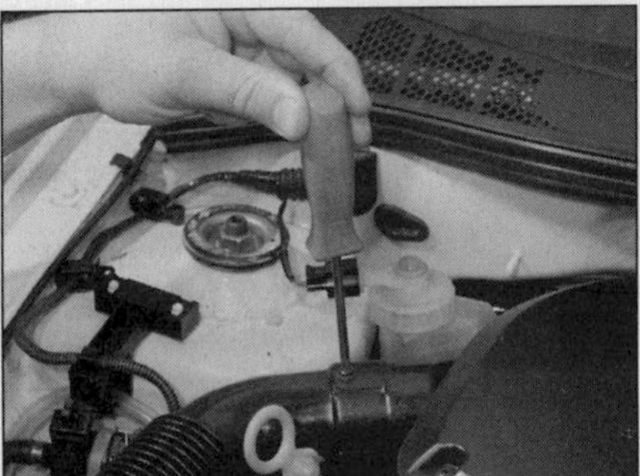

2.4 Slackening the air ducting retaining screw

*and wash off any fuel spilt on bare skin immediately with soap and water. Note that fuel vapour is just as dangerous as liquid fuel - possibly more so; a vessel that has been emptied of liquid fuel will still contain vapour, and can be potentially explosive.*

*Many of the operations described in this Chapter involve the disconnection of fuel lines, which may cause an amount of fuel spillage. Before commencing work, refer to the above Warning and the information in Safety first! at the beginning of this manual.*

*Residual fuel pressure always remains in the fuel system, long after the engine has been switched off. This pressure must be relieved in a controlled manner before work can commence on any component in the fuel system - refer to Section 9 for details.*

*When working with fuel system components, pay particular attention to cleanliness - dirt entering the fuel system may cause blockages, which will lead to poor running.*

*In the interests of personal safety and equipment protection, many of the procedures in this Chapter suggest that the negative lead be removed from the battery terminal. This firstly eliminates the possibility of accidental short-circuits being caused as the vehicle is being worked upon, and secondly prevents damage to electronic components (eg sensors, actuators, ECUs) which are particularly sensitive to the power surges caused by disconnection or reconnection of the wiring harness whilst they are still live.*

*It should be noted, however, that the engine management systems described in this Chapter (and Chapter 5B) have a learning capability, that allows the system to adapt to the engine's running characteristics as it wears with use. This learnt information is lost when the battery is disconnected, and the system will then take a short period of time to re-learn the engine's characteristics - this may be manifested (temporarily) as rough idling, reduced throttle response and possibly a slight increase in fuel consumption, until the system re-adapts. The re-adaptation time will depend on how often the vehicle is used and the driving conditions encountered.*

## 2 Air cleaner and inlet system - removal and refitting

### Removal

**1** On 1.0 litre models, refer to Chapter 2A and remove the engine top cover.

**2** There are eight screws visible on the air cleaner top cover, and four of them are marked 1 to 4 on the top cover - these four screws secure the housing to the inlet manifold **(see illustration)**. The remaining four screws secure the air cleaner top cover to the air cleaner housing, and need only be removed if the filter element is to be renewed. If all eight screws are removed, note that they are of different lengths, so note their locations as they are removed.

**3** If all eight screws have been removed, lift off the air cleaner top cover, and take out the filter element **(see illustration)**.

**4** Slacken the retaining screw and disconnect the air ducting from the air cleaner housing **(see illustration)**.

**5** Unclip the vacuum pipe and charcoal canister hose from the air cleaner housing. Unhook the insulated earth strap leading to the ignition coil, which is hooked into a clip on the right-hand side of the housing **(see illustration)**.

**6** Lift up the air cleaner housing, and disconnect the crankcase breather pipe from the stub. Check the pipe for signs of hardening or splitting, and fit a new pipe if necessary. Pull off the vacuum pipes from the base of the air temperature vacuum switch, noting their locations and colour-coding for use when refitting **(see illustrations)**.

**7** The air cleaner housing can now be removed from the engine compartment. Recover the sealing washer from the base of the housing - it may still be on the throttle body. Examine the seal condition, and renew if it provides a less-than-airtight fit.



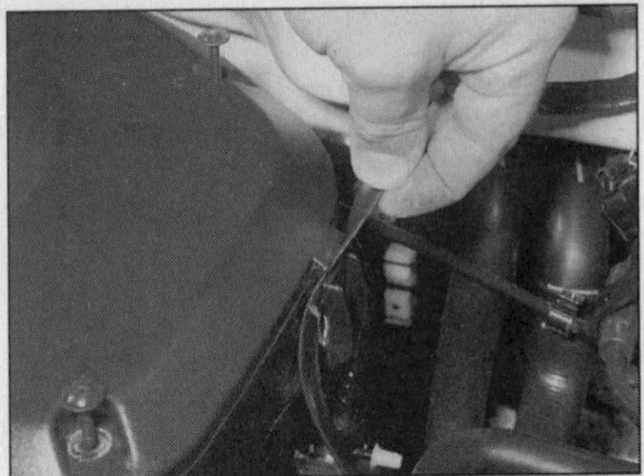

2.5 Unhooking the ignition coil earth strap from the side of the housing

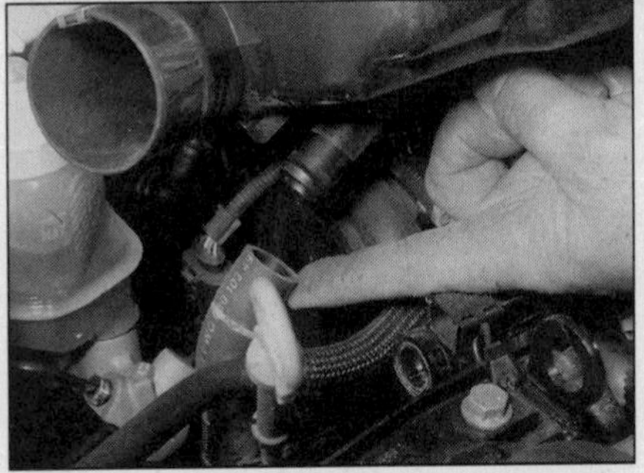

2.6a Disconnecting the crankcase breather pipe from the base of the air cleaner

2.6b The air temperature vacuum switch hose fittings are colour-coded

**2.8a Remove the retaining screws and disconnect the sections of air ducting**

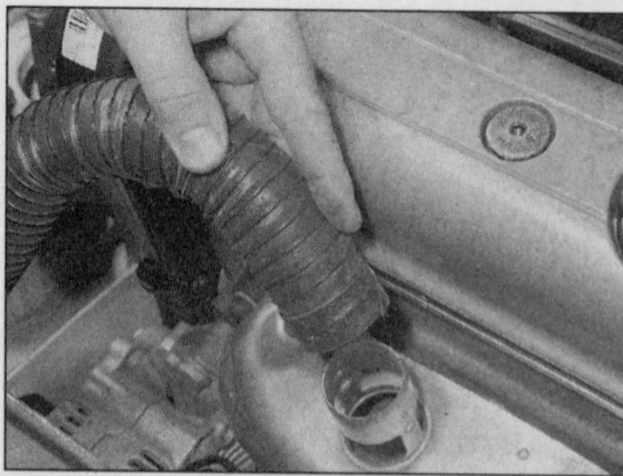

**2.8b The warm-air duct is simply pulled off the collector plate stub**

**8** The removal of the rest of the air inlet trunking is fairly self-evident. The trunking is secured to the air inlet temperature valve housing by a single screw at each end, and the valve housing itself is mounted to the inner wing by a single bolt. The air inlet trumpet is attached to the inner wing by a further bolt; once removed, it can then be pulled from the aperture in the inner wing. The duct to the exhaust manifold warm-air collector plate may have a worm-drive clip securing one end; once this is loosened, the duct is simply pulled off the pipe stubs **(see illustrations)**.

### Refitting

**9** Refit the air cleaner by following the removal procedure in reverse. The air cleaner housing must be correctly mounted on the throttle body, to ensure there is no air leakage.

**2.8c Air cleaner housing and inlet system components**

1 *Air cleaner top cover*
2 *Air filter element*
3 *Air cleaner housing*
4 *Seal*
5 *Crankcase breather hose*
6 *Air inlet trunking*
7 *Warm-air duct*
8 *Air inlet temperature valve housing*

## 3 Inlet air temperature control system - general information

### General information

**1** The inlet air temperature control system consists of a temperature-controlled flap valve, mounted in its own housing in the air cleaner inlet trunking, and a duct to the warm-air collector plate over the exhaust manifold.

**2** The temperature sensor in the flap valve housing senses the temperature of the inlet air, and opens the valve when a preset lower limit is reached. As the flap valve opens, warm air drawn from around the exhaust manifold blends with the inlet air.

**3** As the temperature of the inlet air rises, the sensor closes the flap progressively, until the warm-air supply from the exhaust manifold is completely closed off, and only air at ambient temperature is admitted to the air cleaner.

**4** With the ducting removed from the temperature control flap valve housing, the sensor is visible **(see illustration)**. If a hairdryer and suitable freeze spray is available, the action of the sensor can be tested.

## 4 Accelerator cable - removal, refitting and adjustment

**Note:** *Observe the precautions in Section 1 before working on any component in the fuel system.*

### Removal

**1** Remove the air cleaner housing as described in Section 2.

**2** Remove the metal clip and extract the cable outer from the mounting bracket **(see illustration)**.

**3** At the throttle body, disconnect the accelerator cable inner from the throttle valve spindle **(see illustration)**.

**4** Refer to Chapter 11 and remove the facia trim panels from underneath the steering column.

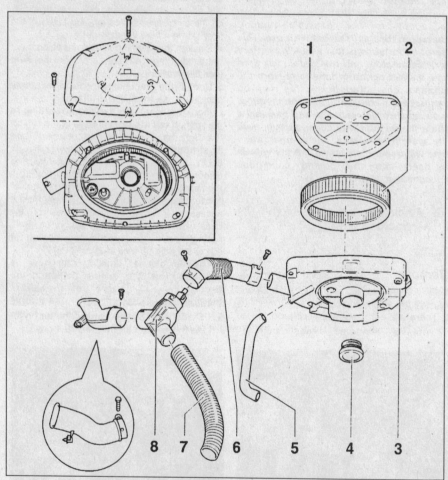

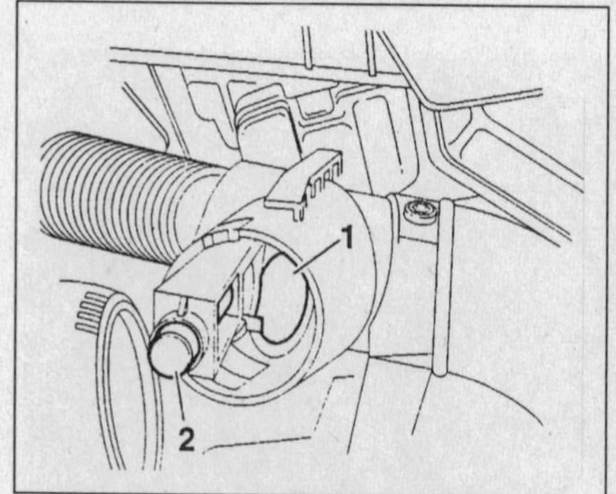


**3.4 Air inlet temperature control flap valve (1) and temperature sensor (2)**

4.2 Extract the metal adjustment clip and pull the cable outer from the mounting bracket

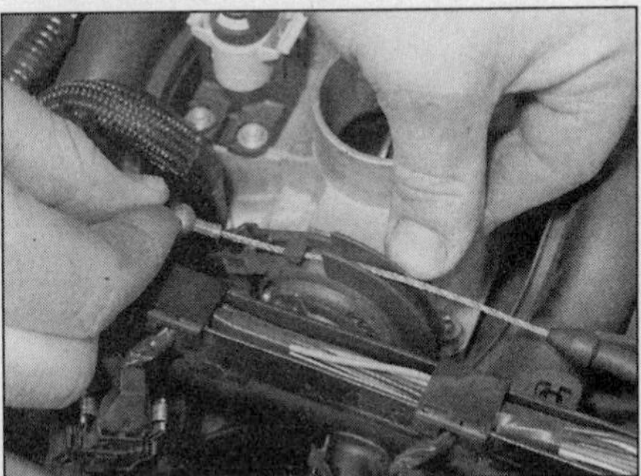

4.3 Disconnect the cable inner from the throttle spindle

4.9 Adjust the accelerator cable, then fix the cable using the metal clip in one of the slots

**5** Depress the accelerator pedal slightly, then unclip the accelerator cable end from the pedal extension lever.

**6** At the point where the cable passes through the bulkhead, unscrew the cap from the two-piece grommet so that the cable can move freely.

**7** Release the cable from its securing clips and guide it out through the bulkhead grommet.

## Refitting

**8** Refit the accelerator cable by following the removal procedure in reverse.

## Adjustment

**9** At the throttle body, fix the position of the cable outer in its mounting bracket by inserting the metal clip in one of the locating slots **(see illustration)**, such that when the accelerator is depressed fully, the throttle valve is just touching its end stop.

# 5 Bosch Motronic system components - removal and refitting

**Note:** *Observe the precautions in Section 1 before working on any component in the fuel system.*

## Throttle body

### Removal

**1** Remove the air cleaner housing as described in Section 2.

**2** Refer to Section 4 and detach the accelerator cable from the throttle valve lever.

**3** Disconnect the battery negative lead, and position it away from the terminal. **Note:** *If the vehicle has a security-coded radio, check that you have a copy of the code number before disconnecting the battery. Refer to your VW dealer if in doubt.*

**4** Unplug the wiring connectors from the throttle potentiometer and from the inlet manifold pressure/air temperature sensor **(see illustrations)**.

**5** Disconnect the hose for the charcoal canister from the port on the throttle body **(see illustration)**.

**6** Slacken and withdraw the through-bolts, then lift the throttle body away from the inlet manifold. Recover and discard the gasket. Note that one of the bolts secures the throttle body earth strap **(see illustrations)**.

**7** If required, refer to the relevant sub-Section and remove the throttle potentiometer.

5.4a Disconnect the throttle potentiometer wiring plug . . .

5.4b . . . and the inlet air pressure/temperature sensor plug

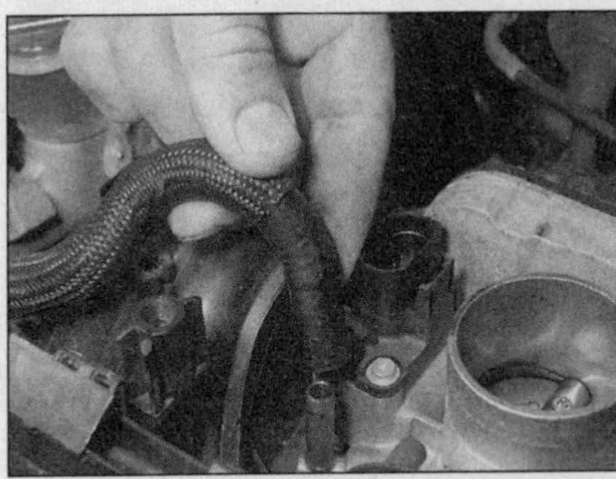

5.5 Disconnect the charcoal canister hose from the stub on the throttle body

4B

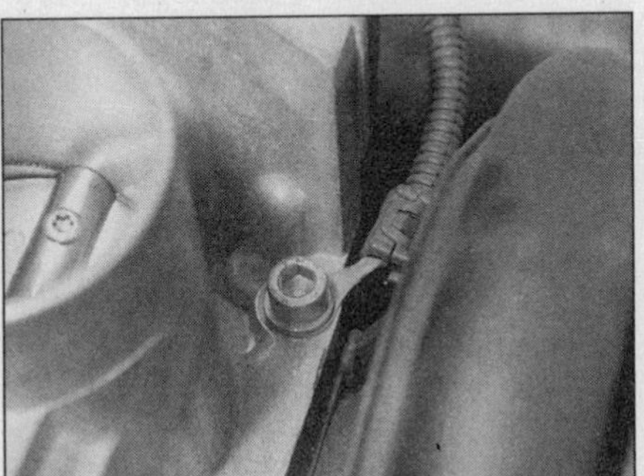

5.6a One of the throttle body through-bolts also secures the earth strap . . .

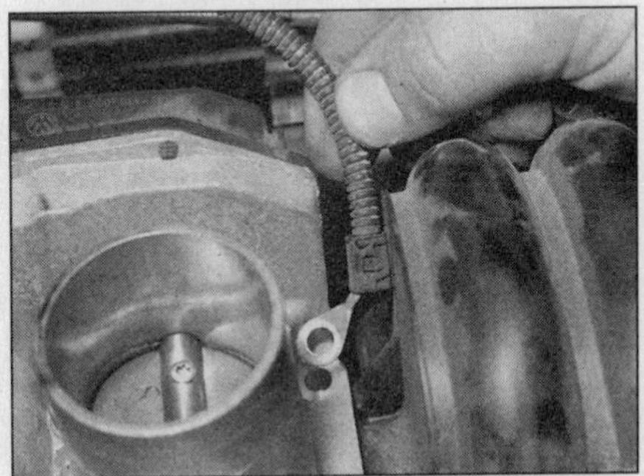

5.6b . . . remove the bolt, and move the strap to one side

5.6c Remove the remaining through-bolts . . .

5.6d . . . lift away the throttle body . . .

5.6e . . . and recover the base gasket

5.10a Disconnect the injector wiring plugs . . .

### Refitting

8 Refitting is a reversal of removal, noting the following:

*a) Use a new throttle body-to-inlet manifold gasket.*

*b) Tighten the throttle body through-bolts securely, to prevent air leaks. A tightening torque for these bolts is not specified by the manufacturers.*

*c) Ensure that all hoses and electrical connectors are refitted securely.*

*d) With reference to Section 4, check and if necessary adjust the accelerator cable.*

## Fuel injectors and fuel rail

**Note:** *Observe the precautions in Section 1 before working on any component in the fuel system. If a faulty injector is suspected, before removing the injectors, it is worth trying the effect of one of the proprietary injector-cleaning treatments. These can be added to the petrol in the tank, and are intended to clean the injectors as you drive.*

### Removal

9 Disconnect the battery negative lead, and position it away from the terminal - refer to the note in paragraph 3.

10 Unplug the injector harness connectors, labelling them to aid correct refitting later. Unclip the wiring harness clips from the top of the fuel rail, and lay the harness to one side **(see illustrations)**.

11 Refer to Section 9 and depressurise the fuel system.

12 Disconnect the vacuum hose from the port on the bottom of the fuel pressure regulator.

13 Slacken the clips and disconnect the fuel supply and return hoses from the end of the fuel rail. *Carefully* note the fitted positions of the hoses - the supply hose is marked with a black or white arrow, and the return hose is marked with a blue arrow **(see illustration)**.

14 Slacken and withdraw the fuel rail mounting bolts, then carefully lift the rail away from the inlet manifold, together with the injectors. Recover the injector lower O-ring seals as they emerge from the manifold **(see illustrations)**.

15 The injectors can be removed individually from the fuel rail by extracting the relevant metal clip and easing the injector out of the rail. Recover the injector upper O-ring seals **(see illustrations)**.

16 If required, remove the fuel pressure regulator, referring to the relevant sub-Section for guidance.

17 Check the electrical resistance of the injector using a multimeter and compare it with the Specifications.

5.10b . . . then unclip the harness retaining clips, and move the wiring harness to one side

5.13 Fuel supply and return connections at the fuel rail - note direction-of-flow arrows and colour-coding

5.14a Lift out the fuel rail . . .

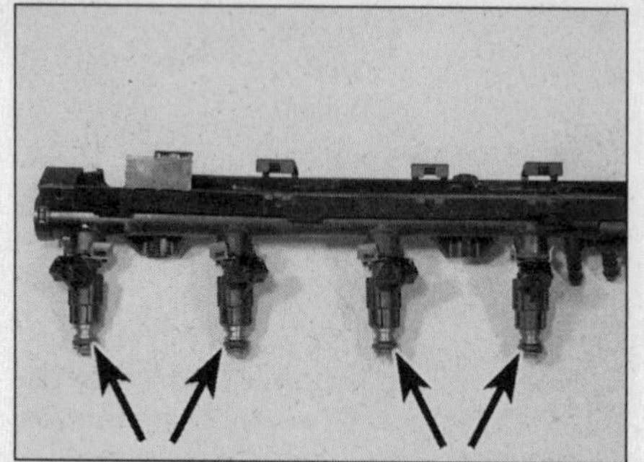
5.14b . . . and recover the injector lower O-ring seals (arrowed)

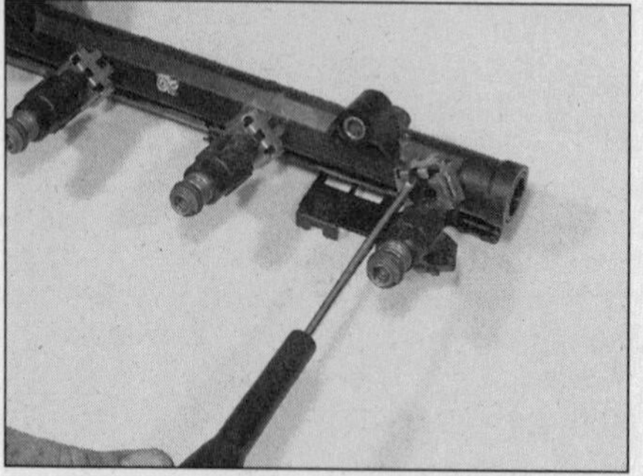
5.15a Using a suitable screwdriver, prise out the injector securing clip . . .

5.15b . . . and remove it from the fuel rail

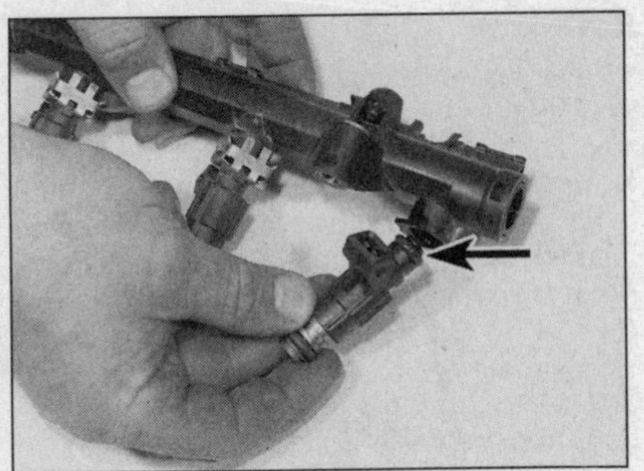
5.15c Ease out the injector, and recover the upper O-ring seal (arrowed)

5.23a The fuel pressure regulator is mounted in the end of the fuel rail (arrowed)

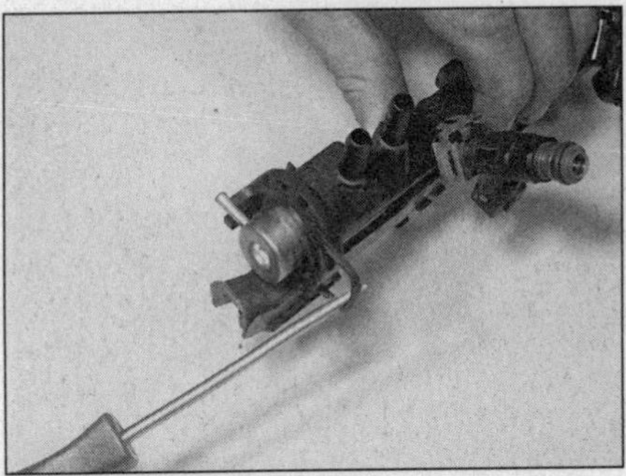
5.23b To remove the pressure regulator, prise out the retaining clip and withdraw it from the fuel rail

### Refitting

**18** Refit the injectors and fuel rail by following the removal procedure in reverse, noting the following points:

*a) Renew the injector O-ring seals if they appear worn or damaged.*
*b) Ensure that the injector retaining clips are securely seated.*
*c) Check that the fuel supply and return hoses are reconnected correctly - refer to the colour coding described in Removal.*
*d) Check that all vacuum and electrical connections are remade correctly and securely.*
*e) On completion, check exhaustively for fuel leaks before bringing the vehicle back into service.*

## Fuel pressure regulator

**Note:** *Observe the precautions in Section 1 before working on any component in the fuel system.*

### Removal

**19** Disconnect the battery negative lead, and position it away from the terminal - refer to the note in paragraph 3.
**20** Refer to Section 9 and depressurise the fuel system.
**21** Disconnect the vacuum hose from the port on the bottom of the fuel pressure regulator.
**22** Slacken the clip and disconnect the fuel supply hose from the end of the fuel rail. This will allow the majority of fuel in the regulator to drain out. Be prepared for an amount of fuel loss - position a small container and some old rags underneath the fuel regulator housing. **Note:** *The supply hose is marked with a black or white arrow.*
**23** Extract the retaining clip from the top of the regulator housing and lift out the regulator body, recovering the O-ring seals **(see illustrations)**.

### Refitting

**24** Refit the fuel pressure regulator by following the removal procedure in reverse, noting the following points:

*a) Renew the O-ring seals if they appear worn or damaged.*
*b) Ensure that the regulator retaining clip is securely seated.*
*c) Refit the regulator vacuum hose securely.*

## Throttle valve potentiometer

**Note:** *The potentiometer is matched to the throttle body during manufacture, and is not available separately - if defective, a complete throttle body assembly will be required.*

### Removal

**25** Disconnect the battery negative lead, and position it away from the terminal - refer to the note in paragraph 3.
**26** Unplug the harness connector from the potentiometer.
**27** Remove the retaining screws and lift the potentiometer away from the throttle body. Recover the gasket.

### Refitting

**28** Refitting is a reversal of removal, noting the following:

*a) Renew the gasket if it is damaged.*
*b) Ensure that the potentiometer drive engages correctly with the throttle spindle extension.*
*c) On vehicles with automatic transmission, the potentiometer must be matched to the automatic transmission Electronic Control Unit (ECU) - this operation requires access to dedicated electronic test equipment, refer to a VW dealer for advice.*

## Inlet manifold temperature sensor

### Removal

**29** The sensor is attached to the right-hand side of the inlet manifold.
**30** Disconnect the battery negative lead, and position it away from the terminal - refer to the note in paragraph 3. Unplug the harness connector from the sensor.
**31** Remove the two securing screws, and pull the sensor from the manifold. Recover the O-ring seal.

### Refitting

**32** Refitting is a reversal of removal, renewing the O-ring seal if necessary, and tightening the securing screws securely.

## Road speed sensor

**33** The road speed sensor is mounted on the transmission - refer to Chapter 7A.

## Coolant temperature sensor

**34** Refer to Chapter 3, Section 6.

## Lambda sensor

### Removal

**35** The lambda sensor is threaded into the exhaust downpipe, ahead of the catalytic converter **(see illustration)**. Refer to Chapter 4D for details.
**36** Disconnect the battery negative lead and position it away from the terminal - refer to the note in paragraph 3. Unplug the wiring harness from the lambda sensor at the connector, located on the right-hand side of the engine rear mounting.
**37** On early models, the sensor is only accessible from below - later models have the sensor situated higher up the downpipe, and it can be accessed from above. Slacken and withdraw the sensor, taking care to avoid damaging the sensor probe as it is removed. **Note:** *As a flying lead remains connected to the sensor after is has been disconnected, if the correct-size spanner is not available, a slotted socket will be required to remove the sensor.*



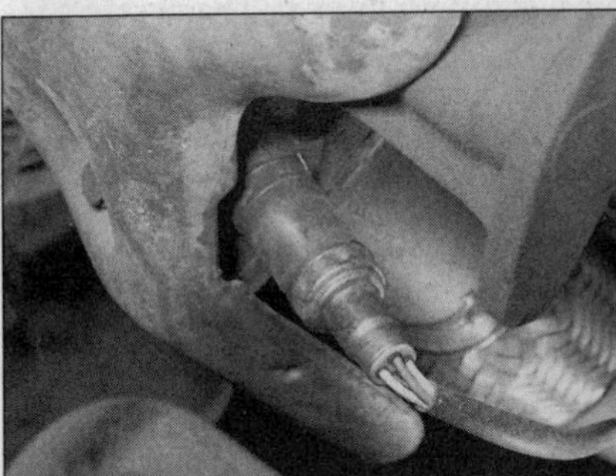
5.35 On later models, the lambda sensor is situated at the top of the exhaust downpipe - on earlier models, the sensor is further down

**5.40 The fuel injection ECU is situated under the windscreen cowl panels**

### Refitting

**38** Apply a little anti-seize grease to the sensor threads - avoid contaminating the probe tip.

**39** Refit the sensor to its housing, tightening it to the correct torque. Restore the harness connection.

### *Electronic control unit (ECU)*

**40** The ECU is located centrally behind the engine compartment bulkhead, under one of the windscreen cowl panels **(see illustration)**. Remove the cowl panel as described in Chapter 12, Section 13. The unit is coded, and should not be removed without consulting a VW dealer, otherwise it may not function correctly when the multi-plug is reconnected.

**10.7a Unscrew the inlet manifold bolts . . .**

## 6 Fuel filter - renewal

**Note:** *Observe the precautions in Section 1 before working on any component in the fuel system.*

Refer to Chapter 1A, Section 28.

## 7 Fuel pump and gauge sender unit - removal and refitting

**Note:** *Observe the precautions in Section 1 before working on any component in the fuel system.*

Refer to the information in Chapter 4A, Section 7.

## 8 Fuel tank - removal and refitting

**Note:** *Observe the precautions in Section 1 before working on any component in the fuel system.*

Refer to the information in Chapter 4A, Section 8.

## 9 Fuel injection system - depressurisation

**Note:** *Observe the precautions in Section 1 before working on any component in the fuel system.*

Refer to the information in Chapter 4A, Section 9.

## 10 Inlet manifold - removal and refitting

**Note:** *Observe the precautions in Section 1 before working on any component in the fuel system.*

### *Removal*

**1** Refer to Section 9 and depressurise the fuel system, then disconnect the battery negative lead and position it away from the terminal. **Note:** *If the vehicle has a security-coded radio, check that you have a copy of the code number before disconnecting the battery. Refer to your VW dealer if in doubt.*

**2** Refer to Section 2 and remove the air cleaner housing.

**3** Refer to Section 5 and remove the throttle body from the inlet manifold.

**4** Unplug the wiring harness from the inlet manifold air temperature/pressure sensor (see Section 5).

**5** Disconnect the brake servo vacuum hose from the port on the side of the inlet manifold. Also disconnect the distributor vacuum supply hose, next to the brake servo vacuum hose.

**6** Refer to Section 5 and remove the fuel rail and fuel injectors. **Note:** *The fuel rail may be moved to one side, leaving the fuel lines connected to it, but take care to avoid straining them.*

**7** Progressively slacken and remove the inlet manifold-to-cylinder head bolts. Move the manifold away from the head, and recover the O-ring seals **(see illustrations)**.

**8** Unclip the fuel supply and return hoses from underneath the manifold **(see illustration)**. If the hoses are disconnected, note their locations and colour-coding identification for refitting. The manifold can now be removed from the engine compartment.

### *Refitting*

**9** Refit the inlet manifold by following the removal procedure in reverse, noting the following points:

*a) Use new manifold O-ring seals **(see illustration)**.*

*b) Tighten the manifold-to-cylinder head bolts to the specified torque.*

*c) Check that all vacuum, electrical and fuel system connections are remade correctly and securely.*

*d) On completion, check exhaustively for fuel leaks before bringing the vehicle back into service.*

**10.7b . . . and withdraw the manifold (and fuel rail) from the cylinder head**

**10.8 Unclip the fuel hoses from the base of the manifold, and remove the manifold from the engine compartment**

**10.9 When refitting the inlet manifold, use new O-ring seals**

## 11 Fuel injection system - testing and adjustment

**1** If a fault appears in the fuel injection system, first ensure that all the system wiring connectors are securely connected and free of corrosion. Then ensure that the fault is not due to poor maintenance; ie, check that the air cleaner filter element is clean, the spark plugs are in good condition and correctly gapped, the cylinder compression pressures are correct, the ignition timing is correct and the engine breather hoses are clear and undamaged, referring to Chapters 1A, 2A, 4D (Section 3) and 5B.

**2** If these checks fail to reveal the cause of the problem, the vehicle should be taken to a suitably-equipped VW dealer for testing. A diagnostic connector is incorporated in the engine management system wiring harness, into which a dedicated electronic test equipment can be plugged. The test equipment is capable of 'interrogating' the engine management system ECU electronically and accessing its internal fault log. In this manner, faults can be pinpointed quickly and simply, even if their occurrence is intermittent. Testing all the system components individually in an attempt to locate the fault by elimination is a time-consuming operation that is unlikely to be fruitful (particularly if the fault occurs dynamically), and carries high risk of damage to the ECU's internal components.

**3** Experienced home mechanics equipped with an accurate tachometer and a carefully-calibrated exhaust gas analyser may be able to check the exhaust gas CO content and the engine idle speed; if these are found to be out of specification, then the vehicle must be taken to a suitably-equipped VW dealer for assessment. Neither the air/fuel mixture (exhaust gas CO content) nor the engine idle speed are manually adjustable; incorrect test results indicate a fault within the fuel injection system.

## 12 Unleaded petrol - general information and usage

**Note:** *The information given in this Chapter is correct at the time of writing, and applies only to petrols currently available in the UK. Check with a VW dealer as more up to date information may be available. If travelling abroad, consult one of the motoring organisations (or a similar authority) for advice on the petrols available and their suitability for your vehicle.*

**1** The fuel recommended by VW is given in the Specifications of this Chapter.

**2** RON and MON are different testing standards; RON stands for Research Octane Number (also written as RM), while MON stands for Motor Octane Number (also written as MM).

# Chapter 4 Part C:
# Fuel system - diesel

## Contents



## Degrees of difficulty

| | | | | |
|---|---|---|---|---|
| **Easy,** suitable for novice with little experience  | **Fairly easy,** suitable for beginner with some experience  | **Fairly difficult,** suitable for competent DIY mechanic | **Difficult,** suitable for experienced DIY mechanic | **Very difficult,** suitable for expert DIY or professional |



## Specifications

### General

| | |
|---|---|
| Firing order | 1-3-4-2 |
| Maximum engine speed (engine code AEF) | 5050 ± 100 rpm |
| Engine idle speed (engine code AEF) | 940 ± 20 rpm |
| Engine idle speed boost (engine code AEF) | 1050 ± 50 rpm |

| **Torque wrench settings** | **Nm** | **lbf ft** |
|---|---|---|
| Fuel cut-off solenoid (except engine code AEF) | 40 | 30 |
| Fuel tank filler neck screws | 4 | 3 |
| Fuel tank retaining bolts | 25 | 18 |
| Injection pump cover screws | 10 | 7 |
| Injection pump fuel supply and return banjo bolts | 25 | 18 |
| Injection pump mounting bolts | 25 | 18 |
| Injection pump sprocket bolts (engine code AEF) | 25 | 18 |
| Injection pump sprocket nut (except engine code AEF) | 55 | 41 |
| Injector fuel pipe unions | 25 | 18 |
| Injector retaining nut/bolt (except engine code AEF) | 20 | 15 |
| Injectors (engine code AEF) | 70 | 52 |

## 1 General information and precautions

### General information

#### Engine code AEF

The fuel system comprises a fuel tank, a fuel injection pump, an engine-bay mounted fuel filter with an integral water separator, fuel supply and return lines, and four fuel injectors.

The injection pump is driven at half crankshaft speed by the camshaft timing belt. Fuel is drawn from the fuel tank, through the filter by the injection pump, which then distributes the fuel under very high pressure to the injectors via separate delivery pipes.

The injectors are spring-loaded mechanical valves, which open when the pressure of the fuel supplied to them exceeds a specific limit. Fuel is then sprayed from the injector nozzle into the cylinder via a swirl chamber (indirect injection). Two-stage injectors are fitted, which open in steps as the supplied fuel pressure rises; this improves the engines combustion characteristics.

The basic injection timing is set by the position of the injection pump on its mounting bracket. When the engine is running, the injection timing is advanced and retarded mechanically by the injection pump itself, and is influenced primarily by the accelerator position and engine speed.

The engine is stopped by means of a solenoid-operated fuel cut-off valve, which interrupts the flow of fuel to the injection pump when de-activated.

When starting from cold, the engine idle speed is raised by means of a vacuum-operated automatic idle boost actuator, mounted on the side of the injection pump.

The fuel injection pump is equipped with an electronic self-diagnosis and fault logging system. Servicing of this system is only possible with dedicated electronic test equipment. Problems with the system's operation should therefore be referred to a VW dealer for assessment. Once the fault has been identified, the removal/refitting sequences detailed in the following Sections will then allow the appropriate component(s) to be renewed as required.

#### Engine codes AHG, AKU and AGD

The direct-injection fuelling system is controlled electronically by a diesel engine management system, comprising an Electronic Control Unit (ECU) and its associated sensors, actuators and wiring.

Basic injection timing is set mechanically by the position of the pump on its mounting bracket. Dynamic timing and injection duration are controlled by the ECU, and are dependent on engine speed, throttle position and rate of opening, inlet air flow , inlet air temperature, coolant temperature, and fuel temperature, received from sensors mounted on and around the engine. Closed-loop control of the injection timing is achieved by means of an injector needle lift sensor, which is fitted to injector No 3.

Two-stage injectors are used, which improve the engine's combustion characteristics, leading to quieter running and better exhaust emissions.

In addition, the ECU manages the operation of the Exhaust Gas Recirculation (EGR) emission control system and the glow plug control system (Chapter 4D).

It should be noted that fault diagnosis of the diesel engine management system fitted to engine codes AHG, AKU and AGD is only possible with dedicated electronic test equipment. Problems with the system's operation should therefore be referred to a VW dealer for assessment. Once the fault has been identified, the removal/refitting sequences detailed in the following Sections will then allow the appropriate component(s) to be renewed as required.

**Note:** *Throughout this Chapter, vehicles are frequently referred to by their engine code, rather than by engine capacity - refer to Chapter 2B for engine code listings.*

### Precautions

Many of the operations described in this Chapter involve the disconnection of fuel lines, which may cause an amount of fuel spillage. Before commencing work, refer to the warnings below and the information in *Safety first!* at the beginning of this manual.

***Warning: When working on any part of the fuel system, avoid direct contact skin contact with diesel fuel - wear protective clothing and gloves when handling fuel system components. Ensure that the work area is well-ventilated, to prevent the build-up of diesel fuel vapour.***

***Fuel injectors operate at extremely high pressures, and the jet of fuel produced at the nozzle is capable of piercing skin, with potentially fatal results. When working with pressurised injectors, take great care to avoid exposing any part of the body to the fuel spray. It is recommended that any pressure testing of the fuel system components should be carried out by a diesel fuel systems specialist.***

***Under no circumstances should diesel fuel be allowed to come into contact with coolant hoses - wipe off accidental spillage immediately. Hoses that have been contaminated with fuel for an extended period should be renewed. Diesel fuel systems are particularly sensitive to contamination from dirt, air and water. Pay particular attention to cleanliness when working on any part of the fuel system, to prevent the ingress of dirt. Thoroughly clean the area around fuel unions before disconnecting them. Store dismantled components in sealed containers, to prevent contamination and the formation of condensation. Only use lint-free cloths and clean fuel for component cleansing. Avoid using compressed air when cleaning components in situ.***

**2.3 Disconnecting the air inlet trunking**

## 2 Air cleaner assembly - removal and refitting

### Removal

**1** The air cleaner housing is mounted under the right-hand side front wing, and is secured in position by two nuts, which are accessed from below.

**2** Remove the air cleaner element, as described in Chapter 1B.

**3** Working in the engine compartment, compress the legs of the large spring clips using pliers, and disconnect the air inlet trunking from the throttle valve housing or inlet manifold cover, as applicable **(see illustration)**.

**4** Similarly, disconnect the opposite end of the air trunking from the top of the air cleaner housing. Pull the air inlet spout nearest the inner wing from the top of the housing, and remove it from the inner wing aperture at the top.

**5** Working in the right-hand front wheel arch, unscrew and remove the two housing securing nuts, and recover the bushes and grommets. Withdraw the housing from below.

### Refitting

**6** Refitting is a reversal of removal.

## 3 Accelerator cable (engine code AEF) - removal, refitting and adjustment

**1** This Section only applies to engine code AEF; all other engine codes are fitted with an electronic accelerator position sensor (see Section 12).

### Removal

**2** Refer to Chapter 11 and remove the facia trim panels from underneath the steering column.

3.5a Unhook the cable end fitting from the injection pump . . .

3.5b . . . and recover the rubber bush

3.6 Using a suitable pair of pliers, pull out the metal clip used to set the cable adjustment

3 Depress the accelerator pedal slightly, then unclip the accelerator cable end from the pedal extension lever.

4 At the point where the cable passes through the bulkhead, unscrew the cap from the two-piece grommet so that the cable can move freely.

5 Working in the engine bay, pull off the end of the accelerator cable inner from the fuel injection pump lever. Recover the rubber bush which fits inside the cable end fitting **(see illustrations)**.

6 Extract the metal securing clip from the grooved accelerator cable outer **(see illustration)**, then disconnect the cable from the mounting bracket.

7 Release the cable from its securing clips and guide it out through the bulkhead grommet.

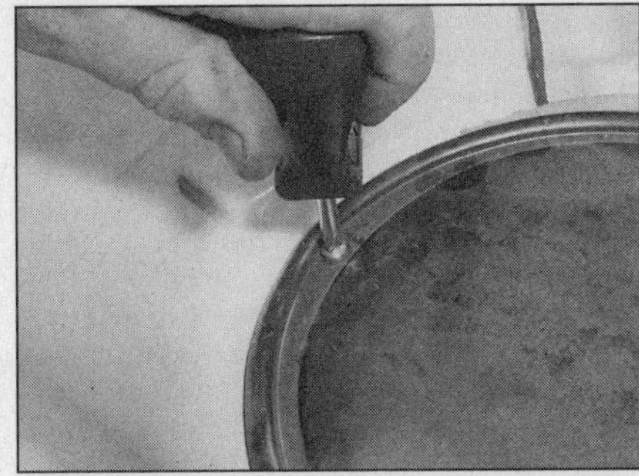
4.5 Slacken the access hatch screws, and lift the hatch away from the floorpan

### Refitting

8 Refit the accelerator cable by following the removal procedure in reverse.

### Adjustment

9 At the fuel injection pump, fix the position of the cable outer in its mounting bracket by inserting the metal clip in one of the locating grooves, such that when the accelerator is depressed fully, the throttle lever just touches its end stop.

## 4 Fuel tank sender unit - removal and refitting

1 The fuel tank sender unit is on the top of the fuel tank, and is accessible via a hatch in the load space floor. The unit provides a variable voltage signal that drives the facia-mounted fuel gauge, and also serves as a connection point for the fuel supply and return hoses.

2 The unit protrudes into the fuel tank, and its removal involves exposing the contents of the tank to the atmosphere.

***Warning: Avoid direct skin contact with diesel fuel - wear protective clothing and gloves when handling fuel system components. Ensure that the work area is well-ventilated, to prevent the build-up of diesel fuel vapour.***

### Removal

3 Ensure that the vehicle is parked on a level surface, then disconnect the battery negative lead and position it away from the terminal. **Note:** *If the vehicle has a security-coded radio, check that you have a copy of the code number before disconnecting the battery. Refer to your VW dealer if in doubt.*

4 Fold the rear seat forwards, and remove the trim from the load space floor.

5 Slacken and withdraw the access hatch screws, and lift the hatch away from the floorpan **(see illustration)**.

6 Unplug the wiring harness connector from the sender unit **(see illustration)**.

7 Pad the area around the supply and return fuel hoses with rags to absorb any spilt fuel, then slacken the hose clips and remove them from the ports at the sender unit **(see illustration)**. Observe the supply and return arrows markings on the ports - label the fuel hoses accordingly to ensure correct refitting. To aid identification, the fuel supply pipe is colour-coded black, and the return pipe is blue.

8 Unscrew the plastic securing ring and lift it out **(see Tool Tip)**. Where applicable, turn the sender unit to the left to release it from its bayonet fitting and lift it out, holding it above the level of the fuel in the tank until the excess fuel has drained out. Recover the rubber seal **(see illustrations)**.

4C

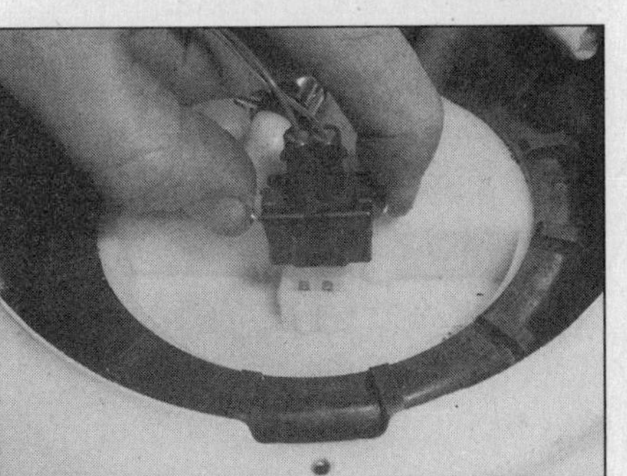
4.6 Unplug the wiring harness connector from the sender unit

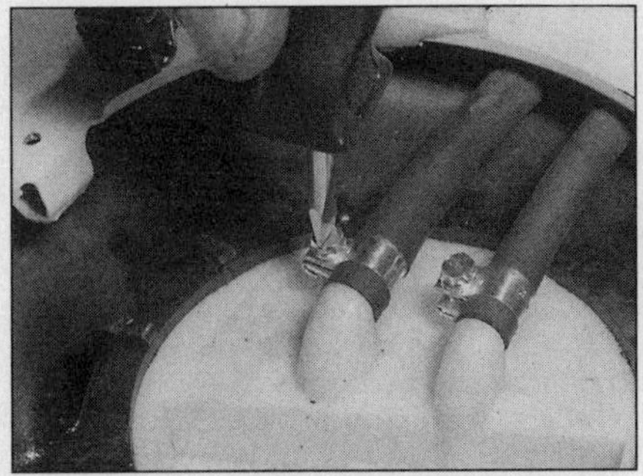
4.7 Slacken the hose clips and remove the fuel pipes from the ports at the sender unit

*Use a pair of water pump pliers to grip and rotate the fuel tank sender unit plastic securing ring*

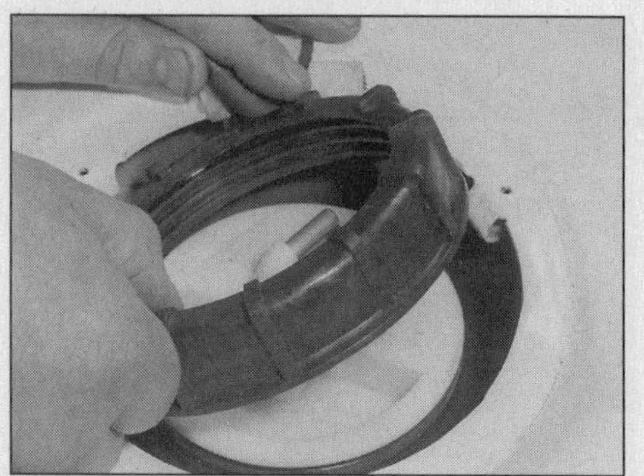

4.8a Unscrew the plastic securing ring and lift it out

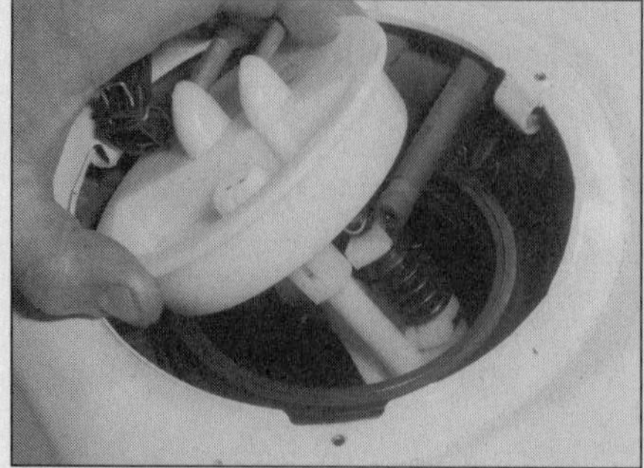

4.8b Lift out the sender unit . . .

4.8c . . . and recover the rubber seal

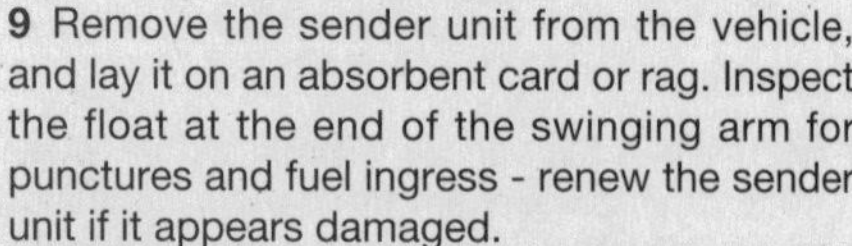

9 Remove the sender unit from the vehicle, and lay it on an absorbent card or rag. Inspect the float at the end of the swinging arm for punctures and fuel ingress - renew the sender unit if it appears damaged.

10 The fuel pick-up incorporated in the sender unit is spring-loaded to ensure that it always draws fuel from the lowest part of the tank. Check that the pick-up is free to move under spring tension with respect to the sender unit body.

11 Recover the rubber seal from the fuel tank aperture and inspect for signs of fatigue - renew it if necessary.

12 Inspect the sender unit wiper and track; clean off any dirt and debris that may have accumulated, and look for breaks in the track **(see illustration)**. An electrical specification for the sender unit is not quoted by VW, but the integrity of the wiper and track may be verified by connecting a multimeter, set to the resistance function, across the sender unit connector terminals. The resistance should vary as the float arm is moved up and down; an open-circuit reading indicates that the sender is faulty and should be renewed.

### Refitting

13 Refitting is a reversal of removal, noting the following points:

a) *The arrow markings on the sender unit body and the fuel tank must be aligned* ***(see illustration)****.*

b) *Smear the tank aperture rubber seal with clean fuel before fitting it in position.*

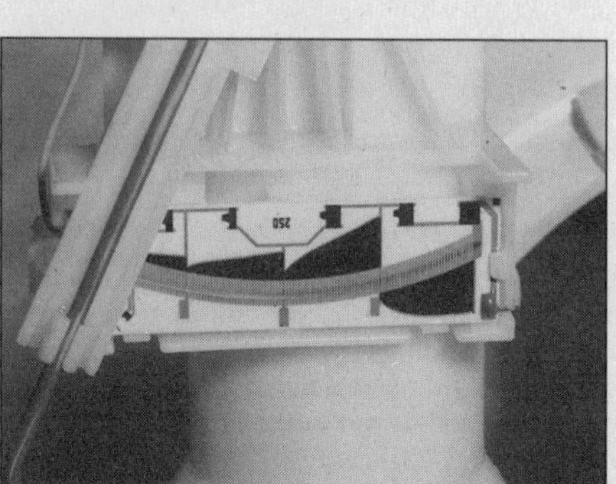

4.12 Look for breaks in the sender unit wiper track

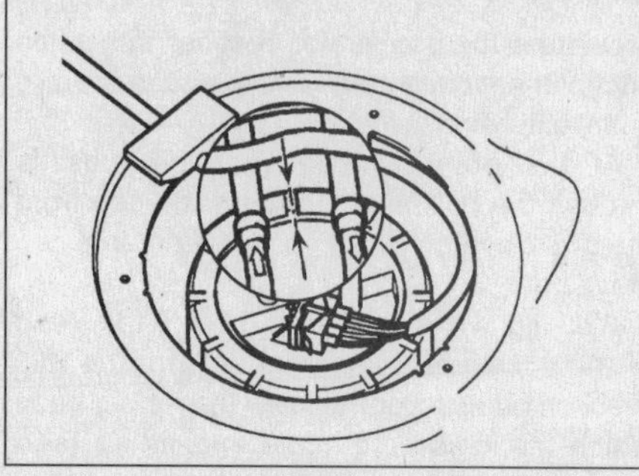

4.13 The arrow marks on the sender unit body and the fuel tank must be aligned

## 5 Fuel tank - removal and refitting

**Note:** *Observe the precautions in Section 1 before working on any component in the fuel system.*

### Removal

1 Before the tank can be removed, it must be drained of as much fuel as possible. As no drain plug is provided, it is preferable to carry out this operation with the tank almost empty.

2 Disconnect the battery negative lead and position it away from the terminal. **Note:** *If the vehicle has a security-coded radio, check that you have a copy of the code number before disconnecting the battery. Refer to your VW dealer if in doubt.*

3 Using a hand pump or syphon, remove any remaining fuel from the bottom of the tank.

4 Refer to Section 4 and carry out the following:

a) *Disconnect the wiring harness from the top of the sender unit at the multiway connector.*

b) *Disconnect the fuel supply and return hoses from the sender unit.*

5 Loosen the right-hand rear wheel bolts, then jack up the rear of the car and remove the right-hand rear wheel.

6 Position a trolley jack under the centre of the tank. Insert a block of wood between the jack head and the tank to prevent damage to the tank surface. Raise the jack until it just takes the weight of the tank.

7 Working inside the rear right-hand wheelarch, slacken and withdraw the bolts that secure the tank filler neck inside of the wheelarch **(see illustration)**. Open the fuel filler flap and peel the rubber sealing flange away from the bodywork.

8 Unhook all the rear exhaust mountings from the body, then lower the exhaust system sufficiently to allow the fuel tank to be lowered. Do not allow the exhaust to hang down unsupported - tie it loosely to the body with wire, or position suitable supports underneath it, to just take its weight.

9 Loosen and remove the retaining bolts around the tank, keeping one hand on the tank to steady it as it is released from its mountings **(see illustration)**. Several of the bolts double as retaining bolts for the exhaust heat shield; recover any sections of shield which are released as the tank is withdrawn.

5.7 Fuel filler neck securing bolts (arrowed) - seen from inside the wheel arch

5.9 Fuel tank strap securing bolt

**10** Lower the jack and tank away from the underside of the vehicle, detaching the filler pipes as the tank is lowered. Locate the earthing strap and breather pipe, and disconnect them from the filler neck.

**11** If the tank is contaminated with sediment or water, remove the sender unit (see Section 4) and swill the tank out with clean fuel. The tank is injection-moulded from a synthetic material and if damaged, it should be renewed. However, in certain cases it may be possible to have small leaks or minor damage repaired. Seek the advice of a suitable specialist before attempting to repair the fuel tank.

### Refitting

**12** Refitting is the reverse of the removal procedure, noting the following points:

a) *When lifting the tank back into position, make sure the heat shield is correctly positioned, and take great care to ensure that none of the hoses become trapped between the tank and vehicle body.*
b) *Ensure that all pipes and hoses are correctly routed and securely held in position with their retaining clips.*
c) *Reconnect the earth strap to its terminal on the filler neck.*
d) *Tighten the tank retaining bolts to the specified torque.*
e) *On completion, refill the tank with fuel and exhaustively check for signs of leakage prior to taking the vehicle out on the road.*

## 6 Fuel injection pump - removal and refitting

**Note 1:** *On engine code AEF, the injection pump timing is checked statically, as is normally the case with diesel engines. The timing would normally be checked using a dial test indicator (DTI) to measure fuel pump lift. However, the injection pump timing setting is expressed as a dimension from the flywheel TDC mark to a fixed point on the engine, and accurate setting must therefore be carried out using dedicated VW equipment.*

**Note 2:** *On engine codes AHG, AKU and AGD, the injection pump commencement-of-injection setting must be checked and if necessary adjusted after refitting. The commencement of injection is controlled by the fuel injection ECU and is influenced by several other engine parameters, including coolant temperature, and engine speed and position. Although the adjustment is a mechanical operation, checking can only be carried out by a VW dealer, as dedicated electronic test equipment is needed to interface with the fuel injection ECU.*

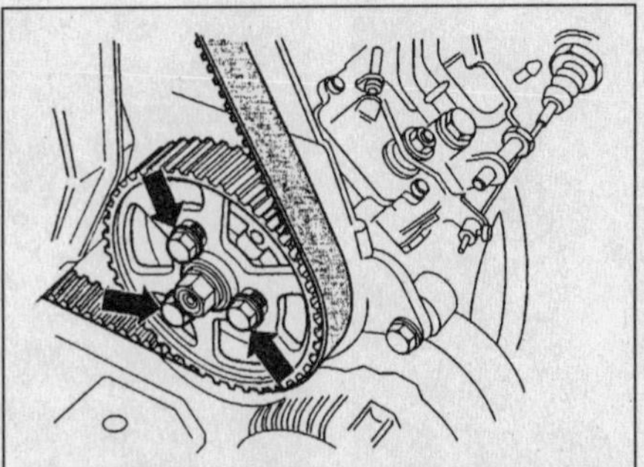

**6.6 Loosen and remove ONLY the three pulley-to-hub bolts (arrowed)**

### Removal

**1** Disconnect the battery negative lead and position it away from the terminal. **Note:** *If the vehicle has a security-coded radio, check that you have a copy of the code number before disconnecting the battery. Refer to your VW dealer if in doubt.*

**2** Remove the air cleaner inlet trunking as described in Section 2.

**3** Owing to the extremely limited working room around the pump, the lock carrier assembly must now be removed - refer to Chapter 2C. The carrier need not be removed completely, just pulled forwards sufficiently to access the pump. Accordingly, the coolant hoses need not be disconnected from the radiator, but the assembly must be adequately supported.

**4** With reference to Chapter 2B, carry out the following:

a) *Remove the camshaft cover and timing belt outer cover.*
b) *Set the engine to TDC on cylinder No 1.*
c) *Remove the timing belt from the camshaft and fuel injection pump sprockets.*

**5** The timing belt sprocket must now be removed from the injection pump shaft. The sprocket must be braced whilst its fixings are loosened - a home-made tool can easily be fabricated for this purpose; refer to Section 5 of Chapter 2B for further details.

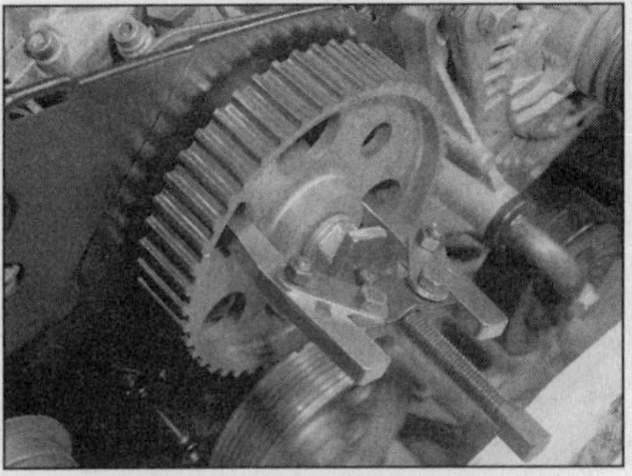

**6.8 Attach a two-legged puller to the injection pump sprocket**

### Engine code AEF

**6** Loosen the three bolts and remove the sprocket from the pump hub **(see illustration)**. ***Caution: On no account should the nut seen at the centre of the sprocket be slackened, as this will alter the basic injection timing.***

### Engine codes AHG, AKU and AGD

**7** Loosen and remove the nut at the centre of the sprocket. To hold the sprocket as the nut is undone, make up a tool similar to the one shown in Chapter 2B, Section 5.

**8** Attach a two-legged puller to the injection pump sprocket, then gradually tighten the puller until the sprocket is under firm tension **(see illustration)**.

***Caution: To prevent damage to the injection pump shaft, insert a piece of scrap metal between the end of the shaft and the puller centre bolt.***

**9** Tap sharply on the puller centre bolt with a hammer - this will free the sprocket from the tapered shaft. Detach the puller, then fully slacken and remove the sprocket fixings, lift off the sprocket and recover the Woodruff key **(see illustrations)**.

### All engines

**10** Disconnect the fuel supply and return hoses from the pump, taking care to minimise fuel loss, and labelling them if necessary for accurate refitting **(see illustration)**. Also disconnect the fuel leak-off hose from the fuel return connection.

4C

**6.9a Lift off the pump sprocket . . .**

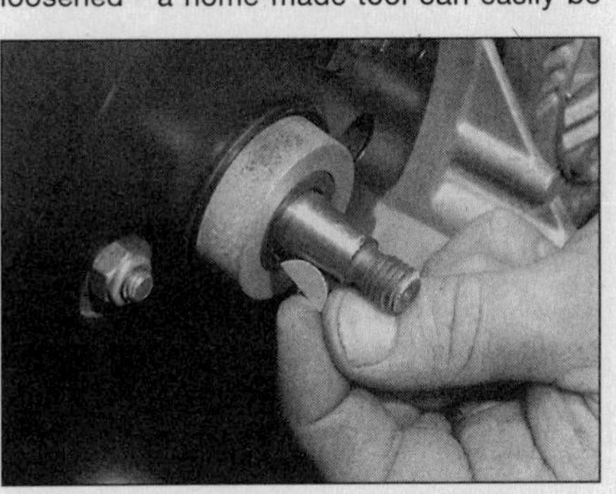

**6.9b . . . and recover the Woodruff key**

**6.10 Fuel supply (top) and return (bottom) hoses**

6.11a Slacken the rigid fuel pipe unions at the rear of the injection pump

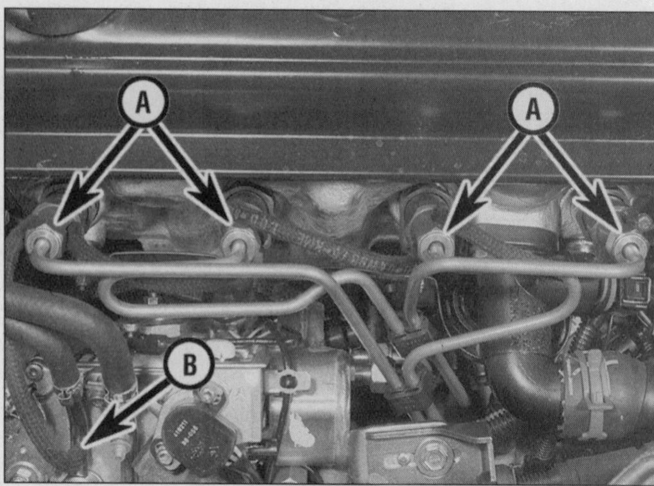


6.11b Fuel injector unions (A) and injector leak-off hose connection (B)

***Haynes Hint 1:** Cut the fingertips from an old pair of rubber gloves and secure them over the fuel ports with elastic bands*

**11** Using a pair of spanners (a slotted ring spanner may be required), slacken the rigid fuel pipe unions on the injection pump and at each end of the injectors, then lift the fuel pipe assembly away from the engine **(see illustrations)**.

***Caution:** Be prepared for some fuel leakage during this operation, position a small container under the union to be slackened and pad the area with old rags, to catch any spilt diesel. Take great care to avoid stressing the rigid fuel pipes as they are removed.*

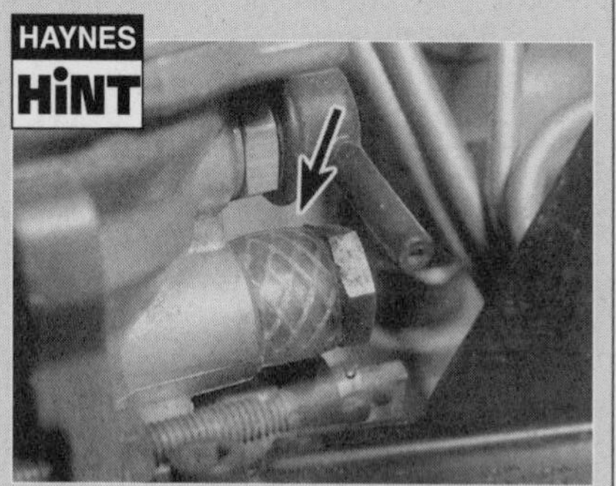


***Haynes Hint 2:** Fit a short length of hose over the banjo bolt (arrowed) so that the drillings are covered, then thread the bolt back into its injection pump port*

**12** Cover the open pipes and ports to prevent the ingress of dirt and excess fuel leakage **(see Haynes Hints 1 and 2)**.

## Engine code AEF

**13** Disconnect the vacuum pipe from the idle speed boost actuator on the injection pump **(see illustration)**.

**14** Disconnect the accelerator cable from the injection pump bracket referring to Section 3.

**15** Disconnect the wiring plugs from the following components/locations, labelling the plugs to aid refitting:

*a) Coolant temperature sender on the coolant elbow at the front of the cylinder head **(see illustration)**.*
*b) Oil pressure switch on the left-hand end of the cylinder head.*
*c) Oil temperature/pressure switch on the oil filter mounting bracket.*
*d) Glow plugs.*
*e) Speedometer sender on the top of the transmission.*
*f) Main harness connector on the left-hand end of the cylinder block, and the earth connection next to it **(see illustration)**.*

**Note:** *New injection pumps are not supplied with harness multiway connector housings. If the pump is to be renewed, then the relevant spade terminal pins must be pushed out of the existing connector housing, to allow those from the new pump to be inserted; refer to the wiring diagrams in Chapter 12 for details of connector pin-outs.*

**16** Before removing the pump, mark the position of the mounting bolts in their elongated holes. The pump can then be refitted in this reference position, to allow an approximate injection timing setting to be achieved when the pump is refitted.

6.13 Disconnecting the idle speed boost actuator vacuum pipe - connection arrowed

6.15a Coolant temperature sender wiring plug (arrowed)

6.15b Main harness wiring connector at left-hand end of cylinder head, and earth connection (arrowed)

17 Loosen and remove the rear support bolt and the three mounting bolts at the sprocket end **(see illustrations)**, supporting the pump as the last is removed. Check that nothing remains connected, then lift the injection pump from the engine bay.

### Engine codes AKU, AHG and AGD

18 Disconnect all wiring plugs from around the injection pump, as listed below. Label the plugs, to aid refitting. Depending on engine code, the exact number and location of the plugs will differ:

*a) Fuel cut-off solenoid valve.*
*b) Commencement-of-injection valve.*
*c) Fuel quantity adjuster.*
*d) Fuel temperature sender.*

19 Before removing the pump, mark the position of the mounting bolts in their elongated holes. The pump can then be refitted in this reference position, to allow an approximate injection timing setting to be achieved when the pump is refitted.

20 Loosen and remove the three mounting nuts/bolts at the sprocket end, and the bolt from the rear support **(see illustrations)**, supporting the pump as the mountings are removed. Check that nothing remains connected, then lift the injection pump from the engine bay.

## Refitting

21 Offer up the injection pump to the engine, then insert the mounting nuts/bolts and tighten to the specified torque. **Note:** *The mounting holes are elongated to allow adjustment - if a new pump is being fitted, then mount it such that the bolts are initially at the centre of the holes, to allow the maximum range of pump timing adjustment. Alternatively, if the existing pump is being refitted, use the markings made during removal for alignment.*

22 Prime the injection pump by fitting a small funnel to the fuel supply and return pipe unions, and filling the cavity with clean diesel. Pad the area around the unions with clean dry rags to absorb any spillage.

23 Reconnect the fuel pipes to the injectors and injection pump, then tighten the unions to the correct torque using a pair of spanners.

**6.17a Injection pump rear support bolt . . .**

24 Reconnect the fuel supply and return pipes to the pump, using new sealing washers. Tighten the banjo bolts to the specified torque.

25 Reconnect all wiring plugs to the engine and injection pump, as applicable, using the labels fitted on disconnection to aid refitting.

### Engine code AEF

26 Reconnect the vacuum pipe to the idle speed boost valve.

27 Referring to Section 3, reconnect and adjust the accelerator cable.

28 Offer up the injection pump sprocket, and fit the three retaining bolts in the centre of the slotted holes. Hand-tighten the bolts at this stage.

29 Lock the injection pump sprocket in position by inserting a bar or bolt through its alignment hole and into the drilling in the pump hub. Ensure that there is minimal play in the sprocket, once it has been locked in position.

30 Refit and tension the timing belt as described in Chapter 2B.

31 The injection pump timing must now be checked and if necessary adjusted by a VW dealer; refer to Note 1 at the start of this Section. If a new pump has been fitted, your VW dealer will need to match the new pump to the electronic immobiliser (where fitted).

32 Check and if necessary adjust the idle speed as described in Chapter 1B, the maximum engine speed (Section 7), and the idle speed boost (Section 8).

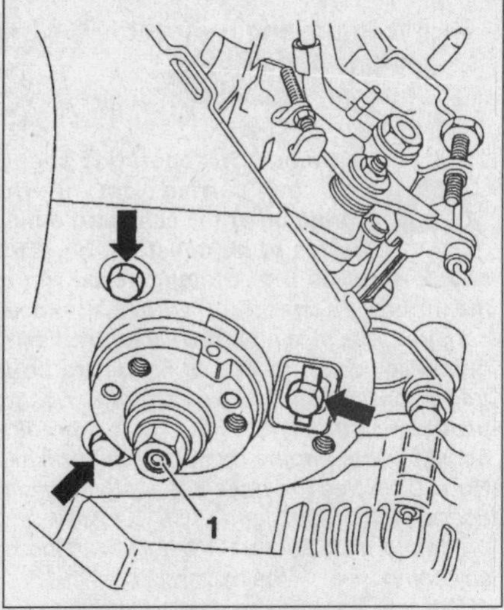


**6.17b . . . and mounting bolts at the sprocket end (arrowed) - engine code AEF**

*On no account loosen the centre nut (1)*

### Engine codes AKU, AHG and AGD

33 Fit the injection pump sprocket to the pump shaft, ensuring that the Woodruff key is correctly seated. Fit the retaining nut and tighten to the specified torque **(see illustration)**.

34 Refit and tension the timing belt as described in Chapter 2B.

35 The commencement-of-injection setting must now be dynamically checked and if necessary adjusted by a VW dealer; refer to Note 2 at the beginning of this Section. If a new pump has been fitted, your VW dealer will need to match the new pump to the electronic immobiliser (where fitted).

### All engines

36 The rest of the refitting procedure is a direct reversal of removal.



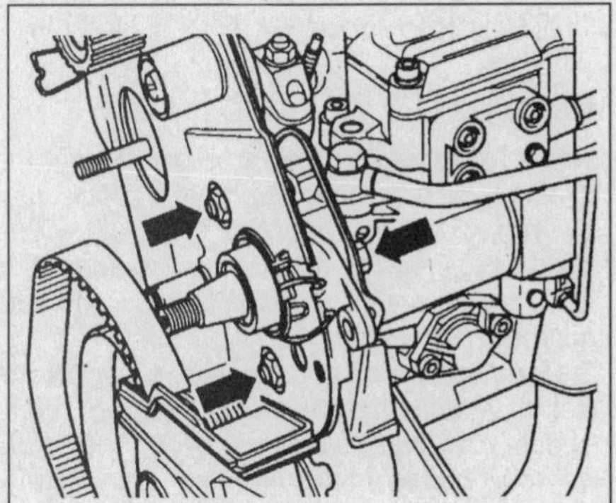

**6.20a Injection pump mounting nuts and bolts at the sprocket end . . .**

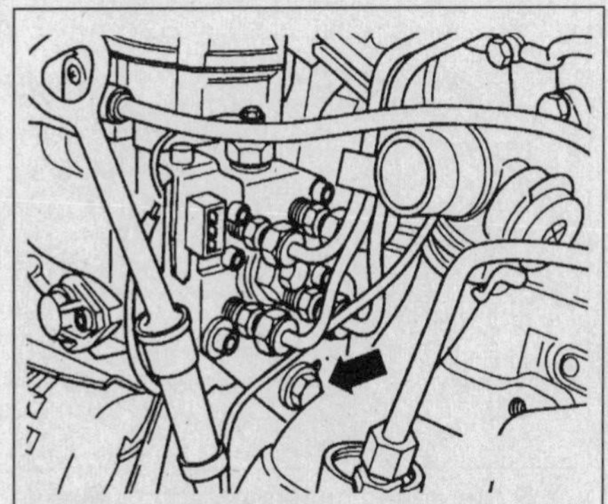

**6.20b . . . and rear support bolt (arrowed) - engine codes AKU, AHG and AGD**

**6.33 Tightening the fuel injection pump sprocket, using a home-made locking tool**

## 7 Maximum engine speed (engine code AEF) - checking and adjustment

***Warning: This operation should not be carried out if the condition of the camshaft timing belt is at all questionable. This check requires that the engine be run at maximum speed, which places considerable strain on the camshaft timing belt. Provided the belt is known to be in good condition, there should be no problem, but if the belt breaks, considerable engine damage would result.***

**Note:** *This Section does not apply to engine codes AHG, AKU and AGD. Observe the precautions in Section 1 before working on any component in the fuel system.*

**1** Start the engine and let it warm up to normal operating temperature.

**2** Ensure that the handbrake is firmly applied and the transmission is in neutral, then have an assistant depress the accelerator fully.

**3** Using a diesel tachometer, check that the maximum engine speed is as quoted in the Specifications.

***Caution: Do not maintain maximum engine speed for more than two or three seconds.***

**4** If adjustment is necessary, remove the locking wire and protective cap from the adjusting screw. Adjust the maximum engine speed by slackening the locknut and rotating the adjusting screw **(see illustration)**.

**5** Re-check the setting, then tighten the locknut. Refit the locking wire and protective cap.

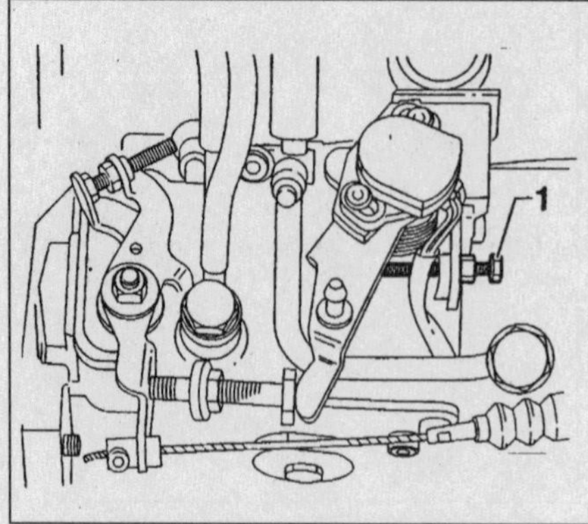


**7.4 Maximum engine speed adjusting screw (1) - engine code AEF**

## 8 Idle speed boost (engine code AEF) - checking

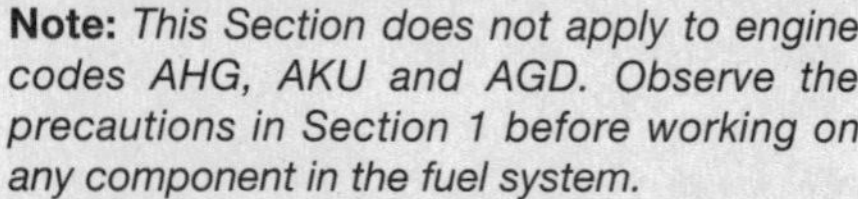

**Note:** *This Section does not apply to engine codes AHG, AKU and AGD. Observe the precautions in Section 1 before working on any component in the fuel system.*

**1** The idle speed boost valve is mounted on the engine compartment bulkhead, next to the EGR solenoid valve **(see illustration)**. It operates when the engine is cold, or when a load is placed on the engine which would normally cause the idle speed to drop (eg switching on the headlights, heated rear window, etc). The system will not necessarily provide a fast idle, such as a choke control might on a petrol engine, but is intended rather to maintain the idle speed, regardless of engine temperature or load. If the system does not appear to be operating properly, check as follows.

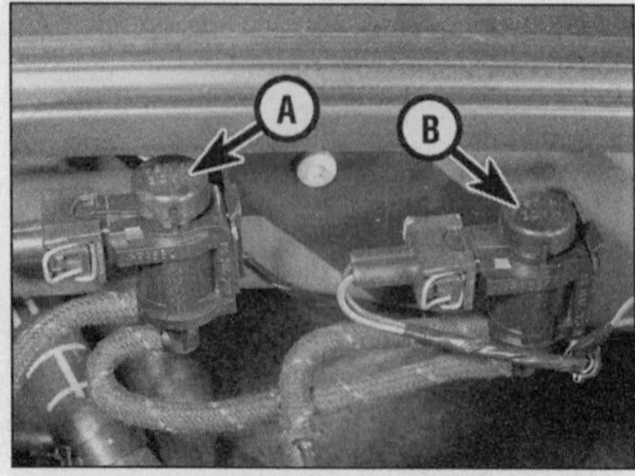


**8.1 Exhaust Gas Recirculation (EGR) solenoid valve (A) and idle speed boost valve (B) on engine compartment bulkhead**

**2** With reference to Chapter 1B, check and if necessary adjust the idle speed.

**3** Start the engine, then switch on as many electrical loads as possible. Provided the battery and charging system are in good condition, the idle speed should not drop significantly.

**4** With the engine warm, pull off the vacuum hose from the boost valve vacuum capsule. The idle speed should rise to the value specified at the start of this Chapter.

**5** The idle speed boost is not adjustable. If the boost valve is not operating correctly, check the vacuum hose for splits, and that the linkage is not binding. The operating cable should be set so that there is slight play between the clamp and the operating lever **(see illustration)**. If the valve is faulty, it should be renewed complete.

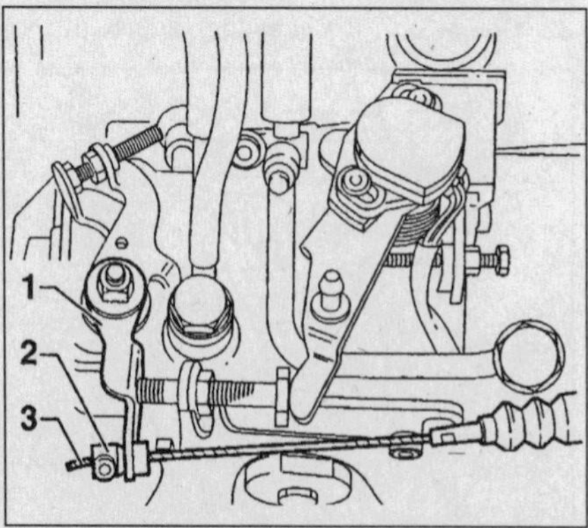


**8.5 Idle speed boost operating linkage**

*1 Operating lever*
*2 Cable clamp*
*3 Operating cable*

## 9 Fuel injection pump timing - testing and adjustment

On engine codes AHG, AKU and AGD, the fuel injection pump timing is controlled electronically by the system ECU, and can only be checked and adjusted using dedicated test equipment. Refer to a VW dealer for advice.

On engine code AEF, checking and setting the injection pump timing using a dial test indicator (DTI) is not possible, since VW do not quote timing figures for use with a DTI - a special VW setting rig is required to set the timing with the necessary degree of accuracy.

## 10 Injectors - general information, removal and refitting

***Warning: Exercise extreme caution when working on the fuel injectors. Never expose the hands or any part of the body to injector spray, as the high working pressure can cause the fuel to penetrate the skin, with possibly fatal results. You are strongly advised to have any work which involves testing the injectors under pressure carried out by a dealer or fuel injection specialist. Refer to the precautions given in Section 1 of this Chapter before proceeding.***

### General information

**1** Injectors do deteriorate with prolonged use, and it is reasonable to expect them to need reconditioning or renewal after 60 000 miles (100 000 km) or so. Accurate testing, overhaul and calibration of the injectors must be left to a specialist. A defective injector which is causing knocking or smoking can be located without dismantling as follows.

**2** Run the engine at a fast idle. Gradually slacken each injector union in turn, placing rag around the union to catch spilt fuel and being careful not to expose the skin to any spray. When the union on the defective injector is slackened, the knocking or smoking will stop.

### Removal

**Note:** *Take great care not to allow dirt into the injectors or fuel pipes during this procedure. Do not drop the injectors, nor allow the needles at their tips to become damaged. The injectors are precision-made to fine limits, and must not be handled roughly.*

**3** Disconnect the battery negative lead. **Note:** *If the vehicle has a security-coded radio, check that you have a copy of the code number before disconnecting the battery. Refer to your VW dealer if in doubt.*

**4** Cover the alternator with a clean cloth or plastic bag, to protect it if fuel is spilt onto it.

10.7a Removing an injector from the cylinder head

5 Carefully clean around the injectors and pipe union nuts, and disconnect the return pipes from the injectors.

6 Wipe clean the pipe unions, then slacken the union nut securing the relevant injector pipes to each injector, and the relevant union nuts securing the pipes to the rear of the injection pump (pipes are removed as one assembly). As each pump union nut is slackened, retain the adapter with a suitable open-ended spanner to prevent it being unscrewed from the pump. With the union nuts undone, remove the injector pipes from the engine. Cover the injector and pipe unions to prevent the entry of dirt into the system.

*Cut the fingertips from an old rubber glove, and secure them over the open unions with elastic bands to prevent dirt ingress (see Section 6).*

### Engine code AEF

7 Unscrew each injector using a 27 mm deep socket or box spanner, and remove from the cylinder head. Recover the heat shield washer, and discard it - new washers must be used when refitting **(see illustrations)**. If the injectors are not being overhauled, label them so they can be refitted in their original positions.

### Engine codes AKU, AHG and AGD

8 Unscrew and remove the retaining nut or bolt, and recover the washer, retaining plate and mounting collar. Note the fitted position of all components, for use when refitting. Withdraw the injector from the cylinder head, and recover the heat shield washer - new washers must be obtained for refitting. If the injectors are not being overhauled, label them so they can be refitted in their original positions; injector No 3 uniquely includes the needle lift sender.

## *Refitting*

### Engine code AEF

9 Fit a new heat shield washer to the cylinder head, noting that it must be fitted with its concave side facing downwards (towards the cylinder head) **(see illustration)**.

10.7b Recover the heat shield washer

10 Screw the injector into position and tighten it to the specified torque **(see illustration)**.

### Engine codes AKU, AHG and AGD

11 Insert the injector into position, using a new heat shield washer.

12 Fit the mounting collar and retaining plate, and secure in position with the nut and washer, tightened to the specified torque.

### All engines

13 Refit the injector pipes, and tighten the union nuts to the specified torque setting. Position any clips attached to the pipes as noted before removal.

14 Reconnect the return pipe to the injector.

15 Restore the battery connection and check the running of the engine.

## 11 Fuel cut-off solenoid valve - removal and refitting

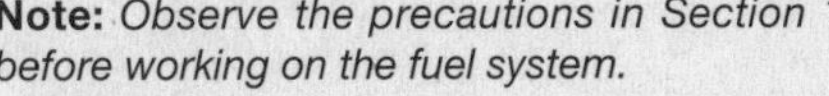

**Note:** *Observe the precautions in Section 1 before working on the fuel system.*

## *Removal*

1 The fuel cut-off solenoid valve, commonly known as the stop solenoid, is located at the rear of the injection pump **(see illustration)**.

2 Disconnect the battery negative lead and position it away from the terminal. **Note:** *If the vehicle has a security-coded radio, check that you have a copy of the code number before disconnecting the battery. Refer to your VW dealer if in doubt.*

10.10 Screw the injector into position and tighten it to the specified torque

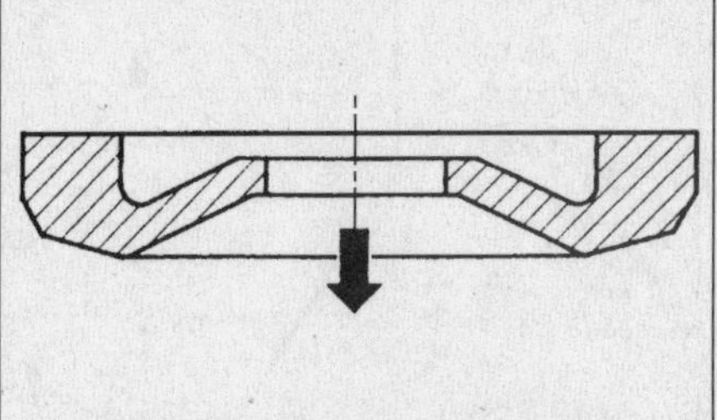
10.9 Cross-section through injector heat shield, to show fitting orientation - engine code AEF

*Arrow points towards cylinder head*

3 Unplug the wiring connector at the top of the valve.

4 Slacken and withdraw the valve body from the injection pump. Recover the O-ring seal, spring and plunger.

## *Refitting*

5 Refitting is a reversal of removal, using a new O-ring seal.

## 12 Diesel engine management system - component removal and refitting

**Note:** *The following procedures apply to vehicles with engine codes AHG, AKU and AGD only.*

**Note:** *Observe the precautions in Section 1 before working on the fuel system.*

## *Accelerator position sensor*

### Removal

1 Disconnect the battery negative lead, and position it away from the terminal. **Note:** *If the vehicle has a security-coded radio, check that you have a copy of the code number before disconnecting the battery. Refer to your VW dealer if in doubt.*

2 Refer to Chapter 11 and remove the trim panels from under the steering column area of the facia, to gain access to the pedal cluster.

3 Unplug the position sensor from the wiring harness at the connector.

11.1 Fuel cut-off valve connector (arrowed) - engine code AGD

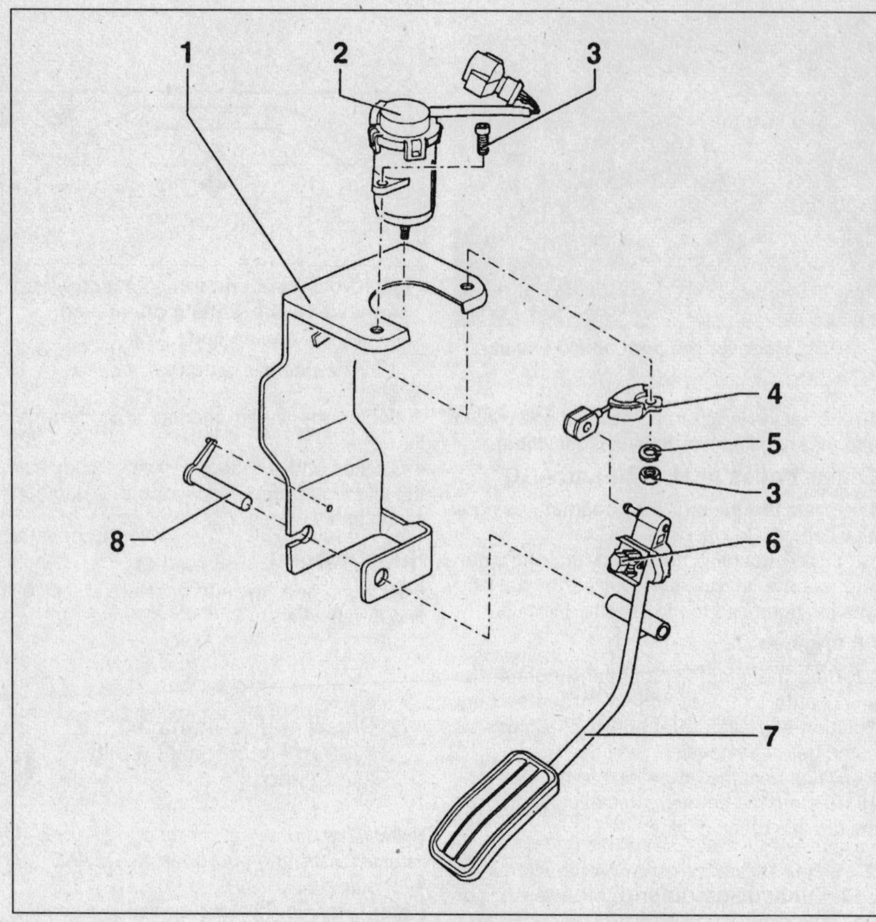


12.4 Accelerator position sensor details

1 Mounting bracket
2 Accelerator position sensor
3 Securing screw
4 Cable cam plate
5 Spring washer
6 Adjustment bolt
7 Accelerator pedal
8 Accelerator pedal spindle

**4** Remove the two screws securing the position sensor mounting bracket, recover the nuts and washers, and lift the sensor out of the car **(see illustration)**.

**5** If wished, the cable cam plate can be unhooked from the accelerator fitting, and removed.

### Refitting

**6** Refitting is a reversal of removal, noting the following points:

a) *The cable cam plate must be fitted to the position sensor spindle according to the dimensions shown* ***(see illustration)****.*

b) *On completion, the adjustment of the position sensor must be verified electronically, using dedicated test equipment - refer to a VW dealer for advice.*

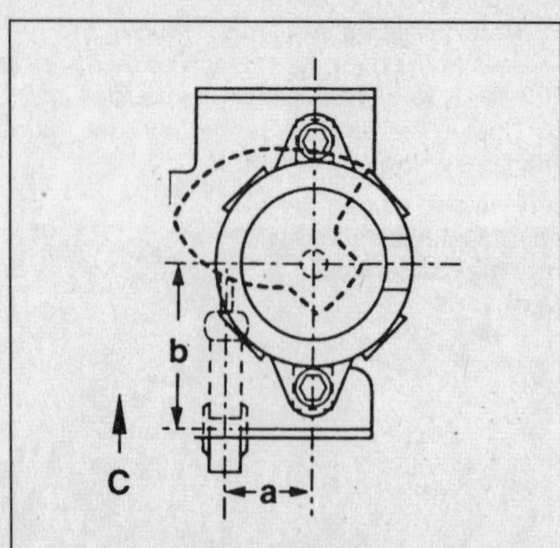


12.6 Accelerator position sensor/cable cam alignment dimensions

a = 22 ± 0.05 mm
b = 41 ± 0.05 mm
C To front of car

## Coolant temperature sensor

**7** Refer to Chapter 3, Section 6.

## Fuel temperature sensor

### Removal

**8** Disconnect the battery negative lead and position it away from the terminal - refer to the note in paragraph 1.

**9** Slacken and withdraw the retaining screws and lift the top cover from the injection pump. Recover the gasket.

**10** Remove the screws and lift out the fuel temperature sensor.

### Refitting

**11** Refitting is a reversal of removal. Tighten the pump top cover screws to the specified torque.

## Inlet air temperature sensor

**12** The air temperature sensor is incorporated into the diesel engine management system ECU, and is not available separately.

## Engine speed signal sensor

### Removal

**13** The engine speed sensor is mounted on the front cylinder block, adjacent to the mating surface of the block and transmission bellhousing.

**14** Disconnect the battery negative lead and position it away from the terminal - refer to the note in paragraph 1.

**15** Unplug the harness connector from the sensor.

**16** Remove the retaining screw and withdraw the sensor from the cylinder block.

### Refitting

**17** Refit the sensor by reversing the removal procedure.

## Throttle valve housing

### Removal

**18** Disconnect the battery negative cable and position it away from the terminal - refer to the note in paragraph 1.

**19** With reference to Section 2 , loosen the clip and disconnect the air trunking from the throttle valve housing.

**20** Pull the vacuum hose off the base of the throttle valve housing, and disconnect the wiring plug **(see illustration)**.

**21** Twist the throttle valve housing towards the front of the car to release it from its bayonet fitting, and remove it from the engine compartment. Recover the O-ring seal from the inlet manifold cover.

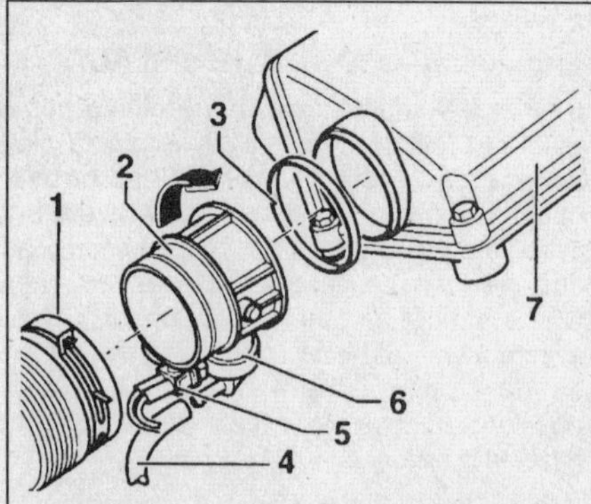


12.20 Throttle valve housing details

1 Inlet air trunking
2 Throttle valve housing
3 O-ring seal
4 Vacuum hose
5 Wiring plug
6 Vacuum unit
7 Inlet manifold cover

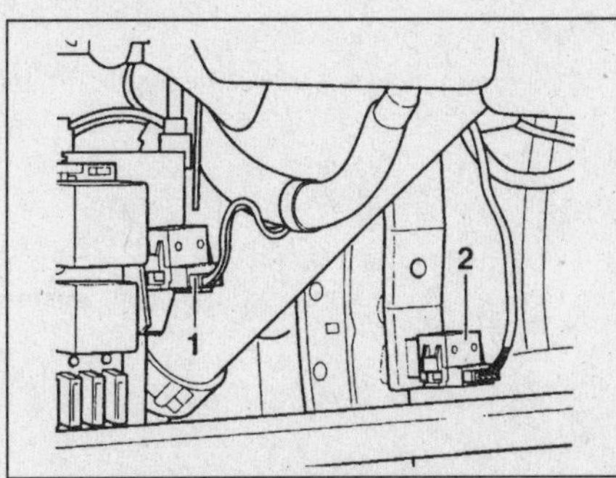


12.23 Clutch pedal switch (1) and brake pedal/brake light switch (2)

### Refitting

**22** Refitting is a reversal of removal. Renew the O-ring seal if it appears damaged.

## *Clutch and brake pedal switches*

### Removal

**23** The clutch and brake pedal switches are clipped to mounting brackets directly above their respective pedals **(see illustration)**.

**24** The brake pedal switch operates as a safety device, in the event of a problem with the accelerator position sensor. If the brake pedal switch is depressed while the accelerator is held at a constant position, the engine speed will drop to idle. Thus, a faulty or incorrectly-adjusted brake pedal switch may result in a running problem.

**25** The clutch pedal switch operation causes the injection pump to momentarily reduce its output while the clutch is disengaged, to permit smoother gear changing.

**26** To remove either switch, refer to Chapter 11 and remove the trim panels from under the steering column area of the facia, to gain access to the pedal cluster.

**27** The switches can be removed by unclipping them from their mountings and disconnecting the wiring plugs.

### Refitting

**28** Refitting is a reversal of removal. On completion, the adjustment of the switches must be verified electronically, using dedicated test equipment - refer to a VW dealer for advice.

## *Electronic control unit (ECU)*

**29** The ECU is located centrally behind the engine compartment bulkhead, under one of the windscreen cowl panels. To remove the cowl panels, refer to Chapter 12, Section 13. The unit is coded, and should not be removed without consulting a VW dealer, otherwise it may not function correctly when the multi-plug is reconnected.

# 13 Inlet manifold cover, air inlet pipes and inlet manifold - removal and refitting

## *Removal*

**1** Loosen and remove the five inlet manifold cover retaining bolts **(see illustration)**.

**2** Pull the breather hose out of the camshaft cover **(see illustration)**, or release the retaining clip and pull the breather hose from the inlet manifold cover.

13.1 Remove the five inlet manifold cover retaining bolts (arrowed)

**3** Release the retaining clip and disconnect the air inlet trunking from the inlet manifold cover **(refer to illustration 2.3)**.

**4** Lift away the inlet manifold cover, tipping it towards the rear of the engine compartment **(see illustration)**. The cover cannot be removed until the air inlet pipes and inlet manifold have been removed. Check the condition of the rubber seal, and fit a new one if necessary.

**5** Loosen and remove the bolts securing the air inlet pipes - these bolts also secure the manifold - and lift the pipes and manifold from the rear of the cylinder head, along with the manifold cover. Recover the manifold gasket.

## *Refitting*

**6** Refitting is a reversal of removal, using a new manifold gasket. Check the breather hose for blockages or signs of splitting, and clean or renew it if necessary.

13.2 Pull the breather hose out of the camshaft cover

13.4 Inlet manifold cover moved aside for access to air inlet pipes and inlet manifold - check the condition of the rubber seal (arrowed)

4C

# Chapter 4 Part D:
# Emission control and exhaust systems

## Contents



## Degrees of difficulty

**Easy,** suitable for novice with little experience 

**Fairly easy,** suitable for beginner with some experience 

**Fairly difficult,** suitable for competent DIY mechanic

**Difficult,** suitable for experienced DIY mechanic 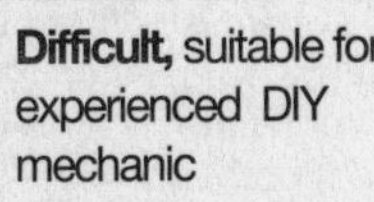

**Very difficult,** suitable for expert DIY or professional 

## Specifications

### Torque wrench settings

| | Nm | lbf ft |
|---|---|---|
| EGR valve clamp screw | 10 | 7 |
| EGR valve-to-exhaust manifold nuts | 25 | 18 |
| EGR valve-to-inlet manifold bolts | 25 | 18 |
| Exhaust downpipe nuts | 25 | 18 |
| Exhaust mounting cross-bracket nuts | 15 | 11 |
| Exhaust rubber mounting bracket-to-body bolts: | | |
| Stage 1 | 20 | 15 |
| Stage 2 | Angle-tighten a further 90° | |
| Exhaust system clamp nuts/bolts | 25 | 18 |

## 1 General information

### *Emission control systems*

All petrol-engined models use unleaded fuel, and are controlled by engine management systems that are tuned to give the best compromise between driveability, fuel consumption and exhaust emission production. In addition, a number of systems are fitted that help to minimise other harmful emissions. All models are fitted with a crankcase emission-control system that reduces the release of pollutants from the engine's lubrication system, and a catalytic converter that reduces exhaust gas pollutants. Petrol engine models have an evaporative loss emission control system that reduces the release of gaseous hydrocarbons from the fuel tank.

All diesel-engined models also have a crankcase emission control system. In addition, all models are fitted with a catalytic converter and an Exhaust Gas Recirculation (EGR) system to reduce exhaust emissions.

### Crankcase emission control

To reduce the emission of unburned hydrocarbons from the crankcase into the atmosphere, the engine is sealed, and the blow-by gases and oil vapour are drawn from inside the crankcase, through a wire mesh oil separator, into the air cleaner, to be burned by the engine during normal combustion.

Under conditions of high manifold depression (idling, deceleration) the gases will be sucked positively out of the crankcase. Under conditions of low manifold depression (acceleration, full-throttle running) the gases are forced out of the crankcase by the (relatively) higher crankcase pressure; if the engine is worn, the raised crankcase pressure (due to increased blow-by) will cause some of the flow to return under all manifold conditions.

### Exhaust emission control - petrol models

To minimise the amount of pollutants which escape into the atmosphere, all models are fitted with a catalytic converter in the exhaust system. The fuelling system is of the closed-loop type, in which a lambda sensor in the exhaust system provides the engine management system ECU with constant feedback, enabling the ECU to adjust the air/fuel mixture to optimise combustion.

The lambda sensor has a heating element built-in that is controlled by the ECU through the lambda sensor relay, to quickly bring the sensor's tip to its optimum operating temperature. The sensor's tip is sensitive to oxygen, and relays a voltage signal to the ECU that varies according to the amount of oxygen in the exhaust gas. If the inlet air/fuel mixture is too rich, the exhaust gases are low in oxygen, so the sensor sends a low-voltage signal, the voltage rising as the mixture weakens and the amount of oxygen rises in the exhaust gases. Peak conversion efficiency of all major pollutants occurs if the inlet air/fuel mixture is maintained at the chemically-correct ratio for the complete combustion of petrol of 14.7 parts (by weight) of air to 1 part of fuel (the stoichiometric ratio). The sensor output voltage alters in a large step at this point, the ECU using the signal change as a reference point, and correcting the inlet air/fuel mixture accordingly by altering the fuel injector pulse width. Details of the lambda sensor removal and refitting are given in Chapter 4A or B, as applicable.

### Exhaust emission control - diesel models

An oxidation catalyst is fitted in the line with the exhaust system of all diesel-engined models. This has the effect of removing a large proportion of the gaseous hydrocarbons, carbon monoxide and particulates present in the exhaust gas.

An Exhaust Gas Recirculation (EGR) system is fitted to all diesel engined models. This reduces the level of nitrogen oxides produced during combustion, by introducing a proportion of the exhaust gas back into the

**2.3 Charcoal canister purge valve wiring connector (arrowed)**

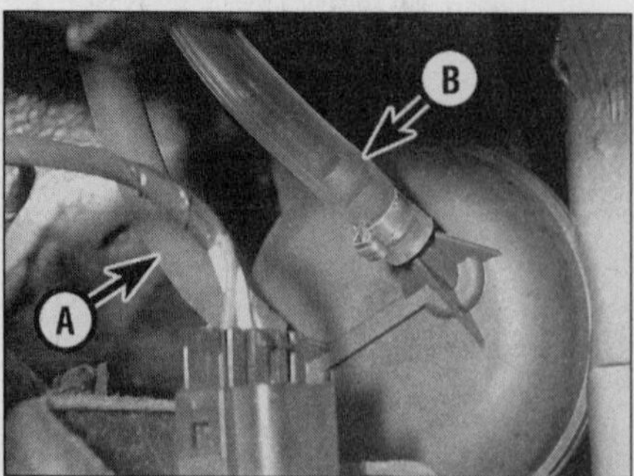


**2.7a Charcoal canister pipe to purge valve (A) and pipe to fuel tank (B)**

inlet manifold, under certain engine operating conditions, via a plunger valve. The system is controlled electronically by the glow plug control module on engine code AEF, or by the diesel engine management ECU on all other diesel engines.

### Evaporative emission control - petrol models

To minimise the escape of unburned hydrocarbons into the atmosphere, an evaporative loss emission control system is fitted to all petrol models. The fuel tank filler cap is sealed, and a charcoal canister is mounted on the right-hand inner wing to collect the petrol vapours released from the fuel contained in the fuel tank. It stores them until they can be drawn from the canister (under the control of the fuel-injection/ignition system ECU) via the purge valve into the inlet tract, where they are then burned by the engine during normal combustion.

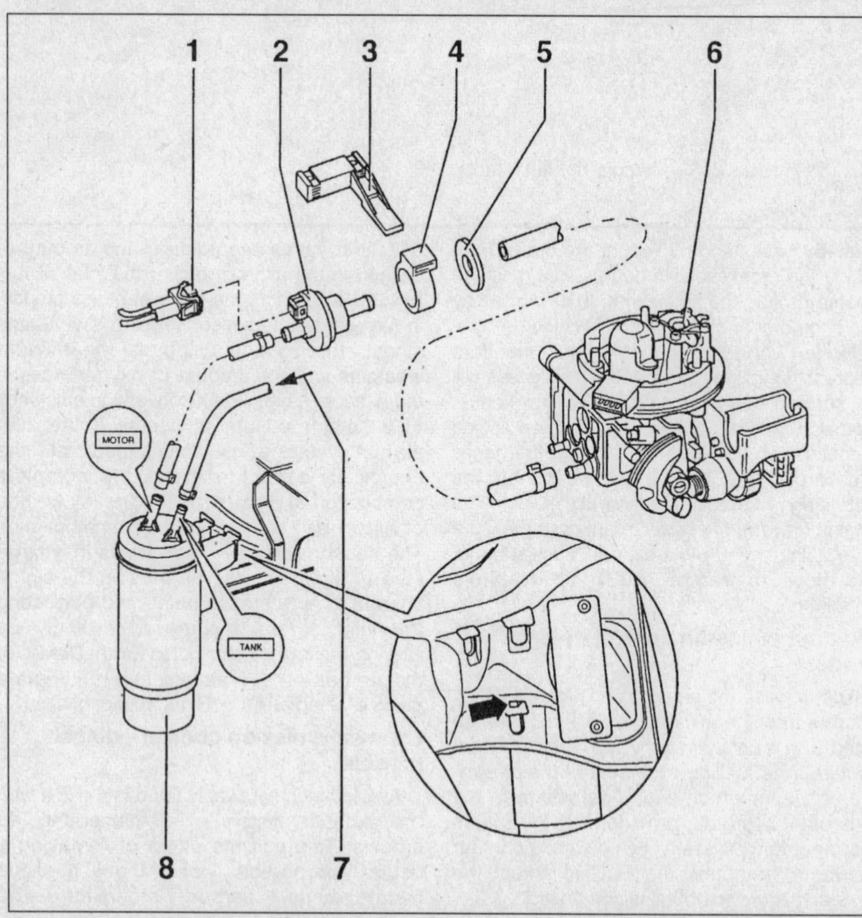


**2.7b Charcoal canister emission control system - early type shown, later type similar**

*1 Wiring connector*
*2 Canister purge solenoid valve*
*3 Mounting bracket*
*4 Purge valve retaining ring*
*5 Washer (early type only)*
*6 Throttle body*
*7 Breather hose from fuel tank*
*8 Charcoal canister*
*Canister securing lug arrowed*

To ensure that the engine runs correctly when it is cold and/or idling, and to protect the catalytic converter from the effects of an over-rich mixture, the purge control valve is not opened by the ECU until the engine has warmed up, and the engine is under load; the valve solenoid is then modulated on and off to allow the stored vapour to pass into the inlet tract.

### Exhaust systems

The exhaust system comprises the exhaust manifold, one or two silencer units (depending on model and specification), a catalytic converter, a number of mounting brackets, and a series of connecting pipes.

## 2 Evaporative loss emission control system - information and component renewal

### Information

**1** The evaporative loss emission control system consists of the purge valve, the activated charcoal filter canister, and a series of connecting hoses.

**2** The purge valve is mounted on a bracket at the top of the right-hand inner wing, and the charcoal canister is mounted lower down the right-hand inner wing.

### Component renewal

#### Purge valve

**3** Ensure that the ignition is switched off, then unplug the wiring harness from the purge valve at the connector **(see illustration)**.

**4** Slacken the clips and pull the hoses off the purge valve ports. Make a note of their orientation to aid refitting later.

**5** Slide the purge valve out of its retaining ring, and remove it from the engine bay.

**6** Refitting is a reversal of removal.

#### Charcoal canister

**7** Locate the canister in the wheel housing. Disconnect the hoses from it, noting which ports they connect to **(see illustrations)**. Release the securing lug and lift the canister out of the wheel housing.

**8** Refitting is a reversal of removal.

## 3 Crankcase emission system - general information

**1** The crankcase emission control system consists of a series of hoses that connect the crankcase vent to the camshaft cover vent (where applicable) and the air cleaner.

**2** An oil separator unit may be fitted on some models. This is a large plastic housing, bolted to the rear of the engine block, and sealed to the block openings by two O-ring seals **(see**

**illustrations)**. If the unit has become blocked, it may be worth trying to clean it out using a suitable solvent before renewing the complete unit. The unit cannot be dismantled for servicing.

**3** The system requires no attention other than to check at regular intervals that the hose(s) are free of blockages and undamaged.

## 4 Exhaust Gas Recirculation (EGR) system - information and component removal

### *Information*

**1** The EGR system consists of the EGR valve, the EGR solenoid valve (engine code AEF) or modulator valve (all other diesel engines) and a connecting vacuum hose.

**2** The EGR valve is mounted on a flange joint at the inlet manifold, and is connected to a second flange joint at the exhaust manifold by a semi-flexible pipe.

**3** The EGR solenoid valve/modulator valve is mounted on a bracket on the engine compartment bulkhead **(see illustration)**.

### *Component renewal*

#### EGR valve

**4** Disconnect the vacuum hose from the port at the top of the EGR valve.

**5** Slacken and withdraw the bolts that secure the EGR valve to the inlet manifold flange **(see illustration)**. Recover and discard the gasket from the joint.

**6** Remove the clamp screw from the EGR valve retaining ring, and lift the EGR valve out of the semi-flexible pipe. If required, unscrew the retaining nuts and disconnect the semi-flexible pipe from the exhaust manifold; recover the gasket.

**7** Refitting is a reversal of removal, noting the following points:

a) *Use a new flange joint gasket.*
b) *If the semi-flexible pipe has been removed, use a new gasket on refitting. Fit the retaining bolts loosely, and ensure that the pipe is unstressed before tightening the bolts to the specified torque.*

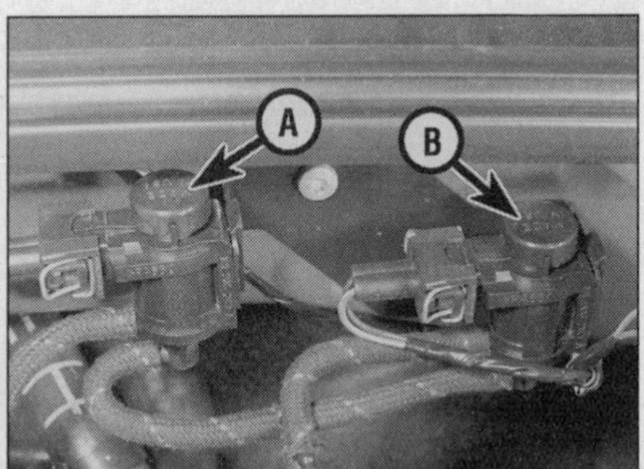


**4.3 Exhaust Gas Recirculation (EGR) solenoid valve (A). Idle speed boost valve (B) is only fitted to models with engine code AEF**

**3.2a Oil separator unit retaining bolts (seen with engine removed, for clarity)**

**3.2b Oil separator unit removed, showing O-ring seals (arrowed)**

#### EGR solenoid valve/Modulator valve

**8** Ensure that the ignition is switched off, then unplug the wiring harness from the valve at the connector.

**9** Slacken the clips and pull the hoses off the valve ports. Make a *careful* note of their orientation to aid refitting later.

**10** Remove the retaining screws and lift off the valve.

**11** Refitting is a reversal of removal.

***Caution: Ensure that the vacuum hoses are refitted correctly; combustion and exhaust smoke production can be drastically affected by an incorrectly operating EGR system.***

## 5 Exhaust manifold - removal and refitting

The exhaust manifold r·moval is described as part of the cylinder head removal sequence; refer to Chapter 2A or B as applicable.

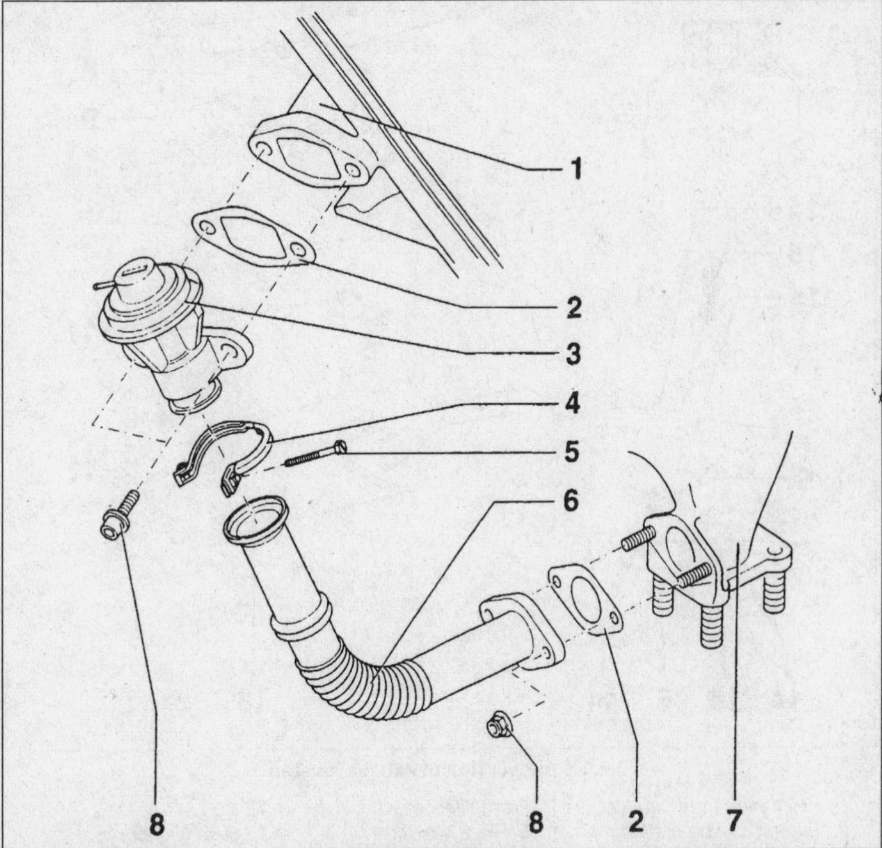


**4.5 EGR valve details**

1 *Inlet manifold*
2 *Gasket*
3 *EGR valve*
4 *Retaining clamp*
5 *Clamp screw*
6 *Connecting pipe*
7 *Exhaust manifold*
8 *Retaining nut*

**6.1 Oxidation catalyst fitted to diesel engine models**

## 6 Exhaust system - general information and component renewal

### General information

**1** On all models, the exhaust system is made up of the downpipe with catalytic converter **(see illustration)**, the front silencer, and the tail section which contains the rear silencer. On some diesel engine models, a flexible coupling is fitted in the downpipe, downstream of the exhaust manifold flange.

**2** The front silencer and tail section are originally fitted as one section, but individual sections are available for repair **(see illustration)**.

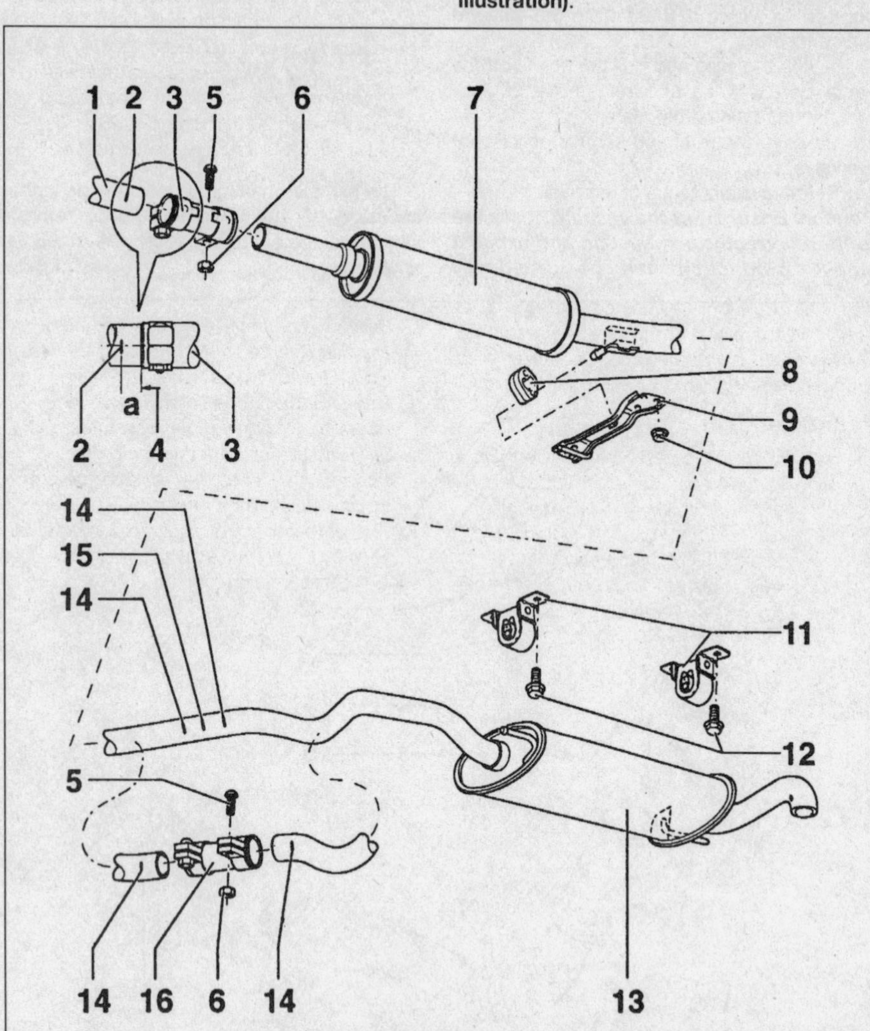


**6.2 Rear section of exhaust system**

1 *Front pipe from catalyst*
2 *Fitted position marking*
3 *Exhaust clamp*
4 *Dimension a = 5 mm approx*
5 *Clamp bolt*
6 *Nut*
7 *Front silencer with balance weight*
8 *Mounting rubber*
9 *Cross-bracket*
10 *Nut*
11 *Rubber mounting bracket*
12 *Bolt*
13 *Rear silencer*
14 *Fitted position marking*
15 *Cutting point for original system*
16 *Exhaust clamp*

**3** On all models, the system is suspended throughout its entire length by rubber mountings, which are secured to the underside of the vehicle by metal brackets **(see illustration)**.

### Removal

***Warning: Allow ample time for the exhaust system to cool before starting work. In particular, the catalytic converter (where applicable) runs at very high temperatures, and severe burns will result if it is carelessly handled. If there is any chance that the system may still be hot, wear suitable gloves.***

**4** Each exhaust section can be removed individually or, alternatively, the complete system can be removed as a unit.

**5** To remove the system or part of the system, first jack up the front or rear of the car and support it on axle stands (see *Jacking and vehicle support*). Alternatively, position the car over an inspection pit or on car ramps.

#### Downpipe and catalytic converter

**6** Place blocks of wood under the front silencer or downpipe to act as a support. Refer to Chapter 4A or B and remove the lambda sensor from the exhaust downpipe.

**7** Slacken and remove the nuts securing the downpipe to the front silencer. Remove the clamp and the bolts.

**8** Undo the nuts and separate the downpipe from the exhaust manifold. Recover the gasket. Unhook the pipe from its mountings, and withdraw the downpipe from underneath the vehicle.

#### Intermediate section/front silencer

**9** Slacken the clamp bolts and disengage the clamp from the intermediate pipe-to-tailpipe joint and the intermediate pipe-to-catalytic converter/downpipe joint **(see illustration)**.

**10** Disengage the intermediate pipe from the tailpipe and the catalytic converter/downpipe. Unhook the pipe from its mountings and remove it from the vehicle.

#### Tailpipe/rear silencer

**11** Slacken the clamping ring bolts and disengage the tailpipe at the joint.

**6.3 Exhaust system rubber mounting at rear of front silencer**

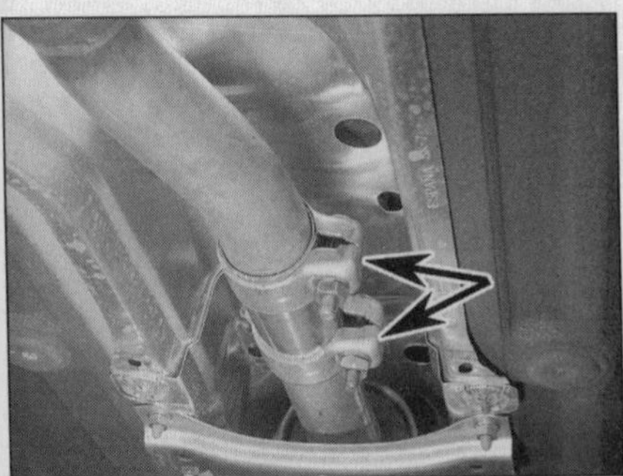

**6.9 Exhaust downpipe-to-intermediate pipe clamp bolts (arrowed)**

**12** Unhook the tailpipe from its mounting rubbers and remove it from the vehicle..

## Complete system

**Note:** *If the original system is being replaced, the silencers in the tail section can be carefully cut from the exhaust system using a hacksaw and renewed individually; refer to a VW dealer or an exhaust specialist for further advice*

**13** Disconnect the front pipe from the manifold - see paragraphs 6 to 8.

**14** With the aid of an assistant, free the system from all its mounting rubbers and manoeuvre it out from underneath the vehicle.

## Heatshield(s)

**15** The heatshields are secured to the underside of the body by a mixture of nuts, bolts and clips. Each shield can be removed once the relevant exhaust section has been removed. Note that if the shield is being removed to gain access to a component located behind it, in some cases it may prove sufficient to remove the retaining nuts and/or bolts and simply lower the shield, removing the need to disturb the exhaust system.

## *Refitting*

**16** Each section is refitted by a reverse of the removal sequence, noting the following points.

a) *Ensure that all traces of corrosion have been removed from the flanges, and renew all necessary gaskets.*
b) *Inspect the rubber mountings for signs of damage or deterioration, and renew as necessary.*
c) *On joints which are secured by clamping rings, apply a smear of exhaust system jointing paste to the joint mating surfaces to ensure an gas-tight seal. Tighten the clamping ring nuts evenly and progressively to the specified torque so that the clearance between the clamp halves is equal on either side.*
d) *Prior to tightening the exhaust system fasteners, ensure that all rubber mountings are correctly located, and that there is adequate clearance between the exhaust system and vehicle underbody.*

## 7 Catalytic converter - general information and precautions

**1** The catalytic converter is a reliable and simple device which needs no maintenance in itself, but there are some facts of which an owner should be aware if the converter is to function properly for its full service life.

## *Petrol models*

a) *DO NOT use leaded (UK 4-star) petrol in a car with a catalytic converter - the lead will coat the precious metals' reagents, reducing their converting efficiency, and will eventually destroy the converter.*
b) *Always keep the ignition and fuel systems well-maintained in accordance with the manufacturer's schedule.*
c) *If the engine develops a misfire, do not drive the car at all (or at least as little as possible) until the fault is cured.*
d) *DO NOT push- or tow-start the car - this will soak the catalytic converter in unburned fuel, causing it to overheat when the engine does start.*
e) *DO NOT switch off the ignition at high engine speeds, ie do not blip the throttle immediately before switching off.*
f) *In some cases a sulphurous smell (like that of rotten eggs) may be noticed from the exhaust. This is common to many catalytic converter-equipped cars and once the car has covered a few thousand miles the problem should disappear. Low-quality fuel with a high sulphur content will exacerbate this effect.*
g) *The catalytic converter, used on a well-maintained and well-driven car, should last between 50 000 and 100 000 miles - if the converter is no longer effective it must be renewed.*

## *Petrol and diesel models*

h) *DO NOT use fuel or engine oil additives - these may contain substances harmful to the catalytic converter.*
i) *DO NOT continue to use the car if the engine burns oil to the extent of leaving a visible trail of blue smoke.*
j) *Remember that the catalytic converter operates at very high temperatures. DO NOT, therefore, park the car in dry undergrowth, over long grass or piles of dead leaves after a long run.*
k) *Remember that the catalytic converter is FRAGILE - do not strike it with tools during servicing work.*

# Chapter 5 Part A:
# Starting and charging systems

## Contents



## Degrees of difficulty

**Easy,** suitable for novice with little experience

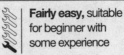

**Fairly easy,** suitable for beginner with some experience

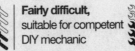

**Fairly difficult,** suitable for competent DIY mechanic

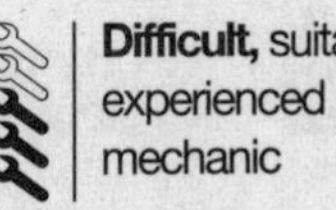

**Difficult,** suitable for experienced DIY mechanic

**Very difficult,** suitable for expert DIY or professional

## Specifications

### General

System type . . . . . . . . . . . . . . . . . . . . . . . . . . . . . . . . . . . . . . . . . . 12-volt, negative earth

### Starter motor

Rating:
- Petrol engines up to and including 1.4 litre . . . . . . . . . . . . . . . . . . 12V, 0.9 kW
- 1.6 litre engines . . . . . . . . . . . . . . . . . . . . . . . . . . . . . . . . . . . . . . 12V, 1.0 kW
- Diesel engines . . . . . . . . . . . . . . . . . . . . . . . . . . . . . . . . . . . . . . . 12V, 1.8 kW

### Battery

Ratings . . . . . . . . . . . . . . . . . . . . . . . . . . . . . . . . . . . . . . . . . . . . . 36 to 110 Ah (depending on model and market)

### Alternator

Minimum brush length . . . . . . . . . . . . . . . . . . . . . . . . . . . . . . . . . . 5 mm (tolerance +1mm, -0 mm)

### Torque wrench settings

| Torque wrench settings | Nm | lbf ft |
|---|---|---|
| Alternator belt tensioner (spring type) | 25 | 18 |
| Alternator mounting bolts | 25 | 18 |
| Alternator mounting bracket-to-block bolts | 55 | 41 |
| Battery clamping plate bolt | 22 | 16 |
| Battery terminal bolts | 6 | 4 |
| Starter motor mounting bolts: | | |
| Petrol engines: | | |
| Lower bolt (M8x160) | 45 | 33 |
| Upper bolts/nut (M8x70) | 60 | 44 |
| Diesel engines (studs) | 60 | 44 |

5A

## 1 General information and precautions

### General information

The engine electrical system consists mainly of the charging and starting systems. Because of their engine-related functions, these are covered separately from the body electrical devices such as the lights, instruments, etc (which are covered in Chapter 12). On petrol engine models refer to Part B of this Chapter for information on the ignition system, and on diesel models refer to Part C for the pre-heating system.

The electrical system is of the 12-volt negative earth type.

The battery may be of the low maintenance or 'maintenance-free' (sealed for life) type and is charged by the alternator, which is belt-driven from the crankshaft pulley.

The starter motor is of the pre-engaged type, with an integral solenoid. On starting, the solenoid moves the drive pinion into engagement with the flywheel ring gear before the starter motor is energised. Once the engine has started, a one-way clutch prevents the motor armature being driven by the engine until the pinion disengages from the flywheel.

Further details of the various systems are given in the relevant Sections of this Chapter. While some repair procedures are given, the usual course of action is to renew the component concerned. The owner whose interest extends beyond mere component renewal should obtain a copy of the *Automobile Electrical & Electronic Systems Manual*, available from the publishers of this manual.

### Precautions

***Warning: It is necessary to take extra care when working on the electrical system to avoid damage to semi-conductor devices (diodes and transistors), and to avoid the risk of personal injury. In addition to the precautions given in Safety first!, observe the following when working on the system:***

***Always remove rings, watches, etc before working on the electrical system.*** Even with the battery disconnected, capacitive discharge could occur if a component's live terminal is earthed through a metal object. This could cause a shock or nasty burn.

***Do not reverse the battery connections.*** Components such as the alternator, electronic control units, or any other components having semi-conductor circuitry could be irreparably damaged.

***Never disconnect the battery terminals, the alternator, any electrical wiring or any test instruments when the engine is running.***

***Do not allow the engine to turn the alternator when the alternator is not connected.***

***Never test for alternator output by flashing the output lead to earth.***

***Always ensure that the battery negative lead is disconnected when working on the electrical system.***

If the engine is being started using jump leads and a slave battery, connect the batteries ***positive-to-positive*** and ***negative-to-negative*** (see *Jump starting*). This also applies when connecting a battery charger.

***Never*** use an ohmmeter of the type incorporating a hand-cranked generator for circuit or continuity testing.

Before using electric-arc welding equipment on the car, ***disconnect the battery, alternator and components such as the electronic control units*** (where applicable) to protect them from the risk of damage.

***Caution: Certain radio/cassettes fitted as standard equipment by VW have a built-in security code to deter thieves. If the power source to the unit is cut, the anti-theft system will activate. Even if the power source is immediately reconnected, the radio/cassette unit will not function until the correct security code has been entered. Therefore, if you do not know the correct security code for the radio/cassette unit do not disconnect the battery negative terminal of the battery or remove the radio/cassette unit from the vehicle. Refer to your VW dealer for further information on whether the unit fitted to your car has a security code.***

## 2 Battery - testing and charging

### Standard and low-maintenance battery - testing

**1** If the vehicle covers a small annual mileage, it is worthwhile checking the specific gravity of the electrolyte every three months to determine the state of charge of the battery. Use a hydrometer to make the check, and compare the results with the following table. Note that the specific gravity readings assume an electrolyte temperature of 15°C (60°F); for every 10°C (18°F) below 15°C (60°F) subtract 0.007. For every 10°C (18°F) above 15°C (60°F) add 0.007.

| | Above 25°C | Below 25°C |
|---|---|---|
| *Fully charged* | *1.210 to 1.230* | *1.270 to 1.290* |
| *70% charged* | *1.170 to 1.190* | *1.230 to 1.250* |
| *Discharged* | *1.050 to 1.070* | *1.110 to 1.130* |

**2** If the battery condition is suspect, first check the specific gravity of electrolyte in each cell. A variation of 0.040 or more between any cells indicates loss of electrolyte or deterioration of the internal plates.

**3** If the specific gravity variation is 0.040 or more, the battery should be renewed. If the cell variation is satisfactory but the battery is discharged, it should be charged as described later in this Section.

### Maintenance-free battery - testing

**4** In cases where a 'sealed for life' maintenance-free battery is fitted, topping-up and testing of the electrolyte in each cell is not possible. The condition of the battery can therefore only be tested using a battery condition indicator or a voltmeter.

**5** Certain models may be fitted with a maintenance-free battery, with a built-in charge condition indicator. The indicator is located in the top of the battery casing, and indicates the condition of the battery from its colour. If the indicator shows green, then the battery is in a good state of charge. If the indicator turns darker, eventually to black, then the battery requires charging, as described later in this Section. If the indicator shows clear/yellow, then the electrolyte level in the battery is too low to allow further use, and the battery should be renewed. **Do not** attempt to charge, load or jump start a battery when the indicator shows clear/yellow.

**6** If testing the battery using a voltmeter, connect the voltmeter across the battery and note the voltage. The test is only accurate if the battery has not been subjected to any kind of charge for the previous six hours. If this is not the case, switch on the headlights for 30 seconds, then wait four to five minutes before testing the battery after switching off the headlights. All other electrical circuits must be switched off, so check that the doors and tailgate are fully shut when making the test.

**7** If the voltage reading is less than 12.2 volts, then the battery is discharged, whilst a reading of 12.2 to 12.4 volts indicates a partially discharged condition.

**8** If the battery is to be charged, remove it from the vehicle and charge it as described later in this Section.

### Standard and low maintenance battery - charging

**Note:** *The following is intended as a guide only. Always refer to the manufacturer's recommendations (often printed on a label attached to the battery) before charging a battery.*

**9** Charge the battery at a rate equivalent to 10% of the battery capacity (eg for a 45 Ah battery charge at 4.5 A) and continue to charge the battery at this rate until no further rise in specific gravity is noted over a four-hour period.

**10** Alternatively, a trickle charger charging at the rate of 1.5 amps can safely be used overnight.

**11** Specially rapid boost charges which are claimed to restore the power of the battery in 1 to 2 hours are not recommended, as they can cause serious damage to the battery plates through overheating. If the battery is completely flat, VW recommend that recharging should take at least 24 hours.

**12** While charging the battery, note that the temperature of the electrolyte should never exceed 37.8°C (100°F).

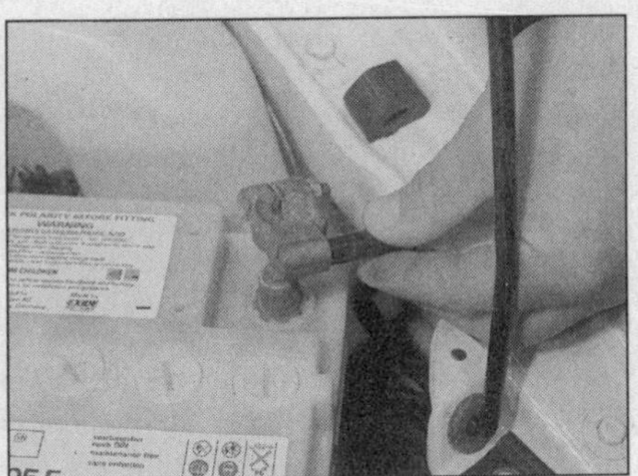
3.2 Loosen the clamp nut and disconnect the battery negative lead

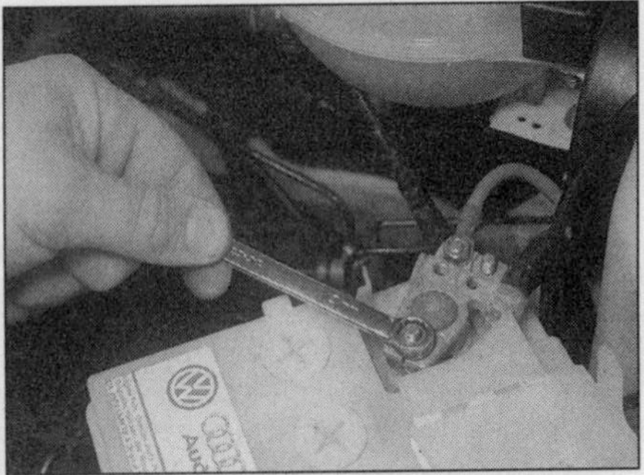
3.3 Similarly, disconnect the battery positive lead

3.4 Open up the fuse cover . . .

### *Maintenance-free battery - charging*

**Note:** *The following is intended as a guide only. Always refer to the manufacturer's recommendations (often printed on a label attached to the battery) before charging a battery.*

**13** This battery type takes considerably longer to fully recharge than the standard type, the time taken being dependent on the extent of discharge, but it can take anything up to three days.

**14** A constant voltage type charger is required, to be set, when connected, to 13.9 to 14.9 volts with a charger current below 25 amps. Using this method, the battery should be useable within three hours, giving a voltage reading of 12.5 volts, but this is for a partially-discharged battery and, as mentioned, full charging can take far longer.

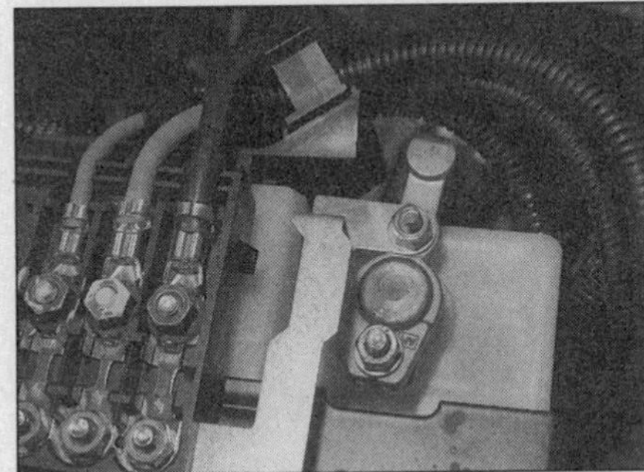
3.5 . . . for access to the battery positive connection and fusible link nuts

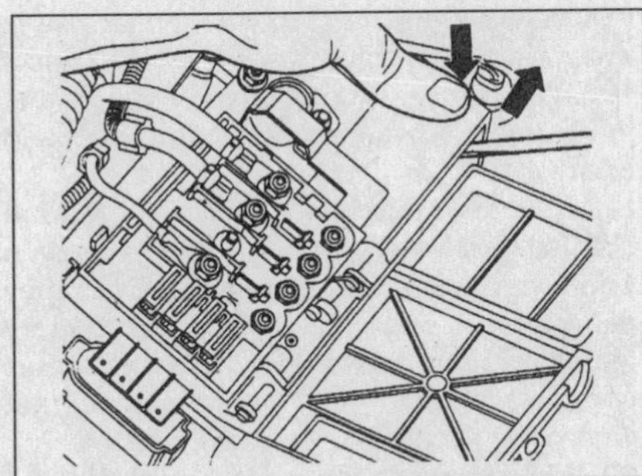
3.8 Releasing the fuse holder from the top of the battery

**15** If the battery is to be charged from a fully-discharged state (condition reading less than 12.2 volts), have it recharged by your VW dealer or local automotive electrician, as the charge rate is higher and constant supervision during charging is necessary.

## 3 Battery - removal and refitting

### *Removal*

**1 Note:** *If the vehicle has a security-coded radio, check that you have a copy of the code number before disconnecting the battery cable; refer to the caution in Section 1.*

**2** Slacken the clamp nut and disconnect the battery negative lead from the terminal **(see illustration)**.

### Models without battery-mounted fuse holder

**3** On models without a fuse holder on top of the battery, unclip the plastic cover and disconnect the battery positive lead in the same manner as the negative lead **(see illustration)**.

### Models with battery-mounted fuse holder

**4** Where a fuse holder is fitted to the top of the battery, squeeze the retaining tabs together and open the fuse cover **(see illustration)**.

**5** Unscrew the nut(s) securing the holder to the battery positive terminal clamp **(see illustration)**.

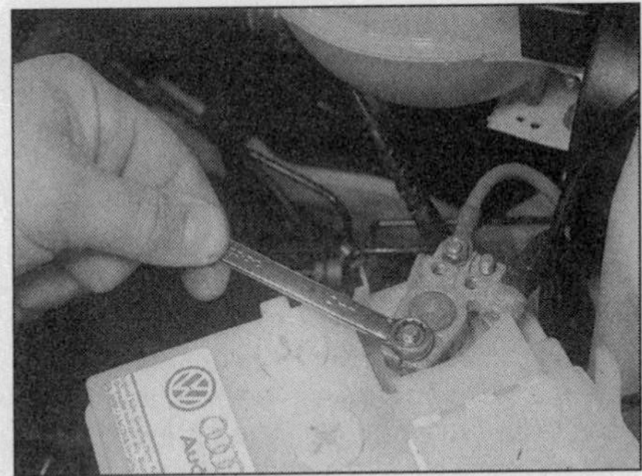
3.9 Unscrew and remove the battery clamp bolt

**6** Unscrew the nuts and disconnect the wiring from the fusible links.

**7** Disconnect the wiring connector from the side of the fuse holder.

**8** Press down on the fuse holder at the positive terminal end, and release the fuse holder from the top of the battery using a small screwdriver **(see illustration)**.

### All models

**9** At the base of the battery, slacken and withdraw the clamp bolt, then lift off the clamping plate **(see illustration)**.

**10** Where applicable, disconnect the vent pipe from the top of the battery, and remove the battery from the engine bay.

**11** If required, the battery tray can be unbolted and removed **(see illustration)**.

### *Refitting*

**12** Refit the battery by following the removal procedure in reverse. Where applicable, make sure the lug at the base of the battery locates in the recess in the battery tray. Tighten the clamp plate bolt to the correct torque.

## 4 Alternator/charging system - testing in vehicle

**Note:** *Refer to Safety first! and Section 1 of this Chapter before starting work.*

**1** If the charge warning light fails to illuminate when the ignition is switched on, first check the alternator wiring connections for security.

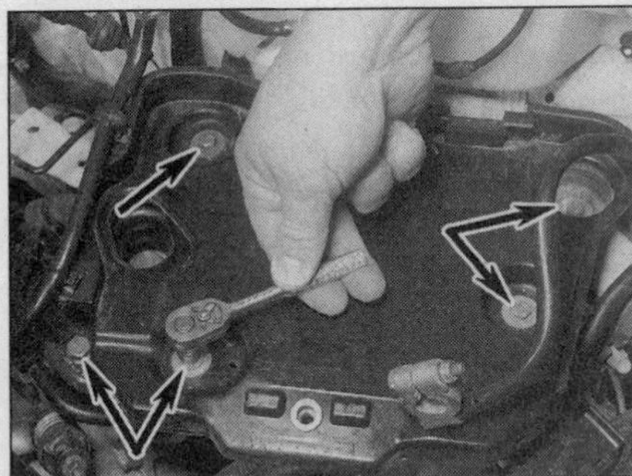
3.11 Battery tray retaining bolts

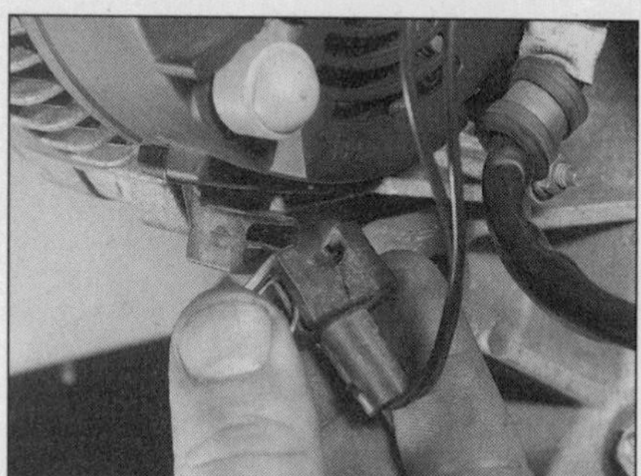
**5.3 Unplug the sense cable from the alternator at the connector (later diesel engine model shown)**

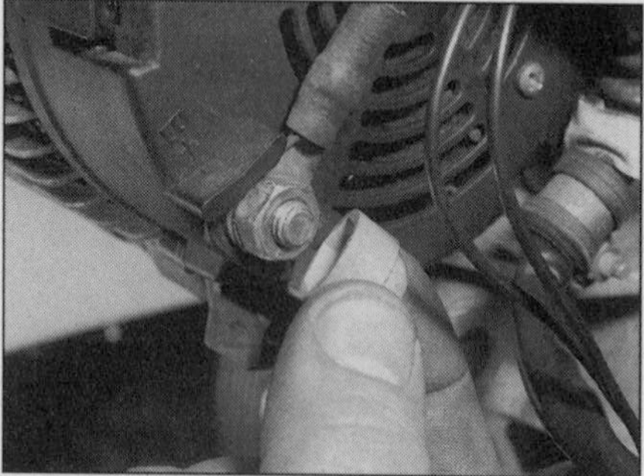
**5.4a Remove the protective cap . . .**

**5.4b . . . remove the nut and washers, then disconnect the power cable**

If the light still fails to illuminate, check the continuity of the warning light feed wire from the alternator to the instrument panel. If all is satisfactory, the alternator is at fault and should be renewed or taken to an auto-electrician for testing and repair.

**2** Similarly, if the charge warning light comes on with the ignition, but is then slow to go out when the engine is started, this may indicate an impending alternator problem. Check all the items listed in the preceding paragraph, and refer to an auto-electrical specialist if no obvious faults are found.

**3** If the charge warning light illuminates when the engine is running, stop the engine and check that the drivebelt is correctly tensioned (see Chapter 1A or 1B) and that the alternator connections are secure. If all is so far satisfactory, check the alternator brushes and slip rings as described in Section 6. If the fault persists, the alternator should be renewed, or taken to an auto-electrician for testing and repair.

**4** If the alternator output is suspect even though the warning light functions correctly, the regulated voltage may be checked as follows.

**5** Connect a voltmeter across the battery terminals, and start the engine.

**6** Increase the engine speed until the voltmeter reading remains steady; the reading should be approximately 12 to 13 volts, and no more than 14 volts.

**7** Switch on as many electrical accessories (eg, the headlights, heated rear window and heater blower) as possible, and check that the alternator maintains the regulated voltage at around 13 to 14 volts.

**8** If the regulated voltage is not as stated, this may be due to worn brushes, weak brush springs, a faulty voltage regulator, a faulty diode, a severed phase winding or worn or damaged slip rings. The brushes and slip rings may be checked (see Section 6), but if the fault persists, the alternator should be renewed or taken to an auto-electrician.

## 5 Alternator - removal and refitting

### Removal

**1** Disconnect the battery negative lead and position it away from the terminal - refer to the caution in Section 1.

**2** Remove the auxiliary drivebelt from the alternator pulley (see Chapter 2A or 2B).

**3** Unplug the sense cable from the alternator at the connector **(see illustration)**.

**4** Remove the protective cap, slacken and withdraw the nut and washers, then disconnect the power cable from the alternator at the screw terminal post. Where applicable, unbolt and remove the cable guide **(see illustrations)**.

**5** Slacken and remove the lower, then the upper bolts **(see illustrations)**, then lift the alternator away from its bracket. Where applicable, pivot the tensioner roller out of the way to gain access to the lower mounting bolt.

**6** Refer to Section 6 if the removal of the brush holder/voltage regulator module is required.

### Refitting

**7** Refitting is a reversal of removal. Refer to Chapter 2A or B as applicable for details of refitting and tensioning the auxiliary drivebelt.

**8** On completion, tighten the alternator mounting bolts to the specified torque.

## 6 Alternator - brush holder/regulator module renewal

**1** Remove the alternator, as described in Section 5.

**2** Place the alternator on a clean work surface, with the pulley facing down.

**3** Remove the retaining screws, then prise open the clips and lift the plastic cover from the rear of the alternator **(see illustrations)**.

**4** Slacken and withdraw the brush holder/voltage regulator module screws, then lift the module away from the alternator **(see illustrations)**.

**5.4c Where applicable, unbolt and remove the cable guide**

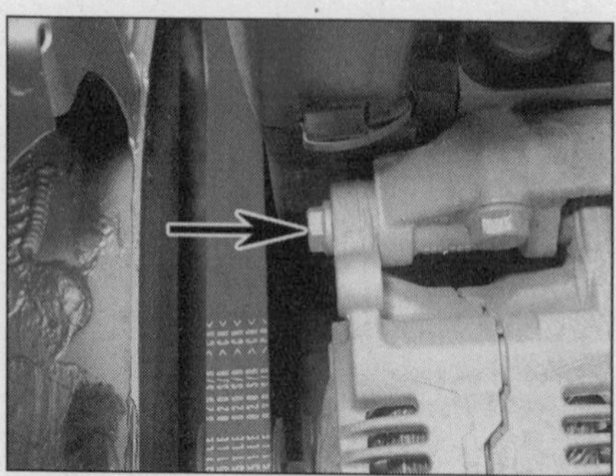
**5.5a Alternator upper mounting bolt . . .**

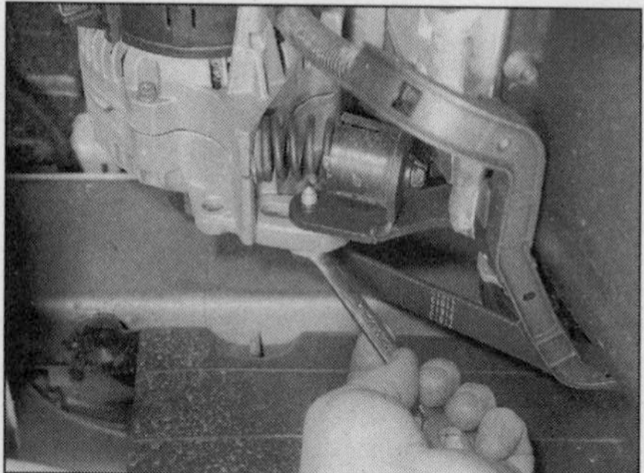
**5.5b . . . and lower mounting bolt**

**6.3a Where applicable, remove the retaining screws (arrowed) . . .**

**5** Measure the free length of the brush contacts - where applicable, take the measurement from the manufacturer's emblem etched on the side of the brush contact, to the shallowest part of the curved end face of the brush **(see illustration)**. Check the measurement with the Specifications; renew the module if the brushes are worn below the minimum limit.

**6** Inspect the surfaces of the slip rings, at the end of the alternator shaft **(see illustration)**. If they appear excessively worn, burnt or pitted, then renewal must be considered; refer to an automobile electrical system specialist for further guidance.

**7** Reassemble the alternator by following the dismantling procedure in reverse. On completion, refer to Section 5 and refit the alternator.

**6.4a Remove the brush holder/voltage regulator module screws . . .**

**6.4b . . . then lift the module away from the alternator**

**6.3b . . . then prise open the clips . . .**

## 7 Starting system - testing

**Note:** *Refer to the precautions given in Safety first! and in Section 1 of this Chapter before starting work.*

**1** If the starter motor fails to operate when the ignition key is turned to the appropriate position, the following possible causes may be to blame:

*a) The battery is faulty.*

*b) The electrical connections between the switch, solenoid, battery and starter motor are somewhere failing to pass the necessary current from the battery through the starter to earth.*

*c) The solenoid is faulty.*

*d) The starter motor is mechanically or electrically defective.*

**2** To check the battery, switch on the headlights. If they dim after a few seconds, this indicates that the battery is discharged - recharge (see Section 2) or renew the battery. If the headlights glow brightly, operate the ignition switch and observe the lights. If they dim, then this indicates that current is reaching the starter motor, therefore the fault must lie in the starter motor. If the lights continue to glow brightly (and no clicking sound can be heard from the starter motor solenoid), this indicates that there is a fault in the circuit or solenoid - see following paragraphs. If the starter motor turns slowly when operated, but the battery is in good condition, then this indicates that either the starter motor is faulty, or there is considerable resistance somewhere in the circuit.

**6.3c . . . and lift the plastic cover from the rear of the alternator**

**3** If a fault in the circuit is suspected, disconnect the battery leads (including the earth connection to the body), the starter/solenoid wiring and the engine/transmission earth strap. Thoroughly clean the connections, and reconnect the leads and wiring, then use a voltmeter or test light to check that full battery voltage is available at the battery positive lead connection to the solenoid, and that the earth is sound. Smear petroleum jelly around the battery terminals to prevent corrosion - corroded connections are amongst the most frequent causes of electrical system faults.

**4** If the battery and all connections are in good condition, check the circuit by disconnecting the wire from the solenoid blade terminal. Connect a voltmeter or test light between the wire end and a good earth (such as the battery negative terminal), and check that the wire is live when the ignition switch is turned to the start position. If it is, then the circuit is sound - if not the circuit wiring can be checked as described in Chapter 12.

**5** The solenoid contacts can be checked by connecting a voltmeter or test light between the battery positive feed connection on the starter side of the solenoid, and earth. When the ignition switch is turned to the start position, there should be a reading or lighted bulb, as applicable. If there is no reading or lighted bulb, the solenoid is faulty and should be renewed.

5A

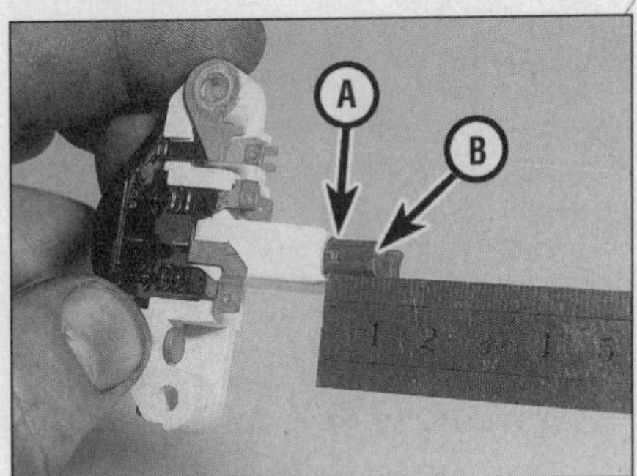


**6.5 Measuring the alternator brush length - for A and B, see text**

**6.6 Inspect the surfaces of the slip rings (arrowed), at the end of the alternator shaft**

8.2 Disconnect the wiring plug . . .

8.4a Loosening one of the starter motor mounting bolts

6 If the circuit and solenoid are proved sound, the fault must lie in the starter motor. Begin checking the starter motor by removing it (see Section 8), and checking the brushes. If the fault does not lie in the brushes, the motor windings must be faulty. In this event, it may be possible to have the starter motor overhauled by a specialist, but check on the availability and cost of spares before proceeding, as it may prove more economical to obtain a new or exchange motor.

## 8 Starter motor - removal and refitting

**Note:** *On petrol engine models, access to the starter motor is difficult from above or below. For clarity, the accompanying photographs were taken after removing the inlet manifold. Whilst this is not essential, it does make the job of removing the starter motor much easier - see the appropriate Part of Chapter 4 for inlet manifold removal details.*

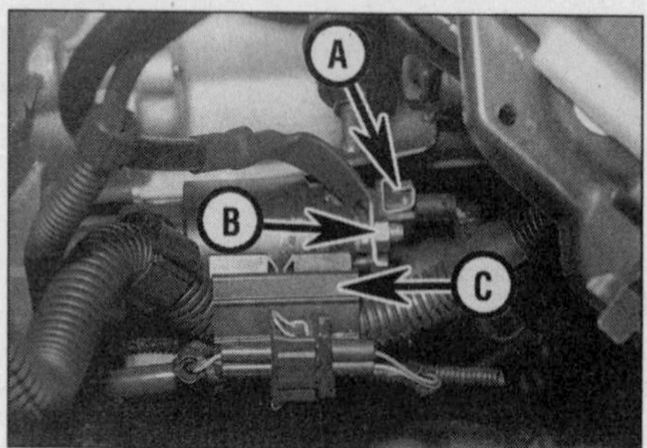


8.6 Starter motor wiring plug (A), wiring retaining nut (B) and harness plastic guide (C) - diesel engine models

8.3a . . . then loosen and remove the nut . . .

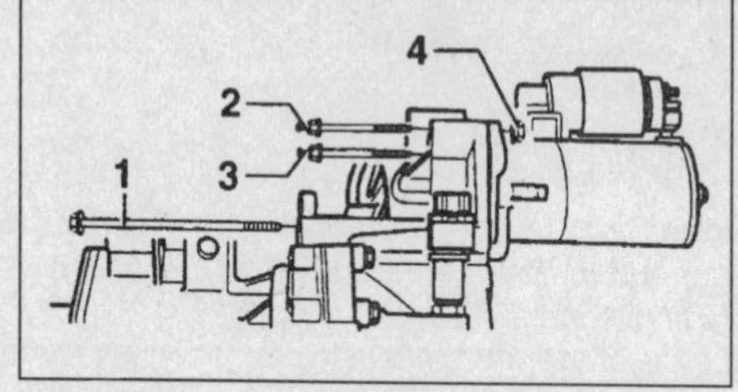


8.4b Starter motor mounting bolts - petrol engine models

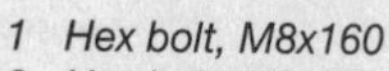

*1 Hex bolt, M8x160*
*2 Hex bolt, M8x70, with nut*
*3 Hex bolt, M8x70*
*4 Nut*

### Removal

1 Disconnect the battery negative lead and position it away from the terminal - refer to the caution in Section 1.

2 Pull off the black plastic cap (where fitted), then disconnect the wiring from the starter solenoid **(see illustration)**.

3 Disconnect the remaining wiring from the starter motor, removing the retaining nuts and washers as necessary **(see illustrations)**.

#### Petrol engine models

4 Remove the longer lower through-bolt, then the two upper bolts. One of the upper bolts is captive, and the other has a nut. Release the starter motor from the bellhousing, and guide it out of the engine compartment **(see illustrations)**.

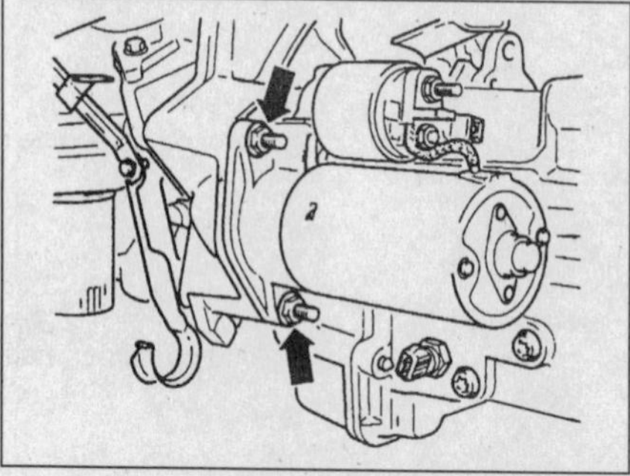

8.8 Starter motor through-bolts (arrowed) - diesel engine models

8.3b . . . and disconnect the remaining wiring

8.4c Removing the starter motor

#### Diesel engine models

5 Move the radiator bottom hose to one side, then unbolt and remove the bottom hose retaining clip.

6 Disconnect the wiring plug, then unscrew the nut and disconnect the cables from the solenoid threaded connection **(see illustration)**.

7 Unclip the wiring harness plastic guide from the front of the starter motor, and move it to one side.

8 Unscrew and remove the threaded studs **(see illustration)**, then release the starter motor from the bellhousing and remove it from the engine compartment.

### Refitting

9 Refit the starter motor by following the removal procedure in reverse. Tighten the mounting bolts to the specified torque.

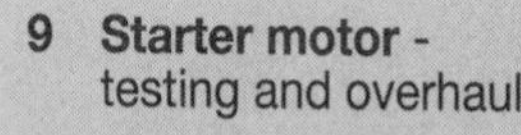

## 9 Starter motor - testing and overhaul

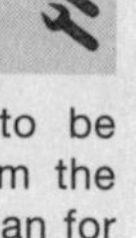

If the starter motor is thought to be defective, it should be removed from the vehicle and taken to an auto-electrician for assessment. In the majority of cases, new starter motor brushes can be fitted at a reasonable cost. However, check the cost of repairs first as it may prove more economical to purchase a new or exchange motor.

# Chapter 5 Part B:
# Ignition system - petrol engines

## Contents



## Degrees of difficulty

| | | | | |
|---|---|---|---|---|
| **Easy,** suitable for novice with little experience 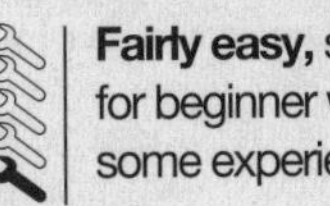 | **Fairly easy,** suitable for beginner with some experience 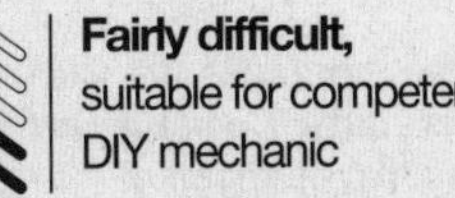 | **Fairly difficult,** suitable for competent DIY mechanic | **Difficult,** suitable for experienced DIY mechanic | **Very difficult,** suitable for expert DIY or professional |

5B

## Specifications

### General

| | |
|---|---|
| Type*: | |
| Engine codes AEV, ADX and AEA | Bosch Mono-Motronic |
| Engine codes AER, ALL, AEX, AKV and ANX | Bosch Motronic |
| Engine code AEE | Magneti-Marelli 1AV |

**Refer to Chapter 2A for engine code listings.*

### Ignition coil

| | |
|---|---|
| Primary winding resistance | 0.5 to 1.2 ohms |
| Secondary resistance | 3000 to 4000 ohms |

### Distributor

| | |
|---|---|
| Type | Breakerless |
| Ignition timing | Controlled by engine management system |

### Spark plugs

See Chapter 1A Specifications

### HT leads

| | |
|---|---|
| Resistance value (nominal) | 30 000 ohms per metre length |

### Torque wrench settings

| | Nm | lbf ft |
|---|---|---|
| Distributor clamp bolts | 10 | 7 |
| Ignition coil mounting bolts | 10 | 7 |
| Knock sensor mounting bolt | 20 | 15 |

## 1 General information

The Bosch Mono-Motronic, Motronic, and Magneti-Marelli 1AV systems are self-contained engine management systems, which control both the fuel injection and ignition. This Chapter deals with the ignition system components only - refer to Chapter 4A or B for details of the fuel system components.

The ignition system comprises four spark plugs, five HT leads, the distributor, an electronic ignition coil, and an Electronic Control Unit (ECU) together with its associated sensors, actuators and wiring. The component layout varies from system to system, but the basic operation is the same for all models.

The basic operation is as follows: the ECU supplies a voltage to the input stage of the ignition coil, which causes the primary windings in the coil to be energised. The supply voltage is periodically interrupted by the ECU, and this results in the collapse of primary magnetic field, which then induces a much larger voltage in the secondary coil, called the HT voltage. This voltage is directed, by the distributor via the HT leads, to the spark plug in the cylinder currently on its ignition stroke. The spark plug electrodes form a gap small enough for the HT voltage to arc across, and the resulting spark ignites the fuel/air mixture in the cylinder. The timing of this sequence of events is critical, and is regulated solely by the ECU.

The ECU calculates and controls the ignition timing and dwell angle primarily according to engine speed, crankshaft position and inlet manifold depression information, received from sensors mounted on and around the engine. Other parameters that affect ignition timing are throttle position and rate of opening, inlet air temperature, coolant temperature and on certain systems, engine knock. Again, these are monitored via sensors mounted on the engine.

Knock control is employed on all engines except code AEV. The knock sensor is mounted on the cylinder block, and has the ability to detect engine pre-ignition (or 'pinking') before it actually becomes audible. If pre-ignition occurs, the ECU retards the ignition timing of the cylinder that is pre-igniting in steps until the pre-ignition ceases. The ECU then advances the ignition timing of that cylinder in steps until it is restored to normal, or until pre-ignition occurs again.

Idle speed control is achieved partly by an electronic throttle valve positioning module, mounted on the side of the throttle body, and partly by the ignition system, which gives fine control of the idle speed by altering the ignition timing. As a result, manual adjustment of the engine idle speed is not necessary or possible.

On certain systems, the ECU has the ability to perform multiple ignition cycles during cold starting. During cranking, each spark plug fires several times per ignition stroke, until the engine starts. This greatly improves the engines cold starting performance.

It should be noted that comprehensive fault diagnosis of all the engine management systems described in this Chapter is only possible with dedicated electronic test equipment. Problems with the system's operation that cannot be pinpointed by following the basic guidelines in Section 2 should therefore be referred to a VW dealer for assessment. Once the fault has been identified, the removal/refitting sequences detailed in the following Sections will then allow the appropriate component(s) to be renewed as required.

## 2 Ignition system - testing

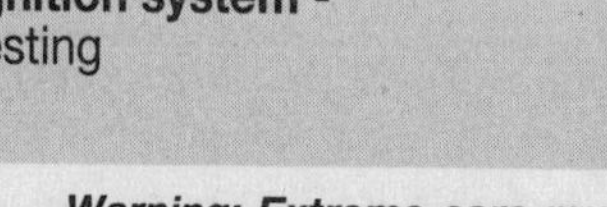

***Warning: Extreme care must be taken when working on the system with the ignition switched on; it is possible to get a substantial electric shock from a vehicle's ignition system. Persons with cardiac pacemaker devices should keep well clear of the ignition circuits, components and test equipment. Always switch off the ignition before disconnecting or connecting any component and when using a multi-meter to check resistances.***

### General

**1** Most ignition system faults are likely to be due to loose or dirty connections or to tracking (unintentional earthing) of HT voltage due to dirt, dampness or damaged insulation, rather than by the failure of any of the system's components. **Always** check all wiring thoroughly before condemning an electrical component, and work methodically to eliminate all other possibilities before deciding that a particular component is faulty.

**2** The old practice of checking for a spark by holding the live end of an HT lead a short distance away from the engine is not recommended; not only is there a high risk of an electric shock, but the HT coil could be damaged. Similarly, **never** try to diagnose misfires by pulling off one HT lead at a time.

### Engine will not start

**3** If the engine either will not turn over at all, or only turns very slowly, check the battery and starter motor. Connect a voltmeter across the battery terminals (meter positive probe to battery positive terminal), disconnect the ignition coil HT lead from the distributor cap and earth it, then note the voltage reading obtained while turning over the engine on the starter for (no more than) ten seconds. If the reading obtained is less than approximately 9.5 volts, first check the battery, starter motor and charging systems (see Chapter 5A).

**4** If the engine turns over at normal speed but will not start, check the HT circuit by connecting a timing light (following the manufacturer's instructions) and turning the engine over on the starter motor; if the light flashes, voltage is reaching the spark plugs, so these should be checked first. If the light does not flash, check the HT leads themselves, followed by the distributor cap, carbon brush and rotor arm.

**5** If there is a spark, check the fuel system for faults, referring to the relevant part of Chapter 4 for further information.

**6** If there is still no spark, then the problem must lie within the engine management system. In these cases, the vehicle should be referred to a VW dealer for assessment.

### Engine misfires

**7** An irregular misfire suggests either a loose connection or intermittent fault on the primary circuit, or an HT fault on the coil side of the rotor arm.

**8** With the ignition switched off, check carefully through the system, ensuring that all connections are clean and securely fastened. If the equipment is available, check the LT circuit as described above.

**9** Check that the HT coil, the distributor cap and the HT leads are clean and dry. Check the leads themselves and the spark plugs (by substitution, if necessary), then check the distributor cap, carbon brush and rotor arm.

**10** Regular misfiring is almost certainly due to a fault in the distributor cap, HT leads or spark plugs. Use a timing light (paragraph 4 above) to check whether HT voltage is present at all leads.

**11** If HT voltage is not present on one particular lead, the fault will be in that lead or in the distributor cap. If HT is present on all leads, the fault will be in the spark plugs; check and renew them if there is any doubt about their condition.

**12** If no HT voltage is present, check the HT coil; its secondary windings may be breaking down under load.

### Other problems

**13** Problems with the system's operation that cannot be pinpointed by following the guidelines in the preceding paragraphs should be referred to a VW dealer for assessment.

### Ignition component check

#### HT leads

**14** The spark plug (HT) leads should be checked whenever new spark plugs are fitted (see Chapter 1A).

**15** Pull the leads from the plugs by gripping the end fitting, not the lead, otherwise the lead connection may be fractured **(see illustration)**.

***Ensure that the leads are numbered before removing them, to avoid confusion when refitting***

2.15 Removing the HT leads and distributor cap as an assembly, for cleaning

16 Check inside the end fitting for signs of corrosion, which will look like a white crusty powder. Push the end fitting back onto the spark plug, ensuring that it is a tight fit on the plug. If not, remove the lead again and use pliers to carefully crimp the metal connector inside the end fitting until it fits securely on the end of the spark plug.

17 Using a clean rag, wipe the entire length of the lead to remove any built-up dirt and grease. Once the lead is clean, check for burns, cracks and other damage. Do not bend the lead too much, nor pull the lead lengthways - the conductor inside might break.

18 Disconnect the other end of the lead from the distributor cap. Again, pull only on the end fitting. Check for corrosion and a tight fit in the same manner as the spark plug end. If an ohmmeter is available, check the resistance of the lead by connecting the meter between the spark plug end of the lead and the segment inside the distributor cap. Refit the lead securely on completion.

19 Check the remaining leads one at a time, in the same way. Do not forget to check the king lead, which runs from the centre terminal of the distributor cap to the coil.

20 If new spark plug (HT) leads are required, buy a set for your specific car and engine.

### Distributor cap

21 Unscrew its retaining screws or release the clips and remove the distributor cap. Wipe it clean, and carefully inspect it inside and out for signs of cracks, black carbon tracks (tracking) and worn, burned or loose contacts; check that the cap's carbon brush is unworn, free to move against spring pressure, and making good contact with the rotor arm. Also inspect the cap seal for signs of wear or damage, and renew if necessary

22 Do not simultaneously remove all the leads from the old cap, or firing order confusion may occur. When refitting, tighten the cap retaining screws securely, or ensure that the cap clips engage correctly.

***When fitting a new cap, remove the leads from the old cap one at a time, and fit them to the new cap in the same location***

23 Even with the ignition system in first-class condition, some engines may still occasionally experience poor starting attributable to damp ignition components. To disperse moisture, a water-dispersant aerosol should be liberally applied.

### Rotor arm

24 With reference to the previous sub-Section, remove the distributor cap.

25 Pull off the rotor arm from the distributor shaft and inspect the rotor arm.

26 Inspect the distributor cap contacts and clean them if necessary.

27 Refitting is a reversal of removal - ensure that the rotor arm alignment lug engages with the recess in the distributor shaft, before refitting the distributor cap.

### Ignition coil

28 Disconnect the LT wiring plug and the HT (king) lead from the ignition coil.

29 Connect a multimeter between terminals 1(–) and 15(+), and check that the resistance of the primary windings is as given in the Specifications.

30 Connect the multimeter between terminals 4 (HT) and 15(+), and check that the resistance of the secondary windings is as given in the Specifications.

31 Reconnect the wiring.

## 3 HT coil - removal and refitting

### *Removal*

1 On all models, the ignition coil is mounted on the engine compartment bulkhead.

2 Disconnect the battery negative lead and position it away from the terminal. **Note:** *If the vehicle has a security-coded radio, check that you have a copy of the code number before disconnecting the battery. Refer to your VW dealer if in doubt.*

3 Unplug the HT lead from the ignition coil at the connector. Note which way round the collar on the lead end fitting is located **(see illustration)**.

4 Disconnect the LT wiring from the ignition coil at the multiway connector **(see illustration)**.

5 Lift up the weatherstrip from the top of the engine compartment bulkhead, and lift up the plastic cowl panel for access to the coil mounting nuts.

6 Slacken and withdraw the mounting nuts or bolts, and remove the ignition coil. Note that one of the mounting bolts is used to retain the coil earth strap **(see illustrations)**.

7 On some models, the coil output stage can be unbolted from the main body and renewed separately if required.

### *Refitting*

8 Refitting is a reversal of removal.

3.3 Unplug the HT lead from the ignition coil at the connector

3.4 Disconnect the LT wiring plug from the ignition coil

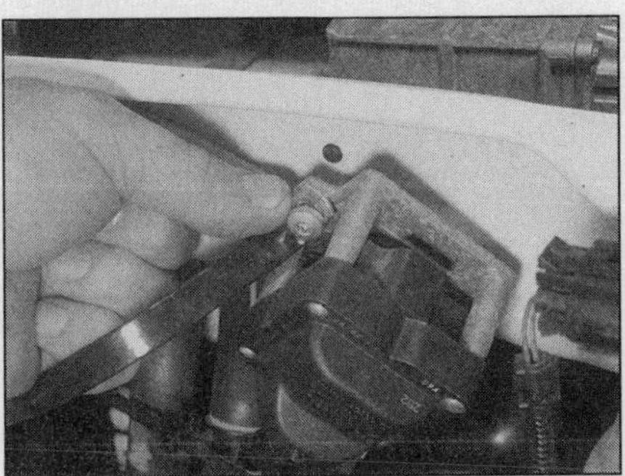

3.6a One of the ignition coil mounting bolts is used to secure the coil earth strap

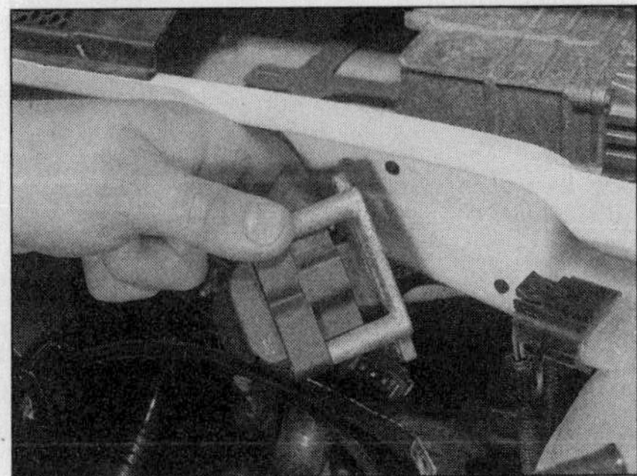

3.6b Removing the ignition coil

4.4 Disconnecting the distributor cap earth braid

## 4 Distributor - removal, inspection and refitting

### Removal

**1** Disconnect the battery negative lead and position it away from the terminal. **Note:** *If the vehicle has a security-coded radio, check that you have a copy of the code number before disconnecting the battery. Refer to your VW dealer if in doubt.*

**2** Set the engine to TDC on cylinder No 1, referring to Section 2 of Chapter 2A for guidance.

**3** If required, unplug all five HT leads from the distributor cap, labelling them to aid refitting later. It is preferable, however, to remove the distributor cap with all leads attached - the leads can then be transferred one at a time to a new cap, if one is being fitted.

4.5 Unplug the Hall sensor cable from the distributor body at the connector

**4** Unplug the earth braid from the metal screening cap **(see illustration)**.

**5** Unplug the Hall sensor cable from the distributor body at the connector **(see illustration)**.

**6** Remove the screws/prise off the retaining clips (as applicable), then lift off the distributor cap **(see illustrations)**. If the HT leads are still attached, lay the cap to one side, ensuring that the leads are not twisted or kinked excessively. Check at this point that the centre of the rotor arm electrode is aligned with the cylinder No 1 marking on the distributor body.

**7** Mark the relationship between the distributor body and the mounting flange by scribing arrows on each, or painting an alignment mark between them **(see illustration)**.

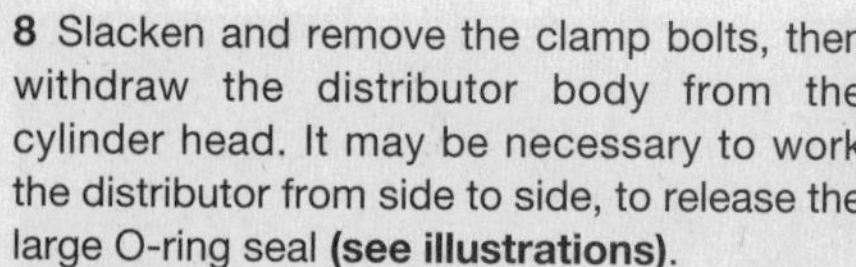

**8** Slacken and remove the clamp bolts, then withdraw the distributor body from the cylinder head. It may be necessary to work the distributor from side to side, to release the large O-ring seal **(see illustrations)**.

### Inspection

**9** Recover the O-ring seal from the bottom of the distributor and inspect it. Renew the seal if it appears at all worn or damaged.

### Refitting

**10** Install the distributor, engaging its drive dog with the hole in the camshaft drive flange, and loosely fit the clamp bolts. Rotate the distributor body such that the alignment marks made during removal line up. The centre of the rotor arm electrode should point directly at the No 1 cylinder mark on the distributor body **(see illustration)**.

**11** Refit the distributor cap, pressing the retaining clips firmly into place/tightening the retaining screws (as applicable).

**12** Reconnect the Hall sensor cabling to the distributor.

**13** Refit the screening cap earth braid.

**14** Working from the No 1 terminal, connect the HT leads between the spark plugs and the distributor cap. The firing order is 1-3-4-2.

**15** Fit the HT king lead between the coil and the centre terminal on the distributor cap.

**16** It may be advisable to have the ignition timing checked and if necessary adjusted, although in fact nothing should have been altered - refer to the notes in Section 5.

4.6a Using a suitable screwdriver, release the spring clips . . .

4.6b . . . and lift away the distributor cap

4.7 Alignment marks (arrowed) painted between distributor body and mounting flange

4.8a Loosen the clamp bolts (arrowed) using an Allen key . . .

4.8b . . . and remove the distributor - note the large O-ring seal (arrowed)

4.10 Rotor arm contact aligned with raised notch in distributor body (arrowed)

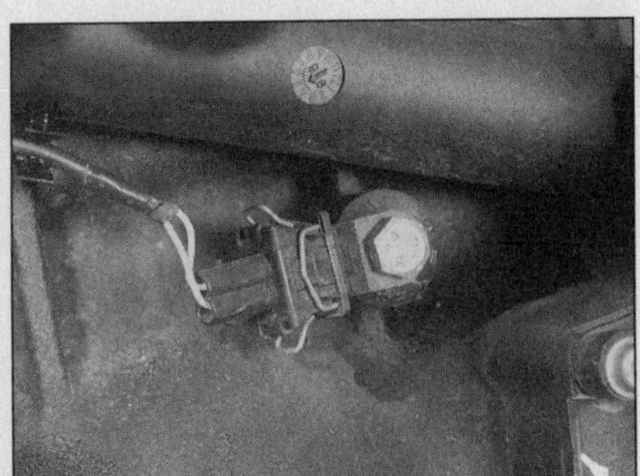
6.4 Knock sensor and wiring plug - seen with engine removed, for clarity

## 5 Ignition timing - checking and adjusting

The ignition timing is under the control of the engine management system ECU, and is not manually adjustable without access to dedicated electronic test equipment. A basic setting cannot be quoted because the ignition timing is constantly being altered to control engine idle speed (see Section 1 for details).

The vehicle must be taken to a VW dealer if the timing requires checking or adjustment.

## 6 Ignition system sensors - removal and refitting

**1** Many of the engine management system sensors provide signals for both the fuel injection and ignition systems. Those specific to the ignition system are detailed in this Section.

**2** Those sensors that are common to both systems are detailed in Chapter 4A or B. These include the coolant temperature sensor, the inlet air temperature sensor, the throttle potentiometer, the road speed sensor, the idle switch and the inlet manifold pressure sensor, as applicable.

7.2 Removing the rotor arm from the end of the distributor shaft

### *Knock sensor*

#### Removal

**3** Disconnect the battery negative lead and position it away from the terminal. **Note:** *If the vehicle has a security-coded radio, check that you have a copy of the code number before disconnecting the battery. Refer to your VW dealer if in doubt.*

**4** The knock sensor is mounted on the rear of the cylinder block, underneath spark plug No 3 and the rigid coolant pipe which runs across the back of the block **(see illustration)**. Access to the sensor is extremely limited from above, and only a little better from below.

**5** Unplug the harness wiring from the sensor at the connector.

**6** Slacken and withdraw the mounting bolt and lift off the sensor.

#### Refitting

**7** Refitting is a reversal of removal, but note that the sensor's operation will be affected if its mounting bolt is not tightened to exactly the right torque.

### *No 1 cylinder Hall-effect sensor*

**8** This sensor is an integral part of the distributor assembly. It can be removed and renewed separately, but dismantling of the distributor will be necessary. It is therefore recommended that this operation is entrusted to a automotive electrical specialist.

## 7 Rotor arm - renewal

**1** With reference to Section 4, remove the distributor cap.

**2** Pull the rotor arm from the end of the distributor shaft **(see illustration)**.

**3** Inspect the distributor cap contacts, and clean them if necessary.

**4** Refitting is a reversal of removal - ensure that the rotor arm alignment lug engages with the recess in the distributor shaft, before refitting the distributor cap.

# Chapter 5 Part C:
# Pre-heating system - diesel models

## Contents



## Degrees of difficulty

| | | | | |
|---|---|---|---|---|
| **Easy,** suitable for novice with little experience  | **Fairly easy,** suitable for beginner with some experience  | **Fairly difficult,** suitable for competent DIY mechanic  | **Difficult,** suitable for experienced DIY mechanic  | **Very difficult,** suitable for expert DIY or professional |

## Specifications

### Glow plugs

| | |
|---|---|
| Electrical resistance: | |
| Engine code AEF | 1.5 ohms (approx) |
| All other engine codes | N/A |
| Current consumption: | |
| Engine code AEF | 8 amps (per glow plug) |
| All other engine codes | N/A |

### Torque wrench settings

| | Nm | lbf ft |
|---|---|---|
| Glow plugs: | | |
| Engine code AEF | 25 | 18 |
| All other engine codes | 15 | 11 |

## 1 General information

To assist cold starting, diesel-engined models are fitted with a pre-heating system, which comprises four glow plugs, a glow plug control unit, a facia-mounted warning light and the associated electrical wiring.

The glow plugs are miniature electric heating elements, encapsulated in a metal case, with a probe at one end and electrical connection at the other. Each swirl chamber/inlet tract has a glow plug threaded into it, the glow plug probe being positioned directly in line with incoming spray of fuel. When the glow plug is energised, the fuel passing over it is heated, allowing its optimum combustion temperature to be achieved more readily when it reaches the cylinder.

The duration of the pre-heating period is governed by the glow plug control unit, which monitors the temperature of the engine via the coolant temperature sensor, and alters the pre-heating time to suit the conditions.

A facia-mounted warning light informs the driver that pre-heating is taking place. The light extinguishes when sufficient pre-heating has taken place to allow the engine to be started, but power will still be supplied to the glow plugs for a further period until the engine is started. If no attempt is made to start the engine, the power supply to the glow plugs is switched off to prevent battery drain and glow plug burn-out. Note that on certain models, the warning light will also illuminate during normal driving if a pre-heating system malfunction occurs.

Generally, pre-heating is triggered by the ignition key being turned to the second position. However, models with engine code AEF (indirect injection engine) are equipped with a pre-heating system that activates when the driver's door is opened, and then shut. Note that the system only functions once each time the engine is started - if the driver's door is opened, shut, and then no attempt is made to start the vehicle within a certain period, subsequent opening and shutting of the door will not reset the system. Refer to the vehicle handbook for further information.

After the engine has been started, the glow plugs continue to operate for a further period of time. This helps to improve fuel combustion whilst the engine is warming up, resulting in quieter, smoother running and reduced exhaust emissions.

## 2 Glow plug control unit (engine code AEF) - removal and refitting

**1** On engine codes except AEF, the pre-heating system is controlled by the diesel engine management system ECU, which is located behind the engine compartment bulkhead, under the windscreen cowl panel.

### Removal

**2** The glow plug control unit is located behind the facia, at the top of the main fuse/relay panel - refer to Chapter 11 and remove the relevant sections of trim to gain access.

**3** Disconnect the battery negative lead and position it away from the terminal. **Note:** *If the vehicle has a security-coded radio, check that you have a copy of the code number before disconnecting the battery. Refer to your VW dealer if in doubt.*

**4** Unplug the control unit and remove it from the relay panel.

### Refitting

**5** Refitting is a reversal of removal.

5C

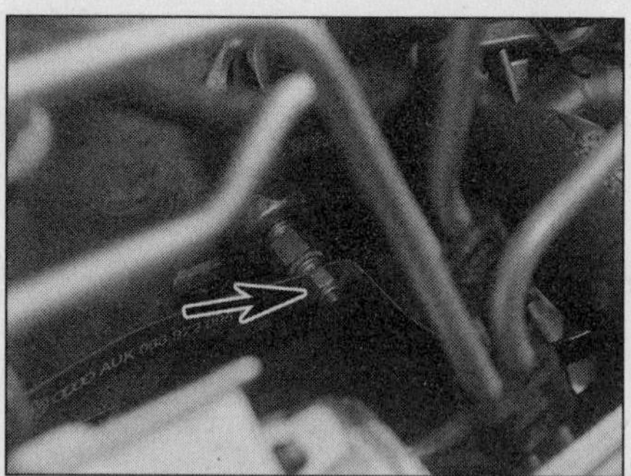

3.4 Glow plug and supply cable retaining nut (arrowed)

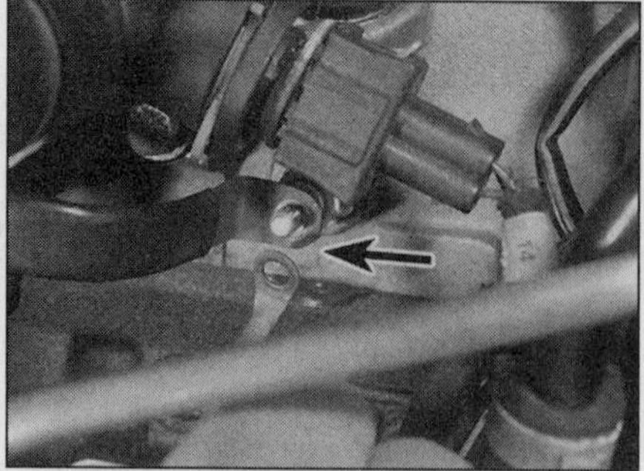

3.6 Supply cable (arrowed) removed from No 4 cylinder glow plug

## 3 Glow plugs - testing, removal and refitting

### Testing

**1** If the system malfunctions, testing is ultimately by substitution of known good units, but some preliminary checks may be made as described in the following paragraphs.

**2** Connect a voltmeter or 12 volt test light to between the glow plug supply cable and a good earth point on the engine.

***Caution: Make sure that the live connection is kept well clear of the engine and bodywork.***

**3** Have an assistant activate the pre-heating system (either using the ignition key, or opening the driver's door, as applicable) and check that a battery voltage is applied to the glow plug electrical connection. (Note that the voltage will drop to zero when the pre-heating period ends).

**4** If no supply voltage can be detected at the glow plug, then either the glow plug relay (where applicable) or the supply cabling must be faulty **(see illustration)**.

**5** To locate a faulty glow plug, first disconnect the battery negative lead and position it away from the terminal. **Note:** *If the vehicle has a security-coded radio, check that you have a copy of the code number before disconnecting the battery. Refer to your VW dealer if in doubt.*

**6** Refer to the next sub-Section and remove the supply cabling from the glow plug terminal **(see illustration)**. Measure the electrical resistance between the glow plug terminal and the engine earth. A reading of anything more than a few ohms indicates that the plug is defective.

**7** If a suitable ammeter is available, connect it between the glow plug and its supply cable, and measure the steady-state current consumption (ignore the initial current surge, which will be about 50% higher). Compare the result with the Specifications - high current consumption (or no current draw at all) indicates a faulty glow plug.

**8** Remove the glow plugs and inspect them visually, as described in the next sub-Section.

**9** There are commercially-produced glow plug testers available which comprise a casing in which the plug is clamped, an ammeter, 12-volt connection leads and a simple timing circuit which illuminates successive LEDs in five-second intervals.

***Warning: Glow plug tips become very hot during testing. Take care to avoid burns, especially from plugs which have only just stopped glowing.***

**10** With the glow plug in place and the leads connected to a 12-volt battery, note the time taken before the tip of the plug begins to glow and the current drops.

**11** Whilst such equipment is available in a commercial workshop, it is too infrequently needed to most owners to justify the purchase price. However, an equivalent test rig can be made up at home at little cost.

**12** Using an ammeter with a range of at least 30A, connect a lead to each ammeter terminal, fitting a crocodile clip at each end. In the interests of safety, fit an in-line fuseholder to one of the leads, using a 30A fuse.

**13** With the suspect glow plug removed from the cylinder head, clamp it with self-locking pliers against its metal body to a sound earth point on the engine. Connect the lead from the positive (+) terminal on the ammeter to the glow plug terminal. Have an assistant ready with a watch so that a running count of seconds elapsed can be made while you watch the glow plug tip.

**14** Connect the remaining crocodile clip from the ammeter negative (-) terminal to the battery positive terminal and start the count. Watch the ammeter needle and the glow plug tip closely. The glow plug tip should start to glow red after about five seconds. After about fifteen seconds, the current reading should drop from around 25A to about 12A.

**15** Note that the above timings and current figures are not precise. If the glow plug under test performs reasonably closely to the above sequence, it is likely to be alright. An abnormally high or low current reading (or a blown fuse) indicates the need for renewal, as does a failure of the tip to glow at all.

***Warning: Under no circumstances should the glow plugs be tested outside the engine. A correctly-functioning glow plug will become red-hot in a very short time!***

### Removal

**16** Disconnect the battery negative lead and position it away from the terminal - refer to the note in paragraph 5.

**17** Remove the nuts and washers from the glow plug terminal. Lift off the bus bar/supply cable **(see illustration)**.

**18** Slacken and withdraw the glow plug **(see illustration)**.

**19** Inspect the glow plug probe for signs of damage. A badly burned or charred probe is usually an indication of a faulty fuel injector - refer to Chapter 4C.

### Refitting

**20** Refitting is a reversal of removal. Tighten the glow plugs to the specified torque **(see illustration)**.

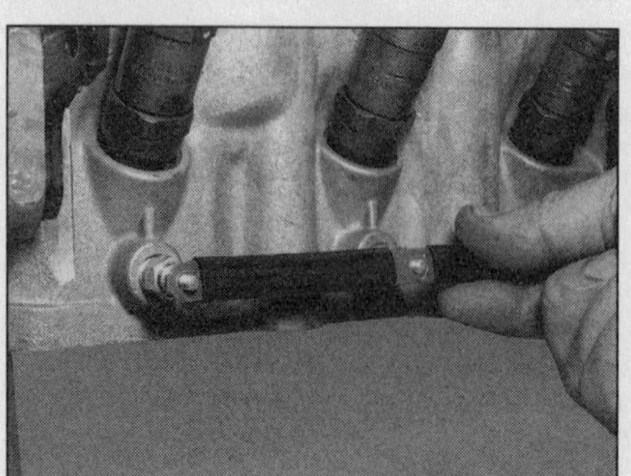

3.17 Remove the nuts and washers from the glow plug terminal. Lift off the bus bar/supply cable

3.18 Slacken and withdraw the glow plug

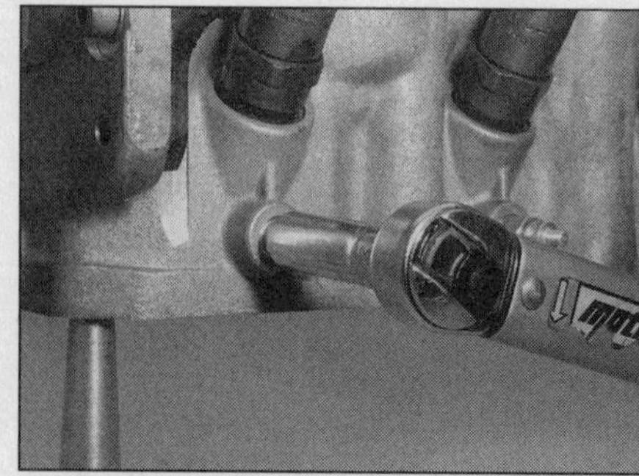

3.20 Tighten the glow plug to the specified torque

# Chapter 6
# Clutch

## Contents



## Degrees of difficulty

| | | | | |
|---|---|---|---|---|
| **Easy,** suitable for novice with little experience  | **Fairly easy,** suitable for beginner with some experience  | **Fairly difficult,** suitable for competent DIY mechanic  | **Difficult,** suitable for experienced DIY mechanic | **Very difficult,** suitable for expert DIY or professional  |

## Specifications

### General

| | |
|---|---|
| Type | Single dry plate, diaphragm spring with spring-loaded hub |
| Operation: | |
| Right-hand-drive models | Cable with automatic adjustment mechanism (up to May 1995), cable with manual adjustment (May 1995 on) |
| Left-hand-drive models | Cable with automatic adjustment mechanism |
| Clutch disc diameter: | |
| Petrol engine models: | |
| Up to and including 1.4 litre engine | 190 mm |
| All 1.6 litre engine models | 200 mm |
| Diesel engine models: | |
| Single-part flywheel | 190 mm |
| Two-part flywheel | 175 mm |

| Torque wrench settings | Nm | lbf ft |
|---|---|---|
| Pedal mounting bracket bolts | 25 | 18 |
| Pedal pivot pin nut | 25 | 18 |
| Pressure plate-to-flywheel bolts: | | |
| Petrol engine models | 20 | 15 |
| Diesel engine: | | |
| Models with single-part flywheel | 20 | 15 |
| Models with two-part flywheel | 13 | 10 |

## 1 General information

Vehicles with manual transmission are fitted with a pedal-operated single dry plate clutch system. When the clutch pedal is depressed, effort is transmitted to the clutch release mechanism mechanically, by means of a cable. The release mechanism transfers effort to the pressure plate diaphragm spring, which withdraws from the flywheel and releases the driven plate.

The flywheel is mounted on the crankshaft, with the pressure plate bolted to it. Some diesel engines are equipped with a two-part flywheel, where the clutch pressure plate is matched to the flywheel and clutch disc during manufacture. Removal of the flywheel is described in Chapter 2A.

## 2 Clutch cable - removal, refitting and adjustment

**Note:** *All models were fitted with an automatic adjustment system up to May 1995. From this date, left-hand-drive models were fitted with a modified automatic adjuster system, while right-hand-drive (eg UK market) models reverted to a manually-adjusted cable. Refer to the relevant sections below, according to your particular model. At the time of writing, it appears that all components are interchangeable - ie if the automatic adjuster should fail, it appears that a manually-adjusted cable can be fitted in its place.*

### *Models with automatic adjustment system - up to May 1995*

#### Removal

**1** Depress the clutch pedal several times, to settle the automatic adjustment mechanism.

6

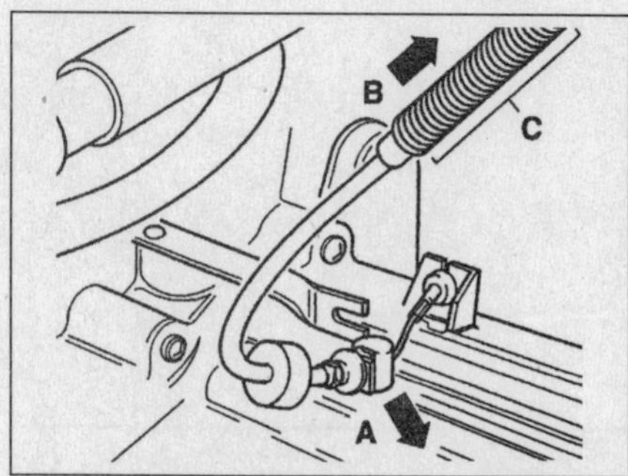


2.2 Clutch cable removal - automatic adjuster models up to May 1995

*A Remove cable outer from release arm*
*B Compress cable bellows in direction of arrow*
*C Cable bellows*

**2** Press the cable outer sideways to release the mounting rubber from the clutch release arm **(see illustration)**.

**3** Push the cable towards the engine compartment bulkhead, so that the cable bellows is compressed. If this proves difficult, have an assistant gently press the clutch pedal to the floor, and try again.

**4** Pull the inner cable end fitting upwards from the gearbox mounting.

**5** Working in the driver's footwell, remove the glovebox and lower trim panel as described in Chapter 11, for access to the foot pedals.

**6** Remove the fuse/relay panel (refer to Chapter 12), but do not disconnect any of the wiring from it.

**7** Remove the clutch pedal cover from the pedal mounting bracket, then unhook the cable end fitting from the top of the clutch pedal, and withdraw the cable into the engine compartment.

**8** Release the cable from its mountings in the engine compartment, and remove the cable from the car.

### Refitting

**9** Refitting is a reversal of removal, noting the following points:

*a) Lubricate all pivot points with a multi-purpose grease.*
*b) Take care that the cable is not kinked as it is fitted.*
*c) When the cable has been fitted, pull the release lever approximately 10 mm in the opposite direction to its normal direction of travel (ie towards the front of the car). The release lever should move freely. If not, carry out the procedure given in paragraphs 2 and 3 above.*

2.13 Compressing the adjustment mechanism using the locking strap

## Models with automatic adjustment system - May 1995 on

### Removal

**10** Depress the clutch pedal several times, to settle the automatic adjustment mechanism.

**11** Working in the engine bay, slide the locking strap down to the top of the adjustment mechanism protective boot.

**12** Pull the release lever approximately 10 mm towards the front of the car - this will compress the adjuster mechanism.

**13** While the mechanism is compressed, hook the ends of the locking strap over the lugs protruding from the side of the adjustment mechanism **(see illustration)**. It may be necessary to enlist the help of an assistant for this. **Note:** *If the locking strap is no longer attached to the clutch cable, a home-made strap can be fabricated using nylon cable-ties or a length of electrical cable.*

**14** Press the cable outer sideways to release the mounting rubber from the clutch release arm.

**15** Pull the inner cable end fitting from the gearbox mounting.

**16** Working in the driver's footwell, remove the glovebox and lower trim panel as described in Chapter 11, for access to the foot pedals.

2.21a Loosen the locknut and adjuster nut . . .

**17** Remove the fuse/relay panel (refer to Chapter 12), but do not disconnect any of the wiring from it.

**18** Remove the clutch pedal cover from the pedal mounting bracket, then unhook the cable end fitting from the top of the clutch pedal, and withdraw the cable into the engine compartment.

**19** Release the cable from its mountings in the engine compartment, and remove the cable from the car.

### Refitting

**20** Refitting is a reversal of removal of removal, noting the following points:

*a) Lubricate all pivot points with a multi-purpose grease.*
*b) Take care that the cable is not kinked as it is fitted.*
*c) Once the cable is attached to the release arm, gearbox mounting and pedal, unhook the locking strap from the adjustment mechanism.*
*d) Check the operation of the adjuster, by pulling the release lever approximately 10 mm in the opposite direction to its normal direction of travel (ie towards the front of the car). The release lever should move freely.*

## Models with manual adjuster

### Removal

**21** At the clutch release lever, loosen the cable adjuster locknut and adjuster nut, then press the cable sideways out of the release lever **(see illustrations)**.

**22** Pull the cable end fitting upwards from the gearbox mounting **(see illustration)**.

2.21b . . . and pull the cable sideways out of the release lever

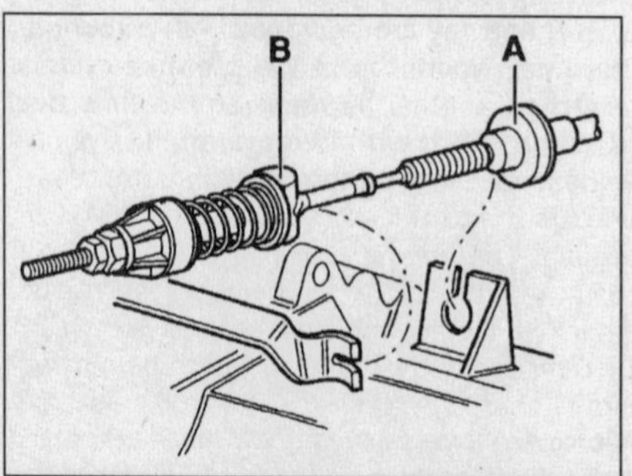


2.21c Clutch cable attachment at gearbox (A) and clutch release lever (B)

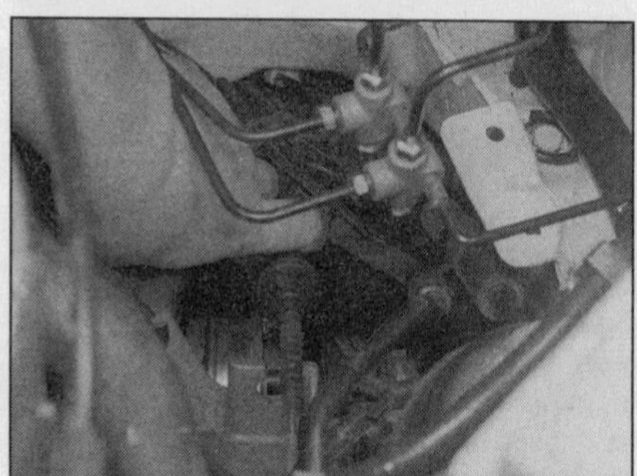

2.22 Pull the cable upwards to release it from the gearbox mounting

23 Working in the driver's footwell, remove the glovebox and lower trim panel as described in Chapter 11, for access to the foot pedals.

24 Remove the fuse/relay panel (refer to Chapter 12), but do not disconnect any of the wiring from it.

25 Remove the clutch pedal cover from the pedal mounting bracket, then unhook the cable end fitting from the top of the clutch pedal, and withdraw the cable into the engine compartment.

26 Release the cable from its mountings in the engine compartment, and remove the cable from the car.

### Refitting

27 Refitting is a reversal of removal, noting the following points:

*a) Lubricate all pivot points with a multi-purpose grease.*

*b) Take care that the cable is not kinked as it is fitted.*

*c) Adjust the cable as described below.*

### Adjustment

28 At the release lever, loosen the adjuster locknut, and turn the adjuster nut to give 15 to 20 mm of free travel at the clutch pedal. Some trial-and-error may be involved before satisfactory clutch operation is achieved. With the handbrake firmly applied, start the engine and select a gear to assess the clutch bite point.

29 When adjustment is complete, tighten the locknut securely, while ensuring the adjuster nut does not move.

## All models

30 On completion, assess the feel of the clutch pedal before bringing the vehicle back into service. If it exhibits any stiffness or shows signs of binding, check the routing of the cable and ensure that there are no sharp bends or kinks along its length.

31 Finally, road test the vehicle and check the operation of the clutch whilst changing up and down through the gears, whilst pulling away from a standstill and from a hill start.

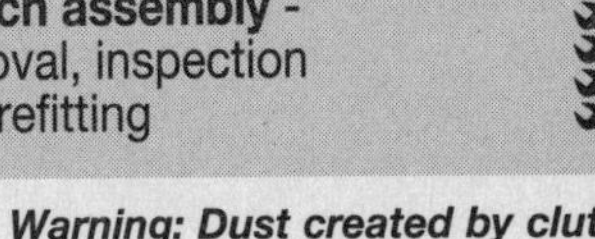

## 3 Clutch assembly - removal, inspection and refitting

***Warning: Dust created by clutch wear and deposited on the clutch components may contain asbestos, which is a health hazard. DO NOT blow it out with compressed air or inhale any of it. DO NOT use petrol or petroleum-based solvents to clean off the dust. Brake system cleaner or methylated spirit should be used to flush the dust into a suitable receptacle. After the clutch components are wiped clean with clean rags, dispose of the contaminated rags and cleaner in a sealed, marked container.***

**Note:** *Some friction materials may no longer contain asbestos, but it is safest to assume they DO, and to take precautions accordingly.*

## Removal

1 Access to the clutch unit is gained by removing the engine and transmission combined, and then separating the two units as described in Chapter 2C, or by removing the transmission as described in Chapter 7A. Unless it is wished to also carry out repairs to the engine, it is preferable to gain access by removing the transmission only.

2 Unclip the release bearing from the release lever, and examine it for signs of terminal wear or damage. Spin it by hand and listen to the bearings; if the bearing sticks or is unduly noisy, it should be renewed.

3 With the transmission separated from the engine, mark the pressure plate and flywheel in relation to each other as a guide for refitting.

4 The flywheel must be held stationary while the pressure plate bolts are loosened - use a screwdriver or home-made tool engaged in the flywheel ring gear for this **(see illustration)**. Progressively slacken the pressure plate bolts in diagonal sequence. With the bolts unscrewed two or three turns, check that the cover is not binding on the dowel pins. If necessary, use a screwdriver to release the cover.

5 Remove all the bolts, then lift the pressure plate and friction disc from the flywheel.

## Inspection

**Note:** *Given the amount of dismantling work required to gain access to the clutch components, it is not advisable to refit any components unless they are known to have been recently fitted, or are obviously in as-new condition. Further, it is common practice when servicing the clutch to buy a complete kit (friction disc, pressure plate and release bearing) rather than just a new friction disc.*

6 Clean the cover, disc, and flywheel. *Do not inhale the dust, as it may contain asbestos which is dangerous to health.*

7 Examine the fingers of the diaphragm spring for wear or scoring. If the depth of any scoring is excessive a new cover assembly must be fitted.

8 Examine the pressure plate for scoring, cracking and discoloration. Light scoring is acceptable, but if excessive, a new cover assembly must be fitted.

9 Examine the friction disc linings for wear, cracking, and for contamination with oil or grease. The linings are worn excessively if they are worn down to, or near, the rivets. Check the disc hub and splines for wear, by temporarily fitting it on the transmission input shaft. Renew the friction disc as necessary.

10 If there is any evidence of contamination by oil or grease, the source of the leak should be traced and rectified before fitting new clutch components, otherwise the new parts will quickly go the same way. There is no satisfactory way to de-grease the friction disc, once contaminated.

**3.4 Home-made flywheel locking tool in use**

11 Examine the flywheel friction surface for scoring, cracking, and discoloration (caused by overheating). If excessive, it may be possible to have the flywheel machined by an engineering works, otherwise it should be renewed.

12 Before refitting the clutch, it is advisable to inspect the condition of the release bearing and lever **(see illustration)**. Spin the release bearing by hand, and check it for any signs of roughness (it is usually considered good practice to renew the bearing at the same time as the friction disc). If the release lever

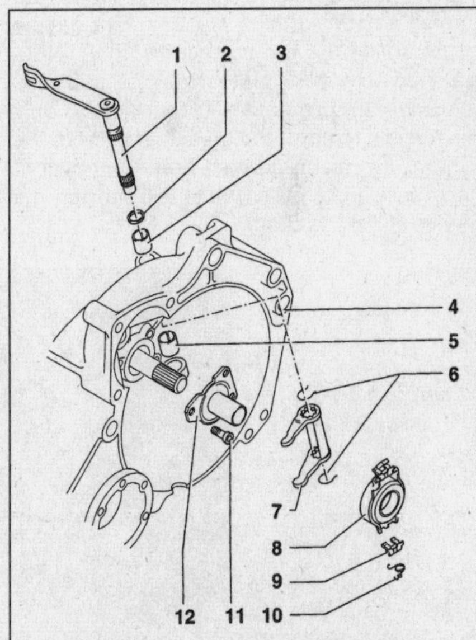


**3.12 Clutch release mechanism components**

*1 Clutch release lever and shaft*
*2 Seal*
*3 Mounting bush*
*4 Clutch bellhousing*
*5 Mounting bush*
*6 Securing clip*
*7 Release bearing lever*
*8 Release bearing*
*9 Retaining clip*
*10 Retaining spring*
*11 Bolt*
*12 Guide sleeve*

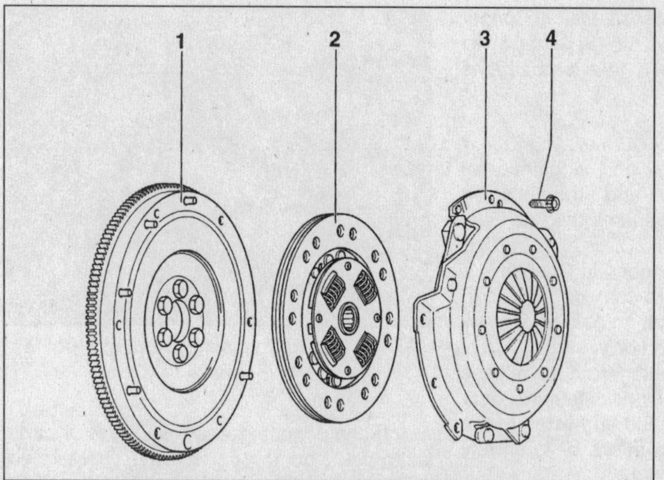


**3.14a Clutch assembly - petrol engine models, and diesel engine models with single-part flywheel**

1 *Flywheel*
2 *Friction disc*
3 *Pressure plate*
4 *Pressure plate bolt*

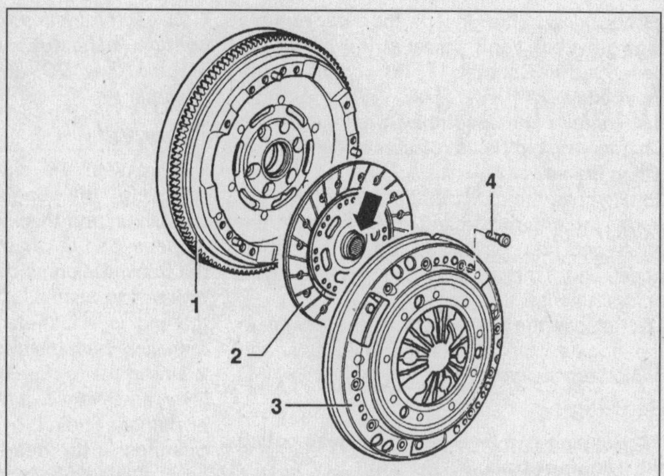


**3.14b Clutch assembly - diesel engine models with two-part flywheel**

1 *Two-part flywheel*
2 *Friction disc (shorter end of hub - arrowed - faces pressure plate)*
3 *Pressure plate*
4 *Pressure plate bolt*

bushes are excessively worn, they can be drifted out and renewed. Lubricate the release lever shaft pivots and release bearing guide sleeve sparingly with high-temperature grease.

## *Refitting*

**13** Ensure that all parts are clean, and free of oil or grease, before reassembling. Apply just a small amount of high melting-point grease to the splines of the friction disc hub. Note that new pressure plates may be supplied coated with protective grease. It is only permissible to clean the grease away from the friction disc lining contact area. Removal of the grease from other areas will shorten the service life of the clutch.

**14** Study the relevant illustration to ensure that the clutch friction disc is fitted the correct way round **(see illustrations)**.

**15** Locate the friction disc into position, then fit the pressure plate on the disc, engaging it onto the location dowels **(see illustrations)**. Hold the disc as central as possible while doing this. If refitting the original cover, make sure that the previously-made marks are aligned.

**16** Insert the bolts finger-tight to hold the cover in position, but to allow movement of the friction disc.

**17** The friction disc must now be centralised, to ensure correct alignment of the transmission input shaft with the clutch components and the spigot bearing in the crankshaft. To do this, a proprietary tool may be used, or alternatively, use a wooden mandrel. Insert the tool through the friction disc into the spigot bearing, and make sure that it is central. Failure to centralise the friction disc will mean that the transmission input shaft will not be able to pass through the clutch components, making reconnecting the engine and transmission impossible. Time spent getting the centralisation correct will be well justified.

**18** Tighten the pressure plate bolts progressively and in diagonal sequence, until the specified torque setting is reached, then remove the centralising tool.

**19** Refit the engine and/or transmission with reference to Chapter 2C or 7A, as applicable.

**3.15a Friction disc orientation - petrol engine model shown**

**3.15b Fitting the clutch friction disc and pressure plate**

# Chapter 7 Part A:
# Manual transmission

## Contents



## Degrees of difficulty

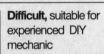

| | | | | |
|---|---|---|---|---|
| **Easy,** suitable for novice with little experience  | **Fairly easy,** suitable for beginner with some experience  | **Fairly difficult,** suitable for competent DIY mechanic | **Difficult,** suitable for experienced DIY mechanic  | **Very difficult,** suitable for expert DIY or professional |

## Specifications

### General

| | |
|---|---|
| Description | Transverse-mounted, front-wheel-drive layout with integral transaxle differential/final drive. 5 forward speeds, 1 reverse speed |
| Transmission type number | 085 |
| Gear selection | Rod or cable operation, depending on model |
| Lubricant capacities | See Chapter 1A or 1B |

### Torque wrench settings

| | Nm | lbf ft |
|---|---|---|
| Angle piece bolts | 15 | 11 |
| Cable mounting bracket bolts | 25 | 18 |
| Cable mounting bracket-to-angle piece bolt | 20 | 15 |
| Cable support bracket nut | 20 | 15 |
| Gate selector finger bolt | 20 | 15 |
| Gate selector rod-to-finger nut | 20 | 15 |
| Gear selector cable-to-selector lever bolt | 20 | 15 |
| Rod-type gear selector finger bolt* | 20 | 15 |
| Transmission bellhousing-to-engine bolts: | | |
| Petrol engine models: | | |
| M7 bolt | 15 | 11 |
| M8 bolts | 20 | 15 |
| M12 bolts | 80 | 59 |
| Diesel engine models: | | |
| M7 bolt | 10 | 7 |
| M10 bolts | 60 | 44 |
| M12 bolts | 80 | 59 |
| Transmission support cable pin | 20 | 15 |

**Use new bolt, with thread-locking fluid*



### 1 General information

The manual transmission is mounted transversely in the engine bay, bolted directly to the engine. This layout has the advantage of providing the shortest possible drive path to the front wheels, as well as locating the transmission in the airflow through engine bay, optimising cooling. The unit is cased in aluminium alloy.

Drive from the crankshaft is transmitted via the clutch to the gearbox input shaft, which is splined to accept the clutch friction plate.

All forward gears are fitted with syncromeshes. When a gear is selected, the movement of the cabin floor-mounted gear lever is communicated to the gearbox either by a selector rod, or gate and gear selector cables, depending on the transmission type. This in turn actuates a series of selector forks inside the gearbox, which are slotted onto the synchromesh sleeves. The sleeves, which are locked to the gearbox shafts but can slide axially by means of splined hubs, press baulk rings into contact with the respective gear/pinion. The coned surfaces between the baulk rings and the pinion/gear act as a friction clutch, that progressively matches the speed of the synchromesh sleeve (and hence the gearbox shaft) with that of the gear/pinion. The dog teeth on the outside of the baulk ring prevent the synchromesh sleeve ring from meshing with the gear/pinion until their speeds are exactly matched; this allows gear changes to be carried out smoothly, and greatly reduces the noise and mechanical wear caused by rapid gear changes.

Drive is transmitted to the differential crownwheel, which rotates the differential case and planetary gears, thus driving the sun gears and driveshafts. The rotation of the planetary gears on their shaft allows the inner roadwheel to rotate at a slower speed than the outer roadwheel during cornering.

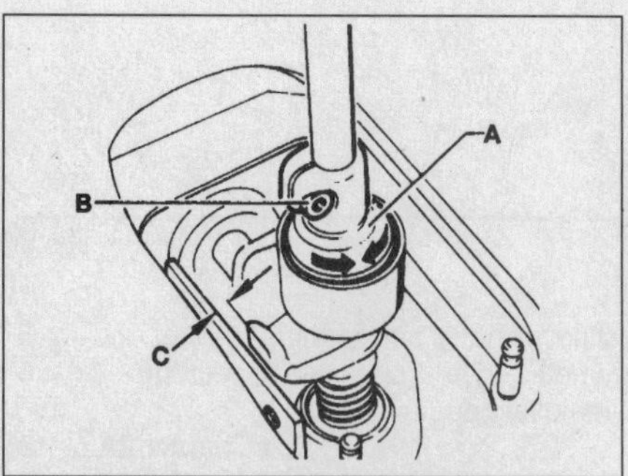


2.4 Gearchange lever adjustment collar - models with rod-type linkage

*A Adjustment collar*
*B Clamp bolt*
*C Clearance less than 1.5 mm*

All models, regardless of whether a rod-type or cable gear linkage is fitted, have a transmission support cable fitted between the transmission and the gear lever housing. The cable, which is under tension, is intended to absorb any movement from the transmission, which would otherwise be transmitted through the gear lever.

## 2 Gearchange linkage - adjustment

### Rod-type linkage

**1** If the gearchange quality proves unsatisfactory following transmission refitting, proceed as described in the following paragraphs.
**2** Refer to Chapter 11 and remove the knob and gaiter from the gear lever, to expose the adjustment collar.
**3** Select first gear, then take up the play in the gear change mechanism by gently pressing the gear lever to the left.
**4** Measure the clearance between the gear lever stop and the side of the lever housing **(see illustration)**.
**5** If the clearance is not between 1 and 2 mm, slacken the adjustment collar clamping bolt and rotate the collar until the correct clearance is achieved **(refer to illustration 2.4)**.
**6** On completion, tighten the clamping bolt.

3.9 Disconnect any wiring harness multi-plugs at the front of the gearbox

3.8a Remove the securing nut . . .

Refit the gear lever gaiter and knob.

### Cable linkage

**7** To accurately adjust the operation of the gate and gear selector cables, precisely-machined jigs are required to set the gear lever in a reference position. It is recommended, therefore that this operation be entrusted to a VW dealer.

## 3 Manual transmission - removal and refitting

### Removal

**1** Select a solid, level surface to park the vehicle upon. Give yourself enough space to move around it easily. Apply the handbrake and chock the rear wheels.
**2** Loosen the front wheel bolts, then raise the front of the vehicle and rest it securely on axle stands (see *Jacking and vehicle support*). Remove the front wheels.
**3** Refer to Chapter 11 and remove the bonnet from its hinges.
**4** Disconnect the battery negative lead and position It away from the terminal. **Note:** *If the vehicle has a security-coded radio, check that you have a copy of the code number before disconnecting the battery.*
**5** The lock carrier is a panel assembly comprising the front valance and bonnet lock mechanism, radiator and grille, cooling fan, and headlight units. Its removal gives greatly-improved access to the engine and transmission, and allows them to be lifted out of the vehicle via the front of the engine bay. Its removal is described at the beginning of the engine removal procedure - refer to Chapter 2C for details.
**6** On diesel engine models, remove the noise insulation tray from under the engine and transmission - see Chapter 1B, Section 3.
**7** Disconnect the clutch cable from the transmission release lever (see Chapter 6).
**8** Unbolt the earth strap from the transmission **(see illustrations)**.
**9** Referring to Sections 5 and 6, disconnect the wiring plugs from the reversing light switch and road speed sensor. Where

3.8b . . . and disconnect the transmission earth strap

applicable, disconnect any additional wiring plugs at the front of the transmission, and release the wiring harness from any securing clips **(see illustration)**.
**10** Referring to Chapter 8, disconnect both driveshafts from the flanges on the transmission - tie both driveshafts up out of the way, with the left-hand driveshaft up as high as possible. Turn the steering wheel to full left lock.

### Models with rod-type gear linkage

**11** Loosen the selector finger bolt, and remove the selector finger from below the transmission **(see illustration)**. Discard the bolt - a new one must be used on refitting.
**12** Prise off the retaining circlip, and lever off the transmission support cable (where fitted) from the transmission housing. Recover the bush from the cable end fitting, and discard it - a new bush must be used on refitting.

### Models with cable gear linkage

**13** Unscrew the through-bolt and disconnect the gear selector cable from the selector lever. Remove the spring clip and detach the gate selector cable from the relay lever. Remove the retaining circlips and detach the cables from the cable support bracket **(see illustrations)**.
**14** Remove the two angle-piece bolts at the rear, and the nut at the front, and lift off the cable support bracket from the top of the transmission **(see illustrations)**. It may be necessary to push the exhaust system over

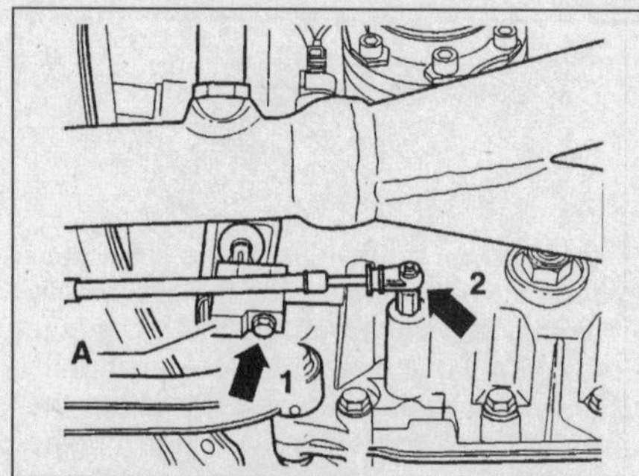


3.11 Gear selector finger (A), retaining bolt (1) and transmission support cable end fitting (2) - models with rod-type gear linkage

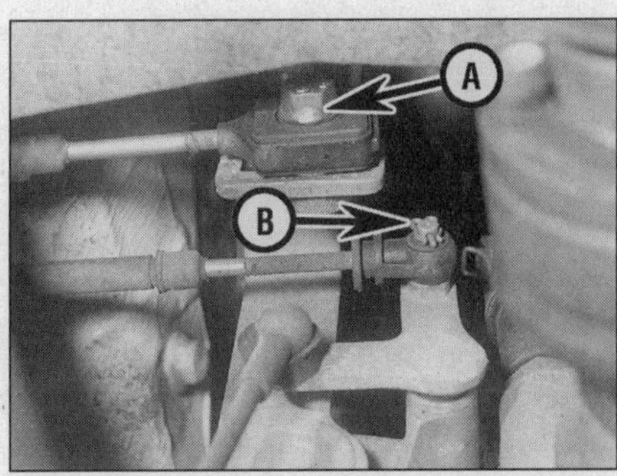

3.13a Gear selector cable through-bolt (A) and gate selector cable spring clip (B)

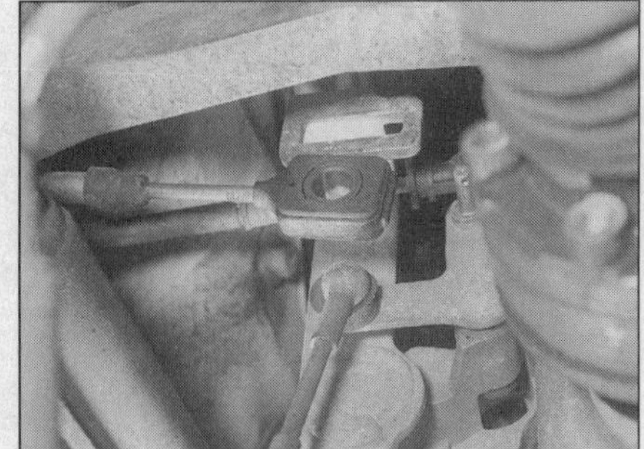
3.13b Gear selector and gate selector cables disconnected

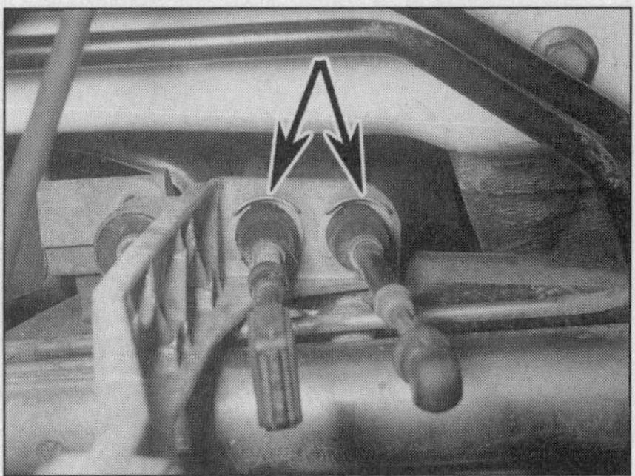
3.13c Cable retaining circlips (arrowed) at the cable support bracket

slightly, to give sufficient clearance to remove the support bracket.

**15** Prise off the retaining circlip, and lever off the transmission support cable (where fitted) from the transmission housing. Recover the bush from the cable end fitting, and discard it - a new bush must be used on refitting **(see illustration)**.

## All models

**16** Unbolt the flywheel shield plate from the underside of the transmission bellhousing.

**17** Position a trolley jack underneath the transmission, and raise it to just take the weight of the unit.

**18** Unscrew and remove the upper bolts securing the transmission bellhousing to the engine, noting the locations of the bolts, as they are of different sizes and lengths.

**19** Referring to Chapter 2A or B as applicable, unbolt and remove the engine/transmission rear mounting.

**20** Where applicable on petrol engine models, unbolt and remove the inlet manifold support bracket.

**21** Refer to Chapter 5A and remove the starter motor.

**22** Ensure that the weight of the engine and transmission is adequately supported, then unscrew and remove the two bolts securing the transmission to the left-hand mounting (refer to Chapter 2A or B, as applicable).

**23** Carefully tilt the engine and transmission assembly down at the transmission end, making sure the weight of the transmission is still adequately supported. Check that nothing remains attached to the transmission housing which would prevent its removal.

**24** Unscrew and remove the lower bolts securing the transmission bellhousing to the engine, again noting the bolt locations, as they are of different sizes and lengths.

**25** Carefully prise the transmission off its locating dowels, and move it to the side, to clear the clutch components.

***Warning: Support the transmission to ensure that it remains steady on the jack head. Keep the transmission level until the input shaft is fully withdrawn from the clutch friction plate.***

**26** When all the locating dowels are clear of their mounting holes, lower the transmission out of the engine bay using the jack.

## Refitting

**27** Refitting the transmission is essentially a reversal of the removal procedure, but note the following points:

*a) Apply a smear of high-melting-point grease to the clutch friction plate splines; take care to avoid contaminating the friction surfaces.*

*b) Tighten the bellhousing bolts to the specified torque*

*c) Refer to Chapter 2A or B (as applicable) and tighten the engine and transmission mounting bolts to the correct torque.*

*d) On models with the rod-type gear linkage, when refitting the selector finger, clean its threaded hole with an M8 tap, and fit a new bolt using thread-locking fluid. The finger should be assembled so that the bolt fits into the forward recess in the inner finger* ***(see illustration)****.*

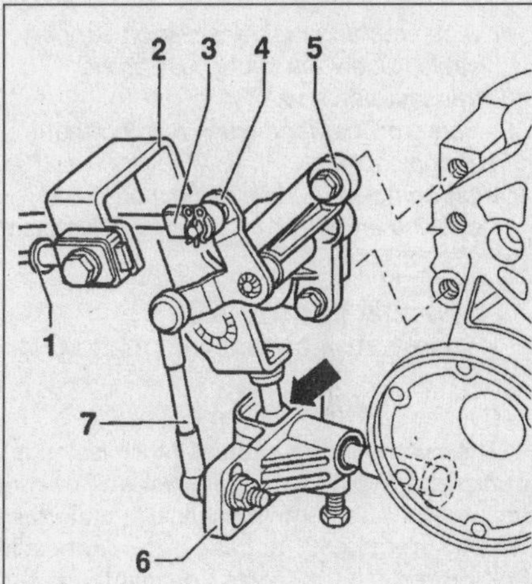

3.13d Selector cables and relay linkage - models with cable gear linkage

*1 Gear selector cable*
*2 Selector lever (fits into selector finger - arrowed)*
*3 Gate selector cable*
*4 Relay lever*
*5 Mounting bracket*
*6 Selector finger*
*7 Gate selector link rod*



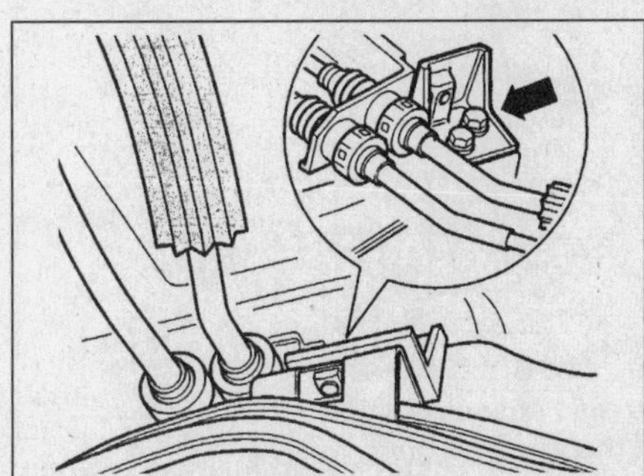
3.14a Remove two bolts from support bracket angle piece . . .

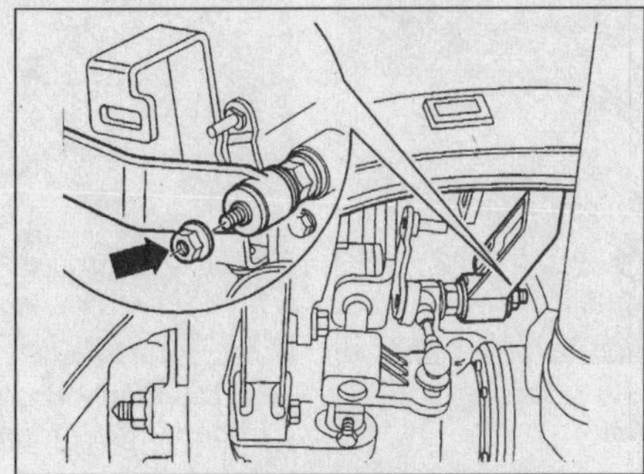
3.14b . . . and nut at front, and remove support bracket

3.15 Prise off the retaining circlip and lever off the transmission support cable - renew bush in cable end fitting (arrowed)

**3.27 Selector finger securing bolt (1) fits into forward recess in inner finger (2) when assembled - rod-type gear linkage**

*e) When refitting the transmission support cable, renew the cable bush at the transmission end.*

*f) Refer to Chapter 6 when refitting the clutch cable.*

*g) On completion, refer to Section 2 and check the gearchange linkage adjustment.*

## 4 Manual transmission overhaul - general information

The overhaul of a manual transmission is a complex (and often expensive) engineering task for the DIY home mechanic to undertake, which requires access to specialist equipment. It involves dismantling and reassembly of many small components, measuring clearances precisely and if necessary, adjusting them by the selection shims and spacers. Internal transmission components are also often difficult to obtain and in many instances, extremely expensive. Because of this, if the transmission develops a fault or becomes noisy, the best course of action is to have the unit overhauled by a specialist repairer or to obtain an exchange reconditioned unit.

Nevertheless, it is not impossible for the more experienced mechanic to overhaul the transmission if the special tools are available and the job is carried out in a deliberate step-by-step manner, to ensure that nothing is overlooked.

The tools necessary for an overhaul include internal and external circlip pliers, bearing pullers, a slide hammer, a set of pin punches, a dial test indicator, and possibly a hydraulic press. In addition, a large, sturdy workbench and a vice will be required.

During dismantling of the transmission, make careful notes of how each component is fitted to make reassembly easier and accurate.

Before dismantling the transmission, it will help if you have some idea of where the problem lies. Certain problems can be closely related to specific areas in the transmission which can make component examination and renewal easier. Refer to the Fault Diagnosis Section in the Reference section of this manual for more information.

## 5 Reversing light switch - testing, removal and refitting

### Testing

**1** Ensure that the ignition switch is turned to the OFF position.

**2** Unplug the wiring harness from the reversing light switch at the connector **(see illustration)**. The switch is located on the front of the transmission casing, with the harness clipped into a retaining bracket above.

**3** Connect the probes of a continuity tester, or multimeter set to the resistance measurement function, across the terminals of the reversing light switch.

**4** The switch contacts are normally open, so with any gear other than reverse selected, the tester/meter should indicate an open circuit. When reverse gear is then selected, the switch contacts should close, causing the tester/meter to indicate a short circuit.

**5** If the switch appears to be constantly open or short circuit, or is intermittent in its operation, it should be renewed.

### Removal

**6** Ensure that the ignition switch is turned to the OFF position.

**7** Unplug the wiring harness from the reversing light switch at the connector.

**8** Slacken the switch body using a ring spanner and withdraw it from the transmission casing. Recover the sealing ring, where fitted.

### Refitting

**9** Refit the switch by reversing the removal procedure.

## 6 Road speed sensor/speedometer drive - removal and refitting

### General information

**1** All transmissions are fitted with an electronic road speed sensor. This device measures the rotational speed of the transmission final drive, and converts the information into an electronic signal, which is then sent to the speedometer module in the instrument panel. On most models, the signal is also used as an input by the engine management system ECU.

### Removal

**2** Ensure that the ignition switch is turned to the OFF position.

**3** Locate the speed sensor, at the top of the transmission casing. Unplug the wiring harness from the sensor, at the connector **(see illustration)**.

**4** Unscrew the transducer using a suitable spanner, and withdraw the unit from the transmission casing.

**5** Recover the sealing ring, where fitted.

### Refitting

**6** Refit the sensor by following the removal procedure in reverse.

**5.2 Disconnecting the reversing light switch**

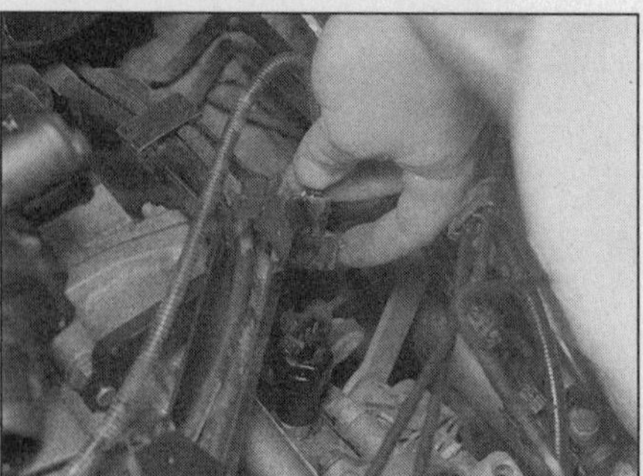

**6.3 Disconnecting the road speed sensor connector on top of the transmission**

# Chapter 7 Part B: Automatic transmission

## Contents



## Degrees of difficulty

| | | | | |
|---|---|---|---|---|
| **Easy,** suitable for novice with little experience  | **Fairly easy,** suitable for beginner with some experience  | **Fairly difficult,** suitable for competent DIY mechanic | **Difficult,** suitable for experienced DIY mechanic  | **Very difficult,** suitable for expert DIY or professional |

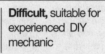

## Specifications

### General

| | |
|---|---|
| Transmission type number | 001 |
| Application | 1.4 and 1.6 litre petrol engine models |
| Description | Electro-hydraulically controlled planetary gearbox providing four forward speeds and one reverse speed. Drive transmitted through hydrokinetic torque converter. Lock-up clutch on top two speeds, electronic control unit (ECU). Two driving modes, selected automatically by ECU |
| Automatic transmission fluid type | See *Lubricants, fluids and tyre pressures* |
| Automatic transmission fluid capacity | See Chapter 1A Specifications |

### Ratios (typical)

| | |
|---|---|
| 1st | 2.875:1 |
| 2nd | 1.512:1 |
| 3rd | 1.000:1 |
| 4th | 0.726:1 |
| Reverse | 2.656:1 |

### Torque wrench settings

| Torque wrench settings | Nm | lbf ft |
|---|---|---|
| Driveshaft-to-swivel hub bolt | 110 | 81 |
| Fluid pan bolts | 8 | 6 |
| Fluid temperature sender unit | 8 | 6 |
| Road speed sensor mounting bolt | 6 | 4 |
| Selector cable-to-selector lever locking bolt | 23 | 17 |
| Selector shaft lever nut | 13 | 10 |
| Series resistance mounting bolt | 6 | 4 |
| Torque converter shield plate nuts | 15 | 11 |
| Torque converter-to-driveplate bolts | 60 | 44 |
| Transmission bellhousing-to-engine bolts: | | |
| M10 bolts | 60 | 44 |
| M12 bolts | 80 | 59 |
| Transmission speed sensor mounting bolt | 6 | 4 |

7B

## 1 General information

The VW type 001 automatic transmission has four forward speeds (and one reverse). The automatic gear changes are electronically controlled, rather than hydraulically as with previous conventional types. The advantage of electronic management is to provide a faster gearchange response. A kickdown facility is also provided, to enable a faster acceleration response when required.

The transmission consists of three main assemblies; the torque converter, which is directly coupled to the engine; the final drive unit, which incorporates the differential unit; and the planetary gearbox, with its multi-disc clutches and brake bands. The transmission is lubricated with automatic transmission fluid (ATF), and is regarded by the manufacturers as being filled for life, with no requirement for the fluid to be changed at regular intervals. No provision is made for DIY checking of the fluid level, either - this must be carried out by a VW dealer, using special equipment capable of monitoring the fluid temperature.

The torque converter incorporates an automatic lock-up feature, which eliminates any possibility of converter slip in the top two gears; this aids performance and economy. In addition to the normal alternative of manual change, two further modes are available - sport or economy mode. In sport mode, upshifts are delayed longer, to make full use of engine power, while in economy mode, upshifts are taken as soon as possible, to permit optimum economy. The decision as to which operating mode to use is determined by the ECU, based on throttle position and its rate of change (this information is derived from the throttle potentiometer signal). In this way, gearchanges can be economy-orientated, but full acceleration is always available on demand.

Another feature of this transmission is the selector lever lock, with which the selector lever can be set in the P or N position when the engine is running, below about 3 mph. Under these conditions, selection from P or N can only be made by depressing the brake pedal. Correct functioning of the brake stop-light switch is therefore vital for this system to work correctly - see Chapter 9.

The transmission kickdown switch, which acts to select a lower gear (where possible) on full-throttle acceleration, is incorporated into the accelerator cable. The switch itself is mounted on the bulkhead in the engine compartment. No adjustment of the switch is possible, beyond ensuring that the basic accelerator cable adjustment is correct - see Chapter 4A or B, as applicable.

A starter inhibitor relay is fitted, to prevent starter motor operation unless the transmission is in P or N. The relay is located above the main fuse/relay panel (see Chapter 12), and is typically marked with the number 53.

Some models also feature a security/safety device which locks the transmission in P when the ignition key is removed (see Section 5).

The transmission is fitted with an electronic road speed sensor **(refer to illustration 2.9)**. This device measures the rotational speed of the transmission final drive, and converts the information into an electronic signal, which is then sent to the speedometer module in the instrument panel. The signal is also used as an input by the engine management system ECU.

A fault diagnosis system is integrated into the control unit, but analysis can only be undertaken with specialised equipment. If a malfunction should occur in the transmission electrical system, automatic gear selection will continue, but the changes will be noticeably jerky. There is also an emergency running mode, in which 4th gear will not be selected. In the event of automatic selection failure, the selection of gears can be made manually. In any event, it is important that any transmission fault be identified and rectified at the earliest possible opportunity. Delay in doing so will only cause further problems. A VW dealer can 'interrogate' the ECU fault memory for stored fault codes, enabling him to pinpoint the fault quickly. Once the fault has been corrected and any fault codes have been cleared, normal transmission operation should be restored.

Because of the need for special test equipment, the complexity of some of the parts, and the need for scrupulous cleanliness when servicing automatic transmissions, the amount which the owner can do is limited. Repairs to the final drive differential are also not recommended. Most major repairs and overhaul operations should be left to a VW dealer, who will be equipped with the necessary equipment for fault diagnosis and repair. The information in this Chapter is therefore limited to a description of the removal and refitting of the transmission as a complete unit. The removal, refitting and adjustment of the selector cable is also described.

In the event of a transmission problem occurring, consult a VW dealer or transmission specialist before removing the transmission from the vehicle, since the majority of fault diagnosis is carried out with the transmission in situ.

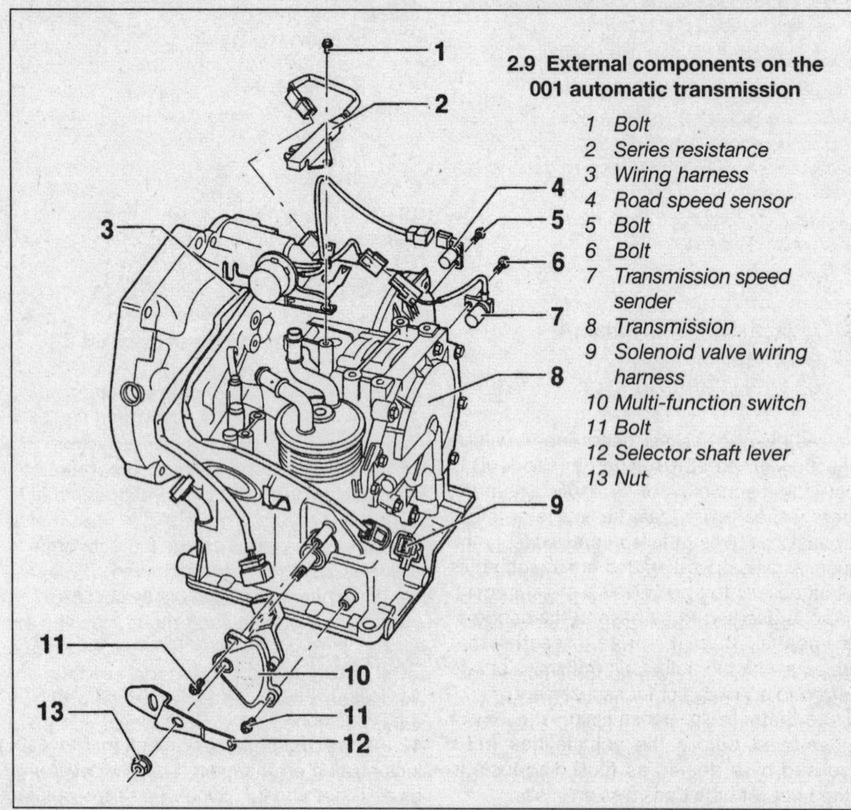


**2.9 External components on the 001 automatic transmission**

*1 Bolt*
*2 Series resistance*
*3 Wiring harness*
*4 Road speed sensor*
*5 Bolt*
*6 Bolt*
*7 Transmission speed sender*
*8 Transmission*
*9 Solenoid valve wiring harness*
*10 Multi-function switch*
*11 Bolt*
*12 Selector shaft lever*
*13 Nut*

## 2 Automatic transmission - removal and refitting

### *Removal*

**1** Select a solid, level surface to park the vehicle upon. Give yourself enough space to move around it easily. Apply the handbrake and chock the rear wheels.

**2** Loosen the front wheel bolts, and the left-hand driveshaft hub nut/bolt, then raise the front of the vehicle and rest it securely on axle stands (see *Jacking and vehicle support*). Remove the front wheels. Allow a suitable working clearance underneath for the eventual withdrawal of the transmission.

**3** Refer to Chapter 11 and remove the bonnet from its hinges.

**4** The lock carrier is a panel assembly comprising the front valance and bonnet lock mechanism, radiator and grille, cooling fan, and headlight units. Its removal gives greatly-improved access to the engine and transmission, and allows them to be lifted out of the vehicle via the front of the engine bay. Its removal is described at the beginning of the engine removal procedure - refer to Chapter 2C for details.

**5** Disconnect the battery negative lead and position It away from the terminal. **Note:** *If the vehicle has a security-coded radio, check that you have a copy of the code number before disconnecting the battery.*

**6** Remove the battery as described in Chapter 5A, then remove the battery tray and the cable guide rail beneath.

**7** Trace the wiring harness back from the radiator cooling fan motor, and remove the radiator fan control unit.

**8** Referring to Chapter 4A or B as applicable, remove the air cleaner housing and air inlet trunking.

**9** Disconnect all the wiring connections from the transmission, labelling them if required for refitting **(see illustration)**.

**10** Using hose clamps, clamp off the fluid hoses at the fluid cooler, and disconnect the hoses.

**11** Referring to Chapter 4D, remove the exhaust front downpipe and catalytic converter.

**12** Referring to Chapter 8, disconnect both driveshafts from the flanges on the transmission - tie the right-hand shaft up out of the way. Remove the left-hand driveshaft completely.

**13** Refer to Chapter 5A and remove the starter motor.

**14** Remove three nuts and take off the torque converter shield plate from the underside of the transmission bellhousing.

**15** Where fitted, remove the transmission sump guard from under the transmission.

**16** Position the selector lever in the P position, then detach the selector cable from the lever on the transmission by unscrewing the shouldered retaining bolt; recover the serrated washer. Detach the cable retaining clip, and move the cable out of the way. The serrated washer should be discarded, and a new one fitted on reassembly.

**17** Where applicable, detach the power steering pump fluid pipes from the radiator - there is no need to disconnect the fluid unions.

**18** Remove the radiator cooling fan as described in Chapter 3.

**19** The weight of the engine must now be supported while the engine/transmission mountings are removed. To do this, attach a lift sling to the engine, and raise it with an engine crane just enough to support the weight of the engine, or support the engine securely from below, taking care not to damage the sump. Alternatively, use an engine support bracket similar to the type which VW mechanics use **(see illustration)**.

**20** In order to create sufficient room for the transmission to be separated and removed, the auxiliary drivebelt and its crankshaft pulley must be removed as described in Chapter 2A.

**21** Position a trolley jack underneath the transmission, and raise it to just take the weight of the unit.

**22** Referring to Chapter 2A, disconnect the engine/transmission rear mounting, and remove the transmission left-hand mounting completely.

**23** Unscrew and remove the upper bolts securing the transmission bellhousing to the engine, noting the locations of the bolts, as they are of different sizes and lengths.

**24** Lower the engine support bar, hoist or jack (as applicable) as far as possible, ensuring that the weight of the engine is still supported.

**25** Unscrew and remove the lower bolts securing the transmission bellhousing to the engine, again noting the bolt locations, as they are of different sizes and lengths.

**26** Check that all fixings and attachments are clear of the transmission. Enlist the aid of an assistant to help in guiding and supporting the transmission during its removal.

**27** The transmission is located on engine alignment dowels, and if stuck on them, it may be necessary to carefully tap and prise the transmission free of the dowels to allow separation. Once the transmission is disconnected from the location dowels, swivel the unit out and lower it out of the car.

***Warning: Support the transmission to ensure that it remains steady on the jack head. Ensure that the torque converter remains in position on its shaft in the torque converter housing.***

**28** With the transmission removed, bolt a suitable bar and spacer across the front face of the torque converter housing, to retain the torque converter in position.

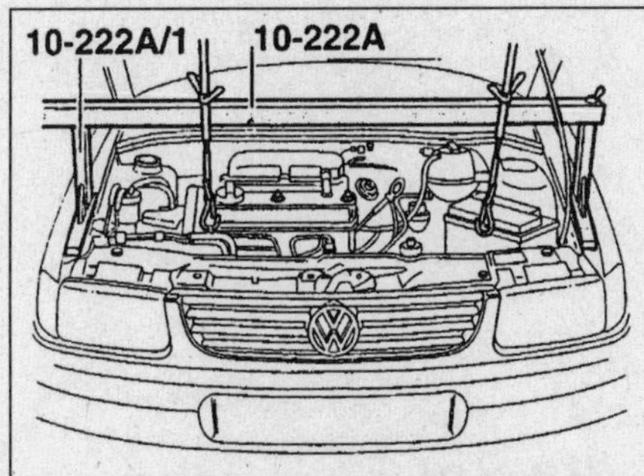


**2.19 Engine/transmission support bar used by VW mechanics**

### Refitting

**29** Refitting is a reversal of the removal procedure, but note the following special points:

*a) When reconnecting the transmission to the engine, ensure that the location dowels are in position, and that the transmission is correctly aligned with them before pushing it fully into engagement with the engine. As the torque converter is refitted, ensure that the drive pins at the centre of the torque converter hub engage with the recesses in the automatic transmission fluid pump inner wheel.*

*b) Tighten all retaining bolts to their specified torque wrench settings.*

*c) Reconnect and adjust the selector cable, as described in Section 4.*

*d) On completion, have the transmission fluid level checked by a VW dealer. If a new transmission unit has been fitted, it may be necessary to have the transmission ECU matched to the engine management ECU electronically, to ensure correct operation - seek the advice of your VW dealer.*

## 3 Automatic transmission overhaul - general information

In the event of a fault occurring, it will be necessary to establish whether the fault is electrical, mechanical or hydraulic in nature, before repair work can be contemplated. Diagnosis requires detailed knowledge of the transmission's operation and construction, as well as access to specialised test equipment, and so is deemed to be beyond the scope of this manual. It is therefore essential that problems with the automatic transmission are referred to a VW dealer for assessment.

Note that a faulty transmission should not be removed before the vehicle has been assessed by a dealer, as fault diagnosis is carried out with the transmission in situ.

## 4 Selector cable - removal, refitting and adjustment

### Removal

**1** Disconnect the battery negative lead and position It away from the terminal. **Note:** *If the vehicle has a security-coded radio, check that you have a copy of the code number before disconnecting the battery.*

**2** Raise and support the vehicle at the front end on axle stands (see *Jacking and vehicle support*). Allow a suitable working clearance underneath the vehicle.

**3** Move the selector lever to the P position.

**4** Undo the screw under the detent button on the lever handle, and lift the handle from the lever **(see illustration overleaf)**.

**5** Detach and lift the selector cover up from the centre console.

**6** Prise free the circlip and detach the cable from the shift mechanism.

**7** Referring to Chapter 4D, remove the exhaust system front downpipe and catalytic converter. Where applicable, detach and remove the sections of exhaust heat shield necessary to gain access to the selector cable.

**8** Withdraw the cable from the selector lever housing, and remove the protective sleeve. If the sleeve is no longer a tight fit in its selector housing aperture, or is in any way damaged, discard it and fit a new one on reassembly. Working along its length, release the cable from the securing clips. Note the cable routing carefully for refitting.

**9** At the transmission end of the cable, undo the locking bolt and detach the cable from the transmission selector shaft. Recover the serrated washer, and discard it - a new one must be used on refitting.

### Refitting

**10** Refit the selector cable by reversing the removal procedure, noting the following points:

*a) Use a new serrated washer when reconnecting the cable to the selector lever, but do not tighten the locking bolt until the cable has been adjusted, as described below.*

*b) Ensure that the cable is correctly routed, as noted on removal, and that it is securely held by its retaining clips.*

*c) Fit the protective sleeve to the selector housing before passing through the selector cable.*

*d) When fitting the cable to the selector lever, use a new circlip.*

*e) Adjust the selector cable as described below.*

### Adjustment

**11** Inside the car, move the selector lever to the P position.

**12** At the transmission, slacken the cable locking bolt on the side of the selector shaft lever (if not already done). Push the selector

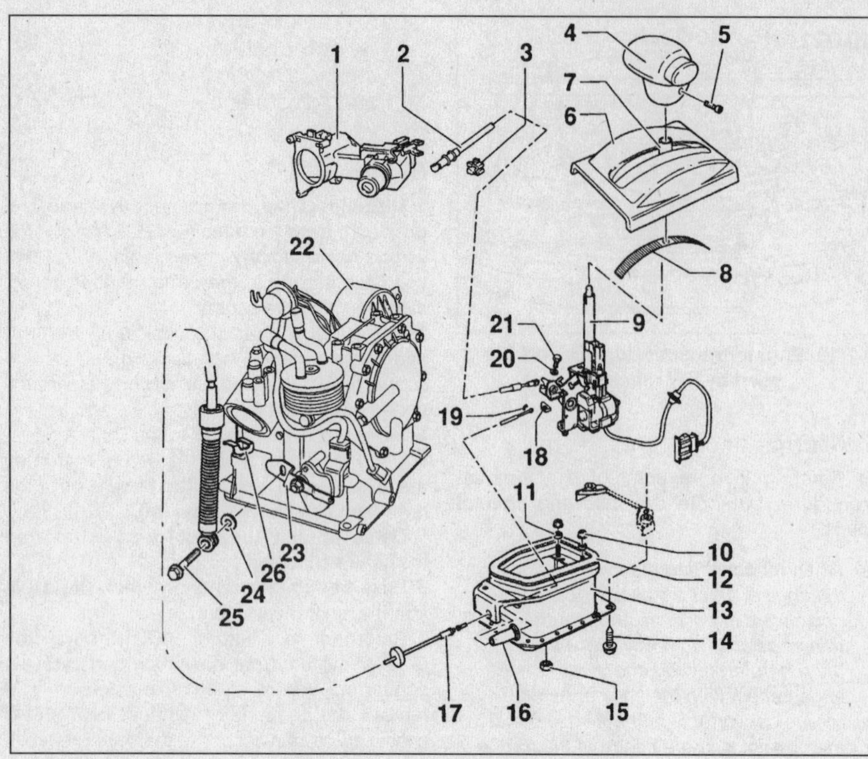


**4.4 Selector lever and cable details**

1 Ignition switch
2 Park locking cable
3 Clip
4 Selector lever handle
5 Screw
6 Selector cover
7 Selector lever sleeve
8 Cover strip
9 Selector lever
10 Nut
11 Distance piece
12 Gasket
13 Selector lever housing
14 Screw
15 Nut
16 Protective sleeve
17 Selector cable
18 Seal
19 Circlip
20 Washer
21 Bolt
22 Transmission
23 Selector shaft lever
24 Washer
25 Locking bolt
26 Serrated washer

shaft up against its end stop, corresponding to the P position, then tighten the locking bolt to the specified torque. If a new cable has not been fitted, check the condition of the serrated washer on the locking bolt, and renew it if it appears to be in less-than-perfect condition.

**13** Verify the operation of the selector lever by shifting through all gear positions and checking that every gear can be selected smoothly and without delay.

## 5 Ignition key Park lock system - description, cable renewal and adjustment

### *Description*

**1** This system is a security/safety device, intended to prevent the vehicle from being left with the transmission in any position other than P. The ignition key cannot be removed from the lock unless P is selected, and once the key has been removed, no other position than P can be selected.

**2** This function is provided by means of a cable fitted to the selector linkage at the selector lever, and to the ignition switch assembly **(refer to illustration 4.4)**.

### *Lock cable*

#### Removal

**3** With reference to Section 4, remove the selector lever handle and cover.

**4** Referring to Chapter 11, remove the centre console for access to the cable run.

**5** At the selector lever, loosen the clamp screw and disconnect the cable outer **(see illustration)**. Unhook the cable eye from the peg on the operating lever.

**6** Referring to Chapter 10, remove the steering wheel and the upper and lower steering column shrouds for access to the ignition switch.

**7** Press the lock cable clip out of its mounting bracket, and prise the cable end fitting off its ballstud **(see illustration)**.

**5.7 Removing the lock cable**

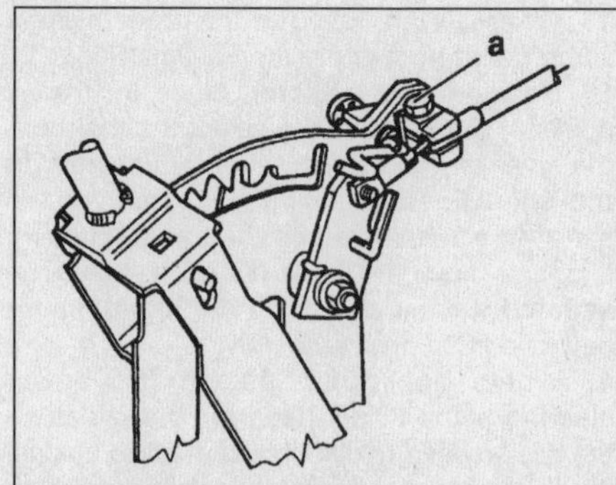


**5.5 Park lock cable clamp screw (a) at selector lever**

**8** The lock cable is now free to be removed from the car. Take careful note of the cable routing, and remove any further trim as necessary to facilitate removal of the cable.

#### Refitting

**9** Refitting is a reversal of removal. Check the cable adjustment as described below.

#### Adjustment

**10** If not already done, refer to paragraphs 3 and 4 to gain access to the cable at the selector lever. Loosen the cable clamp screw at the selector lever.

**11** Apply the handbrake firmly. Place the selector lever in position 1.

**12** Turn the ignition key to the start position, and release it.

**13** Adjust the clearance between the operating lever and the locking pin by moving the cable outer in its clamp, as shown **(see illustration)**.

**14** When the clearance is correct, move the selector lever to P and turn the ignition key to the off position. It should be possible to remove the ignition key - if not, repeat the adjustment procedure, and check the cable for stiffness or kinking. When the system is working correctly, it should only be possible to remove the key with the selector in P, and once the key is removed, it should not be possible to move the lever out of P.

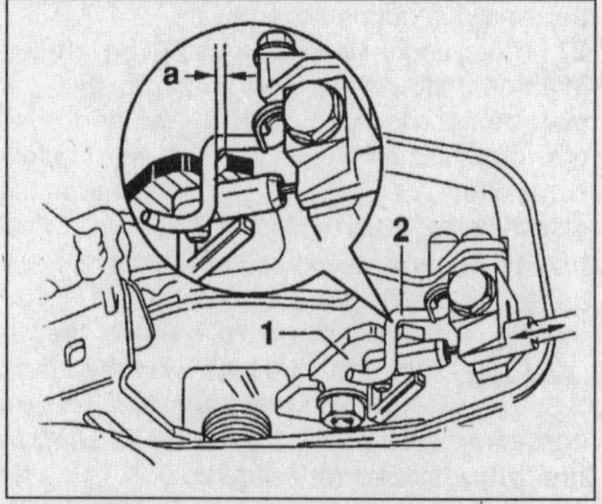


**5.13 Park lock cable adjustment**

1 Operating lever
2 Locking pin
a = 0.7 mm

# Chapter 8
# Driveshafts

## Contents



## Degrees of difficulty

**Easy,** suitable for novice with little experience 

**Fairly easy,** suitable for beginner with some experience 

**Fairly difficult,** suitable for competent DIY mechanic 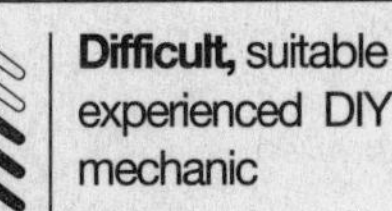

**Difficult,** suitable for experienced DIY mechanic 

**Very difficult,** suitable for expert DIY or professional

## Specifications

**Type** . . . . . . . . . . . . . . . . . . . . . . . . . . . . . . . . . . . . . . . . . . . . . Steel shafts with ball-and-cage type constant velocity joint at each end (certain models have a tripod type inner joint)

| **Torque wrench settings** | **Nm** | **lbf ft** |
|---|---|---|
| Driveshaft retaining bolt (automatic transmission models) | 110 | 81 |
| Driveshaft retaining nut (12-point type): | | |
| Stage 1 | 200 | 148 |
| Slacken the nut by one turn, then: | | |
| Stage 2 | 50 | 37 |
| Stage 3 | Angle-tighten a further 30° | |
| Inner CV joint-to-drive flange bolts: | | |
| Driveshaft with tripod type inner joint (M8 bolt) | 40 | 30 |
| All other driveshafts | 45 | 33 |
| Lower arm balljoint retaining bolts | 35 | 26 |
| Roadwheel bolts | 110 | 81 |

## 1 General information

Drive is transmitted from the differential to the front wheels by means of two driveshafts of unequal length. The right-hand driveshaft is longer than the left-hand, due to the position of the transmission. Depending on engine size and transmission type, there are several different types of driveshaft which may be fitted:

1) *Solid-steel left-hand shaft, tubular right-hand shaft, with ball-and-cage CV joints **(see illustration)**.*
2) *Solid-steel shafts, ball-and-cage outer CV joint, triple-roller (tripod-type) inner CV joint, driveshafts secured to wheel hub with nut **(see illustration)**.*
3) *Solid-steel shafts, ball-and-cage outer CV joint, triple-roller (tripod-type) inner CV joint, driveshafts secured to wheel hub with bolt (automatic transmission models).*

Both driveshafts are splined at their outer ends to accept the wheel hubs, and are threaded so that each hub can be fastened by a large nut or bolt. The inner end of each driveshaft is bolted to the transmission drive flanges.

Constant velocity (CV) joints are fitted to each end of the driveshafts, to ensure the smooth and efficient transmission of drive at all the angles possible as the roadwheels move up and down with the suspension, and as they turn from side to side under steering. As mentioned above, the constant velocity joints are either of the ball-and-cage type or tripod type.

## 2 Driveshaft - removal and refitting

### Removal

**1** Remove the wheel trim/hub cap (as applicable) and slacken the driveshaft retaining nut/bolt with the vehicle resting on its wheels **(see illustration)**. Also slacken the wheel bolts

**2** Chock the rear wheels of the car, firmly apply the handbrake, then jack up the front of the car and support it on axle stands. Remove the relevant front roadwheel.

**3** Remove the CV joint protector plate from the suspension lower arm.

**4** If the right-hand driveshaft is being

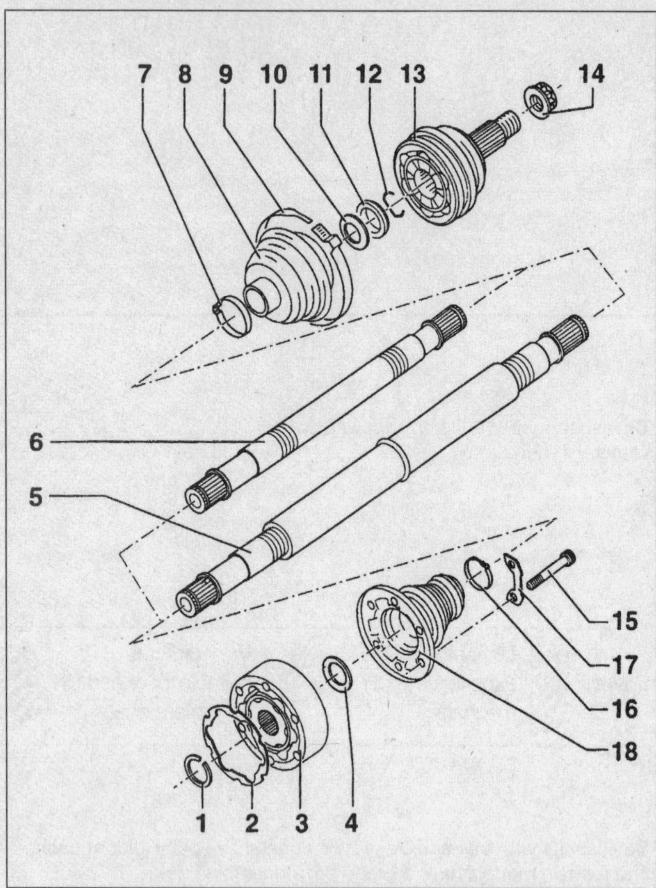


**1.1a Exploded view of driveshaft components - models with ball-and-cage inner CV joint**

1 *Circlip*
2 *Gasket*
3 *Inner CV joint*
4 *Dished washer*
5 *Right-hand driveshaft (tubular)*
6 *Left-hand driveshaft (solid)*
7 *Gaiter securing clip*
8 *Outer CV joint gaiter*
9 *Gaiter securing clip*
10 *Dished washer*
11 *Thrustwasher*
12 *Circlip*
13 *Outer CV joint*
14 *Driveshaft nut*
15 *Driveshaft flange bolt*
16 *Gaiter securing clip*
17 *Plate*
18 *Inner CV joint gaiter*

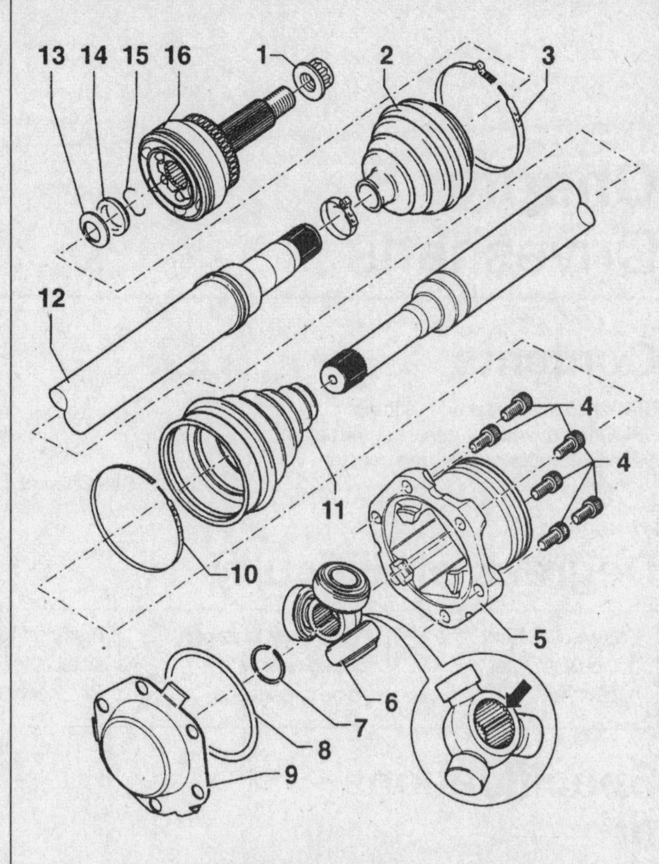


**1.1b Exploded view of driveshaft components - models with tripod-type inner CV joint**

1 *Driveshaft nut (bolt on automatic transmission models)*
2 *Outer CV joint gaiter*
3 *Gaiter securing clip*
4 *Driveshaft flange bolt*
5 *Inner CV joint housing*
6 *Inner CV joint rollers - chamfered end (arrowed) fits onto driveshaft*
7 *Circlip*
8 *Seal*
9 *Inner CV joint cover*
10 *Gaiter securing clip*
11 *Inner CV joint gaiter*
12 *Driveshaft*
13 *Dished washer*
14 *Thrustwasher*
15 *Circlip*
16 *Outer CV joint*

2.1 Remove the trim/hub cap and slacken the driveshaft retaining nut

removed, unbolt and remove the retaining clip for the lambda sensor wiring harness, where applicable. Ensure that the harness is kept clear as the driveshaft is removed/refitted.

**5** Using a suitable marker pen, draw around the end of the suspension lower arm, marking the correct fitted position of the balljoint. Unscrew the balljoint retaining bolts and remove the retaining plate from the top of the lower arm.

**6** Unscrew and remove the driveshaft retaining nut/bolt and (where fitted) remove its washer.

**7** Slacken and remove the splined bolts securing the inner driveshaft joint to the transmission flange and, where necessary, recover the retaining plates from underneath the bolts **(see illustrations)**. Support the driveshaft by suspending it with wire or string - do not allow it to hang under its weight, or the joint may be damaged.

**8** Carefully pull the swivel hub assembly outwards, and withdraw the driveshaft outer constant velocity joint from the hub assembly. The shaft will probably be a very tight fit in the hub; tap the joint out of the hub using a soft-faced mallet. If this fails to free it from the hub, the joint will have to be pressed out using a suitable tool which is bolted to the hub.

**9** Manoeuvre the driveshaft out from underneath the vehicle and (where fitted) recover the gasket from the end of the inner constant velocity joint. Discard the gasket - a new one should be used on refitting.

**10** ***Do not allow the vehicle to rest on its wheels with one or both driveshaft(s) removed, as damage to the wheel bearing(s) may result.*** If moving the vehicle is unavoidable, temporarily insert the outer end of the driveshaft(s) in the hub(s), and tighten the driveshaft retaining nut/bolt(s) to 50 Nm/37 lbf ft; in this case, the inner end(s) of the driveshaft(s) must be supported, for example by suspending with string from the vehicle underbody. ***Do not allow the driveshaft to hang down under its weight, or the joint may be damaged.***

## Refitting

**11** Ensure that the transmission flange and inner joint mating surfaces are clean and dry. Where necessary, fit a new gasket to the joint by peeling off its backing foil and sticking it in position.

**12** Ensure that the outer joint and hub splines are clean and dry.

**13** Manoeuvre the driveshaft into position, and engage the outer joint with the hub. Ensure that the threads are clean, and apply a smear of oil to the contact face of the driveshaft retaining nut/bolt. Although VW do not specifically require that a new nut or bolt be used, it is advisable to consider fitting one, particularly in view of the high torque applied. Fit the washer (where fitted) and the nut/bolt, and draw the joint fully into position. Do not try to fully tighten the driveshaft nut/bolt until the vehicle is resting on its wheels.

**14** Refit the suspension lower arm balljoint retaining bolts, and tighten them to the specified torque setting, using the marks made on removal to ensure that the balljoint is correctly positioned.

**15** Align the driveshaft inner joint with the transmission flange, and refit the retaining plates (where applicable) and the bolts. Tighten the retaining bolts to the specified torque.

**16** Refit the CV joint protector plate to the lower arm. Where removed, refit the lambda sensor wiring harness retaining clip, ensuring that the harness is securely clipped back into place.

**17** Ensure that the outer joint is drawn fully into position, then refit the roadwheel and lower the vehicle to the ground.

**18** Tighten the driveshaft nut/bolt to the specified torque setting **(see Haynes Hint)**.

***Where a 12-point nut is fitted, the angle between each driveshaft retaining nut flat point is 30°. If an angle-tightening gauge is not available, the angle can be accurately measured by making marks on the hub and the nearest nut flat point and tightening the nut so its mark moves by the correct number of points***

**19** Once the driveshaft nut/bolt is correctly tightened, tighten the wheel bolts to the specified torque and refit the wheel trim/hub cap.

## 3 Driveshaft rubber gaiters - renewal

### Outer CV joint gaiter

**1** Remove the driveshaft as described in Section 2.

**2** Secure the driveshaft in a vice equipped with soft jaws, and release the two outer joint gaiter retaining clips. If necessary, the retaining clips can be cut to release them.

**3** Slide the rubber gaiter down the shaft to expose the constant velocity joint, and scoop out excess grease.

**4** Using a soft-faced mallet, tap the joint off the end of the driveshaft.

**5** Remove the circlip from the driveshaft groove, and slide off the thrustwasher and dished washer, noting which way around it is fitted.

**6** Slide the rubber gaiter off the driveshaft and discard it.

2.7a Inner CV joint splined bolts and retaining plates

2.7b Using a suitable key or socket, slacken the splined bolts . . .

2.7c . . . and recover the retaining plates

**7** Thoroughly clean the constant velocity joint(s) using paraffin, or a suitable solvent, and dry thoroughly. Carry out a visual inspection as follows.

**8** Move the inner splined driving member from side to side to expose each ball in turn at the top of its track. Examine the balls for cracks, flat spots or signs of surface pitting.

**9** Inspect the ball tracks on the inner and outer members. If the tracks have widened, the balls will no longer be a tight fit. At the same time, check the ball cage windows for wear or cracking between the windows. If, when carrying out the road test as described in Chapter 1, any noise from the driveshaft joints was apparent, inspect the joints carefully to determine the cause. Re-packing the joint with grease and fitting a new gaiter is unlikely to effect a reduction in noise.

**10** If on inspection any of the constant velocity joint components are found to be worn or damaged, it will be necessary to renew the complete joint assembly. If the joint is in satisfactory condition, obtain a new gaiter and retaining clips, a constant velocity joint circlip and the correct type of grease. Grease is often supplied with the joint repair kit - if not, use a good-quality molybdenum disulphide grease.

**11** Tape over the splines on the end of the driveshaft, to protect the new gaiter as it is slid into place.

**12** Slide the new gaiter onto the end of the driveshaft, then remove the protective tape from the driveshaft splines.

**13** Slide on the dished washer, making sure its convex side is innermost, followed by the thrustwasher.

**14** Fit a new circlip to the driveshaft, then tap the joint onto the driveshaft until the circlip engages in its groove. Make sure that the joint is securely retained by the circlip.

**15** Pack the joint with the specified type of grease. Work the grease well into the bearing tracks whilst twisting the joint, and fill the rubber gaiter with any excess.

**16** Ease the gaiter over the joint, and ensure that the gaiter lips are correctly located on both the driveshaft and constant velocity joint. Lift the outer sealing lip of the gaiter, to equalise air pressure within the gaiter.

**17** Fit the large metal retaining clip to the gaiter. Pull the clip as tight as possible, and locate the hooks on the clip in their slots. Remove any slack in the gaiter retaining clip by carefully compressing the raised section of the clip. In the absence of the special tool, a pair of side cutters may be used, taking care not to cut the clip. Secure the small retaining clip using the same procedure. Some CV gaiter kits now include plastic cable-ties to secure the gaiters - while not as effective as the metal clips, they are adequate for the task. Ensure the ties are pulled as tight as possible, and that the excess is trimmed off.

**18** Check the constant velocity joint moves freely in all directions, then refit the driveshaft to the vehicle, as described in Section 2.

### Inner CV joint gaiter

**19** A hydraulic press and several special tools are required to remove and refit the inner CV joint. Therefore it is recommended that gaiter renewal is entrusted to a VW dealer.

## 4 Driveshaft overhaul - general information

**1** If any of the checks described in Chapter 1 reveal wear in any driveshaft joint, first remove the roadwheel trim or centre cap (as appropriate) and check that the driveshaft retaining nut/bolt is tight.

**2** If the nut/bolt is tight, refit the centre cap or trim. Repeat this check on the remaining driveshaft nut/bolt.

**3** Road test the vehicle, and listen for a metallic clicking from the front as the vehicle is driven slowly in a circle on full lock. This test should be performed in both directions. If a clicking noise is heard, this indicates wear in the outer constant velocity joint. This means that the joint must be renewed; reconditioning is not possible.

**4** If vibration, consistent with road speed, is felt through the car when accelerating, there is a possibility of wear in the inner constant velocity joints.

**5** To check the joints for wear, the driveshaft must be dismantled. The outer constant velocity joint can be removed and checked, but work on the inner joint should be entrusted to a VW dealer (see Section 3); if any wear or free play is found, the affected joint must be renewed.

# Chapter 9
# Braking system

## Contents



## Degrees of difficulty

**Easy,** suitable for novice with little experience 

**Fairly easy,** suitable for beginner with some experience 

**Fairly difficult,** suitable for competent DIY mechanic 

**Difficult,** suitable for experienced DIY mechanic

**Very difficult,** suitable for expert DIY or professional

## Specifications

**System type** . . . . . . . . . . . . . . . . . . . . . . . . . . . . . . . . . . . . . Front disc brakes, rear drums. Dual-circuit, diagonally-split hydraulic system with vacuum servo assistance. Engine-driven vacuum pump on diesel engine models. Mechanical pressure regulator for rear brakes fitted to rear axle. Cable-operated handbrake to rear wheels. Anti-lock Braking System (ABS) optionally available on some models

### Front brakes

| | |
|---|---|
| Disc diameter | 239 mm |
| Disc thickness (new): | |
| Solid disc | 10 mm |
| Ventilated disc | 18 mm |
| Disc thickness (minimum): | |
| Solid disc | 8 mm |
| Ventilated disc | 16 mm |
| Maximum disc runout | 0.1 mm |
| Brake pad thickness (all models): | |
| New | 12 mm |
| Minimum (including backing plate) | 7 mm |

### Rear drum brakes

| | |
|---|---|
| Drum diameter (new): | |
| Models without ABS | 180 mm |
| Models with ABS | 200 mm |
| Drum diameter (wear limit): | |
| Models without ABS | 181.5 mm |
| Models with ABS | 201.5 mm |
| Maximum drum out-of-round | 0.1 mm |
| Brake shoe friction material minimum thickness | 2.5 mm |

## Torque wrench settings

| | Nm | lbf ft |
|---|---|---|
| ABS wheel sensor retaining bolt | 10 | 7 |
| Brake disc splash plate bolts | 10 | 7 |
| Brake fluid hose union | 15 | 11 |
| Brake pedal shaft nut | 25 | 18 |
| Brake pressure regulating valve bolts | 20 | 15 |
| Front brake caliper mounting bolts | 25 | 18 |
| Front caliper air deflector plate bolts | 15 | 11 |
| Handbrake lever mounting nuts | 25 | 18 |
| Master cylinder mounting nuts: | | |
| Models without ABS | 20 | 15 |
| Models with ABS | 25 | 18 |
| Pedal bracket mounting bolts | 25 | 18 |
| Rear brake backplate bolts | 60 | 44 |
| Rear brake wheel cylinder bolts | 10 | 7 |
| Roadwheel bolts | 110 | 81 |
| Servo unit mounting nuts | 20 | 15 |

## 1 General information

The braking system is of the servo-assisted, dual-circuit hydraulic type. The arrangement of the hydraulic system is such that each circuit operates one front and one rear brake from a tandem master cylinder. Under normal circumstances, both circuits operate in unison. However, if there is hydraulic failure in one circuit, full braking force will still be available at two wheels.

All models are fitted with front disc brakes and rear drum brakes. ABS was offered as an option on several models (refer to Section 19 for further information on ABS operation).

The front disc brakes are actuated by single-piston sliding type calipers, which ensure that equal pressure is applied to each disc pad.

The rear drum brakes incorporate leading and trailing shoes, which are actuated by twin-piston wheel cylinders. A self-adjust mechanism is incorporated, to compensate for brake shoe wear.

A pressure-regulating set-up is incorporated in the braking system, this helps to prevent rear wheel lock-up during emergency braking. The system is controlled by a load-dependent valve which is linked to the rear axle.

The handbrake provides an independent mechanical means of rear brake application.

**Note:** *When servicing any part of the system, work carefully and methodically; also observe scrupulous cleanliness when overhauling any part of the hydraulic system. Always renew components (in axle sets, where applicable) if in doubt about their condition, and use only genuine VW replacement parts, or at least those of known good quality. Note the warnings given in Safety first! and at relevant points in this Chapter concerning the dangers of asbestos dust and hydraulic fluid.*

## 2 Hydraulic system - bleeding

***Warning: Hydraulic fluid is poisonous; wash off immediately and thoroughly in the case of skin contact, and seek immediate medical advice if any fluid is swallowed or gets into the eyes. Certain types of hydraulic fluid are flammable, and may ignite when allowed into contact with hot components; when servicing any hydraulic system, it is safest to assume that the fluid is flammable, and to take precautions against the risk of fire as though it is petrol that is being handled. Hydraulic fluid is also an effective paint stripper, and will attack plastics; if any is spilt, it should be washed off immediately, using copious quantities of fresh water. Finally, it is hygroscopic (it absorbs moisture from the air) - old fluid may be contaminated and unfit for further use. When topping-up or renewing the fluid, always use the recommended type, and ensure that it comes from a freshly-opened sealed container.***

### General

**1** The correct operation of any hydraulic system is only possible after removing all air from the components and circuit; this is achieved by bleeding the system.

**2** During the bleeding procedure, add only clean, unused hydraulic fluid of the recommended type; never re-use fluid that has already been bled from the system. Ensure that sufficient fluid is available before starting work.

**3** If there is any possibility of incorrect fluid being already in the system, the brake components and circuit must be flushed completely with uncontaminated, correct fluid, and new seals should be fitted to the various components.

**4** If hydraulic fluid has been lost from the system, or air has entered because of a leak, ensure that the fault is cured before continuing further.

**5** Park the vehicle on level ground, switch off the engine and select first or reverse gear.

**6** Check that all pipes and hoses are secure, unions tight and bleed screws closed. Clean any dirt from around the bleed screws.

**7** Unscrew the master cylinder reservoir cap, and top the master cylinder reservoir up to the MAX level line; refit the cap loosely, and remember to maintain the fluid level at least above the MIN level line throughout the procedure, or there is a risk of further air entering the system.

**8** There are a number of one-man, do-it-yourself brake bleeding kits currently available from motor accessory shops. It is recommended that one of these kits is used whenever possible, as they greatly simplify the bleeding operation, and reduce the risk of expelled air and fluid being drawn back into the system. If such a kit is not available, the basic (two-man) method must be used, which is described in detail below.

**9** If a kit is to be used, prepare the vehicle as described previously, and follow the kit manufacturer's instructions, as the procedure may vary slightly according to the type being used; generally, they are as outlined below in the relevant sub-section.

**10** Whichever method is used, the same sequence must be followed (paragraphs 11 and 12) to ensure the removal of all air from the system.

### Bleeding sequence

**11** If the system has been only partially disconnected, and suitable precautions were taken to minimise fluid loss, it should be necessary only to bleed that part of the system (ie the primary or secondary circuit).

**12** If the complete system is to be bled, then it should be done working in the following sequence:

*a) Right-hand rear brake.*
*b) Left-hand rear brake.*
*c) Right-hand front brake.*
*d) Left-hand front brake.*

***Warning: On models with ABS, under no circumstances should the bleed screws on the ABS hydraulic unit be opened.***

## Bleeding - basic (two-man) method

**13** Collect together a clean glass jar of reasonable size, a suitable length of plastic or rubber tubing which is a tight fit over the bleed screw, and a ring spanner to fit the screw. The help of an assistant will also be required.

**14** Remove the dust cap from the first screw in the sequence **(see illustration)**. Fit the spanner and tube to the screw, place the other end of the tube in the jar, and pour in sufficient fluid to cover the end of the tube.

**15** Ensure that the master cylinder reservoir fluid level is maintained at least above the MIN level line throughout the procedure.

**16** Have the assistant fully depress the brake pedal several times to build up pressure, then maintain it on the final downstroke.

**17** While pedal pressure is maintained, unscrew the bleed screw (approximately one turn) and allow the compressed fluid and air to flow into the jar. The assistant should maintain pedal pressure, following it down to the floor if necessary, and should not release it until instructed to do so. When the flow stops, tighten the bleed screw again, have the assistant release the pedal slowly, and recheck the reservoir fluid level.

**18** Repeat the steps given in paragraphs 16 and 17 until the fluid emerging from the bleed screw is free from air bubbles. If the master cylinder has been drained and refilled, and air is being bled from the first screw in the sequence, allow approximately five seconds between cycles for the master cylinder passages to refill.

**19** When no more air bubbles appear, tighten the bleed screw securely, remove the tube and spanner, and refit the dust cap. Do not overtighten the bleed screw.

**20** Repeat the procedure on the remaining screws in the sequence, until all air is removed from the system and the brake pedal feels firm again.

## Bleeding - using a one-way valve kit

**21** As their name implies, these kits consist of a length of tubing with a one-way valve fitted, to prevent expelled air and fluid being drawn back into the system; some kits include a translucent container, which can be positioned so that the air bubbles can be more easily seen flowing from the end of the tube.

**22** The kit is connected to the bleed screw, which is then opened **(see illustration)**. The user returns to the driver's seat, depresses the brake pedal with a smooth, steady stroke, and slowly releases it; this is repeated until the expelled fluid is clear of air bubbles.

**23** Note that these kits simplify work so much that it is easy to forget the master cylinder reservoir fluid level; ensure that this is maintained at least above the MIN level line at all times.

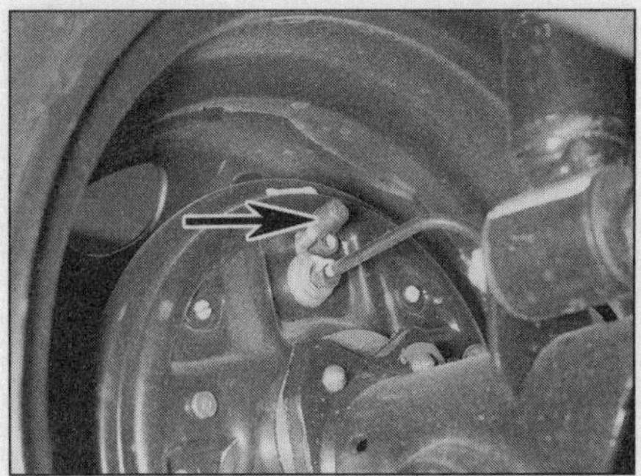

**2.14 Dust cap (arrowed) over bleed screw on rear brake wheel cylinder**

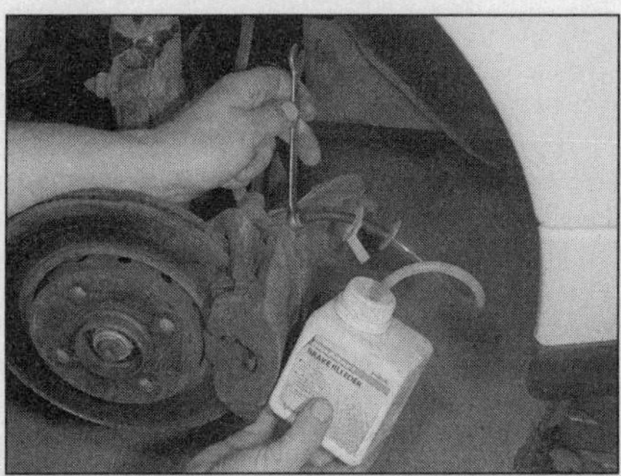

**2.22 Bleeding front brake caliper using a one-way valve brake bleeder kit**

## Bleeding - using a pressure-bleeding kit

**24** These kits are usually operated by the reservoir of pressurised air contained in the spare tyre. However, note that it will probably be necessary to reduce the pressure to a lower level than normal; refer to the instructions supplied with the kit.

**25** By connecting a pressurised, fluid-filled container to the master cylinder reservoir, bleeding can be carried out simply by opening each screw in turn (in the specified sequence), and allowing the fluid to flow out until no more air bubbles can be seen in the expelled fluid.

**26** This method has the advantage that the large reservoir of fluid provides an additional safeguard against air being drawn into the system during bleeding.

**27** Pressure-bleeding is particularly effective when bleeding 'difficult' systems, or when bleeding the complete system at the time of routine fluid renewal.

## All methods

**28** When bleeding is complete, and firm pedal feel is restored, wash off any spilt fluid, tighten the bleed screws securely, and refit their dust caps.

**29** Check the hydraulic fluid level in the master cylinder reservoir, and top-up if necessary (see *Weekly checks*).

**30** Discard any hydraulic fluid that has been bled from the system; it will not be fit for re-use.

**31** Check the feel of the brake pedal. If it feels at all spongy, air must still be present in the system, and further bleeding is required. Failure to bleed satisfactorily after a reasonable repetition of the bleeding procedure may be due to worn master cylinder seals.

## 3 Hydraulic pipes and hoses - renewal

**Note:** *Refer to the note in Section 2 concerning the dangers of hydraulic fluid.*

**1** If any pipe or hose is to be renewed, minimise fluid loss by first removing the master cylinder reservoir cap, then tightening it down onto a piece of polythene to obtain an airtight seal. Alternatively, flexible hoses can be sealed, if required, using a proprietary brake hose clamp; metal brake pipe unions can be plugged (if care is taken not to allow dirt into the system) or capped immediately they are disconnected. Place a wad of rag under any union that is to be disconnected, to catch any spilt fluid.

**2** If a flexible hose is to be disconnected, unscrew the brake pipe union nut before removing the spring clip which secures the hose to its mounting bracket **(see illustration)**.

**3** To unscrew the union nuts, it is preferable to obtain a brake pipe spanner of the correct size; these are available from most large motor accessory shops. Failing this, a close-fitting open-ended spanner will be required, though if the nuts are tight or corroded, their flats may be rounded-off if the spanner slips. In such a case, a self-locking wrench is often the only way to unscrew a stubborn union, but it follows that the pipe and the damaged nuts must be renewed on reassembly. Always clean a union and surrounding area before disconnecting it. If disconnecting a component with more than one union, make a careful note of the connections before disturbing any of them.

**4** If a brake pipe is to be renewed, it can be obtained, cut to length and with the union nuts and end flares in place, from VW dealers. All that is then necessary is to bend it to shape, following the line of the original, before fitting it to the car. Alternatively, most motor accessory shops can make up brake pipes from kits, but this requires very careful measurement of the original, to ensure that the replacement is of the correct length. The safest answer is usually to take the original to the shop as a pattern.

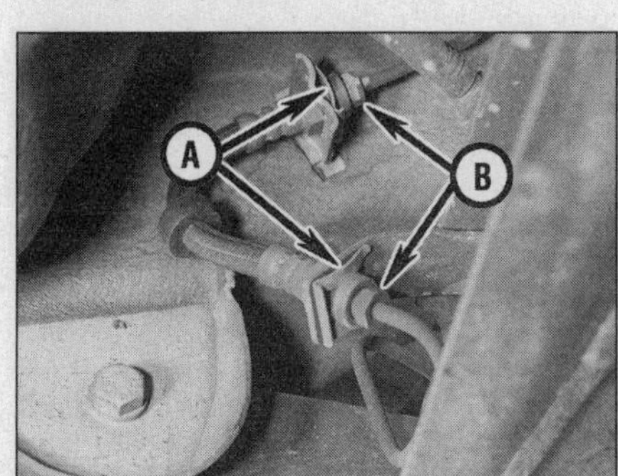


**3.2 Rear brake flexible hose unions showing spring clips (A) and union nuts (B)**

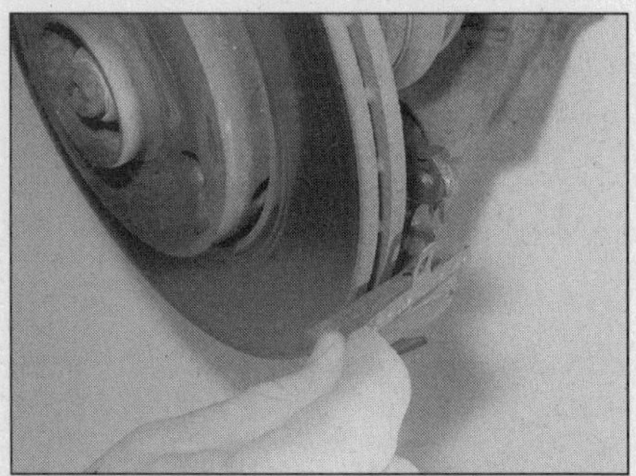

**4.11a Fit the lower anti-rattle spring . . .**

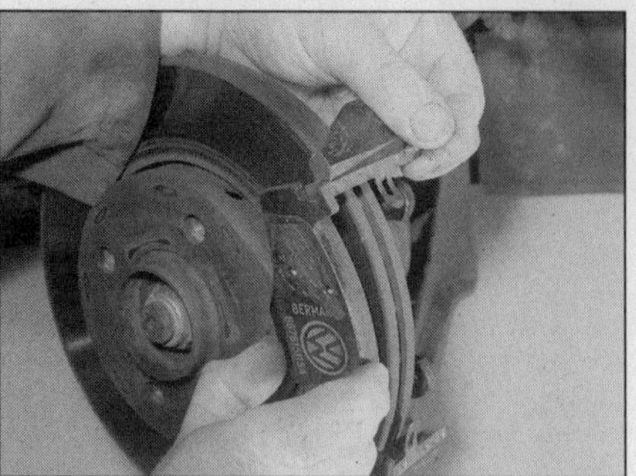

**4.11b . . . then the upper anti-rattle spring and the outer pad . . .**

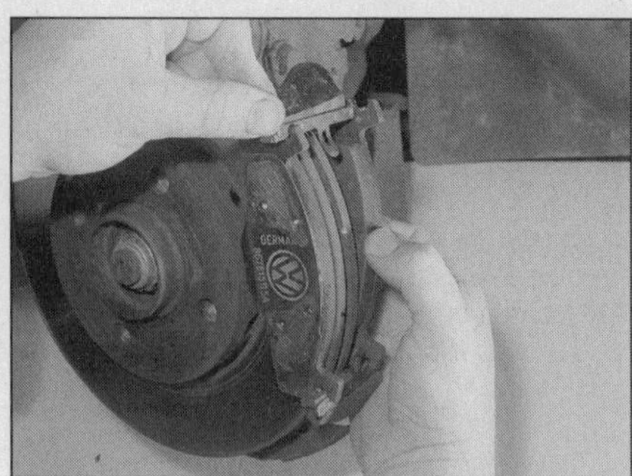

**4.11c . . . followed by the inner pad**

**5** On refitting, do not overtighten the union nuts. It is not necessary to exercise brute force to obtain a sound joint.

**6** Ensure that the pipes and hoses are correctly routed, with no kinks, and that they are secured in the clips or brackets provided. After fitting, remove the polythene from the reservoir, and bleed the hydraulic system as described in Section 2. Wash off any spilt fluid, and check carefully for fluid leaks.

## 4 Front brake pads - renewal

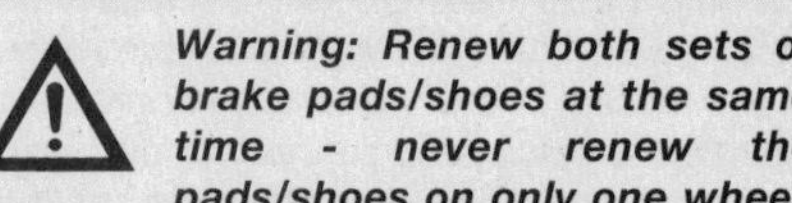

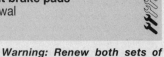

***Warning: Renew both sets of brake pads/shoes at the same time - never renew the pads/shoes on only one wheel, as uneven braking may result. Note that the dust created by wear of the pads may contain asbestos, which is a health hazard. Never blow it out with compressed air, and do not inhale any of it. An approved filtering mask should be worn when working on the brakes. DO NOT use petrol or petroleum-based solvents to clean brake parts; use brake cleaner or methylated spirit only.***

**1** Apply the handbrake, loosen the front wheel bolts, then jack up the front of the vehicle and support it on axle stands. Remove the front roadwheels.

**2** Two different types of calipers and front brake pads are fitted to Polo models. Models fitted with VW type 1 calipers have separate pad retaining/anti-rattle springs fitted at the top and bottom of the caliper; those with the later type 2 calipers have pads with retaining springs riveted to the back of the pads.

### VW type 1 calipers

**3** Although not essential, to improve access, remove the air deflector shield from the caliper.

**4** Using a suitable Allen key or Allen socket, slacken and remove the two caliper mounting bolts.

**5** Lift the caliper away from the brake pads and hub, and tie it to the suspension strut using a suitable piece of wire. Do not allow the caliper to hang unsupported on the flexible brake hose.

**6** Withdraw the two brake pads from the swivel hub and recover the two anti-rattle springs, noting their correct fitted locations. Note that the springs are different, and are not interchangeable.

**7** First measure the thickness of each brake pad (including the backing plate). If either pad is worn at any point to the specified minimum thickness or less, all four pads must be renewed. Also, the pads should be renewed if any are fouled with oil or grease; there is no satisfactory way of degreasing friction material, once contaminated. If any of the brake pads are worn unevenly, or are fouled with oil or grease, trace and rectify the cause before reassembly. New brake pad kits are available from VW dealers.

**8** If the brake pads are still serviceable, carefully clean them using a clean, fine wire brush or similar, paying particular attention to the sides and back of the metal backing. If the pads are glazed (have a shiny appearance) it may be helpful to roughen the surface of the friction material in order to restore the pads' braking effectiveness. Clean out the grooves in the friction material (where applicable), and pick out any large embedded particles of dirt or debris. Carefully clean the pad locations in the caliper body/mounting bracket.

**9** Prior to fitting the pads, check that the spacers are free to slide easily in the caliper body bushes, and are a reasonably tight fit. Brush the dust and dirt from the caliper and piston, but *do not* inhale it, as it is injurious to health. Inspect the dust seal around the piston for damage, and the piston for evidence of fluid leaks, corrosion or damage. If attention to any of these components is necessary, refer to Section 8.

**10** If new brake pads are to be fitted, the caliper piston must be pushed back into the cylinder to make room for them. Either use a G-clamp or similar tool, or use suitable pieces of wood as levers. Provided that the master cylinder reservoir has not been overfilled with hydraulic fluid, there should be no spillage, but keep a careful watch on the fluid level while retracting the piston. If the fluid level rises above the MAX level line at any time, the surplus should be siphoned off or ejected through a plastic tube connected to the bleed screw (see Section 2). **Note:** *Do not syphon the fluid by mouth, as it is poisonous; use a syringe or an old poultry baster.*

**11** Fit the new anti-rattle springs to the hub, making sure they are correctly positioned. Fit the pads, ensuring that the friction material of each pad is against the brake disc **(see illustrations)**.

**12** Position the caliper over the pads, and press into position sufficiently until it is possible to install the caliper mounting bolts **(see illustrations)**. **Note:** *Do not exert excess pressure on the caliper, as this will deform the pad springs, resulting in noisy operation of the brakes.*

**13** Tighten the mounting bolts to the specified torque setting **(see illustration)**.

**14** Where removed, refit the air deflector shield to the caliper.

**15** Depress the brake pedal repeatedly, until the pads are pressed into firm contact with

**4.12a Slide the caliper into position . . .**

**4.12b . . . ensuring that the caliper lugs engage properly with the anti-rattle springs**

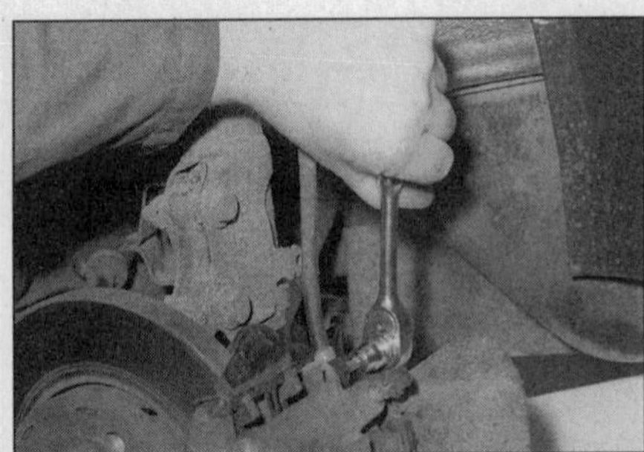

4.13 Using a suitable Allen key or socket, tighten the caliper mounting bolts to the specified torque

the brake disc, and normal (non-assisted) pedal pressure is restored.

16 Repeat the above procedure on the remaining front brake caliper.

17 Refit the roadwheels, then lower the vehicle to the ground and tighten the roadwheel bolts to the specified torque.

18 New pads will not give full braking efficiency until they have bedded-in. Be prepared for this, and avoid hard braking as far as possible for the first hundred miles or so after pad renewal.

19 Check the hydraulic fluid level as described in *Weekly checks*.

## *VW type 2 calipers*

20 Although not essential, to improve access, remove the air deflector shield from the caliper.

21 Using a suitable Allen key or Allen socket, slacken and remove the two caliper mounting bolts **(see illustrations)**.

4.21a Loosen the caliper mounting bolts using an Allen key or socket . . .

4.21b . . . and remove the bolts from the caliper

4.22 Withdraw the caliper and brake pads from the brake disc

22 Lift the caliper and pads away from the hub **(see illustration)**. While the caliper is removed, make sure it is supported at all times, and that the flexible brake hose is not strained or unduly twisted - if the caliper must be left unattended, do not allow it to hang unsupported on the flexible brake hose.

23 Using a flat-bladed screwdriver if necessary, prise the pads out of their locations in the caliper - note that the pad with the larger friction surface is fitted to the outer side of the caliper **(see illustrations)**.

24 First measure the thickness of each brake pad (including the backing plate). If either pad is worn at any point to the specified minimum thickness or less, all four pads must be renewed. Also, the pads should be renewed if any are fouled with oil or grease; there is no satisfactory way of degreasing friction material, once contaminated. If any of the brake pads are worn unevenly, or are fouled with oil or grease, trace and rectify the cause before reassembly.

25 If the brake pads are still serviceable, carefully clean them using a clean, fine wire brush or similar, paying particular attention to the sides and back of the metal backing. If the pads are glazed (have a shiny appearance) it may be helpful to roughen the surface of the friction material in order to restore the pads' braking effectiveness. Clean out the grooves in the friction material (where applicable), and pick out any large embedded particles of dirt or debris. Carefully clean the pad locations in the caliper body/mounting bracket.

26 Prior to fitting the pads, check that the spacers are free to slide easily in the caliper body bushes, and are a reasonably tight fit. Brush the dust and dirt from the caliper and piston, but *do not* inhale it, as it is injurious to health. Inspect the dust seal around the piston for damage, and the piston for evidence of fluid leaks, corrosion or damage. If attention to any of these components is necessary, refer to Section 8.

27 If new brake pads are to be fitted, the caliper piston must be pushed back into the cylinder to make room for them. Either use a G-clamp or similar tool, or use suitable pieces of wood as levers. Provided that the master cylinder reservoir has not been overfilled with hydraulic fluid, there should be no spillage, but keep a careful watch on the fluid level while retracting the piston. If the fluid level rises above the MAX level line at any time, the surplus should be siphoned off or ejected through a plastic tube connected to the bleed screw (see Section 2). **Note:** *Do not syphon the fluid by mouth, as it is poisonous; use a syringe or an old poultry baster.*

28 Press the pads into their locations in the caliper. The inner pad can be pressed in sideways, but the outer pad must be pressed in downwards, as shown **(see illustration)**.

29 Position the caliper and pads over the disc, and press into position sufficiently until it is possible to install caliper mounting bolts. Tighten the mounting bolts to the specified torque setting.

30 Where removed, refit the air deflector shield to the caliper.

31 Depress the brake pedal repeatedly, until the pads are pressed into firm contact with the brake disc, and normal (non-assisted) pedal pressure is restored.

4.23a Prise out the smaller inner pad . . .

4.23b . . . and the larger outer brake pad from the caliper

4.28 Outer brake pad spring clip is most easily engaged in the caliper by pressing in downwards

5.6 Self-adjusting mechanism spring may be attached as shown (arrowed) on some models

**32** Repeat the above procedure on the remaining front brake caliper.

**33** Refit the roadwheels, then lower the vehicle to the ground and tighten the roadwheel bolts to the specified torque.

**34** New pads will not give full braking efficiency until they have bedded-in. Be prepared for this, and avoid hard braking as far as possible for the first hundred miles or so after pad renewal.

**35** Check the hydraulic fluid level as described in *Weekly checks*.

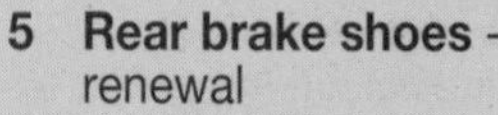

## 5 Rear brake shoes - renewal

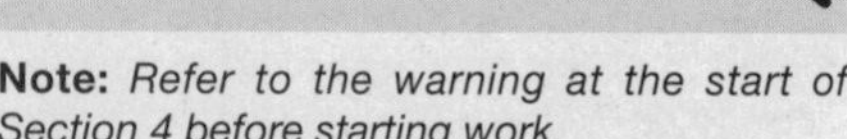

**Note:** *Refer to the warning at the start of Section 4 before starting work.*

**1** Remove the brake drum (see Section 7).

5.8 Unhook the shoes from the lower pivot point, and remove the lower return spring

5.7a Using pliers, remove the spring cup . . .

**2** Working carefully, and taking the necessary precautions, remove all traces of brake dust from the brake drum, backplate and shoes.

**3** Measure the thickness of the friction material of each brake shoe at several points; if either shoe is worn at any point to the specified minimum thickness or less, **all four** shoes must be renewed as a set. The shoes should also be renewed if any are fouled with oil or grease; there is no way of degreasing friction material, once contaminated.

**4** If any of the brake shoes are worn unevenly, or fouled with oil or grease, trace and rectify the cause before reassembly.

**5** To renew the brake shoes, continue as follows. If all is well, refit the brake drum as described in Section 7.

**6** Note the position of the brake shoes and springs, and mark the webs of the shoes, if necessary, to aid refitting. **Note:** *One of the project vehicles seen in the workshop had a slightly different self-adjusting spring arrangement fitted - this should be noted when following the accompanying illustrations in this Section* ***(see illustration)****.*

**7** Using a pair of pliers, remove the shoe retainer spring cups by depressing and turning them through 90°. With the cups removed, lift off the springs and withdraw the retainer pins **(see illustrations)**.

**8** Ease the shoes out one at a time from the lower pivot point, to release the tension of the return spring, then disconnect the lower return spring from both shoes **(see illustration)**.

**9** Ease the upper end of both shoes out from their wheel cylinder locations, taking care not

5.7b . . . then lift off the spring . . .

5.7c . . . and withdraw the retainer pin from the rear of the backplate

to damage the wheel cylinder seals, and disconnect the handbrake cable from the trailing shoe. The brake shoe assembly can then be manoeuvred out of position and away from the backplate. Do not depress the brake pedal until the brakes are reassembled; wrap a strong elastic band around the wheel cylinder pistons to retain them **(see illustrations)**.

**10** Make a note of the correct fitted positions of all components (refer to the Note in paragraph 6, and to illustration 5.6), then unhook the upper return spring, and disengage the wedge key spring **(see illustration)**.

**11** Unhook the tensioning spring, and remove the pushrod from the trailing shoe, together with the wedge key.

**12** Examine all components for signs of wear or damage, and renew as necessary. All return springs should be renewed, regardless of their

5.9a Free the shoes from the wheel cylinder. Note elastic band (arrowed) used to retain pistons . . .

5.9b . . . then detach the handbrake cable and remove the shoe assembly

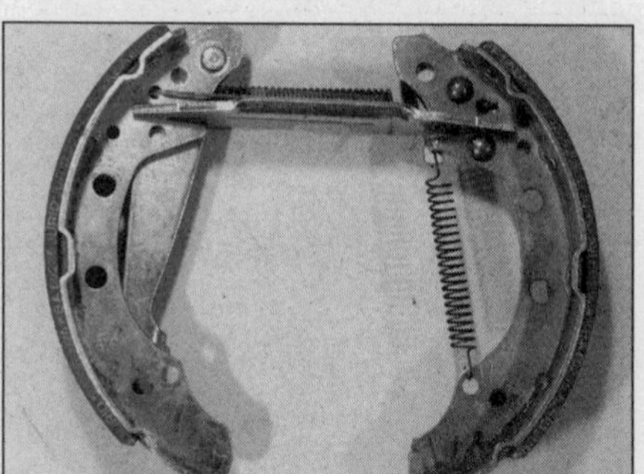

5.10 Prior to dismantling, note the correct fitted location of the shoe components

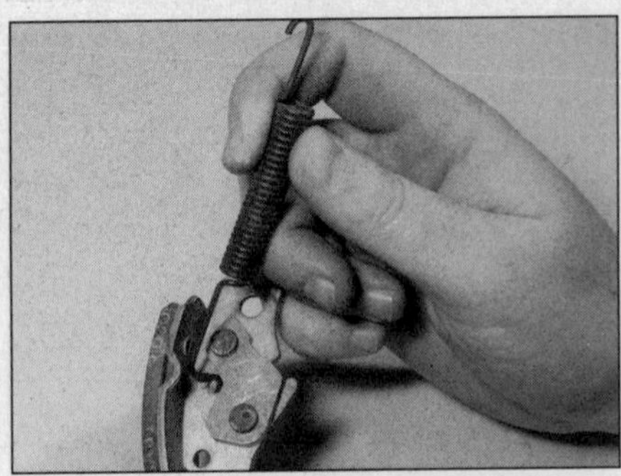
5.15a Hook the tensioning spring into the trailing shoe . . .

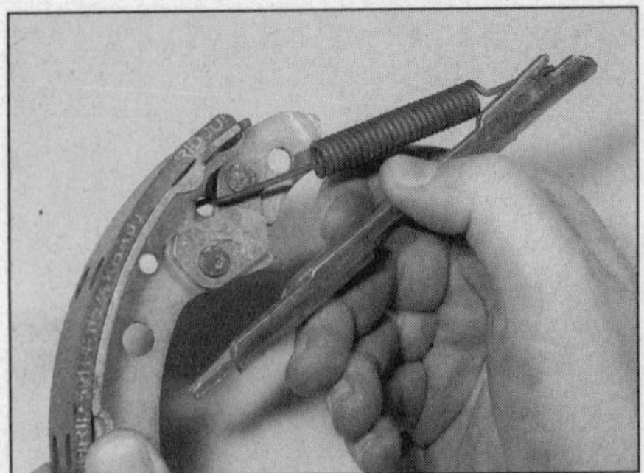
5.15b . . . then engage the pushrod with the opposite end of the spring . . .

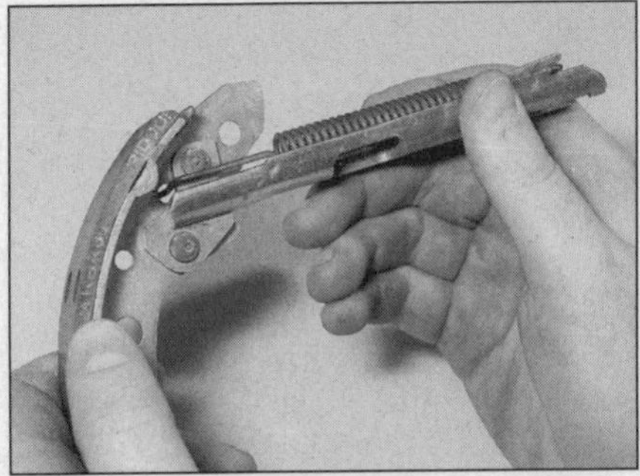
5.15c . . . and pivot the strut into position on the shoe

apparent condition. Although linings are available separately (without shoes) from VW dealers, renewal of the shoes complete with linings is to be preferred, unless the necessary skills and equipment are available to fit new linings to the old shoes.

**13** Peel back the rubber protective caps, and check the wheel cylinder for fluid leaks or other damage; check that both cylinder pistons are free to move easily. Refer to Section 9, if necessary, for information on wheel cylinder overhaul.

**14** Apply a little brake grease to the contact areas of the pushrod and handbrake lever.

**15** Hook the tensioning spring into the trailing shoe. Engage the pushrod with the opposite end of the spring, and pivot the pushrod into position on the trailing shoe **(see illustrations)**.

**16** Fit the wedge key between the trailing shoe and pushrod, making sure it is fitted the correct way around **(see illustration)**.

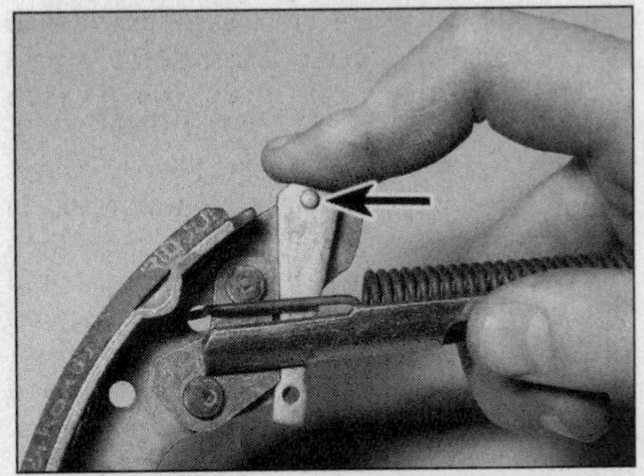
5.16 Slot the wedge key into position. Ensure raised dot (arrowed) is facing away from the shoe

**17** Locate the handbrake lever on the leading shoe in the pushrod, and fit the upper return spring using a pair of pliers **(see illustrations)**.

**18** Fit the spring to the wedge key, and hook it onto the trailing shoe **(see illustration)**.

**19** Prior to installation, clean the backplate, and apply a thin smear of high-temperature brake grease or anti-seize compound to all those surfaces of the backplate which bear on the shoes, particularly the wheel cylinder pistons and lower pivot point. Do not allow the lubricant to foul the friction material.

**20** Remove the elastic band fitted to the wheel cylinder, and offer up the shoe assembly.

**21** Connect the handbrake cable to the handbrake lever, and locate the top of the shoes in the wheel cylinder piston slots.

**22** Fit the lower return spring to the shoes, then lever the bottom of the shoes onto the bottom anchor.

**23** Tap the shoes to centralise them with the backplate, then refit the shoe retainer pins and springs, and secure them in position with the spring cups.

**24** Refit the brake drum as described in Section 7.

**25** Repeat the above procedure on the remaining rear brake.

**26** Once both sets of rear shoes have been renewed, adjust the lining-to-drum clearance by repeatedly depressing the brake pedal until normally (non-assisted) pedal pressure returns.

**27** Check and, if necessary, adjust the handbrake as described in Section 14.

**28** On completion, check the hydraulic fluid level as described in *Weekly checks*.

**29** New shoes will not give full braking efficiency until they have bedded-in. Be prepared for this, and avoid hard braking as far as possible for the first hundred miles or so after shoe renewal.

## 6 Front brake disc - inspection, removal and refitting

**Note:** *Before starting work, refer to the note at the beginning of Section 4 concerning the dangers of asbestos dust.*

### Inspection

**Note:** *If either disc requires renewal, BOTH should be renewed at the same time, to ensure even and consistent braking. New brake pads should also be fitted.*

**1** Apply the handbrake, loosen the front wheel bolts, then jack up the front of the car and support it on axle stands. Remove the appropriate front roadwheel.

**2** Slowly rotate the brake disc so that the full area of both sides can be checked; remove the brake pads if better access is required to the inboard surface. Light scoring is normal in the area swept by the brake pads, but if heavy scoring or cracks are found, the disc must be renewed.

**3** It is normal to find a lip of rust and brake dust around the disc's perimeter; this can be scraped off if required. If, however, a lip has formed due to excessive wear of the brake

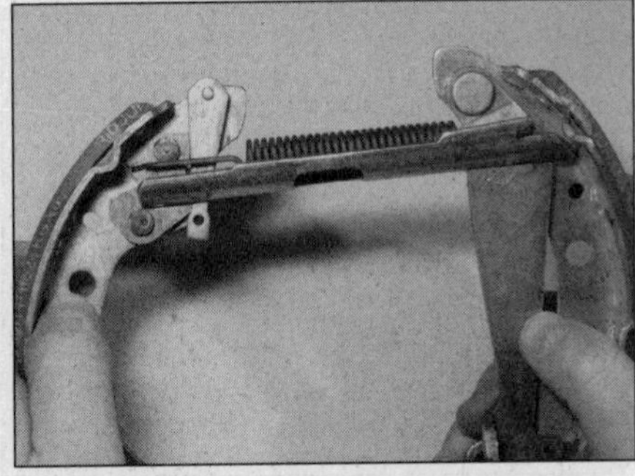
5.17a Locate the leading shoe in the pushrod . . .

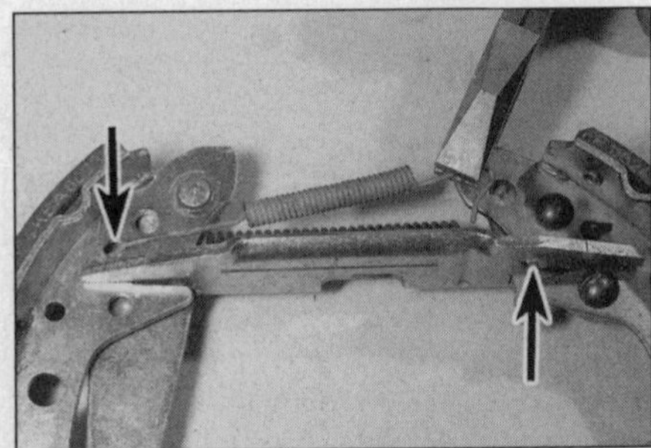
5.17b . . . and hook the upper return spring into the leading shoe and pushrod (arrowed)

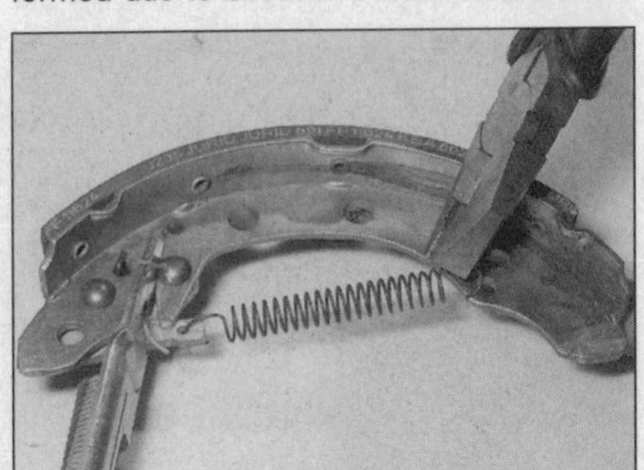
5.18 Fit the spring to the wedge key, and hook it onto the trailing shoe

6.3 Measuring brake disc thickness with a micrometer

6.8a Remove the disc securing screw . . .

6.8b . . . and withdraw the brake disc from the hub

pad swept area, then the disc's thickness must be measured using a micrometer **(see illustration)**. Take measurements at several places around the disc, at the inside and outside of the pad swept area; if the disc has worn at any point to the specified minimum thickness or less, the disc must be renewed.

**4** If the disc is thought to be warped, it can be checked for run-out. Either use a dial gauge mounted on any convenient fixed point, while the disc is slowly rotated, or use feeler blades to measure (at several points all around the disc) the clearance between the disc and a fixed point, such as the caliper mounting bracket. If the measurements obtained are at the specified maximum or beyond, the disc is excessively warped, and must be renewed; however, it is worth checking first that the hub bearing is in good condition (Chapters 1 and/or 10). If the run-out is excessive, the disc must be renewed.

**5** Check the disc for cracks, especially around the wheel bolt holes, and any other wear or damage, and renew if necessary.

7.2 Lever out the cap from the centre of the brake drum

### Removal

**6** On models with VW type 1 calipers, remove the brake pads as described in Section 4.

**7** On models with VW type 2 calipers, unbolt the caliper as described in Section 4, and remove it with the pads. Tie the caliper up to the front suspension coil spring using a piece of wire or string, so that the flexible brake hose is not twisted or strained.

**8** Use chalk or paint to mark the relationship of the disc to the hub, then remove the screw securing the brake disc to the hub, and remove the disc **(see illustrations)**. If it is tight, tap its rear face with a hide or plastic mallet.

### Refitting

**9** Refitting is the reverse of the removal procedure, noting the following points:

*a) Ensure that the mating surfaces of the disc and hub are clean and flat.*
*b) Align (if applicable) the marks made on removal, and securely tighten the disc retaining screw.*
*c) If a new disc has been fitted, use a suitable solvent to wipe any preservative coating from the disc, before refitting the caliper.*
*d) On models with type 2 brake calipers, slide the caliper into position over the disc, making sure the pads pass either side of the disc. Tighten the caliper mounting bolts to the specified torque setting.*
*e) On models with type 1 brake calipers, refit the pads as described in Section 4.*
*f) Refit the roadwheel, then lower the vehicle to the ground and tighten the roadwheel bolts to the specified torque. On completion, repeatedly depress the brake pedal until normal (non-assisted) pedal pressure returns.*

## 7 Rear brake drum - removal, inspection and refitting

**Note:** *Before starting work, refer to the note at the beginning of Section 4 concerning the dangers of asbestos dust.*

### Removal

**1** Chock the front wheels and engage 1st gear (or P). Loosen the rear wheel bolts, then jack up the rear of the vehicle and support it on axle stands. Remove the appropriate rear wheel.

**2** Using a hammer and a large flat-bladed screwdriver, carefully tap and prise the cap out of the centre of the brake drum **(see illustration)**. Discard the cap if it is disfigured during removal.

**3** Extract the split pin from the hub nut, and remove the locking ring **(see illustration)**. Discard the split pin; a new one must be used on refitting.

**4** Slacken and remove the rear hub nut, then slide off the toothed washer and remove the outer bearing from the centre of the drum **(see illustrations)**.

7.3 Remove the split pin and locking cap . . .

7.4a . . . then unscrew the retaining nut and remove the toothed washer

7.4b Withdraw the outer bearing . . .

7.5 . . . and remove the brake drum

7.7a Release the brake shoes by inserting a screwdriver through the drum hole . . .

7.7b . . . and levering the wedge key (arrowed) upwards

**5** It should now be possible to withdraw the brake drum assembly from the stub axle by hand **(see illustration)**. It may be difficult to remove the drum, due to the tightness of the hub bearing on the stub axle, or due to the brake shoes binding on the inner circumference of the drum. If the bearing is tight, tap the periphery of the drum using a hide or plastic mallet, or use a universal puller, secured to the drum with the wheel bolts, to pull it off. If the brake shoes are binding, first check that the handbrake is fully released, then continue as follows.

**6** Referring to Section 14, fully slacken the handbrake adjustment, to obtain maximum free play in the cable.

**7** Insert a screwdriver through one of the wheel bolt holes in the brake drum, and lever up the wedge key in order to allow the brake shoes to retract fully - see Section 5. The brake drum can now be withdrawn **(see illustrations)**.

### Inspection

**Note:** *If either drum requires renewal, BOTH should be renewed at the same time, to ensure even and consistent braking. New brake shoes should also be fitted.*

**8** Working carefully, remove all traces of brake dust from the drum, but avoid inhaling the dust, as it is injurious to health.

**9** Clean the outside of the drum, and check it for obvious signs of wear or damage, such as cracks around the roadwheel bolt holes; renew the drum if necessary.

**10** Examine carefully the inside of the drum. Light scoring of the friction surface is normal, but if heavy scoring is found, the drum must be renewed. It is usual to find a lip on the drum's inboard edge which consists of a mixture of rust and brake dust; this should be scraped away, to leave a smooth surface which can be polished with fine (120- to 150-grade) emery paper. If, however, the lip is due to the friction surface being recessed by wear, then the drum must be renewed.

**11** If the drum is thought to be excessively worn, or oval, its internal diameter must be measured at several points using an internal micrometer. Take measurements in pairs, the second at right-angles to the first, and compare the two, to check for signs of ovality. Provided that it does not enlarge the drum to beyond the specified maximum diameter, it may be possible to have the drum refinished by skimming or grinding; if this is not possible, the drums on both sides must be renewed. Note that if the drum is to be skimmed, BOTH drums must be refinished, to maintain a consistent internal diameter on both sides.

**12** On models with ABS, take the opportunity to inspect the reluctor ring for the wheel sensor, which is pressed into the drum. Examine the ring for signs of damage such as chipped or missing teeth, and renew as necessary.

### Refitting

**13** If a new brake drum is to be installed, use a suitable solvent to remove any preservative coating that may have been applied to its interior. If necessary, install the bearing races, inner bearing and oil seal as described in Chapter 10, and thoroughly grease the outer bearing.

**14** Prior to refitting, fully retract the brakes shoes by lifting up the wedge key.

**15** Apply a smear of grease to the drum oil seal, and carefully slide the assembly onto the stub axle.

**16** Fit the outer bearing and toothed thrustwasher, ensuring its tooth is correctly engaged in the axle slot.

**17** Refit the hub nut, tightening it to the point where it just contacts the washer whilst rotating the brake drum to settle the hub bearings in position. Gradually slacken the hub nut until the position is found where it is just possible to move the toothed washer from side-to-side using a screwdriver. **Note:** *Only a small amount of force should be needed to move the washer.* When the hub nut is correctly positioned, refit the locking cap and secure the nut in position with a new split pin.

**18** Fit the cap to the centre of the brake drum, driving it fully into position.

**19** Depress the footbrake several times to operate the self-adjusting mechanism.

**20** Repeat the above procedure on the remaining rear brake assembly (where necessary), then check and, if necessary, adjust the handbrake cable (see Section 14).

**21** On completion, refit the roadwheel(s), then lower the vehicle to the ground and tighten the wheel bolts to the specified torque.

## 8 Front brake caliper - removal, overhaul and refitting

**Note:** *Before starting work, refer to the note at the beginning of Section 2 concerning the dangers of hydraulic fluid, and to the warning at the beginning of Section 4 concerning the dangers of asbestos dust.*

### Removal

**1** Apply the handbrake, loosen the front wheel bolts, then jack up the front of the vehicle and support it on axle stands. Remove the appropriate roadwheel.

**2** Minimise fluid loss by first removing the master cylinder reservoir cap, and then tightening it down onto a piece of polythene, to obtain an airtight seal. Alternatively, use a brake hose clamp, a G-clamp or a similar tool to clamp the flexible hose.

**3** Clean the area around the union, then loosen the brake hose union nut.

**4** Remove the brake pads as described in Section 4.

**5** Unscrew the caliper from the end of the brake hose, and remove it from the vehicle.

### Overhaul

**6** With the caliper on the bench, wipe away all traces of dust and dirt, but *avoid inhaling the dust, as it is injurious to health.*

**7** Withdraw the partially-ejected piston from the caliper body, and remove the dust seal.

***If the piston cannot be withdrawn by hand, it can be pushed out by applying compressed air to the brake hose union hole. Only low pressure should be required, such as is generated by a foot pump. As the piston is expelled, take great care not to trap your fingers between the piston and caliper.***

9

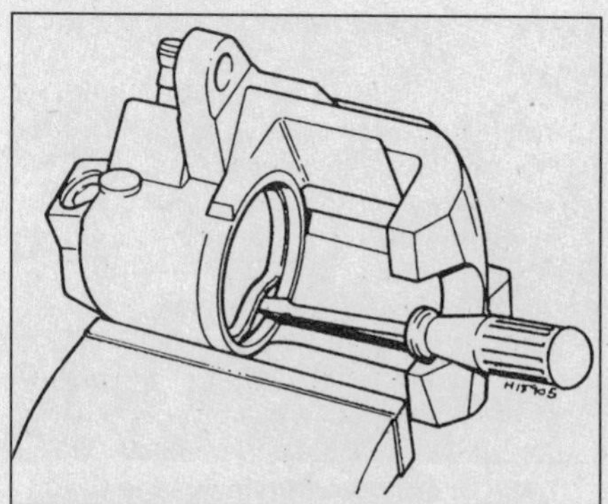

**8.8 Extracting the piston seal - take care not to scratch the surface of the bore**

**8** Using a small screwdriver, extract the piston hydraulic seal, taking great care not to damage the caliper bore **(see illustration)**.

**9** Thoroughly clean all components, using only methylated spirit, isopropyl alcohol or clean hydraulic fluid as a cleaning medium. Never use mineral-based solvents such as petrol or paraffin, as they will attack the hydraulic system's rubber components. Dry the components immediately, using compressed air or a clean, lint-free cloth. Use compressed air to blow clear the fluid passages.

**10** Withdraw the spacers from the caliper body bushes.

**11** Check all components, and renew any that are worn or damaged. Check particularly the cylinder bore and piston; these should be renewed (note that this means the renewal of the complete body assembly) if they are scratched, worn or corroded in any way. Similarly check the condition of the spacers/guide pins and their bushes/bores (as applicable); both spacers/pins should be undamaged and (when cleaned) a reasonably tight sliding fit in their bores. If there is any doubt about the condition of any component, renew it.

**12** If the assembly is fit for further use, obtain the appropriate repair kit; the components are available from VW dealers in various combinations.

**13** Renew all rubber seals, dust covers and caps disturbed on dismantling as a matter of course; these should never be re-used.

**14** On reassembly, ensure that all components are clean and dry.

**15** Soak the piston and the new piston (fluid) seal in clean hydraulic fluid. Smear clean fluid on the cylinder bore surface.

**16** Fit the new piston (fluid) seal, using only your fingers (no tools) to manipulate it into the cylinder bore groove. Fit the new dust seal to the piston, and refit the piston to the cylinder bore using a twisting motion; ensure that the piston enters squarely into the bore. Press the piston fully into the bore, then press the dust seal into the caliper body.

**17** Apply the grease supplied in the repair kit (or a copper-based high-temperature brake grease or anti-seize compound) to the spacers, and insert them into their bushes.

### Refitting

**18** Screw the caliper fully onto the flexible hose union.

**19** Refit the brake pads (see Section 4).

**20** Securely tighten the brake pipe union nut.

**21** Remove the brake hose clamp or polythene, as applicable, and bleed the hydraulic system as described in Section 2. Note that, providing the precautions described were taken to minimise brake fluid loss, it should only be necessary to bleed the relevant front brake.

**22** Refit the roadwheel, then lower the vehicle to the ground and tighten the roadwheel bolts to the specified torque.

## 9 Rear wheel cylinder - removal, overhaul and refitting

**Note:** *Before starting work, refer to the note at the beginning of Section 2 concerning the dangers of hydraulic fluid, and to the warning at the beginning of Section 4 concerning the dangers of asbestos dust.*

### Removal

**1** Remove the brake drum (see Section 7).

**2** Using pliers, carefully unhook the upper brake shoe return spring, and remove it from both brake shoes. Pull the upper ends of the shoes away from the wheel cylinder to disengage them from the pistons.

**3** Minimise fluid loss by first removing the master cylinder reservoir cap, and then tightening it down onto a piece of polythene, to obtain an airtight seal. Alternatively, use a brake hose clamp, a G-clamp or a similar tool to clamp the flexible hose at the nearest convenient point to the wheel cylinder.

**4** Wipe away all traces of dirt around the brake pipe union at the rear of the wheel cylinder, and unscrew the union nut. Carefully ease the pipe out of the wheel cylinder, and plug or tape over its end to prevent dirt entry. Wipe off any spilt immediately.

**5** Unscrew the two wheel cylinder retaining bolts from the rear of the backplate, and remove the cylinder, taking great care not to allow surplus hydraulic fluid to contaminate the brake shoe linings. Later models may be fitted with an aluminium wheel cylinder, which only has one retaining bolt.

### Overhaul

**6** Brush the dirt and dust from the wheel cylinder, but take care not to inhale it.

**7** Pull the rubber dust seals from the ends of the cylinder body.

**8** The pistons will normally be ejected by the pressure of the coil spring, but if they are not, tap the end of the cylinder body on a piece of wood, or apply low air pressure - eg, from a foot pump - to the hydraulic fluid union hole to eject the pistons from their bores.

**9** Inspect the surfaces of the pistons and their bores in the cylinder body for scoring, or evidence of metal-to-metal contact. If evident, renew the complete wheel cylinder assembly. The later aluminium wheel cylinder may be fitted as a direct replacement for the earlier cylinder, if wished - VW state that it is permissible to mix the two types.

**10** If the pistons and bores are in good condition, obtain a repair kit, which will contain all the necessary renewable items.

**11** Remove the seals from the pistons, noting their correct fitted orientation. Lubricate the new piston seals with clean brake fluid, and fit them onto the pistons with their larger diameters innermost.

**12** Dip the pistons in clean brake fluid, then fit the spring to the cylinder.

**13** Insert the pistons into the cylinder bores using a twisting motion.

**14** Fit the dust seals, and check that the pistons can move freely in their bores.

### Refitting

**15** Ensure that the backplate and wheel cylinder mating surfaces are clean, then spread the brake shoes and manoeuvre the wheel cylinder into position.

**16** Engage the brake pipe, and screw in the union nut two or three turns to ensure that the thread has started.

**17** Insert the two wheel cylinder retaining bolts (or the single bolt), and tighten to the specified torque. Now fully tighten the brake pipe union nut.

**18** Remove the clamp from the flexible brake hose, or the polythene from the master cylinder reservoir (as applicable).

**19** Ensure that the brake shoes are correctly located in the cylinder pistons, then refit the brake shoe upper return spring, using a screwdriver to stretch the spring into position.

**20** Refit the brake drum (see Section 7).

**21** Bleed the brake hydraulic system as described in Section 2. Providing suitable precautions were taken to minimise loss of fluid, it should only be necessary to bleed the relevant rear brake.

## 10 Master cylinder - removal, overhaul and refitting

**Note:** *Before starting work, refer to the warning at the beginning of Section 2 concerning the dangers of hydraulic fluid.*

### Removal

**1** Disconnect the battery negative terminal. **Note:** *If the vehicle has a security-coded radio, check that you have a copy of the code number before disconnecting the battery. Refer to your VW dealer if in doubt.*

**2** To improve access to the master cylinder, remove the air cleaner and air inlet trunking (petrol models) or the air inlet trunking and inlet manifold pipe cover (diesel models) as described in the relevant Part of Chapter 4.

**3** Remove the brake fluid reservoir cap, and syphon the hydraulic fluid from the reservoir.

**Note:** *Do not syphon the fluid by mouth, as it is poisonous; use a syringe or an old poultry baster.* Alternatively, open any convenient bleed screw in the system, and gently pump the brake pedal to expel the fluid through a plastic tube connected to the screw (see Section 2). Disconnect the wiring plug from the brake fluid level sender unit.

**4** Wipe clean the area around the brake pipe unions on the side of the master cylinder, and place absorbent rags beneath the pipe unions to catch any surplus fluid. Make a note of the correct fitted positions of the unions, then unscrew the union nuts and carefully withdraw the pipes. Plug or tape over the pipe ends and master cylinder orifices, to minimise the loss of brake fluid, and to prevent the entry of dirt into the system. Wash off any spilt fluid immediately with cold water.

**5** Slacken and remove the two nuts (and washers, where applicable) securing the master cylinder to the vacuum servo unit, then withdraw the unit from the engine compartment. Remove the O-ring from the rear of the master cylinder, and discard it **(see illustration)**.

### Overhaul

**6** If the master cylinder is faulty, it must be renewed. Repair kits are not available from VW dealer, so the cylinder must be treated as a sealed unit.

**7** The only items which can be renewed are the mounting seals for the fluid reservoir; if these show signs of deterioration, pull off the reservoir and remove the old seals. Lubricate the new seals with clean brake fluid, and press them into the master cylinder ports. Ease the fluid reservoir into position, and push it fully home.

### Refitting

**8** Remove all traces of dirt from the master cylinder and servo unit mating surfaces, and fit a new O-ring to the groove on the master cylinder body.

**9** Fit the master cylinder to the servo unit, ensuring that the servo unit pushrod enters the master cylinder bore centrally. Refit the master cylinder mounting nuts (and washers, where fitted) and tighten them to the specified torque.

**10** Wipe clean the brake pipe unions, then refit them to the master cylinder ports and tighten them securely.

**11** Refill the master cylinder reservoir with new fluid, and bleed the complete hydraulic system as described in Section 2.

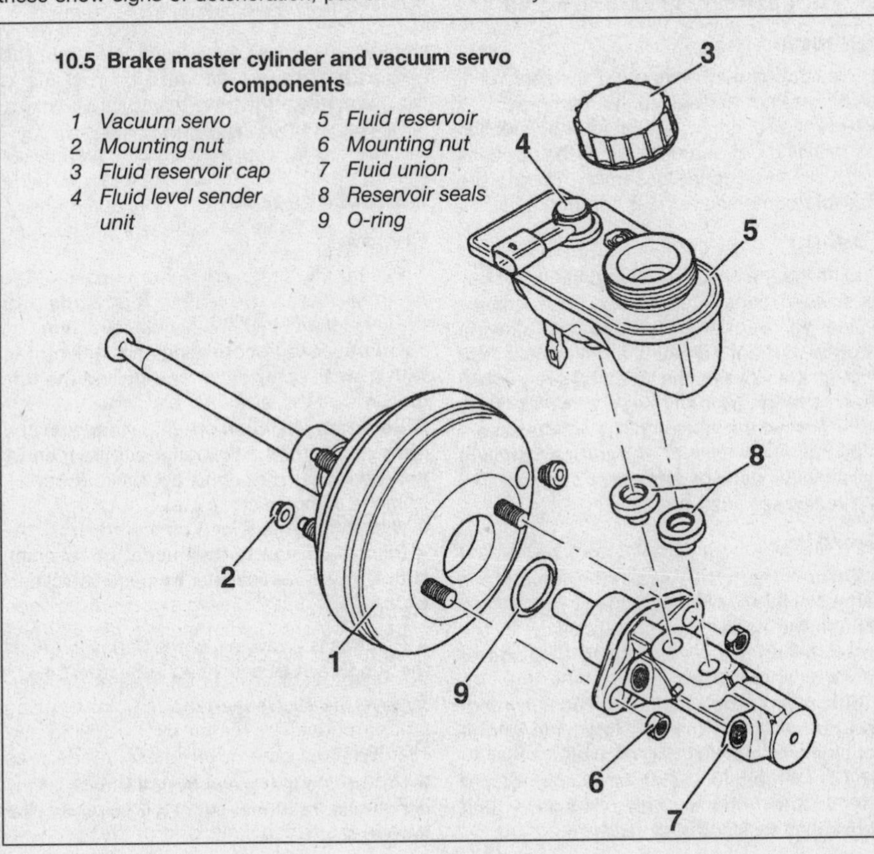


**10.5 Brake master cylinder and vacuum servo components**

1 *Vacuum servo*
2 *Mounting nut*
3 *Fluid reservoir cap*
4 *Fluid level sender unit*
5 *Fluid reservoir*
6 *Mounting nut*
7 *Fluid union*
8 *Reservoir seals*
9 *O-ring*

## 11 Brake pedal - removal and refitting

### Removal

**1** Disconnect the battery negative terminal. **Note:** *If the vehicle has a security-coded radio, check that you have a copy of the code number before disconnecting the battery. Refer to your VW dealer if in doubt.*

**2** Refer to Chapter 11 and remove the driver's side glovebox.

**3** The pedal cluster must be removed complete, in order to allow sufficient room for the brake pedal to be removed.

**4** Remove the stop-light switch (Section 18).

**5** Unhook the clutch and accelerator cables from their respective pedals.

**6** It is now necessary to release the brake pedal from the ball on the vacuum servo pushrod. To do this, reach up behind the pedal and carefully expand the pedal retaining clip lugs until the pedal can be gently pulled off the servo unit pushrod ball.

**7** Drill out the two shear-bolts used to secure the base of the steering column to the pedal bracket.

**8** Unscrew and remove the pedal bracket mounting bolts, and remove the assembly from the car.

**9** Unscrew the nut on the right-hand end of the pedal pivot shaft, and pull the shaft out. Remove the brake pedal.

**10** Carefully clean all components, and renew any that are worn or damaged.

### Refitting

**11** Refitting is a reversal of removal, noting the following points:

a) *Prior to refitting, apply a smear of multi-purpose grease to the pivot shaft and pedal bearing surfaces.*
b) *Fit new shear-bolts and tighten them until their heads break off.*
c) *Press the brake pedal onto the servo pushrod ball, ensuring that it locates correctly.*
d) *Refit the stop-light switch as described in Section 18.*

## 12 Vacuum servo unit - testing, removal and refitting

### Testing

**1** To test the operation of the servo unit, depress the footbrake several times to exhaust the vacuum, then start the engine whilst keeping the pedal firmly depressed. As the engine starts, there should be a noticeable 'give' in the brake pedal as the vacuum builds up. Allow the engine to run for at least two minutes, then switch it off. If the brake pedal is now depressed, it should feel normal, but further applications should result in the pedal feeling firmer, with the pedal stroke decreasing with each application.

**2** If the servo does not operate as described, first inspect the servo unit check valve as described in Section 13. On diesel models, also check the operation of the vacuum pump as described in Section 22.

**3** If the servo unit still fails to operate satisfactorily, the fault lies within the unit itself. Repairs to the unit are not possible - if faulty, the servo unit must be renewed.

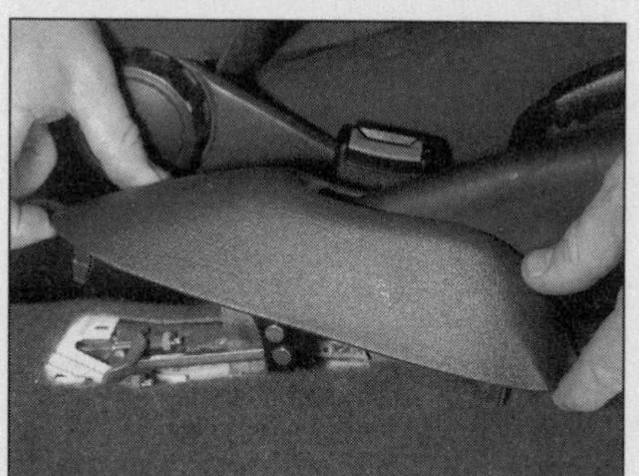
14.4a Pull up the handbrake lever trim . . .

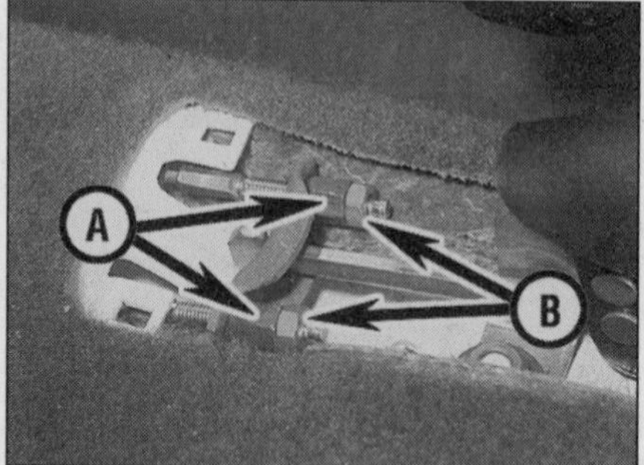

14.4b . . . for access to the cable adjuster nuts (A) and locknuts (B)

### Removal

**Note:** *On left-hand drive models equipped with ABS, it is not possible to remove the vacuum servo unit without first removing the hydraulic unit (see Section 20). Therefore, servo unit removal and refitting should be entrusted to a VW dealer.*

**4** Remove the master cylinder (Section 10).

**5** Carefully ease the vacuum hose out from the servo unit sealing grommet.

**6** From inside the vehicle, remove the stop-light switch as described in Section 18.

**7** Undo the four retaining nuts securing the servo unit to the pedal mounting bracket, then return to the engine compartment and manoeuvre the servo unit out of position, noting the gasket which is fitted to the rear of the unit. As the servo is withdrawn, it will be necessary to release its pushrod ball from the brake pedal spring clip (see paragraph 6 of Section 11).

### Refitting

**8** Check the servo unit vacuum hose sealing grommet for signs of damage or deterioration, and renew if necessary.

**9** Fit a new gasket to the rear of the servo unit, and reposition the unit in the engine compartment.

**10** From inside the vehicle, ensure that the servo unit pushrod is correctly engaged with the brake pedal, and clip the pedal onto the pushrod ball. Check the pedal is securely retained, then refit the servo unit mounting nuts and tighten them to the specified torque.

**11** Carefully ease the vacuum hose back into position in the servo, taking great care not to displace the sealing grommet.

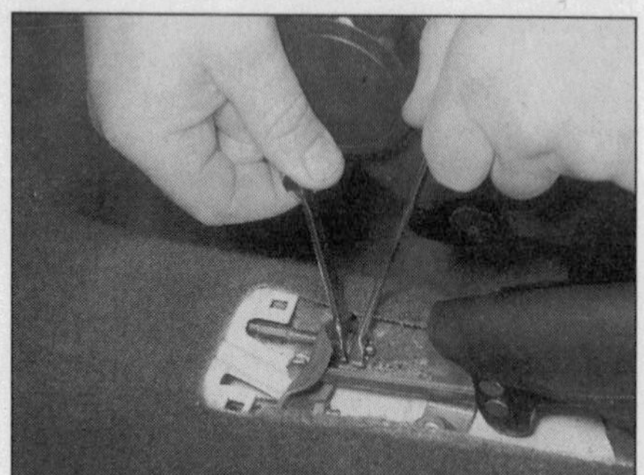
14.5 Adjusting the handbrake cables

**12** Refit the master cylinder as described in Section 10 of this Chapter.

**13** Refit the stop-light switch (Section 18).

**14** On completion, start the engine and check for air leaks at the vacuum hose-to-servo unit connection; check the operation of the braking system.

## 13 Vacuum servo unit check valve - removal, testing and refitting

**1** The check valve is in the vacuum hose from the inlet manifold to the brake servo. If the valve is to be renewed, the complete hose/valve assembly should be replaced.

### Removal

**2** Ease the vacuum hose out of the servo unit, taking care not to displace the grommet.

**3** Note the routing of the hose, then slacken the retaining clip and disconnect the opposite end of the hose assembly from the manifold/pump and remove it from the car.

### Testing

**4** Examine the check valve and vacuum hose for signs of damage, and renew if necessary.

**5** The valve may be tested by blowing through it in both directions. Air should flow through the valve in one direction only - when blown through from the servo unit end of the valve. Renew the valve if this is not the case.

**6** Examine the servo unit rubber sealing grommet for signs of damage or deterioration, and renew as necessary.

### Refitting

**7** Ensure that the sealing grommet is correctly fitted to the servo unit.

**8** Ease the hose union into position in the servo, taking great care not to displace or damage the grommet.

**9** Ensure that the hose is correctly routed, and connect it to the inlet manifold/pump, tightening its retaining clip securely.

**10** On completion, start the engine and check the check valve-to-servo unit connection for signs of air leaks.

## 14 Handbrake - adjustment

**1** To check the handbrake adjustment, first apply the footbrake firmly several times to establish correct shoe-to-drum clearance, then apply and release the handbrake several times.

**2** Applying normal moderate pressure, pull the handbrake lever to the fully-applied position, counting the number of clicks emitted from the handbrake ratchet mechanism. If adjustment is correct, there should be approximately 4 to 7 clicks before the handbrake is fully applied. If this is not the case, adjust as follows.

**3** Chock the front wheels, then jack up the rear of the vehicle and support it on axle stands.

**4** Release the handbrake, then pull up the trim from the rear of the handbrake lever for access to the handbrake cable adjuster nuts **(see illustrations)**.

**5** With the handbrake set on the 4th notch of the ratchet mechanism, slacken the locknuts and rotate the adjusting nuts equally until it is difficult to turn both rear wheels/drums **(see illustration)**. Once this is so, release the handbrake lever, and check that the wheels/hubs rotate freely. Check the adjustment by applying the handbrake fully, counting the clicks from the handbrake ratchet and, if necessary, re-adjust.

**6** Once adjustment is correct, hold the adjusting nuts and securely tighten the locknuts. Refit the handbrake lever trim.

## 15 Handbrake lever and warning light switch - removal and refitting

### Handbrake lever

#### Removal

**1** Pull up the trim piece from the base of the handbrake lever, and remove it upwards over the lever. If required, the handle/lever trim can be removed by depressing the locking lug with a small screwdriver and pulling the trim forwards off the lever.

**2** Referring to Section 14 if necessary, remove both the handbrake cable locknuts and adjusting nuts, and detach the cables from the compensator plate.

**3** Disconnect the wiring connector from the warning light switch, then undo the retaining nuts and remove the lever from the vehicle.

#### Refitting

**4** Refitting is a reversal of the removal. Adjust the handbrake as described in Section 14.

### Warning light switch

#### Removal

**5** Pull up the trim piece from the base of the handbrake lever, and remove it upwards over the lever.

6 Pull the handbrake lever up as far as possible.
7 The switch has a plastic peg moulded into it, which locates through a small hole in the base of the handbrake lever. Press out the peg, and disconnect the wiring plug from the switch **(see illustrations)**.

### Refitting

8 Refitting is a reversal of removal.

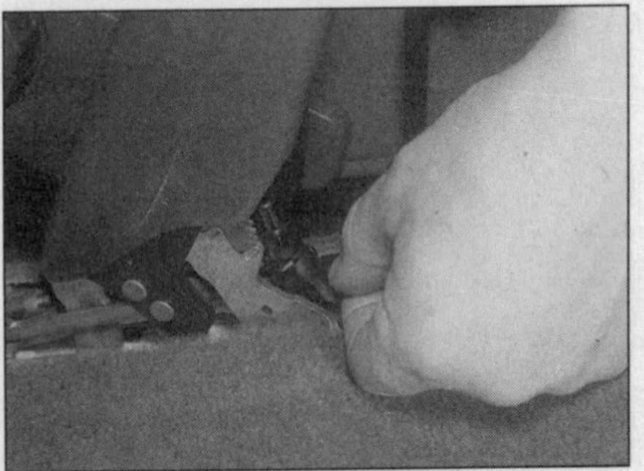

**15.7a Release the handbrake warning light switch from the base of the lever . . .**

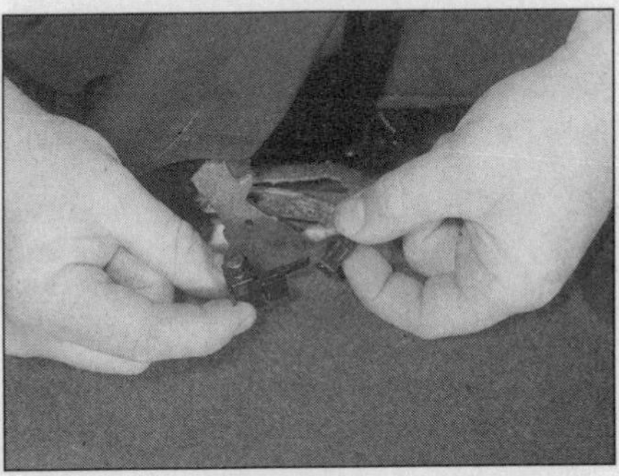

**15.7b . . . and disconnect the wiring plug**

## 16 Handbrake cables - removal and refitting

### Removal

1 The handbrake cable consists of two sections, a right- and a left-hand section, which are linked to the lever by a compensator plate. Each section can be removed individually.
2 Lift up the trim at the base of the handbrake lever to gain access to the cables. Referring to Section 14 if necessary, slacken the relevant handbrake locknut and adjusting nut to obtain maximum free play in the cable, and disengage the inner cable from the handbrake compensator plate.
3 Chock the front wheels, then loosen the relevant rear wheel bolts. Jack up the rear of the car and support it on axle stands.
4 From the vehicle underbody, free the front end of the outer cable from the body, and withdraw the cable from its support guide.
5 Working back along the length of the cable, noting its correct routing, and free it from all the relevant retaining clips **(see illustration)**.
6 Remove the rear brake shoes from the relevant side as described in Section 5. Using a hammer and pin punch, carefully tap the outer cable out from the brake backplate, release it from the backplate cable guide, and remove it from underneath the vehicle.

### Refitting

7 Refitting is a reversal of the removal procedure. Where the cable is clipped to the rear trailing arm, note that genuine VW cables have an indentation in the cable outer, which must lie in the centre of the retaining clip when fitted. On completion, adjust the handbrake as described in Section 14.

## 17 Rear brake pressure-regulating valve - removal and refitting

**Note:** *Before starting work, refer to the warning at the beginning of Section 2 concerning the dangers of hydraulic fluid.*

### Removal

**Note:** *Models with ABS are not fitted with a rear brake pressure-regulating valve; the function is automatically controlled by the ABS unit.*

1 The rear brake pressure-regulating valve is of the load-dependent-type; the valve is mounted in front of the rear axle, attached to the axle by a spring **(see illustration)**. As the load being carried by the vehicle is altered, the suspension moves in relation to the vehicle body, altering the tension in the spring. The spring then adjusts the pressure-regulating valve lever so that the correct pressure is applied to the rear brakes to suit the load being carried.
2 Minimise fluid loss by first removing the master cylinder reservoir cap, and then tightening it down onto a piece of polythene to obtain an airtight seal.
3 Chock the front wheels, then jack up the rear of the car and support it on axle stands.
4 Slacken and remove the nut and bolt securing the valve spring to the axle.
5 Wipe clean the area around the brake pipe unions on the valve, and place rags beneath the pipe unions to catch any surplus fluid. Make identification marks on the brake pipes; these marks can then be used on refitting to ensure each pipe is correctly reconnected.
6 Slacken the union nuts and disconnect the brake pipes from the valve. Plug or tape over the pipe ends and valve orifices, to minimise the loss of brake fluid and to prevent the entry of dirt into the system. Wash off any spilt fluid immediately with cold water.
7 Using a suitable Allen key or Allen socket, undo the regulating valve-to-mounting bracket bolts, and remove the pressure-regulating valve and spring from below the car.

### Refitting

8 Refitting is the reverse of the removal procedure, noting the following points:

*a) If a new valve is being fitted, set the spring adjustment bolt to the same position as the one on the old valve, and tighten it securely.*
*b) Ensure that the brake pipes are correctly connected to the valve, and that their union nuts are securely tightened.*
*c) Coat the ends of the spring with grease prior to installation.*
*d) Tighten the fixings to the specified torque.*
*e) Bleed the braking system (see Section 2).*
*f) On completion, take the vehicle to a VW dealer to have the valve operation checked and if necessary adjusted.*

## 18 Stop-light switch - removal and refitting

### Removal

1 The stop-light switch is located on the pedal bracket below the facia.
2 Referring to Chapter 11, remove the driver's side glovebox.
3 Reach up behind the facia and disconnect the wiring connector from the switch **(see illustration)**.
4 Twist the switch through 90° clockwise and release it from the mounting bracket **(see illustration)**.

**16.5 Handbrake cable securing clip on rear suspension arm**

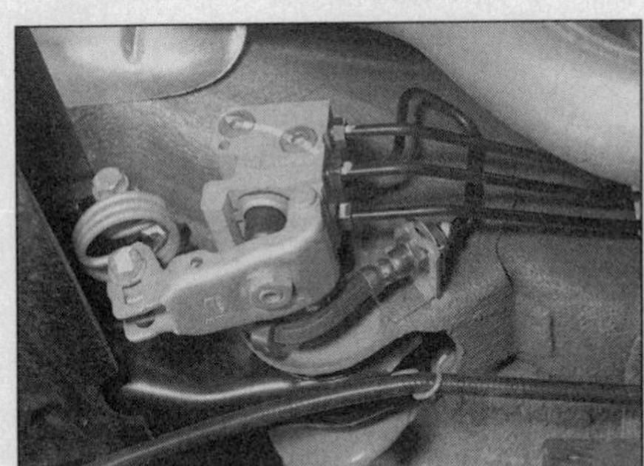

**17.1 Rear brake pressure-regulating valve**

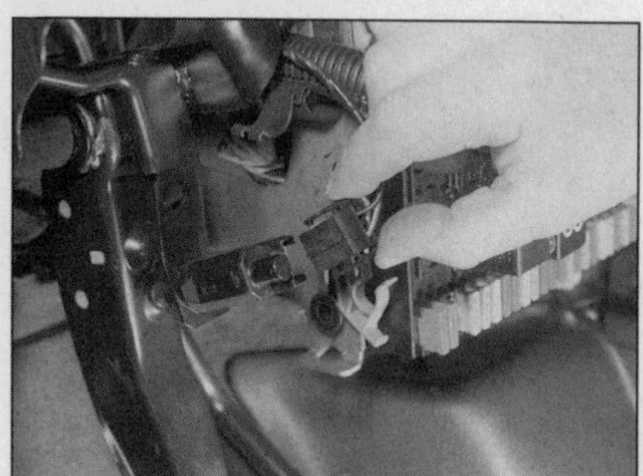

18.3 Disconnect the stop-light switch wiring plug . . .

## Refitting

**5** Prior to installation, fully extend the stop-light switch plunger.

**6** Fully depress and hold the brake pedal, then manoeuvre the switch into position. Secure the switch in position it by twisting it through 90° anti-clockwise, and release the brake pedal.

**7** Reconnect the wiring connector, and check the operation of the stop-lights. The stop-lights should illuminate after the brake pedal has travelled about 5 mm. If the switch is not functioning correctly, it is faulty and must be renewed; no adjustment is possible.

**8** On completion, refit the driver's side glovebox as described in Chapter 11.

# 19 Anti-lock braking system (ABS) - general information

ABS is available as an option on most of the models covered in this manual. The system comprises a hydraulic block (which contains the hydraulic solenoid valves and accumulators), the electrically-driven return pump, and four roadwheel sensors (one fitted to each wheel), and the electronic control unit (ECU). The purpose of the system is to prevent the wheel(s) locking during heavy braking. This is achieved by automatic release of the brake on the relevant wheel, followed by re-application of the brake.

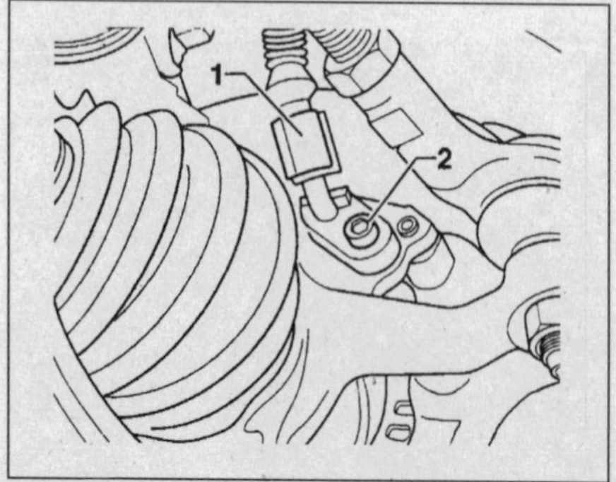


20.5 ABS front wheel sensor wiring plug (1) and retaining bolt (2)

18.4 . . . then twist the switch body 90° clockwise and remove it from the brake pedal

The solenoids are controlled by the ECU, which itself receives signals from the four wheel sensors (one fitted on each hub), which monitor the speed of rotation of each wheel. By comparing these signals, the ECU can determine the speed at which the car is travelling. It can then use this speed to determine when a wheel is decelerating at an abnormal rate, compared to the speed of the car, and therefore predicts when a wheel is about to lock. During normal operation, the system functions in the same way as a non-ABS braking system.

If the ECU senses that a wheel is about to lock, it operates the relevant solenoid valve in the modulator block, which then isolates the brake caliper on the wheel which is about to lock from the master cylinder, effectively sealing-in the hydraulic pressure.

If the speed of rotation of the wheel continues to decrease at an abnormal rate, the ECU switches on the electrically-driven return pump, which pumps the hydraulic fluid back into the master cylinder, releasing pressure on that brake so that the brake is released. Once the speed of rotation of the wheel returns to an acceptable rate, the pump stops; the solenoid valve opens, allowing the hydraulic master cylinder pressure to return to the brake, which then re-applies the brake. This cycle can be carried out at up to 10 times a second.

The action of the solenoid valves and return pump creates pulses in the hydraulic circuit. When the ABS system is functioning, these pulses can be felt through the brake pedal.

The operation of the ABS system is entirely dependent on electrical signals. To prevent the system responding to any inaccurate signals, a built-in safety circuit monitors all signals received by the ECU. If an inaccurate signal or low battery voltage is detected, the ABS system is automatically shut down, and the warning light on the instrument panel is illuminated, to inform the driver that the ABS system is not operational. Normal braking should still be available, however.

If a fault does develop in the ABS system, the car must be taken to a VW dealer for fault diagnosis and repair.

# 20 Anti-lock braking system (ABS) components - removal and refitting

## Hydraulic unit

**1** Removal and refitting of the hydraulic unit should be entrusted to a VW dealer. Great care has to be taken not to allow any fluid to escape from the unit as the pipes are disconnected. If the fluid is allowed to escape, air can enter the unit, causing air locks which cause the hydraulic unit to malfunction.

## Electronic control unit (ECU)

**2** The anti-lock braking system ECU is secured to the hydraulic unit, and can only be separated from it once the pair have been removed as an assembly. This task should be entrusted to a VW dealer.

## Front wheel sensor

### Removal

**3** Chock the rear wheels, then firmly apply the handbrake and loosen the relevant front wheel bolts. Jack up the front of the car and support on axle stands. Remove the appropriate front roadwheel.

**4** Trace the wiring back from the sensor to the connector, freeing it from any retaining clips, and disconnect it from the main loom.

**5** Slacken and remove the bolt securing the sensor to the swivel hub **(see illustration)**, and remove the sensor and lead assembly from the car.

### Refitting

**6** Prior to refitting, apply a thin coat of multi-purpose grease to the sensor body, and to the sensor's location in the swivel hub (VW recommend the use of lubricating paste G 000 650 - available from your dealer).

**7** Fit the sensor to the swivel hub, then refit the retaining bolt and tighten it to the specified torque.

**8** Ensure that the sensor wiring is correctly routed and retained by necessary clips, and reconnect its wiring connector.

**9** Refit the roadwheel, then lower the car to the ground and tighten the roadwheel bolts to the specified torque.

## Rear wheel sensor

### Removal

**10** Chock the front wheels, then loosen the relevant rear wheel bolts. Jack up the rear of the car and support it on axle stands. Remove the appropriate roadwheel.

**11** Fold the rear seat forwards, and lift up any floor covering beneath. Locate the wheel sensor wiring connector, and disconnect it.

**12** Working under the car, unscrew and remove the sensor retaining bolt from the stub axle **(see illustration)**, and withdraw the sensor from the brake.

20.12 ABS rear wheel sensor retaining bolt (arrowed)

13 Trace the sensor wiring back from the sensor, detaching it from the retaining clips. Where the sensor wiring passes into the vehicle interior, prise out the rubber grommet from the vehicle floor, and pull the sensor wiring through. The sensor and its wiring can now be removed from the car.

### Refitting

14 Coat the sensor body and its aperture in the stub axle/brake backplate with a thin coat of multi-purpose grease (VW recommend the use of lubricating paste G 000 650 - available from your dealer).
15 Fit the sensor to the stub axle/brake backplate, then refit the retaining bolt and tighten it to the specified torque.
16 Ensure the sensor wiring is routed correctly, and secured by the retaining clips. Feed the wiring through the hole in the vehicle floor, and seal the hole with the grommet.
17 Inside the car, reconnect the sensor wiring, then refit the floor covering and fold the rear seat upright.
18 Refit the roadwheel, then lower the car to the ground and tighten the roadwheel bolts to the specified torque.

### *Front wheel sensor reluctor rings*

19 The front reluctor rings are fixed onto the rear of wheel hubs. Examine the rings for damage such as chipped or missing teeth. If renewal is necessary, the complete hub assembly must be dismantled as described in Chapter 10.

### *Rear wheel sensor reluctor rings*

20 The rear reluctor rings are pressed onto the inside of the rear brake drum. Examine the rings for signs of damage such as chipped or missing teeth, and renew as necessary. If renewal is necessary, remove the drum as described in Section 7. The reluctor ring can be prised off using two screwdrivers on opposite sides of the ring. Press the new ring on squarely, using a tube or socket of appropriate diameter.

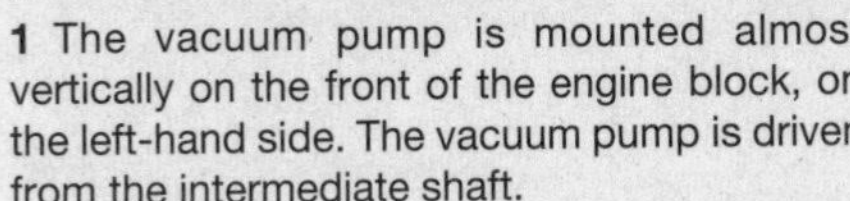

## 21 Vacuum pump (diesel models) - removal and refitting

1 The vacuum pump is mounted almost vertically on the front of the engine block, on the left-hand side. The vacuum pump is driven from the intermediate shaft.
2 The vacuum pump is required to provide a vacuum supply for the servo unit. Diesel engines cannot tap into the inlet manifold for a vacuum supply as on petrol engines, since the manifold is not throttled.

### *Removal*

3 Release the retaining clip, and disconnect the vacuum hose from the top of pump.
4 Slacken and remove the retaining bolt, and remove the pump retaining clamp from the cylinder block.
5 Withdraw the vacuum pump from the cylinder block, and recover the O-ring seal. Examine the O-ring, and obtain a new one for refitting if the old one is damaged or has deteriorated.

### *Refitting*

6 Fit the O-ring to the vacuum pump, and apply a smear of oil to the O-ring to aid installation.
7 Manoeuvre the vacuum pump into position, making sure that the slot in the pump drive gear aligns with the dog on the pump drive gear **(see illustration)**.

21.7 Ensure vacuum pump slot (arrowed) is aligned with the pump drivegear

8 Refit the retaining clamp and tighten its retaining bolt to the specified torque (see Chapter 2B).
9 Reconnect the vacuum hose to the pump, and secure it in position with the retaining clip.

## 22 Vacuum pump (diesel models) - testing and overhaul

1 The operation of the braking system vacuum pump can be checked using a vacuum gauge.
2 Disconnect the vacuum pipe from the pump, and connect the gauge to the pump union using a suitable length of hose.
3 Start the engine and allow it to idle, then measure the vacuum created by the pump. As a guide, after one minute, a minimum of approximately 500 mm Hg should be recorded. If the vacuum registered is significantly less than this, it is likely that the pump is faulty. However, seek the advice of a VW dealer before condemning the pump.
4 Overhaul of the vacuum pump is not possible, since no major components are available separately for it; the only spare part readily available is the pump cover sealing ring. If faulty, the complete pump assembly must be renewed.

# Chapter 10
# Suspension and steering

## Contents



## Degrees of difficulty

**Easy,** suitable for novice with little experience

**Fairly easy,** suitable for beginner with some experience

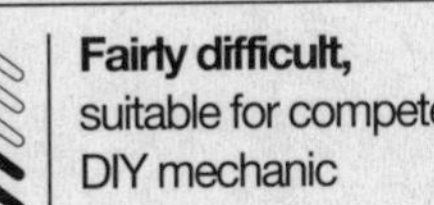

**Fairly difficult,** suitable for competent DIY mechanic

**Difficult,** suitable for experienced DIY mechanic

**Very difficult,** suitable for expert DIY or professional

## Specifications

### General

| | |
|---|---|
| Front suspension type | Independent, with coil spring struts incorporating telescopic shock absorbers; lower wishbones. Anti-roll bar on 1.6 litre and diesel engine models |
| Rear suspension type | Transverse torsion beam with trailing arms. Coil spring struts incorporating telescopic shock absorbers |
| Steering type | Rack-and-pinion. Power assistance on some models |

### Suspension angles/wheel alignment

| | |
|---|---|
| **Front wheels** | |
| Toe-in | 0° ± 10' |
| Camber | -25' ± 20' |
| Castor | +1°20' ± 30' |
| Maximum side-to-side difference: | |
| Camber | 20' |
| Castor | 30' |
| Track angle difference at lock of 20° left and right | -1°05' ± 30' |
| **Rear wheels** | |
| Camber | -1°40' ± 20' |
| Maximum side-to-side difference | 20' |
| Total track (at specified camber) | +20' ± 10' |
| Maximum allowable deviation | 20' |

### Tyre pressures

See end of *Weekly checks*

10

## Torque wrench settings

| | Nm | lbf ft |
|---|---|---|
| **Front suspension** | | |
| Anti-roll bar connecting link nuts | 25 | 18 |
| Anti-roll bar mounting plate bolts | 25 | 18 |
| Brake disc splash shield bolts | 10 | 7 |
| Shock absorber top nut | 60 | 44 |
| Strut upper mounting nut* | 60 | 44 |
| Strut-to-swivel hub mounting nut/bolt* | 95 | 70 |
| Subframe mounting bolt (M12): | | |
| Stage 1 | 50 | 37 |
| Stage 2 | Angle-tighten a further 90° | |
| Wishbone/lower arm balljoint nut | 35 | 26 |
| Wishbone/lower arm balljoint retaining bolts | 35 | 26 |
| Wishbone/lower arm pivot bolt | 70 | 52 |
| Wishbone/lower arm rear mounting through-bolt (M12): | | |
| Stage 1 | 50 | 37 |
| Stage 2 | Angle-tighten a further 90° | |
| **Rear suspension** | | |
| Rear axle pivot bolt nut | 65 | 48 |
| Shock absorber top nuts | 15 | 11 |
| Strut lower mounting nut | 55 | 41 |
| Strut upper mounting nut | 25 | 18 |
| **Manual steering** | | |
| Column height adjuster lever nut (left-hand thread) | 8 | 6 |
| Column height adjuster lever through-bolt (left-hand thread) | 23 | 17 |
| Column lower universal joint (UJ) bolt | 30 | 22 |
| Column upper-to-lower universal joint shaft clamp bolt (up to 1998 model year) | 25 | 18 |
| Horn contact plate bolts* | 7 | 5 |
| Steering gear mounting bolts | 30 | 22 |
| Steering gear pinion clamp bolt | 30 | 22 |
| Steering wheel nut | 50 | 37 |
| Track-rod adjustment locknut | 50 | 37 |
| Track-rod balljoint nut | 35 | 26 |
| **Power steering (where different to manual)** | | |
| Fluid hose banjo bolt | 30 | 22 |
| Fluid reservoir mounting bolts | 5 | 4 |
| Fluid union nuts | 20 | 15 |
| Steering pump mounting bolts | 25 | 18 |
| Steering pump mounting bracket bolts | 45 | 33 |
| Steering pump pulley bolts | 25 | 18 |
| Track-rod-to-steering gear | 80 | 59 |
| **Roadwheels** | | |
| Roadwheel bolts | 110 | 81 |

**Use new nuts/bolts*

## 1 General description

The front suspension is of independent, MacPherson strut and wishbone type. The strut on each side incorporates a telescopic shock absorber and coil spring. The wishbone arms are pivoted from large rubber bushes in the subframe, and are attached to the swivel hubs by a large balljoint. An anti-roll bar is fitted to 1.6 litre and diesel engine models, and is located on the wishbone arms at each end, and also at underbody mountings.

The rear suspension consists of a transverse torsion beam axle with trailing arms. The combined axle and arms pivot from large underbody mountings each side. A coil spring and shock absorber strut are located each side, between the top of the wheel arch and the axle arm at the bottom end, to control axle movement.

Rack-and-pinion steering is fitted, with power assistance on some models. The steering column incorporates a telescopic collapsible section as a safety feature in the event of a collision. A height-adjustable steering column is fitted on some models. Models from 1998 model year onwards have a steering column equipped with a 'torque overload clutch'. This is an additional security device, which ensures that the steering column lock cannot be broken by excessive force. If a torque of more than 100 Nm is applied through the steering wheel, the clutch disengages the column from the front wheels, preventing damage to the lock. The clutch mechanism is overridden when the ignition key is next inserted.

All models except the base 1.0 litre model are equipped with an airbag mounted in the steering wheel. For details, refer to Chapter 12.

## 2 Front suspension strut - removal and refitting

### *Removal*

**1** Chock the rear wheels, apply the handbrake, then loosen the relevant front wheel bolts. Jack up and support the front of the car on axle stands (see *Jacking and vehicle support*). Remove the roadwheel on the side concerned.

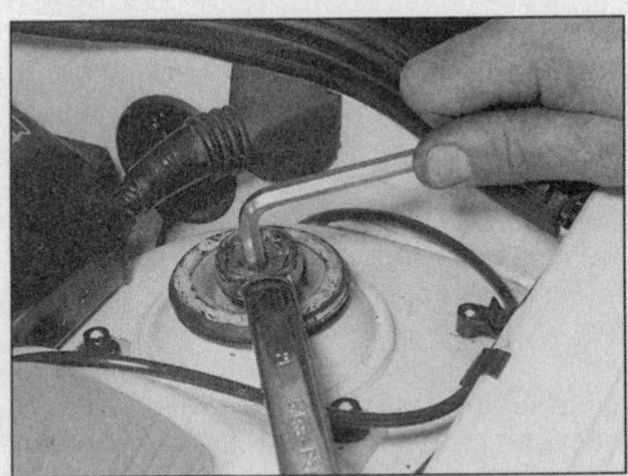

**2.3a Holding the piston rod stationary with an Allen key . . .**

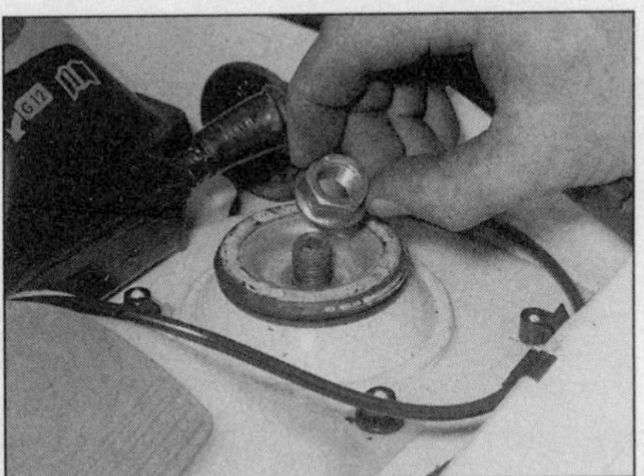

**2.3b . . . loosen and remove the strut upper mounting nut**

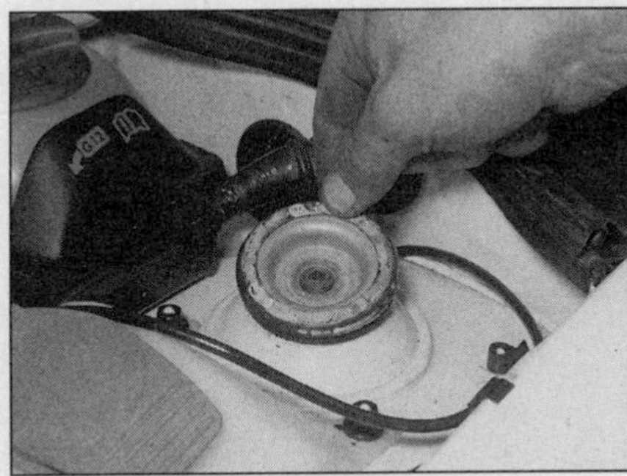

**2.3c Lift off the stop plate from the top of the strut**

**2.4a Loosen and remove the strut-to-swivel hub nuts . . .**

**2.4b . . . and remove the bolts, noting their direction of fitting**

2 Position a jack under the outer end of the wishbone arm for support.

3 In the engine compartment, unscrew and remove the strut upper mounting nut whilst holding the piston rod stationary with a 7 mm Allen key. It is recommended that the self-locking nut be renewed once removed. Lift off the stop plate **(see illustrations)**.

4 Scribe an alignment mark around the periphery of the suspension strut-to-swivel hub location lugs, to ensure accurate positioning when refitting. Also mark the upper and lower retaining bolts to identify one from the other. This is essential, as the fitted position of the strut to swivel hub (and of the bolts) sets the camber angle. It is therefore critical that they be refitted in exactly the same position during reassembly. Undo the retaining nuts (18 mm on project car), and withdraw the two bolts securing the strut at its bottom end to the swivel hub, noting that the bolts are fitted from the front **(see illustrations)**. Renew the self-locking nuts.

5 Disengage the strut from its top mounting, then prise it free from the swivel hub **(see illustration)**.

6 Note that the lower balljoint must not be detached from the wishbone without first referring to Section 6.

### *Refitting*

7 Refitting is a reversal of the removal procedure. Tighten all fasteners to the specified torque **(see illustration)**. Use new self-locking nuts to secure the strut-to-swivel hub bolts. Insert the bolts from the front of the swivel hubs. Ensure the correct realignment of the two units (as marked during removal), to ensure that the camber angle is maintained. If a new strut and/or swivel hub have been fitted, have the camber angle checked and if necessary adjusted by a VW dealer.

## 3 Front suspension strut and coil spring - separation and reassembly

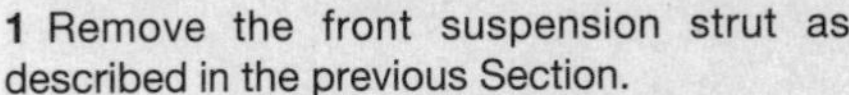

1 Remove the front suspension strut as described in the previous Section.

***Warning: Before attempting to dismantle the suspension strut, a suitable tool to hold the coil spring in compression must be obtained. Adjustable coil spring compressors are readily available, and are***

**2.5 Removing the suspension strut from under the front wheel arch**

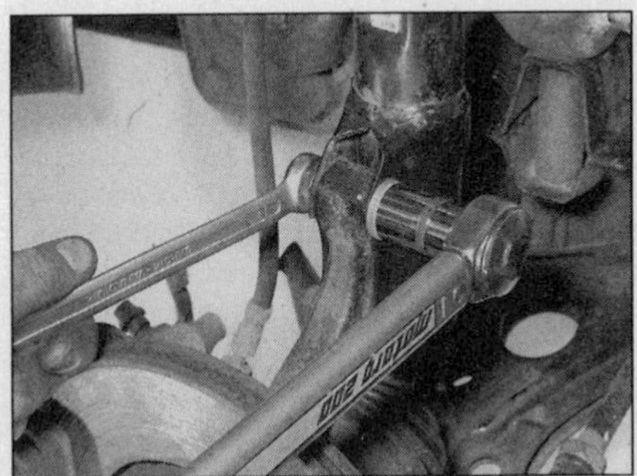

**2.7 Tighten the strut-to-swivel hub nuts/bolts to the specified torque**

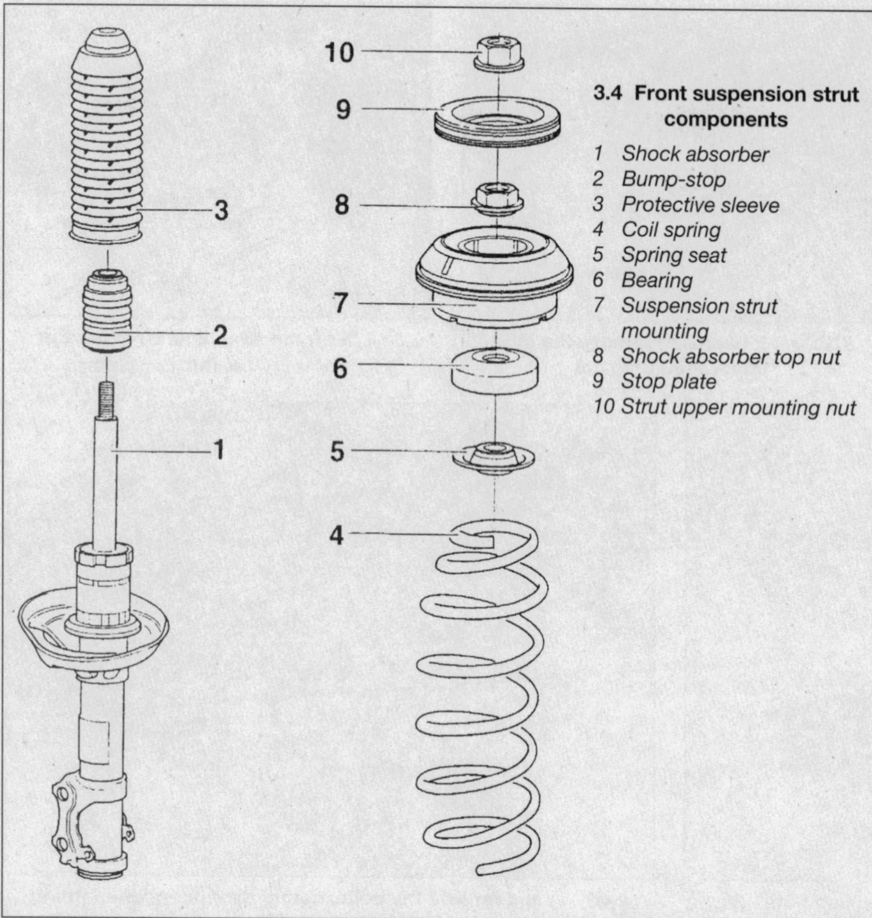


**3.4 Front suspension strut components**

1 *Shock absorber*
2 *Bump-stop*
3 *Protective sleeve*
4 *Coil spring*
5 *Spring seat*
6 *Bearing*
7 *Suspension strut mounting*
8 *Shock absorber top nut*
9 *Stop plate*
10 *Strut upper mounting nut*

***recommended for this operation. Any attempt to dismantle the strut without such a tool is likely to result in damage or personal injury.***

**2** Support the lower end of the strut in a vice, then fit the coil spring compressor into position, and check that it is securely located.

**3** Compress the spring until the upper spring seat is free of tension, then remove the nut from the top of the piston rod. As with removing the strut upper mounting nut, hold the piston rod with a 7 mm Allen key while the nut is unscrewed. The need to hold the piston rod means that an ordinary deep socket cannot readily be used; in the workshop, we used a deep socket with hex flats on it (a box spanner would also work), which could be held using a spanner **(see illustration 3.9i)**. The nut is especially tight - don't expect to use makeshift means to loosen it safely.

**4** Remove the strut mounting, followed by the bearing and the spring seat **(see illustration)**. Note the fitted order and orientation of all components, for use when refitting.

**5** Lift the coil spring from the strut with the compressor still in position. Mark the top of the spring for reference.

**6** Withdraw the protective sleeve and bump-stop from the piston rod, noting their order of removal.

**7** Move the shock absorber piston rod up and down through its complete stroke, and check that the resistance is even and smooth. If there are any signs or seizing or lack of resistance, or if fluid has been leaking excessively, the shock absorber should be renewed.

**3.9a Slide on the bump stop . . .**

**3.9b . . . followed by the protective sleeve**

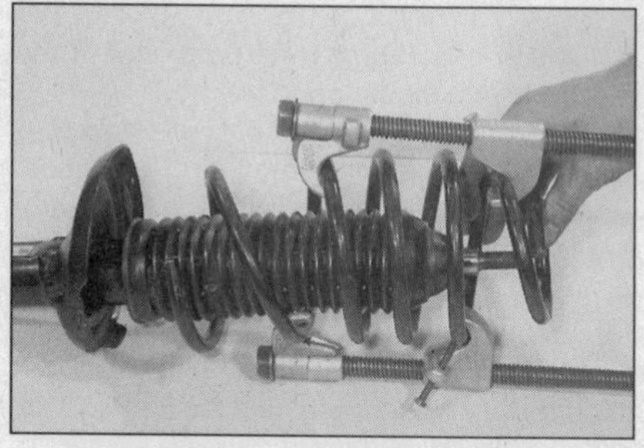

**3.9c Taking care that the spring compressor is not accidentally released, fit the spring over the strut . . .**

**3.9d . . . ensuring that the spring end (arrowed) engages with the recess in the lower spring seat**

**3.9e Fit the upper spring seat . . .**

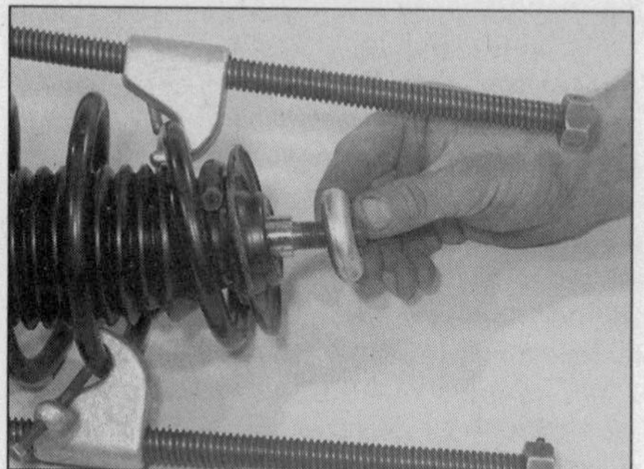

**3.9f . . . strut top bearing . . .**

3.9g . . . and rubber mounting, ensuring that all components are orientated correctly

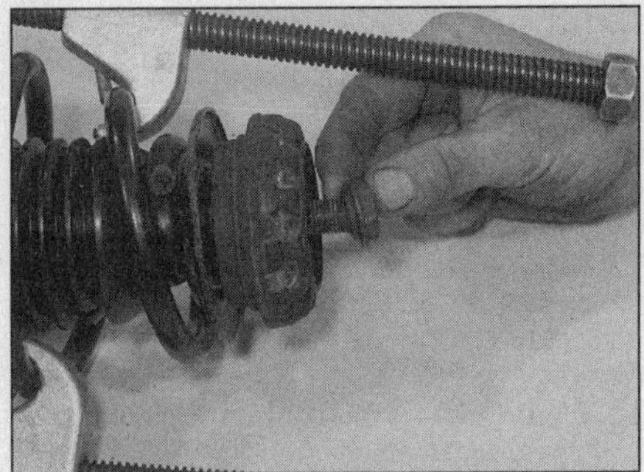

3.9h Fit the shock absorber top nut . . .

3.9i . . . and tighten it to the specified torque, holding the piston rod with an Allen key - note the use of a deep socket with hex flats

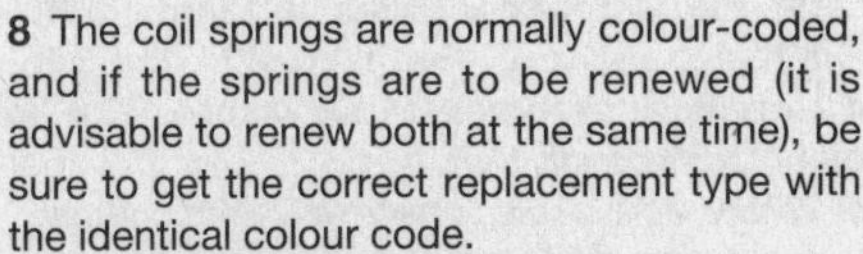

**8** The coil springs are normally colour-coded, and if the springs are to be renewed (it is advisable to renew both at the same time), be sure to get the correct replacement type with the identical colour code.

**9** To reassemble the strut, follow the accompanying photos, beginning with **illustration 3.9a**. Be sure to stay in order, and carefully read the caption underneath each.

## 4 Front swivel hub - removal and refitting

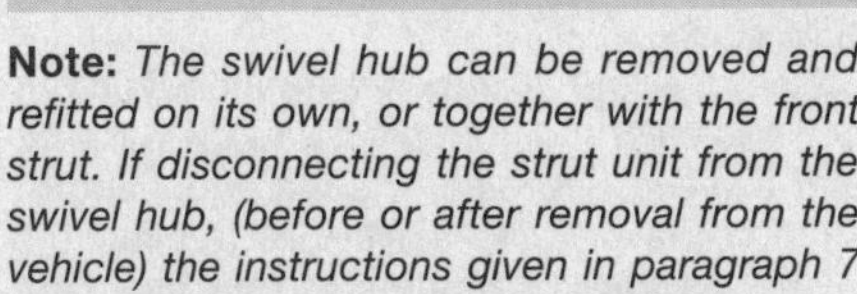

**Note:** *The swivel hub can be removed and refitted on its own, or together with the front strut. If disconnecting the strut unit from the swivel hub, (before or after removal from the vehicle) the instructions given in paragraph 7 of Section 2 must be noted and adhered to.*

### Removal

**1** Firmly apply the handbrake and chock the rear wheels. Where applicable, remove the relevant front wheel trim to gain access to the driveshaft nut or bolt through the centre of the roadwheel.

**2** Loosen, but do not remove, the driveshaft retaining nut or bolt. The weight of the vehicle must be on the ground, as the nut/bolt is tightened to a very high torque, and it would be dangerous to try loosening it with the vehicle raised.

**3** Loosen the relevant front wheel bolts.

**4** Raise the front of the vehicle and support it on axle stands (see *Jacking and vehicle support*). Remove the relevant front roadwheel.

**5** Unscrew and remove the driveshaft nut/bolt, and recover the washer, where applicable **(see illustration)**.

**6** Remove the brake caliper and disc as described in Chapter 9. The brake caliper can be tied up out of the way, leaving the hydraulic hose attached but clear of the strut.

**7** Where applicable, refer to Chapter 9 and remove the ABS front wheel sensor from the side concerned.

**8** Remove the expanding rivets and detach the air deflector from the wishbone/lower arm.

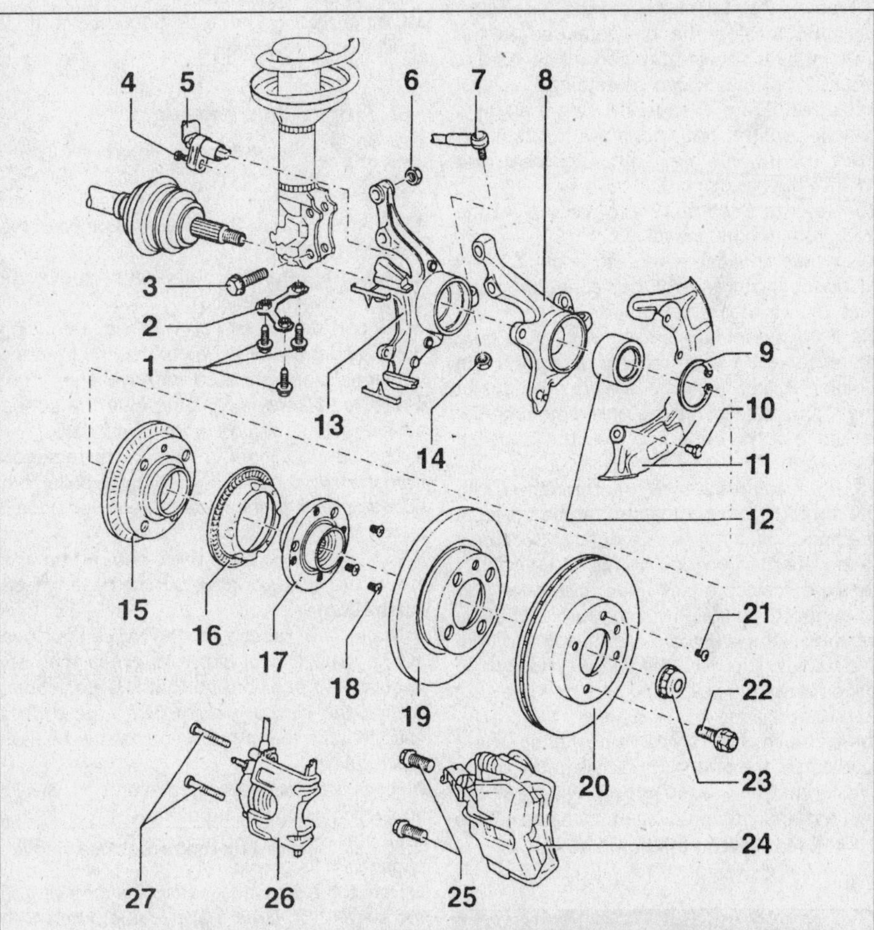


**4.5 Front swivel hub and related components**

1 *Lower balljoint retaining bolts*
2 *Lower balljoint retaining plate*
3 *Strut-to-swivel hub bolt*
4 *ABS wheel sensor retaining bolt*
5 *ABS wheel sensor*
6 *Strut-to-swivel hub nut*
7 *Track rod*
8 *Swivel hub (16-valve models only)*
9 *Wheel bearing retaining circlip*
10 *Brake splash shield retaining bolt*
11 *Brake splash shield*
12 *Wheel bearing*
13 *Swivel hub*
14 *Track rod nut*
15 *Wheel hub with integral ABS rotor*
16 *ABS rotor*
17 *Wheel hub*
18 *Wheel hub-to-ABS rotor screws*
19 *Brake disc (solid type)*
20 *Brake disc (ventilated type)*
21 *Brake disc securing screw*
22 *Roadwheel bolt*
23 *Driveshaft nut*
24 *VW Type 2 brake caliper*
25 *Caliper mounting bolts*
26 *VW Type 1 brake caliper*
27 *Caliper mounting bolts*

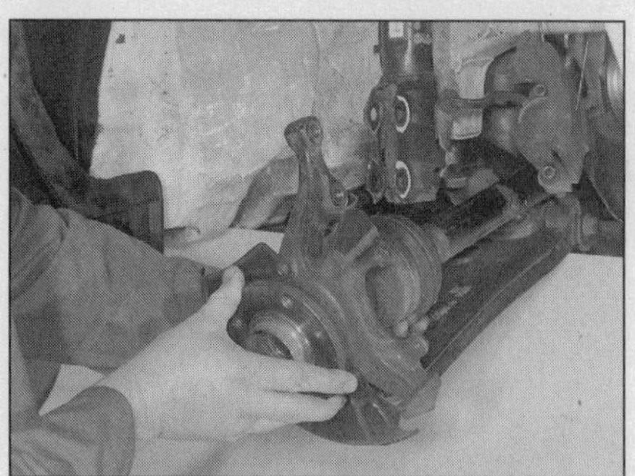

**4.14 Free the swivel hub from the driveshaft splines, and remove it from the car**

**9** Loosen the nut on top of the lower arm balljoint, leaving the nut attached to the balljoint by a couple of threads. If necessary, the balljoint shank can be retained using a cut-down 5 mm Allen key. Using a suitable balljoint splitter tool, separate the balljoint from the swivel hub, then unscrew and remove the balljoint nut.

**10** Refer to Section 19 and disconnect the track-rod from the swivel hub.

**11** Where applicable, refer to Section 7 and disconnect the anti-roll bar connecting link from the wishbone.

**12** If the swivel hub is to be separated from the suspension strut, refer to paragraph 7 in Section 2, and mark the relative positions of the items described before removing the retaining bolts. Prise free the strut from the swivel hub.

**13** If removing the swivel hub together with the strut, disconnect the strut at the top from the body mounting, as described in Section 2. If the suspension coil spring is still under tension, position a jack under the swivel hub to support the weight of the hub and strut; when the strut is detached at the top end from the body, lower the jack slowly to decompress the coil spring and allow the strut to be disengaged from the body.

**14** Remove the swivel hub (and where applicable, the strut), withdrawing it from the driveshaft **(see illustration)**. Withdraw the hub assembly from the shaft, using a suitable puller if necessary, or carefully tap it free.

**5.5 Removing the front wheel bearing retaining circlip**

### *Refitting*

**15** Refitting is a reversal of the removal procedure. Refer to Chapter 8 for details on reconnecting the driveshaft, and Chapter 9 when refitting the wheel sensor, brake disc and caliper.

**16** When reconnecting the suspension strut to the swivel hub, ensure that the two are correctly realigned before tightening the retaining bolts.

**17** When refitting the bottom balljoint nut, hold the balljoint shank stationary using a cut-down 5 mm Allen key.

**18** Do not fully tighten the driveshaft retaining nut/bolt or the anti-roll bar connecting link nut until after the vehicle is lowered, and with its full weight on the wheels.

**19** All fastenings must be tightened to their specified torque settings.

## 5 Front wheel bearing - renewal

**1** Remove the swivel hub, as described in the previous Section.

**2** Undo the retaining bolts, and remove the brake disc splash shield.

**3** Support the swivel hub with the hub facing down, and press or drive out the hub from the housing. Unscrew and remove the three cross-head screws, and remove the speed sensor reluctor ring on models with ABS.

**4** The bearing inner race can be removed from the swivel hub using a suitable puller, but note that the bearing must be renewed once it is removed.

**5** Extract the circlip, then supporting the swivel hub, press or drive out the bearing **(see illustration)**.

**6** Clean the recess in the housing, then support the swivel hub and press the new bearing into position, so that it is positioned behind the circlip groove. If a tube drift is used, ensure that it butts against the bearing outer race only.

**7** Press the inner bearing race onto the swivel hub, using a suitable tube drift.

**8** Fit the circlip, and ensure that it is fully engaged in its groove.

**9** Refit the ABS wheel sensor reluctor ring to the swivel hub (where applicable), then with the swivel hub positioned and supported with its bearing shoulder facing up, press or drive the bearing housing into position.

**10** Refit the brake disc splash shield.

**11** Refit the swivel hub as described in the previous Section.

**12** When the driveshaft nut/bolt and roadwheel bolts have been tightened to the specified torque, raise the car again so that the front wheels are clear of the ground. Referring to Chapter 1 *Suspension and steering check*, rotate the wheels by hand to ensure that they turn freely, without binding. There should be no excessive lateral play.

## 6 Wishbone/lower arm - removal, overhaul and refitting

### *Removal*

**1** Apply the handbrake and chock the rear wheels, then loosen the relevant front roadwheel bolts. Raise and support the front of the vehicle on axle stands (see *Jacking and vehicle support*). Remove the relevant front roadwheel.

**2** Remove the expanding rivets and detach the air deflector plate from the wishbone **(see illustration opposite)**.

**3** Position a jack under the centre of the subframe and raise it to support (not lift) the subframe.

**4** Unbolt and remove the wishbone rear mounting through-bolt.

**5** Where applicable, unscrew the connecting link nut, and detach the anti-roll bar from the wishbone. As it is removed, note that the connecting link-to-wishbone mounting bush is fitted with its conical side towards the wishbone.

**6** Refer to Section 4, paragraph 9 and disconnect the bottom balljoint from the swivel hub.

**7** Unscrew and remove the pivot bolt from the front inboard end of the wishbone arm (to subframe).

**8** Remove the wishbone, manoeuvring it down to clear the front pivot and the balljoint, and twisting it to clear the rear mounting. A suitable lever will assist in freeing the wishbone from its mountings, but take care not to damage adjacent components.

### *Overhaul*

**9** With the wishbone removed, clean it for inspection.

**10** Check the balljoint for excessive wear, and check the pivot bushes for deterioration. Also examine the wishbone arm for damage and distortion. If necessary, the balljoint and bushes should be renewed.

**11** To renew the balljoint, first outline its exact position on the wishbone. This is important as the relative positions of the wishbone and the balljoint are set during production, and the new balljoint must be accurately positioned when fitting it. Unscrew the bolts and remove the balljoint and clamp plate. Fit a new balljoint in the exact outline, and tighten the bolts. If fitting a new wishbone, locate the balljoint centrally in the elongated hole.

**12** To renew the front pivot bush, use a long bolt, together with a metal tube and washers, to pull the bush from the wishbone. Fit the new bush using the same method but, to ease insertion, dip the bush into soapy water first.

**13** The rear mounting rubber bush can be removed in the same manner as the front pivot bush.

14 Press or drive the new mounting bush into position from the top of the wishbone, but ensure that it is positioned correctly, as shown **(see illustration)**.

### *Refitting*

15 Refitting the wishbone is a reverse of removal, noting the following points:

*a) Delay fully tightening the pivot bolts until the weight of the car is on the wheels.*

*b) Tighten all fasteners to the specified torque (where given).*

*c) Refer to Section 4 when reconnecting the balljoint.*

*d) Refer to Section 7 when reconnecting the anti-roll bar.*

*e) Have the front wheel alignment checked and, if necessary, adjusted on completion.*

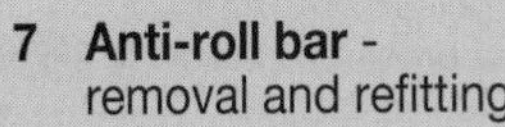

## 7 Anti-roll bar - removal and refitting

### *Removal*

1 Apply the handbrake and chock the rear wheels, then loosen the front roadwheel bolts. Raise and support the front of the vehicle on axle stands (see *Jacking and vehicle support*). For better access, remove the front roadwheels.

2 Unscrew and remove the anti-roll bar mounting plate retaining bolts, then unhook the plates from the subframe locations **(see illustration)**.

3 Unscrew the connecting link nut, and detach the anti-roll bar from the wishbone each side. As they are removed, note that the connecting link-to-wishbone mounting bushes are fitted with their conical side facing the wishbone **(see illustration)**.

4 Lower the anti-roll bar, and remove it from under the vehicle.

5 Renew the anti-roll bar if it is damaged or distorted. Renew the mounting bushes if they are perished or worn.

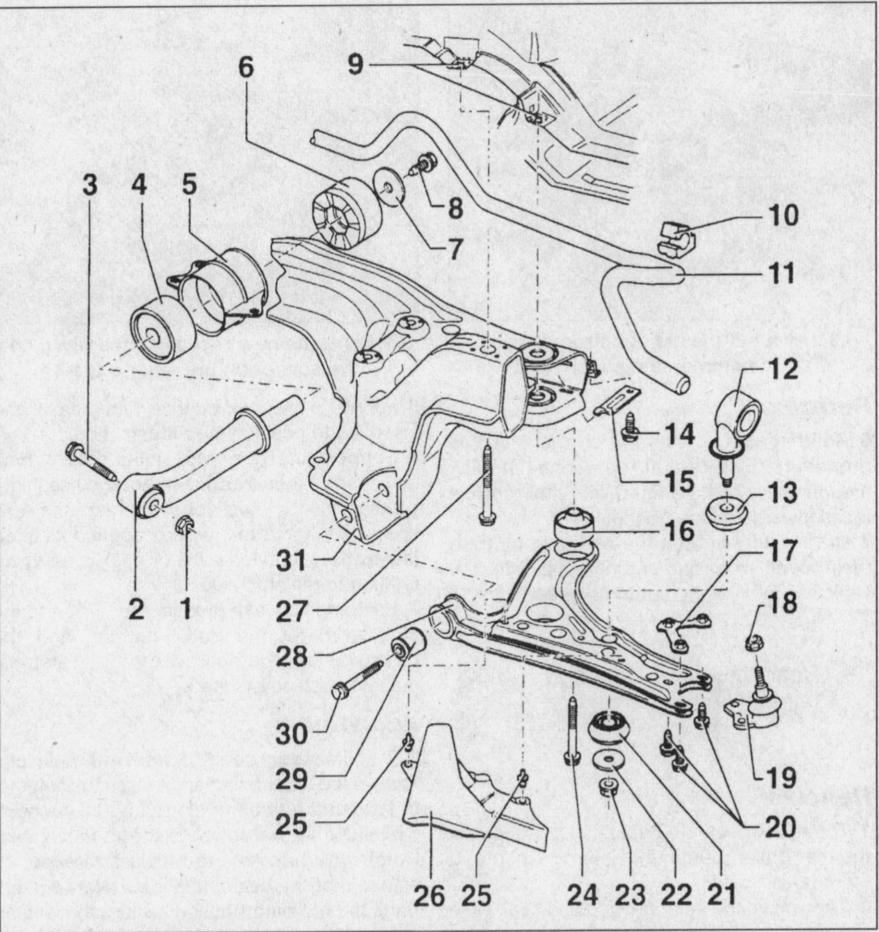


**6.2 Wishbone/lower arm and related components**

*1 Nut*
*2 Engine/transmission rear mounting*
*3 Through-bolt*
*4 Rubber mounting*
*5 Rubber mounting housing*
*6 Rubber mounting*
*7 Washer*
*8 Bolt*
*9 Captive nuts*
*10 Anti-roll bar bush*
*11 Anti-roll bar*
*12 Anti-roll bar connecting link*
*13 Connecting link bush*
*14 Anti-roll bar mounting plate bolt*
*15 Anti-roll bar mounting plate*
*16 Wishbone rear mounting*
*17 Retaining plate*
*18 Lower balljoint nut*
*19 Lower balljoint*
*20 Lower balljoint bolts*
*21 Connecting link bush*
*22 Washer*
*23 Connecting link nut*
*24 Wishbone rear mounting bolt*
*25 Spreader*
*26 Air deflector plate*
*27 Subframe mounting bolt*
*28 Wishbone/lower arm*
*29 Wishbone front mounting bush*
*30 Wishbone front mounting bolt*
*31 Subframe*

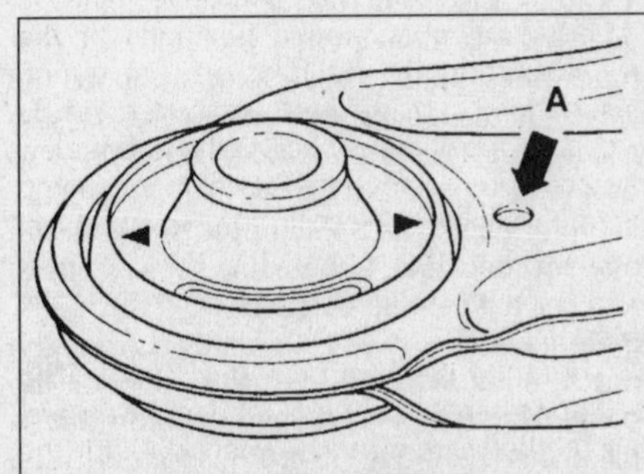


**6.14 Fitted position of wishbone rear mounting**

*One of the embossed arrows must align with the projection (A) on top of the wishbone*

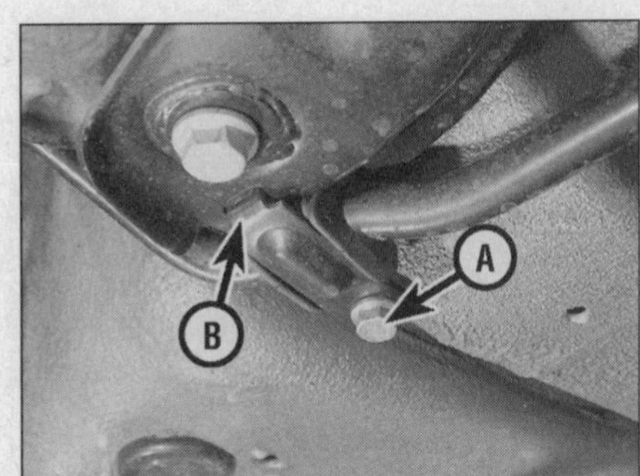


**7.2 Anti-roll bar mounting plate bolt (A) - plate is hooked into subframe at point (B)**

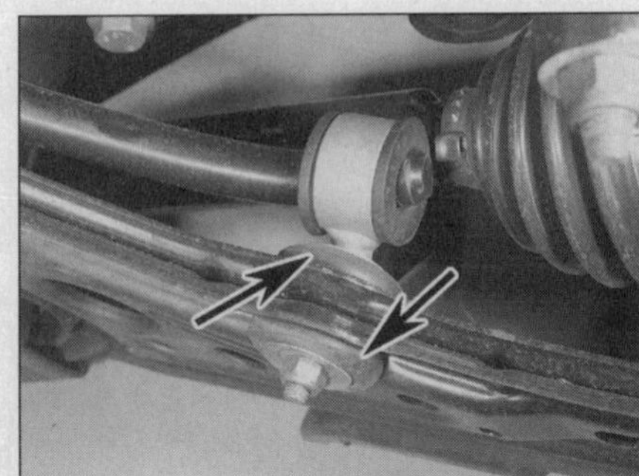

**7.3 Anti-roll bar mounting bushes (arrowed)**

8.3 Drive out the old outer races using a hammer and punch

8.4 Drive the new races in squarely, using a socket on the outer edge

### Refitting

**6** Refitting is a reversal of the removal procedure. Ensure that the connecting link mounting bushes are fitted with their conical faces towards the wishbone.

**7** Do not fully tighten the retaining bolts to their specified torque settings until after the vehicle is fully lowered onto its wheels.

## 8 Rear wheel hub bearings - renewal and adjustment

### Renewal

**1** The rear wheel hub bearings are housed in the rear brake drum/hub. Refer to Chapter 9 for removal details.

**2** Wipe clean the inner bearing and seal. Note the direction of fitting, then lever the seal from the hub. On models with ABS, take care not to damage the speed sensor rotor. Extract the inner bearing from the hub.

**3** The races can be driven out using a suitable soft metal drift, but take care not to damage the hub or ABS speed sensor rotor **(see illustration)**.

**4** Clean the bearing race locations in the hub. Use a tube drift of suitable diameter to drive or press the new races into position in the hub each side **(see illustration)**. Ensure that they are squarely and fully inserted. If using the old bearings, be sure to keep the original bearings and races together. Never interchange new bearings with old races, or vice-versa.

**5** Lubricate the inner bearing with grease, and insert it into position **(see illustration)**.

**6** Support the hub with its outboard face down, and carefully drive the new oil seal into position, taking care not to damage the ABS speed sensor rotor, where applicable **(see illustration)**. Lubricate the oil seal lip ready for refitting to the stub axle.

**7** Pack the hub with grease, then refit it to the stub axle. Fit the outer bearing and the thrustwasher, then screw the hub retaining nut into position by hand.

### Adjustment

**8** If not already done, extract the split pin, remove the locking ring and loosen the hub nut.

**9** Tighten the hub nut slowly, up to the point where it only just touches the thrustwasher. Rotate the hub as the nut is tightened, to ensure that the bearings are correctly seated. Back the nut off a fraction so that the washer can just be seen to move when prodded with a screwdriver. Fit the locking ring and insert a new split pin to secure.

**10** Beware of overtightening the hub nut, as this will cause premature bearing wear. If you are adjusting a bearing which has been in service for some time, when play has been noted, do not overtighten to compensate for wear - this is potentially dangerous and unlikely to effect anything more than a temporary solution.

**11** Smear a liberal amount of grease into the cap, then carefully drive the grease cap into position. If the grease cap is badly dented or distorted, such that it is no longer a tight fit, a new one should be fitted.

8.5 Work grease into the taper-roller inner bearing prior to fitting to the hub

8.6 Grease the lips of the oil seal, and press it into the rear of the hub

**12** If a new bearing has been fitted, it is advisable to check for play after a few hundred miles. Re-adjust the bearing if necessary.

## 9 Rear stub axle - removal and refitting

### Removal

**1** Chock the front roadwheels, engage 1st gear (or P), then loosen the relevant rear roadwheel bolts. Raise the vehicle at the rear and support it on axle stands (see *Jacking and vehicle support*).

**2** Refer to the appropriate Sections in Chapter 9, and proceed with the following:

*a) Remove the brake drum/hub.*
*b) Remove the brake shoe assembly.*
*c) Disconnect the brake hydraulic line from the wheel cylinder.*
*d) Disconnect the handbrake cable.*
*e) On models with ABS, remove the rear wheel sensor.*

**3** Undo the four retaining bolts and remove the brake backplate and stub axle. Note that two of the bolts are used to retain the handbrake cable guide - recover the guide as the bolts are removed, noting its fitted orientation.

### Refitting

**4** Refit in the reverse order of removal.

**5** Refer to the appropriate Sections in Chapter 9 to refit the brake system components. When refitting the drum/hub, adjust the wheel hub bearings as described in Section 8 of this Chapter.

**6** Bleed the brake hydraulic circuit and adjust the handbrake, as described in Chapter 9.

## 10 Rear suspension strut and coil spring - removal and refitting

### Removal

**1** Chock the front roadwheels, engage 1st gear (or P), then loosen the relevant rear roadwheel bolts. Raise and support the vehicle at the rear on axle stands (see *Jacking and vehicle support*). Allow the suspension to extend fully.

**2** From inside the vehicle, tilt forwards the rear seat backrest. Unhook the support straps and pull out the rear parcel shelf.

**3** Remove the two Torx screws from the parcel shelf side support, then unhook the panel from the two retaining lugs on the C-pillar and remove it from the car **(see illustration)**.

**4** If the right-hand rear strut is being removed on models provided with a first aid kit storage compartment, turn the two fasteners through 90° and lower the side trim panel. Otherwise,

10.3 Removing the parcel shelf side support

10.5 Pull off the domed cover from the top of the suspension strut

10.6 Hold the piston rod stationary using a suitable spanner, and unscrew the upper mounting nut

prise out the plastic retainer(s) holding the upper part of the carpeted side trim panel in place, and fold the carpet down for access to the strut upper mounting. It may be helpful to remove, or at least loosen, several peripheral trim panels to achieve improved access - see Chapter 11.

**5** Pull the domed cover off the strut upper mounting for access to the nut beneath **(see illustration)**.

**6** Using a small open-ended spanner on the piston rod flats if necessary, unscrew and remove the upper mounting nut **(see illustration)**. Recover the large dished washer if it is loose.

**7** Working underneath the vehicle, engage a spanner on the nut securing the strut bottom mounting bolt, then unscrew the bolt and remove it. Take care that the ABS wheel sensor wiring is not damaged as the strut is being worked on - if preferred, remove the wheel sensor as described in Chapter 9.

**8** Disengage the strut at the bottom end, and withdraw the strut downwards (complete with coil spring) from the vehicle.

### Refitting

**9** Refit in the reverse order of removal. Ensure that the strut is correctly located at the top end, and then engage the lower end with the trailing arm.

**10** Tighten the retaining bolts to their specified torque settings, but delay full tightening of the upper mounting nut and lower mounting bolt until after the vehicle is lowered fully, and standing on its wheels.

## 11 Rear suspension strut and coil spring - separation and reassembly

**1** The component parts of the strut and coil spring are as shown **(see illustration)**.

***Warning: Before attempting to dismantle the suspension strut, a suitable tool to hold the coil spring in compression must be obtained. Adjustable coil spring compressors are readily available, and are recommended for this operation. Any attempt to dismantle the strut without such a tool is likely to result in damage or personal injury.***

**2** Fit the spring compressor, and ensure that it is fully located. Compress the spring so that the tension on the top mounting retainer is relieved.

**3** Prise free the cover cap and remove the sealing O-ring.

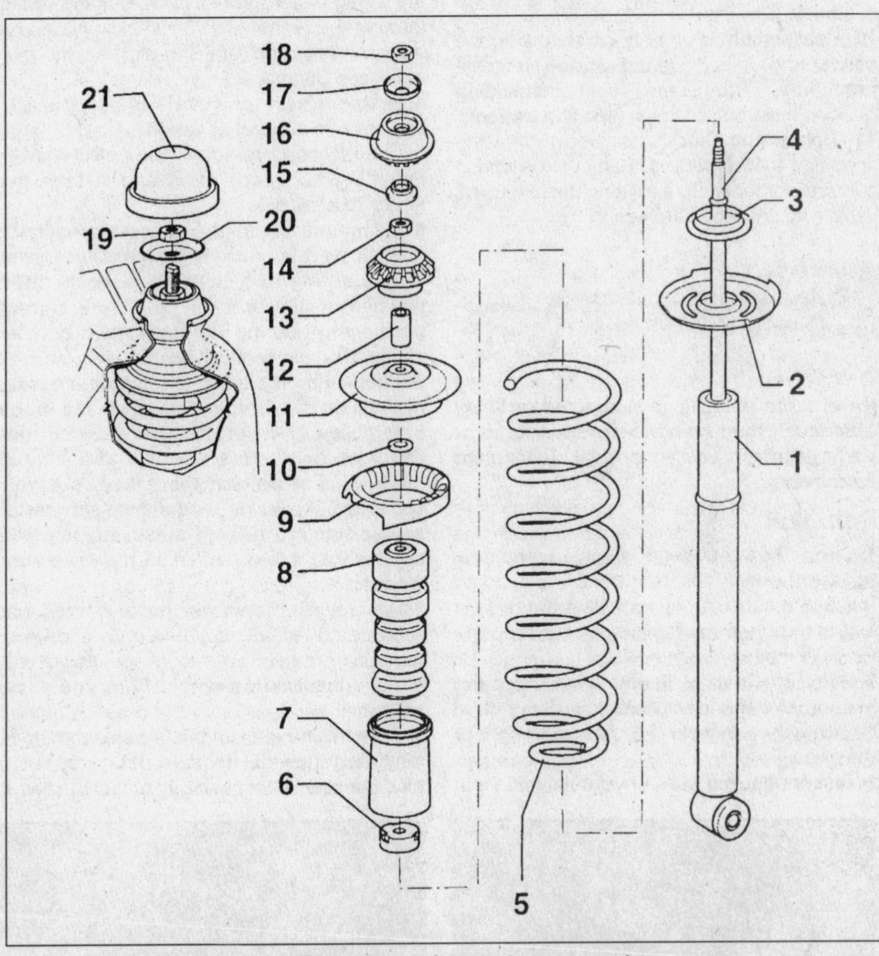


11.1 Rear suspension strut components

1 Shock absorber
2 Lower spring seat
3 Packing piece
4 Piston rod and circlip
5 Coil spring
6 Protective cap
7 Protective tube
8 Bump-stop
9 Upper spring seat
10 Washer
11 Upper spring plate
12 Spacer tube
13 Lower mounting rubber bush
14 Nut
15 Cover
16 Upper mounting rubber bush
17 Cover
18 Nut
19 Upper mounting nut
20 Dished washer
21 Domed cover

4 Unscrew and remove the shock absorber top nut, then remove the large cover, rubber bush, small cover and the nut beneath.
5 Withdraw the spacer tube and washer, the lower bush, spring plate and spring seat.
6 Lift the coil spring from the strut with the compressor still in position. Mark the top of the spring for reference.
7 Remove the bump-stop, tube, and plastic cap. Release the circlip and remove the lower spring seat and packing piece(s).
8 Note that the coil springs are colour-coded, and if renewal is necessary, check that the correct replacement is supplied for your vehicle. It is advisable to renew both rear springs at the same time, to ensure even handling characteristics.
9 Check the operation of the shock absorber in the same manner described for the front units in Section 3, paragraph 7. Renew if necessary, as the shock absorbers cannot be overhauled.
10 Reassembly of the shock absorber and coil spring is a reversal of the removal procedure. The spring seat installation position must be as shown **(see illustration)**.
11 Tighten the shock absorber nuts to the specified torque setting. Remove the spring compressor tool before refitting the unit to the vehicle as described in Section 10.

## 12 Rear torsion beam axle - removal and refitting

**Note:** *If the rear axle is suspected of being distorted, it must be checked in position by a VW garage, using optical alignment equipment.*

### Removal

1 Chock the front wheels, engage 1st gear (or P), then loosen the rear roadwheel bolts. Raise and support the vehicle at the rear on axle stands (see *Jacking and vehicle support*). Remove the rear roadwheels.
2 Refer to Chapter 9 and disconnect the handbrake cable from each rear brake, then detach the cable from the clips securing it to the axle.
3 Disconnect the brake hydraulic line from each rear brake, and from the attachment points on the axle, referring to Chapter 9 for details. Either remove the ABS wheel sensors (where applicable) completely, or disconnect the wiring under the rear seat, pull the wiring through the grommet in the vehicle floor, and detach it from the retaining clips on the rear axle - see Chapter 9.
4 Position jacks or stands under the axle each side to support its weight.
5 Unbolt and remove the strut lower mounting bolt each side, and detach the struts from the axle.
6 Disengage the brake pressure regulator spring from the bracket. If necessary, loosen off the spring bolt, but first mark its fitted position on the bracket, to ensure correct positioning during reassembly, or the regulator adjustment will be lost.
7 Check that all associated fittings are clear of the axle. Cover the stub axles and brake assemblies to ensure that they do not get damaged or dirty as the axle assembly is removed. Ensure that the axle is securely supported. If possible, engage the services of an assistant to help in steadying the axle assembly as it is detached and lowered from the vehicle.
8 Unscrew and remove the pivot bolt nut each side, then withdraw the bolts and lower the axle from the pivot/mountings. Lower and remove the axle assembly from under the vehicle.
9 If the mounting/pivot bushes are worn, they must be renewed. Remove the outer bush, then the inner bush, using a suitable puller. It is important that the mounting is not driven out, or else the seating would be enlarged.
10 Dip the new bushes in soapy water, to lubricate them for ease of fitting. Press each bush in from the outside with a puller, ensuring that the rubber/metal protrusions on the inner face point to the front, and the outer section points to the rear. Insert each half to the point where the conical part is in contact with the axle. Fit each half one at a time.

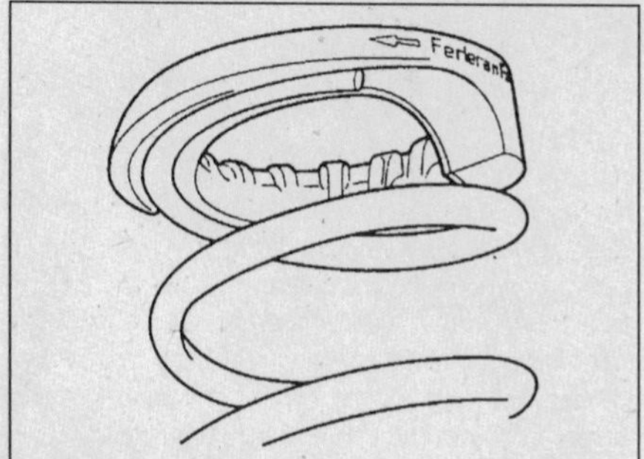

**11.10 The spring seat must be installed so that the arrow aligns with the end of the spring**

### Refitting

11 Refitting is a reversal of the removal procedure. When the axle is raised into position, loosely assemble the retaining bolts and nuts until the axle is fully located before tightening them fully to the specified torque settings.
12 When reconnecting the brake hydraulic lines, handbrake cables and ABS wiring, ensure that everything is correctly routed and secured. Bleed the hydraulic system and adjust the handbrake as described in Chapter 9. When reconnecting the brake pressure regulator spring, its fitted position to the bracket must be as marked during removal.

## 13 Steering wheel - removal and refitting

### Removal

1 Set the front wheels in the straight-ahead position, and release the steering lock by inserting the ignition key. Ensure that the direction indicator lever is in the central 'off' position.

#### Models without an airbag

2 Prise free the horn push-button from the centre of the steering wheel. Note the location of the horn wiring, and disconnect it from the terminals on the cover.
3 Mark the steering wheel and inner column in relation to each other, then unscrew the nut and withdraw the steering wheel. If it is tight, tap it up near the centre, using the palm of your hand, or twist it from side to side, whilst pulling upwards to release it. Remove the washer, where fitted.

#### Models with an airbag

4 Remove the airbag unit from the centre of the steering wheel, as described in Chapter 12.
5 Slacken and remove the two retaining screws underneath, and remove the steering column upper and lower shrouds **(see illustrations)**.
6 Trace the wiring back from the airbag contact unit in the steering wheel, pull up the foam tube, and disconnect the wiring connector **(see illustration)**.
7 Remove the steering wheel as described above in paragraph 3 **(see illustration)**.
8 With the steering wheel removed, rotate the contact unit ring slightly so its wiring connector is at the bottom (steering wheel in

**13.5a Removing the steering column upper shroud . . .**

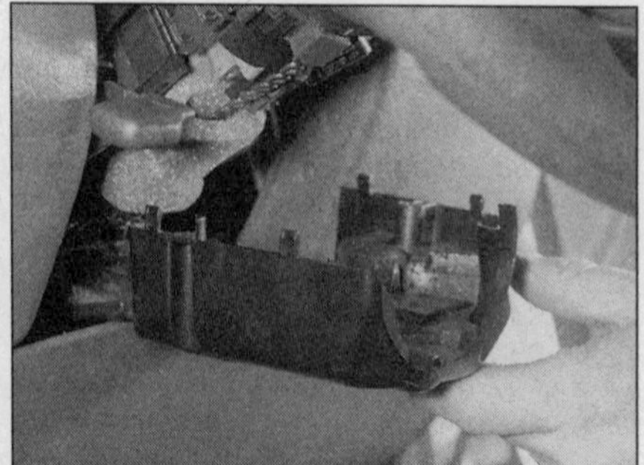

**13.5b . . . and the lower shroud**

the straight-ahead position); this will lock the contact unit in the central position, and prevent it from being turned. Alternatively, tape the wiring connector securely to the steering wheel while the wheel is out of the car.

### *Refitting*

#### Models without an airbag

**9** Refitting is a reversal of removal, but make sure that the direction indicator lever is in its neutral position, otherwise damage may occur in the cancelling arm. Engage the direction indicator lever cancelling ring tongue as the steering wheel is fitted. Tighten the retaining nut to the specified torque.

#### Models with an airbag

**10** Manoeuvre the wheel into position, making sure the wiring connector is correctly positioned, and engage it with the column. Note the points made in paragraph 9.

**11** Reconnect the airbag wiring connector, and refit the steering column shrouds.

**12** Refit the steering wheel retaining nut, and tighten it to the specified torque setting.

**13** Refit the airbag unit as described in Chapter 12.

**13.6 Disconnecting the airbag wiring plug**

**13.7 Loosening the steering wheel nut**

## 14 Steering column - removal and refitting

**Note:** *The steering column was modified for 1998 model year (ie approximately July/August 1997) to incorporate a torque overload clutch assembly. This development may significantly affect the column removal/refitting procedure (and other related tasks). The column upper universal joint (UJ) cannot be separated on the later column - based on our experience of an earlier-type column in the workshop, this suggests that the column cannot be removed from the car, and it certainly cannot be removed from the column tube, without cutting through the column shaft. The torque overload clutch assembly cannot be dismantled.*

**1** Steering column components are shown below **(see illustrations).**

### *Removal*

**2** Disconnect the battery negative lead.

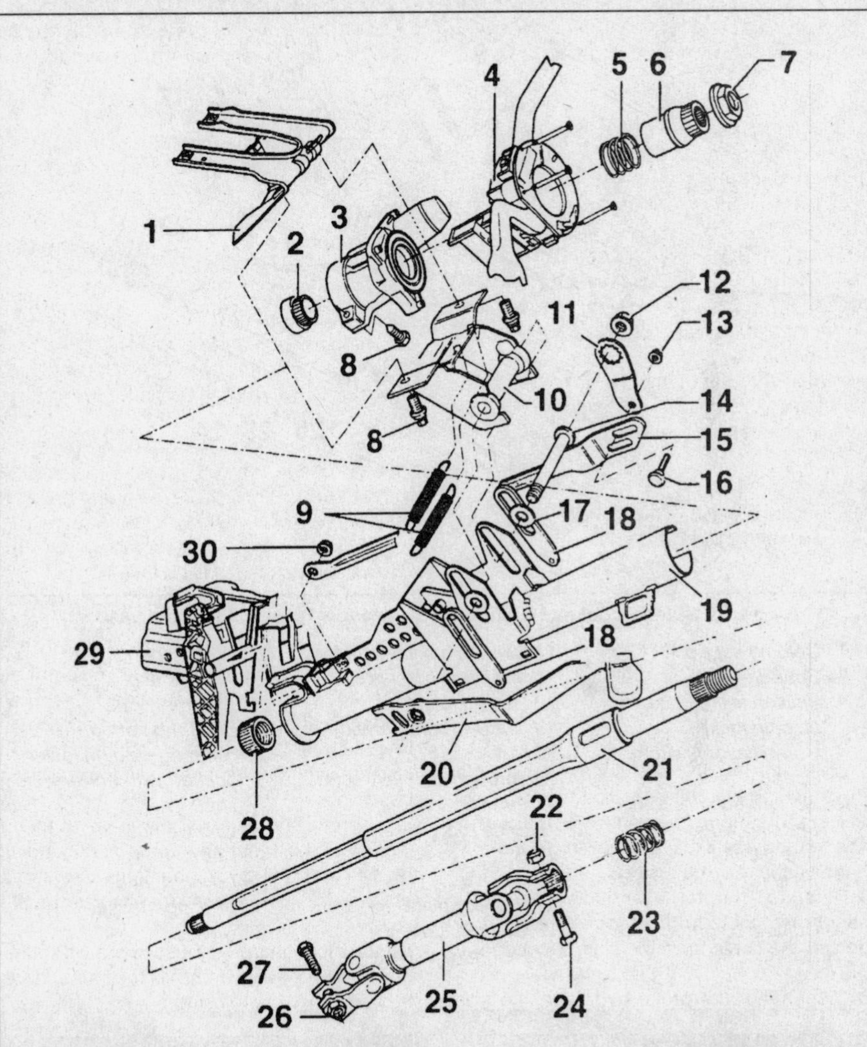


**14.1a Steering column components - models up to 1998 model year**

1 *Column support*
2 *Support ring*
3 *Ignition switch/steering column lock*
4 *Combination switch*
5 *Spring*
6 *Splined adaptor sleeve*
7 *Steering wheel nut*
8 *Shear-bolt*
9 *Column height adjuster spring*
10 *Column height adjuster mounting bracket*
11 *Locking plate*
12 *Nut (left-hand thread)*
13 *Nut*
14 *Through-bolt (left-hand thread)*
15 *Slide rod*
16 *Bolt*
17 *Washer*
18 *Packing plate*
19 *Column tube*
20 *Height adjuster lever*
21 *Steering column*
22 *Self-locking nut*
23 *Lower spring*
24 *Clamp bolt*
25 *Universal joint shaft*
26 *Captive nut*
27 *Clamp bolt*
28 *Lower bearing*
29 *Bearing bracket*
30 *Nut*

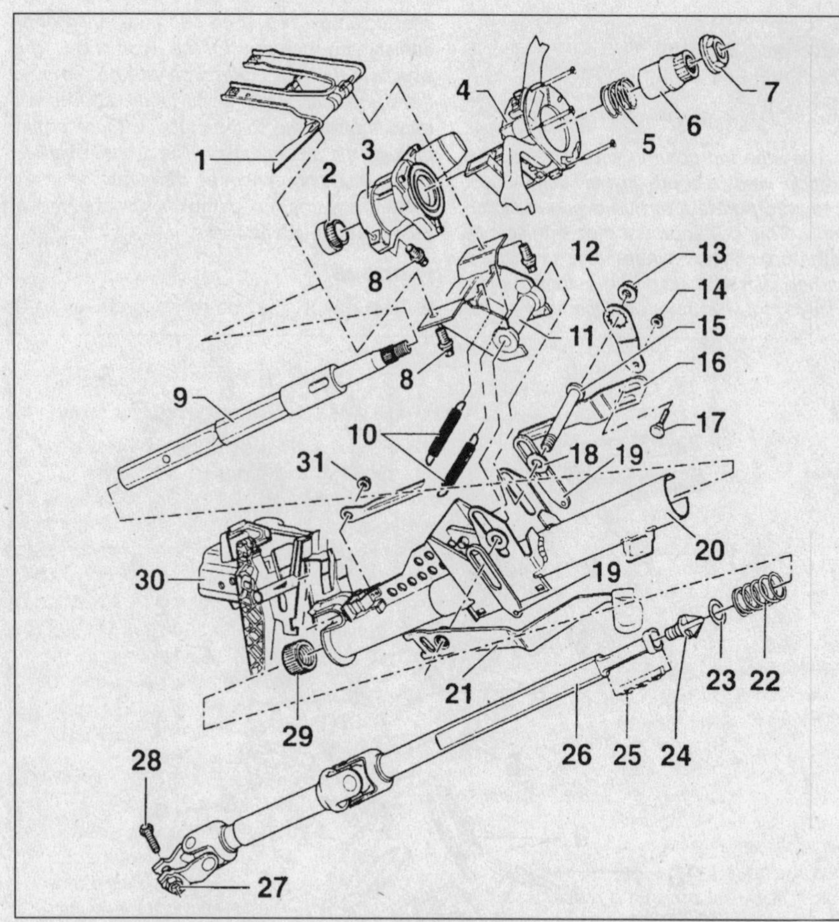


**14.1b Steering column components - models from 1998 model year**

1 *Column support*
2 *Support ring*
3 *Ignition switch/steering column lock*
4 *Combination switch*
5 *Spring*
6 *Splined adaptor sleeve*
7 *Steering wheel nut*
8 *Shear-bolt*
9 *Steering column upper section*
10 *Column height adjuster spring*
11 *Column height adjuster mounting bracket*
12 *Locking plate*
13 *Nut (left-hand thread)*
14 *Nut*
15 *Through-bolt (left-hand thread)*
16 *Slide rod*
17 *Bolt*
18 *Washer*
19 *Packing plate*
20 *Column tube*
21 *Height adjuster lever*
22 *Lower spring*
23 *Rubber ring*
24 *Assembly drift*
25 *Securing spring*
26 *Steering column lower section with universal joint shaft*
27 *Captive nut*
28 *Clamp bolt*
29 *Lower bearing*
30 *Bearing bracket*
31 *Nut*

**14.7a Disconnect the first wiring plug . . .**

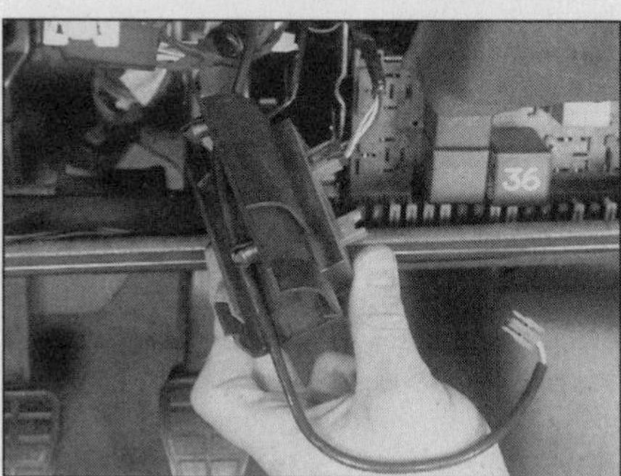

**14.7b . . . unclip the immobiliser control unit from the underside of the column . . .**

**14.7c . . . then disconnect the remaining wiring plug, and remove the control unit**

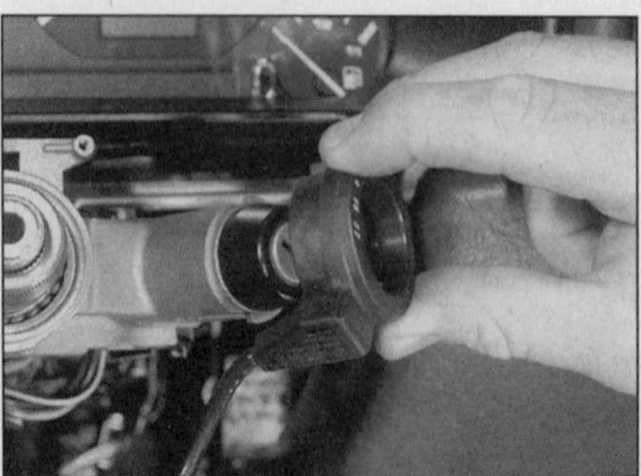

**14.8 On early models, the immobiliser reader coil can be removed from the ignition switch**

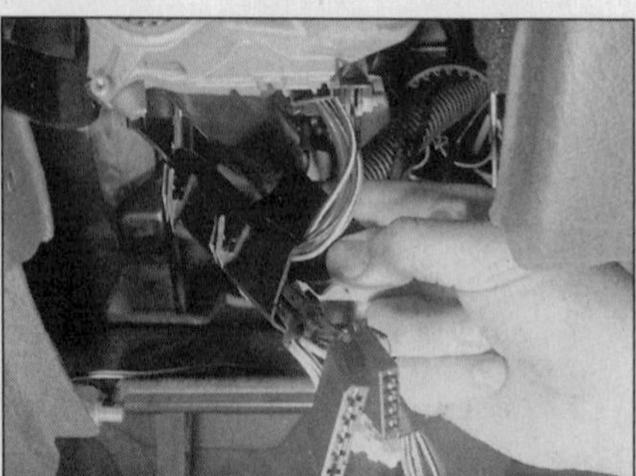

**14.9a Unclip the wiring harness guide from below the column**

**14.9b Unclip and remove the cover from the rear of the ignition switch . . .**

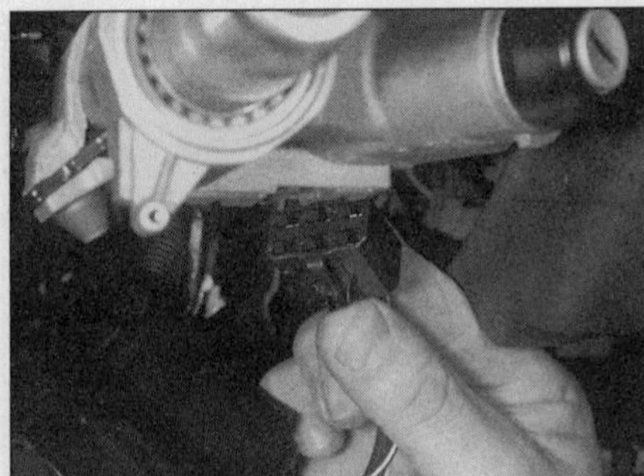
14.9c . . . then disconnect the ignition switch wiring plug

14.10a Unscrew the plastic fasteners (one of two arrowed) . . .

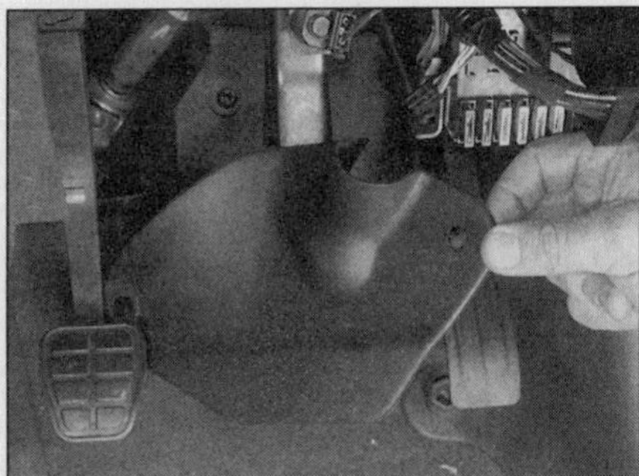
14.10b . . . and remove the lower column cover from behind the pedals

**Note:** *If the vehicle has a security-coded radio, check that you have a copy of the code number before disconnecting the battery. Refer to your VW dealer if in doubt.*

**3** Remove the steering wheel, as described in the previous Section.

**4** If not already done, remove the screws and withdraw the steering column shrouds.

**5** Remove the combination switches as described in Chapter 12.

**6** Remove the driver's side glovebox and lower trim panel as described in Chapter 11, Section 26.

**7** Unclip the ignition immobiliser control unit from the underside of the column, and disconnect its wiring plug from the ignition switch **(see illustrations)**.

**8** On early models, where the immobiliser ignition key reader coil can be removed from the ignition switch, detach the reader coil assembly **(see illustration)**. On later models, the reader coil is integral with the ignition switch.

**9** Unclip the wiring harness plastic guide from the underside of the column, and lower the wiring out of the way. Pull the plastic cover from the rear of the ignition switch, then disconnect the main ignition switch wiring connector **(see illustrations)**.

**10** Unscrew the plastic fasteners and detach and remove the lower column/bulkhead cover from behind the foot pedals **(see illustrations)**.

**11** Remove the column mounting bolts. Shear-type bolts are used - to remove them, it will be necessary to drill out the threaded portion and use a stud extractor, tap them round with a centre-punch, or chisel the heads off **(see illustration)**. Access to one of the bolts may be improved by removing the instrument panel - see Chapter 12.

**12** Unscrew and remove the column upper universal joint clamp bolt - this is only possible on the earlier-type column. It may be possible to remove the later-type column by removing the column lower universal joint clamp bolt, but this approach was unsuccessful when tried on the earlier-type column in the workshop (the only alternative here is to cut through the column to remove it, but consult your VW dealer before doing so). If removing a clamp bolt, it may be necessary to temporarily refit the steering wheel and turn it to bring the clamp bolt into the most accessible position.

**13** Pull the steering column to the rear, to unhook it from the mounting halfway up the column tube, and pull it from the universal joint splines **(see illustrations)**. Withdraw the column tube assembly from the vehicle.

## *Inspection*

**14** Check the various components for excessive wear. If the column has been damaged in any way, it must be renewed as a unit.

**15** The early-type column can be withdrawn upwards through the column tube and removed, noting the fitted positions of all components as it is removed. The later-type column can only be withdrawn from the tube by cutting off the upper universal joint - if a later-type column is to be overhauled, seek the advice of your VW dealer.

### Overhaul - early-type column only

**16** Remove the ignition switch/steering column lock, as described in Chapter 12.

**17** Using a suitable puller, withdraw the splined adaptor sleeve from the shaft.

**18** If the steering column bottom bearing is to be renewed, drive (or draw) it out downwards from the tube. Fit the replacement bearing by driving it into position in the base of the tube, using a suitable tube drift.

**19** Renew any parts which are worn or suspect.

## *Refitting*

**20** Reassembly and refitting is in general a reversal of the dismantling and removal procedure, but note the following points.

*a) When fitting the multi-splined adaptor sleeve, position the sleeve over the column, and then tighten the steering wheel nut against it. Tighten the nut to the specified torque to press the adaptor into position, then remove the nut and continue refitting the column.*

*b) Refit the ignition switch/column lock as described in Chapter 12.*

*c) The captive nut fitted to the lower universal joint should not be re-used if the self-locking threads are no longer effective. The nut should be removed from the UJ, and a replacement self-locking nut obtained.*

*d) When refitting the column tube, hook it onto the mounting bracket halfway up the column tube before engaging the universal joint splines.*

14.11 Using a hammer and chisel to remove the column mounting shear-bolts (arrowed)

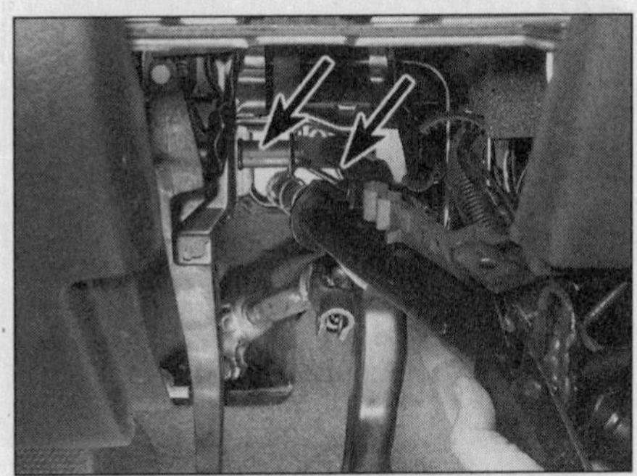
14.13a Unhook the column tube from the mounting (arrowed) . . .

14.13b . . . and disengage the universal joint splines

e) *Tighten the retaining nuts and bolts to the specified torque wrench settings. Fit new shear-bolts and tighten them until their heads break off* **(see illustration)**.

f) *On completion, ensure that the steering action, and the operation of the column switches, is satisfactory.*

## 15 Steering column height adjuster - removal and refitting

**1** The component parts of the height adjuster mechanism are shown in illustrations 14.1a and 14.1b.

**2** The adjuster mechanism components can be removed from the column after the column is lowered from the upper mounting, as described in the previous Section. Note that the lever through-bolt and nut have a left-hand thread - ie they loosen *clockwise* and tighten *anti-clockwise* **(see illustration)**.

**3** Any components in the height adjuster mechanism which are broken or excessively worn must be renewed.

**14.20 Inserting a new steering column shear-bolt (arrowed)**

**4** When refitting the components of the adjuster, note the following points:

a) *Lubricate the sliding surfaces of the adjuster.*

b) *The mounting plate tabs must be guided under the spring pin.*

c) *When refitting the lever, tighten the through-bolt to the specified torque setting with the lever on the upper stop. Refit the locking plate after the bolt is tightened.*

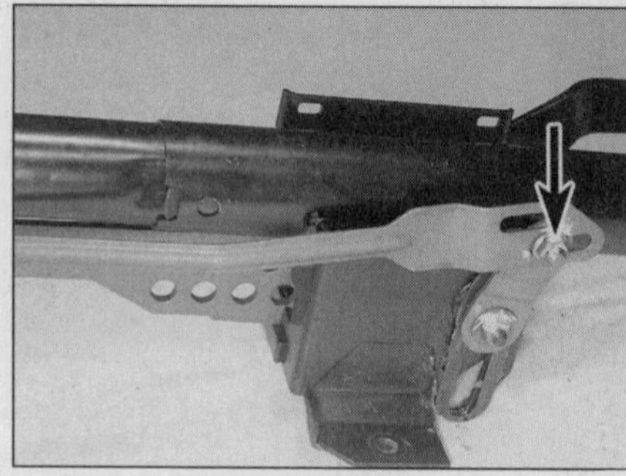

**15.2 General view of the steering column height adjuster mechanism (steering column removed) - nut arrowed has a left-hand thread**

d) *Ensure that the return springs are attached to the mounting bracket.*

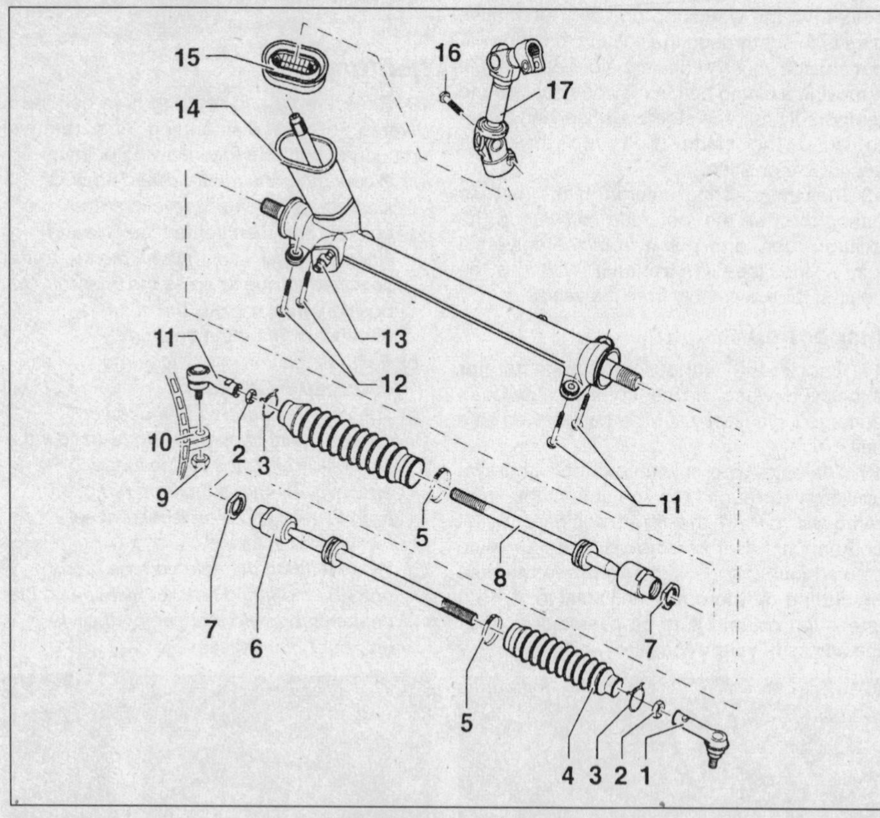


**17.5 Manual steering gear**

1 *Right-hand track-rod end and balljoint*
2 *Track-rod end locknut*
3 *Gaiter securing clip*
4 *Gaiter*
5 *Gaiter securing clip*
6 *Right-hand track-rod*
7 *Locknut*
8 *Left-hand track-rod*
9 *Track-rod balljoint nut*
10 *Steering arm on swivel hub*
11 *Left-hand track-rod end and balljoint*
12 *Steering gear mounting bolts*
13 *Adjustment bolt*
14 *Steering gear*
15 *Grommet*
16 *Clamp bolt*
17 *Steering column universal joint*

## 16 Steering gear gaiters - renewal

**1** The steering gear gaiters can be removed and refitted with the steering gear unit *in situ* or removed from the vehicle.

**2** Measure the exposed amount of adjustment thread showing on the inboard side of the track-rod end balljoint locknut. This will act as a guide to the adjustment position when refitting the balljoint to the rod. Loosen off the locknut, and detach the balljoint from the track-rod as described in Section 19.

**3** Unscrew and remove the locking nut from the track-rod.

**4** Release the retaining clips and withdraw the gaiter from the steering gear and track-rod.

**5** Refit in the reverse order of removal. Smear the inner bore of the gaiter with lubricant prior to fitting, to ease its assembly. Renew the balljoint locknuts.

**6** On completion, have the front wheel alignment checked (see Section 22).

## 17 Steering gear - removal and refitting

**Note:** *If the manual steering gear is being removed because a knocking noise has been noted, refer to Section 18 before proceeding.*

### Removal

**1** Apply the handbrake and chock the rear wheels, then loosen the front roadwheel bolts.

**2** Raise and support the front of the vehicle on axle stands (see *Jacking and vehicle support*). For better access, remove the front roadwheels.

**3** Refer to Section 19, and detach the track-rod end balljoints from the swivel hub.

**4** On power steering models, either clamp the fluid supply and return hoses with suitable hose clamps, or drain the hydraulic system as

17.10a Power steering gear fluid supply and return unions

described in Section 20. Clean the area around the fluid hose connections on the steering gear.

**5** Unscrew and remove the steering column lower universal joint shaft clamp bolt, as described in Section 14, paragraphs 10 and 12. Release the large grommet from the bulkhead on the engine side, and push it forward over the lower joint **(see illustration)**. Note the TOP marking on the grommet, which should face into the passenger compartment when fitted.

**6** Referring to Chapter 4D, unbolt and lower the exhaust system front downpipe.

**7** On manual transmission models, refer to Chapter 7A, Section 3 and disconnect the support cable from the transmission housing.

**8** Unscrew the nut and remove the through-bolt from the engine/transmission rear mounting - see Chapter 2A or B.

**9** Support the subframe from below, using two jacks if available. Loosen, but do not remove, the wishbone/lower arm rear mounting through-bolts and the subframe mounting bolts, then lower the subframe sufficiently to disengage the steering gear pinion from the universal joint splines. Do not lower the subframe any more than is necessary.

**10** On power steering models, disconnect the fluid supply and return lines from the steering gear **(see illustrations)**. Recover the seals and O-rings as they are detached. Drain any fluid remaining in the system into a container for disposal. Position the lines out of the way, and seal off their ends to prevent further leakage and the possible ingress of dirt.

**11** Check that all connections are free and clear of the steering gear, then withdraw it rearwards and manoeuvre it from the vehicle.

**12** If the steering gear is known to be damaged or worn beyond an acceptable level, it may have to be renewed. However, it is possible to have the steering gear overhauled - consult a VW dealer or specialist repairer for further advice.

### Refitting

**13** Refitting is a reversal of the removal procedure, noting the following points:

*a) Centralise the steering rack and the column shaft before connecting them. An assistant will be required to align and engage the two shafts as the subframe and engine are raised. When the two are reconnected and the clamp bolt is tight, make sure the floor sealing grommet is correctly located, to prevent noise and water ingress.*

*b) On power steering models, the fluid lines will also need to be connected as the unit is raised. Take care to keep the connections clean. Use new O-rings and seals when reconnecting the fluid lines.*

*c) Tighten all fasteners to the specified torque wrench settings.*

*d) Refer to Section 19 to reconnect the track-rod ends.*

*e) On power steering models, top up the fluid level as described in Weekly checks and bleed the system as described in Section 20.*

*f) Finally, have the wheel alignment checked and if necessary adjusted (see Section 22).*

## 18 Manual steering gear - adjustment

**Note:** *The power steering gear should not normally require adjustment, and no procedure is given by the manufacturers. Knocking noises from the power steering gear will almost certainly be due to wear, but if a whining or hissing noise is noted, the hydraulic system may need bleeding - see Section 20.*

**1** If there is any undue slackness in the manual steering gear, resulting in noise or rattles, the steering gear can be adjusted as follows.

**2** Apply the handbrake and chock the rear wheels. Raise and support the front of the vehicle on axle stands (see *Jacking and vehicle support*).

**3** With the wheels in the straight-ahead position, tighten the self-locking adjustment screw gradually, while an assistant turns the

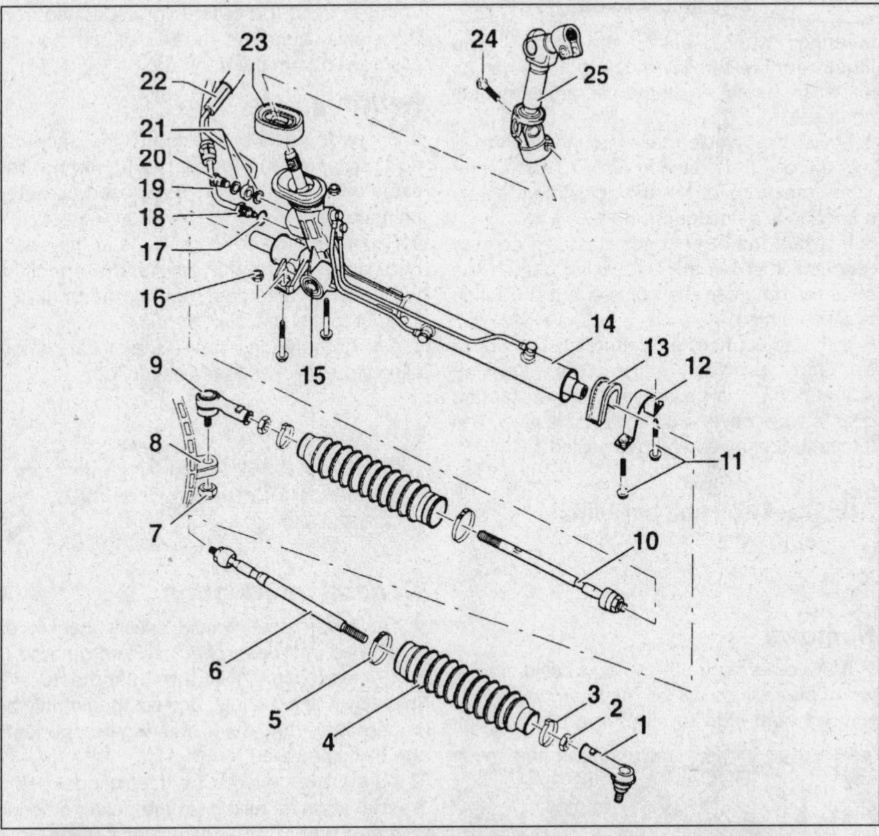


**17.10b Power steering gear**

1 Right-hand track-rod end and balljoint
2 Track-rod end locknut
3 Gaiter securing clip
4 Gaiter
5 Gaiter securing clip
6 Right-hand track-rod
7 Track-rod balljoint nut
8 Steering arm on swivel hub
9 Left-hand track-rod end and balljoint
10 Left-hand track-rod
11 Steering gear mounting bolts
12 Mounting clamp
13 Mounting rubber
14 Steering gear
15 Adjustment bolt
16 Mounting nut
17 O-ring
18 Union nut
19 Return hose
20 Banjo bolt
21 Seal
22 Supply (pressure) hose
23 Grommet
24 Clamp bolt
25 Steering column universal joint

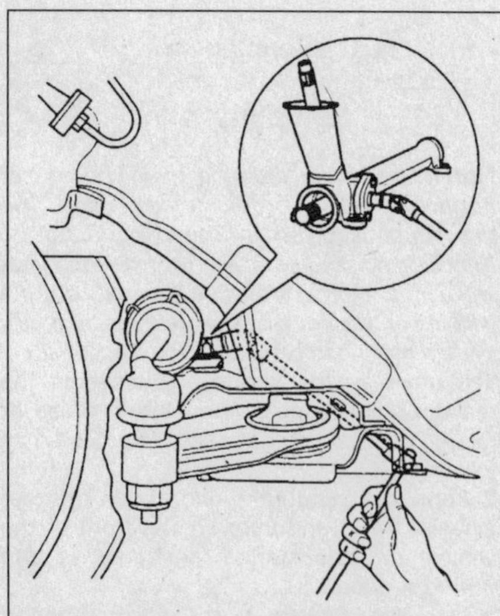

18.3 Using a socket, universal joint and extension to reach the steering gear adjustment screw

steering wheel back and forth **(see illustration)**. When the knocking noise can no longer be heard inside the car, adjustment is complete.

**4** Lower the vehicle to the ground, then road test the car. If the steering fails to self-centre after cornering, loosen the adjustment screw a fraction at a time until it does.

**5** If, when the correct self-centring point is reached, there is still excessive play in the steering, retighten the adjuster nut a fraction to take up the play.

**6** If the adjustment procedures listed above do not provide satisfactory steering adjustment, it is probable that the steering gear is worn beyond an acceptable level, and it must be removed and overhauled.

## 19 Track-rod end balljoints - removal and refitting

### Removal

**1** If the steering track-rod end balljoints are worn, play will be evident as the roadwheel is rocked from side to side, and the balljoint must then be renewed. Make sure, however, that any lateral play noted is not due to a worn wheel bearing - hold your hand over the balljoint while an assistant rocks the roadwheel; play in the balljoint will be readily apparent **(see illustration)**.

19.1 Track-rod end balljoint (arrowed)

**2** Apply the handbrake and chock the rear wheels, then loosen the relevant front roadwheel bolts. Raise and support the front of the vehicle on axle stands (see *Jacking and vehicle support*). Remove the front roadwheel on the side concerned.

**3** Measure the distance of the exposed thread inboard of the locknut. Make a note of the distance, so that the new balljoint can be screwed on to the same position, then loosen the locknut. It is advisable to fit a new locknut if the balljoint is being renewed.

**4** Loosen the balljoint nut on the side concerned, and unscrew it by a few turns - do not remove it at this stage. Use a balljoint separator tool to release the joint from the swivel hub, then remove the nut completely. With the track-rod outer joint separated from the swivel hub, the outer balljoint can be unscrewed from the track-rod.

### Refitting

**5** Screw the new balljoint onto the track-rod so that, when the locknut is tightened, the same amount of thread is exposed as noted on removal.

**6** Reconnect the outer balljoints to the swivel hub, and tighten the nut to the specified torque wrench setting. Tighten the track-rod locknut to the specified torque.

**7** On completion, have the front wheel alignment checked (see Section 22).

## 20 Power steering fluid - general information, draining and refilling

### General information

**1** The power steering fluid level is checked as described in *Weekly checks*. Fluid renewal is not called for by the manufacturer's maintenance schedule, and so should only be necessary if the power steering components are being removed.

**2** All models covered by this manual use a special VW hydraulic oil in the power steering system. When topping-up the system, it is recommended to only use this oil (available from your VW dealer), but the oil is compatible with normal automatic transmission fluid (ATF) and can therefore be mixed in small amounts if required. If the system is being drained and refilled, however, use **only** the recommended oil.

**3** If the system is in need of constant topping-up, check for signs of leakage at the pump, reservoir and steering gear hose unions and make repairs as necessary.

### Draining

**4** To drain the fluid from the system, detach the fluid suction hose at the pump, and drain the fluid into a container for disposal. When draining, turn the steering wheel from lock to lock to expel as much fluid as possible. Do **not** run the engine while this is being done, or the pump will be damaged.

### Refilling and bleeding

**5** After draining off the fluid, reconnect the suction hose to the pump, then fill the reservoir to the top with new fluid. Restart the engine and switch off as soon as it fires, repeating the starting and stopping sequence several times; this will cause fluid to be drawn into the system quickly. As with draining the fluid, do not leave the engine running while the pump is short of fluid, or the pump will be damaged.

**6** Watch the level of fluid, and keep adding fluid so that the reservoir is never sucked dry. When the fluid ceases to drop as a result of the start/stop sequence, start the engine and allow it to run at idle speed.

**7** Turn the steering from lock to lock several times, being careful not to leave the wheels on full lock because this will cause the pressure in the system to build up.

**8** Watch the level of the fluid in the reservoir, and add fluid if necessary to keep the level at the MAX mark.

**9** When the level stops falling and no more air bubbles appear in the reservoir, switch the engine off and fit the reservoir cap. The level of fluid will rise slightly when the engine is switched off.

**10** After the vehicle is next used, re-check the fluid level as described in *Weekly checks*, and top up if necessary.

## 21 Power steering pump - removal and refitting

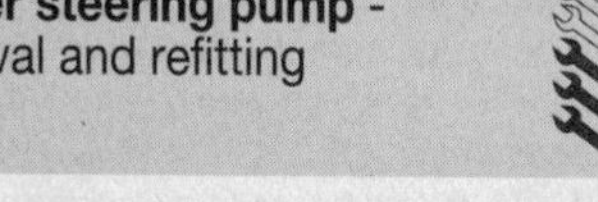

### Removal

**1** If the power steering is suspected of malfunction, have the supply and system pressure checked by your VW dealer. The pump cannot be overhauled or repaired, and if defective, it must be renewed as a unit. Note that the type of pump fitted depends on engine type and equipment level, but removal procedures for each pump are basically the same.

**2** Using brake hose clamps, clamp both the supply and return hoses near the power steering fluid reservoir. This will minimise fluid loss during subsequent operations. Alternatively, drain the fluid from the system as described in Section 20.

**3** Slacken the steering pump pulley retaining bolts - it may be necessary to counterhold the pulley using a large Allen key in the centre of the pulley mounting flange. Working as described in Chapter 2A or B, release the drivebelt tension and unhook the drivebelt from the pump pulley.

4 Unscrew the retaining bolts and remove the pulley from the power steering pump, noting which way around it is fitted **(see illustration)**.
5 Slacken the retaining clip, and disconnect the fluid supply hose from the pump. Where a spring-type clip is still fitted, cut the clip and discard it; replace it with a standard worm-drive hose clip on refitting. Slacken the union bolt, and disconnect the feed pipe from the pump, along with its sealing washers; discard the washers - new ones should be used on refitting. Be prepared for some fluid spillage as the pipe and hose are disconnected, and plug the hose/pipe end and pump unions, to minimise fluid loss and prevent the entry of dirt into the system.
6 Slacken and remove the bolts securing the power steering pump to its mounting bracket, and remove the pump from the engine compartment. On diesel engine models, it will be necessary to disconnect the lock carrier fasteners, and pull the lock carrier forwards slightly, to allow sufficient clearance to withdraw the pump - see Chapter 2C, Section 2.

### Refitting

7 Prior to fitting, ensure that the pump is primed by injecting hydraulic oil in through the supply hose union and rotating the pump shaft. This is especially important if a new or reconditioned pump is being fitted, as it will be supplied dry.
8 Manoeuvre the pump into position and refit the mounting bolts, tightening them to the specified torque setting.
9 Position a new sealing washer on each side of the feed pipe union, then fit the union bolt and tighten it to the specified torque setting. Refit the supply pipe to the pump, and securely tighten its retaining clip. Remove the brake hose clamps, if used.
10 Refit the drive pulley, making sure it is the correct way around, and fit its retaining bolts.
11 Check the condition of the drivebelt as described in Chapter 1A or 1B, as applicable. If a new pump is being fitted, a new drivebelt should be used.
12 Refit the drivebelt to the pump pulley, and tension it as described in Chapter 2A or B. Once the belt is tensioned, tighten the pulley retaining bolts to the specified torque setting.
13 On completion, fill and/or bleed the hydraulic system as described in Section 20.

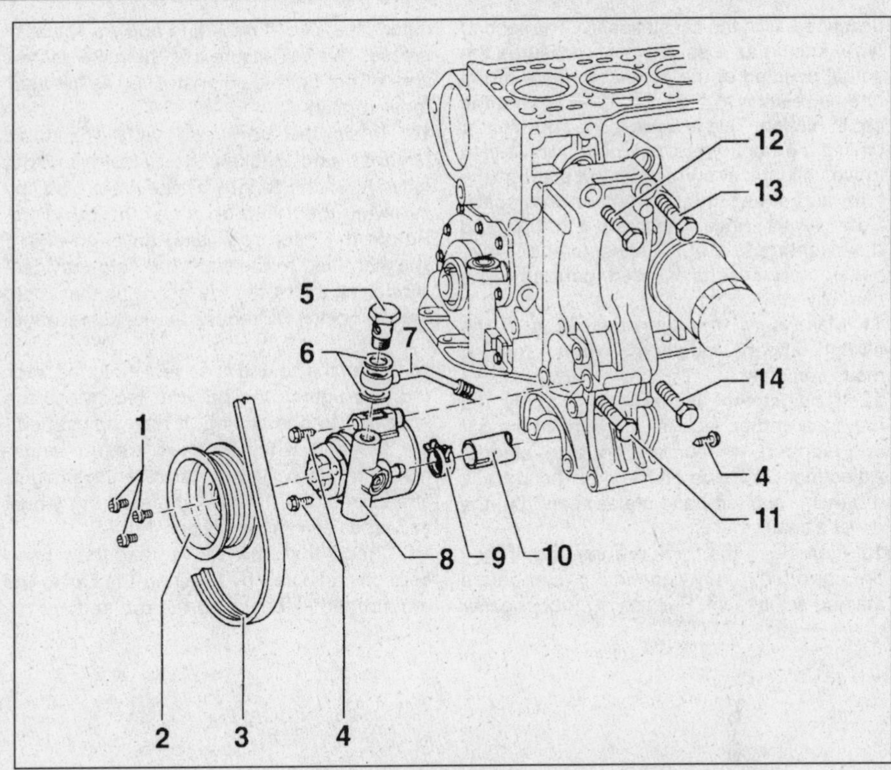


**21.4 Power steering pump and associated components - typical**

*1 Pulley bolts*
*2 Pulley*
*3 Drivebelt*
*4 Pump mounting bolts*
*5 Banjo bolt*
*6 Sealing washers*
*7 Supply (pressure) pipe to steering gear*
*8 Pump*
*9 Spring-type clip*
*10 Hose from fluid reservoir*
*11 to 14 Pump mounting bracket bolts - tighten in sequence: 12, 11, 13, 14*

## 22 Wheel alignment and steering angles - general information

### Definitions

1 A car's steering and suspension geometry is defined in three basic settings - all angles are expressed in degrees (toe settings are also expressed as a measurement); the steering axis is defined as an imaginary line drawn through the axis of the suspension strut, extended where necessary to contact the ground.
2 **Camber** is the angle between each roadwheel and a vertical line drawn through its centre and tyre contact patch, when viewed from the front or rear of the car. Positive camber is when the roadwheels are tilted outwards from the vertical at the top; negative camber is when they are tilted inwards.
3 Camber angle is adjustable, and can be checked using a camber checking gauge.
4 **Castor** is the angle between the steering axis and a vertical line drawn through each roadwheel's centre and tyre contact patch, when viewed from the side of the car. Positive castor is when the steering axis is tilted so that it contacts the ground ahead of the vertical; negative castor is when it contacts the ground behind the vertical.
5 Castor is not adjustable, and is given for reference only; while it can be checked using a castor checking gauge, if the figure obtained is significantly different from that specified, the car must be taken for careful checking by a professional, as the fault can only be caused by wear or damage to the body or suspension components.
6 **Toe** is the difference, viewed from above, between lines drawn through the roadwheel centres and the car's centre-line. Toe-in is when the roadwheels point inwards, towards each other at the front, while toe-out is when they splay outwards from each other at the front.
7 The front wheel toe setting is adjusted by screwing the right-hand track rod in or out of its balljoint, to alter the effective length of the track rod assembly.
8 Rear wheel toe setting is not adjustable, and is given for reference only. While it can be checked, if the figure obtained is significantly different from that specified, the car must be taken for careful checking by a professional, as the fault can only be caused by wear or damage to the body or suspension components.

### Checking and adjustment

#### Front wheel toe setting

9 Due to the special measuring equipment necessary to check the wheel alignment, and the skill required to use it properly, the checking and adjustment of these settings is best left to a VW dealer or similar expert. Note that most tyre-fitting centres now possess sophisticated checking equipment.
10 To check the toe setting, a tracking gauge must first be obtained. Two types of gauge are available, and can be obtained from motor accessory shops. The first type measures the distance between the front and rear inside edges of the roadwheels, as previously

described, with the car stationary. The second type, known as a scuff plate, measures the actual position of the contact surface of the tyre, in relation to the road surface, with the car in motion. This is achieved by pushing or driving the front tyre over a plate, which then moves slightly according to the scuff of the tyre, and shows this movement on a scale. Both types have their advantages and disadvantages, but either can give satisfactory results if used correctly and carefully.

**11** Make sure that the steering is in the straight-ahead position when making measurements.

**12** If adjustment is necessary, apply the handbrake, then jack up the front of the car and support it securely on axle stands. Adjustment is made on the right-hand track rod (right- and left-hand are as seen from the driver's seat).

**13** First clean the track rod threads; if they are corroded, apply penetrating fluid before starting adjustment. Release the rubber gaiter outer clips, peel it back and apply a smear of grease. This will ensure that the gaiter is free, and will not be twisted or strained as the track rod is rotated.

**14** Retain the track rod with a suitable spanner, and slacken the balljoint locknut fully. Alter the length of the track rod, by screwing them into or out of the balljoints. Rotate the track rod using an open-ended spanner fitted to the track rod flats provided; shortening the track rods (screwing them onto their balljoints) will reduce toe-in/increase toe-out.

**15** When the setting is correct, hold the track rod and tighten the balljoint locknut to the specified torque setting. If after adjustment, the steering wheel spokes are no longer horizontal when the wheels are in the straight-ahead position, remove the steering wheel and reposition it (see Section 13).

**16** Check that the toe setting has been correctly adjusted by lowering the car to the ground and re-checking the toe setting; re-adjust if necessary. Ensure that the rubber gaiters are seated correctly and are not twisted or strained, and secure them in position with the retaining clips; where necessary, fit a new retaining clip (refer to Section 16).

## Rear wheel toe setting

**17** The procedure for checking the rear toe setting is the same as described for the front setting in paragraph 10. The setting is not adjustable - see paragraph 8.

## Front wheel camber angle

**18** Checking and adjusting the front wheel camber angle should be entrusted to a VW dealer or other suitably-equipped specialist. Note that most tyre-fitting centres now possess sophisticated checking equipment. For reference, adjustments are made by slackening the suspension strut-to-swivel hub mounting bolts, and repositioning the swivel hub assembly.

# Chapter 11
# Bodywork and fittings

## Contents



## Degrees of difficulty

| **Easy,** suitable for novice with little experience  | **Fairly easy,** suitable for beginner with some experience 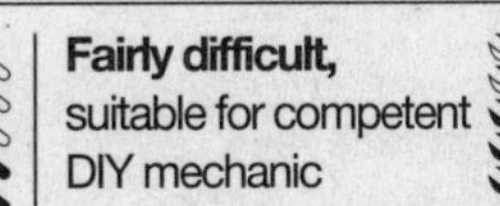 | **Fairly difficult,** suitable for competent DIY mechanic | **Difficult,** suitable for experienced DIY mechanic | **Very difficult,** suitable for expert DIY or professional |
|---|---|---|---|---|

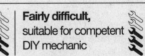

## Specifications

| Torque wrench settings | Nm | lbf ft |
|---|---|---|
| Bonnet hinge bolts | 23 | 17 |
| Bonnet lock retaining bolts (use locking fluid) | 12 | 9 |
| Bumper mounting screws (Torx) | 6 | 4 |
| Door check link pivot bolt nut | 7 | 5 |
| Door handle retaining bolt | 8 | 6 |
| Door hinge pin grub screw | 23 | 18 |
| Door hinge retaining bolts (Torx) | 36 | 27 |
| Door lock retaining bolts | 8 | 6 |
| Door window glass clamp nuts | 10 | 7 |
| Door window glass regulator retaining bolts: | | |
| Electric windows | 23 | 17 |
| Manual windows | 10 | 7 |
| Lock carrier-to-chassis bolts | 23 | 17 |
| Lock carrier-to-front wing bolts | 5 | 4 |
| Rear bumper inner section retaining nuts | 15 | 11 |
| Seat belt height adjuster bolt | 23 | 17 |
| Seat belt mounting bolts | 40 | 30 |
| Tailgate lock screws | 20 | 15 |
| Tailgate strut lower mounting bolts | 10 | 7 |
| Tailgate strut upper mounting ball-stud | 22 | 16 |

## 1 General information

The bodyshell is made of pressed-steel sections, and is available in both three- and five-door Hatchback versions. Most components are welded together, but some use is made of structural adhesives; the front wings are bolted on.

The bonnet, door, and some other vulnerable panels are made of zinc-coated metal, and are further protected by being coated with an anti-chip primer before being sprayed.

Extensive use is made of plastic materials, mainly in the interior, but also in exterior components. The front and rear bumpers and front grille are injection-moulded from a synthetic material that is very strong and yet light. Plastic components such as wheelarch liners are fitted to the underside of the vehicle, to improve the body's resistance to corrosion.

## 2 Maintenance - bodywork and underframe

The general condition of a vehicle's bodywork is the one thing that significantly affects its value. Maintenance is easy, but needs to be regular. Neglect, particularly after minor damage, can lead quickly to further deterioration and costly repair bills. It is important also to keep watch on those parts of the vehicle not immediately visible, for instance the underside, inside all the wheelarches, and the lower part of the engine compartment.

The basic maintenance routine for the bodywork is washing - preferably with a lot of water, from a hose. This will remove all the loose solids which may have stuck to the vehicle. It is important to flush these off in such a way as to prevent grit from scratching the finish. The wheelarches and underframe need washing in the same way, to remove any accumulated mud which will retain moisture and tend to encourage rust. Paradoxically enough, the best time to clean the underframe and wheelarches is in wet weather, when the mud is thoroughly wet and soft. In very wet weather, the underframe is usually cleaned of large accumulations automatically, and this is a good time for inspection.

Periodically, except on vehicles with a wax-based underbody protective coating, it is a good idea to have the whole of the underframe of the vehicle steam-cleaned, engine compartment included, so that a thorough inspection can be carried out to see what minor repairs and renovations are necessary. Steam cleaning is available at many garages, and is necessary for the removal of the accumulation of oily grime, which sometimes is allowed to become thick in certain areas. If steam-cleaning facilities are not available, there are some excellent grease solvents available which can be brush-applied; the dirt can then be simply hosed off. Note that these methods should not be used on vehicles with wax-based underbody protective coating, or the coating will be removed. Such vehicles should be inspected annually, preferably just before Winter, when the underbody should be washed down, and any damage to the wax coating repaired. Ideally, a completely fresh coat should be applied. It would also be worth considering the use of wax-based protection for injection into door panels, sills, box sections, etc, as an additional safeguard against rust damage, where such protection is not provided by the vehicle manufacturer.

After washing paintwork, wipe off with a chamois leather to give an unspotted clear finish. A coat of clear protective wax polish will give added protection against chemical pollutants in the air. If the paintwork sheen has dulled or oxidised, use a cleaner/polisher combination to restore the brilliance of the shine. This requires a little effort, but such dulling is usually caused because regular washing has been neglected. Care needs to be taken with metallic paintwork, as special non-abrasive cleaner/polisher is required to avoid damage to the finish. Always check that the door and ventilator opening drain holes and pipes are completely clear, so that water can be drained out. Brightwork should be treated in the same way as paintwork. Windscreens and windows can be kept clear of the smeary film which often appears, by proprietary glass cleaner. Never use any form of wax or other body or chromium polish on glass.

## 3 Maintenance - upholstery and carpets

Mats and carpets should be brushed or vacuum-cleaned regularly, to keep them free of grit. If they are badly stained, remove them from the vehicle for scrubbing or sponging, and make quite sure they are dry before refitting. Seats and interior trim panels can be kept clean by wiping with a damp cloth. If they do become stained (which can be more apparent on light-coloured upholstery), use a little liquid detergent and a soft nail brush to scour the grime out of the grain of the material. Do not forget to keep the headlining clean in the same way as the upholstery. When using liquid cleaners inside the vehicle, do not over-wet the surfaces being cleaned. Excessive damp could get into the seams and padded interior, causing stains, offensive odours or even rot. If the inside of the vehicle gets wet accidentally, it is worthwhile taking some trouble to dry it out properly, particularly where carpets are involved. *Do not leave oil or electric heaters inside the vehicle for this purpose.*

## 4 Minor body damage - repair

### Repairs of minor scratches in bodywork

If the scratch is very superficial, and does not penetrate to the metal of the bodywork, repair is very simple. Lightly rub the area of the scratch with a paintwork renovator or a very fine cutting paste to remove loose paint from the scratch, and to clear the surrounding bodywork of wax polish. Rinse the area with clean water.

Apply touch-up paint to the scratch using a fine paint brush; continue to apply fine layers of paint until the surface of the paint in the scratch is level with the surrounding paintwork. Allow the new paint at least two weeks to harden, then blend it into the surrounding paintwork by rubbing the scratch area with a paintwork renovator or a very fine cutting paste. Finally, apply wax polish.

Where the scratch has penetrated right through to the metal of the bodywork, causing the metal to rust, a different repair technique is required. Remove any loose rust from the bottom of the scratch with a penknife, then apply rust-inhibiting paint to prevent the formation of rust in the future. Using a rubber or nylon applicator, fill the scratch with bodystopper paste. If required, this paste can be mixed with cellulose thinners to provide a very thin paste which is ideal for filling narrow scratches. Before the stopper-paste in the scratch hardens, wrap a piece of smooth cotton rag around the top of a finger. Dip the finger in cellulose thinners, and quickly sweep it across the surface of the stopper-paste in the scratch; this will ensure that the surface of the stopper-paste is slightly hollowed. The scratch can now be painted over as described earlier in this Section.

### Repairs of dents in bodywork

When deep denting of the vehicle's bodywork has taken place, the first task is to pull the dent out, until the affected bodywork almost attains its original shape. There is little point in trying to restore the original shape completely, as the metal in the damaged area will have stretched on impact, and cannot be reshaped fully to its original contour. It is better to bring the level of the dent up to a point which is about 3 mm below the level of the surrounding bodywork. In cases where the dent is very shallow anyway, it is not worth trying to pull it out at all. If the underside of the dent is accessible, it can be hammered out gently from behind, using a mallet with a wooden or plastic head. Whilst doing this, hold a suitable block of wood firmly against the outside of the panel, to absorb the impact from the hammer blows and thus prevent a large area of the bodywork from being 'belled-out'.

Should the dent be in a section of the bodywork which has a double skin, or some other factor making it inaccessible from behind, a different technique is called for. Drill several small holes through the metal inside the area - particularly in the deeper section. Then screw long self-tapping screws into the holes, just sufficiently for them to gain a good purchase in the metal. Now the dent can be pulled out by pulling on the protruding heads of the screws with a pair of pliers.

The next stage of the repair is the removal of the paint from the damaged area, and from an inch or so of the surrounding 'sound' bodywork. This is accomplished most easily by using a wire brush or abrasive pad on a power drill, although it can be done just as effectively by hand, using sheets of abrasive paper. To complete the preparation for filling, score the surface of the bare metal with a screwdriver or the tang of a file, or alternatively, drill small holes in the affected area. This will provide a good 'key' for the filler paste.

To complete the repair, see the Section on filling and respraying.

### Repairs of rust holes or gashes in bodywork

Remove all paint from the affected area, and from an inch or so of the surrounding 'sound' bodywork, using an abrasive pad or a wire brush on a power drill. If these are not available, a few sheets of abrasive paper will do the job most effectively. With the paint removed, you will be able to judge the severity of the corrosion, and therefore decide whether to renew the whole panel (if this is possible) or to repair the affected area. New body panels are not as expensive as most people think, and it is often quicker and more satisfactory to fit a new panel than to attempt to repair large areas of corrosion.

Remove all fittings from the affected area, except those which will act as a guide to the original shape of the damaged bodywork (eg sill or wheelarch mouldings, etc). Then, using tin snips or a hacksaw blade, remove all loose metal and any other metal badly affected by corrosion. Hammer the edges of the hole inwards, to create a slight depression for the filler paste.

Wire-brush the affected area to remove the powdery rust from the surface of the remaining metal. Paint the affected area with rust-inhibiting paint; if the back of the rusted area is accessible, treat this also.

Before filling can take place, it will be necessary to block the hole in some way. This can be achieved with aluminium or plastic mesh, or aluminium tape.

Aluminium or plastic mesh, or glass-fibre matting, is probably the best material to use for a large hole. Cut a piece to the approximate size and shape of the hole to be filled, then position it in the hole so that its edges are below the level of the surrounding bodywork. It can be retained in position by several blobs of filler paste around its periphery.

Aluminium tape should be used for small or very narrow holes. Pull a piece off the roll, trim it to the approximate size and shape required, then pull off the backing paper (if used) and stick the tape over the hole; it can be overlapped if the thickness of one piece is insufficient. Burnish down the edges of the tape with the handle of a screwdriver or similar, to ensure that the tape is securely attached to the metal underneath.

### Bodywork repairs - filling and respraying

Before using this Section, see the Sections on dent, deep scratch, rust holes and gash repairs.

Many types of bodyfiller are available, but generally speaking, those proprietary kits which contain a tin of filler paste and a tube of resin hardener are best for this type of repair. A wide, flexible plastic or nylon applicator will be found invaluable for imparting a smooth and well-contoured finish to the surface of the filler.

Mix up a little filler on a clean piece of card or board - measure the hardener carefully (follow the maker's instructions on the pack), otherwise the filler will set too rapidly or too slowly. Using the applicator, apply the filler paste to the prepared area; draw the applicator across the surface of the filler to achieve the correct contour and to level the surface. When a contour that approximates to the correct one is achieved, stop working the paste - if you carry on too long, the paste will become sticky and begin to 'pick-up' on the applicator. Continue to add thin layers of filler paste at 20-minute intervals, until the level of the filler is just proud of the surrounding bodywork.

Once the filler has hardened, the excess can be removed using a metal plane or file. From then on, progressively-finer grades of abrasive paper should be used, starting with a 40-grade production paper, and finishing with a 400-grade wet-and-dry paper. Always wrap the abrasive paper around a flat rubber, cork, or wooden block - otherwise the surface of the filler will not be completely flat. During the smoothing of the filler surface, the wet-and-dry paper should be periodically rinsed in water. This will ensure that a very smooth finish is imparted to the filler at the final stage.

At this stage, the dent should be surrounded by a ring of bare metal, which in turn should be encircled by the finely 'feathered' edge of the good paintwork. Rinse the repair area with clean water, until all the dust produced by the rubbing-down operation has gone.

Spray the whole area with a light coat of primer - this will show up any imperfections in the surface of the filler. Repair these imperfections with fresh filler paste or bodystopper, and again smooth the surface with abrasive paper. If bodystopper is used, it can be mixed with cellulose thinners, to form a thin paste which is ideal for filling small holes. Repeat this spray-and-repair procedure until you are satisfied that the surface of the filler, and the feathered edge of the paintwork, are perfect. Clean the repair area with clean water, and allow to dry fully.

The repair area is now ready for final spraying. Paint spraying must be carried out in a warm, dry, windless and dust-free atmosphere. This condition can be created artificially if you have access to a large indoor working area, but if you are forced to work in the open, you will have to pick your day very carefully. If you are working indoors, dousing the floor in the work area with water will help to settle the dust which would otherwise be in the atmosphere. If the repair area is confined to one body panel, mask off the surrounding panels; this will help to minimise the effects of a slight mis-match in paint colours. Bodywork fittings (eg chrome strips, door handles etc) will also need to be masked off. Use genuine masking tape, and several thickness of newspaper, for the masking operations.

Before starting to spray, agitate the aerosol can thoroughly, then spray a test area (an old tin, or similar) until the technique is mastered. Cover the repair area with a thick coat of primer; the thickness should be built up using several thin layers of paint, rather than one thick one. Using 400 grade wet-and-dry paper, rub down the surface of the primer until it is smooth. While doing this, the work area should be thoroughly doused with water, and the wet-and-dry paper periodically rinsed in water. Allow to dry before spraying on more paint.

Spray on the top coat, again building up the thickness by using several thin layers of paint. Start spraying in the centre of the repair area, and then, using a circular motion, work outwards until the whole repair area and about 2 inches of the surrounding original paintwork is covered. Remove all masking material 10 to 15 minutes after spraying on the final coat of paint.

Allow the new paint at least two weeks to harden, then, using a paintwork renovator or a very fine cutting paste, blend the edges of the paint into the existing paintwork. Finally, apply wax polish.

### Plastic components

With the use of more and more plastic body components by the vehicle manufacturers (eg bumpers, spoilers, and in some cases major body panels), rectification of more serious damage to such items has become a matter of either entrusting repair work to a specialist in this field, or renewing complete components. Repair of such damage by the DIY owner is not feasible, owing to the cost of the equipment and materials required for effecting such repairs. The basic technique involves making a groove along the line of the crack in the plastic, using a rotary burr in a power drill. The damaged part is then welded back together, using a hot air gun to heat up and fuse a plastic filler rod into the groove.

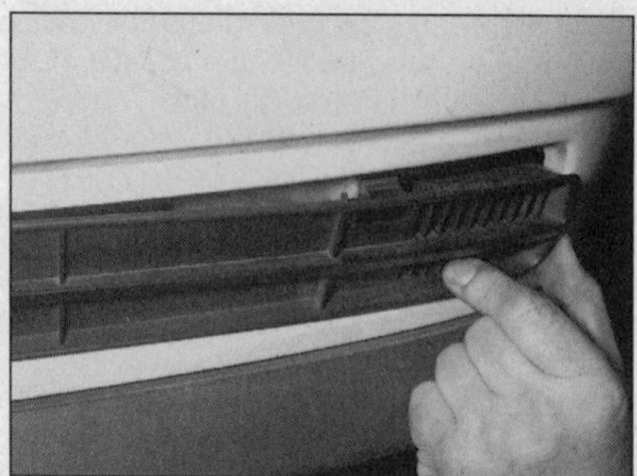

**6.3 Press out the lower grille panel from the bumper**

Any excess plastic is then removed, and the area rubbed down to a smooth finish. It is important that a filler rod of the correct plastic is used, as body components can be made of a variety of different types (eg polycarbonate, ABS, polypropylene).

Damage of a less serious nature (abrasions, minor cracks etc) can be repaired by the DIY owner using a two-part epoxy filler repair material. Once mixed in equal proportions, this is used in similar fashion to the bodywork filler used on metal panels. The filler is usually cured in twenty to thirty minutes, ready for sanding and painting.

If the owner is renewing a complete component himself, or if he has repaired it with epoxy filler, he will be left with the problem of finding a suitable paint for finishing which is compatible with the type of plastic used. At one time, the use of a universal paint was not possible, owing to the complex range of plastics met with in body component applications. Standard paints, generally speaking, will not bond to plastic or rubber satisfactorily, but professional matched paints, to match any plastic or rubber finish, can be obtained from some dealers. However, it is now possible to obtain a plastic body parts finishing kit which consists of a pre-primer treatment, a primer and coloured top coat. Full instructions are normally supplied with a kit, but basically the method of use is to first apply the pre-primer to the component concerned, and allow it to dry for up to 30 minutes. Then the primer is applied, and left to dry for about an hour before finally applying the special-coloured top coat. The result is a correctly coloured component, where the

**6.5a Front bumper upper retaining screw . . .**

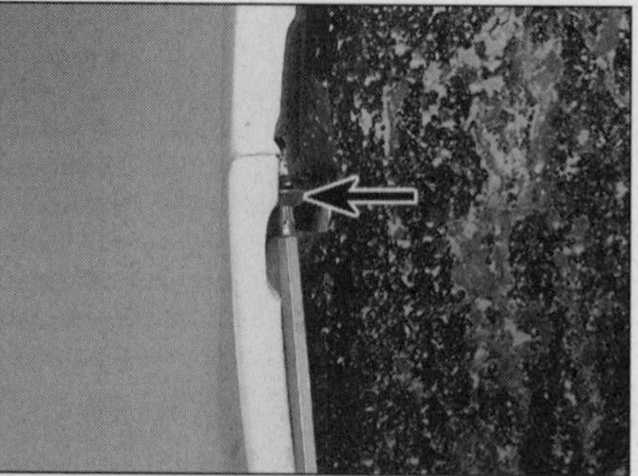

**6.4a Front bumper-to-wheel arch upper screw . . .**

paint will flex with the plastic or rubber, a property that standard paint does not normally possess.

## 5 Major body damage - repair

Where serious damage has occurred, or large areas need renewal due to neglect, it means that complete new panels will need welding-in, and this is best left to professionals. If the damage is due to impact, it will also be necessary to check completely the alignment of the bodyshell, and this can only be carried out accurately by a VW dealer using special jigs. If the body is left misaligned, it is primarily dangerous, as the car will not handle properly, and secondly, uneven stresses will be imposed on the steering, suspension and possibly transmission, causing abnormal wear, or complete failure, particularly to such items as the tyres.

## 6 Front bumper - removal and refitting

### Removal

**1** Apply the handbrake, then jack up the front of the vehicle and support it on axle stands (see *Jacking and vehicle support*).

**2** Remove the radiator grille and the headlight surround as described in Section 29.

**3** Working from behind the bumper, unclip

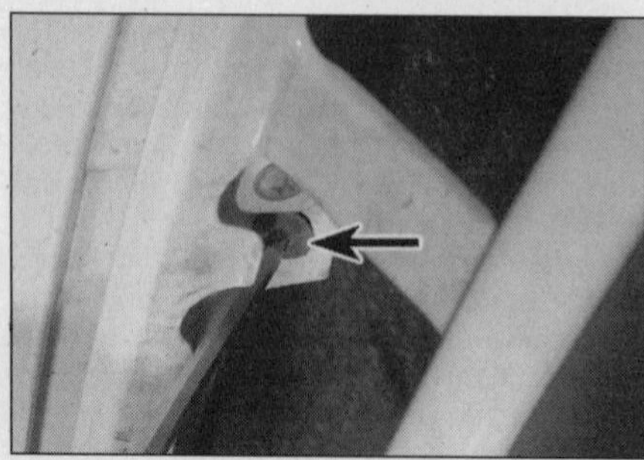

**6.5b . . . and lower screw (arrowed)**

**6.4b . . . and lower screw (arrowed) - wheel arch liner screw also being removed**

and press out the lower grille panel from the bumper, for access to the bumper lower retaining screws **(see illustration)**.

**4** Remove the two screws which secure the ends of the bumper to the front of the front wheel arch. Remove some of the wheel arch liner screws, and move the liner as necessary to release the end of the bumper **(see illustrations)**.

**5** Unscrew and remove the Torx screws (two at the top, four from below) which secure the bumper to the front of the car **(see illustrations)**, and lower the bumper to the ground. Where applicable, disconnect the wiring from the front foglights, and free it from any retaining clips so that the lights are free to be removed with the bumper.

**6** If required, the spoiler fitted to the lower edge of the bumper can be unscrewed or unclipped and removed (this can be achieved with the bumper in place).

### Refitting

**7** Refitting is a reverse of removal. Ensure that any wiring is properly reconnected and secured. Tighten all bumper fixings securely.

## 7 Rear bumper - removal and refitting

### Removal

**1** To improve access, chock the front wheels, then jack up the rear of the vehicle and support it on axle stands (see *Jacking and vehicle support*).

**2** Remove the two screws which secure the ends of the bumper to the rear of the rear wheel arch **(see illustration)**.

**3** Open the tailgate and remove the four Torx screws at the top edge of the bumper **(see illustration)**.

**4** Pull the bumper rearwards off the four locating pins, disconnect the number plate light wiring, and lower to the ground **(see illustration)**.

**5** If the bumper inner section shows signs of damage, it can be removed by unscrewing the four retaining nuts.

7.2 Rear bumper-to-wheel arch screws (arrowed)

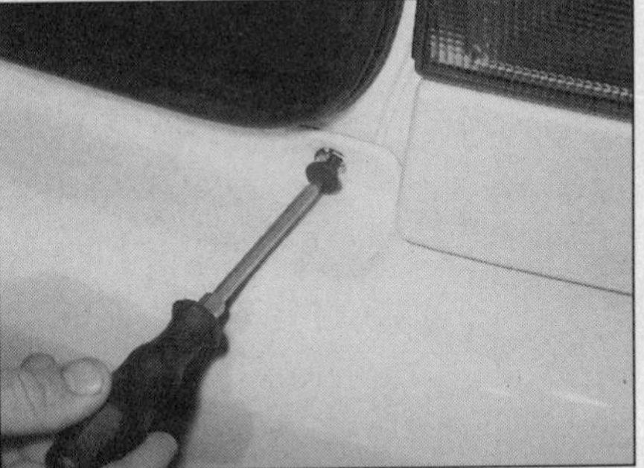
7.3 Removing one of the upper retaining screws

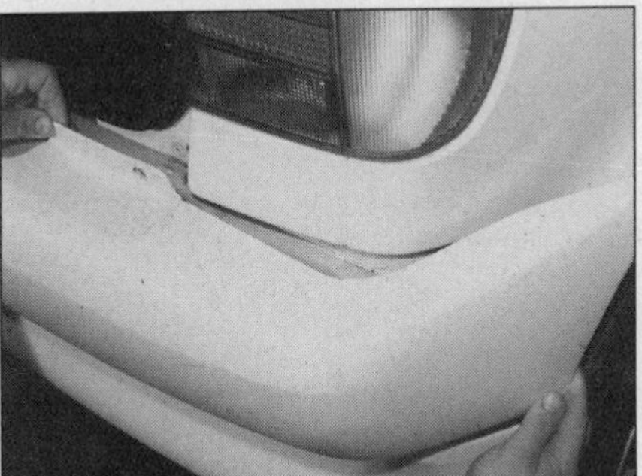
7.4 Pull the bumper rearwards off its retaining pins

### Refitting

**6** Refitting is a reverse of the removal procedure, ensuring that the bumper engages correctly with the locating pins as it is refitted.

## 8 Bonnet - removal, refitting and adjustment

### Removal

**1** Open the bonnet and have an assistant support it. Using a pencil or felt tip pen, mark the outline of each bonnet hinge relative to the bonnet, to use as a guide on refitting.

**2** Disconnect the washer hose from the windscreen washer jets, and from the securing clips on the underside of the bonnet **(see illustration)**. Disconnect the earth strap and undo its retaining nut.

**3** Undo the bonnet retaining bolts and, with the help of an assistant, carefully lift the bonnet clear **(see illustration)**. Store the bonnet out of the way in a safe place.

**4** Inspect the bonnet hinges for signs of wear and free play at the pivots, and if necessary renew. Each hinge is secured to the body by two bolts. Mark the position of the hinge on the body, then undo the retaining bolts and remove it from the vehicle. On refitting, align the new hinge with the marks and securely tighten the retaining bolts.

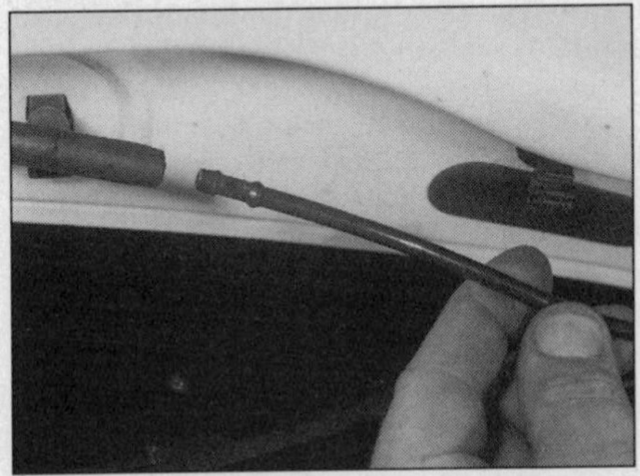
8.2 Unclip the washer hose, and separate it at the rubber connections

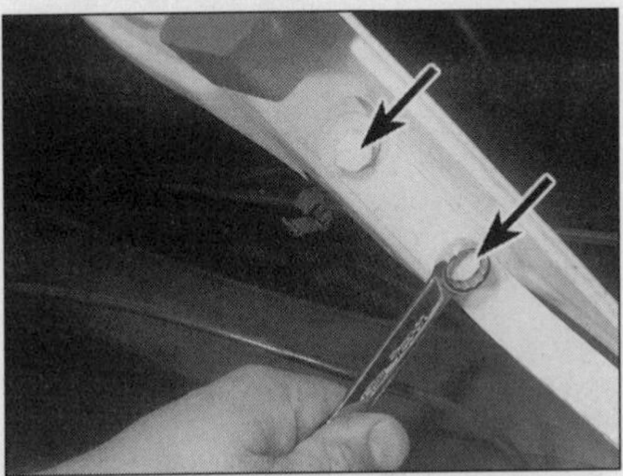
8.3 Bonnet retaining bolts (arrowed)

9.1a Unhook the bonnet release inner cable . . .

### Refitting and adjustment

**5** With the aid of an assistant, offer up the bonnet and loosely fit the retaining bolts. Align the hinges with the marks made on removal, then tighten the retaining bolts securely. Reconnect the earth strap and securely tighten its retaining nut.

**6** Close the bonnet, and check for alignment with the adjacent panels. If necessary, slacken the hinge bolts and re-align the bonnet to suit. Once the bonnet is correctly aligned, securely tighten the hinge bolts. Check that the bonnet fastens and releases satisfactorily.

## 9 Bonnet release cable - removal and refitting

### Removal

**1** Detach the inner cable from the lock body, and release the outer cable from the lock lever **(see illustrations)**.

**2** The cable is in two sections, joined in a plastic housing attached to the right-hand inner wing.

**3** Prise open the housing cover, and disconnect the cable ballstud from the housing **(see illustrations)**. The front section of cable can

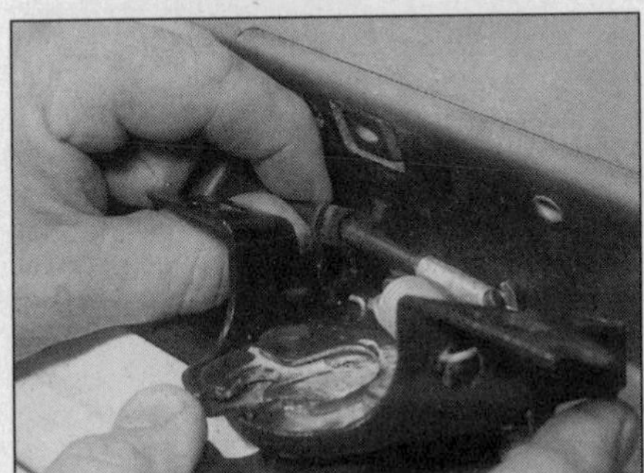
9.1b . . . and the outer cable from the lock

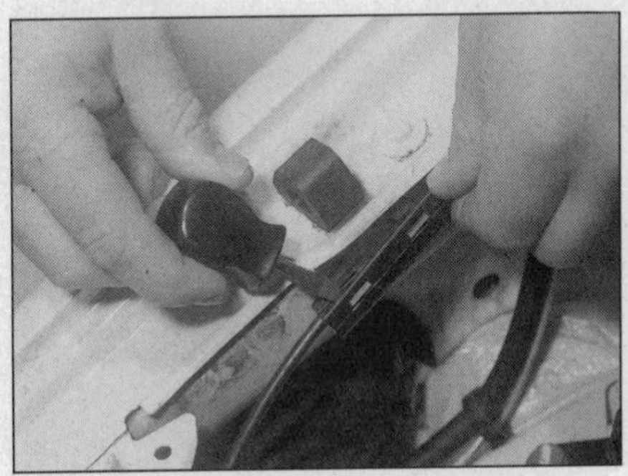
9.3a Unclip the bonnet lock cable connector plastic cover . . .

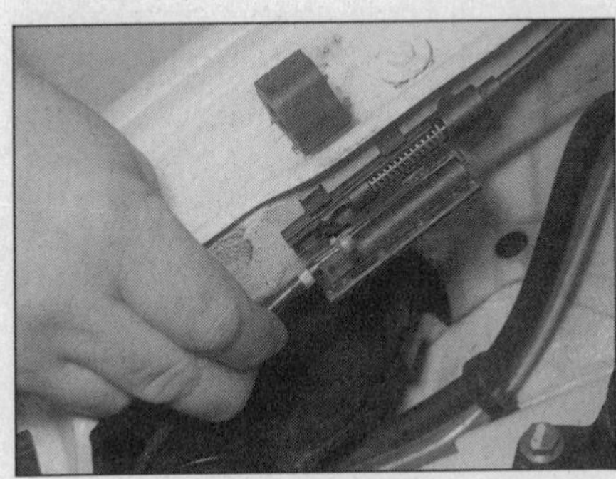
9.3b . . . then unhook the cable end fitting

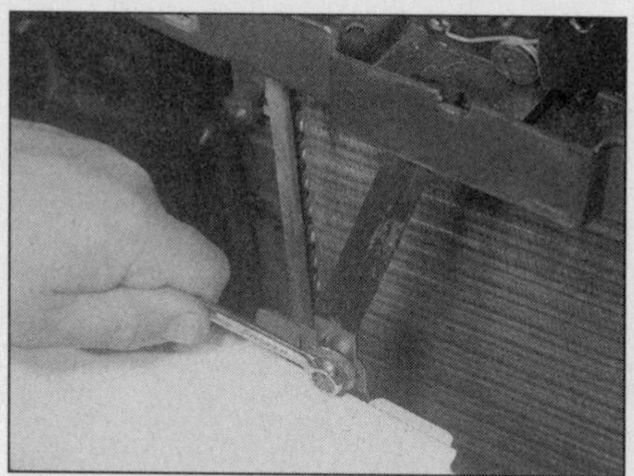

10.2a Remove the bonnet lock support arm securing bolt . . .

be replaced independently, but it may be advisable to renew both sections if one has failed - the other section may be weak.

**4** If required, work back along the cable towards the engine compartment bulkhead, noting its correct routing, and free it from the retaining clips and ties. Tie a length of string to the end of the cable.

**5** From inside the vehicle, slacken and remove the screws securing the bonnet release handle to the vehicle.

**6** Release the cable grommet from the bulkhead, and withdraw the handle and cable assembly. Once the cable is free, untie the string and leave it in position in the vehicle; the string can then be used to draw the new cable back into position.

### Refitting

**7** Tie the inner end of the string to the end of the cable, then use the string to draw the bonnet release cable through into the engine compartment. Once the cable is through, untie the string.

**8** Manoeuvre the bonnet release handle back into position, and securely tighten its retaining screws. Seat the rubber grommet in the bulkhead.

**9** Ensure that the cable is correctly routed, and secured to all the relevant retaining clips.

**10** Clip the cable ballstud into the plastic connector housing on the inner wing, and close the housing cover.

**11** Connect the inner and outer cable to the bonnet lock.

**12** Check that the lock operates smoothly, without any sign of undue resistance. Make sure that the lock is working before closing

10.2b . . . then unhook the arm from the lock carrier, and remove it

the bonnet! Check that the bonnet fastens and releases satisfactorily. If adjustment is necessary, slacken the bonnet lock retaining bolts (see Section 10), and adjust the position of the lock to suit. Once the lock is operating correctly, tighten its retaining bolts to the specified torque.

## 10 Bonnet lock - removal and refitting

### Removal

**1** Remove the radiator grille as described in Section 29.

**2** Unbolt the lock support arm, then unhook and remove it from the lock carrier **(see illustrations)**.

**3** Referring to Section 9, free the release cable outer from the lock lever, then detach the inner cable from the lock bracket.

**4** Using a suitable marker pen, mark the outline of the bonnet lock on the crossmember, then slacken and remove the two lock retaining bolts **(see illustration)**. Remove the lock from the front of the car.

### Refitting

**5** Before refitting, remove all traces of old locking compound from the bonnet retaining bolts and their threads in the body.

**6** Locate the bonnet release inner cable in the lock bracket and reconnect the outer cable to the lever. Seat the lock on the crossmember.

**7** Apply a suitable locking compound (VW recommend the use of locking fluid D 185 400

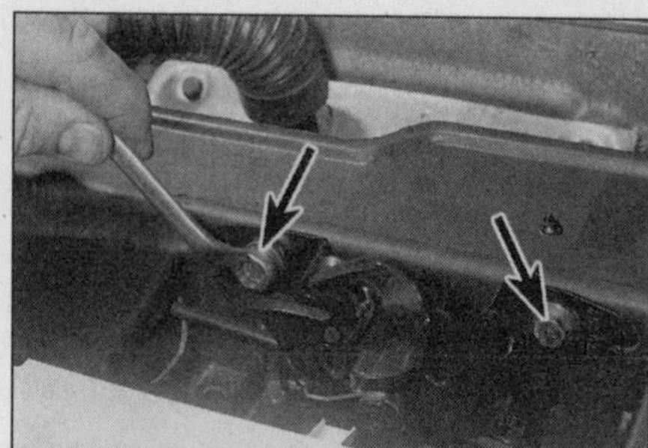

10.4 Unscrew the retaining bolts (arrowed) and remove the bonnet lock from the front of the car

A2 - available from your VW dealer) to the threads of the lock retaining bolts.

**8** Align the lock with the marks made prior to removal, then refit the bolts and tighten them to the specified torque setting.

**9** Hook the lock support arm into through the top of the lock carrier, then insert and tighten the securing bolt at the bottom end.

**10** Clip the radiator grille into position, then check that the lock operates smoothly, without any sign of undue resistance. Make sure that the lock is working before closing the bonnet! Check that the bonnet fastens and releases satisfactorily. If adjustment is necessary, slacken the bonnet lock retaining bolts, and adjust the position of the lock to suit. Once the lock is operating correctly, tighten its retaining bolts to the specified torque.

## 11 Door - removal, refitting and adjustment

### Removal

**1** Disconnect the battery negative terminal. **Note:** *If the vehicle has a security-coded radio, check that you have a copy of the code number before disconnecting the battery. Refer to your VW dealer if in doubt.*

**2** Open the door. On front doors, rotate the wiring connector anti-clockwise and disconnect it from the pillar - a suitable C-spanner may be required for this. When working on rear doors on models equipped with central locking, disengage the gaiter from the door pillar and disconnect the vacuum pipe **(see illustrations)**.

11.2a Unscrew the front door wiring connector using a suitable C-spanner . . .

11.2b . . . and withdraw it from the door pillar

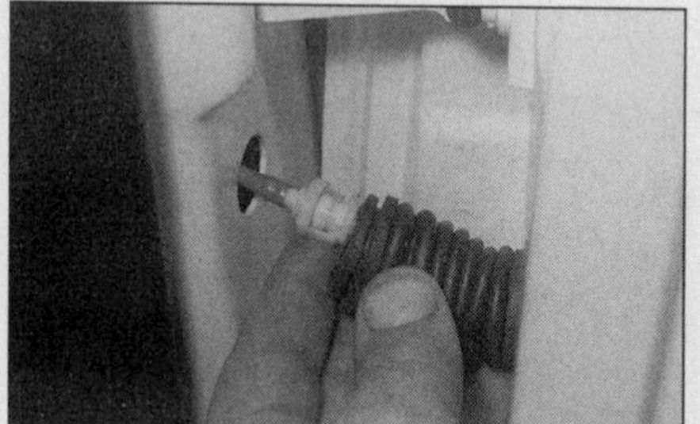

11.2c On 5-door models with central locking, disconnect the vacuum connection to the rear door

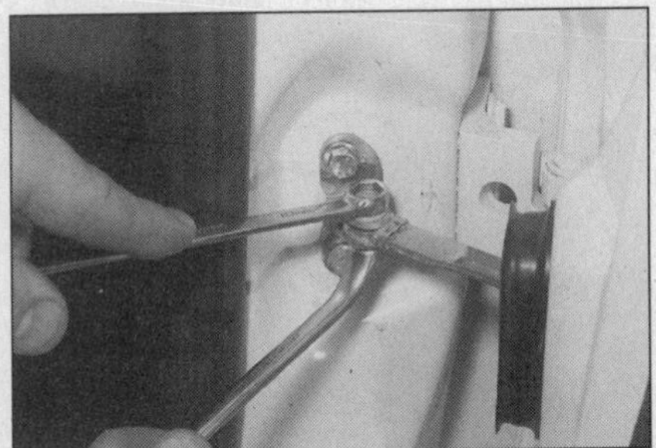

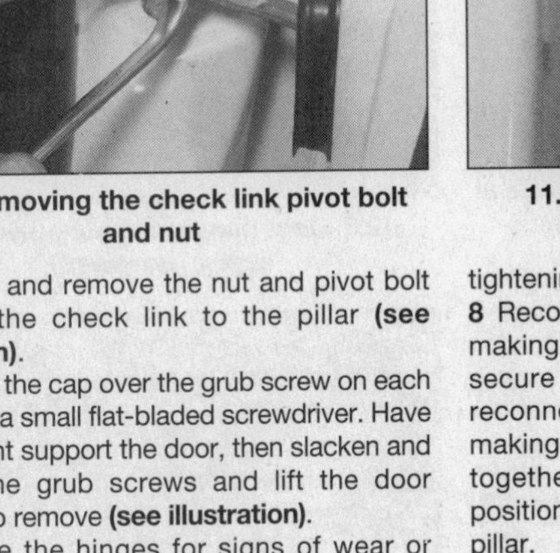

11.3 Removing the check link pivot bolt and nut

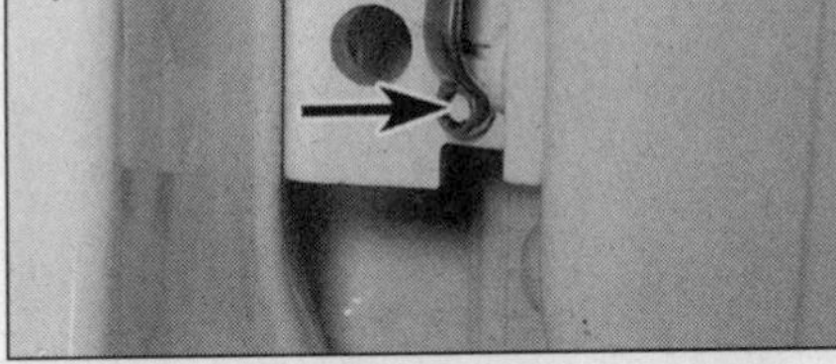

11.4 Loosen the hinge grub screw (arrowed)

3 Slacken and remove the nut and pivot bolt securing the check link to the pillar **(see illustration)**.

4 Prise off the cap over the grub screw on each hinge with a small flat-bladed screwdriver. Have an assistant support the door, then slacken and remove the grub screws and lift the door upwards to remove **(see illustration)**.

5 Examine the hinges for signs of wear or damage. If renewal is necessary, mark the position of the hinge(s) then undo the retaining bolts and remove them from the vehicle. Fit the new hinge(s), align with the marks made before removal and tighten the retaining bolts to the specified torque.

### Refitting

6 Apply a smear of multi-purpose grease to the hinge pins, then, with the aid of an assistant, refit the door to the vehicle. Once the door is correctly positioned, tighten the grub screws to the specified torque.

7 On all models, align the check link with its bracket and refit the pivot bolt and nut, tightening it to the specified torque setting.

8 Reconnect the front door wiring connector, making sure it is correctly reconnected, and secure it in position. Where necessary, reconnect the central locking vacuum pipe, making sure the connection is pushed firmly together. Fold the rubber gaiter back into position, ensuring it is correctly located on the pillar.

9 Check the door alignment and, if necessary, adjust then reconnect the battery negative terminal. If the paintwork around the hinges has been damaged, paint the area with a suitable touch-in brush to prevent corrosion.

### Adjustment

10 Close the door and check the door alignment with surrounding body panels. If necessary, slight adjustment of the door position can be made by slackening the hinge bolts and grub screws and repositioning the hinge/door as necessary. Once the door is correctly positioned, tighten the hinge bolts and grub screws to the specified torque. If the paintwork around the hinges has been damaged, paint the affected area with a suitable touch-in brush to prevent corrosion.

## 12 Door inner trim panel - removal and refitting

### Removal

#### Front door

**Note:** *If the vehicle has a security-coded radio, check that you have a copy of the code number before disconnecting the battery. Refer to your VW dealer if in doubt.*

1 Disconnect the battery negative terminal. Then open the door.

2 Carefully prise out and remove the exterior mirror inner trim panel **(see illustration)**.

3 Unscrew the door lock inner operating knob from its rod **(see illustration)**.

4 On models with manual front windows (or when working on the rear door trim panel), ensure that the window is closed, then slide the spacer behind the regulator handle, to release the retaining clip. The direction in which the spacer must be pushed will vary, as the spacer turns with the handle, but it can easily be done by hand. Pull the handle off the spindle **(see illustrations)**.

5 On models with manual door mirror adjustment, unclip the trim around the mirror adjustment knob, and remove the screw beneath.

6 On models with electric door mirrors, unclip the trim around the switch, and disconnect the wiring connector beneath **(see illustrations)**.

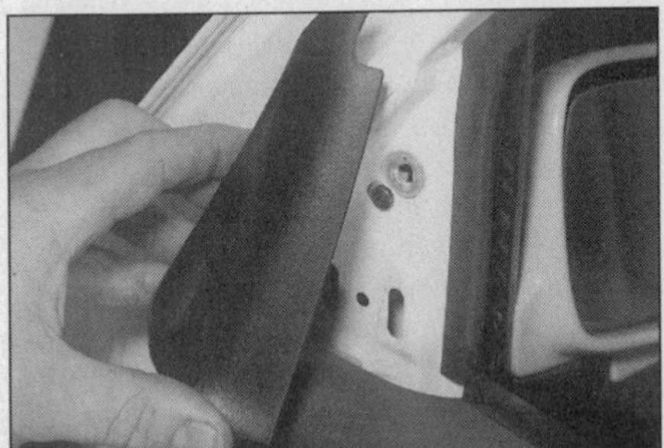

12.2 Removing the mirror trim panel

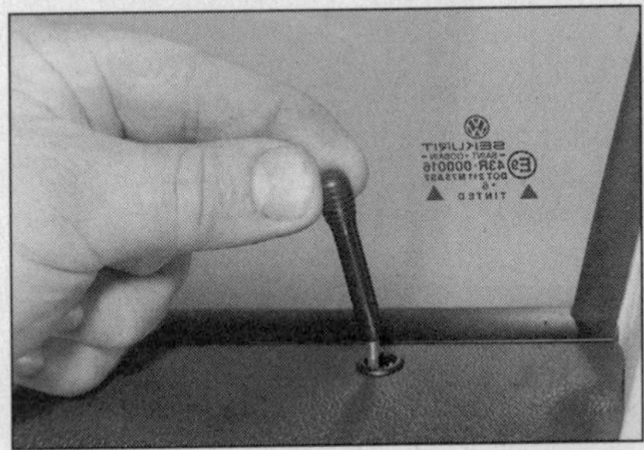

12.3 Remove the door lock operating knob

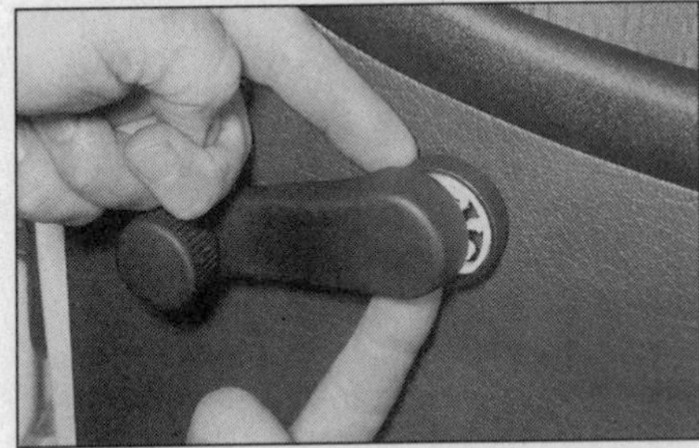

12.4a Slide out the spacer behind the regulator handle (the direction will not necessarily be as shown) . . .

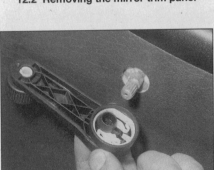

12.4b . . . and remove the handle from the splines

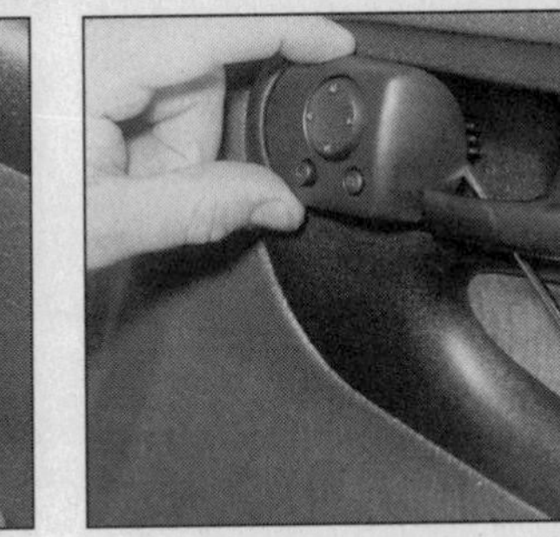

12.6a Unclip the mirror switch trim panel . . .

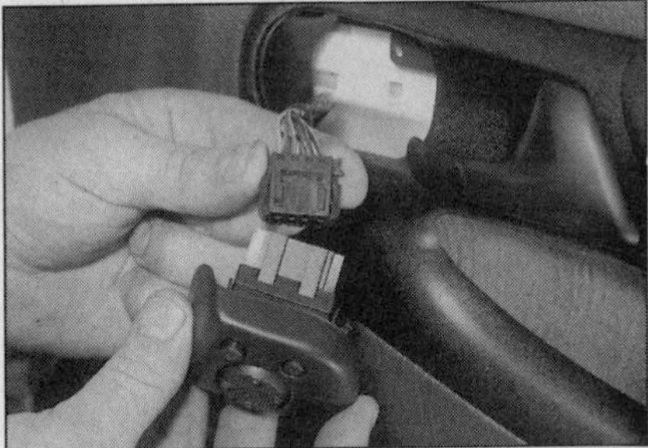

12.6b . . . and disconnect the mirror switch wiring connector

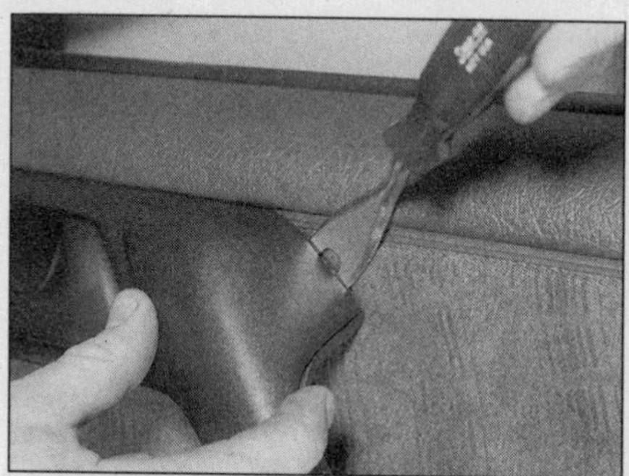
12.7a Unclip the trim cover from the door pull handle . . .

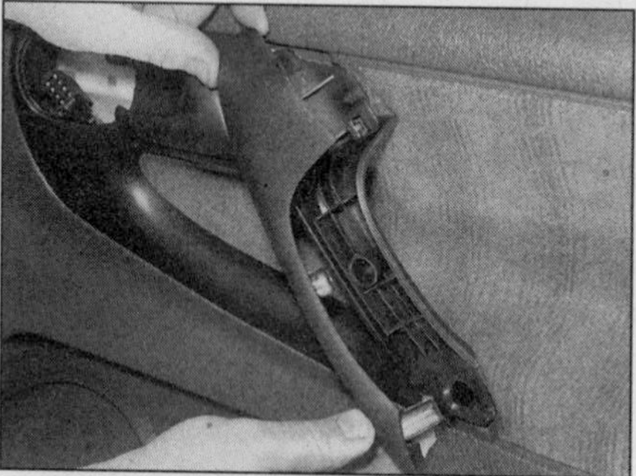
12.7b . . . and remove it from the door

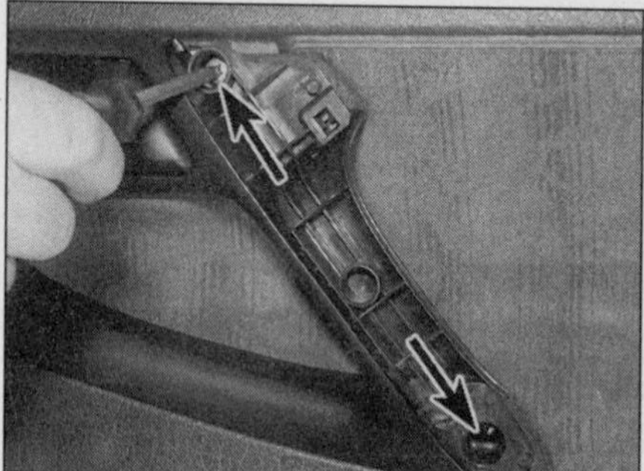
12.8 Door handle surround securing screws (arrowed)

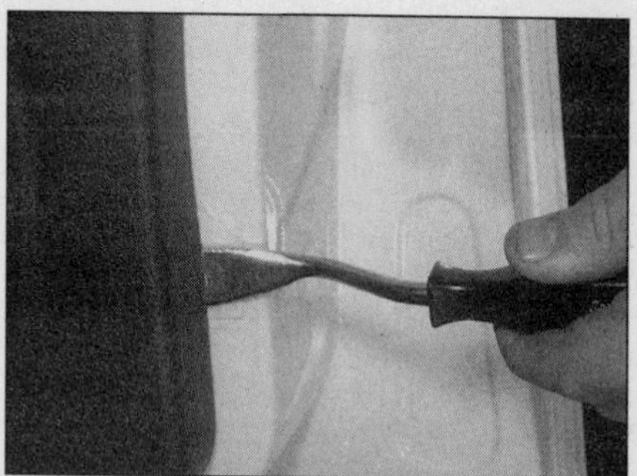
12.9a Lever between the door trim panel and the door to release the trim panel studs . . .

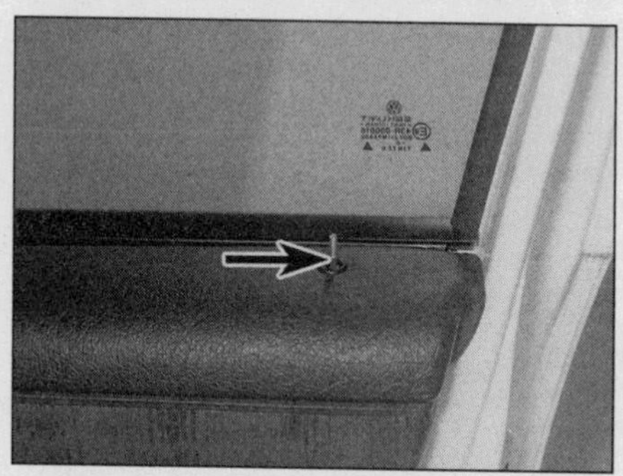
12.9b . . . lift the panel over the door lock operating knob (arrowed) . . .

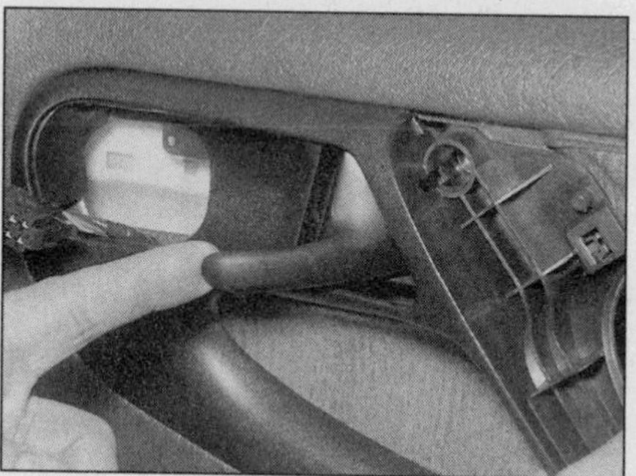
12.9c . . . and release the door panel from the interior lock handle

7 Carefully unclip the upper trim cover from the door pull handle and remove it from the vehicle **(see illustrations)**.

8 Remove the screws securing the interior handle surround **(see illustration)**.

9 Release the door trim panel studs, carefully levering between the panel and door with a flat-bladed screwdriver (or better, a purpose-made tool as shown). Work around the outside of the panel, and when all the studs are released, ease the panel away from the door. Lift the panel over the door lock knob, and release it from the interior lock handle **(see illustrations)**.

### Rear door (where applicable)

10 The procedure for removing the rear door trim panel is very similar to that for the front door panel described previously, ignoring all references to the door mirror.

12.11 If any of the trim panel retaining studs are broken, they should be prised out and renewed

### *Refitting*

11 Refitting the trim panel(s) is the reverse of removal. Before refitting, check whether any of the trim panel retaining studs were broken on removal, and renew them as necessary **(see illustration)**.

## 13 Door handle and lock components - removal and refitting

1 The exterior door handle and lock mechanism were modified for 1998 model year (ie from July 1997 onwards). The later type 'freewheeling' door lock is designed so that the entire lock barrel rotates if excessive force is applied, thereby preventing unauthorised access **(see illustrations)**. It is not recommended that the lock cylinder be removed from the later-type door lock assembly, as a special VW tool is required to reassemble the freewheeling mechanism.

### *Removal*

### Interior door handle

2 Remove the door inner trim panel as described in Section 12.

3 Release the handle retaining clip at the front with a suitable screwdriver, then slide the handle out of the door in a forwards direction, and free it from the end of the link rod **(see illustrations)**.

### Exterior door handle

**Note:** *This task can be performed with the door inner trim panel in position.*

4 If work is being carried out on the front door, insert the key into the lock.

5 Slacken and remove the Torx screw from the rear edge of the door. Move the handle assembly forwards and pivot it out of position. On the front door, as the handle is being removed, rotate the key through 90° (models up to July 1997) or through 45° (models from July 1997) to disengage the handle from the lock operating lever **(see illustrations)**.

6 Recover the handle seals and the lock retaining clips, and inspect them for signs of damage or deterioration; renewing them if necessary. **Note:** *Do not drop the components into the door; if the clip is dropped, it will be necessary to remove the inner trim panel to recover it.*

### Front door lock cylinder (models up to July 1997)

7 Remove the exterior door handle as described in paragraphs 4 to 6.

8 With the key in the lock, unhook the connecting rod from the rear of the lock cylinder and recover the spring.

9 Noting their correct fitted positions, release the coupling plate and spring from the rear of the cylinder, then withdraw the lock cylinder from the handle. Recover the sealing ring from the handle and renew it if damaged.

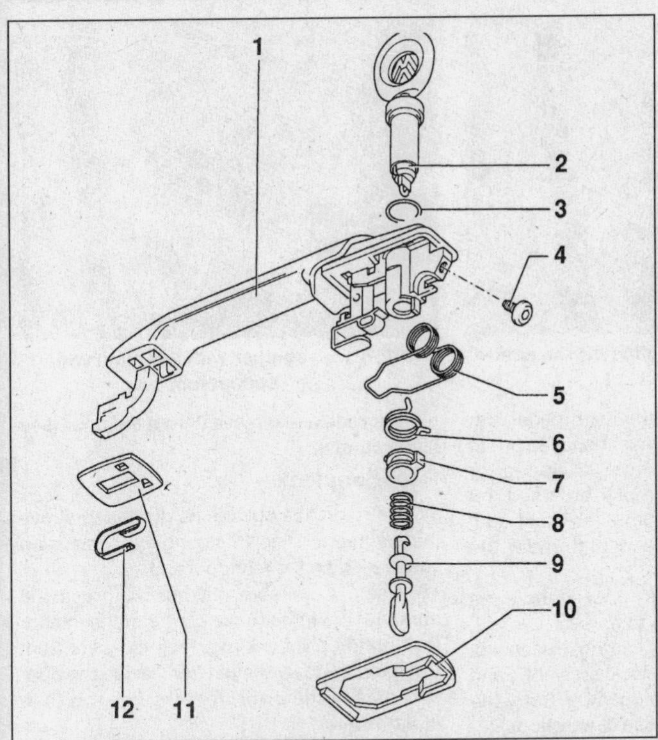


**13.1a Front door handle and lock components - models up to July 1997**

*1 Door handle*
*2 Lock cylinder*
*3 Seal*
*4 Torx screw*
*5 Spring*
*6 Coupling plate spring*
*7 Coupling plate*
*8 Connecting rod spring*
*9 Connecting rod*
*10 Back plate*
*11 Back plate*
*12 Leaf spring*

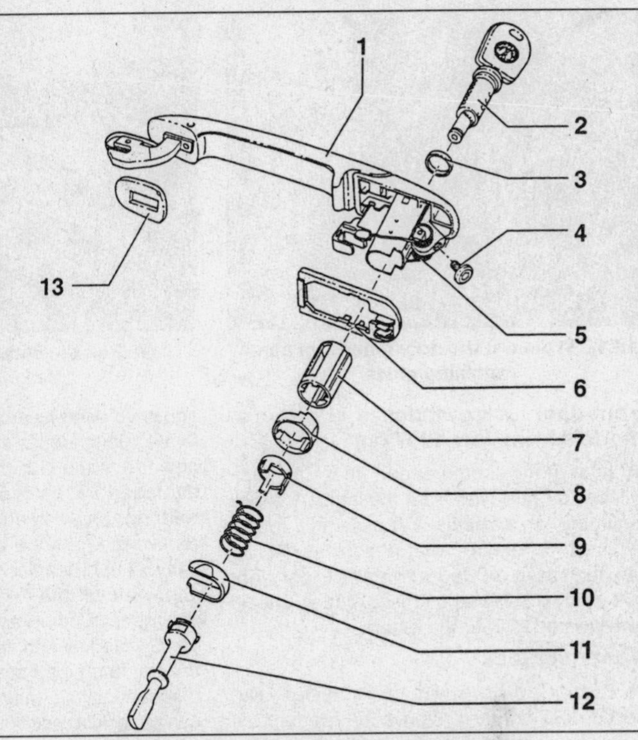


**13.1b Front door handle and lock components - models from July 1997 on**

*1 Door handle*
*2 Lock cylinder*
*3 Seal*
*4 Torx screw*
*5 Spring*
*6 Back plate*
*7 Freewheel sleeve*
*8 Support*
*9 Coupling plate*
*10 Spring*
*11 Locking plate*
*12 Paddle*
*13 Back plate*

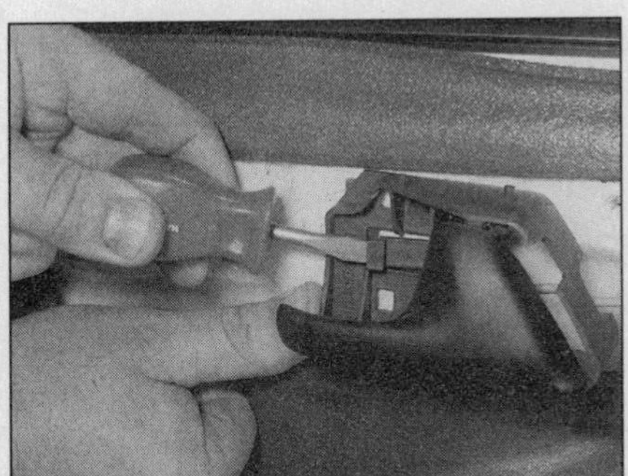

**13.3a Release the interior handle retaining clip using a screwdriver . . .**

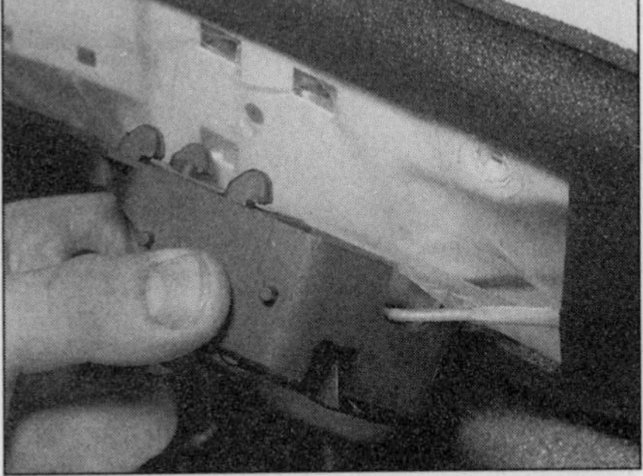

**13.3b . . . then slide the handle out of the door . . .**

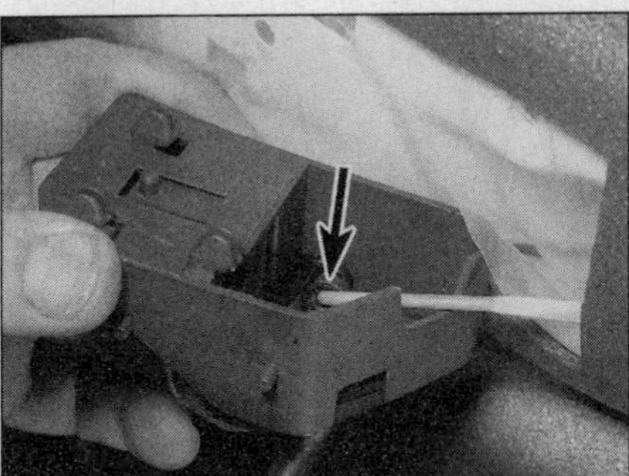

**13.3c . . . and release the link rod (arrowed)**

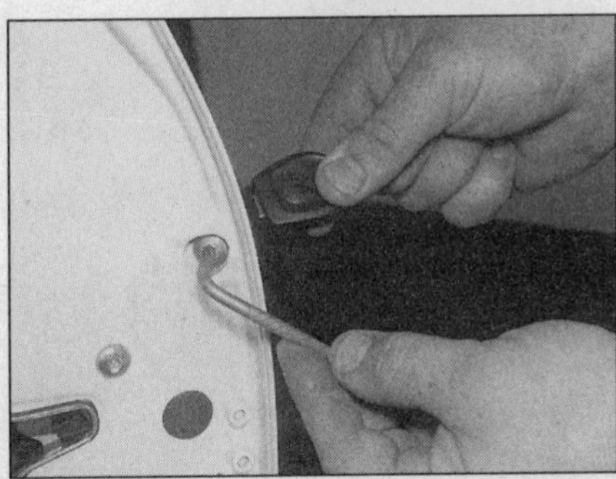

**13.5a Remove the handle securing screw using a Torx key or socket . . .**

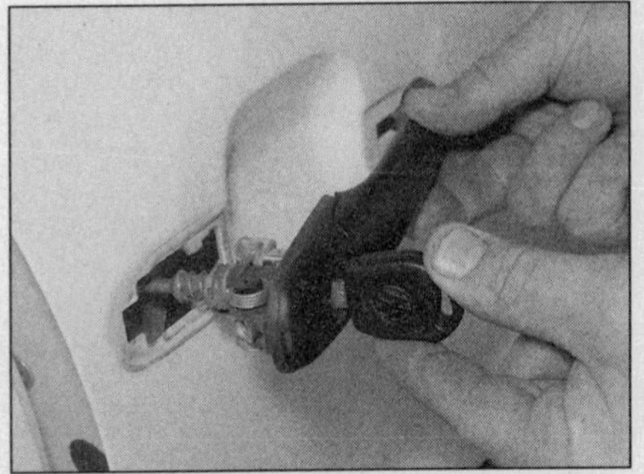

**13.5b . . . then turn the key and disengage the rear end . . .**

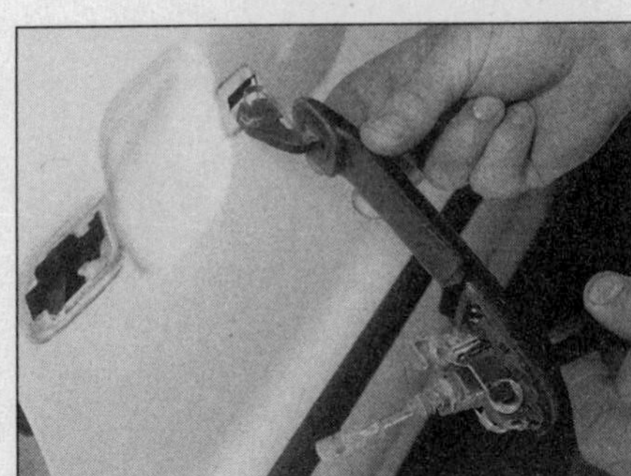

**13.5c . . . and unhook the front end of the handle**

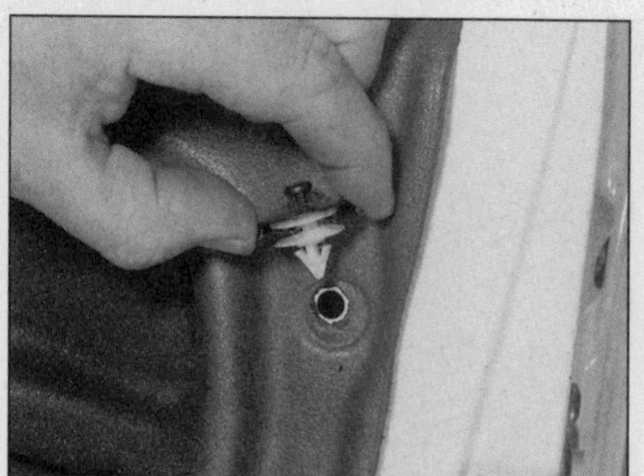
13.12 Prise out the door inner trim panel retaining studs

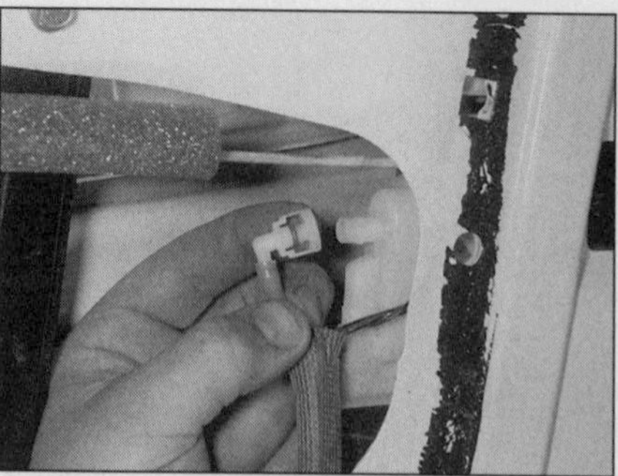
13.15a Pull the vacuum pipe off the central locking unit . . .

13.15b . . . together with the main wiring connector

## Front door lock cylinder (models from July 1997 on)

10 It is not recommended that the lock cylinder be removed from the later-type lock assembly, as a special VW assembly tool is required to ensure that the freewheeling mechanism is refitted correctly. Front door lock cylinder renewal on these models should be entrusted to your VW dealer.

## Front door lock

11 Ensure that the window is in the fully-closed position, then remove the interior door handle as described in paragraphs 2 and 3.

12 Carefully lever out the door trim panel retaining studs from the rear edge of the door **(see illustration)**.

13 Carefully peel the foam insulating panel away from the rear edge of the door (see Section 14). We found that a small trimming knife was useful to slice through the bead of adhesive used to attach the foam panel, but this is a long job, as care must be taken not to cut the panel. If the panel is ripped or damaged, a new one must be used on refitting; any damaged trim clips must also renewed. Continue as described under the relevant sub-heading.

14 Remove the exterior door handle as described in paragraphs 4 to 6.

15 On models with central locking, disconnect the vacuum pipe from the lock assembly, and disconnect the main wiring plug from the central locking positioner **(see illustrations)**.

16 Slacken and remove the lock retaining bolts at the rear edge of the door. Prise out the retaining clips and disconnect the lock link rods from the door frame as necessary. Manoeuvre the lock out through the door inner frame, and disconnect the upper wiring plug from the central locking positioner, where applicable. Disengage the lock from the link rods and remove it from the door **(see illustrations)**.

## Rear door lock

17 Carry out the operations described above in paragraphs 11 to 15, noting that there is no wiring plug on the rear door lock.

18 Using a suitable pin punch, press the spreader pin through the centre of the interior lock button pivot link rod. Free the pivot from the door. Recover the pin from inside the door and detach the pivot from the link rod **(see illustrations)**.

19 Unclip the link rod guide clips from the door.

20 Slacken and remove the lock retaining bolts and manoeuvre the lock and link rod assembly out from the door **(see illustration)**. If necessary, detach the link rods from the lock noting their correct fitted locations; the link rods are different, and must not be interchanged.

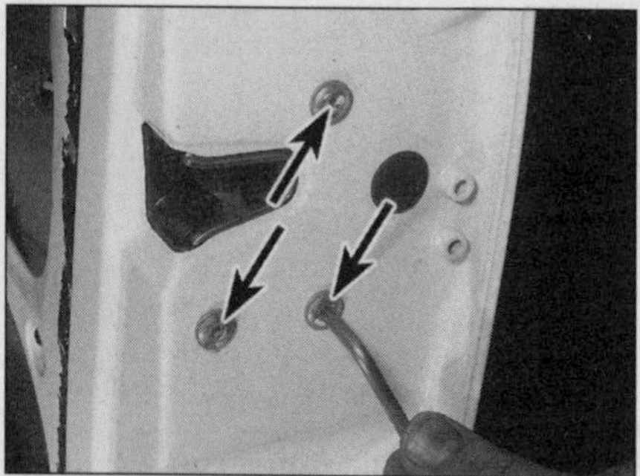
13.16a Unscrew the lock retaining bolts . . .

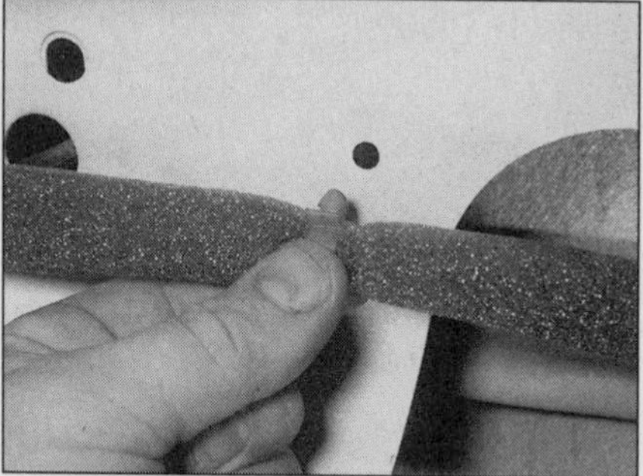
13.16b . . . detach the lock link rod from the door frame . . .

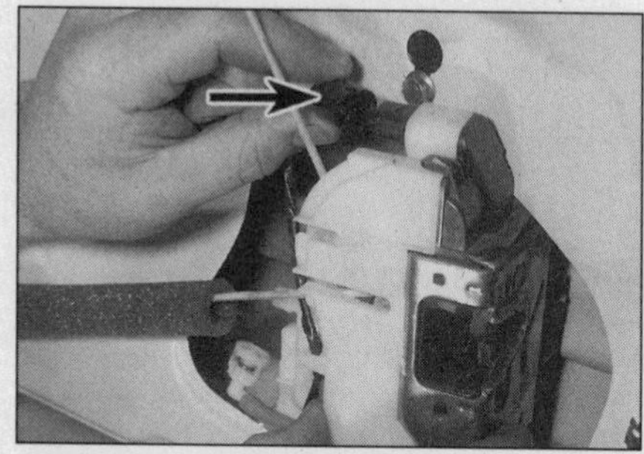
13.16c . . . then pull out the lock and disconnect the upper wiring plug from the central locking unit . . .

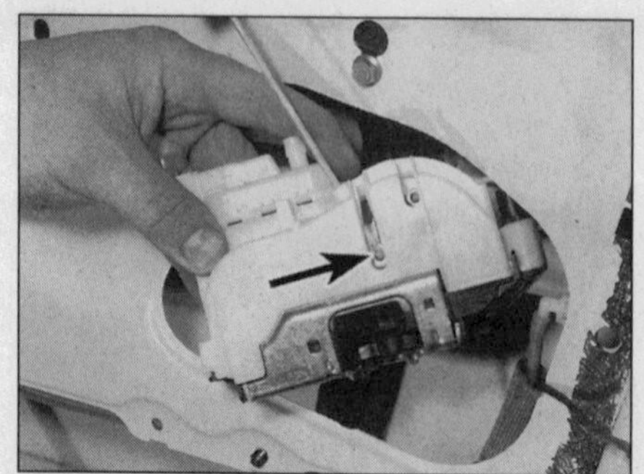
13.16d . . . and disconnect the link rods (arrowed) from the lock

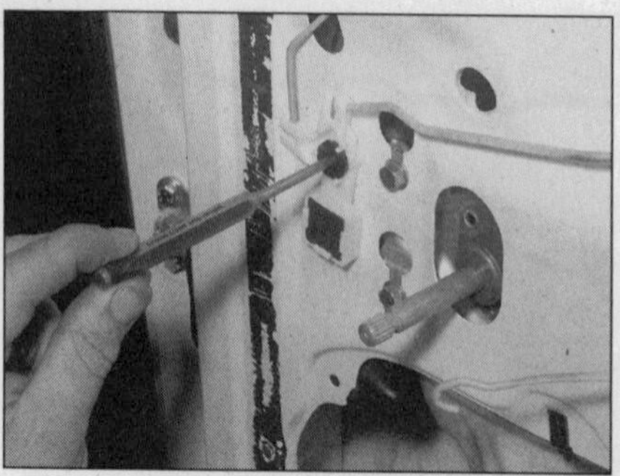
13.18a Using a pin punch, press through the spreader pin . . .

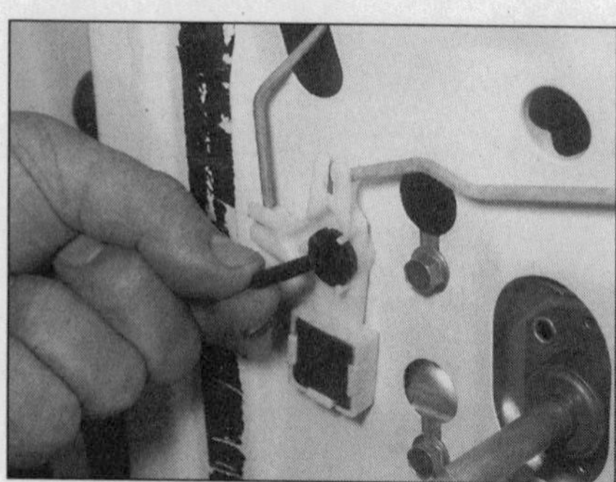
13.18b . . . which fits in the centre of the link rod pivot

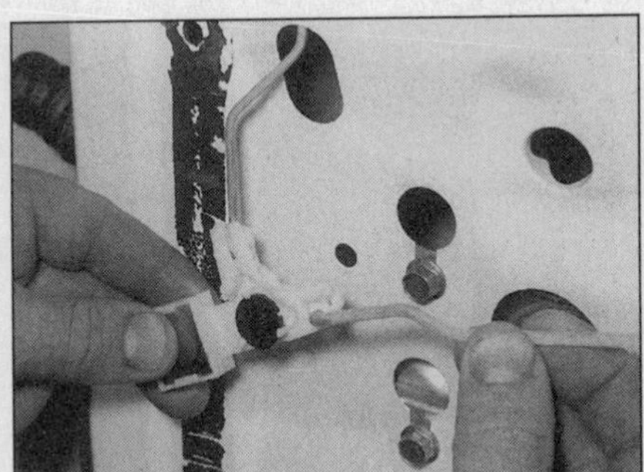

13.18c Unclip the link rods

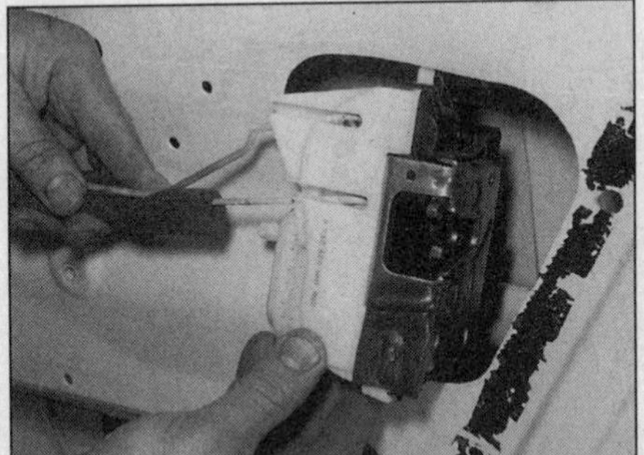

13.20 Removing a rear door lock

13.30 Door lock adjustment screw (arrowed)

## *Refitting*

### Interior door handle

**21** Engage the handle with the link rod, and clip it back into position. Make sure the handle operates correctly, then refit the trim panel as described in Section 12.

### Exterior door handle

**22** Fit the lock retaining clip to the door, and fit the seals to the rear of the handle. **Note:** *Do not drop the clip into the door; if the clip is dropped it will be necessary to remove the inner trim panel to recover it.*

**23** Hook the lock front pivot into place, then clip the rear of the handle into position. On the front door, rotate the key through 90° (models up to July 1997) or through 45° (models from July 1997) to engage the handle with the lock operating lever.

**24** Check the operation of the handle, then refit the Torx screw to the rear edge of the door.

### Front door lock cylinder (models up to July 1997)

**25** Lubricate the outside of the lock cylinder and the locking plates with a suitable lubricant (VW recommend the use of grease G 000 400 - available from your VW dealer).

**26** Fit the sealing ring to the handle, and insert the cylinder.

**27** Refit the coupling plate and spring to the cylinder, making sure they are correctly located, then check the operation of the lock cylinder.

**28** Fit the spring to the connecting rod, and hook the rod onto the rear of the lock cylinder.

**29** Refit the exterior handle as described in paragraphs 22 to 24.

### Front door lock

**30** Before refitting, slacken the lock adjusting (Torx) screw - this screw is normally hidden behind a plastic plug in the rear edge of the door **(see illustration)**. On the right-hand door, this screw has a *left-hand thread* - ie it unscrews *clockwise*.

**31** Manoeuvre the lock assembly into position, and engage it with the link rod.

**32** Refit the lock bolts and tighten them to the specified torque. Where necessary, reconnect the vacuum pipe and wiring connector(s) (as applicable) to the lock assembly.

**33** Refit the exterior handle as described in paragraphs 22 to 24.

**34** Remove the plastic plug from the door to gain access to the lock adjustment screw. Noting that the screw may have a left-hand thread (see paragraph 30), tighten the screw to 3 Nm (2 lbf ft) then refit the plastic plug.

**35** Where necessary, refit the regulator guide rail retaining bolts, and adjust as described in Section 14.

**36** Check the operation of the lock and handle, then press the polythene insulating panel back onto the door and refit the door trim panel retaining clips.

**37** Refit the interior door handle as described in paragraph 21.

### Rear door lock

**38** Refit the link rods to the lock, making sure they are correctly refitted.

**39** Before refitting, slacken the lock adjusting (Torx) screw - this screw is normally hidden behind a plastic plug in the rear edge of the door. On the right-hand door, this screw has a *left-hand thread* - ie it unscrews *clockwise*.

**40** Manoeuvre the lock assembly into position and tighten the retaining bolts to the specified torque. Where necessary, reconnect the vacuum pipe to the lock assembly.

**41** Attach the link rod to the pivot, and clip the pivot into the door. Secure the pivot in position with the spreader pin.

**42** Carry out the operations described in paragraphs 33 to 37, ignoring the remark about the regulator bolts.

## 14 Door window glass and regulator - removal and refitting

## *Removal*

**1** Remove the interior door handle as described in Section 13.

**2** Carefully lever out the door trim panel retaining clips from the door.

**3** On models with front door speakers, remove five screws and lift away the speaker mounting panel. Disconnect the speaker wiring as it becomes accessible **(see illustrations)**.

**4** Carefully peel the foam insulating panel away from the door, and remove the panel, feeding the wiring through the holes provided.

14.3a Remove the five screws (arrowed) . . .

14.3b . . . and lift away the speaker and mounting panel

14.3c Disconnect the wiring from the rear of the speaker

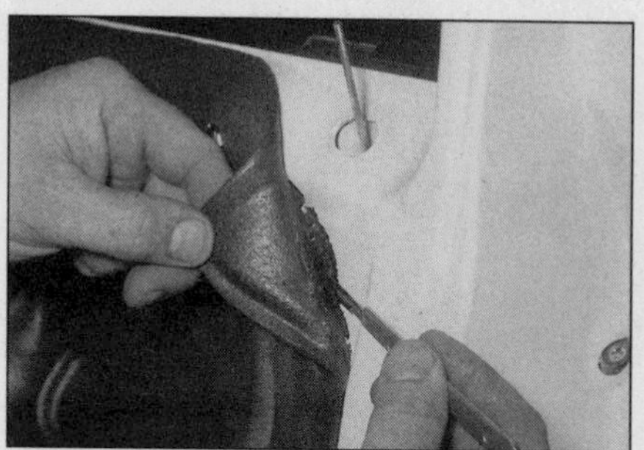
14.4a Using a small knife to slice through the adhesive securing the foam panel to the door

14.4b Removing the foam panel

14.6a Loosen the window clamp bolts . . .

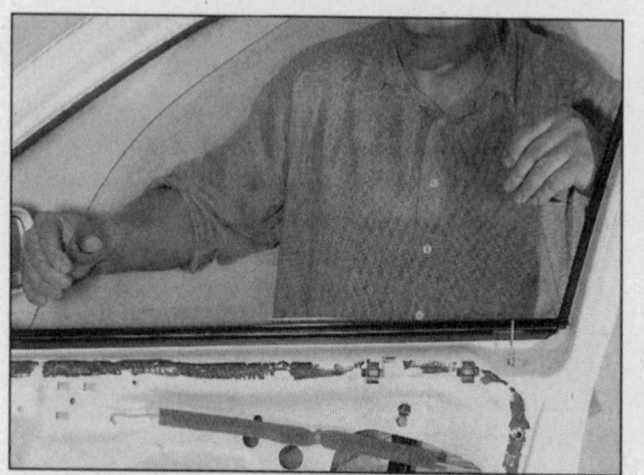
14.6b . . . then lift the window glass upwards and out of the door frame

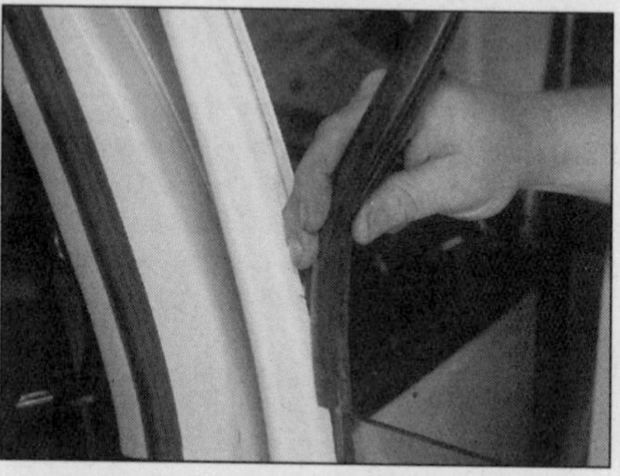
14.10a Pull off the rubber guides in front . . .

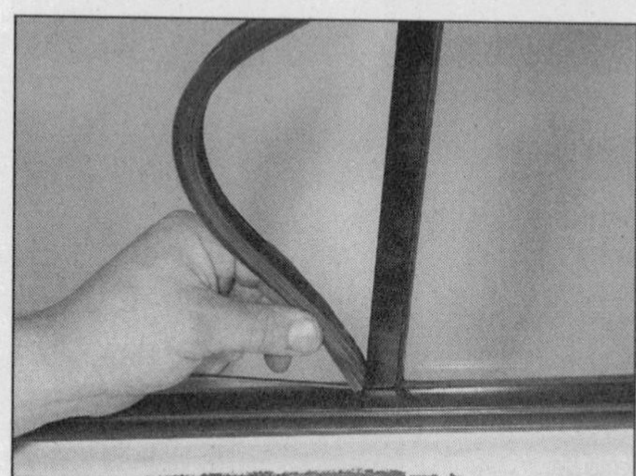
14.10b . . . and to the rear of the rear door window

We found that a small trimming knife was useful to slice through the bead of adhesive used to attach the foam panel, but this is a long job, as care must be taken not to cut the panel **(see illustrations)**. If the panel is ripped or damaged, a new one must be used on refitting; any damaged trim clips must also renewed. Continue as described under the relevant sub-heading.

## Front door window glass

5 Position the window glass so the glass clamps on the regulator mechanism are accessible through the door panel cutaways.

6 Slacken the window clamp bolts, and release the clamps from the glass. Pull the glass upwards, then tilt it towards the front and manoeuvre the window glass out through the top of the door **(see illustrations)**.

## Rear door window glass

7 Remove the interior door handle as described in Section 13.

8 Carefully lever out the door trim panel retaining clips from the door.

9 Carefully peel the foam insulating panel away from the door and remove the panel. We found that a small trimming knife was useful to slice through the bead of adhesive used to attach the foam panel, but this is a long job, as care must be taken not to cut the panel. If the panel is ripped or damaged, a new one must be used on refitting; any damaged trim clips must also renewed. Continue as described under the relevant sub-heading.

10 Pull out the rubber guides in front and to the rear of the window **(see illustrations)**.

11 Remove the rear guide channel upper screw and lower retaining bolt **(see illustrations)**.

12 The window glass is secured to the regulator by a plastic spreader pin and plug - the pin fits inside the plug. Using a 3 mm pin punch, tap out the spreader pin, then use a larger punch to drive out the plug, and recover them both from the door **(see illustration)**.

13 Lift up the window glass to release it from the regulator, and move it down as far as possible.

14 Pull the rear guide channel forwards off the door fixed glass, taking care not to pull off the

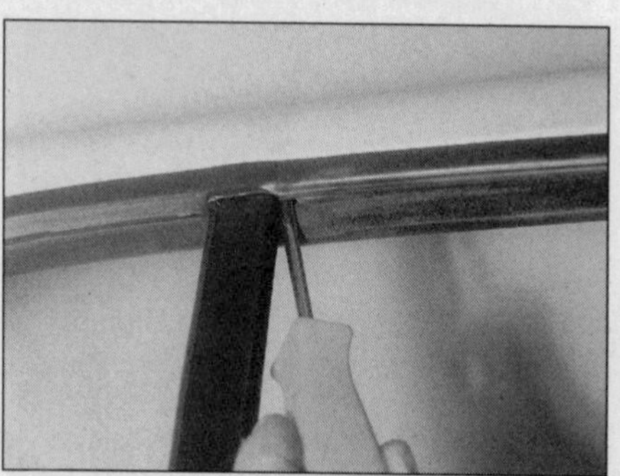
14.11a Remove the rear guide channel upper screw . . .

14.11b . . . and lower retaining bolt

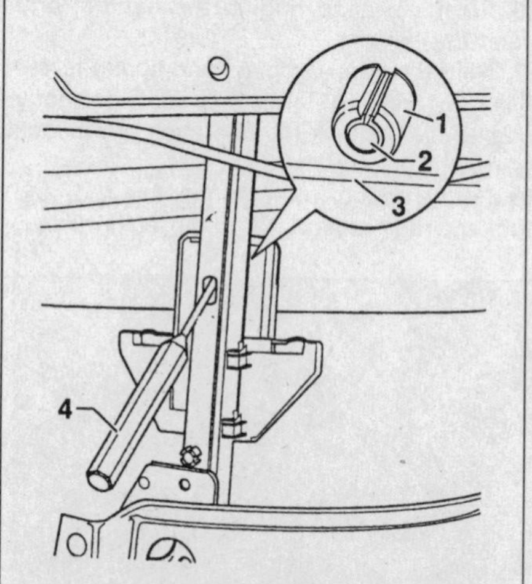

14.12 Rear window glass-to-regulator attachment details

*1 Plastic plug*
*2 Spreader pin*
*3 Window glass*
*4 Pin punch*

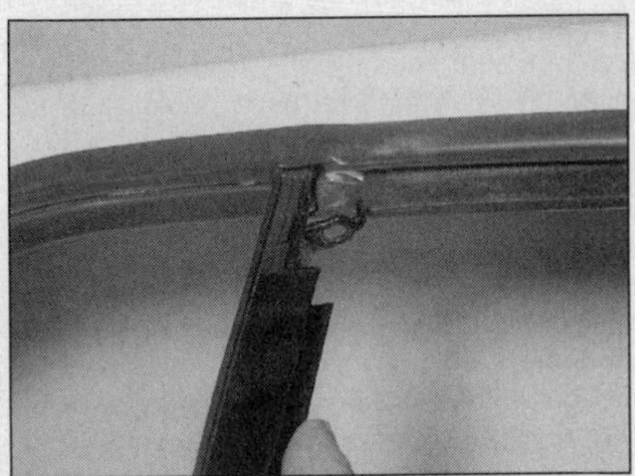

**14.14a Pull the guide channel downwards . . .**

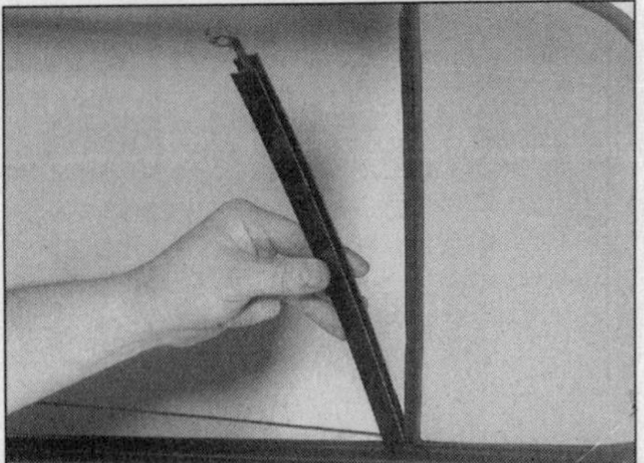

**14.14b . . . then remove it from the door**

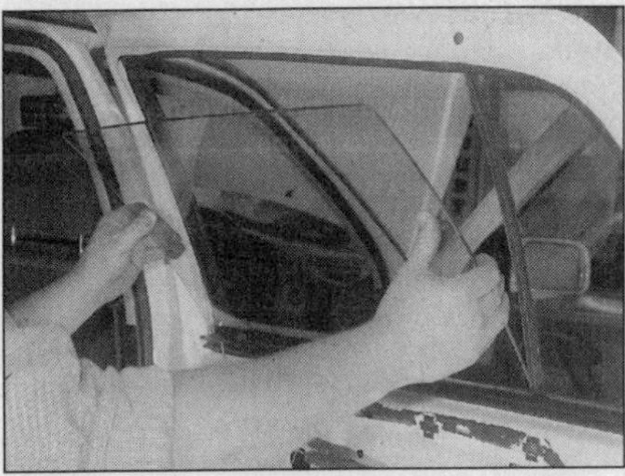

**14.15 Lifting out the rear door window glass**

rubber seal beneath it. Once it is free, pull the channel down a little to release the top from the rubber seal, then remove it upwards from the door **(see illustrations)**.

**15** Pull the window glass upwards out of the door **(see illustration)**.

**16** If necessary, the fixed glass can now be disengaged from the sealing strip and removed from the door.

### Front window regulator

**17** Remove the window glass as described earlier.

**18** Release the retaining clip, and free the regulator cables from the door. On models with electric windows, disconnect the wiring connector from the motor **(see illustration)**.

**19** Loosen the regulator retaining bolts, then lift the regulator slightly so that the bolt heads can be passed through the holes in the inner door **(see illustrations)**.

**20** Manoeuvre the regulator mechanism downwards and out through the door aperture **(see illustration)**.

### Rear window regulator

**21** Remove the window glass as described earlier.

**22** Loosen the regulator retaining bolts, then lift the regulator slightly so that the bolt heads can be passed through the holes in the inner door **(see illustration)**. Recover the foam spacer from the regulator spindle, where fitted.

**23** Manoeuvre the regulator downwards out through the door aperture **(see illustration)**.

## *Refitting*

### Front door window glass

**24** Manoeuvre the window glass into position and engage it with the regulator clamps. Make sure the glass is correctly seated, then lightly tighten the regulator clamp nuts.

**25** Check that the window glass moves smoothly and easily, and closes fully. If necessary, slacken the regulator clamp nuts then reposition the glass as necessary. Once the window operation is correct, tighten the clamp nuts to the specified torque.

**26** Press the foam insulating panel back into position, making sure it is correctly seated, and refit the trim panel clips. Refit the inner trim panel as described in Section 12.

### Rear door window glass

**27** Where removed, ease the fixed glass into position, making sure it is correctly seated in the sealing strip.

**28** Refit the rear guide channel to the fixed glass.

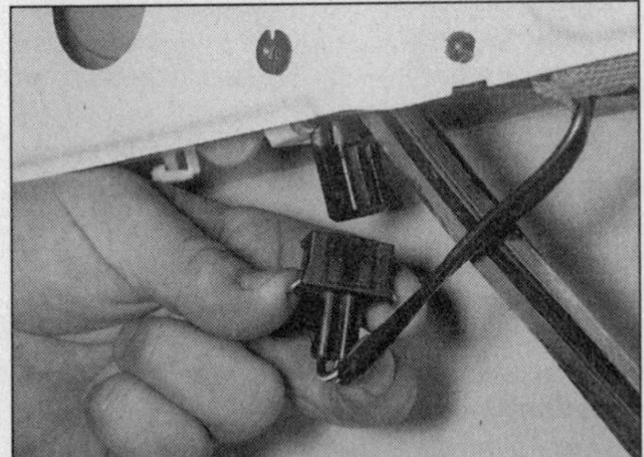

**14.18 Disconnecting the electric window motor wiring plug**

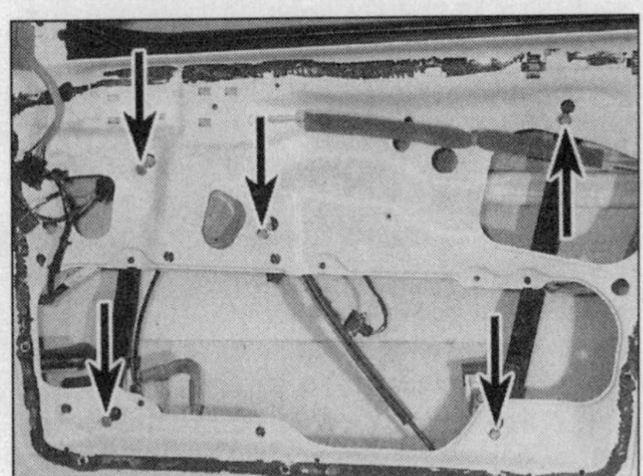

**14.19a Front window regulator bolt locations (arrowed)**

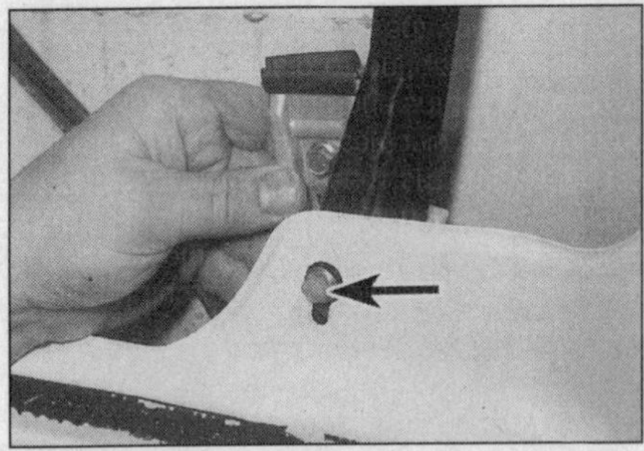

**14.19b Lift the regulator so that the bolt heads (arrowed) can pass through the holes in the door frame**

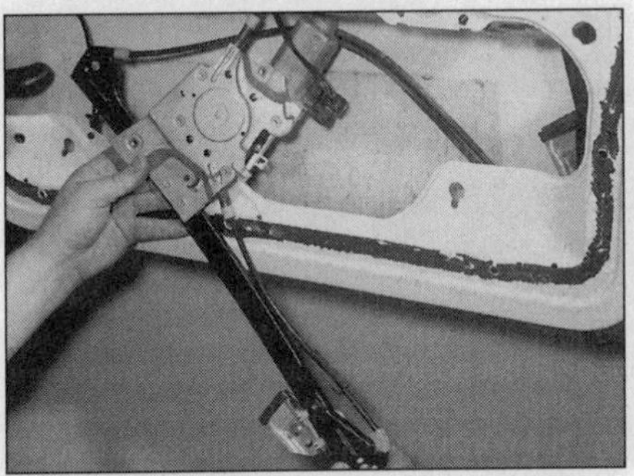

**14.20 Removing the window regulator from a front door**

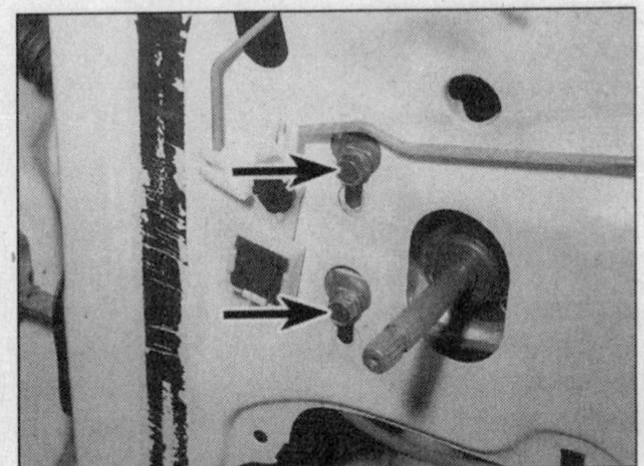

**14.22 Rear door window regulator bolts (two of four arrowed)**

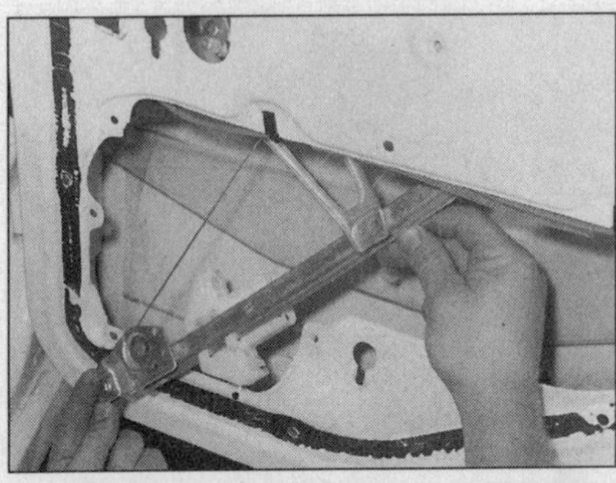

**14.23 Removing the rear door window regulator**

**29** Insert the plastic plug and spreader pin into the window glass, so that the assembly protrudes an equal amount either side of the glass **(see illustration)**.

**30** Guide the window glass into the top of the door, taking care as it is quite difficult to align. Insert the glass into the top of the lifting rail slot, again ensuring that the edge of the glass is central in the slot.

**31** Tap the top of the glass down gently, so that the spreader pin/plug assembly locates in the lifting rail.

**32** Refit the rear guide channel upper and lower retaining screws, then fit the front and rear rubber guides.

**33** Check that the window glass moves smoothly and easily, and closes fully.

**34** Once the window is operating correctly, press the foam insulating panel back into position, making sure it is correctly seated, and refit the trim panel clips. Refit the inner trim panel as described in Section 12.

### Front window regulator

**35** Manoeuvre the regulator into position through the door aperture, hooking the bolt heads into engagement with the inner door. Tighten all its fixings to the specified torque. Where necessary, reconnect the wiring connector to the regulator motor.

**36** Clip the regulator cables into position then refit the glass as described above.

### Rear window regulator

**37** Manoeuvre the regulator into position through the door aperture then refit the retaining bolts and tighten them to the specified torque. Where necessary, reconnect the wiring connector to the regulator motor.

**38** Refit the glass as described above.

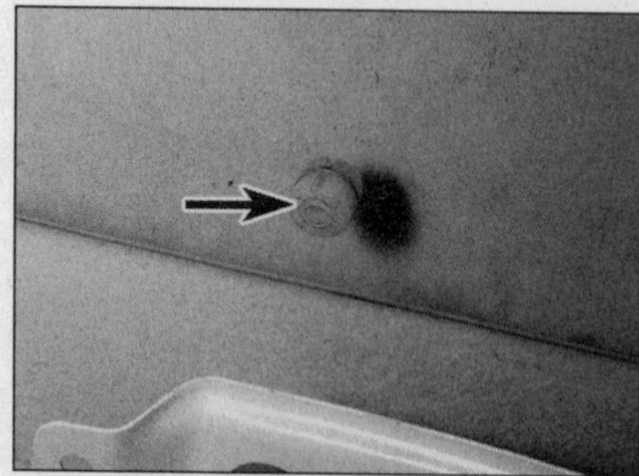

**14.29 Fit the plastic plug and spreader pin (arrowed) so that they protrude an equal amount either side of the glass**

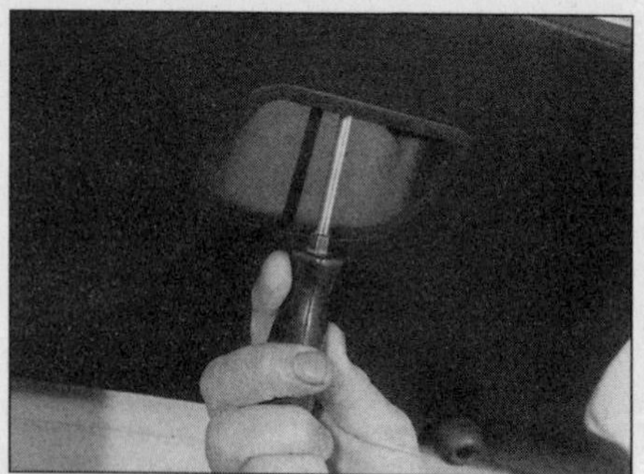

**15.2a Inside the tailgate, remove the handle retaining screw . . .**

## 15 Tailgate and support struts - removal and refitting

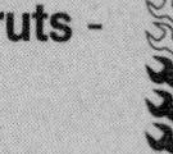

### *Removal*

### Tailgate

**1** Open up the tailgate, then disconnect the battery negative terminal. **Note:** *If the vehicle has a security-coded radio, check that you have a copy of the code number before disconnecting the battery. Refer to your VW dealer if in doubt.*

**2** Slacken and remove the tailgate handle retaining screw, then release the tailgate trim panel clips, carefully levering between the panel and tailgate with a flat-bladed screwdriver. Work around the outside of the panel, and when all the clips are released, remove the panel **(see illustrations)**.

**3** Disconnect the wiring connectors situated behind the trim panel, and free the washer hose from the tailgate wiper motor. Also disconnect the wiring connectors from the heated rear screen terminals, and free the wiring grommets from the tailgate.

**4** Tie a piece of string to each end of the wiring then, noting the correct routing of the wiring harness, release the harness rubber grommets from the tailgate and withdraw the wiring. When the end of the wiring appears, untie the string and leave it in position in the tailgate; it can then be used on refitting to draw the wiring into position.

**5** Using a suitable marker pen, draw around the outline of each hinge, marking its correct position on the tailgate.

**6** Have an assistant support the tailgate, then release the support struts from their balljoint mountings on the tailgate as described in paragraph 10. Slacken and remove the bolts securing the hinges to the tailgate, and remove the tailgate from the vehicle **(see illustration)**. Where necessary, recover the gaskets fitted between the hinge and tailgate.

**7** Inspect the hinges for signs of wear or damage and renew if necessary. The hinges are secured to the vehicle by nuts or bolts (depending on model) which can be accessed once the headlining has been freed from the trim strip and peeled back.

**8** On refitting ensure that the hinge gasket is in good condition, and secure the hinge in position.

### Support struts

**9** Support the tailgate in the open position, using a stout piece of wood, or with the help of an assistant.

**10** Using a small flat-bladed screwdriver, raise the spring clip and pull the support strut off its balljoint mounting on the tailgate **(see illustration)**. Raise the second retaining clip then detach the strut from the balljoint on the body and remove it from the vehicle. If the struts are to be re-used, do not pull the spring clips out completely, or they will be damaged.

### *Refitting*

### Tailgate

**11** Refitting is the reverse of removal, aligning the hinges with the marks made before removal.

**12** On completion, close the tailgate and check its alignment with the surrounding panels. If necessary, slight adjustment can be made by slackening the retaining bolts and repositioning the tailgate slightly on its hinges. If the tailgate buffers are in need of adjustment, continue as follows.

**13** Carefully lever out the retaining pins and

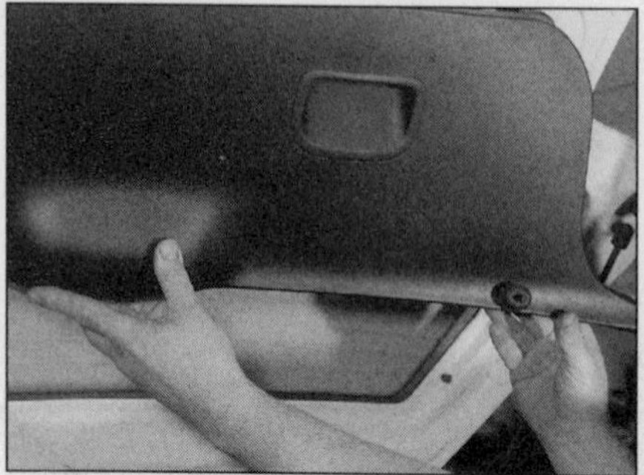

**15.2b . . . then release the securing clips and remove the tailgate trim panel**

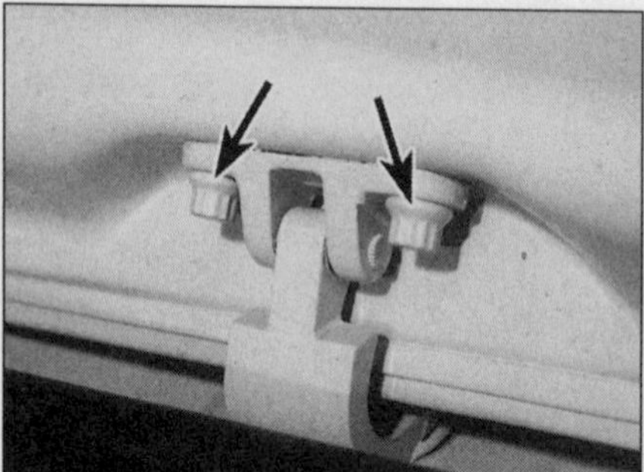

**15.6 Tailgate hinge securing bolts (arrowed)**

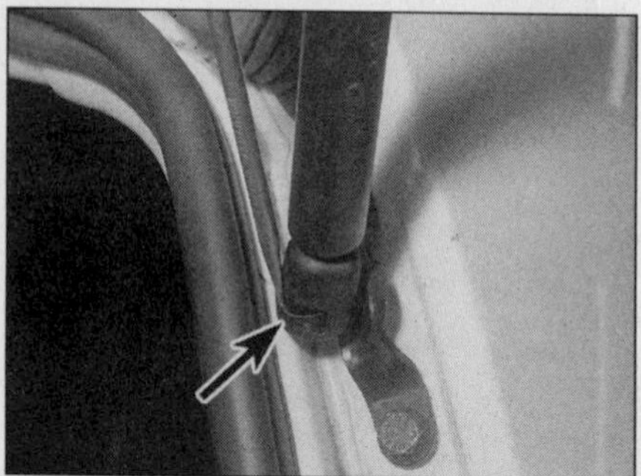

**15.10 Prise out the tailgate support strut spring clip (arrowed)**

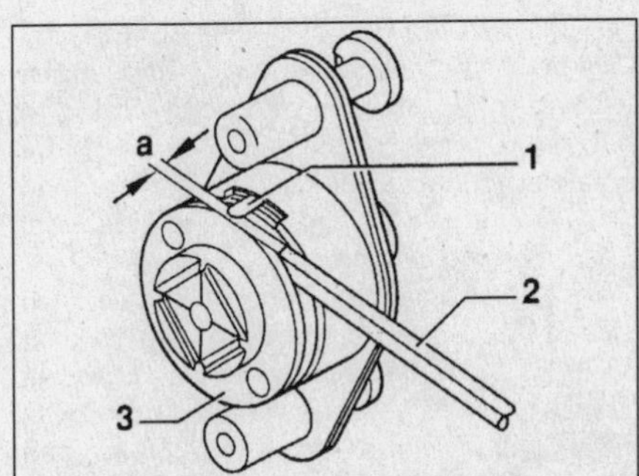


**15.13a Tailgate buffer initial adjustment**

*1 Spacer web*
*2 3 mm Allen key*
*3 Threaded sleeve*
*a = 3 mm*

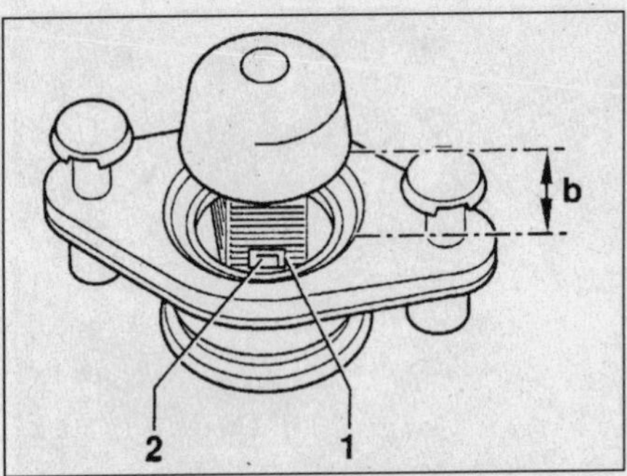


**15.13b Tailgate rubber buffer setting**

*1 Recess*
*2 Locking lugs*
*b = 10 mm*

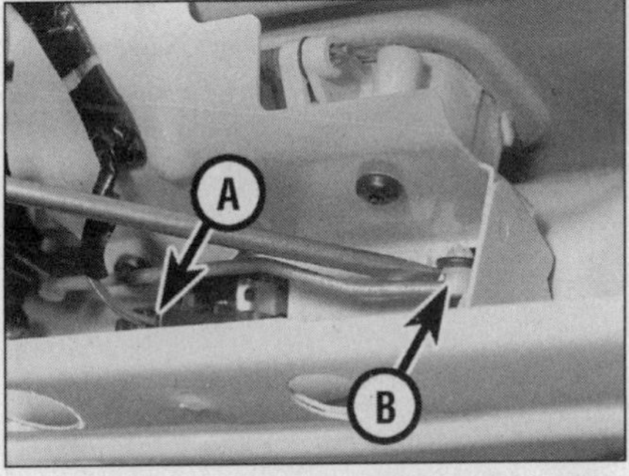


**16.2a Boot light wiring plug (A) and lock operating rod (B)**

remove the buffer from the tailgate. Remove the rubber pad from the buffer to gain access to the clamping screw, then slacken the screw and adjust the *left-hand-threaded* sleeve to provide a 3 mm clearance as shown **(see illustration)**. Refit the rubber pad then pull out the buffer slide then push it back in until the lugs engage with the slots in the slide, the distance between the rubber and buffer should be as shown **(see illustration)**. Refit the buffer to the tailgate and secure it in position with the retaining pins. Close the tailgate to the second lock detent, then open it up again to reset the buffer. Remove the rubber pad and complete the adjustment by tightening the clamp screw lightly (1 to 2 Nm) and refitting the rubber.

### Support struts

**14** Refitting is a reverse of the removal procedure, ensuring that the strut is securely held by its retaining clips.

## 16 Tailgate lock components - removal and refitting

### *Removal*

### Tailgate lock

**1** Open up the tailgate, then remove the tailgate trim panel as described in paragraph 2 of Section 15.

**2** Disconnect the wiring plug for the boot light, then detach the lock and handle operating rod using a suitable flat-bladed screwdriver **(see illustrations)**.

**3** Loosen and remove the lock retaining screws, then manoeuvre the lock out of position **(see illustrations)**.

### Tailgate lock handle

**4** Open up the tailgate, then remove the tailgate trim panel as described in paragraph 2 of Section 15.

**5** Disconnect the pull rod from the handle assembly, and where applicable, unclip the central locking operating rod **(see illustrations)**.

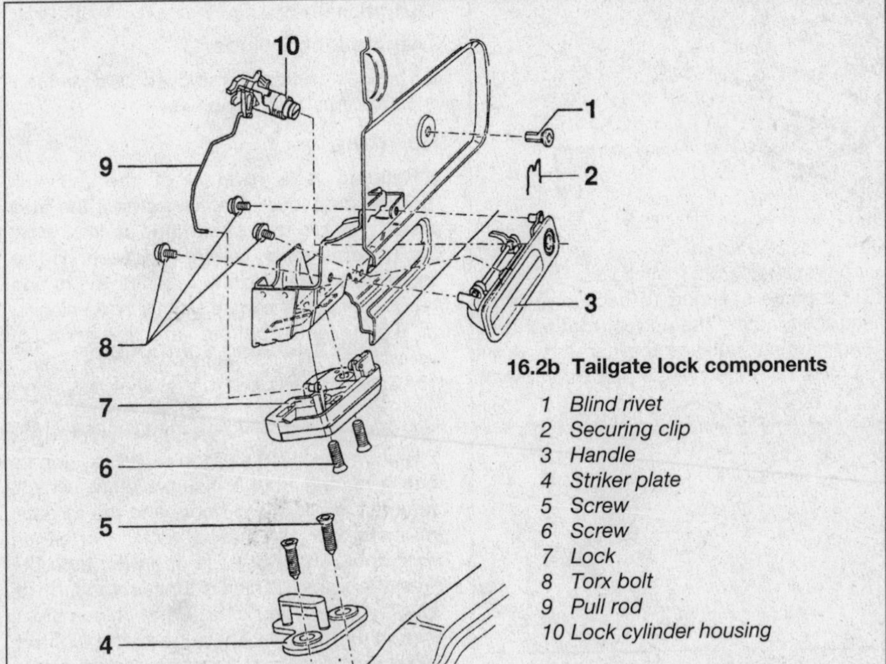


**16.2b Tailgate lock components**

*1 Blind rivet*
*2 Securing clip*
*3 Handle*
*4 Striker plate*
*5 Screw*
*6 Screw*
*7 Lock*
*8 Torx bolt*
*9 Pull rod*
*10 Lock cylinder housing*

**16.3a Tailgate lock retaining screws (arrowed)**

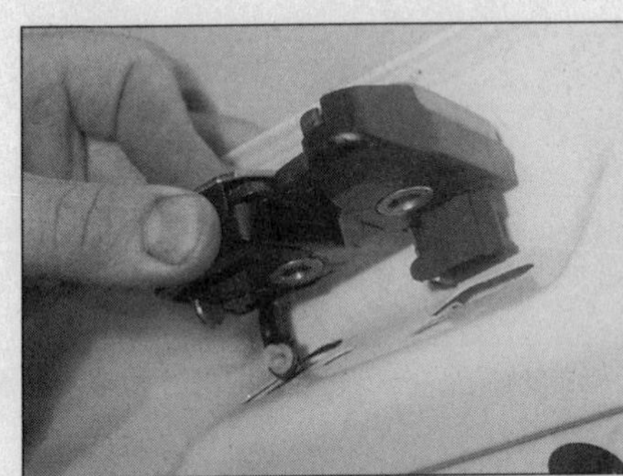

**16.3b Removing the tailgate lock**

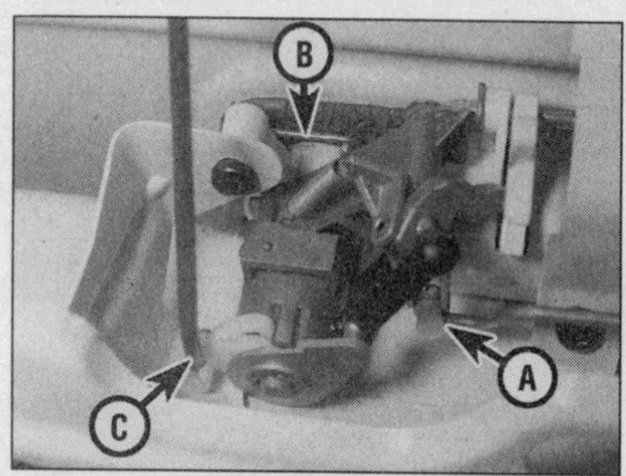

16.5a Tailgate lock cylinder, showing handle pull rod (A), wire clip (B) and central locking rod (C)

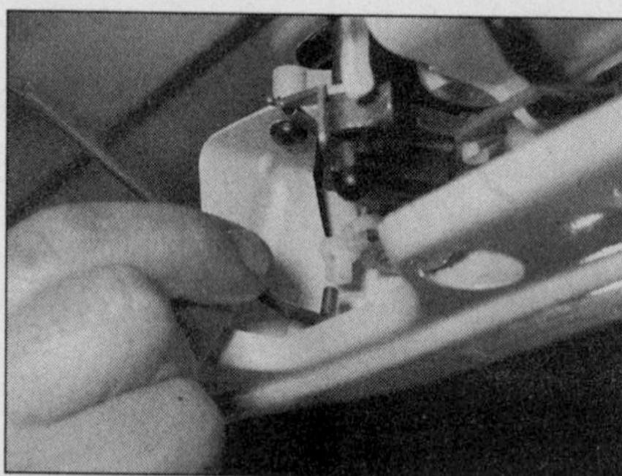
16.5b Disconnecting the central locking operating rod

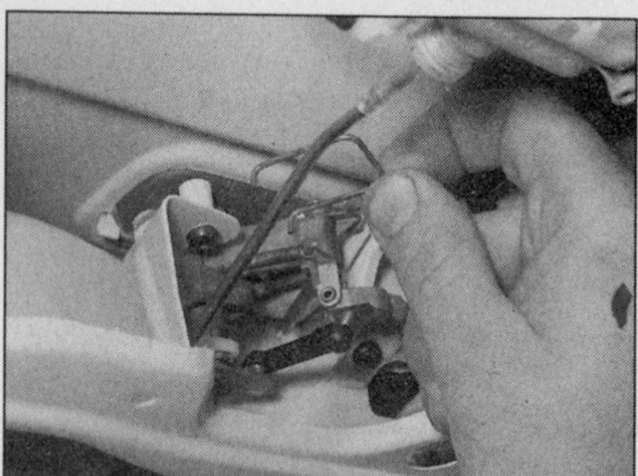
16.6a Prise out the wire clip . . .

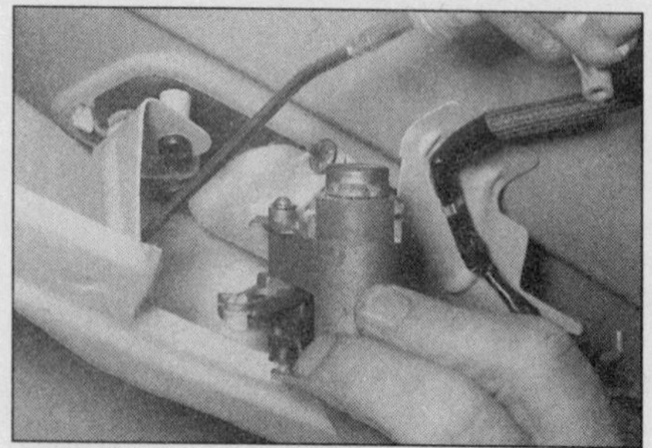
16.6b . . . and withdraw the lock cylinder

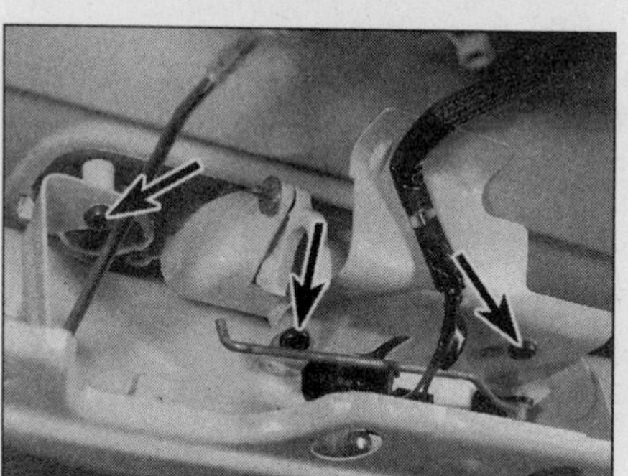
16.7a Unscrew the Torx bolts (arrowed) . . .

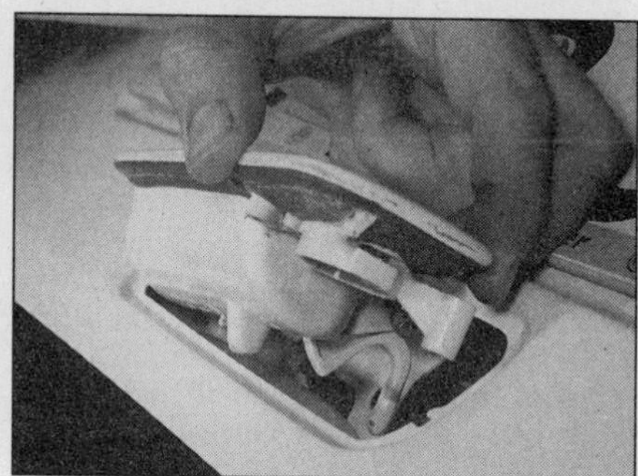
16.7b . . . and withdraw the handle from the tailgate

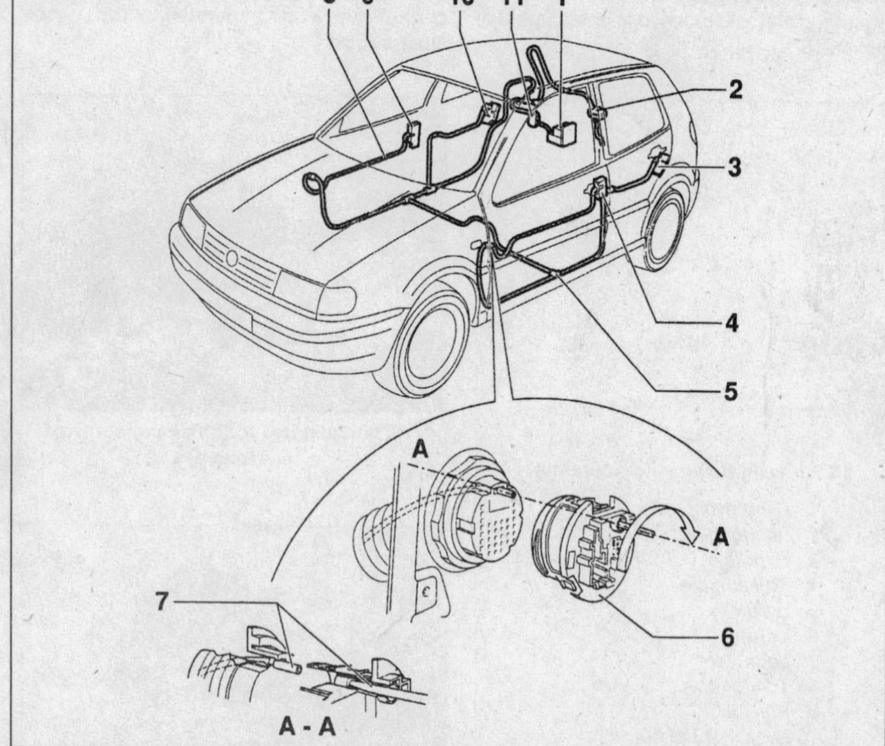

17.1 Central locking system components

1 *Bi-pressure pump*
2 *Tailgate lock positioner*
3 *Rear door lock positioner*
4 *Front door lock positioner*
5 *T-piece*
6 *Door pillar connector*
7 *Pipe connector*
8 *Vacuum pipe*
9 *Front door lock positioner*
10 *Rear door lock positioner*
11 *Fuel filler flap positioner*

**6** Lever out the securing wire clip and detach the lock cylinder from the handle **(see illustrations)**. Recover the O-ring seal.

**7** Remove three Torx retaining bolts and remove the handle from the tailgate **(see illustrations)**.

### Tailgate lock cylinder

**8** The lock cylinder is removed as described in paragraphs 5 and 6 above.

### *Refitting*

**9** Refitting is a reversal of the relevant removal procedure. Before refitting the trim panel, check the operation of the lock components and (where necessary) the central locking system.

## 17 Central locking components - removal and refitting

**1** Higher-specification models are equipped with a central door locking system, which automatically locks all doors and the tailgate in unison with the manual locking of either front door. The system is operated by a bi-pressure pump, which supplies vacuum to lock the doors, and pressure to unlock them **(see illustration)**. Apart from the central locking positioners and the bi-pressure pump, the door locks are identical to those on models without central locking.

**2** Should the system develop a fault, the condition and security of the hoses should first be checked. A leak will cause the bi-

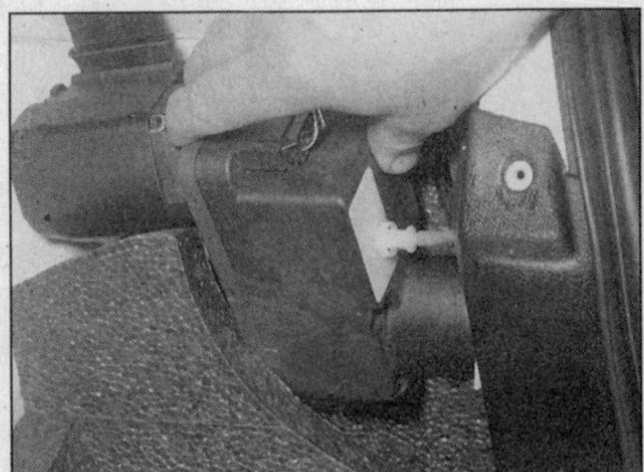

17.5a Pull out the bi-pressure pump . . .

17.5b . . . then disconnect the wiring plug . . .

17.5c . . . and the vacuum connection

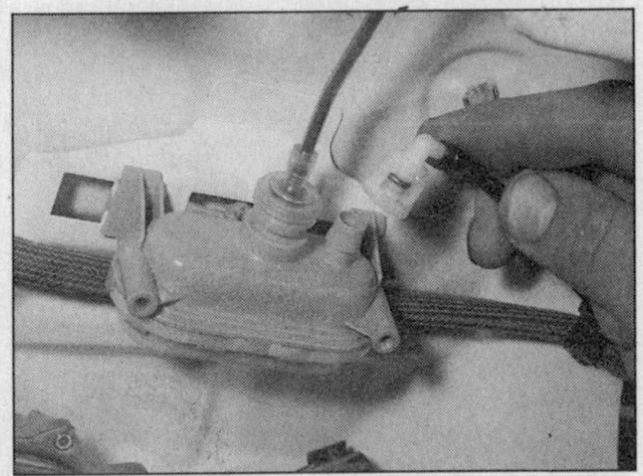

17.9 Pulling off the vacuum pipe from the tailgate lock positioner

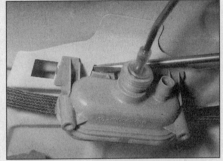

17.11a Lift up the retaining clip . . .

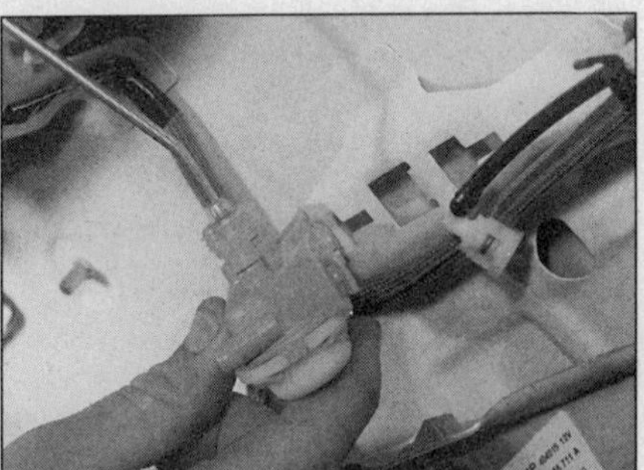

17.11b . . . then slide the positioner to the left and remove

pressure pump to run longer than five seconds, and if it runs for thirty-five seconds, an internal control unit will automatically switch it off.

## Removal

### Central locking pressure pump

**3** The central locking operating pump is located on the right-hand side of the luggage compartment, behind the right-hand side trim panel. Before removal, disconnect the battery negative lead. **Note:** *If the vehicle has a security-coded radio, check that you have a copy of the code number before disconnecting the battery. Refer to your VW dealer if in doubt.*

**4** Open the tailgate, then lower the right-hand side trim panel by turning the two fasteners through 90°.

**5** Lift out the first-aid box tray, where fitted. Lift the pump carefully out of the insulation packing, then disconnect the wiring connector and pressure pipe from the pump, and remove the pump from the vehicle **(see illustrations)**.

### Door lock positioner

**6** The positioner is removed with the door lock, as described in Section 13.

**7** To remove the positioner from the lock, first turn the lock latch to the locked position then pull off the door window stop buffer. Unscrew and remove the positioner retaining Torx screw. Release the retaining clips and remove the positioner from the lock, noting how the positioner plunger is engaged with the lock lever.

### Tailgate lock positioner

**8** Remove the tailgate trim panel as described in paragraph 2 of Section 15.

**9** Disconnect the vacuum pipe from the positioner **(see illustration)**.

**10** Referring to Section 16, disconnect the operating rod from the lock cylinder.

**11** Lift up the retaining clip, and press the positioner to the left to remove it from its location in the tailgate **(see illustrations)**.

### Fuel filler flap positioner

**12** To gain access to the filler flap positioner, remove the pressure pump as described in paragraphs 2 and 3. With the pump removed, take out its insulation packing.

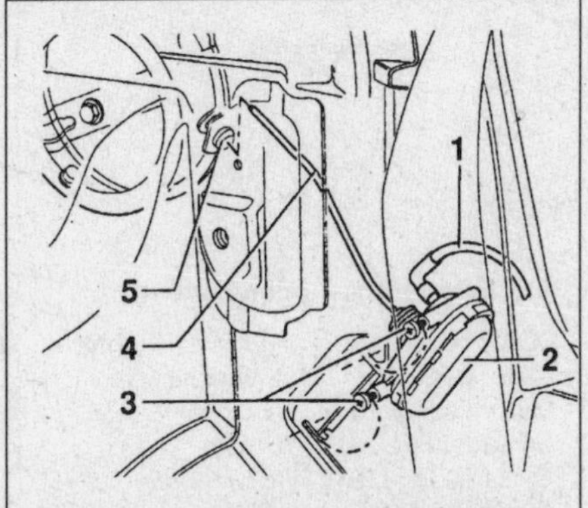


17.13 Fuel filler flap positioner details

*1 Vacuum pipe*
*2 Positioner*
*3 Retaining screws*
*4 Operating rod*
*5 Fuel filler flap*

**13** Slacken and remove the positioner retaining screws **(see illustration)**. Pull the positioner and its operating rod out of its location, disconnecting its vacuum hose as it becomes accessible. Note that the rear light cluster will have to be removed (see Chapter 12) when refitting the positioner, in order to guide the locking rod into the filler cap.

## Refitting

**14** Refitting is a reverse of the relevant removal procedure, making sure all vacuum pipe connections are securely remade. On completion, check the operation of all central locking system components.

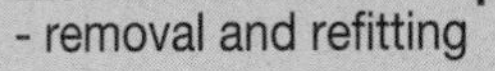

# 18 Electric window components - removal and refitting

## Window switches

**1** Refer to Chapter 12.

## Window motors

### Removal

**2** Remove the regulator assembly as described in Section 14.

**3** Remove the three cross-head motor retaining screws from one side of the motor, and recover the plastic spacer sleeves **(see illustration)**.

**4** Turn the regulator assembly around, and remove the five cable drum securing screws. Open the hinged cover and remove the wiring connector from its location **(see illustration)**.

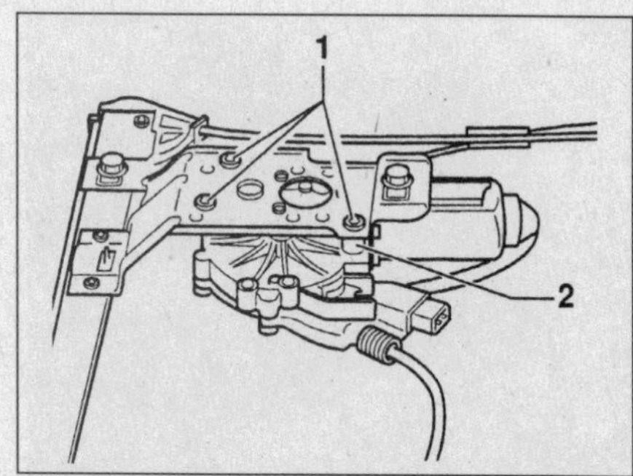


18.3 Electric window motor securing screws (1) and spacer sleeves (2)

5 Pull the cable drum off the gear housing by hand - it may be necessary to rock it loose.

### Refitting

6 If a new motor is being fitted, remove the fitting cover. Pull the drive gear off the old motor shaft, and recover the spacer washer. Fit the drive gear and washer to the cable drum **(see illustration)**.

7 Make sure that the motor drive gear components are sufficiently lubricated (VW recommend grease G 000 450 02 - available from your VW dealer) and free from dust and dirt.

8 Check that the cable is correctly located on the drum, then engage the cable drum with the motor. It may be necessary to turn the drum and motor slightly to achieve satisfactory engagement.

9 Refit the cable drum securing screws, and tighten in the sequence shown **(see illustration)**. Refit the wiring connector, and secure by closing the hinged cover.

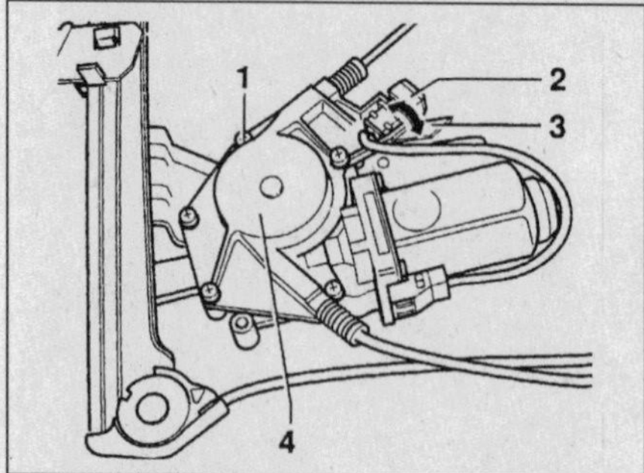


18.4 Electric window motor details

1 *Cable drum securing screws*
2 *Wiring connector*
3 *Hinged cover*
4 *Cable drum*

10 Turn the assembly over, and refit the motor retaining screws.

11 Refit the regulator assembly as described in Section 14.

## 19 Exterior mirrors and associated components - removal and refitting

### *Removal*

### Manually-operated mirror

1 Remove the door inner trim panel as described in Section 12.

2 Remove the insulation from the door frame, then undo the retaining screws and free the mirror adjustment mechanism **(see illustration)**.

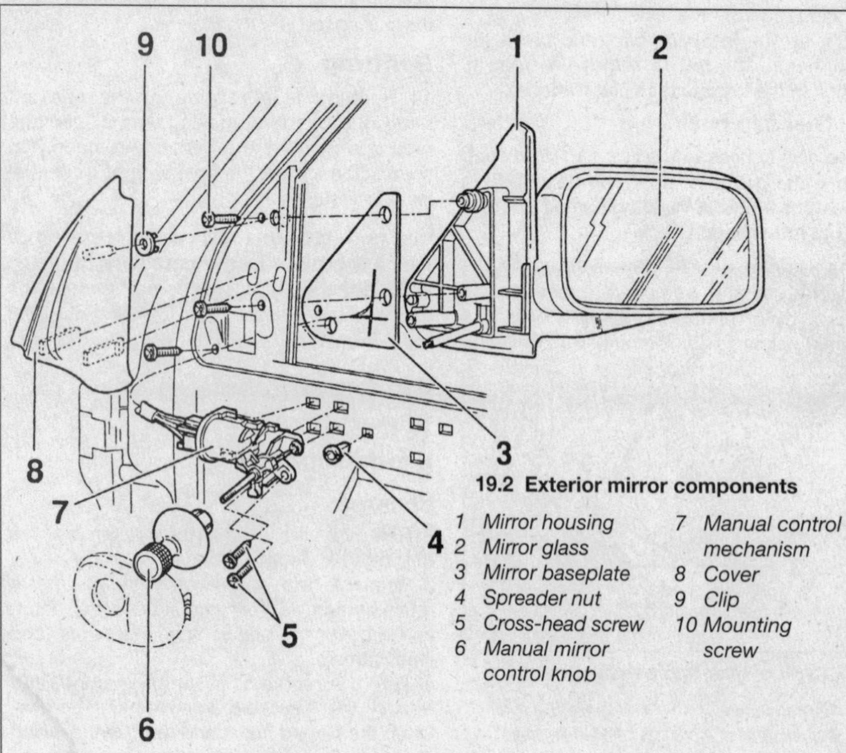


19.2 Exterior mirror components

1 *Mirror housing*
2 *Mirror glass*
3 *Mirror baseplate*
4 *Spreader nut*
5 *Cross-head screw*
6 *Manual mirror control knob*
7 *Manual control mechanism*
8 *Cover*
9 *Clip*
10 *Mounting screw*

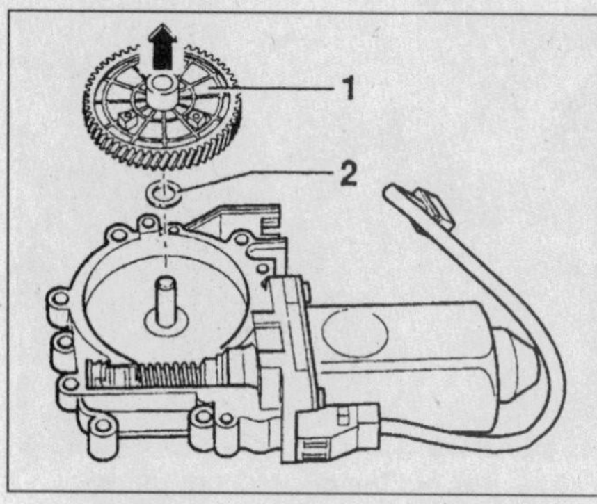


18.6 Fitting the drive gear (2) and spacer washer (1) to the cable drum

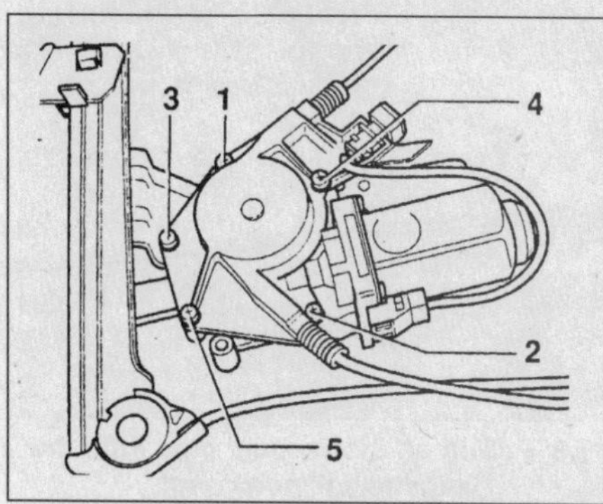


18.9 Cable drum securing screw tightening sequence

3 Slacken and remove the mirror mounting screws and remove the mirror assembly from the door. Recover the mirror baseplate.

### Electrically-operated mirror

4 Remove the door inner trim panel as described in Section 12 and disconnect the mirror wiring connector **(see illustration)**.

5 Remove the insulation from the door frame, then undo the mounting screws and remove the mirror assembly from the door **(see illustrations)**. Recover the baseplate from the mirror.

### Mirror glass

**Note:** *The mirror glass is clipped into place. Removal of the glass without the VW special tool (number 80-200) is likely to result in breakage of the glass.*

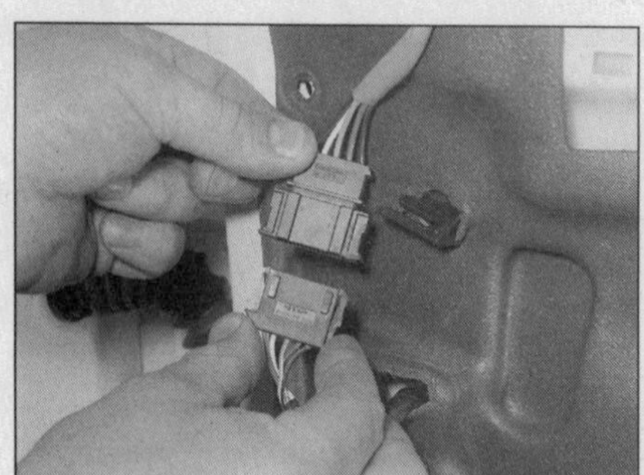

19.4 Disconnecting the mirror wiring plug

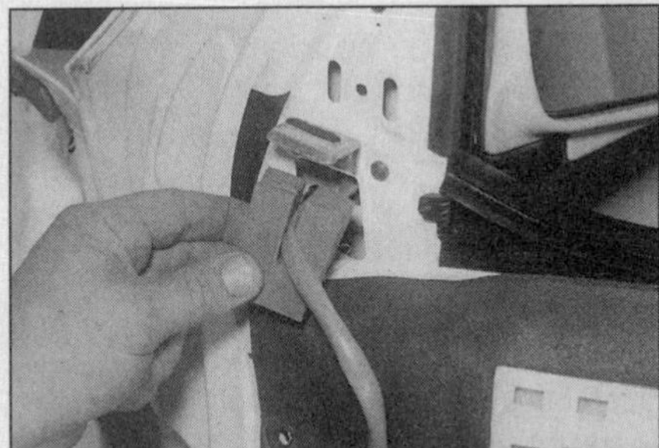

19.5a Mirror wiring is protected from the metal edge of the door frame by a foam insulation block

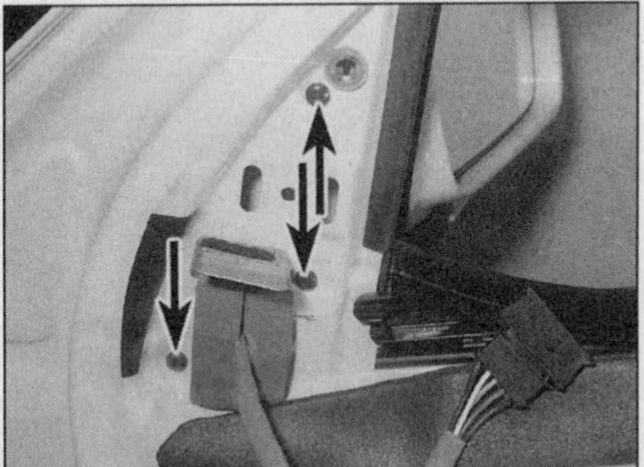

19.5b Remove the three mounting screws (arrowed) . . .

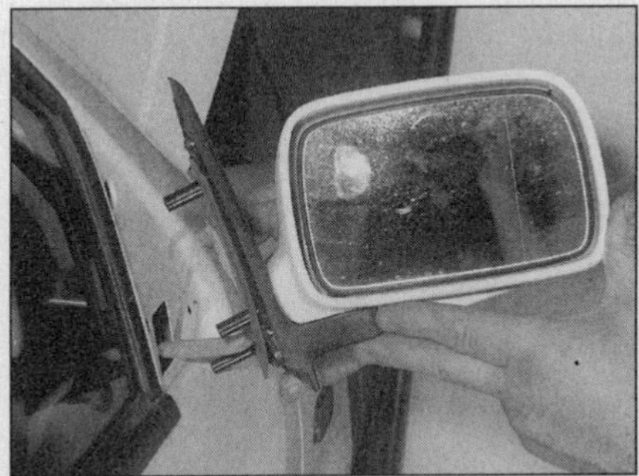

19.5c . . . and remove the mirror from the door

***Warning: Wear thick gloves and eye protection when removing the mirror glass - even if the glass is not broken, it may break during removal***

**6** Insert a wide plastic or wooden wedge between the mirror glass and mirror housing, and carefully prise the glass out. Take great care when removing the glass; do not use excessive force, as the glass is easily broken.

**7** Remove the glass from the mirror. Where applicable, disconnect the wiring connectors from the mirror heating element.

### Mirror switch (electrically-operated mirror)

**8** Refer to Chapter 12.

### Electrically-operated mirror motor

**9** Remove the mirror glass as described above.

**10** Undo the retaining screws and remove the motor, disconnecting its wiring connector as it becomes accessible.

### *Refitting*

**11** Refitting is the reverse of the relevant removal procedure.

## 20 Windscreen, tailgate and fixed rear window glass (3-door models) - general information

These areas of glass are secured by the tight fit of the weatherstrip in the body aperture, and are bonded in position with a special adhesive. Renewal of such fixed glass is a difficult, messy and time-consuming task, which is beyond the scope of the home mechanic. It is difficult, unless one has plenty of practice, to obtain a secure, waterproof fit. Furthermore, the task carries a high risk of breakage; this applies especially to the laminated glass windscreen. In view of this, owners are strongly advised to have this sort of work carried out by one of the many specialist windscreen fitters.

## 21 Sunroof - general information

Due to the complexity of the sunroof mechanism, considerable expertise is needed to repair, replace or adjust the sunroof components successfully. Removal of the roof first requires the headlining to be removed, which is a complex and tedious operation, and not a task to be undertaken lightly. Therefore, any problems with the sunroof should be referred to a VW dealer.

## 22 Body exterior fittings - removal and refitting

### *Wheelarch liners and body under-panels*

**1** The various plastic covers fitted to the underside of the vehicle are secured in position by a mixture of screws, nuts and retaining clips, and removal will be fairly obvious on inspection. Work methodically around the panel, removing its retaining screws and releasing its retaining clips until the panel is free and can be removed from the underside of the vehicle. Most clips used on the vehicle are simply prised out of position.

**2** On refitting, renew any retaining clips that may have been broken on removal, and ensure that the panel is securely retained by all the relevant clips and screws.

### *Body trim strips and badges*

**3** The various body trim strips and badges are held in position with a special adhesive tape. Removal requires the trim/badge to be heated, to soften the adhesive, and then cut away from the surface. Due to the high risk of damage to the vehicle's paintwork during this operation, it is recommended that this task should be entrusted to a VW dealer.

## 23 Seats - removal and refitting

### *Removal*

### Front seat

**1** Slide the seat forwards and unclip the trim cover from the seat inner guide rail. Remove the cover rearwards. Repeat the operation on the outer seat rail **(see illustrations)**.

**2** Slide the seat backwards and remove the rearward travel limiter Allen bolt and nut from the front of the seat centre guide rail **(see illustration)**.

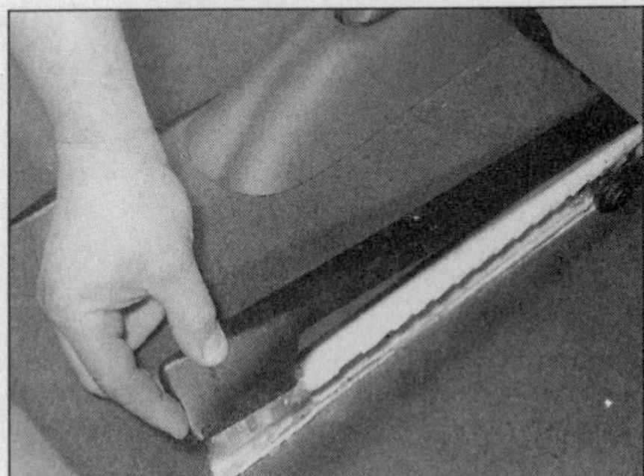

23.1a Unclip the trim cover from the front seat inner rail . . .

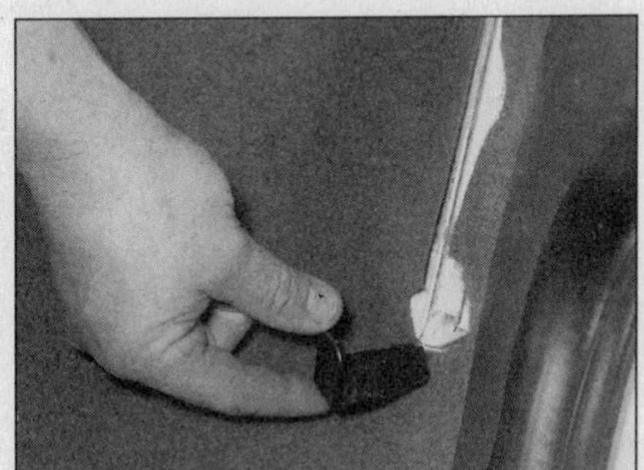

23.1b . . . and the cover or end plug from the outer rail

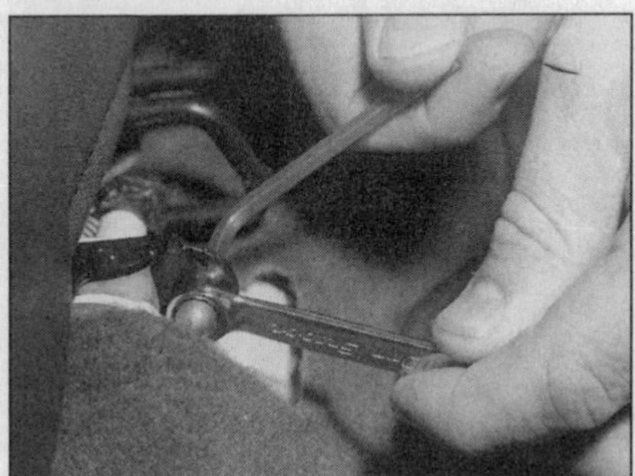

23.2 Removing the rearward travel limiter nut and bolt

3 Slide the seat fully backwards, disengaging it from the outer guide rails and remove it from the vehicle. Recover the plastic guide pieces from each of the seat guides, and renew them if they show signs of damage or deterioration .

### Rear seat assembly

4 Lift up the rear seat cushion(s), then press together the spring legs and release from the hinges. Remove the seat cushion(s) from the vehicle.
5 Fold down the rear seat backrest(s).
6 On models with a split folding rear seat, carefully prise out the double-ended retaining clip out from the top of the centre hinge pivot.
7 Using a small flat-bladed screwdriver, depress the locking hook at the side of the backrest, then move the backrest upwards to release its pivot pin. Disengage the backrest from the centre hinge, or from the other locking hook (as applicable), and remove it from the vehicle. On models with a split folding rear seat, remove the opposite seat back in the same way.

## *Refitting*

### Front seats

8 Before refitting, examine the seat guide pieces for signs of wear or damage, and renew if necessary. Refitting is a reverse of the removal procedure, ensuring that the seat adjustment lever engages correctly with the centre guide locking plunger as the seat is refitted.

### Rear seat assembly

9 Refitting is the reverse of removal, making sure the seat backs and cushions are clipped securely in position.

## 24 Front seat belt tensioning mechanism - general information

Most models covered in this manual are fitted with a front seat belt tensioner system. The system is designed to instantaneously take up any slack in the seat belt in the case of a sudden frontal impact, therefore reducing the possibility of injury to the front seat occupants. Each front seat is fitted with its system, the tensioner being situated behind the sill trim panel.

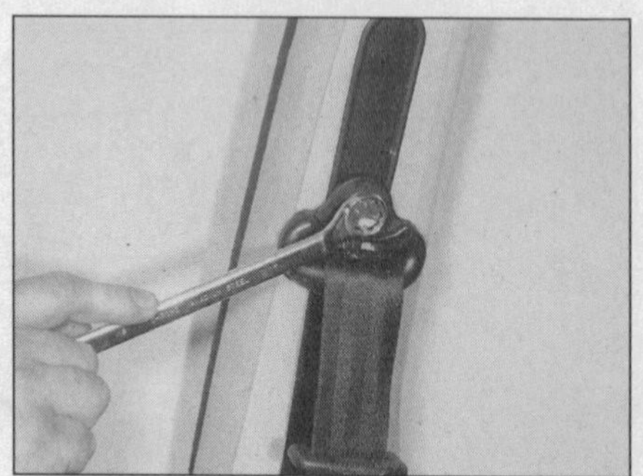

**25.2a . . . loosen the mounting bolt . . .**

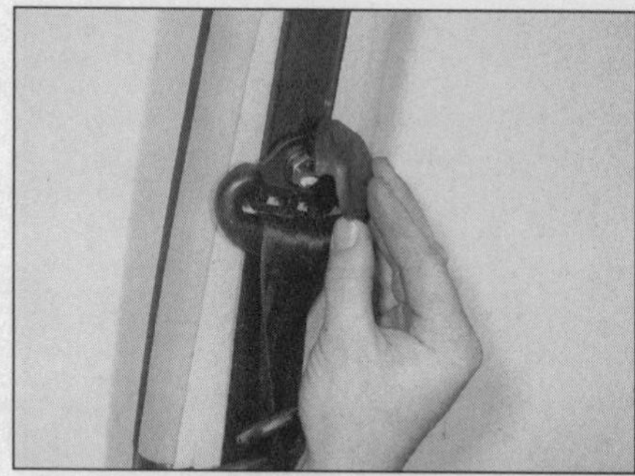

**25.1 Unclip the cover from the seat belt upper mounting . . .**

The seat belt tensioner is triggered by a frontal impact above a pre-determined force. Lesser impacts, including impacts from behind, will not trigger the system.

When the system is triggered, the explosive gas in the tensioner mechanism retracts and locks the seat belt through a cable which acts on the inertia reel. This prevents the seat belt moving and keeps the occupant firmly in position in the seat. Once the tensioner has been triggered, the seat belt will be permanently locked and the assembly must be renewed. If any abnormal rattling noises are heard when pulling out or retracting the belt, this also indicates that the tensioner has been triggered.

There is a risk of injury if the system is triggered inadvertently when working on the vehicle, and it is therefore strongly recommended that any work involving the seat belt tensioner system is entrusted to a VW dealer. Note the following warnings before contemplating any work on the front seat belts.

***Warning: Do not expose the tensioner mechanism to temperatures in excess of 100°C (212°F).***

***If the tensioner mechanism is dropped, it must be renewed, even it has suffered no apparent damage.***

***Do not allow any solvents to come into contact with the tensioner mechanism.***

***Do not attempt to open the tensioner mechanism as it contains explosive gas.***

***Tensioners must be discharged before they are disposed of, but this task should be entrusted to a VW dealer.***

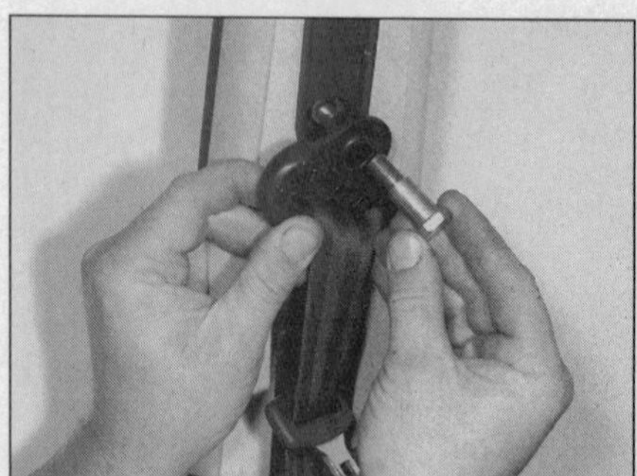

**25.2b . . . and remove it from the car, noting the fitted order of all components**

## 25 Seat belt components - removal and refitting

***Warning: On models equipped with seat belt tensioners refer to Section 24 before proceeding; under no circumstances should you attempt to separate the tensioner assembly from the inertia reel.***

## *Removal*

### Front seat belt - three-door models

1 Pull the cover off the seat belt upper mounting, for access to the mounting bolt beneath **(see illustration)**.
2 Unscrew and remove the upper mounting bolt, recovering any washers or spacers, and noting the correct fitted order of all components **(see illustrations)**.
3 Pull off the rubber door weatherstrip in the area around the B-pillar trim panels. Carefully prise off the B-pillar upper trim panel, releasing it from its clips on the door side first.
4 Remove the screw at the bottom of the door aperture securing the side trim panel to the door sill trim panel. Loosen the sill trim panel in the area where it joins the side trim panel.
5 Fold the rear seat backrest forwards.
6 Unscrew the seat backrest locating pin from the side trim panel.
7 Unscrew the two oval-shaped buttons from the rear of the side trim panel.
8 Working around the edges of the side trim panel, release the panel from its retaining clips and remove it from the car.
9 Remove two cross-head screws and detach the seat belt guide clip from the B-pillar.
10 Loosen and remove the seat belt reel mounting bolt, and remove the belt reel from its location. **Note:** *Removing the reel mounting bolt disables the seat belt tensioner mechanism - do not refit the bolt while the seat belt is removed from the car, as this enables the system once more.*
11 The seat belt side/sliding anchor and the seat belt stalk can be simply unbolted and removed with the seat belt - fold back the carpet for access to the bolts, as required. Note the correct fitted order and position of all bolts and washers, for refitting.

### Front seat belt - five-door models

12 Remove the seat belt upper mounting bolt and B-pillar upper trim panel as described in paragraphs 1 to 3. With the trim panel removed, the seat belt height adjuster can be unbolted and removed, if required **(see illustrations)**.
13 Loosen the door sill trim panels in the area around the base of the B-pillar. Prise off the B-pillar lower trim panel, releasing it from its retaining clips, and pulling it forward off the mounting pin at the base of the panel **(see illustrations)**.

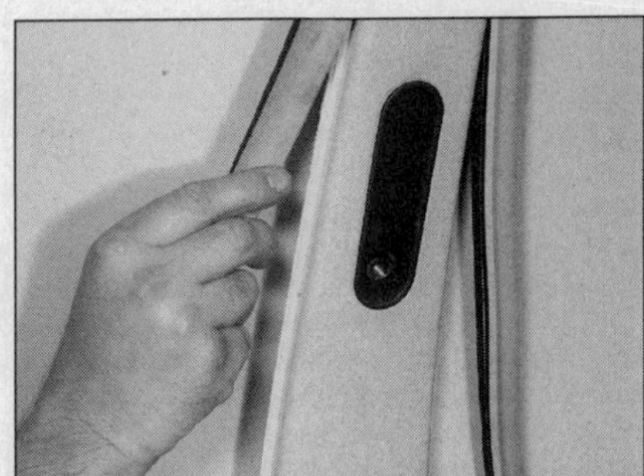

**25.12a Pulling off the weatherstrip from the door aperture**

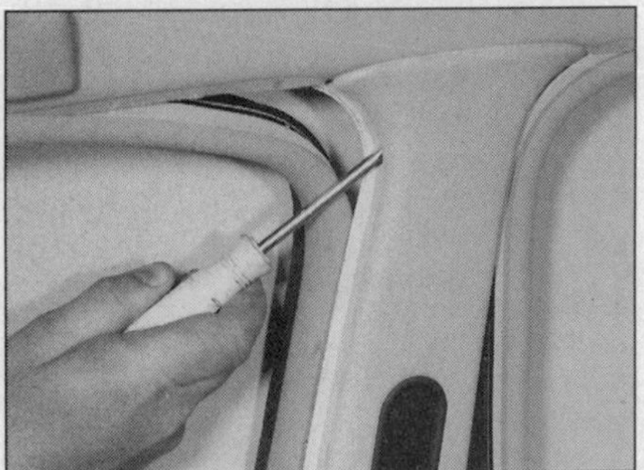

**25.12b Prise off the B-pillar upper trim panel . . .**

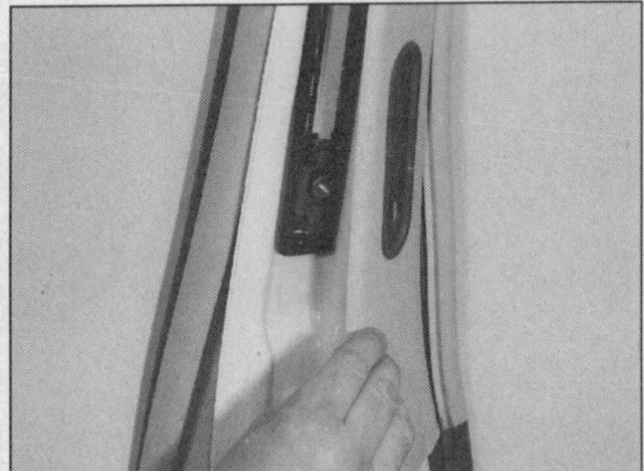

**25.12c . . . and remove it from the car**

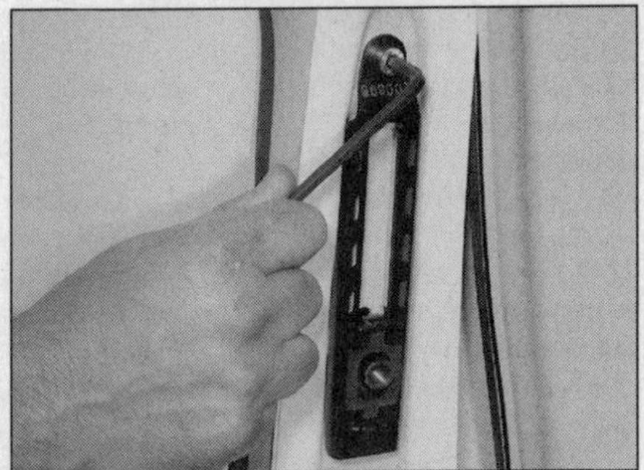

**25.12d If required, the seat belt height adjuster can be unbolted and removed**

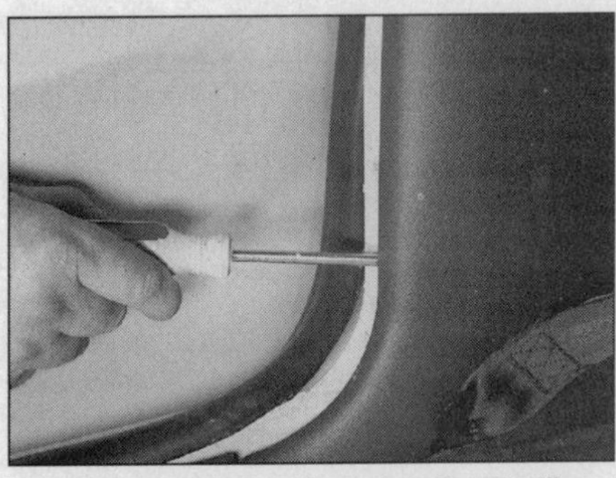

**25.13a Carefully prise away the B-pillar lower trim panel . . .**

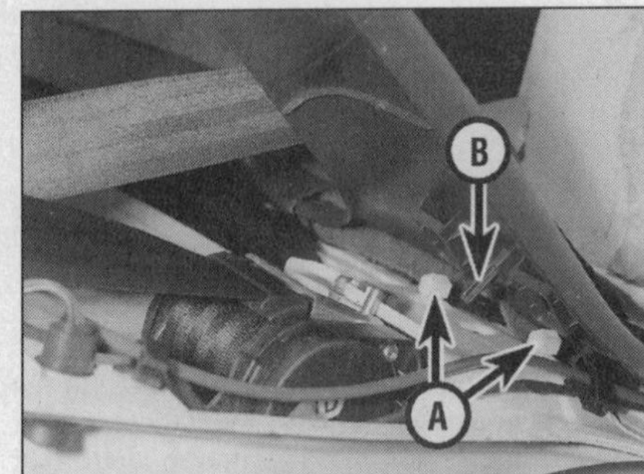


**25.13b . . . to release the retaining clips (A) and the mounting pin (B)**

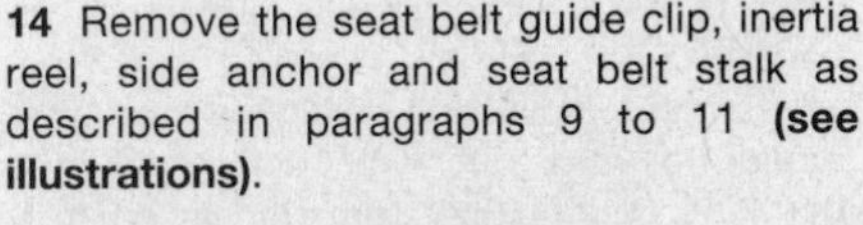

**14** Remove the seat belt guide clip, inertia reel, side anchor and seat belt stalk as described in paragraphs 9 to 11 **(see illustrations)**.

**25.14a Loosening the seat belt side anchor bolt . . .**

## Rear seat belt - three-door models

**15** Remove the rear parcel shelf, and fold the rear seat cushions and backrest forwards.

**16** Remove the side trim panel as described in paragraphs 6 to 8.

**17** Remove the two Torx screws from the parcel shelf side support, then unhook the panel from the two retaining lugs on the C-pillar and remove it from the car.

**18** Unscrew the two nuts from the base of the C-pillar trim panel, then prise off the C-pillar trim panel and remove it from the car.

**19** Depending on model and the amount of access required, it may be necessary to partially remove and fold back the carpeted trim panel from the rear wheel housing.

**20** Pull the cover off the seat belt upper mounting, for access to the mounting bolt beneath **(see illustration)**.

**21** Unscrew and remove the upper mounting bolt, recovering any washers or spacers, and noting the correct fitted order of all components.

**22** Loosen and remove the inertia reel mounting bolt **(see illustration)**, and lower the reel out of position.

**23** The seat belt side anchorages and seat belt stalks can be simply unbolted and removed with the seat belt. Note the correct fitted order and position of all bolts and washers, for refitting.

## Rear seat belt - five-door models

**24** Remove the rear parcel shelf, and fold the rear seat cushions and backrest forwards.

**25** Unscrew the seat backrest locating pin from the rear door aperture trim panel, and unscrew the two oval-shaped buttons.

**26** Working along the panel, release the door aperture trim panel from its retaining clips and remove it from the car.

**25.14b . . . and the inertia reel mounting bolt**

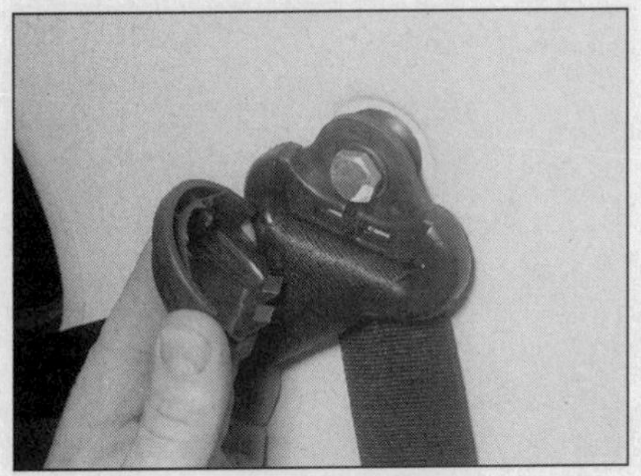

**25.20 Cover removed from rear seat belt upper mounting**

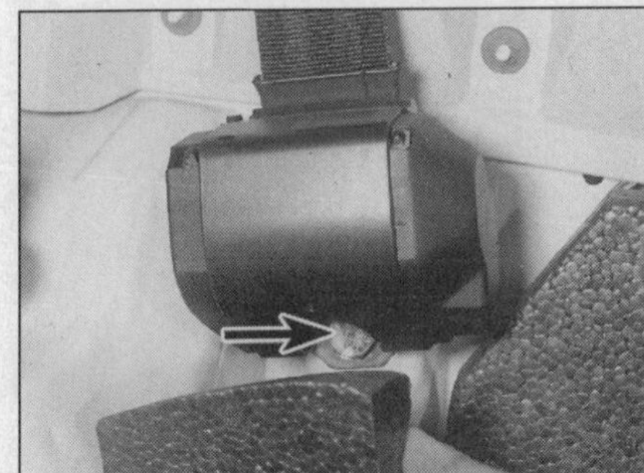

**25.22 Rear seat belt inertia reel mounting bolt (arrowed)**

26.6 Press the glovebox stop legs inwards . . .

26.7 . . . and withdraw the glovebox (seen with steering wheel removed)

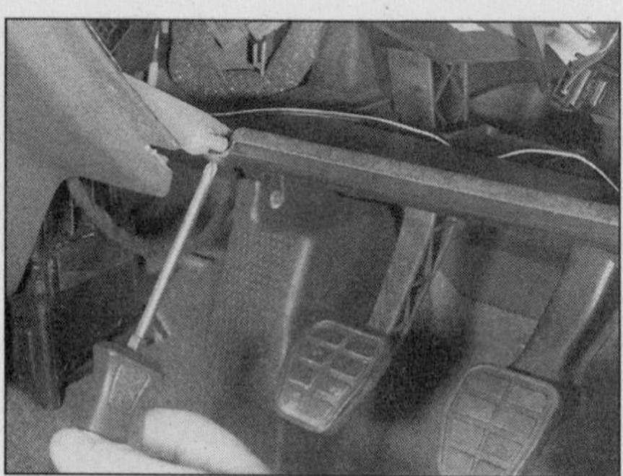
26.8a Remove the cross-head screw at either end . . .

27 The remainder of the removal procedure is as described for three-door models, in paragraphs 17 to 23.

### Refitting

28 Refitting is a reversal of the removal procedure, ensuring that all the seat belt mounting bolts are securely tightened. Also ensure that all disturbed trim panels are correctly located and securely retained by all the relevant retaining clips. When refitting the upper trim panels, the height adjustment lever must engage correctly with the seat belt upper mounting bolt.

## 26 Interior trim - removal and refitting

### Interior trim panels

**Note:** *Specific details for most interior panels are contained within Section 27.*

1 The interior trim panels are secured using either screws or various types of trim fasteners, usually studs or clips.

2 Check that there are no other panels overlapping the one to be removed; usually there is a sequence that has to be followed, and this will only become obvious on close inspection.

3 Remove all obvious fasteners, such as screws. If the panel will not come free, it is held by hidden clips or fasteners. These are usually situated around the edge of the panel, and can be prised up to release them; note, however that they can break quite easily so replacements should be available. The best way of releasing such clips without the correct type of tool, is to use a large flat-bladed screwdriver. Note in many cases that the adjacent sealing strip must be prised back to release a panel.

4 When removing a panel, **never** use excessive force or the panel may be damaged; always check carefully that all fasteners or other relevant components have been removed or released before attempting to withdraw a panel.

5 Refitting is the reverse of the removal procedure; secure the fasteners by pressing them firmly into place and ensure that all disturbed components are correctly secured to prevent rattles.

### Driver's side glovebox

6 Open the glovebox, and press the stop leg at either side inwards so that the glovebox can be lowered right down **(see illustration)**.

7 Pull the glovebox out at the bottom to release it from its lower hinge, and manoeuvre the glovebox out of the facia **(see illustration)**.

8 The driver's side footwell cover can now be removed if required; this is secured by two cross-head screws **(see illustrations)**.

9 Refitting is a reversal of removal.

### Passenger's side glovebox

**Note:** *Models with a passenger airbag do not have a glovebox on the passenger's side. To remove a passenger's side airbag, refer to Chapter 12.*

10 Open the glovebox lid, and remove four screws inside the glove compartment (three at the top, one at the back). One of the screws also retains the glovebox lid catch - recover this as the screw is removed. Remove the screw each side behind the glovebox lid hinge, and withdraw the glovebox from the facia **(see illustrations)**.

11 The passenger's side shelf will either come out with the glovebox, or can be removed by unscrewing the two retaining screws at the top, and pulling the shelf out of its location.

12 Refitting is a reversal of removal.

### Carpets

13 The passenger compartment floor carpet is in one piece and is secured at its edges by screws or clips, usually the same fasteners used to secure the various adjoining trim panels.

14 Carpet removal and refitting is reasonably straightforward but very time-consuming because all adjoining trim panels must be removed first, as must components such as the seats, the centre console and seat belt lower anchorages.

### Headlining

15 The headlining is clipped to the roof and can be withdrawn only once all fittings such as the grab handles, sun visors, sunroof (if fitted), windscreen and rear quarter windows and related trim panels have been removed, and the door, tailgate and sunroof aperture sealing strips have been prised clear.

16 Note that headlining removal requires considerable skill and experience if it is to be carried out without damage, and is therefore best entrusted to an expert.

26.8b . . . and remove the driver's side footwell cover

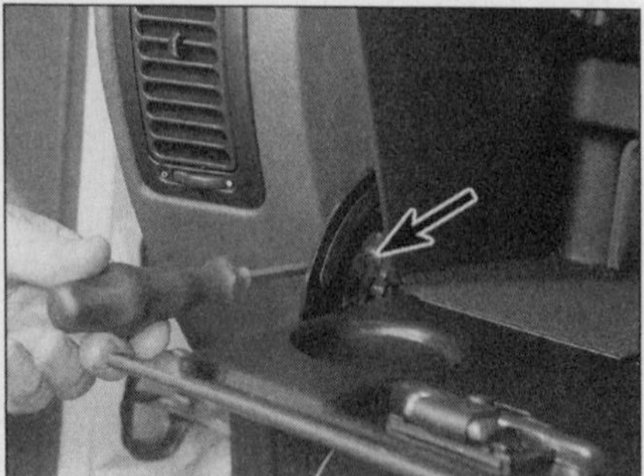
26.10a Remove the screw behind each hinge . . .

26.10b . . . and withdraw the passenger's side glovebox from the facia

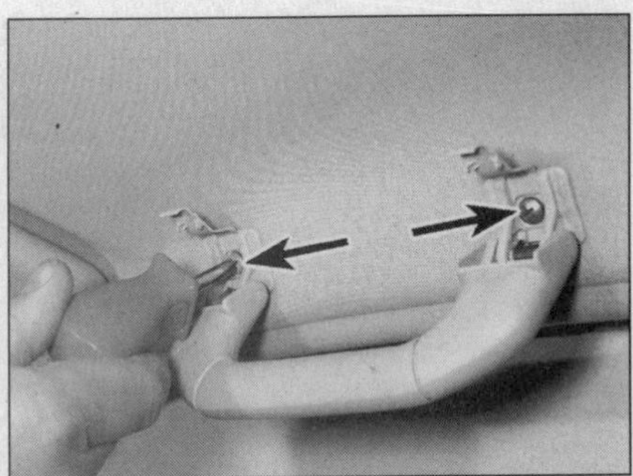

26.18 Removing the grab handle securing screws (arrowed)

27.1a Unclip the gear lever gaiter . . .

27.1b . . . then unclip the console top cover, and lift it over the gear lever

## Grab handles

**17** Pull the grab handle down and hold it in this position.

**18** The grab handle securing screws are located under two flaps, which can be unclipped and swung upwards for access **(see illustration)**.

**19** Remove the two screws and take off the grab handle.

**20** Refitting is a reversal of removal.

## 27 Centre console - removal and refitting

### Removal

**1** On manual transmission models, unclip the gear lever gaiter from the console, and lift it up the gear lever. Unclip the top cover from the centre console, and remove over the gear lever, feeding the gear lever gaiter through the cover **(see illustrations)**.

**2** On automatic transmission models, undo the screw under the detent button on the lever handle, and lift the handle from the lever. Detach and lift the selector cover up from the centre console.

**3** Remove the two plastic nuts at the rear of the console, and the cross-head screw at the very front **(see illustrations)**.

**4** Lift the console upwards, releasing it from the studs at the rear **(see illustration)**. Recover the plastic spacers from the studs once the console is removed.

### Refitting

**5** Refitting is the reverse of removal, making sure all fasteners are securely tightened.

## 28 Facia panel assembly - removal and refitting

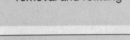

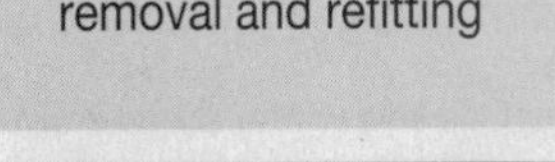

***Label each wiring connector as it is disconnected from its component. The labels will prove useful on refitting, when routing the wiring and feeding the wiring through the facia apertures.***

### Removal

**1** Disconnect the battery negative terminal. **Note:** *If the vehicle has a security-coded radio, check that you have a copy of the code number before disconnecting the battery. Refer to your VW dealer if in doubt.*

**2** Remove the centre console (Section 27).

**3** Remove the steering column (Chapter 10).

**4** Remove the instrument panel assembly and radio/cassette unit as described in Chapter 12. Also remove the front (upper) treble loudspeakers from the facia, where fitted.

**5** On models equipped with a passenger's side airbag, remove the airbag unit (Chapter 12).

**6** On models not equipped with a passenger's side airbag, remove the glovebox as described in Section 26.

**7** If not already done, remove the driver's side glovebox and the footwell cover, as described in Section 26.

**8** Working around the fuse/relay panel, disconnect the aerial plug (which may have a foam insulating cover), then unscrew the nut and detach the earth strap **(see illustrations)**.

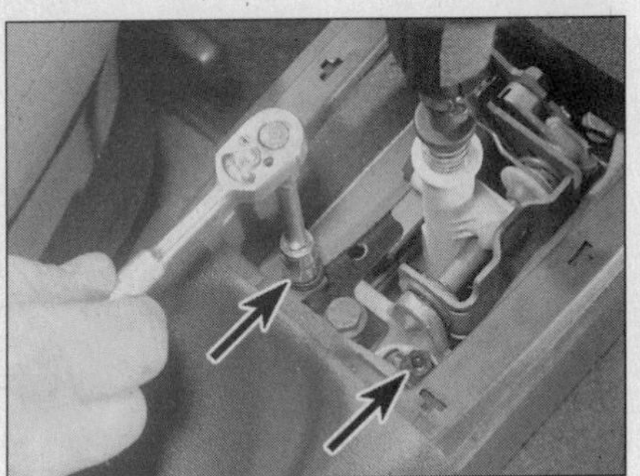

27.3a Remove the two plastic nuts (arrowed) . . .

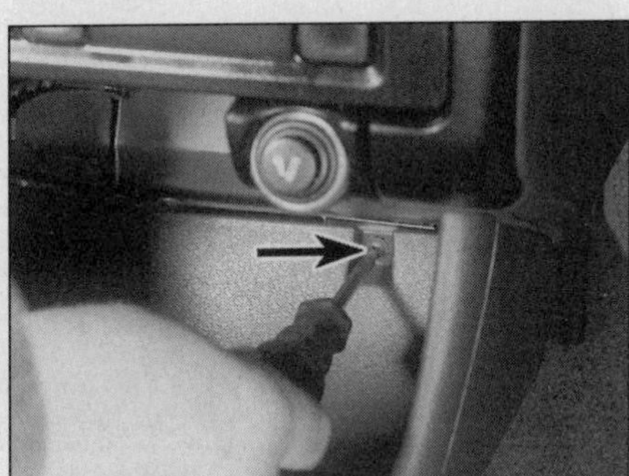

27.3b . . . and the screw at the front of the console (arrowed)

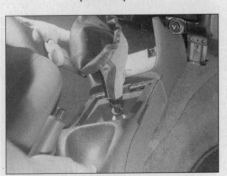

27.4 Removing the centre console

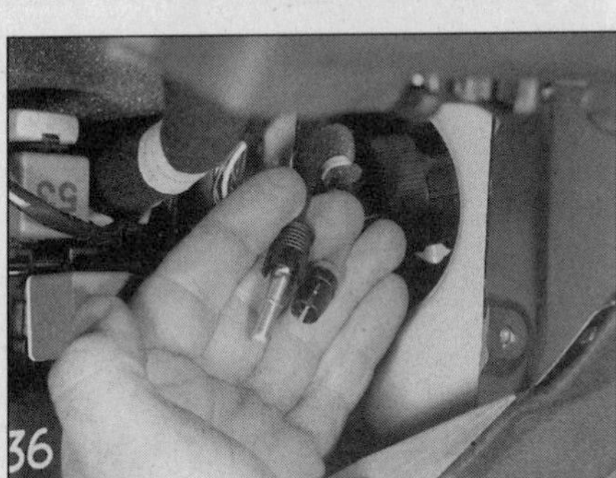

28.8a Disconnect the aerial lead . . .

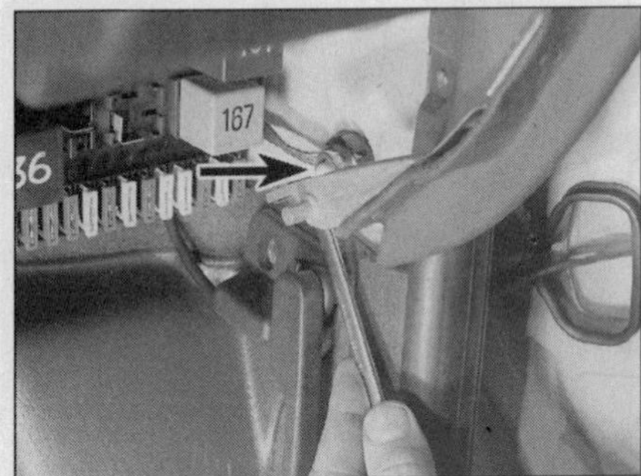

28.8b . . . then unscrew the retaining nut (arrowed) and detach the earth strap

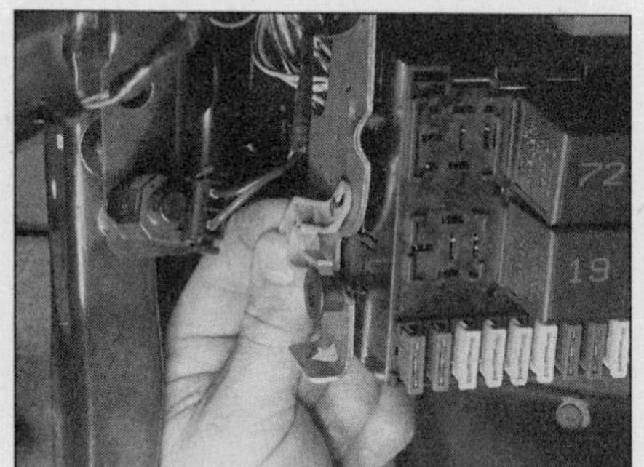

**28.9a Release the retaining clips at each side . . .**

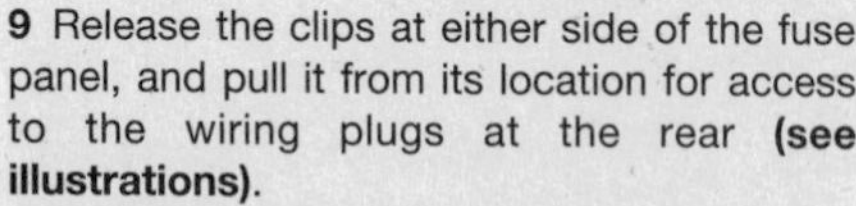

**28.9b . . . then lower the fuse/relay panel**

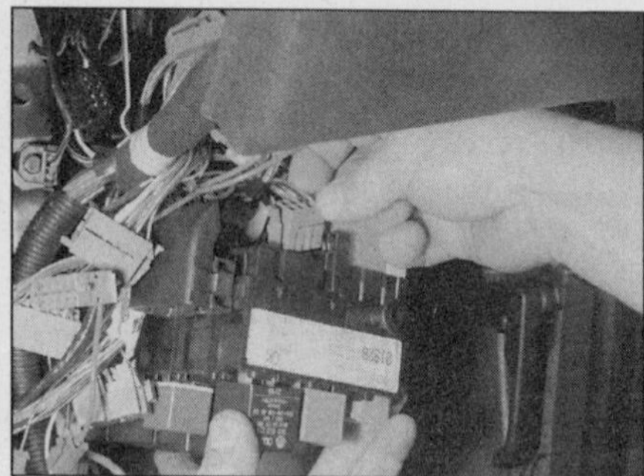

**28.10 Disconnect the wiring plugs from the rear of the panel, noting their locations**

**9** Release the clips at either side of the fuse panel, and pull it from its location for access to the wiring plugs at the rear **(see illustrations)**.

**10** Disconnect all the wiring plugs from the rear of the fuse/relay panel, labelling them for refitting **(see illustration)**. We found that, in practice, the plugs are so designed that they will only fit in one place, but labelling definitely makes reconnecting the plugs much less time-consuming.

**11** Open both front doors, and disconnect the wiring harness connector each side by unscrewing it - a suitable C-spanner may be required. Detach the wiring plug from the door pillar by twisting and releasing its bayonet connecting ring on the door side of the pillar **(see illustrations)**.

**12** Unscrew the nut, and disconnect the earth wire from the lower passenger's side of the facia **(see illustration)**.

**13** Lever off the plastic cap from each end of the facia panel, and remove the bolt beneath **(see illustrations)**.

**14** Refer to Chapter 3, Section 9 and remove the heater control panel. Pull out the shelf or switch panel (depending on model) below the heater controls. Where applicable, disconnect the wiring from the switches **(see illustration)**.

**15** Remove the cross-head screws and the nut, and remove the facia central support from below the heater control panel. Also remove the two screws on the underside of the facia, which secure another support bracket **(see illustration)**.

**16** Reach in through the instrument panel aperture, and disconnect the facia vent plastic duct. Pull the duct to one side, for access to the two facia mounting nuts behind. Have an assistant support the facia, then unscrew and remove the nuts **(see illustrations)**.

**17** Similarly, reach in through the passenger's glovebox aperture, and disconnect the facia vent plastic duct. Pull the duct out of the way (or remove it completely) for access to the two facia mounting nuts behind. Have an assistant support the facia, then remove the nuts **(see illustrations)**.

**18** Carefully ease the facia assembly away from the bulkhead. As it is withdrawn, release the wiring harness from its retaining clips on the rear of the facia, whilst noting its correct routing (see **Haynes Hint** at the start of this Section). Remove the facia assembly from the vehicle. Recover the sealing grommets which are fitted to the facia mounting studs; renew them if they are worn or damaged.

**28.11a Using a C-spanner, turn the harness locking ring . . .**

**28.11b . . . to release its bayonet fitting . . .**

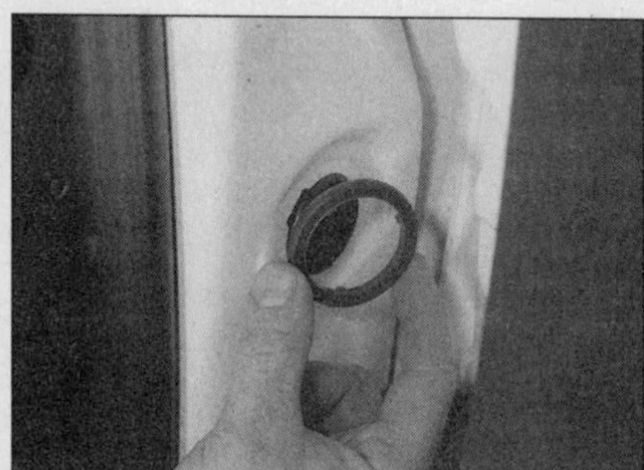

**28.11c . . . then recover the ring from the door pillar**

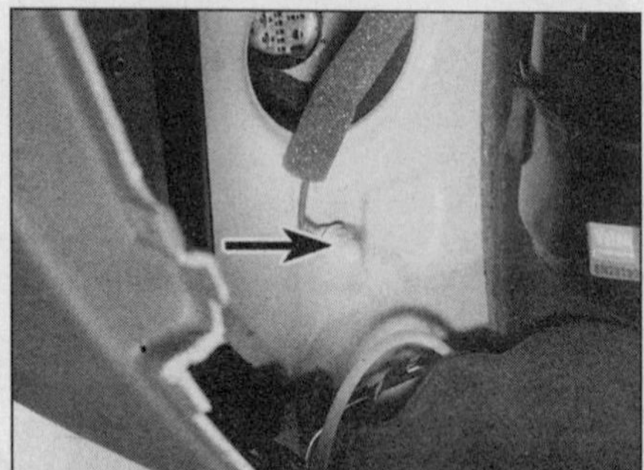

**28.12 Remove the nut (arrowed) and disconnect the earth wire at the passenger's side of the facia**

**28.13a Lever out the plastic end cap . . .**

**28.13b . . . then remove the bolt at each end of the facia**

28.14 Disconnecting the wiring plugs from the switches below the heater controls

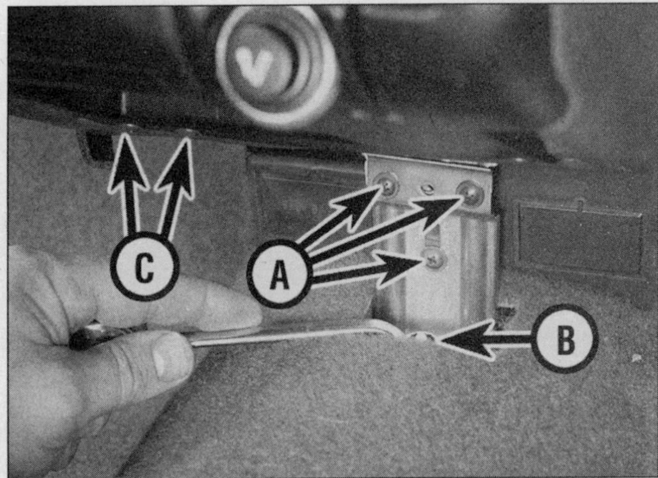


28.15 Facia central support cross-head screws (A), nut (B) and additional support screws (C)

### Refitting

19 Refitting is a reversal of the removal procedure, noting the following points:

a) *Fit the sealing grommets to the facia studs and manoeuvre the facia into position. Using the labels stuck on during removal, ensure that the wiring is correctly routed and securely retained by its facia clips.*

b) *Clip the facia back into position, making sure all the wiring connectors are fed through their respective apertures, then refit all the facia fasteners, and tighten them securely.*

c) *On completion, reconnect the battery and check that all the electrical components and switches function correctly.*

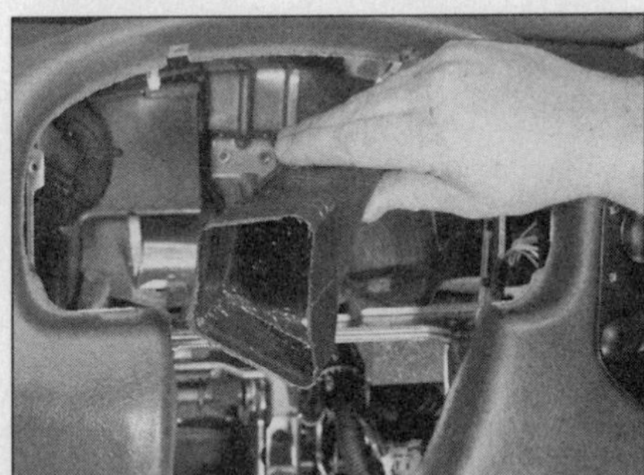

28.16a Removing the driver's side facia vent plastic duct . . .

28.16b . . . for access to the mounting nuts (arrowed)

28.17a Removing the vent duct through the glovebox aperture . . .

28.17b . . . for access to the passenger's side facia mounting nuts (arrowed)

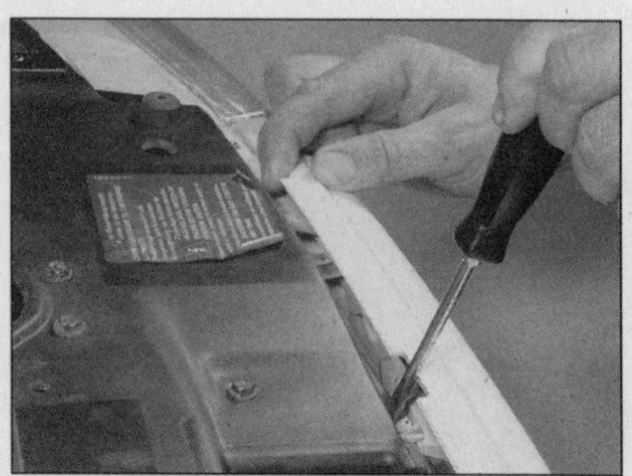
29.2a Release the grille upper retaining lugs . . .

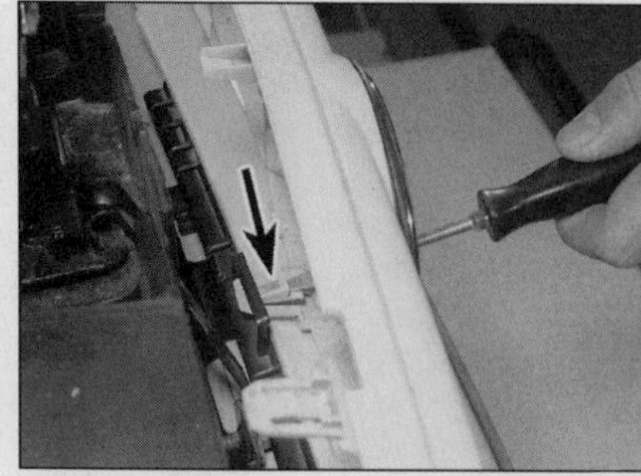
29.2b . . . and the lower retaining lug . . .

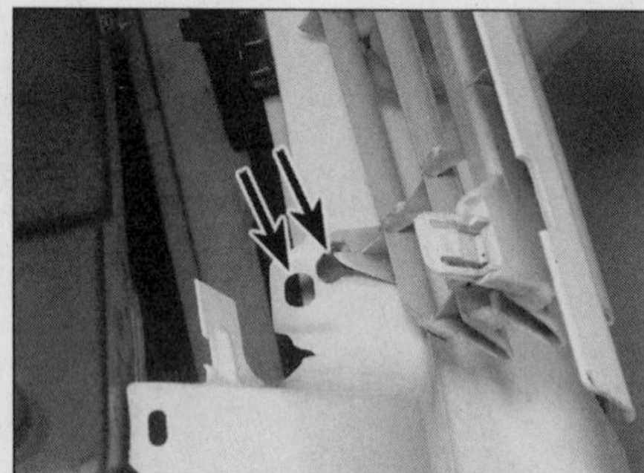
29.2c . . . then lift the grille pegs out of the holes (arrowed) . . .

29.2d . . . and remove the grille from the front of the car

## 29 Radiator grille and headlight surround - removal and refitting

### Removal

**1** Open the bonnet.

**2** Using a suitable screwdriver, carefully release the radiator grille upper and lower retaining lugs (four at the top, one at the bottom), then lift the grille to release the support pegs and remove it forwards from the vehicle **(see illustrations)**.

**3** Refer to Chapter 12 and remove the front direction indicators, for access to the headlight/grille trim retaining screws.

**4** Loosen and remove the retaining screws, release the two central clips, and carefully withdraw the headlight/grille trim from the front of the car **(see illustrations)**.

### Refitting

**5** Refitting is a reversal of removal.

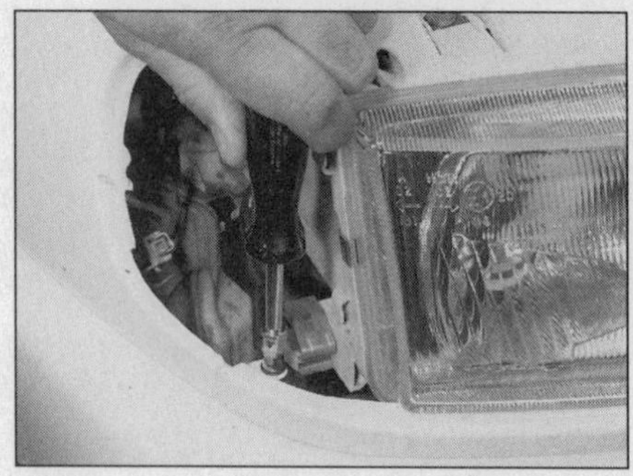
29.4a Remove the retaining screws . . .

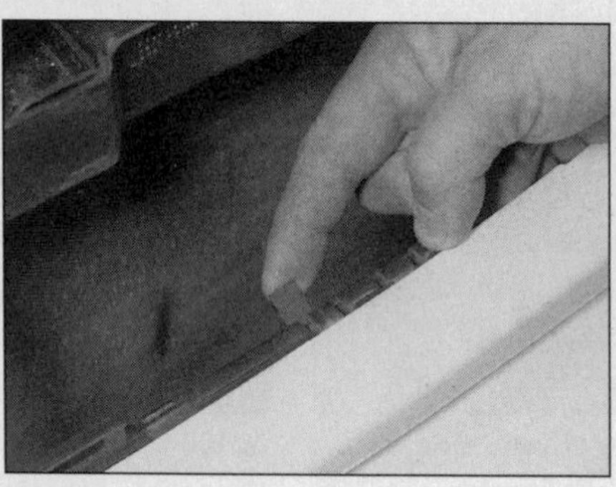
29.4b . . . and release the central clips . . .

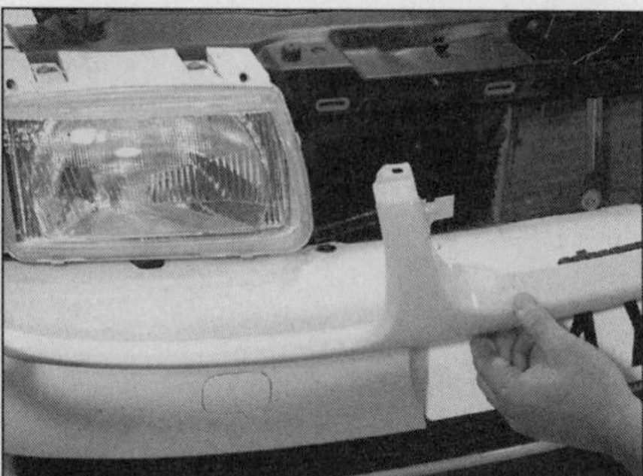
29.4c . . . to remove the headlight/grille trim from the car

# Chapter 12
# Body electrical system

## Contents



## Degrees of difficulty

| **Easy,** suitable for novice with little experience  | **Fairly easy,** suitable for beginner with some experience 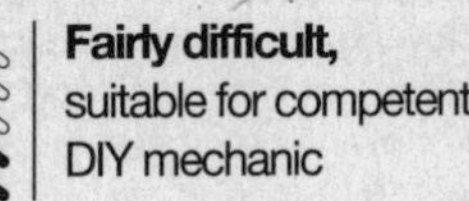 | **Fairly difficult,** suitable for competent DIY mechanic | **Difficult,** suitable for experienced DIY mechanic | **Very difficult,** suitable for expert DIY or professional |
|---|---|---|---|---|

## Specifications

**System type** . . . . . . . . . . . . . . . . . . . . . . 12-volt, negative earth

| **Bulbs** | **Wattage** |
|---|---|
| Headlights | 60/55 (H4 type) |
| Sidelights | 4 |
| Indicators | 21 |
| Foglight (front) | 55 (H3 type) |
| Foglight (rear) | 21 |
| Brake light | 21 |
| High-level brake light | 5 |
| Tail light | 5 |
| Reversing light | 21 |
| Number plate light | 5 |

| **Wiper blades** | |
|---|---|
| Front | Champion X48 |
| Rear | Champion X29 |

| **Torque wrench settings** | **Nm** | **lbf ft** |
|---|---|---|
| Airbag unit securing screws (driver's side) | 7 | 5 |
| Rear wiper arm outer nut | 15 | 11 |
| Rear wiper arm spindle nut | 7 | 5 |
| Rear wiper motor mounting bolts | 5 | 4 |
| Windscreen wiper arm nuts | 20 | 15 |
| Windscreen wiper motor mounting nuts/bolts | 20 | 15 |

## 1 General information and precautions

***Warning: Before carrying out any work on the electrical system, read through the precautions given in Safety first! at the beginning of this manual, and in Chapter 5A.***

The electrical system is of 12-volt negative earth type. Power for the lights and all electrical accessories is supplied by a lead/acid type battery which is charged by the alternator.

This Chapter covers repair and service procedures for the various electrical components not associated with the engine. Information on the battery, alternator and starter motor can be found in Chapter 5A.

It should be noted that prior to working on any component in the electrical system, the battery negative terminal should first be disconnected to prevent the possibility of electrical short-circuits and/or fires. **Note:** *If the vehicle has a security-coded radio, check that you have a copy of the code number before disconnecting the battery. Refer to your VW dealer if in doubt.*

## 2 Electrical fault-finding - general information

**Note:** *Refer to the precautions given in Safety first! and in Chapter 5A before starting work. The following tests relate to testing of the main electrical circuits, and should not be used to test delicate electronic circuits (such as anti-lock braking systems), particularly where an electronic control unit is used.*

### General

**1** A typical electrical circuit consists of an electrical component, any switches, relays, motors, fuses, fusible links or circuit breakers related to that component, and the wiring and connectors which link the component to both the battery and the chassis. To help to pinpoint a problem in an electrical circuit, wiring diagrams are included at the end of this Chapter.

**2** Before attempting to diagnose an electrical fault, first study the appropriate wiring diagram to obtain a complete understanding of the components included in the particular circuit concerned. The possible sources of a fault can be narrowed down by noting if other components related to the circuit are operating properly. If several components or circuits fail at one time, the problem is likely to be related to a shared fuse or earth connection.

**3** Electrical problems usually stem from simple causes, such as loose or corroded connections, a faulty earth connection, a blown fuse, a melted fusible link, or a faulty relay (refer to Section 3 for details of testing relays). Visually inspect the condition of all fuses, wires and connections in a problem circuit before testing the components. Use the wiring diagrams to determine which terminal connections will need to be checked in order to pinpoint the trouble-spot.

**4** The basic tools required for electrical fault-finding include a circuit tester or voltmeter (a 12-volt bulb with a set of test leads can also be used for certain tests); a self-powered test light (sometimes known as a continuity tester); an ohmmeter (to measure resistance); a battery and set of test leads; and a jumper wire, preferably with a circuit breaker or fuse incorporated, which can be used to bypass suspect wires or electrical components. Before attempting to locate a problem with test instruments, use the wiring diagram to determine where to make the connections.

**5** To find the source of an intermittent wiring fault (usually due to a poor or dirty connection, or damaged wiring insulation), a 'wiggle' test can be performed on the wiring. This involves wiggling the wiring by hand to see if the fault occurs as the wiring is moved. It should be possible to narrow down the source of the fault to a particular section of wiring. This method of testing can be used in conjunction with any of the tests described in the following sub-Sections.

**6** Apart from problems due to poor connections, two basic types of fault can occur in an electrical circuit - open-circuit, or short-circuit.

**7** Open-circuit faults are caused by a break somewhere in the circuit, which prevents current from flowing. An open-circuit fault will prevent a component from working, but will not cause the relevant circuit fuse to blow.

**8** Short-circuit faults are caused by a 'short' somewhere in the circuit, which allows the current flowing in the circuit to escape along an alternative route, usually to earth. Short-circuit faults are normally caused by a breakdown in wiring insulation, which allows a feed wire to touch either another wire, or an earthed component such as the bodyshell. A short circuit fault will normally cause the relevant circuit fuse to blow.

### Finding an open-circuit

**9** To check for an open-circuit, connect one lead of a circuit tester or voltmeter to either the negative battery terminal or a known good earth.

**10** Connect the other lead to a connector in the circuit being tested, preferably nearest to the battery or fuse.

**11** Switch on the circuit, bearing in mind that some circuits are live only when the ignition switch is moved to a particular position.

**12** If voltage is present (indicated either by the tester bulb lighting or a voltmeter reading, as applicable), this means that the section of the circuit between the relevant connector and the battery is problem-free.

**13** Continue to check the remainder of the circuit in the same fashion.

**14** When a point is reached at which no voltage is present, the problem must lie between that point and the previous test point with voltage. Most problems can be traced to a broken, corroded or loose connection.

### Finding a short-circuit

**15** To check for a short-circuit, first disconnect the load(s) from the circuit (loads are the components which draw current from a circuit, such as bulbs, motors, heating elements, etc).

**16** Remove the relevant fuse from the circuit, and connect a circuit tester or voltmeter to the fuse connections.

**17** Switch on the circuit, bearing in mind that some circuits are live only when the ignition switch is moved to a particular position.

**18** If voltage is present (indicated either by the tester bulb lighting or a voltmeter reading, as applicable), this means that there is a short-circuit.

**19** If no voltage is present, but the fuse still blows with the load(s) connected, this indicates an internal fault in the load(s).

### Finding an earth fault

**20** The battery negative terminal is connected to earth- the metal of the engine/transmission and the car body - and most systems are wired so that they only receive a positive feed, the current returning through the metal of the car body. This means that the component mounting and the body form part of that circuit. Loose or corroded mountings can therefore cause a range of electrical faults, ranging from total failure of a circuit, to a puzzling partial fault. In particular, lights may shine dimly (especially when another circuit sharing the same earth point is in operation), motors (eg. wiper motors or the radiator cooling fan motor) may run slowly, and the operation of one circuit may have an apparently unrelated effect on another. Note that on many vehicles, earth straps are used between certain components, such as the engine/transmission and the body, usually where there is no metal-to-metal contact between components due to flexible rubber mountings, etc.

**21** To check whether a component is properly earthed, disconnect the battery and connect one lead of an ohmmeter to a known good earth point. Connect the other lead to the wire or earth connection being tested. The resistance reading should be zero; if not, check the connection as follows.

**22** If an earth connection is thought to be faulty, dismantle the connection and clean back to bare metal both the bodyshell and the wire terminal or the component earth connection mating surface. Be careful to remove all traces of dirt and corrosion, then use a knife to trim away any paint, so that a clean metal-to-metal joint is made. On reassembly, tighten the joint fasteners securely; if a wire terminal is being refitted, use serrated washers between the terminal and the bodyshell to ensure a clean and

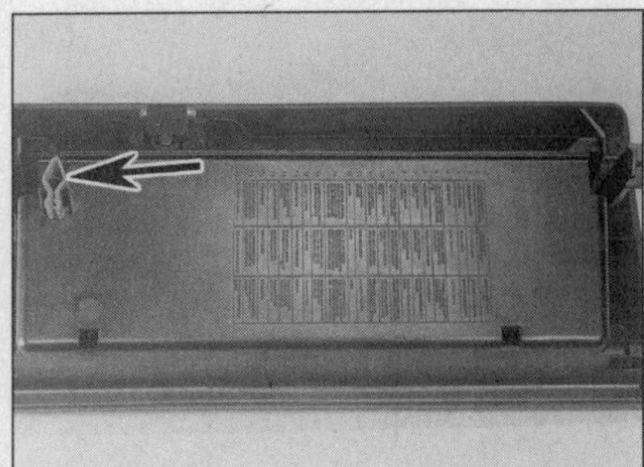

3.6a Rear view of driver's side glovebox, showing fuse table and fuse removal tool (arrowed)

3.6b Removing a fuse from the passenger compartment fusebox, using the removal tool

3.6c Removing a fuse from the engine compartment fusebox, on top of the battery

secure connection. When the connection is remade, prevent the onset of corrosion in the future by applying a coat of petroleum jelly or silicone-based grease or by spraying on (at regular intervals) a proprietary ignition sealer or a water-dispersant lubricant.

## 3 Fuses and relays - general information

### Main fuses

#### Up to 1998 model year

**1** The fuses are located in a row below the relays, on a single panel in the lower facia on the driver's side.

#### 1998 model year onwards

**2** Some of the fuses are located on a panel fixed to the top of the battery in the engine compartment. The rest of the fuses are located in the lower facia on the driver's side.

#### All models

**3** Access to the passenger compartment fuses is gained by removing the driver's side glovebox, as described in Chapter 11, Section 26.

**4** The fuses attached to the top of the battery on later models can be accessed by pressing together the fuse cover locking lugs, and taking off the cover.

**5** All the fuses are numbered, and the circuits which they protect are listed in the wiring diagrams at the end of this Chapter.

3.12 Relays can be pulled from their sockets

**6** To remove a fuse, first switch off the circuit concerned (or the ignition), then pull the fuse out of its terminals. A fuse removal tool is attached to the rear of the glovebox **(see illustrations)**. The wire within the fuse should be visible; if the fuse is blown, it will be broken or melted.

**7** Always renew a fuse with one of an identical rating; never use a fuse with a different rating from the original or substitute anything else. Never renew a fuse more than once without tracing the source of the trouble. The fuse rating is stamped on top of the fuse; note that the fuses are also colour-coded for easy recognition. A list of fuses, and the circuits they protect, appears on the back of the glovebox and in the Specifications at the start of this Chapter.

**8** If a new fuse blows immediately, find the cause before renewing it again; a short to earth as a result of faulty insulation is most likely. Where a fuse protects more than one circuit, try to isolate the defect by switching on each circuit in turn (if possible) until the fuse blows again. Always carry a supply of spare fuses of each relevant rating on the vehicle, a spare of each rating should be clipped into the base of the fusebox.

### Fusible links

**9** If any of the fusible links blows, this indicates a serious wiring fault. Repairing or replacing a fusible link should not be attempted without consulting a VW dealer or automotive electrical specialist - all circuits protected by a fusible link carry a high current, and a fire could result from improper repair.

### Relays

**10** The relays are of sealed construction, and cannot be repaired if faulty. The relays are of the plug-in type, and may be removed by pulling directly from their terminals. On some of the relays located behind the facia, it is necessary to prise the two plastic clips outwards before removing the relay.

**11** If a circuit or system controlled by a relay develops a fault and the relay is suspect, operate the system; if the relay is functioning, it should be possible to hear it click as it is energised. If this is the case, the fault lies with the components or wiring of the system. If the relay is not being energised, then either the relay is not receiving a main supply or a switching voltage, or the relay itself is faulty. Testing is by the substitution of a known good unit, but be careful; while some relays are identical in appearance and in operation, others look similar but perform different functions.

**12** To renew a relay, first ensure that the ignition switch is off. The relay can then simply be pulled out from the socket **(see illustration)** and the new relay pressed in.

### Fuse/relay panel

#### Up to 1998 model year

**13** The fuse/relay panel can be removed by pressing the retaining clip each side so that the engagement pins can be pulled from the recess in the support. The clips can then be swung forward and pulled free from the relay panel pins. Withdraw the fuse/relay unit by prising out the support arms to release the panel pins from the holes in the support arms, and pull the unit free **(see illustration)**.

**14** To detach the multi-pin plug from the rear of the fuse/relay panel, grip and pull the retainer slide out about 5 mm. Press the multi-pin plug securing lug to release the relay panel socket **(see illustration)**.

**15** When refitting the plugs, ensure that they are fitted as far in as possible, and that the securing lugs engage. Fit the lock slide

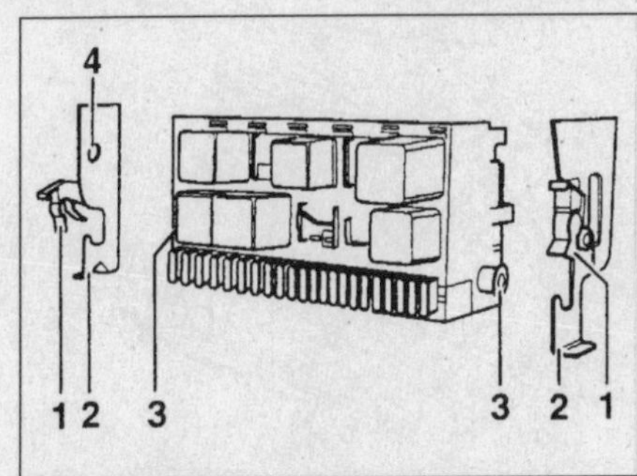


3.13 Fuse and relay unit - up to 1998 model year

*1 Securing clips*
*2 Retainer*
*3 Plate pins*
*4 Support arms*

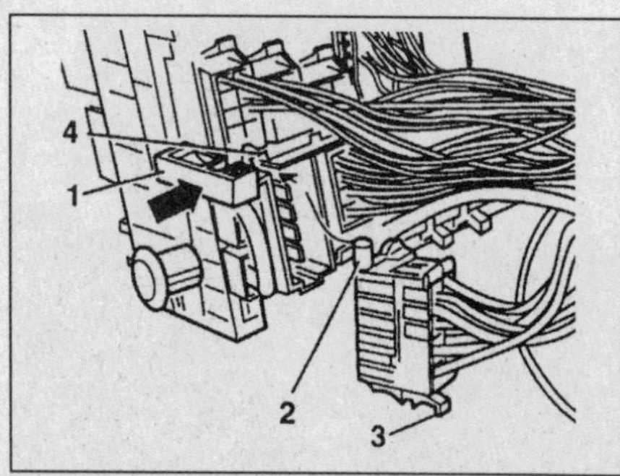


**3.14 Multi-plug installation to fuse/relay panel**

*1 Locking slide (arrow indicates locking direction)*
*2 Lock pins*
*3 Retaining lug*
*4 Lock pin recess*

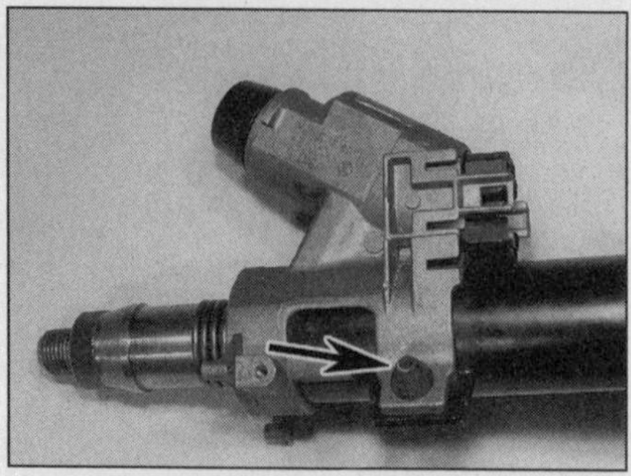

**4.7 Ignition switch/steering column lock shear-bolt (arrowed)**

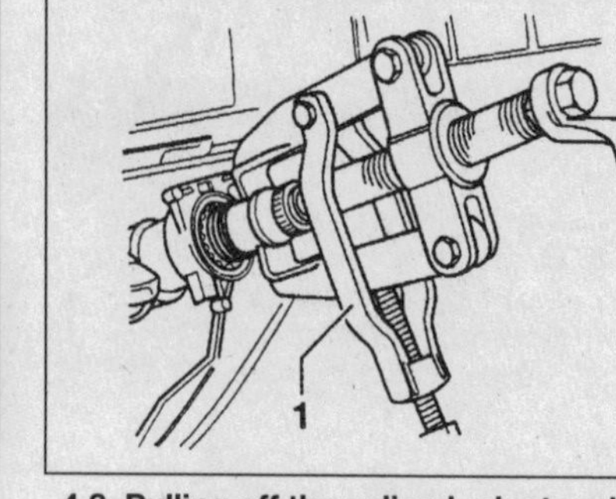


**4.8 Pulling off the splined adapter sleeve from the steering column, using a suitable puller (1)**

against its stop (all of the plugs must be fully engaged to enable the slide to fully enter and lock in position).

### 1998 model year onwards

**16** The passenger compartment fuse panel and relay panel are separate on later models, each panel being secured by two screws. Once the screws are removed, disconnect the wiring plugs from the rear of the panel, labelling the plugs as necessary for refitting.

**17** Removal of the engine compartment fusebox on top of the battery is described in Chapter 5A, as part of the battery removal procedure.

**18** When refitting, ensure that all wiring connections are securely made.

## 4 Ignition switch/steering column lock - removal and refitting

### Removal

**1** Disconnect the battery negative lead (refer to Section 1).

**2** Remove the steering wheel as described in Chapter 10.

**3** Remove the steering column combination switch as described in Section 5.

**4** On models with an immobiliser reader coil which can be detached from the ignition switch, remove the coil from the steering lock housing (see Chapter 10, Section 14).

**5** On models where the immobiliser reader coil is integral with the ignition lock, remove the driver's side glovebox as described in Chapter 11, Section 26. Working under the steering column, disconnect the immobiliser wiring connector, and release the wiring from the retaining clips.

**6** Disconnect the wiring plug from the ignition switch. On models with automatic transmission, press the Park lock cable clip out of its mounting bracket next to the ignition switch, and prise the cable end fitting off its ballstud.

**7** Drill out the shear-bolt securing the ignition switch/steering column lock, or chisel its head off **(see illustration)**.

**8** Pull off the splined adapter sleeve from the top of the steering column, using a suitable two-legged puller **(see illustration)**.

**9** The ignition switch/steering column lock and spring can now be pulled off the column, and removed.

**10** To remove the lock cylinder from the housing, a 3 mm hole must be drilled in the housing **(see illustrations)**. When the hole has been drilled, the lock cylinder retaining spring should be visible. Use the drill bit inserted in the drilled hole to release the lock spring, then pull out the lock cylinder using the ignition key. **Note:** *Once the lock housing has been drilled, it obviously reduces the security of the vehicle, since the lock cylinder could be removed with the housing installed. Consideration should be given to renewing the housing along with the lock cylinder in this instance.*

### Refitting

**11** Insert the new lock cylinder into position in the housing. As it is fitted, turn the key gently in the cylinder to engage the cylinder onto its stop.

**12** Slide the ignition lock housing and spring onto the steering column.

**13** Drive the splined adapter sleeve onto the column using a suitable piece of tubing.

**14** The remainder of refitting is the reverse of removal. Where the column does not project fully from the tube, pull it further up by fitting a nut and spacer washer onto the column, and tighten the washer against the housing to pull the column up so that it projects. Fit a new ignition switch shear-bolt and tighten until the head breaks off.

**15** Refer to Section 5 to refit the steering column combination switch.

**16** Refer to Chapter 10 to refit the steering wheel.

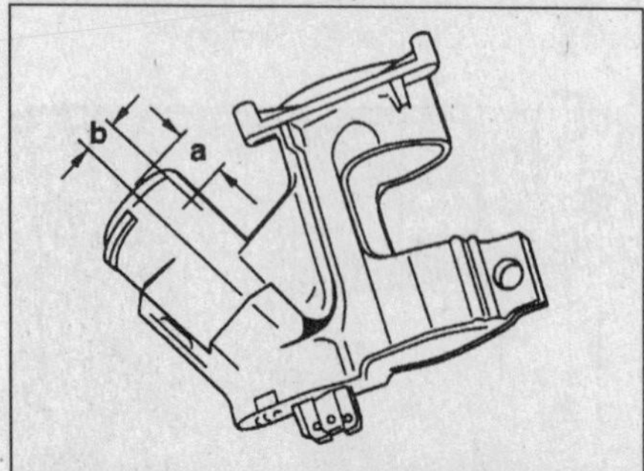


**4.10a Drilling point for removing ignition lock cylinder - models with immobiliser reader coil separate from ignition switch**

*a = 12 mm*    *b = 10 mm*

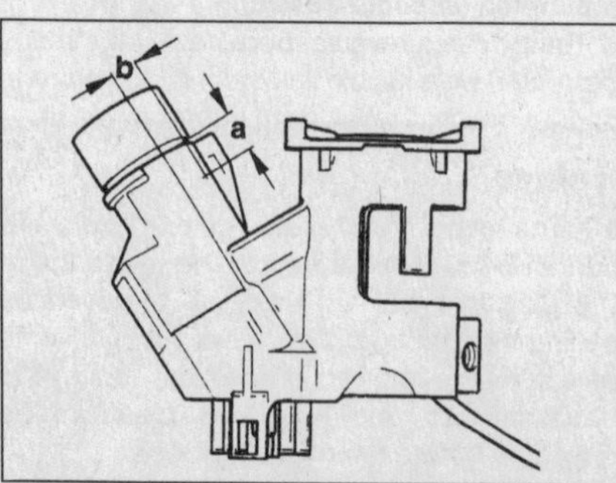


**4.10b Drilling point for removing ignition lock cylinder - models with immobiliser reader coil integral with ignition switch**

*a = 9.5 mm*    *b = 10 mm*

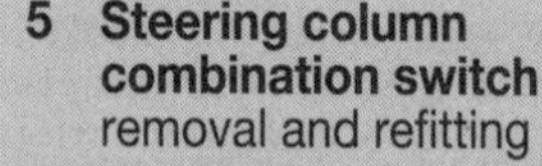

## 5 Steering column combination switch - removal and refitting

### Removal

**1** Disconnect the battery negative lead (refer to Section 1).

**2** Refer to Chapter 10 and remove the steering wheel.

**3** Undo the two retaining screws (from underneath) and remove the upper and lower column shrouds **(see illustration)**.

**4** Undo the three retaining screws and remove the combination switch assembly, and detach all the wiring connectors from it - there may be as many as five plugs **(see illustrations)**.

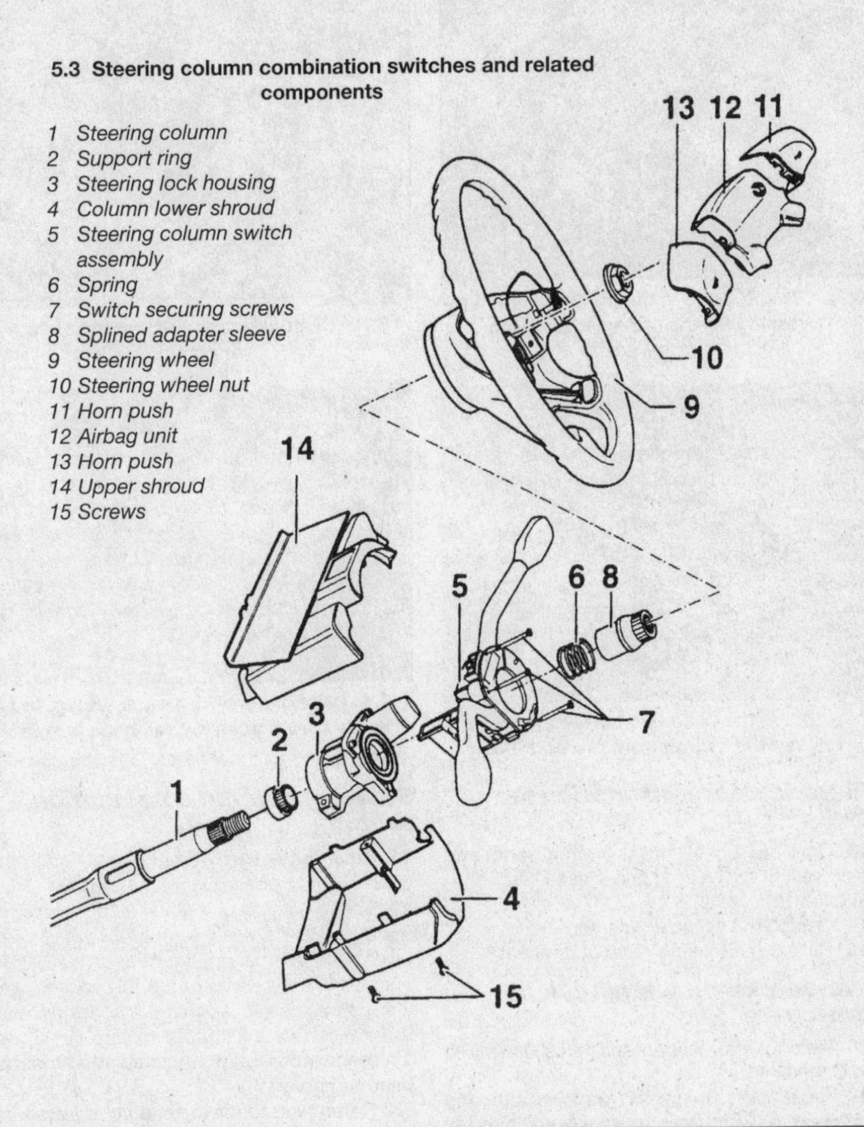


**5.3 Steering column combination switches and related components**

1 *Steering column*
2 *Support ring*
3 *Steering lock housing*
4 *Column lower shroud*
5 *Steering column switch assembly*
6 *Spring*
7 *Switch securing screws*
8 *Splined adapter sleeve*
9 *Steering wheel*
10 *Steering wheel nut*
11 *Horn push*
12 *Airbag unit*
13 *Horn push*
14 *Upper shroud*
15 *Screws*

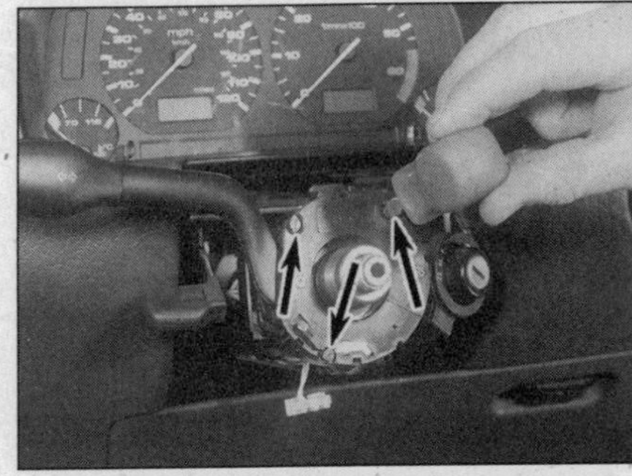

**5.4a Remove the three screws (arrowed) . . .**

**5.4b . . . then remove the direction indicator switch . . .**

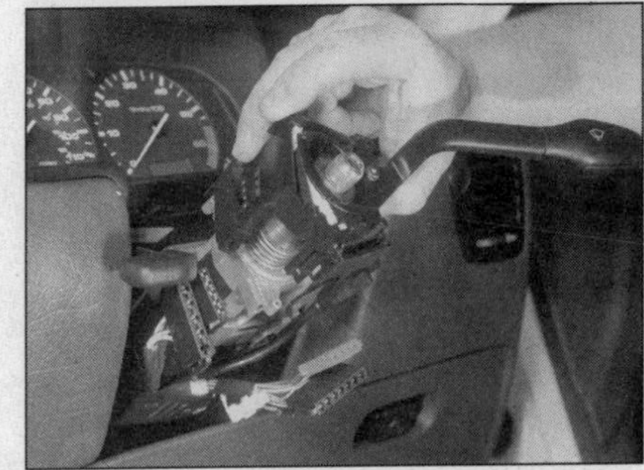

**5.4c . . . and the wiper switch**

### Refitting

**5** Refitting is a reversal of the removal procedure. Ensure that the wiring connections are securely made. Check for satisfactory operation on completion.

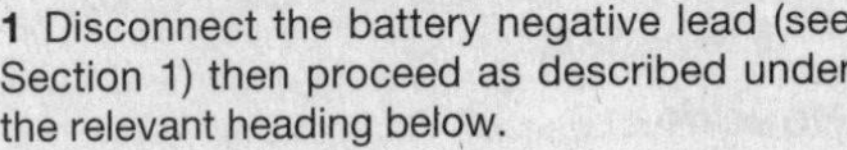

## 6 Switches - removal and refitting

**1** Disconnect the battery negative lead (see Section 1) then proceed as described under the relevant heading below.

### Facia switch

**2** Using a small screwdriver or similar tool, carefully prise the switch out of the facia **(see illustration)**.

**3** Disconnect the multi-plug from the rear of the switch **(see illustration)**.

**4** Refitting is a reversal of removal.

**6.2 Prise the switch out of the facia, taking care not to mark the trim . . .**

### Lighting switch

**5** Remove the driver's side glovebox, as described in Chapter 11, Section 26.

**6.3 . . . and disconnect the wiring plug**

6.6 Reach in through the glovebox aperture . . .

6.7a . . . and remove the lighting switch by pressing up the spring-loaded lug (arrowed)

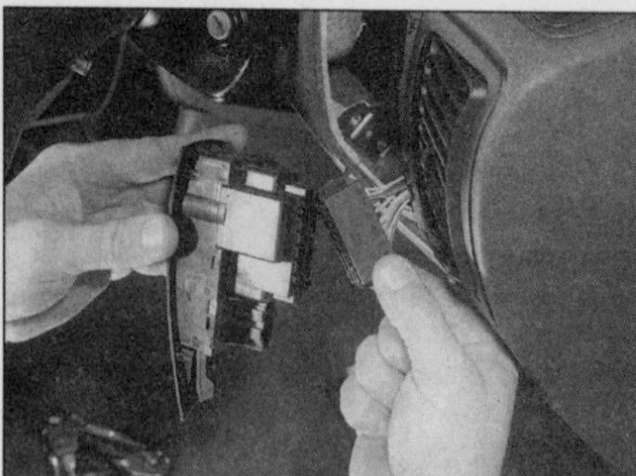

6.7b Disconnecting the lighting switch wiring plug

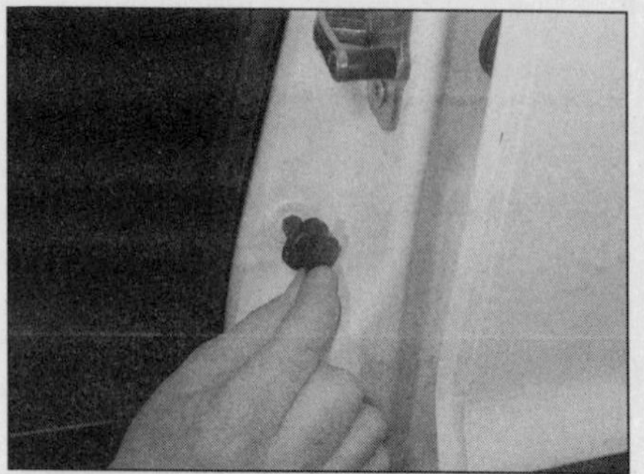

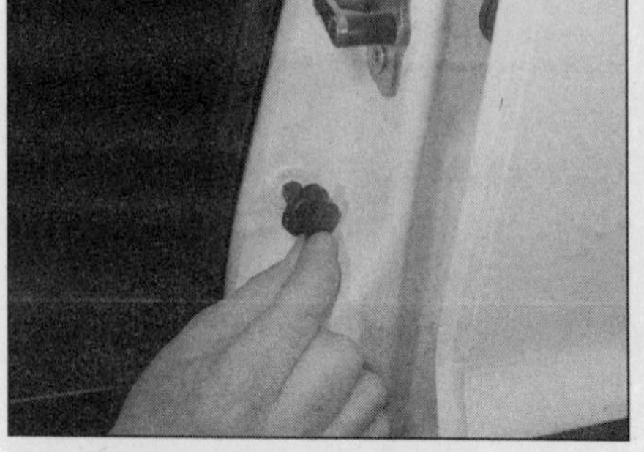

6.9 Pull the rubber cover off the courtesy light switch . . .

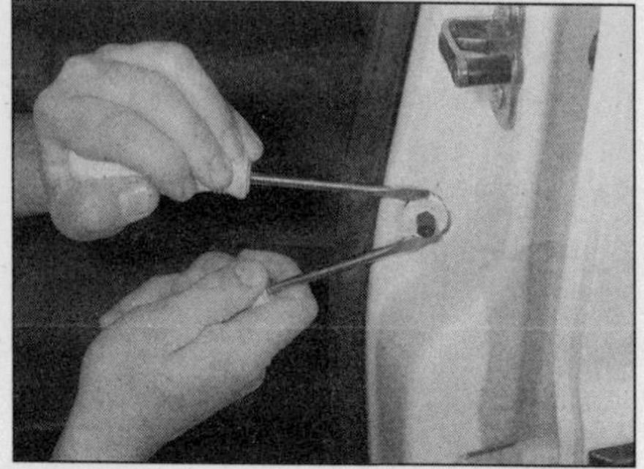

6.10 . . . then use two screwdrivers to release the switch from the door pillar

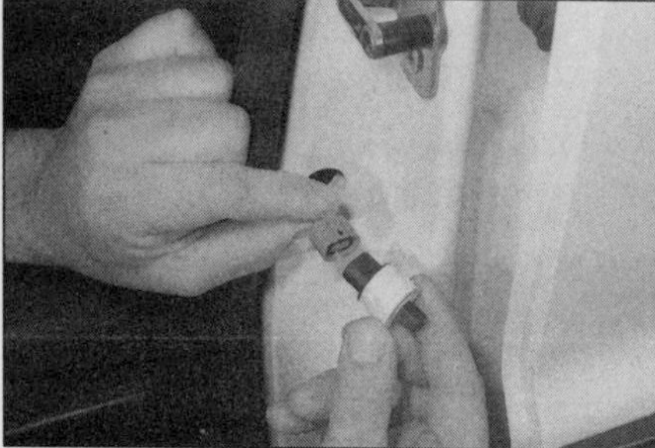

6.11 Disconnect the switch wiring, but make sure it does not fall back into the pillar

6 Reach in through the glovebox aperture, and press the spring-loaded lower retaining lug upwards **(see illustration)**.

7 Pull the lighting switch from the facia panel, and disconnect its wiring connector **(see illustrations)**.

8 Refitting is a reversal of removal.

### Courtesy light switches

9 Pull off the rubber cover **(see illustration)**.

10 Using two small flat-bladed screwdrivers at the prise points indicated by the arrowheads on the switch body, prise the switch out of the door pillar **(see illustration)**.

11 Disconnect the wiring plug and remove the switch **(see illustration)**. Make sure that the wiring does not drop back into the aperture by using tape or string to secure it.

12 Refitting is a reversal of removal. Fit the rubber cover to the switch before reconnecting the wiring and pressing it back into position.

### Electric door mirror adjuster switch

13 Carefully prise out the switch panel and remove it from the door panel (see Chapter 11, Section 12).

14 Detach the wiring connector.

15 Refit in the reverse order of removal.

### Handbrake-on warning light switch

16 Remove the centre console as described in Chapter 11.

17 Press out the switch locating tag and remove the switch from the lever (see Chapter 9, Section 15).

18 Detach the wiring connector from the switch.

19 Refit in the reverse order of removal.

### Stop-light switch

20 Refer to Chapter 9.

### Steering column combination switch

21 Refer to Section 5.

## 7 Exterior light bulbs - renewal

1 Whenever a bulb is renewed, note the following points:

*a) Disconnect the battery negative lead before starting work (see Section 1).*

*b) Remember that if the light has just been in use, the bulb may be extremely hot.*

*c) Always check the bulb contacts and holder, ensuring that there is clean metal-to-metal contact between the bulb and its live(s) and earth. Clean off any corrosion or dirt before fitting a new bulb.*

*d) Wherever bayonet-type bulbs are fitted, ensure that the live contact(s) bear firmly against the bulb contact.*

*e) Always ensure that the new bulb is of the correct rating and that it is completely clean before fitting it; this applies particularly to headlight/foglight bulbs (see below).*

### Headlight

2 Open the bonnet, and release the headlight rear cover by depressing the lug at the top of the cover **(see illustration)**.

3 Pull the wiring connector from the rear of the headlight bulb **(see illustration)**.

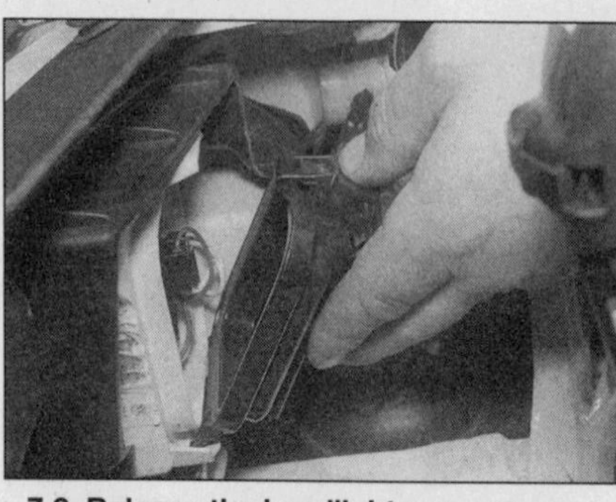

7.2 Release the headlight rear cover . . .

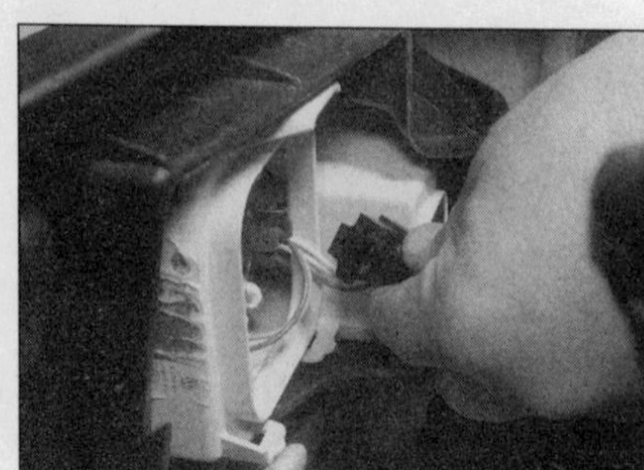

7.3 . . . disconnect the wiring plug . . .

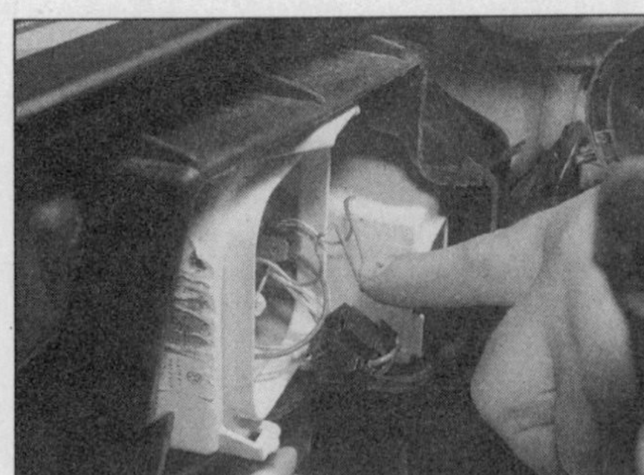
7.4 . . . release the wire retaining clip . . .

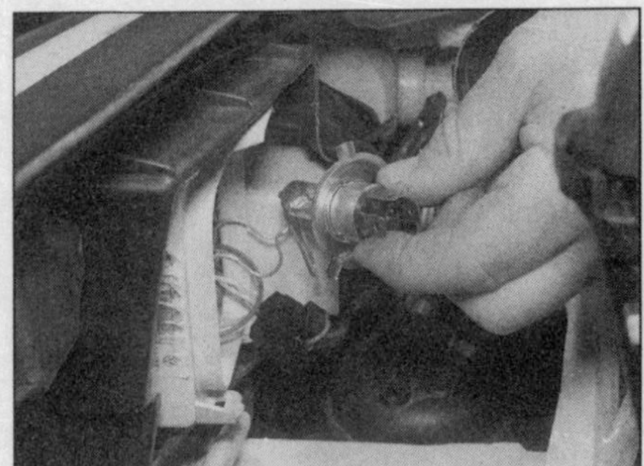
7.5 . . . and pull out the bulb

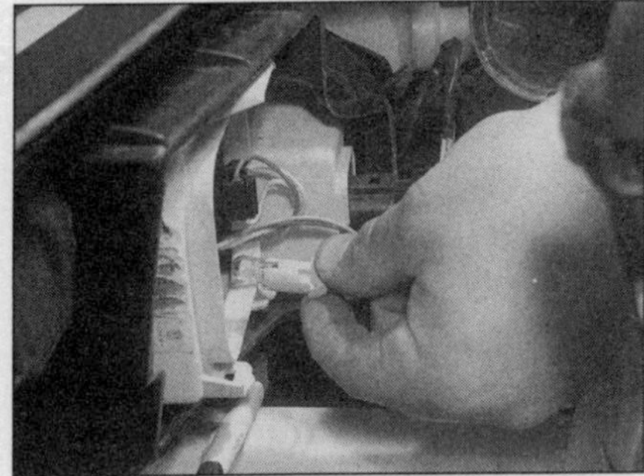
7.8 Pull out the sidelight bulbholder . . .

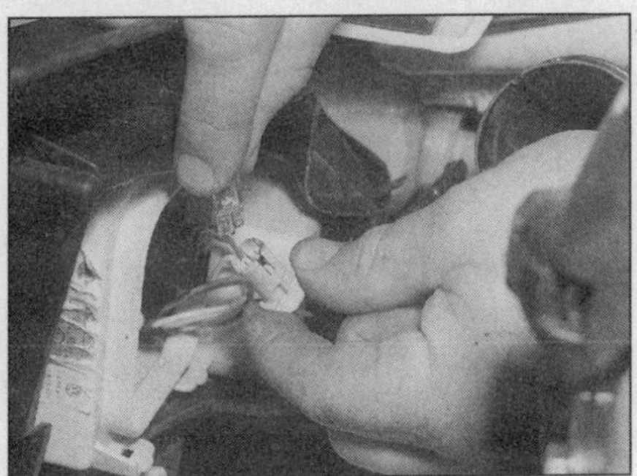
7.9 . . . and pull out the wedge-type bulb

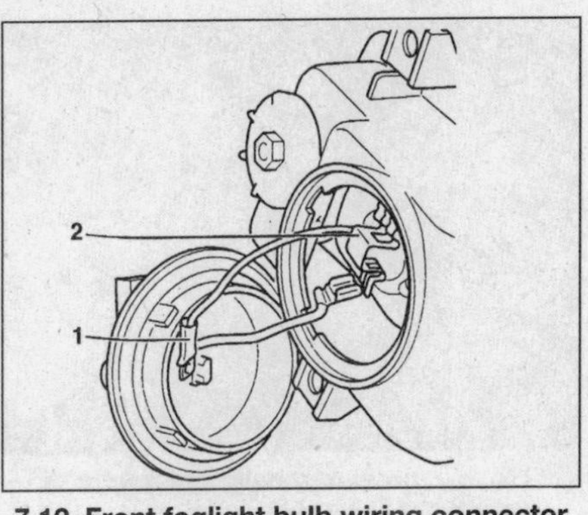

7.12 Front foglight bulb wiring connector (1) and retaining clip (2)

7.15 Remove the indicator securing screw . . .

**4** Unhook the bulb retaining wire clip at the top, and fold the clip down **(see illustration)**.

**5** Withdraw the bulb from the rear of the headlight **(see illustration)**.

**6** Refitting is a reversal of removal. Do not touch the glass of the new headlight bulb with bare fingers. If the glass is accidentally touched, clean it with methylated spirit. Check the light for satisfactory operation, on completion.

## Front sidelight

**7** Remove the plastic cover from the rear of the headlight as described in paragraph 2.

**8** Pull the bulbholder and wiring connector out from the reflector **(see illustration)**.

**9** Pull the wedge-type bulb out and remove it **(see illustration)**.

**10** Refit in the reverse order of removal, and check the light for satisfactory operation.

## Front foglight

**11** Reach in behind the foglight, and twist off the light rear cover anti-clockwise.

**12** Disconnect the wiring plug inside the cap **(see illustration)**, then release the bulb securing clip and remove the H3 bulb from the light unit.

**13** To remove the foglight, refer to Chapter 11 and remove the front bumper components as necessary for access to the foglight securing screws.

**14** Refitting is a reversal of removal. Do not touch the glass of the new bulb with bare fingers. If the glass is accidentally touched, clean it with methylated spirit. Check the light for satisfactory operation, on completion.

## Front direction indicator

**15** Remove the light unit securing screw on the inner wing at the top of the light unit **(see illustration)**.

**16** Pull the direction indicator forwards and disconnect the wiring plug **(see illustrations)**.

**17** Twist the bulbholder approximately 30° anti-clockwise, and pull it from the rear of the light unit.

**18** Depress and twist the bulb to remove it from its holder.

**19** Refit in the reverse order of removal, and check the light for satisfactory operation.

## Direction indicator side repeater light

**20** Push the lens to the rear, then prise it out at the front to release the lens **(see illustration)**.

**21** Turn the bulbholder fully to the right, and extract the bulbholder from the lens **(see illustration)**.

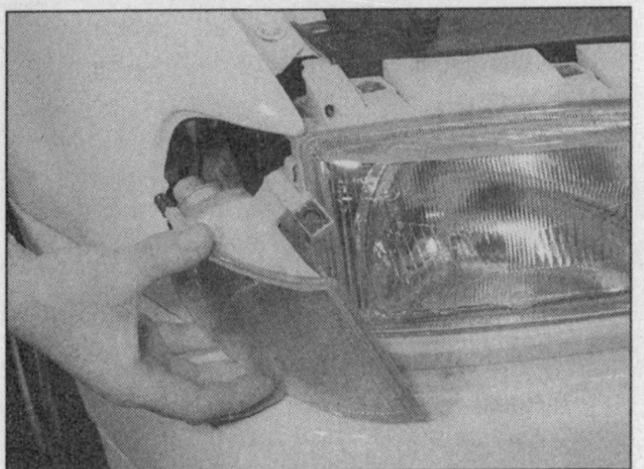
7.16a . . . pull out the light unit . . .

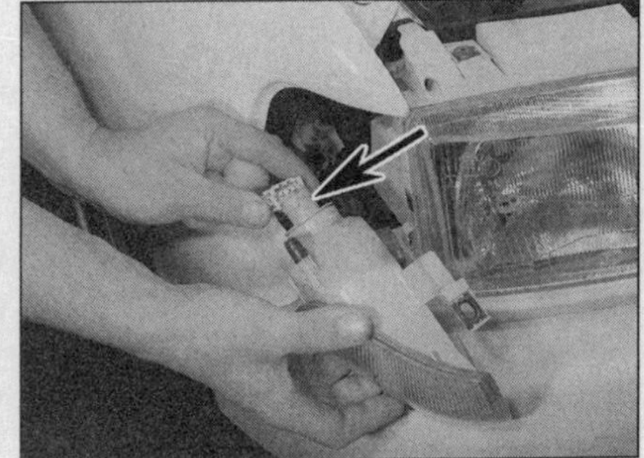
7.16b . . . and disconnect the wiring plug - bulbholder arrowed

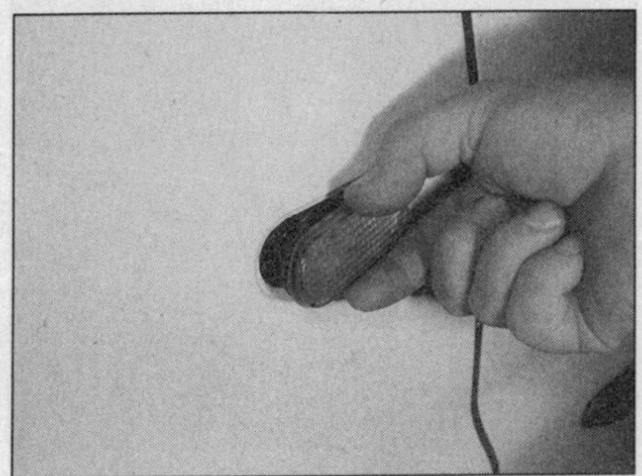
7.20 Push the side repeater light to the rear, and pull out at the front

7.21 Remove the bulbholder from the rear of the light unit

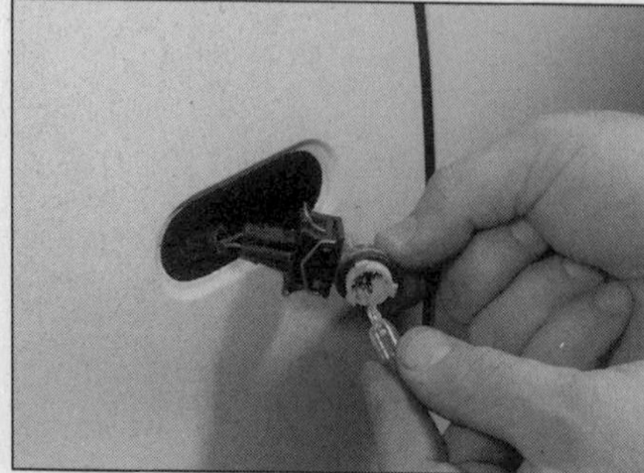
7.22 Pull out the wedge-type bulb

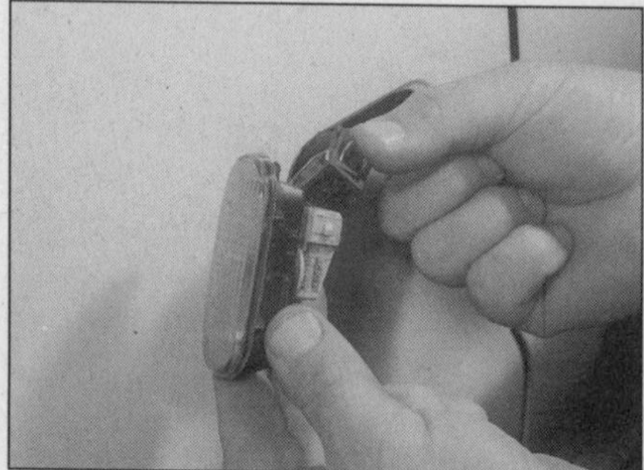
7.23 To remove the light unit, disconnect the wiring plug

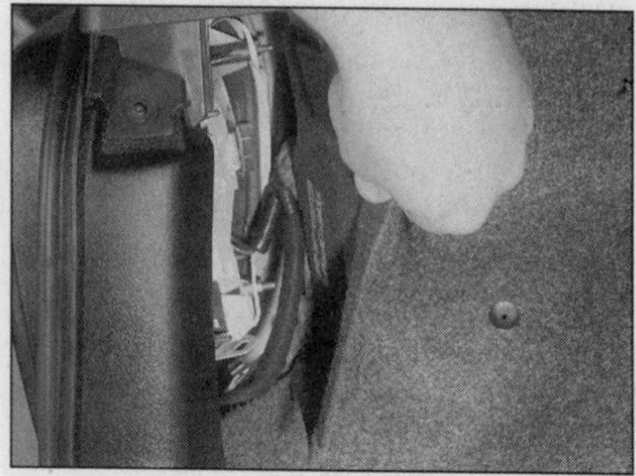
7.25 Pull open the access flap in the luggage area carpet . . .

7.27 . . . press the bulbholder lugs as shown . . .

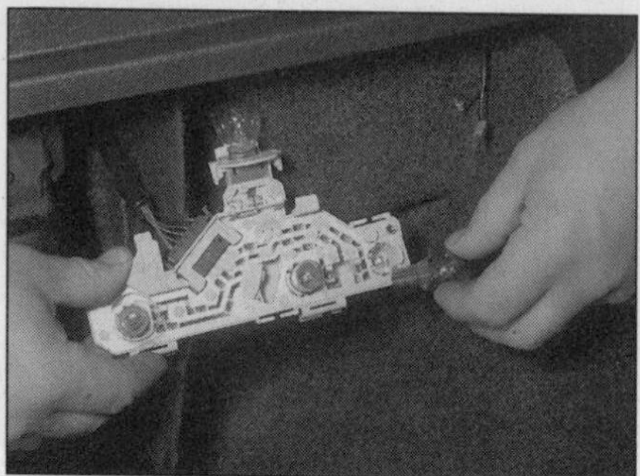
7.28 . . . and withdraw the bulbholder - bulbs are a bayonet fit

**22** Pull the bulb from the holder **(see illustration)**.

**23** To remove the light unit, disconnect the wiring multi-plug **(see illustration)**. Tape the plug or its wire to the wing, to stop it disappearing inside.

**24** Refit in the reverse order of removal, and check the light for satisfactory operation.

## Rear combination lights

**25** On the left-hand rear light, pull open the access flap in the rear luggage area carpet **(see illustration)**.

**26** On the right-hand rear light unit, turn the two trim panel fasteners through 90°, and lower the trim panel for access to the light unit.

**27** Depress the retaining lugs towards the outside of the car, and withdraw the bulbholder **(see illustration)**.

**28** Press and untwist the relevant bulb to remove it **(see illustration)**.

**29** To remove the light unit, disconnect the wiring plug from the bulbholder, then undo three retaining nuts and withdraw the unit from the body **(see illustration)**.

**30** Refit in the reverse order of removal, and check the lights for satisfactory operation.

## High-level stop-light bulbs

**31** Open the tailgate, disconnect the wiring plug, then press in the two retaining tabs through the apertures either side of the bulbholder and release the bulbholder from the light unit.

**32** The bulbs can now be extracted and renewed as necessary.

**33** Refitting is a reversal of removal. Check the light for satisfactory operation.

## Number plate light

**34** Open the tailgate, and carefully prise out the light unit using a small flat-bladed screwdriver in the recess provided **(see illustration)**. Note how the light unit is installed.

**35** Twist and remove the bulbholder from the light unit, then pull out the bulb **(see illustrations)**.

**36** To remove the light unit, disconnect the wiring plug and remove it from the bumper **(see illustration)**.

**37** Refit in the reverse order of removal, and check the light for satisfactory operation.

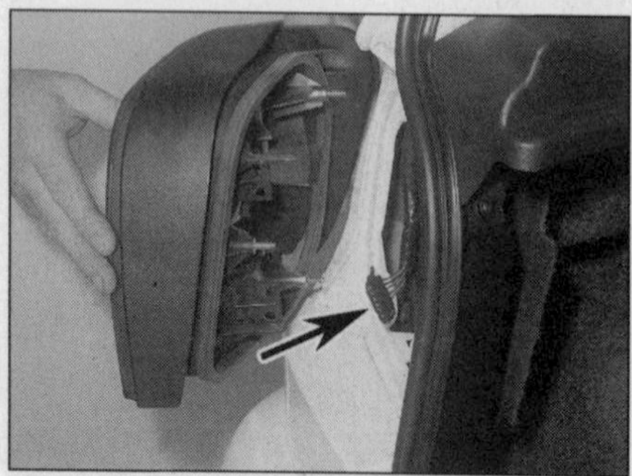
7.29 To remove the rear light unit, undo three nuts and disconnect the wiring plug (arrowed)

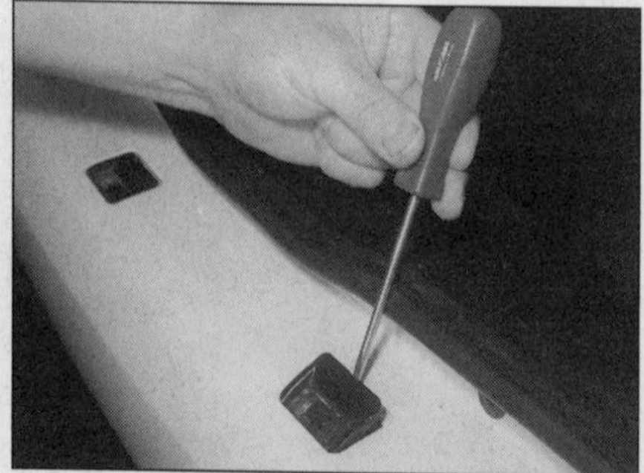
7.34 Prise the light unit out of the bumper . . .

7.35a . . . pull out the bulbholder . . .

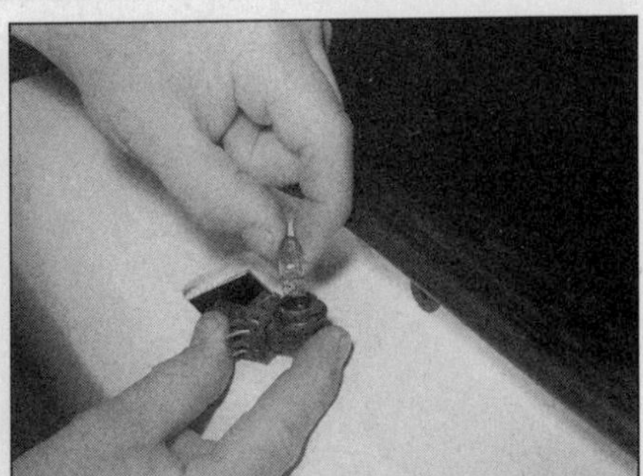

7.35b . . . and extract the wedge-type bulb

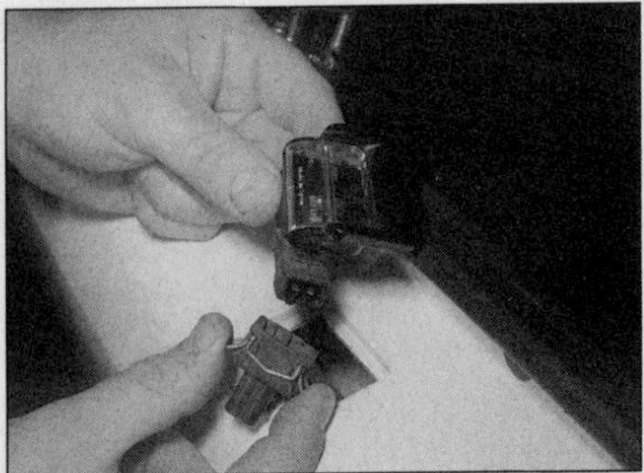

7.36 The light unit may be removed after disconnecting the wiring plug

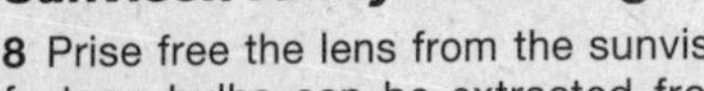

## Sunvisor/vanity mirror light

8 Prise free the lens from the sunvisor. The festoon bulbs can be extracted from their holders in the visor.

9 Refit in the reverse order of removal.

## Instrument panel bulbs

10 Remove the instrument panel as described in Section 10.

### Up to 1998 model year

11 To remove an illumination bulb, untwist or pull out the holder and extract the bulb from it **(see illustrations)**.

12 Refit in the reverse order of removal. Refit the instrument panel as described in Section 10.

### 1998 model year onwards

13 Only the main beam warning light bulb can be renewed, as described in paragraph 11.

14 All other warning light and illumination bulbs are an integral part of the instrument panel, and cannot be removed or renewed separately. If more than one light has failed, check that the multi-pin wiring connectors are securely attached to the rear of the panel, and that all pins are making good contact in the wiring plugs. Refit the instrument panel as described in Section 10.

## Switch illumination bulbs

15 Switch illumination bulbs are usually built into the switch itself, and cannot be renewed separately. Refer to Section 6 and remove the switch - bulb renewal should then be self-evident, if it is possible; otherwise, renew the switch **(see illustration)**.

# 8 Interior light bulbs - renewal

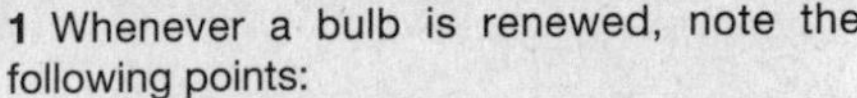

1 Whenever a bulb is renewed, note the following points:

*a) Disconnect the battery negative lead before starting work (see Section 1).*

*b) Remember that if the light has just been in use, the bulb may be extremely hot.*

*c) Always check the bulb contacts and holder, ensuring that there is clean metal-to-metal contact between the bulb and its live(s) and earth. Clean off any corrosion or dirt before fitting a new bulb.*

*d) Wherever bayonet-type bulbs are fitted, ensure that the live contact(s) bear firmly against the bulb contact.*

*e) Always ensure that the new bulb is of the correct rating and that it is completely clean before fitting it.*

## Interior light

2 Using a suitable screwdriver, prise the interior light from the headlining. If wished, the light unit can be removed by disconnecting its wiring plug **(see illustrations)**.

3 Slide the light rear cover upwards in the direction of the arrow moulded into the cover, for access to the bulb **(see illustration)**.

4 Unclip the festoon type bulb from its contacts and remove it **(see illustration)**.

5 Refit in the reverse order of removal.

## Luggage area light

6 Prise free the light lens/unit and extract the festoon bulb from its holder.

7 Refit in the reverse order of removal, and check for satisfactory operation.

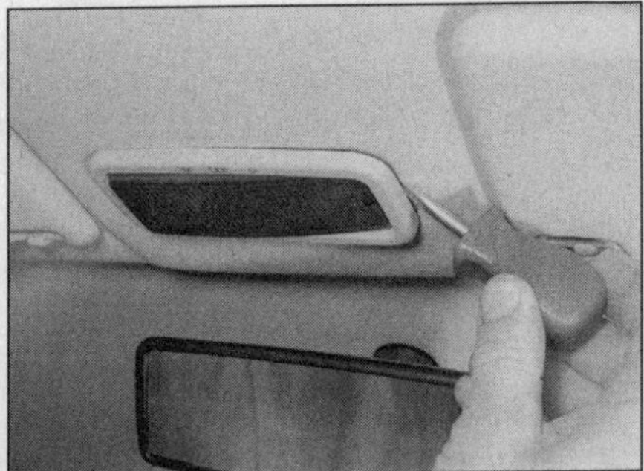

8.2a Prise the interior light out of the headlining . . .

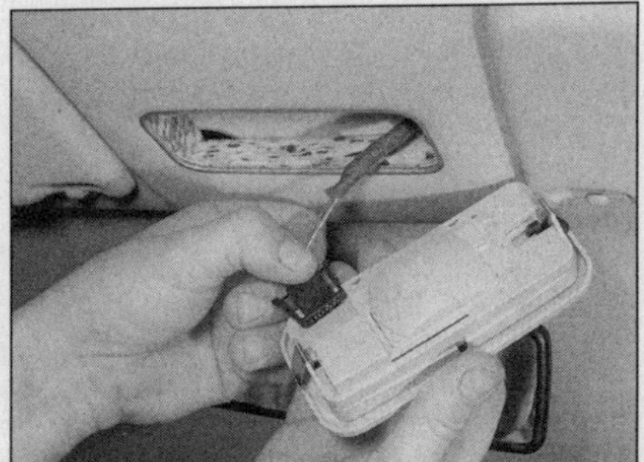

8.2b . . . and disconnect the wiring plug, if required

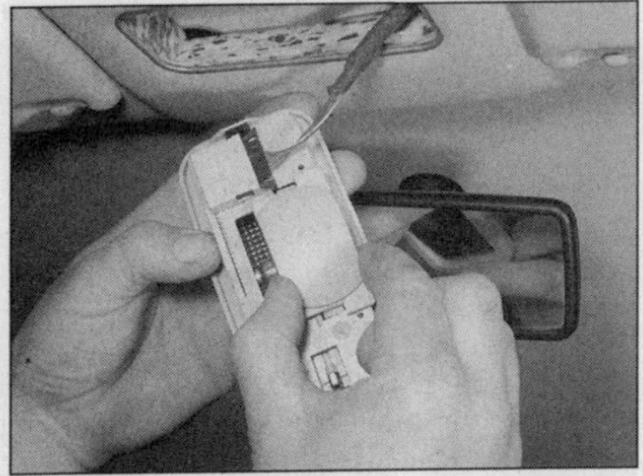

8.3 To renew the bulb, slide up the cover . . .

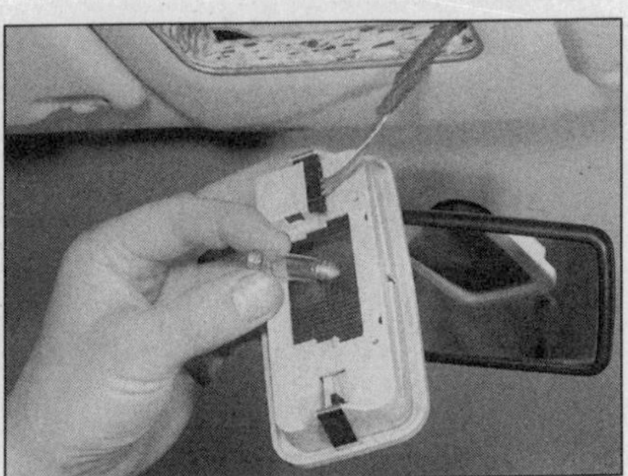

8.4 . . . and pull the festoon-type bulb from the contacts

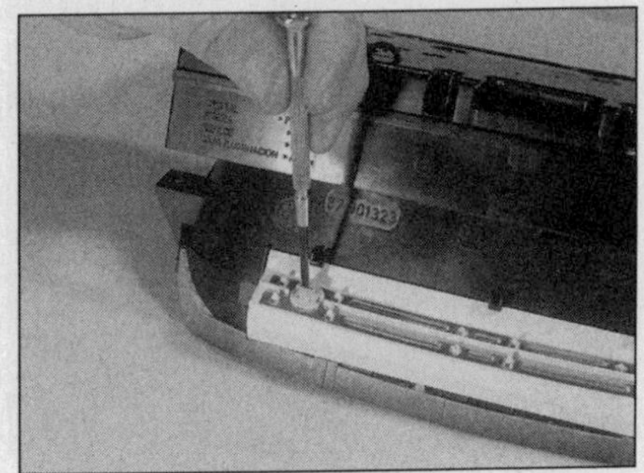

8.11a Turn the bulbholder using a small screwdriver . . .

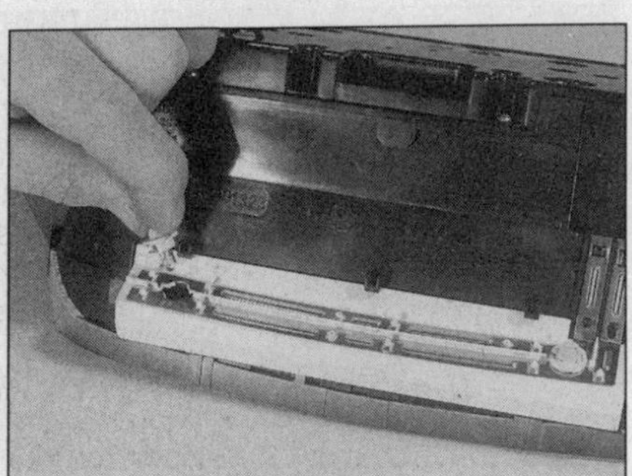

8.11b . . . then pull out the bulbholder

8.15 Bulbholder (arrowed) in the back of the lighting switch

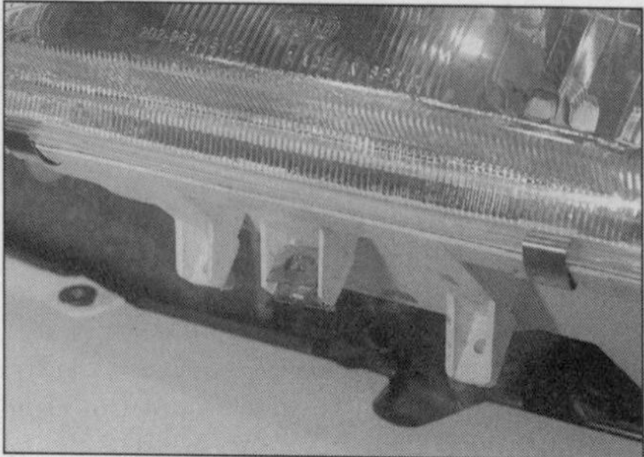

9.2c . . . then lift up the headlight to free the lower lugs



9.6 Headlight beam adjustment screws

*A Horizontal adjustment screw*
*B Vertical adjustment screw*
*C % inclination marking (for use by VW dealer)*

9.2a Remove the two screws at the top (arrowed) . . .

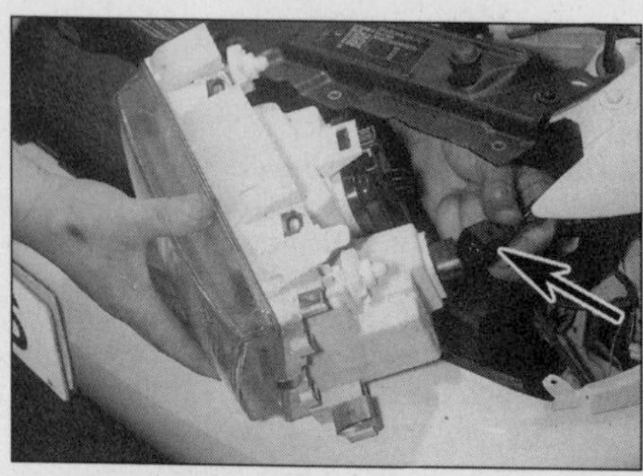

9.3 Disconnect the wiring plug (arrowed) and remove the headlight

### Heater control panel illumination bulb

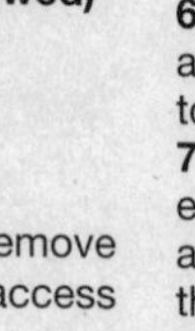

**16** Refer to Chapter 3, Section 9 and remove the heater/ventilation control panel for access to the illumination bulb.

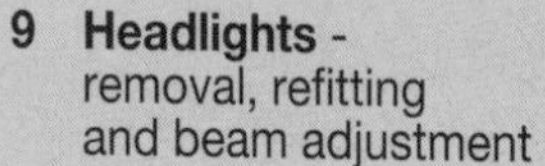

## 9 Headlights - removal, refitting and beam adjustment

### Removal

**1** Remove both the front direction indicators as described in Section 7, then refer to Chapter 11 and remove the radiator grille and the headlight surround.
**2** Remove the three retaining screws, then lift the headlight out of position **(see illustrations)**.
**3** Disconnect the wiring plug from the rear of the headlight, and remove the headlight from the car **(see illustration)**.

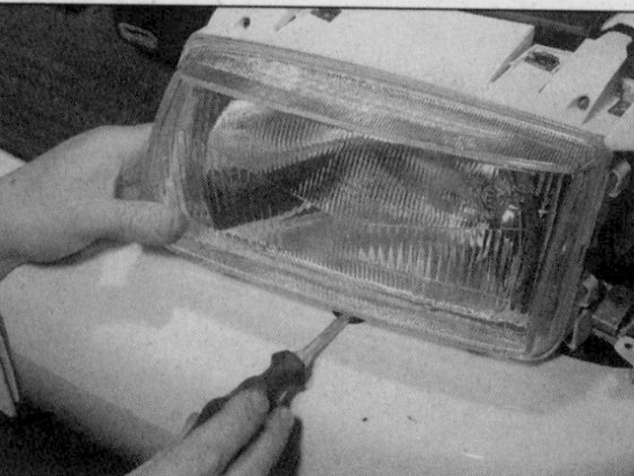

9.2b . . . and the screw at the bottom . . .

### Refitting

**4** Reassembly and refitting is a reversal of the removal procedure. On completion check for satisfactory operation, and have the headlight beam adjustment checked as soon as possible (see below).

### Beam adjustment

**5** Accurate adjustment of the headlight beam is only possible using optical beam-setting equipment, and this work should therefore be carried out by a VW dealer or suitably-equipped workshop.
**6** For reference, the headlights can be adjusted using the adjuster assemblies fitted to the top of each light unit **(see illustration)**.
**7** Some models are equipped with an electrically-operated headlight beam adjustment system, which is controlled through a switch in the facia. On these models, ensure that the switch is set to the basic (–) position before adjusting the headlight aim.

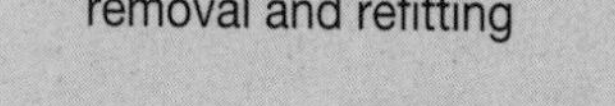

## 10 Instrument panel - removal and refitting

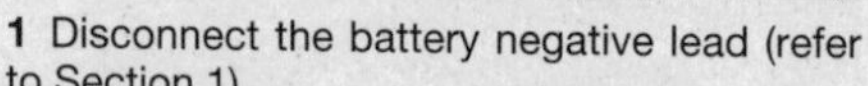

**1** Disconnect the battery negative lead (refer to Section 1).

### Up to 1998 model year

**2** Undo the two upper retaining screws and remove the instrument panel surround **(see illustrations)**.
**3** Remove the screw at either side of the instrument panel, and pull the panel forwards **(see illustrations)**.

10.2a Remove the two screws at the top . . .

10.2b . . . and withdraw the instrument panel surround

10.3a Remove the screw either side . . .

10.3b . . . then pull out the instrument panel

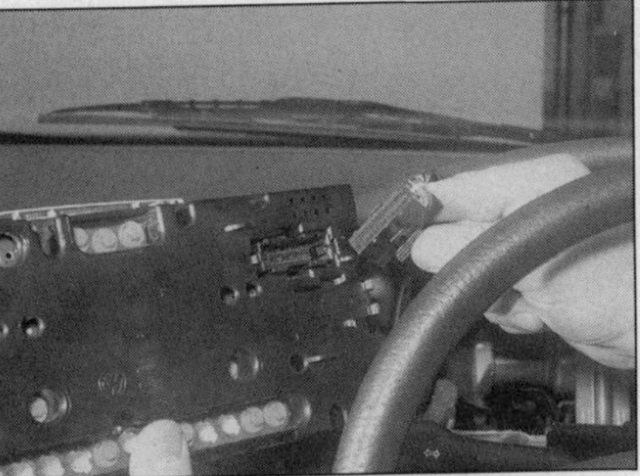
10.4 Disconnecting the multi-plug from the rear of the panel

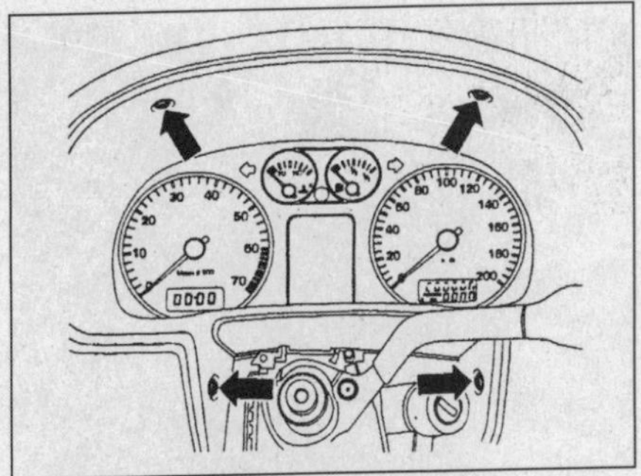
10.8 Instrument panel surround screws (arrowed) - 1998-on models

4 Disconnect the multi-plug from the rear of the instrument panel, and remove the panel from the car **(see illustration)**.

### *1998 model year onwards*

5 Remove the steering wheel as described in Chapter 10. If not already done, remove two screws from below the steering column, and separate and remove the steering column upper and lower shrouds.
6 Remove the steering column combination switch assembly, as described in Section 5.
7 Where applicable, set the steering column height adjuster to its lowest position.
8 Unscrew and remove the four screws securing the instrument panel surround - two at the top, one either side of the steering column **(see illustration)**. Remove the surround from the car.
9 Remove the two upper securing screws **(see illustration)**, and pull the instrument panel forwards.
10 Disconnect the two multi-plugs from the rear of the instrument panel. Seen from the rear, the left-hand multi-plug is green, and the right-hand plug is blue.

### *All models*

11 It is recommended that no attempt is made to dismantle the instrument panel. Any faults with the panel can be diagnosed by a VW dealer, using dedicated fault diagnosis equipment.
12 Refitting the panel is a reversal of removal. Ensure that all wiring connections are correctly and securely made.

## 11 Instruments - removal and refitting

The instrument panel should not be dismantled. In the event of a problem occurring, remove the panel as described in Section 10, and take it to a VW dealer for diagnosis. If a warning light or illumination bulb has failed, refer to Section 8.

## 12 Cigar lighter - removal and refitting

### *Removal*

1 Disconnect the battery negative lead (refer to Section 1).
2 Open the ashtray, then hold down the retaining catch on top, and remove the ashtray from the facia panel **(see illustration)**.
3 The cigar lighter is secured by two clips at the base, and a larger clip at the top.
4 Using a small flat-bladed screwdriver if necessary, release the upper clip, and swing the lighter unit downwards and out of the facia panel **(see illustration)**.
5 Disconnect the wiring from the rear of the lighter assembly, and remove the lighter from the car **(see illustration)**.

### *Refitting*

6 Refit in the reverse order of removal.

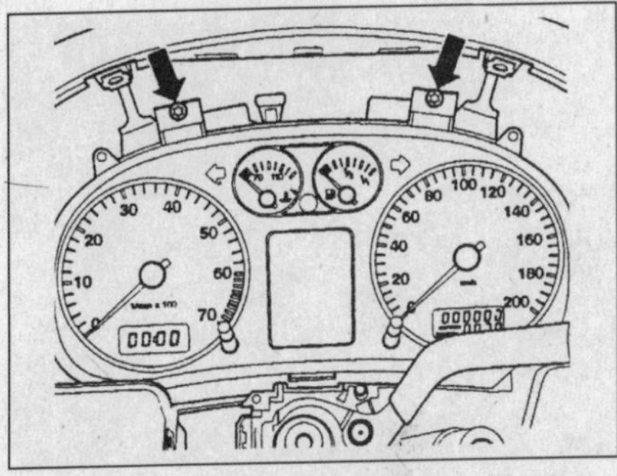
10.9 Instrument panel is secured by two screws (arrowed) at the top on 1998-on models

## 13 Windscreen wiper components - removal and refitting

### *Wiper blades*

1 Refer to *Weekly checks*.

### *Wiper arms*

2 If the wipers are not in their parked position, switch on the ignition, and allow the motor to automatically park. Depending which wiper arm is to be removed, it may be necessary to open the bonnet for access.
3 Before removing an arm, mark its parked position on the glass with a strip of adhesive tape. Prise off the cover and unscrew the outer nut **(see illustrations)**. Remove the

12.2 Removing the ashtray

12.4 Pull the cigar lighter downwards and out of the facia

12.5 Disconnecting the cigar lighter wiring plug

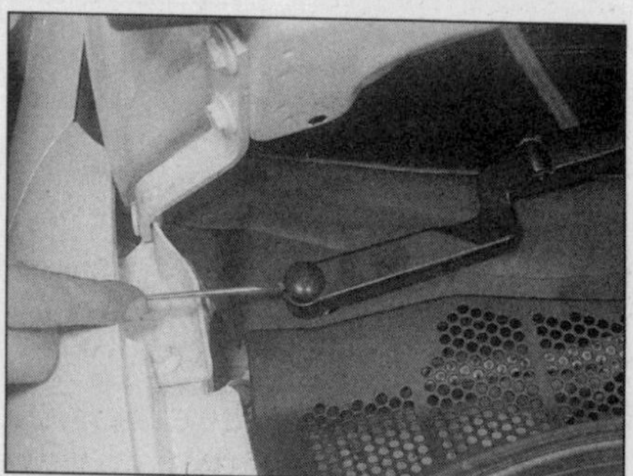

**13.3a Prise off the cover . . .**

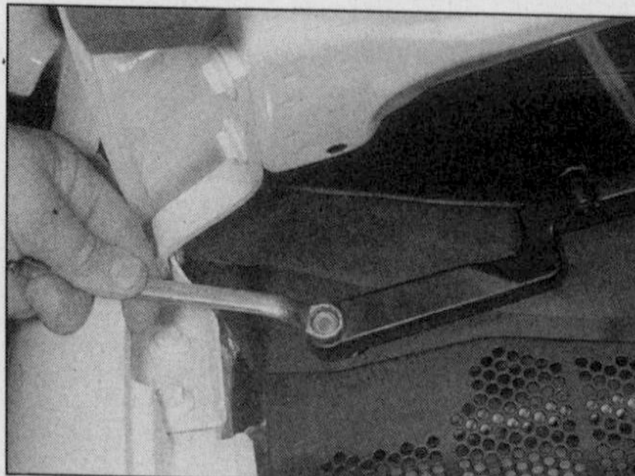

**13.3b . . . then unscrew the nut and remove the wiper arm**

**13.7a Pull off the weatherstrip . . .**

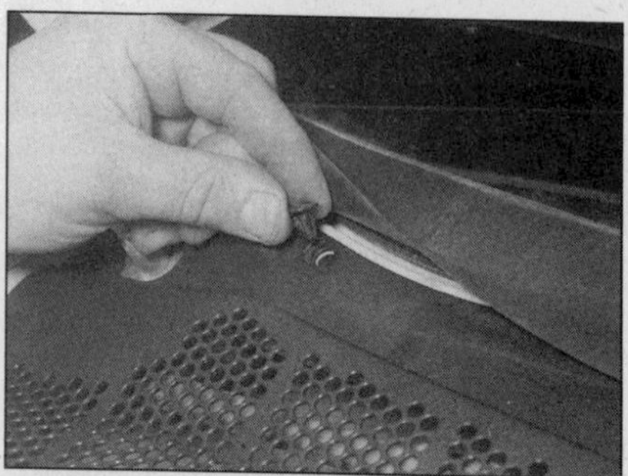

**13.7b . . . then peel back the sealing strip and prise out the cowl panel retaining clips**

**13.7c Removing one of the cowl panels**

**13.8 Wiper motor wiring plug (arrowed)**

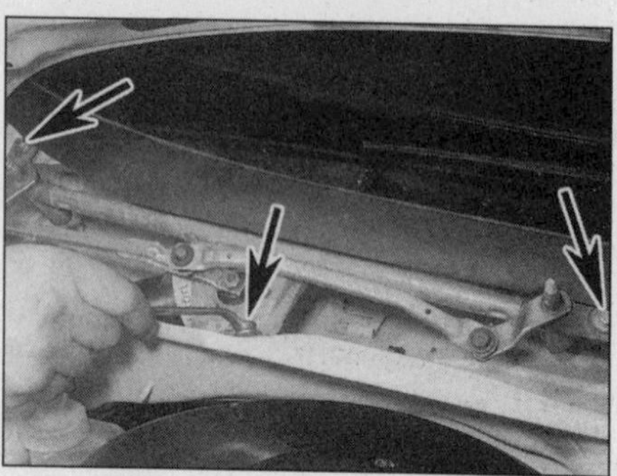

**13.9a Wiper frame-to-body bolts (arrowed)**

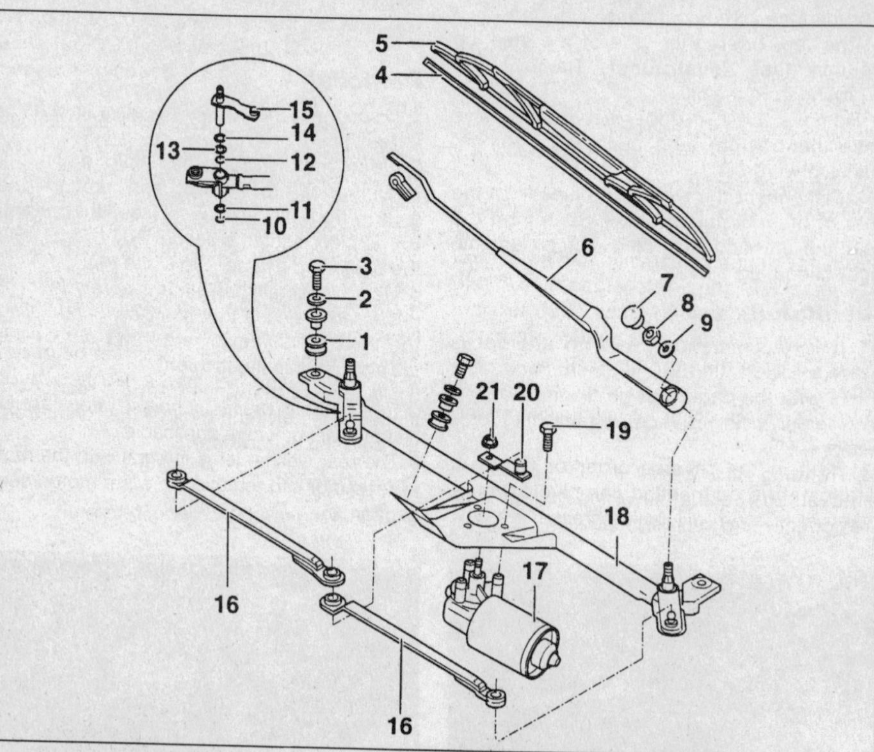


**13.9c Windscreen wiper motor and related components**

*1 Rubber bush*
*2 Washer*
*3 Wiper frame bolt*
*4 Wiper blade rubber*
*5 Wiper blade*
*6 Wiper arm*
*7 Wiper arm nut*
*8 Washer*
*9 Circlip*
*10 Washer*
*11 O-ring*
*12 Spring washer*
*13 Spring washer*
*14 Cover cap*
*15 Connecting lever*
*16 Connecting link*
*17 Wiper motor*
*18 Wiper frame*
*19 Motor mounting bolt*
*20 Crank arm*
*21 Motor mounting nut*

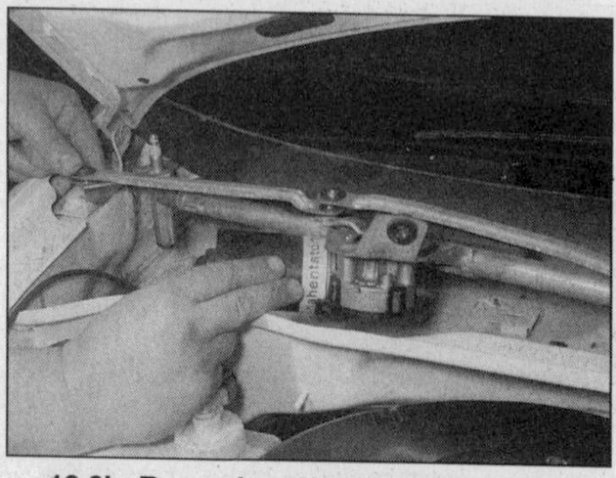

**13.9b Removing the wiper frame and motor assembly**

13.10 Wiper motor-to-frame bolts (arrowed)

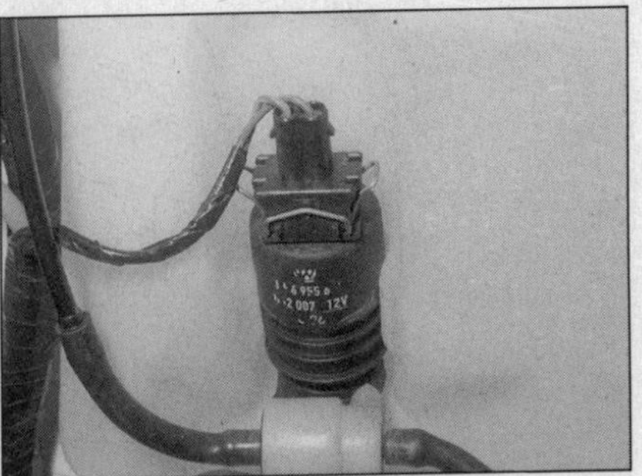
14.2 Washer pump is attached to the side of the washer fluid reservoir

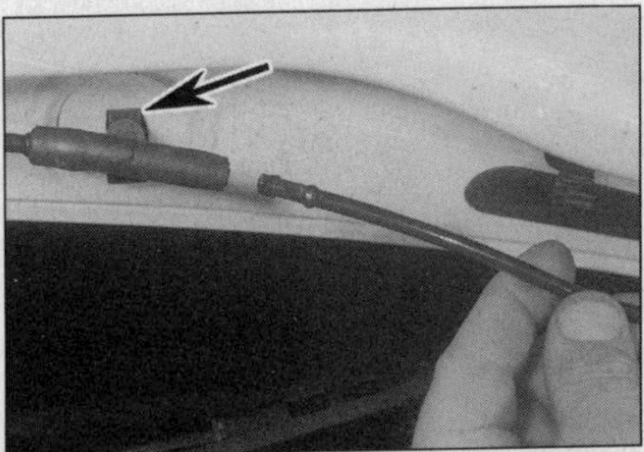
14.4 Disconnecting a washer supply hose from a T-piece connection - washer jet arrowed

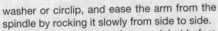

washer or circlip, and ease the arm from the spindle by rocking it slowly from side to side.

**4** Refitting is a reversal of removal, but before tightening the spindle nuts, position the wiper blades on the motor shaft splines so that the blades sit on the glass as marked before removal.

### *Wiper motor*

**5** Disconnect the battery negative lead (refer to Section 1).

**6** Remove the wiper arms as described in paragraphs 2 and 3.

**7** Open the bonnet, then pull off the rubber weatherstrip from the top of the engine compartment bulkhead. Peel back the rubber sealing strip from the base of the windscreen, then prise out the retaining clips and remove the plastic cowling panels from below the windscreen **(see illustrations)**.

**8** Disconnect the wiring plug from the wiper motor **(see illustration)**.

**9** Undo the three wiper frame-to-body bolts (next to the wiper arm spindles, and one beside the motor), noting the fitted order of all washers. Withdraw the wiper motor and mounting frame assembly **(see illustrations)**.

**10** If required, unbolt and remove the motor from the frame **(see illustration)**. If the assembly is to be completely dismantled, note the fitted order of all washers and spacers, etc.

**11** Refit in the reverse order of removal. Lubricate the connecting link pivots with a little molybdenum disulphide grease. If a new wiper motor is being fitted, the crank arm must be set in the parked position.

**12** On completion, check for satisfactory operation.

## 14 Washer system - general

**1** All models are fitted with a windscreen washer system and a tailgate washer.

**2** The fluid reservoir for the windscreen washer and tailgate washer is located in the engine compartment on the left-hand side. The fluid pump is attached to the side of the reservoir body, and can be pulled out once the wiring plug has been disconnected **(see illustration)**.

**3** The reservoir fluid level must be regularly topped up with proper washer fluid containing an antifreeze agent, but not cooling system antifreeze - see *Weekly checks*.

**4** The supply hoses are attached by rubber couplings to their various connections, and if required, can be detached by simply pulling them free from the appropriate connector **(see illustration)**.

**5** The windscreen washer jets can be prised from their locations in the bonnet, after disconnecting the fluid hoses and electric heating wiring, where applicable.

**6** The rear washer jet is integral with the rear wiper motor - to remove the wiper motor, see Section 15.

**7** The washer jets can be cleaned and adjusted using a needle. When adjusted correctly, the jets should be aimed at a point just above the centre of the wiper swept area.

## 15 Tailgate wiper motor - removal and refitting

**1** Disconnect the battery negative lead, with reference to Section 1.

**2** Open the tailgate and detach the trim panel from it. Slacken and remove the tailgate handle retaining screw, then release the tailgate trim panel clips, carefully levering between the panel and tailgate with a flat-bladed screwdriver. Work around the outside of the panel, and when all the clips are released, remove the panel (see Chapter 11, Section 15).

**3** Make sure that the wiper arm is in the parked position by switching the rear wiper on and then off, so that the arm moves through a complete sweep. Mark the position of the wiper blade on the glass by sticking a strip of masking tape along the line of the blade. Lift up the hinged cover from the wiper arm nut, then remove the nut and pull the wiper arm off the splines **(see illustrations)**.

**4** Remove the large nut and trim piece fitted underneath the wiper arm **(see illustrations)**.

**5** Detach the wiring connector from the wiper motor, and pull off the washer fluid pipe **(see illustrations)**.

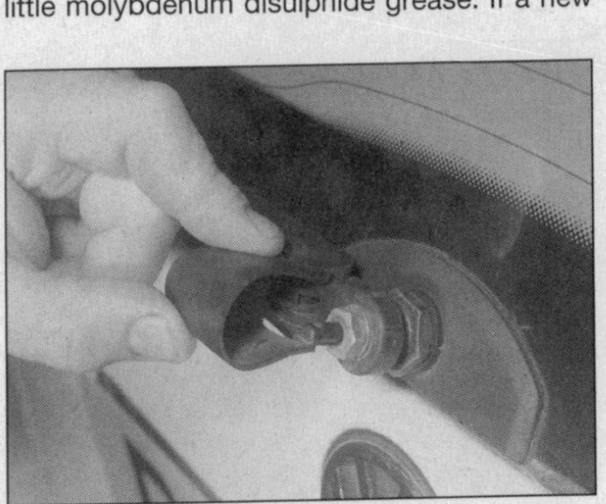
15.3a Lift up the hinged cover . . .

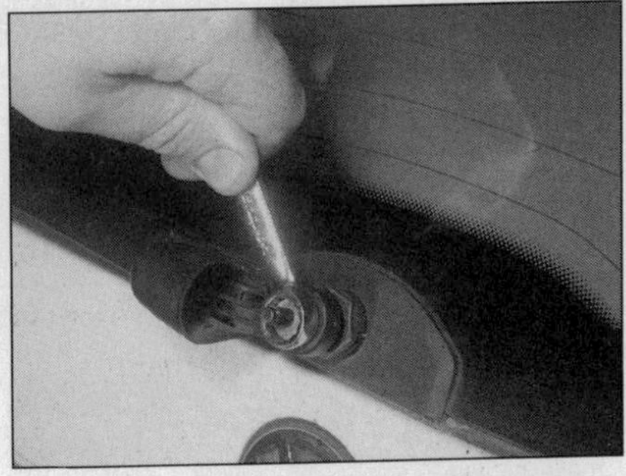
15.3b . . . then remove the wiper arm nut . . .

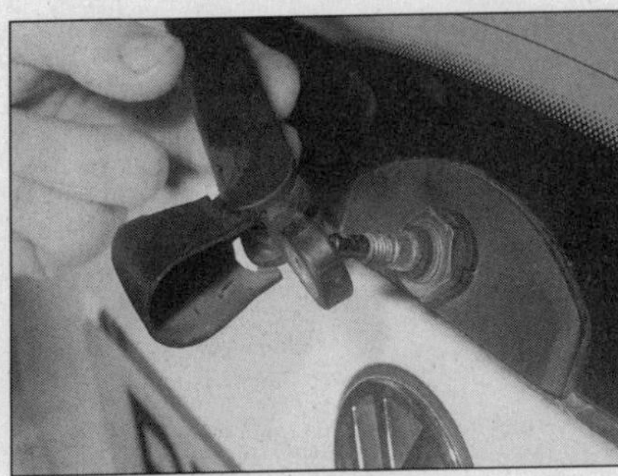
15.3c . . . and pull the wiper arm off the splines

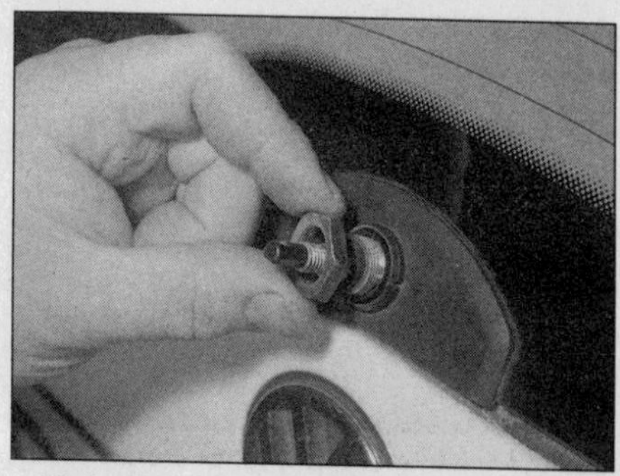

15.4a Unscrew and remove the spindle nut . . .

15.4b . . . and remove the trim piece

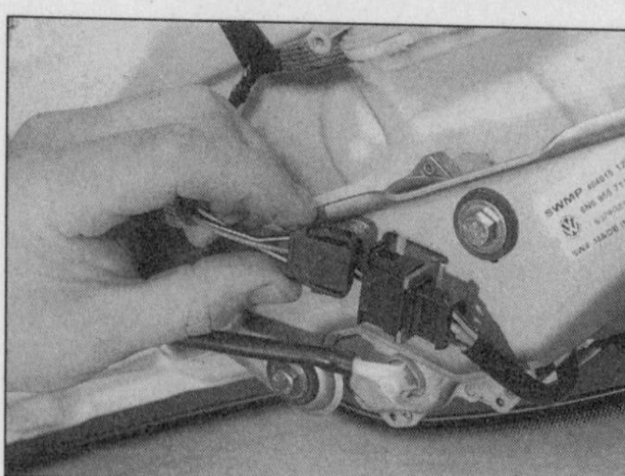

15.5a Disconnecting the motor wiring plug

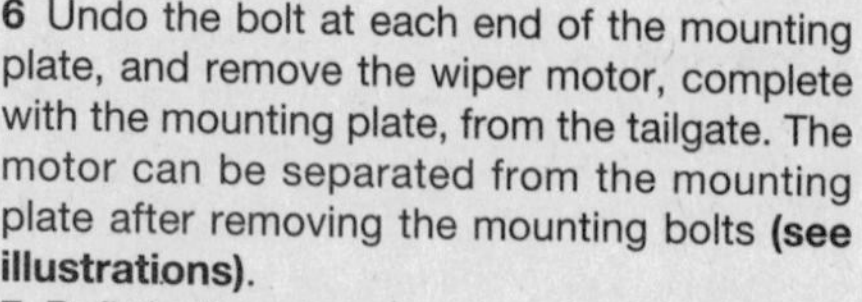

**6** Undo the bolt at each end of the mounting plate, and remove the wiper motor, complete with the mounting plate, from the tailgate. The motor can be separated from the mounting plate after removing the mounting bolts **(see illustrations)**.

**7** Refit in the reverse order of removal. Refit the wiper arm and blade so that the arm is parked correctly.

## 16 Horn - removal and refitting

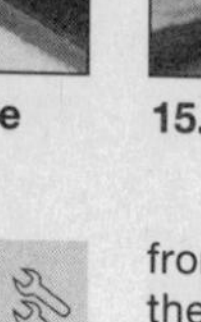

### *Removal*

**1** The horn is located at the front end of the vehicle, on the left-hand side between the front bumper and the inner wing. Access to the horn is best gained from below **(see illustration)**.

**2** Disconnect the battery negative lead (see Section 1).

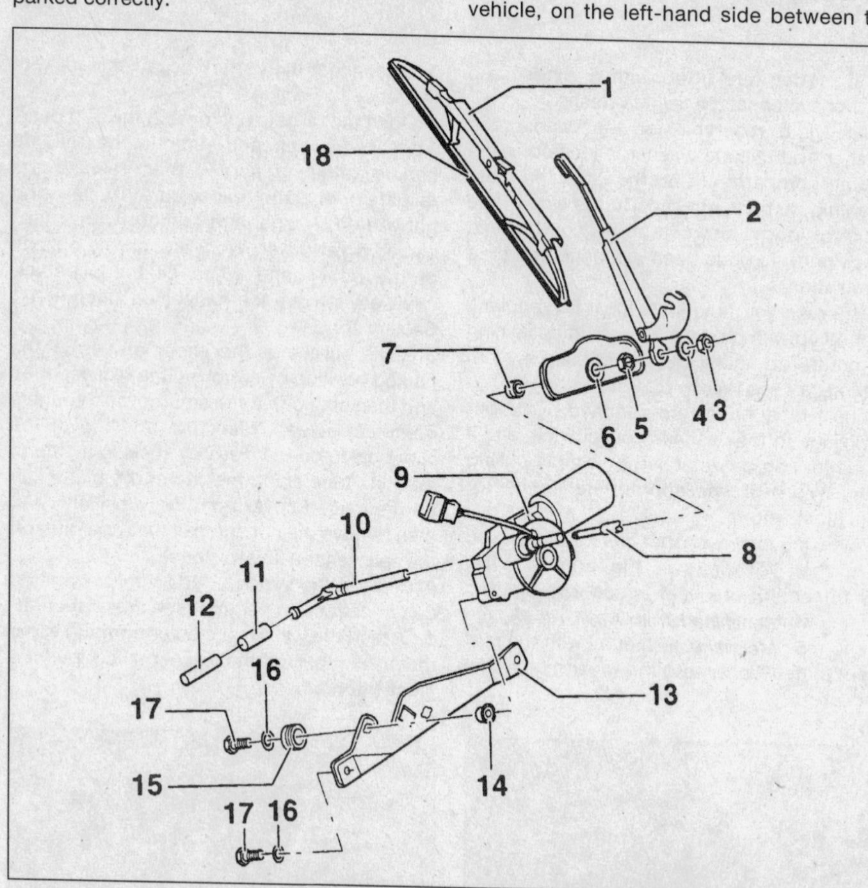



15.5b Tailgate wiper motor and associated components

*1 Wiper blade*
*2 Wiper arm*
*3 Wiper arm mounting nut*
*4 Washer*
*5 Spindle nut*
*6 Cover*
*7 Rubber bush*
*8 Washer jet*
*9 Wiper motor*
*10 Washer jet connecting pipe*
*11 Rubber hose*
*12 Washer supply hose (from engine compartment)*
*13 Wiper motor mounting plate*
*14 Washer*
*15 Rubber bush*
*16 Washer*
*17 Wiper motor/mounting plate bolt*
*18 Wiper blade rubber*

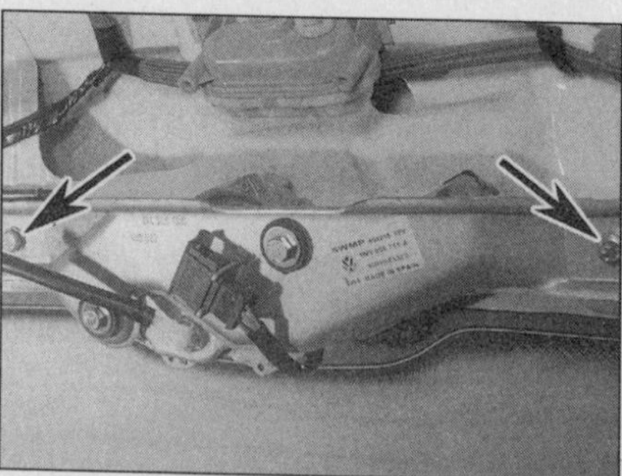

15.6a Wiper motor mounting plate bolts (arrowed)

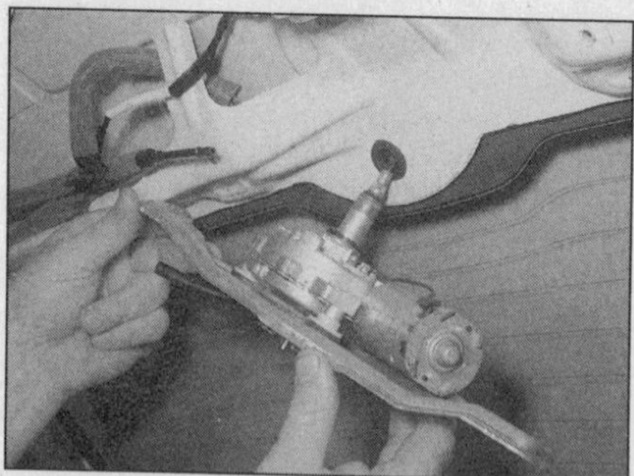

15.6b Removing the wiper motor and mounting plate

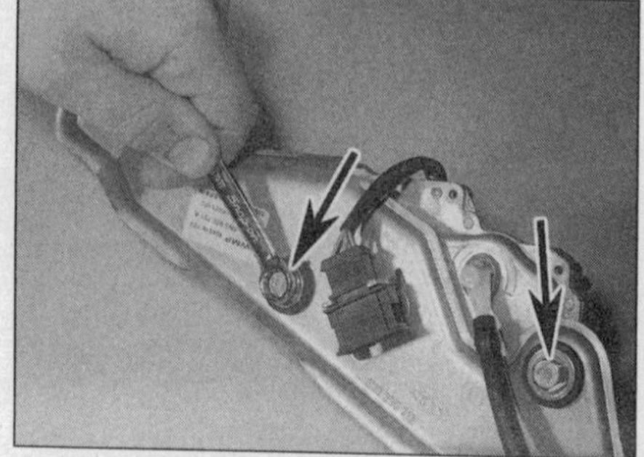

15.6c Wiper motor mounting bolts (arrowed)

**16.1 Horn location under left-hand wing - mounting bolt arrowed**

**3** Apply the handbrake, then jack up the front left-hand corner of the vehicle, and support securely on an axle stand (see *Jacking and vehicle support*).

**4** Disconnect the horn wiring, then unscrew the horn-to-body mounting bolt, and remove the horn unit from under the car.

### Refitting

**5** Refit in the reverse order of removal. Check for satisfactory operation on completion.

## 17 Radio/cassette unit - removal and refitting

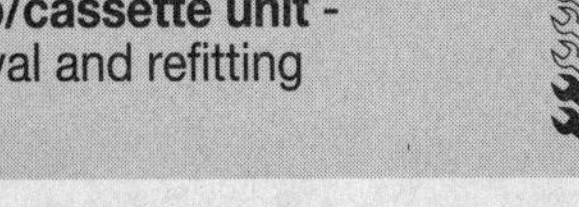

**Note:** *This Section applies only to standard-fit audio equipment.*

### Removal

**1** The radio is fitted with special mounting clips, requiring the use of special removal tools, which should be supplied with the vehicle, or may be obtained from an in-car entertainment specialist. Alternatively, it may be possible to make up some removal tools **(see illustration)**.

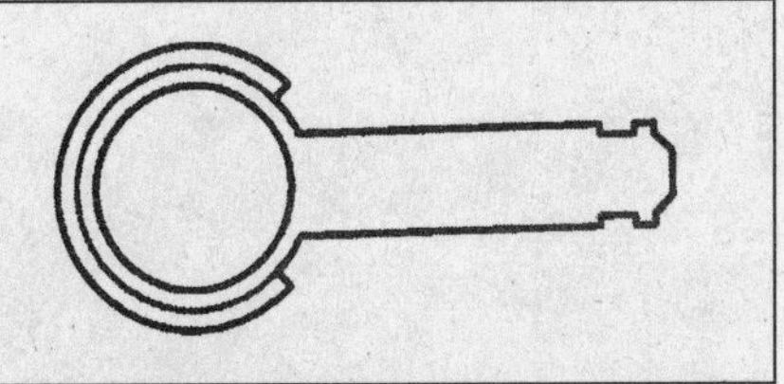

**17.1 Radio/cassette removal tool 3316 - for lower-specification sets**

**2** Disconnect the battery negative lead - refer to Section 1.

**3** Where applicable, first take off the removable front panel. Slide the removal tools into the slots in the radio front panel until they locate, or until the retaining tags are released. On low-specification sets, the removal slots are at either side of the unit. Higher-specification sets have a vertical slot on the right-hand side, and a horizontal slot on the upper left-hand side - in an emergency, a small flat-bladed screwdriver may be used in the slots to release the set.

**4** Withdraw the radio from the mounting case, then disconnect the loudspeaker, supply and aerial plugs **(see illustrations)**. Some units also have a fuse fitted on the rear face.

**17.4a Withdrawing the radio/cassette from the facia - removal tool slots arrowed**

**17.4b Disconnect the aerial lead . . .**

**17.4c . . . and the supply and speaker connector plug, and remove the unit from the facia**

**5** Where applicable, release the radio removal tools once the unit has been withdrawn from the facia panel, by depressing the spring-loaded locating lugs on each side of the radio/cassette unit.

### Refitting

**6** Refitting is a reversal of removal, but push the radio fully into its case until the spring clips are engaged. If the radio is of the security code type, it will be necessary to enter the code number before switching on the radio.

## 18 Radio aerial (roof-mounted) - removal and refitting

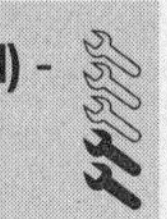

**1** Gaining access to the aerial mounting involves lowering the headlining at the rear. Removing the headlining is not normally a task to be undertaken lightly, and this job may have to be entrusted to a VW dealer. If you are satisfied that this can be accomplished easily, the procedure is given below. The roof-mounted aerial components are as shown - the aerial lead is in two sections, joined behind the facia panel at the left-hand windscreen pillar **(see illustration)**.

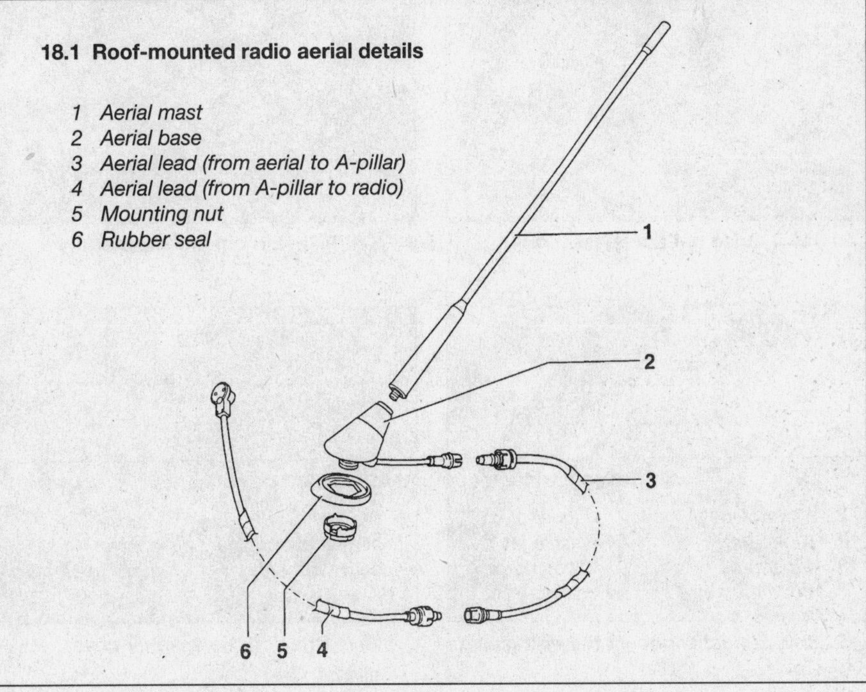


**18.1 Roof-mounted radio aerial details**

1. *Aerial mast*
2. *Aerial base*
3. *Aerial lead (from aerial to A-pillar)*
4. *Aerial lead (from A-pillar to radio)*
5. *Mounting nut*
6. *Rubber seal*

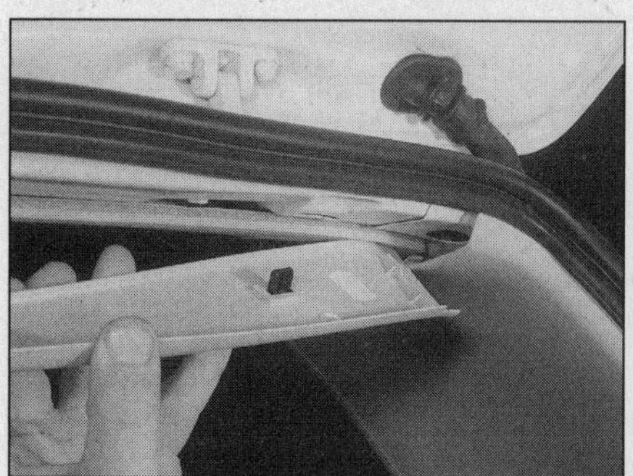
18.4a Release the trim panel from the C-pillar trim . . .

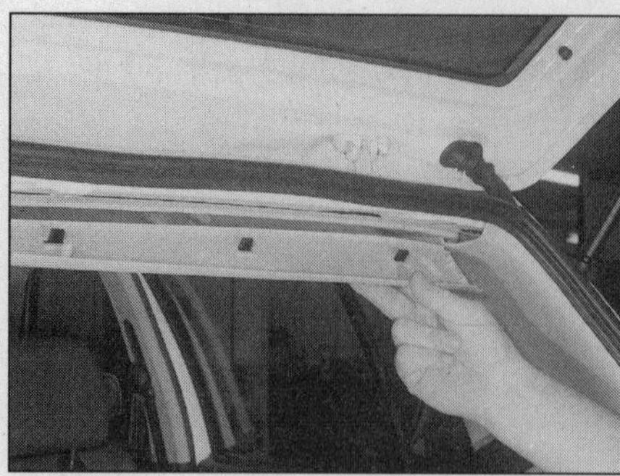
18.4b . . . and remove it from the car

18.5 Pull down the headlining for access to the roof aerial mounting nut

**2** If just the aerial mast has been damaged, this can be unscrewed from the aerial base and replaced separately, with no further dismantling.
**3** To remove the aerial base, open the tailgate and pull down the rubber seal from the top of the tailgate opening.
**4** Prise down the trim panel which fits between the top of the tailgate and the rear of the moulded headlining, releasing its retaining clips. Unhook the panel from the C-pillar trim, and remove it from the car **(see illustrations)**.
**5** Carefully prise down the rear of the headlining for access to the aerial lead and aerial securing nut - don't pull the headlining down more than is necessary **(see illustration)**.
**6** Disconnect the aerial cable at the connector.
**7** If the aerial lead to the front of the car is to be removed, remove its foam insulation, then tie a piece of string to it at the roof aerial end - the string must be long enough to easily reach the front of the car. Remove the radio/cassette unit as described in Section 17. Pull the aerial lead through from the front, until the end of the lead with the string attached appears. Untie the string, and leave it in position in the car - when fitting the new lead, use the string to pull it through into place.
**8** Unscrew the aerial mounting nut from inside the roof. Lift off the aerial base from the top of the roof, pulling the aerial lead through and recovering the roof seal.
**9** Refitting the aerial is a reversal of removal. Check that the aerial works before refitting the headlining, where applicable.

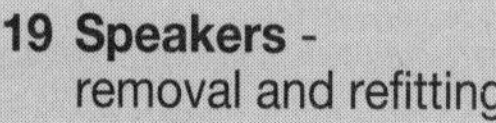

## 19 Speakers - removal and refitting

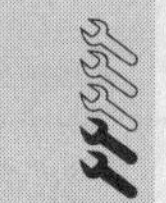

**Note:** *This Section applies only to standard-fit audio equipment.*
**1** Depending on equipment level, two or four speakers will be fitted as standard. Speakers may be fitted at either end of the facia, or in the front door trim panels.

### Facia-mounted speaker

**2** Using a screwdriver, carefully lever out the speaker grille **(see illustration)**. Take care not to damage the facia panel.
**3** The speaker can now be prised out of its location. Detach the wiring connector and remove the speaker from the vehicle **(see illustrations)**.
**4** Refit in the reverse order of removal. Note any direction-of-fitting markings on the rear of the speaker.

### Door-mounted bass speaker

**5** To remove a door-mounted bass speaker, carefully prise off the speaker cover **(see illustration)**.
**6** Undo the four retaining screws **(see illustration)**, remove the speaker, and detach the wiring connectors.
**7** Refit in the reverse order of removal. Note any direction-of-fitting markings on the rear of the speaker.

19.2 Prise out the speaker grille

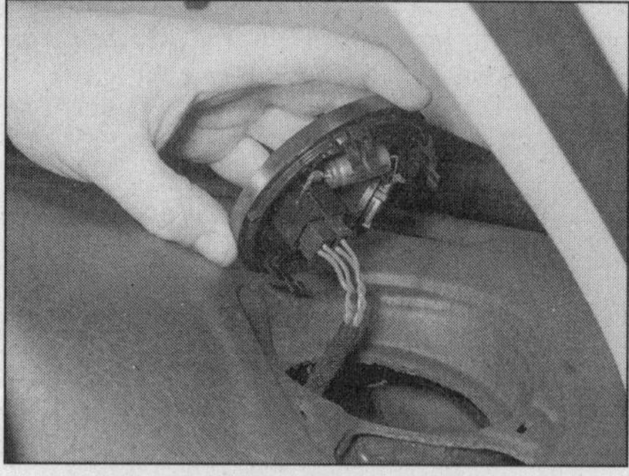
19.3a Lift out the speaker . . .

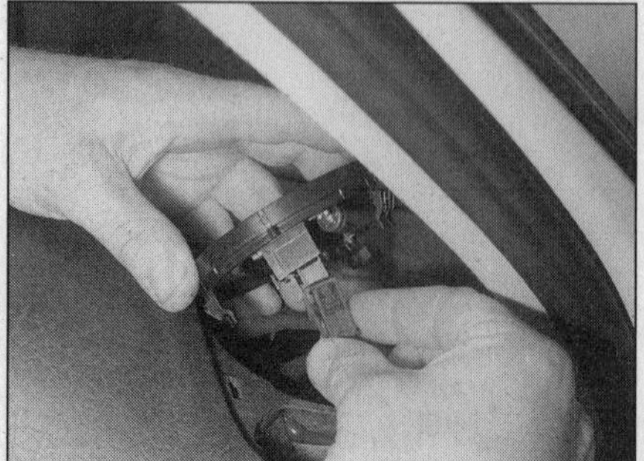
19.3b . . . and disconnect the wiring plug

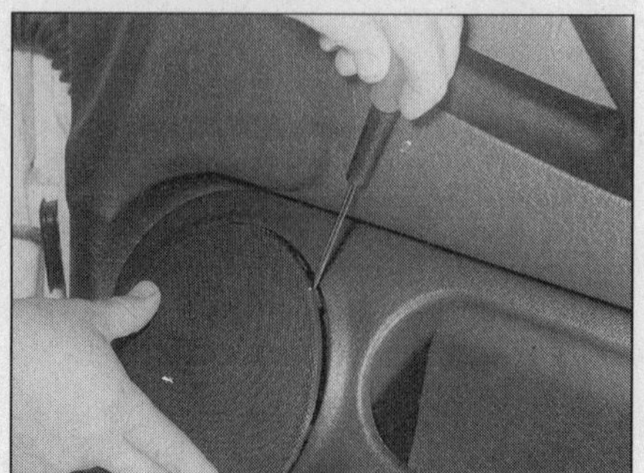
19.5 Prise off the speaker cover . . .

19.6 . . . for access to the speaker retaining screws

## 20 Airbag system - general information and precautions

***Warning: Before carrying out any operations on the airbag system, disconnect the battery negative terminal. When operations are complete, make sure no one is inside the vehicle when the battery is reconnected.***

***Note that the airbag(s) must not be subjected to temperatures in excess of 90°C (194°F). When the airbag is removed, ensure that it is stored the correct way up to prevent possible inflation.***

***Do not allow any solvents or cleaning agents to contact the airbag assemblies. They must be cleaned using only a damp cloth.***

***The airbag(s) and control unit are both sensitive to impact. If either is dropped or damaged they should be renewed.***

***Disconnect the airbag control unit wiring plug prior to using arc-welding equipment on the vehicle.***

**1** A driver's airbag was fitted as standard to all models but the most basic in the Polo range **(see illustration)**; a passenger's side airbag was available as an optional extra. Models fitted with a driver's side airbag have the word AIRBAG stamped on the airbag unit, which is fitted to the centre of the steering wheel. Models also equipped with a passenger's side airbag also have the word AIRBAG stamped on the passenger's end of the facia, in place of the glovebox. The airbag system comprises of the airbag unit (complete with gas generator), an impact sensor, the control unit and a warning light in the instrument panel.

**2** The airbag system is triggered in the event of a heavy frontal impact above a predetermined force; depending on the point of impact. The airbag is inflated within milliseconds, and forms a safety cushion between the driver and the steering wheel or (where applicable) the passenger and the facia. This prevents contact between the upper body and the wheel/facia, and therefore greatly reduces the risk of injury. The airbag then deflates almost immediately.

**3** Every time the ignition is switched on, the airbag control unit performs a self-test. The self-test takes approximately 3 seconds, and during this time the airbag warning light on the facia is illuminated. After the self-test has been completed, the warning light should go out. If the warning light fails to come on, remains illuminated after the initial 3-second period, flashes, or comes on at any time when the vehicle is being driven, there is a fault in the airbag system. The vehicle should then be taken to a VW dealer for examination at the earliest possible opportunity.

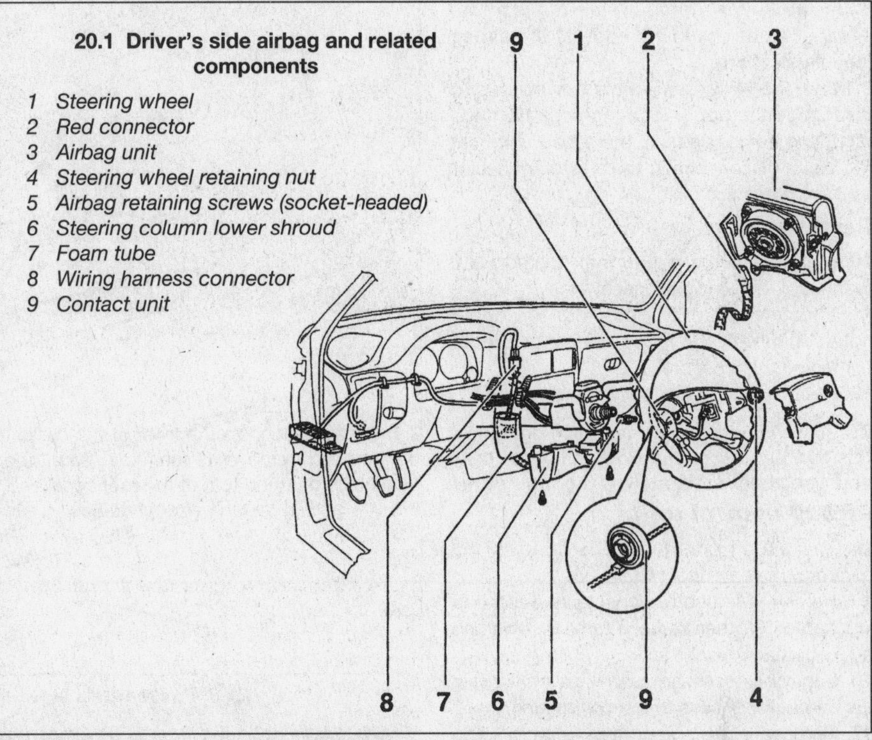


**20.1 Driver's side airbag and related components**

1 *Steering wheel*
2 *Red connector*
3 *Airbag unit*
4 *Steering wheel retaining nut*
5 *Airbag retaining screws (socket-headed)*
6 *Steering column lower shroud*
7 *Foam tube*
8 *Wiring harness connector*
9 *Contact unit*

## 21 Airbag system components - removal and refitting

**Note:** *Refer to the warnings in Section 20 before carrying out the following operations.*

**1** Disconnect the battery negative terminal (see Section 1).

### Driver's side airbag

**Note:** *New airbag retaining screws will be required on refitting.*

#### Removal

**2** Slacken and remove the two Allen screws from the rear of the steering wheel, rotating the wheel as necessary to gain access to the screws **(see illustration)**.

**3** Return the steering wheel to the straight-ahead position, then carefully lift the airbag assembly away from the steering wheel and disconnect the yellow wiring connector from the rear of the unit **(see illustration)**. Note that the airbag must not be knocked or dropped, and should be stored the correct way up with its padded surface uppermost.

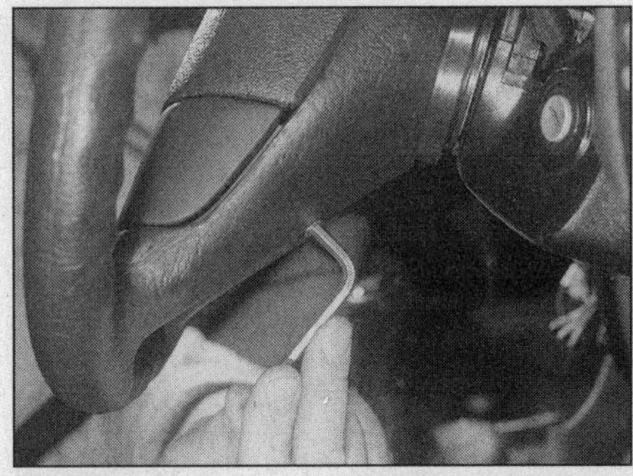

**21.2 Removing an airbag securing screw**

#### Refitting

**4** Make sure that the steering wheel is in the straight-ahead position.

**5** Reconnect the yellow wiring connector and seat the airbag unit in the steering wheel, ensuring that the wire does not become trapped. Fit the new retaining Allen screws, and tighten them securely.

**6** Making sure that no-one is inside the car, switch on the ignition, **then** reconnect the battery negative lead.

### Passenger's side airbag

#### Removal

**7** Slacken and remove the two passenger's side shelf panel upper retaining screws, and remove the panel from the facia.

**21.3 Disconnect the yellow wiring connector and remove the airbag unit from the steering wheel**

**8** Unscrew the three retaining screws, situated along the lower edge of the airbag **(see illustration)**.

**9** Move the airbag assembly downwards to disengage the upper locating pegs from the mounting frame. Remove the airbag unit from the facia, disconnecting the wiring connector as it becomes accessible.

### Refitting

**10** Manoeuvre the airbag into position and reconnect the wiring connector.

**11** Locate the airbag pegs into the upper holes, then refit the lower retaining screws, tightening them securely.

**12** Refit the passenger's side shelf panel.

**13** Making sure that no-one is inside the car, switch on the ignition, **then** reconnect the battery negative lead.

### *Airbag control unit*

**14** The airbag control unit is fitted in the centre of the car, under the facia.

**15** Remove the centre console as described in Chapter 11, then remove three screws and take out the footwell vent.

**16** It may be necessary to make a small cut in the carpet for access to the control unit.

**17** Release the securing catch and disconnect the wiring plug from the side of the unit.

**18** Undo the securing nuts and remove the control unit from the car **(see illustration)**.

**19** Refitting is a reversal of removal.

### *Airbag wiring contact unit*

**20** Remove the airbag unit as described above, and the steering wheel as described in Chapter 10.

**21** Taking care not to rotate the contact unit, undo the three retaining screws and remove it from the steering wheel **(see illustration)**.

**22** On refitting, fit the unit to the steering wheel and securely tighten its retaining screws. If a new contact unit is being fitted, cut the cable-tie which is fitted to prevent the unit accidentally rotating.

**23** Refit the steering wheel as described in Chapter 10, and the airbag unit as described above.

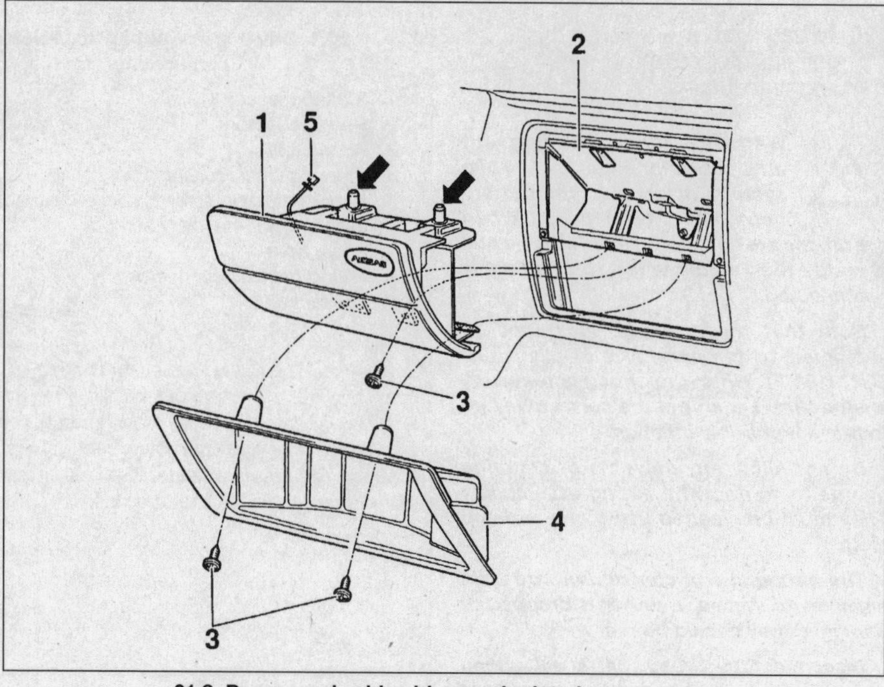


**21.8 Passenger's side airbag and related components**

*1 Airbag unit*
*2 Mounting frame*
*3 Cross-head screws*
*4 Passenger's side shelf panel*
*5 Wiring connector*

## 22 Anti-theft immobiliser system - general information

**Note:** *This information is applicable only to the anti-theft immobiliser system fitted by VW as standard equipment.*

**1** All models are equipped with an electronic immobiliser as standard, which is automatically activated when the ignition key is removed from the ignition switch. A control unit, fitted under the driver's side lower facia next to the fuse/relay panel **(see illustration)**, cuts the ignition circuit (petrol models) or holds the fuel cut-off/stop solenoid closed (diesel models).

**2** The system is disarmed when the ignition key is inserted into the ignition switch, as follows. The head of the ignition key contains a transponder micro-chip, and the ignition lock contains a reader coil. When the key enters the lock, the reader coil recognises the signal from the micro-chip, and de-activates the immobiliser. It is essential that the key tag showing the key number is not lost (this will be supplied with the car when new). Any duplicate keys will have to be obtained from a VW dealer, who will need the key number to supply a duplicate - any keys cut elsewhere will work the door locks, but will not contain the transponder chip necessary to de-activate the immobiliser and allow the engine to be started.

**3** On early models, the immobiliser reader coil could be removed from the ignition switch, after removing the column upper and lower shrouds - on later models, the reader coil is an integral part of the switch. In any case, it is unclear at the time of writing whether a new

**21.18 Airbag control unit**

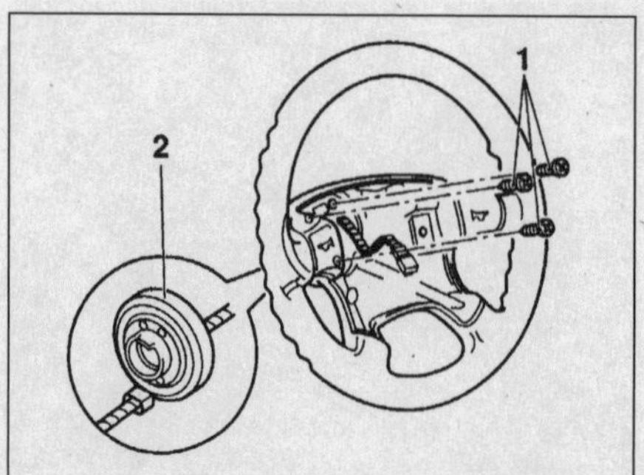


**21.21 Steering wheel airbag contact unit**

*1 Retaining screws 2 Contact unit*

**22.1 Anti-theft immobiliser control unit**

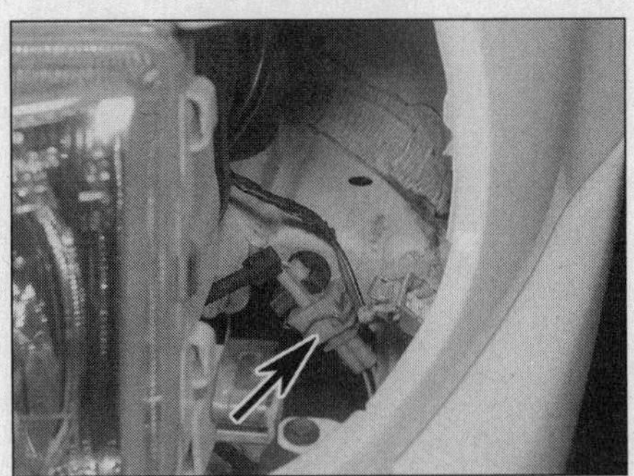

24.2 Dim-dip resistor wiring plug (arrowed) - seen with left-hand front direction indicator light removed

reader coil could be matched to a particular key or control unit. In the case of diesel models, VW state that the entire diesel injection pump and fuel cut-off valve control unit must be replaced in the event of a malfunction with the system.

**4** Any problems or work involving the immobiliser system should be entrusted to a VW dealer, as dedicated electronic equipment is required to diagnose faults, or to match the various components.

## 23 Heated front seat components - removal and refitting

### *Heater mats*

**1** On models equipped with heated front seats, a heater pad is fitted to both the seat back and the seat cushion. Renewal of either heater mat involves peeling back the upholstery, removing the old mat, sticking the new mat in position and then refitting the upholstery. Note that upholstery removal and refitting requires considerable skill and experience if it is to be carried out successfully and is therefore best entrusted to your VW dealer. In practice, it will be very difficult for the home mechanic to carry out the job without ruining the upholstery.

### *Heated seat switches*

**2** Refer to Section 6.

## 24 Dim-dip lighting system (early UK models only) - general information

**1** Early UK market models are equipped with a headlight dim-dip system, to comply with regulations in force when the Polo range was introduced. The purpose of the system is to prevent the car being driven with only the sidelights on.

**2** When the sidelights are switched on with the ignition also on, the headlight dipped beams come on, but at approximately one-sixth of their normal brightness. This is achieved by a relay, which switches the headlight supply across a dropping resistor located behind the left-hand headlight **(see illustration)**.

**3** Later models may not have this system, as it appears that the regulations requiring its fitment may have lapsed.

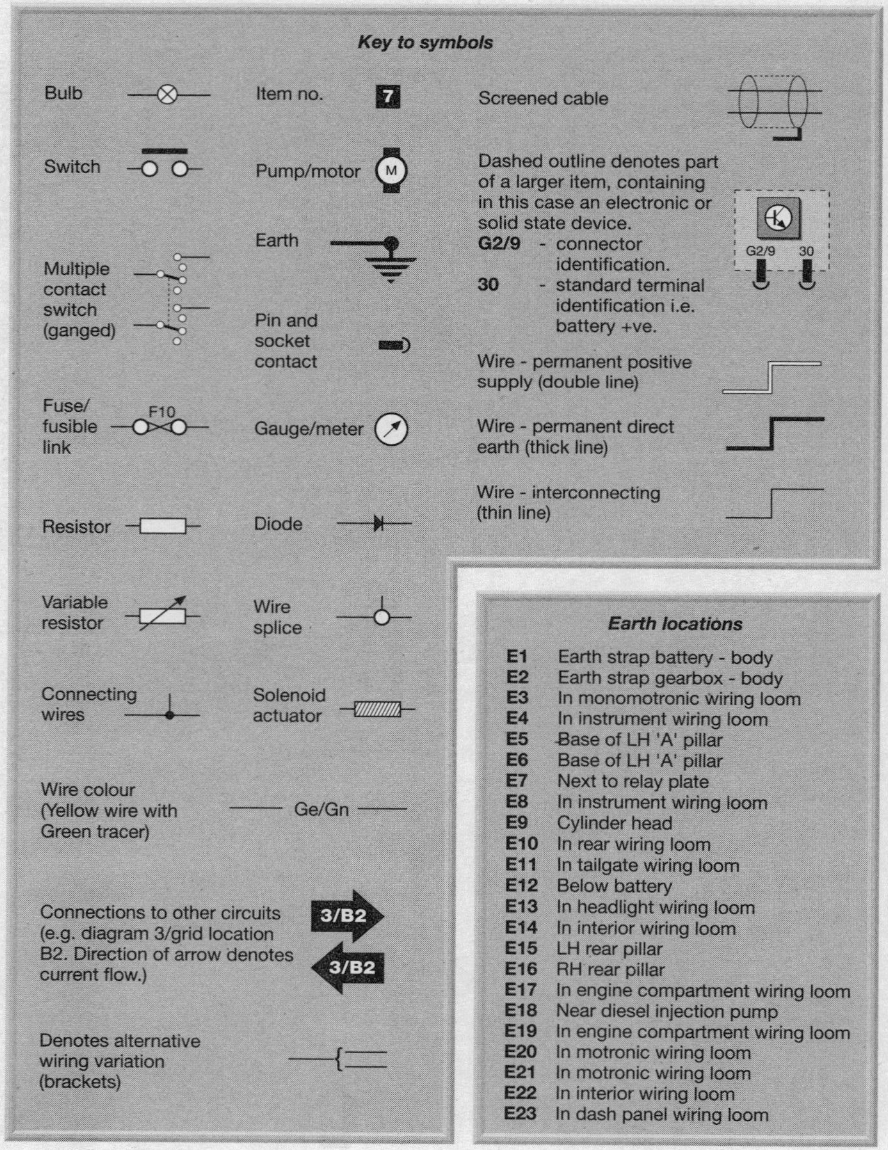

### Key to symbols

| | | | | |
|---|---|---|---|---|
| Bulb | | Item no. | 7 | Screened cable |
| Switch | | Pump/motor | M | Dashed outline denotes part of a larger item, containing in this case an electronic or solid state device. **G2/9** - connector identification. **30** - standard terminal identification i.e. battery +ve. |
| Multiple contact switch (ganged) | | Earth | | |
| | | Pin and socket contact | | Wire - permanent positive supply (double line) |
| Fuse/ fusible link | F10 | Gauge/meter | | Wire - permanent direct earth (thick line) |
| Resistor | | Diode | | Wire - interconnecting (thin line) |
| Variable resistor | | Wire splice | | |
| Connecting wires | | Solenoid actuator | | |
| Wire colour (Yellow wire with Green tracer) | — Ge/Gn — | | | |
| Connections to other circuits (e.g. diagram 3/grid location B2. Direction of arrow denotes current flow.) | 3/B2 3/B2 | | | |
| Denotes alternative wiring variation (brackets) | | | | |

### Earth locations

| | |
|---|---|
| E1 | Earth strap battery - body |
| E2 | Earth strap gearbox - body |
| E3 | In monomotronic wiring loom |
| E4 | In instrument wiring loom |
| E5 | Base of LH 'A' pillar |
| E6 | Base of LH 'A' pillar |
| E7 | Next to relay plate |
| E8 | In instrument wiring loom |
| E9 | Cylinder head |
| E10 | In rear wiring loom |
| E11 | In tailgate wiring loom |
| E12 | Below battery |
| E13 | In headlight wiring loom |
| E14 | In interior wiring loom |
| E15 | LH rear pillar |
| E16 | RH rear pillar |
| E17 | In engine compartment wiring loom |
| E18 | Near diesel injection pump |
| E19 | In engine compartment wiring loom |
| E20 | In motronic wiring loom |
| E21 | In motronic wiring loom |
| E22 | In interior wiring loom |
| E23 | In dash panel wiring loom |

### Standard terminal identification (typical)

| | |
|---|---|
| 15 | Ignition switch 'ignition' position |
| 30 | Battery +ve |
| 31 | Earth |
| 50 | Ignition switch 'start' position |
| 85 | Relay winding input |
| 86 | Relay winding earth |
| 87 | Relay output |
| 87a | Relay output |

### Fuse/relay box

| *Fuse* | *Rating* | *Circuit protected* |
|---|---|---|
| F1 | 10A | Headlight dipped beam and range control (left) |
| F2 | 10A | Headlight dipped beam and range control (right) |
| F3 | 10A | Number plate light |
| F4 | 15A | Rear window wiper |
| F5 | 15A | Windscreen wash/wipe, heated washer jets |
| F6 | 20A | Heater blower motor, air con. |
| F7 | 10A | RH side and tail lights |
| F8 | 10A | RH side and tail lights |
| F9 | 20A | Heated rear window |
| F10 | 15A | Rear fog light |
| F11 | 10A | LH main beam |
| F12 | 10A | RH main beam |
| F13 | 10A | Horn |
| F14 | 15A | Reversing lights |
| F15 | 10A | Engine electrics |
| F16 | 15A | Instrument panel |
| F17 | 10A | Direction indicators |
| F18 | 20A | Fuel pump, lambda sensor |
| F19 | 30A | Engine cooling fan |
| F20 | 10A | Stop lights |
| F21 | 15A | Interior lights, instrument panel, self diagnosis |
| F22 | 10A | Radio/cassette, cigar lighter |

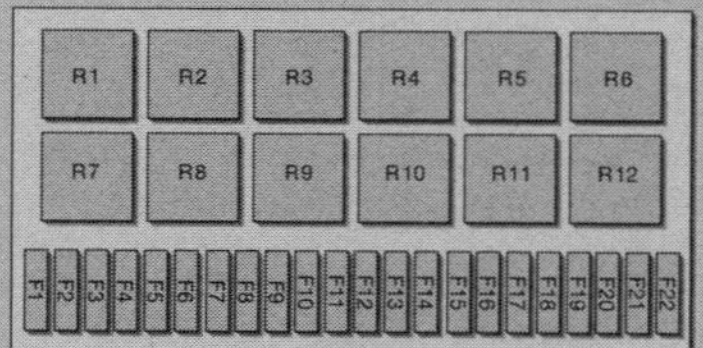

R1 R2 R3 R4 R5 R6
R7 R8 R9 R10 R11 R12
F1 F2 F3 F4 F5 F6 F7 F8 F9 F10 F11 F12 F13 F14 F15 F16 F17 F18 F19 F20 F21 F22

H29829

**Diagram 1 : Information for wiring diagrams - models up to 1998**

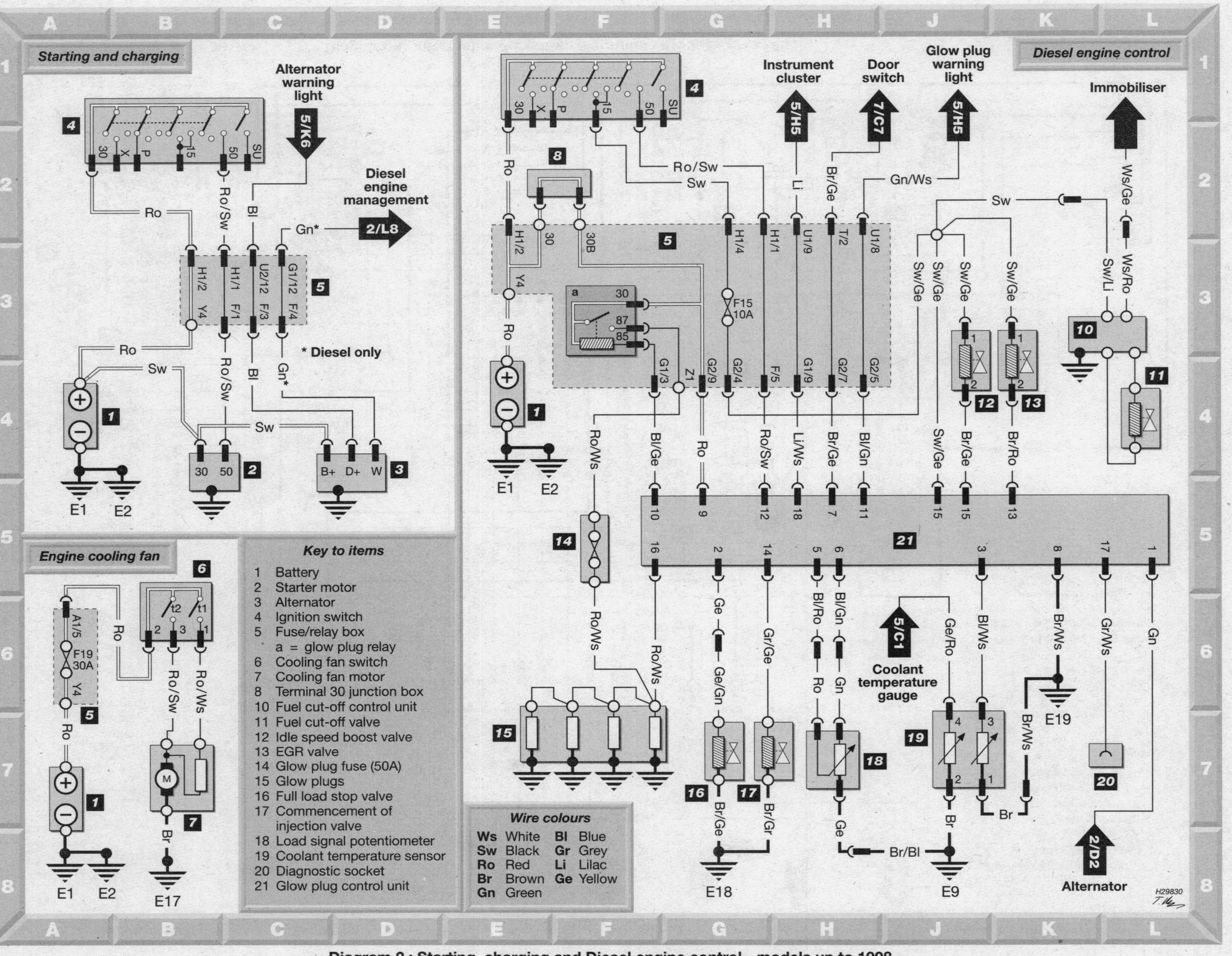

Starting and charging
Alternator warning light
Diesel engine management
* Diesel only
Engine cooling fan
Key to items
1 Battery
2 Starter motor
3 Alternator
4 Ignition switch
5 Fuse/relay box
a = glow plug relay
6 Cooling fan switch
7 Cooling fan motor
8 Terminal 30 junction box
10 Fuel cut-off control unit
11 Fuel cut-off valve
12 Idle speed boost valve
13 EGR valve
14 Glow plug fuse (50A)
15 Glow plugs
16 Full load stop valve
17 Commencement of injection valve
18 Load signal potentiometer
19 Coolant temperature sensor
20 Diagnostic socket
21 Glow plug control unit
Wire colours
Ws White
Sw Black
Ro Red
Br Brown
Gn Green
Bl Blue
Gr Grey
Li Lilac
Ge Yellow
Instrument cluster
Door switch
Glow plug warning light
Diesel engine control
Immobiliser
Coolant temperature gauge
Alternator
H29830


Diagram 2 : Starting, charging and Diesel engine control - models up to 1998

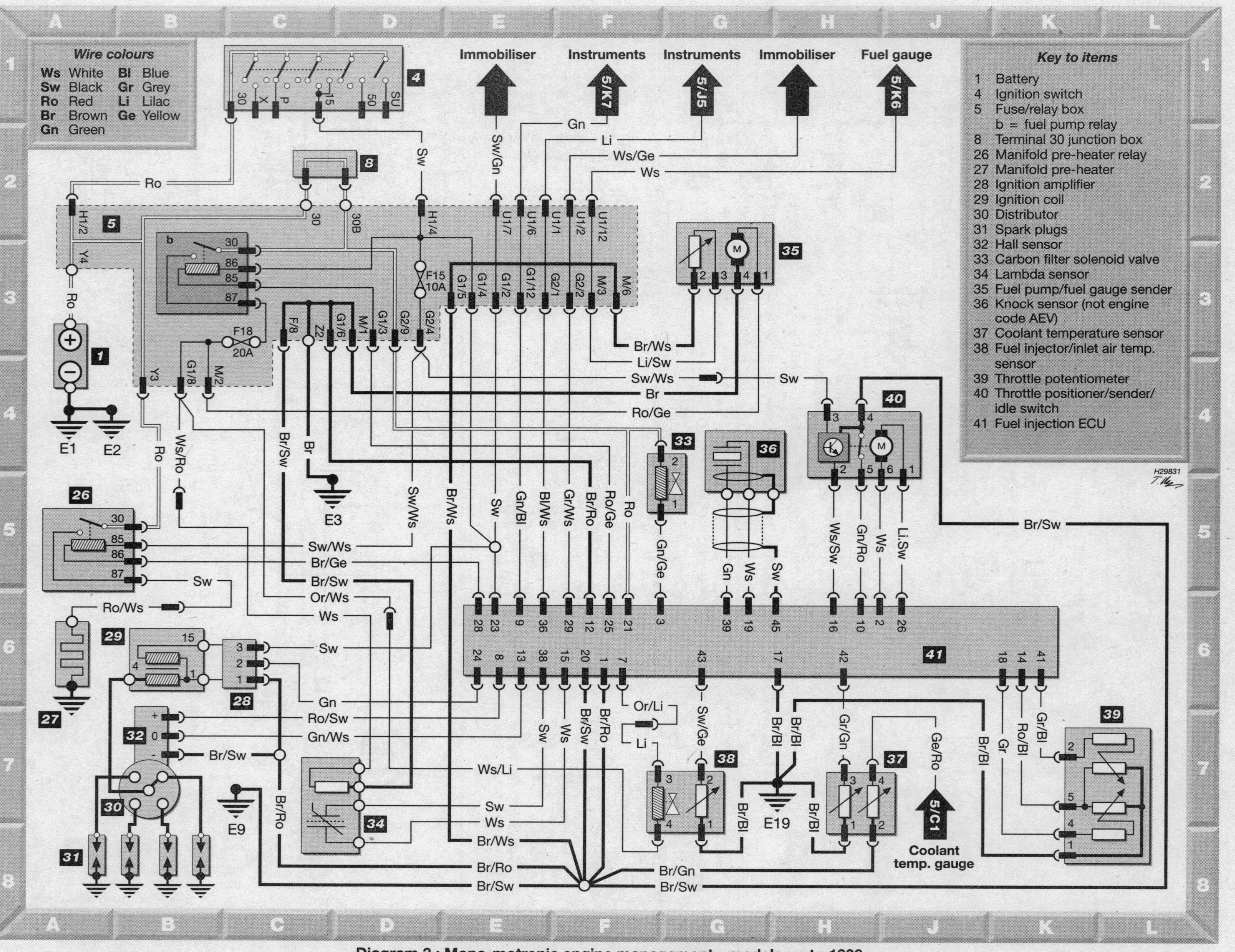

Wire colours
Ws White
Sw Black
Ro Red
Br Brown
Gn Green
Bl Blue
Gr Grey
Li Lilac
Ge Yellow
Immobiliser
Instruments 5/K7
Instruments 5/J5
Immobiliser
Fuel gauge 5/K6
Key to items
1 Battery
4 Ignition switch
5 Fuse/relay box
b = fuel pump relay
8 Terminal 30 junction box
26 Manifold pre-heater relay
27 Manifold pre-heater
28 Ignition amplifier
29 Ignition coil
30 Distributor
31 Spark plugs
32 Hall sensor
33 Carbon filter solenoid valve
34 Lambda sensor
35 Fuel pump/fuel gauge sender
36 Knock sensor (not engine code AEV)
37 Coolant temperature sensor
38 Fuel injector/inlet air temp. sensor
39 Throttle potentiometer
40 Throttle positioner/sender/idle switch
41 Fuel injection ECU
5/C1 Coolant temp. gauge
H29831


Diagram 3 : Mono-motronic engine management - models up to 1998

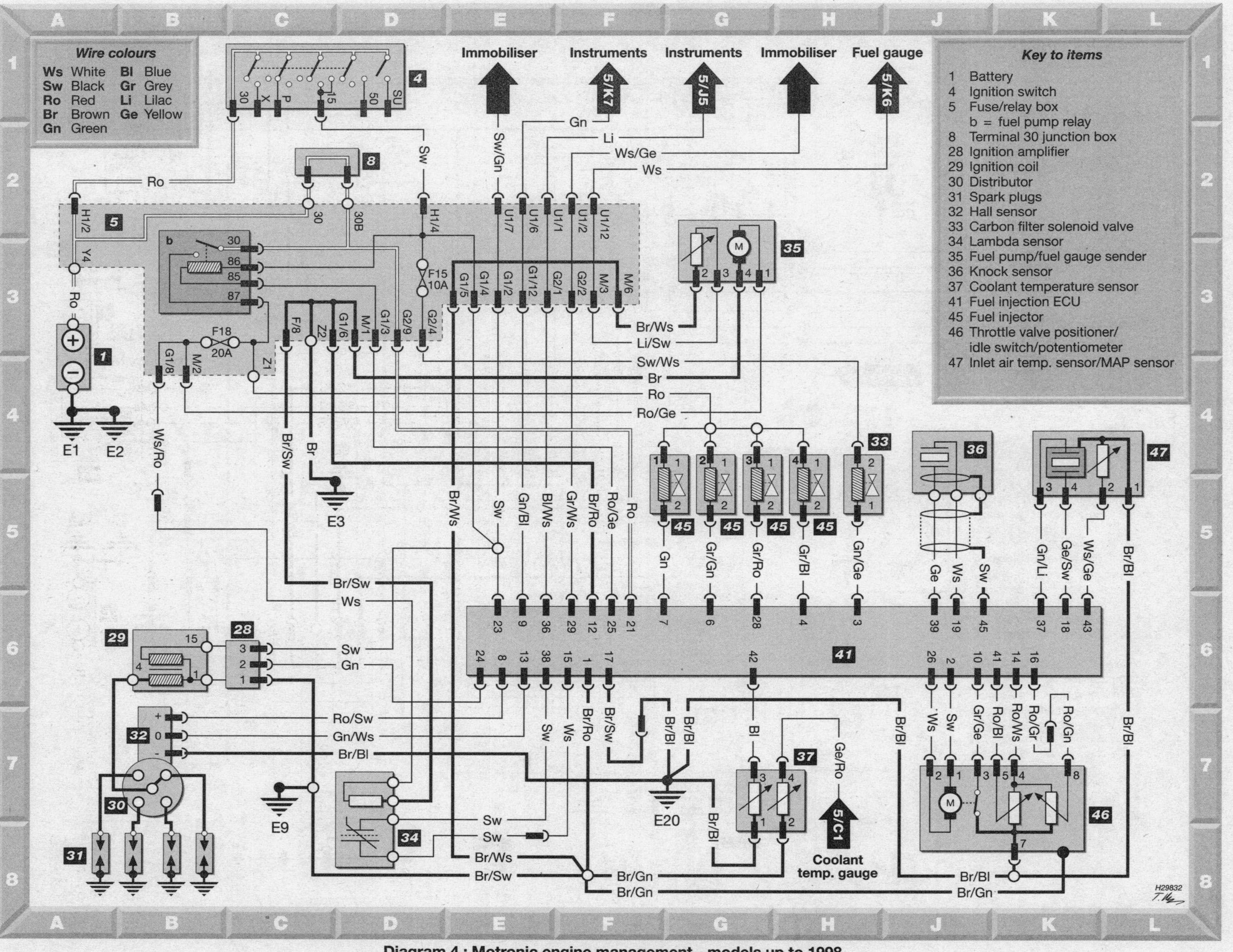


Diagram 4 : Motronic engine management - models up to 1998

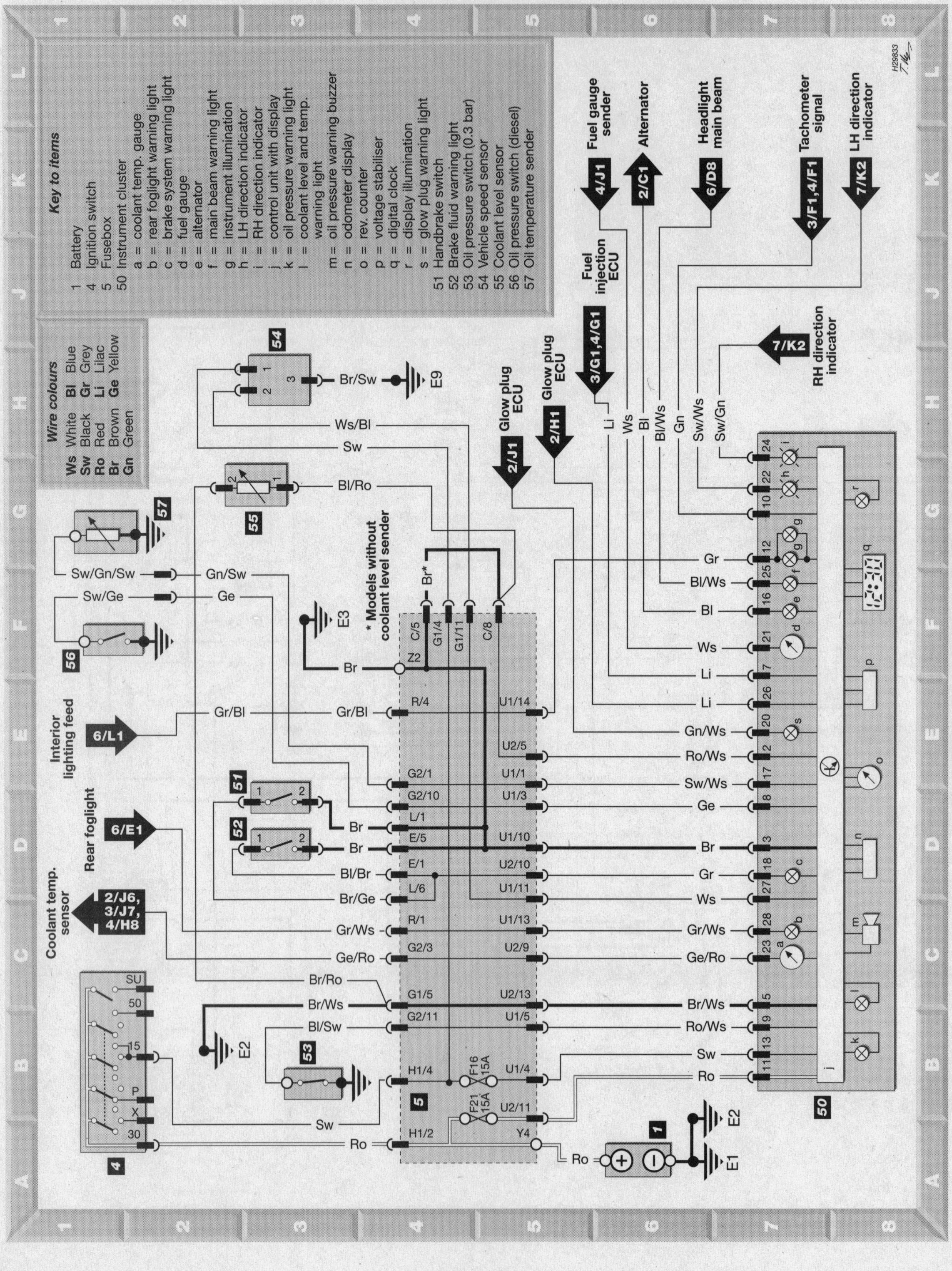
Key to items
1 Battery
4 Ignition switch
5 Fusebox
50 Instrument cluster
a = coolant temp. gauge
b = rear foglight warning light
c = brake system warning light
d = fuel gauge
e = alternator
f = main beam warning light
g = instrument illumination
h = LH direction indicator
i = RH direction indicator
j = control unit with display
k = oil pressure warning light
l = coolant level and temp. warning light
m = oil pressure warning buzzer
n = odometer display
o = rev. counter
p = voltage stabiliser
q = digital clock
r = display illumination
s = glow plug warning light
51 Handbrake switch
52 Brake fluid warning light
53 Oil pressure switch (0.3 bar)
54 Vehicle speed sensor
55 Coolant level sensor
56 Oil pressure switch (diesel)
57 Oil temperature sender
Wire colours
Ws White
Sw Black
Ro Red
Br Brown
Gn Green
Bl Blue
Gr Grey
Li Lilac
Ge Yellow
Fuel gauge sender
Alternator
Headlight main beam
Tachometer signal
LH direction indicator
RH direction indicator
Fuel injection ECU
Glow plug ECU
Interior lighting feed
Rear foglight
Coolant temp. sensor
* Models without coolant level sender
H29833

Diagram 5 : Instrument cluster - models up to 1998

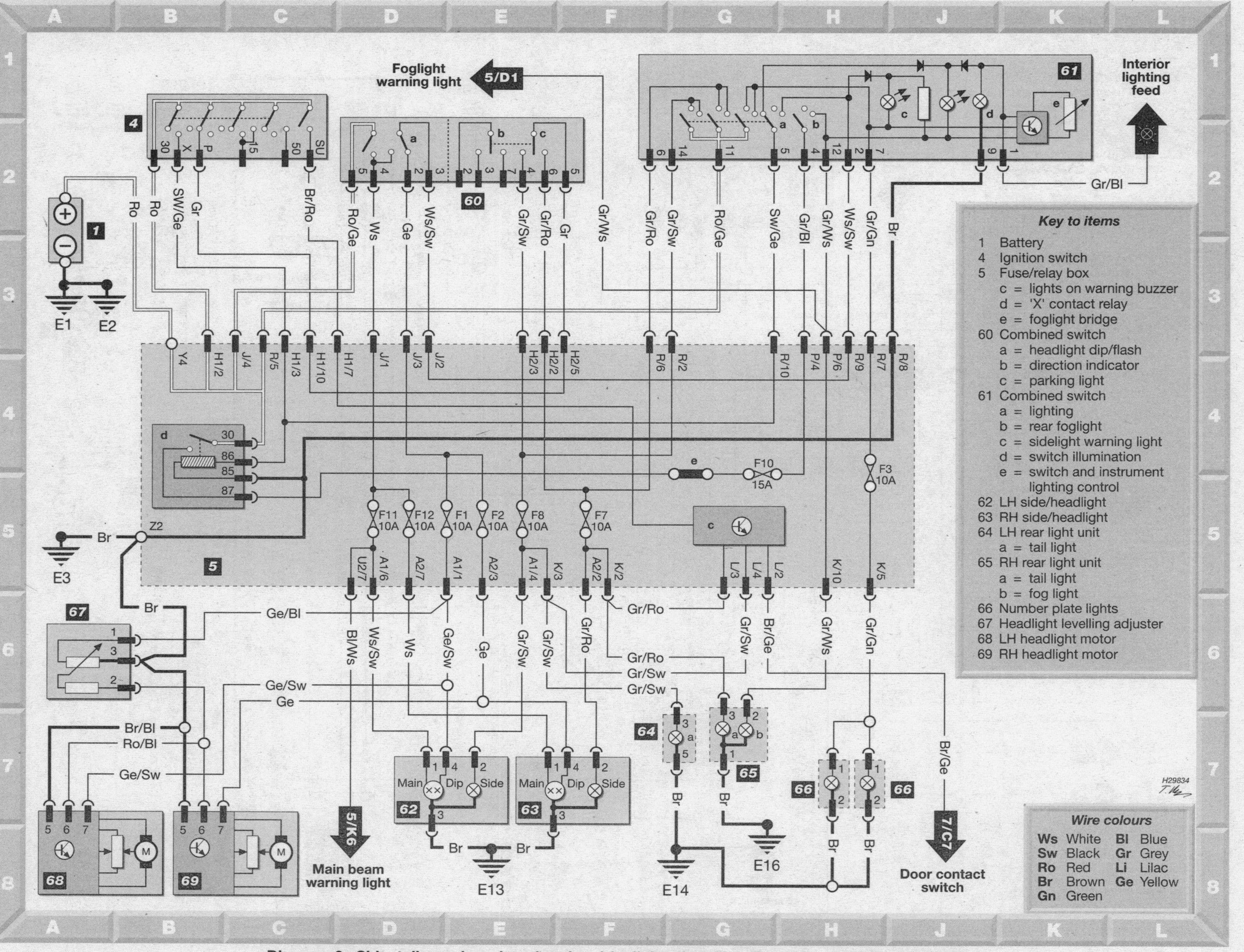

Key to items
1 Battery
4 Ignition switch
5 Fuse/relay box
c = lights on warning buzzer
d = 'X' contact relay
e = foglight bridge
60 Combined switch
a = headlight dip/flash
b = direction indicator
c = parking light
61 Combined switch
a = lighting
b = rear foglight
c = sidelight warning light
d = switch illumination
e = switch and instrument lighting control
62 LH side/headlight
63 RH side/headlight
64 LH rear light unit
a = tail light
65 RH rear light unit
a = tail light
b = fog light
66 Number plate lights
67 Headlight levelling adjuster
68 LH headlight motor
69 RH headlight motor
Wire colours
Ws White
Sw Black
Ro Red
Br Brown
Gn Green
Bl Blue
Gr Grey
Li Lilac
Ge Yellow
Interior lighting feed
Foglight warning light
Door contact switch
Main beam warning light
H29834


Diagram 6 : Side, tail, number plate, head and foglights, headlight levelling - models up to 1998

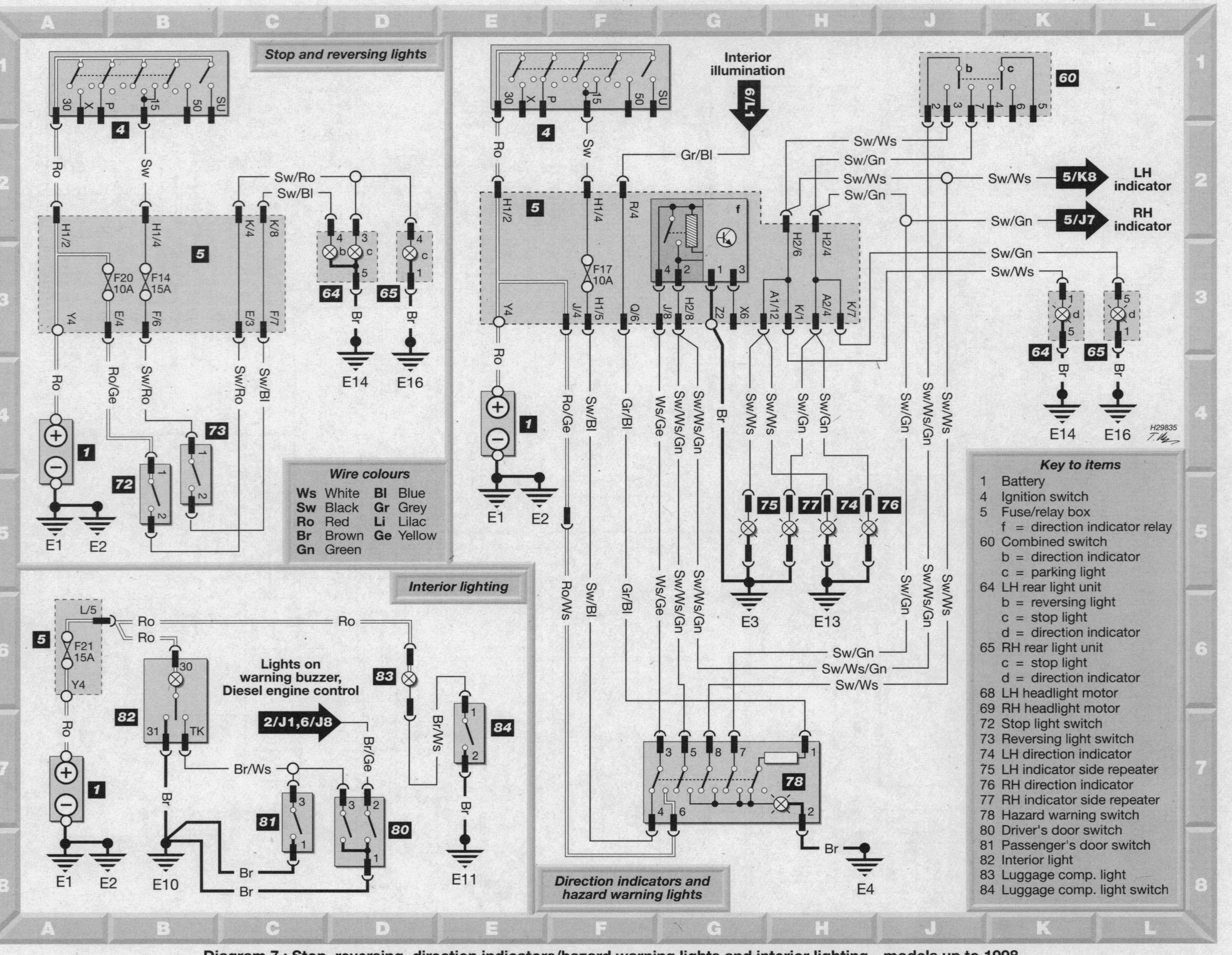

Stop and reversing lights
Interior lighting
Direction indicators and hazard warning lights
Interior illumination
LH indicator
RH indicator
Lights on warning buzzer, Diesel engine control
Wire colours
Ws White
Sw Black
Ro Red
Br Brown
Gn Green
Bl Blue
Gr Grey
Li Lilac
Ge Yellow
Key to items
1 Battery
4 Ignition switch
5 Fuse/relay box
f = direction indicator relay
60 Combined switch
b = direction indicator
c = parking light
64 LH rear light unit
b = reversing light
c = stop light
d = direction indicator
65 RH rear light unit
c = stop light
d = direction indicator
68 LH headlight motor
69 RH headlight motor
72 Stop light switch
73 Reversing light switch
74 LH direction indicator
75 LH indicator side repeater
76 RH direction indicator
77 RH indicator side repeater
78 Hazard warning switch
80 Driver's door switch
81 Passenger's door switch
82 Interior light
83 Luggage comp. light
84 Luggage comp. light switch
H29835


Diagram 7 : Stop, reversing, direction indicators/hazard warning lights and interior lighting - models up to 1998

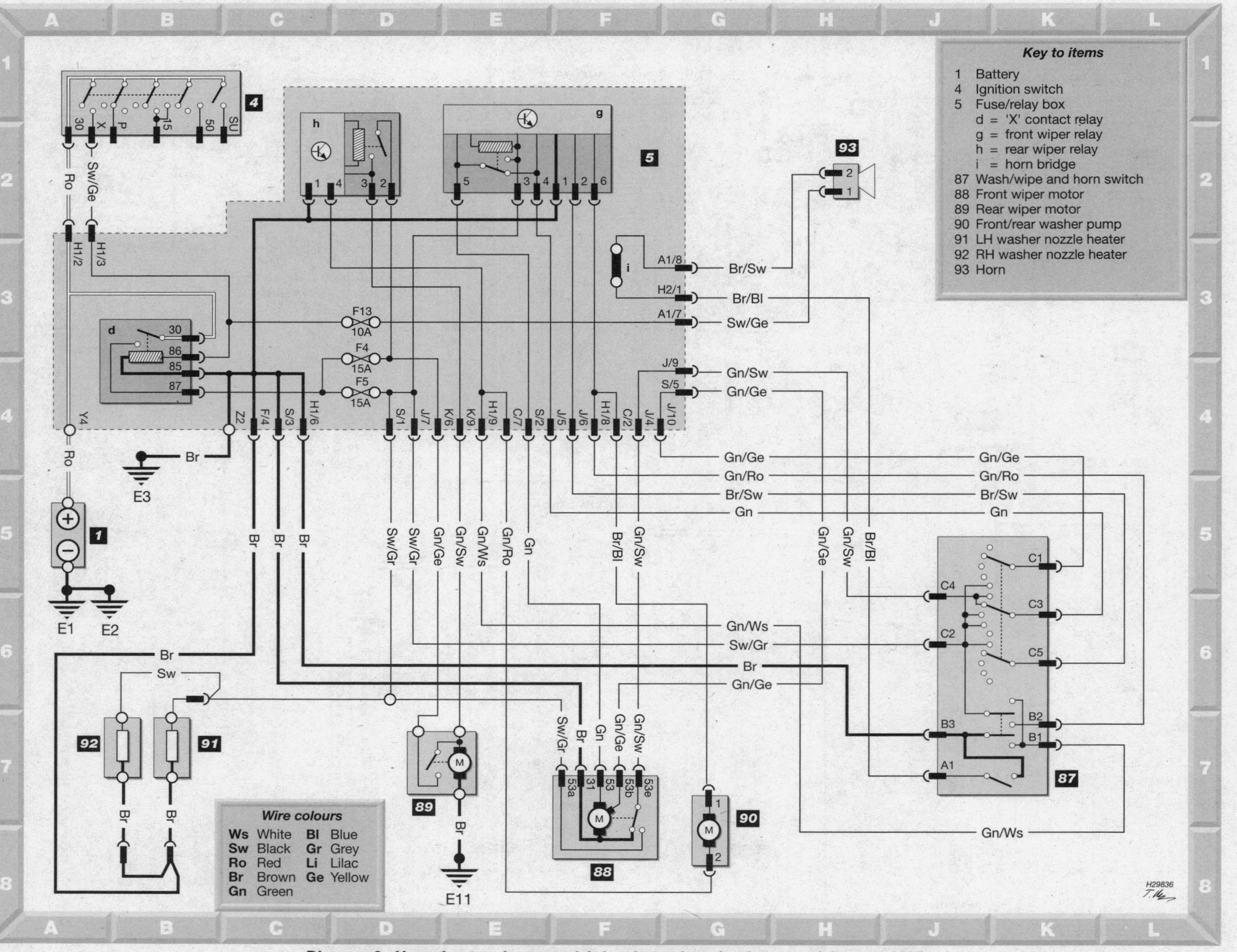

Key to items
1 Battery
4 Ignition switch
5 Fuse/relay box
d = 'X' contact relay
g = front wiper relay
h = rear wiper relay
i = horn bridge
87 Wash/wipe and horn switch
88 Front wiper motor
89 Rear wiper motor
90 Front/rear washer pump
91 LH washer nozzle heater
92 RH washer nozzle heater
93 Horn
Wire colours
Ws White
Sw Black
Ro Red
Br Brown
Gn Green
Bl Blue
Gr Grey
Li Lilac
Ge Yellow
H29836


Diagram 8 : Horn, front and rear wash/wipe, heated washer jets - models up to 1998

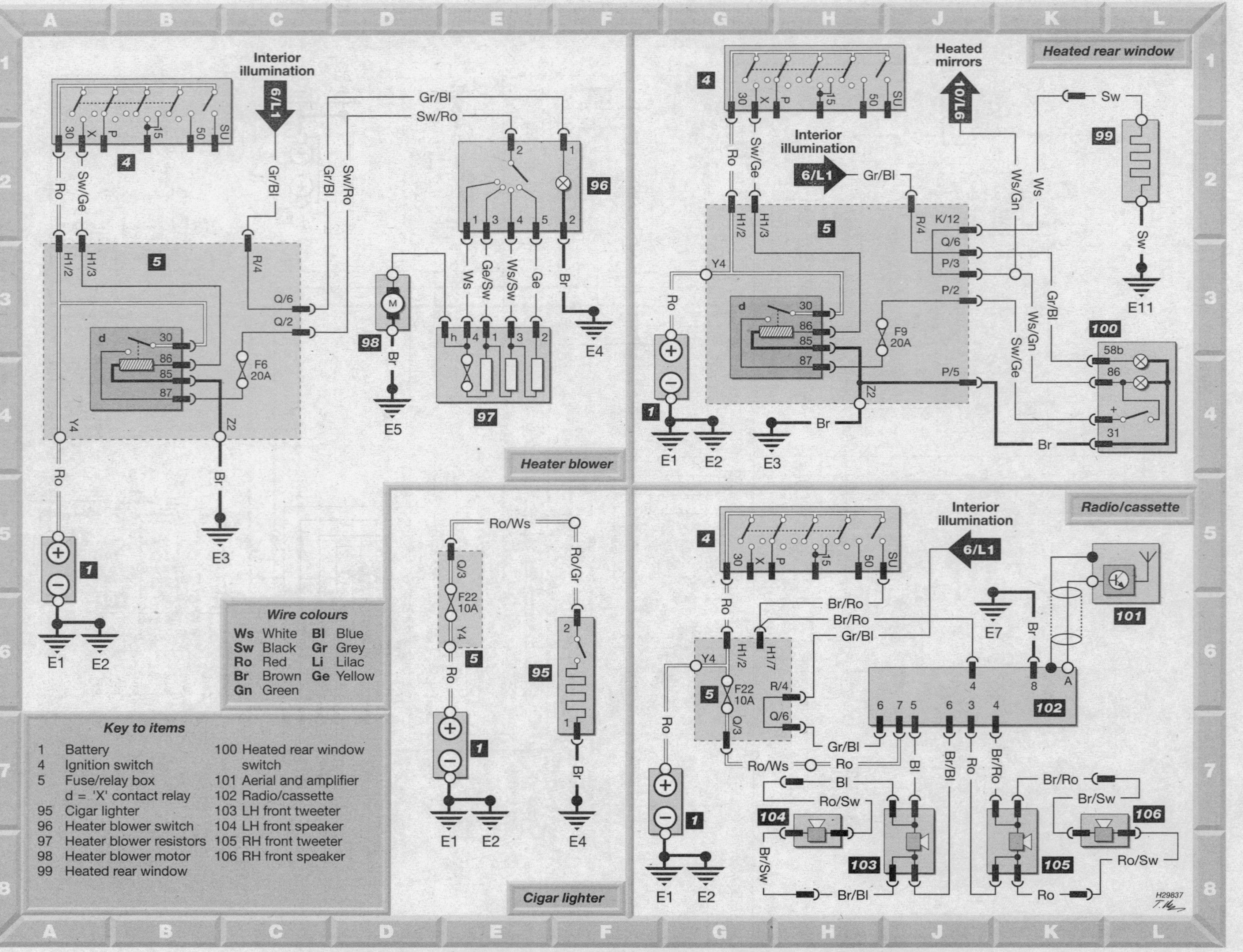


Diagram 9 : Cigar lighter, heater blower and heated rear window - models up to 1998

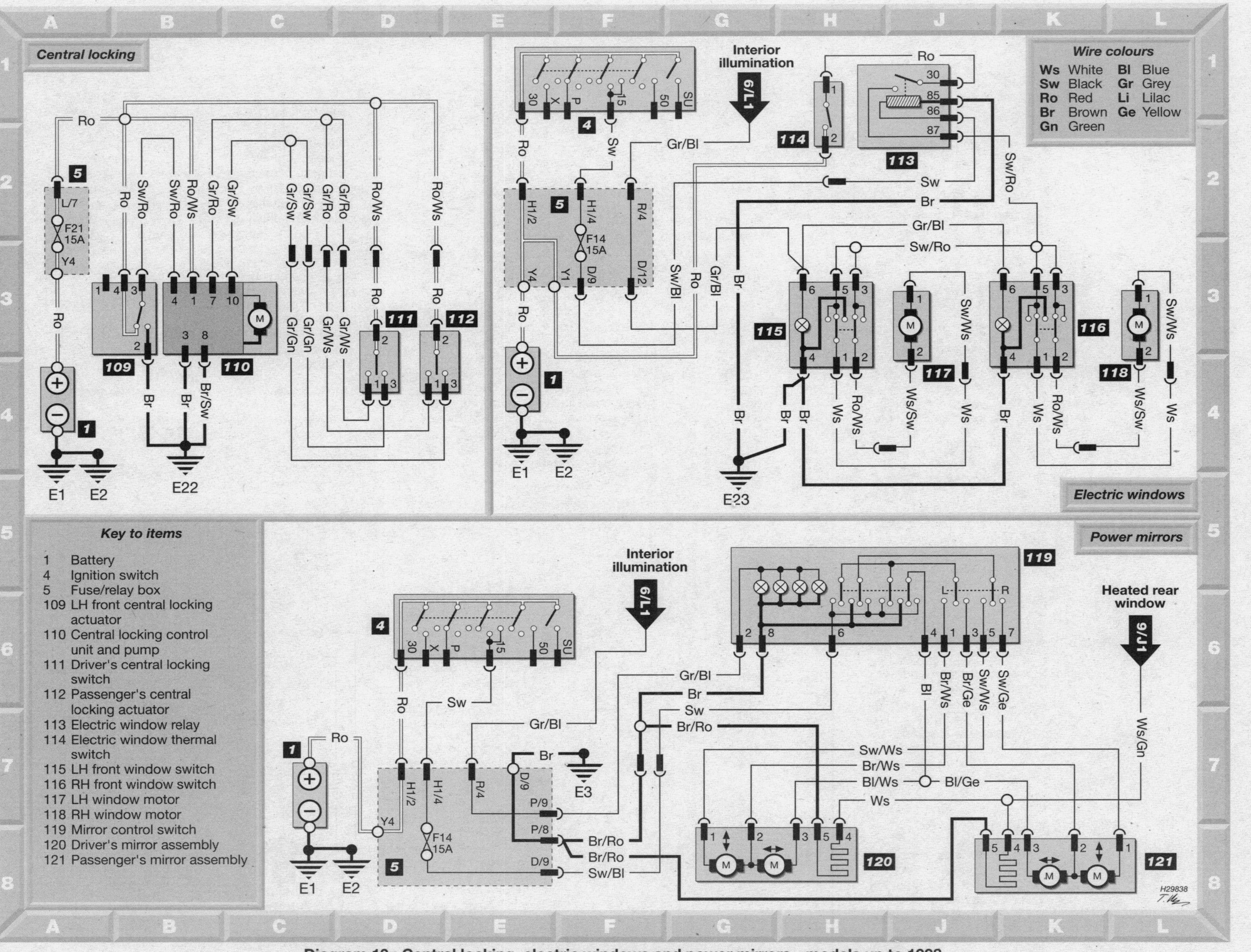


Diagram 10 : Central locking, electric windows and power mirrors - models up to 1998

### Key to symbols

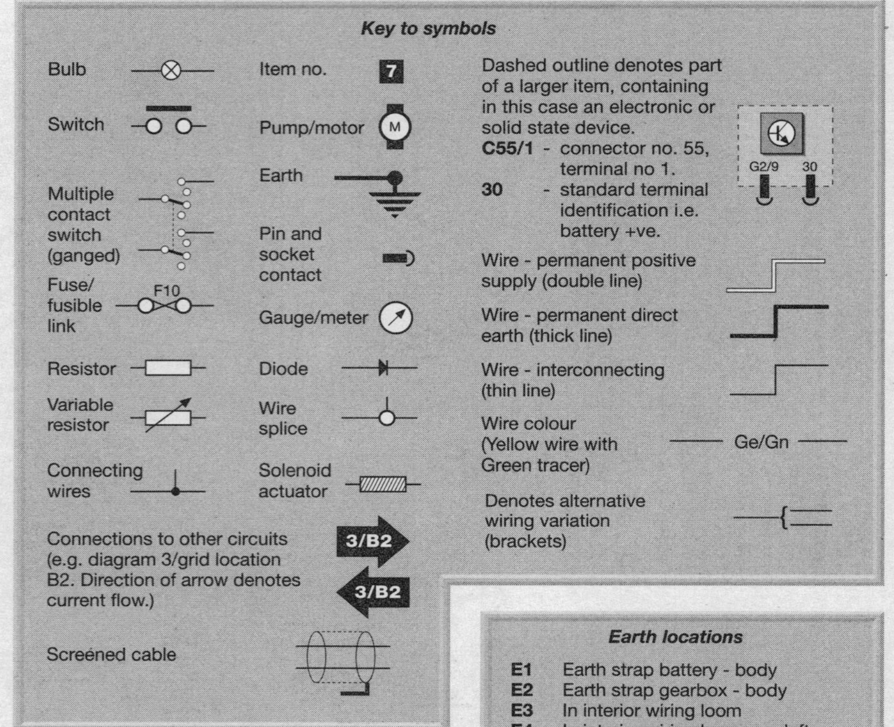


### Battery fusebox

| Fuse | Rating | Circuit protected |
|---|---|---|
| F1 | 110A | Alternator |
| F2 | 80A | Relay supply |
| F3 | 50A | Glow plugs |
| F4 | 50A | Coolant heater elements |
| | 30A | Air conditioning |
| F5 | 30A | ABS control unit |
| F6 | 30A | ABS control unit |
| F7 | 20A | Engine cooling fan |
| F8 | 10A | Air conditioning |

### Earth locations

| | |
|---|---|
| E1 | Earth strap battery - body |
| E2 | Earth strap gearbox - body |
| E3 | In interior wiring loom |
| E4 | In interior wiring loom rear left |
| E5 | In interior wiring loom front left |
| E6 | In engine compartment left |
| E7 | In engine compartment wiring loom |
| E8 | Near gear selector mechanism |
| E9 | In interior wiring harness |
| E10 | In engine compartment wiring loom |
| E11 | Near LH tail light |
| E12 | In tailgate wiring harness |
| E13 | In headlight wiring loom |
| E14 | In engine compartment wiring loom |
| E15 | In headlight wiring loom |
| E16 | Lower RH 'A' pillar |
| E17 | In headlight wiring loom |
| E18 | Near diesel injection pump |
| E19 | On cylinder head |
| E20 | In engine wiring loom |
| E21 | In plenum chamber |
| E22 | In interior wiring loom |
| E23 | In motronic wiring loom |
| E24 | Near RH tail light |
| E25 | Near gear selector mechanism |
| E26 | In driver's door harness |

### Passenger fusebox

| Fuse | Rating | Circuit protected |
|---|---|---|
| F1 | 15A | Engine control unit |
| F2 | 10A | Engine control unit (petrol) Engine electrics (Diesel) |
| F3 | 7.5A | Engine electrics |
| F4 | 15A | Ignition coil |
| F5 | 10A | Auto. gearbox control unit, shift lock |
| F6 | 5A | Auto. gearbox control unit |
| F7 | 5A | ABS control unit |
| F8 | 15A | Injectors, oxygen sensor |
| F9 | 15A | Engine control unit |
| F10 | 15A | Engine control unit (petrol) Engine electrics (Diesel) |
| F11 | 15A | Horn, heated seats |
| F12 | 10A | RH main beam and warning light |
| F13 | 10A | LH main beam |
| F14 | 10A | RH dipped beam and headlight levelling, headlight levelling adjuster |
| F15 | 10A | LH dipped beam and headlight levelling |
| F16 | 5A | RH side/tail light |
| F17 | 5A | LH side/tail light |
| F18 | 7.5A | Reversing lights, heated washer jets, selector illumination |
| F19 | 15A | Front/rear foglights |
| F20 | 10A | Brakelights |
| F21 | 10A | Hazard warning lights |
| F22 | 5A | Direction indicators |
| F23 | 15A | Windscreen wash/wipe |
| F24 | 10A | Rear wiper, heated mirrors |
| F25 | 15A | Heated rear window |
| F26 | 5A | Instruments, immobiliser |
| F27 | 5A | Self-diagnosis, instruments, interior and luggage lights |
| F28 | 15A | Radio, cigarette lighter, central locking |
| F29 | 5A | Interior light, fresh/recircling blower motor |
| F30 | 20A | Fresh air blower |
| F31 | 5A | Number plate lights |
| F32 | 15A | Fuel pump |

### Standard terminal identification (typical)

| | |
|---|---|
| 15 | Ignition switch 'ignition' position |
| 30 | Battery +ve |
| 31 | Earth |
| 50 | Ignition switch 'start' position |
| 85 | Relay winding input |
| 86 | Relay winding earth |
| 87 | Relay output |
| 87a | Relay output |

H29851

**Diagram 11 : Information for wiring diagrams - models from 1998**

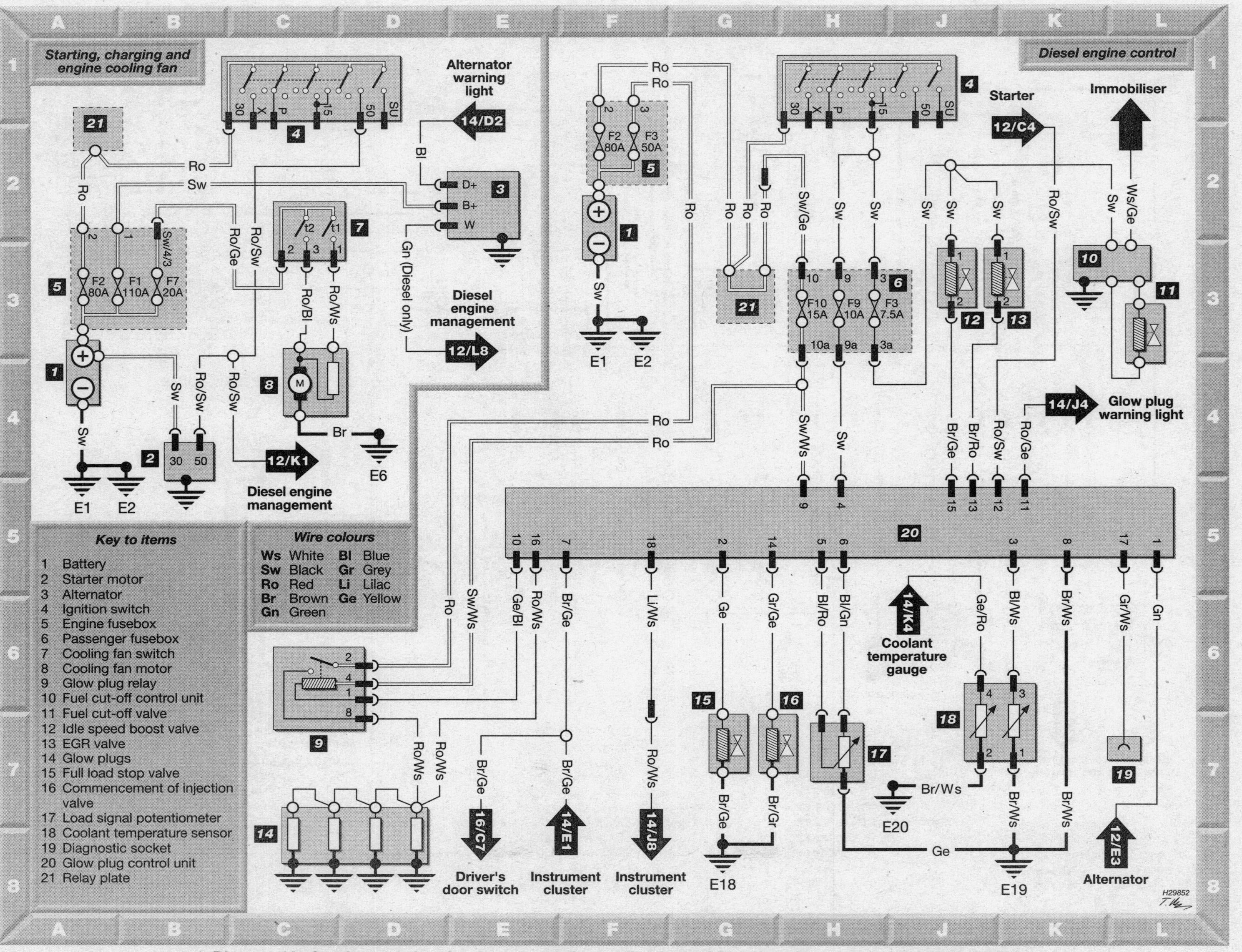

Starting, charging and engine cooling fan
Diesel engine control
Alternator warning light
14/D2
Diesel engine management
12/L8
Gn (Diesel only)
12/K1
Diesel engine management
Starter
12/C4
Immobiliser
14/J4
Glow plug warning light
Coolant temperature gauge
14/K4
16/C7
Driver's door switch
14/E1
Instrument cluster
14/J8
Instrument cluster
12/E3
Alternator
F2 80A
F1 110A
F7 20A
F3 50A
F10 15A
F9 10A
F3 7.5A
E1
E2
E6
E18
E19
E20
Key to items
1 Battery
2 Starter motor
3 Alternator
4 Ignition switch
5 Engine fusebox
6 Passenger fusebox
7 Cooling fan switch
8 Cooling fan motor
9 Glow plug relay
10 Fuel cut-off control unit
11 Fuel cut-off valve
12 Idle speed boost valve
13 EGR valve
14 Glow plugs
15 Full load stop valve
16 Commencement of injection valve
17 Load signal potentiometer
18 Coolant temperature sensor
19 Diagnostic socket
20 Glow plug control unit
21 Relay plate
Wire colours
Ws White
Sw Black
Ro Red
Br Brown
Gn Green
Bl Blue
Gr Grey
Li Lilac
Ge Yellow
H29852

Diagram 12 : Starting and charging systems, engine cooling fan and Diesel engine control - models from 1998

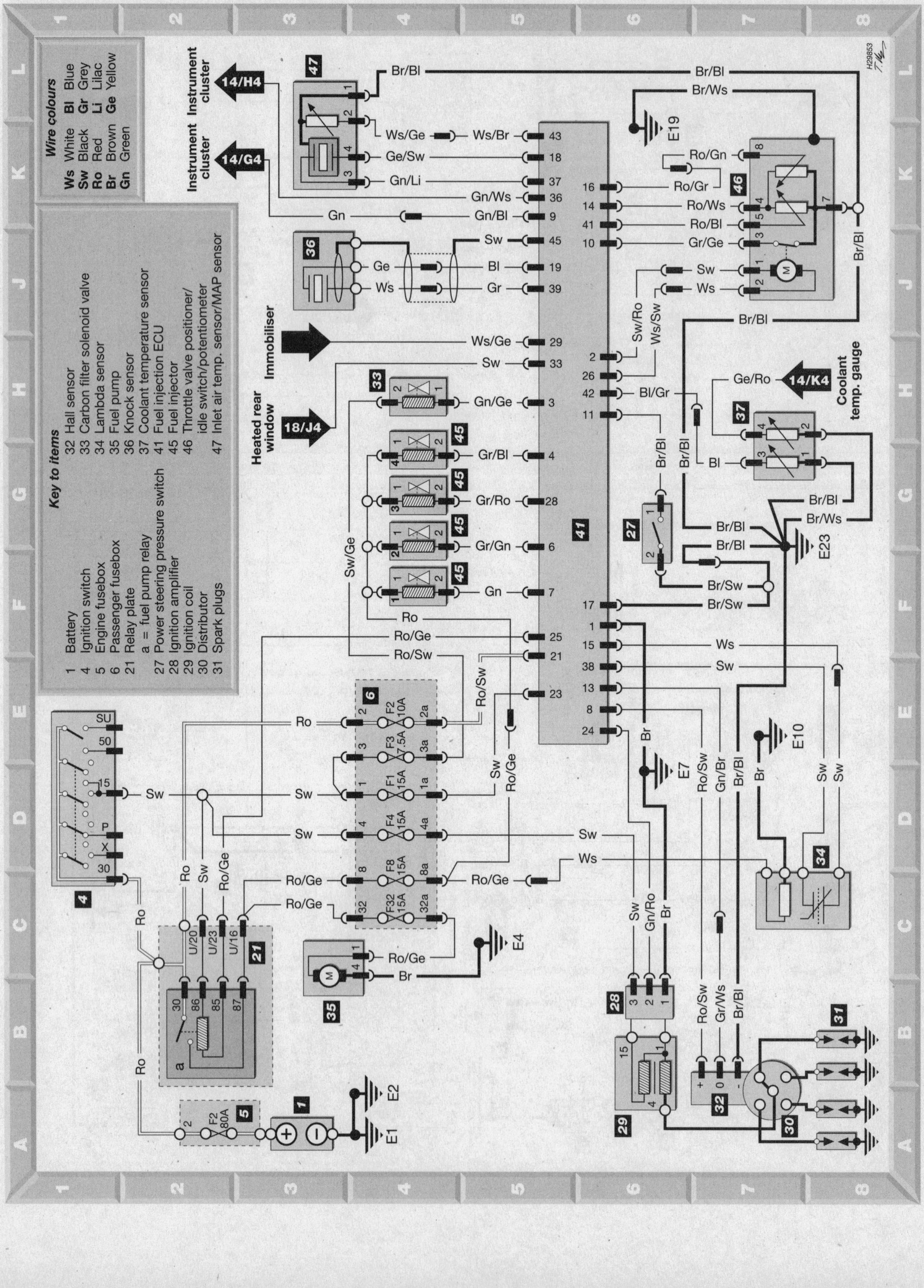

### Key to items

| | | | |
|---|---|---|---|
| 1 | Battery | 32 | Hall sensor |
| 4 | Ignition switch | 33 | Carbon filter solenoid valve |
| 5 | Engine fusebox | 34 | Lambda sensor |
| 6 | Passenger fusebox | 35 | Fuel pump |
| 21 | Relay plate | 36 | Knock sensor |
| | a = fuel pump relay | 37 | Coolant temperature sensor |
| 27 | Power steering pressure switch | 41 | Fuel injection ECU |
| 28 | Ignition amplifier | 45 | Fuel injector |
| 29 | Ignition coil | 46 | Throttle valve positioner/ idle switch/potentiometer |
| 30 | Distributor | 47 | Inlet air temp. sensor/MAP sensor |
| 31 | Spark plugs | | |

### Wire colours

| | | | |
|---|---|---|---|
| **Ws** | White | **Bl** | Blue |
| **Sw** | Black | **Gr** | Grey |
| **Ro** | Red | **Li** | Lilac |
| **Br** | Brown | **Ge** | Yellow |
| **Gn** | Green | | |



**Diagram 13 : Motronic engine management - models from 1998**

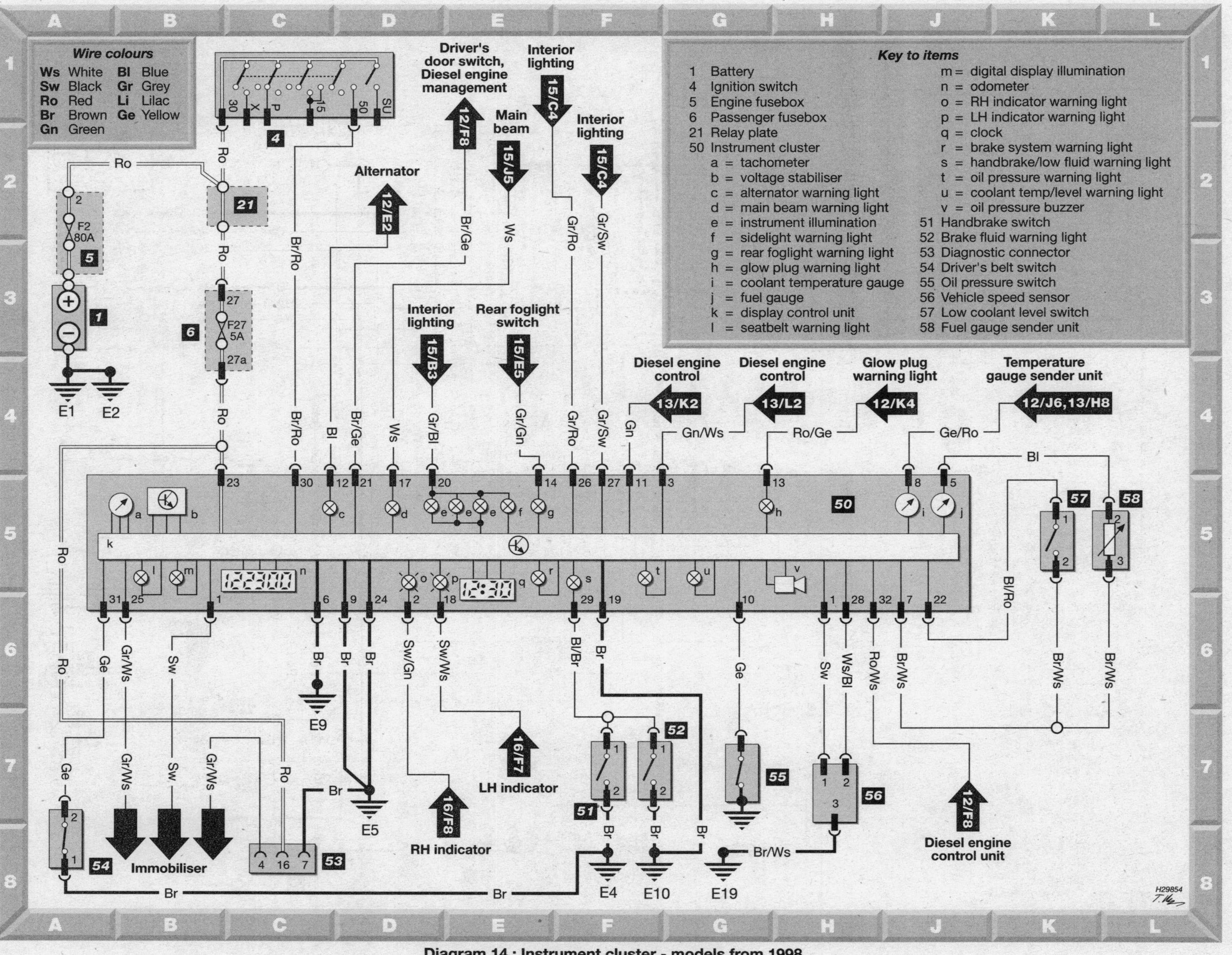

Wire colours
Ws White
Sw Black
Ro Red
Br Brown
Gn Green
Bl Blue
Gr Grey
Li Lilac
Ge Yellow
Key to items
1 Battery
4 Ignition switch
5 Engine fusebox
6 Passenger fusebox
21 Relay plate
50 Instrument cluster
a = tachometer
b = voltage stabiliser
c = alternator warning light
d = main beam warning light
e = instrument illumination
f = sidelight warning light
g = rear foglight warning light
h = glow plug warning light
i = coolant temperature gauge
j = fuel gauge
k = display control unit
l = seatbelt warning light
m = digital display illumination
n = odometer
o = RH indicator warning light
p = LH indicator warning light
q = clock
r = brake system warning light
s = handbrake/low fluid warning light
t = oil pressure warning light
u = coolant temp/level warning light
v = oil pressure buzzer
51 Handbrake switch
52 Brake fluid warning light
53 Diagnostic connector
54 Driver's belt switch
55 Oil pressure switch
56 Vehicle speed sensor
57 Low coolant level switch
58 Fuel gauge sender unit
Driver's door switch, Diesel engine management
Main beam
Interior lighting
Alternator
Rear foglight switch
Diesel engine control
Glow plug warning light
Temperature gauge sender unit
Diesel engine control unit
LH indicator
RH indicator
Immobiliser
12/F8
15/J5
15/C4
15/B3
15/E5
12/E2
13/K2
13/L2
12/K4
12/J6,13/H8
16/F7
16/F8
E1
E2
E4
E5
E9
E10
E19
F2 80A
F27 5A
H29854

Diagram 14 : Instrument cluster - models from 1998

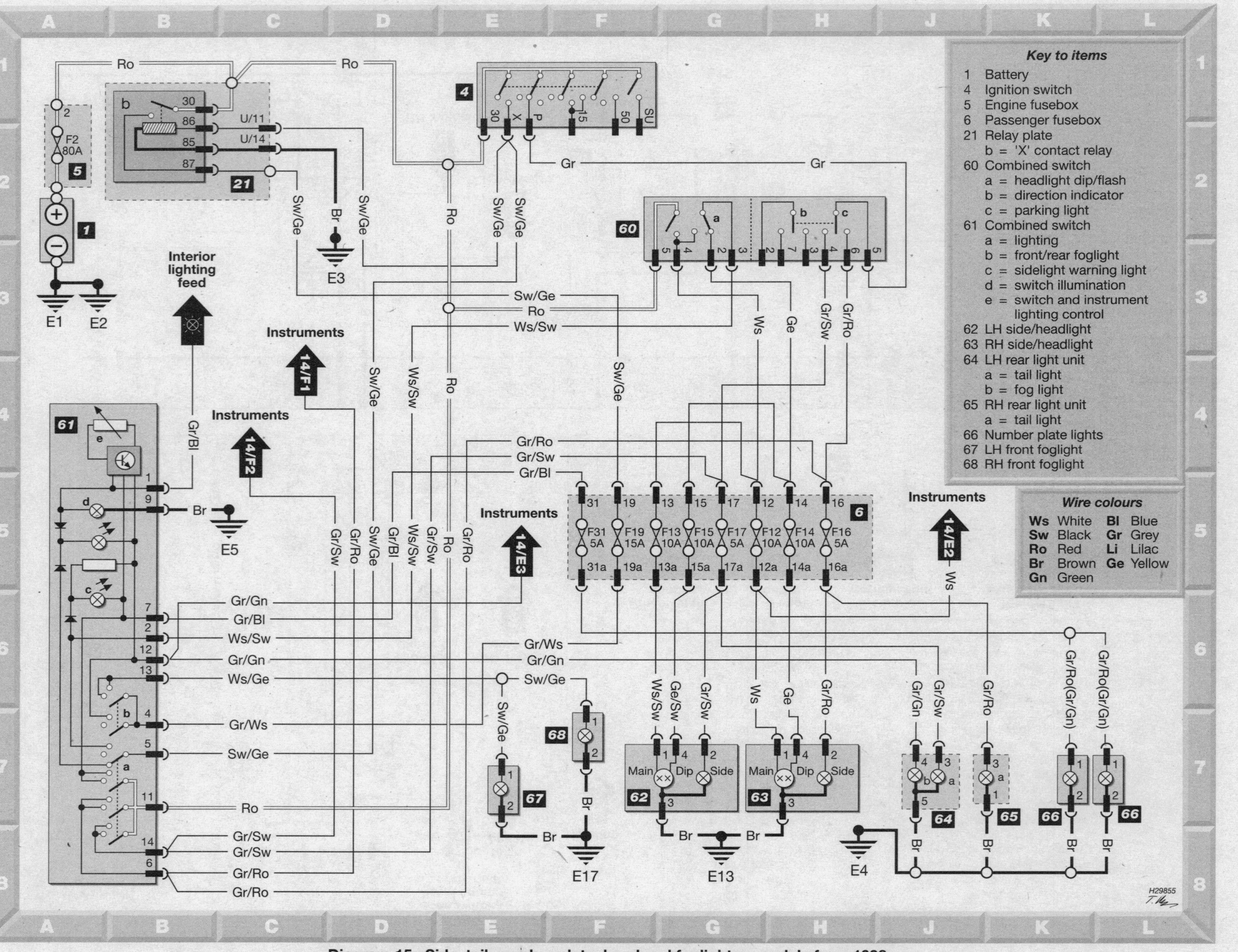

Key to items
1 Battery
4 Ignition switch
5 Engine fusebox
6 Passenger fusebox
21 Relay plate
b = 'X' contact relay
60 Combined switch
a = headlight dip/flash
b = direction indicator
c = parking light
61 Combined switch
a = lighting
b = front/rear foglight
c = sidelight warning light
d = switch illumination
e = switch and instrument lighting control
62 LH side/headlight
63 RH side/headlight
64 LH rear light unit
a = tail light
b = fog light
65 RH rear light unit
a = tail light
66 Number plate lights
67 LH front foglight
68 RH front foglight
Wire colours
Ws White
Sw Black
Ro Red
Br Brown
Gn Green
Bl Blue
Gr Grey
Li Lilac
Ge Yellow
Interior lighting feed
Instruments
14/F1
14/F2
14/E3
14/E2
F2 80A
F31 5A
F19 15A
F13 10A
F15 10A
F17 5A
F12 10A
F14 10A
F16 5A
Main
Dip
Side
E1
E2
E3
E4
E5
E13
E17
H29855


Diagram 15 : Side, tail, number plate, head and foglights - models from 1998

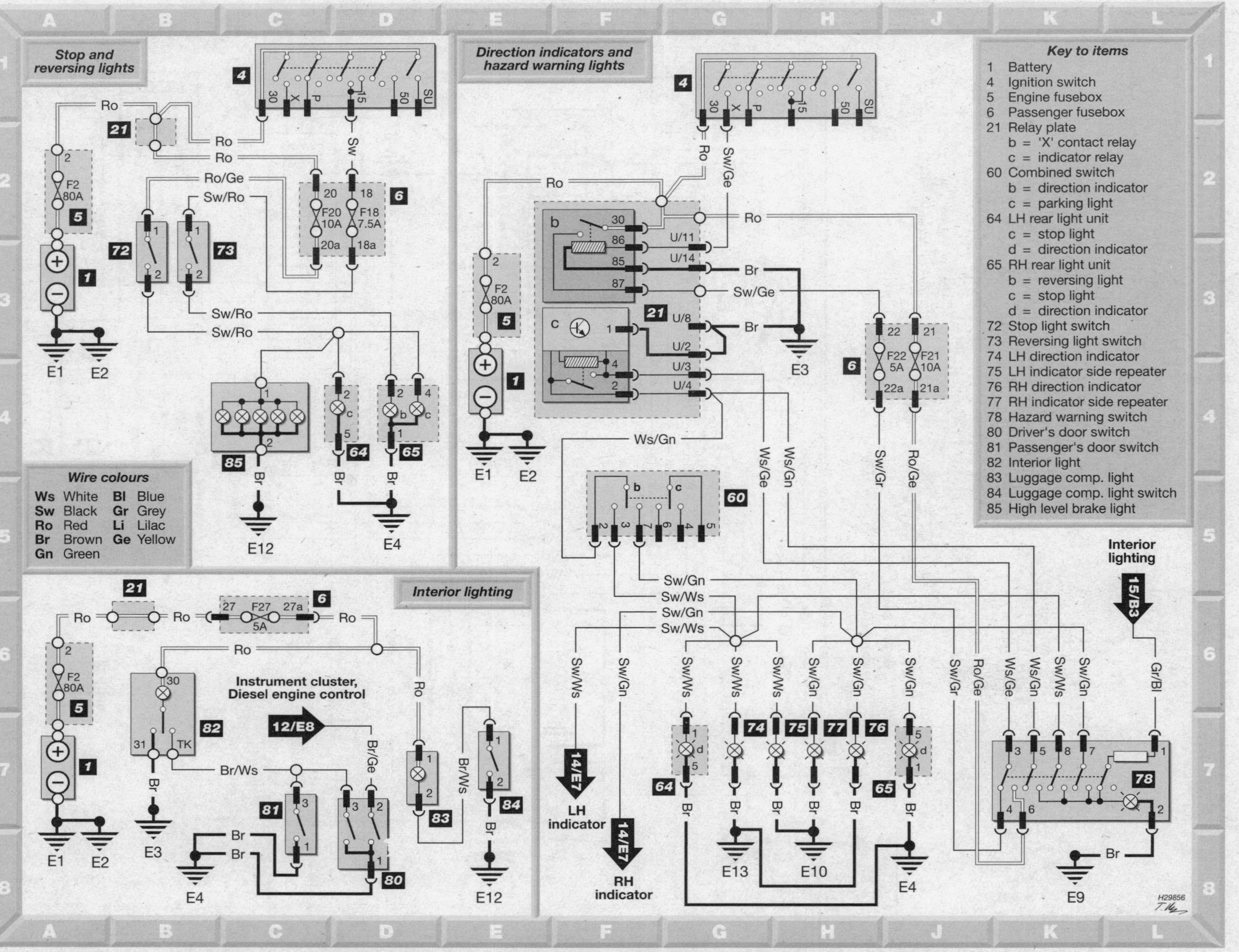


Diagram 16 : Stop, reversing, direction indicators/hazard warning lights and interior lighting - models from 1998

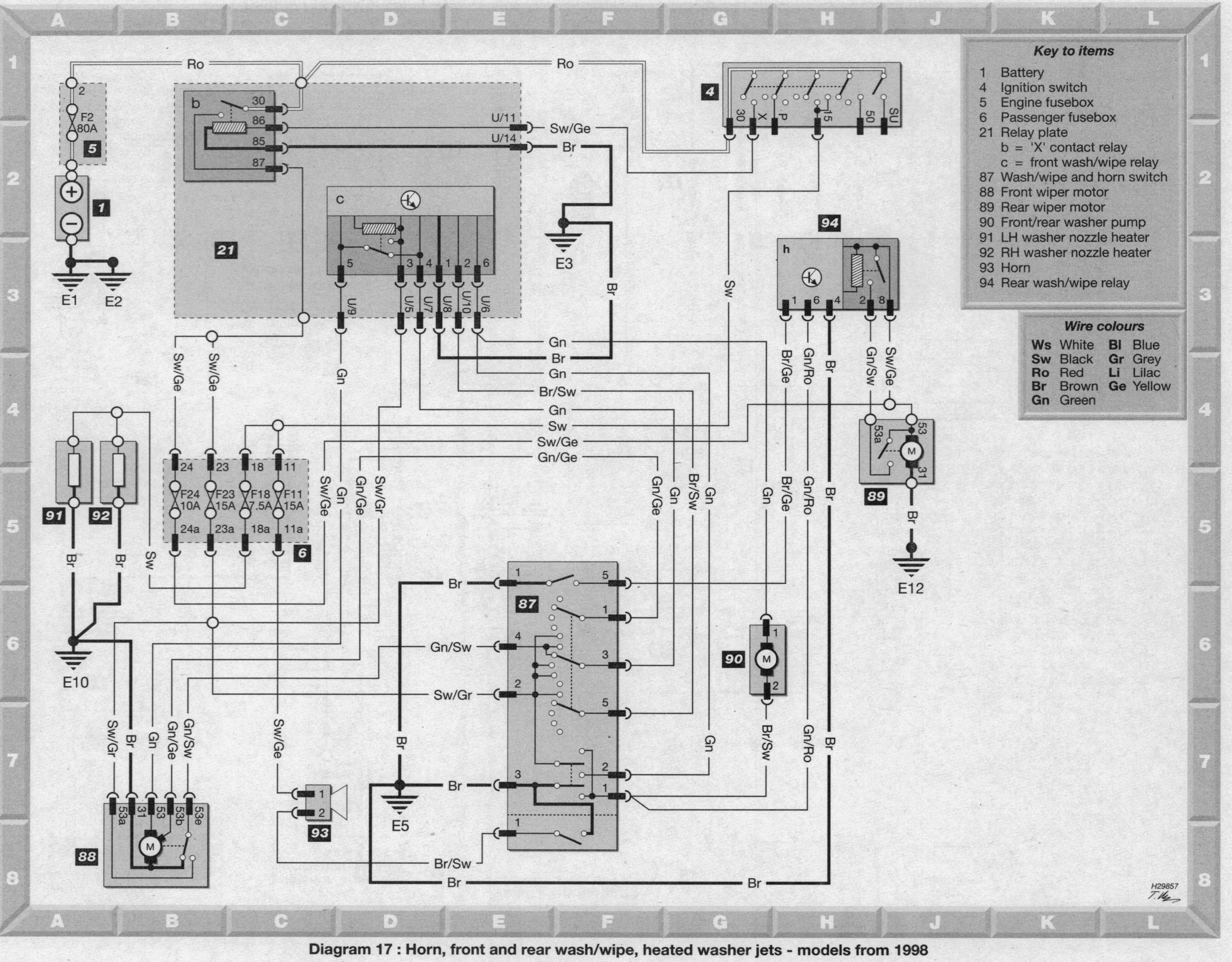


Diagram 17 : Horn, front and rear wash/wipe, heated washer jets - models from 1998

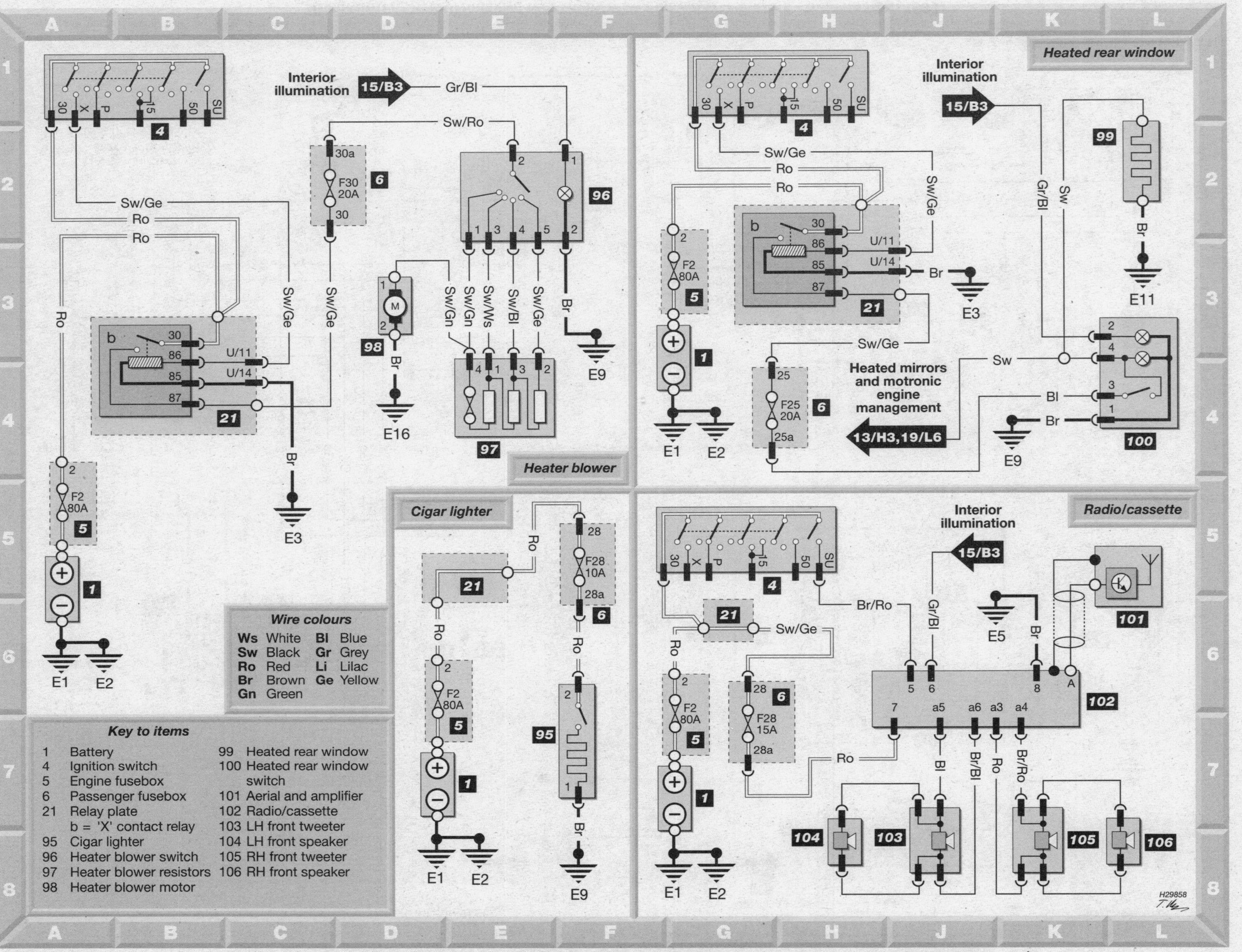


Diagram 18 : Cigar lighter, heater blower, radio/cassette and heated rear window - models from 1998

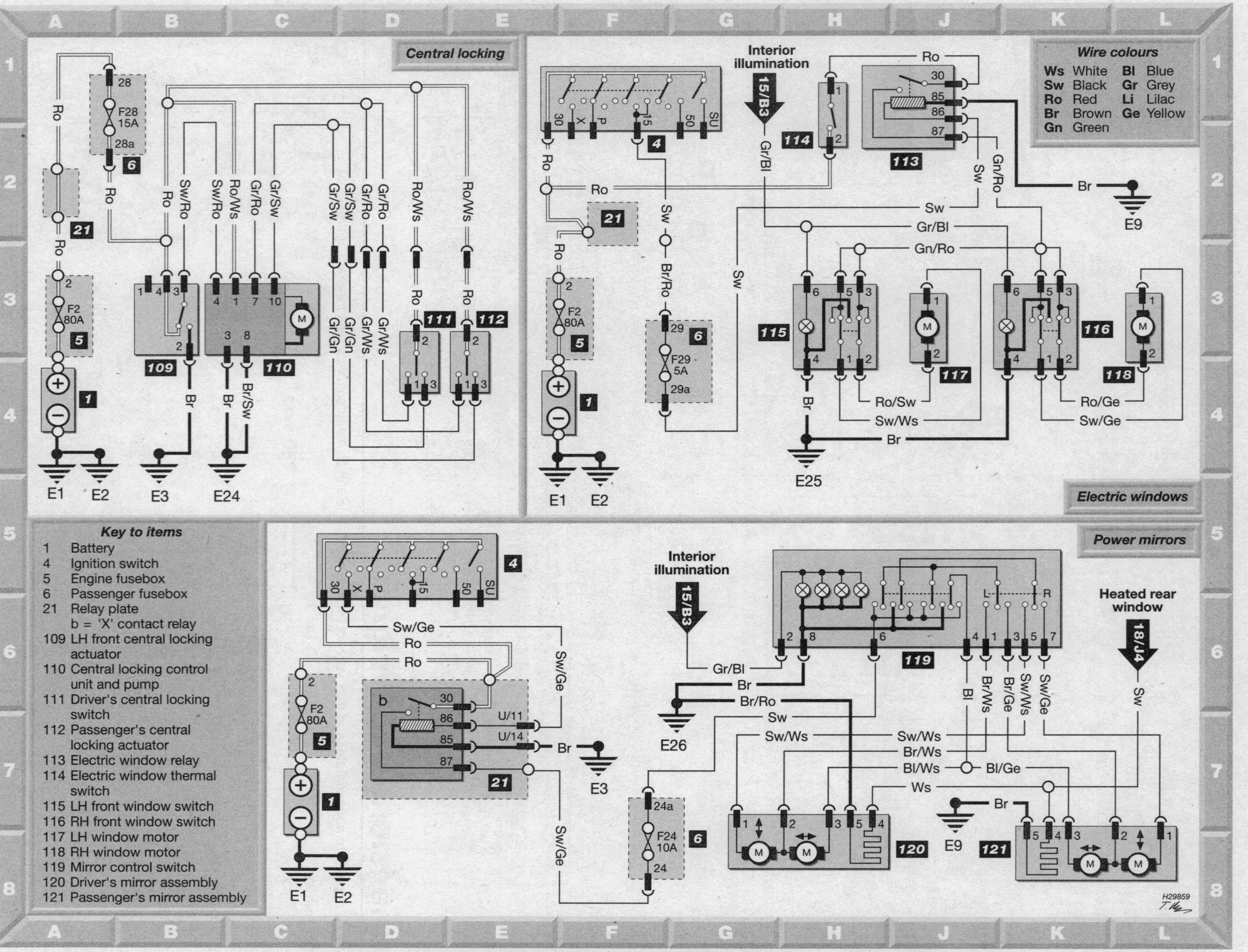

Central locking
Electric windows
Power mirrors
Wire colours
Ws White
Sw Black
Ro Red
Br Brown
Gn Green
Bl Blue
Gr Grey
Li Lilac
Ge Yellow
Interior illumination
15/B3
Heated rear window
18/J4
Key to items
1 Battery
4 Ignition switch
5 Engine fusebox
6 Passenger fusebox
21 Relay plate
b = 'X' contact relay
109 LH front central locking actuator
110 Central locking control unit and pump
111 Driver's central locking switch
112 Passenger's central locking actuator
113 Electric window relay
114 Electric window thermal switch
115 LH front window switch
116 RH front window switch
117 LH window motor
118 RH window motor
119 Mirror control switch
120 Driver's mirror assembly
121 Passenger's mirror assembly
H29859


Diagram 19 : Central locking, electric windows and power mirrors - models from 1998

# Dimensions and weights

**Note:** *All figures are approximate, and may vary according to model. Refer to manufacturer's data for exact figures.*

## Dimensions

| | |
|---|---|
| Overall length | 3715 mm |
| Overall width: | |
| Excluding mirrors | 1655 mm |
| Including mirrors | 1832 mm |
| Overall height (unladen) | 1420 mm |
| Wheelbase | 2406 mm |

## Weights

| | |
|---|---|
| Kerb weight | 880 to 960 kg* |
| Maximum gross vehicle weight** | 1375 to 1435 kg* |
| Maximum roof rack load | 50 kg |
| Maximum towing weight**: | |
| Braked trailer | 650 to 800 kg* |
| Unbraked trailer | 450 kg |
| Maximum trailer nose weight | 50 kg |

**Depending on model and specification.*
***Refer to VW dealer for exact recommendations.*

# Conversion factors

## Length (distance)

| | | | | | |
|---|---|---|---|---|---|
| Inches (in) | x 25.4 | = Millimetres (mm) | x 0.0394 | = | Inches (in) |
| Feet (ft) | x 0.305 | = Metres (m) | x 3.281 | = | Feet (ft) |
| Miles | x 1.609 | = Kilometres (km) | x 0.621 | = | Miles |

## Volume (capacity)

| | | | | | |
|---|---|---|---|---|---|
| Cubic inches (cu in; in³) | x 16.387 | = Cubic centimetres (cc; cm³) | x 0.061 | = | Cubic inches (cu in; in³) |
| Imperial pints (Imp pt) | x 0.568 | = Litres (l) | x 1.76 | = | Imperial pints (Imp pt) |
| Imperial quarts (Imp qt) | x 1.137 | = Litres (l) | x 0.88 | = | Imperial quarts (Imp qt) |
| Imperial quarts (Imp qt) | x 1.201 | = US quarts (US qt) | x 0.833 | = | Imperial quarts (Imp qt) |
| US quarts (US qt) | x 0.946 | = Litres (l) | x 1.057 | = | US quarts (US qt) |
| Imperial gallons (Imp gal) | x 4.546 | = Litres (l) | x 0.22 | = | Imperial gallons (Imp gal) |
| Imperial gallons (Imp gal) | x 1.201 | = US gallons (US gal) | x 0.833 | = | Imperial gallons (Imp gal) |
| US gallons (US gal) | x 3.785 | = Litres (l) | x 0.264 | = | US gallons (US gal) |

## Mass (weight)

| | | | | | |
|---|---|---|---|---|---|
| Ounces (oz) | x 28.35 | = Grams (g) | x 0.035 | = | Ounces (oz) |
| Pounds (lb) | x 0.454 | = Kilograms (kg) | x 2.205 | = | Pounds (lb) |

## Force

| | | | | | |
|---|---|---|---|---|---|
| Ounces-force (ozf; oz) | x 0.278 | = Newtons (N) | x 3.6 | = | Ounces-force (ozf; oz) |
| Pounds-force (lbf; lb) | x 4.448 | = Newtons (N) | x 0.225 | = | Pounds-force (lbf; lb) |
| Newtons (N) | x 0.1 | = Kilograms-force (kgf; kg) | x 9.81 | = | Newtons (N) |

## Pressure

| | | | | | |
|---|---|---|---|---|---|
| Pounds-force per square inch (psi; lbf/in²; lb/in²) | x 0.070 | = Kilograms-force per square centimetre (kgf/cm²; kg/cm²) | x 14.223 | = | Pounds-force per square inch (psi; lbf/in²; lb/in²) |
| Pounds-force per square inch (psi; lbf/in²; lb/in²) | x 0.068 | = Atmospheres (atm) | x 14.696 | = | Pounds-force per square inch (psi; lbf/in²; lb/in²) |
| Pounds-force per square inch (psi; lbf/in²; lb/in²) | x 0.069 | = Bars | x 14.5 | = | Pounds-force per square inch (psi; lbf/in²; lb/in²) |
| Pounds-force per square inch (psi; lbf/in²; lb/in²) | x 6.895 | = Kilopascals (kPa) | x 0.145 | = | Pounds-force per square inch (psi; lbf/in²; lb/in²) |
| Kilopascals (kPa) | x 0.01 | = Kilograms-force per square centimetre (kgf/cm²; kg/cm²) | x 98.1 | = | Kilopascals (kPa) |
| Millibar (mbar) | x 100 | = Pascals (Pa) | x 0.01 | = | Millibar (mbar) |
| Millibar (mbar) | x 0.0145 | = Pounds-force per square inch (psi; lbf/in²; lb/in²) | x 68.947 | = | Millibar (mbar) |
| Millibar (mbar) | x 0.75 | = Millimetres of mercury (mmHg) | x 1.333 | = | Millibar (mbar) |
| Millibar (mbar) | x 0.401 | = Inches of water ($inH_2O$) | x 2.491 | = | Millibar (mbar) |
| Millimetres of mercury (mmHg) | x 0.535 | = Inches of water ($inH_2O$) | x 1.868 | = | Millimetres of mercury (mmHg) |
| Inches of water ($inH_2O$) | x 0.036 | = Pounds-force per square inch (psi; lbf/in²; lb/in²) | x 27.68 | = | Inches of water ($inH_2O$) |

## Torque (moment of force)

| | | | | | |
|---|---|---|---|---|---|
| Pounds-force inches (lbf in; lb in) | x 1.152 | = Kilograms-force centimetre (kgf cm; kg cm) | x 0.868 | = | Pounds-force inches (lbf in; lb in) |
| Pounds-force inches (lbf in; lb in) | x 0.113 | = Newton metres (Nm) | x 8.85 | = | Pounds-force inches (lbf in; lb in) |
| Pounds-force inches (lbf in; lb in) | x 0.083 | = Pounds-force feet (lbf ft; lb ft) | x 12 | = | Pounds-force inches (lbf in; lb in) |
| Pounds-force feet (lbf ft; lb ft) | x 0.138 | = Kilograms-force metres (kgf m; kg m) | x 7.233 | = | Pounds-force feet (lbf ft; lb ft) |
| Pounds-force feet (lbf ft; lb ft) | x 1.356 | = Newton metres (Nm) | x 0.738 | = | Pounds-force feet (lbf ft; lb ft) |
| Newton metres (Nm) | x 0.102 | = Kilograms-force metres (kgf m; kg m) | x 9.804 | = | Newton metres (Nm) |

## Power

| | | | | | |
|---|---|---|---|---|---|
| Horsepower (hp) | x 745.7 | = Watts (W) | x 0.0013 | = | Horsepower (hp) |

## Velocity (speed)

| | | | | | |
|---|---|---|---|---|---|
| Miles per hour (miles/hr; mph) | x 1.609 | = Kilometres per hour (km/hr; kph) | x 0.621 | = | Miles per hour (miles/hr; mph) |

## Fuel consumption*

| | | | | | |
|---|---|---|---|---|---|
| Miles per gallon (mpg) | x 0.354 | = Kilometres per litre (km/l) | x 2.825 | = | Miles per gallon (mpg) |

## Temperature

Degrees Fahrenheit = (°C x 1.8) + 32

Degrees Celsius (Degrees Centigrade; °C) = (°F - 32) x 0.56

** It is common practice to convert from miles per gallon (mpg) to litres/100 kilometres (l/100km), where mpg x l/100 km = 282*

Spare parts are available from many sources, including maker's appointed garages, accessory shops, and motor factors. To be sure of obtaining the correct parts, it may sometimes be necessary to quote the vehicle identification number. If possible, it can also be useful to take the old parts along for positive identification. Items such as starter motors and alternators may be available under a service exchange scheme - any parts returned should always be clean.

Our advice regarding spare part sources is as follows.

## Officially-appointed garages

This is the best source of parts which are peculiar to your car, and are not otherwise generally available (eg badges, interior trim, certain body panels, etc). It is also the only place at which you should buy parts if the vehicle is still under warranty.

## Accessory shops

These are very good places to buy materials and components needed for the maintenance of your car (oil, air and fuel filters, spark plugs, light bulbs, drivebelts, oils and greases, brake pads, touch-up paint, etc). Parts like this sold by a reputable shop are of the same standard as those used by the car manufacturer.

## Motor factors

Good factors will stock all the more important components which wear out comparatively quickly and can sometimes supply individual components needed for the overhaul of a larger assembly. They may also handle work such as cylinder block reboring, crankshaft regrinding and balancing, etc.

## Tyre and exhaust specialists

These outlets may be independent or members of a local or national chain. They frequently offer competitive prices when compared with a main dealer or local garage, but it will pay to obtain several quotes before making a decision. Also ask what extras may be added to the quote - for instance, fitting a new valve and balancing the wheel are both often charged on top of the price of a new tyre.

## Other sources

Beware of parts or materials obtained from market stalls, car boot sales or similar outlets. Such items are not invariably sub-standard, but there is little chance of compensation if they do prove unsatisfactory. In the case of safety-critical components such as brake pads, there is the risk not only of financial loss, but also of an accident causing injury or death.

Second-hand components or assemblies obtained from a car breaker can be a good buy in some circumstances, but this sort of purchase is best made by the experienced DIY mechanic.

# Vehicle identification

Modifications are a continuing and unpublicised process in vehicle manufacture, quite apart from major model changes. Spare parts manuals and lists are compiled upon a numerical basis, the individual vehicle identification numbers being essential to correct identification of the component concerned.

When ordering spare parts, always give as much information as possible. Quote the car model, year of manufacture, body and engine numbers as appropriate.

The vehicle identification number (VIN) plate or chassis number may be found in the engine compartment, on top of the bulkhead or on top of the bonnet lock carrier panel **(see illustrations)**. On some models, this information may appear on the passenger door pillar. Some models may have the chassis number on a small plate on the top of the facia panel (visible VIN).

The vehicle data sticker is on the floor panel to the left of the spare wheel well in the boot.

The engine number is situated on the cylinder block (on some models, it can also be found on a sticker attached to the timing belt cover) and can be found in the following locations:

a) *Petrol engines - stamped on the front of the cylinder block, directly below the cylinder head mating surface **(see illustration)**.*

b) *Diesel engines - stamped on the front of the cylinder block, next to the injection pump **(see illustration)**.*

**Note:** *The first part of the engine number gives the engine code - eg AEF.*

**Vehicle identification number (1) and petrol engine number (2)**

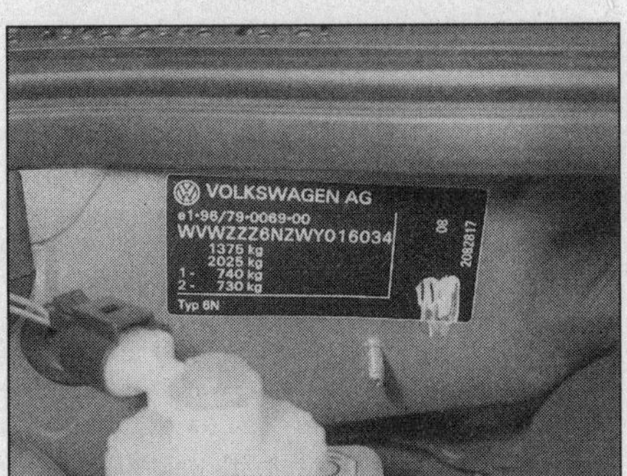

**VIN plate on engine compartment bulkhead**

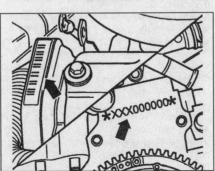

**VIN plate on bonnet lock carrier panel**

**Engine number locations (arrowed) - petrol models**

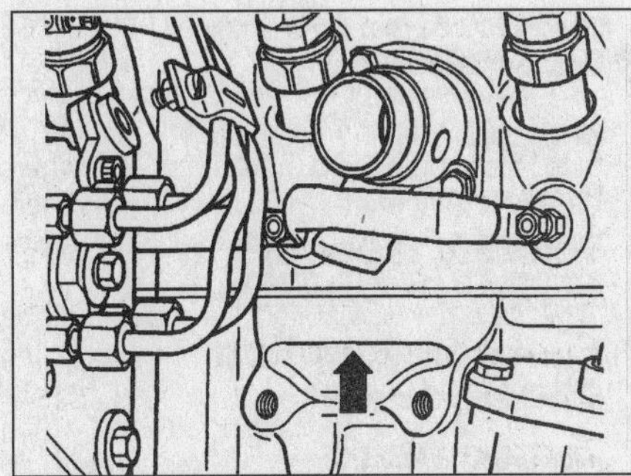
**Engine number location (arrowed) - diesel models**

Whenever servicing, repair or overhaul work is carried out on the car or its components, observe the following procedures and instructions. This will assist in carrying out the operation efficiently and to a professional standard of workmanship.

### Joint mating faces and gaskets

When separating components at their mating faces, never insert screwdrivers or similar implements into the joint between the faces in order to prise them apart. This can cause severe damage which results in oil leaks, coolant leaks, etc upon reassembly. Separation is usually achieved by tapping along the joint with a soft-faced hammer in order to break the seal. However, note that this method may not be suitable where dowels are used for component location.

Where a gasket is used between the mating faces of two components, a new one must be fitted on reassembly; fit it dry unless otherwise stated in the repair procedure. Make sure that the mating faces are clean and dry, with all traces of old gasket removed. When cleaning a joint face, use a tool which is unlikely to score or damage the face, and remove any burrs or nicks with an oilstone or fine file.

Make sure that tapped holes are cleaned with a pipe cleaner, and keep them free of jointing compound, if this is being used, unless specifically instructed otherwise.

Ensure that all orifices, channels or pipes are clear, and blow through them, preferably using compressed air.

### Oil seals

Oil seals can be removed by levering them out with a wide flat-bladed screwdriver or similar implement. Alternatively, a number of self-tapping screws may be screwed into the seal, and these used as a purchase for pliers or some similar device in order to pull the seal free.

Whenever an oil seal is removed from its working location, either individually or as part of an assembly, it should be renewed.

The very fine sealing lip of the seal is easily damaged, and will not seal if the surface it contacts is not completely clean and free from scratches, nicks or grooves. If the original sealing surface of the component cannot be restored, and the manufacturer has not made provision for slight relocation of the seal relative to the sealing surface, the component should be renewed.

Protect the lips of the seal from any surface which may damage them in the course of fitting. Use tape or a conical sleeve where possible. Lubricate the seal lips with oil before fitting and, on dual-lipped seals, fill the space between the lips with grease.

Unless otherwise stated, oil seals must be fitted with their sealing lips toward the lubricant to be sealed.

Use a tubular drift or block of wood of the appropriate size to install the seal and, if the seal housing is shouldered, drive the seal down to the shoulder. If the seal housing is unshouldered, the seal should be fitted with its face flush with the housing top face (unless otherwise instructed).

### Screw threads and fastenings

Seized nuts, bolts and screws are quite a common occurrence where corrosion has set in, and the use of penetrating oil or releasing fluid will often overcome this problem if the offending item is soaked for a while before attempting to release it. The use of an impact driver may also provide a means of releasing such stubborn fastening devices, when used in conjunction with the appropriate screwdriver bit or socket. If none of these methods works, it may be necessary to resort to the careful application of heat, or the use of a hacksaw or nut splitter device.

Studs are usually removed by locking two nuts together on the threaded part, and then using a spanner on the lower nut to unscrew the stud. Studs or bolts which have broken off below the surface of the component in which they are mounted can sometimes be removed using a stud extractor. Always ensure that a blind tapped hole is completely free from oil, grease, water or other fluid before installing the bolt or stud. Failure to do this could cause the housing to crack due to the hydraulic action of the bolt or stud as it is screwed in.

When tightening a castellated nut to accept a split pin, tighten the nut to the specified torque, where applicable, and then tighten further to the next split pin hole. Never slacken the nut to align the split pin hole, unless stated in the repair procedure.

When checking or retightening a nut or bolt to a specified torque setting, slacken the nut or bolt by a quarter of a turn, and then retighten to the specified setting. However, this should not be attempted where angular tightening has been used.

For some screw fastenings, notably cylinder head bolts or nuts, torque wrench settings are no longer specified for the latter stages of tightening, "angle-tightening" being called up instead. Typically, a fairly low torque wrench setting will be applied to the bolts/nuts in the correct sequence, followed by one or more stages of tightening through specified angles.

### Locknuts, locktabs and washers

Any fastening which will rotate against a component or housing during tightening should always have a washer between it and the relevant component or housing.

Spring or split washers should always be renewed when they are used to lock a critical component such as a big-end bearing retaining bolt or nut. Locktabs which are folded over to retain a nut or bolt should always be renewed.

Self-locking nuts can be re-used in non-critical areas, providing resistance can be felt when the locking portion passes over the bolt or stud thread. However, it should be noted that self-locking stiffnuts tend to lose their effectiveness after long periods of use, and should then be renewed as a matter of course.

Split pins must always be replaced with new ones of the correct size for the hole.

When thread-locking compound is found on the threads of a fastener which is to be re-used, it should be cleaned off with a wire brush and solvent, and fresh compound applied on reassembly.

### Special tools

Some repair procedures in this manual entail the use of special tools such as a press, two or three-legged pullers, spring compressors, etc. Wherever possible, suitable readily-available alternatives to the manufacturer's special tools are described, and are shown in use. In some instances, where no alternative is possible, it has been necessary to resort to the use of a manufacturer's tool, and this has been done for reasons of safety as well as the efficient completion of the repair operation. Unless you are highly-skilled and have a thorough understanding of the procedures described, never attempt to bypass the use of any special tool when the procedure described specifies its use. Not only is there a very great risk of personal injury, but expensive damage could be caused to the components involved.

### Environmental considerations

When disposing of used engine oil, brake fluid, antifreeze, etc, give due consideration to any detrimental environmental effects. Do not, for instance, pour any of the above liquids down drains into the general sewage system, or onto the ground to soak away. Many local council refuse tips provide a facility for waste oil disposal, as do some garages. If none of these facilities are available, consult your local Environmental Health Department, or the National Rivers Authority, for further advice.

With the universal tightening-up of legislation regarding the emission of environmentally-harmful substances from motor vehicles, most vehicles have tamperproof devices fitted to the main adjustment points of the fuel system. These devices are primarily designed to prevent unqualified persons from adjusting the fuel/air mixture, with the chance of a consequent increase in toxic emissions. If such devices are found during servicing or overhaul, they should, wherever possible, be renewed or refitted in accordance with the manufacturer's requirements or current legislation.

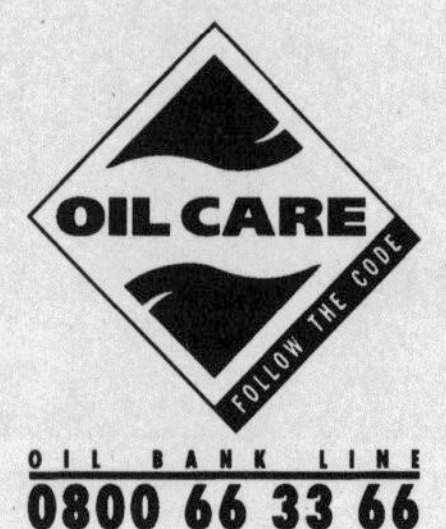

OIL CARE
FOLLOW THE CODE
OIL BANK LINE
0800 66 33 66


***Note: It is antisocial and illegal to dump oil down the drain. To find the location of your local oil recycling bank, call this number free.***

The jack supplied with the vehicle tool kit should only be used for changing the roadwheels - see Wheel changing at the front of this book. When carrying out any other kind of work, raise the vehicle using a hydraulic (or trolley) jack, and always supplement the jack with axle stands positioned under the vehicle jacking points.

When using a hydraulic jack or axle stands, always position the jack head or axle stand head under one of the relevant jacking points.

To raise the front and/or rear of the vehicle, use the jacking/support points at the front and rear ends of the door sills, indicated by the triangular depressions in the sill panel **(see illustration)**. Position a block of wood with a groove cut in it on the jack head to prevent the vehicle weight resting on the sill edge; align the sill edge with the groove in the wood so that the vehicle weight is spread evenly over the surface of the block. Supplement the jack with axle stands (also with slotted blocks of wood) positioned as close as possible to the jacking points **(see illustrations)**.

Do not jack the vehicle under any other part of the sill, sump, floor pan, or any of the steering or suspension components. With the vehicle raised, an axle stand should be positioned beneath the vehicle jack location point on the sill.

**Never** work under, around, or near a raised vehicle, unless it is adequately supported on stands.

**Front and rear jacking points (arrowed)**

**Axle stand and block of wood under front support point**

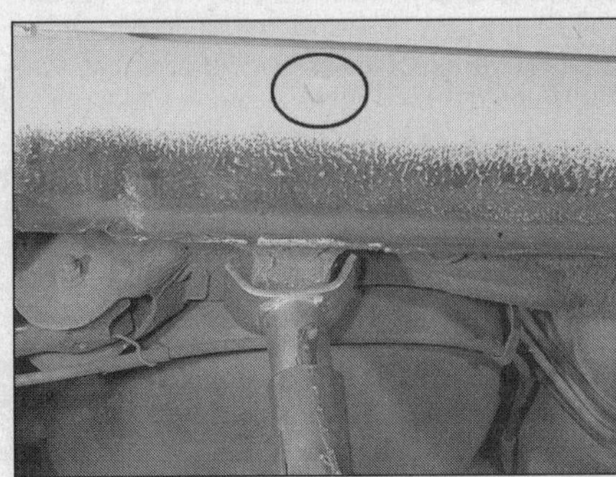

**Axle stand under rear jacking/support point**

# Radio/cassette unit anti-theft system - precaution

The radio/cassette unit fitted by VW may be equipped with a built-in security code, to deter thieves. If the power source to the unit is cut, the anti-theft system will activate. Even if the power source is immediately reconnected, the unit will not function until the correct security code has been entered. Therefore, if you do not know the correct code, DO NOT disconnect the battery negative lead, or remove the radio/cassette unit from the vehicle. The exact procedure for reprogramming a unit which has been disconnected from its power supply varies from model to model. Consult the radio booklet which should have been supplied with the vehicle for specific details.

## Introduction

A selection of good tools is a fundamental requirement for anyone contemplating the maintenance and repair of a motor vehicle. For the owner who does not possess any, their purchase will prove a considerable expense, offsetting some of the savings made by doing-it-yourself. However, provided that the tools purchased meet the relevant national safety standards and are of good quality, they will last for many years and prove an extremely worthwhile investment.

To help the average owner to decide which tools are needed to carry out the various tasks detailed in this manual, we have compiled three lists of tools under the following headings: *Maintenance and minor repair*, *Repair and overhaul*, and *Special*. Newcomers to practical mechanics should start off with the *Maintenance and minor repair* tool kit, and confine themselves to the simpler jobs around the vehicle. Then, as confidence and experience grow, more difficult tasks can be undertaken, with extra tools being purchased as, and when, they are needed. In this way, a *Maintenance and minor repair* tool kit can be built up into a *Repair and overhaul* tool kit over a considerable period of time, without any major cash outlays. The experienced do-it-yourselfer will have a tool kit good enough for most repair and overhaul procedures, and will add tools from the *Special* category when it is felt that the expense is justified by the amount of use to which these tools will be put.

Sockets and reversible ratchet drive

## Maintenance and minor repair tool kit

The tools given in this list should be considered as a minimum requirement if routine maintenance, servicing and minor repair operations are to be undertaken. We recommend the purchase of combination spanners (ring one end, open-ended the other); although more expensive than open-ended ones, they do give the advantages of both types of spanner.

☐ *Combination spanners:*
*Metric - 8 to 19 mm inclusive*
☐ *Adjustable spanner - 35 mm jaw (approx.)*
☐ *Spark plug spanner (with rubber insert) - petrol models*
☐ *Spark plug gap adjustment tool - petrol models*
☐ *Set of feeler gauges*
☐ *Brake bleed nipple spanner*
☐ *Screwdrivers:*
*Flat blade - 100 mm long x 6 mm dia*
*Cross blade - 100 mm long x 6 mm dia*
*Torx - various sizes (not all vehicles)*
☐ *Combination pliers*
☐ *Hacksaw (junior)*
☐ *Tyre pump*
☐ *Tyre pressure gauge*
☐ *Oil can*
☐ *Oil filter removal tool*
☐ *Fine emery cloth*
☐ *Wire brush (small)*
☐ *Funnel (medium size)*
☐ *Sump drain plug key (not all vehicles)*

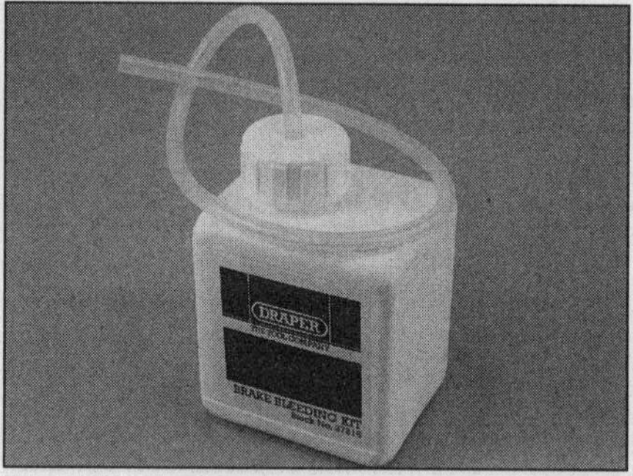

Brake bleeding kit

## Repair and overhaul tool kit

These tools are virtually essential for anyone undertaking any major repairs to a motor vehicle, and are additional to those given in the *Maintenance and minor repair* list. Included in this list is a comprehensive set of sockets. Although these are expensive, they will be found invaluable as they are so versatile - particularly if various drives are included in the set. We recommend the half-inch square-drive type, as this can be used with most proprietary torque wrenches.

The tools in this list will sometimes need to be supplemented by tools from the *Special* list:

☐ *Sockets (or box spanners) to cover range in previous list (including Torx sockets)*
☐ *Reversible ratchet drive (for use with sockets)*
☐ *Extension piece, 250 mm (for use with sockets)*
☐ *Universal joint (for use with sockets)*
☐ *Flexible handle or sliding T "breaker bar" (for use with sockets)*
☐ *Torque wrench (for use with sockets)*
☐ *Self-locking grips*
☐ *Ball pein hammer*
☐ *Soft-faced mallet (plastic or rubber)*
☐ *Screwdrivers:*
*Flat blade - long & sturdy, short (chubby), and narrow (electrician's) types*
*Cross blade – long & sturdy, and short (chubby) types*
☐ *Pliers:*
*Long-nosed*
*Side cutters (electrician's)*
*Circlip (internal and external)*
☐ *Cold chisel - 25 mm*
☐ *Scriber*
☐ *Scraper*
☐ *Centre-punch*
☐ *Pin punch*
☐ *Hacksaw*
☐ *Brake hose clamp*
☐ *Brake/clutch bleeding kit*
☐ *Selection of twist drills*
☐ *Steel rule/straight-edge*
☐ *Allen keys (inc. splined/Torx type)*
☐ *Selection of files*
☐ *Wire brush*
☐ *Axle stands*
☐ *Jack (strong trolley or hydraulic type)*
☐ *Light with extension lead*
☐ *Universal electrical multi-meter*

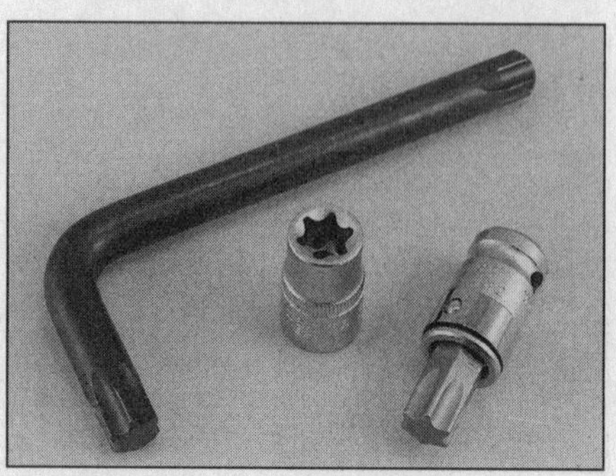
Torx key, socket and bit

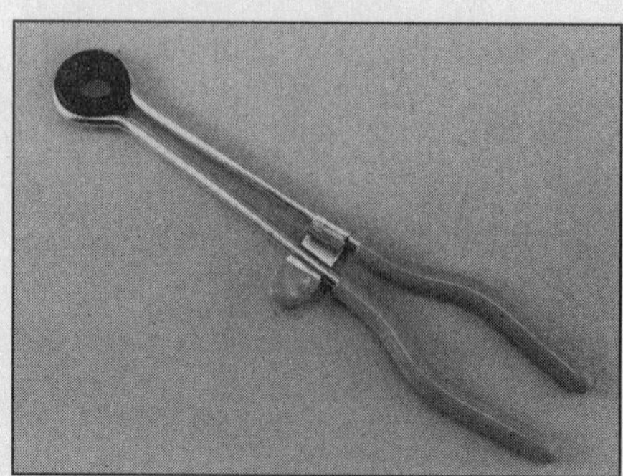
Hose clamp

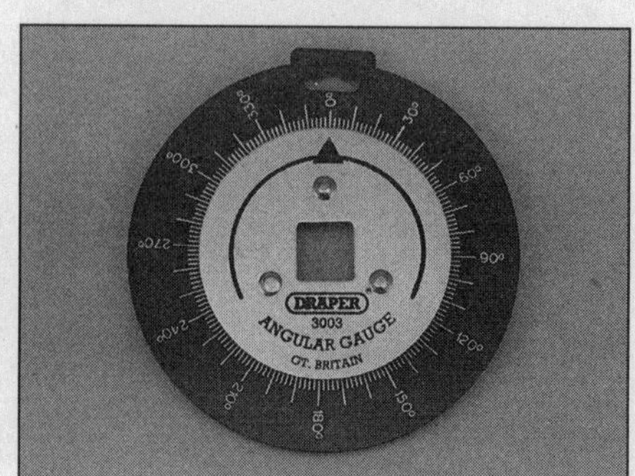

Angular-tightening gauge

## *Special tools*

The tools in this list are those which are not used regularly, are expensive to buy, or which need to be used in accordance with their manufacturers' instructions. Unless relatively difficult mechanical jobs are undertaken frequently, it will not be economic to buy many of these tools. Where this is the case, you could consider clubbing together with friends (or joining a motorists' club) to make a joint purchase, or borrowing the tools against a deposit from a local garage or tool hire specialist. It is worth noting that many of the larger DIY superstores now carry a large range of special tools for hire at modest rates.

The following list contains only those tools and instruments freely available to the public, and not those special tools produced by the vehicle manufacturer specifically for its dealer network. You will find occasional references to these manufacturers' special tools in the text of this manual. Generally, an alternative method of doing the job without the vehicle manufacturers' special tool is given. However, sometimes there is no alternative to using them. Where this is the case and the relevant tool cannot be bought or borrowed, you will have to entrust the work to a dealer.

☐ *Angular-tightening gauge*
☐ *Valve spring compressor*
☐ *Valve grinding tool*
☐ *Piston ring compressor*
☐ *Piston ring removal/installation tool*
☐ *Cylinder bore hone*
☐ *Balljoint separator*
☐ *Coil spring compressors (where applicable)*
☐ *Two/three-legged hub and bearing puller*
☐ *Impact screwdriver*
☐ *Micrometer and/or vernier calipers*
☐ *Dial gauge*
☐ *Stroboscopic timing light*
☐ *Dwell angle meter/tachometer*
☐ *Fault code reader*
☐ *Cylinder compression gauge*
☐ *Hand-operated vacuum pump and gauge*
☐ *Clutch plate alignment set*
☐ *Brake shoe steady spring cup removal tool*
☐ *Bush and bearing removal/installation set*
☐ *Stud extractors*
☐ *Tap and die set*
☐ *Lifting tackle*
☐ *Trolley jack*

## *Buying tools*

Reputable motor accessory shops and superstores often offer excellent quality tools at discount prices, so it pays to shop around.

Remember, you don't have to buy the most expensive items on the shelf, but it is always advisable to steer clear of the very cheap tools. Beware of 'bargains' offered on market stalls or at car boot sales. There are plenty of good tools around at reasonable prices, but always aim to purchase items which meet the relevant national safety standards. If in doubt, ask the proprietor or manager of the shop for advice before making a purchase.

## *Care and maintenance of tools*

Having purchased a reasonable tool kit, it is necessary to keep the tools in a clean and serviceable condition. After use, always wipe off any dirt, grease and metal particles using a clean, dry cloth, before putting the tools away. Never leave them lying around after they have been used. A simple tool rack on the garage or workshop wall for items such as screwdrivers and pliers is a good idea. Store all normal spanners and sockets in a metal box. Any measuring instruments, gauges, meters, etc, must be carefully stored where they cannot be damaged or become rusty.

Take a little care when tools are used. Hammer heads inevitably become marked, and screwdrivers lose the keen edge on their blades from time to time. A little timely attention with emery cloth or a file will soon restore items like this to a good finish.

## *Working facilities*

Not to be forgotten when discussing tools is the workshop itself. If anything more than routine maintenance is to be carried out, a suitable working area becomes essential.

It is appreciated that many an owner-mechanic is forced by circumstances to remove an engine or similar item without the benefit of a garage or workshop. Having done this, any repairs should always be done under the cover of a roof.

Wherever possible, any dismantling should be done on a clean, flat workbench or table at a suitable working height.

Any workbench needs a vice; one with a jaw opening of 100 mm is suitable for most jobs. As mentioned previously, some clean dry storage space is also required for tools, as well as for any lubricants, cleaning fluids, touch-up paints etc, which become necessary.

Another item which may be required, and which has a much more general usage, is an electric drill with a chuck capacity of at least 8 mm. This, together with a good range of twist drills, is virtually essential for fitting accessories.

Last, but not least, always keep a supply of old newspapers and clean, lint-free rags available, and try to keep any working area as clean as possible.

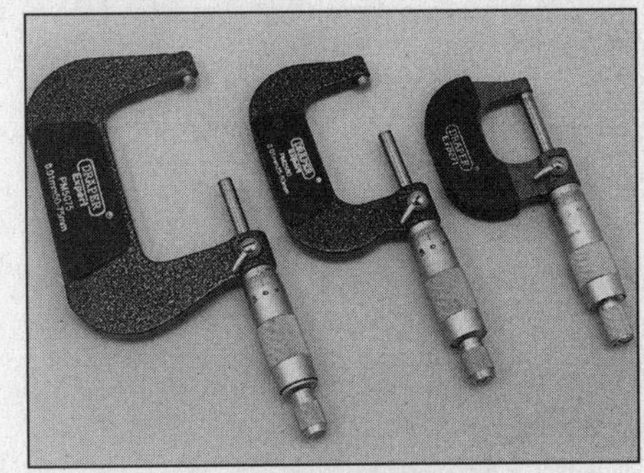

**Micrometers**

**Dial test indicator ("dial gauge")**

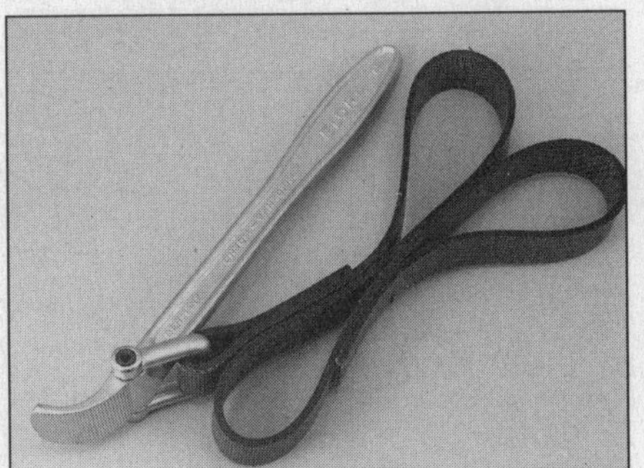

**Strap wrench**

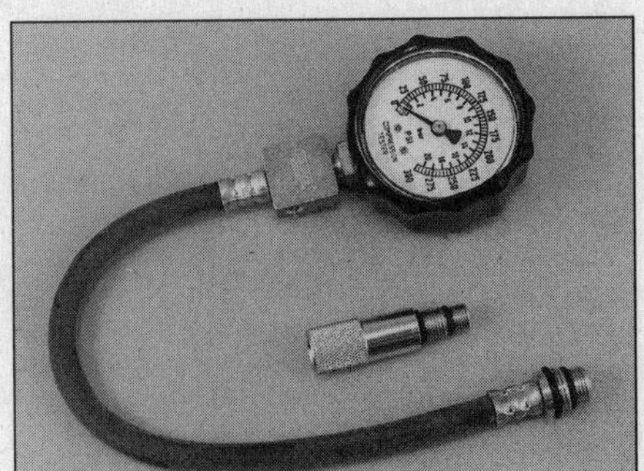

**Compression tester**

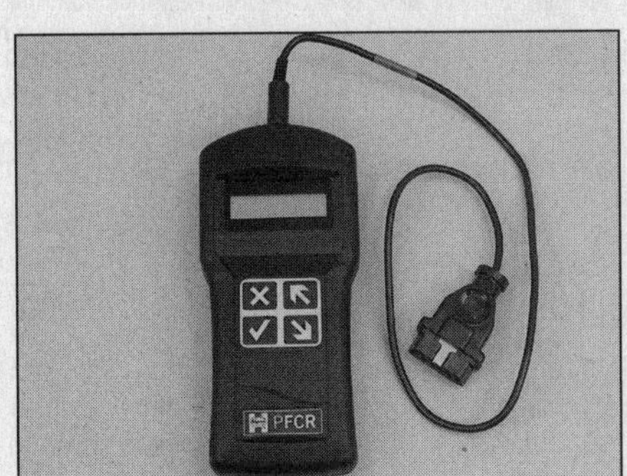


**Fault code reader**

# MOT test checks

This is a guide to getting your vehicle through the MOT test. Obviously it will not be possible to examine the vehicle to the same standard as the professional MOT tester. However, working through the following checks will enable you to identify any problem areas before submitting the vehicle for the test.

Where a testable component is in borderline condition, the tester has discretion in deciding whether to pass or fail it. The basis of such discretion is whether the tester would be happy for a close relative or friend to use the vehicle with the component in that condition. If the vehicle presented is clean and evidently well cared for, the tester may be more inclined to pass a borderline component than if the vehicle is scruffy and apparently neglected.

It has only been possible to summarise the test requirements here, based on the regulations in force at the time of printing. Test standards are becoming increasingly stringent, although there are some exemptions for older vehicles. For full details obtain a copy of the Haynes publication Pass the MOT! (available from stockists of Haynes manuals).

An assistant will be needed to help carry out some of these checks.

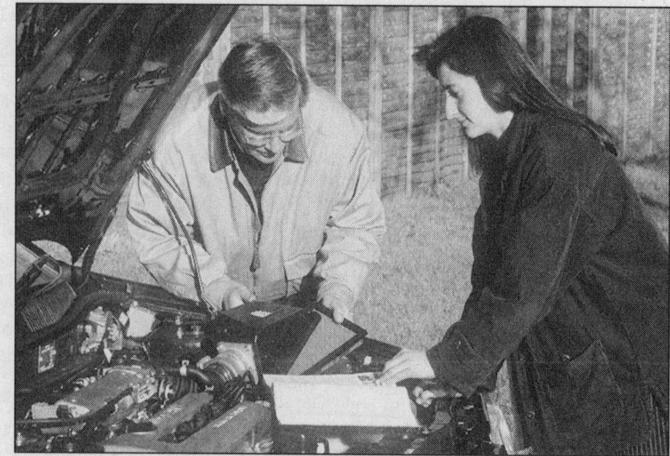

*The checks have been sub-divided into four categories, as follows:*

**1** Checks carried out **FROM THE DRIVER'S SEAT**

**2** Checks carried out **WITH THE VEHICLE ON THE GROUND**

**3** Checks carried out **WITH THE VEHICLE RAISED AND THE WHEELS FREE TO TURN**

**4** Checks carried out on **YOUR VEHICLE'S EXHAUST EMISSION SYSTEM**

## 1 Checks carried out FROM THE DRIVER'S SEAT

### Handbrake

☐ Test the operation of the handbrake. Excessive travel (too many clicks) indicates incorrect brake or cable adjustment.

☐ Check that the handbrake cannot be released by tapping the lever sideways. Check the security of the lever mountings.

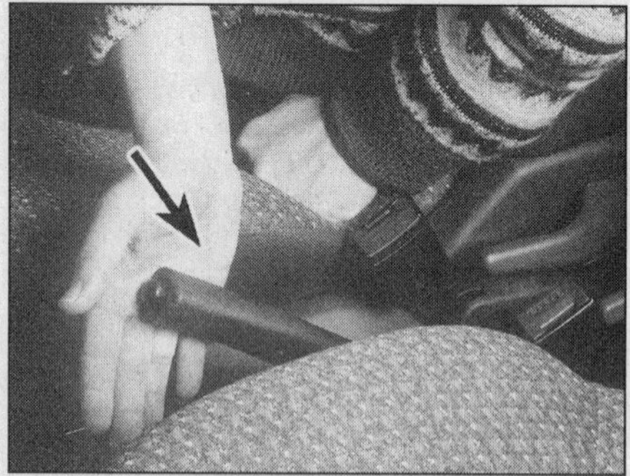

### Footbrake

☐ Depress the brake pedal and check that it does not creep down to the floor, indicating a master cylinder fault. Release the pedal, wait a few seconds, then depress it again. If the pedal travels nearly to the floor before firm resistance is felt, brake adjustment or repair is necessary. If the pedal feels spongy, there is air in the hydraulic system which must be removed by bleeding.

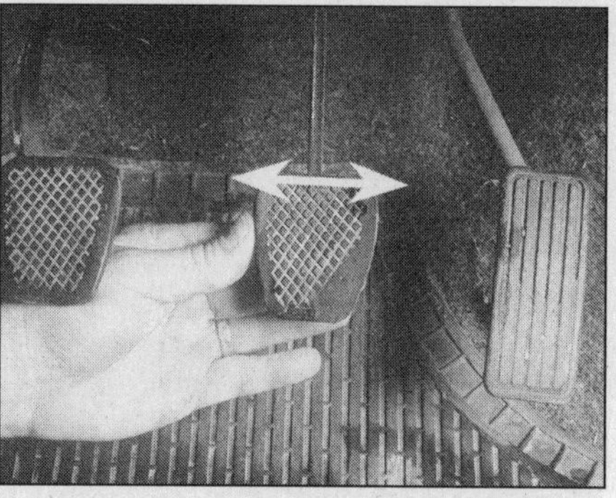

☐ Check that the brake pedal is secure and in good condition. Check also for signs of fluid leaks on the pedal, floor or carpets, which would indicate failed seals in the brake master cylinder.

☐ Check the servo unit (when applicable) by operating the brake pedal several times, then keeping the pedal depressed and starting the engine. As the engine starts, the pedal will move down slightly. If not, the vacuum hose or the servo itself may be faulty.

### Steering wheel and column

☐ Examine the steering wheel for fractures or looseness of the hub, spokes or rim.

☐ Move the steering wheel from side to side and then up and down. Check that the steering wheel is not loose on the column, indicating wear or a loose retaining nut. Continue moving the steering wheel as before, but also turn it slightly from left to right.

☐ Check that the steering wheel is not loose on the column, and that there is no abnormal

movement of the steering wheel, indicating wear in the column support bearings or couplings.

### Windscreen and mirrors

☐ The windscreen must be free of cracks or other significant damage within the driver's field of view. (Small stone chips are acceptable.) Rear view mirrors must be secure, intact, and capable of being adjusted.

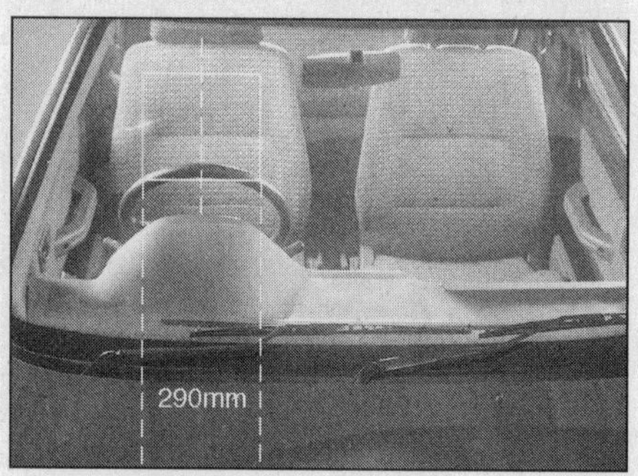

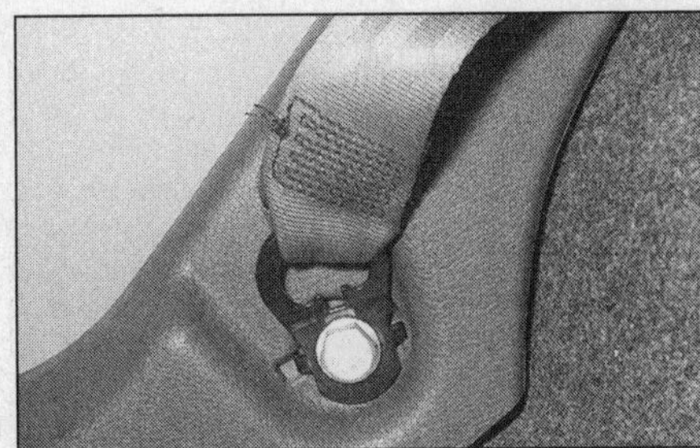

### Seat belts and seats

**Note:** *The following checks are applicable to all seat belts, front and rear.*

☐ Examine the webbing of all the belts (including rear belts if fitted) for cuts, serious fraying or deterioration. Fasten and unfasten each belt to check the buckles. If applicable, check the retracting mechanism. Check the security of all seat belt mountings accessible from inside the vehicle.

☐ The front seats themselves must be securely attached and the backrests must lock in the upright position.

### Doors

☐ Both front doors must be able to be opened and closed from outside and inside, and must latch securely when closed.

## 2 Checks carried out WITH THE VEHICLE ON THE GROUND

### Vehicle identification

☐ Number plates must be in good condition, secure and legible, with letters and numbers correctly spaced – spacing at (A) should be twice that at (B).

☐ The VIN plate and/or homologation plate must be legible.

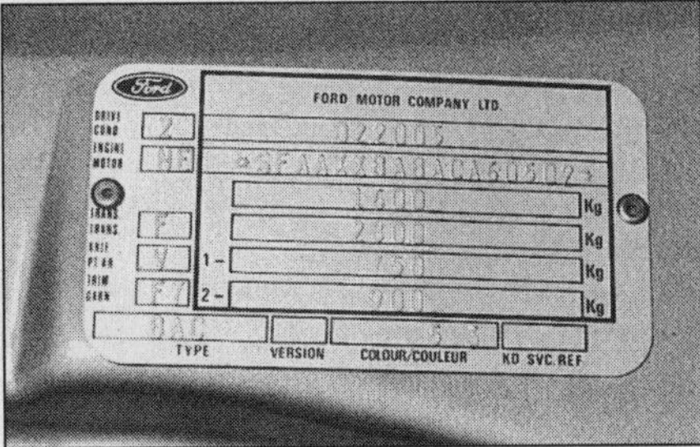


### Electrical equipment

☐ Switch on the ignition and check the operation of the horn.

☐ Check the windscreen washers and wipers, examining the wiper blades; renew damaged or perished blades. Also check the operation of the stop-lights.

☐ Check the operation of the sidelights and number plate lights. The lenses and reflectors must be secure, clean and undamaged.

☐ Check the operation and alignment of the headlights. The headlight reflectors must not be tarnished and the lenses must be undamaged.

☐ Switch on the ignition and check the operation of the direction indicators (including the instrument panel tell-tale) and the hazard warning lights. Operation of the sidelights and stop-lights must not affect the indicators - if it does, the cause is usually a bad earth at the rear light cluster.

☐ Check the operation of the rear foglight(s), including the warning light on the instrument panel or in the switch.

### Footbrake

☐ Examine the master cylinder, brake pipes and servo unit for leaks, loose mountings, corrosion or other damage.

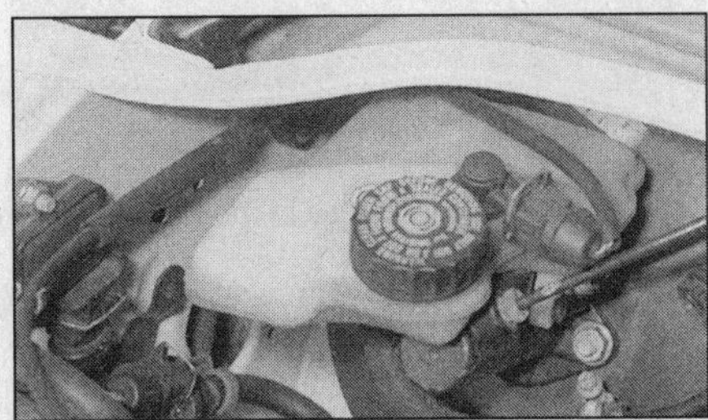

☐ The fluid reservoir must be secure and the fluid level must be between the upper (**A**) and lower (**B**) markings.

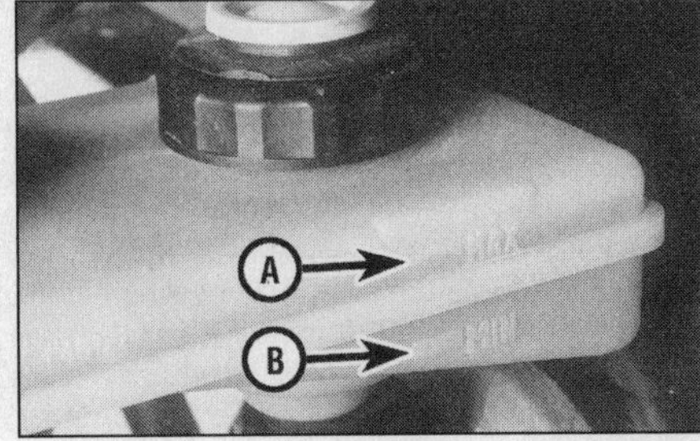


☐ Inspect both front brake flexible hoses for cracks or deterioration of the rubber. Turn the steering from lock to lock, and ensure that the hoses do not contact the wheel, tyre, or any part of the steering or suspension mechanism. With the brake pedal firmly depressed, check the hoses for bulges or leaks under pressure.

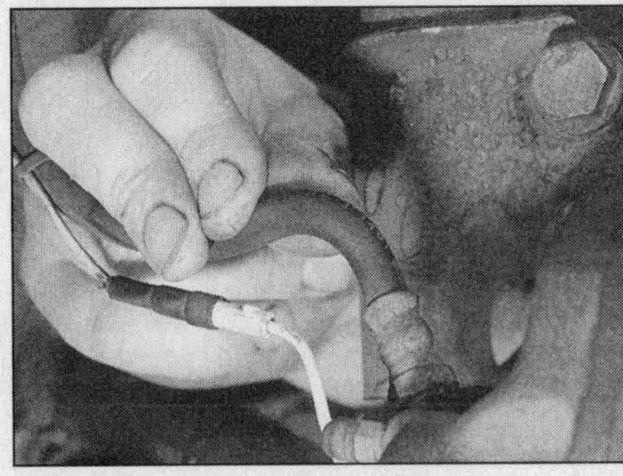

### Steering and suspension

☐ Have your assistant turn the steering wheel from side to side slightly, up to the point where the steering gear just begins to transmit this movement to the roadwheels. Check for excessive free play between the steering wheel and the steering gear, indicating wear or insecurity of the steering column joints, the column-to-steering gear coupling, or the steering gear itself.

☐ Have your assistant turn the steering wheel more vigorously in each direction, so that the roadwheels just begin to turn. As this is done, examine all the steering joints, linkages, fittings and attachments. Renew any component that shows signs of wear or damage. On vehicles with power steering, check the security and condition of the steering pump, drivebelt and hoses.

☐ Check that the vehicle is standing level, and at approximately the correct ride height.

### Shock absorbers

☐ Depress each corner of the vehicle in turn, then release it. The vehicle should rise and then settle in its normal position. If the vehicle continues to rise and fall, the shock absorber is defective. A shock absorber which has seized will also cause the vehicle to fail.

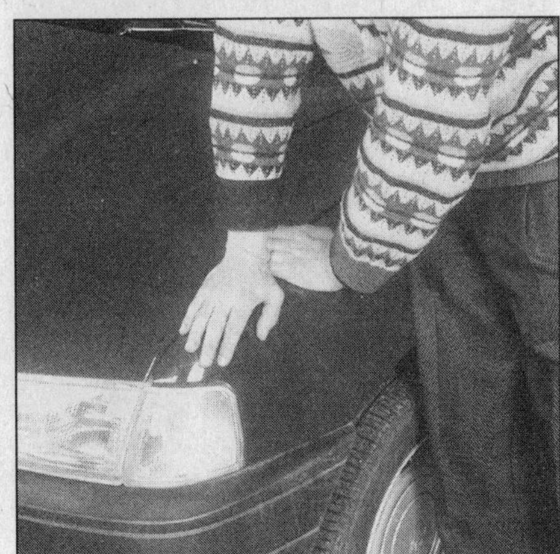

### Exhaust system

☐ Start the engine. With your assistant holding a rag over the tailpipe, check the entire system for leaks. Repair or renew leaking sections.

## 3 Checks carried out WITH THE VEHICLE RAISED AND THE WHEELS FREE TO TURN

***Jack up the front and rear of the vehicle, and securely support it on axle stands. Position the stands clear of the suspension assemblies. Ensure that the wheels are clear of the ground and that the steering can be turned from lock to lock.***

### Steering mechanism

☐ Have your assistant turn the steering from lock to lock. Check that the steering turns smoothly, and that no part of the steering mechanism, including a wheel or tyre, fouls any brake hose or pipe or any part of the body structure.

☐ Examine the steering rack rubber gaiters for damage or insecurity of the retaining clips. If power steering is fitted, check for signs of damage or leakage of the fluid hoses, pipes or connections. Also check for excessive stiffness or binding of the steering, a missing split pin or locking device, or severe corrosion of the body structure within 30 cm of any steering component attachment point.

### Front and rear suspension and wheel bearings

☐ Starting at the front right-hand side, grasp the roadwheel at the 3 o'clock and 9 o'clock positions and shake it vigorously. Check for free play or insecurity at the wheel bearings, suspension balljoints, or suspension mountings, pivots and attachments.

☐ Now grasp the wheel at the 12 o'clock and 6 o'clock positions and repeat the previous inspection. Spin the wheel, and check for roughness or tightness of the front wheel bearing.

☐ If excess free play is suspected at a component pivot point, this can be confirmed by using a large screwdriver or similar tool and levering between the mounting and the component attachment. This will confirm whether the wear is in the pivot bush, its retaining bolt, or in the mounting itself (the bolt holes can often become elongated).

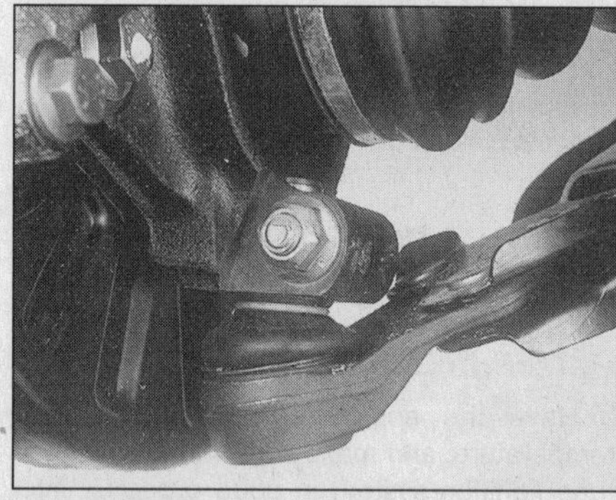

☐ Carry out all the above checks at the other front wheel, and then at both rear wheels.

### Springs and shock absorbers

☐ Examine the suspension struts (when applicable) for serious fluid leakage, corrosion, or damage to the casing. Also check the security of the mounting points.

☐ If coil springs are fitted, check that the spring ends locate in their seats, and that the spring is not corroded, cracked or broken.

☐ If leaf springs are fitted, check that all leaves are intact, that the axle is securely attached to each spring, and that there is no deterioration of the spring eye mountings, bushes, and shackles.

☐ The same general checks apply to vehicles fitted with other suspension types, such as torsion bars, hydraulic displacer units, etc. Ensure that all mountings and attachments are secure, that there are no signs of excessive wear, corrosion or damage, and (on hydraulic types) that there are no fluid leaks or damaged pipes.

☐ Inspect the shock absorbers for signs of serious fluid leakage. Check for wear of the mounting bushes or attachments, or damage to the body of the unit.

### Driveshafts (fwd vehicles only)

☐ Rotate each front wheel in turn and inspect the constant velocity joint gaiters for splits or damage. Also check that each driveshaft is straight and undamaged.

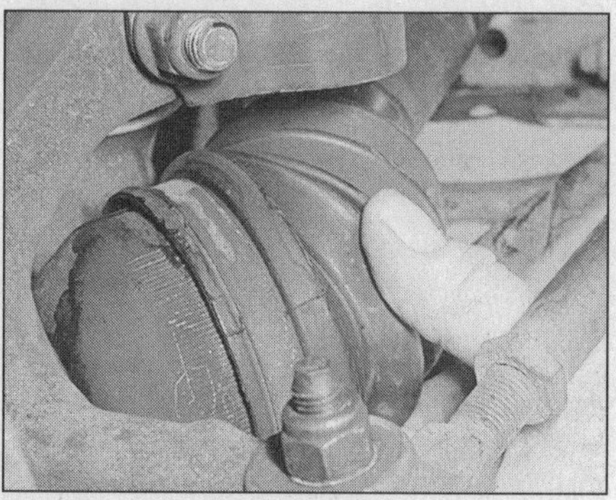

### Braking system

☐ If possible without dismantling, check brake pad wear and disc condition. Ensure that the friction lining material has not worn excessively, (A) and that the discs are not fractured, pitted, scored or badly worn (B).

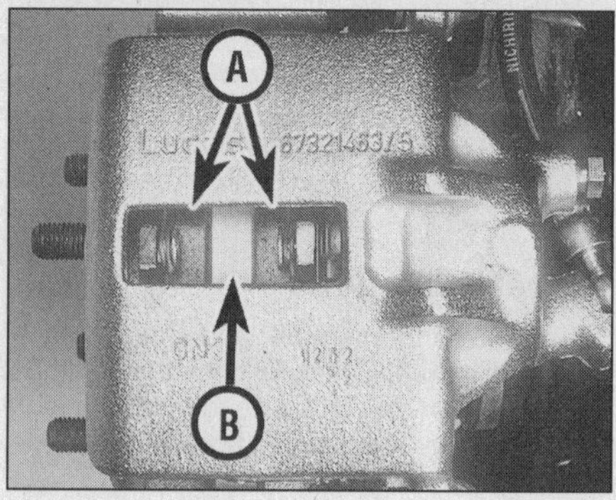


☐ Examine all the rigid brake pipes underneath the vehicle, and the flexible hose(s) at the rear. Look for corrosion, chafing or insecurity of the pipes, and for signs of bulging under pressure, chafing, splits or deterioration of the flexible hoses.

☐ Look for signs of fluid leaks at the brake calipers or on the brake backplates. Repair or renew leaking components.

☐ Slowly spin each wheel, while your assistant depresses and releases the footbrake. Ensure that each brake is operating and does not bind when the pedal is released.

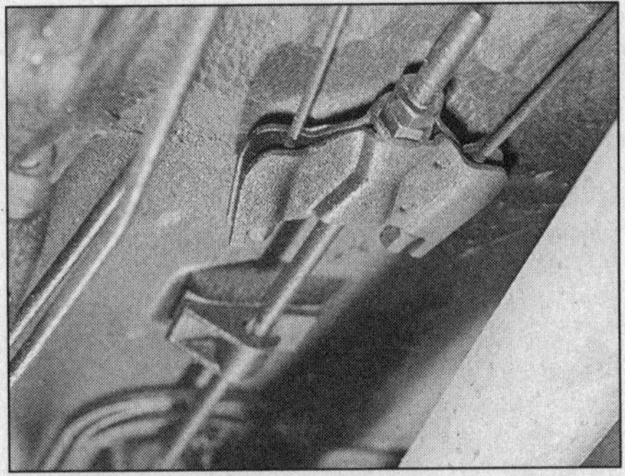

☐ Examine the handbrake mechanism, checking for frayed or broken cables, excessive corrosion, or wear or insecurity of the linkage. Check that the mechanism works on each relevant wheel, and releases fully, without binding.

☐ It is not possible to test brake efficiency without special equipment, but a road test can be carried out later to check that the vehicle pulls up in a straight line.

### Fuel and exhaust systems

☐ Inspect the fuel tank (including the filler cap), fuel pipes, hoses and unions. All components must be secure and free from leaks.

☐ Examine the exhaust system over its entire length, checking for any damaged, broken or missing mountings, security of the retaining clamps and rust or corrosion.

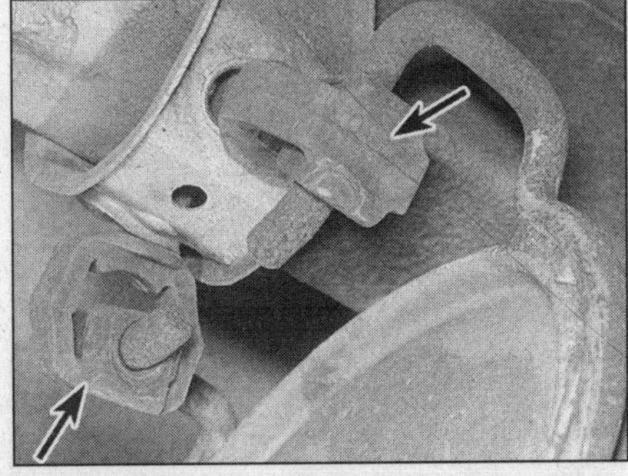

### Wheels and tyres

☐ Examine the sidewalls and tread area of each tyre in turn. Check for cuts, tears, lumps, bulges, separation of the tread, and exposure of the ply or cord due to wear or damage. Check that the tyre bead is correctly seated on the wheel rim, that the valve is sound and

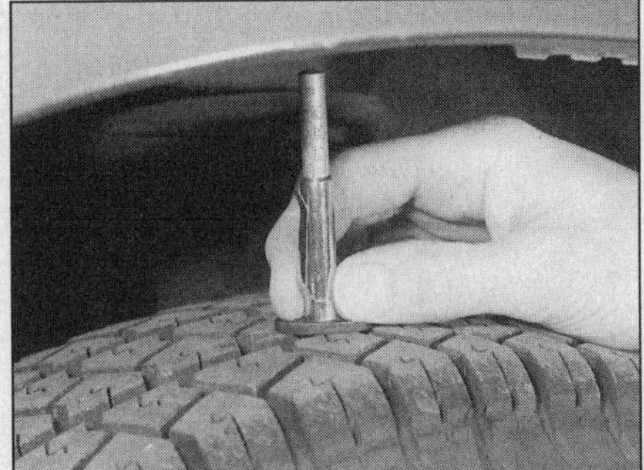

properly seated, and that the wheel is not distorted or damaged.

☐ Check that the tyres are of the correct size for the vehicle, that they are of the same size and type on each axle, and that the pressures are correct.

☐ Check the tyre tread depth. The legal minimum at the time of writing is 1.6 mm over at least three-quarters of the tread width. Abnormal tread wear may indicate incorrect front wheel alignment.

### Body corrosion

☐ Check the condition of the entire vehicle structure for signs of corrosion in load-bearing areas. (These include chassis box sections, side sills, cross-members, pillars, and all suspension, steering, braking system and seat belt mountings and anchorages.) Any corrosion which has seriously reduced the thickness of a load-bearing area is likely to cause the vehicle to fail. In this case professional repairs are likely to be needed.

☐ Damage or corrosion which causes sharp or otherwise dangerous edges to be exposed will also cause the vehicle to fail.

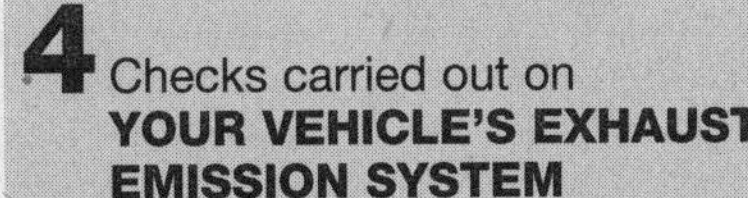

## 4 Checks carried out on YOUR VEHICLE'S EXHAUST EMISSION SYSTEM

### Petrol models

☐ Have the engine at normal operating temperature, and make sure that it is in good tune (ignition system in good order, air filter element clean, etc).

☐ Before any measurements are carried out, raise the engine speed to around 2500 rpm, and hold it at this speed for 20 seconds. Allow the engine speed to return to idle, and watch for smoke emissions from the exhaust tailpipe. If the idle speed is obviously much too high, or if dense blue or clearly-visible black smoke comes from the tailpipe for more than 5 seconds, the vehicle will fail. As a rule of thumb, blue smoke signifies oil being burnt (engine wear) while black smoke signifies unburnt fuel (dirty air cleaner element, or other carburettor or fuel system fault).

☐ An exhaust gas analyser capable of measuring carbon monoxide (CO) and hydrocarbons (HC) is now needed. If such an instrument cannot be hired or borrowed, a local garage may agree to perform the check for a small fee.

### CO emissions (mixture)

☐ At the time of writing, the maximum CO level at idle is 3.5% for vehicles first used after August 1986 and 4.5% for older vehicles. From January 1996 a much tighter limit (around 0.5%) applies to catalyst-equipped vehicles first used from August 1992. If the CO level cannot be reduced far enough to pass the test (and the fuel and ignition systems are otherwise in good condition) then the carburettor is badly worn, or there is some problem in the fuel injection system or catalytic converter (as applicable).

### HC emissions

☐ With the CO emissions within limits, HC emissions must be no more than 1200 ppm (parts per million). If the vehicle fails this test at idle, it can be re-tested at around 2000 rpm; if the HC level is then 1200 ppm or less, this counts as a pass.

☐ Excessive HC emissions can be caused by oil being burnt, but they are more likely to be due to unburnt fuel.

### Diesel models

☐ The only emission test applicable to Diesel engines is the measuring of exhaust smoke density. The test involves accelerating the engine several times to its maximum unloaded speed.

**Note:** *It is of the utmost importance that the engine timing belt is in good condition before the test is carried out.*

☐ Excessive smoke can be caused by a dirty air cleaner element. Otherwise, professional advice may be needed to find the cause.

### Engine

- ☐ Engine fails to rotate when attempting to start
- ☐ Engine rotates, but will not start
- ☐ Engine difficult to start when cold
- ☐ Engine difficult to start when hot
- ☐ Starter motor noisy or excessively-rough in engagement
- ☐ Engine starts, but stops immediately
- ☐ Engine idles erratically
- ☐ Engine misfires at idle speed
- ☐ Engine misfires throughout the driving speed range
- ☐ Engine hesitates on acceleration
- ☐ Engine stalls
- ☐ Engine lacks power
- ☐ Engine backfires
- ☐ Oil pressure warning light illuminated with engine running
- ☐ Engine runs-on after switching off
- ☐ Engine noises

### Cooling system

- ☐ Overheating
- ☐ Overcooling
- ☐ External coolant leakage
- ☐ Internal coolant leakage
- ☐ Corrosion

### Fuel and exhaust systems

- ☐ Excessive fuel consumption
- ☐ Fuel leakage and/or fuel odour
- ☐ Excessive noise or fumes from exhaust system

### Clutch

- ☐ Pedal travels to floor - no pressure or very little resistance
- ☐ Clutch fails to disengage (unable to select gears)
- ☐ Clutch slips (engine speed increases, with no increase in vehicle speed)
- ☐ Judder as clutch is engaged
- ☐ Noise when depressing or releasing clutch pedal

### Manual transmission

- ☐ Noisy in neutral with engine running
- ☐ Noisy in one particular gear
- ☐ Difficulty engaging gears
- ☐ Jumps out of gear
- ☐ Vibration
- ☐ Lubricant leaks

### Automatic transmission

- ☐ Fluid leakage
- ☐ Transmission fluid brown, or has burned smell
- ☐ General gear selection problems
- ☐ Transmission will not downshift (kickdown) with accelerator fully depressed
- ☐ Engine will not start in any gear, or starts in gears other than Park or Neutral
- ☐ Transmission slips, shifts roughly, is noisy, or has no drive in forward or reverse gears

### Driveshafts

- ☐ Clicking or knocking noise on turns (at slow speed on full-lock)
- ☐ Vibration when accelerating or decelerating

### Braking system

- ☐ Vehicle pulls to one side under braking
- ☐ Noise (grinding or high-pitched squeal) when brakes applied
- ☐ Excessive brake pedal travel
- ☐ Brake pedal feels spongy when depressed
- ☐ Excessive brake pedal effort required to stop vehicle
- ☐ Judder felt through brake pedal or steering wheel when braking
- ☐ Brakes binding
- ☐ Rear wheels locking under normal braking

### Suspension and steering systems

- ☐ Vehicle pulls to one side
- ☐ Wheel wobble and vibration
- ☐ Excessive pitching and/or rolling around corners, or during braking
- ☐ Wandering or general instability
- ☐ Excessively-stiff steering
- ☐ Excessive play in steering
- ☐ Lack of power assistance
- ☐ Tyre wear excessive

### Electrical system

- ☐ Battery will not hold a charge for more than a few days
- ☐ Ignition/no-charge warning light remains illuminated with engine running
- ☐ Ignition/no-charge warning light fails to come on
- ☐ Lights inoperative
- ☐ Instrument readings inaccurate or erratic
- ☐ Horn inoperative, or unsatisfactory in operation
- ☐ Windscreen/tailgate wipers inoperative, or unsatisfactory in operation
- ☐ Windscreen/tailgate washers inoperative, or unsatisfactory in operation
- ☐ Electric windows inoperative, or unsatisfactory in operation
- ☐ Central locking system inoperative, or unsatisfactory in operation

## Introduction

The vehicle owner who does his or her own maintenance according to the recommended service schedules should not have to use this section of the manual very often. Modern component reliability is such that, provided those items subject to wear or deterioration are inspected or renewed at the specified intervals, sudden failure is comparatively rare. Faults do not usually just happen as a result of sudden failure, but develop over a period of time. Major mechanical failures in particular are usually preceded by characteristic symptoms over hundreds or even thousands of miles. Those components which do occasionally fail without warning are often small and easily carried in the vehicle.

With any fault-finding, the first step is to decide where to begin investigations. Sometimes this is obvious, but on other occasions, a little detective work will be necessary. The owner who makes half a dozen haphazard adjustments or replacements may be successful in curing a fault (or its symptoms), but will be none the wiser if the fault recurs, and ultimately may have spent more time and money than was necessary. A calm and logical approach will be found to be more satisfactory in the long run. Always take into account any warning signs or abnormalities that may have been noticed in the period preceding the fault - power loss, high or low gauge readings, unusual smells, etc - and remember that failure of components such as fuses or spark plugs may only be pointers to some underlying fault.

These pages provide an easy-reference guide to the more common problems which may occur during the vehicle's life. These problems and their possible causes are grouped under headings such as Engine, Cooling system, etc. The Chapter and/or Section which deals with the problem is also shown in brackets. Whatever the fault, certain basic principles apply. These are as follows:

*Verify the fault.* This is simply a matter of being sure you know exactly what the symptoms are before starting work. This is particularly important if you are investigating a fault for someone else, who may not have described it very accurately.

*Don't overlook the obvious.* For example, if it won't start, is there fuel in the tank? (Don't take anyone else's word on this particular point, and don't trust the fuel gauge either!) If an electrical fault is indicated, look for loose or broken wires before digging out the test gear.

*Cure the disease, not the symptom.* Substituting a flat battery with a fully-charged one will get you off the hard shoulder, but if the underlying cause is not attended to, the new battery will go the same way. Similarly, changing oil-fouled spark plugs (petrol models) for a new set will get you moving again, but remember that the reason for the fouling (if it wasn't simply an incorrect grade of plug) will have to be established and corrected.

*Don't take anything for granted.* Particularly, don't forget that a new component may itself be defective (especially if its been rattling around in the boot for months), and don't leave components out of a fault diagnosis sequence just because they are new or recently-fitted. When you do finally diagnose a difficult fault, you'll probably realise that all the evidence was there from the start.

# Engine

### *Engine fails to rotate when attempting to start*

- ☐ Battery terminal connections loose or corroded (*Weekly checks*).
- ☐ Battery discharged or faulty (Chapter 5A).
- ☐ Broken, loose or disconnected wiring in the starting circuit (Chapter 5A).
- ☐ Automatic transmission not in P or N (Chapter 7B)
- ☐ Defective starter solenoid or switch (Chapter 5A).
- ☐ Defective starter motor (Chapter 5A).
- ☐ Starter pinion or flywheel ring gear teeth loose or broken (Chapters 2A, 2B, 2C and 5A).
- ☐ Engine earth strap broken or disconnected (Chapter 5A).

### *Engine rotates, but will not start*

- ☐ Fuel tank empty.
- ☐ Battery discharged (engine rotates slowly) (Chapter 5A).
- ☐ Battery terminal connections loose or corroded (*Weekly checks*).
- ☐ Immobiliser fault (Chapter 12).
- ☐ Ignition components damp or damaged - petrol models (Chapters 1 and 5B).
- ☐ Ignition timing incorrect (Chapter 5B)
- ☐ Broken, loose or disconnected wiring in the ignition circuit - petrol models (Chapter 5B).
- ☐ Worn, faulty or incorrectly-gapped spark plugs - petrol models (Chapter 1).
- ☐ Preheating system faulty - diesel models (Chapter 5C).
- ☐ Fuel injection system faulty - petrol models (Chapter 4A or 4B).
- ☐ Fuel cut-off (stop) solenoid faulty - diesel models (Chapter 4C).
- ☐ Air in fuel system - diesel models (Chapter 4C).
- ☐ Major mechanical failure (eg camshaft drive) (Chapter 2A, 2B or 2C).

### *Engine difficult to start when cold*

- ☐ Battery discharged (Chapter 5A).
- ☐ Ignition timing incorrect (Chapter 5B)
- ☐ Battery terminal connections loose or corroded (*Weekly checks*).
- ☐ Worn, faulty or incorrectly-gapped spark plugs - petrol models (Chapter 1).
- ☐ Preheating system faulty - diesel models (Chapter 5C).
- ☐ Fuel injection system fault - petrol models (Chapter 4A or 4B).
- ☐ Other ignition system fault - petrol models (Chapter 5B).
- ☐ Low cylinder compressions (Chapter 2A or 2B).

### *Engine difficult to start when hot*

- ☐ Air filter element dirty or clogged (Chapter 1).
- ☐ Fuel injection system fault - petrol models (Chapter 4A or 4B).
- ☐ Low cylinder compressions (Chapter 2A or 2B).
- ☐ Ignition timing incorrect (Chapter 5B)

### *Starter motor noisy or excessively-rough in engagement*

- ☐ Starter pinion or flywheel ring gear teeth loose or broken (Chapters 2A, 2B and 5A).
- ☐ Starter motor mounting bolts loose or missing (Chapter 5A).
- ☐ Starter motor internal components worn or damaged (Chapter 5A).

### *Engine starts, but stops immediately*

- ☐ Loose or faulty electrical connections in the ignition circuit - petrol models (Chapter 5B).
- ☐ Vacuum leak at the throttle body or inlet manifold - petrol models (Chapter 4A or 4B).
- ☐ Blocked injector/fuel injection system fault - petrol models (Chapter 4A or 4B).

### *Engine idles erratically*

- ☐ Air filter element clogged (Chapter 1).
- ☐ Vacuum leak at the throttle body, inlet manifold or associated hoses - petrol models (Chapter 4A or 4B).
- ☐ Worn, faulty or incorrectly-gapped spark plugs - petrol models (Chapter 1).
- ☐ Uneven or low cylinder compressions (Chapter 2A or 2B).
- ☐ Camshaft lobes worn (Chapter 2A or 2B).
- ☐ Timing belt incorrectly tensioned (Chapter 2A or 2B).
- ☐ Blocked injector/fuel injection system fault - petrol models (Chapter 4A or 4B).
- ☐ Faulty injector(s) - diesel models (Chapter 4C).

### *Engine misfires at idle speed*

- ☐ Worn, faulty or incorrectly-gapped spark plugs - petrol models (Chapter 1).
- ☐ Faulty spark plug HT leads - petrol models (Chapter 5B).
- ☐ Vacuum leak at the throttle body, inlet manifold or associated hoses - petrol models (Chapter 4A or 4B).
- ☐ Blocked injector/fuel injection system fault - petrol models (Chapter 4A or 4B).
- ☐ Faulty injector(s) - diesel models (Chapter 4C).
- ☐ Distributor cap cracked or tracking internally - petrol models (where applicable) (Chapter 5B).
- ☐ Uneven or low cylinder compressions (Chapter 2A or 2B).
- ☐ Disconnected, leaking, or perished crankcase ventilation hoses (Chapter 4D).

### *Engine misfires throughout the driving speed range*

- ☐ Fuel filter choked (Chapter 1).
- ☐ Fuel pump faulty, or delivery pressure low - petrol models (Chapter 4A or 4B).
- ☐ Fuel tank vent blocked, or fuel pipes restricted (Chapter 4A, 4B or 4C).
- ☐ Vacuum leak at the throttle body, inlet manifold or associated hoses - petrol models (Chapter 4A or 4B).
- ☐ Worn, faulty or incorrectly-gapped spark plugs - petrol models (Chapter 1).
- ☐ Faulty spark plug HT leads - petrol models (Chapter 5B).
- ☐ Faulty injector(s) - diesel models (Chapter 4C).
- ☐ Distributor cap cracked or tracking internally - petrol models (where applicable) (Chapter 5B).
- ☐ Faulty ignition coil - petrol models (Chapter 5B).
- ☐ Uneven or low cylinder compressions (Chapter 2A or 2B).
- ☐ Blocked injector/fuel injection system fault - petrol models (Chapter 4A or 4B).

# Engine (continued)

### Engine hesitates on acceleration

- ☐ Worn, faulty or incorrectly-gapped spark plugs - petrol models (Chapter 1).
- ☐ Vacuum leak at the throttle body, inlet manifold or associated hoses - petrol models (Chapter 4A or 4B).
- ☐ Blocked injector/fuel injection system fault - petrol models (Chapter 4A or 4B).
- ☐ Faulty injector(s) - diesel models (Chapter 4C).

### Engine stalls

- ☐ Vacuum leak at the throttle body, inlet manifold or associated hoses - petrol models (Chapter 4A or 4B).
- ☐ Fuel filter choked (Chapter 1).
- ☐ Fuel pump faulty, or delivery pressure low - petrol models (Chapter 4A or 4B).
- ☐ Fuel tank vent blocked, or fuel pipes restricted (Chapter 4A, 4B or 4C).
- ☐ Blocked injector/fuel injection system fault - petrol models (Chapter 4A or 4B).
- ☐ Faulty injector(s) - diesel models (Chapter 4C).

### Engine lacks power

- ☐ Timing belt incorrectly fitted or tensioned (Chapter 2A or 2B).
- ☐ Fuel filter choked (Chapter 1).
- ☐ Ignition timing incorrect (Chapter 5B)
- ☐ Fuel pump faulty, or delivery pressure low - petrol models (Chapter 4A or 4B).
- ☐ Uneven or low cylinder compressions (Chapter 2A or 2B).
- ☐ Worn, faulty or incorrectly-gapped spark plugs - petrol models (Chapter 1).
- ☐ Vacuum leak at the throttle body, inlet manifold or associated hoses - petrol models (Chapter 4A or 4B).
- ☐ Blocked injector/fuel injection system fault - petrol models (Chapter 4A or 4B).
- ☐ Faulty injector(s) - diesel models (Chapter 4C).
- ☐ Injection pump timing incorrect - diesel models (Chapter 4C).
- ☐ Brakes binding (Chapters 1 and 9).
- ☐ Clutch slipping (Chapter 6).

### Engine backfires

- ☐ Timing belt incorrectly fitted or tensioned (Chapter 2A or 2B).
- ☐ Vacuum leak at the throttle body, inlet manifold or associated hoses - petrol models (Chapter 4A or 4B).
- ☐ Blocked injector/fuel injection system fault - petrol models (Chapter 4A or 4B).
- ☐ Ignition timing incorrect (Chapter 5B)

### Oil pressure warning light illuminated with engine running

- ☐ Low oil level, or incorrect oil grade (*Weekly checks*).
- ☐ Worn engine bearings and/or oil pump (Chapter 2C).
- ☐ High engine operating temperature (Chapter 3).
- ☐ Oil pressure relief valve defective (Chapter 2A or 2B).
- ☐ Oil pick-up strainer clogged (Chapter 2A or 2B).

### Engine runs-on after switching off

- ☐ Excessive carbon build-up in engine (Chapter 2C).
- ☐ High engine operating temperature (Chapter 3).
- ☐ Fuel injection system fault - petrol models (Chapter 4A or 4B).
- ☐ Faulty fuel cut-off (stop) solenoid - diesel models (Chapter 4C).

### Engine noises

#### Pre-ignition (pinking) or knocking during acceleration or under load

- ☐ Ignition timing incorrect/ignition system fault - petrol models (Chapter 5B).
- ☐ Incorrect grade of spark plug - petrol models (Chapter 1).
- ☐ Incorrect grade of fuel (Chapter 1).
- ☐ Vacuum leak at the throttle body, inlet manifold or associated hoses - petrol models (Chapter 4A or 4B).
- ☐ Excessive carbon build-up in engine (Chapter 2C).
- ☐ Blocked injector/fuel injection system fault - petrol models (Chapter 4A or 4B).

#### Whistling or wheezing noises

- ☐ Leaking inlet manifold or throttle body gasket - petrol models (Chapter 4A or 4B).
- ☐ Leaking exhaust manifold gasket or pipe-to-manifold joint (Chapter 4A, 4B or 4C).
- ☐ Leaking vacuum hose (Chapters 4, 5B and 9).
- ☐ Blowing cylinder head gasket (Chapter 2A or 2B).

#### Tapping or rattling noises

- ☐ Worn hydraulic tappet or camshaft (Chapter 2A or 2B).
- ☐ Ancillary component fault (water pump, alternator, etc) (Chapters 3, 5A, etc).

#### Knocking or thumping noises

- ☐ Worn big-end bearings (regular heavy knocking, perhaps less under load) (Chapter 2C).
- ☐ Worn main bearings (rumbling and knocking, perhaps worsening under load) (Chapter 2C).
- ☐ Piston slap (most noticeable when cold) (Chapter 2C).
- ☐ Ancillary component fault (water pump, alternator, etc) (Chapters 3, 5A, etc).

# Cooling system

### Overheating

- ☐ Insufficient coolant in system (*Weekly checks*).
- ☐ Auxiliary drivebelt broken or drivebelt tensioner faulty (Chapter 1 or 2)
- ☐ Thermostat faulty (Chapter 3).
- ☐ Radiator core blocked, or grille restricted (Chapter 3).
- ☐ Electric cooling fan or thermoswitch faulty (Chapter 3).
- ☐ Pressure cap faulty (Chapter 3).
- ☐ Ignition timing incorrect/ignition system fault - petrol models (Chapter 5B).
- ☐ Inaccurate temperature gauge sender unit (Chapter 3).
- ☐ Airlock in cooling system (Chapter 1).

### Overcooling

- ☐ Thermostat faulty (Chapter 3).
- ☐ Inaccurate temperature gauge sender unit (Chapter 3).

### External coolant leakage

- ☐ Deteriorated or damaged hoses or hose clips (Chapter 1).
- ☐ Radiator core or heater matrix leaking (Chapter 3).
- ☐ Pressure cap faulty (Chapter 3).
- ☐ Water pump seal leaking (Chapter 3).
- ☐ Boiling due to overheating (Chapter 3).
- ☐ Core plug leaking (Chapter 2C).

### Internal coolant leakage

- ☐ Leaking cylinder head gasket (Chapter 2A or 2B).
- ☐ Cracked cylinder head or cylinder bore (Chapter 2A or 2B).

### Corrosion

- ☐ Infrequent draining and flushing (Chapter 1).
- ☐ Incorrect coolant mixture or inappropriate coolant type (Chapter 1).

# Fuel and exhaust systems

### *Excessive fuel consumption*

- ☐ Air filter element dirty or clogged (Chapter 1).
- ☐ Fuel injection system fault - petrol models (Chapter 4A or 4B).
- ☐ Faulty injector(s) - diesel models (Chapter 4C).
- ☐ Ignition timing incorrect/ignition system fault - petrol models (Chapter 5B).
- ☐ Tyres under-inflated (*Weekly checks*).
- ☐ Brakes binding (Chapter 9).

### *Fuel leakage and/or fuel odour*

- ☐ Damaged or corroded fuel tank, pipes or connections (Chapter 4).

### *Excessive noise or fumes from exhaust system*

- ☐ Leaking exhaust system or manifold joints (Chapters 1 and 4).
- ☐ Leaking, corroded or damaged silencers or pipe (Chapters 1 and 4).
- ☐ Broken mountings causing body or suspension contact (Chapter 1).

# Clutch

### *Pedal travels to floor - no pressure or very little resistance*

- ☐ Broken clutch cable (Chapter 6).
- ☐ Cable automatic adjuster faulty, or cable out of adjustment (Chapter 6).
- ☐ Broken clutch release bearing or fork (Chapter 6).
- ☐ Broken diaphragm spring in clutch pressure plate (Chapter 6).

### *Clutch fails to disengage (unable to select gears)*

- ☐ Cable automatic adjuster faulty, or cable out of adjustment (Chapter 6).
- ☐ Clutch disc sticking on gearbox input shaft splines (Chapter 6).
- ☐ Clutch disc sticking to flywheel or pressure plate (Chapter 6).
- ☐ Faulty pressure plate assembly (Chapter 6).
- ☐ Clutch release mechanism worn or incorrectly assembled (Chapter 6).

### *Clutch slips (engine speed increases, with no increase in vehicle speed)*

- ☐ Cable automatic adjuster faulty, or cable out of adjustment (Chapter 6).
- ☐ Clutch disc linings excessively worn (Chapter 6).
- ☐ Clutch disc linings contaminated with oil or grease (Chapter 6).
- ☐ Faulty pressure plate or weak diaphragm spring (Chapter 6).

### *Judder as clutch is engaged*

- ☐ Clutch disc linings contaminated with oil or grease (Chapter 6).
- ☐ Clutch disc linings excessively worn (Chapter 6).
- ☐ Clutch cable sticking or frayed - cable-operated clutch (Chapter 6).
- ☐ Faulty or distorted pressure plate or diaphragm spring (Chapter 6).
- ☐ Worn or loose engine or gearbox mountings (Chapter 2A or 2B).
- ☐ Clutch disc hub or gearbox input shaft splines worn (Chapter 6).

### *Noise when depressing or releasing clutch pedal*

- ☐ Worn clutch release bearing (Chapter 6).
- ☐ Worn or dry clutch pedal bushes (Chapter 6).
- ☐ Faulty pressure plate assembly (Chapter 6).
- ☐ Pressure plate diaphragm spring broken (Chapter 6).
- ☐ Broken clutch disc cushioning springs (Chapter 6).

# Manual transmission

### *Noisy in neutral with engine running*

- ☐ Input shaft bearings worn (noise apparent with clutch pedal released, but not when depressed) (Chapter 7A).*
- ☐ Clutch release bearing worn (noise apparent with clutch pedal depressed, possibly less when released) (Chapter 6).

### *Noisy in one particular gear*

- ☐ Worn, damaged or chipped gear teeth (Chapter 7A).*

### *Difficulty engaging gears*

- ☐ Clutch fault (Chapter 6).
- ☐ Worn or damaged gearchange linkage/cable (Chapter 7A).
- ☐ Incorrectly-adjusted gearchange linkage/cable (Chapter 7A).
- ☐ Worn synchroniser units (Chapter 7A).*

### *Jumps out of gear*

- ☐ Worn or damaged gearchange linkage/cable (Chapter 7A).
- ☐ Incorrectly-adjusted gearchange linkage/cable (Chapter 7A).
- ☐ Worn synchroniser units (Chapter 7A).*
- ☐ Worn selector forks (Chapter 7A).*

### *Vibration*

- ☐ Lack of oil (Chapter 1).
- ☐ Worn bearings (Chapter 7A).*

### *Lubricant leaks*

- ☐ Leaking differential output oil seal (Chapter 7A).
- ☐ Leaking housing joint (Chapter 7A).*
- ☐ Leaking input shaft oil seal (Chapter 7A).*

**Although the corrective action necessary to remedy the symptoms described is beyond the scope of the home mechanic, the above information should be helpful in isolating the cause of the condition, so that the owner can communicate clearly with a professional mechanic.*

# Automatic transmission

**Note:** *Due to the complexity of the automatic transmission, it is difficult for the home mechanic to properly diagnose and service this unit. For problems other than the following, the vehicle should be taken to a dealer service department or automatic transmission specialist. Do not be too hasty in removing the transmission if a fault is suspected, as most of the testing is carried out with the unit still fitted.*

### Fluid leakage

- ☐ Automatic transmission fluid is usually dark in colour. Fluid leaks should not be confused with engine oil, which can easily be blown onto the transmission by airflow.
- ☐ To determine the source of a leak, first remove all built-up dirt and grime from the transmission housing and surrounding areas using a degreasing agent, or by steam-cleaning. Drive the vehicle at low speed, so airflow will not blow the leak far from its source. Raise and support the vehicle, and determine where the leak is coming from.

### General gear selection problems

- ☐ Chapter 7B deals with checking and adjusting the selector cable on automatic transmissions. The following are common problems which may be caused by a poorly-adjusted cable:
  - *a) Engine starting in gears other than Park or Neutral.*
  - *b) Indicator panel indicating a gear other than the one actually being used.*
  - *c) Vehicle moves when in Park or Neutral.*
  - *d) Poor gear shift quality or erratic gear changes.*
- ☐ Refer to Chapter 7B for the selector cable adjustment procedure.

### Transmission will not downshift (kickdown) with accelerator pedal fully depressed

- ☐ Low transmission fluid level (Chapter 1).
- ☐ Incorrect selector cable adjustment (Chapter 7B).

### Engine will not start in any gear, or starts in gears other than Park or Neutral

- ☐ Incorrect selector cable adjustment (Chapter 7B).

### Transmission slips, shifts roughly, is noisy, or has no drive in forward or reverse gears

- ☐ There are many probable causes for the above problems, but unless there is a very obvious reason (such as a loose or corroded wiring plug connection on or near the transmission), the car should be taken to a VW dealer for the fault to be diagnosed. The transmission control unit incorporates a self-diagnosis facility, and any fault codes can quickly be read and interpreted by a VW dealer with the proper diagnostic equipment.

# Driveshafts

### Clicking or knocking noise on turns (at slow speed on full-lock)

- ☐ Lack of constant velocity joint lubricant, possibly due to damaged gaiter (Chapter 8).
- ☐ Worn outer constant velocity joint (Chapter 8).

### Vibration when accelerating or decelerating

- ☐ Worn inner constant velocity joint (Chapter 8).
- ☐ Bent or distorted driveshaft (Chapter 8).

# Braking system

**Note:** *Before assuming that a brake problem exists, make sure that the tyres are in good condition and correctly inflated, that the front wheel alignment is correct, the front wheels are balanced, and that the vehicle is not loaded with weight in an unequal manner. Apart from checking the condition of all pipe and hose connections, any faults occurring on the anti-lock braking system should be referred to a VW dealer for diagnosis.*

### Vehicle pulls to one side under braking

- ☐ Worn, defective, damaged or contaminated brake pads/shoes on one side (Chapters 1 and 9).
- ☐ Seized or partially-seized front brake caliper/wheel cylinder piston (Chapters 1 and 9).
- ☐ A mixture of brake pad/shoe lining materials fitted between sides (Chapters 1 and 9).
- ☐ Brake caliper or backplate mounting bolts loose (Chapter 9).
- ☐ Worn or damaged steering or suspension components (Chapters 1 and 10).

### Noise (grinding or high-pitched squeal) when brakes applied

- ☐ Brake pad or shoe friction lining material worn down to metal backing (Chapters 1 and 9).
- ☐ Excessive corrosion of brake disc or drum. (May be apparent after the vehicle has been standing for some time (Chapters 1 and 9).
- ☐ Foreign object (stone chipping, etc) trapped between brake disc and shield (Chapters 1 and 9).

### Excessive brake pedal travel

- ☐ Inoperative rear brake self-adjust mechanism - drum brakes (Chapters 1 and 9).
- ☐ Faulty master cylinder (Chapter 9).
- ☐ Air in hydraulic system (Chapters 1 and 9).
- ☐ Faulty vacuum servo unit (Chapter 9).

### Brake pedal feels spongy when depressed

- ☐ Air in hydraulic system (Chapters 1 and 9).
- ☐ Deteriorated flexible rubber brake hoses (Chapters 1 and 9).
- ☐ Master cylinder mounting nuts loose (Chapter 9).
- ☐ Faulty master cylinder (Chapter 9).

### Excessive brake pedal effort required to stop vehicle

- ☐ Faulty vacuum servo unit (Chapter 9).
- ☐ Faulty vacuum pump - diesel models (Chapter 9).
- ☐ Disconnected, damaged or insecure brake servo vacuum hose (Chapter 9).
- ☐ Primary or secondary hydraulic circuit failure (Chapter 9).
- ☐ Seized brake caliper or wheel cylinder piston(s) (Chapter 9).
- ☐ Brake pads or brake shoes incorrectly fitted (Chapters 1 and 9).
- ☐ Incorrect grade of brake pads or brake shoes fitted (Chapters 1 and 9).
- ☐ Brake pads or brake shoe linings contaminated (Chapters 1 and 9).

### Judder felt through brake pedal or steering wheel when braking

- ☐ Excessive run-out or distortion of discs/drums (Chapters 1 and 9).
- ☐ Brake pad or brake shoe linings worn (Chapters 1 and 9).
- ☐ Brake caliper or brake backplate mounting bolts loose (Chapter 9).
- ☐ Wear in suspension or steering components or mountings (Chapters 1 and 10).
- ☐ Vibration through pedal - Anti-lock Braking System (ABS) in operation - no fault (models with ABS).

### Brakes binding

- ☐ Seized brake caliper or wheel cylinder piston(s) (Chapter 9).
- ☐ Incorrectly-adjusted handbrake mechanism (Chapter 9).
- ☐ Faulty master cylinder (Chapter 9).

### Rear wheels locking under normal braking

- ☐ Rear brake shoe linings contaminated (Chapters 1 and 9).
- ☐ Faulty brake pressure regulator (Chapter 9).

## Suspension and steering

**Note:** *Before diagnosing suspension or steering faults, be sure that the trouble is not due to incorrect tyre pressures, mixtures of tyre types, worn tyres, or binding brakes.*

### Vehicle pulls to one side

- ☐ Defective or worn tyre (*Weekly checks*).
- ☐ Tyre pressure low on one side of the car (*Weekly checks*).
- ☐ Excessive wear in suspension or steering components (Chapters 1 and 10).
- ☐ Incorrect front wheel alignment (Chapter 10).
- ☐ Accident damage to steering or suspension components (Chapter 1).

### Wheel wobble and vibration

- ☐ Front roadwheels out of balance (vibration felt mainly through the steering wheel) (*Weekly checks*).
- ☐ Rear roadwheels out of balance (vibration felt throughout the vehicle) (*Weekly checks*).
- ☐ Roadwheels damaged or distorted (*Weekly checks*).
- ☐ Faulty, worn or damaged tyre (*Weekly checks*).
- ☐ Worn steering or suspension joints, bushes or components (Chapters 1 and 10).
- ☐ Wheel bolts loose (Chapter 1).

### Excessive pitching and/or rolling around corners, or during braking

- ☐ Defective shock absorbers (Chapters 1 and 10).
- ☐ Broken or weak spring and/or suspension component (Chapters 1 and 10).
- ☐ Worn or damaged anti-roll bar or mountings (Chapter 10).

### Wandering or general instability

- ☐ Incorrect front wheel alignment (Chapter 10).
- ☐ Worn steering or suspension joints, bushes or components (Chapters 1 and 10).
- ☐ Roadwheels out of balance (*Weekly checks*).
- ☐ Faulty or damaged tyre (*Weekly checks*).
- ☐ Wheel bolts loose (Chapter 1).
- ☐ Defective shock absorbers (Chapters 1 and 10).

### Excessively-stiff steering

- ☐ Incorrect power steering fluid level (*Weekly checks*).
- ☐ Lack of steering gear lubricant (Chapter 10).
- ☐ Seized track rod end balljoint or suspension balljoint (Chapters 1 and 10).
- ☐ Broken auxiliary drivebelt or drivebelt tensioner fault - power steering (Chapter 1).
- ☐ Incorrect front wheel alignment (Chapter 10).
- ☐ Steering rack or column bent or damaged (Chapter 10).

### Excessive play in steering

- ☐ Worn steering column intermediate shaft universal joint (Chapter 10).
- ☐ Worn steering track rod end balljoints (Chapters 1 and 10).
- ☐ Worn rack-and-pinion steering gear (Chapter 10).
- ☐ Worn steering or suspension joints, bushes or components (Chapters 1 and 10).

### Lack of power assistance

- ☐ Broken or incorrectly-adjusted auxiliary drivebelt (Chapter 1 or 2).
- ☐ Incorrect power steering fluid level (*Weekly checks*).
- ☐ Restriction in power steering fluid hoses (Chapter 1).
- ☐ Faulty power steering pump (Chapter 10).
- ☐ Faulty rack-and-pinion steering gear (Chapter 10).

### Tyre wear excessive

#### Tyres worn on inside or outside edges

- ☐ Tyres under-inflated (wear on both edges) (*Weekly checks*).
- ☐ Incorrect camber or castor angles (wear on one edge only) (Chapter 10).
- ☐ Worn steering or suspension joints, bushes or components (Chapters 1 and 10).
- ☐ Excessively-hard cornering.
- ☐ Accident damage.

#### Tyre treads exhibit feathered edges

- ☐ Incorrect toe setting (Chapter 10).

#### Tyres worn in centre of tread

- ☐ Tyres over-inflated (*Weekly checks*).

#### Tyres worn unevenly

- ☐ Tyres/wheels out of balance (*Weekly checks*).
- ☐ Excessive wheel or tyre run-out (*Weekly checks*).
- ☐ Worn shock absorbers (Chapters 1 and 10).
- ☐ Faulty tyre (*Weekly checks*).

## Electrical system

**Note:** *For problems associated with the starting system, refer to the faults listed under Engine earlier in this Section.*

### *Battery will not hold a charge for more than a few days*

- ☐ Battery defective internally (Chapter 5A).
- ☐ Battery terminal connections loose or corroded (*Weekly checks*).
- ☐ Auxiliary drivebelt worn or incorrectly adjusted (Chapter 1 or 2).
- ☐ Alternator not charging at correct output (Chapter 5A).
- ☐ Alternator or voltage regulator faulty (Chapter 5A).
- ☐ Short-circuit causing continual battery drain (Chapters 5A and 12).

### *Ignition/no-charge warning light remains illuminated with engine running*

- ☐ Auxiliary drivebelt broken, worn, or incorrectly adjusted (Chapter 1).
- ☐ Alternator brushes worn, sticking, or dirty (Chapter 5A).
- ☐ Alternator brush springs weak or broken (Chapter 5A).
- ☐ Internal fault in alternator or voltage regulator (Chapter 5A).
- ☐ Broken, disconnected, or loose wiring in charging circuit (Chapter 5A).

### *Ignition/no-charge warning light fails to come on*

- ☐ Warning light bulb blown (Chapter 12).
- ☐ Broken, disconnected, or loose wiring in warning light circuit (Chapter 12).
- ☐ Alternator faulty (Chapter 5A).

### *Lights inoperative*

- ☐ Bulb blown (Chapter 12).
- ☐ Corrosion of bulb or bulbholder contacts (Chapter 12).
- ☐ Blown fuse (Chapter 12).
- ☐ Faulty relay (Chapter 12).
- ☐ Broken, loose, or disconnected wiring (Chapter 12).
- ☐ Faulty switch (Chapter 12).

### *Instrument readings inaccurate or erratic*

#### Instrument readings increase with engine speed

- ☐ Faulty voltage stabiliser (Chapter 12).

#### Fuel or temperature gauges give no reading

- ☐ Faulty gauge sender unit (Chapters 3 and 4A, 4B or 4C).
- ☐ Wiring open-circuit (Chapter 12).
- ☐ Faulty gauge (Chapter 12).

#### Fuel or temperature gauges give continuous maximum reading

- ☐ Faulty gauge sender unit (Chapters 3 and 4A, 4B or 4C).
- ☐ Wiring short-circuit (Chapter 12).
- ☐ Faulty gauge (Chapter 12).

### *Horn inoperative, or unsatisfactory in operation*

#### Horn operates all the time

- ☐ Horn push either earthed or stuck down (Chapter 12).
- ☐ Horn cable-to-horn push earthed (Chapter 12).

#### Horn fails to operate

- ☐ Blown fuse (Chapter 12).
- ☐ Cable or cable connections loose, broken or disconnected (Chapter 12).
- ☐ Faulty horn (Chapter 12).

#### Horn emits intermittent or unsatisfactory sound

- ☐ Cable connections loose (Chapter 12).
- ☐ Horn mountings loose (Chapter 12).
- ☐ Faulty horn (Chapter 12).

### *Windscreen/tailgate wipers inoperative, or unsatisfactory in operation*

#### Wipers fail to operate, or operate very slowly

- ☐ Wiper blades stuck to screen, or linkage seized or binding (*Weekly checks* or Chapter 12).
- ☐ Blown fuse (*Weekly checks* or Chapter 12).
- ☐ Cable or cable connections loose, broken or disconnected (Chapter 12).
- ☐ Faulty relay (Chapter 12).
- ☐ Faulty wiper motor (Chapter 12).

#### Wiper blades sweep over too large or too small an area of the glass

- ☐ Wiper arms incorrectly positioned on spindles (Chapter 12).
- ☐ Excessive wear of wiper linkage (Chapter 12).
- ☐ Wiper motor or linkage mountings loose or insecure (Chapter 12).

#### Wiper blades fail to clean the glass effectively

- ☐ Wiper blade rubbers worn or perished (*Weekly checks*).
- ☐ Wiper arm tension springs broken, or arm pivots seized (Chapter 12).
- ☐ Insufficient windscreen washer additive to adequately remove road film (*Weekly checks*).

### *Windscreen/tailgate washers inoperative, or unsatisfactory in operation*

#### One or more washer jets inoperative

- ☐ Blocked washer jet (Chapter 1).
- ☐ Disconnected, kinked or restricted fluid hose (Chapter 12).
- ☐ Insufficient fluid in washer reservoir (*Weekly checks*).

#### Washer pump fails to operate

- ☐ Broken or disconnected wiring or connections (Chapter 12).
- ☐ Blown fuse (*Weekly checks* or Chapter 12).
- ☐ Faulty washer switch (Chapter 12).
- ☐ Faulty washer pump (Chapter 12).

#### Washer pump runs for some time before fluid is emitted from jets

- ☐ Faulty one-way valve in fluid supply hose (Chapter 12).

### *Electric windows inoperative, or unsatisfactory in operation*

#### Window glass will only move in one direction

- ☐ Faulty switch (Chapter 12).

#### Window glass slow to move

- ☐ Regulator seized or damaged, or in need of lubrication (Chapter 11).
- ☐ Door internal components or trim fouling regulator (Chapter 11).
- ☐ Faulty motor (Chapter 11).

#### *Window glass fails to move*

- ☐ Blown fuse (Chapter 12).
- ☐ Faulty relay (Chapter 12).
- ☐ Broken or disconnected wiring or connections (Chapter 12).
- ☐ Faulty motor (Chapter 11).

### *Central locking system inoperative, or unsatisfactory in operation*

#### Complete system failure

- ☐ Blown fuse (*Weekly checks* or Chapter 12).
- ☐ Faulty relay (Chapter 12).
- ☐ Broken or disconnected wiring or connections (Chapter 12).
- ☐ Faulty bi-pressure pump (Chapter 11).

#### Latch locks but will not unlock, or unlocks but will not lock

- ☐ Broken or disconnected latch operating rods or levers (Chapter 11).
- ☐ Faulty relay (Chapter 12).
- ☐ Faulty bi-pressure pump (Chapter 11).

#### One solenoid/motor fails to operate

- ☐ Broken or disconnected wiring or connections (Chapter 12).
- ☐ Faulty operating assembly (Chapter 11).
- ☐ Broken, binding or disconnected latch operating rods or levers (Chapter 11).
- ☐ Fault in door latch (Chapter 11).

## A

**ABS (Anti-lock brake system)** A system, usually electronically controlled, that senses incipient wheel lockup during braking and relieves hydraulic pressure at wheels that are about to skid.

**Air bag** An inflatable bag hidden in the steering wheel (driver's side) or the dash or glovebox (passenger side). In a head-on collision, the bags inflate, preventing the driver and front passenger from being thrown forward into the steering wheel or windscreen.

**Air cleaner** A metal or plastic housing, containing a filter element, which removes dust and dirt from the air being drawn into the engine.

**Air filter element** The actual filter in an air cleaner system, usually manufactured from pleated paper and requiring renewal at regular intervals.

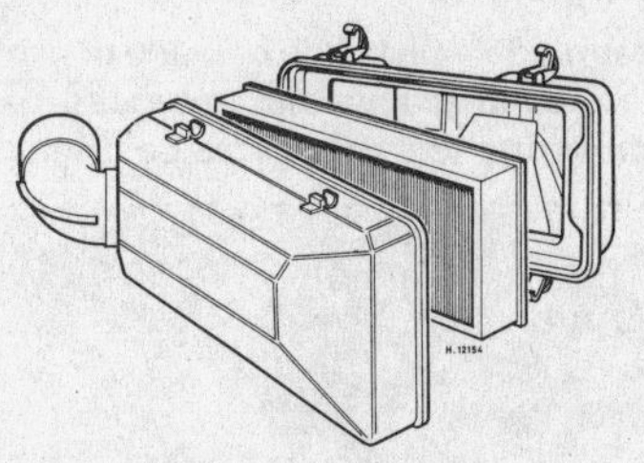

*Air filter*

**Allen key** A hexagonal wrench which fits into a recessed hexagonal hole.

**Alligator clip** A long-nosed spring-loaded metal clip with meshing teeth. Used to make temporary electrical connections.

**Alternator** A component in the electrical system which converts mechanical energy from a drivebelt into electrical energy to charge the battery and to operate the starting system, ignition system and electrical accessories.

**Ampere (amp)** A unit of measurement for the flow of electric current. One amp is the amount of current produced by one volt acting through a resistance of one ohm.

**Anaerobic sealer** A substance used to prevent bolts and screws from loosening. Anaerobic means that it does not require oxygen for activation. The Loctite brand is widely used.

**Antifreeze** A substance (usually ethylene glycol) mixed with water, and added to a vehicle's cooling system, to prevent freezing of the coolant in winter. Antifreeze also contains chemicals to inhibit corrosion and the formation of rust and other deposits that would tend to clog the radiator and coolant passages and reduce cooling efficiency.

**Anti-seize compound** A coating that reduces the risk of seizing on fasteners that are subjected to high temperatures, such as exhaust manifold bolts and nuts.

**Asbestos** A natural fibrous mineral with great heat resistance, commonly used in the composition of brake friction materials. Asbestos is a health hazard and the dust created by brake systems should never be inhaled or ingested.

**Axle** A shaft on which a wheel revolves, or which revolves with a wheel. Also, a solid beam that connects the two wheels at one end of the vehicle. An axle which also transmits power to the wheels is known as a live axle.

**Axleshaft** A single rotating shaft, on either side of the differential, which delivers power from the final drive assembly to the drive wheels. Also called a driveshaft or a halfshaft.

## B

**Ball bearing** An anti-friction bearing consisting of a hardened inner and outer race with hardened steel balls between two races.

**Bearing** The curved surface on a shaft or in a bore, or the part assembled into either, that permits relative motion between them with minimum wear and friction.

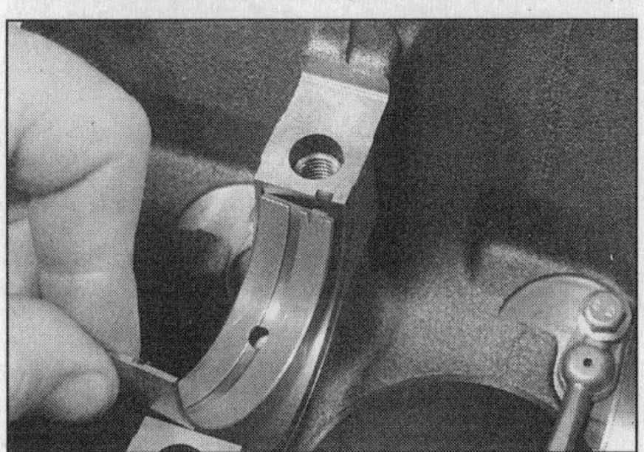

*Bearing*

**Big-end bearing** The bearing in the end of the connecting rod that's attached to the crankshaft.

**Bleed nipple** A valve on a brake wheel cylinder, caliper or other hydraulic component that is opened to purge the hydraulic system of air. Also called a bleed screw.

**Brake bleeding** Procedure for removing air from lines of a hydraulic brake system.

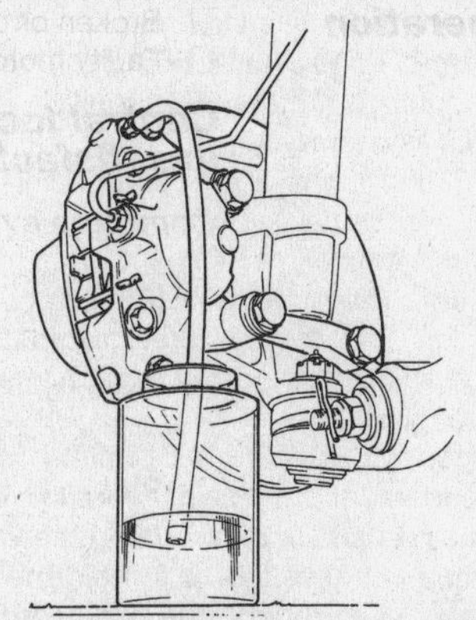

*Brake bleeding*

**Brake disc** The component of a disc brake that rotates with the wheels.

**Brake drum** The component of a drum brake that rotates with the wheels.

**Brake linings** The friction material which contacts the brake disc or drum to retard the vehicle's speed. The linings are bonded or riveted to the brake pads or shoes.

**Brake pads** The replaceable friction pads that pinch the brake disc when the brakes are applied. Brake pads consist of a friction material bonded or riveted to a rigid backing plate.

**Brake shoe** The crescent-shaped carrier to which the brake linings are mounted and which forces the lining against the rotating drum during braking.

**Braking systems** For more information on braking systems, consult the *Haynes Automotive Brake Manual*.

**Breaker bar** A long socket wrench handle providing greater leverage.

**Bulkhead** The insulated partition between the engine and the passenger compartment.

## C

**Caliper** The non-rotating part of a disc-brake assembly that straddles the disc and carries the brake pads. The caliper also contains the hydraulic components that cause the pads to pinch the disc when the brakes are applied. A caliper is also a measuring tool that can be set to measure inside or outside dimensions of an object.

**Camshaft** A rotating shaft on which a series of cam lobes operate the valve mechanisms. The camshaft may be driven by gears, by sprockets and chain or by sprockets and a belt.

**Canister** A container in an evaporative emission control system; contains activated charcoal granules to trap vapours from the fuel system.

*Canister*

**Carburettor** A device which mixes fuel with air in the proper proportions to provide a desired power output from a spark ignition internal combustion engine.

**Castellated** Resembling the parapets along the top of a castle wall. For example, a castellated balljoint stud nut.

**Castor** In wheel alignment, the backward or forward tilt of the steering axis. Castor is positive when the steering axis is inclined rearward at the top.

**Catalytic converter** A silencer-like device in the exhaust system which converts certain pollutants in the exhaust gases into less harmful substances.

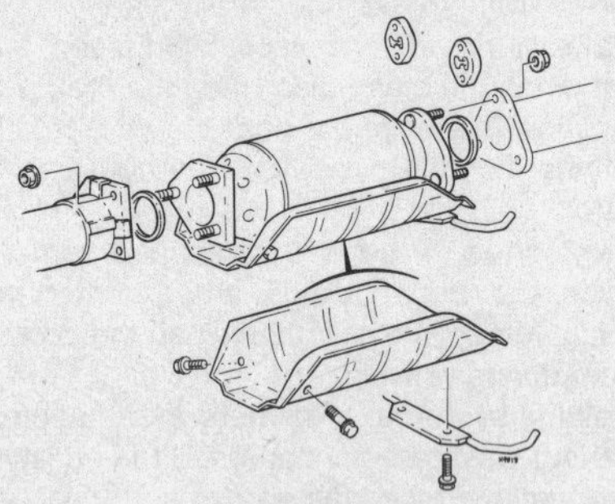

*Catalytic converter*

**Circlip** A ring-shaped clip used to prevent endwise movement of cylindrical parts and shafts. An internal circlip is installed in a groove in a housing; an external circlip fits into a groove on the outside of a cylindrical piece such as a shaft.

**Clearance** The amount of space between two parts. For example, between a piston and a cylinder, between a bearing and a journal, etc.

**Coil spring** A spiral of elastic steel found in various sizes throughout a vehicle, for example as a springing medium in the suspension and in the valve train.

**Compression** Reduction in volume, and increase in pressure and temperature, of a gas, caused by squeezing it into a smaller space.

**Compression ratio** The relationship between cylinder volume when the piston is at top dead centre and cylinder volume when the piston is at bottom dead centre.

**Constant velocity (CV) joint** A type of universal joint that cancels out vibrations caused by driving power being transmitted through an angle.

**Core plug** A disc or cup-shaped metal device inserted in a hole in a casting through which core was removed when the casting was formed. Also known as a freeze plug or expansion plug.

**Crankcase** The lower part of the engine block in which the crankshaft rotates.

**Crankshaft** The main rotating member, or shaft, running the length of the crankcase, with offset "throws" to which the connecting rods are attached.

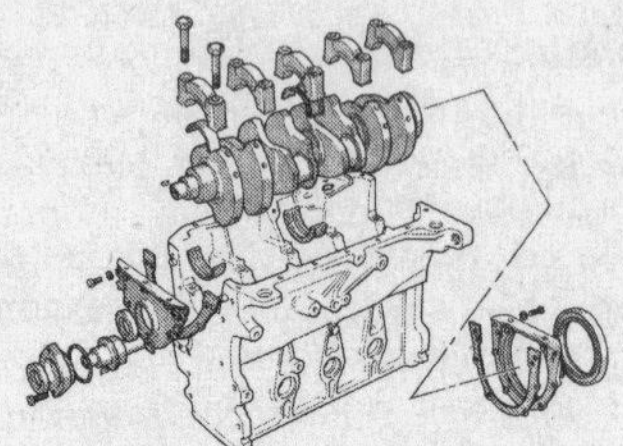

*Crankshaft assembly*

**Crocodile clip** See Alligator clip

## D

**Diagnostic code** Code numbers obtained by accessing the diagnostic mode of an engine management computer. This code can be used to determine the area in the system where a malfunction may be located.

**Disc brake** A brake design incorporating a rotating disc onto which brake pads are squeezed. The resulting friction converts the energy of a moving vehicle into heat.

**Double-overhead cam (DOHC)** An engine that uses two overhead camshafts, usually one for the intake valves and one for the exhaust valves.

**Drivebelt(s)** The belt(s) used to drive accessories such as the alternator, water pump, power steering pump, air conditioning compressor, etc. off the crankshaft pulley.

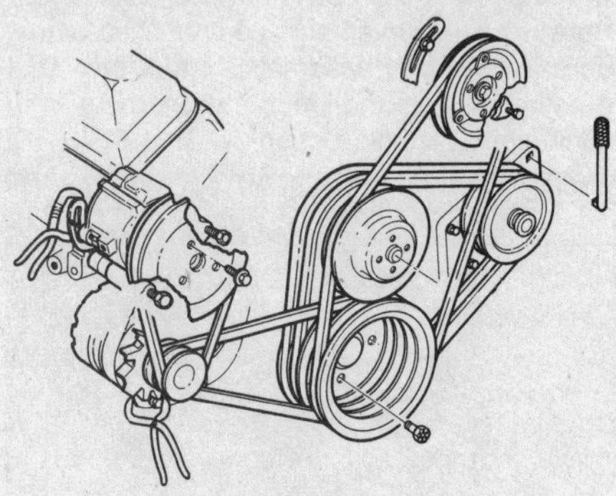

*Accessory drivebelts*

**Driveshaft** Any shaft used to transmit motion. Commonly used when referring to the axleshafts on a front wheel drive vehicle.

**Drum brake** A type of brake using a drum-shaped metal cylinder attached to the inner surface of the wheel. When the brake pedal is pressed, curved brake shoes with friction linings press against the inside of the drum to slow or stop the vehicle.

## E

**EGR valve** A valve used to introduce exhaust gases into the intake air stream.

**Electronic control unit (ECU)** A computer which controls (for instance) ignition and fuel injection systems, or an anti-lock braking system. For more information refer to the *Haynes Automotive Electrical and Electronic Systems Manual.*

**Electronic Fuel Injection (EFI)** A computer controlled fuel system that distributes fuel through an injector located in each intake port of the engine.

**Emergency brake** A braking system, independent of the main hydraulic system, that can be used to slow or stop the vehicle if the primary brakes fail, or to hold the vehicle stationary even though the brake pedal isn't depressed. It usually consists of a hand lever that actuates either front or rear brakes mechanically through a series of cables and linkages. Also known as a handbrake or parking brake.

**Endfloat** The amount of lengthwise movement between two parts. As applied to a crankshaft, the distance that the crankshaft can move forward and back in the cylinder block.

**Engine management system (EMS)** A computer controlled system which manages the fuel injection and the ignition systems in an integrated fashion.

**Exhaust manifold** A part with several passages through which exhaust gases leave the engine combustion chambers and enter the exhaust pipe.

## F

**Fan clutch** A viscous (fluid) drive coupling device which permits variable engine fan speeds in relation to engine speeds.

**Feeler blade** A thin strip or blade of hardened steel, ground to an exact thickness, used to check or measure clearances between parts.

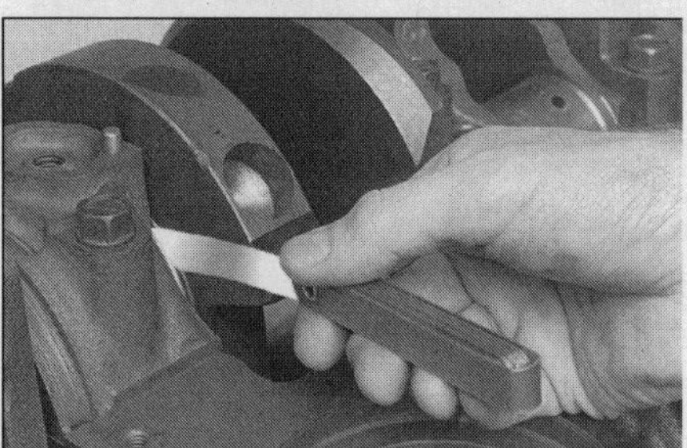

*Feeler blade*

**Firing order** The order in which the engine cylinders fire, or deliver their power strokes, beginning with the number one cylinder.

**Flywheel** A heavy spinning wheel in which energy is absorbed and stored by means of momentum. On cars, the flywheel is attached to the crankshaft to smooth out firing impulses.

**Free play** The amount of travel before any action takes place. The "looseness" in a linkage, or an assembly of parts, between the initial application of force and actual movement. For example, the distance the brake pedal moves before the pistons in the master cylinder are actuated.

**Fuse** An electrical device which protects a circuit against accidental overload. The typical fuse contains a soft piece of metal which is calibrated to melt at a predetermined current flow (expressed as amps) and break the circuit.

**Fusible link** A circuit protection device consisting of a conductor surrounded by heat-resistant insulation. The conductor is smaller than the wire it protects, so it acts as the weakest link in the circuit. Unlike a blown fuse, a failed fusible link must frequently be cut from the wire for replacement.

## G

**Gap** The distance the spark must travel in jumping from the centre electrode to the side electrode in a spark plug. Also refers to the spacing between the points in a contact breaker assembly in a conventional points-type ignition, or to the distance between the reluctor or rotor and the pickup coil in an electronic ignition.

*Adjusting spark plug gap*

**Gasket** Any thin, soft material - usually cork, cardboard, asbestos or soft metal - installed between two metal surfaces to ensure a good seal. For instance, the cylinder head gasket seals the joint between the block and the cylinder head.

*Gasket*

**Gauge** An instrument panel display used to monitor engine conditions. A gauge with a movable pointer on a dial or a fixed scale is an analogue gauge. A gauge with a numerical readout is called a digital gauge.

## H

**Halfshaft** A rotating shaft that transmits power from the final drive unit to a drive wheel, usually when referring to a live rear axle.

**Harmonic balancer** A device designed to reduce torsion or twisting vibration in the crankshaft. May be incorporated in the crankshaft pulley. Also known as a vibration damper.

**Hone** An abrasive tool for correcting small irregularities or differences in diameter in an engine cylinder, brake cylinder, etc.

**Hydraulic tappet** A tappet that utilises hydraulic pressure from the engine's lubrication system to maintain zero clearance (constant contact with both camshaft and valve stem). Automatically adjusts to variation in valve stem length. Hydraulic tappets also reduce valve noise.

## I

**Ignition timing** The moment at which the spark plug fires, usually expressed in the number of crankshaft degrees before the piston reaches the top of its stroke.

**Inlet manifold** A tube or housing with passages through which flows the air-fuel mixture (carburettor vehicles and vehicles with throttle body injection) or air only (port fuel-injected vehicles) to the port openings in the cylinder head.

## J

**Jump start** Starting the engine of a vehicle with a discharged or weak battery by attaching jump leads from the weak battery to a charged or helper battery.

## L

**Load Sensing Proportioning Valve (LSPV)** A brake hydraulic system control valve that works like a proportioning valve, but also takes into consideration the amount of weight carried by the rear axle.

**Locknut** A nut used to lock an adjustment nut, or other threaded component, in place. For example, a locknut is employed to keep the adjusting nut on the rocker arm in position.

**Lockwasher** A form of washer designed to prevent an attaching nut from working loose.

## M

**MacPherson strut** A type of front suspension system devised by Earle MacPherson at Ford of England. In its original form, a simple lateral link with the anti-roll bar creates the lower control arm. A long strut - an integral coil spring and shock absorber - is mounted between the body and the steering knuckle. Many modern so-called MacPherson strut systems use a conventional lower A-arm and don't rely on the anti-roll bar for location.

**Multimeter** An electrical test instrument with the capability to measure voltage, current and resistance.

## N

**NOx** Oxides of Nitrogen. A common toxic pollutant emitted by petrol and diesel engines at higher temperatures.

## O

**Ohm** The unit of electrical resistance. One volt applied to a resistance of one ohm will produce a current of one amp.

**Ohmmeter** An instrument for measuring electrical resistance.

**O-ring** A type of sealing ring made of a special rubber-like material; in use, the O-ring is compressed into a groove to provide the sealing action.

**Overhead cam (ohc) engine** An engine with the camshaft(s) located on top of the cylinder head(s).

**Overhead valve (ohv) engine** An engine with the valves located in the cylinder head, but with the camshaft located in the engine block.

**Oxygen sensor** A device installed in the engine exhaust manifold, which senses the oxygen content in the exhaust and converts this information into an electric current. Also called a Lambda sensor.

## P

**Phillips screw** A type of screw head having a cross instead of a slot for a corresponding type of screwdriver.

**Plastigage** A thin strip of plastic thread, available in different sizes, used for measuring clearances. For example, a strip of Plastigage is laid across a bearing journal. The parts are assembled and dismantled; the width of the crushed strip indicates the clearance between journal and bearing.

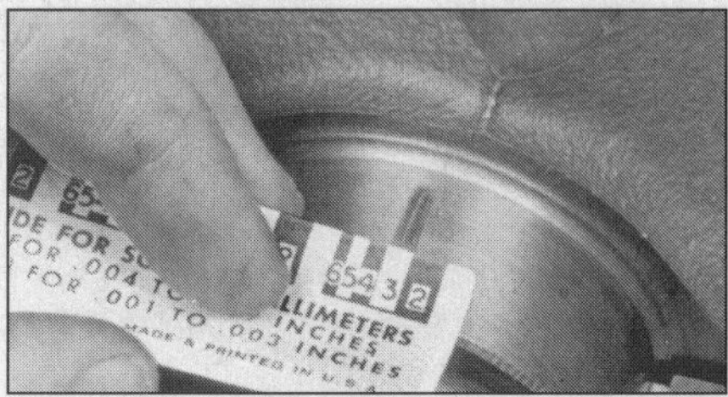

*Plastigage*

**Propeller shaft** The long hollow tube with universal joints at both ends that carries power from the transmission to the differential on front-engined rear wheel drive vehicles.

**Proportioning valve** A hydraulic control valve which limits the amount of pressure to the rear brakes during panic stops to prevent wheel lock-up.

## R

**Rack-and-pinion steering** A steering system with a pinion gear on the end of the steering shaft that mates with a rack (think of a geared wheel opened up and laid flat). When the steering wheel is turned, the pinion turns, moving the rack to the left or right. This movement is transmitted through the track rods to the steering arms at the wheels.

**Radiator** A liquid-to-air heat transfer device designed to reduce the temperature of the coolant in an internal combustion engine cooling system.

**Refrigerant** Any substance used as a heat transfer agent in an air-conditioning system. R-12 has been the principle refrigerant for many years; recently, however, manufacturers have begun using R-134a, a non-CFC substance that is considered less harmful to the ozone in the upper atmosphere.

**Rocker arm** A lever arm that rocks on a shaft or pivots on a stud. In an overhead valve engine, the rocker arm converts the upward movement of the pushrod into a downward movement to open a valve.

**Rotor** In a distributor, the rotating device inside the cap that connects the centre electrode and the outer terminals as it turns, distributing the high voltage from the coil secondary winding to the proper spark plug. Also, that part of an alternator which rotates inside the stator. Also, the rotating assembly of a turbocharger, including the compressor wheel, shaft and turbine wheel.

**Runout** The amount of wobble (in-and-out movement) of a gear or wheel as it's rotated. The amount a shaft rotates "out-of-true." The out-of-round condition of a rotating part.

# S

**Sealant** A liquid or paste used to prevent leakage at a joint. Sometimes used in conjunction with a gasket.

**Sealed beam lamp** An older headlight design which integrates the reflector, lens and filaments into a hermetically-sealed one-piece unit. When a filament burns out or the lens cracks, the entire unit is simply replaced.

**Serpentine drivebelt** A single, long, wide accessory drivebelt that's used on some newer vehicles to drive all the accessories, instead of a series of smaller, shorter belts. Serpentine drivebelts are usually tensioned by an automatic tensioner.

*Serpentine drivebelt*

**Shim** Thin spacer, commonly used to adjust the clearance or relative positions between two parts. For example, shims inserted into or under bucket tappets control valve clearances. Clearance is adjusted by changing the thickness of the shim.

**Slide hammer** A special puller that screws into or hooks onto a component such as a shaft or bearing; a heavy sliding handle on the shaft bottoms against the end of the shaft to knock the component free.

**Sprocket** A tooth or projection on the periphery of a wheel, shaped to engage with a chain or drivebelt. Commonly used to refer to the sprocket wheel itself.

**Starter inhibitor switch** On vehicles with an automatic transmission, a switch that prevents starting if the vehicle is not in Neutral or Park.

**Strut** See MacPherson strut.

# T

**Tappet** A cylindrical component which transmits motion from the cam to the valve stem, either directly or via a pushrod and rocker arm. Also called a cam follower.

**Thermostat** A heat-controlled valve that regulates the flow of coolant between the cylinder block and the radiator, so maintaining optimum engine operating temperature. A thermostat is also used in some air cleaners in which the temperature is regulated.

**Thrust bearing** The bearing in the clutch assembly that is moved in to the release levers by clutch pedal action to disengage the clutch. Also referred to as a release bearing.

**Timing belt** A toothed belt which drives the camshaft. Serious engine damage may result if it breaks in service.

**Timing chain** A chain which drives the camshaft.

**Toe-in** The amount the front wheels are closer together at the front than at the rear. On rear wheel drive vehicles, a slight amount of toe-in is usually specified to keep the front wheels running parallel on the road by offsetting other forces that tend to spread the wheels apart.

**Toe-out** The amount the front wheels are closer together at the rear than at the front. On front wheel drive vehicles, a slight amount of toe-out is usually specified.

**Tools** For full information on choosing and using tools, refer to the *Haynes Automotive Tools Manual.*

**Tracer** A stripe of a second colour applied to a wire insulator to distinguish that wire from another one with the same colour insulator.

**Tune-up** A process of accurate and careful adjustments and parts replacement to obtain the best possible engine performance.

**Turbocharger** A centrifugal device, driven by exhaust gases, that pressurises the intake air. Normally used to increase the power output from a given engine displacement, but can also be used primarily to reduce exhaust emissions (as on VW's "Umwelt" Diesel engine).

# U

**Universal joint or U-joint** A double-pivoted connection for transmitting power from a driving to a driven shaft through an angle. A U-joint consists of two Y-shaped yokes and a cross-shaped member called the spider.

# V

**Valve** A device through which the flow of liquid, gas, vacuum, or loose material in bulk may be started, stopped, or regulated by a movable part that opens, shuts, or partially obstructs one or more ports or passageways. A valve is also the movable part of such a device.

**Valve clearance** The clearance between the valve tip (the end of the valve stem) and the rocker arm or tappet. The valve clearance is measured when the valve is closed.

**Vernier caliper** A precision measuring instrument that measures inside and outside dimensions. Not quite as accurate as a micrometer, but more convenient.

**Viscosity** The thickness of a liquid or its resistance to flow.

**Volt** A unit for expressing electrical "pressure" in a circuit. One volt that will produce a current of one ampere through a resistance of one ohm.

# W

**Welding** Various processes used to join metal items by heating the areas to be joined to a molten state and fusing them together. For more information refer to the *Haynes Automotive Welding Manual.*

**Wiring diagram** A drawing portraying the components and wires in a vehicle's electrical system, using standardised symbols. For more information refer to the *Haynes Automotive Electrical and Electronic Systems Manual.*

**Note:** *References throughout this index are in the form "**Chapter number**" • "**Page number**"*

# Haynes Manuals – The Complete List

| Title | Book No. |
|---|---|
| **ALFA ROMEO** | |
| Alfa Romeo Alfasud/Sprint (74 - 88) up to F | 0292 |
| Alfa Romeo Alfetta (73 - 87) up to E | 0531 |
| **AUDI** | |
| Audi 80 (72 - Feb 79) up to T | 0207 |
| Audi 80, 90 (79 - Oct 86) up to D & Coupe (81 - Nov 88) up to F | 0605 |
| Audi 80, 90 (Oct 86 - 90) D to H & Coupe (Nov 88 - 90) F to H | 1491 |
| Audi 100 (Oct 82 - 90) up to H & 200 (Feb 84 - Oct 89) A to G | 0907 |
| Audi 100 & A6 Petrol & Diesel (May 91 - May 97) H to P | 3504 |
| Audi A4 (95 - Feb 00) M to V | 3575 |
| **AUSTIN** | |
| Austin A35 & A40 (56 - 67) * | 0118 |
| Austin Allegro 1100, 1300, 1.0, 1.1 & 1.3 (73 - 82)* | 0164 |
| Austin Healey 100/6 & 3000 (56 - 68) * | 0049 |
| Austin/MG/Rover Maestro 1.3 & 1.6 (83 - May 95) up to M | 0922 |
| Austin/MG Metro (80 - May 90) up to G | 0718 |
| Austin/Rover Montego 1.3 & 1.6 (84 - 94) A to L | 1066 |
| Austin/MG/Rover Montego 2.0 (84 - 95) A to M | 1067 |
| Mini (59 - 69) up to H | 0527 |
| Mini (69 - Oct 96) up to P | 0646 |
| Austin/Rover 2.0 litre Diesel Engine (86 - 93) C to L | 1857 |
| **BEDFORD** | |
| Bedford CF (69 - 87) up to E | 0163 |
| Bedford/Vauxhall Rascal & Suzuki Supercarry (86 - Oct 94) C to M | 3015 |
| **BMW** | |
| BMW 1500, 1502, 1600, 1602, 2000 & 2002 (59 - 77)* | 0240 |
| BMW 316, 320 & 320i (4-cyl) (75 - Feb 83) up to Y | 0276 |
| BMW 320, 320i, 323i & 325i (6-cyl) (Oct 77 - Sept 87) up to E | 0815 |
| BMW 3-Series (Apr 91 - 96) H to N | 3210 |
| BMW 3- & 5-Series (sohc) (81 - 91) up to J | 1948 |
| BMW 520i & 525e (Oct 81 - June 88) up to E | 1560 |
| BMW 525, 528 & 528i (73 - Sept 81) up to X | 0632 |
| **CITROËN** | |
| Citroën 2CV, Ami & Dyane (67 - 90) up to H | 0196 |
| Citroën AX Petrol & Diesel (87 - 97) D to P | 3014 |
| Citroën BX (83 - 94) A to L | 0908 |
| Citroën C15 Van Petrol & Diesel (89 - Oct 98) F to S | 3509 |
| Citroën CX (75 - 88) up to F | 0528 |
| Citroën Saxo Petrol & Diesel (96 - 01) N to X | 3506 |
| Citroën Visa (79 - 88) up to F | 0620 |
| Citroën Xantia Petrol & Diesel (93 - 98) K to S | 3082 |
| Citroën XM Petrol & Diesel (89 - 00) G to X | 3451 |
| Citroën Xsara Petrol & Diesel (97 - Sept 00) R to W | 3751 |
| Citroën ZX Diesel (91 - 98) J to S | 1922 |
| Citroën ZX Petrol (91 - 98) H to S | 1881 |
| Citroën 1.7 & 1.9 litre Diesel Engine (84 - 96) A to N | 1379 |
| **FIAT** | |
| Fiat 126 (73 - 87) * | 0305 |
| Fiat 500 (57 - 73) up to M | 0090 |
| Fiat Bravo & Brava (95 - 00) N to W | 3572 |
| Fiat Cinquecento (93 - 98) K to R | 3501 |
| Fiat Panda (81 - 95) up to M | 0793 |
| Fiat Punto Petrol & Diesel (94 - Oct 99) L to V | 3251 |
| Fiat Regata (84 - 88) A to F | 1167 |
| Fiat Tipo (88 - 91) E to J | 1625 |
| Fiat Uno (83 - 95) up to M | 0923 |
| Fiat X1/9 (74 - 89) up to G | 0273 |
| **FORD** | |
| Ford Anglia (59 - 68) * | 0001 |
| Ford Capri II (& III) 1.6 & 2.0 (74 - 87) up to E | 0283 |
| Ford Capri II (& III) 2.8 & 3.0 (74 - 87) up to E | 1309 |
| Ford Cortina Mk III 1300 & 1600 (70 - 76) * | 0070 |
| Ford Cortina Mk IV (& V) 1.6 & 2.0 (76 - 83) * | 0343 |
| Ford Cortina Mk IV (& V) 2.3 V6 (77 - 83) * | 0426 |
| Ford Escort Mk I 1100 & 1300 (68 - 74) * | 0171 |
| Ford Escort Mk I Mexico, RS 1600 & RS 2000 (70 - 74)* | 0139 |
| Ford Escort Mk II Mexico, RS 1800 & RS 2000 (75 - 80)* | 0735 |
| Ford Escort (75 - Aug 80) * | 0280 |
| Ford Escort (Sept 80 - Sept 90) up to H | 0686 |
| Ford Escort & Orion (Sept 90 - 00) H to X | 1737 |
| Ford Fiesta (76 - Aug 83) up to Y | 0334 |
| Ford Fiesta (Aug 83 - Feb 89) A to F | 1030 |
| Ford Fiesta (Feb 89 - Oct 95) F to N | 1595 |
| Ford Fiesta (Oct 95 - 01) N-reg. onwards | 3397 |
| Ford Focus (98 - 01) S to Y | 3759 |
| Ford Granada (Sept 77 - Feb 85) up to B | 0481 |
| Ford Granada & Scorpio (Mar 85 - 94) B to M | 1245 |
| Ford Ka (96 - 02) P-reg. onwards | 3570 |
| Ford Mondeo Petrol (93 - 99) K to T | 1923 |
| Ford Mondeo Diesel (93 - 96) L to N | 3465 |
| Ford Orion (83 - Sept 90) up to H | 1009 |
| Ford Sierra 4 cyl. (82 - 93) up to K | 0903 |
| Ford Sierra V6 (82 - 91) up to J | 0904 |
| Ford Transit Petrol (Mk 2) (78 - Jan 86) up to C | 0719 |
| Ford Transit Petrol (Mk 3) (Feb 86 - 89) C to G | 1468 |
| Ford Transit Diesel (Feb 86 - 99) C to T | 3019 |
| Ford 1.6 & 1.8 litre Diesel Engine (84 - 96) A to N | 1172 |
| Ford 2.1, 2.3 & 2.5 litre Diesel Engine (77 - 90) up to H | 1606 |
| **FREIGHT ROVER** | |
| Freight Rover Sherpa (74 - 87) up to E | 0463 |
| **HILLMAN** | |
| Hillman Avenger (70 - 82) up to Y | 0037 |
| Hillman Imp (63 - 76) * | 0022 |
| **HONDA** | |
| Honda Accord (76 - Feb 84) up to A | 0351 |
| Honda Civic (Feb 84 - Oct 87) A to E | 1226 |
| Honda Civic (Nov 91 - 96) J to N | 3199 |
| **HYUNDAI** | |
| Hyundai Pony (85 - 94) C to M | 3398 |
| **JAGUAR** | |
| Jaguar E Type (61 - 72) up to L | 0140 |
| Jaguar MkI & II, 240 & 340 (55 - 69) * | 0098 |
| Jaguar XJ6, XJ & Sovereign; Daimler Sovereign (68 - Oct 86) up to D | 0242 |
| Jaguar XJ6 & Sovereign (Oct 86 - Sept 94) D to M | 3261 |
| Jaguar XJ12, XJS & Sovereign; Daimler Double Six (72 - 88) up to F | 0478 |
| **JEEP** | |
| Jeep Cherokee Petrol (93 - 96) K to N | 1943 |
| **LADA** | |
| Lada 1200, 1300, 1500 & 1600 (74 - 91) up to J | 0413 |
| Lada Samara (87 - 91) D to J | 1610 |
| **LAND ROVER** | |
| Land Rover 90, 110 & Defender Diesel (83 - 95) up to N | 3017 |
| Land Rover Discovery Petrol & Diesel (89 - 98) G to S | 3016 |
| Land Rover Series IIA & III Diesel (58 - 85) up to C | 0529 |
| Land Rover Series II, IIA & III Petrol (58 - 85) up to C | 0314 |
| **MAZDA** | |
| Mazda 323 (Mar 81 - Oct 89) up to G | 1608 |
| Mazda 323 (Oct 89 - 98) G to R | 3455 |
| Mazda 626 (May 83 - Sept 87) up to E | 0929 |
| Mazda B-1600, B-1800 & B-2000 Pick-up (72 - 88) up to F | 0267 |
| Mazda RX-7 (79 - 85) * | 0460 |
| **MERCEDES-BENZ** | |
| Mercedes-Benz 190, 190E & 190D Petrol & Diesel (83 - 93) A to L | 3450 |
| Mercedes-Benz 200, 240, 300 Diesel (Oct 76 - 85) up to C | 1114 |
| Mercedes-Benz 250 & 280 (68 - 72) up to L | 0346 |
| Mercedes-Benz 250 & 280 (123 Series) (Oct 76 - 84) up to B | 0677 |
| Mercedes-Benz 124 Series (85 - Aug 93) C to K | 3253 |
| Mercedes-Benz C-Class Petrol & Diesel (93 - Aug 00) L to W | 3511 |
| **MG** | |
| MGA (55 - 62) * | 0475 |
| MGB (62 - 80) up to W | 0111 |
| MG Midget & AH Sprite (58 - 80) up to W | 0265 |
| **MITSUBISHI** | |
| Mitsubishi Shogun & L200 Pick-Ups (83 - 94) up to M | 1944 |
| **MORRIS** | |
| Morris Ital 1.3 (80 - 84) up to B | 0705 |
| Morris Minor 1000 (56 - 71) up to K | 0024 |
| **NISSAN** | |
| Nissan Bluebird (May 84 - Mar 86) A to C | 1223 |
| Nissan Bluebird (Mar 86 - 90) C to H | 1473 |
| Nissan Cherry (Sept 82 - 86) up to D | 1031 |
| Nissan Micra (83 - Jan 93) up to K | 0931 |
| Nissan Micra (93 - 99) K to T | 3254 |
| Nissan Primera (90 - Aug 99) H to T | 1851 |
| Nissan Stanza (82 - 86) up to D | 0824 |
| Nissan Sunny (May 82 - Oct 86) up to D | 0895 |
| Nissan Sunny (Oct 86 - Mar 91) D to H | 1378 |
| Nissan Sunny (Apr 91 - 95) H to N | 3219 |
| **OPEL** | |
| Opel Ascona & Manta (B Series) (Sept 75 - 88) up to F | 0316 |
| Opel Ascona (81 - 88) *(Not available in UK see Vauxhall Cavalier 0812)* | 3215 |
| Opel Astra (Oct 91 - Feb 98) *(Not available in UK see Vauxhall Astra 1832)* | 3156 |
| Opel Astra & Zafira Diesel (Feb 98 - Sept 00) *(See Astra & Zafira Diesel Book No. 3797)* | |
| Opel Astra & Zafira Petrol (Feb 98 - Sept 00) *(See Vauxhall/Opel Astra & Zafira Petrol Book No. 3758)* | |
| Opel Calibra (90 - 98) *(See Vauxhall/Opel Calibra Book No. 3502)* | |
| Opel Corsa (83 - Mar 93) *(Not available in UK see Vauxhall Nova 0909)* | 3160 |
| Opel Corsa (Mar 93 - 97) *(Not available in UK see Vauxhall Corsa 1985)* | 3159 |
| Opel Frontera Petrol & Diesel (91 - 98) *(See Vauxhall/Opel Frontera Book No. 3454)* | |
| Opel Kadett (Nov 79 - Oct 84) up to B | 0634 |
| Opel Kadett (Oct 84 - Oct 91) *(Not available in UK see Vauxhall Astra & Belmont 1136)* | 3196 |
| Opel Omega & Senator (86 - 94) *(Not available in UK see Vauxhall Carlton & Senator 1469)* | 3157 |
| Opel Omega (94 - 99) *(See Vauxhall/Opel Omega Book No. 3510)* | |
| Opel Rekord (Feb 78 - Oct 86) up to D | 0543 |
| Opel Vectra (Oct 88 - Oct 95) *(Not available in UK see Vauxhall Cavalier 1570)* | 3158 |
| Opel Vectra Petrol & Diesel (95 - 98) *(Not available in UK see Vauxhall Vectra 3396)* | 3523 |
| **PEUGEOT** | |
| Peugeot 106 Petrol & Diesel (91 - 01) J to X | 1882 |
| Peugeot 205 Petrol (83 - 97) A to P | 0932 |
| Peugeot 206 Petrol and Diesel (98 - 01) S to X | 3757 |
| Peugeot 305 (78 - 89) up to G | 0538 |

* Classic reprint

| Title | Book No. |
|---|---|
| Peugeot 306 Petrol & Diesel (93 - 99) K to T | 3073 |
| Peugeot 309 (86 - 93) C to K | 1266 |
| Peugeot 405 Petrol (88 - 97) E to P | 1559 |
| Peugeot 405 Diesel (88 - 97) E to P | 3198 |
| Peugeot 406 Petrol & Diesel (96 - 97) N to R | 3394 |
| Peugeot 505 (79 - 89) up to G | 0762 |
| Peugeot 1.7/1.8 & 1.9 litre Diesel Engine (82 - 96) up to N | 0950 |
| Peugeot 2.0, 2.1, 2.3 & 2.5 litre Diesel Engines (74 - 90) up to H | 1607 |
| **PORSCHE** | |
| Porsche 911 (65 - 85) up to C | 0264 |
| Porsche 924 & 924 Turbo (76 - 85) up to C | 0397 |
| **PROTON** | |
| Proton (89 - 97) F to P | 3255 |
| **RANGE ROVER** | |
| Range Rover V8 (70 - Oct 92) up to K | 0606 |
| **RELIANT** | |
| Reliant Robin & Kitten (73 - 83) up to A | 0436 |
| **RENAULT** | |
| Renault 4 (61 - 86) * | 0072 |
| Renault 5 (Feb 85 - 96) B to N | 1219 |
| Renault 9 & 11 (82 - 89) up to F | 0822 |
| Renault 18 (79 - 86) up to D | 0598 |
| Renault 19 Petrol (89 - 94) F to M | 1646 |
| Renault 19 Diesel (89 - 96) F to N | 1946 |
| Renault 21 (86 - 94) C to M | 1397 |
| Renault 25 (84 - 92) B to K | 1228 |
| Renault Clio Petrol (91 - May 98) H to R | 1853 |
| Renault Clio Diesel (91 - June 96) H to N | 3031 |
| Renault Clio Petrol & Diesel (May 98 - May 01) R to Y | 3906 |
| Renault Espace Petrol & Diesel (85 - 96) C to N | 3197 |
| Renault Fuego (80 - 86) * | 0764 |
| Renault Laguna Petrol & Diesel (94 - 00) L to W | 3252 |
| Renault Mégane & Scénic Petrol & Diesel (96 - 98) N to R | 3395 |
| Renault Mégane & Scénic (Apr 99 - 02) T-reg onwards | 3916 |
| **ROVER** | |
| Rover 213 & 216 (84 - 89) A to G | 1116 |
| Rover 214 & 414 (89 - 96) G to N | 1689 |
| Rover 216 & 416 (89 - 96) G to N | 1830 |
| Rover 211, 214, 216, 218 & 220 Petrol & Diesel (Dec 95 - 98) N to R | 3399 |
| Rover 414, 416 & 420 Petrol & Diesel (May 95 - 98) M to R | 3453 |
| Rover 618, 620 & 623 (93 - 97) K to P | 3257 |
| Rover 820, 825 & 827 (86 - 95) D to N | 1380 |
| Rover 3500 (76 - 87) up to E | 0365 |
| Rover Metro, 111 & 114 (May 90 - 98) G to S | 1711 |
| **SAAB** | |
| Saab 90, 99 & 900 (79 - Oct 93) up to L | 0765 |
| Saab 95 & 96 (66 - 76) * | 0198 |
| Saab 99 (69 - 79) * | 0247 |
| Saab 900 (Oct 93 - 98) L to R | 3512 |
| Saab 9000 (4-cyl) (85 - 98) C to S | 1686 |
| **SEAT** | |
| Seat Ibiza & Cordoba Petrol & Diesel (Oct 93 - Oct 99) L to V | 3571 |
| Seat Ibiza & Malaga (85 - 92) B to K | 1609 |
| **SKODA** | |
| Skoda Estelle (77 - 89) up to G | 0604 |
| Skoda Favorit (89 - 96) F to N | 1801 |
| Skoda Felicia Petrol & Diesel (95 - 01) M to X | 3505 |
| **SUBARU** | |
| Subaru 1600 & 1800 (Nov 79 - 90) up to H | 0995 |
| **SUNBEAM** | |
| Sunbeam Alpine, Rapier & H120 (67 - 76) * | 0051 |
| **SUZUKI** | |
| Suzuki SJ Series, Samurai & Vitara (4-cyl) (82 - 97) up to P | 1942 |
| Suzuki Supercarry & Bedford/Vauxhall Rascal (86 - Oct 94) C to M | 3015 |
| **TALBOT** | |
| Talbot Alpine, Solara, Minx & Rapier (75 - 86) up to D | 0337 |
| Talbot Horizon (78 - 86) up to D | 0473 |
| Talbot Samba (82 - 86) up to D | 0823 |
| **TOYOTA** | |
| Toyota Carina E (May 92 - 97) J to P | 3256 |
| Toyota Corolla (Sept 83 - Sept 87) A to E | 1024 |
| Toyota Corolla (80 - 85) up to C | 0683 |
| Toyota Corolla (Sept 87 - Aug 92) E to K | 1683 |
| Toyota Corolla (Aug 92 - 97) K to P | 3259 |
| Toyota Hi-Ace & Hi-Lux (69 - Oct 83) up to A | 0304 |
| **TRIUMPH** | |
| Triumph Acclaim (81 - 84) * | 0792 |
| Triumph GT6 & Vitesse (62 - 74) * | 0112 |
| Triumph Herald (59 - 71) * | 0010 |
| Triumph Spitfire (62 - 81) up to X | 0113 |
| Triumph Stag (70 - 78) up to T | 0441 |
| Triumph TR2, TR3, TR3A, TR4 & TR4A (52 - 67)* | 0028 |
| Triumph TR5 & 6 (67 - 75) * | 0031 |
| Triumph TR7 (75 - 82) * | 0322 |
| **VAUXHALL** | |
| Vauxhall Astra (80 - Oct 84) up to B | 0635 |
| Vauxhall Astra & Belmont (Oct 84 - Oct 91) B to J | 1136 |
| Vauxhall Astra (Oct 91 - Feb 98) J to R | 1832 |
| Vauxhall/Opel Astra & Zafira Diesel (Feb 98 - Sept 00) R to W | 3797 |
| Vauxhall/Opel Astra & Zafira Petrol (Feb 98 - Sept 00) R to W | 3758 |
| Vauxhall/Opel Calibra (90 - 98) G to S | 3502 |
| Vauxhall Carlton (Oct 78 - Oct 86) up to D | 0480 |
| Vauxhall Carlton & Senator (Nov 86 - 94) D to L | 1469 |
| Vauxhall Cavalier 1300 (77 - July 81) * | 0461 |
| Vauxhall Cavalier 1600, 1900 & 2000 (75 - July 81) up to W | 0315 |
| Vauxhall Cavalier (81 - Oct 88) up to F | 0812 |
| Vauxhall Cavalier (Oct 88 - 95) F to N | 1570 |
| Vauxhall Chevette (75 - 84) up to B | 0285 |
| Vauxhall Corsa (Mar 93 - 97) K to R | 1985 |
| Vauxhall/Opel Corsa (Apr 97 - Oct 00) P to X | 3921 |
| Vauxhall/Opel Frontera Petrol & Diesel (91 - Sept 98) J to S | 3454 |
| Vauxhall Nova (83 - 93) up to K | 0909 |
| Vauxhall/Opel Omega (94 - 99) L to T | 3510 |
| Vauxhall Vectra Petrol & Diesel (95 - 98) N to R | 3396 |
| Vauxhall/Opel 1.5, 1.6 & 1.7 litre Diesel Engine (82 - 96) up to N | 1222 |
| **VOLKSWAGEN** | |
| Volkswagen 411 & 412 (68 - 75) * | 0091 |
| Volkswagen Beetle 1200 (54 - 77) up to S | 0036 |
| Volkswagen Beetle 1300 & 1500 (65 - 75) up to P | 0039 |
| Volkswagen Beetle 1302 & 1302S (70 - 72) up to L | 0110 |
| Volkswagen Beetle 1303, 1303S & GT (72 - 75) up to P | 0159 |
| Volkswagen Beetle Petrol & Diesel (Apr 99 - 01) T reg onwards | 3798 |
| Volkswagen Golf & Bora Petrol & Diesel (April 98 - 00) R to X | 3727 |
| Volkswagen Golf & Jetta Mk 1 1.1 & 1.3 (74 - 84) up to A | 0716 |
| Volkswagen Golf, Jetta & Scirocco Mk 1 1.5, 1.6 & 1.8 (74 - 84) up to A | 0726 |
| Volkswagen Golf & Jetta Mk 1 Diesel (78 - 84) up to A | 0451 |
| Volkswagen Golf & Jetta Mk 2 (Mar 84 - Feb 92) A to J | 1081 |
| Volkswagen Golf & Vento Petrol & Diesel (Feb 92 - 96) J to N | 3097 |
| Volkswagen LT vans & light trucks (76 - 87) up to E | 0637 |
| Volkswagen Passat & Santana (Sept 81 - May 88) up to E | 0814 |
| Volkswagen Passat Petrol & Diesel (May 88 - 96) E to P | 3498 |
| Volkswagen Passat 4-cyl Petrol & Diesel (Dec 96 - Nov 00) P to X | 3917 |
| Volkswagen Polo & Derby (76 - Jan 82) up to X | 0335 |
| Volkswagen Polo (82 - Oct 90) up to H | 0813 |
| Volkswagen Polo (Nov 90 - Aug 94) H to L | 3245 |
| Volkswagen Polo Hatchback Petrol & Diesel (94 - 99) M to S | 3500 |
| Volkswagen Scirocco (82 - 90) up to H | 1224 |
| Volkswagen Transporter 1600 (68 - 79) up to V | 0082 |
| Volkswagen Transporter 1700, 1800 & 2000 (72 - 79) up to V | 0226 |
| Volkswagen Transporter (air-cooled) (79 - 82) up to Y | 0638 |
| Volkswagen Transporter (water-cooled) (82 - 90) up to H | 3452 |
| Volkswagen Type 3 (63 - 73) * | 0084 |
| **VOLVO** | |
| Volvo 120 & 130 Series (& P1800) (61 - 73) * | 0203 |
| Volvo 142, 144 & 145 (66 - 74) up to N | 0129 |
| Volvo 240 Series (74 - 93) up to K | 0270 |
| Volvo 262, 264 & 260/265 (75 - 85) * | 0400 |
| Volvo 340, 343, 345 & 360 (76 - 91) up to J | 0715 |
| Volvo 440, 460 & 480 (87 - 97) D to P | 1691 |
| Volvo 740 & 760 (82 - 91) up to J | 1258 |
| Volvo 850 (92 - 96) J to P | 3260 |
| Volvo 940 (90 - 96) H to N | 3249 |
| Volvo S40 & V40 (96 - 99) N to V | 3569 |
| Volvo S70, V70 & C70 (96 - 99) P to V | 3573 |
| **AUTOMOTIVE TECHBOOKS** | |
| Automotive Air Conditioning Systems | 3740 |
| Automotive Brake Manual | 3050 |
| Automotive Carburettor Manual | 3288 |
| Automotive Diagnostic Fault Codes Manual | 3472 |
| Automotive Diesel Engine Service Guide | 3286 |
| Automotive Electrical and Electronic Systems Manual | 3049 |
| Automotive Engine Management and Fuel Injection Systems Manual | 3344 |
| Automotive Gearbox Overhaul Manual | 3473 |
| Automotive Service Summaries Manual | 3475 |
| Automotive Timing Belts Manual – Austin/Rover | 3549 |
| Automotive Timing Belts Manual – Ford | 3474 |
| Automotive Timing Belts Manual – Peugeot/Citroën | 3568 |
| Automotive Timing Belts Manual – Vauxhall/Opel | 3577 |
| Automotive Welding Manual | 3053 |
| In-Car Entertainment Manual (3rd Edition) | 3363 |

* Classic reprint

CL13.4/02

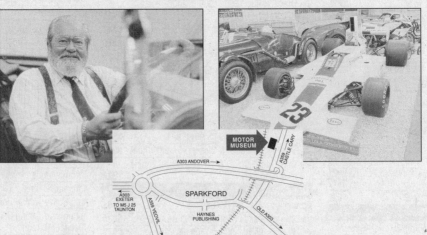